HEALTH INSURANCE TODAY

A Practical Approach

Seventh Edition

Janet I. Beik, AA, BA, MEd
Southeastern Community College (retired), Administrative Instructor,
Medical Assistant Program, West Burlington, Iowa

Julie K. Pepper, CMA (AAMA), BS
Chippewa Valley Technical College, Program Director – Health Navigator
Program, Instructor – Medical Assistant Program, Eau Claire, Wisconsin

ELSEVIER

Elsevier
3251 Riverport Lane
St. Louis, Missouri 63043

HEALTH INSURANCE TODAY: A PRACTICAL APPROACH, SEVENTH EDITION   ISBN: 978-0-323-65553-8

Previous editions copyrighted 2018, 2015, 2013, 2011, 2009, 2007.

Library of Congress Control Number: 2020941247

Senior Content Strategist: Linda Woodard
Senior Content Development Manager: Luke Held
Senior Content Development Specialist: Maria Broeker
Publishing Services Manager: Julie Eddy
Senior Project Manager: Tracey Schriefer
Design Direction: Margaret Reid

Printed in China

Last digit is the print number: 9 8 7 6 5 4 3 2 1

Reviewers

Kathleen Archer, BA, AS, CMA (AAMA)
Professor
Palm Beach State College
Lake Worth, Florida

Victoria Marie Conerly, CEHRS, CBCS, MBE, AABE
Medical Coder, Medical Biller, Medical Instructor
Ventura Cardiology Consultant
Ventura, California

Tiffany Cooper, CPC
Medical Office Systems Instructor, Business Sciences
Isothermal Community College
Rutherford, North Carolina

Roberta A. Pell, CPC, CEHRS
Program Director, Medical Billing and Coding
Western Technical College
El Paso, Texas

Preface

As in the previous editions, this edition follows our objective to present the complex issues of health insurance in a manner that allows students to focus on what they need to know and how to function as a health insurance professional without excessive miscellaneous information that, although informative, can become burdensome to the reader.

Health Insurance Today: A Practical Approach, seventh edition, begins by introducing students to the history of insurance, providing some general facts on its origin, and describing the metamorphosis of health insurance into what we know it to be today.

Although the textbook and workbook continue to address completing insurance claims using the universal paper claim form, the CMS-1500, this edition focuses on electronic claims.

Organization of the chapters:
- Chapter Outline
- Chapter Objectives
- Chapter Terms
- Opening Scenario
- Chapter Content
- Summary Checkpoints
- Closing Scenario
- Chapter Review Questions
- Websites to Explore

SPECIAL CHAPTER FEATURES

WHAT DID YOU LEARN?

The chapters are broken into easy-to-learn sections; after each section, the students are asked, "What Did You Learn?" Several review questions that reflect important "focus points" of that section are presented.

Example:

 What Did You Learn?

1. Besides their health problems, what do patients bring with them to the healthcare office?
2. List four issues that affect patient expectations.
3. Why is a clean, well-kept reception room important?
4. What is the rationale of explaining policies and fees up front to patients?

IMAGINE THIS!

The "Imagine This!" scenarios allow students to apply information to real-life situations, many of which have been taken from our actual experiences in healthcare facilities. By applying what has been presented in each "Imagine This!" scenario, students can easily understand the importance of the scenario and how it fits into real life, as well as determine the involved medical setting expectations.

Example:

 Imagine This!

Greg Manning was diagnosed with prostate cancer, and the options his provider gave him held a high probability of impotence, which was unacceptable to Greg. He logged on to the Internet and began an extensive search for possible alternatives. He found a clinic in another state where the medical staff offered a relatively new, noninvasive procedure that was highly successful in patients with similar malignancies. Greg traveled to the clinic and met with the staff providers to discuss the procedure. Greg was happy with the alternative they presented and subsequently underwent the new procedure successfully.

STOP AND THINK

The "Stop and Think" exercises ask the students to read and study a paragraph and then apply critical-thinking skills to resolve a problem or answer a question. Critical thinking is vital to individuals in the workplace, especially in a medical setting, where members of the healthcare team are often asked to think "on their feet" to resolve problems.

Example:

 Stop and Think

You notice that Theodore Simpson's account balance is $365, and he has not made a payment for 45 days. Office policy is to telephone patients 15 days after the last statement has been sent. How will you handle this? Create a telephone scenario of your conversation with Mr. Simpson.

HIPAA TIP

A federal law, the Health Insurance Portability and Accountability Act (HIPAA), has presented challenges to both healthcare workers and patients. Although this textbook does not attempt to cover all information included in HIPAA, it does give periodic applicable tips to help students better understand this important law.

Example:

 HIPAA Tip

Basic patient rights under HIPAA include the following:
1. Right to notice of privacy practices
2. Right to access to protected health information (PHI)
3. Right to an accounting of how PHI has been disclosed outside normal patient care channels
4. Right to request an amendment or correction to PHI

PATIENT'S POINT OF VIEW

The "Patient's Point of View" boxes challenge the students to look at a given situation from the patient's perspective and determine how they can best help that patient. The student should use empathy and active listening skills in these situations.

Example:

 Patient's Point of View

The terminology involved in discussing health insurance can be confusing for patients, especially when it comes to cost-sharing. Joy has developed a short glossary of terms for patients that includes an explanation of *deductible, coinsurance,* and *copayment:*

Deductible: A specific dollar amount that the patient must pay each year toward his or her medical expenses before the insurance company will pay for covered services.

Coinsurance: After the deductible has been met, the insured pays a certain percentage of the bill, and the insurance company pays the remaining percentage. An 80/20 split is common. The insurance company will pay 80% of the bill, and the insured is responsible for the remaining 20%.

Copayment: A specific dollar amount that the patient must pay for each office visit or other specified service, such as a visit to the emergency department.

APPENDIXES

There are three appendixes: Appendix A, Appendix B, and Appendix C. Appendix A is an example of a blank CMS-1500 (02/12) form. Appendix B presents nine examples of completed claim forms for a variety of payers, along with step-by-step completion instructions. Appendix C presents the UB-04 institutional (hospital) claim form and completion instructions.

STUDENT MATERIALS

WORKBOOK

A comprehensive Student Workbook accompanies the textbook and is intended to supplement the material presented in the book. Each chapter follows a precise structure, beginning with a short introduction, workbook chapter objectives, and a list of chapter terms, followed by a review test that allows the student to recall information presented in the book.

Each workbook chapter ends with application and enrichment activities in which students can apply what they have learned to today's healthcare environment. Most workbook chapters present at least one "performance objective." A performance (or learning) objective is a statement of what the students are expected to do when they have completed a specified course of instruction. It sets the conditions, behavior (action), and standard of task performance for the training setting. Performance objectives must be mastered to the predetermined criteria set by the instructor, institution, or organization. If the course is competency based, performance objectives may be repeated up to three times or until the student successfully meets the predetermined grading criteria.

One of the application exercises included in the Student Workbook involves creating a health insurance professional's notebook. The purpose of this notebook is to allow the student to access information quickly and accurately when preparing insurance claims for some of the major third-party payers. If kept current, it will be an excellent resource later, on the job.

EVOLVE RESOURCES

The Evolve website (http://evolve.elsevier.com/Beik/today/) is a free (with new textbook purchase) interactive learning resource that works in coordination with the textbook. For students, it provides content-related resources that give them a chance to enhance their knowledge and practice their skills. The Evolve website gives students the chance to:
- Access specific web links on the Internet to research topics and websites indicated in the "Websites to Explore" section at the end of each chapter
- Assess their progress with each chapter by working through the Chapter Review Questions
- Use Elsevier's educational EHR program, SimChart for the Medical Office (available in an optional upgrade package), and the supplied SimChart for the Medical Office insurance cases to practice completing duties that students would encounter while working in a medical office

The Evolve website also includes the following two distinct software offerings that support the teachings presented in this textbook:
- Electronic forms
- Guided completion

Electronic Forms

Within the CMS-1500 software, common health insurance forms, such as the CMS-1500 (02/12) claim form and ledger card, are formatted in a very simple and straightforward way to complete exercises in the Student Workbook electronically. Using these basic forms, students can complete their exercises and turn in clean forms that are easier for the instructor to grade.

Guided Completion

A guided process to completing a CMS-1500 (02/12) claim form, this software element corrects students as they complete a CMS-1500 (02/12) claim form block by block. If any incorrect information is provided, the program corrects the student immediately. This software offers both direction and insight to students on how to complete a claim form correctly. This element accompanies select exercises and serves as an introduction to completing a CMS-1500 (02/12) claim form. In addition to the CMS-1500 software there is a UB-04 Form Filler software element, which provides students with an opportunity to practice filling out sample UB-04 forms when provided with specific case studies and real-world examples.

INSTRUCTOR RESOURCES

TEACH INSTRUCTOR'S RESOURCE MANUAL

This text is written in such a way that it can be used in courses that range from 6 weeks in length to the more traditional 16-week semester. The TEACH Manual includes specific lesson plans and PowerPoint slides to aid instructors in their classroom planning. If an instructor thinks that a particular chapter is not a good fit for his or her class, it can be eliminated from the course outline and substituted with other course material. Also, chapters do not have to be taught in the sequence presented in the textbook.

The TEACH Manual contains an extensive amount of information and resources for both experienced and newer instructors. The manual is a culmination of our education, work, and teaching experiences over the past 26 years. It answers questions such as:

- "Where do I begin?"
- "How do I assess my students' work?"
- "Are the students learning what they need to learn to successfully perform in the real world?"

The manual should be used to supplement the textbook and Student Workbook, which have been created for use in the following programs:

- Medical Assisting
- Health Information Management
- Medical Reimbursement Specialist
- Billing and Coding Specialist
- Medical Office Administration

Teaching is a complex task, and this manual (the lesson plans, PowerPoint slides, and answer key) assists with instructional planning, delivery, and evaluation. A successful instructor must understand the various steps involved in effective teaching. To get the full benefit of this manual, new and experienced instructors can adopt or adapt various teaching aids from the examples included in the various sections.

Also included with the TEACH Manual is an answer key that provides answers to all Student Workbook questions, as well as all questions posed in the many boxes and questions throughout the textbook.

TEST BANK

A comprehensive, customizable test bank can be found on the Evolve website; it includes true and false, multiple choice, and matching questions. Using ExamView, instructors can create customized tests or quizzes.

POWERPOINT PRESENTATIONS

As mentioned, PowerPoint slides are included with the TEACH Manual on the Evolve website. These slides are best used as visual summaries of chapter information to supplement oral presentations. Instructors are cautioned against using PowerPoint slides to completely replace lecture and interactive learning.

EVOLVE RESOURCES

The Evolve website is a free interactive learning resource (with new textbook purchase) that works in coordination with the textbook. In addition to the assets listed and described earlier, the outstanding instructor Evolve features include the ability to do the following:

- Post class syllabi, outlines, and lecture notes
- Set up virtual "office hours" and email communication
- Share important dates and information through the online class calendar
- Encourage student participation through chat rooms and discussion boards

Evolve can play an integral part in how instructors teach, as well as how they interact with students, and it is our sincere hope that instructors will take advantage of all of the free interactive Evolve resources available to them.

http://evolve.elsevier.com/Beik/today/

Janet I. Beik, AA, BA, MEd
Julie K. Pepper, CMA (AAMA), BS

A Word About HIPAA

HIPAA rings a bell for most people, but many do not know much about it other than that they may have signed a form that contained this acronym when they visited their doctor. Those who are new to the world of health insurance and intend to make a career in healthcare need to know HIPAA's particulars.

HIPAA is an acronym for the Health Insurance Portability and Accountability Act of 1996 (August 21), Public Law 104-191, which amended the Internal Revenue Service Code of 1986. Also known as the *Kennedy-Kassebaum Act*, HIPAA includes a section, Title II, titled "Administrative Simplification" that requires the following:

- Improved efficiency in healthcare delivery by standardizing electronic data interchange
- Protection of confidentiality and security of health data through setting and enforcing standards

More specifically, HIPAA called on the US Department of Health and Human Services (HHS) to publish new rules that ensure the following:

- Standardization of electronic patient health, administrative, and financial data
- Unique health identifiers for individuals, employers, health plans, and healthcare providers
- Security standards protecting the confidentiality and integrity of "individually identifiable health information," past, present, and future

The bottom line is that HIPAA has resulted in extensive changes in most healthcare transaction and administrative information systems. Virtually all healthcare organizations are affected, including all healthcare providers, health plans, public health authorities, healthcare clearinghouses, and self-insured employers, as well as life insurers, information systems vendors, various service organizations, and colleges and universities.

To improve the efficiency and effectiveness of the healthcare system, HIPAA included "Administrative Simplification" provisions that required HHS to adopt national standards for electronic healthcare transactions. At the same time, Congress recognized that advances in electronic technology could erode the privacy of health information. Consequently, Congress incorporated provisions that mandated the adoption of federal privacy protections for individually identifiable or protected health information (PHI) within HIPAA.

When Congress enacted HIPAA in 1996, one of its main purposes was to protect private individual health information from being disclosed to anyone without the consent of the individual. Except under unusual circumstances, this consent needs to be in writing.

Title I of HIPAA protects health insurance coverage for workers and their families when they lose or change their jobs. According to Title II of HIPAA, the "Administrative Simplification" provisions require the establishment of national standards for electronic healthcare transactions and national identifiers for providers, health insurance plans, and employers. The "Administrative Simplification" provisions also address the security and privacy of health data. The purpose of all of these standards is to improve the efficiency and effectiveness of the nation's healthcare system by encouraging the widespread use of electronic data interchange in healthcare.

Like everything else associated with healthcare, HIPAA introduces updates periodically. One modification in 2016 dealt with a firearms background check system. This rule applies to only a small subset of HIPAA-covered entities that make mental health determinations and does not allow reporting of diagnostic, clinical, or other mental health treatment information. There have been no major rule changes that apply to most treating providers. The following website will help keep you current with HIPAA: http://www.hhs.gov/ocr/privacy/index.html.

About the Authors

Janet Beik began her career in the healthcare field in 1964, when she was employed as a medical secretary and transcriptionist at the University of Iowa's Department of Medicine. After that, she worked as an administrative assistant in various medical facilities, where she gained experience and expertise in all facets of "front office" work, including the preparation and submission of all types of insurance claims. In 1993 she began her teaching career as the administrative instructor in the Medical Assistant Program at Southeastern Community College in West Burlington, Iowa. During her tenure there, she acquired a master's degree in higher education from Iowa State University. After retiring in 2003, Ms. Beik began a career as a writer, first authoring several children's books, winning an achievement award for her story "Dolbee Creek—Elberta Trotsworth" from the National League of American Pen Women, Inc., Quad-Cities Branch. She was also a master presenter at the National Institute for Staff and Organizational Development (NISOD) at the University of Texas at Austin in May 2000 for her master's thesis titled "Saving the Endangered Student."

Julie Pepper began her career in healthcare as a certified medical assistant. She spent more than 20 years working in various healthcare facilities and a brief time working for an insurance company in claims adjudication. Her experience in healthcare facilities ranged from solo practitioners to large multispecialty clinics. While working in the clinical side of medical assisting, Julie recognized the need to have a solid understanding of how health insurance affected both patients and the organization. While working in the administrative side of medical assisting, she gained an even greater understanding of how she could help patients with issues related to health insurance. In 2002 she started her teaching career in the Medical Assistant Program at Chippewa Valley Technical College in Eau Claire, Wisconsin. In 2013 Julie received the Fuerstenberg Teaching Excellence Award, and in 2019 she became the program director for the Health Navigator program. The Medical Assistant Program was new to the college when Julie started teaching there, and she was able to develop the curriculum for many of the courses offered, including Medical Office Insurance and Finance. It was during the ongoing development of that course that she found *Health Insurance Today: A Practical Approach*. In 2012 she was approached by Elsevier to be involved in the electronic health record project, SimChart for the Medical Office. Since the development of that project, Julie has written two textbooks related to SimChart for the Medical Office and has been part of a team of authors for two comprehensive medical assistant textbooks. In 2018 she was asked to work with Janet Beik on the seventh edition of *Health Insurance Today: A Practical Approach* and jumped at the opportunity to collaborate with an author whom she so thoroughly respects.

Acknowledgments

I am pleased to present the seventh edition of my textbook, *Health Insurance Today: A Practical Approach*. I would like to thank the reviewers and the Elsevier staff, particularly Linda Woodard, Tracey Schriefer, and Maggie Reid, who have provided valuable insight and guidance in preparing this seventh edition, which I greatly appreciate. In addition, I would like to sincerely thank Kelly Skelton, Content Development Specialist.

In addition, I would like to thank my daughter, Cynthia Bowen, a frequent collaborator and constant cheerleader, who assisted with the editing and updating of this seventh edition.

A word of acknowledgment also should go out to my son, Jim, a computer engineer, who keeps my computers and printers running smoothly and resolves real and potential problems quickly and efficiently.

Last, but not least, thanks to my patient husband, whose encouragement and pragmatism keep me on track and focused.

Janet I. Beik, AA, BA, MEd

I was so pleased when I was asked to be involved in the seventh edition of *Health Insurance Today: A Practical Approach.* I have used this textbook for many years and have a great deal of respect for Janet Beik and the staff at Elsevier. At Elsevier, I especially want to thank Linda Woodard, for trusting me to work on this project, and Kelly Skelton, for answering my many questions. My biggest thanks go to Janet Beik, for challenging me to provide the best content for students in a way that keeps them engaged. She has made me a better teacher and writer.

I also have to thank my family for supporting me during the writing of this textbook. Jeff, Megan, Jon, and Callie, you have all been very understanding of the time needed for this project. Everything that you all have done—listening to me talk through ideas, making sure I eat and play, and just being there—is appreciated beyond measure.

Julie Pepper, CMA (AAMA), BS

Contents

The Origins of Health Insurance

1

Chapter Outline

I. **What Is Insurance?**
II. **History**
III. **Metamorphosis of Health Insurance**
IV. **Key Health Insurance Issues**
   A. Access to Health Insurance
   B. Access to Health Insurance and the Law
      1. *Patient Protection and Affordable Care Act*
      2. *Health Insurance Portability and Accountability Act*
      3. *The Affordable Care Act (ACA) and Consolidated Omnibus Budget Reconciliation Act (COBRA)*
      4. *State Programs for the Uninsured*

C. Controlling Healthcare Costs
D. Healthcare Expenditures
   1. *Americans Are Living Longer Than Ever Before*
   2. *Advances in Medical Technology*
   3. *Rise in Chronic Diseases*
   4. *More Demand for Healthcare*
   5. *Media Intervention*
   6. *Rising Medical Malpractice Premiums*
E. Cost-Sharing
V. **Basic Health Insurance Plans**

Chapter Objectives

After completion of this chapter, the student should be able to:
1. Explain health insurance.
2. Discuss the history of health insurance in the United States.
3. Outline the important changes in the evolution of health insurance.

4. List and explain today's key health insurance issues.
5. Explain how the Affordable Care Act affects the uninsured's access to health insurance.
6. Examine issues affecting the cost of healthcare, as well as explain cost-sharing.
7. Identify the basic types of health insurance plans.

Chapter Terms

Accountable Care Organization (ACO)
Consolidated Omnibus Budget Reconciliation Act (COBRA)
cost-sharing
deductible
entity/entities
fee-for-service
health insurance
health insurance exchanges

Health Insurance Portability and Accountability Act (HIPAA)
Health Maintenance Organization (HMO) Act
indemnify
indemnity insurance
indigent
insured
insurer
maintenance of effort (MOE)
managed healthcare

Patient Protection and Affordable Care Act
Patient-Centered Medical Home (PCMH)
policy
preexisting conditions
premium
preventive medicine
subsidies
tiering

Joy Cassabaum has worked at Walden-Martin Family Medical Clinic for more than 10 years and truly enjoys her position as a health insurance specialist. She has seen this field grow and change significantly during her time at Walden-Martin. The many changes in how people can obtain health insurance and the different laws that affect health insurance have made this a very challenging field. Joy has found it to be rewarding to be able to help the patients of Walden-Martin understand the complex world of health insurance. Joy also has found that by having a strong understanding of healthcare legislation, she has been able to keep reimbursements at a high level.

WHAT IS INSURANCE?

To understand **health insurance**, you must know a little about insurance in general. First, let's look at a typical definition of insurance:

> "The act or business, through legal means (normally a written contract), of protecting an individual's person or property against loss or harm arising out of specified circumstances in return for payment, which is called a premium."

The insuring party (called the **insurer**) agrees to **indemnify** (or reimburse) the **insured** for loss that occurs under the terms of the insurance contract.

Now that we know that insurance is basically financial protection against loss or harm, let's break it into smaller pieces. Insurance, as we know it, is a written agreement called a **policy**, between two parties (or **entities**), whereby one entity (the insurance company) promises to pay a specific sum of money to a second entity (often an individual, or it could be another company) if certain specified undesirable events occur. Examples of undesirable events include a windstorm blowing a tree over on a house, a car being stolen, or—as in the case of health insurance—an illness or injury. In return for this promise for financial protection against loss, the second entity (the insured) periodically pays a specific sum of money (**premium**) to the insurance company in exchange for this protection.

John and Anna Smith buy a house for $150,000. That's a lot of money, and the Smiths have worked hard to save up for this purchase. Now, they look at the house and wonder, what if a strong wind blows the roof off? Or, worse yet, what if there is an electrical malfunction and the house catches on fire? Along comes a neighbor who says, "Hey, I work for Colossus Insurance Company, and I'll write up an agreement saying that if you pay me $1000 a year, Colossus will foot the bills for any repair or replacement your house suffers in case of a storm, a fire, or most other bad stuff that can happen." The Smiths think, "This is great," and agree to the neighbor's offer. So a contract (the insurance policy) is drawn up, John and Anna pay Colossus Insurance Company $1000 to satisfy their mortgage lender's requirement, their worries about their new house are relieved, and they sleep soundly each night. Homeowners' insurance protects people from having to pay large sums of money out of their own pockets to repair or replace their homes in the event of fire, storm, theft, or other hazards.

With your understanding of what insurance is in general, let's look at health insurance. Health insurance narrows down the "undesirable events" mentioned earlier to illnesses and injuries. The insurance company promises to pay part (or sometimes all, depending on the policy) of the financial expenses incurred as a result of medical procedures, services, and certain supplies performed or provided by healthcare professionals if and when an individual becomes sick or injured. Some insurance policies also pay medical expenses even if the individual is not sick or injured. Healthcare providers and companies that sell health insurance have determined that it is often less costly to keep an individual well or to catch an emerging illness in its early stages, when it is more treatable, than to pay more exorbitant expenses later on should that individual become seriously ill. This practice is referred to as **preventive medicine**.

The term *health insurance* should not cause students to become uneasy when they hear it. A good analogy to put health insurance into perspective might be to compare it with a picture puzzle. When the individual puzzle pieces are dumped onto a table, there is little meaning or continuity to the jumble of pieces lying haphazardly on the tabletop. Then slowly, as the pieces are assembled, a picture begins to take shape and the puzzle starts making sense. Similarly, health insurance can be perplexing as individual concepts are presented, but when you "look at the whole picture," it becomes clearer and more understandable. As we begin to appreciate how the puzzle pieces fit together, we can understand the whole picture more easily when the puzzle is at last completed. Fig. 1.1 illustrates how the "health insurance puzzle" is assembled.

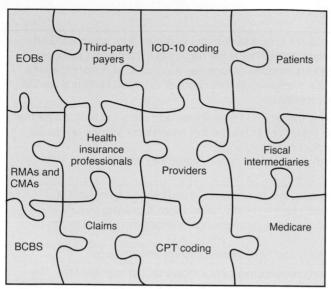

Fig. 1.1 The insurance "puzzle." *BCBS, Blue Cross Blue Shield; CMA, certified medical assistant; CPT, Current Procedural Terminology; EOB, explanation of benefits; ICD, International Classification of Diseases; RMA, registered medical assistant.*

! Stop and Think

Reread the paragraph comparing health insurance with a picture puzzle. Can you think of other applicable analogies that would help make the various components of health insurance more understandable at this point?

? What Did You Learn?

1. Give a brief definition of insurance.
2. Health insurance narrows down "undesirable events" to what two categories?
3. What is the term used when medical services and procedures are performed to keep a person well or prevent a catastrophic illness?

HISTORY

Insurance is not a recent phenomenon. The word *insurance* is derived from the Latin word *securitas*, which translates to the English word *security*.

From the beginning of time, people have looked for ways to ease some of the hardships of human existence. It has been common knowledge down through the ages that it has been difficult for any one individual to survive for long on his or her own. Prehistoric humans quickly learned that to survive, the resources of others must be pooled.

The beginnings of modern health insurance occurred in England in 1850, when a company offered coverage for medical expenses for bodily injuries that did not result in death. By the end of that same year in the United States, the Franklin Health Assurance Company of Massachusetts began offering medical expense

Imagine This!

It's ancient Babylon. Merchants are constantly being robbed or captured for ransom as their caravans cross the desert or as their ships sail off to trade with Egypt, India, and China. One wealthy businessman who made loans to the traders—we'll call him Ali-baba Gosmere—conceived a clever plan. As the traders came to him to borrow money for their journeys, he told the merchants, "For two additional gold coins, I'll forgive your loan if you're robbed!" The traders thought, "Wow! How can we lose with this deal?" This clever lender, by collecting these "premiums" from many such traders, was able to absorb the losses of the few unfortunate ones who were robbed. (According to documented history, this practice was later legalized in the Code of Hammurabi.)

coverage on a basis resembling health insurance as we know it now. By 1866 many other insurance companies began writing health insurance policies. These early policies were mostly for loss of income and provided health benefits for a few of the serious diseases that were common at that time—typhus, typhoid, scarlet fever, smallpox, diphtheria, and diabetes. People did not refer to these arrangements as insurance, but the concept was the same.

In the United States the birth of health insurance came in 1929 when Justin Ford Kimball, an official at Baylor University in Dallas, Texas, introduced a plan to guarantee schoolteachers 21 days of hospital care for $6 a year. Other employee groups in Dallas soon joined the plan, and the idea caught on nationwide. This plan eventually evolved into what we now know as Blue Cross. The Blue Shield concept grew out of the lumber and mining camps of the Pacific Northwest at the turn of the 20th century. Employers, wanting to provide medical care for their workers, paid monthly fees to "medical service bureaus," which were composed of groups of physicians. The Blue Cross and Blue Shield plans traditionally established premiums by community rating—that is, everybody in the community paid the same premium.

To explore more interesting and detailed facts related to the history of insurance, refer to "Websites to Explore" at the end of this chapter.

? What Did You Learn?

1. What is the Latin word for insurance, and what is its literal English translation?
2. State when and where the birth of health insurance occurred in the United States.
3. What did early insurance policies in the United States typically cover?

METAMORPHOSIS OF HEALTH INSURANCE

If you ever took a biology course, you may remember how certain insects go through several stages—from the caterpillar to the pupa and from the pupa to the

Table 1.1	**Health Insurance Timeline**
1900s	American Medical Association (AMA) becomes a powerful national force. Membership increases from about 8000 physicians in 1900 to 70,000 in 1910—half of them in the United States. This is the beginning of "organized medicine." Surgery is becoming more common. Physicians are no longer expected to provide free services to all hospital patients. United States lags behind European countries in finding value in insuring against costs of sickness. Railroads are the leading industry to develop extensive employee medical programs.
1910s	US hospitals are now modern scientific institutions, valuing antiseptics and cleanliness, and using medications for the relief of pain. American Association for Labor Legislation (AALL) organizes the first national conference on "social insurance." Progressive reformers begin gaining support for health insurance. Opposition from physicians and other interest groups and the entry of the United States into World War I in 1917 undermine the reform front.
1920s	Reformers emphasize the cost of medical care instead of wages lost to sickness—the relatively higher cost of medical care is a new and dramatic development, especially for the middle class. There is growing cultural influence of the medical profession—physicians' incomes are higher, and prestige is established. Rural health facilities are seen by many as inadequate. Penicillin is discovered, but it will be 20 years before it is widely used to combat infection and disease.
1930s	The Depression changes priorities, with greater emphasis on unemployment insurance and "old age" benefits. The Social Security Act is passed, omitting health insurance. Against the advice of insurance professionals, Blue Cross begins offering private coverage for hospital care in dozens of states.
1940s	Penicillin comes into use. Prepaid group healthcare begins and is seen as radical. To compete for workers, companies begin to offer health benefits, giving rise to the employer-based system in place today. Congress is asked to pass an "economic bill of rights," including the right to adequate medical care. The president offers a single-system, national health program plan that would include all Americans.
1950s	Attention turns to Korea and away from health reform; the United States has a system of private insurance for people who can afford it and welfare services for the poor. Federal responsibility for the sick is firmly established. Many more medications are available now to treat a range of diseases, including infections, glaucoma, and arthritis, and new vaccines that prevent dreaded childhood diseases, such as polio, become available. The first successful organ transplantation is performed.
1960s	In the 1950s, the price of hospital care doubled. Now in the early 1960s, people outside the workplace, especially the elderly, have difficulty affording insurance. More than 700 insurance companies sell health insurance. Major insurance endorses high-cost medicine. The president signs Medicare and Medicaid into law. The number of physicians reporting themselves as full-time specialists grows from 55% in 1960 to 69%.
1970s	Prepaid group healthcare plans are renamed health maintenance organizations (HMOs) with legislation that provides federal endorsement, certification, and assistance. Healthcare costs escalate rapidly; US medicine is now seen as in crisis. Healthcare costs rise at double the rate of inflation. Expansion of managed care helps moderate increases in healthcare costs.
1980s	Overall, there is a shift toward privatization and corporatization of healthcare. Under President Reagan, Medicare shifts to payment by diagnosis-related groups instead of by treatment. Private plans quickly follow suit. A specific fee or payment amount per patient (capitation) to physicians becomes more common.
1990s	Healthcare costs rise at double the rate of inflation. Expansion of managed care helps moderate increases in healthcare costs. By the end of the decade, 44 million Americans—16% of the nation—have no health insurance at all. Human Genome Project to identify all of the >100,000 genes in human DNA gets under way. By June 1990, 139,765 people in the United States have HIV/AIDS with a 60% mortality rate.
2000s	Healthcare costs continue to rise. Medicare is viewed by some as unsustainable under the present structure and must be "rescued." Changing demographics of the workplace lead many to believe the employer-based system of insurance cannot last. Human Genome Project's identification of all of the >100,000 genes in human DNA is completed in 2003, and all individual chromosome papers are completed in 2006; papers analyzing the genome continue to be published. Direct-to-consumer advertising for pharmaceuticals and medical devices is on the rise.
2010s	2010: A Patient's Bill of Rights goes into effect, protecting American consumers from abuses of the insurance industry. Cost-free preventive services begin.
	2011: Medicare enrollees can get key preventive services for free and receive a 50% discount on brand-name drugs in the Medicare "donut hole."

Adapted from http://www.pbs.org/healthcarecrisis/history.htm. Accessed April 17, 2019.

Table 1.1	Health Insurance Timeline—cont'd
2012: Accountable Care Organizations and other programs help healthcare providers work together to deliver better care.	
2013: Open enrollment in the Health Insurance Marketplace begins October 1.	
2014: Americans will have access to affordable health insurance options. • Middle- and low-income families will get tax credits that cover a significant portion of the cost of coverage. • The Medicaid program expands to cover more low-income Americans. • Discrimination due to preexisting conditions or gender is prohibited. • Annual limits on insurance coverage are eliminated. • Coverage for individuals participating in clinical trials is ensured.	

adult butterfly. This is called *metamorphosis*. By definition, metamorphosis is "a profound change in form from one stage to the next in the life history of an organism." The transformation of health insurance from what it was in the beginning to what we know it to be today can be compared with this metamorphosis, although the transformation of health insurance as it was in the beginning into what it has evolved to in the 21st century certainly does not resemble that of a caterpillar into a beautiful butterfly—perhaps more that of an ugly duckling into a beautiful swan. To illustrate this changing process, Table 1.1 presents a health insurance timeline.

You should now be familiar with how health insurance got started and how it developed into what we know as modern health insurance today. It is also important to know how it has changed throughout history and what caused these changes. As you might imagine, politics has played a big role in the development of health insurance in the United States. Support for government health insurance began when Theodore Roosevelt made national health insurance one of the major propositions of the Progressive Party during the 1912 presidential campaign, but the plan was eventually defeated. After 1920 opposition to government-sponsored plans was led by the American Medical Association (AMA) out of concern that government involvement in healthcare would lead to socialized medicine—a public tax-supported national healthcare system. Passage of the Social Security Act in 1935 became a vehicle for the development of a nationalized health insurance plan. During the middle of the 20th century it became obvious that something needed to be done to provide medical care for the elderly. In 1965, during President Lyndon B. Johnson's administration, federal legislation was enacted, resulting in *Medicare* for the elderly and *Medicaid* for the **indigent** (those having insufficient income or assets to be able to pay for adequate medical care). Since 1966 public and private health insurance has played a key role in financing healthcare costs in the United States. Medicare and Medicaid are examined more closely in later chapters.

Figs. 1.2 and 1.3 illustrate where US health dollars come from and how they are spent.

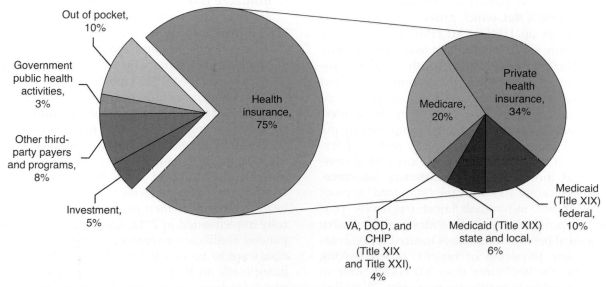

Fig. 1.2 Pie chart of "The Nation's Health Dollar: 2018 (Where It Came From)." *CHIP, Children's Health Insurance Program; DOD, US Department of Defense; VA,* Veterans Affairs.[S10] (From Centers for Medicare and Medicaid Services, Office of the Actuary, National Health Statistics Group.)

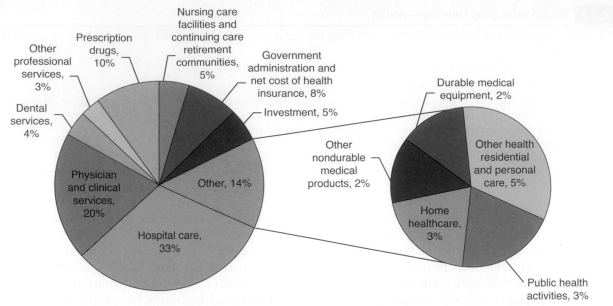

Fig. 1.3 Pie chart of "The Nation's Health Dollar: 2018 (Where It Went)." (From Centers for Medicare and Medicaid Services, Office of the Actuary, National Health Statistics Group.)

The structure and system of care that is known today as *managed care* traces its history to a series of alternative healthcare arrangements that appeared in various communities across the United States in the 19th century. The goal of these arrangements was to help meet the healthcare needs of select groups of people, including rural residents and workers and families in the lumber, mining, and railroad industries. The enrollees paid a set fee to healthcare providers, who delivered care under the terms of their agreement. In urban areas, such groups often were paid by charitable organizations to provide care to their members or charges. These prepaid group practices were a model for later entities that came to be known as *health maintenance organizations* (HMOs).

In 1973 Congress passed the **Health Maintenance Organization (HMO) Act**, which provided grants to employers who set up HMOs. An HMO is a plan that provides healthcare to its enrollees from specific physicians and hospitals that contract with the plan. Usually there are no **deductibles** (the amount of covered expenses that must be incurred and paid by the insured before benefits become payable by the insurer) to be met and no claim forms to be completed by the enrollee, and there is a geographically restricted service area. HMOs were intended to be low-cost alternatives to the more traditional **indemnity insurance**, which until recently has been the "standard" type of health insurance individuals most frequently purchased. Indemnity insurance provides comprehensive major medical benefits and allows insured individuals to choose any physician or hospital when seeking medical care. By 1997 more than 600 HMOs were in existence, providing healthcare to nearly 70 million people in the United States. By 2010 the number of people enrolled in HMO and managed care plans had

decreased significantly as more alternative plan options became available. Currently about 66 million people are covered by HMO health insurance policies. More detailed information on managed healthcare and HMOs is presented in Chapter 9.

In recent years the buzzword in healthcare was "reform." In 2010 two healthcare laws were enacted, the **Patient Protection and Affordable Care Act** (Public Law No. 111-148, **hereafter referred to as the ACA**) and the Health Care and Education Reconciliation Act (Public Law No. 111-152). These acts cover a number of issues and represent significant changes in America's healthcare industry. Although the ACA legislation involves many pages, the following three major changes went into effect immediately:

1. Insurance companies could no longer deny coverage to children with preexisting illnesses.
2. Children were allowed to remain on their parent's insurance policies until age 26.
3. Medicare recipients who fell into a specific coverage gap received a $250 rebate.

Other changes included a rule that individuals who have not had health insurance for 6 months received a subsidy allowing them to enroll in high-risk insurance pools run by the states. All new insurance plans sold must exempt preventive care and specific screenings from deductibles, and small businesses with fewer than 25 employees received a tax credit for providing health insurance to their employees. The ACA became fully implemented in 2014, adding provisions that expanded healthcare coverage. All parts of the legislation were to be enacted by 2018, with the last part being a tax on high-cost employer-sponsored health plans. Students can acquire details of the ACA by accessing the links listed in "Websites to Explore" at the end of this chapter.

Note: The ACA has faced some changes and criticism since it was signed into law in 2010 and has been partially repealed. However, although some key provisions of the ACA are gone, large portions remain intact. To review the current status of the ACA, refer to "Websites to Explore" or use applicable search words in your Internet search engine.

? What Did You Learn?

1. How is the transformation of health insurance from what it was in the beginning to what it is today comparable with the transformation of an ugly duckling into a beautiful swan?
2. Why are some people and certain organizations in the United States opposed to the government getting involved in health insurance?
3. What two federal programs got their start in the 1960s during President Johnson's administration?
4. List the three major changes made to healthcare in 2010.

KEY HEALTH INSURANCE ISSUES

With the passage of the ACA, some former issues were resolved; however, because health insurance is constantly evolving, there will no doubt always be issues to face. Some of the earlier issues included the following:

- Keeping costs down
- Regulating the health insurance industry
- Introducing more effective medications and treatments
- Stabilizing use of emergency departments
- Preventing chronic diseases
- Protecting patients' privacy
- Expanding the use of electronic health records (EHRs)

Predicting the future of healthcare and health policy is difficult. We know that the earlier issues already mentioned have affected our health policy, and several issues continue to challenge policymakers. Today we have new and reemerging issues that will create new challenges, such as the "tiering" of healthcare, new and emerging infectious diseases, the threat of terrorism, and the rediscovery of lifestyle-related health issues.

THE "TIERING" OF HEALTHCARE
A current trend in healthcare is **tiering**. This occurs when people with higher incomes are able to afford a wider range of services than those of the middle- and lower-income classes.

NEW AND REEMERGING INFECTIOUS DISEASES
Infectious diseases that are resistant to antibiotics are a serious threat, such as the Ebola threat in 2014. These occurrences will likely lead to greater emphasis in specialization in infectious disease and in rebuilding the public health system.

THE THREAT OF TERRORISM
The challenges faced by healthcare systems in dealing with the aftermath of terrorist attacks will generate considerable pressure to improve the capacity of local public health systems to ensure that they are adequately prepared.

REDISCOVERY OF LIFESTYLE-RELATED HEALTH ISSUES
Positive incentives to engage in or maintain healthy behaviors—for example, discounted health club memberships and/or free smoking cessation programs—are being offered by an increasing number of businesses.

Future issues might revolve around safeguarding individuals from the improper use of genetic information, creating precise definitions of "genetic tests" and "genetic information," genotherapy, and cloning. Meanwhile, this book focuses on healthcare issues that currently affect everyone.

ACCESS TO HEALTH INSURANCE

Most people who have health insurance get it from one of two major sources: (1) the government or (2) private organizations. The government provides health insurance programs to specific groups, such as the elderly, the disabled, and people who qualify because their income is below the federal poverty level. Many Americans get private health insurance through their employers. Still others purchase and pay for it themselves.

ACCESS TO HEALTH INSURANCE AND THE LAW

Patient Protection and Affordable Care Act
The Patient Protection and Affordable Care Act (ACA), nicknamed Obamacare, is a US federal statute enacted by the 111th US Congress and signed into law by President Barack Obama on March 23, 2010. Together with the Health Care and Education Reconciliation Act of 2010 amendment, it represented the US healthcare system's most significant overhaul and expansion of coverage since the passage of Medicare and Medicaid in 1965 (see Chapters 10 and 11). Part of the original ACA was the assessment of a penalty for anyone not buying insurance. In 2019 this penalty was eliminated; however, most other parts of the law remain intact.

Before the passage of the ACA, millions of Americans—particularly those who did not have job-based coverage—were without health insurance. The ACA provided for individual states to set up **health insurance exchanges**—a set of government-regulated, standardized plans eligible for federal **subsidies** (financial assistance) from which individuals can purchase low-cost health insurance. These healthcare exchanges were to be fully certified and operational by January 1, 2014. Also, beginning in 2014, the law made it illegal for any health insurance plan to use **preexisting conditions** to exclude, limit, or set unrealistic rates on coverage for adults. Preexisting conditions are certain illnesses that were diagnosed or injuries that occurred before the effective date of the insurance policy.

As of this writing, 10 states—California, Colorado, Connecticut, Hawaii, Maryland, Massachusetts, Minnesota, New York, Oregon, and Vermont—as well as the District of Columbia have kept the provisions of the ACA intact. They've set up their own insurance marketplaces, expanded Medicaid coverage, and enacted most or all of the law's insurance-industry reforms. Thirty-two states are helping the federal government enforce at least one of the ACA's insurance reforms, such as family coverage for those under age 26, no penalties for preexisting conditions, and essential benefits in all health plans. Three of those states—Maine, South Dakota, and Virginia—are fully implementing the insurance reforms even as they decline to expand Medicaid or manage their own health insurance marketplaces. Although the ACA is still in force today, the healthcare law's future looks uncertain. Students should keep up to date with any changes in the ACA by logging on to the Internet frequently and using search words such as "changes in the Affordable Care Act" or similar phrases. See also "Websites to Explore" at the end of this chapter.

 Imagine This!

Susan Broaden lost her job as office manager with the Canal county attorney's office where she was covered under a comprehensive employer-provided healthcare plan. After scrupulously researching alternative private health plans, Susan realized that the premium of a similar plan would be between $900 and $1100 a month, and her deductible would range from $2500 to $5500 a year. Eventually, she discovered that she was eligible for the "exchange" in the state in which she resided with a monthly premium of $55. Even if Susan was successful in obtaining another job, her premium would not increase as long as her income did not exceed the limited annual amount, which in 2019 was $51,000.

Health Insurance Portability and Accountability Act

The ACA is not the only law that addresses preexisting conditions. In 1996 Congress introduced the **Health Insurance Portability and Accountability Act (HIPAA)**, which (among other things) required most employer-sponsored group health insurance plans to accept transfers from other group plans without imposing a preexisting condition clause. Additional information on HIPAA is presented in this book's preface and in Chapter 3.

 HIPAA Tip

The four main provisions of HIPAA are that it:
1. Allows portability of health insurance coverage.
2. Protects workers and their families from preexisting conditions when they change or lose their jobs.
3. Establishes national standards for electronic healthcare transactions and national identifiers for providers, health plans, and employers.
4. Addresses the security and privacy of health data.

Adopting these standards is intended to improve the efficiency and effectiveness of healthcare in the United States. (For more information on HIPAA, go to https://www.HHS.gov.)

The Affordable Care Act and Consolidated Omnibus Budget Reconciliation Act

Another provision that serves to prevent people from losing their healthcare coverage is the **Consolidated Omnibus Budget Reconciliation Act (COBRA)**, a health benefit act that Congress passed in 1986. Under COBRA, when an employee quits his or her job or is laid off (or work hours are reduced) from a company with 20 or more workers, the law requires the employer to extend group health coverage to the employee and his or her dependents at group rates for 18 months and in some cases up to 36 months. Group health coverage for COBRA participants is usually more expensive than health coverage for active employees because the employer usually pays a part of the premium for active employees, whereas COBRA participants generally pay the entire premium themselves. However, coverage under COBRA is normally less expensive than individual health coverage. The ACA does not eliminate or change COBRA's rules. Students interested in learning more detailed information about COBRA can find an applicable link at the end of this chapter under "Websites to Explore."

 HIPAA Tip

HIPAA amended the Employee Retirement Income Security Act (ERISA) to provide new rights and protections for participants and beneficiaries in group health plans. The *P* in HIPAA stands for portability. This protects the employee's right to keep certain benefits when switching employers or when retiring, making those benefits portable. Understanding this amendment is important in decisions about future health coverage. HIPAA contains protections for health coverage offered in connection with employment (group health plans) and for individual insurance policies sold by insurance companies (individual policies).

State Programs for the Uninsured

Medicaid and the Children's Health Insurance Program (CHIP) are two common state programs for the uninsured. The ACA expands coverage to people who did not previously qualify for state Medicaid programs. Effective in 2014, all Americans with incomes up to 133% of federal poverty guidelines are covered under this expanded program. Before the ACA, states shared the cost of the Medicaid program with the federal government; however, under the law, the federal government provides states with 100% financing for those individuals newly eligible for Medicaid for the first 3 years. This percentage decreases incrementally each year until 2020, at which time the federal government's share drops to 90%. For more information on Medicaid, see Chapter 10.

CHIP provides insurance for qualifying children who are ineligible for Medicaid but cannot afford private insurance. States receive a higher federal match to pay for CHIP coverage than for their Medicaid programs. All 50 states and the District of Columbia use

Medicaid or CHIP to provide coverage beyond federal standards. The ACA extended funding for CHIP through fiscal year 2015 and continued the authority for the program through 2019. The ACA also requires **maintenance of effort (MOE)**—a requirement that states spend at least a specified amount of state funds for federal assistance program purposes—for CHIP programs. Eligibility levels for children that were in place on March 23, 2010, continued through 2019.

CHIP covers approximately 9 million children nationwide, with the federal government covering most of the cost until recently. Unless Congress renews funding for this program, states no longer will receive this additional federal funding that helps keep CHIP sustainable. To keep current on CHIP, log on to the Internet periodically and use appropriate search words. See also "Websites to Explore" at the end of this chapter.

CONTROLLING HEALTHCARE COSTS

The intent of the ACA was not only to help uninsured Americans acquire healthcare coverage, but also to help reduce healthcare costs for families, businesses, and government. Following are some of the ways it proposed to do this:

- Stop insurance company abuses.
- Crack down on Medicare waste and fraud.
- Eliminate certain subsidies to private insurance companies.
- Introduce payment reforms that allow providers to deliver care more effectively.
- Offer tax credits to small businesses to help cover health insurance premiums for their employees. (In 2014 small businesses were eligible for tax credits of up to 50% of their premiums.)
- Make affordable insurance exchanges available for individuals and families purchasing coverage in the health insurance market.
- Provide tax relief that cuts the cost of insurance while guaranteeing access to basic health benefits.

HEALTHCARE EXPENDITURES

We all know that the costs of healthcare have increased in recent years. Fig. 1.4 shows the change in national health expenditures beginning in 1980 through the projected expenditures up to 2022.

Many factors are to blame for increases in healthcare costs. Because of the complexity of the problem and the issues involved, it is easy to jump to conclusions that are not based on careful consideration of all the facts. Some blame the insurance companies for these rising costs, but one of the largest health insurance companies in the United States claims that, contrary to common opinion, administrative costs of processing claims and providing customer service for members amount to only a small portion of escalating premium dollars. The lion's share goes to pay for the medical care that members receive, and because the cost of this care keeps increasing, members' premiums keep increasing. Some reasons and explanations experts give to try to explain the increasing cost of healthcare are presented in the following paragraphs.

Americans Are Living Longer Than Ever Before

In 1900 the average life expectancy of Americans was about 50 years. In 2016 life expectancy was 78.6 years. You may have heard the phrase "the graying of America." During the 20th century, the number of people in the United States who were 65 years or older increased 11-fold. Because elderly people typically require more healthcare, when they join an insured group, the entire group's healthcare risks, along with the costs, rise accordingly.

Advances in Medical Technology

Until recent years, when individuals had a serious disease, such as cancer or heart disease, there were no effective ways to treat it, and often they just died. Today, new technology (chemotherapy and organ and bone marrow transplants) and equipment (magnetic

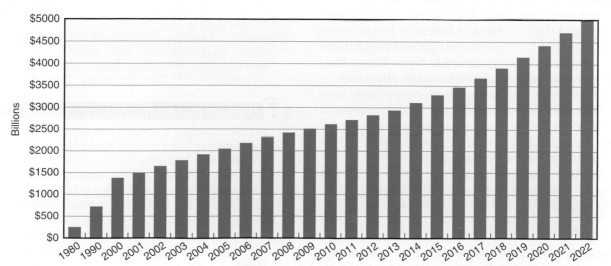

Fig. 1.4 Chart showing growth in national healthcare expenditures beginning in 1980 through the projected expenditures in 2022. (Data from Centers for Medicare and Medicaid Services, Office of the Actuary, National Health Statistics Group.)

resonance imaging and robotics) provide treatments for medical conditions that were previously untreatable, but these new treatments are expensive.

Rise in Chronic Diseases

Some experts estimate that healthcare costs for chronic disease treatment account for more than 75% of national health expenditures. In particular, there has been a tremendous focus on the rise in rates of overweight and obesity and their contribution to chronic illnesses and healthcare spending. The changing nature of illness has sparked a renewed interest in the possible role for prevention to help control costs.

More Demand for Healthcare

In years past, many people would treat their illnesses at home, reluctant to go to physicians, and many were actually afraid of hospitals. People tended to accept certain physical problems, such as sexual dysfunction, attention deficit disorder, and depression, as their "lot in life." More treatments for these disorders have been developed and accepted. In addition, it seems that the trend is to see a healthcare provider for even minor medical problems. This increase in the general population's demand for healthcare has resulted in higher medical costs.

Media Intervention

Media that use direct-to-consumer marketing are partly to blame. How many of us have watched a commercial on television or seen an advertisement on the Internet, in which someone has an ache or a pain? A charismatic voice announces that if you are suffering from this or that ailment, some new drug might be the answer, so "Ask your doctor if *Cure-It-All* is right for you!"

Rising Medical Malpractice Premiums

The increase in medical malpractice premiums has also become an issue of increasing concern for healthcare providers, policymakers, and the general public. Premiums may influence physicians' decisions to join and leave the labor force, their choice of a medical specialty, and their decision of where to locate, creating the potential for underserved patient populations in certain specialties or geographic areas. Rising malpractice premiums may also encourage physicians to practice "defensive medicine," performing more tests and procedures than necessary to reduce exposure to lawsuits. Both rising malpractice premiums and defensive medicine practices may contribute to the increase in health insurance premiums.

A link that provides more information on factors driving up healthcare costs can be found under "Websites to Explore" at the end of this chapter.

COST-SHARING

Cost-sharing is a situation in which insured individuals pay a portion of the healthcare costs, such as deductibles, coinsurance, or copayment amounts. It is one method of curbing the rising cost of health insurance

premiums. Most covered workers are in health plans that require a deductible to be met before most plan benefits are provided, after which the individual must pay a copayment or a percentage of coinsurance per encounter. In the past a typical deductible was in the range of $250 to $500, and coinsurance was 10% to 20%. Today deductible and copayment amounts depend on the plan type. The ACA helps make prevention of certain diseases and conditions affordable and accessible for all Americans by requiring health insurance plans to cover recommended preventive services without cost-sharing. For example, under the ACA, women's preventive healthcare services (such as mammograms, screenings for cervical cancer, and other services) are covered with no cost-sharing under some plans. The ACA also made recommended preventive services free for people on Medicare. In 2011 the US Department of Health and Human Services (HHS) adopted additional Guidelines for Women's Preventive Services. In addition, many private plans must cover regular well-baby and well-child visits without cost-sharing.

 Stop and Think

Compare the concept of today's health insurance "cost-sharing" with the insurance for ancient sailors of Babylon.

 Patient's Point of View

The terminology involved in discussing health insurance can be confusing for patients, especially when it comes to cost-sharing. Joy has developed a short glossary of terms for patients that includes an explanation of *deductible*, *coinsurance*, and *copayment*:

Deductible: A specific dollar amount that the patient must pay each year toward his or her medical expenses before the insurance company will pay for covered services.

Coinsurance: After the deductible has been met, the insured pays a certain percentage of the bill, and the insurance company pays the remaining percentage. An 80/20 split is common. The insurance company will pay 80% of the bill, and the insured is responsible for the remaining 20%.

Copayment: A specific dollar amount that the patient must pay for each office visit or other specified service, such as a visit to the emergency department.

? **What Did You Learn?**

1. List five of today's key health insurance issues.
2. Name the two major sources from which most people acquire health insurance.
3. A set of government-regulated, standardized healthcare plans eligible for federal subsidies from which individuals can purchase low-cost health insurance describes a

   _____.
4. Name four key factors that drive up healthcare costs.
5. Name four ways the ACA helps keep healthcare costs down.
6. How does "cost-sharing" help keep healthcare costs down?

BASIC HEALTH INSURANCE PLANS

The two main categories of private insurance plans are indemnity plans and managed care plans. The indemnity plan (also called **fee-for-service**) is the type of plan most Americans were covered under until the past 2 decades. Under this type of plan, patients can go to any healthcare provider or hospital they choose, medical bills are sent to the insurance carrier, and the patient (or healthcare provider) is reimbursed according to rules of the policy. Managed care plans function differently.

Any system of healthcare payment or delivery arrangement in which the health plan attempts to control or coordinate use of health services by its enrolled members to contain health expenditures, improve quality, or both falls under the category of **managed healthcare**. Arrangements often involve a defined delivery system of providers with some form of contractual arrangement with the plan. Under managed healthcare plans, patients see designated providers, and benefits are paid according to the structure of the managed care plan. With both types of plans, patients and the insurance company share the cost of services rendered. Initially managed healthcare plans were quite restrictive. This has changed over time, with some plans allowing their enrollees to choose from a range of providers who may not be directly employed by the plan. Managed care is discussed in detail in Chapter 9.

In addition to private healthcare plans, there are three government-funded plans: (1) Medicare, which provides healthcare coverage for individuals age 65 and older and individuals with certain disabilities; (2) Medicaid, which provides healthcare coverage for qualifying low-income individuals; and (3) Tricare, which provides coverage for uniformed service members and their families. All of these plans are discussed individually and in more detail in later chapters.

Recent healthcare reform has introduced health insurance exchanges, a model intended to create a more organized and competitive market for health insurance by offering a choice of plans with common rules governing how each plan is offered and its cost and by providing information to help consumers better understand the choices available to them.

Another healthcare model introduced in recent years is the **Accountable Care Organization (ACO)**. Authors of this coverage structure have formulated ACOs to provide a more efficient way to deliver care. Similar to an HMO, an ACO is a network of doctors and hospitals that shares responsibility for providing care to patients. Under the healthcare law, ACOs would agree to manage all of the healthcare needs of a minimum of 5000 Medicare beneficiaries for at least 3 years. Goals for an ACO are to determine how to successfully:

- Keep patients within the ACO and encourage them to stay healthy and take more responsibility for their own healthcare
- Encourage patients to use healthcare providers that are part of the ACO network to keep down the overall costs within the organization

A treatment model that developed out of the ACA is the concept of the **Patient-Centered Medical Home (PCMH)**. PCMH is designed to improve quality of care while increasing efficiency in the delivery of care and reducing healthcare costs for that care. The basic concept of the PCMH is that patients' treatment is coordinated through their primary care physicians to ensure that patients receive the care they need when and where they need and want it and that care is delivered in a culturally and linguistically appropriate manner. The objective is to have a centralized setting that facilitates partnerships between individual patients and their personal physicians and, when appropriate, the patient's family. Care is further facilitated through the use of information technology, a health information exchange, and other means to ensure that patients get adequate, appropriate, and cost-effective healthcare.

 What Did You Learn?

1. Provide your opinion of why people need health insurance.
2. Name the two basic categories of health insurance.
3. Briefly describe an ACO.

SUMMARY CHECKPOINTS

- Health insurance can be defined as financial protection from loss or harm as a result of medical care and treatment caused by illness and injuries. When an individual purchases an insurance policy, the insuring company promises to pay a portion of the financial expenses incurred (as outlined in the policy) resulting from any medical procedures, services, and certain supplies performed or provided by healthcare professionals if and when the insured or his or her dependents become sick or injured. In return for this financial protection, the insured individual pays a monthly (or periodic) premium.
- The roots of modern health insurance began in England in 1850, when a company offered coverage for medical expenses for bodily injuries that did not result in death. Health insurance in the United States began shortly after the turn of the 20th century as a result of a contract between schoolteachers and a hospital in Texas wherein the hospital agreed to provide certain services for a set number of days for a nominal fee.
- Health insurance has gone through many stages to evolve into what we know it to be today. Politics has played a big role in this growth and change and is responsible for the advent of major government-sponsored plans—Medicare and Medicaid—and HMOs. Important changes include the following:
  - Employer-sponsored group health plans
  - Creation of Medicare and Medicaid
  - Development of managed care
  - HIPAA
  - Healthcare reform and the Affordable Care Act
- A number of formerly unresolved issues regarding access to healthcare represent significant changes in

America's healthcare industry. The ACA and the Health Care and Education Reconciliation Act address significant issues and changes in America's healthcare industry. The ACA became fully implemented in 2014, adding provisions that expanded healthcare coverage to more Americans.

- Historically, many people had access to health insurance through an employer-sponsored group plan, government-sponsored programs, or private organizations. Those who could not afford it went without health insurance. Today, all Americans (with certain exceptions) are required to have health insurance or face a penalty in the form of a tax. For those who do not have affordable healthcare, the ACA provides for individual states to set up health insurance exchanges from which individuals can purchase low-cost health insurance. Individuals within 133% of the federal poverty line are eligible for government assistance.

- Reasons why healthcare costs and premiums have increased significantly in recent years include:
  - Americans are living longer than ever before
  - Advances in medical technology, leading to more expensive equipment and methods of treatment
  - Rise in chronic diseases
  - More demand for healthcare
  - Media intervention

- Some of the ways the ACA cuts costs:
  - Stops insurance company abuses.
  - Cracks down on Medicare waste and fraud.
  - Eliminates certain subsidies to private insurance companies.
  - Introduces payment reforms that allow providers to deliver care more effectively.
  - Offers tax credits to small businesses to help cover health insurance premiums for their employees. (In 2015 small businesses were eligible for tax credits of up to 50% of their premiums.)
  - Makes affordable insurance exchanges available for individuals and families purchasing coverage in the health insurance market.

- The two basic types of health insurance plans are fee-for-service (indemnity) and managed care. Other health insurance structures include health insurance exchanges and ACOs.

Closing Scenario

As you have just read, Joy was accurate in her description of her position as a health insurance specialist. It truly is a challenging and rewarding position. Joy continues to stay up to date with all of the changes that occur in the world of health insurance by maintaining her membership in her professional organization, obtaining and reading all of the updates published by the government-sponsored plans and private health insurance companies, and attending training sessions offered. Having a comprehensive understanding of health insurance has made Joy a valuable employee of Walden-Martin Family Medical Clinic.

CHAPTER REVIEW QUESTIONS

1. Financial protection against loss describes which term?
   a. Indemnity
   b. Insurance
   c. Managed care
   d. HIPAA

2. The birth of health insurance in the United States occurred in what year?
   a. 1850
   b. 1929
   c. 1965
   d. 2010

3. A healthcare plan that has no deductibles and does not require claim forms to be completed is:
   a. An indemnity plan
   b. Fee-for-service
   c. A health maintenance organization
   d. Medicare

4. The government-sponsored plan for the indigent is:
   a. Medicare
   b. A health maintenance organization
   c. An indemnity plan
   d. Medicaid

5. Key health insurance issues include:
   a. Access to health insurance
   b. Controlling healthcare costs
   c. Healthcare expenditures
   d. All of the above

6. The type of insurance plan where patients can go to any healthcare provider or hospital they choose is:
   a. Managed care
   b. Patient-centered medical home
   c. Fee-for-service
   d. None of the above

7. The law that requires most employer-sponsored group health insurance plans to accept transfers from other group plans without imposing a preexisting condition clause is:
   a. The Affordable Care Act
   b. The Health Insurance Portability and Accountability Act
   c. The Health Maintenance Organization Act
   d. None of the above

8. The plan that provides coverage for children who do not qualify for Medicaid but cannot afford private health insurance is:
   a. Medicare
   b. Health Maintenance Organizations
   c. Children's Health Insurance Program
   d. Blue Shield

9. The term that refers to a specific dollar amount that a patient must pay each year toward his or her medical expenses before the insurance company will pay for covered services is:
   a. Deductible
   b. Coinsurance
   c. Copayment
   d. Premium

10. Keeping an individual well or catching an emerging illness in its early stages is:
    a. Preventive medicine
    b. Patient-centered medical home
    c. Preexisting condition
    d. All of the above

WEBSITES TO EXPLORE

- For live links to the following websites, please visit the Evolve website at http://evolve.elsevier.com/Beik/today.
- If you are interested in learning more about the evolution of health insurance in the United States, log on to the PBS website and study the Healthcare Timeline table: http://www.pbs.org/healthcarecrisis/history.htm.
- The ACA became law in March 2010. To learn more about this important legislation, log on to http://www.healthcare.gov/.
- For more information on HIPAA, log on to the following website: https://www.hhs.gov/hipaa/index.html.
- It is important for the health insurance professional to know about COBRA. The following URL will direct your search to an informative website that includes the full text of COBRA: https://www.dol.gov/general/topic/health-plans/cobra.
- This website provides more detailed information on healthcare reform: https://www.healthcare.gov/.
- Additional websites of interest:
  http://kff.org/health-costs/
  https://www.cms.gov/CCIIO/Resources/Fact-Sheets-and-FAQs/ratereview

Author's Note: Due to the dynamic nature of the Internet, web addresses and/or links provided in this chapter may have changed since publication and may no longer be valid. In such cases, students should select comparable search words to access related sites.

2 Tools of the Trade: A Career as a Health Insurance Professional

Chapter Outline

I. **Your Future as a Health Insurance Professional**
  A. Required Skills and Interests
    1. *Education*
    2. *Preparation*
II. **Job Duties and Responsibilities**
III. **Career Prospects**
  A. Occupational Trends and Future Outlook
  B. What to Expect as a Health Insurance Professional
    1. *Home-Based Careers*
  C. Rewards

IV. **Is a Career in Healthcare Right for You?**
V. **Certification Possibilities**
VI. **Career Focus for the Health Insurance Professional**
  A. Electronic Claims
  B. CMS-1500 (02/12) Universal Paper Form

Chapter Objectives

After completion of this chapter, the student should be able to:

1. List the entry-level skills necessary for success in the health insurance professional's career.
2. Discuss college courses typically included in a medical insurance billing and coding program.
3. Explain the importance of effective study skills and proper preparation to maximize learning.
4. Demonstrate the importance of time management by developing and using a time management chart.
5. Identify desirable personality traits and on-the-job skills health insurance professionals should possess to optimize career success.

6. Classify various job titles and their corresponding duties included under the general umbrella of "health insurance professional."
7. Explore career prospects and job opportunities for health insurance professionals.
8. Predict possible rewards of a career in medical-related fields.
9. Investigate certification possibilities related to the field of insurance billing and coding.
10. Compare the two methods of submitting insurance claims.

Chapter Terms

adjudicated	covered entity	objectivity
application	diagnosis	paraphrase
autonomy	diligence	prioritize
certification	electronic data interchange (EDI)	professional ethics
CMS-1500 claim form	enthusiasm	trading partners
communication	initiative	
comprehension	integrity	

Rachel Butler has recently made the decision to make a career change. She has not felt challenged in her current job and is excited about the opportunities in the healthcare field. Although she greatly enjoys working with people, she is not really interested in the clinical side of healthcare.

The responsibilities of a health insurance professional appeal to her attention to detail and her problem-solving skills. She has undertaken the education necessary for this profession and understands the need for lifelong learning in her new career. She will be working as a health insurance professional at Walden-Martin Family Medicine Clinic and looks forward to learning how the organization handles the complex world of health insurance.

YOUR FUTURE AS A HEALTH INSURANCE PROFESSIONAL

Before you begin any college or vocational program, you might want to ask yourself, "Where will this take me, and what career opportunities are available to a graduate of this type of program?" You should think about several things. Naturally, the first question in many individuals' minds is, "How much money can I make?" That question is logical, but other factors should be considered when choosing a career. One wise person said, "If you choose a job you love, you will never have to work a day the rest of your life."

Although there are many different career paths you can choose in the area of healthcare, this chapter refers to the domain of medical expertise of a "health insurance professional," sometimes referred to as a *health insurance specialist* or *medical billing and coding specialist*. The administrative health insurance professional plays a crucial role in healthcare—one that is increasingly in demand. Qualified health insurance professionals are experts in generating, submitting, and tracking insurance claims for a variety of payers and ensuring that insurance companies reimburse the healthcare provider (and/or patient) appropriately and in a timely manner for services rendered. Those trained as health insurance professionals are vital not only to healthcare providers but to health insurance companies as well. They also play an important role in patient advocacy. Although

job opportunities in this career field are increasing because of the relatively complex nature of health insurance in general (particularly the coding process), the industry is placing great emphasis on training and experience. Certification is recommended and is available for various specialties in the allied health field. Certification tells prospective employers that the individual possesses the skills necessary in a particular area, which helps the office run efficiently and effectively and provides for each patient's specific needs (see "Certification Possibilities" later in this chapter).

It should be noted that although we refer to this career field as "health insurance professional," there is no nationally recognized title or acronym for this broad specialty.

REQUIRED SKILLS AND INTERESTS

Success as a health insurance professional requires a certain degree of competency or knowledge in general educational areas. To increase the potential for success, candidates entering this field should possess college entry-level skills in the following areas:

- Reading and **comprehension** (understanding what you have read)
- Basic business math
- English and grammar
- Oral and written **communication** (sending and receiving information through speech, writing, or signs that are mutually understood)
- Keyboarding and office skills
- Computer **application** skills (ability to use computer hardware and software, including Windows and Microsoft Word [or similar word processing software], and ability to use the Internet)

Education

Many community colleges and career training schools offer programs that provide graduates with the skills to become specialists in the health insurance field. Typically, students begin the program with core courses that are built on in the later stages of the program. They receive extensive hands-on training and practice in health insurance billing and coding and in computerized patient account management. Box 2.1 lists courses included in a typical insurance billing professional program.

Program length for a health insurance professional is 2 to 4 years at community colleges and technical schools and 4 to 9 months at a career school. Most community colleges offer a 2-year associate degree in this discipline. A 4-year college typically awards a Bachelor of Science degree in health science, healthcare management, or whatever specific health fields are offered. Diplomas and certificates also can be obtained from online courses and independent study programs. A graduate of a health insurance professional or billing and coding program has opportunities for entry-level employment as a medical biller,

Box 2.1   **Courses in a Typical Insurance Billing Professional Program**

CORE COURSES
Anatomy and Physiology
Medical Terminology
Keyboarding
Word Processing
Business English
Business Math
Medical Office Administrative Skills

SPECIALIZED COURSES
Medical Transcription (optional in some programs)
Medical Records Management
Current Procedural Terminology (CPT) Coding
International Classification of Diseases, 10th revision, Clinical Modification (ICD-10-CM) Coding
Medical Insurance Billing
Information Technology and Computers
Bookkeeping/Accounting

medical coder, or other health insurance–related position in hospitals, nursing homes, physicians' offices, ambulatory care facilities, medical or surgical supply companies, or billing service companies.

Preparation

Another important key for success in any career, besides basic entry-level skills and applicable education, is proper preparation. Many people entering the health insurance professional field have been out of school for several years. Sharp study skills are needed for this type of program. To succeed in any formal college or training program, you must have good study skills.

"Lifelong learning" is essential to being successful when working in healthcare. This means that learning will not stop when you graduate from the college or career program you have chosen, but that you will continue to learn for the rest of your career—or, ideally, the rest of your life. In healthcare, this is especially true because this discipline is constantly changing. Many students who have been out of school for several years find that their study skills may be a little rusty. Even if you have been out of school for only a short time, you still may need help to "get back in the groove" of studying. The following is a list of suggestions that may help you develop effective study skills to enhance your chances of success:

1. **Prioritize Your Life.** Develop a weekly time management schedule in which tasks and activities are **prioritized** (organized by importance). Make sure this schedule:
   • Allows time for studying each specific subject
   • Spreads out study times throughout the week
   • Permits time for recreation and rest and family
   • Grants periodic "rewards," such as social media or lunch out with friends

Make a list of the things you need to do (just as you make a list before you go grocery shopping). Do not create a schedule that is too detailed or rigid. As you progress, make adjustments as needed. Table 2.1 provides an example of a time management schedule.

2. **Learn How to Study.** Choose a quiet, suitable area where you:
   • Can concentrate
   • Will have minimal interruptions
   • Can be comfortable enough to focus on your work
   • Are close to resources (e.g., computer, reference materials)

3. **Develop Positive Personality Traits.** Not everyone is suited to working in the healthcare field. Following is a list of desirable personality traits and qualities of character that experts believe an individual should possess to be successful in this field:
   • Self-discipline
   • A positive attitude
   • **Diligence** (sticking with a task until it is finished)
   • **Integrity** (having honest ethical and moral principles)
   • **Objectivity** (not influenced by personal feelings, biases, or prejudices)
   • **Initiative** (readiness and ability to take action)
   • **Enthusiasm** (positive motivation to fulfill assigned duties and responsibilities)

 Stop and Think

Reread the personality traits listed. Do you understand what each one means? Review the definition for each. Do you think you possess all of these personality traits? If there are any traits that you think you do not have or that you might need to improve on, list them along with ideas on how to develop these traits or make them better.

4. **Prepare for Class.** Getting the most out of the courses you take involves effort on your part. The time and effort you invest in your preparation before class and the time you spend in class greatly affect what you get out of your schooling:
   • Attend every class and be on time.
   • Become an active participant—ask questions and take notes.
   • Learn to recognize important points in the text and from lectures.
   • Outline, underline, highlight, or make notes in the text margins.
   • Work through questions and examples until you understand them.
   • Communicate with your instructor and other students.

Table 2.1   **Time Management Schedule**

TIME	SUN	MON	TUES	WED	THURS	FRI	SAT
6:00	Sleep	Shower/eat	Shower/eat	Shower/eat	Shower/eat	Shower/eat	Sleep
7:00	Personal	Personal	Personal	Personal	Personal	Personal	
8:00	Breakfast	Bus	Bus	Bus	Bus	Bus	Personal/ breakfast
9:00	Family	Group discussion	Computer Lab	Group discussion	Computer Lab	Group discussion	Chores
10:00	Business Policy	Marketing Communications	Business Policy	Marketing Communications	Business Policy		
11:00	Self	Marketing Research	Library	Marketing Research	Library	Marketing Research	Self
12:00	Lunch	Lunch	Lunch	Lunch			
1:00	Lunch	Writing Lab	Lunch	Writing Lab	Lunch	Writing Lab	Chores
2:00	Group study	Group study/ research	Group study/ research	Shopping			
3:00	Expository Writing	Business and Professional Speaking	Expository Writing	Business and Professional Speaking	Expository Writing		
4:00	Chores	Bus	Sales Management	Bus	Sales Management	Bus	Recreation and rest
5:00	Dinner/ recreation and rest	Bus	Dinner/ recreation and rest	Bus	Dinner/ recreation and rest		
6:00	Dinner	Chores	Dinner/ recreation and rest	Chores	Dinner/ recreation and rest	Write paper for Expository Writing	Family
7:00	Study	Study	Bus/shopping	Study	Chores	Recreation and rest	

- Become a good listener.
- Complete all homework and assigned readings on time.
- Develop the ability to concentrate.
- Enhance your reading comprehension. (After you read a section of the text, stop and ask yourself, "What are they trying to get across to me?")
- **Paraphrase** (write down in your own words) important facts from lectures and readings.

! Stop and Think

Think about each of the bulleted points. Why do you think each one is important to your success as a student and as a career professional? Develop a plan for effective studying. Compare your study plan with the plans of your peers and share ideas. Keep working on your study plan until you have developed one that works for you.

In addition to the previously listed classroom skills, individuals experienced in working as health insurance professionals suggest that candidates for this field should be able to do the following:

- Pay attention to detail.
- Follow directions.
- Work independently without supervision.
- Understand the need for and possess a strong sense of **professional ethics** (moral principles associated with a specific vocation).
- Understand the need for and possess strong people skills (ability to communicate effectively with all types of individuals at all levels).
- Demonstrate patience and an even temperament.
- Be empathetic without being sympathetic.
- Be organized but flexible.
- Be conscientious.
- Demonstrate a sense of responsibility.
- Possess manual dexterity.
- Understand and respect the importance of confidentiality.
- Demonstrate a willingness to learn.

It is also important that a health insurance professional be proficient in using the computer and software programs, such as Word and Excel, for letter writing and creating reports.

 What Did You Learn?

1. List five required classroom skills that help ensure success as a health insurance professional.
2. Why is "preparation" an important key to success?
3. List five "on-the-job" skills that experienced health insurance professionals should possess.

Imagine This!

Sandra Bence-Franklin works for New Beauty Products, Inc., a large cosmetics firm, where her responsibilities are limited to handling incoming calls on a complicated telephone system and greeting and directing customers. Although the pay and benefits are good, she has quickly become bored and disillusioned with her job. She desires more challenge and variety. Her cousin Lisa, a health insurance professional, has recently been hired at Walden-Martin Family Medicine Clinic. Lisa talks constantly about the variety and challenges of her new job, remarking, "I'm doing something different every day. I'm learning so much, and it's so interesting! I really feel I'm making a difference when I help a patient understand the confusing issues of health insurance."

After thinking about what Lisa had told her, Sandra muses, "Maybe I should look into what a career as a health insurance professional has to offer me."

JOB DUTIES AND RESPONSIBILITIES

We mentioned earlier that there are different career options you can choose that are covered under the general umbrella term *health insurance*. The title we have chosen is "health insurance professional," which includes the knowledge and expertise associated with that of medical billing, generating insurance claims, and coding. Table 2.2 lists the various job titles under this specialty and their corresponding duties.

Another positive aspect of the health insurance professional's career is the variety of tasks and responsibilities it offers. These vary from office to office, depending on the number of employees, the degree of job specialization, and the type of practice; however, the variety of roles and job **autonomy** (working without direct supervision) make this profession attractive to many individuals. Typical duties of health insurance professionals might include, but are not limited to, the following:

- Scheduling appointments
- Bookkeeping and other administrative duties
- Explaining insurance benefits to patients
- Handling day-to-day medical billing procedures
- Adhering to each insurance carrier's guidelines
- Documenting all activities using correct techniques and medical terminology
- Keeping current on coding and compliance

Table 2.2 Job Titles Included Under the Umbrella of the Health Insurance Professional

JOB TITLE	ROLE/DUTIES
Claims Assistant Professional (CAP)	Assists patients/consumers in obtaining full benefits from healthcare coverage under private or government health insurance and coordinates with healthcare providers to avoid duplication of payment and overpayment.
Medical Coder/ Coding Specialist	Possesses expertise in assigning diagnostic and procedural codes using common coding manuals (ICD-10-CM, ICD-10-PCS, and CPT).
Medical Claims Processor	Prepares and transmits claims by paper and electronically using the computer.
Reimbursement Specialist	Checks and verifies records, prepares insurance claims, posts ledger and general journal entries, balances accounts payable and accounts receivable records, and follows up on claims and delinquent reimbursements.
Billing Coordinator	Responsible for maintaining patient accounts and for collecting money. Also may create and file insurance claims and handle accounts receivable.
Patient Account Representative	Obtains patient insurance information, confirms appointments, verifies insurance eligibility, and enters/ updates insurance information in the records and computer.
Medical Claims Reviewer	Analyzes claims for "medical necessity" and valid policy coverage. Performs audits on charge entry for accuracy and HIPAA and Office of Inspector General compliance. Supports/maintains all forms of billing, payment posting, refunds, and credentialing and system issues.
Medical Claims Analyst	Assists with claim rule setup and maintenance, medical claim–related data mapping, claim analysis, and other tasks related to supporting client claims and medical coding.
Electronic Claims Processor	Sets up and implements electronic claims processing (in standardized formats) via electronic modes and transmits claims to third-party payers.
Medical Collector	Handles inquiries regarding patient account balances and insurance submission dates. Proficient in collection laws and collection techniques used to settle delinquent accounts and maximize reimbursements.

CPT, Current Procedural Terminology; *HIPAA*, Health Insurance Portability and Accountability Act; *ICD-10-CM*, International Classification of Diseases, 10th revision, Clinical Modification; *ICD-10-PCS*, International Classification of Diseases, 10th revision, Procedure Coding System.

- Completing insurance forms promptly and accurately
- Knowing and complying with laws and regulations
- Entering computer data
- Interpreting explanations of benefits (EOBs)
- Posting payments to patient accounts
- Corresponding with patients and insurance companies

? What Did You Learn?

1. List at least eight of the specialized fields that are included under the general umbrella of a health insurance professional.
2. Why do you think autonomy might be attractive to some career-minded individuals?
3. List six typical duties of a health insurance professional.

CAREER PROSPECTS

Individuals who choose a career in a healthcare field, such as health insurance, have an opportunity to work in a variety of professional locations, including the following:

- Physicians' or dentists' offices
- Hospitals and urgent care facilities
- Pharmacies
- Nursing homes
- Home health agencies
- Mental health facilities
- Physical therapy and rehabilitation centers
- Insurance companies
- Managed care organizations
- Consulting firms
- Health data organizations

Successful completion of a health insurance program gives the student the training and skills to become a health insurance professional, which includes the various subspecialties. If an individual decides to become a medical coder, the education and knowledge of healthcare and disease processes that he or she learned while taking educational courses or on the job gives the individual a good background if he or she chooses to become certified in this specialty. In the past, many coders were employed in hospitals; however, the growth of ambulatory care facilities and outpatient clinics has greatly increased the demand for employees with a solid background in coding and excellent computer skills.

 HIPAA Tip

One goal of the administrative simplification provisions of the Health Insurance Portability and Accountability Act (HIPAA) is to reduce the number of forms and methods of completing claims and other payment-related documents through the efficient use of computer-to-computer methods of exchanging standard healthcare information.

 Stop and Think

The text stated that the numbers of ambulatory care facilities and outpatient clinics are increasing. What do you think has triggered this growth, and how does it affect health insurance professionals?

OCCUPATIONAL TRENDS AND FUTURE OUTLOOK

Most healthcare providers in the United States today rely heavily on health insurance professionals and medical billing and coding specialists for better customer relations, as well as assistance in maximum third-party reimbursement for their professional services. It is therefore important that those individuals wishing to enter this medical career specialty clearly understand the educational requirements, training, earning potential, and home business options. They should also be aware of any potential "downsides" of a career as a health insurance professional. Knowing what to expect and where the challenges lie will provide students with the right tools and give them the best chance to succeed in their chosen career path.

Following are some factors currently affecting careers as health insurance professionals and medical billers or coders:

- *Expanding electronic health record adoption:* In 2011 the National Center for Health Statistics found that 55% of physicians had adopted an electronic health record (EHR) system. Today, almost 9 in 10 (86%) office-based physicians report that they have adopted some type of EHR system.
- *Evolution of coding:* The development and adoption of the International Classification of Diseases, 10th revision (ICD-10) coding system, which provides greater specificity to diagnoses, allows policymakers, healthcare providers, and third-party payers to improve reimbursement systems. ICD-10 means more accurate medical billing and coding, which translates to more jobs with higher salaries as providers make the transition to ICD-10.
- *Advancing information technology (IT):* Although IT continues to advance healthcare in a positive way, it will not completely replace human expertise. Advancement opportunities in a health insurance career are virtually unlimited. Employment prospects exist in medical facilities ranging in size from a small staff of one or two healthcare providers to several hundred providers in a multispecialty group practice. An American Hospital Association survey showed that nearly 18% of billing and coding positions are unfilled because of a lack of qualified candidates.

The US Bureau of Labor Statistics reports that employment for medical records and health information technicians will grow by 13% through 2026. Overall, careers in healthcare occupations have a bright future in continuing to help the US healthcare system save money, improve patient care, and enhance efficiency.

As an alternative to working in a medical office as an employee, the health insurance professional has the option of working independently from a home-based office. Many electronic billing programs are available and can be set up through home office computers. This, however, can be a challenge for beginners, because it takes time and experience to learn the rules and to become accustomed to the various third-party claims processes. Also, there is the possibility of becoming an independent insurance specialist or consultant, who contracts to do coding and claims submission for healthcare providers who do not have the ability or workforce to do it themselves. Another possibility is to work as a consultant to help patients understand their insurance bills and what they should be paying.

The Health Insurance Portability and Accountability Act (HIPAA) of 1996 has encouraged the healthcare industry to move from paper claims transactions to electronic transactions using one national standard format. This situation has created tremendous job opportunities for health insurance professionals to help noncompliant providers achieve HIPAA compliance. More information can be learned about HIPAA by logging on to and studying the "Websites to Explore" at the end of this chapter.

◎ HIPAA Tip

HIPAA, created to reduce healthcare costs and protect patient privacy (through the use of an electronic data interchange [EDI]), has established rigorous standards and requirements for the maintenance and transmission of healthcare information. Healthcare providers, insurers, and clearinghouses need specialists with HIPAA training and HIPAA certification to ensure that medical facilities are in compliance with HIPAA's rules and regulations to help them avoid federal penalties.

WHAT TO EXPECT AS A HEALTH INSURANCE PROFESSIONAL

Following are nine steps explaining how to pursue a career as a health insurance professional and what to expect. These steps are provided for students to use as a guideline for success.

Step 1: Research duties and responsibilities. As mentioned previously, the student should be aware of the duties and responsibilities required to become a successful health insurance professional. When a patient receives healthcare services, each office visit and/or procedure performed must be assigned a specific code. Also, the patient's **diagnosis** (the reason he or she sought medical care) must be assigned a code. These codes, along with the corresponding charges, are submitted to the insurance company for payment decisions. After the insurer makes its decision, both the provider and the patient receive notification of how the claim was **adjudicated** (payment determination).

An EOB document is provided by the insurer that indicates the amount of the insurance payment and any remaining balance for which the patient is responsible. The health insurance professional is involved throughout this entire process.

Step 2: Enroll in a formal training program. Education for health insurance professionals can vary, ranging from a diploma or certificate to an associate degree. Many community colleges and career schools offer a variety of allied health programs, both online classes and day, evening, and weekend classes, in an institutional environment. Associate of applied science degrees, which normally take 2 years to complete, can lead to higher salaries and expanded career opportunities.

Step 3: Become certified. Numerous options are available for certification, depending on the employer's preferences and the individual's career goals. The American Medical Billing Association (AMBA) (http://www.ambanet.net/AMBA.htm) offers an examination to qualify as a Certified Medical Reimbursement Specialist (CMRS). An entry-level certification called *Certified Coding Associate (CCA)* is also available from the American Health Information Management Association (AHIMA) (http://www.ahima.org/).

The American Academy of Professional Coders (AAPC) also offers certifications for hospital, outpatient, and payer employees who use coding in their work (see "Certification Possibilities" later in the chapter for further certification opportunities).

Step 4: Obtain employment. In addition to physicians' offices, insurance companies, hospitals, pharmacies, and government entities make use of health insurance professionals. An individual trained in this field but not yet certified may be able to acquire an entry-level position and pursue certification later. After acquiring a position within a medical facility, the person must work diligently to gain the experience needed to specialize in the field of health insurance professional. He or she should also be willing to learn and acquire new skills outside the job duties to enhance advancement opportunities.

Step 5: Learn and perform your job duties. It is important to study and learn the claims submission process from beginning to end. If a claim is rejected, determine the reason by reviewing the claim. The insurance company usually offers a code that explains the specific reason for the rejection. Make any corrections or adjustments necessary and resubmit all related charges. Making sure the claim is "clean" before submission will help you avoid losing valuable time. Always verify the correct spelling of the patient's (and the insured's) name, date of birth, sex, and insurance identification number. Contact the patient if the information is not available in the file.

Step 6: Posting payments. All payments received, either from the insurer or from the patient, should be posted promptly to the patient's account, and any contractual adjustments should be made as required by law. Sometimes insurance companies make errors when calculating payments; therefore it is important to check these amounts during the posting process to ensure accuracy. Follow the specific guidelines of the insurer for submitting original or corrected claims and for appealing rejected claims.

Step 7: Reporting denied charges to a coding specialist. The law requires that only certified coders make changes to a patient's medical codes once it is determined that an error has occurred. If the health insurance professional is not a certified coder, all denied charges caused by coding errors should be referred to the coding specialist in the appropriate department.

Step 8: Generate and maintain a log. It is recommended that health insurance professionals keep a detailed log of all conversations with either the patient or the insurance company. Such a log will provide detailed information to anyone who needs to examine the account for an accurate and up-to-date report of the status of the account. Many patient accounting software programs have features that allow this process.

Step 9: Benefit from job security and flexibility. Advances in electronic billing have made it possible for some health insurance professionals and medical billing specialists to work from their homes. An experienced professional may be able to start a home business to provide insurance, billing, and coding services on a contractual basis. Home-based careers are discussed in more detail in the next section.

Home-Based Careers

With the advent of more sophisticated computer technology and the Internet, career opportunities in home-based medical billing and coding, as both part-time and full-time endeavors, are growing. Numerous online courses in this subspecialty are offered, as are courses in career schools. Experts in this field suggest that if the idea of self-employment appeals to you, do some thorough research before you begin this venture.

The basics to get started are a personal computer (ideally no more than 2 years old) and access to the Internet via the most recent version of a web browser (e.g., Google Chrome, Mozilla Firefox, Opera, Microsoft Edge, or Apple Safari) and antivirus software such as Bitdefender or Norton Antivirus Plus. Minimum requirements vary depending on personal preference and usage, but for basic email, Internet access, word processing, and spreadsheet generation, at least a 1-GHz processor (or better), a 2-GB minimum of memory (RAM), and a 250-GB hard drive are considered adequate. Keep in mind that these minimum requirements are upgraded every year or more often and that keeping your system as up to date as possible will enhance performance. After that, you need to find clients to support your home-based business. Consult with organizations for medical claims processors or medical billing businesses and with doctors in your community. Ask them the following about the medical billing field:

- How much of a need is there for this type of work?
- How much work does medical billing entail?
- What kind of training is required?
- Do they know anything about the promotion or promoter that you are interested in?

Be aware of unsubstantiated dollar-earning possibilities, though. The Federal Trade Commission (FTC) has brought charges against promoters of medical billing opportunities for misrepresenting the earnings potential of their businesses and for failing to provide key preinvestment information required by law.

For additional information on home-based careers, see "Websites to Explore" at the end of this chapter.

REWARDS

Individuals working as health insurance professionals enjoy many benefits, such as job security, a good income, personal satisfaction, and challenges. One of the biggest rewards is the knowledge that they are helping people. As for earnings, a graduate of a health insurance professional program can expect to earn $12 to $15 per hour upon entry to the workforce, depending on his or her geographic area of the United States. This base wage typically increases rapidly as the individual gains experience and success in the field. Certified coders, at the same time, can expect to earn between $30,000 and $60,000 per year, depending on experience, credentials, location, and education. For income ranges in various allied health occupations, refer to the Bureau of Labor Statistics website listed in "Websites to Explore" at the end of this chapter.

> **? What Did You Learn?**
>
> 1. How has HIPAA opened up opportunities for health insurance professionals?
> 2. What does the text suggest might be the biggest reward for health insurance professionals?

IS A CAREER IN HEALTHCARE RIGHT FOR YOU?

Health-related professions offer an exciting and satisfying career with exceptional challenges and opportunities for growth. With dozens of specialized health careers, an individual can use almost any talent he or she has. With such a variety of choices and specializations, there is a place in healthcare for anyone who chooses to follow this career path.

To see whether healthcare is a good career choice for you, take the short quiz in Box 2.2. When you are finished, add up the number of times you selected "yes." If you checked seven or more boxes "yes," a career in healthcare may be right for you!

Box **2.2**	Is Healthcare Right for You?

YES	NO	
☐	☐	I am interested in health and science classes.
☐	☐	I am an active listener.
☐	☐	I enjoy helping people.
☐	☐	I might like helping people who are sick or injured.
☐	☐	I find working with equipment and technology appealing.
☐	☐	I am an even-tempered person.
☐	☐	I take satisfaction in working as a member of a team.
☐	☐	I find having responsibilities inviting.
☐	☐	I am an effective communicator.
☐	☐	I fare well under stress.
☐	☐	I perform competently in math.
☐	☐	I would prefer to have flexibility in my work schedule.
☐	☐	I enjoy meeting new people.
☐	☐	I am fascinated about the human body and how it works.
☐	☐	I delight in solving problems.
☐	☐	I take pleasure in carrying out instructions acceptably.
☐	☐	I am able to follow directions.
☐	☐	I aspire to work in a laboratory.

CERTIFICATION POSSIBILITIES

Graduates of a health insurance professional program can be eligible for many different professional certifications that would enhance their careers. **Certification** is the culmination of a process of formal recognition of the competence possessed by an individual. In many vocational training institutions, certification is rewarded as recognition of the successful completion of a vocational training process, based on the time of training and practice and on the evaluated contents. Certification possibilities available to the health insurance professional include, but are not necessarily limited to, the following:

- Certified Medical Assistant (CMA)
- Registered Medical Assistant (RMA)
- Professional Association of Healthcare Coding Specialists (PAHCS)
- American Academy of Professional Coders (AAPC)
- Certified Professional Coder (CPC)
- Certified Professional Coder for Hospitals (CPC-H)
- American Health Information Management Association (AHIMA)
- Certified Coding Specialist (CCS)
- Certified Coding Associate (CCA)
- Certified Coding Specialist for Physicians (CCS-P)

Additional national certifications for the health insurance professional are the Nationally Certified Insurance and Coding Specialist (NCICS) through the National Center for Competency Testing (NCCT), and Certified Medical Reimbursement Specialist (CMRS) offered by the American Medical Billing Association (AMBA).

AHIMA also offers certification in the other areas, such as:

- Health Information Management
- Registered Health Information Administrator (RHIA)
- Registered Health Information Technician (RHIT)
- Certified Health Data Analyst (CHDA)
- Certified in Healthcare Privacy and Security (CHPS)
- Certified Documentation Improvement Practitioner (CDIP)
- Certified Professional in Health Informatics (CPHI)

For additional possibilities of career-related certifications, see "Websites to Explore" at the end of this chapter.

Individuals who are trained and certified as health insurance professionals, coders, and collection specialists have a basic goal: *to ensure that providers (and patients) get paid correctly the first time, every time, on time.* The ever-increasing complexity of diagnosis and treatment codes, coupled with the confusing and often seemingly contradictory guidelines for what various insurance carriers will accept as a claim, makes it almost impossible for healthcare providers to stay on top of the constantly changing healthcare scene and still maintain maximum cash flow.

The US Department of Labor states that continued employment growth for health insurance professionals is spurred by the increased medical needs of an aging population and the number of healthcare practitioners. Federal regulations and confusing health insurance policies also have created a strong demand for professionals who can comprehend and perform successfully the demanding role of compliance and provider education. The Department of Labor posts current statistics and quick facts by job description on its Occupational Outlook Handbook at http://www.bls.gov/ooh/a-z-index.htm.

Computers have dramatically transformed the health insurance industry by enabling the health insurance professional to focus on accuracy and efficiency instead of the cumbersome task of manually processing each claim. This change has brought health insurance billing into the limelight as one of the fastest-growing disciplines in the workforce today. Health insurance professionals not only are in high demand but also have a secure future in the world of medicine.

[?] What Did You Learn?

1. List at least four certification possibilities available to health insurance professionals.
2. What is the basic goal of health insurance professionals, coders, and collection specialists?
3. True or false: Computers have reduced the demand for health insurance professionals.

CAREER FOCUS FOR THE HEALTH INSURANCE PROFESSIONAL

The focus of your career as a health insurance professional is the insurance claim. After completion of this course, you will be able to identify each major health insurance payer; its individual rules, guidelines, and procedures; and the relevant information that must be collected to submit a claim. Basically, there are two methods of claims submission: electronic and paper.

ELECTRONIC CLAIMS

Since 2003 the Centers for Medicare and Medicaid Services (CMS)—the US federal agency that administers Medicare, Medicaid, and the Children's Health Insurance Program (CHIP)—has required all physicians, providers, and suppliers who bill Medicare carriers, fiscal intermediaries (FIs), Medicare Administrative Contractors (MACs) for Parts A and B, and Durable Medical Equipment MACs (DME MACs) for services provided to Medicare beneficiaries to submit claims electronically (with a few exceptions) (see Box 6.1, "Exceptions to HIPAA's Electronic Claim Submission Requirements," in Chapter 6). In March 2009 the secretary of the US Department of Health and Human Services (HHS) adopted ASC X12 5010 (Version 5010) as the next standard for HIPAA-covered transactions. This change accommodated the expanded diagnostic coding system, International Classification of Diseases, 10th revision (ICD-10), which was implemented on October 1, 2015. The date on which all covered entities were to be in full compliance with Version 5010 was June 30, 2012.

Level I compliance means that a **covered entity** (a healthcare provider, a health plan, or a healthcare claims clearinghouse) can clearly demonstrate the ability to successfully create and receive compliant transactions using the 5010 version.

Level II compliance means that a covered entity has completed "end-to-end testing" with each of its **trading partners** (any business entity engaging in **electronic data interchange (EDI)**—the computer-to-computer exchange of structured information) and is able to consistently transmit claims electronically using the newer version of the standards.

Electronic claims submission using Version 5010 and the ICD-10 diagnostic coding system is discussed in more detail later in the text. For an overview of Version 5010, visit the cms.gov website. As mentioned, the date for all covered entities to be in compliance with Version 5010 was June 30, 2012.

CMS-1500 (02/12) UNIVERSAL PAPER FORM

Even though CMS mandates that insurance claims be submitted electronically using the specific format as discussed in the previous section, there are exceptions to this rule. If a paper claim form is going to be submitted, it must be the **CMS-1500 claim form**, which is the standard insurance form used by all government and most commercial insurance payers. It is also known as the universal claim form. The information required on a paper claim form is the same as that required in the electronic format. The CMS-1500 claim form will be discussed further in Chapter 6. For an overview of the CMS-1500 claim form visit the cms.gov website.

? What Did You Learn?

1. True or false: CMS mandates that insurance claims be submitted electronically.
2. The universal form accepted for submitting paper claims is the _____.

SUMMARY CHECKPOINTS

- College entry-level skills necessary for success as a health insurance professional include reading and comprehension, basic business math, English and grammar, oral and written communication, keyboarding and office skills, and computer application skills.
- College courses that typically comprise a health insurance billing and coding program include, but are not limited to, the following:
  - Medical Terminology
  - Anatomy and Physiology
  - Medical Law and Ethics
  - Medical Records Management
  - Current Procedural Terminology (CPT) Coding
  - International Classification of Diseases, 10th revision, Clinical Modification (ICD-10-CM) Coding
  - Medical Insurance Billing
  - Information Technology and Computers
- Effective study skills and proper preparation are important components for getting the most out of an education and optimizing career potential. Success in these areas assists "lifelong learning."
- An effective plan that organizes and prioritizes study time along with other activities is important to the overall learning process. Time management schedules are excellent tools to help students develop better study skills, but they should not be too detailed or rigid. Allow for adjustments as needed to accommodate time not only for studying but also for relaxation and rewards. It is suggested that students develop a time management chart and continue it through their employment.
- Some of the personality traits and on-the-job skills that health insurance professionals should possess to optimize career success include:
  - Self-discipline
  - A positive attitude
  - Diligence
  - Integrity
  - Objectivity
  - Initiative
  - Enthusiasm

- Several different job titles, each with its corresponding duties, are included under the general umbrella of "health insurance professional." Job titles and duties vary from office to office, depending on the number of employees, the type of medical practice, and the degree of job specialization. Refer to Table 2.2 for a classification of various job titles and the duties associated with them.
- Career prospects and job opportunities for health insurance professionals include, but are not limited to, physicians' or dentists' offices, hospitals, pharmacies, nursing homes, mental health facilities, rehabilitation centers, insurance companies, managed care organizations, consulting firms, and health data organizations.
- Health insurance professionals and similar healthcare careers offer job security, good income, personal satisfaction, challenges, and satisfying experiences as possible rewards, plus the most important reward of all—helping people.
- Professional certifications that enhance the careers of health insurance professionals include CPC certification, the AHIMA CCS and CCA certifications, and NCCT and NCICS certification.
- Two methods of submitting insurance claims are:
  - Electronic submission using Version 5010 as required by CMS (with certain exceptions)
  - CMS-1500 (02/12) universal paper form

🔍 Closing Scenario

Rachel spent a fair amount of time investigating the different options available for certification as a health insurance professional. She chose an accredited program that would give her a credential that would be well accepted in her community. She also took the time to investigate the various job titles and responsibilities to find the right fit. Her job at Walden-Martin Family Medicine Clinic may allow her to work from home in the future, and this is one of the reasons she was drawn to the position.

Her education prepared her well for the job by providing her with a strong understanding of the electronic claims process that is vital for ensuring the proper reimbursement for her employer.

Rachel is very satisfied with her career change and is looking forward to the challenges provided by being a health insurance professional.

CHAPTER REVIEW QUESTIONS

1. Important computer application skills for a health insurance professional include the ability to use all of the following except:
   a. Windows
   b. Internet
   c. Google
   d. Microsoft Word

2. Insurance billing professional programs include core courses and specialized courses. An example of a specialized course is:
   a. Medical Terminology
   b. Anatomy and Physiology
   c. Keyboarding
   d. Current Procedural Terminology (CPT) Coding

3. What is the definition of "lifelong learning"?
   a. Learning about the different lifespan stages.
   b. Continuing to learn throughout your career.
   c. Using your education during the span of your career.
   d. Starting college after the age of 30.

4. Sticking with a task until it is finished is the definition of:
   a. Diligence
   b. Integrity
   c. Objectivity
   d. Initiative

5. Health insurance professionals have a great deal of autonomy in their jobs. What is the definition of autonomy?
   a. Having honest ethical and moral principles.
   b. Working without direct supervision.
   c. Readiness and ability to take action.
   d. Positive motivation to fulfill assigned duties and responsibilities.

6. How many office-based physicians have adopted some type of EHR system?
   a. 55%
   b. 64%
   c. 72%
   d. 86%

7. The basic goal for health insurance professionals, coders, and collection specialists is:
   a. To ensure that their training is up to date.
   b. To ensure that providers and patients get paid correctly the first time, every time, on time.
   c. To ensure that HIPAA is not violated.
   d. To ensure that patient statements are generated in a timely fashion.

8. What is the format required by CMS for electronic claim submission?
   a. Version 5010
   b. CMS-1500
   c. UB-04
   d. None of the above

9. The universal claim form is:
   a. Version 5010
   b. CMS-1500
   c. UB-04
   d. None of the above

10. Computer-to-computer exchange of structured information is the definition of:
    a. HIPAA
    b. EDI
    c. CMS
    d. FTC

WEBSITES TO EXPLORE

- For live links to the following websites, please visit the Evolve website at http://evolve.elsevier.com/Beik/today.
- For a listing of health-related careers and occupations, go to http://www.bls.gov/ooh/.
- AHIMA has a good website for health information technology careers. For more information, log on to http://www.ahima.org/ and use the key words "health information technology careers."
- You also may want to explore medical billing and coding blogs: https://blog.feedspot.com/medical_billing_and_coding_blogs/.
- For additional possibilities of career-related certifications, explore these websites:
  http://www.aapc.com
  http://www.pmimd.com
  http://www.ahima.org/

- For a complete account of the HIPAA of 1996, log on to and peruse the following websites:
  https://www.hhs.gov/hipaa/index.html
  http://whatishipaa.org/.
- Additional websites to explore for certification possibilities:
  http://www.aama-ntl.org/
  http://www.americanmedtech.org

Author's Note: Due to the dynamic nature of the Internet, web addresses and/or links provided in this chapter may have changed since publication and may no longer be valid. In such cases, students should select comparable search words to access related sites.

3

The Legal and Ethical Side of Health Insurance

Chapter Outline

Chapter Objectives

After completion of this chapter, the student should be able to:

1. Discuss employer and employee liability.
2. List and explain the elements of a legal contract.
3. Name and briefly discuss important legislative acts affecting health insurance.
4. Compare and contrast medical ethics and medical etiquette and explain their importance in the workplace.
5. State the basic purposes and components of a medical health record.
6. Describe the issues of medical health record ownership, retention, access, and release.
7. Discuss the requirements of appropriate medical health record documentation.
8. List legal and ethical responsibilities of ancillary staff members.
9. Identify HIPAA's primary objectives.
10. Discuss HIPAA's impact on healthcare personnel and patients, providers, and businesses.
11. Demonstrate an understanding of privacy and confidentiality laws.
12. List the exceptions to privacy and confidentiality laws.
13. Define and contrast fraud and abuse.
14. Analyze cause and effect of fraud and abuse in healthcare.
15. List ways to prevent fraud and abuse in the medical office.

Chapter Terms

abandonment	etiquette	offer
abuse	fraud	party of the first part (first party)
acceptance	implied contract	party of the second part (second party)
accountability	implied promises	
ancillary	incidental disclosure	party of the third part (third party)
binds	Joint Commission, The	portability
breach of confidentiality	litigious	privacy
confidentiality	medical ethics	privacy statement
consideration	medical etiquette	*respondeat superior*
durable power of attorney	medical (health) record	*subpoena duces tecum*
emancipated minor	mentally competent	
ethics	negligence	

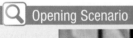 Opening Scenario

Callie Casper has been working at Walden-Martin Family Medical Clinic for several years as a health insurance professional. She truly enjoys the work she does and finds the laws associated with this area of healthcare really interesting. She recognizes how important it is for her to stay current and observant of those laws. The healthcare facility could be put at risk if she even inadvertently does something wrong.

Having a good understanding of the laws and what constitutes fraud and abuse has allowed Callie to obtain the highest level of reimbursement for Walden-Martin Family Medical Clinic. She has also seen how that understanding can help her explain to patients why things are done in a certain way. This open communication has helped to build positive relationships with the patients.

The subject of medical law and ethics would fill volumes of books. So as not to overwhelm you, this chapter attempts to zero in on what we think a health insurance professional should know to perform his or her job accurately and efficiently while maintaining confidentiality and sensitivity to patients' rights.

The practice of medicine is, after all, a business—not unlike an auto body shop. The auto body shop's goal is to fix cars; the healthcare facility's goal is to fix people. Although the healthcare facility may be more charitable, the bottom line of both (unless the healthcare facility qualifies as a nonprofit organization) is to produce revenue.

The primary goals of the health insurance professional are to complete and submit insurance claims and to conduct billing and collection procedures that enable him or her to generate as much money for the practice as legally and ethically possible that the medical health record will support in the least amount of time. To do this, the health insurance professional must be knowledgeable in the area of medical law and liability.

MEDICAL LAW AND LIABILITY

Medical law and liability can vary widely from state to state; however, some rules and regulations affect healthcare facilities in the United States as a whole. The health insurance professional should become familiar with the medical laws and liability issues in his or her state and should follow them conscientiously. The following sections discuss various aspects of medical law and liability.

EMPLOYER LIABILITY

In our **litigious** (quick to bring lawsuits) society, people tend to hold physicians to a higher standard than those in other professions, and the slightest breach of healthcare can end up as a malpractice lawsuit. Often these lawsuits are settled out of court—not because the healthcare provider was afraid that he or she would be found negligent and wanted to avoid publicity, but because of cost.

 Imagine This!

A well-known medical talk show host tells of a situation in which his TV crew was filming a critically ill patient in a California hospital. A woman in Texas saw the episode and sued, claiming that the hospital patient was her mother who had recently died. The film did not show the woman from the front, but the camera clearly showed items that accurately identified the hospital where the actual filming took place. The talk show host won the lawsuit, but it cost nearly $20,000 in court costs and legal fees to clear everything up.

EMPLOYEE LIABILITY

No matter what the employee's position is or how much education he or she has had, direct and indirect patient contact involves ethical and legal responsibility. Although we all know that professional healthcare providers have a responsibility for their own actions, what about the health insurance professional? Can he or she be a party to a legal action in the event of error or omission? The answer is yes!

You may have heard the Latin term *respondeat superior (ree-spond-dee-at superior)*. The English translation is "Let the master answer." *Respondeat superior* is a key principle in business law that says that an employer is responsible for the actions of his or her employees in the "course of employment." For instance, if a truck driver for Express Delivery, Inc., hits a child in the street because of **negligence** (failure to exercise a reasonable degree of care), the company for which the driver works (Express Delivery) most likely would have the primary burden of liability for the injuries. This does not let the driver off the hook completely. He or she could also be sued.

Like the truck driver, the **ancillary** members of the medical team (e.g., nurses, medical assistants, health insurance professionals, technicians) cannot avoid legal responsibility altogether. They also can be named as parties to a lawsuit. However, it is usually the healthcare provider who bears the financial brunt of legal action because he or she is what is referred to as the "deep pocket," or the person or corporation with the most money.

 Stop and Think

Marcy Knox worked as a health insurance professional in a large medical center where there were many professional offices. One day, as she was delivering some paperwork to a psychiatrist's office on the same floor, she spotted a former teacher waiting in the reception area. At lunch, Marcy met Sherry, a former classmate. "You'll never guess who I saw in Dr. Pilova's office yesterday!" Marcy confided excitedly. Eager to share the news, Marcy didn't wait for her lunch partner to respond. "Our old instructor at Grassland Community College, Mrs. Bitterhaven!" Because Marcy was not actually employed by the psychiatrist's office, was she guilty of a breach of confidentiality in divulging this information to her friend?

 What Did You Learn?

1. What is the primary goal of the health insurance professional?
2. What does the Latin term *respondeat superior* mean?
3. List members of the healthcare team who would typically make up the "ancillary" staff.

INSURANCE AND CONTRACT LAW

Because a health insurance policy and the relationship between a healthcare provider and a patient are considered legal contracts, it is important that the health insurance professional become familiar with the basic concepts of contract law.

ELEMENTS OF A LEGAL CONTRACT

To understand insurance of any kind, you need to have a reasonable knowledge base of the legal framework surrounding it. In other words, you must learn some basic concepts about the law of contracts. For a health insurance policy to be a legally binding contract, it must contain certain elements. These elements are as follows:
1. Offer and acceptance
2. Consideration
3. Legal object (also referred to as "legal subject matter")
4. Competent parties (also referred to as "competency and capacity")
5. Legal form (written contracts only)

Let's take a closer look at each of these five contract elements and apply them to the health insurance contract. We will follow a fictitious character—Jerry Dawson, a self-employed computer consultant—through this process.

Offer and Acceptance

Jerry visits Ned Nelson of Acme Insurance Company and tells him that he wants to purchase a health insurance policy for his family. Jerry completes a lengthy application form detailing his family's medical history. Here, Jerry is making the **offer**—a proposition to create a contract with Ned's company. Ned sends the application to his home office; after verifying the information, someone at the home office might say, "This guy and his family are okay; we'll insure them." This is the **acceptance**; Acme Insurance has agreed to take on Jerry's proposition, or offer. The acceptance occurs when the insurance company **binds** (agrees to accept the individual[s] for benefits) coverage or when the policy is issued.

Consideration

Jerry receives his new insurance contract from Acme. The binding force in any contract that gives it legal status is the **consideration**—the *thing of value* that each party gives to the other. In a health insurance contract, the consideration of the insurance company lies in the promises that make up the contract (e.g., the promise to pay all or part of the insured individual's *covered medical expenses* as set forth in the contract). The promise to pay the premium is the consideration of the individual seeking health insurance coverage.

Legal Object

A contract must be *legal* before it can be enforced. If an individual contracts with another to commit murder for a specified amount of money, that contract would be unenforceable in court because its intent is not legal (murder is against the law). Are we confident that this insurance policy between Jerry, our computer expert, and Acme Insurance Company is legal? We can rest assured that a contract is legal if it contains all of the necessary elements and whatever is being contracted (the object) is not breaking any laws.

Competent Parties (Competency and Capacity)

The parties to the contractual agreement must be **mentally competent**, which means they are capable of understanding the legal implications of entering into a contract in the eyes of the law. Competency typically enters the picture in the case of minors and individuals who are mentally handicapped, except for **emancipated minors**—individuals younger than 18 years who are independent and living away from home. The courts have ruled that if individuals in either of these two categories (mentally handicapped and minors who are not emancipated) enter into a contractual agreement, it is not enforceable because the individuals might not understand all of the legal ramifications involved. To learn more about this competency and capacity, see the applicable link(s) under "Websites to Explore" at the end of this chapter.

Note: The Infirm Persons Act defines a mentally incompetent person as someone whose mind is affected from birth, disease, or injury or by a disorder to such a degree that the person requires care, supervision, and control for his or her own protection, the protection of others, or the protection of his or her property.

Legal Form

Most states require that all types of insurance policies be filed with and approved by the state regulatory authorities before the policy may be sold in that state. This procedure determines whether the policy meets the legal requirements of the state and protects policyholders from unscrupulous insurance companies that might take advantage of them.

TERMINATION OF CONTRACTS

A contract between an insurance company and the insured party can be terminated on mutual agreement or if either party defaults on the provisions in the policy. The insurance company can terminate the policy for nonpayment of premiums or fraudulent action. The insured individual usually can terminate the policy at his or her discretion.

The contract between a healthcare provider and a patient (referred to as an *implied contract*, discussed in the next section) can be terminated by either party; however, when the provider enters into this contractual relationship, he or she must render care for as long as the patient needs it and follows the provider's instructions. The patient can terminate the contract simply by paying all incurred charges and not returning to the practice. The provider must have good reason to withdraw from a particular case and must follow specific guidelines in doing so. Some common reasons for a healthcare provider to stop providing care to a patient are:

- The patient consistently fails to keep appointments.
- The patient's account becomes delinquent (typically 90 days) and he or she makes no effort to arrange for payment.
- The patient refuses to follow the physician's advice.

If it is determined that the provider desires to withdraw from a particular case for a particular reason, it is prudent that he or she:

- Notify the patient in writing of such a decision via certified mail with a return receipt to ensure that the patient is aware of the decision
- Give the patient the names of other qualified healthcare providers, if the patient needs further treatment
- Explain the medical problems that need continued treatment
- State in writing the specific date of the termination, allowing enough time for the patient to find a new healthcare provider

It is important that these steps be followed to avoid a lawsuit for **abandonment**, because abandoning a patient—ceasing to provide care—is considered a breach of contract.

? What Did You Learn?

1. Name and explain the necessary elements that make a contract legally binding.
2. "Competency" enters the picture when what two categories of individuals are considered?
3. What governing bodies typically approve insurance contracts?

MEDICAL LAW AND ETHICS APPLICABLE TO HEALTH INSURANCE

Now that some of the fundamentals of contract law have been presented, we will take a brief look at basic medical law and liability as it applies to health insurance. First, it is important that the health insurance professional understand that the provider-patient relationship is a different kind of contract. The contract (or policy) between our computer consultant and Acme Insurance was a written contract. The relationship between a healthcare provider and a patient is an **implied contract**—meaning that it is not in writing but it has all the components of a legal contract and is just as binding. You have the *offer* (the patient enters the provider's office in anticipation of receiving medical treatment) and the *acceptance* (the provider accepts by granting professional services). The *consideration* here lies in the provider's **implied promises** (promises that are neither spoken nor written but implicated by the individual's actions and performance) to render professional care to the patient to the best of his or her ability (this does not have to be in writing), and the patient's consideration is the promise to pay the provider for these services. This implied contract meets the *legal object* requirement because granting medical care and paying for it are within the limits of the law. The healthcare provider, of legal age and sound mind, and the patient (or the patient's parent or legal guardian, in the case of a minor or mentally handicapped individual) would constitute the competent parties—individuals with the necessary mental capacity or those old enough to enter into a contract. In an implied contract, however, there would be no *legal form* because it is not in writing.

 Stop and Think

Eleanor Stevens is a health insurance professional for Halcyon Medical Clinic. Clara Bartlett, a patient of the clinic, comes in for a sore throat and fever. After the examination, Mrs. Bartlett approaches Eleanor and says, "Hon, I have a really high deductible, but I do have 100% coverage for preventive care. So, I'll have to pay today's charge out of my own pocket. I'm a little short on money this month—the high cost of utilities and all—you understand, don't you? (Sigh.) I'm wondering if you could help me out just a little by fudging something on my claim so that my insurance will pay." How might Eleanor handle this situation?

You might have heard an insurance company referred to as a *third party*. In the implied contract between the physician and patient, the patient is referred to as the **party of the first part (first party)** in legal language and the healthcare provider is the **party of the second part (second party)**. Because insurance companies often are involved in this contract indirectly, they are considered the **party of the third part (third party)**.

 Stop and Think

Ned Farnsworth takes a prescription to the local pharmacy. Ned lives in a small town where everyone knows everybody else, and he frequently plays golf with Archie, the pharmacist. After Archie fills Ned's prescription, Ned says, "Just put this on my bill, Arch. See you next Saturday on the links." Is this transaction a legally binding contract? If so, (1) what kind of a contract took place, and (2) can you identify the four necessary components of this contract?

 Stop and Think

In our scenario with Ned and Archie, identify the party of the first part and the party of the second part. Would there likely be a "third party" involved in this transaction; if so, who would it be?

? What Did You Learn?

1. What is an *implied* contract?
2. True or false: An *implied* contract must be in writing to be enforceable.
3. Explain the function of a *third party* in a contract.

IMPORTANT LEGISLATION AFFECTING HEALTH INSURANCE

Several federal laws have evolved over the past few decades that regulate and act as "watchdogs" over the complicated and confusing world of health insurance.

FEDERAL OMNIBUS BUDGET RECONCILIATION ACT OF 1980

The federal Omnibus Budget Reconciliation Act (OBRA) of 1980 states that Medicare is the secondary payer in the case of an automobile or liability insurance policy. However, if the automobile or liability insurer refuses to pay because of a "Medicare primary clause" in the policy, Medicare becomes the primary payer. If the automobile or liability insurer makes payment after Medicare has paid, the provider (or the patient) must refund the Medicare payment.

TAX EQUITY AND FISCAL RESPONSIBILITY ACT OF 1982

The Tax Equity and Fiscal Responsibility Act (TEFRA) of 1982 made Medicare benefits secondary to benefits payable under employer group health plans for employees age 65 through 69 years and their spouses of the same age group.

CONSOLIDATED OMNIBUS BUDGET RECONCILIATION ACT OF 1986

The Consolidated Omnibus Budget Reconciliation Act (COBRA) of 1986 allows individuals to purchase temporary continuation of group health plan coverage if they are laid off, fired for any reason (other than gross misconduct), or must quit because of an injury or illness. This coverage is temporary (18 months for the employee and 36 months for the spouse) and generally required by companies with 20 or more employees. The former employee is responsible for paying the total cost of the health insurance coverage during the time COBRA is in effect.

FEDERAL FALSE CLAIM AMENDMENTS ACT OF 1986

The False Claims Amendments Act originally was enacted in 1863 because of reports of widespread corruption and fraud in the sale of supplies and provisions to the Union government during the Civil War. This act expands the government's ability to control fraud and abuse in healthcare insurance. Its purpose is to amend the existing civil false claims statute to strengthen and clarify the government's ability to detect and prosecute civil fraud and to recover damages suffered by the government as a result of such fraud. Fraud and abuse are also addressed in the Health Insurance Portability and Accountability Act (HIPAA), discussed later in this chapter.

FRAUD AND ABUSE ACT

The Fraud and Abuse Act addresses the prevention of healthcare fraud and abuse of patients eligible for Medicare and Medicaid benefits. It states that any person who knowingly and willfully breaks the law could be fined, imprisoned, or both. Penalties can result from the following:

- Intentionally using incorrect codes that result in greater payment than appropriate (upcoding)
- Submitting claims for a service or product that is not medically necessary
- Offering payment (or other compensation) to persuade an individual to order from a particular provider or supplier who receives Medicare or state health funds

Federal criminal penalties are established for individuals who:

- Knowingly or purposely defraud a healthcare program
- Knowingly embezzle, steal, or misapply a healthcare benefit program

FEDERAL OMNIBUS BUDGET RECONCILIATION ACT OF 1987

The federal OBRA of 1987 allows current or former employees or dependents younger than 65 years to become eligible for Medicare because of end-stage renal disease (ESRD). When the individual is diagnosed with ESRD and becomes eligible for Medicare, the employer-sponsored group plan is primary (pays first) for a period of up to 12 consecutive months, which begins when a regular course of dialysis is initiated or, in the case of a kidney transplant, in the first month in which the individual becomes entitled to Medicare. If the individual's condition is resulting from a disability other than ESRD, group coverage is primary and Medicare is secondary. (This applies only if the company has at least 100 full-time employees.)

HIPAA'S PRIVACY RULE

HIPAA regulations are divided into four standards or rules: (1) privacy, (2) security, (3) identifiers, and (4) transactions and code sets. The privacy rule is the most complex of the four, setting standards for how protected health information (PHI) "in any form or medium" should be controlled. Privacy rule protections extend to every patient whose information is collected, used, or disclosed by covered entities—healthcare providers, healthcare plans, and healthcare clearinghouses (discussed in a later chapter). The privacy rule imposes responsibilities on the entire workforce of a covered entity—including all employees and volunteers—to secure those rights. It also requires contractual agreements for any business associates of healthcare institutions that handle healthcare information on a covered entity's behalf.

Note: HIPAA is discussed in the preface of this book, and because it affects all facets of health insurance, it will be discussed frequently throughout this chapter as it affects the various elements of health insurance law and ethics (see http://www.HHS.gov for more details on HIPAA's four standards).

THE PATIENT PROTECTION AND AFFORDABLE CARE ACT

The Patient Protection and Affordable Care Act (more commonly referred to as the *Affordable Care Act*) is a federal statute that was signed into law in March 2010. This act and the Health Care and Education Reconciliation Act of 2010 (also signed into law in March 2010) make up the healthcare reform of 2010. These laws focus on reform of the private health insurance market, provide better coverage for those with preexisting conditions, improve prescription drug coverage in Medicare, and extend the life of the Medicare trust fund by at least 12 years. An important component of the act was the removal of the "preexisting condition" regulation that most health insurance policies previously included in their language. The healthcare reform acts have also provided for a patient's bill of rights. To learn more about this legislation and the patient's bill of rights, see the applicable link(s) under "Websites to Explore" at the end of this chapter.

THE SOCIAL SECURITY NUMBER PROTECTION ACT OF 2010

The Social Security Number Protection Act of 2010 prohibits the display of the Social Security account number on any check issued by a federal, state, or local agency. This was done to limit the access to Social Security account numbers and to prevent identity theft.

THE SOCIAL SECURITY NUMBER PROTECTION ACT OF 2011

The Social Security Number Protection Act of 2011 requires the elimination of unnecessary collection, use, and display of Social Security account numbers of Medicare beneficiaries on Medicare identification cards and communications. As a result of this legislation, all Medicare beneficiaries were issued new Medicare identification cards with new numbers, now called Medicare Beneficiary Identifier (MBI). See Chapter 11 for more information.

? What Did You Learn?

1. What legislation established that Medicare is the secondary payer in the case of an automobile or liability insurance policy?
2. For OBRA of 1987 to be applicable, how many employees must the employer have?
3. What is the name of the act that allows individuals the option of continuing their group coverage in case they are laid off or quit their jobs?
4. What did TEFRA of 1982 make Medicare benefits secondary to?

MEDICAL ETHICS AND MEDICAL ETIQUETTE

Most of us are familiar with the Hippocratic Oath. It is a brief description of principles for physicians' conduct that dates to the 5th century BCE. Statements in the oath protect the rights of the patient and oblige the physician to behave voluntarily in a humane and selfless manner toward patients. Although there is no such written or recorded oath for health insurance professionals, certain codes of conduct—referred to as *medical ethics* and *medical etiquette*—are expected of all individuals who work in healthcare.

MEDICAL ETHICS

The word *ethics* comes from the Greek word *ethos*, meaning "character." Broadly speaking, **ethics** are the standards of human conduct—sometimes called *morals* (from the Latin word *mores*, meaning "customs")—of a particular group or culture. Although the terms *ethics* and *morals* often are used interchangeably, they are not the same. *Morals* refer to actions; *ethics* refer to the reasoning behind such actions. Ethics are not the same as laws, and if a member of a particular group or culture breaches one of these principles or customs, he or she probably would not be arrested; however, the group can levy a sanction (punishment) against this person, such as fines, suspension, or even expulsion from the group.

Ethics are a code of conduct of a particular group of people or culture. **Medical ethics** are the code of conduct for the healthcare profession. The American Medical Association (AMA) has long supported certain principles of medical ethics developed primarily for the benefit of patients. These are not laws but socially acceptable principles of conduct, which define the essentials of honorable behavior for healthcare providers. Fig. 3.1 provides a list of professional ethics from the AMA website.

The field of medical ethics is a current area of concern for practitioners and consumers. From the time an individual is conceived until death, there are ethical questions regarding healthcare at every juncture, such as:

- Abortion
- Improving access to care
- Patient relationships
- End-of-life issues
- Patient confidentiality

It is often difficult to distinguish between absolute right and wrong in controversial medical issues. Although laws are universal rules to be observed by everyone, different cultures follow different moral and ethical codes. Who is to say whether these codes are right or wrong? It is sufficient to state here that it is important that all healthcare professionals follow the established standards of conduct issued by these professional organizations to guide their future course of action.

I. A physician shall be dedicated to providing competent medical care, with compassion and respect for human dignity and rights.

II. A physician shall uphold the standards of professionalism, be honest in all professional interactions, and strive to report physicians deficient in character or competence, or engaging in fraud or deception, to appropriate entities.

III. A physician shall respect the law and also recognize a responsibility to seek changes in those requirements, which are contrary to the best interests of the patient.

IV. A physician shall respect the rights of patients, colleagues, and other health professionals, and shall safeguard patient confidences and privacy within the constraints of the law.

V. A physician shall continue to study, apply, and advance scientific knowledge, maintain a commitment to medical education, make relevant information available to patients, colleagues, and the public, obtain consultation, and use the talents of other health professionals when indicated.

VI. A physician shall, in the provision of appropriate patient care, except in emergencies, be free to choose whom to serve, with whom to associate, and the environment in which to provide medical care.

VII. A physician shall recognize a responsibility to participate in activities contributing to the improvement of the community and the betterment of public health.

VIII. A physician shall, while caring for a patient, regard responsibility to the patient as paramount.

IX. A physician shall support access to medical care for all people.

Fig. 3.1 Principles of medical ethics. (From American Medical Association. *Principles of medical ethics.* Revised and adopted by the AMA House of Delegates, June 17, 2001. HSA:10-0390:9/10phy. http://www.ama-assn.org.)

Imagine This!

Marian Grube worked in the spinal and brain injuries ward at Blessing Memorial Hospital. Often, she would relate the sad story of patients who lay there in a vegetative state, dying by inches, to close friends and family members. One such patient was a young man who had been severely injured in a motorcycle accident. As a result of her experiences, Marian became an advocate for wearing helmets while riding motorcycles and bicycles. Once, during a public speaking engagement, she referred to this patient not by name but by condition, using him as an example to drive her point home. The patient's family members complained, and Marian lost her job.

 Stop and Think

Mary Ann was in the hospital for a dilation and curettage and a tubal ligation. Samantha, the nurse on duty, was preparing Mary Ann for the procedure. "Mary Ann," Samantha began, "do you really think that you're doing the right thing?"

"What do you mean?" asked Mary Ann.

"Well," Samantha said, "you're still a young woman, and I notice in the chart that you have only one child. If you go through with this procedure, you will probably never have any more children." Samantha sighed and continued with a note of bitterness, "There are thousands of women in the world who would give anything to become a mother. I know—I'm one of them."

Was Samantha acting ethically? If not, what particular area of ethical conduct was she violating? How do you think this situation should be handled?

MEDICAL ETIQUETTE

Although etiquette and ethics are closely related, there is a difference in their meaning. **Etiquette** consists of the rules and conventions governing correct or polite behavior in society in general or in a particular social or professional group or situation. In our society, for example, etiquette dictates that we do not belch at the table. In the medical office, good etiquette is reflected in how the receptionist answers the telephone and greets patients. The health insurance professional can perform his or her duties well within the limits of medical ethics, but this does not mean that he or she does so in a well-mannered way. If the patient completes the information form incorrectly, causing a delay or rejection of the claim, the healthcare professional can resolve the situation in an ethical manner, but if he or she is rude or impatient with the patient in doing so, a breach of **medical etiquette** will have occurred.

Ethics and etiquette are constantly evolving. What is acceptable behavior today might not have been okay 20, or even 10, years ago. In today's healthcare environment, patients are considered "customers," and they should be treated with respect and courtesy.

 What Did You Learn?

1. Explain the difference between ethics and laws.
2. Explain the difference between ethics and etiquette.
3. List some current ethical issues facing society today.

MEDICAL HEALTH RECORD

The medical record (or health record) is an account of a patient's medical assessment, investigation, and course of treatment. It is a source of information and one component in the quality of patient care. The medical record is a chronological listing of medical-related facts regarding the dates of an individual's injuries and illnesses; dates of treatment; and all notes, diagnostic test results, correspondence, and any other pertinent information regarding the medical care and treatment of the patient.

PURPOSES OF A MEDICAL HEALTH RECORD

The medical health record serves several important functions:

- It enables the healthcare provider to render medical care to the best of his or her ability.
- It provides statistical information for research.
- It offers legal protection for the healthcare team.
- It provides support for third-party reimbursement.

COMPLETE MEDICAL HEALTH RECORD

The Joint Commission (an independent, not-for-profit organization that administers voluntary accreditation programs for hospitals and other healthcare organizations in the United States) emphasizes four factors that improve the quality and usefulness of medical records, as follows:

- *Timeliness* (entries, such as history and physical exam, must be made and updated as necessary within 24 hours of the encounter)
- *Completeness* (documentation of patient problems and concerns, diagnostic tests performed and their results, diagnosis, treatment or recommended treatment, and prognosis)
- *Accuracy*
- *Confidentiality*

Typical components of a medical record include the following:

- Demographic information (patient information form, including insurance information)
- Current release-of-information form (signed and dated)
- Drug or other allergy flags
- Medical or health history
- Physical examination
- Chronological chart (progress) notes for all subsequent visits
- Medication sheet showing all prescriptions and over-the-counter drugs

- Results of diagnostic tests (x-rays, laboratory tests, electrocardiograms)
- Hospital records (if applicable)
- Correspondence

WHO OWNS MEDICAL HEALTH RECORDS?

There is some controversy regarding who owns the medical record. It has become an accepted opinion, however, that even though medical records contain patients' personal and confidential information, medical records are the property of the physician providing the care or the corporate entity that employs the provider. The information contained in the record is technically the patient's and is considered privileged communication because it cannot be divulged to anyone without the patient's written consent. It is important to keep in mind that medical records are considered legal documents, and their use is limited by universal laws. See http://www.HHS.gov for further information on the use of medical records. For more information on the medical records ownership law by state, see "Websites to Explore" at the end of this chapter.

 Patient's Point of View

Noemi Rodriguez stops in at Walden-Martin Family Medical Clinic because she has a question about her bill and how much her insurance has paid. The insurance company has requested additional information before paying the claim. Callie explains that because Noemi has now signed a release-of-information form allowing the clinic to send the information to the insurance company, the information would be sent that afternoon. Noemi states that she now understands why she had to sign the release-of-information form, as she actually owns the medical health record and Walden-Martin would need her permission to send the information. Callie explains that although Noemi has control over what happens with the information in the medical health record, the record actually belongs to Walden-Martin Family Medical Clinic. The clinic needs Noemi's permission to release any information from the medical health record, but the clinic owns the medical health record.

Noemi thanks Callie for clarifying the difference and states that she now has a better understanding of how information in a medical health record is owned and who has control over that information.

RETENTION OF MEDICAL HEALTH RECORDS

It is important that a healthcare facility have a policy regarding the retention of medical health records. According to the AMA, physicians have an obligation to retain patient records that may reasonably be of value to a patient and that may offer guidelines to assist physicians in meeting their ethical and legal obligations to good patient care.

Statutes of limitation and other federal or state regulations may affect time requirements for retaining medical health records. Other factors that affect record retention include:

- Expansion rate of records in the practice
- Space available for storage

- Volume of postactive uses
- Costs of alternatives

How long medical health records are kept and how they are stored or disposed of vary from practice to practice and state to state. The records of any patient covered by Medicare (Title XVIII) should be kept for 5 years. Medicaid (Title XIX) and Maternal and Child Health (Title V) records should be kept for at least 6 years.

Some states do not have a statutory requirement for record retention. In California, for example, the following criteria have been adopted as minimum standards, although this is not a state law:

- Adult patients: 10 years from the date the patient was last seen
- Minor patients: 28 years from the patient's date of birth
- Deceased patients: 5 years from the patient's date of death

Another question that arises is how long billing records, telephone calls and messages, and appointment books should be kept.

- Billing records in all states should be retained for 7 years according to Internal Revenue Service standards. They may be kept in a separate file.
- Telephone calls and messages that pertain to medical care should be documented in the medical record and kept according to the previously mentioned medical practice's retention guidelines.
- Appointment books may be kept for 1 year.

 Imagine This!

Indiana law states that a provider must maintain health records for at least 7 years. A minor younger than 6 years of age has until the minor's eighth birthday to file a claim, however. It is advisable to know the statute of limitations for minors in your state and to retain medical health records accordingly.

Most healthcare facilities periodically archive records that have had no activity for a certain number of years. With electronic health records, this can be done by moving the records to another server. This allows for the records to be accessed if needed but frees up space on the main server. Paper records are put into storage in another part of the building. In all cases, medical records should be kept for at least as long as the statute of limitations for medical malpractice claims. The statute of limitations is typically 3 or more years, depending on the state law. State medical associations and insurance carriers are the best resources for this information.

HIPAA Tip

Every medical office should establish a policy for retention, storage, and disposal of old or inactive records. The health insurance professional should become familiar with the laws in his or her state that deal with retention of medical health records and adhere to them. Check with the medical licensing board or medical society in your state for this information.

ACCESS TO MEDICAL HEALTH RECORDS

As governed by The Joint Commission, access to medical records within an institution or practice is limited to situations involving the following:

1. Treatment
2. Quality assurance
3. Utilization review
4. Education
5. Research

RELEASING MEDICAL HEALTH RECORD INFORMATION

Under no circumstances should any information from a patient's medical record (or from other sources) be divulged to any third party without the *written* consent of the patient (parent or guardian in the case of a minor or intellectually disabled adult). The HIPAA rules allow billing of third-party insurers without patients' written authorization. This is referred to as *Treatment, Payment, and Healthcare Operations (TPO)*. Even though it is allowed by HIPAA, many healthcare facilities include a place on the patient information form where the patient can sign to release the information necessary to complete the insurance claim. It is a good idea to advise the patient to specify the name of the insurer on the form. For information to be released to any other third party, a separate release of information should be used. Fig. 3.2 shows a typical information release form that can be used for a range of reasons.

Stop and Think

Ellen Porter walks out of an examination room and overhears a provider talking to a patient about treatment as they exit from the adjacent room. Is this a violation of the privacy law?

Stop and Think

A patient waiting at the pharmacy pickup counter overhears a pharmacist talking to another patient about her prescription. Is this a violation of HIPAA privacy standards?

? What Did You Learn?

1. List four purposes of a medical health record.
2. According to The Joint Commission, what are the four factors that improve the quality and usefulness of medical health records?
3. What items should be included in a medical health record?
4. Who owns medical health records?
5. Why is a retention policy important?

DOCUMENTATION AND MAINTENANCE OF PATIENT MEDICAL HEALTH RECORDS

A **medical (health) record** is a clinical, scientific, administrative, and legal document of facts containing statements relating to a patient. It incorporates scientific data and scientific events in chronological order regarding the case history, clinical examination, investigative procedures, diagnosis, treatment, and response to the treatment. Medical health records are extremely valuable, not only to healthcare providers and the scientific community, but also to patients and third-party carriers. Properly documented medical health records expand knowledge and improve the standard of medical care.

Medical health records are kept for two basic purposes:

1. They document the interaction between the healthcare provider and the patient so that a permanent record of what was said and done exists.
2. They show the ongoing process of patient care.

Note: Electronic medical records are discussed in depth in Chapter 16.

POLICY AND PERFORMANCE

Every medical facility should have a policy in place to ensure that medical health record entries are accurately documented and signed in a timely manner. If additional information needs to be added to the record, it should be in the form of an appropriate addendum that has been prepared in accordance with this policy. Fig. 3.3 shows the correct method of correcting an erroneous health record entry.

The provider does not always perform all patient record documentation. Some medical practices assign the task of documenting the chief complaint (CC) and history of present illness (HPI) to ancillary staff members. In such cases, it is important that the staff member understands the process of evaluation and management (E/M) coding. (Chapters 14 and 15 provide an in-depth look at diagnostic coding and procedural coding that includes E/M coding.) Adequate and complete documentation helps establish medical necessity for the visit and the level of service, which justifies the fee charged.

In addition to charting the CC and HPI, documentation that the ancillary medical staff might be responsible for includes the following:

- Patient contact, such as office visits and telephone calls
- Routine vital signs: blood pressure, pulse, respirations, weight, and height
- Applicable patient education—verbal instructions and written materials
- Communication or follow-up (either by phone or in writing) with patients who have failed to keep appointments, referrals, or scheduled tests
- Prescription refills authorized by the healthcare provider (some states require the physician's initials in the chart for every prescription refill)

The medical staff also should verify that all laboratory and diagnostic test results are read and signed by the healthcare provider and filed in the patient's chart in a timely manner. (The Office of Inspector General [OIG] interprets "timely" as 24 hours.)

MEDICAL RECORD	**Authorization for the Release of Medical Information**

INSTRUCTIONS: Complete this form in its entirety and forward the original to the address below:

NATIONAL INSTITUTES OF HEALTH
ATTN: MEDICAL RECORD DEPARTMENT
MEDICOLEGAL SECTION
10 CENTER DRIVE, MSC 1192   TELEPHONE: (888) 790-2133 (outside)
BLDG 10, ROOM 1N205   (301) 496-3331 (local)
BETHESDA, MD 20892-1192   FACSIMILE: (301) 480-9982

IDENTIFYING INFORMATION:

Patient Name	Daytime Telephone	Date of Birth

REQUEST INFORMATION: Information is to be released to the following individual or party:

Name	Telephone
Address	

The purpose or need for disclosure (charges will be determined based on purpose of disclosure):
_____

Date Range of Information to be Released: from _____ to _____

Please check specific information to be released:

☐ Discharge Summary   ☐ Radiology Reports   ☐ EKG Reports
☐ History & Physical   ☐ Radiology Films   ☐ Echocardiogram Reports
☐ Operative Reports   ☐ Tissue Exam Reports   ☐ Heart Diagnostic Reports
☐ Outpatient Progress Notes ☐ Tissue Slides   ☐ Nuclear Medicine Reports
☐ Length of Stay Verification ☐ Lab Results   ☐ Nuclear Medicine Scans

☐ Other (Please Specify): _____

_____

AUTHORIZATION: Permission is hereby granted to the Warren Grant Magnuson Clinical Center to release medical information to the individual/organization as identified above.
(Note: submission of this form authorizes the release of the information specified within one year from date of signature.)

Patient/Authorized Signature	Print Name	Date

If other than patient, specify relationship: _____

Patient Identification	Authorization for the Release of Medical Information
	NIH-527 (02-01)
	P.A. 09-25-0099
	File in Section 4: Correspondence

Fig. 3.2 National Institutes of Health (NIH) release-of-information authorization form. (From Clinical Center, National Institutes of Health, US Department of Health and Human Services.)

sprained left ankle FA 12/27/20xx

12/23/20xx   Rachel is seen again in the office today for follow-up of her ~~sprained right ankle~~. She is able to put some weight on it, and swelling has subsided. Gradually increase activity. Continue ibuprofen for pain as needed. Recheck in two weeks. (s) Frances Akers, MD

Fig. 3.3 Example of a properly corrected chart entry.

1. All medical record entries should be complete, accurate, and legible and contain the date the entry was made.
2. Only authorized individuals will make entries into medical records.
3. Entries should be made using a black ink (not felt tip) pen.
4. The author of every medical record entry shall be identified in the entry, and all clinical entries shall be individually authenticated by the responsible practitioner. Other entries will be authenticated as specified by medical staff bylaws or as required by state or federal law or regulation.
5. All authorized individuals who make entries into medical records will make every effort to create such entries in accordance with this policy, applicable medical staff bylaw provisions, and all applicable state and federal laws, regulations, and guidelines. Any questions concerning creation of medical record entries should be directed to appropriate personnel for clarification.
6. All final diagnoses and complications should be recorded without the use of symbols or abbreviations.
7. Only the abbreviations, signs, and symbols approved by the medical staff shall be used in medical records.

Fig. 3.4 Principles of documentation.

Appropriate documentation serves as the basis for the defense of malpractice claims and lawsuits (Fig. 3.4). Many insurance carriers now conduct record reviews in an effort to ensure proper documentation of services billed. Lack of proper documentation could result in reduced or denied claim payments. A common saying among healthcare professionals is "If it isn't documented, it didn't happen."

> **? What Did You Learn?**
>
> 1. What is the process of recording information in a patient's health record called?
> 2. Who shares the responsibility of documentation?
> 3. List the types of documentation that typically fall into the realm of the ancillary medical staff.
> 4. What problems can be the result of poorly maintained or inaccurate medical records?

HEALTH INSURANCE PORTABILITY AND ACCOUNTABILITY ACT AND COMPLIANCE

Even though HIPAA legislation was passed in 1996, it is important to review the four primary objectives of this law, which are:
1. To ensure health insurance portability
2. To reduce healthcare fraud and abuse
3. To enforce standards for health information
4. To guarantee security and privacy of health information for patients

The word **portability** means that people with preexisting medical conditions cannot be denied health insurance coverage when moving from one employer-sponsored group healthcare plan to another. This law also helps individuals who need to switch health insurance companies in the event of job termination, job relocation, or quitting a job. **Accountability** refers to the responsibility that the healthcare profession has to others, specifically to patients, so that a feeling of confidence exists between patient and provider. Accountability applies more to patient rights, the billing process, and other aspects of the medical office.

Fig. 3.5 shows a flow chart illustrating who must comply with HIPAA standards. The series of easy "yes" and "no" questions is designed to be a simple test to help providers determine whether they must comply with the privacy, security, transactions, and other related standards of HIPAA. Note: The Affordable Care Act does not affect HIPAA.

IMPACT OF HIPAA

HIPAA's regulations affect more than just the healthcare provider and his or her patients. The impact is felt across the board in professional, business, and private worlds. The following paragraphs discuss some of the more pertinent areas.

Impact on the Health Insurance Professional

Health insurance professionals who work in an office with more than 10 employees are likely to submit insurance claims to major government payers (Medicare and Medicaid) using a standardized electronic format, simplifying and creating efficiency via HIPAA's "Electronic Health Transactions Standards." These standards affect health insurance claims processing, health plan eligibility, payments, and other related transactions. The idea behind these standards is to make processing these records more efficient, more accurate, and less costly. In the past, most health, financial, and insurance records in medical offices were paper documents. Because more and more records are becoming computerized, concern has been raised regarding patient privacy and how it will be maintained in electronic media. Under HIPAA, patients have the ability to view their medical health records and to be informed about who else has viewed them and why. For these reasons, the "Standards for Privacy"—a set of specific rules to ensure confidentiality—should be considered.

Because HIPAA imposes specific responsibilities on everyone who works in the healthcare field, major changes were required for healthcare facilities to become HIPAA compliant. Changes were needed on all levels—management of information, patient records, patient care, security, and coding. The health insurance professional must be aware of what these requirements are and why they are necessary. Examples include but are not limited to the following:
- Arranging patient charts in the receptacle outside the examination room door in such a way that patient names are not visible
- Locking the physician's office door when confidential laboratory reports and other documents are placed on his or her desk for review
- Closing the window separating the reception area from the waiting room when not in use

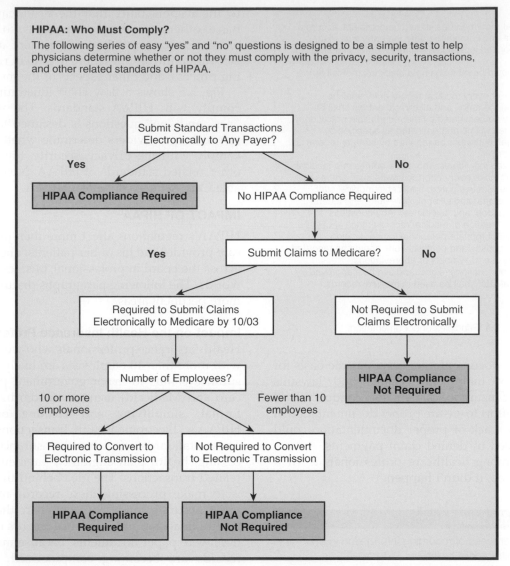

Fig. 3.5 Health Insurance Portability and Accountability Act *(HIPAA)*: Who must comply? (From the American Medical Association, http://www.ama-assn.org/ama.)

- Positioning computer screens so that someone standing at the reception desk cannot view them
- Changing computer security passwords routinely
- Avoiding transfer of confidential information via fax or electronic methods to unsecured locations, such as schools, hotel lobbies, and businesses

 HIPAA Tip

Healthcare providers are not required to monitor actively the means by which a business associate carries out the safeguards of the contract.

Impact on Patients

When patients see their healthcare providers, they are given a **privacy statement** at each location they visit. Patients are asked to read it, ask necessary questions for clarification, and sign the statement. Beyond that,

there is little obvious evidence of any change from the patient's standpoint.

The privacy statement includes not only information about who the physician or pharmacy shares health information with and why, but also what rights patients have to access their own health information. The only real change brought about by HIPAA is in presentation. Patients were able to do all of those things before HIPAA came into effect, but it was not brought to their attention in this manner and in printed form. Another way HIPAA has changed patient routines in many offices is that when patients sign in at the reception desk, they may no longer see a clipboard with the names of people who have signed in before them (commonly referred to as the "community sign-in sheet"). If medical personnel call the patient by name, that kind of exposure is called **incidental disclosure**, which is specifically allowed under HIPAA.

In the long run, HIPAA regulations benefit patients by ensuring that their medical information is not accessible by anyone who is not entitled to view it. They also benefit patients by ensuring confidentiality.

 Stop and Think

Sally Sergeant is seen in the physician's office for confirmation of a suspected pregnancy. After Sally leaves, her husband phones and inquires as to the results of the examination. Can any member of the medical staff give Sally's husband these results?

Impact on Providers

Providers are required to have business associate agreements with every company they exchange patient information with, including insurance companies, attorneys, financial institutions, and other providers. The idea behind these agreements is to reassure providers that the people they do business with are also complying with HIPAA regulations.

 HIPAA Tip

Employers should determine what type of computer security, such as a device that blocks unauthorized access, needs to be put into place for risk management purposes to ensure that health information is not used in the employment process.

Impact on Private Businesses

Businesses have the same obligation to protect medical records as government, medical, and human resource officials. Businesses need to ensure that there is uniformity in application of HIPAA requirements. Employees typically receive a letter notifying them of any changes stemming from HIPAA. One of the most significant changes is that health records must now be kept separate from routine personnel records. Some companies were already doing that. Although the average worker might not have felt the effects of the HIPAA privacy requirements on the job, he or she no doubt felt them indirectly in the wallets.

 HIPAA Tip

Health insurance professionals need to know how to apply for new provider identification numbers for physicians and other healthcare providers. Health insurance professionals also might be in charge of security measures for computers, which include virus protection, password maintenance, and ensuring that confidential information stays secure.

 What Did You Learn?

1. Name the four primary objectives of HIPAA.
2. How does HIPAA affect claims submission and processing?
3. Define *incidental disclosure*.
4. How does HIPAA benefit patients?

ENFORCEMENT OF CONFIDENTIALITY REGULATIONS OF HIPAA

One of the primary purposes of HIPAA is to provide standards for health information transactions and confidentiality and security of patient data. This confidentiality portion has had a considerable impact on the day-to-day workflow among medical institutions. HIPAA is complaint driven, however. If no one complains, there probably would not be an investigation. If a deliberate violation of the regulations were found, action would be taken. The Office of Civil Rights enforces the HIPAA regulations, and there are civil penalties of $100 per violation up to $50,000 per year. Criminal penalties are also possible, including $50,000 or 1 year in prison or both for wrongful disclosure, or $250,000 or 10 years in prison or both for the intent to sell information. To keep up to date on HIPAA, go to the website listed at the end of this chapter or type "HIPAA" into your search engine.

DEVELOPING A COMPLIANCE PLAN

A written compliance plan can help protect a medical practice and can be the best defense against possible problems. Compliance programs are a significant tool in reducing the potential for healthcare fraud and abuse; however, they must be adapted and implemented appropriately to be effective. The OIG recommends that the medical facility periodically review its existing standards and procedures to determine whether it is in compliance with HIPAA laws and regulations.

 What Did You Learn?

1. What is the best defense against committing violations of HIPAA guidelines?
2. What entity recommends that all medical facilities review standards and procedures to determine whether they are in compliance?

CONFIDENTIALITY AND PRIVACY

The words *confidentiality* and *privacy* are sometimes used interchangeably, but there is a distinction between the two. **Privacy** denotes a "zone of inaccessibility" of mind or body—the right to be left alone and to maintain individual autonomy, solitude, intimacy, and control over information about oneself. **Confidentiality** concerns the communication of private and personal information from one person to another. The key ingredients of confidentiality are trust and loyalty. Professionals rely on the promise of confidentiality to inspire trust in their clients and patients. In the case of healthcare providers, lawyers, and clergy, communications are legally designated "privileged." The following paragraphs examine these two terms separately as they affect healthcare.

CONFIDENTIALITY

Confidentiality is the foundation for trust in the provider-patient relationship. Providers have always had an ethical duty to keep their patients' confidences. Even before HIPAA came into being, the AMA's *Code of Medical Ethics* stated that information disclosed to a physician during the course of the physician-patient relationship or discovered in connection with the treatment of a patient is strictly confidential. The basic reason for this is so that the patient feels comfortable to disclose, fully and frankly, any and all information to the provider. This full disclosure enables the healthcare provider to diagnose conditions more effectively and to treat the patient appropriately.

Confidentiality extends to all health professionals, including health insurance professionals. Each member of the healthcare team has a responsibility to uphold confidentiality for patients. In a busy medical office setting or clinic, maintaining confidentiality might be difficult. Voices carry from the reception work area to waiting patients in chairs and through thin walls of examination rooms. Elevator or cafeteria discussions of Mrs. Brown's cancer or Mr. Lewis's heart attack are common, and this careless practice is prohibited. The person next to you could be a patient's friend, relative, or someone else who is not entitled to this privileged information. Permission must be received from the patient before *any* disclosure.

Any information the health insurance professional learns while caring for a patient or performing administrative duties, such as completing insurance claims, must remain strictly confidential unless the professional is authorized in writing by the patient or ordered by law to reveal it. Section 164.506 of the HIPAA privacy regulations permits release of information for treatment, payment, or healthcare operation purposes *without a specific patient authorization*. However, most healthcare facilities believe it is good practice to have the patient's written authorization to release information necessary to process an insurance claim or to complete a treatment report for precertification, and there may be circumstances when authorization is required.

PRIVACY

As mentioned, privacy is different from confidentiality. It refers to an individual's right to keep some information to himself or herself and to have it used only with his or her approval. The American public's privacy concerns are of more recent origin, dating back to events in the 1960s and early 1970s that led to the Privacy Act of 1974.

Under HIPAA, physicians must use and disclose only the minimum amount of patient information needed for the purpose in question. Patients can request a copy of their medical records and can request amendments to incorrect records. In addition, patients must receive notification of their privacy rights.

SECURITY

HIPAA also requires administrative procedures for guarding data confidentiality, integrity, and availability with formal procedures for implementation. Physical safeguards are required and include the following:
- Maintaining a system for keeping and storing critical data safe, such as locked, fireproof file cabinets
- Reporting and responding to any attempts to "hack" into the system
- Assessing the security risks of the system
- Developing a contingency plan for data backup and disaster recovery
- Training in security awareness
- Ensuring that the data are secure by monitoring access and protecting the use of passwords or other methods used to ensure security

EXCEPTIONS TO CONFIDENTIALITY

Certain situations and classes of patients do not come under the umbrella of confidentiality. In addition, certain medical information by law must be reported to state and local governments, where it is maintained in databases for research and public safety. Exceptions to confidentiality include but are not limited to the following:
- Treatment of minors (Note: There are some exceptional circumstances in which youth under 18 years of age can be treated without parental consent)
- Human immunodeficiency virus (HIV)–positive patients and healthcare workers
- Abuse of a child (or, in most states, an adult)
- Injuries caused by firearms or other weapons
- Communicable diseases
- Billing TPO insurance

Note: Although HIPAA regulations allow billing insurance companies without a written release of information, most medical facilities still require it.

 Imagine This!

A California psychologist requested that University of California campus police arrest a patient of his who he believed was going to kill a woman. The patient was arrested but subsequently released after assuring the police that he would stay away from the woman. The woman was never notified of the impending danger, and the patient killed her 2 months later *(Tarasoff v. Regents of the University of California).*

Some states allow disclosure of certain types of mental health information without patient consent to:
- Other treatment providers
- Healthcare services payers or other sources of financial assistance to the patient
- Third parties that the mental health professional feels might be endangered by the patient
- Researchers

- Agencies charged with oversight of the healthcare system or the system's practitioners
- Families under certain circumstances
- Law enforcement officials under certain circumstances
- Public health officials

AUTHORIZATION TO RELEASE INFORMATION

Earlier in this chapter we discussed the importance of obtaining a signed release of information before any information is divulged to any third party. Most states agree on the typical elements of a valid general release of information, which are as follows:

- Patient's name and identifying information
- Address of the healthcare professional or institution directed to release the information
- Description of the information to be released
- Identity of the party to be furnished the information
- Language authorizing release of information
- Signature of patient or authorized individual
- Time period for which the release remains valid

Generally, the authorization for release of health information form in cases of alcohol or drug treatment, mental health information, and confidential HIV/AIDS-related information differs from a general release-of-information form.

Failure to obtain an appropriate release for disclosing medical health records information to a third party can result in serious consequences. Twenty-one states punish disclosure of confidential information by revoking a physician's medical license or taking other serious disciplinary action.

EXCEPTIONS FOR SIGNED RELEASE OF INFORMATION

In a few situations, a signed release of information is not always required, as discussed in the following paragraphs.

Medicaid-Eligible Patients and Workers' Compensation Cases

When completing an insurance claim form for a Medicaid recipient or a patient being treated as a result of an on-the-job illness or injury (workers' compensation), a written release of information is not usually required. The reason is that the contract in these cases is between the healthcare provider and the government agency sponsoring that specific program, and the patient is the third party. In both cases, however, the patient cannot be billed for medical procedures or services unless it is determined that he or she is ineligible for benefits for those particular dates of service. More information on Medicaid and workers' compensation is given in later chapters.

Inpatient-Only Treatment

Another group of patients for which the normally required signed release of information for filing insurance claims is waived consists of those who are seen in the hospital but do not come to the office for follow-up care. It is considered that the release of information signed by the patient for hospital services also covers the physician's services, and the health insurance professional can simply insert the phrase "Signature on file" in block 12 of the CMS-1500 claim form. An example would be when the healthcare provider sees a patient only for consultation purposes.

Court Order

If a patient's record is subpoenaed by a court of law as evidence in a lawsuit, it may be released to the court without the patient's approval. A **subpoena** *duces tecum* is a legal document that requires an individual to appear in court with a piece of evidence that can be used or inspected by the court. The judge determines whether the evidence is relevant to the controversy or issues that must be resolved between the parties of the lawsuit.

BREACH OF CONFIDENTIALITY

When confidential information is disclosed to a third party without patient consent or court order, a **breach of confidentiality** has occurred. The disclosure violation can be oral or written, made by telephone, faxed, or transmitted electronically. As mentioned earlier, the release of PHI in a patient's medical health record to third parties is allowed only if the patient has consented, in writing, to such disclosure. This rule includes the following categories of individuals:

- Attorneys
- Clergy
- Insurance companies
- Relatives (except when a relative has a **durable power of attorney**, meaning that he or she has been named as an agent to handle the individual's affairs if the patient becomes incapacitated; when a relative has a healthcare power or attorney to make healthcare decisions for the individual)
- Employers (except in the case of workers' compensation cases)
- All other third parties

State law governs who can give permission to release medical record information. Usually the authority to release medical information is granted to:

- The patient, if he or she is a competent adult or emancipated minor
- A legal guardian or parent, if the patient is a minor child or is incompetent
- An individual to whom the patient has granted power of attorney possessing legal authority to act for the patient in legal and business matters to make such decisions
- The administrator or executor of the patient's estate if the patient is deceased

Stop and Think

You receive a phone call from Abner L. Smith, a local attorney. He is representing Patricia Lane, a patient of your practice, who was recently involved in a rear-end auto collision. Mr. Smith wants to know the results of Ms. Lane's recent magnetic resonance imaging (MRI) of her neck because it is important to the case. He tells you that Ms. Lane is sitting in his office and says it's okay for you to give him this information. What should you do?

 Stop and Think

Mrs. Ayers is being seen in your clinic for migraines. Dr. Smithers, another provider in your clinic, is also seeing Mrs. Ayers for severe acne and needs additional information regarding her medications. Can you provide this information to Dr. Smithers without Mrs. Ayers' written consent?

 What Did You Learn?

1. What is the term for the foundation of trust in the provider–patient relationship?
2. Define *confidentiality*.
3. Whose responsibility is it to uphold patient confidentiality?
4. List the exceptions to confidentiality.
5. Before divulging confidential patient information to any third party, what must the health insurance professional do?

HEALTHCARE FRAUD AND ABUSE

Stories about the growing incidence of healthcare fraud and abuse can be found in newspapers and on television. Fraud and abuse in healthcare are widespread and costly to the US healthcare system. Federal investigations have identified fraud and abuse in all areas of healthcare, including providers' offices and clinics, hospitals, clinical laboratories, durable medical equipment suppliers, hospices, and home health agencies. Medicare and Medicaid scams cost taxpayers billions of dollars a year. More recent legislation has enhanced enforcement capabilities, and even more government enforcement activity is expected in the future. Because providers and members of their healthcare teams are not immune to such government actions, they (and others involved in providing patient care) need to know how to comply with the federal laws to guard against potential liability in fraud enforcement actions.

DEFINING FRAUD AND ABUSE

Fraud can be defined any number of ways. The National Health Care Anti-Fraud Association (NHCAA) defines fraud as an intentional deception or misrepresentation that the individual or entity makes, knowing that the misrepresentation could result in some unauthorized benefit to the individual, the entity, or another party.

Examples of health insurance fraud include billing for services that were not rendered and falsifying a patient's diagnosis to justify tests, surgery, or other procedures that are not medically necessary.

Abuse, although similar to fraud, is considered less serious when applied to healthcare. Abuse can be defined as improper or harmful procedures or methods of doing business that are contradictory to accepted business practices. Often it is impossible to establish that the abusive acts were done with intent to deceive the insurance carrier.

Examples of health insurance abuse include charging for services that were not medically necessary, do not conform to recognized standards, or are unfairly priced. Another example of abuse is performing a laboratory test on large numbers of patients when only a few patients should have had the test.

Although no exact dollar amount can be determined, some authorities contend that health insurance fraud and abuse constitute a $100 billion/year problem. The US General Accountability Office (GAO) estimates that $1 of every $7 spent on Medicare is lost to fraud and abuse and that, in 1 year, Medicare typically loses nearly $12 billion to fraudulent or unnecessary claims. Private insurers estimate the dollar amount lost to health insurance fraud and abuse to be 3% to 5% of total healthcare dollars spent.

 Imagine This!

A man in Los Angeles billed Medicare more than $1 million for motorized wheelchairs that people didn't need. One person who got a wheelchair was blind and later testified that he couldn't see to operate it. In another incident, two individuals allegedly submitted $9 million in false and fraudulent claims to Medicare for services that were never provided, offering cash and other rewards to beneficiaries who visited their clinic and signed forms that said they received services that they never actually got.

Who Commits Healthcare Insurance Fraud?

Just about anyone can commit health insurance fraud—physicians, hospitals, medical suppliers, pharmacies, nursing homes—the list goes on and on. Dishonest healthcare providers are not the only ones who commit fraud. Patients and insured individuals also commit health insurance fraud and abuse. Most healthcare providers, however, are caring, honest, and ethical professionals.

How Is Healthcare Fraud Committed?

The most popular schemes for committing healthcare fraud include the following:

• Billing for services, procedures, and supplies that were not provided to the patient. *Example:* Billing for a diagnostic test that was *not* performed
• Upcoding—billing for a more expensive service or procedure than what was provided. *Example:* Charging for a comprehensive office visit when a shorter, routine visit occurred

- Unbundling of charges or code fragmentation—billing services separately when these services are usually included in a single service fee. *Example:* Making separate charges for each component of a total abdominal hysterectomy; this operation typically has one code, which includes preoperative and postoperative procedures and has a lesser fee than occurs by coding each component separately
- Misrepresenting services—misrepresenting or falsifying the diagnosis to obtain insurance payment on something that is not covered. *Example:* Using a diagnosis of benign cataracts for a routine eye examination with refraction because many insurance policies do not cover this procedure

How Do Consumers Commit Healthcare Insurance Fraud?

The patient can agree to or encourage the provider to inflate or misrepresent the services provided. An example is a patient who is seeing a psychiatrist who charges $150 for 1 hour of therapy. The patient, whose policy covers only 50% of psychotherapy charges, suggests that the therapy session be coded for $150 or 2 hours so that the insurer pays more of the charges. Other methods consumers use to commit fraud are creating fake receipts and claims and modifying an actual receipt to gain more claim dollars.

PREVENTING FRAUD AND ABUSE

As a health insurance professional, you can do your part to prevent fraud and abuse in the medical office. The following are some general principles to follow:

- Create a file for every major third-party payer your office deals with, and keep current providers' manuals, claims completion guidelines, and publications up to date to aid you in generating timely and accurate claims.
- Develop a list of "hot" phone numbers of these carriers to use when questions arise.
- Use the most current coding manuals, and code to the greatest specificity.
- Take advantage of every opportunity to improve your coding skills by attending seminars, continuing education, or both.
- Discuss questions or potential problems regarding diagnoses, procedures and services, and fees charged with the physician or other healthcare provider.
- Notify your superior immediately if you suspect fraud or abuse.

? What Did You Learn?

1. How does fraud differ from abuse?
2. Who typically commits healthcare fraud?
3. List several common ways that fraud is committed.
4. How can the health insurance professional prevent fraud and abuse?

SUMMARY CHECKPOINTS

- *Respondeat superior* is a key principle in business law that says that an employer is responsible for the actions of his or her employees in the "course of employment." However, the health insurance professional should have a basic knowledge of medical law and ethics to aid in accurate claims completion and submission and conduct himself or herself appropriately in and out of the medical facility.
- The elements necessary to constitute a legal contract are:
  - Offer and acceptance
  - Consideration
  - Legal object (also referred to as "legal subject matter")
  - Competent parties (also referred to as "competency and capacity")
  - Legal form (written contracts only)

  The relationship between patient and healthcare provider is an implied contract, meaning it is not in writing but is just as legally binding in the eyes of the law.

  The federal laws that regulate health insurance include the following:
  - OBRA (1980)
  - TEFRA (1982)
  - COBRA (1986)
  - Federal False Claim Amendments Act of 1986
  - Fraud and Abuse Act
  - OBRA (1987)
  - HIPAA's Privacy Rule
  - The Patient Protection and Affordable Care Act
  - The Social Security Number Protection Act of 2010
  - The Social Security Number Protection Act of 2011
- Displaying proper medical ethics and etiquette in the workplace is important for the protection and well-being of the patients and the entire healthcare team. In today's complicated healthcare world, experts recommend that patients be regarded as "customers" who are vital to the practice and should be treated with courtesy and respect. When proper medical ethics and etiquette are shown in the workplace, the practice is more likely to avoid potential legal problems.
- Accurate, complete, and concise documentation in medical health records is essential to the delivery of quality medical care and serves the following important purposes:
  - It provides information about the patient's condition, the treatment, the patient's response to this treatment, and the patient's progress.
  - It serves as a legal document, which can protect and defend the provider in the event of legal action.
  - It provides information necessary for third-party reimbursement.

- It can be used in clinical research under certain circumstances.
- It is accepted in the industry that medical records are the property of the provider providing the care or the corporate entity where the provider is employed. The information contained in the record is technically the patient's, however, because it cannot be divulged to anyone without the patient's written consent. All healthcare facilities should have a policy regarding the retention of medical records. Statutes of limitation and other federal or state regulations may affect time requirements for retaining medical records.
- The physician does not always perform all patient record documentation. Some medical practices assign the task of documenting the CC and HPI to ancillary staff members. In such cases, it is important that the staff member understands the process of evaluation and management coding. Adequate and complete documentation helps establish medical necessity for the visit and the level of service, which justify the fee charged.
- The four primary objectives of HIPAA are to:
  - Ensure health insurance portability
  - Reduce healthcare fraud and abuse
  - Enforce standards for health information
  - Guarantee security and privacy of health information for patients
- HIPAA affects various categories of people involved with healthcare, including:
  - Health insurance professionals
  - Patients
  - Healthcare providers
  - Private business entities
- Confidentiality is the foundation for trust in the provider–patient relationship. Every healthcare organization and provider must guarantee confidentiality and privacy of the healthcare information they collect, maintain, use, and transmit. This obligation of confidentiality extends to every member of the healthcare team.
- Exceptions to confidentiality include:
  - Minors (under specific circumstances)
  - HIV-positive patients and HIV-positive healthcare workers
  - Abuse of a child or adult
  - Injuries inflicted by firearms or other weapons
  - Communicable diseases
  - TPO insurance
- Fraud can be defined as an intentional deception or misrepresentation that the individual or entity makes, knowing that the misrepresentation could result in some unauthorized benefit to the individual, the entity, or another party. Abuse can be defined as improper or harmful procedures or methods of doing business that are contradictory to accepted business practices.

- Fraud and abuse are widespread in the US healthcare system. Not only healthcare providers, but also consumers, commit fraud and abuse; however, most providers and consumers are honest and ethical. Fraud and abuse result in millions of wasted healthcare dollars.
- Health insurance professionals can do their part to prevent fraud and abuse in the medical office in numerous ways, such as:
  - Creating and maintaining a file for each major third-party payer's guidelines
  - Developing a list of "hot" phone numbers to use when questions arise
  - Using the most current coding manuals and coding to the greatest specificity
  - Improving coding skills by attending seminars, continuing education, or both
  - Discussing questions or potential problems with healthcare providers
  - Reporting suspected fraud or abuse

Closing Scenario

As you can see, it is vitally important for a health insurance professional to understand the laws that affect health insurance and healthcare facilities. Callie has been able to better help patients understand why certain forms need to be signed and specific information gathered. She is better prepared to deal with the complex world of health insurance and to help her providers obtain the best reimbursement possible for services provided.

Staying current with all changes in the laws is a challenge, but Callie has taken advantage of any workshops provided and stays current in her field by reading journals and newsletters on those relevant topics.

The area of medical ethics has always been of interest to Callie. By being familiar with the laws about fraud and abuse, Callie is able to use that knowledge when she is asked to change how something is billed and to recognize when there is a honest mistake that could be construed as abuse. By following an ethical code, Callie is helping to maintain the integrity of Walden-Martin Family Medical Clinic.

CHAPTER REVIEW QUESTIONS

1. The term that means "Let the master answer" and applies to employee liability is:
   a. Litigious
   b. Party of the second part
   c. *Respondeat superior*
   d. Accountability
2. Which is not an element of a legally binding contract?
   a. Offer and acceptance
   b. Consideration
   c. Competent parties
   d. Consideration
   e. All of the above are elements of a legally binding contract.

3. Which is considered the third party in a contract in a healthcare facility?
   a. The healthcare provider
   b. The patient
   c. The health insurance professional
   d. The insurance company

4. Which law states that Medicare is the secondary payer in the case of automobile accident?
   a. Federal Omnibus Reconciliation Act of 1980
   b. Tax Equity and Fiscal Responsibility Act of 1982
   c. Consolidated Omnibus Budget Reconciliation Act of 1986
   d. Federal Omnibus Reconciliation Act of 1987

5. Which law required the Centers for Medicare and Medicaid Services (CMS) to reissue Medicare cards to all beneficiaries?
   a. Tax Equity and Fiscal Responsibility Act of 1982
   b. The Social Security Number Protection Act of 2011
   c. Consolidated Omnibus Budget Reconciliation Act of 1986
   d. Federal Omnibus Reconciliation Act of 1987

6. What statement best describes the ownership of the medical health record?
   a. The patient owns and has complete control of the medical health record.
   b. The healthcare facility has ownership of the medical health record, but the patient has control over what information is released and to whom.
   c. The healthcare facility owns and has complete control of the medical health record.
   d. The patient has ownership of the medical health record, but the healthcare facility has control over what information is released and to whom.

7. HIPAA requires that a patient's privacy be protected. What term describes what occurs when a patient's name is used when calling him or her to the exam room?
   a. Negligence
   b. Ancillary
   c. Incidental disclosure
   d. Medical etiquette

8. The penalty for violations of the HIPAA regulations includes civil penalties of up to:
   a. $1000
   b. $16,000
   c. $50,000
   d. $250,000

9. Which of the following would be an exception to confidentiality?
   a. Abuse of a child
   b. Injuries caused by a firearm
   c. Communicable diseases
   d. All of the above

10. An intentional deception or misrepresentation made knowing that it could result in some unauthorized benefit is:
    a. Consideration
    b. Abuse
    c. Litigious
    d. Fraud

WEBSITES TO EXPLORE

- For live links to the following websites, please visit the Evolve site at http://evolve.elsevier.com/Beik/today.
- For extensive and up-to-date information on HIPAA, log on to the following website: http://www.hhs.gov/ocr/privacy/.
- For further clarification on competency and capacity go to: https://lawprofessors.typepad.com/elder_law/2006/01/competence_vs_c.html.
- The activities of the GAO are designed to ensure the executive branch's accountability to Congress under the Constitution and the government's accountability to the American people. You will find many interesting facts and information on medical insurance and healthcare on its website at http://www.gao.gov/.
- To learn more about medical records ownership laws by state, go to: http://www.healthinfolaw.org/comparative-analysis/who-owns-medical-records-50-state-comparison.
- To learn more about healthcare fraud and abuse, log on to the following website and use the search words "fraud and abuse": http://oig.hhs.gov/reports-and-publications/hcfac/index.asp.
- To learn more about exceptions to HIPAA confidentiality laws, go to the following website: https://www.universalclass.com/articles/medicine/exceptions-to-the-hipaa-privacy-policy.htm.
- To access AHIMA's article on defining the legal health record, go to http://library.ahima.org/xpedio/groups/public/documents/ahima/bok1_048604.hcsp?dDocName=bok1_048604/.

Author's Note: Due to the dynamic nature of the Internet, web addresses and/or links provided in this chapter may have changed since publication and may no longer be valid. In such cases, students should select comparable search words to access related sites.

4 Healthcare Reform: Coverage Types and Sources

Chapter Outline

I. **The Changing Face of Health Insurance**
  A. Reimbursement Models
   1. *Fee-for-Service (Indemnity)*
      a. *Discounted Fee-for-Service*
   2. *Capitation*
   3. *Resource-Based Relative Value Scale*
   4. *Value-Based Care*
   5. *Episode-of-Care*
  B. The Affordable Care Act of 2010: Major Reforms
   1. *Out-of-Pocket Maximum and Lifetime Limits*
   2. *Levels of Coverage*
   3. *Limitations and Exclusions*
   4. *Preventive Services*
   5. *Standardized Benefits and Coverage Rule*
  C. Managed Care
II. **The Health Insurance Marketplace**
III. **Major Healthcare Payers**
  A. Medicaid
  B. Medicare
  C. TRICARE/CHAMPVA
  D. Disability Insurance
   1. *Private*
   2. *Social Security Disability Insurance*
   3. *Workers' Compensation*

IV. **Miscellaneous Healthcare Coverage Options**
  A. Health Savings Account
  B. Flexible Spending Account
  C. Health Reimbursement Arrangements
  D. Premium Reimbursement Arrangement
  E. Health Insurance Exchanges
  F. Accountable Care Organizations
  G. Long-Term Care Insurance
  H. Dental Care
  I. Vision Care
V. **CMS-1500 Claim Form**
VI. **Consolidated Omnibus Budget Reconciliation Act**
VII. **Health Insurance "Watchdogs"**
VIII. **Other Terms Common to Third-Party Carriers**
  A. Birthday Rule
  B. Coordination of Benefits
  C. Medical Necessity
  D. UCR and Balance Billing
  E. Participating Versus Nonparticipating Providers
  F. Miscellaneous Terms

Chapter Objectives

After completion of this chapter, the student should be able to:

1. Discuss the major reforms that have transformed health insurance in recent years.
2. Explain the health insurance marketplace and its role in today's healthcare system.
3. List the major healthcare payers and briefly describe each.
4. Compare and contrast the alternative healthcare coverage options.
5. Name the universal insurance claim form.
6. Discuss the purpose and role of the Consolidated Omnibus Budget Reconciliation Act (COBRA).
7. Evaluate the importance of the health insurance "watchdogs."
8. Provide brief definitions for the terms common to third-party carriers.

Chapter Terms

accountable care organization (ACO)
Affordable Care Act (ACA)
annual dollar limit
balance billing
birthday rule
cafeteria plan
capitation

Civilian Health and Medical Program of the Department of Veterans Affairs (CHAMPVA)
CMS-1500 claim form
coinsurance
comprehensive plan
Consolidated Omnibus Budget Reconciliation Act (COBRA)

coordination of benefits (COB)
copayment
cost-sharing
deductible
disability insurance
enrollees
episode-of-care
essential health benefits

exclusions
fee-for-service (FFS)
flexible spending account (FSA)
grandfathered plans
group plan
hardship exemption
health insurance exchanges
health insurance marketplace
health reimbursement
    arrangements (HRAs)
health savings account (HSA)
insured
lifetime limit
long-term care

managed care
Medicaid
medical savings account (MSA)
medically necessary
Medicare
Medicare Supplement plans
Medigap
metal plans (metal levels)
nonparticipating (nonPAR) provider
out-of-pocket maximum
participating (PAR) provider
policyholder
preexisting condition
premium

premium reimbursement
    arrangement (PRA)
preventive services
resource-based relative value scale
    (RBRVS)
Social Security Disability Insurance
    (SSDI)
TRICARE
usual, customary, and reasonable
    (UCR)
value-based care
workers' compensation

Opening Scenario

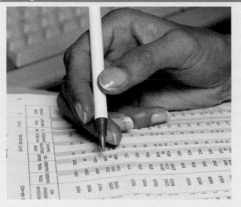

Rachel Butler really enjoys her work at Walden-Martin Family Medical Clinic. She has been working as a health insurance professional for several months now and is starting to feel very comfortable in that role. Rachel would like to give back to her community and has volunteered to work two evenings a week for the free clinic in her rural community. The physician in charge recognizes Rachel's skills in billing and insurance and puts her to work in that area in the free clinic. Rachel watched how the current health insurance professional handles things at the free clinic and is feeling confident that she can do the work required. She will be responsible for completing and submitting claims.

At first, the work is challenging, but Rachel becomes more comfortable each day that she works at the clinic. Rachel enjoys helping new patients fill out the patient information form and is able to guide them and answer questions relating to primary and secondary insurance coverage. She is especially diligent about each patient having an up-to-date release of information in his or her record and confidently explains the rationale of this important document to patients who inquire. It surprises her that so many patients are willing to put their signature on a document without really knowing the reason why.

Being able to relate her work experiences at Walden-Martin to the work in the clinic has made her better at both jobs. Patient education is quickly becoming her area of special interest because it is obvious that many patients do not know their rights.

THE CHANGING FACE OF HEALTH INSURANCE

Most people in the United States know how important it is to have health insurance in today's world of increasing medical costs. You may have heard a lot of confusing terms when people speak of health insurance, such as *Affordable Care Act, essential health benefits, health insurance marketplace,* and *managed care.* Acronyms such as HMOs, PPOs, and POS make things even more confusing. Note: A complete glossary of healthcare terms can be found at https://www.healthcare.gov/glossary/.

In Chapter 1, we learned how insurance got its start. Chapter 2 discussed the education and preparation necessary for becoming a health insurance professional and what job duties and responsibilities are common in this field. Chapter 2 also explained various career opportunities and certification possibilities. Chapter 3 provided a solid background on medical law and ethics. Here, in Chapter 4, we take a closer look at healthcare reform, namely the **Affordable Care Act (ACA)**, the major changes included in it, and how it affects the American people. Some of the more common types of health insurance models are also explained, as are insurance terms common to all third-party carriers.

The health insurance industry is constantly changing. What is trending in one region may be different in other areas of the country. Healthcare options available in rural communities can be vastly different from those accessible in large cities. Many independent rural clinics are being purchased and run by large hospitals or closed down completely. As a result, instead of having billers in each clinic, billing is centralized. Jobs tend to be more narrowly focused (such as billing electrocardiograms), and the depth of overall knowledge and capabilities required a couple of years ago might not be used today or tomorrow.

Note: It is important to keep in mind that as a result of a time lapse between the writing of these chapters and publication, some of the information, dates, and so on, contained may become outdated. It is difficult to be comprehensive when trends change so frequently. Students should be aware of the dynamics of health insurance and judiciously use the Internet for up-to-date information that affects the state or area in which they are employed.

REIMBURSEMENT MODELS

Fee-for-Service (Indemnity)

The traditional healthcare delivery system relies heavily on the **fee-for-service (FFS)** payment method in which a provider is paid a fee for rendering a specific service.

Under this healthcare reimbursement model, patients can choose any healthcare provider or hospital they want (including specialists) and change physicians at any time. Most types of insurance require the **insured** (or **policyholder**—the individual in whose name the policy is written) to pay a periodic fee (generally monthly or quarterly) called a **premium**. Premiums are based on the policy type and coverage, and the better the coverage, the higher the premium. With FFS policies, the patient also pays a certain amount of money up front each year toward his or her covered medical expenses, known as the **deductible**, before the insurance company begins paying benefits. These dollar amounts vary widely depending on the type of plan chosen (e.g., bronze, silver, gold, or platinum). The ACA has set limits on out-of-pocket (OOP) costs, and currently insurance policies have an annual OOP limit—or cap—on the dollar amount that the patient is responsible for. Under the act, most health plans are required to cover certain preventive care services at no OOP costs. These services do not require patients to meet their deductible or other limits first. (See "The Affordable Care Act of 2010: Major Reforms" and "Levels of Coverage" later in this chapter.) Under FFS, payment is traditionally based on what is referred to as **usual, customary, and reasonable (UCR)** rates. UCR rates are the part of a provider's charge that the insurance carrier allows as covered expenses. The UCR value of the provider's service is based on historical data developed from the following criteria:

- How much the provider charges his or her patients for the same or a similar service
- The variance in the charges by most providers for the same service in the same geographic area
- Whether the procedure requires more time, skill, or experience than it usually requires
- The value of the procedure in comparison with that of other services

Discounted fee-for-service

A variation on the FFS model is the discounted FFS. With this model the provider is paid for each service but requires the provider to give a discount on their typical fee. This model is used when the provider has a contract with certain types of managed care organizations, such as a preferred provider organization (PPO).

Capitation

Capitation refers to a form of healthcare reimbursement. In a capitation model, typically used in managed care plans such as health maintenance organizations (HMOs), the insurer (or other payer) contracts to pay the healthcare provider a specific dollar amount per patient during a particular period of time (e.g., 1 year). For example, if an insurer negotiates to pay a healthcare provider $300 per year for each of the 1000 people enrolled in the plan, the provider would receive a total of $300,000 for that year, and the provider would be expected to supply all medical services necessary to those 1000 people. The amount paid to the provider is not affected by the number of times the patient is seen by the provider.

Resource-Based Relative Value Scale

Another payment system that has become more widely used is the **resource-based relative value scale (RBRVS)**, a formula established by the Centers for Medicare and Medicaid Services (CMS) that assigns a value to every medical procedure to calculate Medicare's fee schedule allowance. In the RBRVS system, payments for services are determined by the resource costs needed to provide them. The cost of providing each service is divided into three components: (1) physician work, (2) practice expense, and (3) professional liability insurance. Payments are calculated by multiplying the combined costs of a service by a conversion factor (a monetary amount that is determined by CMS). Payments are also adjusted for geographic differences in resource costs. RBRVS is used by many health plans in negotiating fee schedules with in-network physicians. RBRVS is discussed in detail in Chapter 17.

Value-Based Care

We are currently in the process of transitioning from the traditional FFS model to **value-based care**. With value-based care, instead of providers being paid by the number of visits and tests they order for a patient (as with FFS), payments are based on the "value" of care they deliver. The target with value-based care is better healthcare at a lower cost. To learn more, type "value-based care" in your Internet search engine.

Episode-of-Care

Medicare uses both FFS methods and an **episode-of-care** method called a *prospective payment system (PPS)*. The PPS uses diagnosis-related groups (DRGs) to classify services, which can be bundled together into a single payment for an episode. Episode-of-care is defined as when a single provider is paid a set amount for all services rendered by that provider during a defined "episode." For example, a provider may be paid a predetermined amount for a patient undergoing a kidney transplant.

Note: Additional reimbursement models are discussed in Chapter 17.

THE AFFORDABLE CARE ACT OF 2010: MAJOR REFORMS

This landmark law (which we will frequently refer to simply as the act) transformed health insurance in the United States from what it was before the passing of this bill to what it is today. According to experts, many Americans are now receiving better care and more value for their healthcare dollar as a result of major changes in the way we insure the nation's health. Although the components of the act are constantly changing and will continue to do so in the foreseeable future, the major reforms are as follows:

1. Before healthcare reform, a health insurance company could deny certain coverage or exclude condition-specific benefits if an individual had a life-threatening or chronic health condition. Beginning in 2014, no insurer can charge more or deny coverage based on a person's current health status or a **preexisting condition**—a physical or mental illness or disorder that existed before the issuance of an insurance policy. (This provision went into effect for children younger than 19 years on September 23, 2010.)

2. All health plans issued after September 23, 2010, must offer a wide range of in-network **preventive services**—certain routine healthcare that includes checkups, patient counseling, and screenings to prevent illness, disease, and other health-related problems—and treatments for adults and children with no OOP costs such as copayments, coinsurance, or the need to meet a deductible. For example, there is no patient responsibility, such as a copayment, for a mammogram or colonoscopy.

    Note: **Coinsurance** is the percentage amount a patient is required to pay out of pocket toward the cost of healthcare when a health insurance claim is filed. Coinsurance commonly is 20/80, meaning that the patient pays 20% of the allowable charge and the insurance policy pays 80%. A **copayment** is a specific dollar amount (e.g., $30) that a patient must pay out of pocket for a healthcare encounter. The coinsurance or copayment is usually in addition to the deductible.

3. Lifetime limits are no longer imposed for **essential health benefits**—minimum coverage requirements for all plans in the **health insurance marketplace** (including **grandfathered plans**) in 2010—and annual limits were prohibited on new health insurance plans beginning in 2014. Health insurance marketplaces, also called *health exchanges,* are organizations set up to facilitate the purchase of health insurance in each state in accordance with the act.

    Grandfathered plans are those that were in effect before March 23, 2010, when the act was signed into law. These plans are allowed to offer the same coverage that was in place before the act.

4. Cost controls, called *medical loss ratios,* require insurers to spend at least 80% of individual plan premium dollars (85% for group plans) on actual medical care rather than administrative costs and profits. If insurers do not spend the required amount, they must send rebates to policyholders.

5. It is now illegal for insurers to cancel a policy except in the case of outright false or incomplete information on an application or nonpayment of premiums.

    Private insurers must explain why a claim was denied and the steps that can be taken to challenge their decision. If the insurer still denies coverage after its required internal review, the patient can request an external review by an independent organization with the power to overturn the decision.

Out-of-Pocket Maximum and Lifetime Limits

Most policies generally have an **out-of-pocket maximum**, which is the most the policyholder must pay for covered essential health benefits during a policy period (usually 1 year) before the health insurance plan starts to pay 100%. This dollar limit includes deductibles, coinsurance, copayments, and any other expenditure the individual must pay that is considered a qualified medical expense.

Under the act, the maximum OOP cost for any marketplace plan for 2020 can be no more than $8200 for an individual plan and $16,400 for a family plan. In May 2015, the government branches that oversee the ACA established the rule that, beginning in 2016, non-grandfathered health plans—including self-funded and large-group plans—must apply an "embedded self-only out-of-pocket (OOP)" maximum to each individual enrolled in family coverage if the plan's family OOP maximum exceeds the ACA's OOP limit for self-only coverage: $8200.

The act bans **annual dollar limits** that all job-related plans and individual health insurance plans can put on most covered health benefits. Before the enactment of the healthcare law, many health plans set an annual limit—a dollar limit on yearly reimbursement for covered benefits—after which patients were required to pay the cost of all care exceeding those limits. Some exceptions apply to the annual dollar limit under the act:

- Plans can put an annual dollar limit and a lifetime dollar limit on spending for healthcare services that are not considered essential health benefits.
- Grandfathered individual health insurance policies are not required to follow the rules on annual limits.

As mentioned, essential health benefits are minimum requirements for all plans in the marketplace; however, some plans may offer additional coverage. Essential health benefits include at least the following items and services:

- Ambulatory patient services (outpatient care one gets without being admitted to a hospital)
- Emergency services
- Hospitalization (such as surgery)
- Pregnancy, maternity, and newborn care
- Mental health and substance use disorder services, including behavioral health treatment, such as counseling and psychotherapy
- Prescription drugs

- Rehabilitative and habilitative services and devices (services and devices to help people with injuries, disabilities, or chronic conditions gain or recover mental and physical skills)
- Laboratory services
- Preventive and wellness services and chronic disease management
- Pediatric services, including oral and vision care

Note: All marketplace plans must offer pediatric dental and vision care for children 18 years and younger but not for adults.

Previously, many healthcare plans set a **lifetime limit**—a dollar limit on what a patient would spend for covered benefits during the entire time he or she was enrolled in that plan. Then, the patient was required to pay the cost of all care exceeding those limits. Under the act, lifetime limits on essential benefits are prohibited in any health plan or insurance policy. Insurance companies can, however, still put yearly or lifetime dollar limits on spending for healthcare services that are not considered essential health benefits.

Levels of Coverage

Before the introduction of the act, we referred to levels of healthcare coverage as "basic," "major medical," and "comprehensive." Basic is a low-cost, limited coverage that typically includes common medical expenses such as doctors' visits, laboratory tests, and certain surgical procedures. Major medical covers most serious medical expenses up to a maximum limit, usually after a deductible and coinsurance have been met. A **comprehensive plan** combines the benefits of both basic and major medical, typically covering a patient's total healthcare needs.

Levels of coverage have changed to some degree under the ACA. Now, health plans are still grouped by levels of coverage—how much the plan will pay for healthcare and what services are covered; however, each level is named after a type of metal: bronze, silver, gold, or platinum, sometimes referred to as "**metal plans**" or "**metal levels**." "Basic" coverage is similar to a bronze plan, which has the fewest benefits, lowest premium, and highest OOP costs. A silver-level plan can be compared with major medical coverage. It is in the middle range for coverage. A gold-level plan has a higher level of coverage than bronze or silver. Platinum plans have the most comprehensive coverage of all four plans. The "metal" plans vary by the percentage of costs the enrollee has to pay on average toward the healthcare services they receive and by the choice of providers. The average percentages that **enrollees** (people who are covered under the managed care plan) typically pay OOP for healthcare costs for each type of plan are as follows:

- Bronze: 60% covered by the plan; 40% by the consumer
- Silver: 70% covered by the plan; 30% by the consumer
- Gold: 80% covered by the plan; 20% by the consumer
- Platinum: 90% covered by the plan; 10% by the consumer

A fifth type of care is the "catastrophic plan," which pays less than 60% of the total cost of care on average. This plan protects the individual from worst-case medical scenarios, such as serious accidents and illnesses. The entire deductible must be paid first before the plan pays. However, preventive care and three primary care visits per year are free from deductibles. Catastrophic plans are available only to people who are under 30 years old or have a **hardship exemption**. A hardship exemption can be acquired for certain life situations that prevent an individual from being able to afford health insurance, such as foreclosure of or eviction from the person's home or incurring substantial debt as a result of high medical expenses.

Those who enroll in the silver plan and whose incomes fall below 250% of the federal poverty level receive cost-sharing subsidies. These subsidies are in addition to any tax credit for which they may be eligible. **Cost-sharing**, in which patients pay a portion of their healthcare costs, such as through a deductible or copayment, is automatically applied based on income. Fig. 4.1

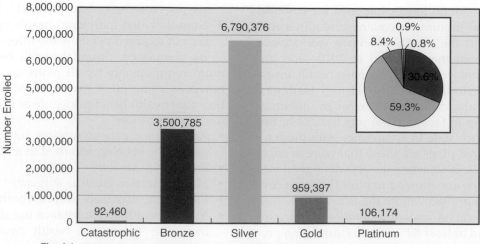

Fig. 4.1 Affordable Care Act enrollment by metal plan type. (Data from healthcare.gov.)

shows enrollment in the various metal plans as of March 2019.

Limitations and Exclusions

Sometimes the insurance policy does not cover certain medical conditions. These are known as **exclusions** (illnesses or injuries not covered by the policy). Historically, many exclusions were due to a preexisting condition. No health insurance plan covers everything, and every plan includes a section called the *limitations and exclusions*. Following is a list of medical services and equipment the patient's health plan may not pay for. Keep in mind, however, that exclusions vary from one plan to another and according to the level of benefits included in the plan. Common services excluded by most (but not necessarily all) health plans include:

- Long-term care
- Eyeglasses or contact lenses
- Adult dental services
- Fertility treatment
- Cosmetic surgery
- Acupuncture
- Private nursing care
- Weight loss surgery[a]

The ACA now makes it illegal for health insurance companies to deny coverage to any applicant with a preexisting condition. Further, insurers cannot charge any more for that applicant's health insurance than they would for any healthy applicant. The requirement for insurers to cover children with preexisting conditions was implemented soon after passage of the law in 2010. Immediately after the law was passed, children could no longer be denied coverage by the insurer that covered their parents and must be included in family coverage. The part of the law that covers adults with preexisting conditions was not in force until 2014.

 Imagine This!

Larry Burton and his wife, Marjorie, want to have a baby; however, after several years of trying, Marjorie has not been able to get pregnant. One of Marjorie's friends suggested they try in vitro fertilization (IVF), because she was successful in having a child using this method. "Isn't that expensive?" Marjorie asked. "Oh, our insurance paid for 80% of the cost," her friend responded. What might Larry and Marjorie consider as far as insurance coverage is concerned before undergoing IVF?

Preventive Services

Under the ACA, people may be eligible for some important preventive services, which can help avoid

[a]Different plans have different rules regarding coverage for weight loss programs, treatment, medications, or surgery. Each state must cover certain essential benefits, but it gets to decide what's included in those benefits. Check healthcare.gov or your state's marketplace to find out what is covered.

illness and improve health at no additional cost. Insurance plans that are subject to these requirements provide certain benefits for free. In other words, people do not have to pay a copayment, coinsurance, or deductible to receive recommended preventive health services, such as screenings, vaccinations, and counseling. For example, depending on age, individuals covered under qualifying policies have access to preventive services such as:

- Blood pressure, diabetes, and cholesterol tests
- Common cancer screenings, including mammograms and colonoscopies
- Counseling on such topics as quitting smoking, losing weight, eating healthfully, treating depression, and reducing alcohol use
- Regular well-baby and well-child visits, from birth to age 21 years
- Routine vaccinations against diseases, such as measles, polio, or meningitis
- Counseling, screening, and vaccines to ensure healthy pregnancies
- Flu and pneumonia shots

Note: The preventive services provision applies only to people enrolled in job-related health plans or individual health insurance policies created after March 23, 2010.

Standardized Benefits and Coverage Rule

In August 2011, the US Department of Health and Human Services (HHS) announced a rule that will help consumers choose new health insurance policies or better understand their existing ones. Starting in March 2012, all insurance vendors were required to provide consumers with a standard four-page "Summary of Benefits and Coverage (SBC)," along with a universal glossary of common health insurance terms (e.g., "deductible," "copay"). The summary must spell out specific elements: what the policy does and does not cover and the cost of the periodic premium and cost-sharing requirements, such as what the annual deductible is, how much an individual should expect to pay in OOP costs (e.g., coinsurance and copayments), and information on any exceptions, reductions, or limitations under the coverage. The rule is part of the ACA, disclosed by CMS.

Under this rule, if an insurance company wants to make major changes to a policy, policyholders would have to be notified of the changes 60 days in advance. Before the rule, insurers offered policy information in a lengthy, often difficult-to-understand document called a *certificate of coverage*, which was generally provided after the policy was purchased. The SBC also contains real-life examples, such as having a baby, treating breast cancer, and managing diabetes, explaining what proportion of healthcare expenses a policy will cover. Those who are shopping for or enrolled in a healthcare plan can request a copy of the SBC and must receive it within 7 days. The uniform glossary is made available on request, as well as in a link provided in the coverage label by the plan or insurance company. Refer to the Evolve website for links to the uniform glossary. To view this document, log on to the HealthCare.gov website and use the key words "Summary of Benefits and Coverage."

It is safe to say that the ACA is a "work in progress," and it is important to keep up with the changes. For example, a provision effective January 1, 2015, tied physician payments to the quality of care these physicians provide. Physicians' payments will be modified so that those who provide higher-value care will receive higher payments than those who provide lower-quality care. A good Internet source for keeping abreast of the latest news on healthcare is http://www.hhs.gov/healthcare/index.html.

MANAGED CARE

The term *managed care* is often heard on the news to describe certain medical plans, and many people do not know what it means. **Managed care** is medical care that is provided by a corporation established under state and federal laws. This corporation makes medical decisions for its enrollees. Managed care organizations contract with healthcare providers and medical facilities to provide care to their members at reduced cost. A managed care provider tells patients which physicians they can see, monitors the medications and treatments prescribed, and ensures that enrollees' costs will remain as low as possible. For these services, enrollees pay a set insurance premium each year and a small copayment with each visit. To perform these services satisfactorily, the corporation typically hires a medical staff (physicians, nurses, and other healthcare providers). These "employees" are under contract and to some degree take their orders from corporate management. Many types of managed care organizations are available. For more detailed information on managed care, see Chapter 9.

? What Did You Learn?

1. The traditional healthcare delivery system in which payment is made to the provider for each specific service performed is _____.
2. Name the reimbursement model in which providers are paid based on the "value" of care they deliver.
3. List five major reforms of the Affordable Care Act.
4. What effect did the Affordable Care Act have on preexisting conditions?
5. What are the various levels of coverage under the Affordable Care Act?
6. Under the act, individuals enrolled in job-related health plans have access to preventive services such as _____. (Name at least four.)
7. Explain the Standardized Benefits and Coverage rule.
8. How is managed care different from more traditional healthcare models?

THE HEALTH INSURANCE MARKETPLACE

There are different types of health insurance plans designed to meet different needs. Some types of plans restrict or encourage people to get care from the plan's network of physicians, hospitals, pharmacies, and other medical service providers. Patients pay a greater share of costs for providers outside the plan's network. Plan types you'll find in the health insurance marketplace include the following:

- *Exclusive Provider Organization (EPO):* A plan composed of a network of individual (or groups of) healthcare providers who have entered into written agreements with a third-party insurer to provide health insurance coverage to those individuals enrolled in the plan. Enrollees are reimbursed only if the medical expenses are rendered by this designated network of providers, who in turn provide patients with services at significantly lower rates than they would have been under more traditional reimbursement models.
- *Health Maintenance Organization (HMO):* A type of plan that typically limits healthcare coverage from providers who work for or contract with the HMO. It generally will not cover out-of-network care except in an emergency. An HMO may require an enrollee to live or work in its service area to be eligible for coverage. HMOs often provide integrated care and focus on prevention and wellness.
- *Point of Service (POS):* A type of managed care plan that combines characteristics of the HMO and the preferred provider organization (PPO). A major difference is that POS plans allow their policyholders to receive medical care outside the network, although use of facilities and physicians within the network is encouraged since medical costs may be lower. Members of a POS plan do not make a choice about which system to use until the point at which the service is being used. POS plans require a referral from your primary care doctor to see a specialist.
- *Preferred Provider Organization (PPO):* A group of healthcare providers who contract with a private insurer and agree to render particular services to the plan's enrollees. These services may be furnished at discounted rates if the patients receive their care from member providers rather than select a provider outside the network. PPOs also offer more flexibility by allowing visits to out-of-network professionals, although at a greater expense to the patient. Patients usually have a primary care physician (PCP) within the network who arranges any necessary referrals to specialists that will be covered by the PPO.

Individuals can obtain healthcare coverage in today's insurance markets in several ways. Many are eligible for coverage through their employers offering a group plan. A group plan is a contract of insurance made with a company, a corporation, or other groups of common interest wherein all employees or individuals (and their eligible dependents) are insured under a single policy. Self-employed individuals and individuals who are ineligible for coverage through their employer should contact a professional health insurance agent and apply for a private policy. In addition, government programs, such as Medicare and Medicaid, are available for qualifying individuals.

> ### [?] What Did You Learn?
>
> 1. Name four alternative types of health plans available in the health insurance marketplace.
> 2. What is the difference between an HMO and a PPO?
> 3. True or false: In a POS plan, patients are not allowed to see a healthcare provider outside the network of plan providers under any circumstances.
> 4. A healthcare plan in which an insurer contracts with a company, a corporation, or other groups of common interest wherein all employees (and their eligible dependents) are insured under a single policy is a
> _____.

MAJOR HEALTHCARE PAYERS

This book dedicates four chapters (10, 11, 12, and 13) to presenting detailed information on the following major healthcare payers.

MEDICAID

Medicaid covers some low-income individuals (particularly children and pregnant women) and certain disabled individuals. Medicaid is a joint federal–state health program that is administered by the individual states. Medicaid coverage differs from state to state. See Chapter 10 for more extensive information on Medicaid.

MEDICARE

Medicare is a federal health insurance program that provides benefits to individuals 65 years or older and to individuals younger than 65 years who have certain disabilities. In many parts of the United States, Medicare-eligible patients now have a choice between managed care and indemnity plans. For individuals who enroll in the traditional Medicare plan, private insurance options help cover some of the gaps in Medicare coverage. These supplemental policies are called **Medigap** or **Medicare Supplement plans**. These policies must cover certain expenses, such as deductibles and the daily coinsurance amount for hospitalization. Some Medicare managed care policies may offer additional benefits, such as coverage for preventive medical care, prescription drugs, or at-home recovery that original Medicare does not cover. For more details on Medicare, Medigap, and Medicare Supplement plans, see Chapter 11.

TRICARE/CHAMPVA

TRICARE is the US military's comprehensive healthcare program for active-duty personnel and eligible family members, retirees, and family members younger than 65 years and survivors of all uniformed services (i.e., Army, Air Force, Marines, and Navy). The TRICARE program is managed by the military in partnership with civilian hospitals and clinics. It is designed to expand access to care, ensure high-quality care, and promote medical readiness. All military hospitals and clinics are part of the TRICARE program.

The **Civilian Health and Medical Program of the Department of Veterans Affairs (CHAMPVA)** is a health benefits program in which the Department of Veterans Affairs (VA) shares the cost of certain healthcare services and supplies with eligible beneficiaries. CHAMPVA is managed by the VA's Health Administration Center in Denver, Colorado, where applications are processed, eligibility is determined, benefits are authorized, and medical claims are processed. Military insurance programs are discussed in detail in Chapter 12.

DISABILITY INSURANCE

Disability insurance is a form of insurance that pays the policyholder a specific sum of money in place of his or her usual income if the policyholder cannot work because of illness or accident. It is not health insurance coverage per se. Usually policies begin paying after a waiting period stipulated in the policy and pay a certain percentage of the policyholder's usual income. Sometimes disability insurance is provided by employers, but it also is available as individual private coverage. Several types of disability insurance are available.

Private

An individual can purchase a private disability insurance policy or can be covered by a disability policy offered by his or her employer. Disability insurance does not cover illnesses or injuries related to one's employment. It is designed to replace 45% to 60% of an individual's gross income on a tax-free basis should an illness unrelated to the job prevent him or her from earning an income. Disability insurance policies vary from one insurance company to another. Disability insurance can provide short-term or long-term benefits, depending on the stipulations of the policy. Private disability insurance can be costly; however, some employers offer it to their employees at more reasonable rates. There is often a waiting period (e.g., 30 days) before benefits begin.

Social Security Disability Insurance

Social Security Disability Insurance (SSDI) is an insurance program for individuals who become unable to work. It is administered by the Social Security Administration (SSA) and is funded by Federal Insurance Contributions Act (FICA) tax withheld from workers' pay and by matching employer contributions. SSDI pays qualifying disabled workers cash and healthcare benefits. If you are age 31 or older, you must have worked and paid FICA tax for at least 5 of the past 10 years to pass the recent work test. Put another way, you will need to have earned 20 credits (one quarter of work equals one credit) in the 10 years immediately before you became disabled to be covered by SSDI. Younger workers can qualify with fewer years of work. A person can apply for SSDI benefits at any SSA office. There is a 5-month waiting period before an individual can begin receiving SSDI benefits. This is to ensure that benefits are paid only to those who have long-term disabilities. A free booklet titled *Social Security Disability Benefits* (SSA Publication No. 05-10029) is available at any Social Security office or through the SSA toll-free phone number: 800-772-1213. Individuals can apply via the Internet at http://www.ssa.gov/.

The supplemental security income disability program has marked similarities to SSDI. Both programs are run by the SSA, both offer disability benefits, and both use the same legal definition of "disability." The programs differ significantly, however, in their financial qualifications and benefits.

Workers' Compensation

Workers' compensation insurance pays workers who are injured or disabled on the job or have job-related illnesses. Laws governing workers' compensation are designed to ensure that employees who are injured or disabled on the job are provided with fixed monetary awards, eliminating the need for litigation. These laws also provide benefits for dependents of workers who die as a result of work-related accidents or illnesses. Some laws also protect employers and fellow workers by limiting the amount an injured employee can recover from an employer and by eliminating the liability of coworkers in most accidents. State workers' compensation statutes establish this framework for most employment and differ from state to state. Federal statutes are limited to federal employees or workers employed in some significant aspect of interstate commerce.

The Federal Employees' Compensation Act provides workers' compensation for nonmilitary federal employees. Many of its provisions are typical of most workers' compensation laws. Awards are limited to "disability or death" sustained while in the performance of the employee's duties but not caused willfully by the employee or by intoxication. The act covers medical expenses resulting from the disability and may require the employee to undergo job retraining. In other words, if the employee is unable to return to his or her original position because of a particular disability, the employee is trained to perform in a different

position, ideally at an equal level of pay. A disabled employee receives two-thirds of his or her normal monthly salary during the disability period and may receive more for permanent physical injuries or if he or she has dependents. The act provides compensation for survivors of employees who are killed. The Office of Workers' Compensation Programs administers the act.

The Federal Employers' Liability Act, although not a workers' compensation statute, provides that railroads engaged in interstate commerce are liable for injuries to their employees if they have been negligent. Disability insurance and workers' compensation are discussed in Chapter 13.

What Did You Learn?

1. What classes of people are covered by Medicaid?
2. The federal health insurance program that provides benefits to individuals 65 years or older and individuals younger than 65 years with certain disabilities is _____.
3. Name the US military's comprehensive healthcare program for active-duty personnel and eligible family members, retirees, and family members younger than 65 years and survivors of all uniformed services.
4. _____ is an insurance program for individuals who become unable to work.
5. True or false: Workers' compensation laws were created to eliminate the need for litigation.
6. How does disability insurance differ from workers' compensation?

MISCELLANEOUS HEALTHCARE COVERAGE OPTIONS

The next few subsections describe various healthcare coverage options that are available to people instead of or in addition to group or individual policies. Some options have been around for a while; some are relatively new. It's important to point out that no one type is universally better than the others.

HEALTH SAVINGS ACCOUNT

A **health savings account (HSA)**, sometimes referred to as a **medical savings account (MSA)**, is a special tax shelter set up for the purpose of paying medical bills. It is similar to an individual retirement account (IRA), which allows an individual to make tax-deferred contributions to a personal retirement fund, and works in conjunction with a special low-cost, high-deductible health insurance policy to provide comprehensive healthcare coverage at the lowest possible net cost for individuals who qualify.

Here's how an HSA works. Instead of buying high-priced health insurance with low copayments and a low deductible, the individual or business purchases a low-cost policy with a high deductible for the big bills and saves the difference in the HSA to cover smaller bills. Money deposited into the HSA is 100% tax deductible (as with a traditional IRA) and can be easily accessed by check or debit card to pay most medical bills tax free (even expenses not covered by insurance, such as dental and vision care). The funds that are not used for medical bills stay in the HSA and keep growing on a tax-favored basis to cover future medical bills or to supplement retirement. An HSA plan in combination with a high-deductible health insurance plan offers (1) lower premiums, (2) lower taxes, (3) freedom of choice, and (4) more cash at retirement.

Funds can be withdrawn for other purposes, but if that is done, the individual will face both increased income taxes and penalties. (Currently, the penalty does not apply to people over age 65.)

HIPAA Tip

Health savings accounts (HSAs) under the Health Insurance Portability and Accountability Act (HIPAA) provide federal tax deductions for contributions to multiyear savings accounts established for medical purposes.

FLEXIBLE SPENDING ACCOUNT

The **flexible spending account (FSA)** is an Internal Revenue Service (IRS) Section 125 **cafeteria plan**. A plan falls into the cafeteria category when the cost of the plan (premium) is deducted from the employee's wages before withholding taxes are deducted. This allows employees the option of pretax payroll deduction for some insurance premiums, unreimbursed medical expenses, and child or dependent care expenses. Cafeteria plans are among the fastest-growing employee benefits. Employers save when employees elect for pretax payroll deduction because lower adjusted gross income also reduces matching FICA and federal unemployment tax. Employees benefit because expenses for such items as health insurance premiums and unreimbursed medical, vision, dental, and child or dependent care expenses paid before the tax deduction result in immediate tax savings. When employees switch expenses to "before tax," they save on Social Security tax, federal income tax, and state and local tax (in most states). There are obvious advantages associated with FSAs. Consequently, the government has placed certain restrictions on plans of this type in exchange for the favorable tax treatment.

During the year, FSA participants may change the amount of their contribution designation only if there is a change in the health premium or the employee's family status. Participants should also be aware that funds in a FSA generally do not roll from year to year. Calculating how much to put into this type plan should be done carefully. If the funds are not used up by December 31, they are lost to the participant.

HEALTH REIMBURSEMENT ARRANGEMENTS

Health reimbursement arrangements (HRAs), also known as *health reimbursement accounts* or *personal care accounts,* are a type of health insurance plan that reimburses employees for certain qualifying medical expenses. HRAs consist of funds set aside by employers to reimburse employees for "qualified" medical expenses.

An HRA provides "first-dollar" medical coverage until funds are used up. First-dollar coverage means that the individual does not have any deductible or copayments—expenses are paid beginning with the first dollar charged for care. For example, if an employee incurs a $250 qualifying medical expense, the full amount will be covered by the HRA if there is enough money in the account. Under an HRA, the employer, rather than the employee, provides the funds. All unused funds are retained in the account at the end of the year. Former employees, including retirees, can have continued access to unused reimbursement amounts; however, HRAs remain with the originating employer and do not follow an employee to new employment. Employers can deduct the cost of the HRA as a business expense under IRS rules.

PREMIUM REIMBURSEMENT ARRANGEMENT

The **premium reimbursement arrangement (PRA),** or premium-only plan, is a relatively new option in employee health benefits. This option is often a choice of businesses that do not offer health benefits to their employees or when a new business is started. With a PRA health plan, employers allow their employees to reimburse themselves for their individual health insurance costs with pretax wages. This results in an immediate savings on their health insurance premiums. At the same time, the company realizes a savings in FICA taxes on all reimbursements. This savings can also offset any setup or monthly fees. The PRA can reimburse any expense considered a qualified medical expense by the IRS; however, employers may restrict the list of reimbursable expenses the IRS allows. There is no limit to the amount of money an employer can contribute to an employee's benefits.

Table 4.1 compares key features of HSAs, FSAs, HRAs, and PRAs. It is important to note that rules and dollar amounts are subject to change annually.

Imagine This!

Donald Barker begins working for Chase Instruments, which offers a premium reimbursement arrangement (PRA) to its employees. After he begins work, Donald selects a personal health policy for himself and his dependents, after which he is reimbursed, tax free, for his current health plan premiums, as well as for specific medical expenses allowed by his employer and the Internal Revenue Service (IRS).

HEALTH INSURANCE EXCHANGES

As discussed in Chapter 1, due to the ACA, additional types of healthcare plans are now available through **health insurance exchanges**—a state-provided health

Table 4.1 Comparison of Key Features of Health Spending Accounts (2020)

	HEALTH REIMBURSEMENT ARRANGEMENT (HRA)	HEALTH SAVINGS ACCOUNT (HSA)	FLEXIBLE SPENDING ACCOUNT (FSA)	PREMIUM REIMBURSEMENT ARRANGEMENT (PRA)
Who may contribute	Employer only	Employer or employee	Employer or employee	Employee (final rules pending)
Maximum annual contribution	No maximum	$3550 (single) $7100 (family)	Determined by employer; capped at $2750	Determined by employer; usually total compensation
Eligibility requirements	None or determined by employer	Must have high deductible health plan (HDHP)	None or determined by employer	None or determined by employer
Employee bank account required	No	Yes	No	No
Tax treatment	Tax free	Tax free	Tax free	Tax free
Medical expenses allowed	Health insurance premiums + IRS Code 213d[a] expenses as determined by employer	IRS Code 213d expenses with no employer limitations	IRS Code 213d expenses but no personal health insurance	Personal health insurance only
Use for nonmedical expenses	None	None	None	None
Carryover for unused funds to next year	Determined by employer	Yes	No	No
Portability after termination of employment	Determined by employer	Yes	No	No
Administrator	Determined by employer	Employee	Determined by employer	Determined by employer

[a]An eligible medical expense as defined in Internal Revenue Service (IRS) Code Section 213d.

Adapted from US Department of Labor Statistics: *Health spending accounts* (website). http://www.bls.gov/opub/mlr/cwc/health-spending-accounts.pdf.

plan that is federally subsidized. The intention of this model is to create a more organized and competitive market for health insurance by offering a choice of plans with common rules governing how each plan is offered and its cost and providing information to help consumers better understand the choices available to them.

Exchanges do not provide insurance. The state programs select insurance companies to participate in the exchanges based on consumer needs and a determination that each insurance company's goal is cost efficiency. The concept of exchanges is to spread high costs for select healthcare users over a wider base of insured members. This practice lowers the cost for the insured who are at high risk for disease or those insured while undergoing expensive health treatment and care.

ACCOUNTABLE CARE ORGANIZATIONS

Another healthcare model is the **accountable care organization (ACO)**. The intention of this coverage model is to provide a more efficient way to deliver care. Similar to an HMO, an ACO is a network of doctors and hospitals that shares responsibility for providing care to patients. Under the healthcare law, ACOs agree to

manage all healthcare needs of a minimum of 5000 Medicare beneficiaries for at least 3 years. Goals for an ACO are to determine how to successfully:
- Keep patients within the ACO, encouraging them to stay healthy and take more responsibility for their own healthcare
- Encourage patients to use healthcare providers that are part of the ACO network to keep the overall costs down within the organization

LONG-TERM CARE INSURANCE

When we are healthy, it is easy to take activities of daily living (ADLs), such as bathing, dressing, and feeding ourselves, for granted. When an individual is stricken with a degenerative condition, however, such as a stroke or Alzheimer disease, performing these ADLs becomes impossible without the assistance of another person. This type of care is referred to as **long-term care**; it is ongoing and quickly becomes expensive. Long-term care is not medical care but rather custodial care. Custodial care involves providing an individual with assistance with or supervision of (or both) ADLs that he or she no longer can perform.

Today, long-term care insurance typically covers a broad range of services, including nursing home care, assisted living facilities, certain types of home healthcare, and adult day care. Similar to any insurance product, long-term care insurance allows the insured to pay an affordable premium to protect himself or herself in case of an unaffordable catastrophic event.

DENTAL CARE

A health insurance plan may or may not cover dental care. Even if it does, it might not cover all procedures, such as orthodontics (teeth straightening) and cosmetic dentistry. Because dental care can be expensive, a separate dental insurance policy can be purchased. Health insurance plans typically cover dental restoration work needed because of disease or accident. As mentioned, all marketplace plans must offer pediatric dental and vision care for children age 18 and younger but not for adults.

VISION CARE

As with dental care, a health insurance plan may or may not cover vision care. General eye care, such as refractions (vision tests), are typically provided by an optometrist, a professional who is trained and licensed to examine eyes, check for eye diseases and problems, and prescribe corrective lenses. More serious vision problems are normally handled by an ophthalmologist—a medical doctor specializing in eye diseases.

◎ HIPAA Tip

The Health Insurance Reform Act, incorporated within the Health Insurance Portability and Accountability Act (HIPAA), includes consumer protections for purchasers of long-term care insurance and clarifications that make treatment of private long-term care insurance identical to that of health insurance coverage.

? What Did You Learn?

1. List four types of healthcare options.
2. What is a health insurance exchange?
3. Explain how an HSA operates.
4. What are the benefits of an FSA?
5. What type of healthcare typically falls in the category of long-term care?

CMS-1500 CLAIM FORM

For medical bills to be paid, the patient or the healthcare provider must fill out forms and send them to the insurance carrier (payer). The form most commonly used is referred to as the **CMS-1500 claim form** (version 02/12), a universal form created by the government for Medicare claims and since adopted by most third-party carriers. The CMS-1500 may be submitted in paper form (under specific circumstances) or electronically. To view the CMS-1500, see Appendix A. Detailed information

on the CMS-1500 paper form is provided in Chapter 6. The CMS-1500 is updated periodically, so it is important to use the most recent version of the form when submitting claims. It is recommended that when completing a claim, the guidelines set forth by the National Uniform Claim Committee be followed. These detailed guidelines can be found at http://nucc.org/.

Medicare claims may be electronically submitted from a provider's office using a computer with software that meets electronic filing requirements as established by the HIPAA claim standard. In certain circumstances, providers can submit paper claims if they meet the qualifications. These qualifications can be found in Chapter 11 under "Exceptions to Mandatory Electronic Claim Submission." For all other claims, follow the guidelines as directed by the specific payer.

? What Did You Learn?

1. The form most commonly used to submit paper claims is referred to as the _____.
2. True or false: This universal form must be submitted only electronically to be eligible for reimbursement.
3. What is the name of the organization that provides guidelines for completing the form?
4. Software used to submit claims must meet the electronic filing requirements established by _____.

CONSOLIDATED OMNIBUS BUDGET RECONCILIATION ACT

Congress passed the **Consolidated Omnibus Budget Reconciliation Act (COBRA)** health benefit provisions in 1986. The law amends the Employee Retirement Income Security Act, the Internal Revenue Code, and the Public Health Service Act to provide continuation of group health coverage that otherwise would be terminated when an individual leaves his or her place of employment. The law generally covers group health plans maintained by employers with 20 or more employees in the prior year. It applies to plans in the private sector and plans sponsored by state and local governments. The law does not apply, however, to plans sponsored by the US government and certain church-related organizations. Under COBRA, a group health plan is ordinarily defined as a plan that provides medical benefits for the employer's own employees and their dependents through insurance or otherwise (e.g., a trust, HMO, self-funded pay-as-you-go basis, reimbursement, or combination of these).

COBRA contains provisions that give certain former employees and retirees, as well as their spouses and dependent children, the right to temporary continuation of health coverage at group rates. Currently, most people working for qualifying employers can continue their coverage for 18 months under the COBRA program when they lose their jobs. COBRA premiums can be expensive, however, because the ex-employee must pay the share of premiums once covered by the employer as well as his or her own share from the previous group health plan. Events that can cause workers and their family members to lose group health coverage and that may result in the right to COBRA coverage include the following:

- Voluntary or involuntary termination of the covered employee's employment for reasons other than gross misconduct
- Reduced hours of work for the covered employee
- Covered employee becoming entitled to Medicare
- Divorce or legal separation of a covered employee
- Death of a covered employee
- Loss of status as a dependent child under plan rules

Employee or retiree entitlement to Medicare does not apply because entitlement to Medicare does not result in loss of coverage.

 Imagine This!

Mary is an employee covered under Southeast Medical Clinic's group health plan. When her employment terminates, she elects COBRA. Her maximum coverage period is 18 months. On the last day of the tenth month of her COBRA coverage, Mary gives birth. Her child is a qualified beneficiary. The child's maximum coverage period is the remaining 8 months of Mary's maximum coverage period.

Medical benefits provided under the terms of the plan and available to COBRA beneficiaries may include, but are not necessarily limited to, the following:

- Inpatient and outpatient hospital care
- Physician care
- Surgery and other major medical benefits
- Prescription drugs
- Any other medical benefits, such as dental and vision care

It is important to note that the ACA did not change the COBRA rules.

 HIPAA Tip

The Health Insurance Portability and Accountability Act (HIPAA) does not set premium rates, but it does prohibit healthcare plans and issuers from charging an individual more than similarly situated individuals in the same plan because of health status. Plans may offer premium discounts or rebates for participation in wellness programs.

 What Did You Learn?

1. To whom does the COBRA law generally apply?
2. List the various events that qualify an employee for COBRA coverage.
3. What medical benefits are included under COBRA?

HEALTH INSURANCE "WATCHDOGS"

The following organizations are instrumental in recognizing and assessing healthcare plans and certifying the quality of the care they provide, functioning as "watchdogs":

- The Joint Commission—Evaluates and accredits nearly 20,000 healthcare organizations and programs, including almost 12,000 hospitals and home care organizations, and more than 7000 other healthcare organizations that provide long-term care, behavioral healthcare, and laboratory and ambulatory care services. The Joint Commission also accredits health plans, integrated delivery networks, and other managed care entities.
- National Committee for Quality Assurance (NCQA)—Accredits HMOs and other managed care organizations.
- American Accreditation HealthCare Commission (formerly Utilization Review Accreditation Commission [URAC])—Accredits PPOs and other managed care networks.
- Accreditation Association for Ambulatory Health Care—Accredits outpatient healthcare settings, such as ambulatory surgery centers, radiation oncology centers, and student health centers.
- Community Health Accreditation Partner—Accredits community, home health, and hospice programs; public health departments; and nursing centers.
- Consumer Coalition for Quality Health Care—A national, nonprofit organization of consumer groups advocating for consumer protections and quality assurance programs and policies.

Several of these organizations are discussed in later chapters.

 What Did You Learn?

1. What is the function of The Joint Commission?
2. List the names of the organizations that function as health insurance "watchdogs."

OTHER TERMS COMMON TO THIRD-PARTY CARRIERS

Many terms are used commonly in the medical provider, hospital, and healthcare industries. A few of the more commonly used terms are discussed here. In "Websites to Explore" at the end of this chapter, several URLs for accessing a comprehensive list of health insurance terms and their definitions are given.

BIRTHDAY RULE

The **birthday rule** is an informal procedure used in the health insurance industry to help determine which health plan is considered "primary" when individuals (usually children) are listed as dependents on more than one health plan. Sometimes parents include their children on each other's insurance plan to maximize coverage and, if they are divorced, to ensure that the children will be covered when visiting the other parent. The insurance plans need to coordinate benefits so that the claim is paid properly. To prevent overpayment, one parent's plan is designated as the primary plan and the other as a secondary plan. The birthday rule determines which plan is primary. It states that *the health plan of the parent whose birthday comes first in the calendar year will be considered the primary plan.*

When parents have the same birthday, the parent who has had his or her plan longer pays first. When parents are divorced or separated, the plan of the parent who has legal custody is considered primary. If the custodial parent remarries, the new spouse's plan would be considered secondary. The plan of the parent without custody would pay any additional expenses not covered. If one spouse is currently employed and has insurance and the other spouse has coverage through a former employer (COBRA), the plan of the currently employed spouse would be primary. Group plans are considered primary over individual plans.

It is important to keep in mind that these practices are common among insurance companies, but they are not governed by law. Practices may vary from one insurer to another. It is important that people read their policies carefully to make sure that they understand how their insurance company handles dual coverage. In addition, a prudent health insurance professional should discuss this situation with the patient's parent or guardian as it arises.

⚠ Stop and Think

Helen and Paul Jackson are recently divorced. Hunter, their 7-year-old son, comes to the office with a broken wrist. Helen informs the health insurance professional that she is the custodial parent, but the court has named Paul as the party responsible for all medical bills. After the divorce, Helen had quit her job to become a stay-at-home mom, and she and Hunter are still covered on a COBRA policy through Packers United; Paul is covered by a Blue Cross Blue Shield PPO group plan. Helen's birth date is listed on the patient information form as May 24, 1984. Hunter's father's birth date is September 5, 1979. To which third-party insurer should the insurance claim be sent first?

COORDINATION OF BENEFITS

In the past, it was not unusual for a husband and wife to each have the same or similar group health insurance benefits but on different policies. This was commonly referred to as *overinsurance.* Possible sources of overinsurance occurred when:

- The husband and the wife were employed and eligible for group health coverage, and each listed the other as a dependent
- A person was employed in two jobs, both of which provided group health insurance coverage

- A salaried or professional person who had group health insurance coverage with an employer also had an association group health plan

The historical concept of **coordination of benefits (COB)** has been to limit the total benefits an insured individual can receive from both group plans to not more than 100% of the allowable expenses. This prevents the policyholders from making a profit on health insurance claims.

Under COB, the primary plan pays benefits up to its limit; then the secondary plan pays the difference between the primary insurer's benefits and the total incurred allowable expenses (historically 100% of the allowed expenses) up to the secondary insurer's limit. Each state may have different COB regulations based on the National Association of Insurance Commissioners and variations in the language used to assist consistent claim administration. When this situation arises, the health insurance professional must rely on the patient (or his or her parent or guardian if a minor) to state which policy is primary. It is not the health insurance professional's responsibility to make this determination.

💡 Imagine This!

Mason and Tamara Oliver both work for the Appanoose Community College. Both are eligible for the group policy provided by the college. The college's policy is to pay one-half of its employees' premiums. To avoid a coordination of benefits (COB) situation, Mason lists Tamara and their two children on his policy. Because Tamara is technically eligible for her own policy as an employee of the college, the college reimburses her a dollar amount equal to one-half of the premiums she would be charged if she had a separate but identical policy.

MEDICAL NECESSITY

Most third-party payers do not pay for medical services, procedures, or supplies unless:

- They are proper and needed for the diagnosis or treatment of a patient's medical condition
- They are provided for the diagnosis, direct care, and treatment of a medical condition
- They meet the standards of good medical practice in the local area
- They are not mainly for the convenience of the patient or the healthcare provider

When medical services, procedures, or supplies meet these criteria, they are said to be **medically necessary** or meet the standards of "medical necessity." For treatment of Medicare patients, it is sometimes necessary to complete a certificate of medical necessity (Fig. 4.2).

UCR AND BALANCE BILLING

We learned earlier in this chapter that a UCR fee is a calculation of what certain third-party payers believe

U.S. DEPARTMENT OF HEALTH & HUMAN SERVICES
CENTERS FOR MEDICARE & MEDICAID SERVICES

FORM APPROVED
OMB NO. 0938-0679

CERTIFICATE OF MEDICAL NECESSITY

DMERC 01.02A

HOSPITAL BEDS

SECTION A   Certification Type/Date: INITIAL ___/___./___.   REVISED ___/___./___.

PATIENT NAME, ADDRESS, TELEPHONE and HIC NUMBER	SUPPLIER NAME, ADDRESS, TELEPHONE and NSC NUMBER
(_ _ _)_ _ _ -_ _ _ _ HICN _____	(_ _ _)_ _ _ -_ _ _ _ NSC # _____

| PLACE OF SERVICE _____
NAME and ADDRESS of FACILITY if applicable (See reverse) | HCPCS CODE
_____
_____
_____
_____ | PT DOB ___/___./___.; Sex ____ (M/F); HT. ____ (in.); WT.____ (lbs.)
PHYSICIAN NAME, ADDRESS (Printed or Typed)

PHYSICIAN'S UPIN: _____
PHYSICIAN'S TELEPHONE #: (_ _ _)_ _ _ _ -_ _ _ _ |

SECTION B   Information in this Section May Not Be Completed by the Supplier of the Items/Supplies.

EST. LENGTH OF NEED (# OF MONTHS): _____ 1-99 (99=LIFETIME) | DIAGNOSIS CODES (ICD-9): _____ _____ _____ _____

ANSWERS	ANSWER QUESTIONS 1, AND 3-7 FOR HOSPITAL BEDS
	(Circle **Y** for Yes, **N** for No, or **D** for Does Not Apply)
	QUESTION 2 RESERVED FOR OTHER OR FUTURE USE.
Y N D	1. Does the patient require positioning of the body in ways not feasible with an ordinary bed due to a medical condition which is expected to last at least one month?
Y N D	3. Does the patient require, for the alleviation of pain, positioning of the body in ways not feasible with an ordinary bed?
Y N D	4. Does the patient require the head of the bed to be elevated <u>more than 30 degrees</u> most of the time due to congestive heart failure, chronic pulmonary disease, or aspiration?
Y N D	5. Does the patient require traction which can only be attached to a hospital bed?
Y N D	6. Does the patient require a bed height different than a fixed height hospital bed to permit transfers to chair, wheelchair, or standing position?
Y N D	7. Does the patient require frequent changes in body position and/or have an immediate need for a change in body position?

NAME OF PERSON ANSWERING SECTION B QUESTIONS, IF OTHER THAN PHYSICIAN (Please Print):
NAME: _____ TITLE: _____ EMPLOYER: _____

SECTION C   **Narrative Description Of Equipment And Cost**

(1) <u>Narrative</u> description of all items, accessories and options ordered; **(2)** Supplier's charge; and **(3)** Medicare Fee Schedule Allowance for <u>each</u> item, accessory, and option. *(See Instructions On Back)*

SECTION D   **Physician Attestation and Signature/Date**

I certify that I am the physician identified in Section A of this form. I have received Sections A, B and C of the Certificate of Medical Necessity (including charges for items ordered). Any statement on my letterhead attached hereto, has been reviewed and signed by me. I certify that the medical necessity information in Section B is true, accurate and complete, to the best of my knowledge, and I understand that any falsification, omission, or concealment of material fact in that section may subject me to civil or criminal liability.

PHYSICIAN'S SIGNATURE _____ DATE ____/____/____ (SIGNATURE AND DATE STAMPS ARE NOT ACCEPTABLE)

CMS-841 (04/96)

A

Fig. 4.2 Certificate of medical necessity. (A) Front. (From US Department of Health and Human Services, Centers for Medicare bund Medicaid Services, Baltimore, MD.)

SECTION A:	**(May be completed by the supplier)**
CERTIFICATION TYPE/DATE:	If this is an initial certification for this patient, indicate this by placing date (MM/DD/YY) needed initially in the space marked "INITIAL." If this is a revised certification (to be completed when the physician changes the order, based on the patient's changing clinical needs), indicate the initial date needed in the space marked "INITIAL," <u>and also</u> indicate the recertification date in the space marked "REVISED." If this is a recertification, indicate the initial date needed in the space marked "INITIAL," <u>and also</u> indicate the recertification date in the space marked "RECERTIFICATION." Whether submitting a REVISED or a RECERTIFIED CMN, be sure to always furnish the INITIAL date as well as the REVISED <u>or</u> RECERTIFICATION date.
PATIENT INFORMATION:	Indicate the patient's name, permanent legal address, telephone number and his/her health insurance claim number (HICN) as it appears on his/her Medicare card and on the claim form.
SUPPLIER INFORMATION:	Indicate the name of your company (supplier name), address and telephone number along with the Medicare Supplier Number assigned to you by the National Supplier Clearinghouse (NSC).
PLACE OF SERVICE:	Indicate the place in which the item is being used; i.e., patient's home is 12, skilled nursing facility (SNF) is 31, End Stage Renal Disease (ESRD) facility is 65, etc. Refer to the DMERC supplier manual for a complete list.
FACILITY NAME:	If the place of service is a facility, indicate the name and complete address of the facility.
HCPCS CODES:	List all HCPCS procedure codes for items ordered that require a CMN. Procedure codes that do not require certification should not be listed on the CMN.
PATIENT DOB, HEIGHT, WEIGHT AND SEX:	Indicate patient's date of birth (MM/DD/YY) and sex (male or female); height in inches and weight in pounds, if requested.
PHYSICIAN NAME, ADDRESS:	Indicate the physician's name and complete mailing address.
UPIN:	Accurately indicate the ordering physician's Unique Physician Identification Number (UPIN). UPINs and surrogate UPINs may still be used to identify ordering and referring providers. http://www.feemedicare.info/are-upin-numbers-still-used/.
PHYSICIAN'S TELEPHONE NO:	Indicate the telephone number where the physician can be contacted (preferable where records would be accessible pertaining to this patient) if more information is needed.
SECTION B:	**(May not be completed by the supplier. While this section may be completed by a non-physician clinician, or a physician employee, it must be reviewed, and the CMN signed (in Section D) by the ordering physician.)**
EST. LENGTH OF NEED:	Indicate the estimated length of need (the length of time the physician expects the patient to require use of the ordered item) by filling in the appropriate number of months. If the physician expects that the patient will require the item for the duration of his/her life, then enter 99.
DIAGNOSIS CODES:	In the first space, list the diagnosis code that represents the primary reason for ordering this item. List any additional ICD9 codes that would further describe the medical need for the item (up to 3 codes).
QUESTION SECTION:	This section is used to gather clinical information to determine medical necessity. Answer each question which applies to the items ordered, circling "Y" for yes, "N" for no, "D" for does not apply, a number if this is offered as an answer option, or fill in the blank if other information is requested.
NAME OF PERSON ANSWERING SECTION B QUESTIONS:	If a clinical professional other than the ordering physician (e.g., home health nurse, physical therapist, dietician), or a physician employee answers the questions of Section B, he/she must <u>print</u> his/her name, give his/her professional title and the name of his/her employer where indicated. If the <u>physician</u> is answering the questions, this space may be left blank.
SECTION C:	**(To be completed by the supplier)**
NARRATIVE DESCRIPTION OF EQUIPMENT & COST:	Supplier gives **(1)** a narrative description of the item(s) ordered, as well as all options, accessories, supplies and drugs; **(2)** the supplier's charge for each item, option, accessory, supply and drug; and **(3)** the Medicare fee schedule allowance for each item/option/accessory/supply/drug, if applicable.
SECTION D:	**(To be completed by the physician)**
PHYSICIAN ATTESTATION:	The physician's signature certifies **(1)** the CMN which he/she is reviewing includes Sections A, B, C and D; **(2)** the answers in Section B are correct; and **(3)** the self-identifying information in Section A is correct.
PHYSICIAN SIGNATURE	After completion and/or review <u>by the physician</u> of Sections A, B and C, the physician must sign and date the CMN in Section D, verifying the Attestation appearing in this Section. The physician's signature also certifies the items ordered are medically necessary for this patient. Signature and date stamps are not acceptable.

B

Fig. 4.2, cont'd (B) Back.

is the appropriate fee for healthcare providers to charge for a specific service or procedure in a certain geographic area. The fee is based on a consensus of what most local hospitals, physicians, or laboratories typically charge for a similar procedure or service in the geographic area in which the provider practices. The state and federal governments do not regulate UCR charges, but Medicare publishes its own fee schedules using RBRVS.

Healthcare providers' actual charges may be different from the UCR (allowable) charge of the third-party payer. When an insurance carrier has a UCR charge that is below the actual provider's charge, the patient may be responsible for paying this difference. This is called **balance billing**.

PARTICIPATING VERSUS NONPARTICIPATING PROVIDERS

A **participating (PAR) provider** is one who contracts with the third-party payer and agrees to abide by certain rules and regulations of that carrier. In doing so, the provider usually must accept the insurance carrier's allowable fee as payment in full (after patient deductibles and coinsurance are met) and may not bill the patient for the balance. Some insurance companies offer certain incentives to providers if they agree to become PARs, such as processing claims more quickly and furnishing claims with preidentifying information. Another advantage of becoming a PAR is that payment from the insurer is paid directly to the provider rather than to the patient.

A **nonparticipating (nonPAR) provider** has no contractual agreement with the insurance carrier; the provider does not have to accept an insurance company's reimbursement as payment in full. Patients can be billed for the difference between the insurance carrier's allowed fee and the provider's actual fee. (Medicare limits how much a nonPAR provider can charge, however.) One disadvantage of being nonPAR is that, typically, insurance payments are sent to the patient rather than to the provider. If a nonPAR provider accepts assignment, they are paid directly.

MISCELLANEOUS TERMS

Copayment—A way of sharing medical costs often associated with managed care. Here, the patient pays a flat fee every time he or she receives a medical service (e.g., $25 for every visit to the doctor). The healthcare plan typically pays the rest of covered expenses.

Covered expenses—Covered healthcare services are those medical procedures the health plan (insurer) agrees to pay, which are listed in the health insurance policy.

Noncancellable policy—A policy that guarantees the patient or insured can receive health insurance coverage as long as the premiums are paid on time—also called a *guaranteed renewable policy*.

Primary care physician or provider (PCP)—A family physician, internist, obstetrician-gynecologist, pediatrician, physician's assistant, or nurse practitioner who is usually the patient's first contact for healthcare. A PCP monitors the patient's health and diagnoses, treats routine health problems, and refers the patient to a specialist if another level of healthcare is needed. Note: Many health plans pay for a specialist only if the patient is referred by his or her PCP.

Provider—Any person (doctor, physician's assistant, nurse practitioner, nurse, dentist) or institution (hospital or clinic) that provides medical care.

Third-party payer—Any payer for healthcare services other than the patient. This can be an insurance company, a managed care organization (HMO or PPO), or the federal government.

? **What Did You Learn?**

1. When a child is listed on both parents' health plans, which one pays first?
2. List some exceptions to the birthday rule.
3. What are some possible sources of overinsurance?
4. Name the four stipulations that determine medical necessity.

SUMMARY CHECKPOINTS

- The major reforms of the ACA include the following:
  - No healthcare insurer can charge more or deny coverage based on a person's current health status or a preexisting condition.
  - All health plans issued after September 23, 2010, must offer a wide range of in-network preventive services and treatments for adults and children with no OOP costs such as copayments, coinsurance, or the need to meet a deductible.
  - Lifetime limits are no longer imposed for essential health benefits in the health insurance marketplace (including grandfathered plans), and annual limits were prohibited on health insurance plans beginning in 2014.
  - Cost controls, called *medical loss ratios*, require insurers to spend at least 80% of individual plan premium dollars (85% for group plans) on actual medical care rather than administrative costs and profits. If insurers do not spend the required amount, they must send rebates to policyholders.
  - It is now illegal for insurers to cancel a policy except in the case of outright false or incomplete information on an application or nonpayment of premiums.
  - Private insurers must explain why a claim was denied and the steps that can be taken to challenge their decision. If the insurer still denies coverage after its required internal review, the

patient can request an external review by an independent organization with the power to overturn the decision.

- Health insurance marketplaces, also called *health exchanges*, are organizations set up to facilitate the purchase of health insurance in each state in accordance with the act.
- The major healthcare payers are as follows:
  - *Medicaid*—A joint federal–state health insurance program that is run by the individual states. Medicaid covers some low-income individuals and certain categories of disabled individuals.
  - *Medicare*—A federal health insurance program for individuals 65 years old and older and individuals younger than 65 years with certain disabilities.
  - *TRICARE/CHAMPVA*—TRICARE is the US military's comprehensive healthcare program. TRICARE covers active-duty personnel and their eligible family members and retirees and their qualifying family members. CHAMPVA is a healthcare benefits program for the spouse or widow (or widower) and children of certain qualifying categories of veterans.
  - *Disability insurance*—Insurance that is designed to replace a portion of an individual's gross income in the case of an accident or illness that is unrelated to his or her employment.
  - *SSDI*—An insurance program administered by the SSA and funded by a combination of FICA taxes withheld from employees' pay and matching contributions of the employer. SSDI pays healthcare benefits to qualifying disabled workers.
  - *Workers' compensation*—A type of insurance that pays workers who are injured or disabled on the job or suffer from job-related illnesses.
- Alternative healthcare coverage options include:
  - *HSA*—A health insurance option for certain qualifying self-employed individuals and small businesses consisting of two components: (1) a low-cost, high-deductible insurance policy and (2) a tax-advantaged savings account. Individuals pay for their own healthcare up to the annual deductible by withdrawing funds from the savings account or paying medical bills OOP. The insurance policy then pays for most or all costs of covered services after the deductible is met.
  - *FSA*—Offers tax advantages to the employer and the employee. Provides reimbursement for medical expenses that are not typically covered by a high-deductible, major medical policy (e.g., insurance premiums, dental, vision, and child care).
  - *HRA*—An employer-sponsored and employer-funded health insurance plan that reimburses employees for qualified medical expenses, including health insurance premiums. Funds contributed to an HRA are the property of the employer, and unused contributions cannot be moved when an employee moves to a new employer.
  - *PRA*—A contribution health plan wherein employers let their employees reimburse themselves for their individual health insurance costs with their pretax salary. An option for businesses that don't offer health benefits or are starting a new business.
  - *Health insurance exchange*—Proposes a choice of plans with common rules governing how the plan is offered and its cost and providing information to help consumers better understand the choices available to them.
  - *ACOs*—A network of doctors and hospitals similar to an HMO that shares responsibility for providing care to patients. ACOs would agree to manage all of the healthcare needs of a minimum of 5000 Medicare beneficiaries for at least 3 years. Goals for an ACO are to determine how to successfully:
    - Keep patients within the ACO, encouraging them to stay healthy and take more responsibility for their own healthcare
    - Encourage patients to use healthcare providers that are part of the ACO network to keep the overall costs down within the organization
- The form most commonly used to submit healthcare claims is referred to as the *CMS-1500* (version 02/12), a universal form created by the government for Medicare claims and since adopted by most third-party carriers. The CMS-1500 may be submitted in paper form or electronically.
- COBRA gives workers and their dependents who lose their health insurance benefits the right to continue group coverage temporarily under the same group health plan sponsored by their employer in certain instances when coverage under the plan would otherwise end. The law generally covers group health plans maintained by employers with 20 or more employees in the prior year.
- Health insurance "watchdogs" include the following:
  - The Joint Commission evaluates and accredits healthcare organizations and programs, including hospitals, home care organizations, and other healthcare organizations that provide long-term care, behavioral care, and laboratory and ambulatory care services.
  - NCQA accredits HMOs and other managed care organizations.
  - American Accreditation HealthCare Commission/URAC accredits PPOs and other managed care networks.
  - Accreditation Association for Ambulatory Health Care accredits outpatient healthcare settings, such as ambulatory surgery centers, radiation oncology centers, and student health centers.
  - Community Health Accreditation Partner accredits community, home health, and hospice

programs; public health departments; and nursing centers.

- Consumer Coalition for Quality Health Care is a national, nonprofit organization of consumer groups advocating for consumer protections and quality assurance programs and policies.
- Terms common to third-party payers include:
  - Birthday rule—An informal procedure used in the health insurance industry to help determine which health plan is considered "primary" when individuals (usually children) are listed as dependents on more than one health plan.
  - COB—When an individual is covered under two separate insurance policies, the total benefits an insured can receive from both plans are limited to no more than 100% of the allowable expenses.
  - Medical necessity—When medical services, procedures, or supplies meet these criteria, they are said to meet the standards of "medical necessity":
    - They are proper and needed for the diagnosis or treatment of a patient's medical condition.
    - They are provided for the diagnosis, direct care, and treatment of a medical condition.
    - They meet the standards of good medical practice in the local area.
    - They are not mainly for the convenience of the patient or the healthcare provider.
  - UCR and balance billing—Balance billing is when an insurance carrier has a UCR charge that is below the actual provider's charge; the patient may be responsible for paying the difference.

Closing Scenario

Rachel has learned that she needs to brush up a bit on the Health Insurance Portability and Accountability Act (HIPAA) rules and regulations as they pertain to the free clinic. Rachel has run into some situations that are quite different from what she encounters at Walden-Martin, especially in the area of releasing information. She is often handling phone calls with requests for information, and she is being very careful to make sure that she can actually release the information to the caller.

Rachel has found it very rewarding to be able to help explain to the patients, at both the free clinic and Walden-Martin, some of the terminology used with health insurance. The patients have expressed their gratitude for her taking the time to make sure that they understand what their financial responsibility is and why. The providers at both organizations have noticed it as well and have made sure to include those comments in her evaluations.

All in all, Rachel is extremely happy with her chosen career.

CHAPTER REVIEW QUESTIONS

1. UCR is based on which of the following?
   a. How much the provider charges his or her patients for the same or similar service.
   b. Whether the procedure requires more time, skill, or experience than it usually requires.
   c. The value of the procedure in comparison with that of other services.
   d. All of the above.
2. The reimbursement model that pays the provider a specific dollar amount per patient for a specific period of time is:
   a. Fee-for-service
   b. Capitation
   c. Resource-based relative value scale
   d. Episode-of-care
3. The episode-of-care model of reimbursement is also known as:
   a. Prospective payment system
   b. Capitation
   c. Resource-based relative value scale
   d. None of the above
4. The Affordable Care Act states that no insurer can charge more or deny coverage based on a person's current health status. It also states that preventive services are subject to copayment and deductible.
   a. Both statements are true.
   b. Both statements are false.
   c. The first statement is true, and the second statement is false.
   d. The first statement is false, and the second statement is true.
5. Which of the following is not considered an essential health benefit under the Affordable Care Act?
   a. Pregnancy, maternity, and newborn care
   b. Adult oral care
   c. Laboratory services
   d. Pediatric vision care
6. In the silver level of healthcare coverage, the patient pays what percentage of healthcare costs?
   a. 30%
   b. 40%
   c. 70%
   d. 90%
7. The type of plan you can find on the health insurance marketplace that includes a group of healthcare providers who contract with the managed care organization to provide services to the plan's enrollees is:
   a. POS
   b. EPO
   c. PPO
   d. HMO

8. The government health plan that covers some low-income individuals and certain disabled individuals is:
   a. TRICARE
   b. Medicare
   c. CHAMPVA
   d. Medicaid

9. The type of policy that provides income replacement when someone cannot work because of illness or an accident is:
   a. Workers' compensation
   b. EPO
   c. Disability insurance
   d. Medicare

10. This option that allows the patient to use tax-deferred dollars, which are contributed to a personal retirement fund, to pay for medical bills is used in conjunction with a high-deductible insurance plan.
    a. Premium reimbursement arrangement
    b. Health reimbursement arrangement
    c. Flexible spending account
    d. Health savings account

WEBSITES TO EXPLORE

- For a comprehensive list of health insurance terms and their definitions, log on to the following websites: http://www.cms.gov/apps/glossary/ and https://www.healthcare.gov/glossary/.
- For more information on healthcare in general, explore these websites: http://www.cms.gov/, http://www.ahima.org/, and http://www.hhs.gov/ocr/privacy/index.html.
- Browse this CMS website to learn more about HIPAA: http://www.hhs.gov/ocr/privacy/hipaa/understanding/.
- The following website is helpful and offers further clarification on healthcare: http://www.healthcare.gov.

Author's Note: Due to the dynamic nature of the Internet, web addresses and/or links provided in this chapter may have changed since publication and may no longer be valid. In such cases, students should select comparable search words to access related sites.

5 The Patient and the Billing Process

Chapter Outline

Chapter Objectives

After completion of this chapter, the student should be able to:

1. List and discuss various patient expectations.
2. Name two future trends in the patient–practice relationship.
3. Explain various regulations in the Health Insurance Portability and Accountability Act (HIPAA) that affect patient billing.
4. Outline appropriate patient billing policies and practices.
5. Discuss billing and collection strategies in healthcare practices.
6. List federal regulations affecting credit and collection.
7. Explain two conventional collection methods.
8. Assess the benefits of a billing service.
9. Compare the advantages and disadvantages of using a collection agency.
10. Outline the steps involved in the small claims litigation process.

Chapter Terms

accounts receivable

alternate billing cycle

assignment of benefits

billing cycle

coinsurance

collection agency

collection ratio

copayment

daily journal

deductible

defendant

deidentified

disbursements journal

Equal Credit Opportunity Act

Fair Credit Billing Act (FCBA)

Fair Credit Reporting Act

Fair Debt Collection Practices Act

general journal

general ledger

HIPAA-covered entities

intangible

meaningful use

patient information form

patient ledger

payroll journal

plaintiff

protected health information (PHI)

self-pay patient

small claims litigation

surrogates

treatment, payment, or healthcare operations (TPO)

Truth in Lending Act

Opening Scenario

Callie Foster has worked for Walden-Martin Family Medical Clinic for several years as a health insurance professional. She enjoys working with the patients and providers in this challenging field. Patients come to the clinic with certain expectations of how they will be treated. If those expectations are met, the patient has a positive experience. If they are not met, it can be a very negative experience, which is not good for the patient or the healthcare facility. Callie has seen firsthand how empathy and listening have created a better relationship with both patients and providers. Being able to see both the patient's side and the insurance company's side of issues has helped Callie come up with solutions that both sides were agreeable to.

When working to collect balances that are due to Walden-Martin, Callie can empathize with the patient who is struggling to make ends meet. By listening to what the patient says about his or her situation, Callie is able to work within the Walden-Martin policies and come up with a payment plan that works for both parties.

Callie recognizes that she needs to stay current with and abide by not only the Walden-Martin policies, but also state and federal regulations such as the Health Insurance Portability and Accountability Act (HIPAA). When she is working on setting up credit payment plans or collecting a past due balance, there are many things to be aware of so that the clinic will not be put at risk for a lawsuit.

Callie feels that all of these moving parts make her position at Walden-Martin a very challenging and rewarding one.

PATIENT EXPECTATIONS

When patients visit a healthcare practice, they bring something with them that may not be obvious to the healthcare team. Besides sore throats, broken legs, or heart palpitations, they bring a set of expectations with them. These expectations were created by previous experiences with other healthcare providers, the media, and the opinions of friends and family. If the healthcare provider and office staff members are oblivious to those expectations, the entire practice risks being perceived as cold and unfeeling. If the healthcare staff is successful in meeting or exceeding these expectations, the patient is likely to be pleased with the care he or she receives.+

The first step in creating a good patient–staff relationship begins when the individual telephones for an appointment. How this encounter is handled can have a lasting impression on how the patient perceives the entire practice, including the healthcare providers. If the rapport between the providers and the medical team is strained and uneasy, patients sense this and are likely to feel tension also. The bottom line is that overlooking patients' needs and expectations can be costly to the practice. Without patients, there is no practice.

It is also important to be up front with office policies and procedures. When patients are sick or hurting, they usually do not feel up to questioning the medical staff about their policies or procedures. They usually are reacting to their physical symptoms, and their lack of questions or interest is caused by the fear of the unknown. Some conditions can be frightening, such as a burning chest pain or a breast lump. It is the responsibility of the medical staff to find out what patients' expectations are by asking questions. Being open with patients, anticipating their concerns, and creating an environment in which patients feel that they can discuss their needs safely are comforting and affirming.

Patient expectations vary from office to office. The following are some issues to consider when evaluating new patient protocol.

PROFESSIONAL OFFICE SETTING

When individuals walk into a hardware or clothing store, they are looking for physical items—tangible things they can pick up, examine, and put into their shopping cart. If they are unhappy with the hammer or sweater purchased, they can voice a complaint or return the item for a refund. Most services offered by a healthcare facility are considered **intangible**—individuals cannot see or feel them. When individuals buy intangible services, they compensate by looking for **surrogates**, or substitutes, to put their mind at ease. Surrogates that patients look for in a healthcare office may be the office location, size, layout, and staff enthusiasm. The color of the walls and the appearance of the reception area can affect a new patient's initial judgment about the quality of care that office provides. A shabby and cluttered reception room may suggest inferior care.

RELEVANT FORMS AND QUESTIONS

A substantial number of forms typically must be completed, and many questions need to be answered when seeing a healthcare provider for the first time. Besides being brief and of high quality, forms should seem relevant to the reason for the patient's visit. Personal questions, such as whether a patient smokes or drinks, how many pregnancies a female patient has had, and whether a patient is divorced or widowed, should be asked privately out of hearing from office staff members and other patients. It also might be necessary to explain how these forms and questions relate to the individual's care and treatment. Although new patients expect to complete some forms, filling out multiple pages can become frustrating and tiresome, especially if they're not feeling well to begin with. Often the forms can be completed before the patient arrives at the healthcare facility. These forms may be completed on paper and brought to the appointment or completed electronically on the provider's secure website.

HONORING APPOINTMENT TIMES

Time is a valuable commodity, and staying on schedule communicates respect for the patient's time. Because the encounter may be a new experience for a patient, when he or she phones for an appointment, time management experts recommend that the medical receptionist explain approximately how long an initial visit will take and what to expect. If the healthcare provider gets behind schedule, which occurs frequently, patients can become annoyed—glancing at their watches, shifting in their seats, and looking at the receptionist expectantly for explanations. Out of courtesy, the receptionist should keep the patient advised as to the length of the delay and the reason for it. For example, the patient might be told, "Dr. Khan has been delayed because of an emergency, so you may have to wait another 10 or 15 minutes." The patient should be kept apprised of the anticipated time he or she will be seen: "Dr. Khan has just left the hospital and will be here in approximately 10 minutes." If it looks like the wait is going to be lengthy, the receptionist should offer to reschedule the patient's appointment or, if it is practical for the specific situation, ask if the patient would like to see another provider. Many individuals today believe that their time is equally as valuable as the provider's, especially if they have taken time off work for their appointment. Delays often cannot be avoided; however, be empathetic to the patient's situation.

 Imagine This!

Jennifer Cooper had a 2 PM appointment with Dr. Shirley Bennet, a gynecologist. She arrived about 10 minutes early, as the receptionist recommended when she made the appointment. After completing all of the necessary new patient forms, the receptionist advised Jennifer that Dr. Bennet had been called out on an emergency cesarean section and would be about a half-hour late. The staff gave Jennifer the option of waiting or rescheduling. Jennifer, already having waited nearly 2 weeks for an opening in Dr. Bennet's schedule, chose to stay. Dr. Bennet kept the reception staff informed periodically as to how things were progressing, and this information was quickly and quietly passed on to Jennifer. In addition, she was offered a choice of coffee or a cold soda. The reception room atmosphere was comfortable with pleasant background music and an assortment of recent issues of magazines to browse through. Although Jennifer ended up waiting nearly 45 minutes for her appointment with Dr. Bennet, she did not become irritated or impatient because she was kept apprised of Dr. Bennet's schedule and was treated courteously by the staff.

 Imagine This!

Lurvis Burke, a civil engineer with a consulting engineering firm, took time out of his busy schedule to visit a cardiologist for a routine stress test, recommended by his family physician. Lurvis had a 9 AM appointment with Dr. Harlan Solomon and arrived shortly before his appointment time, filled out the new patient forms, and sat down to wait. Two hours later, his name was called, and a member of the medical staff ushered him to an examination room without a word. When Dr. Solomon entered the examination room where Lurvis was waiting, he found an angry patient who informed him that he did not appreciate the long wait and that he considered his time just as important as the physician's. Lurvis vowed not to return to Dr. Solomon's office in the future. Compare this patient's experience with that of Jennifer Cooper.

 Stop and Think

Reread the "Imagine This!" scenario featuring Lurvis Burke. Do you think Mr. Burke is justified in his decision to not return to this office? How would you have handled this situation if you were the front desk receptionist?

PATIENT LOAD

A new patient often draws conclusions about the competency of the healthcare provider and the entire healthcare team by observing how many others are waiting in the reception area. If the reception area is empty when the patient enters, he or she may think, "Why aren't there more people here? Maybe this doctor isn't very good." To avoid this negative reaction, some experts suggest scheduling new patients during a time when the practice is busiest. This can be a workable solution as long as it does not result in a longer wait for established patients.

 Imagine This!

Beverly Tweedy, who transferred to a new city due to her employment, found the name of William Salvatore, an internist, from an Internet search for providers in her area. When she telephoned Dr. Salvatore's office, she was surprised that she was able to get an appointment the next day. Upon arriving at Dr. Salvatore's office, she noticed that she was the only person in the reception area. After a short wait, she was escorted to an examination room. Some months later, a newspaper article appeared in the local paper citing Dr. Salvatore with failure to keep adequate patient records and Medicare fraud.

 Imagine This!

Juanita Lindo, the medical receptionist for Anthony Park, a neurosurgeon, informed new patients when scheduling appointments that Dr. Park preferred reserving an ample amount of time for the encounter. The physician allowed a half-hour before the examination, an hour for the examination, and a half-hour after to answer all questions and ensure that the patient and family members were comfortable and well informed of their options before leaving his office. When a patient arrived for an appointment, he or she was already aware of how long the encounter would take, explaining the absence of a reception room full of waiting patients.

GETTING COMFORTABLE WITH THE HEALTHCARE PROVIDER

It is human nature for patients to want to like their providers as much as respect them. Perceptive patients expect their providers to reveal enough information about themselves so that they can identify with them. The provider and staff members do not need to discuss their personal lives with patients, but sharing some personal information promotes a good provider–patient relationship and often tends to relieve anxiety if the provider and staff members compare a personal experience that is relevant to what the patient is experiencing.

 Imagine This!

Dottie Shrike visited Dr. Forrest Carpenter, her family practitioner, for treatment of an episode of anxiety and mild depression after being fired from her job as a teacher's aide. Dr. Carpenter, attempting to alleviate some of Dottie's angst, related a story about an experience he had had before becoming a physician. He was working for a trucking firm and had lost his job because of noncompliance with company policy. He was young then, like Dottie, and the experience left him feeling humiliated and vulnerable. Relating this story to Dottie allowed her to feel as if he really understood her problem, reinforcing the provider–patient relationship.

PRIVACY AND CONFIDENTIALITY

If the medical professional wants patients to reveal their personal health-related problems, patients must feel confident that this information will be kept private and confidential. If patients who are waiting in the reception room hear the front desk staff talking about other patients, it can lead them to believe that their own information will be treated casually, too. The office staff must make every effort possible to assure patients that any personal information they divulge will be held in the strictest confidence. When making and receiving telephone calls, staff members should speak quietly or close the glass partition (which is recommended by HIPAA regulations) so that conversations do not carry into the reception area. Also, the entire medical staff should be cautioned when talking among themselves or to patients in examining rooms. Walls are often thin, allowing voices to carry into adjacent rooms.

FINANCIAL ISSUES

Most patients have an idea of what their medical care and treatment should cost before they make an appointment. Some patients even do "comparison shopping." Although many patients may be embarrassed or uneasy discussing fees, especially ahead of time, it is good business practice to discuss the financial ramifications of the healthcare encounter. Most providers prefer to leave the subject of fees to their reception staff. When a new patient telephones for an appointment and explains his or her condition or symptoms that prompted the call, giving the individual a range of what the initial fee would be is considered appropriate. Healthcare consumers do not object if the cost of their services or procedures is addressed up front.

 Stop and Think

Mary Ellen Brown calls Dr. Bennet's office for an appointment. She explains that she is new in the area and is looking for a "good OB-GYN" because she thinks she may be pregnant. What kind of information might the medical receptionist give Mrs. Brown?

? What Did You Learn?

1. Besides their health problems, what do patients bring with them to the healthcare office?
2. List four issues that affect patient expectations.
3. Why is a clean, well-kept reception room important?
4. What is the rationale of explaining policies and fees up front to patients?

FUTURE TRENDS

Most healthcare experts agree that healthcare today bears little resemblance to healthcare a decade ago. The United States is faced with a rapidly changing healthcare environment, and individuals who are involved in the healthcare field must identify and anticipate future trends—from new technology to changing directions and demographics. Some of these topics were examined in Chapter 1, so the following discussions will be brief.

AGING POPULATION

Due to the changes in healthcare, life expectancy in the United States has increased. One hundred years ago people would expect to live to the age of about 51. Currently the Centers for Disease Control and Prevention (CDC) estimate that life expectancy is 78.6 years. Healthcare facilities will need to be prepared to handle a growing volume of elderly patients; these elderly patients will have different medical needs than young adult or pediatric patients. Healthcare staff members should be aware of, or even specially trained in, particular skills for interacting with this demographic. Many local medical organizations or community colleges offer continuing education courses in the care and treatment of elderly patients.

INTERNET AS A HEALTHCARE TOOL

The Internet offers access to a great deal of relevant, quality healthcare information. Websites deliver large amounts of healthcare knowledge to consumers, allowing them to form their own opinions and expectations. More and more people are becoming involved in the process of self-education that was not possible before the advent of the Internet. Websites can help individuals find providers and hospitals that offer certain procedures; other websites offer lifestyle advice, plus educational details and references for a multitude of health conditions.

Internet tools that can be used to reach the computer-oriented consumer can help healthcare facilities serve patients better. Some successful online patient-centered topics include:

• Provider–patient communication
• Online scheduling (e.g., examinations, procedures)
• Online billing services
• Provider biographies
• Procedural information

It is predicted that patients, in the future, will rely more and more on the Internet, and healthcare providers will have to adapt their practices to meet these state-of-the-art electronic requirements. As the healthcare industry moves toward adopting more technology, telehealth programs are becoming available across the country. Some online facilities believe that their telehealth systems keep patients connected and improve care quality. For more information on healthcare technology online, access the website listed in "Websites to Explore" at the end of this chapter.

Imagine This!

Greg Manning was diagnosed with prostate cancer, and the options his provider gave him held a high probability of impotence, which was unacceptable to Greg. He logged on to the Internet and began an extensive search for possible alternatives. He found a clinic in another state where the medical staff offered a relatively new, noninvasive procedure that was highly successful in patients with similar malignancies. Greg traveled to the clinic and met with the staff providers to discuss the procedure. Greg was happy with the alternative they presented and subsequently underwent the new procedure successfully.

PATIENTS AS CONSUMERS

As evidenced by the increase in medical news on television and in advertising, radio broadcasts, periodicals, and Internet sites, the healthcare industry must acknowledge a new type of patient—one who is more educated, more aware of choices, and more likely to take an active part in his or her own healthcare decisions. Experts say that patients should be considered "consumers" rather than "patients." Today, Americans are exposed daily to a vast amount of medical information through various media outlets. Some of this information can be misleading and confusing. Whether or not patients are correctly informed, however, healthcare providers are expected to take the time to satisfy patients' questions about diagnosis, treatment, and therapy options.

A set of healthcare consumer essentials has been developed, and experts believe it should become mandatory for any healthcare facility that endeavors to provide patient-centered service. These essentials include:

• Choice
• Control (self-care, self-management)
• Shared medical decision making
• Customer service
• Information

Similar to other types of consumers, patients today are likely to switch healthcare plans or healthcare providers if they believe they are not getting the quality service they desire.

HIPAA REQUIREMENTS

HIPAA has had a big impact on healthcare, in particular, where confidentiality is concerned. What is contained in a patient's health record has always been confidential, dating back to the wording of the Hippocratic Oath. However, HIPAA has refined the rules of confidentiality for covered entities in a much more comprehensive way.

AUTHORIZATION TO RELEASE INFORMATION

The release of any information contained in a patient's health record to a third party, with certain exceptions, is prohibited by law. Civil and criminal penalties exist for the unauthorized release of such information. A healthcare provider can be allowed to release confidential information from an individual's health records only with the consent of the individual or the person authorized to give consent for that individual. However, patient consent is not required if the information is used or disclosed for **treatment, payment, or healthcare operations (TPO)**.

HIPAA AND COVERED ENTITIES

HIPAA is a federal law designed to protect the privacy of individuals' health information. A major component of HIPAA addresses this privacy by establishing a nationwide federal standard concerning the privacy of health information and how health information can be used and disclosed. This federal standard generally preempts all state privacy laws except for those that establish stronger protections. HIPAA privacy laws became effective on April 14, 2003.

HIPAA requires all employees and staff (including volunteers) at healthcare facilities to sign a confidentiality agreement to protect patients' privacy. To view an example of a confidentiality agreement, see "Websites to Explore" at the end of this chapter.

HIPAA-covered entities consist of healthcare providers, health plans (including employer-sponsored plans), and healthcare clearinghouses (including billing agents). These covered entities must comply with HIPAA rules for any health information of identifiable individuals. Health information that is protected under HIPAA is referred to as *individually identifiable health information* or, more commonly, **protected health information (PHI)**. PHI refers not only to data that are explicitly linked to a particular individual, but also to health information with data items that reasonably could be expected to allow individual identification. PHI includes medical records, medical billing records, any clinical or research databases, and tissue bank samples. HIPAA regulations allow researchers to access and use PHI when necessary to conduct research. However, HIPAA affects only research that uses, creates, or discloses PHI that will be entered into the medical record or will be used for healthcare services, such as TPO. Covered entities generally are unable to communicate or transfer PHI to noncovered entities (who do not come under HIPAA rules) without violating HIPAA.

Potential identifiers that can link information to a particular individual include obvious ones, such as name and Social Security number. Note: The covered entity may assign a code or other means of identification to allow deidentified information if it later becomes necessary to reidentify the information. When the identifiable elements are removed, the information is considered **deidentified** under most circumstances.

HIPAA Tip

Covered entities (such as health plans, healthcare providers, and claims clearinghouses) must comply with HIPAA rules. Other businesses may comply voluntarily with the standards, but the law does not require them to do so.

HIPAA REQUIREMENTS FOR COVERED ENTITIES

The Administrative Simplification standards adopted by the US Department of Health and Human Services (HHS) under HIPAA apply to any entity that is a:
- Healthcare provider that conducts certain transactions in electronic form (called here a *covered healthcare provider*)
- Healthcare clearinghouse
- Health plan

An entity that is one or more of these types of entities is referred to as a *covered entity* in the Administrative Simplification regulations.

HIPAA's Administrative Simplification provisions require the HHS to adopt national standards for electronic healthcare transactions and national identifiers for providers, health plans, and employers. Provisions under the Affordable Care Act of 2010 will further these increases and include requirements to adopt:
- Operating rules for each of the HIPAA-covered transactions
- A unique, standard health plan identifier
- A standard and operating rules for electronic funds transfer (EFT) and electronic remittance advice (ERA) and claims attachments

In addition, health plans will be required to certify their compliance. The act provides for substantial penalties for failure to certify or comply with the standards and operating rules.

HIPAA 5010 Transaction Standards

The Administrative Simplification provisions require all physicians, providers, and suppliers who bill

Medicare carriers, fiscal intermediaries, Medicare administrative contractors (MACs) for Parts A and B, and durable medical equipment MACs for services provided to Medicare beneficiaries to submit claims electronically, with certain exceptions. The Centers for Medicare and Medicaid Services (CMS) introduced the HIPAA 5010 Transaction Standards, which replaced Version 4010/4010A as of January 1, 2012. This change allowed for the use of International Statistical Classification of Diseases and Related Health Problems, 10th revision (ICD-10) codes (discussed in Chapter 14). The 5010 Transaction Standards affect the data that are transmitted via the 837P, which is the electronic data set equivalent to the paper CMS-1500 (02/12) form.

It is important that health insurance professionals keep abreast of these and other potential changes involving electronic claims transactions. The CMS website is a good resource for keeping up to date.

Changes to the CMS-1500 Form

As a result of the conversion to the 5010 Transaction Standards and the ICD-10 diagnosis codes, the National Uniform Claim Committee (NUCC) proposed certain data-reporting revisions in the Version 005010 837 professional electronic claim transaction that affected the paper CMS-1500 form. After considering several options for completely revising the form, the NUCC decided to make "minor changes" to the existing form. Also, a revised NUCC 1500 Reference Instruction Manual was developed for the revised form. To view the current version of the CMS-1500 (02/12) form, visit the NUCC website at http://www.nucc.org/.

Health insurance professionals should keep up to date with future changes to the 1500 form by periodically logging on to the NUCC website. Visit the NUCC or the CMS website periodically for updates on the implementation deadline.

PATIENT'S RIGHT OF ACCESS AND CORRECTION

The HIPAA Privacy Rules provide for the patient's right to correct or amend his or her medical record. Although HIPAA rules limit this right by reasonable protections for the covered entity that controls the protected information, a patient has a right to ask for corrections or amendments to his or her medical record and to place an explanation into the record if that request is denied. The privacy notice that a medical practice gives to patients must specify how they should make requests to amend their records (e.g., in writing). The practice may refuse such a request for several reasons, including that the patient's record is accurate and complete. However, the patient has the right to appeal. If the practice agrees to amend the patient's record, it must notify the individual and others to whom the information was provided that the record has been amended. However, the rules do not include a requirement that incorrect information be removed from the record; rather, it should be labeled as corrected, and the correction should be appended.

HIPAA provides a limited public policy exception for PHI disclosure involving public health issues, judicial and administrative proceedings, law enforcement purposes, and others as required by law.

In 2011 the HHS proposed a rule that requires hospitals, physicians' offices, and insurance companies to advise a patient, if requested, of anyone who has accessed the patient's electronic medical record (EMR). Under this rule, healthcare-related businesses must list everyone in their firms—from physicians to data-entry clerks—who has accessed a patient's EMR and when.

⊚ HIPAA Tip

Basic patient rights under HIPAA include the following:
1. Right to notice of privacy practices
2. Right to access to protected health information (PHI)
3. Right to an accounting of how PHI has been disclosed outside normal patient care channels
4. Right to request an amendment or correction to PHI

AFFORDABLE CARE ACT'S PATIENT'S BILL OF RIGHTS

The Affordable Care Act introduced a "Patient's Bill of Rights" that gives Americans more stability and flexibility to make informed choices about their health. The following list describes the elements included in the Affordable Care Act's Patient's Bill of Rights:

- Provides coverage to Americans with preexisting conditions.
- Protects the individual's choice of healthcare providers.
- Allows eligible young adults to retain coverage under a parent's health plan until age 26.
- Ends lifetime limits on coverage. (Lifetime limits on most benefits are banned for all new health insurance plans.)
- Ends preexisting condition exclusions for children under age 19.
- Bans arbitrary withdrawals of insurance coverage. (Insurers can no longer cancel policies due to an honest mistake.)
- Reviews premium increases. (Insurance companies must now publicly justify any unreasonable rate hikes.)
- Helps Americans get the most from their premium dollars. (Premium dollars must be spent primarily on healthcare, not on administrative costs.)
- Restricts annual dollar limits on coverage. (Annual limits on health benefits were phased out in 2014.)
- Removes insurance company barriers to emergency services. (Patients can seek emergency care at a hospital outside their health plan's network.)
- Covers preventive care at no cost. (Individuals may be eligible for recommended preventive health services with no copayment.)
- Guarantees patients' right to appeal. (Allows patients to ask the insurer to reconsider a denial of payment.)

ACCESSING INFORMATION THROUGH PATIENT AUTHORIZATION

HIPAA states that when an authorization to release information (Fig. 5.1) is required from a patient, it must include the following elements:

- A description that identifies the information in a specific and meaningful fashion
- The name of the person authorized to make the requested use or disclosure
- The name of the person to whom the covered entity may make the requested use or disclosure
- A description of each purpose of the requested use or disclosure

WALDEN-MARTIN
FAMILY MEDICAL CLINIC
1234 ANYSTREET | ANYTOWN, ANYSTATE 12345
PHONE 123-123-1234 | FAX 123-123-5678

Instructor: Kelly Albright

Medical Records Release

Patient Name: _____ Date of Birth: _____
SSN: _____ Phone: _____
Address:

I, _____ authorize _____
to disclose/release the following information (check all applicable):

☐ All Records ☐ Abstract/Summary
☐ Laboratory/pathology records ☐ Pharmacy/prescription records
☐ X-ray/radiology records ☐ Other
☐ Billing records

Note: If these records contain any information from previous providers or information about HIV/AIDS status, cancer diagnosis, drug alcohol abuse, or sexually transmitted disease, you are hereby authorizing disclosure of this information. A copy of this signed authorization must be given to the individual.

These records are for services provided on the following date(s): _____

Please send the records listed above to (use additional sheets if necessary):

Name: _____ Phone: _____
Address: Fax: _____

The information may be used/disclosed for each of the following purposes:

☐ At patient's request ☐ For employment purposes
☐ For patient's health care ☐ Other
☐ For payment/insurance

This authorization shall expire no later than _____ or upon the following event _____ , and may not: be valid for greater than one year from the date of signature for medical records.

I understand that after the custodian of records discloses my health information, it may no longer be protected by federal privacy laws. I understand that this authorization is voluntary and I may refuse to sign this authorization which will not affect my ability to obtain treatment; receive payment; or eligibility for benefits unless allowed by law. By signing below I represent and warrant that I have authority to sign this document and authorize the use or disclosure of protected health information and that there are no claims or orders that would prohibit, limit, or otherwise restrict my ability to authorize the use or disclosure of this protected health information.

_____ _____
Patient signature Date
(or patient's personal representative)

_____ _____
Printed name of patient representative Representative's authority to sign for patient
(i.e. parent, guardian, power of attorney, executor)

Fig. 5.1 Health Insurance Portability and Accountability Act (HIPAA)–approved release of information form from SimChart for the Medical Office.

- An expiration date or event that relates to the purpose of the use or disclosure
- A statement of the individual's right to revoke the authorization in writing and the exceptions to the right to revoke, with a description of how the individual may revoke the authorization
- A statement that information used may be subject to additional disclosure by the recipient and no longer be protected by this rule
- Signature of the individual and date signed
- A description of a representative's authority to act for an individual if the authorization is signed by a personal representative of the individual

HIPAA Tip

Uses and disclosures not requiring patient consent include:
- To carry out treatment, payment, or healthcare operations (TPO)
- For public health, health oversight, judicial or administrative proceedings, coroners and medical examiners, and law enforcement

ACCESSING INFORMATION THROUGH DEIDENTIFICATION

Covered entities can release deidentified health information without patient authorization. PHI can be deidentified through a general deletion of specific identifiers, such as name, address, telephone number, Social Security number, medical record number, and any other of the 18 elements that may identify a patient. To release the information without patient authorization, the covered entity cannot have actual information that could be used alone or in combination with other information to identify an individual.

APPLYING FOR HEALTHCARE ASSISTANCE UNDER THE AFFORDABLE CARE ACT

The paper application for acquiring healthcare assistance under the Affordable Care Act has been shortened from a complicated 24-page form that covered all applicants to one that covers the most common, basic cases of those who apply for insurance assistance. Different forms are available for the more complex cases.

The revised Affordable Care Act application form streamlines the enrollment process, making it more user friendly, and it significantly increases the likelihood that more people will get enrolled to gain access to affordable health coverage.

Americans also will be able to get insurance coverage under the healthcare law by applying online. Others can get assistance in filling out the form from "consumer guides" whose job it is to help applicants—many of whom will be buying insurance coverage for the first time—figure out which option works best for them.

 Stop and Think

What information in the following documentation should be removed to deidentify this patient?

Frasier, Eric
DOB 1/13/1977
Patient #12112
6/10/20XX
History: Eric presents to the clinic today for chief complaint of an abrasion on the right knee after a fall yesterday. According to the patient, he has had this soft tissue lesion for some time, and when he fell, he abraded the lower half of the lesion. He is here for reevaluation and possible excision of the lesion.
Pain assessment: Scale 0 to 10, 1
Allergies: Meperidine (Demerol)
Current medications: None
Physical examination: NAD; ambulatory; appears well
Vital signs: Blood pressure 120/74 mm Hg; weight 150 lbs
Right knee examination: The patient has a tibial prominence, and just above that there is what appears to be a 1.5-cm epidermal inclusion cyst with an abraded area inferiorly. There is mild erythema and serous drainage but no purulence. There is no appreciable edema. Just lateral to the lesion is a small superficial abrasion. The knee examination was normal.
IMP: Epidermal inclusion cyst measuring 1.5 to 2 cm of the right knee, traumatized with abrasion
Plan: The patient was empirically started on cephalexin (Keflex) 500 mg 1 po bid. He was given instructions on home care and is to follow up this week for excision of the lesion. Routine follow-up as noted. Return as needed.
Frederick Mahoney, MD
Friendly Family Clinic

bid, Twice a day; *DOB,* date of birth; *IMP,* impression, *NAD,* no acute distress; *PO,* by mouth.

What Did You Learn?

1. What three entities are covered under HIPAA?
2. List at least six elements that make a patient health record identifiable.
3. How does a patient health record become deidentifiable?
4. Name three exceptions to the confidentiality rule.
5. True or false: All Americans wishing to acquire assistance with healthcare coverage must fill out a 24-page form.

BILLING POLICIES AND PRACTICES

Although specific billing policies and procedures differ from one practice to another, the goals are similar. Many healthcare facilities anticipate that the patient will pay for services or procedures on the same day they are rendered, especially if they do not have insurance. If the patient does not have insurance, he or she may be expected to pay in full at the time of the visit or make payment arrangements if the office policy allows this option. If the patient has insurance, there are three cost-sharing factors for which patients could be responsible. The first is a **deductible**—a specific dollar amount that the patient must pay before the insurance company benefits begin. Many policies are "high-deductible" plans, with deductibles starting at $1350 per year for an individual policy and $2700 for a family policy. The second factor is **coinsurance**—after the deductible has been met, the insurance company pays a percentage and the patient pays a percentage, typically 10% to 25%. The third factor is a **copayment**—a specific dollar amount that the patient is responsible for when office visits and emergency department (ED) visits occur. Most offices collect the copayment or at least a partial payment of the coinsurance on the day of the visit. Some third-party carriers indicate the amount of copayment the patient must make on the face of the insurance identification card. Healthcare facilities are in business to make a profit; procedures and policies should be in place to protect the financial success of the practice.

ASSIGNMENT OF BENEFITS

An **assignment of benefits** is an arrangement by which a patient requests that his or her health insurance benefit payments be made directly to a designated person or facility, such as a physician or hospital. When new patients come to the healthcare office, they are typically requested to fill out a form providing their name, address, employer, and health insurance information. Usually, at the bottom of the page is a place for the patient's signature or, in the case of a minor or an individual with an intellectual disability, the signature of a parent or legal guardian. This form is commonly referred to as the **patient information form**.

On many patient information forms, in addition to the authorization to release information, there is terminology above the patient's signature that provides for the assignment of benefits, authorizing the transfer of payment from the insured to the healthcare provider. Sometimes the assignment of benefits is a separate document. Not all insurers allow assignment of benefits. In such cases, if a medical provider obtains patient permission to receive payment directly from the third-party insurer, the insurer is not bound to honor the agreement. In Florida and Louisiana, however, state laws order an insurance company to accept assignment of benefits even if it is against their company policy. Medical providers, on the other hand, have the right to refuse to accept assignment of benefits if they prefer to bill their patients directly.

Many healthcare providers participate in a health maintenance organization, a preferred provider organization (PPO), or some similar managed care organization. These practitioners are referred to as *participating providers*. When a provider is a participating provider, or PAR, assigning benefits on the insurance claim or on the patient information form is unnecessary because there is a contractual agreement between the provider and the third-party carrier that payment automatically is sent directly to the provider. That is one of the benefits to becoming a PAR.

KEEPING PATIENTS INFORMED

It is important that patients understand the patient accounting policies and procedures of the healthcare practice, such as:

- Approximately how much the medical service or procedure will cost
- When patients are expected to pay for services
- If the practice is willing to submit claims to insurance carriers

Discussing professional fees with patients is an important step that requires a sensitive and balanced approach by the health insurance professional. Patients should not be intimidated or offended when discussing fees and payment policies; however, the health insurance professional should ensure that patients are clear about their responsibilities. Most patients appreciate having billing information presented clearly and matter of factly yet always in a pleasant and courteous manner. The healthcare office staff should encourage patients to ask questions about their bills or the payment or insurance process. Many offices have printed materials available, such as an informational brochure stating or reinforcing the financial policies and procedures of the practice. This written information can be helpful in collecting fees.

ESTABLISHING A BILLING POLICY

Establishing sound billing practices is important in a healthcare office. Although medical practitioners are dedicated to the health and well-being of their patients, they are ultimately running a business for the purpose of making a profit. Keeping accurate financial records is just as important as keeping accurate patient health records.

The ultimate goal in healthcare office billing is reimbursement or payment for the medical services provided to patients. A satisfactory **collection ratio** (the total amount collected divided by the total amount charged) can be challenging at times. Some healthcare offices display a sign that payment for services rendered is expected on the day on which services are provided. In other words, patients are expected to pay as they go, just as retail stores expect customers to pay for a tube of toothpaste or a can of soup at the time of purchase.

The receptionist should request payment on the day of the visit, either before or after the encounter is concluded. Experts consider this the most effective payment policy. Patients who put off paying for their services are historically more difficult to collect from. It is common practice for the receptionist to ask for a percentage—often 20%—of the current charge; 20% is a common coinsurance amount.

ACCOUNTING METHODS

There is a good chance that the office where the health insurance professional finds employment uses a computerized patient accounting system for financial records. This is not always the case, however, and the health insurance professional should be aware of how paper accounting records are generated and maintained. A typical paper method of accounting includes a series of journals and ledgers such as the following:

- A **daily journal** (or day sheet) (Fig. 5.2) is a chronological record of all patient transactions, including previous balances, charges, payments, and current balances for that day.
- A **disbursements journal** (Fig. 5.3) is a listing of all expenses paid out to vendors, such as building rent, office supplies, and salaries. Some offices maintain

JOURNAL OF DAILY CHARGES, PAYMENTS & DEPOSITS

PLACE FIRST PEG HERE

	DATE	PROFESSIONAL SERVICE	FEE	PAYMENT	ADJUST-MENT	NEW BALANCE	OLD BALANCE	PATIENT'S NAME
1								
2								
3								
4								
5								
6								
7								
8								
9								
10								
11								
12								
13								
14								
15								
16								Totals this page
17								Totals previous page
18								Totals to date

COLUMN A   COLUMN B   COLUMN C   COLUMN D   COLUMN E

MEMO _____

DAILY - FROM LINE 31

ARITHMETIC POSTING PROOF	
Column E	$
Plus Column A	
Sub-Total	
Minus Column B	
Sub-Total	
Minus Column C	
Equals Column D	

MONTH - FROM LINE 31

ACCOUNTS RECEIVABLE PROOF	
Accts. Receivable Previous Day	$
Plus Column A	
Sub-Total	
Minus Column B	
Sub-Total	
Minus Column C	
Accts. Receivable End of Day	

Fig. 5.2 Example of a day sheet.

a separate **payroll journal** (Fig. 5.4) for wages and salaries.

- A **general journal**, the most basic of journals, is a chronological listing of transactions. It has a specific format for recording each transaction. Each transaction is recorded separately and consists of:
  - A date
  - All accounts that receive a debit entry (these are typically listed first with an amount in the appropriate column)
  - All accounts that receive a credit entry (these are indented and listed next with an amount in the appropriate column)
  - A clear description of each transaction

- A **general ledger** is the core of the practice's financial records. The general ledger constitutes the central "books" of an accounting system; every transaction flows through the general ledger. These records are a permanent tracking of the history of all financial transactions from day 1 of the life of a practice. The general ledger can be used to prepare a range of periodic financial statements, such as income statements and balance sheets.

- A **patient ledger** (Fig. 5.5) is a chronological accounting of activities of a particular patient (or family), including all charges and payments. The entire group of patient ledgers is referred to as **accounts receivable.**

FEBRUARY 20XX

DATE	DESCRIPTION	CHECK NUMBER	AMOUNT	PER CAPITA	RENT	PHONE	OFFICE SUPPLIES	POSTAGE	OFFICERS' EXPENSE	NEWS LETTER
1-FEB	ABC Realty	291	475.00		475.00					
1-FEB	AFT	292	2,301.60	2,301.60						
1-FEB	State Fed	293	1,288.60	1,288.60						
1-FEB	Central Labor Council	294	75.60	75.60						
1-FEB	Bell Telephone	295	131.00			131.00				
7-FEB	State Fed	296	1,828.60	1,828.60						
21-FEB	Sue Smith, Sec'y	297	50.00						50.00	
28-FEB	Mary Jones, Petty Cash	298	18.50				16.00	2.50		
			6,168.90	5,494.40	475.00	131.00	16.00	2.50	50.00	0.00

Fig. 5.3 Sample cash disbursements journal.

Date	Employee	Hourly Rate	Regular Hours	Overtime Hours	Net Pay	Check Number	Federal Withholding	OASI	Insurance	Retirement	Other	Gross Pay	Fund	Account

Fig. 5.4 Sample payroll journal.

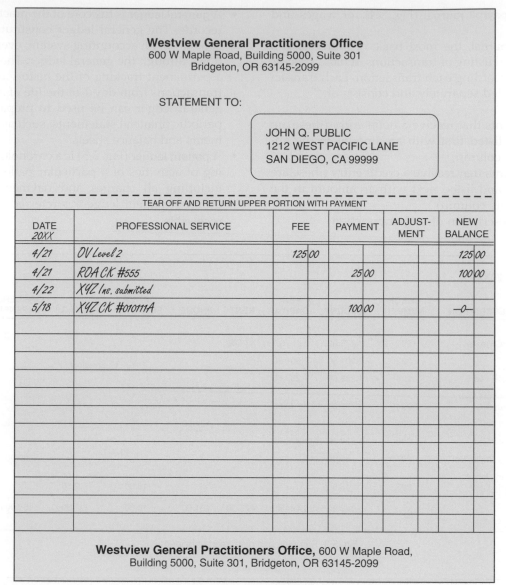

Fig. 5.5 Sample patient ledger card.

The ledger card shown contains:

Westview General Practitioners Office
600 W Maple Road, Building 5000, Suite 301
Bridgeton, OR 63145-2099

STATEMENT TO:

JOHN Q. PUBLIC
1212 WEST PACIFIC LANE
SAN DIEGO, CA 99999

– –
TEAR OFF AND RETURN UPPER PORTION WITH PAYMENT

DATE 20XX	PROFESSIONAL SERVICE	FEE	PAYMENT	ADJUST-MENT	NEW BALANCE
4/21	OV Level 2	125 00			125 00
4/21	ROA CK #555		25 00		100 00
4/22	XYZ Ins. submitted				
5/18	XYZ CK #010111A		100 00		–0–

Westview General Practitioners Office, 600 W Maple Road,
Building 5000, Suite 301, Bridgeton, OR 63145-2099

Electronic Patient Accounting Software

Most healthcare offices are now computerized and use some type of electronic patient accounting software program. Previous barriers to computerization have been largely overcome by the introduction of cost-effective and user-friendly systems for the management of clinical records and appointments. Computerized patient billing software typically includes accounts receivable, appointment scheduling, insurance billing, and practice management modules. Many of the same forms seen in a paper system can be found in an electronic system as well.

Computerized patient accounting typically begins with inputting the demographic patient data (i.e., name, address, birth date) and creating a patient "account" within the software program. When all patient data have been entered into the system, patient lists and many other documents can be generated in several ways. A list of patient appointments by day and by provider and an encounter form for each one can be printed. When the patient encounter is concluded, the health insurance professional inputs the information from the encounter form, including date, diagnosis code, procedure code, and charges. Also, any payments can be posted to the computer program. A current copy of the patient ledger can be printed and given to the patient as a statement or receipt. Appointments can be scheduled, deleted, and adjusted within the accounting system. Periodic statements, aging reports, and insurance claims can be generated.

The computer program performs all phases of the accounting process quickly and accurately. However, any system, whether computerized or manual, is only as good as the individual who inputs the information. Accuracy is crucial. A backup system is also imperative in case of power fluctuations or failure. Without a dependable backup system, all electronic data could be lost as a result of electrical problems or human error. Daily backups should be made and stored offline or in a fireproof vault to prevent loss of patient records.

Relatively inexpensive technology that protects data against a hard disk crash is widely available and simple to use. Exterior hardware with multiple disk drives protects data even if one of the hard disks fails.

ELECTRONIC MEDICAL RECORDS

An EMR (frequently referred to as an *electronic health record [EHR]*) stores a patient's health history and medical information in electronic format rather than on paper, eliminating the need for bulky files and space-consuming storage facilities. With an EMR, healthcare providers and other clinical staff members enter essential patient data—providers' orders, prescriptions, and other important information—directly into a computer using a highly secure network. This process allows for better coordination of patient care through immediate access to secure data.

In 2009 congressional legislation established a program that provided incentives to physicians and hospitals that use certified EMR technology in a meaningful manner, referred to as **meaningful use**. Meaningful use incentives seek to encourage widespread EMR adoptions and ensure that healthcare providers are using EMRs properly in their day-to-day operations. The goals were to reduce medical errors, improve overall patient care, and save money. In 2018 the CMS finalized a rule that overhauled the meaningful use program. It has been renamed to Promoting Interoperability, and the focus is now on advancing health data exchange among providers. EMRs are discussed in more detail in Chapter 16.

> ### ? What Did You Learn?
> 1. What is an assignment of benefits?
> 2. Name three things that are important for patients to know about a healthcare practice.
> 3. What are the four elements that must be included in each transaction in a general journal?
> 4. A computerized patient accounting system can generate many kinds of documents. Name four.

BILLING AND COLLECTION

Individuals who work in healthcare offices claim that collecting past due accounts is one of the least pleasant aspects of the job. Healthcare practices that maintain a high collection ratio say that the most effective way to collect money is to establish a formal financial policy that is clear to patients and that is enforced by healthcare staff members. Patients need to know that it is important to pay in full and on time, and the medical staff needs to know what is expected of them. The health insurance professional sometimes must take a firm stand, and the situation can become uncomfortable. An assertive approach to account collection does not have a negative effect on developing good rapport with patients. A collection policy that is fair and clear to patients and staff members results in fewer misunderstandings (Fig. 5.6).

Following is a list of suggestions that some healthcare practices use to aid their financial success. These items are often included in the practice's policy manual.

- Have a written payment and credit policy. Give a copy to each patient and discuss it with him or her. Ensure that each point is understood.
- Do not ignore overdue bills. The older the bill, the more uncollectible it becomes. Begin a plan of action as soon as the account becomes 30 days old.
- Rebill promptly. Some experts suggest rebilling every 15 days, rather than the traditional 30 days. Stamp or place a sticker on the second statement with the words "Second Notice."
- Telephone or write a letter. This action can be effective if the second statement does not get a response from the patient.
- Do not apologize when telephoning or writing about delinquent bills. Simply ask the customer to write a check today for the full amount owed. If the patient is agreeable and the practice has the capability, immediate payment can be taken over the phone using a credit or debit card.
- Be pleasant and courteous. There is never a reason to get into an argument, even if the patient becomes hostile. Listen patiently to what the individual has to say without interrupting; try to be understanding.
- Ask for the full amount, not just a partial payment. If a patient owes $500, ask for the full $500. If the patient says he or she will send a partial payment, ask what the exact amount will be and what date the payment will be sent. Do not accept vague statements such as, "I'll send you something in a couple of days." Also, ask for a precise date when the remainder of the bill will be paid.
- Negotiate the terms but not the amount. If you believe the patient truly has a problem paying, offer to work out a payment plan, but do not make this offer right away; do this only as a last resort. Also, always adhere to the office policy when negotiating terms.
- Use the services of a small claims court. If patient promises are not kept or if the account ages past a certain time period (e.g., 60 days, depending on office policy), small claims litigation is an alternative.

> ### Stop and Think
> You notice that Theodore Simpson's account balance is $365, and he has not made a payment for 45 days. Office policy is to telephone patients 15 days after the last statement has been sent. How will you handle this? Create a telephone scenario of your conversation with Mr. Simpson.

BILLING CYCLE

Sending statements to patients on a regular basis is necessary to maintain cash flow for the practice and an

Payment Policy

Thank you for choosing our practice! We are committed to the success of your medical treatment and care. Please understand that payment of your bill is part of this treatment and care.

For your convenience, we have answered a variety of commonly asked financial policy questions below. If you need further information about any of these policies, please ask to speak with a Billing Specialist or the Practice Manager.

How May I Pay?
We accept payment by cash, check, VISA, Mastercard, American Express and Discover.

Do I Need A Referral?
If you have an HMO plan with which we are contracted, you need a referral authorization from your primary care physician. If we have not received an authorization prior to your arrival at the office, we have a telephone available for you to call your primary care physician to obtain it. If you are unable to obtain the referral at that time, you will be rescheduled.

Which Plans Do You Contract With?
Please see attached list.

What Is My Financial Responsibility for Services?
Your financial responsibility depends on a variety of factors, explained below.

Office Visits and Office Services

If you have:	You are Responsible for:	Our staff will:
Commercial Insurance Also known as indemnity, "regular" insurance, or "80%/20% coverage."	Payment of the patient responsibility for all office visit, x-ray, injection, and other charges at the time of office visit.	Call your insurance company ahead of time to determine deductibles and coinsurance. File an insurance claim as a courtesy to you.
Medicare HMO	All applicable copays and deductibles at the time of the office visit.	File the claim on your behalf, as well as any claims to your secondary insurance.
Workers' Compensation	If we have verified the claim with your carrier No payment is necessary at the time of the visit. If we are not able to verify your claim Payment in full is requested at the time of the visit.	Call your carrier ahead of time to verify the accident date, claim number, primary care physician, employer information, and referral procedures.
Workers' Compensation (Out of State)	Payment in full is requested at the time of the visit.	Provide you a receipt so you can file the claim with your carrier.
Occupational Injury	Payment in full is requested at the time of the visit.	Provide you a receipt so you can file the claim with your carrier.
No Insurance	Payment in full at the time of the visit.	Work with you to settle your account. Please ask to speak with our staff if you need assistance.

Fig. 5.6 Payment policy. *HMO,* Health maintenance organization.

acceptable collection ratio. Every healthcare office has its own routine for sending statements. Typically, statements are mailed every 30 days. This process is called a **billing cycle**. In large practices, one 30-day mass billing for all patients is a cumbersome task. Such facilities often use an **alternate billing cycle**—a billing system that incorporates the mailing of a partial group of statements at spaced intervals during the month. With an alternate billing cycle, the breakdown of accounts is frequently determined by an alphabetical list of last names or by account numbers. For example, patients with last names ending in "A" through "F" would be sent statements on the first of the month, patients with last names ending with "G" through "L" would receive statements on the tenth day of the month, and so forth. One advantage to an alternate billing cycle is that cash flow is distributed throughout the entire month, whereas billing only once a month generates a large amount of receipts at one time. No one specific method is considered best for all healthcare practices. Each practice must establish its own system that works well.

Note: If the patient has valid insurance coverage, it is important to make sure that the insurance carrier was billed appropriately and that the claim was denied before sending statements asking for the full amount.

ARRANGING CREDIT OR PAYMENT PLANS

The cost of some medical treatments or procedures can be thousands of dollars, and the patient might not have adequate insurance coverage (or may have no insurance at all) to pay the medical fees. Many healthcare facilities offer patient financing plans, which allow patients to get treatments or procedures and pay for them in periodic installments—similar to buying a car. A comprehensive range of plan options that offer low, or at least manageable, monthly payments to fit almost every budget is available in healthcare facilities across the United States.

Self-Pay Patients

Some patients may have inadequate health insurance coverage or no insurance at all. These are referred to as **self-pay patients**. Just because patients are self-pay does not mean they would deliberately try to avoid paying their bills. Some individuals who do not carry health insurance are still able to pay their medical bills in a timely manner.

As mentioned previously, the patient should be provided with the policies and expectations of the healthcare practice early in the encounter. Under most state laws, full payment for medical services is due and payable at the time the service is provided. However, healthcare providers often take the initiative to temper this mandate as they see fit.

When a patient completes the patient information form and no insurance is listed, the health insurance professional should inquire about the reason. It is possible that the insurance section was overlooked. If the patient has no insurance, it is prudent to inquire tactfully how the patient intends to pay for the service. Some healthcare offices ask the patient whether he or she has insurance when the appointment is made, and if there is no insurance, the patient must make at least a partial payment in advance.

Ideally, the practice should have an established credit plan for self-pay patients because it is mandatory that every patient be treated equally. Equally as important, the healthcare office cannot refuse to see an established patient because of an outstanding debt.

Terminating the Patient–Provider Relationship

There is a procedure whereby (if carried out within the confines of the law) a healthcare provider can terminate the patient–provider relationship. This procedure involves sending a certified letter to the patient, with a return receipt to confirm that the patient received the letter, communicating that the patient can no longer be treated (for whatever reason spelled out in the letter) and giving the patient a specified amount of time to find alternative care. The provider might also suggest one or two alternative caregivers to aid the patient in continuing his or her healthcare. (This information must be thoroughly documented in the patient's medical health record.) Following this structured method of notifying the patient that the practice will no longer accept him or her as a patient and spelling out the reason why limits the practice's liability in the event of legal action brought by the patient accusing the practice of "abandonment."

Establishing Credit

When patients cannot make payment in full, credit is sometimes arranged, and a payment plan is established (Fig. 5.7). Some medical facilities offer a credit arrangement whereby the patient can pay the fee, interest free, in several installments. Other medical

5   Financial Arrangements

Payment is expected at time of service.

For your convenience, we offer the following methods of payment. Please check the option which you prefer.

_____ Cash

_____ Personal Check

_____ Credit Card _____ Visa _____ Mastercard

_____ I wish to make arrangements with an office manager today.

Late Charges

I realize that failure to keep this account current may result in you being unable to provide additional services except for emergencies or where there is prepayment for additional services. In the case of default on payment of this account, I agree to pay collection costs and reasonable attorney fees incurred in attempting to collect on this amount or any future outstanding account balances.

Thank you for filling out this form completely.
The information you have provided will help us serve your healthcare needs more effectively and efficiently.
If you have any questions at any time, please ask – we are always happy to help.

Fig. 5.7 Sample of financial arrangement plan.

facilities allow more flexibility for self-paying patients by offering an installment plan with interest rates lower than those of most major credit cards.

An installment payment plan of more than four payments comes under the federal Truth in Lending Act of 1968, Regulation Z. Regulation Z applies to each individual or business that offers or extends consumer credit if the following four conditions are met:

1. The credit is offered to consumers.
2. Credit is offered on a regular basis.
3. The credit is subject to a finance charge (i.e., interest) or must be paid in more than four installments according to a written agreement.
4. The credit is primarily for personal, family, or household purposes.

The Truth in Lending Act of 1968 and Regulation Z are discussed in more detail later in this chapter.

More information on this act can be found by accessing the applicable website listed in the "Websites to Explore" section at the end of this chapter.

PROBLEM PATIENTS

Sometimes the health insurance professional may know or have reason to believe that it will be difficult to collect fees from a particular patient. A policy should be in place for "problem" patients such as these or for patients who, for whatever reason, "send up a red flag." Following are some suggestions to maximize collection success from problem or questionable patients:

- Contact a local credit bureau or view the patient's credit report and score online to find out if the patient is creditworthy.
- Discuss the credit policy with the patient before the encounter and establish a payment that is affordable for the patient.
- Have the patient sign a written agreement.
- Ask the patient to make a down payment of at least 20%.
- Arrange with the patient and his or her bank for automatic withdrawals if the patient has an account where that is a viable option.
- Charge interest (if that is practice policy) or a "carrying fee" to give the patient added incentive to make regular payments and pay off the balance promptly.

   Note: Even if the practice does not charge interest, if it is mutually agreed that the account will be paid off in more than four payments, the practice by law must provide the patient with a copy of the Truth in Lending Act, if the patients requests it.
- Arrange to have payments automatically deducted each month on a presigned credit card form.
- Do not allow the payments to extend past the treatment program, or 12 months, whichever is the shorter time.
- Provide the patient with a self-addressed, stamped return envelope in each bill.

Keep a copy of the signed agreement on file so that the office staff can refer to it for specific monthly payments or fees for missed payments. Most healthcare offices keep these agreements in a separate file rather than in the patient's health record.

When setting up payment arrangements, be considerate but firm. The health insurance professional should explain the payment plan clearly, emphasizing that payments must not be missed and that the payment must be received on or before the due date.

Starting in January 2013, the Affordable Care Act requires medical practices to automate patient eligibility. This should dramatically decrease issues in account collection because patients will know their financial responsibility immediately.

> ### ? What Did You Learn?
>
> 1. List five things a healthcare practice can do to aid in its financial success.
> 2. Explain how an alternate billing cycle can be used.
> 3. What is meant by a self-pay patient?
> 4. Name the four conditions that must be met under Regulation Z when a business extends credit.

LAWS AFFECTING CREDIT AND COLLECTION

Because healthcare offices typically extend credit to their patients, they need to comply with federal consumer credit laws. It is important that the health insurance professional become acquainted with collection laws. The relevant federal laws dealing with consumer credit are introduced in this section.

TRUTH IN LENDING ACT

The **Truth in Lending Act** (TILA) helps consumers of all kinds. It requires the person or business entity to disclose the exact credit terms when extending credit to applicants and regulates how the business advertises consumer credit. The following items must be disclosed to a consumer who buys on credit:

- The monthly finance charge
- The annual interest rate
- When payments are due
- The total sale price (the cash price of the item or service, plus all other charges)
- The amount of any late payment charges and when they will be imposed

FAIR CREDIT BILLING ACT

The **Fair Credit Billing Act (FCBA)** sets guidelines for disputing what a consumer believes to be an error on his or her credit card statement. The FCBA applies only to accounts considered to be open-end accounts, such as credit card accounts and charge accounts issued by department stores. The FCBA does not apply to installment loans. The FCBA would apply to medical practices if the practice allows patients to pay with credit cards.

In addition to advising how to handle billing disputes, the FCBA requires that the entity granting credit tell consumers (in periodic mailings) what their rights are.

EQUAL CREDIT OPPORTUNITY ACT

The **Equal Credit Opportunity Act** states that a business entity may not discriminate against a credit applicant on the basis of race, color, religion, national origin, age, sex, or marital status. The Equal Credit Opportunity Act does allow freedom to consider legitimate factors in granting credit, such as the applicant's financial status (earnings and savings) and credit record. Despite the prohibition on age discrimination, a consumer who has not reached the legal age for entering into contracts can be rejected.

FAIR CREDIT REPORTING ACT

The **Fair Credit Reporting Act** deals primarily with credit reports issued by credit reporting agencies. It is intended to protect consumers from having their eligibility for credit damaged by incomplete or misleading credit report information. The law gives consumers the right to a copy of their credit reports. If they see an inaccurate item, they can ask that it be corrected or removed. If the business entity reporting the credit problem does not agree to a change or deletion, or if the credit bureau refuses to make it, the consumer can add a 100-word statement to the file explaining his or her side of the story. This statement becomes a part of any future credit report.

FAIR DEBT COLLECTION PRACTICES ACT

The **Fair Debt Collection Practices Act** addresses abusive methods used by third-party collectors—bill collectors hired to collect overdue bills. Small businesses are more directly affected by state laws that apply directly to collection methods used by a creditor. The Fair Debt Collection Practices Act states that unless a debtor consents or a court order permits, debt collectors may not call to collect a debt:

- At any time or place that is unusual or known to be inconvenient to the consumer (8 AM to 9 PM is presumed to be convenient)
- When the creditor is aware that the debtor is represented by an attorney with respect to the debt, unless the attorney fails to respond to the communication in a reasonable time period
- At work if the creditor is aware that the patient's employer prohibits such contacts

? What Did You Learn?

1. List the five federal laws that affect credit and collection.
2. What can a consumer do if they find inaccurate information on their credit report?
3. What does the Equal Credit Opportunity Act address?
4. Name the three telephone limitations upheld by the Fair Debt Collection Practices Act.

COLLECTION METHODS

No matter how experienced, how resourceful, or how persuasive the health insurance professional or collection manager is, there always will be some bad debts in a healthcare practice. Two common methods that healthcare offices use for collecting bad debts are collection by telephone and collection by letter.

COLLECTION BY TELEPHONE

Collecting overdue accounts by phone is a job that many healthcare office employees would prefer not to do. It is so much easier to write a collection letter than to call a patient about a delinquent account, but the collection call is considered far more effective because patients usually respond more readily to a friendly voice than they do to a letter. Many offices have found that the collection call, when done correctly, is an inexpensive and effective collection technique. It costs money to continue sending statements and letters.

Making collection calls throughout the day with special emphasis from 5 PM to 8 PM is recommended whenever possible. Most offices report that more patients can be reached between 5 PM and 7 PM than at any other time during the day. The health insurance professional should be aware of the legal limits of telephone collection calls as spelled out in the Fair Debt Collection Practices Act. For more information on this act, see the website listed in "Websites to Explore" at the end of this chapter.

Timetable for Calling

A workable telephoning timetable needs to be specific and must be followed consistently to get results. This may be one-half of the list per week or per month, depending on the size of the practice. Random calling tends not to work as well.

Do not wait too long to get aggressive with collections. Many offices wait 4, 5, or 6 months before making the first collection call; such a policy yields a very low return. Collection specialists claim that calling closer to the time of service results in greater payoffs. The longer an account is left without follow-up calls, the less chance there is of collecting the fees.

Selecting Which Patients to Call

The next step is to select which patients to call. Some offices believe that it is not cost effective to call accounts that are less than a certain amount (e.g., $30 to $45). A large practice with thousands of patient visits per month may not find it cost effective to call accounts that are less than $100. Fig. 5.8 shows examples of typical conversation scenarios and how the health insurance professional might handle the situation.

COLLECTION BY LETTER

Collecting delinquent accounts by letter has been successful for some healthcare practices. The timing and

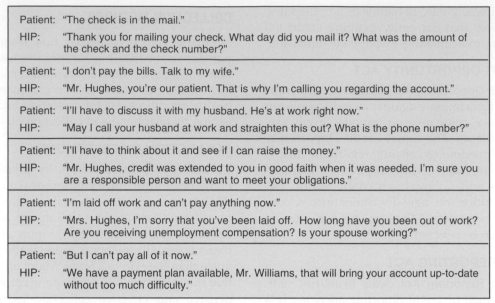

Patient:	"The check is in the mail."
HIP:	"Thank you for mailing your check. What day did you mail it? What was the amount of the check and the check number?"
Patient:	"I don't pay the bills. Talk to my wife."
HIP:	"Mr. Hughes, you're our patient. That is why I'm calling you regarding the account."
Patient:	"I'll have to discuss it with my husband. He's at work right now."
HIP:	"May I call your husband at work and straighten this out? What is the phone number?"
Patient:	"I'll have to think about it and see if I can raise the money."
HIP:	"Mr. Hughes, credit was extended to you in good faith when it was needed. I'm sure you are a responsible person and want to meet your obligations."
Patient:	"I'm laid off work and can't pay anything now."
HIP:	"Mrs. Hughes, I'm sorry that you've been laid off. How long have you been out of work? Are you receiving unemployment compensation? Is your spouse working?"
Patient:	"But I can't pay all of it now."
HIP:	"We have a payment plan available, Mr. Williams, that will bring your account up-to-date without too much difficulty."

Fig. 5.8 Sample phone conversations. *HIP,* Health insurance professional.

wording of written communications with patients should be based on numerous factors, including the size of the balance owed, the payment history of the patient, and the philosophy and policy of the practice.

When composing collection letters, be careful with the wording used so as not to anger or upset the patient. Be matter of fact and nonthreatening. Adopt the attitude that the patient has simply overlooked the bill and will make a payment because of this reminder letter. Fig. 5.9 shows examples of collection letters. These letters can be tailored to fit the particular needs of the practice and the patients. Additional letters or phone calls can be used to extend the time between communications. The key is to stay in constant communication with overdue accounts, rather than adopting a "wait until tomorrow" attitude or assuming that the account will need to be written off or turned over for collection.

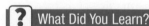

What Did You Learn?

1. Why might a telephone call be more effective in collecting delinquent accounts than a letter?
2. When should the healthcare practice make its first collection call?
3. What minimum amount warrants a telephone call?

BILLING SERVICES

Some healthcare practices "outsource" their medical billing by hiring a separate professional medical billing service. A reputable medical billing service can provide comprehensive, cost-effective, HIPAA-compliant medical billing solutions for healthcare professionals nationwide. Medical billing services are

typically organized and run by medical billing professionals who design, implement, and manage the accounts receivable portion of the healthcare practice. A well-run medical billing service can help a healthcare practice run more efficiently by eliminating staffing issues, undisciplined medical billing and collection processes, outdated medical billing systems, and archaic reporting tools that result in poor collection ratios. Billing services can perform multiple functions for the healthcare practice, such as:

- Preparing and submitting insurance claims
- Providing data entry of patient demographics, insurance information, charges, payments, and adjustments
- Tracking payments from patients and third-party payers
- Producing practice management reports
- Collecting delinquent accounts

Usually a computer, modem, and Internet access are all that is necessary to access a billing service's network, after which the medical facility can retrieve up-to-the-minute patient information and practice management reports at any time on a secure server. Many billing services are available locally and nationwide. With the advent of the Internet, a healthcare office can interact with a professional billing service anywhere in the United States. Care should be taken, however, when choosing a billing service. The service should be thoroughly researched, and references checked out with several of its current customers.

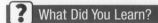

What Did You Learn?

1. What is a billing service?
2. List five functions of a billing service.

Example Letter 1: Send when the account is past 30 days.	Example Letter 2: Send 15 days after letter #1 if no payment is made.
Dear Mrs. Williams: Your account balance of $340.50 is now overdue. Please send your payment to the above address at your earliest convenience. If you have questions, you can reach our bookkeeper at xxx-xxxx between 8 a.m. and 5 p.m. weekdays. Sincerely, XYZ Family Clinic	Dear Mrs. Williams: Despite several communications, we have not received payment for your overdue balance in the amount of $340.50. Your account is now seriously past due. Please send your payment to the above address or contact our bookkeeper at xxx-xxxx if you have questions. We will contact you by telephone if we do not hear from you within 7 days. Sincerely, XYZ Family Practice
Example Letter 3: Send 15 days after letter #2 if no payment is made.	Example Letter 4: Send 15 days after letter #3 if no payment is made.
Dear Mrs. Williams: We have made all reasonable attempts to work with you to reduce your seriously overdue balance with our clinic. You have not met the terms of the payment plan that we agreed upon. Professional services have been provided to your family in good faith, and payment of your account will protect your status as a family in good standing. We must hear from you within 15 days of the date of this letter. Our bookkeeper is available on weekdays between the hours of 8 a.m. and 5 p.m. Sincerely, XYZ Family Clinic	CERTIFIED MAIL RETURN RECEIPT REQUESTED Dear Mrs. Williams: You have failed to pay or satisfactorily reduce your severely delinquent balance despite our many efforts to work with you. Therefore, XYZ Family Clinic will no longer be providing medical care for you and your children. You should place your family under the care of another physician as soon as possible. You may contact XYZ Family Clinic or the County Medical Society for a referral to a new physician. When you have selected another physician, please send us a signed authorization so that we can provide a copy of your children's medical charts or a summary of its contents to your new physician. XYZ Family Clinic will remain available to treat your children for a short time, which will be no more than 30 days from the date of this letter. Please make the transfer to a new physician as soon as possible within that period. Sincerely, XYZ Family Clinic

Fig. 5.9 Sample letter series for delinquent accounts.

COLLECTION AGENCIES

A **collection agency** is an organization that obtains or arranges for payment of money owed to a third party—in this case, a healthcare office. Many healthcare practices use collection agencies to help collect delinquent accounts. Collection agencies provide a service to businesses that:

- Are too small to have a collection department of their own
- Lack the expertise to collect delinquent accounts themselves
- Think a collection agency would get faster results
- Simply do not want to deal with the hassle of collections

Most collection agencies request at least 50% of the money they collect. Experts suggest that delinquent bills should be turned over for collection only when it is obvious that payment by any other means is a dead issue. When to go to a collection agency is a business decision made within each healthcare practice.

If the decision is made to turn delinquent accounts over to a collection agency, care should be taken when choosing the agency. Experts say that a credible collection agency should be a member of a national trade association, such as the Consumer Data Industry Association (formerly Associated Credit Bureaus) and American Collectors Association. These organizations provide all-important standards and training. When choosing a collector, choose one that specializes in collecting medical accounts. Also, use standard business practices such as talking with associates; checking references, credentials, and local professional or trade memberships; and touching base with state or local licensing authorities and perhaps the Better Business Bureau. In addition to checking references and credentials, the healthcare practice should ensure that the agency chosen:

- Employs trained, certified collectors who understand and abide by the Fair Debt Collection Practices Act and follow the requirements of state laws
- Is insured, licensed, and bonded
- Is able to collect in other states

HIPAA Tip

The Health Insurance Portability and Accountability Act (HIPAA) Privacy Rule does not require consent from a patient before turning in his or her account for collection. Covered providers still must be cautious when using protected health information (PHI) for collection purposes in determining just how much PHI is needed to accomplish the specific goal of satisfying their account receivables.

? What Did You Learn?

1. What is a collection agency?
2. List four reasons why a healthcare practice might hire a collection agency.
3. What two trade organizations do experts suggest contacting when choosing a collection agency?
4. Name three things to look for in a reputable collection agency.

SMALL CLAIMS LITIGATION

Small claims litigation is an alternative to turning accounts over for collection. Filing a small claims suit can be effective for a healthcare practice to collect delinquent accounts. Before making the decision to take a delinquent patient to small claims court, however, the cost should be weighed against the monetary gain. The cost of generating a small claims lawsuit is typically $30 to $50 for filing fees and another $20 to $100 for an enforcement officer or process server, so the account ideally should total enough to offset this expense. The process is administered by the services at local county or district courts, but the individual initiating the small claims lawsuit must prepare the paperwork.

The small claims process is set up to make it easy for individuals or businesses to recover legitimate debts without using expensive legal advisors. The claim is usually heard by a judge in chambers (or, in some cases, an appointed arbitrator) with the parties presenting their sides in person. The individual or business entity that initiates the legal process must pay the initial costs such as filing and serving fees, but

these fees usually can be recovered from the debtor if the case is won. Small claims suits can be for any amount of money up to a limiting threshold, which varies by state, usually $3000 to $5000; however, there is ongoing legislation in many states to increase these limits.

WHO CAN USE SMALL CLAIMS

Generally, any person of legal age or any business entity can file a small claims lawsuit if there is a legitimate claim against someone who owes money and is refusing to pay. All that is necessary is proof that the debt exists. In the case of a healthcare office, this is usually some sort of written evidence such as a patient ledger. It is important that there is full and proper documentation. The most prolonged and expensive disputes generally result from inadequate paperwork and a lack of attention to detail.

Before a claim can proceed, the court expects the **plaintiff** (the party bringing the lawsuit) to have explored all other avenues of settlement. This means that the plaintiff should allow the other side (in this case, the patient) a "reasonable period of time" to make a payment before resorting to legal action.

HOW THE SMALL CLAIMS PROCESS WORKS

The procedure starts with the plaintiff filling out a standard form, which outlines details about the claim and the various parties. The following information needs to appear on the form:

1. Name of the party being sued
2. Current address of that party
3. Amount of the plaintiff's claim
4. Basis, or proof, of the claim

The completed form is returned to the court office with the appropriate filing and serving fees. A copy of the form is "served" to the **defendant** (the party being sued), who may choose to pay the debt in full plus all accrued fees before the process goes any further. He or she also may dispute the claim in its entirety.

If the claim, or any part of it, is disputed, the matter goes to a court hearing where the evidence is heard in informal surroundings, usually around the table in a judge's chambers. The plaintiff and defendant are given an opportunity to introduce evidence, ask questions, and explain to the judge (or arbitrator) why judgment should be entered in his or her favor. The judge usually makes an immediate decision, and the parties involved get a full and final result on the day of the hearing. The judgment of the court is an official statement in the court's records that the defendant owes the plaintiff a certain amount of money with interest. The judgment must be enforced out of the defendant's assets. More simply put, if the judgment is in favor of the plaintiff, the defendant must pay immediately. If the defendant does not pay after judgment, the plaintiff can "attach," or gain ownership of the defendant's assets, such as a paycheck, a bank account, or a car.

Small claims litigation can be successful, but it is time consuming and can be costly if there are a lot of claims. If the healthcare practice has someone on staff who is able and willing to prepare all of the proper documents and attend court hearings, this process can have positive results. Filing and serving fees can be far less than the typical 50% of the outstanding debt kept back by a collection agency.

> **? What Did You Learn?**
>
> 1. What was the initial intent of the small claims process?
> 2. What is a typical monetary threshold for a small claims suit?
> 3. What is the first step in initiating a small claims suit?
> 4. List the four elements of information that must appear on the small claims form.

SUMMARY CHECKPOINTS

- Patients typically come to a healthcare office expecting certain things, such as the following:
  - Professional office setting: Because patients cannot see and touch an intangible service such as healthcare, they look for substitutes to put their mind at ease, such as the office location, size, and layout and staff enthusiasm.
  - Relevant forms and questions: Patients prefer forms to be brief, of high quality, and relevant to the encounter. Patients should be given reasons why these forms and questions are important to their care and treatment.
  - Honoring appointment times: Time is a valuable commodity in everyone's life; if the schedule lags, the patient should be told the reason for the delay and offered alternatives to waiting.
  - Patient load: Negative conclusions about the competency of the entire healthcare team can be offset by explaining to the patient why the reception room has no or few patients waiting.
  - Getting comfortable with the healthcare provider: Sharing a relevant personal experience or information promotes a good provider–patient relationship and can relieve patient anxiety.
  - Privacy and confidentiality: Patients must feel confident that any personal information they divulge would be kept private and confidential.
  - Financial issues: Discuss financial issues and practice policies up front with patients so that they know what to expect.
- Future trends in the patient–practice relationship include the following:
  - An aging population: Over the next 30 years, the number of Americans older than age 65 will increase, and healthcare facilities should be prepared to handle an increasing volume of elderly patients.
  - Using the Internet as a healthcare tool: Patients will rely more on the Internet, and healthcare providers will have to adapt their practices to meet these state-of-the-art electronic requirements.
  - Seeing patients as consumers: Similar to other types of consumers, patients today are likely to switch healthcare plans or healthcare providers or both if they think they are not getting quality service.
- Any individual or any business involved in transferring data or carrying out transactions related to patient PHI is a HIPAA-covered entity. The law applies to three groups:
  - Healthcare providers: Any provider of healthcare services or supplies who transmits any health information in electronic form in connection with a transaction for which standard requirements have been adopted
  - Health plans: Any individual or group plan that provides or pays the cost of healthcare
  - Healthcare clearinghouses: Any public or private entity that transforms healthcare transactions from one format to another
- Personally identifiable information includes information about an individual collected by the covered entity that could be used to identify the individual, regardless of the source of such information or the medium in which it is recorded (e.g., name, address, email address, telephone number, birth date, and Social Security number).
- When all identifiable elements are removed, the information under most circumstances is considered deidentified.
- Two common methods of accounting are used in healthcare facilities today:
  - Paper accounting system: This system uses several accounting forms to capture information, including a daily journal, a disbursements journal, a general journal, a general ledger, and a patient ledger.
  - Electronic patient accounting software: A computer software program can perform all phases of the accounting process quickly and accurately. It allows the input of demographic data, creating a patient "account" from which many documents can be generated, such as a list of appointments by day and by provider and an encounter form for each. Appointments also can be scheduled, deleted, and adjusted within the accounting system. Periodic statements, aging reports, and insurance claims can be generated.
- Some things a healthcare practice might do to increase its financial success include, but are not limited to, the following:
  - Establish a written credit policy.
  - Discuss payment and practice policies up front with patients.

- Bill promptly.
- Plan an action for bills more than 30 days old.
- Telephone (or send a letter) after the second statement.
- Use the services of a collection agency or small claims court.
- Laws affecting credit and collection include:
  - The Truth in Lending Act
  - The Fair Credit Billing Act
  - The Equal Credit Opportunity Act
  - The Fair Credit Reporting Act
  - The Fair Debt Collection Practices Act
- Collecting by telephone and using small claims litigation are two common methods for collecting delinquent accounts. A reputable medical billing service can provide comprehensive, cost-effective, HIPAA-compliant medical billing solutions for healthcare professionals nationwide. Billing services can perform multiple functions for the practice.
- Collection agencies provide a valuable service to medical practices; however, most keep 50% of the fees they collect.
- The steps involved in small claims litigation are as follows:
  - Acquire the proper forms from the local county or district court, along with instructions on how to fill them out properly.
  - Include the following information on the original form: (1) the name of the defendant, (2) the current address of the defendant, (3) the amount of the plaintiff's claim, and (4) the basis of the claim.
  - Attach documentation that provides proof that the money is owed.
  - Return the completed form (and the required number of copies) to the court office with the appropriate filing and serving fees.
  - Appear in court on the date indicated to substantiate the case.

Closing Scenario

Callie Foster recently had to use small claims court to collect a balance owed by a patient. She found this process interesting, but it left her wondering how things could have been done differently to avoid going to court. She is going to review the Walden-Martin payment policy to see if it needs updating. She is also going to ask the office manager if there could be training for all staff on how to help collect payment when the patient is still in the office.

CHAPTER REVIEW QUESTIONS

1. The forms that the patient is required to complete should:
   a. Be complex and contain medical terminology.
   b. Be relevant to the reason the patient is at the clinic.
   c. Be very abbreviated.
   d. Be offered only in a paper format.
2. The discussion of fees is often the responsibility of:
   a. The provider.
   b. A billing service.
   c. The reception staff.
   d. All of the above.
3. Future trends in healthcare include:
   a. Aging population
   b. Internet as a healthcare tool
   c. Patients as consumers
   d. All of the above
4. HIPAA-covered entities include:
   a. Collection agencies
   b. Patients
   c. Healthcare clearinghouses
   d. The cleaning service
5. When certain data items are removed from PHI, it is considered:
   a. Deidentified.
   b. CMS compliant.
   c. Protected.
   d. HIPAA approved.
6. HIPAA 5010 Transaction Standards addressed:
   a. The use of ICD-10 codes.
   b. The use of NPI numbers.
   c. The use of CPT codes.
   d. The use of the CMS-1500 form.
7. HIPAA requires which elements on an authorization to release information?
   a. The purpose of the disclosure
   b. An expiration date
   c. Signature of the patient and the date
   d. All of the above
8. Which term describes the specific dollar amount that the patient is responsible for when an office visit or ED visit occurs?
   a. Deductible
   b. Coinsurance
   c. Copayment
   d. None of the above
9. Which term describes when the insurance company pays a certain percentage of the fee and the patient pays the remaining percentage?
   a. Deductible
   b. Coinsurance
   c. Copayment
   d. None of the above

10. Collection telephone calls are most effective when made between:
    a. 8:00 AM and 11:00 AM.
    b. 11:00 AM and 2:00 PM.
    c. 2:00 PM and 5:00 PM.
    d. 5:00 PM and 8:00 PM.

WEBSITES TO EXPLORE

- For live links to the following websites, please visit the Evolve website at http://evolve.elsevier.com/Beik/today.
- For information on HIPAA regulations, go to https://www.hhs.gov/hipaa/for-professionals/privacy/laws-regulations/index.html.
- To view a sample patient confidentiality agreement, visit https://www.hcms.org/tmaimis/HARRIS/Practice_Resources/Tools_and_Resources/Letters-Templates.aspx?WebsiteKey=0a784a46-1152-4b41-8e5d-3545a059ff7f.
- For more information on financial policies for healthcare offices, go to https://www.verywellhealth.com/balance-billing-what-it-is-how-it-works-1738460.

- For more detailed information and to keep up to date on the Truth in Lending Act, Regulation Z, visit http://www.federalreserve.gov/boarddocs/supmanual/cch/200601/til.pdf.
- For more information on laws regarding credit and collection, visit http://www.ftc.gov/bcp/edu/pubs/consumer/credit/cre18.shtm.
- For more information on fair debt collection, visit http://www.fair-debt-collection.com.
- For more information on the Consumer Data Industry Association, go to https://www.cdiaonline.org/.
- For more information on the American Collectors Association, go to http://www.acainternational.org.
- For more information on small claims procedures and forms for individual states, go to http://www.uslegalforms.com/smallclaims/.
- For more information on healthcare technology online, go to https://mobidev.biz/blog/technology-trends-healthcare-digital-transformation.

Author's Note: Due to the dynamic nature of the Internet, web addresses and/or links provided in this chapter may have changed since publication and may no longer be valid. In such cases, students should select comparable search words to access related sites.

6 Claim Submission Methods

Chapter Outline

Chapter Objectives

After completion of this chapter, the student should be able to:

1. Provide a brief overview of the health insurance claims process.
2. Explain the development and expansion of electronic claims.
3. Discuss the HIPAA Administrative Simplification Compliance Act (ASCA) and its impact on electronic claims.
4. Determine the rationale for the HIPAA 5010 Standards.
5. Outline the electronic billing process, and list essential elements for claim submission.
6. List the advantages of submitting electronic claims.
7. Name the two ways to submit electronic claims.
8. Discuss the CMS-1500 universal claim form.
9. Explain the rationale for understanding both paper and electronic claims submission.
10. Identify sources for general guidelines for completing the CMS-1500 paper claim form.

Chapter Terms

American Standard Code for Information Interchange (ASCII)
assign(s) benefits
beneficiary
claim attachments
claims clearinghouse
clean claims
CMS-1500 form
demographic information

dial-ups
electronic protected health information (ePHI)
employer identification number (EIN)
encounter form
guarantor
HIPAA-covered entity
insurance billing cycle
medical necessity

national provider identifier (NPI)
optical character recognition (OCR)
patient ledger card
practice management software
protected health information (PHI)
release of information
small (entity) provider
third-party payer
waiver

Latisha Howard started working for Walden-Martin Family Medical Clinic right after completing her health insurance professional course work about 5 years ago. While taking classes, she didn't really understand why she had to learn the paper format for claims, but now she can see how that information relates to the information needed to submit electronic claims. She also realizes that having a solid understanding of the Health Insurance Portability and Accountability Act (HIPAA) and other laws helps her do her job. Patients often are confused about why certain information is needed, and Latisha is able to reassure them that all information is kept confidential and also why it is necessary to getting their claims paid.

OVERVIEW OF THE HEALTH INSURANCE CLAIMS SUBMISSION PROCESS

The health insurance claims submission process is an interaction between the healthcare provider and an insurance company (**third-party payer**). Sometimes referred to as the **insurance billing cycle**, this interaction can take anywhere from several days to several months to complete, depending on the number of exchanges in communication required. The cycle begins when a patient visits a healthcare provider, where a medical health record is created or an existing one is updated. This record contains **demographic information**, including but not limited to the patient's name, address, Social Security number (SSN) (optional), date of birth, sex, telephone numbers, and insurance identification (ID) numbers. Also included in the record are examination details, medications prescribed, diagnoses, and suggested treatment. If the patient is a minor, information for the **guarantor** (a parent or an adult related to or legally responsible for the patient) is recorded. The medical health record can be paper, electronic, or a combination of both. It is a legal document, and the information it contains is protected by privacy laws.

Once the patient visit is over, the health insurance professional (or medical biller) transmits information from the record to the insurance company in the form of a claim. Historically, claims were submitted using a paper form—the **CMS-1500 form**—named for its originator, the Centers for Medicare and Medicaid Services

Box 6.1 Exceptions to HIPAA's Electronic Claims Submission Requirement

- A small provider billing a Medicare Administrative Contractor (MAC) that has fewer than 25 FTE employees and a physician, practitioner, or supplier with fewer than 10 FTEs that bills a Medicare carrier
- A dentist
- A participant in a Medicare demonstration project in which paper claim filing is required to report data essential for the demonstration
- A provider that conducts mass immunizations, such as flu injections, and may be permitted to submit paper roster bills
- A provider that submits claims when more than one other payer is responsible for payment before Medicare payment
- A provider that furnishes services only outside the United States
- A provider experiencing a disruption in electricity and communication connections that are beyond its control
- A provider that can establish the existence of an "unusual circumstance" that precludes electronic submission of claims

FTE, Full-time equivalent; *HIPAA*, Health Insurance Portability and Accountability Act.

(CMS) (discussed later). After the federal Health Insurance Portability and Accountability Act (HIPAA) was passed in 1996, CMS directed providers who submitted claims to Medicare to do so electronically with few exceptions. However, some providers (e.g., dentists and small, rural practices) may still be using the paper form (Box 6.1).

After the insurance company receives the claim, it is reviewed, evaluated for validity—patient eligibility, provider credentials, and **medical necessity**—and processed. (To meet the medical necessity criteria, services or supplies must be appropriate and necessary for the symptoms, diagnosis, and/or treatment of the medical condition, and they must meet the standards of good medical practice.) For those providers who have contracted with the insurance carrier, approved claims are reimbursed according to prenegotiated rates between the provider and the insurance contract. (It is important to note, however, that not all providers contract with all insurance carriers.) Failed claims are rejected, and notice is sent to both the provider and the patient. An explanation of benefits (EOB) or a remittance advice (RA) is generated for both approved and rejected claims. EOBs and RAs are discussed in Chapter 7.

TWO BASIC CLAIMS SUBMISSION METHODS

In this chapter, the two basic methods of submitting health insurance claims, electronic and paper, are discussed. Submission of claims has gone through a metamorphosis just as health insurance itself has. Before the electronic age, providers submitted claims on paper through the mail. Every insurance carrier had its own specialized type of paperwork for submitting claims. Imagine the frustration a health insurance professional must have felt trying to figure out how to complete all of these different forms properly. Then, in the mid-1970s, the Health Care Financing Administration (HCFA, pronounced "hick-fa") created a new form for Medicare claims, called the *HCFA-1500*. The form was approved by the American Medical Association Council on Medical Service and was subsequently adopted by all government healthcare programs. Although the HCFA-1500 originally was developed for submitting Medicare claims, it eventually was accepted by most commercial and private insurance carriers to assist with the standardization of the claims process. Because HCFA is now called CMS, the form is called the *CMS-1500*; however, it is basically the same document as the original. Because many medical offices currently submit claims electronically, the electronic claims submission process is discussed first; because some providers still use the paper claim form, submission of claims using the CMS-1500 is also briefly discussed. The information needed for claims processing, however, is the same whether it is a paper or electronic claim.

REVISIONS TO THE CMS-1500 FORM

The CMS-1500 has gone through several updates, the most recent being CMS-1500 (02/12), which went into effect in 2014. Specific changes that were made to the form include the addition of eight diagnosis codes and better support of the use of the International Classification of Diseases, 10th revision (ICD-10) diagnosis code set in Item Number 21 (for a total of 12) and the addition of the quick response (QR) code at the top left of the form. The QR code provides a link to a National Uniform Claim Committee (NUCC) landing page that provides information about the form. It also helps align the form for the reader. A copy of the CMS-1500 (02/12) claim form can be found in Appendix A.

CLAIM FORM COMPLETION INSTRUCTIONS

The NUCC's goal in developing the *1500 Claim Form Reference Instruction Manual* is to help standardize the manner in which the form is completed. The NUCC's general instructions for completing the 1500 Health Insurance Claim Form are intended only as a guide and not as definitive instructions for this purpose. It is recognized that some payers require different instructions on how to complete specific item numbers (or blocks) on the form. Providers should refer to the most current federal, state, or other payer instructions for specific requirements applicable to using the 1500 Health Insurance Claim Form.

The NUCC releases an updated version of its *1500 Claim Form Reference Instruction Manual* annually, which is available at the NUCC's website, http://www.nucc.org, under the "1500 Claim Form" tab.

? What Did You Learn?

1. The health insurance claims submission process is an interaction between _____ and _____.
2. After the patient visit, information from the record is transmitted to the insurance company in the form of a _____.
3. Provide an accurate definition for "medical necessity."
4. Name the two basic claim submission methods.

ELECTRONIC CLAIMS

With the development and growth of computer technology, specifically medical **practice management software** (a type of software that deals with the day-to-day operations of a medical practice), the way in which claims are generated and processed has changed. Practice management software allows users to enter patient demographic information, schedule appointments, maintain lists of insurance payers, perform billing tasks, and generate reports. Also known as *health information systems,* this category of software has made it possible to manage large numbers of insurance claims with various payers accurately and efficiently. Currently, many companies offer such software programs. Computer technology has also made claims submission faster and more accurate at a cost savings to the practice using it.

Although new technologies improved some facets in the administration of healthcare, others made it more complex. Just as in dealing with the many types of paper insurance claim forms and specific standards for completing each, payers once more developed individualized methods for providers to submit claims electronically. The result was added administrative costs for providers and the need for their staffs to learn various, often complicated, computer programs.

HEALTH INSURANCE PORTABILITY AND ACCOUNTABILITY ACT

A very significant change that affected medical billing was the legislation passed by Congress in 1996—the Health Insurance Portability and Accountability Act (HIPAA). HIPAA initiated changes to promote uniformity in healthcare claim submission by adopting standards for electronic health information transactions. This adoption eliminated most of the unique forms used by individual health insurance carriers and the different requirements for processing claims. By October 2003, every **HIPAA-covered entity** (healthcare plans, healthcare providers, and healthcare clearinghouses) was asked to begin using these standard formats for processing claims and payments, as well as for the maintenance and transmission of electronic healthcare information and data.

Before HIPAA, there were more than 400 different ways to submit a claim. With HIPAA, there are only two: submitting them electronically using the standard transaction formats (currently ASC X12 5010 [Version 5010]) or, if the provider meets certain criteria, using the universal CMS-1500 paper form. This standardization of submitting claims and simplifying the processes involved makes getting paid quicker, easier, and less costly. The HIPAA mandates also help providers take advantage of new technologies, ultimately improving their overall business practices.

As a result of HIPAA, CMS directed all healthcare providers to submit Medicare claims electronically in a HIPAA-compliant format beginning in October 2003. Recognizing that this ruling could generate some challenging situations, the Administrative Simplification Compliance Act (ASCA) of 2001 identified limited exceptions to this requirement, which include:

- Roster billing of Medicare-covered vaccinations
- Dental claims
- Claims in which there are two or more primary plans and Medicare is secondary
- Service interruptions beyond the control of the provider

Also qualifying for exemption are **small entities**, or **small providers**—those with 25 or fewer full-time equivalent (FTE) employees—and physicians, practitioners, and suppliers with 10 or fewer FTEs. This small-entity exemption applies only to billing Medicare electronically, not to implementing HIPAA transactions and code sets.

The intent of HIPAA's Administrative Simplification law was to provide consumers with greater access to healthcare insurance, to protect the privacy of healthcare data, and to promote more standardization and efficiency in the healthcare industry. Although HIPAA covers a number of important healthcare issues, this chapter focuses on the Administrative Simplification portion of the law—specifically HIPAA's Electronic Transactions and Code Sets requirements. There are four parts to HIPAA's Administrative Simplification:

- Electronic transactions and code sets standards requirements
- Privacy requirements
- Security requirements
- National identifier requirements

The following sections briefly summarize each of these four parts.

 HIPAA Tip

An organization that routinely handles **protected health information (PHI)** in any capacity is, in all probability, considered a covered entity.

 Imagine This!

The Rolling Prairie Health Clinic holds a senior health fair every fall. Many Medicare beneficiaries come to the clinic for their annual flu and/or pneumonia shots. Amelia, Rolling Prairie's health insurance professional, uses roster billing as a quick and convenient way to bill Medicare for these vaccinations. Nina, the clinic manager, reminds Amelia that when submitting a roster bill, the provider must have given the same type of vaccination to five or more people on the same date of service and that each type of vaccination must be billed on a separate roster bill. Amelia cannot combine pneumococcal pneumonia vaccines and flu vaccines on the same roster bill.

ELECTRONIC TRANSACTIONS AND CODE SET REQUIREMENTS

HIPAA requires every provider who conducts business electronically to use the same healthcare transactions, code sets, and identifiers. HIPAA has identified 10 standard transactions for electronic data interchange (EDI) for the transmission of healthcare data. Claims and encounter information, payment and remittance advice (RA), and claims status and inquiry are some of these standard transactions that affect medical billing and claim submission. The ICD-10 codes and Current Procedural Terminology, 4th edition (CPT-4) (see Chapters 14 and 15) are examples of code sets for diagnosis and procedure coding, respectively. Other code sets adopted under the Administrative Simplification provisions of HIPAA include those used for claims involving medical supplies, dental services, and drugs.

PRIVACY REQUIREMENTS

The *Standards for Privacy of Individually Identifiable Health Information* (Privacy Rule) establishes a set of national standards for the protection of certain health information. The US Department of Health and Human Services (HHS) issued the Privacy Rule to implement one of HIPAA's main requirements. These standards address the use and disclosure of an individual's PHI—as introduced in the HIPAA Tip earlier—as well as standards for an individual's privacy rights to understand and control how his or her health information is used. Within HHS, the Office for Civil Rights is responsible for implementing and enforcing the Privacy Rule in regard to voluntary compliance procedures and civil penalties.

A major goal of the Privacy Rule is to ensure that individuals' health information is properly protected while allowing the flow of health information needed to provide and promote high-quality healthcare and to protect the public's health and well-being. The objective is to strike a balance between the uses of information and protecting a patient's privacy.

SECURITY REQUIREMENTS

The *Security Standards for the Protection of Electronic Protected Health Information* (Security Rule) established a national set of security standards for protecting certain health information that is held or transferred in electronic form. This rule addresses the technical and nontechnical safeguards that covered entities must put in place to secure individuals' **electronic protected health information (ePHI)**. As with the Privacy Rule, the Office for Civil Rights is responsible for enforcing the Security Rule.

A major goal of the Security Rule is to protect the privacy of individuals' health information while allowing covered entities to adopt new technologies to improve the quality and efficiency of patient care.

NATIONAL IDENTIFIER REQUIREMENTS

HIPAA requires the adoption of a standard unique identifier for every healthcare provider, health plan, and employer that identifies the entity on standard transactions. The Final Rule, issued in January 2004, adopted the **national provider identifier (NPI)** as this standard. The NPI is a 10-digit *intelligence-free* number, meaning that the number does not carry any information about the provider, such as the state in which he or she practices or the type of specialization. The NPI replaced all healthcare identifiers used before the onset of this rule. Version 5010 guidelines emphasize uniform reporting of NPIs to all payers. Previously, many providers had to submit NPIs differently based on the requirement of each health plan involved with their practice. After Version 5010 took effect, providers who previously used more than one NPI had to decide which one to use to submit claims. Then they had to notify all health plans they submitted claims to of their selected identifier. The NPI of the organization with which the provider is associated should now be used on claims. Individual NPIs will only be allowed as the billing NPI when services were performed by and will be paid to an independent, nonincorporated individual. The NPI should not be confused with the **employer identification number (EIN)**, which is a unique, nine-digit number issued to businesses for use by the Internal Revenue Service in the administration of tax laws. Both the NPI and the EIN are used in claims submission.

For more detailed information on HIPAA's Administrative Simplification Act, choose the applicable web link in the "Websites to Explore" section at the end of this chapter.

? What Did You Learn?

1. What type of software was instrumental in the expansion of electronic claims?
2. Name the important legislation Congress passed in 1996 that significantly affected medical billing and claims submission.
3. List who is included in the designation "covered entity."
4. What are the four exceptions to ASCA's electronic claims submission requirement?
5. Name the four parts to HIPAA's Administration Simplification Act.
6. True or false: The NPI and the EIN are basically the same and can be used interchangeably on claims.

HIPAA VERSION 5010 TRANSACTIONS AND CODE STANDARDS

Version 5010 is the set of standards that regulate the electronic transmission of specific healthcare transactions, including eligibility, claim submission, claim status, referrals, and remittances. Covered entities (health plans, healthcare claims clearinghouses, and healthcare providers) are required by law to conform to Version 5010, which went into effect on January 1, 2012. This version focuses on the electronic transactions that transfer healthcare information from one party to another. A typical example would be a healthcare provider sending claims to an insurance carrier for payment.

The 1996 HIPAA law established certain standards to govern specific electronic transactions, which include:

- Claims and patient visit information
- Claim status inquiries
- Patient eligibility verifications
- Insurance payments and EOBs
- Patient insurance plan enrollment and disenrollment
- Patient referrals and prior authorizations

MAJOR IMPROVEMENTS IN VERSION 5010

A number of major improvements are built into Version 5010 electronic transaction standards, which are listed in Box 6.2.

Box 6.2   Major Improvements in Version 5010

- Supports new-use cases introduced by the healthcare industry
- Clarifies misleading and/or uncertain content contained in the previous version
- Improves definition of required data elements
- Provides consistency across transactions
- Supports the NPI regulation
- Eliminates obsolete data contents
- Supports the three to seven digits necessary for ICD-10 codes
- Expands the number of diagnosis codes to 12
- Disallows the use of a post office box as the billing provider address
- Requires a nine-digit ZIP code for the billing and service provider(s)
- Allows use of assignment or plan participation to accept assignment with payers (previously used to indicate Medicare participation status only)
- Deletes approved and allowed amounts from AMT (estimated amount due/estimated amount paid) segments for coordination of benefits claims
- Requires the date-of-service range only when "from" and "to" dates are different
- Requires the pay-to-provider address when different from that of the billing provider
- Improves the way businesses function in general

ICD-10, International Classification of Diseases, 10th revision; *NPI*, national provider identifier.

The 5010 upgrade was necessary to implement some unforeseen issues and requirements discovered while the former version (4010) was in use. Furthermore, 5010 accommodates the mandatory switchover from ICD-9-CM diagnostic coding to ICD-10-CM and ICD-10-PCS code sets. ICD-10 is the upgraded version of ICD-9 diagnosis codes. The ICD-10 codes have a different format and length than the ICD-9 codes, and the format of ICD-10 codes could not be reported in the previous version of the transaction standards.

All of these standards were put in place in 1996 when the HIPAA laws were enacted, and many are now outdated. Version 5010 updates the standards for electronic transactions to incorporate all of the changes that needed to occur when ICD-10 was implemented. It took into account all of the changes that occurred in the healthcare industry since HIPAA took effect, including updates to patient privacy, stricter security practices, and faster transaction processing.

Version 5010 regulations implemented more than 850 changes to electronic claims transactions and data entry. As mentioned, many of these changes resolved problems that occurred in the earlier Version 4010. Version 5010 has reduced transaction costs, minimized manual claims processing, and reduced personnel needs.

The most important change with Version 5010 that affected the health insurance professional (medical coder) is the increased field size for patient diagnosis to accommodate the three- to seven-digit ICD-10 codes. ICD-9 codes were all three to five digits. Version 5010 increases the allowable field size of the diagnosis code box to seven digits, creating room for the longer ICD-10 codes.

The Version 5010 regulations also included specific built-in rules to make unusual circumstances (which require CMS review) more understandable. (An unusual circumstance might be when a claim requires a paper attachment for proper adjudication.) Version 5010 also helped covered entities better understand such things as claim reversals and corrections, recoupment of claims payments, and claim refund processing.

These regulations have increased revenue for the medical industry resulting from the benefits listed previously, as well as made it easier to understand NPI instructions, provided information requirements on eligibility verifications, and reduced denials due to data error messages. By making electronic transactions easier, Version 5010 has improved the functioning of the entire medical industry.

To learn more, visit the CMS website, where up-to-date information and resources related to the 5010 and ICD-10 can be found.

MEDICARE'S CLAIM SUBMISSION REQUIREMENT

Although HIPAA does not require healthcare providers to use electronic transactions, ASCA imposes such a requirement for those who bill Medicare. ASCA requires that all claims submitted to the Medicare program be submitted in electronic form with limited exceptions. The implication of this requirement is that because the claims are submitted electronically, they are also required to comply with HIPAA. Physicians who qualify for exemption under the small-provider exemption may continue sending paper claims. A small provider or supplier is defined as *a provider of services with fewer than 25 FTE employees or a physician, practitioner, facility, or supplier (other than a provider of services) with fewer than 10 FTE employees* (see Box 6.1).

For more detailed information about Version 5010, read the CMS article in *MLN Matters* titled "An Introductory Overview of the HIPAA 5010." The link can be found in "Websites to Explore" at the end of this chapter.

◎ HIPAA Tip

Small providers who can use paper forms (i.e., CMS-1500 and UB-04) for submitting claims can continue to do so because the most recent versions of these paper claim forms accommodate the relevant data reported in Version 5010.

? What Did You Learn?

1. After January 2012, providers who submit claims electronically must use Standard Version _____.
2. The Standard Version supports the reporting of _____ and _____ codes.
3. True or false: ASCA requires that all claims submitted to the Medicare program be submitted in electronic form, with no exceptions.
4. Physicians who qualify for exclusion under the _____ exemption may continue sending paper claims.

THE ELECTRONIC INSURANCE CLAIMS PROCESS

Regardless of how claims are submitted, the insurance claims process begins when the patient arrives at the medical facility, at which time he or she is given various forms to read and fill out. The front office staff then enters the information into the medical facility's computer using the practice management software that meets electronic filing requirements as established by the current HIPAA claim standards. It is from this information that the claim is generated through the internal functioning of the software.

ESSENTIAL INFORMATION FOR CLAIMS PROCESSING

The following sections discuss the various forms and documents from which necessary data for generating claims are gathered, along with illustrations showing sample data entry screens.

WALDEN-MARTIN
FAMILY MEDICAL CLINIC
1234 ANYSTREET | ANYTOWN, ANYSTATE 12345
PHONE 123-123-1234 | FAX 123-123-5678

JULIE WALDEN MD
JAMES MARTIN MD
DAVID KAHN MD
ANGELA PEREZ MD
PATRICK TAYLOR DDS
JEAN BURKE NP

PATIENT INFORMATION

First Name		MI	Last Name		Date of Birth		Sex

SSN		Home Phone		Work Phone		Cell

Home Address		City		State	Zip

Marital Status		Employer		Driver's License #

Emergency Contact		Relationship to Patient		Phone Number

RESPONSIBLE PARTY INFORMATION   SELF ☐

First Name		MI	Last Name		Date of Birth		Sex

SSN		Home Phone		Work Phone		Cell

Home Address		City		State	Zip

Employer			Relationship to Patient	

INSURANCE INFORMATION

Primary Insurance Carrier		Phone Number

Address		City		State	Zip

Policy Holder Name (if different from patient)		Phone		Date of Birth		Sex

Policy Number		Group Number	

Secondary Insurance Carrier		Phone Number

Address		City		State	Zip

Policy Holder Name (if different from patient)		Phone		Date of Birth		Sex

Policy Number		Group Number	

I hereby give lifetime authorization for payment of insurance benefits to be made directly to Walden-Martin Medical Group, and any assisting physicians, for services rendered. I understand that I am financially responsible for all charges whether or not they are covered by insurance. In the event of default, I agree to pay all costs of collection, and reasonable attorney's fees. I hereby authorize this healthcare provider to release all information necessary to secure the payment of benefits. I further agree that a photocopy of this agreement shall be as valid as the original.

Signature		Date

Fig. 6.1 A typical patient information form. (From Elsevier: *Practice management for the medical office powered by SimChart for the Medical Office,* St. Louis, 2016, Elsevier.)

Patient Information Form

A *patient information form,* sometimes referred to as a *patient registration form,* is a document (typically one page) that patients are asked to complete for the following reasons:

1. To gather all necessary demographic information to aid the healthcare professional in providing appropriate treatment
2. To have a record of current insurance information for claim preparation and submission
3. To keep medical health records up to date
4. To give the physician or provider authorization to release medical information and to accept assignment for insurance benefits

When the form is completed, it becomes an integral part of the patient's medical health record. This information form is considered a legal document, and the information should be updated at least once a year. It is a good idea to ask returning patients whether there have been any changes since they were last in the office. Fig. 6.1 shows a typical patient information form.

New patient information. Look at this section in the example patient information form in Fig. 6.1. Note that it asks for general demographic information, such as name, address, and employment. Financial status and self-pay amounts may also need to be identified and communicated completely, clearly, and accurately. The front office staff is also responsible for obtaining treatment consents, release of information consents, necessary authorizations, and assignments. Fig. 6.2 illustrates how demographic information appears on the patient entry screen in a typical type of practice management software.

Medical facilities sometimes request that patients provide their SSNs. In this age of identity theft, patients may appear reluctant to do so. If a healthcare provider asks for the patient's SSN, it is the responsibility of the health insurance professional, or whoever is gathering personal data, to assure the patient that all information will remain strictly confidential.

Until healthcare providers are required by law to collect SSNs, there is currently no existing law or reason for them to force patients to provide their SSNs if those patients use only private insurance. If a patient refuses to provide his or her SSN to office personnel, however, he or she may be at risk of being rejected as a patient.

The following are a few suggestions to offer patients who are reluctant to provide their SSNs:

- Ask for a portion of the SSN—perhaps the last four digits.
- Ask for another piece of identifying information, such as a driver's license or a passport.
- Ask them to pay cash for the service.

ⓘ Stop and Think

The question frequently arises as to whether people are required to provide their Social Security number (SSN) to government agencies. The answer depends on the agency. Some government agencies, including tax authorities, welfare offices, and state Departments of Motor Vehicles, can require a person's SSN as mandated by federal law. Others may *request* the SSN, leading people to believe they must provide it.

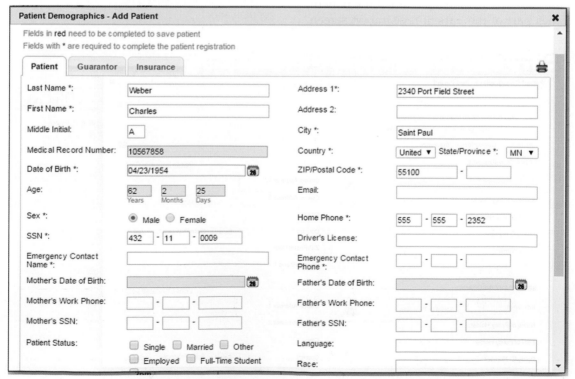

Fig. 6.2 Patient entry screen using SimChart for the Medical Office.

The Privacy Act of 1974 requires all government agencies—federal, state, and local—that request SSNs to provide a "disclosure" statement on the form. The statement explains whether you are required to provide your SSN or if it's optional, how the SSN will be used, and under what statutory or other authority the number is requested. The US Office of Management and Budget, Office of Information and Regulatory Affairs (OIRA) provides guidance on and oversight of the Privacy Act of 1974. The Privacy Act states that you cannot be denied a government benefit or service if you refuse to disclose your SSN unless the disclosure is required by federal law or the disclosure is to an agency that has been using SSNs since before January 1975, when the Privacy Act went into effect. There are other exceptions as well. More information on the Privacy Act can be found at https://www.privacyrights.org/.

Insurance section. Another section in the patient information form contains questions regarding the patient's insurance. Having the patient fill out this section is important, but it is also necessary to request and make photocopies of or scan the front and back of the patient's insurance ID card. The ID card often lists additional information that patients might not routinely include on the form, such as telephone numbers for preauthorization or precertification. Also, it is common for patients to transpose or omit identifying alphabetical characters, numbers, or both. It is also recommended to make a copy of the patient's driver's license or other picture ID for verification to make certain that the person is not using someone else's insurance card. Some electronic medical records (EMRs) will allow the provider to take a picture of the patient, and it becomes part of the patient registration screen.

This allows for immediate identification of the patient when the EMR is accessed.

Additional insurance. In some cases, patients may be covered under more than one insurance policy. For example, a Medicare patient may have supplemental coverage through another payer. Most patient information forms have a separate section where additional insurance is listed. Information from a secondary insurance policy should be noted in this section, including the name of the policy, the policyholder's name, and the policy numbers. It is important for the health insurance professional to confirm that the "additional insurance" is secondary. Some patients, particularly elderly ones, can become confused over the technicalities of dual insurance coverage. If the patient is uncertain which of the policies is primary and which is secondary, the health insurance professional may have to do some detective work, such as telephoning one or both of the insuring agencies, to find out. Fig. 6.3 shows the screen where insurance information is entered.

Patient's Point of View

Latisha is working with Mr. Casper. He is 80 years old and is covered by Medicare and a supplemental policy. Mr. Casper doesn't understand why he has to pay anything when he has two insurance policies. Latisha explains to Mr. Casper that both Medicare and his supplemental policy have a deductible and coinsurance. That means that although he has very good coverage, it does not cover everything at 100%. After Latisha explained how each company determined what was paid and what was the patient responsibility, Mr. Casper felt much better and thanked her for taking the time to help him understand.

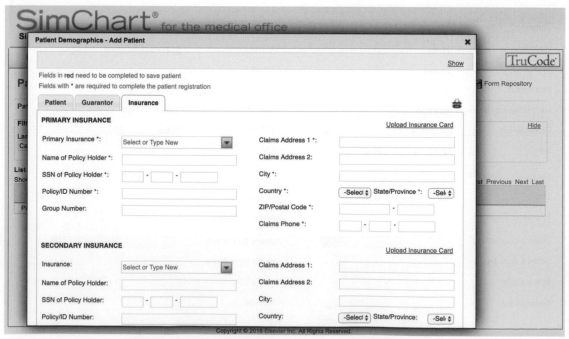

Fig. 6.3 Insurance information using SimChart for the Medical Office.

Insurance authorization and assignment. The section on insurance authorization and assignment should be completed and signed by the patient or responsible party in the case of a minor or mentally disabled individual. This section gives the healthcare professional the authorization to release the information necessary to complete the insurance claim form. It also **assigns benefits**—that is, it authorizes the insurance company to send the payment directly to the healthcare professional. This authorization should be updated at least once a year, unless it is a "lifetime" **release of information** worded specifically for Medicare claims.

Patient Insurance Identification Card

Every insurance company has a unique ID card that it issues to its subscribers. With Medicare, every individual (referred to as a **beneficiary**) has his or her own individual card. Other insurers, such as Blue Cross and Blue Shield, may issue a card that covers not only the subscriber but also his or her spouse and any dependents included on the policy; this arrangement is referred to as a *family plan*. As mentioned, when the patient completes the information form, the health insurance professional should ask to see the patient's insurance ID card and make a photocopy or scan of it to keep in the medical health record. It is important to always make sure to copy both front and back of the ID card if there is information on the back. On subsequent visits, the health insurance professional should ask the patient whether there is any change in coverage. If there has been a change, the professional should ask for and make a copy of the new card. The rationale for this procedure is to have complete and correct insurance information on file for the purpose of accurate claims submission. It is also helpful for obtaining telephone numbers to contact for preauthorization or precertification from the carrier if certain procedures or inpatient hospitalization is required. Fig. 6.4 shows the front and back of a typical insurance ID card.

Patient Medical Health Record

After the patient information form is completed, the health insurance professional should examine it to ensure that all necessary information has been entered and that the entries are legible. The form is customarily either placed in the patient's paper medical health record near the front or scanned into an EMR after the information is typed into the data fields of the EMR so that the health insurance professional has easy access to it when it is time to complete and submit a claim. Details of the patient medical record are discussed in Chapter 3. To review, a medical health record is an account of a patient's medical assessment, investigation, and course of treatment. It is a source of information and a vital component in quality patient care. A complete medical health record should:

- Outline the reason for the patient's visit to the healthcare professional
- Document the healthcare professional's findings
- Include a detailed discussion of the recommended treatment
- Provide information to any referring physician or other healthcare provider
- Serve as a teaching or research tool (or both)
- Provide a means for assessing the quality of care by the practitioner or other healthcare provider

The clinical chart note illustrated in Fig. 6.5 is a typical example taken from a patient's medical health record.

Encounter Form

We have discussed three of the items necessary for generating an insurance claim. Now we look at a document used by most medical practices that is often referred to as the **encounter form**. This multipurpose billing form is known by many names (e.g., superbill, routing form, patient service slip). The encounter form can be customized to medical specialties and preprinted with common diagnoses and procedures for that particular specialty. Encounter forms can be either

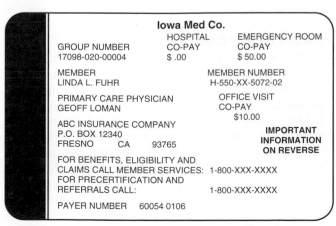

Fig. 6.4 Insurance identification (ID) card.

Fig. 6.5 Clinical notes from a patient's medical health record using SimChart for the Medical Office.

paper or electronic. Fig. 6.6 shows an example of a paper encounter form; Fig. 6.7 illustrates an electronic version of this form.

Typically the encounter form is clipped to the front of the patient's paper medical health record before the patient is seen in the clinical area. (If the medical facility uses EMRs, this information is available on the selected screen.) Note the variety of information included on the forms shown in both figures:

- Demographic
- Accounting
- Professional services rendered
- Procedure (CPT) codes
- Professional fees
- Return appointment information

It is important that the sections dealing with professional services and diagnostic and procedure codes be updated annually so that revised codes are changed, new codes are added, and old codes are deleted.

The following is a typical routine in many medical offices. Each morning, the medical records clerk (or whichever member of the healthcare team is in charge of this task) prepares the medical health records for the patients who are to be seen that day. An encounter form is attached to the front of each record, and any areas on the form regarding the date of service, patient demographics, and accounting information are filled out. (If computerized patient accounting software is used, this information is printed automatically on the form.) Each encounter form has a number (usually at the top) that serves as an identifier for that particular patient visit.

As each patient is seen in the clinical area, the healthcare provider indicates on the form what services or procedures were performed, along with the corresponding fees. The provider signs the encounter form and indicates whether and when the patient needs to return or have any follow-up tests. It is important that the encounter form is checked for accuracy, after which the front office staff totals the day's

charges, enters any payment received, and calculates the balance due. The patient receives a copy of the completed encounter form, and a copy is retained in the medical office for accounting purposes and future reference in case any question comes up regarding that particular visit. Many offices file these forms by number within files that are separated into months and days.

If the medical facility is using an electronic encounter form, the provider will complete it when the patient's visit is done. They will indicate the diagnosis and the services provided. The health insurance professional may need to review the medical health record to ensure that all services have been accounted for on the encounter form.

Medical offices are subject to accounting and insurance audits. The original encounter form can be requested by auditors to verify services rendered to any patient or on any date of service. If practice management software is used, the information from the encounter form is entered into the computer and is computed automatically. A statement can immediately be printed for the patient showing the payments and current balance, if any. This information can be used for audit purposes. Fig. 6.8 is a sample statement printout.

Patient Ledger Card

In offices that do not use practice management software, patient charges and payments are kept track of on a **patient ledger card**. Fig. 6.9 is an example of a ledger card from a paper system, Fig. 6.10 shows a ledger from an electronic system. A ledger card is an accounting form on which professional service descriptions, charges, payments, adjustments, and current balance are posted chronologically. Although most medical offices are becoming computerized, there are still some that are not, so to become a well-rounded healthcare professional, you should be familiar with manual accounting methods.

Tri-State Medical Group   008112

400 North 4th Street • Anytown, Iowa 50622
Phone: 319-555-5734 • Fax: 319-555-5758
Fed. Tax I.D. # 42-1435XXX

ACCOUNT NO.	DOB	DATE OF SERVICE
PATIENT NAME	PROVIDER	
INSURANCE ID #-PRIMARY	SECONDARY	

DESCRIPTION	CODE		FEE	DESCRIPTION	CODE	FEE	DESCRIPTION	CODE	FEE
OFFICE VISIT	NEW	ESTAB.		DT, Pediatric	90702		Removal Skin Tags up to 15 Lesions	*11200	
Minimum	99201	99211		MMR	90707		Exc. Malignant Lesion, Trunk, Arm or Leg		
Brief	99202	99212		Oral Polio	90712		Exc. Malignant Lesion, Face, Ear, Eyelid, Nose		
Limited	99203	99213		IVP Polio	90713		Exc. Malignant Lesion, Scalp, Hand, Neck, Feet		
Extended	99204	99214		Varicella	90716		Lacer, Repair 2.5cm or Less/Location:	*12001	
Comprehensive	99205	99215		Td, Adult	90718		Scalp, Nk, Axille, Ext. Genitalia, Trk, Hands/Feet		
Prenatal Care		59400		DTP & HIB	90720		Lacer, Repair 2.5cm or Less/Location:	*12011	
Global		99024		Influenza	90659		Face, Ears, Eyelids, Nose, Lips & Mucous Mem.		
PREVENTIVE	NEW	ESTAB.		Hepatitis B, Newborn to 11 Years	90744		Burn w/Dressing, w/o Anesth. Small	16020	
Infant	99381	99391		Hepatitis B, 11-19 Years	90747		Wart Removal	*17110	
Age 1-4	99382	99392		Hepatitis B, 20 Years & Above	90746		Removal FB Conjunct. Ext. Eye	*65205	
Age 5-11	99383	99393		Pneumococcal	90732		Removal FB Ext. Auditory Canal	69200	
Age 12-17	99384	99394		Hemophilus Infl. B	90645		Ear Lavage	69210	
Age 18-39	99385	99395		Therapeutic:	90782		Tympanometry	92567	
Age 40-64	99386	99396		Allergy Inject Single	95115		EKG Tracing Only w/o Interp. & Rept	93005	
Age 65 & Over	99387	99397		Allergy Inject Multiple	95117		Nebulizer Therapy (x)	94640	
OFFICE CONSULTATION				B-12	J3420		Pulse Oximetry	94760	
Limited		99241		Injection / Aspiration	20600		Cryosurgery		
Intermediate		99242		Small joint-Finger, Toes, Ganglion			Debridement	11041	
Extended		99243		Injection / Aspiration	20605		Excise Ingrown Toenail	11730	
Comprehensive		99244		Intermediate jt-Wrist, Elbow, Ankle			Colposcopy w/Biopsy	57454	
Complex		99245		Injection / Aspiration	20610		Leep	57460	
LABORATORY PROCEDURES				Major jt. - Shoulder, Hip, Knee			Endometrial Bx	58100	
Venipuncture		36415		Inject Tendon/Ligament	20550		Cryotherapy	57511	
Routine Urinalysis w/o Microscopy		81002		Aristacort	J3302		Peak Flow Measurement	94160-52	
Hemoccult		82270		Depo Provera	J1055		Intradermal Tests CMI # Doses =	95025	
Glucose Blood Reagent Strip		82948		Rocephin	J0696		Intradermal Tests/Allergens	95024	
Wet Mount		87210		OFFICE PROCEDURE / MINOR SURGERY			Intravenous Access	36000	
PAP Smear		88155		I & D Abscess	10060		Immunotherapy/Single Injection	95120	
Urine Pregnancy		81025		Removal FB Subcutaneous	*10120		Immunotherapy/Double Injection	95125	
Other:		99000		I & D Hematoma	10140		Regular Spirometry	94010	
X-RAY				Puncture Aspiration Abscess	10160		Spirometry Read by Physician	94010-26	
X-ray Cervical Spine		75052		Exc. Ben. Lesion #:			Spirometry w/pre & Post Bronchodilator	94060	
X-ray Thoracic Spine		72070		Location:			Spirometry/Bronchodilator read by Doctor	94060-26	
X-ray Lumbar Spine (2)		72100		Exc. Ben. Lesion #:			Skin Prick Test: # of Tests =	95004	
X-ray Lumbar Spine (Comp)		72110		Location:			Vial Preparation	95165	
X-ray Pelvis (1 view)		72170		HOSPITAL ORDERS					
X-ray Sacrum & Coccyx		72220		OB Non-Stress Test	Cystogram		Physical Therapy		
X-ray Clavicle (Complete)		73000		OB Ultrasound-Diagnostic	MRI				
X-ray Shoulder (2) or		73030		OB Ultrasound-Routine	CT Scan		Diet Consultation		
X-ray Humerus (2 views)		73060		Biophysical Profile	Chest X-ray				
X-ray Elbow (AP & LATE)		73070		Mammogram-Diagnostic	X-ray				
X-ray Forearm (AP & LA)		73090		Mammogram-Routine	Bone Densitometry		Laboratory		
X-ray Wrist (AP & LATE)		73100			EKG				
X-ray Wrist (3 Views)		73110		Ultrasound	Holter Monitor				
X-ray Hand (2 Views)		73120		Gallbladder Ultrasound	Echocardiogram				
X-ray Hand (3 Views)		73130		Pelvic Ultrasound	Treadmill				
X-ray Finger (2 Views)		73140		Doppler Studies	Thallium Stress Test				
X-ray Hip (2 Views)		73510			Doppler Studies				
X-ray Hips (Bilateral)		73520		IVP	PFT-Partial				
X-ray Scoliosis (2 AP & LA)		72069		Upper GI	PFT-Complete				
X-ray Femur (AP & LATE)		73550		Lower GI	Cardiac Rehab				
X-ray Knee (AP & LATE)		73560		Barium Enema					
X-ray Knee (3 Views)		73564		Barium Swallow					
X-ray Tibia & Fibula		73590							
X-ray Ankle (3 Views)		73610							
X-ray Foot (AP & LATER)		73620							
X-ray Foot (AP. LA.,)		73630							
X-ray Calcaneus (2 Views)		73650							
X-ray Toes		73660							
X-ray Pelvis & Hip Inf		73540							
Elbow, Minimum of 3 Views		73080							
IMMUNIZATIONS & INJECTIONS									
PPD Intradermal TB Tine		86580							
DTaP		90700							

AUTHORIZATION TO PAY BENEFITS AND RELEASE INFORMATION TO TRI-STATE MEDICAL GROUP: I hereby authorize payment directly to the undersigned Physician of all Surgical and / or Medical Benefits, if any, otherwise payable to me for his / her services as described above. I have read and understand the Financial Policy and that I am financially responsible for charges not covered by this insurance. I also authorize the undersigned Physician to release any information acquired in the course of my examination or treatment.

Signed: _____

Date: _____

Provider's Signature _____   Date

PREVIOUS BALANCE	
CHARGES TODAY	
TOTAL	
AMOUNT PAID	
BALANCE DUE	

DX or Other Information

Samples:

Your next appointment is:

BILLING COPY

Fig. 6.6 Sample paper encounter form.

Fig. 6.7 Sample electronic encounter form using SimChart for the Medical Office.

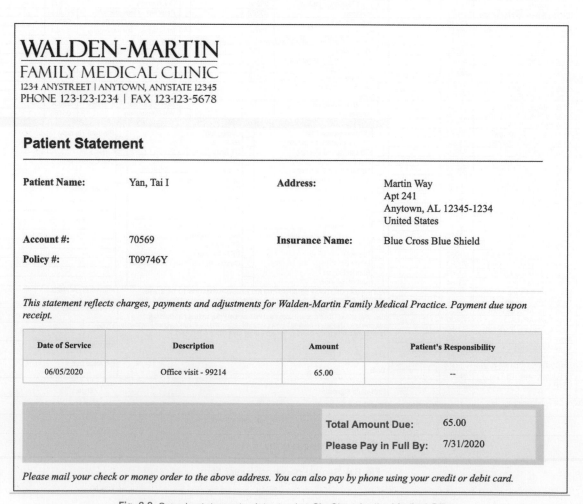

Fig. 6.8 Sample statement printout using SimChart for the Medical Office.

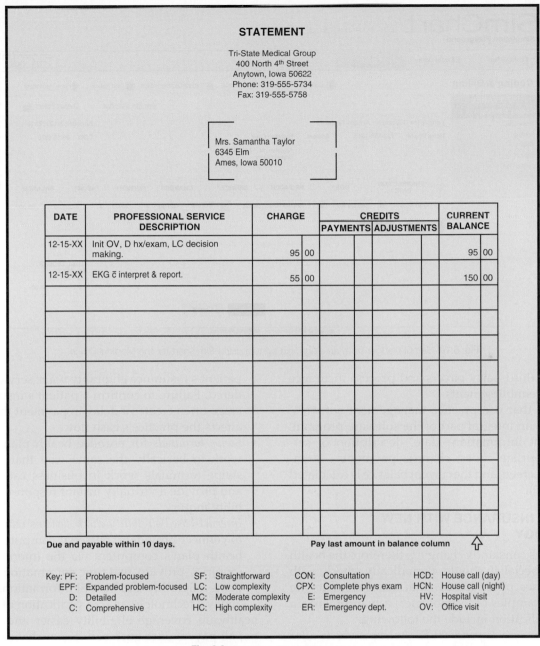

STATEMENT

Tri-State Medical Group
400 North 4th Street
Anytown, Iowa 50622
Phone: 319-555-5734
Fax: 319-555-5758

Mrs. Samantha Taylor
6345 Elm
Ames, Iowa 50010

DATE	PROFESSIONAL SERVICE DESCRIPTION	CHARGE		CREDITS				CURRENT BALANCE	
				PAYMENTS		ADJUSTMENTS			
12-15-XX	Init OV, D hx/exam, LC decision making.	95	00					95	00
12-15-XX	EKG c̄ interpret & report.	55	00					150	00

Due and payable within 10 days.   Pay last amount in balance column ⇧

Key: PF: Problem-focused   SF: Straightforward   CON: Consultation   HCD: House call (day)
EPF: Expanded problem-focused   LC: Low complexity   CPX: Complete phys exam HCN: House call (night)
D: Detailed   MC: Moderate complexity   E: Emergency   HV: Hospital visit
C: Comprehensive   HC: High complexity   ER: Emergency dept.   OV: Office visit

Fig. 6.9 Sample patient ledger card.

A patient ledger card is prepared for each new patient. In some medical offices, particularly family practice facilities, one ledger card is set up for the head of household, and all dependent family members are included on it. This makes sense because it not only saves time and space in the ledger file, but also addresses statements to parents and guardians of minor children, who are usually not responsible for their own bills. Caution must be used, however, in the case of divorced parents because it is important that the parent who is financially responsible for the child be billed. More information is given on the maintenance of the patient ledger card as we proceed through the

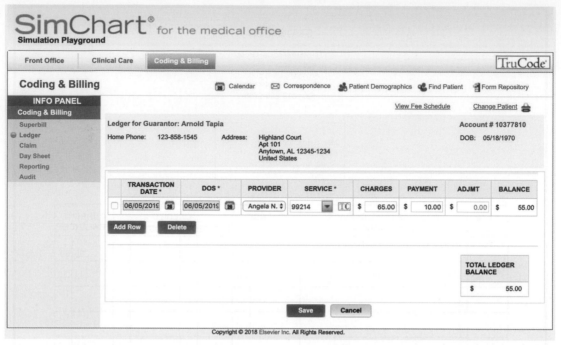

Fig. 6.10 Sample ledger from an electronic system using SimChart for the Medical Office.

chapters on third-party payers and process insurance claims and reimbursements.

In offices that use practice management software, the ledger is an integral part of the software program. All pertinent information—date, description of services, appropriate codes, charges, payments—is entered onto a screen, and the current balance is calculated (see Fig. 6.10).

VERIFYING INSURANCE WITH NEW TECHNOLOGY

Technology is constantly changing; therefore the health insurance specialist should periodically check with each insurance payer to see what advancements are available. Examples of technological advancements in enrollee verification include the following:

- *Interactive voice response (IVR) systems*, which offer solutions customized for explicit business needs. IVR systems typically use the telephone to interact directly with a database, and information can be passed to an existing personal computer or a web application through customized software. IVR systems offer automated customer care and customer relationship management applications, which make verification of patient insurance eligibility easier and faster for medical practices. IVR systems also can reduce collection time and enhance customer service. IVR systems can be purchased independently, and some insurance companies offer this technology; however, there is little uniformity among systems. It is recommended that healthcare providers take advantage of these services if and when they are available. It is simply good business practice to do whatever is necessary to verify a

patient's insurance eligibility *before* services are rendered. Failure to confirm a patient's insurance coverage often creates a delay in payment that, in turn, affects the practice's cash flow.
- *Swipe terminals* for enrollee health plan cards that work in basically the same way that credit card swipe terminals work in business establishments and provide a virtually instant response to an eligibility inquiry.
- *Internet-based eligibility check systems* using software to connect providers' personal computers with the health plan's computers via the Internet. Internet inquiries provide real-time information about patients' eligibility and benefit information.

Today's technology makes verification of a patient's healthcare coverage eligibility easier and faster, but not all payers offer such services or devices. As mentioned, there is little uniformity among systems; however, medical practices are encouraged to use whatever technology is available. Although enrollee verification may be time consuming, failure to do so could harm the practice's cash flow.

> ### ❓ What Did You Learn?
>
> 1. When does the insurance claims process begin?
> 2. List the information and documents essential for claims processing.
> 3. Explain why it is important to photocopy or scan both back and front of the ID card.
> 4. What types of information are typically included on an encounter form?
> 5. Explain the rationale for verifying a patient's insurance coverage.

HIPAA Tip

Patients:
- Must be told in writing how their protected health information (PHI) may be used
- Have a right to see their medical records
- Have a right to amend incorrect or incomplete information in their record
- Must give authorization before PHI is released (with a few exceptions)
- Have a right to complain formally if they feel that their privacy was not protected

ADVANTAGES OF ELECTRONIC CLAIMS

Most practices submit their claims electronically, not only because some major payers demand it, but also because of the time and money savings that result. Experts tell practitioners that processing insurance claims electronically (1) improves cash flow, (2) reduces the expense of claims processing, and (3) streamlines internal processes, allowing them to focus more on patient care. On average, a paper insurance claim typically takes 30 to 45 days for reimbursement, whereas the average payment time for electronic claims is approximately 10 to 14 days. This reduction in insurance reimbursement time results in a significant increase in cash available for other practice expenses. As with everything, however, there is a tradeoff because often the expense of setting up for an electronic process is not taken into account. First, the office must purchase adequate equipment—computers, printers, and software programs. In addition, everyone involved in the claims process must become computer literate. Depending on the size and needs of the practice, computer hardware and software can cost from $10,000 to $250,000. Also, an intensive training program may be necessary to teach staff how to use the equipment and become adept at operating the software.

TWO WAYS TO SUBMIT ELECTRONIC CLAIMS

There are basically two ways to submit claims electronically: (1) through an electronic claims clearinghouse and (2) directly to an insurance carrier. Many large practices can be set up to support both methods. Whether a practice chooses to use a clearinghouse or to submit claims directly to the carrier, it usually must go through an enrollment process before submitting electronic claims. The enrollment process is required so that the company the practice has hired can "set up" information about the practice on its computer system. Most government and many commercial carriers require such an enrollment. Some also require that the practice sign a contract with them. The enrollment process typically takes 6 to 7 weeks to complete. The biggest obstacle in getting set up for electronic claims

processing is the time it takes for approval from state, federal, and, in some cases, commercial and health maintenance organization carriers.

HIPAA Tip

For entities that choose to transmit claims electronically, practice management software or a clearinghouse is necessary to handle the conversion of data to meet Health Insurance Portability and Accountability Act (HIPAA) requirements.

CLAIMS CLEARINGHOUSES

A **claims clearinghouse** is a company that receives claims from healthcare providers and specializes in consolidating the claims so that they can send one transmission containing batches of claims to each third-party payer. A clearinghouse typically is an independent, centralized service available to healthcare providers for the purpose of simplifying medical insurance claims submission for multiple carriers. HIPAA defines a healthcare clearinghouse as "a public or private entity that processes or facilitates the processing of nonstandard data elements of health information into standard data elements." The clearinghouse acts as a simple point of entry for paper and electronic claims from providers. Clearinghouse personnel edit each claim for validity and accuracy before routing the edited claim to the appropriate third-party carrier for payment. A medical practice can send all completed claims to one central location rather than to multiple payers. If the clearinghouse finds errors on the claim that would cause the claim to be rejected or denied, it sends the claim back to the provider for correction and resubmission.

Clearinghouses also are capable of translating data from one format to another (e.g., electronic to paper and vice versa). Many private clearinghouses that facilitate electronic and paper claims processing are available to healthcare providers and payers. Payers also can act as clearinghouses for claims of other payers.

DIRECT CLAIMS

Submitting electronic claims directly to an insurance carrier is a little more complicated. As explained previously, the healthcare provider first must enroll with the carrier. Most government carriers and many commercial carriers require that providers enroll with them before submitting claims electronically to them. The provider also needs some additional software from each insurance carrier to which the practice will submit claims. This method will also require staff to be trained on the various software programs to ensure that claims are submitted correctly. Many carriers have their own software or can refer the health insurance professional to someone who supports direct transmissions in the area.

CLEARINGHOUSES VERSUS DIRECT

When deciding whether to send claims electronically through a clearinghouse or direct to the carrier, several things must be considered. Sending claims direct to the carrier is usually less expensive if the medical practice submits most claims to just one carrier. When multiple carriers are used, however, a clearinghouse is generally less expensive. With a clearinghouse, the health insurance professional needs to connect to, or dial into, only one location. If the decision is made to go direct to the carrier, there will be multiple **dial-ups**. (In this context, a "dial-up" occurs when a computer is programmed to automatically connect to another computer—for example, that of a third-party payer—via the Internet using a modem and a telephone line [or other telecommunication device].)

When a clearinghouse is used, all claims can be submitted in one transmission, and the convenience of sending all claims to one location should not be underestimated. Submitting claims to multiple insurance carriers requires members of the health insurance team to become experts in each of the claims submission software applications used. Because each one is unique, the health insurance professional must be adequately trained and available to submit all varieties of claims. Clearinghouses typically generate a separate confirmation report for each carrier to which claims are submitted directly.

As to which method of electronic claims submission is better, if a medical practice submits insurance claims to multiple carriers and has someone who is well trained technically to handle the task of electronic claims submission, an electronic claims clearinghouse might be the better choice. If claims are sent primarily to one carrier, the practice should consider using direct submission to that carrier. Whichever method is selected, it is a proven fact that claims are processed much faster and reimbursement time is shortened with the use of electronic claims submission.

? What Did You Learn?

1. What is a claims clearinghouse?
2. List two advantages of submitting claims electronically.
3. Explain the process for submitting direct claims.
4. Which of the two electronic submission processes (clearinghouse or direct) is better?

THE UNIVERSAL CLAIM FORM (CMS-1500)

The second way to submit a health insurance claim is with the CMS-1500 paper form. This form was considered a major innovation that made the process of health insurance claims submission simpler. As discussed earlier, before the development of this universal form, every insurance carrier had its own specialized type of paperwork for submitting claims. The NUCC and the National Uniform Billing Committee (NUBC)

are responsible for updating and revising the CMS-1500 universal form. The most recent revision is the CMS-1500 (02/12) form. The 02/12 revision is similar to the previous revision (08/05) but incorporates a few changes to accommodate HIPAA's Version 5010 transaction standards and ICD-10 codes. The official CMS-1500 (02/12) is shown in Appendix A. Additional information on the revised form is available at the NUCC website, which is listed under "Websites to Explore" at the end of this chapter.

As previously mentioned, the NUCC's *1500 Health Insurance Claim Form Reference Instruction Manual* Version 2.0 07/14 (for Form Version 02/12) provides current detailed step-by-step claims completion instructions. The NUCC developed this general instruction manual for completing the CMS-1500 form, and it is intended to be a guide, not definitive instructions for this purpose. Users of this manual should refer to the most current federal, state, or individual payers for specific requirements applicable for using and completing the 1500 claim form. Any interim changes, clarifications, or corrections to the instructions after this release will be posted on the NUCC website. The link to this manual is listed in the "Websites to Explore" section. Log on to http://nucc.org periodically to keep up to date with any changes to these instructions.

Examples of Item 21, illustrating the difference between the former CMS-1500 (08/05) and the revised CMS-1500 (02/12) claim forms, are shown in Fig. 6.11.

The CMS-1500 (02/12) revised form included the implementation of an indicator system for Item (Block) 21, which allowed differentiation between ICD-9 and ICD-10 codes—9 for ICD-9 codes; 0 for ICD-10 codes. This numerical differentiation helped insurance companies, claims clearinghouses, and medical billing practices distinguish between ICD-9 and ICD-10 codes. The compliance date for use of ICD-10 diagnostic codes was October 1, 2015. Until that date, providers were allowed to use ICD-9 codes.

 HIPAA Tip

Any person or organization that furnishes bills or is paid for healthcare electronically in the normal course of business is bound by Health Insurance Portability and Accountability Act (HIPAA) rules and regulations.

OPTICAL CHARACTER RECOGNITION

In most instances, when the paper CMS-1500 claim form is prepared for submission, **optical character recognition (OCR)** formatting guidelines should be used. OCR is the recognition of printed or written *text characters* by a computer. This involves photo scanning of the text character by character, analysis of the scanned-in image, and translation of the character image into character codes, such as **American Standard Code for**

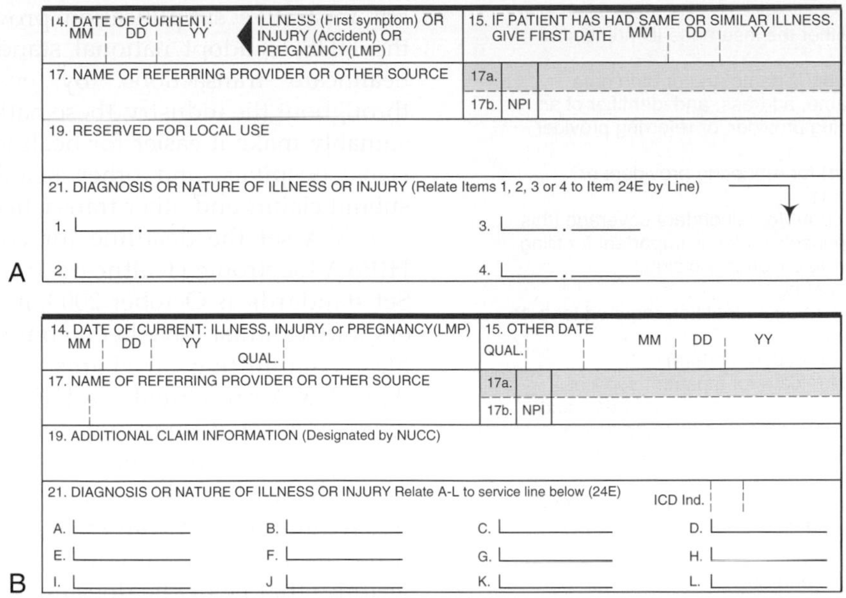
14. DATE OF CURRENT: MM | DD | YY ◀ ILLNESS (First symptom) OR INJURY (Accident) OR PREGNANCY(LMP)
15. IF PATIENT HAS HAD SAME OR SIMILAR ILLNESS. GIVE FIRST DATE MM | DD | YY
17. NAME OF REFERRING PROVIDER OR OTHER SOURCE
17a.
17b. NPI
19. RESERVED FOR LOCAL USE
21. DIAGNOSIS OR NATURE OF ILLNESS OR INJURY (Relate Items 1, 2, 3 or 4 to Item 24E by Line)
1. 3.
2. 4.
A

14. DATE OF CURRENT: ILLNESS, INJURY, or PREGNANCY(LMP) MM | DD | YY QUAL.
15. OTHER DATE QUAL. MM | DD | YY
17. NAME OF REFERRING PROVIDER OR OTHER SOURCE
17a.
17b. NPI
19. ADDITIONAL CLAIM INFORMATION (Designated by NUCC)
21. DIAGNOSIS OR NATURE OF ILLNESS OR INJURY Relate A-L to service line below (24E) ICD Ind.
A. B. C. D.
E. F. G. H.
I. J K. L.
B

Fig. 6.11 Comparison of Block 21 on the CMS-1500 forms. (A) Block 21 from the obsolete CMS-1500 form (08/04). (B) Block 21 from the current CMS-1500 form (02/12). (From US Centers for Medicare & Medicaid Services, Baltimore, MD.)

Information Interchange (ASCII). ASCII is the most common *format* used for *text files* in computers and on the Internet.

In OCR processing, the scanned-in image is analyzed for light and dark areas to identify each alphabetical letter or numerical digit. When a character is recognized, it is converted to an ASCII code. Special circuit boards and computer chips designed expressly for OCR are used to speed up the recognition process. The CMS-1500 is printed in a special red ink to optimize this OCR process. When the form is scanned, everything in red "drops out," and the computer reads the information printed within the blocks.

The following are specific guidelines for preparing OCR scannable claims:

- Use all uppercase (capital) letters.
- Omit all punctuation.
- Use the MM DD YYYY format (with a space—not a dash—between each set of digits) for date of birth.
- Use a *space* instead of the usual punctuation or symbols for each of the following situations:
    - Dollar signs and decimal points in fee charges and ICD codes
    - Dash preceding a procedure code modifier
    - Parentheses around the telephone area code
- Omit titles and other designations, such as Sr., Jr., II, or III, unless they appear on the patient's ID card.
- Use two zeros in the cents column when the charge is expressed in whole dollars.
- Do not use lift-off tape, correction tape, or a white-out type fluid.
- Photocopied forms and forms printed from a color printer are not acceptable.

A section of the CMS-1500 form showing the proper OCR format is shown in Fig. 6.12.

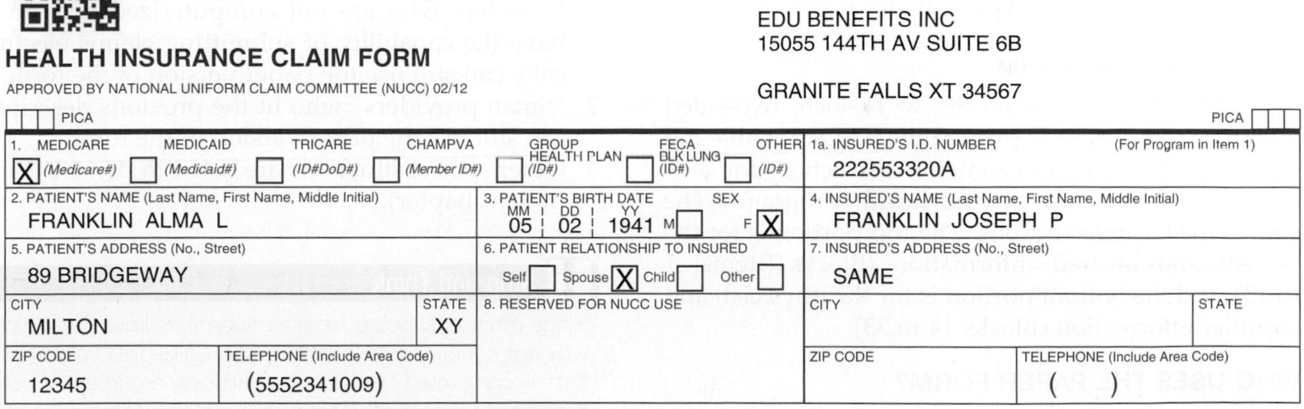
HEALTH INSURANCE CLAIM FORM
APPROVED BY NATIONAL UNIFORM CLAIM COMMITTEE (NUCC) 02/12
EDU BENEFITS INC
15055 144TH AV SUITE 6B
GRANITE FALLS XT 34567
PICA PICA
1. MEDICARE [X] (Medicare#) MEDICAID (Medicaid#) TRICARE (ID#DoD#) CHAMPVA (Member ID#) GROUP HEALTH PLAN (ID#) FECA BLK LUNG (ID#) OTHER (ID#)
1a. INSURED'S I.D. NUMBER (For Program in Item 1): 222553320A
2. PATIENT'S NAME (Last Name, First Name, Middle Initial): FRANKLIN ALMA L
3. PATIENT'S BIRTH DATE MM DD YY: 05 02 1941 SEX M [ ] F [X]
4. INSURED'S NAME (Last Name, First Name, Middle Initial): FRANKLIN JOSEPH P
5. PATIENT'S ADDRESS (No., Street): 89 BRIDGEWAY
6. PATIENT RELATIONSHIP TO INSURED: Self [ ] Spouse [X] Child [ ] Other [ ]
7. INSURED'S ADDRESS (No., Street): SAME
CITY: MILTON STATE: XY
8. RESERVED FOR NUCC USE
CITY STATE
ZIP CODE: 12345 TELEPHONE (Include Area Code): (5552341009)
ZIP CODE TELEPHONE (Include Area Code) ( )

Fig. 6.12 Section of the CMS-1500 form illustrating proper optical character recognition (OCR) format. (Form from US Centers for Medicare & Medicaid Services, Baltimore, MD.)

- Improper ID of patient, either the insurance ID number or name
- Missing or invalid subscriber's name and/or birth date
- Missing or incomplete name, address, and identifier of an ordering provider, rendering provider, or referring provider (or others)
- Invalid NPI (when needed) for rendering providers or referring providers or others
- Missing "insurance type code" for secondary coverage (this information, such as a spouse's payer, is important for filing primary claims in addition to secondary claims)
- Preauthorization codes missing
- Missing payer name and/or payer identifier, required for both primary and secondary payers
- Invalid diagnostic and/or procedure code(s)
- Missing or invalid admission date for inpatient services
- Missing or incomplete service facility name, address, and identification for services rendered outside the office or home, including invalid ZIP codes or two-letter state abbreviations
- Failing to include necessary documentation when needed
- Filing the claim after the deadline date

Fig. 6.13 List of common errors and omissions on the CMS-1500 claim form. *ID*, Identification; *NPI*, national provider identifier.

When the health insurance professional has completed the claim form, it is important that the form be thoroughly examined for errors and omissions. A health insurance professional who is new to the profession should ask coworkers or supervisors to proofread forms before submission until he or she acquires the necessary proficiency in the claims process. The most important task that the health insurance professional is responsible for is to obtain the maximum amount of reimbursement in the minimal amount of time that the medical record supports. Fig. 6.13 shows common CMS-1500 claim form errors and omissions.

If a claim is being resubmitted, most carriers require a new one using the original (red print) CMS-1500 form. Additional tips for submitting paper claims include the following:

- Do not include any handwritten data (other than signatures) on the forms.
- Do not staple anything to the form.

Completed CMS-1500 paper forms for various major payers, along with step-by-step completion instructions, can be viewed in Appendix B.

FORMAT OF THE FORM

The CMS-1500 form is an 8½ × 11–inch, two-sided document. The front is printed in OCR scannable red ink; the back of the form contains instructions for various government and private health programs. The CMS-1500 has two sections. The top portion is for the patient and insured information (Blocks [Items] 1 to 13), and the bottom portion is for the physician and supplier information (Blocks 14 to 33).

WHO USES THE PAPER FORM?

To improve the efficiency and effectiveness of the healthcare system, HIPAA includes a series of administrative simplification provisions that require the HHS to adopt national standards for electronic healthcare transactions. By ensuring consistency throughout the industry, these national standards presumably make it easier for healthcare carriers, physicians, hospitals, and other healthcare providers to submit claims and other transactions electronically.

ASCA set the deadline for compliance with the HIPAA Electronic Healthcare Transactions and Code Set standards as October 2003, meaning that providers' offices must have been computerized and capable of submitting all claims electronically by that date. ASCA prohibited the HHS from paying Medicare claims that were not submitted electronically after this date, unless the secretary of the HHS (hereafter referred to as the secretary) granted a **waiver** for this requirement. A waiver, in this case, would occur if the secretary formally tells a provider (usually in writing) that he or she does not have to comply with this regulation. ASCA further stated that the secretary must grant such a waiver if a provider had no method available for the submission of claims in electronic form or if the facility submitting the claim was a small provider of services or supplies. As noted earlier, a small provider or supplier is defined as a provider of services with fewer than 25 FTE employees or a physician, practitioner, facility, or supplier (other than a provider of services) with fewer than 10 FTE employees.

This provision does not prevent providers from submitting paper claims to other health plans, but if a provider transmits any claim electronically, it is subject to the HIPAA Administrative Simplification requirements, regardless of size. In other words, if a provider's office submits *any* claims electronically, ASCA says that it must submit *all* claims electronically. It cannot submit some claims on paper and some electronically.

So, who uses the paper CMS-1500 form? If the provider falls into one of the following categories, the paper CMS-1500 form can be used, but it must be used exclusively with all carriers that have the capability of receiving electronic transmissions:

1. Providers who are not computerized and do not have the capability of submitting claims electronically can still use the paper version of the form.
2. "Small providers" who fit the previous description can still use the paper version of the form.
3. Other special situations are listed in Box 6.1 (earlier in this chapter).

! Stop and Think

Since most healthcare facilities submit claims electronically, why is it necessary to learn how the CMS-1500 paper claim form is completed? Provide a convincing argument substantiating the reasons for learning the precise completion steps for the CMS-1500 paper form.

HIPAA Tip

The "under 10" rule applies only to Medicare and Medicaid. If a medical facility has only one employee but is doing anything electronic, the office must be in compliance with the Health Insurance Portability and Accountability Act's (HIPAA's) privacy rules and regulations.

HIPAA Tip

The Health Insurance Portability and Accountability Act's (HIPAA's) 5010 transaction standards affect only electronic claim submissions. Paper claims are not affected.

! Stop and Think

We learned in this section that two categories of providers are exempt from the Administrative Simplification Compliance Act (ASCA) mandate that by October 2003, all claims must be submitted electronically. In your opinion, why are providers in these categories allowed to use the CMS-1500 paper form?

PROOFREADING

After the paper form has been completed according to the applicable payer guidelines, it should be proofread meticulously for accuracy. The goal is always to submit **clean claims**—claims that can be processed for payment quickly without being returned. Returned or rejected claims delay the payment process and cost the practice and the patient money. On average, nearly one-quarter of the claims submitted by medical practices to insurers are rejected because they contain some type of error. One national professional association estimates that resubmitting a paper claim could cost a medical practice between $24 and $42.

A claim that is rejected for missing or invalid information must be corrected and resubmitted by the provider. Common examples of claim rejections include the following:

- Incomplete or invalid patient diagnosis code
- Diagnosis code that does not justify the procedure code
- Missing or incorrect modifiers
- Omitted or inaccurate provider information or NPI
- Insured's subscriber or group number missing or incorrect
- Charges not itemized
- Provider signature missing

When claims are submitted electronically, the health insurance professional should review all patient data that were entered into the practice management software to make sure that there are no errors. Because the process is electronic and the claim is generated internally, there is normally no hard copy to proofread. This is why comparing the information on the form the patient fills out initially with what has been entered into the computer system is so important. If something has been entered into the practice software incorrectly, there is an original source document with which to compare it.

GENERAL GUIDELINES FOR COMPLETING THE CMS-1500 FORM

Steps for completing the universal CMS-1500 claim form for generic commercial carriers and the major payers—Medicaid, Medicare, and TRICARE/CHAMPVA—are available in Appendix B and on the NUCC website. A link to the NUCC website, which provides step-by-step guidelines for completing the CMS-1500 (02/12) claim form, can be found in the "Websites to Explore" section at the end of this chapter.

Box 6.3 lists some general guidelines for preparing all paper claims. Earlier chapters also stressed the importance of strict adherence to payer-specific guidelines when preparing claims. In addition, the NUCC *1500 Health Insurance Claim Form Reference Instruction Manual for Version 02/12 Revised Form* provides detailed information, is updated periodically, and is available

Box 6.3 General Guidelines for Completing the CMS-1500 Paper Claim Form

- Use the preprinted red and white CMS-1500 claim form only.
- Follow the optical character recognition (OCR) guidelines.
- Submit claims that are legible, using computer-generated or typed entries.
- Submit only six line items (24a) per claim. Do not compress two lines of information on one line.
- Send paper claims unfolded in large envelopes.
- Use standard fonts (preferably Courier) in 10-point or 12-point size.
- Type within each block and not outside the block. Characters out of alignment will cause the claim to be returned as misaligned.
- Follow payer guidelines regarding where to type the insurance carrier's name and address. Do not submit a narrative description of the ICD code(s) in Item 21.
- Do not submit procedure codes with negative charges in Item 24d.
- Do not report a telephone number in the NPI(a) or non-NPI(b) portion of the field in Item 33.
- Do not highlight information. Instead, underline information that you want to bring to the payer's attention on attachments.
- Remove pin-feed strips on pin-fed claims at the perforations only. Do not cut the strips because doing so may alter the document size.
- Do not tape, glue, or staple attachments to the CMS-1500 claim form. Do not tear, bend, or fold corners of the claim form with attachments.
- Attachments should be the same size as the paper claim form (8½ × 11 inches).

ICD, International Classification of Diseases; *NPI,* national provider identifier.

on the NUCC website. Keep in mind that the NUCC instructions are intended to be a guide only, and the health insurance professional should follow specific federal, state, or other payer guidelines for more definitive claims completion instructions.

CLAIM ATTACHMENTS

Claim attachments are supplemental documents that provide additional medical information to the claims processor that cannot be included within the electronic claim format. These documents are sometimes necessary to support the services and procedures reported on the claim. Common attachments are certificates of medical necessity, discharge summaries, and operative reports. When a paper form is used, attachments are sent to the insurance carrier with the original claim.

Because HIPAA standards do not accommodate supplemental documents with electronic claims submission, it became necessary to develop standard claims attachment forms. In 1997 the American National Standards Institute attempted to develop standardized electronic claims attachments. In September 2005, the HHS published a Notice of Proposed Rule Making for electronic claims attachments in the *Federal Register,* the daily journal of the US government. The intent of this rule was to propose standards to implement some of the requirements of HIPAA.

The Patient Protection and Affordable Care Act (ACA) has established a time frame for standardizing claim attachments. CMS published the Claims Attachment Operating Rule in 2012, and the statutory compliance date for use of the rule was January 1, 2016; however, some changes were expected before this deadline. For example, given the evolving state of attachments and the ACA statutory deadlines, the healthcare industry was expected to coordinate in 2012 and 2013 to (1) identify the standards and operating rules that it will propose for inclusion in this regulation, (2) agree on the rationale, and (3) demonstrate practicality. For updates on this rule, log on to http://www.CMS.gov and insert "Claims Attachment Operating Rule" in the search box.

So, how have providers been submitting claim attachments for electronic claims when needed? Some carriers ask providers to send the attachments by mail using an attachment control number that, on arrival, can be matched with the appropriate claim. Alternatively, some providers use companies like National Electronic Attachment, Inc. (NEA), to send attachments electronically using software such as FastAttach. With this method, the healthcare office scans an image of the attachment into its computer (or captures an image already in the computer) through FastAttach. Then the image is transported to NEA's computer "storehouse." NEA immediately sends a report back to the provider's office with an NEA number for each file. The healthcare office then submits the claim electronically with the NEA number in the appropriate section

of the claim form. This is done automatically for those users with access to the FastAttach link. Some carriers' software programs allow providers to submit claims electronically with attachments using the direct data entry functionality through their online service center. An electronic copy of the attachment(s) can be uploaded with the claim, much like a document is attached to an email.

It is important to note that guidelines for electronic claim attachments vary from one carrier to the next; therefore it is a good habit to contact the carrier in question for their specific guidelines for electronic claim attachments. Be aware, however, that standardization of submitting claim attachments is likely coming soon.

? What Did You Learn?

1. What is a "clean" claim?
2. True or false: There is no way the health insurance professional can "proofread" an electronic claim before submission.
3. Discuss two methods that might be used if an electronic claim requires an "attachment."
4. Identify a major difference between OCR and NUCC claims completion guidelines.
5. Name two categories of providers who can use the CMS-1500 paper form.

SUMMARY CHECKPOINTS

- The health insurance claims process is an interaction between the healthcare provider and an insurance company. The cycle begins when the patient visits a provider and a medical health record is generated or updated. When the visit is complete, services or procedures rendered by the healthcare provider are communicated to the insurance company in the form of a claim. The two methods for submitting health insurance claims are electronic, using practice management software, and the paper CMS-1500 form.
- The electronic claims submission process was born out of the development and growth of computer technology and medical practice management software. Practice management software allows users to enter patient information, schedule appointments, maintain lists of insurance payers, perform billing tasks, and generate reports. Also known as *health information systems*, this category of software has made it possible to manage large numbers of insurance claims with various payers accurately and efficiently. Computer technology has also made claims submission faster, more accurate, and less costly to the practice.
- HIPAA initiated changes to promote uniformity in healthcare claim submission by adopting standards for electronic health information transactions. This

step eliminated most of the unique forms used by individual health insurance carriers and the requirements that each had for processing claims. Currently, all HIPAA-covered entities (healthcare plans, healthcare providers, and healthcare clearinghouses) are required to use these standard formats for processing claims and payments, as well as for the maintenance and transmission of electronic healthcare information and data. This standardization of submitting claims and simplifying the processes involved makes getting paid quicker, easier, and less costly.

- HIPAA requires the use of standard transactions to report and inquire about healthcare services. Starting in January 2012, providers who submitted claims electronically are required to use Version 5010. Version 5010 addresses many of the limitations in the former version and supports the reporting of NPIs and ICD-10 codes (see Chapter 14).
- The electronic billing claims process begins when a patient arrives at the medical facility. The front office staff enters patient information into the medical facility's practice management software. It is from this information that the claim is generated through the internal functioning of the software. Once the patient visit is over, the health insurance professional transmits information to the insurance company in the form of a claim. The documents necessary for generating a claim are as follows:
  - The *patient information form,* which supplies demographic and insurance information and provides the necessary signed release of information
  - The *patient's insurance ID card,* which contains current subscriber numbers and other information necessary for preauthorization of certain procedures and inpatient hospitalization
  - The *patient's medical health record,* which contains detailed documentation of the reason for the patient's visit, the physician's findings, and a discussion of the recommended treatment
  - The *encounter form,* which includes the professional services rendered and corresponding procedure and diagnostic codes
  - The *patient ledger card,* which documents the fees charged for the services
- Advantages of the electronic claims process include:
  - Faster claims payment
  - Fewer errors and rejected claims
  - Improved cash flow
  - Reduced cost of claims processing
  - More streamlined internal processes
- These advantages allow providers to focus more on patient care.
- There are basically two ways to submit claims electronically: (1) through an electronic claims clearinghouse and (2) directly to an insurance carrier. There

are advantages and disadvantages to each method. If a medical practice submits claims to multiple carriers, a clearinghouse might be the better choice. If claims are sent primarily to one carrier, the practice may consider using direct submission to that carrier.

- The NUCC and the NUBC are responsible for updating and revising the CMS-1500 universal paper claim form. The most recent revision is the CMS-1500 (02/12) form. The 02/12 revision is similar to the previous revision (08/05) but incorporates a few changes to accommodate HIPAA's Version 5010 transaction standards and ICD-10 codes.

Closing Scenario

Latisha finds that she uses so much of what she learned in school on a daily basis. By having an understanding of what information is required for a clean claim the first time, Latisha is very careful when entering data into the practice management system and the EMR. She has seen claims rejected due to inaccurate data entry.

Latisha also makes sure that she is staying current with all of the changes that occur with the insurance companies that Walden-Martin sees, including Medicare. She can then prevent rejections and denials, which in turn increases the revenue for the clinic.

CHAPTER REVIEW

1. The type of software that deals with the day-to-day operations of a medical practice is:
   a. EDI.
   b. Electronic medical records.
   c. Spreadsheet software.
   d. Practice management software.
2. HIPAA-covered entities include:
   a. Healthcare plans.
   b. Healthcare providers.
   c. Healthcare clearinghouses.
   d. All of the above.
3. ICD-10 codes are considered part of:
   a. HIPAA PHI.
   b. HIPAA code set requirements.
   c. HIPAA business associates.
   d. HIPAA-covered entities.
4. The employer identification number (EIN) is assigned by:
   a. the IRS.
   b. HIPAA.
   c. HHS.
   d. None of the above.
5. What change in standards allowed for the use of ICD-10 codes?
   a. HIPAA
   b. Version 5010
   c. CMS-1500 (02/12)
   d. ASC X12 4010/4010A

6. The term that refers to authorizing payment from the insurance company to be made directly to the provider is:
   a. Release of information.
   b. Assignment of benefits.
   c. Coordination of benefits.
   d. Secondary payer.
7. All patient charges and payments are kept track of in a(n):
   a. Encounter form.
   b. Ledger.
   c. Claim.
   d. Aging report.
8. Insurance covered for patients can be verified using:
   a. Interactive voice response (IVR) systems.
   b. Swipe terminals.
   c. Internet-based eligibility check systems.
   d. All of the above.
9. When submitting claims electronically, the process that involves consolidating claims from various healthcare providers and sending one transmission to the insurance carrier is:
   a. Direct billing.
   b. Claims clearinghouse.
   c. EDI.
   d. HIPAA 5010.
10. When submitting a paper claim, the provider must use:
   a. HIPAA 5010.
   b. EDI.
   c. CMS-1500.
   d. NUBC.

WEBSITES TO EXPLORE

- For live links to the following websites, please visit the Evolve website at http://evolve.elsevier.com/Beik/today.
- For detailed step-by-step guidelines for completing the CMS-1500 (02/12) paper claim form, see http://www.nucc.org/index.php?option=com_content&view=featured&Itemid5101.
- The NUCC updated instruction manual for the updated CMS-1500 (02/12) claim form can be found at http://www.nucc.org/images/stories/PDF/draft_version_0212_nucc_1500_claim_form_instruction_manual.pdf.
- For more information on HIPAA, visit https://www.hhs.gov/hipaa/index.html.
- For general information on claims processing, visit http://www.ama-assn.org.
- For links to individual state insurance offices, visit http://www.naic.org/state_web_map.htm.
- The code sets for use with HIPAA 276/277 Health Care Claim Status Category Codes and Health Care Claim Status Codes can be found at http://www.cms.gov/Outreach-and-Education/Medicare-Learning-Network-MLN/MLNMattersArticles/downloads/MM3361.pdf.
- To learn more about the Medicare appeals process, check the following websites using "appeals" as the search word: http://www.cms.gov and http://www.medicare.gov.

Author's Note: Due to the dynamic nature of the Internet, web addresses and/or links provided in this chapter may have changed since publication and may no longer be valid. In such cases, students should select comparable search words to access related sites.

Claims Management

Chapter Outline

Chapter Objectives

1. List and explain the five keys to successful claims.
2. Determine the role of HIPAA and the National Standard employer identification number (EIN) in claims processing.
3. Identify and provide brief explanations of the six steps of the claims process.
4. Outline the process for processing secondary claims.
5. List suggestions for optimizing the billing and claims process.
6. Discuss the process for appealing incorrect payments and denied claims.

Chapter Terms

adjudication process
appeal
birthday rule
charge-to-collection ratio
clean claim
coordination of benefits (COB)

correct code initiative
downcoding
employer identification number (EIN)
explanation of benefits (EOB)
insurance claims register (log)

Medicare secondary payer (MSP) claims
real-time claims adjudication (RTCA)
secondary claim
suspension file

Zoey Edwards, confined to a wheelchair after an automobile accident at the age of 12, was looking for a career opportunity that allowed her to work out of her home. She noticed an article in a flyer from a local community college about a healthcare billing and insurance program. The article listed the career possibilities for graduates of this program, along with testimonials from several former students who had established successful home-based businesses in healthcare billing and insurance. Zoey decided that a career in this field might meet her needs. Through a state-of-the-art communications network and with the help of the student services staff at the college, Zoey was able to participate in classes from the comfort of her own home, traveling to campus only for major examinations.

After completing her degree Zoey was hired by Walden-Martin Family Medical Clinic to handle some of the claims submission and management duties. They were willing to work with her and develop a home-based operation. This has worked well for both Zoey and Walden-Martin. Zoey works with specific insurance companies and ensures that claims are being submitted properly for those companies. She also tracks the claims submitted and follows up with the insurance companies when payment hasn't been made or if there is a question about a payment.

OVERVIEW OF THE CLAIMS MANAGEMENT PROCESS

In Chapter 6 we learned that there are two basic methods for submitting health insurance claims: paper and electronic. We also learned that there are limited exceptions to this mandate. In addition, more and more nongovernment payers are requiring claims to be submitted electronically. Now we are going to look at how to manage the claims process so that payment can be received quickly and smoothly.

KEYS TO SUCCESSFUL CLAIMS

Claims processing involves many steps, and each step must be performed thoroughly and accurately to receive the maximum payment that the medical health record documentation substantiates. This process begins with the patient appointment and ends with the subsequent payment by the carrier. Understanding how this process works allows the health insurance professional to file claims properly, resulting in full and timely reimbursement. Fig. 7.1 illustrates the five "keys" to successful claims processing. These "keys" are applicable to both paper claims and the electronic claims processes.

FIRST KEY: COLLECT AND VERIFY PATIENT INFORMATION

Unless a patient visits the healthcare facility on a regular basis (e.g., weekly allergy shots or blood pressure checks), the health insurance professional should verify the patient's information each time he or she visits the office. New patients must complete a patient information form on the first visit. Established patients should be required to update the form at least annually. This is because within a year's time the patient

Fig. 7.1 Five keys to successful claims processing.

could have remarried, moved to a new address, changed jobs, or, most important to the health insurance professional, changed insurance companies. In addition to demographic data (e.g., name, address, age, gender), the patient information form should include basic items, such as the insurance carrier's name, policy and group numbers (if applicable), the insured's name (if different from the patient), effective date of coverage, and any secondary insurance information. Some practices with a high volume of Medicare patients may have a separate information form for these patients.

After the patient information form is completed, the health insurance professional should check it to ensure that the correct information has been entered in the required blanks and all information is legible. One key to successful claims submission is to have the patient provide as much information as possible, and the health insurance professional should verify this information. It is very important to make sure that all information that is entered into the patient's electronic medical record be entered correctly. This includes all demographic and billing information. When working with cither a paper system or an electronic system, all work should be proofread to prevent any errors in billing.

In some situations, more than one insurer is involved. Such cases might occur when the patient and his or her spouse are covered under separate employer group plans or when the parents of a minor patient are divorced, and each parent has his or her own insurance policy. In the latter case, if the primary carrier is not designated on the information form, the health insurance professional should obtain this information from the parent who accompanies the child to the office.

⊚ HIPAA Tip

Patients have certain rights and protections against the misuse or disclosure of their medical health records. All patients should receive a Notice of Privacy Practices that informs them of their rights and of the legal duties of the healthcare practice with respect to protected health information.

In addition to the standard demographic and insurance questions asked on the patient information form, many healthcare practices include a section (often at the bottom of the form) for the patient to sign a release of information and an assignment of benefits. Other practices use separate forms for these functions. Although the Health Insurance Portability and Accountability Act (HIPAA) says it is unnecessary for treatment, payment, or healthcare operations (TPO), most healthcare facilities request that patients sign and date a valid release of information before they submit an insurance claim. Most facilities also require that patients sign an assignment of benefits,

authorizing the insurance carrier to send payment directly to the healthcare provider.

Verifying a patient's current insurance coverage (e.g., enrollment and copayments) is one of the most important administrative duties of the health insurance professional. Accurate verification has a direct impact on the promptness and correctness of claim payments. Many third-party payment delays are caused by inaccurate verification on the part of the practitioner's office or missed information at the time of the verification. Many insurance companies offer online services for providers to exchange eligibility and benefits information on their patients electronically. After obtaining a complete and accurate patient information form, the health insurance professional should make a photocopy of the patient's insurance identification (ID) card and place it in an easily accessible location in the patient's medical health record, such as inside the front cover. Many insurance ID cards also have information on the back. The health insurance professional should always check the back of the card for information and make a photocopy of it as well. Many healthcare facilities also ask for and make a copy of the patient's driver's license to ascertain the patient's identity, which helps prevent fraud.

💡 Imagine This!

Shirley Gibson, a health insurance professional for Walden-Martin Family Medical Clinic, updates all demographic and insurance information when patients come to the office for an appointment. In addition, she checks to ensure that the release of information and assignment of benefits forms are signed, dated, and current. After the patient completes the new information form, Shirley checks it for accuracy and legibility. If two insurance companies are listed, she asks the patient which is primary. In some cases, Shirley must call either the employer or the insurance carrier to verify which is the primary carrier. "It is important for smooth, efficient, and timely claims processing to have all information current and accurate before the claim is prepared for submission," Shirley says. "It is surprising," she adds, "how much people move around, change jobs, and change insurers these days."

SECOND KEY: OBTAIN NECESSARY PREAUTHORIZATION AND/OR PRECERTIFICATION

The health insurance professional should be familiar with the rules regarding preauthorization and precertification, because it has been discussed in earlier chapters. To review, some third-party payers reject certain types of claims if they do not know about and approve a service or procedure beforehand. Services that most often require preauthorization or precertification include inpatient hospitalizations, new or experimental procedures, and certain diagnostic studies. Emergency services typically do not need prior authorization, but they often require some type of follow-up with the insurance company—typically within 24 to 48 hours. Although the provider's front office staff often handles this requirement, it is ultimately the patient's responsibility to know when and how to notify the insurance company for preauthorization or precertification; however, the health insurance professional should advise the patient when this process is necessary to avoid rejected claims. Also, if the patient is incapacitated in any way, the health insurance professional or a member of the healthcare staff should notify the patient's insurer to acquire the necessary preauthorization. Telephone numbers for contacting the carrier are usually on the back of the patient's ID card. Fig. 7.2 shows the back of an insurance ID card with a toll-free number to call when precertification or preauthorization is necessary. Some carriers issue a "prior authorization" number, which should be indicated in Block 23 of the CMS-1500 form.

Reminder: Medicare (fee-for-service) does not need prior authorization to provide medically necessary services.

 Stop and Think

Helen Rigdon was admitted as an inpatient to Memorial East Hospital after a visit to the emergency department for a bleeding ulcer. After Helen was discharged, she received an explanation of benefits (EOB) from her insurance carrier stating that they were denying the claim because there had been no preauthorization for the hospital admission. In this case, whose responsibility was it to contact the insurance company to obtain the required preauthorization?

THIRD KEY: DOCUMENTATION

It is the healthcare provider's responsibility to document appropriate comments in the patient's medical health record. Each entry must indicate clearly the history, physical examination, and medical decision making for the patient. The provider also fills out an encounter form, indicating the proper procedure codes

---

IMPORTANT PHONE NUMBER INFORMATION

For pre-admission certification, OB and emergency admissions call 1-800-558-xxxx.

To locate a participating provider call 1-800-810-xxxx or access BlueCard website @ www.bcbs.com.

Providers - Please submit all claims to your local Blue Cross and Blue Shield Plan.

Pharmacists - Pharmacy Benefits Manager (PBM) is AdvancePCS. For assistance call 1-800-600-xxxx.

Wellmark Blue Cross and Blue Shield of Iowa, an independent licensee of the Blue Cross and Blue Shield Association.

Fig. 7.2 Back of insurance identification (ID) card.

(CPT-4 or HCPCS Level II) and diagnosis codes (ICD-10-CM) to describe the patient's condition and the services that were rendered. These codes should be checked before transferring them to the claim, because when in a hurry some practitioners may indicate the wrong ones. The health insurance professional places the appropriate diagnosis codes, procedure codes, charges, and any other pertinent information in the proper boxes on the claim. Whether claims are submitted on paper or in electronic format, each required field on the claim helps determine if it is "clean." Claims that are not clean are returned for more information or are denied. It is important that the claim shows the exact diagnosis that is documented in the medical health record.

FOURTH KEY: FOLLOW PAYER GUIDELINES

Some major payers (Medicaid, Medicare, Blue Cross and Blue Shield, TRICARE/CHAMPVA) have slightly different guidelines for completing the CMS-1500 claim form. The health insurance professional must obtain the most recent guidelines from each of these major payers to complete the claim exactly to their specifications. The guidelines provided in this chapter follow those provided in the National Uniform Claim Committee (NUCC) website, except for punctuation allowances. Where punctuation is concerned, the optical character recognition (OCR) guidelines are adhered to. The guidelines for electronic claim submission should be uniform as designated by HIPAA.

FIFTH KEY: SUBMIT A CLEAN CLAIM

The most important process in the healthcare insurance cycle is submitting a clean claim to the third-party payer. A **clean claim** means that all information necessary for processing the claim has been entered on the claim form and the information is correct. Clean claims are usually paid in a timely manner. Paying careful attention to what information should be entered in each field helps produce clean claims. For electronic claims this starts with proper entry of information in the practice management system. Refer to Appendix B at the back of this book for examples of completed claims. Box 7.1 lists some common errors that cause a claim to be rejected or denied.

Stop and Think

Silver River Medical Center has a higher-than-average number of rejected claims. The billing and insurance staff consist of four health insurance professionals; each individual handles approximately 50 to 55 claims per day. Many of the claims are rejected or denied because of simple errors—transposed numbers, misspelled patient names, incorrect charges, or an omitted provider signature. What might the billing and insurance staff do to resolve this problem?

Box 7.1   Common Errors Made on Claims

1. Patient's insurance ID number is incorrect.
2. Patient information is incomplete.
3. Patient or insured name and address do not match the insurance carrier's records.
4. Physician's EIN, provider number, NPI, or Social Security number is incorrect or missing.
5. There is little or no information regarding primary or secondary coverage.
6. Physician's (or authorized person's) signature has been omitted.
7. Dates of service are incorrect or do not correlate with information from other providers (e.g., hospital, nursing homes).
8. The fee column is blank, not itemized, and not totaled.
9. The CPT or ICD codes are invalid, or the diagnostic codes are not linked to the correct services or procedures.
10. The claim is illegible.
11. Preauthorization or precertification was not obtained before services were rendered.

CPT, Current Procedural Technology; *EIN,* employer identification number; *ICD,* International Statistical Classification of Diseases and Related Health Problems; *ID,* identification; *NPI,* national provider identifier.

REJECTED CLAIMS VERSUS DENIED CLAIMS

A claim that does not successfully pass through the **adjudication process** to the payment system is rejected. The adjudication process involves the payer's examination of a claim and determining the amount of payment, if any. Examples of why a claim is rejected include provider was not found, member was not found, incorrect address was used, or more than one rendering provider submitted a claim. A claim that is denied is passed through to a payment system but is not payable for numerous reasons, including but not limited to member is ineligible, benefit is not covered, or benefit maximum has been met. A rejected claim must be researched differently than a denied claim. Questions regarding rejected claims should be directed to the carrier or clearinghouse. Questions regarding denied claims should be directed to the carrier's customer service department.

Patient's Point of View

Charles Johnson called to talk to Zoey about his claim that had been denied by his insurance company. He had been seen for a sore throat, but while he was in the office his provider decided to check his blood sugar since Charles has type 2 diabetes. As Zoey was reviewing the claim, she noticed that the blood glucose charge was submitted with the sore throat diagnosis. The insurance carrier denied that charge as not medically necessary. Zoey was able to resubmit the claim with the correct diagnosis, and the charge was paid.

What Did You Learn?

1. Why is it important to update the patient information form with each patient visit?
2. What is the result of failing to obtain preauthorization or precertification for certain procedures such as inpatient hospitalization?
3. Whose responsibility is it to document appropriate comments in the medical health record?
4. What is a "clean claim"?

HIPAA AND NATIONAL STANDARD EMPLOYER IDENTIFICATION NUMBER

An **employer identification number (EIN)** is used by the federal government to identify each employer for a variety of federal reporting requirements, including income taxes. The Secretary of the Department of Health and Human Services (HHS) requires that the EIN assigned by the Internal Revenue Service (IRS) also be used as the employer identifier standard for all electronic healthcare transactions as required by HIPAA. The ruling requires the following:

1. Health plans must accept the EIN on all electronic transactions that require an employer identifier.
2. Healthcare clearinghouses must use the EIN on all electronic transactions that require an employer identifier.
3. Healthcare providers must use the EIN on all transactions, wherever required, that are transmitted electronically.
4. Employers must disclose their EIN when requested to do so by an entity that conducts standard electronic transactions requiring that employer's identifier.

An EIN consists of nine digits, with the first two digits separated by a hyphen (e.g., 00-1234567). The IRS assigns EINs to employers, who can obtain an EIN by submitting IRS Form SS-4 (Application for Employer Identification Number). Business entities that pay wages to one or more employees are required to have an EIN as their taxpayer identifying number; most employers already have an EIN assigned to them.

The HHS issued a final rule in May 2002 to standardize the identifying numbers assigned to employers in the healthcare industry by using the existing EIN. (This EIN should appear in Block [or Item] 25 of the CMS-1500 claim form. The NUCC guidelines for the 02/12 revised form say to enter these numbers left justified in this field without a space or hyphen.) Most covered entities were to have been in compliance with the EIN standard by July 30, 2004. Although small healthcare facilities were allowed an additional year to comply, all providers should now be in compliance.

NATIONAL UNIFORM CLAIM COMMITTEE GUIDELINES FOR REPORTING THE EMPLOYER IDENTIFICATION NUMBER ON THE CMS-1500

The NUCC guidelines for Item Number 25 on the CMS-1500 paper claim state the following:

Enter the "Federal Tax ID Number" (employer ID or Social Security number [SSN]) of the Billing Provider identified in Item Number 33. This is the tax ID number intended to be used for 1099 reporting purposes. Enter an X in the appropriate box to indicate which number is being reported. Only one box can be marked. Do not enter hyphens with numbers. Enter numbers left justified in the field. Description: The "Federal Tax ID Number" is the unique identifier assigned by a federal or state agency.

? What Did You Learn?

1. What is the format of an EIN?
2. How does a provider acquire an EIN?
3. True or false: NUCC allows either the provider's EIN or SSN in Block 25 on the CMS-1500.

CLAIMS PROCESS

After a claim has been received by a third-party payer, it is reviewed, and the carrier makes payment decisions. As explained previously, this process is referred to as *adjudication*. If the claim is clean, it continues through several more steps to the reimbursement process, and ideally the insurance carrier pays up to the allowed amount (according to the patient's policy) for the services that have been billed. However, the carrier can reduce payment or deny the claim completely. If any information is missing or if there are errors on the claim, the process is stopped, and the claim is returned to the healthcare office where it originated. Fig. 7.3 is a flow chart that illustrates how a paper claim progresses through the various steps after it is received at the payer's facility. The steps discussed in the following sections and listed in Fig. 7.4 are for both paper and electronic claims.

STEP ONE: CLAIM IS RECEIVED

When the insurance carrier receives a paper claim, it is dated, and the claim is processed through an OCR

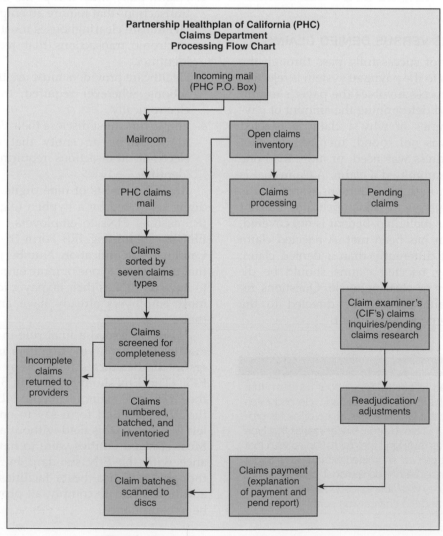

Fig. 7.3 Claims department processing flow chart.

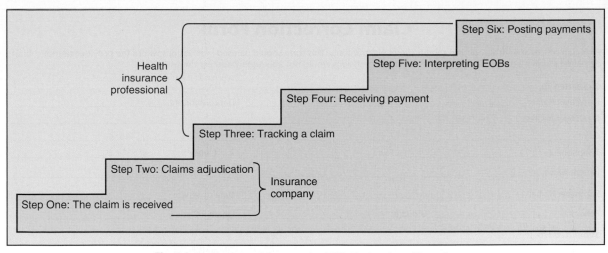

Fig. 7.4 Steps of the claim process. *EOB,* Explanation of benefits.

scanner. If any attachments accompanied the claim, the practice name, provider or group number, address, and telephone number should appear on each attached document. Providing this information on each attachment helps prevent claim denial in case the attachments get separated from the claim during the adjudication process.

When an electronic claim is submitted, it will be electronically date and time stamped and will enter the insurance company's computer system for processing.

STEP TWO: CLAIMS ADJUDICATION

After the data are entered into the payer's computer system, if the claim is clean, it is approved and proceeds on to be paid. However, it first must pass through a series of edits to verify the patient's coverage and eligibility and check for medical necessity, exclusions, and noncovered services contained in the patient's policy. If the claim requires additional information, the insurer contacts the healthcare practice or the patient. In the case of a paper claim, this contact usually is accomplished by mail, but it also can be by telephone. If the claim is not clean, it is rejected and returned to the provider.

When a claims error that could result, or already has resulted, in inaccurate reimbursement is discovered, a corrected claim should be prepared and submitted. For a paper claim, the health insurance professional should mark the corrected claim as a "corrected billing" and not a "duplicate claim." It also is advisable to include a note describing the error plus any additional documentation necessary to support the correction. Some practices use a claims correction form (Fig. 7.5) for submitting corrected claims. The form is filled out, attached to a corrected claim, and resubmitted to the payer.

 HIPAA Tip

The Health Insurance Portability and Accountability Act (HIPAA) has developed a transaction that allows payers to request additional information to support claims. This transaction uses Logical Observation Identifiers Names and Codes (LOINC) to request the clinical information that is required to process healthcare claims.

STEP THREE: TRACKING CLAIMS

Many practices use some sort of claims follow-up system so that claims can be tracked and delinquent claims resolved before it is too late to resubmit them (as in the case of a lost claim). Most practice management software includes a claims tracking function that allows reports to be generated showing outstanding claims by date, by carrier, or by some other sorting function. For medical offices that still use paper claims, an example of a claims follow-up system is an insurance log or insurance register. The insurance log or register should include various entries, such as the patient's name, insurance company's name, date the claim was filed, status of the claim (e.g., paid, pending, denied), date of EOB or payment receipt, and resubmission date. A claims follow-up system can be set up manually or electronically. It is a helpful tool for the health insurance professional and the provider because it ultimately leads to an increase in payments to the practice. Insurance claims can be overlooked if a tracking system is not in place, leading to lost revenue. Fig. 7.6 shows an example of an insurance log. Fig. 7.7 is an example of a practice management software screen listing outstanding claims on a primary insurance aging report. Some practices use a form similar to the one in Fig. 7.8 for claims follow-up.

Claim Correction Form

Physician offices are encouraged to submit claims electronically. This form should be used in situations where the provider cannot submit corrected claims electronically or where electronic submissions would not adequately address the issue.

Submitted To:

Plan/Payer Name: _____   Date Submitted: _____

Plan/Payer Address: _____

City _____ State: _____ Zip: _____

Telephone: (_____) _____ Fax: (_____) _____ E-mail: _____

Patient Name: _____   D.O.B.: _____
               First   M.I.   Last

Subscriber Name: _____   Date of Service: _____

Policy #: _____   Group #: _____   Original Claim #: _____

Submitted From:

Provider Name: _____   TIN or ID #: _____

Contact: _____   Telephone: (_____) _____   Ext. _____

Fax: (_____) _____   E-mail: _____

THE FOLLOWING WAS CORRECTED ON THIS CLAIM:

❑   The patient's policy/group number was incorrect. The correct number(s) are shown above.

❑   The correct CPT code is _____ instead of _____

❑   Wrong date of service was filed. The correct date is _____

❑   Visits were denied based on the diagnosis given. Proper diagnosis code is _____ instead of _____

❑   Visit: ❑ Procedure: denied as over carrier's utilization limits. Please see attached letter to justify extensions of these limits.

❑   Carrier indicated that the patient is covered by another plan that is Primary. This is incorrect. Patient indicates you are Primary.

❑   The secondary carrier is: _____   ❑ There is no secondary carrier.

❑   The procedure was denied as medically not necessary. Documentation to support the medical necessity of this service is attached.

❑   Our clerk: ❑ Carrier's clerk: failed to enter correct number of times (units) procedure was performed. Correct units are as follows:

    D.O.S.: _____   Code: _____   Units: _____   Charge Total $: _____

❑   Multiple Surgical Procedures:

    ❑ Carrier failed to approve any procedure at 100%.   ❑ Carrier approved incorrect procedure at 100%.

    Carrier should have approved code _____ @ 100%/50% instead of _____

    Carrier should have approved code _____ @ 100%/50% instead of _____

    Carrier should have approved code _____ @ 100%/50% instead of _____

❑   Modifiers should be attached to code(s)

	Code	Code			Code	Code
❑ -50	_____	_____		❑ -51	_____	_____
❑ -58	_____	_____		❑ -59	_____	_____
❑ -79	_____	_____		❑ -GA	_____	_____
❑ __	_____	_____		❑ __	_____	_____

❑   The following E/M visit was denied as included in the global surgical fee. In fact, the service was a significant separately identifiable service provided above and beyond the procedure and submitted with appropriate E/M modifier. Please reconsider with attached documentation:

    Code: _____   with modifier(s): ❑ -24 ❑ -25   Charge $: _____

❑   UPIN information for code _____ was omitted. Physician name: _____   UPIN: _____

❑   Plan specific provider I.D. omitted. The I.D. # is _____

❑   CLIA number was omitted. The CLIA number is _____

❑   The place of service was incorrect. The place of service should be _____

❑   The service was rendered at the physician's physical location listed in Box 32 of the claim form.

❑   Failed to attach EOB from Primary carrier. The EOB is attached to this form.

❑   Failed to enter correct information on indicated line of claim form.

    Line #: _____   Correct Information: _____

❑   Other reason for claim correction: _____

❑   Comment: _____

June 2003

Fig. 7.5 Example of a claim correction form.

Creating a Suspension File System

For offices filing paper claims, some sort of claims tracking system, such as a suspension file, is recommended. A **suspension file** is a series of files set up chronologically and labeled according to the number of days since the claim was submitted. Claims in a file labeled "current" might be 30 days or less, a second series might be labeled "claims over 30 days," and so forth. Another type of follow-up system that works well is one in which claims are filed according to the date they are submitted.

Patient Name	Carrier Name	Date Filed	Claim Amount	Date of Payment/EOB	Payment Amount	Claim Status	Action Taken/Date
Anderson, Joseph L.	Metropolitan Life	01/12/XX	1450.00			Pending	Telephone call to Met Life 2/12/XX
Siverly, Penelope R.	Medicare	01/23/XX	125.00	02/13/XX	64.50		
Loper, Michael C.	Medicaid	01/25/XX	65.00			Denied	Appeal Letter to Medicaid 2/16/XX
Carpenter, Susan	BCBS	01/27/XX	255.00			Lost Claim	Resubmitted on 2/22/XX

Fig. 7.6 Sample insurance claims tracking form.

Instructor: Hannah Melvin

WALDEN-MARTIN
FAMILY MEDICAL CLINIC
1234 ANYSTREET | ANYTOWN, ANYSTATE 12345
PHONE 123-123-1234 | FAX 123-123-5678

Patient Aging by Date of Service

Date Of Service	Procedure	Current 0 - 30	Past 31 - 60	Past 61 - 90	Past 91 - 120	Past 121 - -->	Payment Collected	Total Balance
Aetna								

Guarantor: Simpson, Tanus   04/04/1968

12418281   Simpson, Tanus   04/04/1968   Initial Billing Date: 07/18/20xx   Policy: GG93GXTA   Group: 99999

07/18/20xx	81000	50.00						50.00
07/18/20xx	99213	86.00						86.00
		136.00	00.00	00.00	00.00	00.00	00.00	136.00

Report Aging Totals		136.00	0.00	0.00	0.00	0.00	0.00	136.00

Fig. 7.7 An electronic insurance aging report using SimChart for the Medical Office.

Imagine This!

Laurence Benson visits his family physician, Dr. Myron Peters, yearly for annual wellness examinations. Every 3 years, Dr. Peters orders an electrocardiogram for Laurence as part of his routine examination. Normally, Laurence's insurance carrier, XYZ Health Indemnity, pays within 2 to 3 weeks. It is Dr. Peters' office policy to send a statement to the patient if the insurance carrier does not pay within 60 days. When Laurence received an overdue statement, he called Dr. Peters' office and asked the health insurance professional to check into the matter. When she did, she was told that the claim was "pending" because the individual who reviewed it saw something on the attached electrocardiogram that required further assessment by the medical review committee, but the committee was "bogged down" with a backlog of claims to review.

Stop and Think

Reread the Imagine This! box concerning Dr. Peters. How might Dr. Peters' health insurance professional modify her routine to avoid future problems similar to the one experienced by Mr. Benson?

Claim copies should be removed systematically as they are finalized. Paid claims can be filed in a permanent folder or binder under each major payer. If payment has not been received, some sort of follow-up procedure can be initiated. Claims follow-up should be given a high priority and become a regularly scheduled part of the health insurance professional's workweek.

Prompt Payment Tracking Form

Practice/Physician Information (complaint by)

Name: _____

Address: _____

City, Zip _____

Phone: _____ Fax: _____

E-Mail: _____

Insurance Company and Claim Information

Original Submission Date: _____

Company: _____ Phone: _____

Date(s) of Services: _____ Claims Rep (if known): _____

Submitted via: ❑ Paper ❑ Electronic

Action by Insurance Company

Date of Initial Response from Ins. Co.: _____

❑Denied ❑Requested Additional Information ❑Reduced Payment ❑Other (see attached)

Insurance Company Response: _____

_____

_____

Current Status of Claim: _____

_____

_____

Fig. 7.8 Example of a claims tracking form.

Experienced health insurance professionals who deal with Medicare and Medicaid carriers recommend making inquiries in writing or using the forms specifically created for follow-up. Inquiries to commercial carriers often are handled more efficiently by a telephone call. If a claim has been rejected for a simple reason, without notification, a quick phone call is time well spent. In the case of resubmission, always attach a note with the date, the contact person's name, and a description of the conversation. Keep a copy of all correspondence as documented proof of response.

Creating an Insurance Claims Register System

An alternative to the suspension file is to record claims information on a columnar form known as an **insurance claims register** or **log** (Fig. 7.9). When a claim is

INSURANCE CLAIMS REGISTER

Filing Date	Chart Number	Patient's Name	Name & Address Where Claim Submitted	Amount Billed	Amount Paid	Difference	Status or Comment
10/6	1221	Matthew Kramer	First Insurance 1st Avenue Newark, NJ 12345	$525			10/21 busy 10/30 busy 11/6 busy
10/6	1350	Luke Myers	Better Insurance 3rd Avenue New York City, NY 02110	$1200	$700	$500	Requested Review 10/30
10/6	1098	Christi Wilson	County Farm Ins 6th Avenue New Era, IA 45678	$125	$50	$75	$75 deductible. Bill Patient
10/6	1352	Rose Larson	Last Insurance 7th Avenue New Hope, MS 56789	$1500	0		Sent to Medical Review 10/30

Fig. 7.9 Example of an insurance claims register.

submitted, the health insurance professional records the filing date, the patient's name and chart number, the name and address of the payer, and the amount billed. As payments are received, the original copy of the claim form is removed from the follow-up file and compared with the EOB. The amount paid is recorded in the applicable column along with any difference from the amount billed as shown on the log sheet. Any notations, such as "claim sent to review" or "claim rejected for additional information," should be recorded in the status column along with the date the notice was received. If a claim is resubmitted, that date should be recorded on the log as well.

STEP FOUR: RECEIVING PAYMENT

The insurer sends the payment for services and the EOB—sometimes called a *remittance advice (RA)*—back to the provider's office. (Whether or not there is a payment, there is always an EOB or RA.) If the practice submits claims electronically, the EOB or RA also may be in an electronic format. Each EOB should be checked thoroughly to ensure that the payment is consistent with the fee schedule or contracted amount from the insurance company (Table 7.1). Claims that have been denied or rejected for any reason or that have been reduced in payment should be reviewed to determine the source of the denial or payment reduction. A

Table 7.1 **Common Payment Errors**

RESULT	REASON
A service is reduced	The adjudicator may have downcoded the claim for lack of documentation. Current Procedural Terminology (CPT) code was converted to a relative value scale code that did not directly correlate with CPT.
Reimbursement is made at a much-reduced rate	Possibly a data entry error. Compare the CPT code submitted with the code paid.
Low reimbursement	Precertification was not completed. Insufficient documentation to establish medical necessity.
Multiple units are paid as one unit	The insurer "missed" a number in the unit column.
Reimbursement for a procedure or service suddenly decreases	This could mean a recalculation of the allowable fee or an error. Phone the payer.
Payment is not received	Claim is lost or "caught in the system." Begin your inquiry.
Multiple procedures were not paid	The insurance company either ignored the additional procedures or lumped them in with the primary procedure.

decision must be made whether to pursue the claim further.

STEP FIVE: INTERPRETING THE EXPLANATION OF BENEFITS

The **explanation of benefits (EOB)** is the document sent by the insurance carrier to the provider and the patient explaining how the claim was adjudicated. The EOB is the key to knowing how much of the claim was paid, how much was not, and why—in other words, adjudicated. Sometimes understanding what this document means can be challenging. Every payer has a different EOB format. The EOB has a unique vocabulary, such as "applied to deductible," "above usual and customary," "patient copay," and "allowable." Codes are often used, and the health insurance professional must determine what each code means. Deciphering the EOB language and codes reveals the following:

1. Date received
2. Date processed
3. Amount of billed charges
4. Charges allowed by the carrier
5. How much of the claim was applied to the patient's deductible
6. How much of the patient's annual deductible has been met
7. Why a service was reduced or denied

Knowing how to read the EOB is important, because it aids in collecting full reimbursement, including any balance owed by the patient. Fig. 7.10 shows an EOB from a commercial insurance company and an explanation of what each code means.

Troubleshooting the Explanation of Benefits

As discussed, an EOB explains the outcome of the claim that was submitted for payment processing. If the payment was reduced or rejected, the EOB itemizes the reason. By reading the EOB and following the instructions, the health insurance professional can analyze the situation. If an error has been made on the claim and it is correctable, it should be done so in a timely manner. If it is believed that the insurance carrier made the error, it should be reported to the carrier immediately.

Initially, there are several things to evaluate when looking over an EOB that indicates no payment or a reduced payment. The first thing is to compare the totals billed on the EOB and the claim that was submitted. If they do not match, it is a good indication that the insurer missed a procedure. If the totals match but the number of line items (actual procedure codes performed) do not, more than likely the insurer bundled one procedure into another, without listing them as "duplicate."

The odds are that if a claim is reduced or rejected, the problem lies with the provider's office. However, this is not always the case, and the health insurance professional should be vigilant in analyzing the EOB.

One billing professional suggests keeping copies of sample EOB files for procedures that the medical practice performs regularly for each payer. A payment discrepancy would stand out when compared with the sample EOB file. This "example" file can be used for appealing claims as long as all patient identification is deleted.

 Imagine This!

Dr. Edwin Carter, a podiatrist, performed three arthroplasties on Priscilla Fortune's toes at $500 for each procedure. When the EOB was received, the total charge was $1500, but there were only two codes of 28285 listed. This meant that Ms. Fortune's insurance carrier had bundled two of the procedures into one, but the fee schedule was considered for only one. To clear things up, Wayne Thomas, Dr. Carter's health insurance professional, had to contact the insurer and explain that there were three distinct procedures performed on three individual toes and not two, as the carrier had assumed.

Downcoding

Downcoding by an insurance company occurs when claims are submitted with outdated, deleted, or nonexistent Current Procedural Terminology (CPT) codes. When this happens, the payer assigns a substitute code it thinks best fits the services performed. Often the healthcare practice does not agree with the choice because the substituted code results in a lesser payment. Similar problems occur when an insurer's payment system is based on CPT codes and a relative value scale code is submitted that does not directly translate to CPT. When these claims are reviewed by a claims adjuster, he or she assigns a valid CPT code. Coding accurately and knowing which coding systems payers use help to avoid these downcoding problems. (See Chapter 17 for more information on the relative value scale.)

If the claims adjuster changes a valid procedure code that was submitted on the claim, the health insurance professional should contact the claims adjuster and ask for the reason. If the contact is by mail, documentation that supports the code submitted should be included. In some cases, a procedure is denied because the insurer states that it is considered "integral to the main procedure." In other cases, a modifier that was submitted on the claim was dropped or the claim was subject to a **correct code initiative** edit. Correct code initiative edits are the result of the National Correct Coding Initiative, which develops correct coding methods for the Centers for Medicare and Medicaid Services (CMS). The edits are intended to reduce overpayments that result from improper coding. If the denial was due to a correct code initiative edit, documentation supporting why the procedure was distinct and not related to another procedure must be submitted.

EXPLANATION OF BENEFITS

EMPLOYEE BENEFIT PLAN ADMINISTRATION SERVICES

EMPLOYER/GROUP NAME	SOUTHEAST IOWA SCHOOLS		DATE PREPARED	08–06–XX
PLAN/LOCATION NUMBER	10000000 14008020 02		SOCIAL SECURITY I.D. NUMBER	
EMPLOYEE/MEMBER NAME	BEIK JANET I		CONTROL #	8470.0
PATIENT NAME	BEIK JANET I		EOB #	9808060048

JANET I BEIK
545 IOWA CITY RD
SOMEWHERE IA 00506

SOUTHEAST IOWA SCHOOLS
SOMEWHERE IA 00506

PROVIDER NAME and TYPE OF SERVICE	DATES FROM/THRU	AMOUNT CHARGED	AMOUNT COVERED	EXPL. CODE	COVERED AT 100 %	COVERED AT %	COVERED AT %
HAYS, ANDERSON, DIAGNOSTIC LABORATORY	06–22–XX	15.00	15.00	099 514	15.00		
ADJUSTMENTS TO BENEFITS	TOTAL →	15.00	15.00		15.00		
			Less Deductible				
			Balance		15.00		
			Benefit %		AT 100%	AT %	AT %
			Plan Benefits		15.00		
			Total Benefit		15.00		

099   THIS PREFERRED PROVIDER ACCEPTS THE "AMOUNT COVERED" AND HAS AGREED NOT TO
099   BILL PATIENTS FOR MORE THAN DEDUCTIBLES, COPAYS & NONCOVERED CHARGES.
514   THIS WORKSHEET WAS PROCESSED BY JENNIFER

DEDUCTIBLE SATISFIED: 1000.00

PAYMENTS HAVE BEEN ISSUED TO THE FOLLOWING BASED ON ABOVE EXPENSES.

HAYS, ANDERSON   15.00

Fig. 7.10 Example of an explanation of benefits (EOB).

STEP SIX: POSTING PAYMENTS

After the EOB has been reconciled with the patient's account, the health insurance professional (or other staff member) posts the payment received from the insurance carrier to the patient ledger and bills the patient for any applicable outstanding copayments or deductible amounts. Participating providers (PARs) cannot bill the patient for the balance because they have signed an agreement with the insurer to that effect, but nonparticipating providers (nonPARs) for commercial claims are allowed to bill the patient for any balance the insurance carrier does not pay. It is against the law to waive Medicare copayments unless financial hardship has been established and documented. Fig. 7.11 illustrates a payment entry on a patient ledger. (Note: Contractual adjustments are discussed in Chapter 17.)

TIME LIMITS

As stated previously, claims should be submitted to the insurance carrier as soon as possible, ideally within 30 days or sooner of the conclusion of treatment.

STATEMENT

Westlake Medical Clinic
2604 Spindle Center
Cherokee, XY 23133
231-555-1212

Stanley P. Grady
1234 Old Colony Road
Calamus City, XY 23232

DATE	REFERENCE	DESCRIPTION	CHARGES	CREDITS PYMNTS.	CREDITS ADJ.	BALANCE
20XX		BALANCE FORWARD ⟶				26 00
1/10	Stanley	99214, ROA	135 00	8 00		153 00
3/21	Stanley	99214, ROA	135 00	8 00		280 00
5/18	Stanley	99214, ROA	135 00	8 00		407 00
5/20		XYZ Ins. Claim				
6/24		XYZ Ins. Ck 319116		324 00		83 00
6/24		Contr. Adj XYZ			50 00	33 00

B40BC-2   PLEASE PAY LAST AMOUNT IN BALANCE COLUMN ⟶

Fig. 7.11 Example of a patient ledger card with entries.

Claims for patients who receive ongoing treatment typically are submitted on a periodic basis—every 15 to 30 days, depending on the policy of the healthcare practice. Most third-party payers have time limits for when claims can be submitted to be considered for payment. The time limit for each of the major carriers discussed in this book is addressed in the corresponding chapters.

Most third-party payers do not pay a claim if the time limit for claim submission has been exceeded. Not all payers deny late claims but instead levy a fine or penalty because of lateness or "past timely filing" status. The time limit in which to file a claim varies from carrier to carrier and often depends on various circumstances, such as the following:

- Whether the provider of the services participates (or is contracted) with the insurer
- Whether the provider of services does not participate (or is not contracted) with the insurer

- The method in which the claim was submitted for payment (e.g., electronic or paper)
- The type of provider who is billing for services (e.g., physician, hospital)
- When coordination of benefits (COB) applies

Generally, an insurer allows a maximum of 1 year from the date of service for submitting a claim; however, some commercial carriers allow 180 days. If there is any question about time limits, the health insurance professional should contact the carrier. It is a good idea to include time limits for each major payer in the same file that contains their claims submission guidelines.

Most insurance companies also have a time limit for filing appeals. The time limit varies from carrier to carrier, and it is important that the health insurance professional keep this information on file so that it is readily available when and if needed.

The health insurance professional should establish a routine for completing and submitting insurance claims (e.g., the end of every week, the 15th and 30th of each month). How often claims are submitted varies depending on:

- The size of the practice
- Office staffing
- The type of claim (e.g., workers' compensation, supplemental security income [SSI], Medicare)
- How the claims are submitted (electronically or paper)
- Whether claims are sent directly or a clearinghouse is used
- The major carriers involved

 Imagine This!

Maise Smyth is employed as a billing and insurance clerk for a family practice physician, Dr. Isaac Finnes, at the Gulf Coast Medical Clinic. Dr. Finnes sees approximately 25 patients a day. The clinic is not yet computerized, so all claims are submitted on paper. To accomplish this challenging workload, Maise has set up a routine for submitting preparation. At the end of each day, she sorts the medical health records by insurer name. Following is Maise's schedule for claims preparation:

1. Monday—Blue Cross and Blue Shield
2. Tuesday—Medicare and Medicaid
3. Wednesday—TRICARE/CHAMPVA
4. Thursday—Magna Insurance (a major carrier in the area)
5. Friday—All miscellaneous carriers, plus claims follow-up

By the end of the day on Friday, all claims for patients seen that week have been prepared and submitted. Because there are only a few miscellaneous carriers, Maise has time on Friday afternoon to do any necessary claims tracking.

 What Did You Learn?

1. What is typically the first thing that happens to a claim when it is received by the insurer?
2. If the insurer determines that a claim is "unclean," what happens to it?
3. Name the two suggested methods for tracking claims.
4. List four common payment errors.
5. Why is it important for the health insurance professional to know how to interpret EOBs?

PROCESSING SECONDARY CLAIMS

It is not unusual for a patient to be covered under two insurance plans. In this situation, the health insurance professional may have to prepare and submit a primary claim and a **secondary claim**. The insurer who pays first is the primary payer, and that payer receives the first claim. The insurance company that pays after the primary carrier is referred to as the *secondary insurer*. This second carrier receives a claim after the primary carrier pays its monetary obligations.

As previously stated, the health insurance professional must determine which coverage is primary and which is secondary. If it is not immediately obvious which payer is primary, the health insurance professional should first ask the patient. If the patient does not know, a telephone call to one of the insurance companies should answer the question quickly and easily.

When using paper claims, if Block 11d is marked "YES," complete fields 9, 9a, and 9d; otherwise, leave these blocks blank. When additional group health coverage exists, enter the other insured's full last name, first name, and middle initial if it is different from that shown in Block 2. If the insured uses a last name suffix (Jr., Sr.), enter it after the last name and before the first name. Titles (Sister, Capt., Dr.) and professional suffixes (PhD, MD) should not be included with the name. The NUCC guidelines allow the use of a comma to separate the last name, first name, and middle initial; however, some third-party payers still do not allow punctuation. Periods are not allowed within the name. A hyphen can be used for hyphenated names.

Occasionally a patient and spouse (or parent) are covered under two separate employer group policies, resulting in what is referred to as **coordination of benefits (COB)**. When a COB situation exists, the health insurance professional should:

- Verify which payer is primary and which is secondary
- Send a copy of the EOB from the primary payer along with the claim to the secondary carrier (if the EOB is not included, the claim is likely to be rejected or delayed pending COB determination)

The rule of thumb for dependent children covered under more than one policy is as follows: the payer whose subscriber has the earlier birthday in the calendar year is generally primary. This is referred to as the **birthday rule**. In the case of divorce, the birthday rule may not apply. The custodial parent's policy may be primary, depending on the legal arrangement ordered by the court.

Medicare secondary payer (MSP) claims are claims that are submitted to another insurance company before they are submitted to Medicare. When a Medicare beneficiary has other insurance coverage that is primary to Medicare, the other insurer's payment information must be included on the claim that is submitted to Medicare; otherwise, Medicare may deny payment for the services. The health insurance professional should check the current guidelines of the specific payer in question when a secondary policy is involved. See Chapter 11 for more information on submitting MSP claims.

 Stop and Think

Fran and Ted Washburn and their two children have been coming to Walden-Martin Family Medical Clinic on a regular basis for nearly 2 years. Shortly before the last office visit, Fran and Ted divorced; Ted changed jobs and moved to a different address in a nearby town. Fran and Ted are both employed, and each is covered under a separate employer group policy. Ted's date of birth is 09/06/85 and Fran's is 08/16/86. Which parent's policy should be considered primary?

What Did You Learn?

1. What is a secondary claim?
2. What document typically must accompany a secondary claim?
3. Explain what is meant by the "birthday rule."

OPTIMIZING THE BILLING AND CLAIMS PROCESS

One of the major problems that healthcare facilities have always faced is the ability to maintain a satisfactory **charge-to-collection ratio**—the total amount of money collected divided by the total amount charged (also referred to as a *collection ratio*.) The following tips can help medical practices improve their billing and claims process, improve office efficiency, and increase revenues:

1. *Create a consistent scheduling plan:* Experts say this is the first step in optimizing billing success. Using an appointment-only scheduling structure promotes insurance verification before services are rendered. It also leads to greater accuracy in acquiring necessary billing information. Facilities that have initiated self-service online scheduling claim that this process has improved its charge-to-collection ratio.

2. *Verify insurance coverage:* Verifying insurance prior to the time of service also boosts the practice's income. Ideally, each patient's insurance should be verified a day or two before his or her scheduled appointment. This process gives the health insurance professional time to reschedule the patient if the insurance cannot be verified. (Methods for verifying insurance are discussed earlier in the chapter.) Designate a single staff member to be the "insurance verification specialist" so that he or she can be free of distractions and more easily identify potential problems before the patient's appointment.

3. *Collect at the time of service:* The chances of collecting patient fees decrease by 40% as soon as they leave your office. Time of service collection techniques include but are not limited to copayments, coinsurances, projected deductibles, and collecting past due balances. Again, to optimize the opportunity for collection at the time of service, experts strongly recommend implementing a structured patient checkout process. By formalizing the checkout process, practices create a key opportunity to collect before the patient exits the office.

4. *Use technology:* With the technological capabilities of electronic medical records and billing software programs, many daily billing functions and decisions can be automated. Many medical billing programs offer automated eligibility checking, charge entry, and claims edits. (See Chapter 16 for more information on the role of computers in health insurance.)

5. *Generate clean claims:* Clean claims are those that are error free and can be processed without any additional information. The more claims that leave the practice clean the first time, the greater the overall financial health of the practice will be.

REAL-TIME CLAIMS ADJUDICATION

Real-time claims adjudication (RTCA) is a means of electronic communication that allows instant adjudication of an insurance claim, including the third-party insurer's payment, adjustment, and patient responsibility. RTCA typically reduces the time frame of claims submission to adjudication from the traditional 2 to 6 weeks to just a few seconds. Healthcare providers are becoming increasingly concerned about the impact that consumer-directed healthcare plans and high-deductible plans have on their ability to collect timely payment from their patients. Because these plans require patients to pay more out-of-pocket costs, some providers believe that collecting payment from patients may become increasingly difficult. Many payers are asking providers not to collect copayments at the time of service; the reason for this is that any attempt to collect at the time of service may create credit balances or patient dissatisfaction. RTCA enables a provider to bill for services before the patient leaves the office and to receive a fully adjudicated response from the insurer at the time of service. With this technology, the provider can send out the inquiry and receive and print the response, displaying total and allowable charges and the patient's responsibility (coinsurance, deductible, and copayment). Providers can be certain of the amount the patient should pay at the time of service.

HIPAA ELECTRONIC CLAIMS STATUS INQUIRY/RESPONSE

An effective way for providers to receive information electronically regarding the status of claims is to use the HIPAA ASC X12N 276/277 Health Care Claim Status Inquiry/Response system. Such inquiries can be conducted through a standard personal computer linked to the Internet. Here's how it works: The provider uses the Health Care Claim Status Inquiry (276 transaction) to request claim status information. The payer then responds to the request through the Health Care Claim Status Response (277 transaction) using the claim status category codes. Claim status category codes indicate the general category of the status (accepted, rejected, additional information requested, etc.), which is then further detailed in the claim status codes. The claim status category codes and claim status codes can be found on the CMS website. The link for this website is listed in "Websites to Explore" at the end of this chapter.

HIPAA requires all payers to use the applicable healthcare claim status category codes and claim status codes. Medicare carriers and fiscal intermediaries (FIs) must update their claims system periodically with the most current codes for use with the ASC

X12N 276/277 Health Care Claim Status Inquiry/ Response. Providers also need to be aware of the new codes that may appear on the response to a claim status inquiry.

? What Did You Learn?

1. Explain what is meant by the "charge-to-collection ratio."
2. True or false: RTCA reduces the time frame of claims submission to adjudication from 2 to 6 weeks to just a few seconds.
3. What is the benefit of RTCA to healthcare providers?
4. What is the name of HIPAA's method for providers to receive information electronically regarding the status of claims?

APPEALS

An **appeal**, as defined in insurance language, is the process of calling for a review of a decision made by a third-party carrier. In many instances, providers of services and patients have the right to appeal a rejected insurance claim or a payment made that the provider or patient (or both) believes is incorrect.

INCORRECT PAYMENTS

Before appealing a payment or a claim, whether with Medicare or a private commercial insurer, the health insurance professional should notify the insurer in writing that there has been an error. Many payers have a set time limit for claim appeals and often print it on their EOB.

A basic rule for appealing a claim is to include a copy of the original claim, EOB or RA, and any additional documentation necessary to provide evidence for the appeal. Cover letters are also effective for appeals and provide the claims reviewer with all necessary information regarding the reason for the appeal. If the payer does not respond to an appeal, the health insurance professional can pursue other alternatives, such as contacting the state's insurance commissioner and sending a clear, well-documented account of the discrepancy. See "Websites to Explore" at the end of this chapter for links to individual state insurance departments.

DENIED CLAIMS

If the health insurance professional believes that a claim has been wrongly denied, an appeal can be filed. The appeal process differs from carrier to carrier; however, appeals generally must be in writing and initiated within a specified number of days—usually 30 to 60. The appeal letter should identify the claim and the reason the health insurance professional believes the claim should be approved.

The appeal is usually sent directly to the carrier with any written comments, documents, records, or other information relating to the claim, even if such information was not submitted with the original claim. The carrier typically reviews the appeal within 30 calendar days. Sometimes the insurance carrier's review committee allows the provider (or their representative) to present the case in person or over the telephone, which allows the individual or committee members conducting the review to ask questions to clarify the reason why the provider (or the provider's representative) thinks the claim is valid. The outcome of the appeal is determined, and the provider is notified verbally or in writing of the decision. This decision is usually final; however, some carriers allow second-level or third-level appeals. The health insurance professional should consult guidelines of individual carriers regarding the steps to take when initiating an appeal.

If the claim remains unpaid after all levels of appeal are exhausted, some options are still open. If there have been repeated problems with a particular carrier, the state insurance commission can be contacted, and the problem case can be outlined in a letter. A second option is to file a complaint with HIPAA. Also, it may be important to get the patient involved because he or she often can make helpful contributions.

HIPAA Tip

The Health Insurance Portability and Accountability Act (HIPAA) provides an online health plan complaint form so that healthcare providers and their staff members can report administrative and payment disputes with health insurers and third-party payers. The form is designed to collect information from physicians on health plan and third-party payer noncompliance with the provisions of the HIPAA Transaction and Code Set Standards.

APPEALING A MEDICARE CLAIM

PARs, suppliers, and patients have the right to appeal any decision about Medicare services, regardless of whether the patient is enrolled in original Medicare, a Medicare managed care plan (Medicare Part C), or a Medicare prescription drug plan (Medicare Part D). (Providers and suppliers who do not accept assignment on claims typically have limited appeal rights.) The type of Medicare coverage dictates the specific appeal filing process. The five levels of the Medicare appeals process are discussed in Chapter 11.

HIPAA Tip

According to Health Insurance Portability and Accountability Act (HIPAA) privacy regulations, documents relating to uses and disclosures, authorization forms, business partner contracts, notices of information practice, responses to a patient who wants to amend or correct his or her information, the patient's statement of disagreement, and a complaint record must be maintained for 6 years.

1. What can the health insurance professional do if he or she believes that a claim has been wrongly denied?
2. If a payer does not respond to an appeal, what alternative does the health insurance professional have?
3. True or false: A Medicare claim cannot be appealed if the provider is a PAR.

SUMMARY CHECKPOINTS

- The five keys to successful claims are as follows:
  - *Verify patient information:* It is important to keep patient information and a signed release of information current to generate clean claims, process them expeditiously, and minimize claim delay or denial because of misinformation. Also, if there is a second insurance carrier, primary status must be determined.
  - *Obtain necessary preauthorization or precertification:* Most insurance carriers have a rule that when a patient is to be hospitalized or undergo certain procedures or diagnostic studies, preauthorization or precertification must be acquired beforehand. If this is not done, the claim is likely to be denied. (Medicare does not require preauthorization for medically necessary services.)
  - *Documentation:* The healthcare provider must document accurate and appropriate information in the patient's medical health record to substantiate the procedures and diagnoses listed on the claim form.
  - *Follow payer guidelines:* Because every third-party payer has slightly different guidelines for completing and submitting claims, the health insurance professional should create and maintain a file for each payer's current guidelines and follow those guidelines to the letter when preparing claims.
  - *Submit a clean claim:* The ultimate goal in the healthcare insurance process is to submit a clean claim, meaning that all necessary, correct information appears on the claim. Clean claims typically are processed quickly.
- An EIN is used by the federal government to identify each employer for a variety of federal reporting requirements. The Secretary of HHS requires that the EIN assigned by the IRS be used as the employer identifier standard for all electronic healthcare transactions as required by HIPAA.
- The claims process includes several steps:
  - When the claim is received by the third-party payer, the claim is dated, attachments (if any) are confirmed, and the claim is processed through an OCR scanner.
  - The claim passes through a series of edits and is compared with the patient's policy to verify coverage, eligibility, medical necessity, exclusions, and noncovered services. "Clean" claims are approved and proceed for payment if payment is due. If there is a problem with the claim, the provider is notified by mail or by telephone.
  - If a claim is not paid and no communication has been received explaining the delay, it needs to be followed up. A mechanism should be in place for tracking claims so that no claim "falls through the cracks." This tracking mechanism could be a suspension filing system or an insurance claims log system.
  - Whether or not a payment is made against a claim, there is always an EOB. Each EOB should be checked to ensure that no error has been made by the insurance carrier. If the claim is denied or there has been a payment reduction, a decision must be made whether to appeal.
  - Interpreting the EOB is key to understanding how the claim was adjudicated. Accurately interpreting an EOB aids in collecting full reimbursement, including any balance owed by the patient.
  - After the EOB has been reconciled, the payment is posted to the patient's account ledger. Participating providers cannot bill the patient for the balance beyond deductibles and copayments; nonparticipating providers can bill for the balance. Medicare copayments cannot be waived except in a legitimate case of financial hardship.
  - Time limits for submitting claims vary with insurance carriers; however, most allow 1 year after the date of service. The health insurance professional should file all claims in a timely manner for the benefit of the practice and the patient.
- The insurance company that pays after the primary carrier is referred to as the *secondary insurer.* This second carrier receives a claim after the primary carrier pays its monetary obligations. Complete the claim for the primary carrier, checking "YES" in Block 11d on the CMS-1500 claim form and completing Blocks 9, 9a, and 9d. Usually the process for sending a claim to the secondary carrier is to include the EOB from the primary carrier with the claim.
- Suggestions for optimizing the billing and claims process include the following:
  - Creating a consistent scheduling plan
  - Verifying insurance coverage
  - Collecting fees at the time of service
  - Using technology
  - Generating clean claims
- The first step in appealing a denied claim (or a claim where the payment has been reduced) is to notify the insurance carrier. Most payers have time limits for appealing claims. The health insurance

professional should check the payer-specific guidelines in appealing claims. If all efforts of appeal are exhausted without success and the health insurance professional is certain that the claim is valid, a remaining option is to contact the state insurance commissioner's office.

Closing Scenario

Zoey has found that following the five keys to successful claims results in fewer errors in claim submissions and has increased the payment rate from insurance companies. Understanding what happens to a claim after it reaches the payer's office has given Zoey insight on how to handle claims that have not been paid in a timely manner.

Zoey also understands the importance of the appeals process. One of the most rewarding aspects of her job is to help patients with filing an appeal for a claim that they feel was not adjudicated properly. She understands the documentation needed to help the insurance company understand why an appeal is being requested.

CHAPTER REVIEW QUESTIONS

1. The first key to successful claims involves:
   a. Obtaining and verifying patient demographic and billing information.
   b. Ensuring that all services provided were documented on the encounter form.
   c. Following all payer guidelines.
   d. Proofreading to ensure that a clean claim is submitted.
2. Preauthorization and/or precertification is only required for:
   a. Fee-for-service policies.
   b. Managed care policies.
   c. Medicare.
   d. All of the above.
3. A clean claim is:
   a. One that is submitted on a CMS-1500 claim form.
   b. One that is submitted electronically.
   c. One that has all of the information necessary for processing, and the information is correct.
   d. One that has the correct EIN on it.
4. A claim is rejected because:
   a. A service is not covered by the policy.
   b. The member is not found.
   c. A maximum benefit has been met.
   d. All of the above.
5. Adjudication refers to:
   a. The health insurance professional's review of a claim before submission.
   b. The payer's examination of a claim and determination of payment.
   c. The clearinghouse's determination of a clean claim.
   d. The insurance company's final decision on an appealed claim.

6. An EIN is assigned by:
   a. Office of the Inspector General.
   b. Centers for Medicare and Medicaid Services.
   c. Department of Health and Human Services.
   d. Internal Revenue Service.
7. Information found on an EOB includes all of the following except:
   a. Amount of billed charges.
   b. Why a service was denied.
   c. Test results.
   d. Date received.
8. Downcoding occurs when:
   a. A provider wants to give a patient a discount on services provided.
   b. An insurance company assigns a substitute code because a provider submitted an out-of-date code.
   c. A provider submits a code for services that are not medically necessary.
   d. None of the above.
9. Ideally claims should be submitted:
   a. Within 30 days of the conclusion of treatment.
   b. Within 120 days of the conclusion of treatment.
   c. Within 1 year of the conclusion of treatment.
   d. There is no time limit for the submission of claims.
10. Sarah and Mitch both carry family policies through their employers. Sarah's birthday is 1/7/1987, and Mitch's birthday is 5/12/1984. Whose policy would be considered primary for their children?
    a. Sarah's policy
    b. Mitch's policy
    c. Whichever policy has the best coverage
    d. Whichever policy is the oldest

WEBSITES TO EXPLORE

- For live links to the following websites, please visit the Evolve website at http://evolve.elsevier.com/Beik/today.
- For detailed, step-by-step guidelines for completing the CMS-1500 (02/12) paper claim form, see http://www.nucc.org/index.php?option=com_content&view=featured&Itemid=101.
- The NUCC updated instruction manual for the updated CMS-1500 (02/12) claim form can be found at http://www.nucc.org/images/stories/PDF/draft_version_0212_nucc_1500_claim_form_instruction_manual.pdf.
- For more information on HIPAA, visit https://www.hhs.gov/hipaa/index.html.
- For general information on claims processing, visit http://www.ama-assn.org.
- For links to individual state insurance offices, visit http://www.naic.org/state_web_map.htm.
- The code sets for use with HIPAA 276/277 Health Care Claim status category codes and Health Care

Claim status codes can be found at http://www. cms.gov/Outreach-and-Education/Medicare-Learning-Network-MLN/MLNMattersArticles/downloads/MM3361.pdf.

- To learn more about the Medicare appeals process, check the following websites using "appeals" as the search word: http://www.cms.gov and http://www.medicare.gov.

Author's Note: Due to the dynamic nature of the Internet, web addresses and/or links provided in this chapter may have changed since publication and may no longer be valid. In such cases, students should select comparable search words to access related sites.

Reimbursement Models

Chapter Outline

I. **Fee-for-Service/Indemnity Insurance**
II. **Managed Care Insurance**
III. **Minimum Essential Coverage and the Marketplace**
IV. **Standard Costs Associated With Insurance Plans**
V. **How Medical Fees Are Determined**
   A. Reasonable and Customary Fee
   B. Resource-Based Relative Value Scale
   C. Value-Based Healthcare
VI. **The Changing Structure of Healthcare in the United States**
   A. Phasing Out Fee-for-Service
   B. New Models of Healthcare Delivery
      1. *Integrated Delivery System*
      2. *Accountable Care Organization*
      3. *Patient-Centered Medical Home*
      4. *Shared Savings*
      5. *Episode of Care/Bundled Payments*
      6. *Partial or Blended Capitation*
   C. On the Horizon
      1. *Single-Payer Proposals*
      2. *Public Option Proposals*
      3. *Medicare Buy-In Proposals*
VII. **Healthcare Reform and Preexisting Conditions**
VIII. **HIPAA and Healthcare Reform**
IX. **Commercial or Private Health Insurance**
   A. Who Pays for Commercial Insurance?
   B. Federal Employees Health Benefits Program
      1. *Federal Employee Program*

C. Employer Coverage Mandate
D. Health Insurance Exchanges
E. What Is Self-Insurance?
   1. *Employee Retirement Income Security Act of 1974*
   2. *Third-Party Administrators/Administrative Services Organizations*
F. Single or Specialty Service Plans
X. **Largest Commercial Insurance Companies**
   A. UnitedHealth Group
   B. Anthem, Inc.
   C. Aetna
   D. Cigna
   E. Humana
   F. Blue Cross and Blue Shield
XI. **Coverage When Traveling Abroad**
XII. **Participating Versus Nonparticipating Providers**
XIII. **Submitting Commercial Claims**
   A. Timely Filing
   B. Filing Electronic Claims
XIV. **Commercial Claims Involving Secondary Coverage**
   A. Explanation of Benefits
   B. Electronic Remittance Advice

Chapter Objectives

After completing this chapter, the student should be able to:

1. Describe fee-for-service (FFS; indemnity) insurance.
2. Explain minimum essential coverage and how it correlates with the insurance marketplace under the Affordable Care Act (ACA).
3. Identify the standard costs associated with health insurance plans.
4. Explain how medical fees are determined using UCR and RBRVS.
5. Describe some of the newer models of care delivery that are changing the structure of healthcare in the United States.

6. Discuss healthcare reform under the ACA and how it modifies previous preexisting condition exclusions.
7. Assess the correlation between HIPAA and healthcare reform.
8. Explain the various characteristics of commercial (private) health insurance.
9. Differentiate between participating providers (PARs) and nonparticipating providers (nonPARs).
10. Review submission guidelines for commercial claims.
11. Outline the procedure for submitting claims involving secondary coverage.

Chapter Terms

accountable care organization
  (ACO)
administrative services organization
  (ASO)
Blue Cross and Blue Shield Federal
  Employee Program (FEP)
carrier
carve-out
coinsurance
commercial health insurance
copayment
credible coverage
data analytics
deductible
electronic remittance advice (ERA)
Employee Retirement Income
  Security Act (ERISA) of 1974
episode of care/bundled payment
ERISA plans

explanation of benefits (EOB)
Federal Employees Health Benefits
  (FEHB) Program
fee-for-service (FFS), or indemnity,
  insurance
fee schedule
grandfathered
group insurance
health insurance exchange
health maintenance organization
  (HMO)
individual market
integrated delivery system (IDS)
minimum essential coverage (MEC)
partial (blended) capitation
participating provider (PAR)
patient-centered medical home
  (PCMH)
pay for performance

point of service (POS) plan
policyholder
preexisting conditions
preferred provider organization
  (PPO)
premium
reasonable and customary fee
resource-based relative value scale
  (RBRVS)
self-insured
single or specialty service plans
supplemental coverage
third-party administrator (TPA)
third-party payer
usual, customary, and reasonable
  (UCR)
value-based healthcare

Opening Scenario

The subject matter of this chapter is traditional fee-for-service (FFS) insurance, sometimes referred to as *indemnity*, *private*, or *commercial insurance*. Emilio Sanchez has worked as a health insurance professional for several years and has seen many changes occur in the health insurance industry. His employer recognizes and appreciates that Emilio is staying current with all of these changes and with the new models of healthcare delivery. Walden-Martin Family Medical Clinic is implementing the patient-centered medical home model, and Emilio has been instrumental in making sure that the policies and procedures are in place to support that.

Patients have expressed appreciation for Emilio's understanding of the ins and outs of FFS insurance. He has been able to explain how the insurance determined what the payment would be and how the patient responsibility is determined.

FEE-FOR-SERVICE/INDEMNITY INSURANCE

Fee-for-service (FFS), or indemnity, insurance has been the traditional type of healthcare policy for many years. FFS medical plans have made up the majority of employer-provided health plans in private industry. To review, FFS insurance pays fees for whatever services are provided to the individuals covered by the policy. As discussed in an earlier chapter, this type of health insurance offers the most choices of physicians and hospitals. Typically, patients can choose any physician they want and can change physicians at any time. In addition, they can go to any hospital in any part of the United States and still be covered. The "Blues"—Blue Cross Blue Shield (BCBS)—are among the best-known providers of FFS health insurance, although they are not the only ones.

We know why people need health insurance. Today's healthcare costs are continually rising, and individuals need to protect themselves from catastrophic financial losses that result from serious illnesses or injuries. If you have health insurance, a **third-party payer** covers a major portion of your medical expenses. A third-party payer is any organization (e.g., BCBS, Medicare, Medicaid, commercial insurance company) that provides payment for specified coverages provided under the health insurance plan. Many Americans obtain health insurance through their employment, through what is referred to as **group insurance**. Group insurance is a contract between an insurance company and an employer (or other entity) that covers eligible employees or members. Group insurance is generally the least expensive kind. The employer pays part or, in some cases, all of the cost.

MANAGED CARE INSURANCE

Another reimbursement model is managed care insurance. With managed care insurance the insurance company contracts with the healthcare facilities to provide care for its members at a reduced cost. The out-of-pocket expenses for members are usually lower than with an FFS policy.

In this model the insurance company controls more aspects of patient care. The member could be limited to certain providers, known as the network. If a provider outside of the network is seen, there may be reduced coverage or no coverage at all. Managed care insurance includes **health maintenance organizations (HMOs), preferred provider organizations (PPOs), point of service (POS) plans**, and several others.

Managed care is discussed in more detail in Chapter 9.

MINIMUM ESSENTIAL COVERAGE AND THE MARKETPLACE

Under the Affordable Care Act (hereafter referred to as the ACA), people who were covered under an employer-sponsored group plan before the enforcement of the act can usually keep their group coverage as long as the plan meets the **minimum essential coverage (MEC)** rule. MEC is the type of coverage people need to have to meet the individual responsibility requirement under the ACA. This includes not only job-based plans but also retiree plans, COBRA coverage, **individual market** policies, Medicare Parts A and C, most Medicaid coverage, the Children's Health Insurance Program (CHIP), TRICARE, and certain other coverage.

An individual market in the context of healthcare means the market for health insurance coverage offered to individuals other than in connection with a group health plan. An individual market policy normally has higher premiums and deductibles than employer-provided plans, and the coverage offered under individual market policies is generally less comprehensive. **Premiums** are the dollar amount that **policyholders** (the individual or firm in whose name an insurance policy is written) must pay the insurance company for healthcare coverage. **Deductibles** are the total amount of medical expenses that the patient must pay out of pocket before the insurance company will begin paying.

The individual mandate rule under the ACA states that everyone must have minimal essential coverage beginning January 1, 2014. The rationale behind this requirement is to spread the risk of the cost incurred for medical treatment of illness or injury. It is important to know that the ACA requires that health insurance plans sold to individuals and small businesses provide a minimum package of services in 10 benefit categories called *essential health benefits,* which include the following:

1. Ambulatory patient services
2. Emergency services
3. Hospitalization
4. Laboratory services
5. Pregnancy, maternity, and newborn care
6. Mental health and substance use disorder services, including behavioral health treatment
7. Pediatric services, including oral and vision care
8. Prescription drugs
9. Preventive and wellness services and chronic disease management
10. Rehabilitative and habilitative services and devices

Well-known marketplace providers from which individual plans are available include but are not limited to:

- BCBS
- Aetna
- UnitedHealth Group
- Humana
- Cigna
- Kaiser

There are different types of marketplace health insurance plans designed to meet different needs. Some types of plans restrict individuals to get care from the plan's network of physicians, hospitals, pharmacies, and other medical service providers. Others might pay a greater share of costs for providers outside the plan's network. Several of these plan types were discussed in Chapter 4 under "The Health Insurance Marketplace."

 Imagine This!

Maria Solaris is 52 years old and has worked out of her home as a self-employed health insurance professional for 10 years. In January 2015, Maria became employed at Mid-Prairie Health Clinic; she joined the clinic's group health plan, which had a $1000 deductible clause in the policy. Because of a family history of colon cancer, Maria decided to have a colonoscopy in February of that same year. In keeping with the rules of the healthcare reform bill, even though she had not yet met her deductible, the clinic's policy paid for the procedure up to the allowed amount without making Maria meet her deductible first.

STANDARD COSTS ASSOCIATED WITH INSURANCE PLANS

Although it is hard to predict the actual annual cost of healthcare under an insurance plan, a few costs are relatively standard, as follows:

• A periodic payment (monthly or quarterly), called a *health insurance policy premium*

• A yearly deductible (out-of-pocket payment) before the insurance company (the company that issues and assumes the risk of the policy) begins to contribute

• A per-visit **coinsurance** (percentage of healthcare expenses) or **copayment** (specified dollar amount per visit)

To help clarify the concept of deductibles and coinsurance, if a medical expense is covered by the patient's healthcare plan, he or she might still be responsible for 100% or a portion of the cost; however, any amount paid will count toward the deductible or coinsurance. In other situations, the plan might cover 100% of the cost. As long as the plan's benefits apply to the item or service, it is considered a covered benefit. The extent to which the item or service is covered depends on what it is and on the particular health insurance plan. It is important to note that covered benefits vary from one health plan to the next. For example, one policy might cover trips to the chiropractor with a $20 copayment. Another policy might not cover chiropractic care at all, and any chiropractor visits would have to be paid entirely out of pocket (and the payments would not count toward a deductible or out-of-pocket limit). In general, the more comprehensive the plan (i.e., plans that cover more benefits), the more expensive it will be.

It is important to keep in mind that coinsurance and copayments are not the same thing. A copayment is a specific dollar amount—for example, $20 per visit to an in-network provider or $40 for an out-of-network provider—that the patient is required to pay at the time the service is rendered. Coinsurance is a percentage of the fee that the plan requires the patient to pay. For example, many plans have an 80/20 clause,

meaning that the plan pays 80% of the allowable charge and the patient pays 20% after the deductible has been met. In many cases, copayments are not subject to the deductible, which means that the deductible does not have to be met before copayments can be applied. As a rule, healthcare services that are not covered by the health insurance policy, as well as premiums and copayments, do not count toward satisfying the deductible, but all health plan rules are not the same.

Under the ACA, health plans must provide four levels of coverage: bronze, silver, gold, and platinum (see Chapter 4). Limits have been placed on the maximum amount of out-of-pocket costs that an individual or family must pay per year. In addition, the act has set minimum essential coverage for certain plan types, and no plan can apply a deductible or charge any cost-sharing for specified preventive health services.

The cost of the health insurance coverage plan varies with the level of coverage chosen—the better the coverage, the higher the premiums, and the higher the deductible, the lower the premium. Although today's insurance plans offer choice and security, these advantages are reflected in the cost of the coverage.

HOW MEDICAL FEES ARE DETERMINED

Fees charged for medical services are determined using various methods. A comprehensive listing of medical charges is commonly referred to as a **fee schedule**. A fee schedule is a complete listing of fees set by commercial payers, Medicare, and other government payers to reimburse physicians or other providers/suppliers, typically on an FFS basis. The Centers for Medicare & Medicaid Services (CMS) develops fee schedules for physicians; ambulance services; clinical laboratory services; and durable medical equipment, prosthetics, orthotics, and supplies. These fees are published in regularly updated fee schedules that are made available to healthcare providers.

Although healthcare providers are free to set their fees at whatever level they feel is reasonable, they are obligated to accept no more than the agreed-upon fee schedule when they contract to provide services to the covered beneficiaries of third-party payers. The terms of the contract obligate the payer to reimburse the healthcare provider for either the actual fee charged or the contracted fee, whichever is less.

REASONABLE AND CUSTOMARY FEE

Historically, most insurance plans' reimbursement rates were based on **reasonable and customary fees** (or **usual, customary, and reasonable [UCR]**) for a particular service. The term *reasonable and customary* refers to the commonly charged or prevailing fees for health services within a geographic area. A fee is generally considered reasonable if it falls within the parameters of the average or commonly charged fee for the particular service within that specific community. If the healthcare provider charges $1000 for a specific procedure but most other providers in the same geographic area charge only $600, the policyholder may be billed for the $400 difference. If the provider is a **participating provider (PAR)**, one who participates through a contractual arrangement with a healthcare service contractor in the type of health insurance in question, he or she agrees to accept the amount allowed by the **carrier** as payment in full. The policyholder does not have to pay the $400 difference—it is adjusted off, or deducted from, the patient's dollar balance, which means that the provider absorbs this difference in cost.

 Imagine This!

Jim Benson is seen at Walden-Martin Family Medical Clinic by Dr. Kahn for the removal of a benign cyst of the right hand and is charged $125 for the procedure; however, his insurance company's allowed fee for this procedure is only $95. Jim has an 80/20 coverage plan and has met his yearly deductible. The difference between the two charges, or $30, is deducted from the original charged amount, resulting in an insurance payment of $76. If Dr. Kahn is a participating provider (PAR) with Jim's insurance company, the $30 difference between the original charge and the insurance company's allowed charge would have to be adjusted off of Jim's bill. If Dr. Kahn is a nonparticipating provider (nonPAR), he could bill Jim for this difference. Jim is still responsible for his 20% share of the allowed charge, or $19.

 Stop and Think

Dr. Martin, a family practitioner, asks you, his health insurance professional, for your opinion as to whether he should sign a contract and become a participating provider (PAR) for Western United Insurance. Olympia Products, a manufacturing plant employing 1350 people in the same city, has a group policy with Western United. What is your opinion?

RESOURCE-BASED RELATIVE VALUE SCALE

Resource-based relative value scale (RBRVS) is a system of payments established by the CMS to reimburse healthcare providers for treating Medicare patients. RBRVS takes into account (1) the work done by the physicians; (2) the cost of malpractice insurance; and (3) practice expenses, including staff salaries, overhead, and supplies. To ensure that physician services

across all specialties are well represented, the American Medical Association (AMA) established the AMA/Specialty Society Relative Value Scale Update Committee (RUC). The RUC makes annual recommendations regarding new and revised physician services to the CMS and reviews the RBRVS every 5 years. (RBRVS is discussed again in Chapter 17.)

VALUE-BASED HEALTHCARE

Value-based healthcare is a reimbursement model in which providers are paid based on patient outcomes. The goal is to provide better care to patients and better health for populations, all at a lower cost. A key component of value-based healthcare is care coordination. The primary provider will likely collaborate with other providers to create a plan of care for a patient. By using **data analytics**, the science of analyzing raw data to make conclusions, certain at-risk patient populations can be determined. Once the patients have been identified, steps can be taken to ensure that they are getting the specialized care they need. Analytics can also help to identify gaps in care, such as missed immunizations or patients who have not been in for an annual physical examination.

Incentives are paid to providers who institute measures to identify patients most in need and then provide care to help prevent their health from becoming compromised. To learn more about value-based healthcare, select the applicable link under "Websites to Explore" at the end of this chapter.

? What Did You Learn?

1. A comprehensive listing of medical charges is commonly referred to as a _____.
2. Explain how fees are determined under UCR.
3. With a PAR, what happens to any balance owed after the patient has paid his or her deductible and coinsurance and the insurer has paid the "allowable" fee?
4. What three things does the RBRVS take into consideration when establishing fees?

THE CHANGING STRUCTURE OF HEALTHCARE IN THE UNITED STATES

Today most Americans want access to affordable healthcare services. Accessibility to healthcare is no longer viewed as a privilege but as a right. The question is no longer whether quality healthcare should or will be available, nor even whether the public and private sectors should cooperate in programs of health protection. The question now is how health protection is to be financed; how it is to be made available to all people, including the poor, the disadvantaged, the emotionally troubled, the chronically ill, and the addicted; and how services can be delivered at the right time and place and at manageable costs.

PHASING OUT FEE-FOR-SERVICE

During the years before World War II, FFS originated as "traditional indemnity" health insurance. Under the FFS model, the patient received a service and submitted a claim, and the insurer paid for the expenses incurred in accordance with the patient's insurance policy, which were usually quite comprehensive. With the advent of healthcare reform, FFS insurance is now becoming obsolete. Some experts, in fact, claim that this outdated model of paying for care is partly to blame for the excessive growth in healthcare costs. Under FFS, little was done to discourage unnecessary services. Although most patients were protected from the direct cost of healthcare by insurance, providers tended to practice defensive medicine due to fear of lawsuits and were inclined to order any and all diagnostic tests, whether or not they were necessary.

Shifting from FFS to other types of payment requires realigning the care delivery and payment incentives in the healthcare system. Today, insurers are encouraged to structure their reimbursement models based on the quality and utility of care provided, rather than on the sheer volume of services. The idea of paying for "value over volume" or "paying for performance" is now a common catchphrase in the world of health policy. Some experts even go so far as to say that too much care can be detrimental to health, such as unnecessary or redundant medical imaging scans that expose patients to excessive radiation. Examples of delivery and payment models that move away from FFS are discussed in the following paragraphs.

NEW MODELS OF HEALTHCARE DELIVERY

Due to recent healthcare reform, new models of care delivery that aid the transition away from FFS are being used across the nation. To ensure that our healthcare system is sustainable, change that provides a logical plan to **pay for performance** must occur across all ranges of care, meaning that we need a provider structure capable of accountability, coordination, and timely, data-driven self-evaluation. Accountable care organizations (ACOs) and patient-centered medical homes (PCMHs) are two frequently cited examples of care models, but there are many other options, depending on the preference of the payer, provider, and patient.

Integrated Delivery System

As the healthcare industry changes, one of the results has been the formation of **integrated delivery systems (IDSs),** or integrated care. An IDS is a network of healthcare providers and organizations that provides a coordinated range of services to a defined population and is willing to be held clinically and financially accountable for the clinical outcomes and health status of the population served. A single IDS is responsible for providing all health services, including delivery of care, payment, and risk management. Consumers are provided with a consistent point of access to all services, and their care is coordinated and managed by the IDS. IDS networks focus on improving the health status of the entire community. Important objectives of an IDS include the following:

- Improving quality of care while lowering patient cost
- Reducing administrative and overhead costs
- Sharing risk
- Reducing inappropriate and unnecessary resource use

Although integrated care seems promising, only time will tell whether it will be successful in lowering costs while improving healthcare.

Accountable Care Organization

An **accountable care organization (ACO)** is one of the latest models for delivering health services. It is made up of groups of physicians, hospitals, and other healthcare providers who come together voluntarily to provide coordinated, high-quality care to their patients. In turn, they are provided with financial incentives to provide high-quality care to patients while keeping down costs. The goal of coordinated care is to ensure that patients, especially the chronically ill, get the right care at the right time while avoiding unnecessary duplication of services and preventing medical errors. ACOs are moving rapidly into the private sector and Medicare. In 2019 ACOs served approximately 12.3 million people in the United States.

Patient-Centered Medical Home

The **patient-centered medical home (PCMH)** is a model of care in which a primary provider manages and coordinates the care of all elements of a patient's health with a team of healthcare providers. The PCMH aims to transform the delivery of comprehensive primary care to children, adolescents, and adults. Through the medical home model, healthcare practices seek to improve the quality, effectiveness, and efficiency of the care they deliver while responding to each patient's unique needs and preferences. The PCMH model can lead to higher quality and lower costs and can improve patients' and providers' experience of care.

> ### Patient's Point of View
>
> Charles Johnson, a patient at Walden-Martin Family Medical Clinic, was recently diagnosed with type 2 diabetes. Walden-Martin has adopted the patient-centered medical home model and was able to coordinate all of Mr. Johnson's care within their clinic. Mr. Johnson was able to talk to a dietitian about his new meal plans and to a diabetes nurse educator about how this diagnosis will affect his care plan going forward. Mr. Johnson also met with Emilio to discuss whether his insurance will pay for all of the supplies he needs to monitor his diabetes. In that meeting Mr. Johnson expressed appreciation for his care team. He has family members and friends that have not had that kind of support.

Shared Savings

The Medicare ACO program from the ACA uses a shared savings payment model. A shared savings plan financially rewards providers who come in under a yearly "target" spending goal and adhere to quality standards. Although this model preserves some of the traditional FFS structure, it realigns incentives to encourage quality improvement and cost control.

Episode of Care/Bundled Payments

Instead of reimbursing per service as in FFS, bundled payments give providers a lump sum that represents expected costs for a particular **episode of care**. A **bundled payment** is defined as the reimbursement to healthcare providers based on expected costs for a clinically defined episode of care. Examples of episodes of care for which a single bundled payment can be made include all physician, inpatient, and outpatient care for procedures such as a knee or hip replacement, pregnancy and delivery, or heart attack. Savings can be realized in three ways: (1) by negotiating a payment so that the total cost will be less than with the FFS model; (2) by agreeing with providers that any savings that arise because total expenditures under episode-of-care payment are less than they would have been under FFS will be shared between the payer and providers; and/or (3) from savings that arise because no additional payments will be made for the cost of treating complications of care, as would normally be the case under FFS. This model encourages providers to eliminate unnecessary tests and services while still achieving a good outcome for the patient's health issue. To learn more about episode of care/bundled payments, select the applicable link under "Websites to Explore" at the end of this chapter.

Partial or Blended Capitation

Traditional capitated models of reimbursement pay healthcare providers a flat per-patient fee. Under **partial (blended) capitation** models, only certain categories of services are paid on a capitated basis. A typical scenario in which partial capitation might apply would be where a fixed amount is paid to a primary care practice for primary care services and, in some cases, ancillary services provided under the direction of the primary care practice. Alternatively, specialists may be paid on a capitated basis for services they provide, whereas the primary care services in that same scenario are paid using FFS. Ideally, the partial capitation model encourages providers to be more cost conscious and stay within budget, allowing for more effective care coordination and better risk adjustment mechanisms, and encourages fair compensation to providers who take on sicker patients. In addition, improved health information technology and data sharing enable greater clinical efficiency.

ON THE HORIZON

The discussion on how to best provide health insurance coverage for more people is ongoing. At the time of writing this text, three main categories are being discussed: single-payer proposals, public option proposals, and Medicare buy-in proposals.

Single-Payer Proposals

This option, also known as Medicare for all, involves having a single government-operated healthcare system that would replace the entire health insurance system that we have today. Many other countries have systems like this that have worked well. Some proposals still provide an option to purchase private insurance.

Public Option Proposals

This option allows more people access to our current government-run programs. One proposal would allow individuals to pay a premium to participate in Medicare or Medicaid. Another proposal would create a new public plan, run by the government. These options would be available to certain qualifying individuals. The qualifications have yet to be determined.

Medicare Buy-In Proposals

With the Medicare buy-in proposals, more people could obtain Medicare coverage. One of the options would be to lower the age requirement to allow people ages 50 to 64 years into the program. With this plan, the enrollees would pay the premiums. These proposals would keep the current health insurance system in place.

? **What Did You Learn?**

1. Accessibility to healthcare is no longer viewed as a _____ but as a _____.
2. True or false: Today, insurers are encouraged to reimburse based on the quality and utility of care provided, rather than on the sheer volume of services.
3. Name two new models of healthcare delivery.
4. A network of healthcare providers that provides a coordinated range of services to a defined population, including delivery of care, payment, and risk management, is a(n) _____.
5. Explain the advantages of the PCMH model of care.
6. Bundled payments give providers a lump sum that represents expected costs for a particular _____.

HEALTHCARE REFORM AND PREEXISTING CONDITIONS

We discussed **preexisting conditions**—physical or mental disorders that existed before a health insurance policy was issued for which the applicant (or one of his or her dependents) received treatment by a healthcare provider—in Chapter 4. Prior to the ACA, preexisting conditions were excluded from coverage under some policies, or a specified length of time had to elapse before the condition was covered, typically anywhere from 30 days to 2 years. The ACA changed the preexisting condition requirements. Effective in September 2010, children younger than 19 years with preexisting conditions could not be denied access to their parents' health plan because of a preexisting condition. In line with this change, insurers are no longer allowed to insure a child and, at the same time, exclude healthcare services for that child's preexisting condition. Beginning in 2014, this provision applied to adults as well. Until 2014, however, the preexisting condition exclusion factor was still applicable for adults, and health plans could issue a policy conditionally by providing a preexisting condition exclusion period.

 Imagine This!

Example 1: Eleanor R. is a 46-year-old woman who works as a medical biller/coder in a small rural clinic that does not offer healthcare coverage for its employees. She has hypertension (high blood pressure), but it is well controlled by medication. In 2012 she decided to purchase a private health insurance policy that included drug coverage. The only affordable plan she could find had a 12-month exclusion period for her preexisting condition—hypertension. For the first year of her policy, all claims (including visits to her doctor and her medication) related to her condition were denied. However, within that first year of coverage, she was diagnosed with a heart arrhythmia and type 2 diabetes. Both of these new conditions were covered completely because they were not considered preexisting.

Example 2: Martin F., a 24-year-old man, was employed in 2013 as a health insurance professional at Mid-Prairie Health Clinic. Mid-Prairie allows employees to participate in its group health plan after a 90-day waiting period. Martin has back problems caused by an old sports injury; however, he had never seen a healthcare professional or taken any prescription medications for this condition. He therefore was not subject to any exclusion period for his preexisting condition. Shortly after he started working at Mid-Prairie, his back problem worsened; he was fully covered for all back-related care.

 HIPAA Tip

The Health Insurance Portability and Accountability Act (HIPAA) limits the use of preexisting condition exclusions.

 What Did You Learn?

1. What is a "preexisting condition"?
2. How did the ACA change how insurance plans dealt with a preexisting condition?
3. True or false: Today, the preexisting condition provision under the ACA applies to only children.

HIPAA AND HEALTHCARE REFORM

Prior to the passage of the ACA, the Health Insurance Portability and Accountability Act (HIPAA) provided some protection when people needed to buy, change, or continue health insurance coverage, which included:

- Limiting insurers on the use of preexisting condition exclusions
- Preventing many health plans from denying coverage or charging more for coverage based on the insured's (or a dependent's) health problems
- Guaranteeing, under most circumstances, that when an individual loses a job along with coverage, he or she has the right to purchase new health insurance for himself or herself and the family
- Guaranteeing, in most situations, that when health insurance is purchased, the policy can be renewed, regardless of any of the policyholder's (or dependents') health conditions, as long as premiums are paid

Although HIPAA does not apply in all situations, the law decreases the chance that a person will lose existing coverage, makes it easier for people to switch health plans, and helps someone who has lost coverage through a job-related health plan to purchase new coverage.

The ACA includes amendments to certain provisions of HIPAA to conform to the requirements of the act. For example, HIPAA's rules for demonstrating **credible coverage** (health insurance coverage a person has before enrolling in a new health plan that has been in effect for a specific waiting period) have been replaced by the act's prevention of preexisting condition exclusions. The waiting period limitation applied to health insurance issuers (i.e., state-licensed insurance companies that issue group health products) and insured and self-funded group health plans, whether or not they were **grandfathered**. This took effect for policy and plan years beginning on or after January 1, 2014.

Note: *Grandfathered* means to exempt an individual or a business from new regulations; for example, a new law restricts the size of billboards along a highway to no larger than 4 × 6 feet, but it allows (or grandfathers) larger ones that were erected before the passage of the law to remain.

 What Did You Learn?

1. True or false: The HIPAA law did not address preexisting conditions.
2. True or false: The Affordable Care Act left HIPAA's "credible coverage" rule unchanged.
3. Explain the term *grandfathered*.

COMMERCIAL OR PRIVATE HEALTH INSURANCE

Commercial health insurance (also called *private* health insurance) is any kind of health insurance paid for by someone other than the government. Medicare, Medicaid, TRICARE, and CHAMPVA are all government programs and do not fall into the category of commercial or private plans.

Government health insurance is relatively standard for each program it sponsors, but commercial health insurance includes many variations in price and the kinds of benefits that the policy covers. The rules about a health insurance policy, such as what benefits are received and what rights the individuals covered under the policy have, depend on two things: the type of insurance (e.g., HMO, FFS) and who is paying for it.

 HIPAA Tip

The Health Insurance Portability and Accountability Act (HIPAA) protects millions of American workers by offering portability and continuity of health insurance coverage when they change jobs.

WHO PAYS FOR COMMERCIAL INSURANCE?

The premium for commercial health insurance is usually paid by an employer, a union, an employee and employer who share the cost, or an individual. When the cost of health insurance is shared, the cost to the patient is much less than if he or she were buying health insurance as an individual. Not all jobs come with health insurance, and sometimes individuals are between jobs and not eligible for group coverage. In these situations, it may be necessary to consider a private insurance policy to maintain healthcare coverage.

FEDERAL EMPLOYEES HEALTH BENEFITS PROGRAM

There is one kind of commercial insurance that the government pays for—the **Federal Employees Health Benefits (FEHB) Program**, which is health insurance coverage for the federal government's own civilian employees. Established in 1960, the FEHB Program is the largest employer-sponsored health benefits program in the United States. Federal employees, retirees, and dependents can participate in the program. Approximately 85% of federal employees are enrolled, including covered federally employed spouses and approximately 90% of retirees. Under this program, eligible members of the participating insurance companies have access to a wide variety of healthcare plans. Choices include various types of plans, as follows:

- FFS plans (PPO and non-PPO)
- HMO
- HMO plans offering a POS product
- Consumer-driven health plans (CDHPs)
- High-deductible health plan (HDHP)
- Health reimbursement arrangement
- Health savings account (HSA)

Choices among healthcare plans are available to employees during an open enrollment period, after which the employee will be covered fully in any plan that he or she chooses without limitations regarding preexisting conditions. Premiums vary from plan to plan and are paid in part by the employer (the US government agency that the employee works for); the remainder is paid by the employee.

The FEHB Program under the ACA now covers more than 400,000 young people between the ages of 22 and 26 through their parents' employer-based coverage. In addition, Native American tribes and tribal organizations can buy health coverage for their employees through the FEHB Program. The FEHB Program continues to offer comprehensive preventive services at no cost to the enrollee, and a number of plans have added incentives to enrollees to participate in wellness activities.

Federal Employee Program

The BCBS government-wide Service Benefit Plan, also known as the **Blue Cross and Blue Shield Federal Employee Program (FEP)**, has been part of the FEHB Program since its beginning in 1960. FEP covers roughly 4.5 million federal employees, retirees, and their families out of the nearly 8 million people (enrollees and their dependents), amounting to nearly 60% of those receiving their benefits through the FEHB Program. Blue Cross Blue Shield Association (BCBSA) works with the Office of Personnel Management (OPM) to administer the Service Benefit Plan on behalf of all independent BCBS companies.

 HIPAA Tip

Under the Health Insurance Portability and Accountability Act (HIPAA), group health plans cannot deny an application for coverage solely on the basis of the individual's health status. It also limits exclusions for preexisting conditions.

EMPLOYER COVERAGE MANDATE

Under the ACA, certain business establishments with 50 or more full-time workers must offer affordable health insurance to at least 95% of their full-time equivalent employees (FTEs) and their dependents up to 26 years of age or pay a fee. (An FTE is one who works at least 30 hours a week.) The mandate does not apply to employers with 49 or fewer FTEs. On December 28, 2015, the federal government extended the ACA 2015 reporting deadlines to give employers more time to meet the requirements. The first information returns were due no later than March 1, 2016, or March 31, 2016, if filing electronically. The first individual statements were due no later than February 1, 2016.

Employer group plans must now pass two tests to meet this mandate—they must be affordable and meet the minimum value standard. To be *affordable*, premiums

Table 8.1	Employer Coverage Mandate: 2020 Penalties that Apply for Noncompliance	
NONCOMPLIANCE WITH MANDATE	**PENALTY**	
Company does not offer coverage	$2570 per full-time employee (minus first 30) applies if one full-time employee receives federal premium subsidy for marketplace coverage	
Coverage is not affordable (≤9.86% of income) Plan does not provide "minimum value" (≥60% of total allowed costs)	Lesser of $3860 per full-time employee receiving subsidy or $2570 per full-time employee (minus first 30)	

cannot cost a worker more than 9.78% of his or her income. (This applies only to employee-only coverage because the health reform law does not consider the affordability of family coverage.) To meet the *minimum value standard,* the policy must pay for at least 60% of the employee's collective medical expenses and cover an array of essential health benefits, such as prescriptions and maternity care.

Those companies that do not comply with the coverage mandate face substantial penalties if they do not offer healthcare coverage. This penalty will be assessed even if just one of their workers gets subsidized insurance through an individual exchange. For plan years beginning in 2015, the penalty was $2000 for each full-time employee minus the first 80 employees. For plan years beginning in 2016 and beyond, employers can exclude 30 employees from the penalty calculation. That penalty can be higher if the company offers insurance that is not considered affordable or comprehensive. Table 8.1 explains the requirements under the mandate and the penalties that apply if the firm does not comply.

HEALTH INSURANCE EXCHANGES

Health insurance exchanges, shortened to "exchanges," are a set of state-regulated and standardized healthcare plans from which individuals may purchase coverage that is eligible for federal subsidies. Exchanges are one of the main focuses of the ACA and offer a variety of insurance coverage options for both individuals and small businesses. Exchanges allow people to shop and compare before enrolling in a healthcare plan. State-based exchanges were scheduled to become available in all states by 2014, and earlier in some states. In 2014, when the exchanges were offered, federal assistance was also available for some people, depending on their income level. To learn more about the ACA and health insurance exchanges, select the applicable link under "Websites to Explore" at the end of this chapter.

WHAT IS SELF-INSURANCE?

Some employers are **self-insured,** which means that when an employee needs healthcare, the employer, not an insurance company, is responsible for the cost of medical services. Most organizations that are self-insured are large entities that can draw from hundreds or thousands of enrollees. As with most other areas of health insurance, the ACA has imposed a significant number of requirements regarding both the eligibility for plan membership and the scope of some of the benefits that self-insured plans must provide. What makes self-insured health plans popular is that they are exempt from many of the taxes and mandates that the ACA otherwise imposes on businesses and individuals. In addition, those firms that choose to self-insure can tailor their health benefits to meet the needs of their workers. They do not have to pay for services that their employees neither need nor want.

Employee Retirement Income Security Act of 1974

Self-insured plans are sometimes called **ERISA plans.** The **Employee Retirement Income Security Act (ERISA) of 1974** sets minimum standards for pension plans in private industry, which are how most self-insured employers fund their programs.

Self-insured employers typically set up plans that provide benefits to employees in the form of life, disability, and health insurance; severance pay; and pensions. These benefits are funded through the purchase of insurance policies or through the establishment of trusts, paid for by the employer or by the employer and employee together. The trust money is then invested, and the employer takes a tax deduction for its contribution to the trust. If an employer maintains a pension plan, ERISA applies very specific provisions, most of which are effective for plan years beginning on or after January 1, 1975.

Third-Party Administrators/Administrative Services Organizations

Many self-insured groups hire **third-party administrators (TPAs)** or **administrative services organizations (ASOs)** to manage and pay their claims. A TPA is a person or organization that processes claims and performs other contractual administrative services. An ASO, similar to a TPA, provides a wide variety of health insurance administrative services for organizations that have chosen to self-fund their health benefits. TPAs and ASOs are neither health plans nor insurers but rather organizations that provide claims-paying functions for the clients they service. Although historically TPAs and ASOs only paid claims, their functions are expanding. They now typically perform additional functions, such as:
- General administrative tasks
- Planning
- Marketing
- Human resources management
- Financing and accounting

SINGLE OR SPECIALTY SERVICE PLANS

Single or specialty service plans are health plans that provide services only in certain health specialties, such as vision or dental plans. These specialty plans developed as people realized that eliminating a specific category of healthcare might slow the rate of increasing costs for healthcare in general and assist the management of care within these specialties. Eliminating a certain specialty of services from coverage under the healthcare policy is referred to as a **carve-out**. Vision and dental plans have often been add-on or **supplemental coverage** to health plans. Single or specialty service plans do not fall under the rules of the ACA.

◎ HIPAA Tip

There is one major exception to the Health Insurance Portability and Accountability Act (HIPAA) rule on insurance portability: it provides no protection for switching from one individual health plan to another individual plan.

? What Did You Learn?

1. Who pays for commercial insurance?
2. Name the one kind of commercial insurance the government pays for.
3. What role does BCBS play in the FEP?
4. Explain the "employer coverage mandate."
5. Employer group plans must now pass two tests to meet the employer coverage mandate; they must be _____ and _____.
6. True or false: Companies with fewer than 50 people on staff, which make up the largest percentage of businesses, are not subject to the employer coverage mandate.
7. A _____ is a set of state-regulated and standardized healthcare plans from which individuals may purchase coverage that is eligible for federal subsidies.

LARGEST COMMERCIAL INSURANCE COMPANIES

The insurance industry is ever changing, as are the top insurance companies. In this section we take a look at the largest insurance companies, at this time, providing commercial insurance. Most have been around for many years and have adapted to the changing world of health insurance. They offer traditional insurance as well as managed care options. In this chapter we focus on the traditional insurance offerings.

UNITEDHEALTH GROUP

In 1977 UnitedHealthcare was founded. The name was changed to UnitedHealth Group in 1988. The American Association of Retired Persons (AARP) chose UnitedHealth Group to provide coverage to its members in 1997. The company provides insurance coverage for long-term care, Medicaid participants, elderly individuals, and people with chronic illnesses.

In addition to providing health insurance plans, UnitedHealth Group also provides benchmarking tools for providers so that they can improve the quality of care provided to patients. In 2018 it had 49.5 million members.

ANTHEM, INC.

This company was formed when WellPoint Health Networks Inc. and Anthem Inc. merged in 2004. The company was known as WellPoint, Inc. until December 2014, when the name was changed to Anthem, Inc. In 1993 Anthem merged with BCBS of Kentucky. This was the first cross-state merger of two Blue plans. Anthem is now an independent licensee of BCBSA in 14 states. In addition to providing health insurance plans, it also offers life and disability insurance benefits, dental, vision, behavioral health benefit services, long-term care insurance, and flexible spending accounts. In 2020 it had 70 million members.

AETNA

Aetna started out as a life insurance company in 1850. It wasn't until 1899 that it entered the health insurance business. At that time, you could obtain the health insurance only if you had a life or accident policy. In addition to health insurance, Aetna provides liability insurance, workers' compensation policies, and financial planning services. In 1966 it paid the first Medicare claim. In 2020 it had 22.1 million members.

CIGNA

Cigna is the result of a 1982 merger between Connecticut General Life Insurance Company (CG) and INA Corporation. Both organizations have their roots in life insurance and liability protection. In 1937 CG became a leader in providing group health insurance policies covering hospital and surgery charges. In 1950, for the first time in the United States, CG offered major medical insurance. In 2004 Cigna turned its focus to health insurance products. In 2020 it had 20.4 million members.

HUMANA

Humana was founded in 1961 and was known as Extendicare. Under this name it was a nursing home company. In 1974 the name was changed to Humana, and the focus changed to running hospitals. In 1984 Humana created its own health insurance plan while continuing to run hospitals. In 2006 Humana started RightSource, a mail-order pharmacy business. In 2020 it had 16.6 million members.

BLUE CROSS AND BLUE SHIELD

For more than 80 years, BCBS companies have been leaders in healthcare coverage for Americans. BCBSA is a federation of 36 separate organizations and companies. Although it is no longer one of the 5 top insurance companies in the United States, it provides health insurance to more than 106 million people. Initially, the two entities developed separately in the early 20th century, with Blue Cross providing coverage for hospital services and Blue Shield covering physicians' services. BCBS companies continue to provide local leadership and solutions to promote safe, high-quality, and affordable care. To learn more about BCBS and its history, see "Websites to Explore" at the end of this chapter.

 What Did You Learn?

1. What are the top three largest commercial insurance companies?
2. Which company started a mail-order pharmacy business?
3. Which company works closely with BCBSA?
4. Which company has the most members as of 2018?

COVERAGE WHEN TRAVELING ABROAD

Do health insurance companies cover their members when they travel abroad? Many Americans are unclear whether their domestic health insurance will pay providers' charges while traveling outside of the United States. Experts advise that before traveling out of the country, you should inquire with the customer service department as to the limitations of your health plan and verify whether your emergency medical coverage extends outside the United States. For example:

• If I get sick or injured abroad, will my policy cover me?
• Does my policy cover preexisting conditions outside the United States?
• Will I have to pay health expenses out-of-pocket and then file a claim for reimbursement?

PARTICIPATING VERSUS NONPARTICIPATING PROVIDERS

To review what was covered in Chapter 4, a PAR enters into a contractual agreement with a carrier and agrees to follow certain rules involving claims and payment in return for advantages granted by the carrier. Not all insurance companies offer such contracts to healthcare providers, but many do. A PAR agrees to:

• File claims (within the time limit stated in the contract) for all patients insured by that company
• Accept the "allowed" fee as payment in full and write off (adjust) any differences between the fee charged and that which is allowed by the insurance company

In turn, under this contractual agreement, the insurance company agrees to:

• Send payments directly to the provider
• Host periodic staff training seminars
• Offer guides and newsletters at no charge

• Provide assistance with claim problems
• Publish the practice's information in the PAR directory

Providers who are not a part of the previously described contractual agreement are referred to as *nonPARs*. NonPARs do not have to file patient claims and can bill the patient for the difference between their charges and allowed charges. The downside is that in many cases the insurance company mails payments to the patient rather than the provider, and the health insurance professional must collect the fees directly from the patient unless the patient agrees to assign benefits (in writing). Benefits can be assigned by having the patient sign either Block 13 on the CMS-1500 form or a separate assignment of benefits form. Assigning benefits authorizes the third-party carrier to send the payment directly to the provider.

 Imagine This!

Dr. Mueller is a nonparticipating provider (nonPAR) with Blue Cross Blue Shield (BCBS). The medical receptionist neglected to ask new patient Agnes Blank to assign benefits, so BCBS sent the payment for Agnes's medical services directly to her. Agnes cashes the insurance check but fails to pay Dr. Mueller's bill. Statements mailed to Agnes are returned stamped "moved; no forwarding address."

What Did You Learn?

1. Name two things a PAR must agree to.
2. What special benefits are extended to PARs?

SUBMITTING COMMERCIAL CLAIMS

Step-by-step guidelines for completing commercial claims using the CMS-1500 claim form differ widely. The best thing to do is contact the carrier and follow the recommended guidelines for that particular carrier. Some insurers provide step-by-step claims completion guidelines on their website. Other carriers indicate that the National Uniform Claim Committee (NUCC) guidelines be followed. Whatever the case, it is important that the healthcare professional follow the correct guidelines and update the instructions for completing the CMS-1500 form periodically to ensure that any changes are noted. When a patient is covered by an insurance company with which the health information professional is unfamiliar, the carrier should be called and guidelines requested to assist in claims submission and to avoid claim delays and rejections.

Most insurance company member offices publish specialty-specific billing guides to help health insurance professionals code and bill specific services, such as physical medicine, eye care, and home medical equipment. For example, BCBS of Illinois posts a "Guide for Completing the CMS-1500 Claim Form" on its website. These guides can be viewed online under "Provider Guides" on most member websites. Paper copies also are available on request. Keep in mind that claims completion requirements can differ from one commercial carrier to another—even from one BCBS member office to another. Refer to Fig. B.1 in Appendix B for an example of a completed claim for a patient with BCBS health insurance coverage.

TIMELY FILING

The time limit for filing claims varies among third-party payers. Normally, PARs must file claims within 365 days of the last date of service provided to the patient; however, the health insurance professional should be aware of the specific timely filing guidelines stated in the contract, because claim-filing deadlines may differ among commercial insurance payers. If a claim is not filed within the specified filing period, insurance companies normally do not allow benefits for the claim. If payment on the claim is denied for this reason, the provider cannot collect payment from the patient. Unusual circumstances may allow the provider to request payment past the deadline. Situations such as these are handled on a case-by-case basis. If a claim is denied as "untimely" and the provider did submit it on time, an appeal should be filed with proof of timely filing attached to the appeal documents and forwarded to the payer. (Health insurance professionals should visit the website of the specific carrier to determine the deadline for submitting claims.)

FILING ELECTRONIC CLAIMS

If the provider's office is set up for electronic claims filing, the health insurance professional should contact the carrier before submitting the claims directly to find out what format will be compatible. If the provider uses a claims clearinghouse, the clearinghouse manages this process. The Health Insurance Portability and Accountability Act – Administrative Simplification (HIPAA-AS), passed by Congress in 1996, set standards for the electronic transmission of healthcare data and to protect the privacy of individually identifiable healthcare information. It is important that these standards be adhered to.

To make sure that electronic claims have been received by the payer (or clearinghouse) for processing within the timely filing limits, the health insurance professional should review the electronic claims receipt, a report that the carrier normally sends after each electronic transmission. This report is usually available to review within 24 to 48 hours after transmission and confirms timely filing. It also provides a summary of all claims that are accepted, are rejected, and/or contain errors. Accepted claims are passed on to the insurer's internal claims processing system(s) for consideration. Rejected claims appear individually on the report with the reason for rejection. To be considered for further processing, claims with errors must first be corrected and then resubmitted electronically.

> ## ? What Did You Learn?
>
> 1. What is the usual filing deadline for submitting claims?
> 2. If the provider's office is set up for electronic claims filing, how can the health insurance professional find out whether his or her facility is compatible with the carrier's electronic standards?
> 3. What federal legislation set standards for the electronic transmission of healthcare data and to protect the privacy of individually identifiable healthcare information?
> 4. Name the document that guarantees that claims reached the payer or clearinghouse on time.

COMMERCIAL CLAIMS INVOLVING SECONDARY COVERAGE

It is not unusual for a patient to be covered under a second insurance policy. A typical situation occurs when spouses are employed by companies who offer paid, or partially paid, group insurance plans. Because of the rising costs of health insurance, however, dual coverage is becoming less common. When a situation such as this arises, it is important to find out which policy is primary and to submit the claim to that carrier first. Normally, when spouses are covered under separate policies, primary coverage follows the patient. To determine which policy is primary, the health insurance professional should call the employer or contact the third-party payer directly.

EXPLANATION OF BENEFITS

When the primary carrier has processed the claim and payment is determined, a new claim is sent to the secondary carrier with the **explanation of benefits (EOB)** from the primary carrier attached. An EOB, also called a *remittance notice* or *remittance advice*, is a document prepared by the carrier that gives details of how the claim was adjudicated (the process of determining how a claim should be paid or denied after comparing it to the coverage stipulated in the healthcare policy).

An EOB typically includes a comprehensive listing of patient information, dates of service, payments, or reasons for nonpayment (Fig. 8.1). In some situations, as with patients who have both Medicare and Medicaid, there is what is called a *crossover*—that is, the claim is filed first with Medicare, during which any deductible and/or coinsurance is applied, and then it is automatically forwarded to Medicaid. Providers do not bill Medicaid separately. This automatic crossover process is the same for patients with both Medicare and Medigap policies (see Chapter 11).

Explanation of Health Care Benefits

THIS IS NOT A BILL

Page Number
1

Identification No.:	111-23-4567
Patient Name:	Sarah M. White
Provider Name:	Dean P. Locks, MD

MURRAY L. WHITE
3434 West Covington Place
Somewhere, XY 12345

Benefits Summary

Billed Charges	Provider Savings	Other Insurance Settlement	Blue Cross Blue Shield Settlement	Amount You Owe
136.00				136.00

Claim Details

		Notes		Notes		Notes		Notes
Place of Service	OFFICE		OFFICE		OFFICE		OFFICE	
Description of Service	MEDICAL CARE		LABORATORY		LABORATORY		LABORATORY	
Service Date: From/To	12/11 12/11/XX		12/11 12/11/XX		12/11 12/11/XX		12/11 12/11/XX	
Billed Charge	90.00		18.00		18.00		10.00	
Provider Savings (-)								
Contract Limitations (-)			11.00		11.00		6.25	
Copayment (-)								
Deductible (-)	90.00		7.00		7.00		3.75	
Sub-Total				1		1		1
Coinsurance								

Please see the back of this form for the "Definition of Terms."

Group Number	Claim Number	Account Number	Provider Number	Date Received	Date Processed
000059999–2104	05040190981500	A–0000960	17437	01–19–XX	01–20–XX

NOTES

1– YOU MAY BE MISSING OUT ON SAVINGS THAT YOU WOULD RECEIVE IF SERVICES HAD BEEN
   PERFORMED BY A BLUE CROSS AND BLUE SHIELD PARTICIPATING PROVIDER. (Z183)

$107.75 OF THIS CLAIM HAS BEEN APPLIED TO YOUR BASIC BLUE CROSS AND BLUE SHIELD
DEDUCTIBLE. FOR THE PERIOD BEGINNING ON 10/01/XX THROUGH 12/31/XX, THIS PATIENT HAS
SATISFIED $2969.42 OF THE $5000.00 DEDUCTIBLE. (Z551)

530-409 C-5356 (MD) 7/02

Fig. 8.1 Sample explanation of benefits.

NOTES KEY

A. Your benefit plan covers accidental injury, medical emergency and surgical care. Other medical care received in the hospital's outpatient department or practitioner's office is not covered by your benefit plan.

B. The services identified on this claim do not meet the criteria of a medical emergency as defined in your benefit plan.

C. These services and/or supplies are not a benefit for the diagnosis, symptom or condition given on the claim.

D. These services are not covered by your benefit plan as described in the *Services Not Covered* section.

E. Routine physical exams and related services are not covered by your benefit plan as described in the *Services Not Covered* section.

F. These services were not performed within the time limit for treatment of accidental injury.

G. Routine vision examinations, eyeglasses, or examinations for their prescription or fittings are not covered by your benefit plan as described in the *Services Not Covered* section.

H. The services of this provider are not covered by your benefit plan.

I. These services exceed the maximum allowed by your benefit plan as described in the *Summary of Payment* section.

J. These services were received before you satisfied the waiting period required by your benefit plan as described in *Your Payment Obligations* section.

K. These services were not submitted within timely filing limits. Timely filing requires that we receive claims within 365 days after the end of the calendar year you receive services.

L. Using the identification number provided, we are unable to identify you as a member.

M. These services were performed before your benefit plan became effective.

N. These services were performed after your benefit plan was cancelled.

O. This individual is not covered by your benefit plan.

P. This individual may be eligible for Medicare. File this claim first with Medicare, if the individual has no other group health coverage as primary.

Q. The Plan in the state where these services were received will process this claim. Your claim has been sent to that Plan for processing.

R. These services have been billed to the wrong plan. Please forward your claim to the plan named on your identification card for processing.

S. These services are a duplication of a previously considered claim.

T. All or part of these services were paid by another insurance company or Medicare.

U. We have received no response to our request for additional information. Until this information is received, the claim is denied.

V. Personal convenience items or hospital-billed non-covered services are not covered by your benefit plan as described in the *Services Not Covered* section.

W. Services covered by Worker's Compensation are not covered by your benefit plan as described in the *Services Not Covered* section.

X. These services should be billed to the carrier that provides your hospital or medical coverage.

DEFINITION OF TERMS

Billed Charge: The total amount billed by your provider. *(If your coverage is Select and you receive covered services in the office of a Select provider, your coinsurance is based on this amount).*

Coinsurance: The amount, calculated using a fixed percentage, you pay each time you receive certain covered services.

Copayment: The fixed dollar amount you pay for certain covered services.

Deductible: The fixed dollar amount you pay for covered services before benefits are available.

Sub-Total: The amount reached by subtracting from the billed charge the following applicable amounts: provider savings; contract limitations; copayment and deductible. Your coinsurance is calculated on this amount *(unless your coverage is Select and you receive covered services in the office of a Select provider. In this case, your coinsurance is based on billed charge).*

Settlement: The total amount fulfilled by us as a result of our agreement with the provider; or the amount we pay directly to you.

Other Insurance Settlement: The total amount settled by another carrier (or us) because you are covered by more than one health plan.

Provider Savings: The amount saved because of our contracts with providers. For some inpatient hospital services, this amount may be an estimate. See explanation of payment arrangements in your benefits certificate.

Contract Limitations: Amounts for which you are responsible based on your contractual obligations with us. Examples of contract limitations include all of the following:
- Amounts for services that are not medically necessary.
- Amounts for services that are not covered by this certificate.
- Amounts for services that have reached contract maximums.
- If you receive services from a nonparticipating provider, any difference between the billed charge and usual, customary, and reasonable (UCR) amount.
- Penalty amounts for services that are not properly precertified.
- Penalty amounts for receiving inpatient hospital services from a nonparticipating hospital.

NOTICE OF RIGHT TO APPEAL AND ERISA RIGHTS

If you disagree with the denial, or partial denial of a claim, you are entitled to a full and fair review.

1. Submit a WRITTEN request for a review within 180 days OF THE DATE OF THIS NOTICE. Your request should include:
   - Date of your request;
   - Your printed name and address (and name and address of authorized representative if you have designated one);
   - The identification number and claim number from your Explanation of Health Care Benefits;
   - The date of service in question.

2. Send your request to:

Fig. 8.1, cont'd For legend see opposite page.

Stop and Think

Carol Bolton is a computer programmer for American Commuter Services, Inc. She and her dependents are covered under an employer-sponsored group policy, and American Commuter Services, Inc. pays the entire premium. Jim Bolton, her husband, is employed by ESI Repairs and is covered under a similar family plan through his employer. How might it be determined which policy is primary when Carol is seen in the office for her yearly physical?

ELECTRONIC REMITTANCE ADVICE

To save time and money, providers can enroll in an interface program wherein they can receive an **electronic remittance advice (ERA)** that allows payments to be posted to patients' accounts automatically, eliminating manual posting of claim payments to both electronic and paper claims. The ERA is based on a provider's payment cycle and then delivered to an electronic mailbox. As with most electronic processes, the provider must first enroll in the program by completing an ERA form. As a complement to ERA, electronic funds transfer (EFT) is also available from BCBS providers. EFT is a direct deposit method that allows the transfer of payments directly into a provider's designated bank account. It may be necessary to coordinate these electronic interface processes with the provider's software vendor. More information on the ERA is provided in Chapter 16.

What Did You Learn?

1. What is the best way to determine primary coverage for a patient who has two insurance policies?
2. What is the purpose of an EOB?
3. How might the ERA process benefit a healthcare provider?

SUMMARY CHECKPOINTS

- FFS, or indemnity, insurance is a traditional kind of healthcare policy. The insurance company pays a specific percentage of the fees for the services provided to the insured individuals covered by the policy. FFS health insurance offers the most choices of physicians and hospitals. Typically, patients can choose any physician they want and can change physicians at any time. In addition, they can go to any hospital in any part of the United States and still be covered.

- Under the managed care model of reimbursement, the insurance company determines what providers the patient can see. If a provider outside of the network is used, there may be reduced coverage or no coverage at all. If a network provider is used, the out-of-pocket expenses for the patient are usually less than when an FFS model is used.

- Under the ACA, minimum essential coverage is the type of coverage people need to meet the individual responsibility requirement under the act. This includes not only job-based plans but also retiree plans, COBRA coverage, individual market policies, Medicare Parts A and C, most Medicaid coverage, CHIP, TRICARE, and certain other coverage. An individual market means the market for health insurance coverage offered to individuals other than in connection with a group health plan. An individual market policy normally has higher premiums and deductibles than employer-provided plans, and the coverage offered under the individual market policy is generally less comprehensive.

- Common standard patient costs of healthcare under most insurance plans include the following:
  - A periodic payment (monthly or quarterly), called a *health insurance policy premium*
  - A yearly deductible (out-of-pocket payment) before the insurance company begins to contribute
  - A per-visit coinsurance percentage (or a specific dollar amount—copayment) of healthcare expenses

- Two common methods for determining medical fees are UCR and RBRVS. UCR refers to the commonly charged or prevailing fees for health services within a geographic area. A fee is generally considered reasonable if it falls within the parameters of the average or commonly charged fee for the particular service within that specific community. RBRVS is a system of payments established by the CMS to reimburse healthcare providers for treating Medicare patients. RBRVS takes into account (1) the work done by the physicians; (2) the cost of malpractice insurance; and (3) practice expenses, including staff salaries, overhead, and supplies.

- Value-based healthcare is being used more frequently. Under this method providers are paid based on patient outcomes. This provides incentives for the provider to keep the patient healthy. Data analytics are used to determine what patients need to have additional care.

- To ensure that our healthcare system is sustainable, change must occur across all ranges of healthcare that provides a logical plan for paying for performance, meaning that we need a provider structure capable of accountability, coordination, and timely, data-driven self-evaluation. Some of the new models of care delivery being introduced to achieve this goal include but are not limited to:
  - *Integrated delivery system:* A network of healthcare providers and organizations that provides a coordinated range of services to a defined population and is held clinically and financially accountable for the clinical outcomes and health status of the population served.

- *Accountable care organization:* Groups of healthcare providers who team up to provide coordinated, high-quality patient care and, in turn, receive financial incentives to keep costs down. The goal of ACOs is to ensure that patients, especially the chronically ill, get the right care at the right time, while avoiding unnecessary duplication of services and preventing medical errors.
- *Patient-centered medical home:* Through this model, healthcare practices attempt to improve the quality, effectiveness, and efficiency of the care they deliver while responding to each patient's unique needs and preferences, ideally leading to higher quality and lower costs while improving both patients' and providers' experience of care.
- *Shared savings:* Financially rewards providers who come in under a yearly "target" spending goal and adhere to quality standards. Although this model preserves some of the traditional FFS structure, it realigns incentives to encourage quality improvement and cost control.
- *Episode of care/bundled payments:* Instead of reimbursing per service, bundled payments give providers a lump sum that represents expected costs for a particular episode of care. A bundled payment is defined as the reimbursement to healthcare providers based on expected costs for a clinically defined episode of care (e.g., cancer, heart attack, or hip replacement).
- *Partial or blended capitation:* A combination of the traditional capitated model of reimbursement that pays healthcare providers a flat per-patient fee for certain categories of services with payment for ancillary or other services in that same scenario using the FFS payment model.
- The ACA changed the preexisting condition requirements. Effective in September 2010, children younger than age 19 years with preexisting conditions could not be denied access to their parents' health plan because of a preexisting condition. In line with this change, insurers are no longer allowed to insure a child and, at the same time, exclude healthcare services for that child's preexisting condition. Beginning in 2014, this provision applied to adults as well.
- Commercial health insurance (also called *private* health insurance) is any kind of health insurance paid for by someone other than the government. Medicare, Medicaid, TRICARE, and CHAMPVA are all government programs and do not fall into the category of commercial or private plans. There is one kind of commercial insurance, however, that the government does pay for—the FEHB Program, which is government health insurance coverage for its own civilian employees. BCBS also falls into the category of commercial insurance.

- There are many different commercial insurance companies in the United States. The top five companies as of 2018 are:
  - UnitedHealth Group
  - Anthem, Inc.
  - Aetna
  - Cigna
  - Humana
- PARs enter into a contractual agreement with the carrier and agree to follow the payer's specific guidelines for claims and payment in turn for certain advantages granted by the payer. Providers who do not enter into such a contractual agreement with the payer are referred to as *nonPARs.*
- Claims usually must be filed within 365 days after the last date of service provided to the patient; however, the timely filing deadline can vary among payers. Health insurance professionals should follow provider-payer contract guidelines.
- For people who are covered by two different commercial insurance policies, a claim is sent to the primary carrier first. After it has been processed and payment is determined, an EOB, along with a payment (if any), is sent to the provider. A new claim is sent to the secondary carrier with the EOB from the primary carrier attached. In some situations, as with patients who have both Medicare and Medicaid, there is what is called a *crossover;* that is, the claim is filed first with Medicare, for which any deductible and/or coinsurance is applied, and then it is automatically forwarded to Medicaid. Providers do not bill Medicaid separately. This automatic crossover process is the same for patients with both Medicare and Medigap policies.

Closing Scenario

Emilio has been spending some time investigating self-insurance, as Walden-Martin Family Medical Clinic is looking at all options for providing health insurance for their employees. During this research Emilio has discovered that many of their patients are covered by these types of policies. His research is not only benefiting Walden-Martin, but also providing additional information that can be shared with patients.

Walden-Martin has been approached by several large insurance companies that have members in the community about becoming a participating provider (PAR). Walden-Martin has been a PAR for Medicare for many years. Emilio has been asked to look into the benefits of becoming a PAR for these other insurance companies. Given the large number of Walden-Martin patients that are covered by these insurance companies, it would seem to be in the clinic's best interest to become a PAR. It addition, there are many benefits for the patients covered under those policies.

Having an expanded understanding of fee-for-service (FFS) policies has enabled Emilio to better serve the patients of Walden-Martin and to ensure that Walden-Martin is getting compensated at the highest level possible.

CHAPTER REVIEW

1. An example of a third-party payer would be:
   a. A physician.
   b. A hospital.
   c. An insurance company.
   d. An attorney.
2. The reimbursement model that allows for the most choice of providers is:
   a. A health maintenance organization.
   b. A preferred provider organization.
   c. A point-of-service plan.
   d. A fee-for-service policy.
3. Minimum essential coverage includes all of the following except:
   a. Adult vision care.
   b. Emergency services.
   c. Prescription drugs.
   d. Ambulatory patient services.
4. A percentage of healthcare expenses that is the patient's responsibility is the:
   a. Premium.
   b. Deductible.
   c. Coinsurance.
   d. Copayment.
5. A specified dollar amount for each provider visit that the patient is responsible is the:
   a. Premium.
   b. Deductible.
   c. Coinsurance.
   d. Copayment.
6. The system used by the CMS to reimburse providers for treating Medicare patients is:
   a. UCR.
   b. RBRVS.
   c. Value-based healthcare.
   d. None of the above.
7. The model of healthcare delivery that involves a primary care provider, with a team of healthcare providers, managing and coordinating the care of all elements of a patient's health is:
   a. Integrated delivery system.
   b. Accountable care organization.
   c. Patient-centered medical home.
   d. Shared savings.
8. When an employer, rather than an insurance company, is responsible for the cost of medical services provided to an employee, this is called:
   a. Federal Employees Health Benefits Program.
   b. Health insurance exchanges.
   c. Self-insurance.
   d. All of the above.
9. A patient sees a participating provider for a minor surgical procedure and the fee is $350. The insurance company's allowed amount is $300. The deductible has been met, and the patient has 80/20 coinsurance. The insurance company has sent the payment to the provider. How much can the provider bill the patient?
   a. $60
   b. $240
   c. $300
   d. $350
10. A patient sees a nonparticipating provider for a minor surgical procedure, and the fee is $350. The insurance company's allowed amount is $300. The deductible has been met, and the patient has 80/20 coinsurance. The insurance company has sent the payment to the patient. How much can the provider bill the patient?
    a. $60
    b. $240
    c. $300
    d. $350

WEBSITES TO EXPLORE

- For live links to the following websites, please visit the Evolve site at http://evolve.elsevier.com/Beik/today.
- To learn more about the ACA and health insurance exchanges, log on to the following website: https://www.healthcarereformmagazine.com/?s=health+insurance+exchange.
- For more information about value-based healthcare, log on to the following website: https://searchhealthit.techtarget.com/definition/value-based-healthcare.
- For more information about episode of care/bundled payments, log on to the following website: https://innovation.cms.gov/initiatives/bundled-payments/.
- For more information on the BCBS FEP, log on to http://fepblue.org/benefitplans/index.jsp.
- For more information on HIPAA-AS, search the following websites or use "HIPAA Administrative Simplification (HIPAA-AS)" as search words: http://www.hhs.gov/ocr/privacy/hipaa/administrative/index.html and https://www.cms.gov/regulations-and-guidance/administrative-simplification/hipaa-aca/index.html.

- For more information on BCBS, go to the following websites:
  https://web.archive.org/web/20090926122415/
    http://www.bcbs.com/about/history/1980s.html
    and
  https://www.thebalance.com/blue-cross-blue-
    shield-insurance-company-review-1969885.

- To learn about the changes happening to healthcare, go to https://www.ncbi.nlm.nih.gov/pmc/articles/PMC5902765/.

  Author's Note: Due to the dynamic nature of the Internet, web addresses and/or links provided in this chapter may have changed since publication and may no longer be valid. In such cases, students should select comparable search words to access related sites.

9

The Changing Face of Managed Care

Chapter Outline

Chapter Objectives

After completion of this chapter, the student should be able to:

1. Explain the concept of managed care.
2. Discuss the origins of managed care.
3. List the goals of managed care.
4. Identify ways in which managed care is adapting to changes in healthcare.
5. Emphasize challenges that managed care is currently facing.
6. Discuss preferred provider organizations (PPOs), as well as provide names and descriptions of various models of health maintenance organizations (HMOs).
7. Describe other types of managed care organizations (MCOs), as well as define and discuss primary care PPOs and integrated delivery systems.
8. Explain how government-sponsored health programs integrate managed care concepts into their plans.
9. Assess the correlation between managed care and the Affordable Care Act (ACA).
10. Specify organizations that accredit and regulate MCOs.
11. Evaluate the purpose of preauthorization, precertification, predetermination, and referrals.
12. Discuss HIPAA's influence on managed care.
13. Describe the impact of managed care on the physician–patient relationship, as well as on healthcare providers.
14. Analyze the future predictions of managed care.

Chapter Terms

capitation

closed-panel HMO

consultation

copayment

covered entities

direct contract model

enrollees

exclusive provider organization (EPO)

full-service HMO

gatekeepers

group model

health information exchange (HIE)

health maintenance organization (HMO)

high-deductible plans (HDPs)

iatrogenic effects

independent practice association (IPA)

insurance marketplace

integrated delivery system (IDS)

The Joint Commission

managed behavioral healthcare organization (MBHO)

managed care

meaningful use

mixed model

National Committee for Quality Assurance (NCQA)

network

network model

open-panel plan

point of service (POS)

preauthorization

precertification

predetermination of benefits

preferred provider organization (PPO)

primary care physician (PCP)

primary care preferred provider organizations

provider-sponsored organization (PSO)

referral

specialist

staff model

URAC

utilization review

Opening Scenario

Ann Lillian has worked with health insurance for many years. She has seen the changes that managed care has made to how healthcare is provided. She has seen the positives for patients, including lower out-of-pocket expenses. She has also heard the stories on the news about medical cases gone wrong because of a health maintenance organization's (HMO's) refusal to pay for certain services.

Over the years Ann has seen her provider become a participating provider in several preferred provider organizations (PPOs). It has been important for her to understand each plan's requirement for preauthorization. She has developed a list of procedures for each insurance company that requires preauthorization or precertification and is always willing to contact the insurance company if a there is any question. Ann understands that it is in the best interest of the patient and her provider to make sure that everything possible is done to ensure that proper payment is made by the insurance carrier.

WHAT IS MANAGED CARE?

No doubt you have heard the term **managed care**. It became the "buzzword" in healthcare after the enactment of the Health Maintenance Organization Act of 1973. But what exactly is managed care, what is its origin, how has the Affordable Care Act (ACA) affected this type of reimbursement model, what are its challenges in today's insurance marketplace, and what are the current and future trends? This chapter attempts to answer these questions.

Before we go further, it is important that you understand what the **insurance marketplace** is. It is a key provision of the ACA and can be defined as an organization established to provide a selection of structured and competitive options for purchasing health coverage. Also called an *exchange,* the health insurance marketplace offers standardized health insurance plans to individuals, families, and small businesses. Different types of marketplace health insurance plans are available to consumers and are designed to meet different needs. Some types of plans may restrict or encourage you to get care from the plan's network of doctors, hospitals, pharmacies, and other medical service providers. Other plans pay a lesser share of costs for providers outside the plan's network. Depending on how many plans are offered in your area, you may find plans of all or any of these types at each metal level—bronze, silver, gold, and platinum—as well as catastrophic plans (see Chapter 4). Examples of plan types that are included in the marketplace are discussed throughout this chapter, such as an exclusive provider organization (EPO), health maintenance organization (HMO), point of service (POS), and preferred provider organization (PPO).

Managed care is a complex healthcare system in which physicians, hospitals, and other healthcare professionals organize an interrelated system of people and facilities that communicate with one another and work together as a unit, commonly referred to as a **network**. This network coordinates and arranges healthcare services and benefits for a specific group of individuals, referred to as **enrollees**, for the purpose of managing cost, quality, and access to healthcare.

Managed care organizations (MCOs) typically perform three main functions:

- Set up the contracts and organizations of the healthcare providers who furnish medical care to the enrollees
- Establish the list of covered benefits tied to managed care rules
- Oversee the healthcare they provide

Managed care has strongly influenced the practice of medicine. The principles of managed healthcare shown in Fig. 9.1 represent key components in promoting effective managed care techniques that are fair and equitable to physicians in ensuring that high-quality healthcare services are delivered to patients. MCOs and third-party payers are strongly encouraged to use these guidelines in developing their own policies and procedures. In addition, any public or private entities that evaluate MCOs or their contracted associations for purposes of certification or accreditation are encouraged to use these principles in conducting their evaluations.

According to the United States National Library of Medicine, the term *managed care* encompasses programs that are intended to reduce unnecessary healthcare costs through a variety of methods, including:

- Economic incentives for physicians and patients to select cheaper forms of care
- Programs for reviewing the medical necessity of specific services
- Increased beneficiary cost-sharing
- Controls on inpatient admissions and lengths of stay
- The establishment of cost-sharing incentives for outpatient surgery
- Selective contracting with healthcare providers

1. Managed care organizations (MCOs) should encourage access to health coverage—including those individuals with the greatest health risk.
2. MCOs must recognize physicians' principal role in making medical decisions and guarantee strong physician leadership.
3. MCOs should promote members' health by ascertaining that health plans and providers have incentives to provide high-quality medical care.
4. MCOs should be accountable for the health of members by preventing, as well as managing, diseases and illnesses.
5. MCOs are ultimately accountable for the health of the enrollees and for the outcomes of the treatment they receive.
6. MCOs should communicate the outcomes of their services based on valid measures of medical quality.
7. To fulfill their responsibility to society and the communities they serve, MCOs should work together with public-sector agencies to resolve gaps between commercial insurance and "safety net" programs.
8. MCOs can help the government fulfill its responsibility to ensure healthcare for all through the provision of a more cost-effective and comprehensive system of care.

Fig. 9.1 Principles of managed healthcare.

- The intensive management of high-cost healthcare cases

The programs may be provided in a variety of settings, such as HMOs and PPOs.

? What Did You Learn?

1. A key provision of the ACA that can be defined as an organization established to provide a selection of structured and competitive options for purchasing health coverage is known as the _____, also referred to as a(n) _____.
2. _____ is a complex healthcare system in which healthcare providers organize an interrelated system of people and facilities that communicate with one another and work together as a unit, commonly referred to as a _____.
3. The term *managed care* encompasses programs that are intended to reduce unnecessary healthcare costs through a variety of methods. Name at least four of these methods.

ORIGINS OF MANAGED CARE

The origins of managed care actually date back to the 19th century, when the system was introduced to take care of the health needs of specific groups, such as rural residents and lumber, mining, and railway workers and their families. In those early days, enrollees paid a fixed amount to the doctor, who then provided healthcare services under a specific agreement. This fee could be charged monthly or annually and would cover certain services provided by healthcare providers. This concept, however, was not fully endorsed by the American Medical Association (AMA). It took until the 1970s for managed care to gain acceptance and respect among both physicians and the general public. The popularity of managed care was largely due to increasing concern regarding rising healthcare costs, which led to the search for cost-effective healthcare services. In addition, the increase in competition in the healthcare market prompted many healthcare organizations to use this reimbursement model to increase their profits, which caused some misunderstanding of the exact meaning and value of managed care.

It is important to understand that today just about all health coverage plans under the ACA are some type of managed care plan. The days of traditional fee-for-service (FFS, or indemnity) insurance in which patients chose their own doctors, paid for their care, and were reimbursed by their insurance company for some or all of their doctor's bills are disappearing.

? What Did You Learn?

1. Briefly explain the origins of managed care.
2. What was the main reason that managed care became popular?
3. True or false: Today, nearly all health coverage plans under the ACA are some type of managed care plan.

GOALS OF MANAGED CARE

Managed care includes processes by which delivery of proper healthcare is administered and maintained at low costs. The primary aim of managed care is to limit the per-capita spending on healthcare by individuals, which in turn reduces the amount spent on healthcare in the country. Managed care can be defined to include either of the following two components:

- Techniques that help reduce the cost of providing health benefits while improving the quality of healthcare to those organizations using such techniques or providing them as services to other organizations
- A system whereby people who are enrolled can benefit from the healthcare services offered, as well as from financial savings for such services, which are regulated and covered by managed care concepts

The chief goals of managed care include the following:

- To provide adequate and quality healthcare to all enrollees at reduced or controlled costs
- To ensure that the healthcare provided is necessary and suitable for the patient's medical condition
- To ensure that the services are provided by qualified healthcare clinicians
- To ensure that the entire process, as well as the environment, is not restrictive in any way

> **? What Did You Learn?**
> 1. The processes by which delivery of proper healthcare is managed and maintained at low costs can be defined as _____.
> 2. List the chief goals of managed care.

THE CHANGING FACE OF MANAGED CARE

Managed care plans are making important shifts in their overall business strategy to hold on to their share in the new insurance markets. Managed care plans historically have relied on two key strategies to enable them to offer expanded benefits with limited expenditure for consumers and cost control for employers and other customers. One strategy is to use traditional managed care technology to control costs through limited provider networks and primary care **gatekeepers**. (A gatekeeper is a primary care physician [PCP], typically one who is a family practice clinician, such as an internist, or a pediatrician.) This healthcare professional manages the patient's total care, determines medical necessity, and provides access to specialists when needed. The second key strategy is to increase membership enrollment that enables the organization to become more effective in provider negotiations to obtain cost advantages.

> **? What Did You Learn?**
> 1. True or false: Managed care plans are making important shifts in their overall business strategy to maintain their share of today's insurance market.
> 2. Identify the two key strategies that enable managed care organizations to offer expanded benefits with limited expenditure for consumers and cost control for employers.
> 3. The healthcare professional who manages a patient's total care, determines medical necessity, and provides access to specialists when needed is called a _____.

MANAGED CARE'S CHALLENGES

Managed care plans face the challenge of meeting today's marketplace preferences for less restrictive care while still holding down costs. As a result, managed care plans are making important changes in their overall business policies. These less restrictive plans are offering products and services that answer consumer demands for more choice and greater flexibility. In addition, because consumers prefer networks that require plans to include rather than exclude a wider choice of providers, plans are looking for contractual relationships with healthcare providers that are more flexible than in the past. Following are some of the challenges that managed care plans are facing in today's insurance marketplace:

1. **The role of state and federal government:** Government support, intervention, and regulation are having an increasing impact on payer's operations, costs, and marketplace strategies.
2. **Healthcare reform:** Reform legislation is resulting in dozens of new agencies and grant programs in addition to adjustments to the insurance market and resulting reimbursement.
3. **Value-based reimbursement:** The transition to a value-based reimbursement (see Chapter 8) model is going to be a slow one. Most business remains FFS. The infrastructure needed to support value-based reimbursement is quite different from what has been used in the past.
4. **Using big data to improve quality and reduce costs:** This issue goes hand in hand with value-based reimbursement. Good data are needed for the value-based reimbursement model. Even when a more traditional model is used, having good, reliable data can help reduce costs and improve the quality of care.
5. **Consumer response to healthcare changes:** The year 2010 saw many consumers voicing their opinion on product offerings, costs, networks, and reform. Consumers now demand integration between web-based technology and administrative services to improve their total healthcare experience.
6. **Health information exchanges:** An electronic **health information exchange (HIE)** allows healthcare

providers and patients to securely access and share a patient's vital medical information electronically, improving the speed, quality, safety, and cost of patient care. HIEs are a key component of the Health Information Technology for Economic and Clinical Health (HITECH) Act of 2009. The purpose of this act was to encourage healthcare providers in the United States to begin using electronic health records (EHRs).

The HITECH Act outlined the intended plans for the adoption of EHRs through **meaningful use**. (Meaningful use means "providers need to show they are using certified EHR technology in ways that can be measured significantly in quality and in quantity.") Under meaningful use, EHR incentive payments are given to eligible professionals (EPs) and eligible hospitals as they adopt, implement, upgrade, or demonstrate meaningful use of certified EHR technology. In 2018 the meaningful use program was renamed to *Promoting Interoperability*. The focus is now patient health data access and interoperability. The four objectives for 2019 were:

- *Electronic prescribing:* Generate and transmit permissible discharge prescriptions electronically.
- *Health information exchange:* Encourage and leverage interoperability on a broader scale and promote health information technology (IT)–based care coordination.
- *Provider to patient exchange:* Provide patients with electronic access to their health information.
- *Public health and clinical data exchange:* Measures that an eligible hospital or critical access hospital attests to being in active engagement with a public health agency or clinical data registry to submit electronic public health data in a meaningful way using certified EHR technology.

🔆 Imagine This!

Managed care is not a new idea or even a recent one. Its origins can be traced back to the 1880s, when German Chancellor Otto von Bismarck developed a form of prepaid health insurance for his workers as a means of warding off plans for a government-run insurance program in Germany. Here in the United States, the original form of managed care dates back to 1933, when a young California surgeon accepted the invitation of Henry Kaiser to provide his workers with healthcare on a prepaid basis. The Permanente Foundation Hospital was established. The hospital was named after the Permanente River, which never ran dry (*permanente* means "everlasting" in Spanish). Today, Kaiser Permanente is the largest health maintenance organization (HMO) in the United States.

More information on EHRs and meaningful use is provided in Chapters 5 and 16 and on http://www.cms.gov using the search terms "EHR incentive programs" and "meaningful use."

TYPES OF MANAGED CARE ORGANIZATIONS

Although there are many forms of managed healthcare, we are going to concentrate on the major types of managed care plans.

PPOs, HMOs, and POS, three common types of MCOs, are compared with traditional (FFS) insurance in Fig. 9.2.

PREFERRED PROVIDER ORGANIZATIONS

Preferred provider organizations (PPOs) are popular throughout the United States. PPOs typically provide a high level of healthcare and offer a variety of medical facilities to everyone who chooses to participate in them.

Here's how a PPO functions: A group of healthcare providers works under one umbrella, the PPO, to provide medical services at a discount to the individuals who participate in the PPO. The PPO contracts with this network of providers, who agree to offer medical services to the PPO members at lower rates (smaller and lower coinsurance limits) in exchange for being part of the network. This agreement allows the PPO to reduce overall healthcare costs. Two things about PPOs make them popular:

- Members do not have to choose a **primary care physician (PCP)**, a specific provider who oversees the member's total healthcare treatment.
- Participants do not need authorization from the PCP, commonly called a **referral**, to visit any physician, hospital, or other healthcare provider who belongs to the network.

Plan members can visit physicians and hospitals outside the network. However, visits to healthcare providers who do not belong to the PPO network do not have the same coverage as visits to providers within the network, and the amount of money the patient has to pay out of his or her own pocket, the **copayment**, is higher. The deductible normally does not change if and when a PPO member sees a provider outside the network.

Other advantages of PPOs include the following:
- PPO networks are not as tightly controlled by laws and regulations as HMOs.
- Many PPOs offer a wider choice of treatments to members with fewer restrictions than HMOs.

Disadvantages include the following:
- Loosely controlled PPOs are often not much better at controlling costs than traditional FFS (indemnity) health insurance, resulting in higher premiums over time.

PLAN COST	PROVIDER SELECTION	CONSULTS/SPECIALIST	MEMBER OUT-OF-POCKET COSTS
Traditional Insurance	Patient can select any physician, hospital, or healthcare provider (HCP).	Patient can use any specialist. However, some plans require preapproval for certain procedures performed by specialists.	Patients may have to pay an annual deductible. This amount depends on what plan they choose. Patients may also be responsible for coinsurance payments (typically 20% to 40%). Coverage for routine care and drugs varies with the policy.
Preferred Provider Organization	Patients may select any HCP in the network. If they use a provider outside of the network, they pay a larger portion (up to 50%) of the fee.	Patients may use any specialist in the network, but if they use a provider outside of the network, they will pay a larger portion of the fee.	Patients may have to pay copayments for network doctor visits and drugs. When using a provider outside the network, there may be a deductible and then the plan will reimburse at a previously determined percentage of the costs— usually 60% to 70%.
Health Maintenance Organization (HMO)	Patients may only select providers in the network. If they select a provider outside the network without HMO approval, they will pay the entire bill.	The primary care physician (PCP) determines the need for a specialist—if approval is not received, the patient is responsible for the entire bill.	Patients may have to pay copayments for doctor visits and drugs. Patients may be charged copayments for hospital stays and emergency room visits. Usually there are no deductibles.
Point of Service	Patients designate an in-network PCP but may also go outside of the provider network for services.	PCP would refer to an in-network provider, but the patient can choose to go to one outside of the network. The PCP may also refer to a specialist outside of the network if one is not available in-network.	Patients who see in-network providers typically do not have a deductible. Services outside of the network are subject to the deductible, coinsurance, and copayments.

Fig. 9.2 Comparison of types of healthcare plans, providers, consultants, and costs.

- More tightly controlled PPOs come at the expense of the patients' ability to manage their own healthcare treatments.
- The fact that an individual belongs to a PPO may lead the individual to believe that he or she is paying lower premiums than he or she would for traditional healthcare when this may not be the case at all.

! Stop and Think

Ellen Comstock's health insurance carrier is a preferred provider organization (PPO). Soon after her second child is born, Ellen learns that Dr. Susan Wallingford, her obstetrician, has severed her contractual affiliation with the PPO network. Ellen wants to continue seeing Dr. Wallingford. What ramifications should Ellen consider in seeing a provider outside her PPO network?

HEALTH MAINTENANCE ORGANIZATIONS

Under the federal Health Maintenance Organization Act, a business entity must have the following three characteristics to call itself a **health maintenance organization (HMO)**:

- An organized system for providing healthcare or otherwise ensuring healthcare delivery in a geographic area
- An agreed-on set of basic and supplemental health maintenance and treatment services
- A voluntarily enrolled group of people

HMOs provide members with basic healthcare services for a fixed price and for a given period. In return, the participant receives medical services, including physician visits, hospitalization, and surgery, at no additional cost other than a relatively small per-encounter copayment, which is typically $25 to $30 per visit and sometimes less than that.

Each HMO has a network of physicians who participate in the HMO system. When an individual first enrolls in the HMO, he or she chooses a PCP from the HMO network. This PCP serves as caretaker for the enrollee's future medical needs and is the first person that the patient calls when he or she needs medical care. PCPs are usually physicians who practice family medicine, internal medicine, or pediatrics. The PCP determines whether the patient's problem warrants a referral to a **specialist**, a physician who is trained in a certain area of medicine (e.g., a cardiologist, who specializes in diseases and conditions of the heart). If an enrollee sees a specialist withou t the PCP's approval, the HMO normally does not pay the specialist's fees, even if the specialist practices within the network.

HMOs are more tightly controlled by government regulations than PPOs. Members must use the HMO's healthcare providers and facilities, and medical care outside the system usually is not covered except in emergencies. HMOs typically have no deductibles or plan limits. As mentioned earlier, the member pays only a small fee, or copayment, for each visit or sometimes pays nothing at all. Because the HMO provides all of a member's healthcare for one set monthly premium, it is considered in everyone's best interest to emphasize preventive healthcare.

Some HMOs operate their own facilities, staffed with salaried physicians; others contract with individual physicians and hospitals to be part of the HMO. A few do both. An HMO can be a good choice for some individuals; however, there are many restrictions. If its facilities are convenient and the individual wants to avoid most out-of-pocket expenses and paperwork, an HMO might be a good healthcare option. One problem exists, however. Some states, especially those that are predominantly rural, offer few HMO choices. Iowa, for instance, had only 31 functioning HMOs in July 2011, compared with 106 in California. At that time, there were a total of 564 HMOs in the entire United States. In 2016 the total number of HMOs in the United States totaled 472. (Data take into account all licensed HMOs, which may include Medicaid- and/or Medicare-only HMOs.)

Several types of managed care come under the HMO umbrella. We'll look at some of the more common types in the following paragraphs.

Staff Model

A **staff model** HMO is a multispecialty group practice in which all healthcare services are provided within the building(s) owned by the HMO. The staff model is a **closed-panel HMO**, meaning that other healthcare providers in the community generally cannot participate. Providers participating in the HMO are salaried employees who spend their time providing services only to the HMO enrollees. All routine medical care is furnished, or authorized, by a member's PCP. Preauthorization is necessary for referrals to specialists. In a staff model HMO, the HMO bears the financial risk for the entire cost of healthcare services furnished to the HMO's members.

Group Model

In the **group model**, the physicians are not salaried employees of the HMO but rather are under contract with the HMO to receive a certain fee for each patient they see who is enrolled in the HMO's program. Once the HMO has paid the contracted rate, it is up to the physicians' group to decide how money will be dispersed to each individual healthcare provider in the group. Because the group model HMO is owned by the physicians, as opposed to the HMO itself, the group can increase or reduce the size of its staff in any way it sees fit, without first getting the approval of the HMO, contrary to the policies of a staff model. Group physicians receive reimbursement in the form of **capitation**, a reimbursement system in which healthcare providers receive a fixed fee for every patient enrolled in the plan, regardless of how many or few services the patient uses. (The word *capitation* comes from the Latin phrase *per capita*, meaning "each head.")

Imagine This!

Rolling Hills Urgent Care Clinic is a group model health maintenance organization (HMO). The managed care (HMO) insurer has negotiated an agreement with the clinic to pay $100 per month to care for each of the clinic's patients enrolled in the plan, regardless of the amount of services each enrollee uses. The HMO insurer pays the clinic a lump sum each month, and the clinic in turn decides how to distribute the money among each of its member healthcare providers.

Network Model

The **network model** HMO allows multiple provider arrangements, including staff, group, and independent practice association (IPA) structures. It is similar to the group model HMO, but services are provided at multiple sites by multiple groups so that a wider geographic area is served. A network model HMO usually allows the healthcare provider to be paid on an FFS basis, whereas the group practices in the network typically receive a capitation payment from the healthcare plan. The network model is the most common type of HMO.

Mixed Model

Mixed model describes certain HMO plans in which the provider network is a combination of delivery systems. An example of this would be if a staff model HMO decided to contract with either a group model or an IPA (see discussion later) to expand the kinds of treatments it could provide to its patients. In general, a mixed model HMO offers the widest variety of choices and the broadest geographic coverage to its members. Patients often have choices of clinics, laboratories, pharmacies, and hospitals as their providers of care.

Direct Contract Model

The **direct contract model** HMO is similar to an IPA except the HMO contracts directly with the individual physicians. The HMO recruits a variety of community healthcare providers, including PCPs and specialists.

Independent Practice Association

In an **independent practice association (IPA)**, services are provided by outpatient networks composed of individual healthcare providers who provide all needed healthcare services for the HMO. The providers maintain their own offices and identities and see both patients who belong to the HMO and patients who do not. This is an **open-panel plan** because healthcare providers in the community may participate if they meet certain HMO/IPA standards. IPA reimbursement methods vary from plan to plan. This particular model also offers a wide choice to its patients but is the least organized of the HMO models.

Full-Service HMO

A **full-service HMO** is one that provides physical and mental health services. However, most people who have health insurance receive their mental health services through a different organization known as a **managed behavioral healthcare organization (MBHO)**.

Managed Behavioral Healthcare Organization

Many insurance plans contract with MBHOs to provide all of the covered services related to mental healthcare. This arrangement is known as a *carve-out*. For example, if your child needs mental health services, you may need to get a special referral from your primary care doctor before seeing the MBHO provider. If your health plan uses an MBHO, you should be sure that your child's doctor and mental health provider communicate about your child's treatment.

 What Did You Learn?

1. List four types of managed care.
2. Explain how a PPO works.
3. List the main differences between PPOs and HMOs.
4. What is the function of a PCP?

POINT OF SERVICE

The **point of service (POS)** model is a "hybrid" type of managed care (sometimes referred to as an *open-ended HMO*) that allows patients to either use the HMO provider or go outside the plan and use any provider they choose. When individuals enroll in a POS plan, they are required to choose a PCP to monitor their healthcare. This PCP must be chosen from within the healthcare network and becomes the person's "point of service." One disadvantage with POS plans is that some services require claims to be submitted, whereas an HMO does not. However, POS plans are much more flexible than HMOs because enrollees can use physicians who are out of network and still remain covered; however, the coverage may not be as good as when an in-network provider is used, and copayments and deductibles are usually higher than if the individual had remained in the network.

OTHER TYPES OF MANAGED CARE ORGANIZATIONS

Several other kinds of health plans fall under the category of managed care besides PPOs, HMOs, and POS. Keep in mind that "managed" basically means that the plan is usually able to offer more affordable health insurance because it has negotiated in advance with hospitals and doctors. The following paragraphs discuss other types of managed care plans.

Provider-Sponsored Organization

A **provider-sponsored organization (PSO)** is a type of MCO that falls under the Medicare Part C provision of the Balanced Budget Act of 1997. Now referred to as *Medicare Advantage plans*, PSOs provide Medicare beneficiaries with alternatives to original Medicare. The PSO receives a fixed monthly payment from the federal government to provide care for Medicare beneficiaries enrolled in the plan and accepts full risk for the lives of these patients. PSOs may be developed as for-profit or not-for-profit entities, of which at least 51% must be owned and governed by healthcare providers (physicians, hospitals, or allied health professionals), and they may be organized as either public or private companies. A PSO must supply at least 70% of all medical services required by Medicare law and must do so primarily through its network. The remaining services may come from contracts with other providers if necessary.

Exclusive Provider Organization

An **exclusive provider organization (EPO)** is a network of individual (or groups of) healthcare providers who have entered mutually beneficial relationships with an insurer to provide health insurance to subscribers. Similar to other managed care models, the insurer reimburses the EPO enrollee only if the medical expenses are received from the designated network of providers who, in turn, provide medical services at significantly lower rates than they would have under normal circumstances. In exchange for reduced rates for services, medical care providers typically have a steady stream of business.

High-Deductible Plans

High-deductible plans (HDPs), also known as *consumer-directed health plans (CDHPs)*, are becoming increasingly common as employers and health plans shift more payment responsibility to the plan member. HDPs include large deductibles that the family or patient is financially responsible for. For 2020 the Internal Revenue Service (IRS) defines an HDP as any plan with a deductible of at least $1400 for an individual or $2800 for a family. Once the deductible is met, insurance benefits will kick in. The ACA mandates that HDPs purchased after March 2010 provide free preventive services even if the deductible has not been met.

 Patient's Point of View

Ann recently met with a patient, Julia Berkley, whose employer-sponsored health insurance was recently changed to a high-deductible plan. Julia's new deductible is $1500. Julia has questions about what services she will have to pay for out-of-pocket before her deductible is met. Ann assured her that her preventive services would not be subject to the deductible, but services that are not considered preventive would be. Julia's employer has also set up a health savings account (HSA) (see Chapter 4). Her employer makes an annual contribution to help cover the cost of the $1500 deductible. Ann tells Julia that if she needs services before she meets the deductible, a payment plan can be set up.

NEW MANAGED CARE PRODUCTS

The ACA contains many provisions that attempt to link the quality of care with the cost of care. This is a response, in part, to research demonstrating that a single focus on reducing cost is not the entire answer. Instead, it is important to ask what our healthcare dollars are purchasing and how that investment contributes to improved health for consumers. The current system does not assign the responsibility for the overall quality and coordination of the patient's care to any one entity. By creating incentives for integrated care delivery models and paying for coordination and quality of care, the law seeks to rebalance the system's resource allocation and reward the value of care over volume of care.

Primary Care Preferred Provider Organizations

These types of POS plans are hybrids of more traditional HMO and PPO models, though they are licensed as PPOs. The following are characteristics of **primary care preferred provider organizations**:

- PCPs may be reimbursed through capitation payments (i.e., a fixed payment per member per month) or other performance-based reimbursement methods.
- A dollar amount may be withheld from physician compensation that is paid contingent upon achievement of utilization or cost targets.
- The PCP acts as a gatekeeper for referral and institutional medical services.

- The member retains some coverage for services rendered that either are not authorized by the PCP or are delivered by nonparticipating providers. Such coverage is typically significantly lower than coverage for authorized services delivered by participating providers (e.g., 100% compared with 60%).

Integrated Delivery Systems

There are several types of **integrated delivery systems (IDSs)**; some of the more common forms are discussed in this chapter and some in Chapter 8. To review, an IDS represents providers coming together in some type of legal structure for purposes of managing healthcare and contracting with health plans such as HMOs, PPOs, or health insurance enterprises. The IPA, as discussed earlier, is an IDS. Although some IDSs combine different types of providers, the common denominator is the physician. Many types of organizations can exist for the purposes of managing healthcare and contracting with health plans that do not involve physicians (e.g., a multifacility hospital system with affiliated ancillary services), but unless there is a significant physician component (specifically, physicians other than the paid hospital staff), they would not be considered IDSs.

Fig. 9.3 shows how one determines the type of medical plan employers offer. Table 9.1 compares the requirements of four common managed care plans.

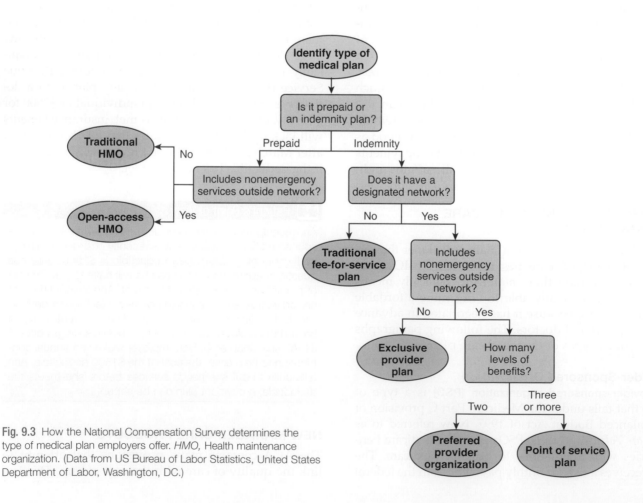

Fig. 9.3 How the National Compensation Survey determines the type of medical plan employers offer. *HMO,* Health maintenance organization. (Data from US Bureau of Labor Statistics, United States Department of Labor, Washington, DC.)

| Table 9.1 | Comparison of the Requirements of Four Common Managed Care Plans |

	REQUIRES PCP	REQUIRES REFERRALS	REQUIRES PREAUTHORIZATION	PAYS FOR OUT-OF-NETWORK CARE	COST-SHARING	DO YOU HAVE TO FILE CLAIM PAPERWORK?
HMO	Yes	Yes	Not usually required. If required, PCP does it.	No	Low	No
POS	Yes	Yes	Not usually. If required, PCP likely does it. Out-of-network care may have different rules.	Yes, but requires PCP referral.	Low for in-network care, high for out-of-network care	Only for out-of-network claims
EPO	No	No	Yes	No	Low	No
PPO	No	No	Yes	Yes	High, especially for out-of-network care	Only for out-of-network claims

EPO, Exclusive provider organization; *HMO*, health maintenance organization; *PCP*, primary care physician; *POS*, point of service; *PPO*, preferred provider organization.

? What Did You Learn?

1. Explain a POS plan.
2. True or false: With an EPO, plan enrollees are reimbursed for medical expenses even when services are received from providers outside the network.
3. True or false: The ACA mandates that HDPs purchased after March 2010 provide free preventive services even if the deductible has not been met.
4. List the primary characteristics of a primary care PPO.
5. A(n) _____ represents providers coming together in some type of legal structure for the purposes of managing healthcare and contracting with health plans such as HMOs, PPOs, or insurance enterprises.

MANAGED CARE AND GOVERNMENT-SPONSORED HEALTH PLANS

The Centers for Medicare and Medicaid Services (CMS) offers managed care plans to Medicare beneficiaries and those who qualify for Medicaid benefits. The following paragraphs briefly discuss managed care and these two government programs.

MANAGED CARE AND MEDICAID

Medicaid managed care provides for the delivery of Medicaid health benefits and additional services through contracted arrangements between state Medicaid agencies and MCOs that accept a set per-member, per-month (capitation) payment for these services. By contracting with various types of MCOs to deliver Medicaid program healthcare services to their beneficiaries, states can reduce Medicaid program costs and better manage the use of health services. As of 2017, 80% of Medicaid enrollees receive their benefits through an MCO, according to Data.Medicaid.gov. Improvement in health plan performance, healthcare quality, and outcomes are key objectives of Medicaid managed care. Updated data for applications, eligibility determinations, and enrollment numbers can be found at http://www.medicaid.gov. Medicaid is discussed in detail in Chapter 10.

MANAGED CARE AND MEDICARE

A Medicare managed care plan is a type of Medicare health plan offered by a private company that contracts with Medicare to provide the beneficiary with all Part A and Part B benefits. Medicare Advantage plans include HMOs, PPOs, private FFS plans, special needs plans, and Medicare medical savings account (MSA) plans. When enrolled in a Medicare Advantage plan, most Medicare services are covered through the plan as opposed to being paid for under original Medicare. Most Medicare Advantage plans offer prescription drug coverage. Plans must be approved by Medicare. Availability and costs may vary by location and carrier.

MEDICARE MANAGED CARE PLANS VERSUS MEDIGAP INSURANCE

Medicare managed care plans fill the gaps in basic Medicare, as do Medigap (Medicare Supplement) policies. However, Medicare managed care plans and Medigap policies operate in different ways. Medigap policies work alongside Medicare to pay the bills: medical bills are sent both to Medicare and to a Medigap insurer, and each pays a portion of the approved charges. Medicare managed care plans, on the other hand, provide all coverage themselves, including all basic Medicare coverage plus other coverage to fill the gaps in Medicare coverage. The extent of coverage beyond Medicare, the size of premiums and copayments, and decisions about paying for treatment are all controlled by the managed care plan itself, not by Medicare. Table 9.2 summarizes the types of Medicare MCOs. Refer to Chapter 11 for more detailed information on Medicare.

! Stop and Think

Imagine you are employed as a health insurance professional with a multispecialty medical group. Mr. Washburn, a new patient, says to you, "I hear a lot of bad things about managed care organizations. Are they all true?" What would you tell him?

Table 9.2 Types of Medicare Managed Care Organizations

TYPE OF MANAGED CARE ORGANIZATION (MCO)	DESCRIPTION
Health maintenance organization (HMO)	Insurers contract with groups of physicians, hospitals, and other providers to provide medical care to their members. Members must use only network providers and are required to select a primary care physician (PCP). Access to specialists requires referral from the PCP. Most services require small or no copayments.
Preferred provider organization (PPO)	Insurers contract with groups of physicians, hospitals, and other providers to provide medical care to their members. Members are not required to select a PCP. Plan's permission is not required for a member to see a specialist for a Medicare-covered service. A small copayment is associated with use of a network provider. Costs are higher for use of an out-of-network provider.
Point of service (POS) plan	Allows members to use medical providers that are not part of the managed care plan's provider network at an additional fee. Plan will pay a percentage of cost for use of services of a healthcare provider outside the network. Member may need plan's approval to receive out-of-network services.
Provider-sponsored organization (PSO)	A plan owned by physicians and hospital(s). Physicians and hospital(s) agree to provide the majority of Medicare-covered services. If unable to provide services directly, they must arrange with other medical providers to furnish needed care.
Private fee-for-service plan	Private insurance companies, approved by the Centers for Medicare and Medicaid Services (CMS), offer their fee-for-service plans to Medicare beneficiaries. Members may use any provider who agrees to the payment terms of the plan or may use other providers and pay the difference between the provider charges and the plan fees.
Medicare medical savings accounts (MSAs)	High-deductible health insurance plan. Members must satisfy the annual deductible through the MSA or personal savings before the health plan pays for medical expenses. CMS will contribute money to the savings account every year. The funds collect interest and carry over each year. The money may be used to pay for medical expenses to satisfy the annual deductible or to cover medical expenses not covered by original Medicare, such as prescription drugs. Either a managed care plan or a fee-for-service plan. Members may not end enrollment until December 31 of each year.

? What Did You Learn?

1. CMS offers managed care plans to beneficiaries enrolled in _____ and _____.
2. Provide some examples of Medicare's managed care plans.
3. True or false: Most Medicare managed care plans offer some type of prescription drug coverage.
4. Medicare managed care plans cover all "gaps" in Medicare, so beneficiaries do not need a _____ (or Medicare Supplement) policy.

MANAGED CARE AND THE AFFORDABLE CARE ACT

We know that one of the major goals of the ACA is to provide quality, affordable care for all Americans. In addition, the act promotes wellness through prevention of disease and early intervention. How does this fit in with managed care? Because wellness and prevention are the mission of most MCOs, experts believe that healthcare reform ultimately will lead to some form of a managed care model with limits on spending, and highly integrated healthcare systems will be in the best position to produce more efficient care that provides value and addresses three dominant healthcare issues: (1) access, (2) cost, and (3) quality.

There have been substantial increases in Medicaid managed care plans, especially in those states that are participating in the Medicaid expansion plan. Across all states, there was an increase of more than 20% between January 1, 2014, and December 31, 2016. Experts who have studied this issue claim that Medicaid-managed long-term services and supports, in particular, offer better patient care along with greater ability to control costs. In the past few years, Medicaid-managed care has witnessed extreme growth in this area. A few years ago, only a few states were using managed care for long-term services. Now, about half of states have shifted from FFS programs to managed care for some or all of their long-term services and supports. The focus is said to be on capitated managed care in which states hire an MCO to run the program and assume most of the risk of caring for people. In addition, a number of states have used their managed care program to expand home- and community-based services. It may be too soon to determine how this will all turn out, but by all indications, as a result of the ACA, managed care will be the future trend.

 HIPAA Tip

The health reform law added to the rights and protections under the Health Insurance Portability and Accountability Act (HIPAA), but the most significant ones didn't take effect until 2014.

What Did You Learn?

1. How did the ACA affect managed care?
2. Identify the type of care predicted to be the focus of future healthcare.

MANAGED CARE ACCREDITATION AND REGULATION

There are many reasons why MCOs need to pay particular attention to the quality of care and service they provide. MCOs are expected to build on and improve their performance every year. Most are regulated from three areas: from states, from the federal government, and from voluntary accreditation. States usually regulate HMOs and other forms of managed care through their department of insurance. Although the states look at areas such as enrollment and utilization review, they are also interested in quality. A majority of states ask HMOs to have specific quality assurance (QA) plans and to take corrective action when problems are noted.

The federal government also has the responsibility for overseeing specific MCOs, particularly plans enrolling Medicaid or Medicare beneficiaries. The federal statute outlines a comprehensive set of benefits that HMOs must provide, as well as specific requirements for the HMO, including reporting on utilization patterns, availability, and accessibility. CMS has specific requirements that must be part of any Medicare or Medicaid contract with MCOs.

Although most MCOs are not required to obtain formal accreditation, the competition from other accredited organizations encourages them to do so. In the area of voluntary accreditation, there are three primary organizations: the National Committee for Quality Assurance (NCQA), The Joint Commission, and the Utilization Review Accreditation Commission (URAC). We look as these three organizations briefly in the following paragraphs.

NATIONAL COMMITTEE FOR QUALITY ASSURANCE

The **National Committee for Quality Assurance (NCQA)** is the predominant accrediting body in managed care today. It is an independent nonprofit organization that measures, assesses, and reports on the quality of care and service in MCOs. NCQA standards are particularly useful in focusing on the MCO's quality program and helping to prioritize important initiatives. In recent years, many businesses and industries are requiring NCQA accreditation.

HIPAA Tip

The Standards and Guidelines for the Accreditation of MCOs, which went into effect in July 2003, make the National Committee for Quality Assurance's (NCQA's) privacy and confidentiality requirements reflect key elements of the Health Insurance Portability and Accountability Act (HIPAA).

THE JOINT COMMISSION

The Joint Commission also evaluates and accredits healthcare organizations. Like the NCQA, The Joint Commission is an independent, not-for-profit organization and is considered the predominant standards-setting and accrediting body in healthcare in the United States. The Joint Commission's standards outline performance expectations for activities that affect the safety and quality of patient care. The Joint Commission is governed by a board of commissioners that includes nurses, physicians, consumers, medical directors, administrators, providers, employers, a labor representative, health plan leaders, quality experts, ethicists, a health insurance administrator, and educators. Its mission is "to continuously improve healthcare for the public, in collaboration with other stakeholders, by evaluating healthcare organizations and inspiring them to excel in providing safe and effective care of the highest quality and value."

The Joint Commission's accreditation is nationally recognized as a symbol of quality that reflects an organization's commitment to meeting quality performance standards. To earn and maintain accreditation, an organization must undergo an onsite survey by a Joint Commission survey team every 2 to 3 years, depending on the type of facility.

HIPAA Tip

Both The Joint Commission and the National Committee for Quality Assurance (NCQA) have incorporated the Health Insurance Portability and Accountability Act (HIPAA) standards into their own accreditation criteria.

URAC

URAC, formerly known as the *Utilization Review Accreditation Commission,* is a nonprofit organization promoting healthcare quality by accrediting many types of healthcare organizations, depending on the functions they carry out. Any organization that meets the URAC standards, including hospitals, HMOs, PPOs, third-party administrators (TPAs), and provider groups, can seek accreditation. Accreditation adds value to these programs by providing an external seal of approval and by promoting quality improvement within the organization as part of the accreditation process.

UTILIZATION REVIEW

Utilization review, sometimes referred to as *utilization management,* is a system designed to determine the medical necessity and appropriateness of a requested medical service, procedure, or hospital admission before, during, or after the event. Utilization review is used in managed care plans to reduce unnecessary medical inpatient or outpatient services. The review is generally performed by the third-party payer's professional staff (nurses and physicians) using standardized medical research data from across the United States and reviewing patient health records in an attempt to make fair and reasonable decisions on behalf of the patients and the third-party payers. Deciding whether or not a service, procedure, or hospital admission is "appropriate" can also be influenced by what is covered in the individual's health insurance plan.

COMPLAINT MANAGEMENT

The individual's right to file a complaint with any managed care carrier about any aspect of health insurance coverage, the carrier's network, and the services provided by healthcare providers is a right guaranteed by federal and/or state government. If the individual prefers, he or she may, upon consent, have the provider file the complaint instead if the provider is willing to do so. A carrier is required to respond to complaints filed by or on behalf of a covered individual within a reasonable period, typically up to 30 days (depending on state law) after the date the carrier received the complaint. Carriers are required to establish a complaint system and to provide covered individuals with a written explanation about the process for filing a complaint.

The organization that handles complaints from consumers and healthcare providers regarding coverage and/or payment under a managed care plan also addresses complaints regarding marketing practices and policy provisions. In addition to filing a complaint, an individual who disagrees with the decision of the carrier to deny, terminate, or limit access to a covered service or benefits for that service has the right to appeal that decision. If a healthcare provider has a specific complaint about how a claim is being handled, the provider may file a claims payment appeal with the carrier in an effort to resolve the situation. A provider must file the appeal within the specified number of days after a claims determination.

Fig. 9.4 shows an example of one state's insurance complaint system. You can research your state's health insurance complaint index by logging on to the Internet and using applicable key words along with the name of your state to locate this information.

 Imagine This!

Texas was the first state to post information about complaints filed against health maintenance organizations (HMOs) and other insurers on the Internet. The Internet Complaint Information System, launched by the state's department of insurance, also includes complaints against automobile and property insurers. The information is updated quarterly, and only complaints that have been investigated and resolved are included. The most common complaints from members concerned prescription coverage, reimbursement, and denial or nonpayment for emergency care. Most provider complaints were related to denial or delay of payment.

A Review of Michigan's Insurance Complaint System

Michigan's Office of Financial and Insurance Services (OFIS) contracted with two organizations to act as independent review organizations to review residents' complaints. The system was put into effect in May 2002. The external review process followed strict policies and procedures; the independent review organizations had 14 days to process the review request. The independent review panel was staffed with qualified, trained, and licensed clinicians, as well as other health professionals who were experts in the treatment of the medical condition that is the subject of the external review.

Findings: During the first 16 months of the insurance complaint program, 418 requests for claim reviews were filed with Michigan's OFIS. From the initial 418 requests, 309 cases went to internal review organizations for adjudication. Of these 309 cases, 143 cases were resolved in favor of the patient. A total of 36 cases were dismissed, resulted in a split decision, or have yet to be decided. The OFIS staff resolved the remaining 72 cases internally, thus avoiding the need for external review. One request for external review was withdrawn.

Fig. 9.4 A review of Michigan's insurance complaint system.

? What Did You Learn?

1. From what three areas are MCOs regulated?
2. Name the organizations from which MCOs typically receive their accreditation.
3. Identify The Joint Commission's mission.
4. What is a utilization review?

CLAIMS MANAGEMENT

The AMA recommends that physicians review health insurance company contracts to confirm the insurer's definition of claims management terms and the verification processes used for cost containment. Insurers often require preauthorization for outpatient diagnostic and surgical procedures. Precertification is required for hospital admission and surgical procedures. Preauthorization and precertification confirm medical necessity before the insurer approves or pays a claim. Predetermination confirms that the patient's policy covers a specific service.

PREAUTHORIZATION, PRECERTIFICATION, PREDETERMINATION, AND REFERRALS

A common method many healthcare payers use to monitor and control healthcare costs is evaluating the need for a medical service before it is performed. Most commercial healthcare organizations and MCOs now request that they be made aware of and consent to certain procedures or services before their enrollees undergo or receive them. Preauthorization and precertification are two cost-containment features whereby the insured must contact the insurer before a hospitalization or surgery and must receive prior approval for the service.

PREAUTHORIZATION AND PRECERTIFICATION

Preauthorization and *precertification* are terms that are often used interchangeably, but both refer to specific processes in a health insurance or healthcare environment. Most commonly, **preauthorization** and **precertification** refer to the method by which a patient is preapproved for coverage of a specific medical service, procedure, or prescription drug. Health insurance companies may require that patients meet certain criteria before they will extend coverage for some diagnostic tests, surgeries, or certain drugs.

The term *precertification* may also be used in the process by which a hospital notifies a health insurance company of an inpatient admission. This may also be referred to as *preadmission authorization.* (It should be noted, however, that definitions of certain terms may vary among insurance companies.)

Preauthorization and/or precertification usually works as follows: The healthcare provider or a member of his or her staff contacts the healthcare plan by phone, fax, email, or online portal or in writing and requests permission to perform the treatment or service proposed. To preapprove a particular procedure or service, the insurance company generally requires that the patient's doctor submit notes and/or laboratory results documenting the patient's condition and treatment history. The plan's representative then either authorizes the service or procedure or does not, depending on what the plan covers and whether the procedure or service is considered medically necessary and appropriate. Often, when a procedure or service is authorized, the insurance carrier assigns a specific identifying number or code, which is included on the claim submission. Insurance carriers also may require diagnosis and procedure codes. Figs. 9.5 and 9.6 are generic examples of a preauthorization form and a precertification form, respectively.

HIPAA Tip

Before transmitting any patient information via fax or email, the health insurance professional must make sure that the individual on the receiving end of the transmission has a "medical right to know" and that the destination location has a security system in place. The Health Insurance Portability and Accountability Act (HIPAA) requires that a "confidentiality statement" be included with each transmittal.

PREDETERMINATION OF BENEFITS

The **predetermination of benefits** process allows the medical provider—at the patient's request—to send the insurance company a statement explaining a proposed treatment or test or the planned purchase of medical equipment. This process makes it possible for the patient to review the cost and possible reimbursement for treatments or tests in advance, which allows him or her to make an appropriate decision before the test or procedure is performed. In addition, if there is a significant difference between the estimated cost and possible reimbursement or if the insurer determines that the test or procedure is not covered under the policy, the predetermination of benefits process offers an opportunity for the patient to discuss the economic issues with the healthcare provider and/or the insurer in advance. The predetermination of benefits process is particularly helpful in a nonemergency situation that involves significant cost, such as elective surgery, expensive medical tests, or the purchase of medical equipment. In such cases, the predetermination of benefits process can help prevent situations in which the patient may be forced to pay significant out-of-pocket costs.

Predetermination Letter

Insurers tell providers which medical services require predetermination letters—whether they include cosmetic, investigational, or experimental procedures—and many insurers ask that these letters be submitted on the provider's letterhead. The purpose of the letter is to request advance verification that the patient is covered for the particular medical service. Failure to submit a precertification letter can result in denial of the claim for payment. The AMA recommends that physicians also submit predetermination letters for services and procedures that an insurer frequently denies as not medically necessary.

Imagine This!

Harold Jenkins had two small growths on his back surgically removed at the same time. When the surgery was completed, the healthcare provider sent Harold a bill for the cost of removing the growths. However, because the growths were both removed at the same time, Harold's managed care organization (MCO) insurer provided reimbursement for less than half of the total bill, claiming that the removal of the second growth was incidental to the removal of the first growth. As a result, Harold was left with a large bill for which he was responsible. The predetermination of benefits process would have given Harold information about billing and reimbursement in advance, after which Harold no doubt would have been compelled to discuss the matter with the provider and the insurer before the surgery.

REFERRALS

A referral is a request by a healthcare provider for a patient under his or her care to be evaluated or treated by another provider, usually a specialist. The purpose of a referral by a PCP to a specialist is to:

- Inform a specialist that the patient needs to be seen for care (or a second opinion) in his or her field of specialty
- Inform the insurance company that the PCP has approved the visit to a specialist because most managed care companies would not pay for care that has not been authorized with a referral

Tri-State Medical Group

PREAUTHORIZATION REQUEST FORM

PATIENT INFORMATION

Last Name: _____ First Name: _____

DOB: _____ Member #: **R**_____ Group #: _____

PREAUTHORIZATION REQUEST INFORMATION

Please list *both* procedure/product code <u>and</u> narrative description:

CPT / HCPCS Code(s): _____ Durable Medical Equipment: ☐ Rental ☐ Purchase

Description: _____

_____

Date of Service: _____ Length of Stay (if applicable): _____

Place of Service or Vendor Name: _____

Assistant Surgeon Requested? ☐ Yes ☐ No **Please list *both* diagnosis(es) code <u>and</u> narrative description:**

1. ICD-10 Code: _____

   Description: _____

2. ICD-10 Code: _____

   Description: _____

Ordering Physician/Provider: _____ Office Location: _____
FIRST <u>AND</u> LAST NAMES PLEASE

Referring Physician/Provider: _____
FIRST <u>AND</u> LAST NAMES PLEASE; REQUIRED FOR PRIME PLANS

Date: _____ Contact Person: _____ Phone: _____

> ***Please Note: Incomplete forms will delay the preauthorization process.***
> ***Requests received after 3:00 PM are processed the next working day.***
>
> **PacificSource responds to preauthorization requests within 2 working days.**
> **A determination notice will be mailed to the requesting provider, facility, and patient.**
>
> **Please attach pertinent chart notes as appropriate.**

FOR INTERNAL OFFICE USE ONLY:

STATUS: APPROVED / DENIED / PENDING / EXPLANATION

DATE: _____ **ACUITY:** _____ **INITIALS:** _____

Reason/Status _____

_____

Field 11 Notes _____ LOS Approved _____

☐ Chart notes filed with preauthorization

Notes _____

Field 10 Facility Copy _____

PO Box 5555 • Somewhere OR 00908 • (541) 555-5584 • (800) 555-6052 x 2584

MEDICAL AFFAIRS DEPARTMENT CONFIDENTIAL FAX: (541) 555-2051

9/8/2003

Fig. 9.5 Generic preauthorization form.

Tri-State Medical Group

FAX Request Form for Precertification Review

To:_____Date:_____

(Area Code) Fax:_____

(Area Code) Phone:_____

Attn:_____

From:_____Fax:_____

Number of Pages (Including Cover Sheet):_____
If there is problem with the receipt of this fax, please call _____.Thank you.

Recipient/Patient Name:_____
Complete Recipient
Address _____

_____

ID Number:_____ CAMA ☐ Yes ☐ No

Requested Admit Date:_____ Diagnosis Code(s):_____

Procedure Date(s): _____

Days Requested: _____ Procedure Code(s):_____

New Admit? ( ) Transfer ( )

Recertification Review? Y( ) If So, Par/Reference #_____

Setting: ☐ Inpatient   ☐ Physician Office
                       ☐ Outpatient   ☐ Out of State

Admit Type: ☐ Non-urgent/Emergent   ☐ Urgent/Emergent

Physician Name:_____ Phone:_____
                                                Fax:_____

Facility:_____ Phone:_____
                                                Fax:_____

Clinical Information:_____
_____
_____
_____
_____
_____

Fig. 9.6 Generic precertification form.

How a Patient Obtains a Referral

The patient schedules a visit with the PCP, who evaluates the problem. If the PCP decides that the patient's condition or symptoms warrant a specialist's opinion, a referral form is completed (Fig. 9.7). In most managed care situations, for the insurance company to recognize the referral, it must come from the patient's designated PCP or a provider who is covering for the PCP. If an orthopedic physician refers a patient to a physical therapist, for example, the patient must also obtain a referral from his or her PCP to process through the insurance company.

Walden-Martin Family Medical Clinic

Date Referred:_____

Referred By:_____ Supervising MD _____ Phone: _____ Fax: _____

Referred To:_____ Fax #:_____

Office Address: _____ Phone #: _____

Patient Name:_____ DOB:_____ Gender: F / M

  Parent's Name (if patient is a minor): _____

Home Phone: _____ Work Phone: _____ Cell Phone: _____

Patient's Address:_____

Authorization: ☐ Not Required ☐ Requested/Pending ☐ Requested/Obtained Auth # _____

Primary Medical Insurance: _____ Subscriber ID#:_____

Secondary Medical Insurance: _____ Subscriber ID#:_____

Worker's Comp Insurance (if any):_____ Employer:_____

  Adjustor: _____ Claim #: _____ Date of Injury: _____

  Comp Address: _____ Comp Telephone: _____

<u>**For Urgent Referrals**</u> (need to be seen within a week), **the referring clinician should call the specialist.**

☐ **Reason for Referral (Symptoms of Concern)** (<u>also</u> send related medical records or dictated summary)

  ☐ Please advise on the patient's care ☐ Please assume care of this patient
  Please ask patient to provide related records from other specialists, if any.

☐ **Relevant lab test and imaging results** (also send related medical records)

☐ **Medications and Dosages tried and outcomes** (if not specifically noted in medical records sent with referral)
  Please ask patient to bring his/her complete medication list with dosages (or bring the meds themselves) to their appointment.

Appointment is scheduled with: _____ on _____ at _____ arrival time

Prior to appointment please obtain the following information, tests, etc: Date faxed to referring clinician:_____

☐ We will contact patient to schedule   ☐ Please have patient call to schedule   ☐ Please call patient to schedule

CONFIDENTIAL NOTICE: This facsimile, including any attachments, is for the sole use of the intended recipient(s) and may contain confidential and privileged information or otherwise protected by law. Any unauthorized review, use, disclosure or distribution is prohibited. If you are not the intended recipient, please contact the sender and destroy all copies of the original facsimile.

Rev 10/10/06

Fig. 9.7 Universal referral form.

Referrals Versus Consultations

There is a significant difference between a referral and a **consultation**. A consultation occurs when the PCP sends a patient to another healthcare provider, usually a specialist, so that the consulting physician may render his or her expert opinion on the patient's condition. The intent of a consultation is usually to obtain an expert opinion only, and the PCP does not relinquish the care of the patient to the consulting provider. In the case of a referral, the PCP typically relinquishes care of the patient, or at least a specific portion of care, to the specialist. The insurance professional must determine whether the visit is a consultation or a referral because this status will affect accurate Current Procedural Terminology (CPT) code selection for the visit.

 Imagine This!

Daniel Bowers visited Dr. Adler, his primary care physician (PCP), with complaints of back pain and numbness in his left leg radiating down to his left foot. Dr. Adler x-rayed Daniel's spinal column, discovered a degenerative disk condition, and subsequently referred him to Dr. Langford, who specializes in degenerative disk disease.

Susan Lane, another patient of Dr. Adler, complained of heart palpitations during an office visit for treatment of a severe case of poison ivy. After performing an electrocardiogram, Dr. Adler informed Susan that he was sending her to Dr. Woodley for a stress electrocardiogram and an echocardiogram to determine whether her palpitations represented a serious cardiac problem.

While in the hospital for a hip replacement, Evelyn Conner was diagnosed with diabetes. Dr. Blake, her surgeon, asked Dr. Martin, a specialist in endocrinology, to manage Mrs. Conner's diabetic condition.

 Stop and Think

Study the three cases in Imagine This! Decide whether each one is a consultation or a referral.

 What Did You Learn?

1. Explain the difference between preauthorization and predetermination of benefits.
2. List some of the typical things that a plan's representative takes into consideration when precertifying a procedure or service.
3. Explain the difference between a referral and a consultation.

HIPAA AND MANAGED CARE

The Health Insurance Portability and Accountability Act (HIPAA), an important federal act introduced in 1996, was intended to improve the efficiency of healthcare delivery, reduce administrative costs, and protect patient privacy. In general, the law required **covered entities** (most health plans, healthcare clearinghouses,

and healthcare providers who engage in certain electronic transactions) to come into compliance with HIPAA standards within a specific period. For the electronic transaction and code sets rule only, Congress enacted legislation in 2001 extending the deadline to October 16, 2003, for all covered entities, including small health plans. The legislative extension did not affect the compliance dates for the health information privacy rule, which was April 14, 2003, for most covered entities (and April 14, 2004, for small health plans).

HIPAA regulations affect the following four areas of healthcare:

- Maintaining patient confidentiality
- Implementing standards for electronic transmission of transactions and code sets
- Establishing national provider and employer identifiers
- Resolving security and privacy issues arising from the storage and transmission of healthcare data

How do these regulations affect managed healthcare? Some experts claim that the cost of complying with HIPAA is in the billions. The repercussions of this high cost likely affect all healthcare, not just managed care. Large medical facilities for the most part were able to shoulder the expense of becoming HIPAA compliant; however, many small one- or two-physician practices found it very difficult. HIPAA zeros in on electronic health information. Even if a solo practitioner has all paper records, as soon as he or she starts dealing electronically with the billing of third-party payers, he or she encounters HIPAA's strict regulations.

 Imagine This!

Elliot Larson was the sole proprietor of a small podiatry practice in southcentral Iowa. He employed two full-time staff members, a receptionist, and an assistant who was a licensed practical nurse. When the Health Insurance Portability and Accountability Act (HIPAA) was enacted, his office was already computerized and submitting claims electronically to a certain major carrier. Dr. Larson's financial advisor calculated that it would cost approximately $50,000 to upgrade his office to HIPAA compliance. Dr. Larson did not want to revert to a manual accounting system; plus, he was under contract to submit claims electronically to the major carrier under which most of his patients had coverage. To justify the cost to upgrade to HIPAA's regulations, he would have to raise his fees. The socioeconomic area in which he practiced was predominantly agricultural, where the farmers and rural people could not afford increased charges. Dr. Larson closed his practice in the small rural town where he'd been practicing for 10 years and joined a multispecialty group in Des Moines.

The consequences of noncompliance are the legal penalties that HIPAA provides for failure to adopt its standards. Fines range from $100 for violating a general requirement to $50,000 or more for more serious offenses, such as wrongful disclosure of individually identifiable health information.

HIPAA Tip

The Health Insurance Portability and Accountability Act's (HIPAA's) impact on managed care organizations (MCOs) is the same as that on fee-for-service (FFS)–type structures. HIPAA does not have a separate set of rules and regulations for MCOs.

 What Did You Learn?

1. List four areas of healthcare affected by HIPAA regulations.
2. True or false: If a practice has all paper records, as soon as it starts billing third-party payers electronically, it encounters HIPAA's strict regulations.
3. What are the consequences of HIPAA noncompliance?

IMPACT OF MANAGED CARE

Since the 1990s, the United States has witnessed a transformation in all phases of the healthcare system, from financing to the way in which healthcare services are organized and delivered. The driving force in this transformation, experts say, is the shift from traditional FFS systems to managed care networks. These changes in the US healthcare system came in response to market forces for cost control, to regulatory initiatives on cost and quality, and to consumer demands for quality care and greater flexibility in provider choice. Because these changes occurred so rapidly and extensively, little is known about the long-term effects of managed care on access to care, cost, and quality of care.

The Agency for Health Care Policy and Research (AHCPR) is the leading federal agency charged with supporting and conducting health services research. The AHCPR's studies are designed to produce information that ultimately will improve consumer choice, improve the quality and value of healthcare services, and support and improve the healthcare marketplace. Most research on managed care has been conducted in HMOs.

IMPACT OF MANAGED CARE ON THE PHYSICIAN–PATIENT RELATIONSHIP

Managed care can affect relationships between physicians and patients in various ways. First, it may change the way in which such relationships begin and end. The typical HMO pays only for care provided by its own physicians. Preferred provider groups restrict access to physicians by paying a smaller percentage of the cost of care when patients go for care outside the network. These restrictions can limit patients' ability to establish a relationship with the physician of their choice. Termination of physician–patient relationships can also occur without patients' choosing. When employers shift managed care health plans that mandate the determination of PCPs, employees may have no choice but to sever ties with the PCP of the previous plan and establish a relationship with a new one.

Managed care arrangements often control patients' access to medical specialists, restricting patients' freedom to choose providers and obtain the medical services they desire. In HMOs, PCPs function as "gatekeepers" who authorize patient referrals to medical specialists. Critics of managed care claim that this gatekeeping lowers the quality of care, whereas supporters believe that gatekeeping yields benefits such as reducing **iatrogenic effects** (a symptom or illness brought on unintentionally by something that a physician does or says), promoting rigorous review of standards of care, and emphasizing low-technology, care-oriented services.

Seeing a physician and the practice as a whole is the main experience of the managed care plan for most patients. If that experience is difficult or substandard, the patient is likely to blame the practice. Whatever help a practice can give its patients in navigating the waters of managed care can reduce problems for everybody.

 Imagine This!

Arnold Talbott is a fabrication specialist with Jones Implement. Employees were covered under a group health insurance contract with Superior Healthcare Systems, a health maintenance organization (HMO), when Arnold first started working for Jones Implement in 1993. Over the years, Arnold and his family established a mutually satisfying patient–provider relationship with Dr. VanHorn, their primary care physician (PCP). In 2004 Jones changed carriers and switched their group coverage to Ideal Health Maintenance Group. Because Dr. VanHorn was not a part of Ideal's network, Arnold and his family had to choose a new PCP and have all of their health records transferred.

IMPACT OF MANAGED CARE ON HEALTHCARE PROVIDERS

Most healthcare providers believe that the shift within the healthcare industry from FFS toward managed care is requiring providers to:

1. Become participants in larger provider practice structures (e.g., single-specialty or, preferably, multispecialty group practices, or IPAs)
2. Become participants in IDSs, which may include acquisition of physician practices by a hospital system
3. Become employees and service providers for large insurance organizations, HMOs, or both.

With the establishment of managed care, such acquisitions are being considered necessary more often by smaller-scale healthcare providers (e.g., sole practitioners, small partnerships and group practices) to satisfy the increasing demands of managed care contracting. Large employers, insurance organizations, and HMOs view this as appealing and seek to contract with healthcare providers who can offer a complete package of "seamless" healthcare services, which satisfies most medical needs within a single IDS. Providers within these more integrated medical organizations are likely to experience greater economic viability as managed care continues to transform the medical environment.

The PCP is considered by most within the medical sector of the healthcare industry to be the future controller of patient flow and revenue-generating potential for fellow practitioners. Functioning in the role of gatekeeper, the PCP is likely to be required to perform a higher level of services that formerly were referred to specialists to control healthcare costs in capitation model healthcare plans.

? What Did You Learn?

1. What is AHCPR, and how does it relate to managed care?
2. How does managed care affect the patient–physician relationship?
3. List ways that managed care affects healthcare providers.

FUTURE OF MANAGED CARE

Many changes are expected to occur with the passage of healthcare reform laws, and managed care programs certainly will be affected. Before the ACA, it was estimated that 48 million Americans were uninsured. Nearly 20 million people gained coverage with the ACA. Although cost and efficiency still will be important selling points, quality of services also will come into play. One expert has gone so far as to suggest that along with new systems of managed care and continuing systems of indemnity plans, healthcare providers may even organize and offer services directly to employers, thus eliminating the intermediaries. This development may be beneficial to all involved—employers would pay less, providers would be better compensated, and patients would receive better care. Implementation of the ACA may result in changes to employment-based medical plans. As the data from employers continue to be collected and the findings reported, new plan names may arise and new plan features may be identified. The US Bureau of Labor Statistics will collect and update the data as needed to monitor this ever-changing health insurance scenario.

Managed care is evolving and is very much a work in progress. It will be interesting to see what the future brings.

? What Did You Learn?

1. Name some of the changes predicted for managed care.
2. What do you think is meant by this statement: "Managed care is evolving and is very much a work in progress"?

SUMMARY CHECKPOINTS

- Managed care is a healthcare system in which insurance companies attempt to control the cost, quality, and access of medical care provided to individuals enrolled in their plan by limiting the reimbursement levels paid to providers, by reducing utilization, or both.
- The origins of managed care date back to the 19th century. It was introduced to take care of the health needs of specific groups. Enrollees paid a fixed fee monthly or annually to physicians who then provided healthcare services under a specific agreement.
- The chief goals of managed care include the following:
  - To provide adequate and quality healthcare to all enrollees at reduced or controlled costs
  - To ensure that the healthcare provided is necessary and suitable for the patient's medical condition
  - To ensure that the services are provided by qualified healthcare clinicians
  - To ensure that the entire process, as well as the environment, is not restrictive in any way
- Managed care plans are making important shifts in their overall business strategy to adapt to changes brought on by the ACA to hold on to their share in the new insurance markets. They face the challenge of meeting today's marketplace preferences for less restrictive care while still holding down costs. These less restrictive plans are offering products and services that meet consumer demands for more choice and greater flexibility.
- Some of the challenges that managed care plans are facing in today's insurance marketplace include:
  - Government support, intervention, and regulation
  - Healthcare reform
  - Value-based reimbursement and using big data to improve quality and reduce costs
  - Consumer response to healthcare changes
  - The capabilities of the new health information exchanges
- Common types of MCOs include:
  - PPO: A group of hospitals and physicians that agree to render particular services to a group of people, generally under contract with a private insurer, at discounted rates if the members receive their healthcare from member providers. Services received from providers outside the organization may result in higher out-of-pocket expenses.
  - HMO: Enrollees receive comprehensive preventive, hospital, and medical care from specific medical providers who receive a prepaid fee. Members select a PCP or medical group from the HMO's list of affiliated physicians

who coordinates the patient's total care. When using medical services, members pay a small copayment. Several types of plans fall under the HMO umbrella (e.g., staff models, group models).

- POS: A "hybrid" type of managed care (sometimes referred to as an *open-ended HMO*) that allows patients to either use the HMO provider or go outside the plan and use any provider they choose. Patients are required to choose a PCP from within the network to monitor their healthcare.

Numerous other types of MCOs are discussed in the chapter.

- The CMS offers managed care plans to Medicare beneficiaries and those who qualify for Medicaid benefits. Medicaid MCOs provide for the delivery of health benefits and additional services through contracted arrangements between state Medicaid agencies and MCOs that accept a set per-member, per-month (capitation) payment for these services. A Medicare managed care plan (called a *Medicare Advantage plan*) is a type of health plan offered by a private company that contracts with Medicare to provide the beneficiary with all Part A and Part B benefits. Most Medicare Advantage plans offer prescription drug coverage. Availability and costs may vary by location and carrier.

- The major goals of the ACA are to provide high-quality, affordable care for all Americans and to promote wellness through prevention of disease and early intervention. Because wellness and prevention are the mission of most MCOs, experts believe that healthcare reform ultimately will lead to some form of a managed care model with limits on spending, and highly integrated healthcare systems will be in the best position to produce more efficient care that provides value and addresses three dominant healthcare issues: (1) access, (2) cost, and (3) quality.

- Accreditation adds value to these programs by providing an external seal of approval and by promoting quality improvement within the organization as part of the accreditation process.

- Most MCOs are regulated from three areas: from states, from the federal government, and from voluntary accreditation. MCOs receive their accreditation mainly from the following three organizations:
  - The NCQA, a private, not-for-profit organization dedicated to improving healthcare quality. For an organization to become accredited by NCQA, it must undergo a rigorous survey and meet certain standards designed to evaluate the health plan's clinical and administrative systems. In particular, NCQA evaluates health plans in the areas of patient safety, confidentiality, consumer protection, access, service, and continuous improvement.
  - The Joint Commission is a private, independent, nonprofit organization that evaluates medical facility compliance based on a focused set of standards that are long known as essential to the delivery of good patient care. Its standards are guidelines for achieving "quality" patient care that include the rights and treatment of patients and quality of patient care.
  - URAC promotes healthcare quality by accrediting many types of healthcare organizations, depending on the functions they carry out. Any organization that meets the URAC standards, including hospitals, HMOs, PPOs, and provider groups, can seek accreditation.

- Physicians review health insurance company contracts to confirm the insurer's definition of claims management terms and the verification processes used for cost containment. This is accomplished through preauthorization and/or precertification—a process whereby certain tests, procedures, or inpatient hospitalizations are ascertained as "medically necessary" before a service or procedure is performed.

- HIPAA affected MCOs much the same as it did FFS plans. One of the most important protections under HIPAA is for those with preexisting conditions to get healthcare coverage. HIPAA's regulations affect other areas of healthcare—both traditional healthcare plans and MCOs.

- Managed care can affect relationships between physicians and patients in various ways. The typical HMO pays only for care provided by its own physicians. PPOs restrict access to physicians by paying a smaller percentage of the cost of care when patients go outside the network for care. Managed care arrangements often control patients' access to medical specialists, restricting patients' freedom to choose providers and obtain the medical services they desire. In HMOs, PCPs function as "gatekeepers" who authorize patient referrals to medical specialists.

- Many changes are expected to occur with the passage of healthcare reform laws, and managed care programs certainly will be affected. It is predicted that they will compete among themselves and establish new types of plans. Although cost and efficiency still will be important selling points, preventive care and quality of services will remain central to the theme of MCOs. It is important to keep in mind that managed care is evolving and is very much a work in progress. It will be interesting to see what the future brings.

To maintain her certification as a medical assistant, Ann has been learning more about health maintenance organizations (HMOs). Her current employer is not part of an HMO, but in her work as a health insurance specialist she has had questions from patients regarding HMOs. She was surprised to learn that there are so many different types of HMOs. With her better understanding of how the HMO system works, she is better able to answer her patient's questions.

To help patients better understand, Ann developed an information sheet for patients that explains managed care in simple terms, comparing it with the more familiar fee-for-service (FFS) structure and including the pros and cons of both. With all of the changes in health insurance that have occurred with the Affordable Care Act (ACA), Ann is seeing more patients with Medicare and Medicaid managed care plans. Her information sheet helps these patients as well.

Being a health insurance professional has taken on a new meaning: it's not just knowing how to complete an insurance form and submitting it; it's also knowing how to build positive relationships with all members of the healthcare team and the patients. Ann knows that all jobs at the clinic are inter-related and that everyone has to work together for the entire system to work efficiently.

CHAPTER REVIEW QUESTIONS

1. An organization established to provide a selection of structured and competitive options for purchasing health coverage is the definition of:
   a. The Joint Commission.
   b. Managed care.
   c. The insurance marketplace.
   d. An exclusive provider organization.
2. Managed care organizations perform which of the following functions?
   a. Establish the list of covered benefits tied to managed care rules
   b. Oversee the healthcare they provide
   c. Set up the contracts and organizations of the healthcare providers who furnish medical care to the enrollees
   d. All of the above
3. The primary goal of managed care is to:
   a. Reduce the cost of healthcare in this country by reducing the spending by individuals.
   b. Increase reimbursement to providers.
   c. Reduce the number of people enrolled in Medicaid.
   d. Increase the use of electronic health records and electronic claim submission.
4. One way in which managed care plans control costs is through the use of gatekeepers, also known as:
   a. POS.
   b. PCPs.
   c. PPOs.
   d. PSOs.

5. The meaningful use program is now known as:
   a. HIPPA.
   b. Health information exchange.
   c. Promoting Interoperability.
   d. Utilization review.
6. The type of managed care organization in which a patient must choose a PCP and can see only providers within a certain network is a(n):
   a. PPO.
   b. HMO.
   c. POS.
   d. IPA.
7. An example of a closed-panel HMO is:
   a. Staff model.
   b. Group model.
   c. Network model.
   d. Independent practice association.
8. The type of managed care organization that falls under Medicare Part C is a:
   a. PPO.
   b. POS.
   c. PSO.
   d. PCP.
9. Managed care plans can be accredited by which of the following organizations?
   a. NCQA
   b. The Joint Commission
   c. URAC
   d. All of the above
10. Dr. Walden has a patient that has type 1 diabetes and has not been able to bring his blood sugars under control. Dr. Walden has asked the patient to see an endocrinologist for treatment of the diabetes. This is considered a:
    a. Consultation.
    b. Referral.
    c. Preauthorization.
    d. Precertification.

WEBSITES TO EXPLORE

- For live links to the following websites, please visit the Evolve site at http://evolve.elsevier.com/Beik/today.
- To learn more about managed care, visit the websites of the groups that evaluate MCOs in the United States: the National Committee for Quality Assurance (NCQA) at http://www.ncqa.org/, The Joint Commission at http://www.jointcommission.org/, and URAC at http://www.urac.org/about-urac/about-urac/.

Author's Note: Due to the dynamic nature of the Internet, web addresses and/or links provided in this chapter may have changed since publication and may no longer be valid. In such cases, students should select comparable search words to access related sites.

10 Understanding Medicaid

Chapter Outline

Chapter Objectives

After completion of this chapter, the student should be able to:

1. Summarize the development and structure of the Medicaid program.
2. Describe how the Affordable Care Act affected Medicaid.
3. Discuss Medicaid benefits and the two major population groups eligible for benefits.
4. Identify criteria that qualify beneficiaries for the dual eligible program.
5. List and briefly discuss key Medicaid programs.
6. Identify Medicaid groups that are affected by premiums and cost-sharing.
7. Explain how payment for Medicaid beneficiaries' prescription drugs requirements is determined.
8. Discuss the Emergency Medical Treatment and Labor Act regulations.
9. Specify the various methods for accepting Medicaid patients and verifying Medicaid eligibility.
10. Differentiate the Medicare versus Medicaid program benefits.
11. Outline the Medicaid claim process.
12. Interpret third-party liability as it relates to Medicaid.
13. Demonstrate an understanding of the standard Medicaid remittance advice.
14. Explain special notes and terminology associated with the billing process.
15. Review the meanings of fraud and abuse and how they affect the Medicaid program.
16. Examine Medicaid quality practices.
17. Analyze the health insurance professional's role in optimizing Medicaid's implementation.

Chapter Terms

abuse
adjudicated
Affordable Care Act (ACA)
balance billing
capitation
categorically needy
Children's Health Insurance Program (CHIP)
community call plan
Community First Choice (CFC) Option
cost avoid(ance)
cost-sharing
crossover claims
dual eligibility
Early and Periodic Screening, Diagnosis, and Treatment (EPSDT)
Emergency Medical Treatment and Labor Act (EMTALA)

fraud
Home and Community-Based Services (HCBS) Waivers programs
mandated (or mandatory) services
Maternal and Child Health (MCH) Services
Medicaid
Medicaid contractor
Medicaid expansion
Medicaid Integrity Program (MIP)
Medicaid secondary claim
Medicaid "simple" claim
medically necessary
medically needy
Medicare Savings Programs (MSPs)
Medicare-Medicaid (Medi-Medi)
modified adjusted gross income (MAGI)
participating provider

pay-and-chase claims
payer of last resort
Plan to Achieve Self-Support (PASS)
preferred drug list
Program of All-Inclusive Care for the Elderly (PACE)
reciprocity
remittance advice (RA)
retroactive eligibility
spend down
subsidies
Supplemental Security Income (SSI)
Temporary Assistance for Needy Families (TANF)
third-party liability (TPL)
Ticket to Work
urgent care centers

Opening Scenario

Nela Karnama has been employed as a medical receptionist in a multispecialty medical practice for 9 years and has recently been promoted to a health insurance specialist. She has specialized in working with Medicaid. In her personal life, she has experience with Medicaid; after her husband was killed in an automobile accident, she and her children became eligible for benefits. In her training for this position, she learned that there are multiple patient populations that would qualify for Medicaid, especially since her state has taken part in the Medicaid expansion made possible through the Affordable Care Act. Nela works hard to stay current with any changes in Medicaid at the federal level as well as the state level. She knows that she is best able to serve her patients by knowing as much as she can about the various Medicaid programs and the changes that frequently occur.

WHAT IS MEDICAID?

Medicaid is a medical assistance program funded by the US federal and state governments designed to provide comprehensive and quality medical care for people who are unable to pay some or all of their own medical expenses. Special emphasis is on children, pregnant women, the elderly, the disabled, and parents with dependent children who have no other way to pay for healthcare. Congress established the Medicaid program under Title XIX of the Social Security Act of 1965. The program is administered by the Centers for Medicare and Medicaid Services (CMS) under the general direction of the Department of Health and Human Services (HHS). The secretary of the federal HHS is charged with determining whether a state is in compliance with Medicaid benefit and eligibility standards. Within the guidelines set forth by the federal government, each state establishes its own eligibility standards; determines the type, amount, duration, and scope of services; sets the rate of payment for services; and administers its own program. As a result of each state's ability to modify eligibility, benefits, and other aspects of its programs, state programs vary widely. Each state has a federally approved Medicaid plan that outlines eligibility and benefit categories, as well as other aspects of its Medicaid program.

DEVELOPMENT OF MEDICAID

Medicaid originally was created to give certain groups of low-income Americans access to healthcare. Since its beginning, Medicaid has evolved from a narrowly defined program available only to individuals eligible for cash assistance (welfare) into a large insurance program with complex eligibility rules. Today, Medicaid is a major social welfare program and is administered by the CMS, formerly called the *Health Care Financing Administration.* Medicaid has the responsibility of overseeing other assistance programs. A link to a "timeline" illustrating the milestones of Medicare and Medicaid can be found under "Websites to Explore" at the end of this chapter.

FEDERAL AND STATE GUIDELINES

According to the national Medicaid guidelines, federal and state governments must each contribute a specified percentage of total healthcare expenditures. The federal government establishes general guidelines for eligibility and mandatory services, and each state then is allowed to expand its own guidelines regarding eligibility, services, benefits package, payment rates, and program administration within the broad federal guidelines. Flexibility to set eligibility levels has been limited over time by increases in federal minimum levels for children and pregnant women and more recently by eligibility protections established under the American Recovery and Reinvestment Act and the Patient Protection and Affordable Care Act (PPACA; hereafter referred to as the **Affordable Care Act [ACA]**). Medicaid benefits vary from state to state, and although state participation in Medicaid is optional, all states have Medicaid programs. As a result, there are essentially 56 different Medicaid programs—one for each state, each territory, and the District of Columbia. Not all states call their programs Medicaid. For example, in California the program is called *Medi-Cal,* in Arizona it's *AHCSS* (pronounced "access"), in Massachusetts it's *MassHealth,* in Washington state it's *Washington Apple Health,* and in Tennessee it's *TennCare.* States may combine the administration of Medicaid with that of other programs, such as the **Children's Health Insurance Program (CHIP)**, so the same organization that manages Medicaid may also manage other programs. Most state Medicaid programs have both fee-for-service (FFS) and managed care coverage options. CHIP and other Medicaid programs are discussed later in the chapter. To learn more about your state Medicaid program and other options, visit the Medicaid.gov website.

STATE PARTICIPATION

For many years, Medicaid law has required participating states to cover specific needy and "at-risk" populations while giving them the option of extending coverage to other groups. State participation in programs other than those mandated by the federal government is technically optional; however, all states participate in the Medicaid program. Although eligibility varies widely among states, all states must meet federal minimum requirements, such as covering certain categories of people and offering specific benefits; however, they may choose to cover additional "optional" people and services as well, as discussed previously. Provisions of the ACA expanded Medicaid to all Americans under age 65 whose family income is at or below 138% of the federal poverty level (FPL). Under the expanded Medicaid provision, 138% of the FPL for a family of three was $29,435 in 2019 and for an individual was $17,236. (The 100% FPL for a family of three in 2019 was $21,330.)

For many eligibility groups, income is calculated in relation to a percentage of the FPL. Many states have expanded coverage, particularly for children, above the federal minimums. For other groups, income standards are based on income or other nonfinancial criteria standards for other programs, such as the Supplemental Security Income (SSI) program.

Health insurance subsidies such as the premium tax credit, the cost-sharing subsidy, and the subsidy to reduce the out-of-pocket maximum are available only to people with incomes between 100% and 400% of FPL. A table showing FPL limits of 100%, 125%, and 150% for fiscal year 2019 are shown in Table 10.1.

Note: The qualifying dollar amounts for Medicaid eligibility are subject to change annually. Keep up to date with changes through the *Federal Register* or CMS.

| Table 10.1 | Federal Poverty Level (FPL) Guidelines: Maximum Income Levels for Program Year 2020 |

| | 12 MONTHS' INCOME | | |
FAMILY SIZE	100% POVERTY GUIDELINE	125% POVERTY GUIDELINE	150% POVERTY GUIDELINE
1	$12,760	$15,950	$19,140
2	$17,240	$21,550	$25,860
3	$21,720	$27,150	$32,580
4	$26,200	$32,750	$39,300
5	$30,680	$38,350	$46,020
6	$35,160	$43,950	$52,740
7	$39,640	$49,500	$59,460
8	$44,120	$55,150	$66,180
For each additional household member, add: $4480			

Data from Office of the Assistant Secretary for Planning and Evaluation, Washington, DC.

? What Did You Learn?

1. What is Medicaid?
2. When was the Medicaid program established?
3. The Medicaid program is administered by the _____ under the general direction of the _____.
4. True or false: The federal government establishes general guidelines for eligibility and mandatory services, and each state is allowed to expand its own guidelines within the broad federal guidelines.
5. Provisions of the _____ expanded Medicaid to all Americans under age 65 whose family income is at or below 138% of the FPL by January 1, 2015.

MEDICAID AND HEALTHCARE REFORM

We learned in an earlier chapter that the ACA provides Americans with opportunities for better healthcare by putting in place comprehensive health insurance reforms that:

- Expand coverage
- Lower healthcare costs
- Guarantee more choices in healthcare coverage
- Hold insurance companies accountable
- Improve the overall quality of care for Americans

We have also learned that the ACA is made up of two separate pieces of legislation: the PPACA and the Health Care and Education Reconciliation Act of 2010. Together, these acts expand Medicaid coverage to millions of low-income Americans and introduce improvements to both Medicaid and CHIP.

Since the law was enacted in March 2010, the CMS has worked with states to identify key priorities and provide the guidance needed to carry out the important changes to Medicaid and CHIP that became effective on January 1, 2014. In 2019 the Medicaid and CHIP programs together provided health coverage to nearly 72.5 million Americans, including half of all low-income children in the United States. As mentioned previously, the federal government sets minimum guidelines for Medicaid eligibility, but states can choose to expand coverage beyond the federal minimum threshold. See the following section on Medicaid eligibility.

MEDICAID ELIGIBILITY

As a result of the Medicaid expansion, the total number of individuals enrolled in Medicaid and CHIP totaled approximately 72.5 million people in the United States. Before the ACA, each state sets its own Medicaid eligibility rules under broad federal guidelines, but in general, state programs *must* cover the following groups of children, families, and pregnant women:

- Infants born to Medicaid-eligible pregnant women
- Children up to age 19 and pregnant women with family incomes at or below 138% of the FPL
- Children and certain adults who would be eligible for cash assistance under pre–welfare reform rules in effect in July 1996
- Children and certain adults with incomes below 185% of the FPL ($40,182 for a family of three in 2020) in families that are leaving welfare for work as transitional medical assistance
- Children in foster care or an adoption assistance program

States have the option of making children, families, and pregnant women with incomes above the mandatory coverage limits eligible for Medicaid. For example, most states cover children with incomes up to 200% of the FPL under their Medicaid programs or through Medicaid and CHIP.

State programs *must* cover elderly and disabled individuals receiving cash benefits under the SSI program (or aged, blind, or disabled individuals who meet state criteria that were in place in a state as of January 1972 and are more restrictive than SSI's eligibility criteria). In addition, beginning in 2014, most adults under age 65 with individual incomes up to about $15,000 per year qualify for Medicaid in every state. These dollar limits are subject to change annually. Even when people's income exceeds Medicaid income levels in their state, they may become eligible under Medicaid spend down rules. Spend down is discussed later in this chapter.

Certain severely impaired individuals who are working and have earnings above the SSI eligibility limits are permitted to continue receiving Medicaid benefits, despite the loss of SSI coverage. (SSI is discussed later in this chapter.) States have the option of allowing individuals with disabilities with incomes up to 250% of the FPL to continue receiving Medicaid while working.

The ACA would have extended Medicaid eligibility to all individuals under age 65 living in families with incomes under 133% of the FPL starting in 2014. However, in June 2012, the US Supreme Court decided that the federal government cannot make all federal Medicaid funding for a state's Medicaid program contingent on a state implementing the ACA Medicaid expansion. As a result of this decision, states were allowed to choose not to expand the program to newly eligible adults without losing their federal Medicaid funding for other eligible populations.

All children enrolled in Medicaid are entitled to the comprehensive set of healthcare services known as *Early and Periodic Screening, Diagnosis, and Treatment (EPSDT)*. CHIP also ensures a comprehensive set of benefits for children, but states have flexibility to design the benefit package.

Other eligibility criteria also apply, such as documentation of US citizenship, immigration status, and residency. State Medicaid and CHIP income eligibility standards tables are available on the Medicaid.gov website.

MEDICAID EXPANSION UNDER THE ACA

Medicaid expansion is the process of increasing the number of people enrolled in Medicaid by making it easier for people to qualify for Medicaid. It is called *Medicaid expansion* because enrolling more people expands the list of those receiving Medicaid benefits. The expansion of Medicaid under the ACA is one of the biggest changes in healthcare reform, expanding Medicaid to cover nearly half of uninsured Americans. The law previously required states to cover their poorest (categorically needy and medically needy) or lose federal funding, which covered 90% to 100% of state costs. Under the ACA, states can choose to take advantage of the Medicaid expansion, or they can choose not to—referred to as *opting out*.

Until the ACA was passed, every state had different eligibility requirements for Medicaid based on income, age, gender, dependents, and other specific requirements. Now, more people can qualify for Medicaid under expanded eligibility rules; for example:

- Starting in 2014, states that expanded Medicaid increased eligibility levels to 138% of the FPL.
- All states that expanded Medicaid have uniform eligibility requirements.
- Because every state covers those who have no income, expansion almost exclusively covers the working poor and their families.
- Medicaid expansion helps cover gaps between current Medicaid eligibility and families being able to afford private health insurance using marketplace **subsidies**. Subsidies are types of cost assistance that lower the amount an individual spends on monthly premiums or reduces out-of-pocket costs for copayments, coinsurance, deductibles, and out-of-pocket maximum (cost-sharing reduction).
- If all states would take advantage of the Medicaid expansion, about half of the uninsured in America would have medical coverage.

Table 10.2 illustrates the realignment of Medicaid eligibility groups after the Medicaid expansion under the ACA final rule. Learn more about the Medicaid expansion law by logging on to the cms.gov website and clicking on the Medicaid/CHIP tab.

> ◎ **HIPAA Tip**
>
> The Medicaid Health Insurance Portability and Accountability Act (HIPAA)–Compliant Concept Model shows how HIPAA affects Medicaid and provides practical tools to help a state determine the best course of action for analyzing HIPAA's impact, determine implementation strategies, determine best practices, and validate what a state has accomplished.

Table 10.2 Realignment of Medicaid Eligibility Groups

BEFORE	AFTER THE AFFORDABLE CARE ACT RULE		
MANDATORY MEDICAID ELIGIBILITY GROUPS (PRE–AFFORDABLE CARE ACT)	PARENTS/CARETAKER RELATIVES	PREGNANT WOMEN	CHILDREN UNDER 19
Low-income families	X	X	X
Qualified pregnant women and children under age 19		X	X
Poverty-level related pregnant women and infants		X	X
Poverty-level related children ages 1–5			X
Poverty-level related children ages 6–18			X
OPTIONAL MEDICAID ELIGIBILITY GROUPS (PRE–AFFORDABLE CARE ACT)	PARENTS/CARETAKER RELATIVES	PREGNANT WOMEN	CHILDREN UNDER 19
Families and children financially eligible for AFDC		X	
Families and children who would be eligible for AFDC if not institutionalized		X	X
Poverty-level related pregnant women and infants		X	X

AFDC, Aid to Families with Dependent Children.
Data from Centers for Medicare and Medicaid Services, Baltimore, MD.

NEW ELIGIBILITY GROUP

To review, before the ACA took effect, Medicaid eligibility rules were strict. To qualify for Medicaid, an individual had to meet low-income criteria and have limited assets. In addition, many states required the individual to be a member of a particular "at-risk" group to qualify. These groups included the elderly, disabled, blind, pregnant women, children, or parents caring for young children.

With the passage of the ACA, the Medicaid program expanded benefits to a new group: low-income adults without children, including everyone with incomes at or below 138% of the FPL and younger than 65 years old. As a result, every state now manages its state Medicaid programs, providing healthcare coverage with a specific focus on individuals in the lower-income levels, families and youngsters, and the elderly, as well as those with disabilities.

Adding this new group was initially mandatory for each state if the original version of the ACA was upheld; however, the Supreme Court decided that individual states could choose whether to take advantage of this expansion. Consequently, many states opted out, choosing not to include this expanded group of Americans, leaving them without healthcare coverage. Other states made it possible for childless adults to receive benefits through the state's medical assistance program.

Beginning in 2014, states that decided to take advantage of Medicaid expansion were allowed to enroll childless adults who previously were unable to enroll in Medicaid. Before health reform, parents in more than 30 states did not qualify for coverage even if their children did because the income guidelines were set extremely low for parents—for example, $1100 per month.

Also beginning in 2014, coverage for the newly eligible adults was to be fully financed through the federal government for 3 years, phasing down to 90% by 2020. Federal financing for CHIP has been extended to 2023. Extra federal financing is also available for primary care, preventive care, and community-based long-term services to improve quality and revamp delivery systems to accommodate the increase in Medicaid applications for newly qualifying individuals. Beginning in 2014, the majority of people under age 65, along with those earning less than $15,000 per year, became eligible for a state Medicaid program. It is important to keep in mind that the qualification rules with regard to Medicaid eligibility vary for each state. Additional information on CHIP and Medicaid eligibility is provided later in this chapter.

Note: In a December 2015 bulletin, CMS announced that the 90% federal match would be permanently extended.

CALCULATING ELIGIBILITY USING MAGI

The ACA provides a simplified method for calculating income eligibility for Medicaid, CHIP, and other financial assistance programs available through the health insurance marketplace. This method calculates eligibility for all programs based on what is called **modified adjusted gross income (MAGI)**. Generally, MAGI is a person's adjusted gross income plus any tax-exempt Social Security, interest, or other income. By using one set of income eligibility rules across all insurance affordability programs, this law makes it easier for people to apply for health coverage through one application and enroll in the appropriate program. CMS has worked with states to convert their Medicaid and CHIP eligibility levels to be based on MAGI as required by the act as of October 1, 2014. These levels are presented as a percentage of the FPL and provide the eligibility levels in dollar amounts for annual income calculated for a family size of one, two, three, and four. Not all populations that are enrolled in Medicaid and CHIP will have their eligibility determined based on MAGI. The key groups include children, pregnant women, parents and caretaker relatives, and other adults whose eligibility was MAGI-based beginning in 2014. MAGI and non-MAGI eligibility groups are shown in Table 10.3.

See "Websites to Explore" at the end of this chapter for a table listing individual state Medicaid and CHIP income eligibility standards for MAGI groups based on state decisions as of January 2020.

RETROACTIVE ELIGIBILITY

Retroactive eligibility for benefits may be available to Medicaid applicants who did not apply for assistance until after they received care, either because they were unaware of Medicaid or because the nature of their illness prevented the filing of an application. Retroactive eligibility is available when there is an unpaid medical bill for a service provided for 3 full months immediately before the month of application, providing the individual meets all eligibility criteria. An applicant does not need to be eligible in the month of application (or current month) to be eligible for one or more months of retroactive Medicaid. The individual requesting retroactive Medicaid must meet all requirements for the Medicaid category, both financial and nonfinancial.

Imagine This!

Gwendolyn Banks, a 74-year-old woman, consulted her healthcare provider on May 14, 2020, for health problems (e.g., unexplained weight loss, numbness and tingling in her extremities). After her treatment, it was discovered that Gwen qualified for Medicaid benefits; however, because she had little contact with the outside world, she was not aware of the Medicaid program and that she was financially eligible for benefits. In July 2020 a caseworker assisted Gwen in completing a Medicaid application, resulting in Medicaid paying for the medical expenses that were incurred in May and June.

Table 10.3   MAGI and Non-MAGI Eligibility Groups

MAGI ELIGIBILITY GROUPS	NON-MAGI ELIGIBILITY GROUPS
Pregnant women • Presumptive for pregnant women	SSI • SSI recipients • State supplement only
Infants and children under age 19 • Infants less than 1 year of age • Child 1: 5 years of age • Child 6: 18 years of age (two levels)	SSI-related medically needy • Aged • Disabled • Blind
New adult group • Childless adults, which includes individuals who are not pregnant, are ages 19–64 (19- and 20-year-olds living alone), do not have Medicare, and could be certified disabled but do not yet have Medicare	ADC-related medically needy • Pregnant women • Parent or caretaker relatives • Under 21 years of age
PARENTS/CARETAKER RELATIVES	**COBRA**
19- and 20-year-olds living with parents	Medicare Savings Program (MSP)
Family Planning Benefit Program (FPBP; if applying through the New York Marketplace and are eligible for FPBP only)	AIDS Health Insurance Program (AHIP) Foster care
Child in foster care • MAGI administered in welfare management system (WMS)	Medicaid Buy-In for Working People With Disabilities (Basic and Medical Improvement Groups) Medicaid Cancer Treatment Program Individual under 26 years of age who was in foster care and in receipt of Medicaid on 18th birthday Resident of home for adults

ADC, Adult disabled children; *COBRA,* Consolidated Omnibus Budget Reconciliation Act (continuation of healthcare coverage); *MAGI,* modified adjusted gross income; *SSI,* Supplemental Security Income.
Data from Centers for Medicare and Medicaid Services, Baltimore, MD.

? What Did You Learn?

1. Name the five comprehensive health insurance reforms put in place by the ACA.
2. List the groups of people that the federal government mandates states' Medicaid programs cover.
3. Explain the Medicaid expansion process.
4. With the passage of the ACA, the Medicaid program has expanded benefits to what new group?
5. What is MAGI and how is it used?

MEDICAID BENEFITS

It was pointed out earlier in this chapter that states establish and administer their own Medicaid programs and determine the type, amount, duration, and scope of services within broad federal guidelines. States are required to cover certain "mandatory benefits" and can choose to provide other "optional benefits" through the Medicaid program.

MANDATED SERVICES

Title XIX of the Social Security Act requires that for a state to receive federal matching funds for their Medicaid programs, certain basic services (referred to as **mandated [or mandatory] services**) must be offered to the categorically needy population in the state's program. These basic services are listed in Table 10.4.

OPTIONAL SERVICES

As mentioned earlier, states establish and administer their own Medicaid programs and determine the type, amount, duration, and scope of services within broad federal guidelines. States are required to cover certain mandatory benefits and can choose to provide other optional benefits through the Medicaid program. A list of optional benefits is included in Table 10.4. These services can vary by state. A website showing a full list of both mandatory and optional benefits for Medicaid and CHIP can be found under "Websites to Explore" at the end of this chapter.

Categorically Needy

Categorically needy is a classification of individuals who fall into a specific category (or criteria) of mandatory Medicaid eligibility established by the federal government. For example, low-income families, qualifying pregnant women, newborns, and SSI recipients would meet the categorically needy criteria. Subject to medical necessity, Medicaid programs *must* cover the following services for categorically eligible populations:

• Hospital services (inpatient and outpatient)
• Physicians' services
• Medical and surgical dental services
• Nursing facility (NF) services for individuals age 21 or older

Table 10.4 Medicaid Mandatory and Optional Benefits

MANDATORY BENEFITS	OPTIONAL BENEFITS
• Inpatient hospital services	• Prescription drugs
• Outpatient hospital services	• Clinic services
• EPSDT: Early and Periodic Screening, Diagnostic, and Treatment Services	• Physical and occupational therapy
• Nursing facility services	• Speech, hearing, and language disorder services
• Home health services	• Respiratory care services
• Physician services	• Other diagnostic, screening, preventive, and rehabilitative services
• Rural health clinic services	• Podiatry services
• Federally qualified health center services	• Optometry services
• Laboratory and x-ray services	• Dental services
• Family planning services	• Dentures
• Nurse midwife services	• Prosthetics
• Certified pediatric and family nurse practitioner services	• Eyeglasses
• Freestanding birth center services (when licensed or otherwise recognized by the state)	• Chiropractic services
• Transportation to medical care	• Private duty nursing services
• Tobacco cessation counseling for pregnant women	• Personal care
	• Hospice
	• Case management
	• State plan home and community-based services 1915(i)
	• Community First Choice Option 1915(k)
	• Other services approved by the secretary[a]

[a]These include services furnished in a religious nonmedical healthcare institution, emergency hospital services by a non-Medicare certified hospital, and critical access hospital (CAH).

Data from Centers for Medicare and Medicaid Services, Baltimore, MD.

• Home healthcare for persons eligible for NF services
• Family planning services and supplies

Medically Needy

Medically needy is an optional eligibility category. States that allow medically needy individuals to qualify for Medicaid deduct the cost of the person's medical care from his or her income when determining eligibility. The concept of the **spend down** process, or "spending down" to Medicaid eligibility, often applies to elderly individuals who have high medical expenses. The opportunity to spend down may be particularly important for those who are elderly and reside in a nursing home. Also, children and adults with disabilities who live in the community may have high prescription drug, medical equipment, or other healthcare expenses that would allow them to meet the medically needy criteria.

As with many other components of the Medicaid program, eligibility criteria, qualifying services, and benefits can change, so it is very important to keep up to date with your state's rules and regulations.

Imagine This!

Inez Burke, a widow, resides in a nursing home and has complications of diabetes and cellulitis. Six years ago, Inez's husband died, leaving her with a modest savings account. The homestead on which she and her husband raised their family had earlier been divided into parcels for the three children with the arrangement that Inez would receive life estate in the property. In just a few years, the bills that were generated as a result of her medical condition depleted her savings account. Realizing that she could no longer live alone, Inez's son arranged for her care at the Sunset Care Center. Because Inez's savings were used up to pay her medical bills, Inez qualified for Medicaid. Her monthly Social Security check is applied toward her care at Sunset; other than that, Medicaid pays her room and board plus any medical care she receives from the staff that Medicare does not pay.

Stop and Think

Refer to the Inez Burke scenario in Imagine This! What Medicaid category does this individual fall into?

The Affordable Care Act (ACA) significantly expands the number of people in the United States who are eligible for Medicaid. This expansion may cover many of the people who currently are in a medically needy program. The chart in Fig. 10.1 shows how ACA enrollment and spending drive Medicaid growth. To learn more about the ACA, see "Websites to Explore" at the end of this chapter.

Imagine This!

Jim Norton has monthly income of $723. If the Medicaid income limit is $623, then Jim is over the limit by $100. If Jim has monthly medical expenses of more than $100, he can be eligible for Medicaid with a "spend down" of $100. (Then he must spend $100 per month on his medical expenses before Medicaid will begin paying.)

MEDICAID COST-SHARING

People who fall in the medically needy category may be required to share in the cost of their medical care. Cost-sharing options vary by beneficiary category, income level, and the type of service. **Cost-sharing** is when beneficiaries are required to pay a portion of the cost of medical services (e.g., copayments and premiums) for Medicaid. Cost-sharing varies by state, but because of the limited income of most individuals eligible for Medicaid, Medicaid's laws and regulations place strict limits on cost-sharing. Premium charges are prohibited under traditional Medicaid for most eligibility groups. Similarly, service-related cost-sharing (e.g., copayments and coinsurance) is prohibited for certain eligibility groups and services.

States that offer a medically needy program must cover medically needy pregnant women and children under age 18. States also have the option to cover children up to age 21, parents and other caretaker relatives, certain elderly individuals, and those with disabilities. Maximum allowable cost-sharing amounts are shown in Table 10.5.

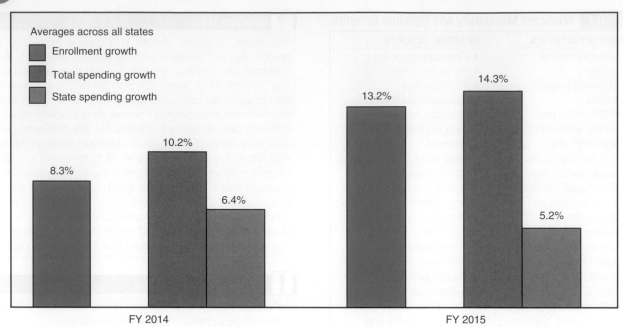

Fig. 10.1 Affordable Care Act (ACA)–related enrollment and overall expenditure growth. *FY,* Fiscal year. (Adapted from the Kaiser Family Foundation, San Francisco, California.)

A comprehensive list of Medicaid eligibility groups, both mandatory and optional, as well as medically needy groups, can be found on the Medicaid.gov website.

[?] What Did You Learn?

1. Name the federal act that requires states that receive federal matching funds for their Medicaid programs to offer certain basic (or mandated) services.
2. True or false: "Optional" services offered by a Medicare program can vary from state to state.
3. The two classifications (or categories) of Medicaid eligibility are _____ and _____.
4. Subject to medical necessity, Medicaid programs *must* cover certain services for categorically eligible populations. Name at least four.
5. Explain how an individual can qualify for the "medically needy" category through the "spend down" process.
6. What is meant by "cost-sharing"?

DUAL ELIGIBLE BENEFICIARIES

Dual eligibility is a term that is often heard but not always understood. To qualify for dual eligibility, an individual must meet the requirements for both Medicare and Medicaid. Historically, individuals meet the requirements for only one or the other; however, there is a growing number of Medicare beneficiaries who also meet Medicaid guidelines based on income and assets. Some people qualify for Medicare and partial dual eligibility, meaning that they have Medicare coverage and can receive Medicaid benefits if they pay a small monthly premium, or cost-share. Others qualify for total dual eligibility, meaning that they can be covered by both Medicare and Medicaid and, because their income and assets are below a certain point, they do not have to pay Medicaid premiums.

The importance of having both Medicare and Medicaid is that they cover different things. When an individual—especially one with a low income—qualifies

Table 10.5 | **Maximum Allowable Medicaid Cost-Sharing**

MAXIMUM ALLOWABLE MEDICAID COST-SHARING VARIES BY INCOME[a]			
	<100% FPL	100%–150% FPL	>150% FPL
Outpatient services	$4	10% of the cost state pays	20% of the cost state pays
Nonemergency ER	$8	$8	No limit
Prescription drugs	Preferred: $4 Nonpreferred: $8	Preferred: $4 Nonpreferred: $8	Preferred: $4 Nonpreferred: 20% of cost state pays
Inpatient services	$75 per stay	10% of the total cost state pays for the entire stay	20% of the total cost state pays for the entire stay

[a]Any cost-sharing in the state plan applies to all eligibility categories (unless exempt), with the exception of certain targeted cost-sharing. Also, targeted cost-sharing may only be applied to individuals with incomes above 100% FML.
ER, Emergency room; *FPL,* federal poverty level.
Data from Centers for Medicare and Medicaid Services, Baltimore, MD.

for both programs through dual coverage, they are basically covered for hospital care, as well as visits to physicians and medication, with low or no copayments. In addition, certain features of dual coverage may help pay Medicare Part D premiums for prescription drugs.

DUAL ELIGIBLE PROGRAMS

Dual eligible beneficiaries include individuals who receive full Medicaid benefits, as well as those who receive only assistance with Medicare costs (e.g., premiums and deductibles). To qualify as dual eligible, the individual must meet certain income and resource requirements, be entitled to Medicare Part A and/or Part B, and receive full Medicaid benefits or be enrolled in the Medicare Savings Program (MSP). Dual eligible beneficiaries may choose coverage under FFS Medicare or a Medicare Advantage (MA) plan.

Medicare-covered services under the dual eligible status are paid first by Medicare because *Medicaid is always the* **payer of last resort**, meaning that all other available third-party resources must meet their legal obligations to pay claims before the Medicaid program pays for the care of an individual eligible for Medicaid. Medicaid may cover the cost of prescription drugs and other care that Medicare does not cover. Individuals who have Medicare and full Medicaid coverage have most of their healthcare costs paid. For more information about dual coverage, how it works, what states provide it, and who qualifies, visit the CMS website at https://www.cms.gov/Outreach-and-Education/Medicare-Learning-Network-MLN/MLNProducts/Downloads/Medicare_Beneficiaries_Dual_Eligibles_At_a_Glance.pdf.

Patient's Point of View

Tai Yan is meeting with Nela, as she will soon be eligible for Medicare but has concerns about the amount of money owed after Medicare pays. She has no other insurance and has very little income to purchase additional coverage. Nela explained to Tai that she may be eligible for Medicare and Medicaid. She does qualify for both Medicare Part A and Part B; Nela looked up the income requirements in her state, and it appears that Tai would be eligible for the dual eligible program. Nela helped Tai contact a state program representative and set up an appointment. Nela also made sure that Tai had transportation to that appointment.

Tai left her meeting with Nela with hope that there was assistance for her medical expenses as she heads into retirement.

Medicare Savings Programs

All **Medicare Savings Programs (MSPs)**, also known as *Medicare buy-in programs*, save the Medicare beneficiary money by paying for the Part B premium. MSPs may also pay for Part A premiums, depending on income and assets. For most people, Part A is free, but if the beneficiary or the beneficiary's spouse has not worked enough to qualify for free Part A, he or she must pay a Part A premium. There are several different MSPs; for example:

- Qualified Medicare Beneficiary (QMB) Program
- Specified Low-Income Medicare Beneficiary (SLMB) Program
- Qualifying Individual (QI) Program
- Qualified Disabled and Working Individuals (QDWI) Program

Table 10.6 lists these programs along with what they pay and eligibility requirement limits through 2020. More information on MSPs can be found on the Medicaid.gov website.

Table **10.6**	MSPs by Name, What They Pay, and Eligibility Requirements	
MSP NAME	**WHAT IT PAYS**	**ELIGIBILITY REQUIREMENTS**
Qualified Medicare Beneficiary (QMB)	Pays both Medicare Part A and Part B premiums, deductibles, coinsurance, and copayments	Income limits: Up to 100% of the FPL + $20 and resources under $7860 if single or $11,800 if married: Single person – $1084/month Married couple – $1457/month
Specified Low-Income Medicare Beneficiary (SLMB)	Pays Medicare Part B premiums only	Income limits: Less than 120% of the FPL + $20 and resources under $7860 if single or $11,800 if married: Single person – $1296/month Married couple – $1744/month
Qualifying Individual (QI) Program	Pays Part B premiums only	Income limits: Less than 135% of the FPL + $20 and resources under $7860 if single or $11,800 if married: Single person – $1456/month Married couple – $1960/month
Qualified Disabled and Working Individuals (QDWI) Program	Helps pay for Part A premium	Income limits: Resources under $4000 if single or $6000 if married: Single person – $4339/month Married couple – $5833/month

FPL, Federal poverty limit; *MSP,* Medicare Savings Program.

OTHER MEDICAID PROGRAMS

There are multiple special programs under the broad umbrella of Medicaid, two of which are discussed in the following sections.

TEMPORARY ASSISTANCE FOR NEEDY FAMILIES

Temporary Assistance for Needy Families (TANF) is a federally funded grant program that allows states to create and administer their own "safety net" social assistance programs. TANF replaced the federal program previously known as *Aid to Families with Dependent Children (AFDC)*. TANF enables states to offer a wide variety of social services to those who meet the eligibility criteria. The goal of TANF is to provide needy families with a combination of financial assistance and work opportunities. TANF is administered by the Office of Family Assistance, which is part of the Administration for Children and Families, and each state has its own local TANF office. However, as with Medicaid, the titles of TANF programs vary from state to state.

One significant change from the former AFDC system is that TANF recipients must participate in work activities to receive benefits. This means that parents receiving TANF must be employed in some capacity, be working toward employment, or be taking classes that increase their long-term employability prospects. TANF recipients may also be eligible for:
- Women, Infants, and Children (WIC): A supplemental nutrition program administered by the Food and Nutrition Service (FNS) division of the US Department of Agriculture.
- Supplemental Nutrition Assistance Program (SNAP): A relatively new name for what used to be known as the *federal Food Stamp Program*. Individuals who are eligible for this program receive a SNAP electronic benefits transfer (EBT) card, which works like a debit card. With a SNAP EBT card, qualifying individuals can pay for food at grocery stores that accept SNAP payments.

TANF is not an "entitlement" program. It is funded by the federal government through block grants to states and must be renewed each year. A link to help you find the TANF program in your area is listed under "Websites to Explore" at the end of this chapter.

CHILDREN'S HEALTH INSURANCE PROGRAM

Enacted as part of the Balanced Budget Act of 1997, the State Children's Health Insurance Program (SCHIP)—now known more simply as *CHIP*—provides federal matching funds for states to implement health insurance programs for children in families that earn too much to qualify for Medicaid but too little to reasonably afford private health coverage. With CHIP, states can provide coverage through two different options:
- Creation of a separate children's health program that meets the requirements specified under Section 2103 of the act, an option known as *separate* or *stand-alone* CHIP
- Expansion of eligibility for benefits under the state's Medicaid plan under Title XIX of the act, an option known as *Medicaid expansion* CHIP

States can operate either of these options alone or in combination.

Within federal guidelines, each state determines the design of its CHIP program, eligibility groups, benefit packages, payment levels for coverage, and administrative and operating procedures. Eligibility levels range from 138% to 300% of FPL, depending on the state and the age of the child. These percentage levels are subject to change annually.

CHIP health benefits typically cover physician, hospital, well-baby, and well-child care; prescription drugs; and limited behavioral and personal care services. In contrast with Medicaid, private-duty nursing, personal care, and orthodontia usually are not covered by CHIP.

Many CHIP programs require small premiums and copayments, but federal law prohibits cost-sharing from exceeding 5% of a family's income. CHIP typically has a multilevel cost-sharing approach, with greater cost-sharing for families with higher incomes (e.g., above 150% of the FPL). Copayments range from $1 for a generic drug prescription to $100 for an inpatient hospital stay and can vary by state.

SUPPLEMENTAL SECURITY INCOME

In 1972 federal law established the **Supplemental Security Income (SSI)** program, which provides federally funded cash assistance to qualifying elderly and disabled poor. Under the SSI program, the Social Security Administration (SSA) determines eligibility criteria and sets the cash benefit amounts for SSI. SSI is a cash benefit program controlled by the SSA; however, it is not related to the Social Security program. States may choose to supplement federal SSI payments with state funds.

SSI Eligibility

To be eligible for SSI, an individual must be at least 65 years old or blind or disabled and must have limited assets (or resources). Income is determined by the standards set forth in the FPL guidelines. The figures below represent the income of the individual or family. These guidelines serve as one of the indicators for determining eligibility in a wide variety of federal and state programs. The income benefits limit for SSI eligibility is $783 per month for an individual and $1175 for a couple (2020 figures). The HHS issues new FPL guidelines in January or February of each year. In most states, SSI beneficiaries also can get medical assistance (Medicaid) to pay for hospital stays, doctor bills, prescription drugs, and other health costs. In addition, to receive SSI, a person must:

- Be a resident of the United States
- Not be absent from the country for more than 30 consecutive days
- Be either a US citizen or a US national or in one of certain categories of eligible noncitizens
- Apply for any other cash benefits or payments for which he or she may be eligible (e.g., pensions, Social Security benefits).

In addition, for those participating in the Plan to Achieve Self-Support (PASS) program (see discussion later), SSI allows funds to be set aside to help return to work; these funds do not count toward the income or asset limit for SSI. Many states add money to the federal SSI payment. This additional payment is called a *state supplement,* meaning that the allowed income levels, as well as the SSI payments, are higher than the federal maximums in those states. Every state except Arizona, Arkansas, Georgia, Mississippi, Oregon, Tennessee, Texas, and West Virginia has a state supplement. For SSI updates, see the appropriate weblink in "Websites to Explore" at the end of this chapter.

Many people who are eligible for SSI also may be entitled to receive Social Security benefits. In fact, the application for SSI is also an application for Social Security benefits. Unlike Social Security benefits, SSI benefits are not based on prior work or a family member's prior work. It is easy to confuse SSI benefits with Social Security benefits. Refer to Box 10.1 for a comparison of the two programs.

SSI Work Incentives

Work incentives make it easier for adults with disabilities to work and still receive benefits from Social Security. The goal of work incentives is to help people with disabilities achieve independence by helping them take advantage of employment opportunities, thus minimizing the risk of losing their SSI or Medicaid benefits. Work incentives allow individuals to control their finances and healthcare during transition to work and financial independence. For more information on work incentives, go to http://www.socialsecurity.gov/work.

Ticket to Work

The **Ticket to Work** and Work Incentives Improvement Act of 1999 provides several important opportunities for people ages 18 through 64 who receive Social Security disability or SSI benefits and who want to go to work or increase their earnings. One of the opportunities provided by this law is the "Ticket" program, which is available in all states. Under the Ticket program, individuals are eligible to receive free employment services from an approved employment support service provider of their choice, or individuals can choose to work with their state vocational rehabilitation agency.

The term for an approved service provider is *employment network.* The employment network works with program enrollees to come up with a plan designed to help attain their goals. The program pays the employment networks for helping participants achieve certain earnings-related milestones and outcomes at no cost to the individual. The ultimate goal is to help program members find good jobs that lead to successful careers and ultimately to better self-supporting

---

Box **10.1**	Supplemental Security Income and Social Security Benefits

How Is Supplemental Security Income Different From Social Security Benefits?	How Is Supplemental Security Income Like Social Security Benefits?
Many people who are eligible for SSI may also be entitled to receive Social Security benefits. In fact, the application for SSI is also an application for Social Security benefits. • Unlike Social Security benefits, SSI benefits are not based on a person's (or a family member's) prior work. • SSI is financed by general funds of the US Treasury—from personal income taxes, corporate taxes, and other taxes. Social Security taxes are withheld under FICA or SECA and do not fund the SSI program. • In most states, SSI beneficiaries also can get medical assistance (Medicaid) to pay for hospital stays, doctor bills, prescription drugs, and other healthcare costs. • SSI beneficiaries may also be eligible for food assistance (except in California). In some states, an application for SSI benefits also serves as an application for food assistance. • To receive SSI benefits, a person must be disabled, blind, or at least 65 years old and must have "limited" income and resources.	• Both programs pay monthly benefits. • The medical standards for disability are the same in the two programs for individuals age 18 or older. There is a separate definition of disability under SSI for children from birth to age 18. • SSA administers both programs.

FICA, Federal Insurance Contributions Act; *SECA,* Self-Employment Contributions Act; *SSA,* Social Security Administration; *SSI,* Supplemental Security Income.
From Social Security Administration: *Understanding Supplemental Security Income (SSI) overview—2019 edition* (website). http://www.ssa.gov/ssi/text-over-ussi.htm.

futures. While participating in the Ticket program, SSI ceases disability reviews to monitor disabling conditions.

Plan to Achieve Self-Support

Plan to Achieve Self-Support (PASS) is an SSI provision to help individuals with disabilities return to work. PASS allows disabled individuals to set aside money and/or resources and assets to pay for items or services needed to achieve a specific work goal. PASS applicants must determine what training, items, or services are needed to reach their work goals and verify how much these items and services will cost. PASS then helps the person save to pay these costs and allows money to be set aside for payments for things like a vehicle, wheelchair, or computer if needed to reach the work goal.

COMMUNITY FIRST CHOICE OPTION

The **Community First Choice (CFC) Option** was established under the ACA of 2010 and became available on October 1, 2011. This option provides a 6% increase in federal matching payments to states for service expenditures related to this option. The CFC gives individuals with disabilities who are eligible for nursing homes and other institutional settings options to receive community-based services. CFC provides qualifying Medicaid beneficiaries the choice to leave facilities and institutions (e.g., nursing homes) for care in their own homes and communities with appropriate, cost-effective services and supports. CFC also helps address state waiting lists for services by providing qualified individuals with access to a community-based benefit within Medicaid. The option does not allow caps on the number of individuals served, nor does it allow waiting lists for these services. States noted as "currently participating" are approved to participate or have a state plan amendment under official review by CMS.

MATERNAL AND CHILD HEALTH SERVICES

Maternal and Child Health (MCH) Services programs promote the development of local systems of healthcare for pregnant women, children ages 0 to 21, and their families and support the continued improvement in the health, safety, and well-being of all mothers and children, especially low-income and at-risk families. Fundamental to MCH programs are services that are family centered, community based, collaborative, comprehensive, flexible, coordinated, and culturally competent and developmentally appropriate. In addition, local grantees are expected to make a special effort to build community capacity to deliver such enabling services as care coordination, transportation, home visiting, and nutrition counseling, which complement and help ensure the success of CHIP and other medical assistance programs.

EARLY AND PERIODIC SCREENING, DIAGNOSIS, AND TREATMENT PROGRAM

Medicaid's child health component, known as the **Early and Periodic Screening, Diagnosis, and Treatment (EPSDT)** program (see earlier), was developed to fit the standards of pediatric care and to meet the special physical, emotional, and developmental needs of children from low-income families. Federal law, including statutes, regulations, and guidelines, requires that Medicaid cover a comprehensive set of benefits and services for children that are different from adult benefits. EPSDT offers an important way to ensure that young children receive appropriate health, mental health, and developmental services.

PROGRAM OF ALL-INCLUSIVE CARE FOR THE ELDERLY

In addition to mandatory and optional services, there are other program options, such as the **Program of All-Inclusive Care for the Elderly (PACE)** program option. This program provides comprehensive alternative care for noninstitutionalized elderly people who otherwise would be in a nursing home. PACE is centered on the belief that it is better for the well-being of elderly with long-term care needs and their families to be served in the community where they live whenever possible. PACE serves individuals who are age 55 or older, certified by their state to need nursing home care, able to live safely in the community at the time of enrollment, and live in a PACE service area. Although all PACE participants must be certified to need nursing home care to enroll in PACE, only a small percentage of PACE participants reside in nursing homes nationally. If a PACE enrollee does need nursing home care, the PACE program pays for it and continues to coordinate his or her care.

MEDICAID HOME AND COMMUNITY-BASED SERVICES WAIVERS

Medicaid **Home and Community-Based Services (HCBS) Waivers programs** are the federally approved Medicaid programs authorized by Title XIX of the Social Security Act that provide services in the home for persons who would otherwise require institutional care in a hospital, nursing facility, or intermediate care facility. In January 2014, the CMS issued a final rule for home and community-based programs. The rule contains requirements that ensure persons who receive Medicaid home and community-based services do so from providers who:

- Help them to be active in the community
- Provide a homelike environment if a person lives in a group home, assisted living facility, or adult family care home
- Enable them to make personal choices

In addition, the rule requires the agency to provide an opportunity for the public to comment on its transition plan and any changes the state proposes to its HCBS Waivers and state plan programs.

> **?** **What Did You Learn?**

1. TANF replaced the federal program known as
   _____.
2. What are some of the services typically covered by CHIP?
3. True or false: The SSI program is the same as the Social Security program.
4. List the requirements for SSI eligibility.
5. Identify the choice(s) offered in the CFC Option.
6. What does the EPSDT program offer and to what population group?
7. Name the program that is centered on the belief that the elderly with long-term care needs are better served in their own community.

MEDICAID PREMIUMS AND COST-SHARING

Recognizing the limited family budgets of low-income individuals, federal rules set limitations in Medicaid and CHIP on the amount of premiums and cost-sharing (copayments, coinsurance, and deductibles) that states may charge. Consistent with federal rules, premiums and cost-sharing for selected services generally remain low in Medicaid and CHIP. Even when they are allowed to charge premiums and cost-sharing, many states limit charges in their programs to minimize barriers so that enrollees can obtain care at affordable costs and to reduce complicated administrative functions for state agencies.

Maximum allowable amounts of premiums and cost-sharing in Medicaid vary by income and group. Medicaid enrollees, including children, pregnant women, qualifying parents, and the adult expansion group with incomes below 150% of the FPL may not be charged premiums. Cost-sharing generally is not allowed for children with incomes below 133% of the FPL. Adults enrolled in Medicaid may have to pay cost-sharing fees, but charges for those below 100% of the FPL are limited to small amounts. Medicaid enrollees (both children and adults) with incomes above 150% of the FPL can be charged premiums and higher cost-sharing compared with those at lower income levels.

Cost-sharing cannot be charged for preventive services for children or for emergency services, family planning, and pregnancy-related services in Medicaid. Overall premium and cost-sharing amounts for family members enrolled in Medicaid may not exceed 5% of household income. States have somewhat greater flexibility to charge premiums and cost-sharing for children covered by CHIP, although there are federal limits on the amounts that can be charged, including the overall 5% cap. CMS released final rules that streamlined and simplified existing regulations around premiums and cost-sharing while also making some changes to regulations for cost-sharing. (Note: Cost-sharing amounts, FPLs, and percentages of FPLs are subject to annual changes.)

The Deficit Reduction Act of 2005 allows providers in most states to withhold care or services from individuals who do not meet their cost-sharing obligations, except for those whose income is at or below 100% of the FPL. In addition, states have the option to terminate coverage if a recipient fails to make premium payments for periods longer than 60 days. States may waive this penalty in cases in which it would impose "undue hardship."

PRESCRIPTION DRUGS

Anyone eligible for Medicaid coverage may also receive the benefit of coverage for their prescription drug needs unless they are also receiving Medicare. If the Medicaid beneficiary is receiving Medicare, that coverage takes care of prescription needs (see discussion later). There may be exceptions to this ruling, such as when an individual state decides to cover a medication that is not covered by Medicare Part D. Although pharmacy coverage is an optional benefit under federal Medicaid law, all states currently provide coverage for outpatient prescription drugs to all categorically eligible individuals and most other enrollees within their state Medicaid programs.

Under Medicaid, states have the ability to use out-of-pocket charges to promote the most cost-effective use of prescription drugs. To encourage the use of lower-cost drugs, states may establish different copayments for generic versus brand name drugs or for drugs included on a **preferred drug list**. For people with incomes above 150% of the FPL, copayments for nonpreferred drugs may be as high as 20% of the cost of the drug. For people with income at or below 150% of the FPL, copayments are limited to smaller amounts. States must specify which drugs are considered either "preferred" or "nonpreferred." States also have the option to establish different copayments for mail-order drugs and for drugs sold in a pharmacy.

MEDICAID DRUG REBATE PROGRAM

The Medicaid Drug Rebate Program is a program that includes CMS, state Medicaid agencies, and participating drug manufacturers and helps offset the federal and state costs of most outpatient prescription drugs dispensed to Medicaid patients. Approximately 600 drug manufacturers currently participate in this program. All 50 states and the District of Columbia cover prescription drugs under the Medicaid Drug Rebate Program, which is authorized by Section 1927 of the Social Security Act.

PRESCRIPTION DRUGS FOR DUAL ELIGIBLES

Beginning January 1, 2006, full-benefit dual eligible individuals began receiving drug coverage through the Medicare Prescription Drug Benefit (Part D) of the Medicare Prescription Drug, Improvement, and Modernization Act of 2003 rather than through their state Medicaid programs. However, certain drugs are excluded from coverage under the Medicare Prescription Drug Benefit. The secretary of HHS is responsible for automatically enrolling dual eligible individuals into Part D plans if they do not sign up on their own.

To the extent that state Medicaid programs cover the excluded drugs for Medicaid recipients who are not full-benefit dual eligibles, states are required to cover the excluded drugs for full-benefit dual eligibles with federal financial participation. More information on the Medicare Prescription Drug Plan is available in Chapter 11.

EMERGENCY MEDICAL TREATMENT AND LABOR ACT

Congress enacted the **Emergency Medical Treatment and Labor Act (EMTALA)** in 1986 to make sure that the public has access to emergency services regardless of ability to pay. Section 1867 of the Social Security Act states that if a patient arrives at the emergency department of a Medicare-participating hospital that offers emergency services, the hospital must provide a medical screening examination and/or treatment for any emergent medical condition, including active labor, regardless of an individual's ability to pay. (An emergent medical situation is one that arises suddenly and unexpectedly that calls for quick medical judgment to determine if it is an actual emergency.) Hospitals are then required to stabilize patients with emergency medical conditions. If a hospital is unable to stabilize a patient within its capability, or if the patient requests it, he or she should be transported to an appropriate alternative facility.

COMMUNITY CALL PLAN AND EMERGENCY WAIVER

In March 2015 the CMS issued clarification for three significant changes to EMTALA. These changes involve community call plans, EMTALA waivers in times of national emergency, and transfer obligations related to hospitals with specialized capabilities. A **community call plan** is when two or more hospitals participate in a formal agreement to develop and implement a plan to coordinate on-call physician coverage in a specific geographic area (i.e., community).

During a national emergency, the secretary of the HHS may temporarily *waive* (set aside) EMTALA restrictions to allow hospitals to implement their disaster plans to provide healthcare services in a disaster area. In such cases, the hospital must notify the appropriate state agency so that CMS can track the number and locations of hospitals using waivers.

For detailed information on EMTALA, go to the cms.gov website and use "EMTALA" in the search box.

NONEMERGENCY USE OF EMERGENCY DEPARTMENTS

States have the option to charge higher copayments for Medicaid recipients who visit a hospital emergency department for treatment of a condition that is not considered a true emergency. This copayment is limited to nonemergency services, because emergency services are exempt from all out-of-pocket cost-sharing. For people with incomes above 150% of the FPL, copayment amounts for such improper use of an emergency department can be as high as the established cost for the service.

URGENT CARE CENTERS

Some states (e.g., Oregon) are limiting emergency department visits to certain medical conditions. As an option, Medicaid and other healthcare payers are encouraging patients to use **urgent care centers** as an alternative. Urgent care centers offer immediate outpatient medical care for the treatment of acute and chronic illness and injury. Urgent care does not replace a primary care physician, but it can be a convenient option when a person's regular physician is on vacation or unable to offer a timely appointment or when illness strikes outside of regular office hours. Urgent care offers a less costly alternative to a hospital emergency department visit.

> **? What Did You Learn?**
> 1. Explain cost-sharing.
> 2. What types of items are typically included in cost-sharing?
> 3. True or false: States can charge limited premiums and enrollment fees on certain groups of Medicaid enrollees.
> 4. True or false: All groups of Medicare enrollees must be charged the same premium.
> 5. Name three types of services that are exempt from out-of-pocket costs.
> 6. True or false: Medicaid recipients cannot be seen in hospital emergency departments.

ACCEPTING MEDICAID PATIENTS

Physicians have the choice of whether to accept Medicaid patients—that is, patients with Medicaid coverage only or those with coverage by any combination of Medicaid and other health insurance (OHI). (Keep in mind that Medicaid is *always* the payer of last resort.) In an emergency, or if it cannot be determined whether the patient has Medicaid at the time of treatment, the patient must be informed as soon as possible after

Medicaid coverage has been identified whether the practice will accept him or her as a Medicaid patient.

In most states, physicians can limit the number of Medicaid patients they accept, as long as there is no discrimination by age, sex, race, religious preference, or national origin, in addition to the limits of their scope of practice. If a practice sees only children, refusing to accept adult patients is not considered discrimination. If a patient has Medicare and Medicaid coverage, however, and the practice does not accept the Medicaid coverage, the health insurance professional must make sure that the patient understands this *before* treatment. The patient then has the opportunity to find a physician who would accept the patient's Medicaid coverage.

If a Medicaid recipient insists on being treated by a nonparticipating healthcare provider (one who does not accept Medicaid), it is recommended that the health insurance professional ask the patient to sign a form verifying his or her understanding that the practice does not accept Medicaid and that he or she will be responsible for paying the deductible and coinsurance amounts.

VERIFYING ELIGIBILITY

Before providing services, Medicaid providers should always make sure that Medicaid will pay for patients' medical care, determine eligibility for the current date, and discover any limitations to the recipient's coverage. Because most states grant eligibility a month at a time for most Medicaid-eligible patients, eligibility should be verified for every month in which the patient visits the practice. If a patient is being seen more often, such as for weekly allergy injections or frequent monitoring for some other condition, verifying eligibility on a monthly basis is probably often enough; however, the health insurance professional might want to check with the local Medicaid contractor. Several methods of verification are available in most states; the health insurance professional may be able to verify eligibility by using one or more of the following:

- The patient's Medicaid identification (ID) card
- An automated voice response (AVR) system
- Electronic data interchange (EDI)
- A point-of-sale device
- A computer software program

Medicaid Identification Card

A common method for verifying a patient's Medicaid eligibility is the ID card. Many states now use a plastic Medicaid ID card that is smaller than the former paper document and easier for clients to carry in their wallet. Because cards are issued by the individual states, they will look different depending on the state in which it is issued. Using plastic, credit card–size IDs rather than a larger piece of paper mailed on a monthly basis is expected to save Medicaid programs money in printing and mailing costs.

Cards are normally issued on a one-time basis; however, lost cards can be replaced, or a new card may be issued in special circumstances. The card should be presented to the healthcare provider when Medicaid recipients seek healthcare services. The cards have a magnetic strip, much like a credit card, that the healthcare provider can swipe in a "reader" to access the member ID. Providers then can use a web-based system to verify eligibility. The following steps are suggestions for eligibility verification:

- Ensure that the patient's name is on the ID card.
- Request another form of ID to confirm the patient's identity, unless he or she is known to office personnel.
- Check the eligibility period or issue date on the card.
- Look for insurance information. (In the example shown in Fig. 10.2, if the Medicaid recipient had another health plan, its name and phone number would be listed in the space indicated.)
- Examine the card closely to see whether the patient is enrolled in a special program or has special coverage.
- Photocopy the document if a paper ID is still used in your state.
- Enter any new information in the patient's record.
- Verify eligibility, because a Medicaid card does not necessarily guarantee that the patient is still in the program.

Some states color-code ID cards, and the color of the card tells the health insurance professional which type of Medicaid program the recipient is enrolled in. Keep in mind that Medicaid cards are issued by the individual states, and each is different. Fig. 10.3 is an example of South Carolina's Medicaid (Healthy Connections) ID card, which shows the beneficiary name, date of birth, and ID number.

It is important for the health insurance professional to obtain a provider's guide from the Medicaid contractor in his or her state for assistance in interpreting the information and codes on the Medicaid ID card.

Automated Voice Response System

The AVR system allows a touch-tone phone call to be used to obtain eligibility information. For this method of verification, the health insurance professional needs to know the patient's Medicaid ID number or Social Security number and date of birth. The AVR system can provide a variety of eligibility information, including the following:

- Eligibility for specific dates of service
- The type of coverage or special programs in which the patient is enrolled
- Whether the patient is covered under Medicare Part A and Part B
- Information known by Medicaid concerning other insurance coverage

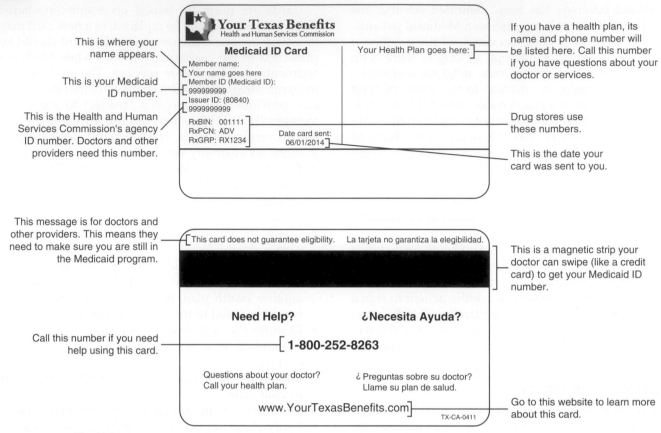

This is where your name appears.

This is your Medicaid ID number.

This is the Health and Human Services Commission's agency ID number. Doctors and other providers need this number.

Your Texas Benefits
Health and Human Services Commission

Medicaid ID Card

Your Health Plan goes here:

Member name:
Your name goes here
Member ID (Medicaid ID):
999999999
Issuer ID: (80840)
9999999999

RxBIN: 001111
RxPCN: ADV
RxGRP: RX1234

Date card sent:
06/01/2014

If you have a health plan, its name and phone number will be listed here. Call this number if you have questions about your doctor or services.

Drug stores use these numbers.

This is the date your card was sent to you.

This message is for doctors and other providers. This means they need to make sure you are still in the Medicaid program.

This card does not guarantee eligibility. La tarjeta no garantiza la elegibilidad.

This is a magnetic strip your doctor can swipe (like a credit card) to get your Medicaid ID number.

Call this number if you need help using this card.

Need Help?   **¿Necesita Ayuda?**

1-800-252-8263

Questions about your doctor? Call your health plan.

¿ Preguntas sobre su doctor? Llame su plan de salud.

www.YourTexasBenefits.com

TX-CA-0411

Go to this website to learn more about this card.

Fig. 10.2 Medicaid identification *(ID)* card. (From Texas Department of Health and Human Services Commission.)

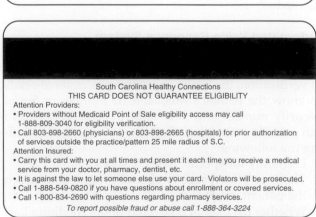

South Carolina
Healthy Connections

SUBSCRIBER NAME
DOB   12/20/2020
Medicaid Member Number: 1234567890

South Carolina Healthy Connections
THIS CARD DOES NOT GUARANTEE ELIGIBILITY
Attention Providers:
• Providers without Medicaid Point of Sale eligibility access may call 1-888-809-3040 for eligibility verification.
• Call 803-898-2660 (physicians) or 803-898-2665 (hospitals) for prior authorization of services outside the practice/pattern 25 mile radius of S.C.
Attention Insured:
• Carry this card with you at all times and present it each time you receive a medical service from your doctor, pharmacy, dentist, etc.
• It is against the law to let someone else use your card. Violators will be prosecuted.
• Call 1-888-549-0820 if you have questions about enrollment or covered services.
• Call 1-800-834-2690 with questions regarding pharmacy services.
To report possible fraud or abuse call 1-888-364-3224

Fig. 10.3 South Carolina's Medicaid identification (ID) card, showing the beneficiary name and ID number. (From South Carolina Healthy Connections.)

If the medical practice has access to this type of eligibility verification, the health insurance professional should know how to use it correctly and should keep current by requesting and reading periodic updates.

Electronic Data Interchange

Providers may obtain Medicaid eligibility information electronically. Online, interactive eligibility verification is available from EDI vendors (sometimes referred to as *clearinghouses*). Use of an EDI vendor is voluntary to providers. EDI vendors interface directly with the Medicaid recipient database maintained by an electronic data service for claims processing. The database is updated every day from the state's master eligibility file. This service is available 24 hours a day, 7 days a week, except for periods when it is down for system maintenance. EDI vendors normally charge a fee for their services, and providers might be required to pay a transaction fee to the state's Medicaid contractor.

Point-of-Sale Device

With a point-of-sale device, the patient is issued an ID card that is similar in size and design to a credit card. Through the information on the magnetic strip, the provider can swipe the card through the card reader device and receive an accurate return of eligibility information within a matter of seconds.

Computer Software Program

With eligibility verification through a computer software program, the provider can key the patient's information into the program and in a short time have an accurate return of eligibility information. Most state Medicaid offices provide the necessary software at no charge to enrolled providers.

BENEFITS OF ELIGIBILITY VERIFICATION SYSTEMS

By using one of these eligibility verification system methods, providers can reduce the number of denied claims by verifying recipient eligibility and insurance information before services are provided. Up-front verification using an eligibility verification system results in the submission of more accurate claims and decreases eligibility-related claims denials.

 HIPAA Tip

Medicaid providers and their vendors who bill electronically need to verify that their systems accept Health Insurance Portability and Accountability Act (HIPAA)–compliant Medicaid transactions.

PAYMENT FOR MEDICAID SERVICES

States establish their own Medicaid provider payment rates within federal requirements. States generally pay for services through FFS or managed care arrangements.

Under FFS, states pay providers directly for services rendered. Payment rates are based on:

- The costs of providing the service
- A review of what commercial payers pay in the private market
- A percentage of what Medicare pays for equivalent services

Under managed care arrangements, states contract with organizations to deliver care through networks and pay providers. Approximately 70% of Medicaid enrollees are served through managed care delivery systems, in which providers are typically paid on a monthly **capitation** payment rate.

Payment rates are often updated based on specific trending factors, such as the Medicare Economic Index or a Medicaid-specific trend factor that uses a state-determined inflation adjustment rate. Providers participating in Medicaid must accept the Medicaid reimbursement as payment in full. Each state is free to determine (within certain federal restrictions) how reimbursements are calculated and the resulting rates for services, with a few exceptions, such as institutional (hospital) services and hospice care.

Note: CMS has released a guide that has been used for Medicaid managed care rates since January 1, 2016. You can review this guide as well as an updated Medicaid Managed Care Rate Development Guide for rating periods starting between January 1, 2019, and June 30, 2020, at Medicaid.gov using the search words "Medicaid Managed Care Rate Development Guide."

MEDICALLY NECESSARY

As a general rule, Medicaid pays only for services that are determined to be **medically necessary**. For a procedure or service to be considered medically necessary, it typically must be consistent with the diagnosis and, in accordance with the standards of good medical practice, performed at the proper level and provided in the most appropriate setting. If the health insurance professional questions whether a service or procedure is medically necessary, he or she should consult the current Medicaid provider handbook provided by the state in which he or she is employed or should telephone the contractor that administers local Medicaid programs. This action should be taken before the service or procedure is performed to avoid problems with collecting payment from Medicaid or the patient after the fact.

PARTICIPATING PROVIDERS

As stated before, the healthcare provider can elect to accept or refuse Medicaid patients; however, many state regulations say that if a Medicaid **participating provider** elects to treat one Medicaid patient, the provider must accept all Medicaid patients in his or her particular specialty; the provider cannot single out which Medicaid patients to treat. However, providers can put a cap on the total number of new patients, including Medicaid patients, that they will accept. In addition, providers must agree to accept what Medicaid pays as payment in full for covered services (with the exception of any cost-sharing obligations on the part of the patient) and are prohibited by law to balance-bill Medicaid patients for these services. The healthcare professional should know beforehand whether a particular service or procedure is covered by Medicaid. If the patient insists on being treated for a particular noncovered service, it is recommended that he or she sign a waiver that spells out that the service is not covered by Medicaid and that the patient acknowledges responsibility for payment. Some practices even ask the patient to pay for noncovered services in advance.

 Stop and Think

As a general rule, Dr. Vandenberg accepts Medicaid patients in her family practice. After seeing Harold Apple, a patient with an unpleasant personality, Dr. Vandenberg advises the medical receptionist not to schedule any follow-up appointments for Mr. Apple. Is Dr. Vandenberg violating any Medicaid principles?

MEDICARE/MEDICAID RELATIONSHIP

Earlier in the chapter, we learned that most elderly or disabled individuals who are very poor are covered under Medicaid and Medicare, commonly referred to as *dual eligibility*—also called *dual coverage* or **Medicare-Medicaid (Medi-Medi)**. These individuals may receive Medicare services for which they are entitled and other services available under that state's Medicaid program. Because each state sets up its own Medicaid program, certain services typically not covered by Medicare (e.g., hearing aids, eyeglasses, nursing facility care beyond the 100 days covered by Medicare) may be provided to these individuals through the state's Medicaid program. In addition, the Medicaid program pays all of the cost-sharing portions (deductibles and coinsurance) of Medicare Part A and Part B for these dually eligible beneficiaries. Medicare Parts A and B are discussed in Chapter 11.

In all cases, Medicaid is always the payer of last resort. If an individual is a Medicare beneficiary, payments for any services covered by Medicare are made by the Medicare program before any payments are made by the Medicaid program. The bottom line: Medicaid pays last.

MEDICARE AND MEDICAID DIFFERENCES EXPLAINED

People are often confused about the differences between Medicare and Medicaid. Eligibility for Medicare is not tied to individual need. Rather, it is an *entitlement* program. Individuals are entitled to it because they or their spouses paid for it through Social Security taxes withheld from their wages. Medicaid is a federal *assistance* program for low-income, financially needy individuals set up by the federal government and administered differently in each state. Although an individual may qualify and receive coverage from Medicare and Medicaid, there are separate eligibility requirements for each program, and being eligible for one program does not mean that an individual is eligible for the other.

Table 10.7 provides a brief summary of the major differences between the two programs.

Table 10.7 Medicare and Medicaid: Two Different Programs

MEDICARE	MEDICAID
Provision of healthcare insurance for disabled individuals, individuals age 65 years and older, and individuals of any age with end-stage renal disease	Needs-based healthcare program
Individuals must have contributed to Medicare system (deductions from wages) to be eligible	Payment for long-term care for qualifying individuals
Payment for primary hospital care and related medically necessary services	Individuals must meet income and financial limitations to be eligible for certain programs
Generally, individuals must be older than age 65 to be eligible	Individuals must be 65 years of age or older, or disabled, or blind to qualify for coverage
There may be a copayment provision, depending on the services received	Requires mandatory contribution of *all* of a recipient's income in certain programs
A federally controlled, uniform application across the United States	Individual state-by-state plan options create a different program in each state (generally similar but may be different in specific application)
Title XVIII	Title XIX
Federal administration	State administration with federal oversight
Work history affects eligibility	Eligibility based on need
Public insurance	Public assistance
For aged, blind, and disabled	For aged, blind, disabled, pregnant women, children, and caretaker relatives
Funded by Social Security and Medicare payroll tax deductions	Funded by federal general fund appropriations combined with individual state funds

PROCESSING MEDICAID CLAIMS

As a rule, Medicaid does not process claims. Instead, individual states contract with an organization specializing in administering government healthcare programs. These contracting organizations, formerly called *fiscal intermediaries*, are now more commonly referred to as **Medicaid contractors**. Medicaid contractors process all healthcare claims on behalf of the Medicaid program. Some states have more than one contractor—one for FFS claims and a second one for managed care claims. Before a contractor is selected by the state, there is a bidding process similar to the bidding done by construction contractors for the job of building a bridge or road.

Responsibilities of a Medicaid contractor may differ from state to state; however, more common responsibilities are as follows:

- Process claims
- Provide information for healthcare providers for the particular government program involved
- Generate guidelines for providers to facilitate the claims process
- Answer beneficiary questions about benefits, claims processing, appeals, and the explanation of benefits (EOB; remittance advice [RA]) document

The health insurance professional should know the name and telephone number of his or her state Medicaid contractor and keep it handy, because this organization can offer a wealth of information on healthcare claims and administration of the Medicaid program. In addition, if and when questions arise regarding claims, help is available from the contractor.

In certain cases, Medicaid recipients can submit claims for covered Medicaid expenses on their own if their healthcare provider does not participate in the Medicaid program. Medicaid must receive claims within the required time frame. Deadlines to submit Medicaid claims vary by state, and most states' Medicaid programs do not pay late claims (see discussion later).

COMPLETING THE CMS-1500 USING MEDICAID GUIDELINES

The guidelines for completing a **Medicaid "simple" claim**—that is, the patient has Medicaid coverage only and no secondary insurance—can be found in Appendix B along with an example of a completed Medicaid simple claim. Keep in mind that these guidelines are generic, and the health insurance professional must follow the exact guidelines for completing the CMS-1500 form issued by the Medicaid contractor in his or her state.

SUBMITTING MEDICAID CLAIMS

The method for submitting Medicaid claims varies from state to state. Whereas most state Medicaid programs require electronic claim submission, nearly all Medicaid contractors accept paper claims, using either the universal CMS-1500 form or their own form if certain conditions apply. These exceptions depend on the individual state, and the health insurance professional should be knowledgeable of what exceptions to electronic claim filing apply in his or her state.

All providers who submit claims electronically—whether through a clearinghouse or directly to a Medicaid contractor—must do so using software obtained from an approved vendor. All electronic transactions must be compliant with the Health Insurance Portability and Accountability Act (HIPAA). Providers and clearinghouses that bill HIPAA-compliant transactions directly are normally required to complete and submit a certification agreement that binds the provider to the requirements stated in the agreement. This certification process helps prevent providers from submitting fraudulent claims.

There is no one specific computer program or universal requirement for submitting Medicaid claims except for the prerequisite of following HIPAA standards for electronic data submission. All states have their own software and guidelines, and some will provide this software to enrolled providers at no charge after providers complete an enrollment form and submit it to the appropriate Medicaid contractor. As with all third-party payers, the health insurance professional should contact the Medicaid contractor in his or her state for claims completion instructions and should make sure to have the current guidelines on hand.

TIME LIMIT FOR FILING MEDICAID CLAIMS

The time limit for filing Medicaid claims varies from state to state, anywhere from 2 months to 1 year from the date of service. The health insurance professional should check with the Medicaid contractor in his or her state for the "timely filing" deadline. It is good practice, however, to file all claims in a timely manner—typically right after the service has been performed, unless additional services are anticipated within the same month or eligibility period. If denial of a claim is received because of failure to meet the state's timely filing deadlines, the provider cannot bill the patient. Most Medicaid contractors no longer issue paper checks for claims payment, instead using electronic automatic deposit into the account specified by the provider.

MEDICAID SECONDARY CLAIMS

A **Medicaid secondary claim** occurs when the beneficiary has more than one type of healthcare coverage—Medicare, TRICARE, and/or OHI coverage (such as commercial or group policies) or dual coverage with traditional (original) Medicare enrollment. It is important that the health insurance professional determine which type of claim is being submitted, because Medicaid simple and **crossover claims** are often sent to different addresses and are processed differently. A crossover claim is the transfer, usually electronic, of claim data from one insurer (e.g., Medicare) to another insurer. The recipient of the information might be Medicaid, a state agency, or a private insurance company. If a claim is submitted to the wrong address, it may be processed incorrectly or denied. *Remember that Medicaid is always paid last.*

RESUBMISSION OF MEDICAID CLAIMS

When errors or omissions are detected on a Medicaid claim, it is typically rejected and returned to the provider for correction and resubmission. Although every Medicaid contractor may have different guidelines for correcting and resubmitting claims, most require a resubmission code and/or reference number, which is usually reported in Block 22 of the CMS-1500 claim form. In some states, Medicaid contractors offer online, real-time claims processing and resubmission capabilities. Every health insurance professional should be aware of the Medicaid resubmission rules applicable in his or her state.

RECIPROCITY

A simple dictionary definition of **reciprocity** is the occurrence of a situation in which individuals or entities offer certain rights to each other in return for the rights being given to them. In the field of healthcare insurance and coverage, when one state allows Medicaid beneficiaries from other states (usually states that are adjacent) to be treated in its medical facilities, this exchange of privileges is referred to as *reciprocity*. Health insurance professionals should be aware of which states, if any, offer reciprocity for Medicaid claims in their states.

 Imagine This!

Ellen Statler is a single mother of two dependent children living in a small Illinois town along the Mississippi River. Ellen is covered under Illinois Medicaid; however, because the nearest Illinois town where there is a healthcare provider who accepts Medicaid patients is 35 miles away, Ellen travels across the bridge into Iowa and receives care from a family practice clinic there, which is 2 miles from her home. This arrangement works out much more favorably for Ellen because both of her children have acute asthma, and periodic emergency visits are common. The Iowa provider is paid by Illinois Medicaid because a reciprocity agreement is in place.

COMMON MEDICAID BILLING ERRORS

The primary goal of the health insurance professional is to create and submit insurance claims so that the

---

Missing or erroneous:
• Provider and patient identification numbers
• Birthdates
• Diagnostic information
• Prior authorization information

Fig. 10.4 Common billing errors on Medicaid claims. (Data from Office of the Inspector General, Department of Health and Human Services: *Medicaid claims processing safeguards.* Available at https://oig.hhs.gov/oei/reports/oei-05-99-00071.pdf. Accessed October 16, 2019.)

maximum benefits the medical record supports are received in the minimal amount of time. This is a learned process, however, and it takes an experienced individual to avoid making common errors that cause a claim to be delayed or rejected. Fig. 10.4 lists some of the things to do to avoid billing errors.

 What Did You Learn?

1. What is a Medicaid "simple" claim?
2. What is the usual time limit for filing Medicaid claims?
3. Define a Medicaid secondary claim.
4. What is meant by a "crossover claim"?
5. Explain what is meant by "reciprocity."
6. List four common billing errors.

MEDICAID AND THIRD-PARTY LIABILITY

Third-party liability (TPL) refers to the legal obligation of third parties to pay all or part of the expenditures for medical assistance furnished under a state plan. Earlier in this chapter, we discussed the fact that the Medicaid program, by law, is intended to be the payer of last resort. Examples of third parties that may be liable to pay for services before Medicaid include but are not limited to the following:

• Group health plans
• Self-insured plans
• Employment-related health insurance
• Court-ordered health insurance by a noncustodial parent
• Workers' compensation
• Long-term care insurance
• Other state and federal programs (unless specifically excluded by federal statute)

The contract language between the individual state Medicaid agency and a managed care organization (MCO) dictates the terms and conditions under which the MCO assumes TPL responsibility. Generally, any TPL administration and performance activities by the MCO will be set by the state and should be supervised by the state.

Medicaid pays the bills when due and does not put the burden of collection from a third party on the Medicaid client. Individuals eligible for Medicaid assign their rights to third-party payments to the state Medicaid agency. States are required to take all reasonable measures to ensure that the legal liability of third parties to pay for care and services is met before funds are made available under the state Medicaid plan. Healthcare providers are obligated to inform Medicaid of any known third parties who might have liability.

When states have determined that a potentially liable third party exists, the state is required to **cost avoid** or **pay-and-chase claims**. Cost avoidance is the process by which the healthcare provider bills and collects from liable third parties before sending the claim to Medicaid. Pay-and-chase is used when the state Medicaid agency goes ahead and pays the medical bills and then attempts to recover these paid funds from liable third parties. States generally are required to cost avoid claims unless they have a waiver approved by CMS that allows them to use the pay-and-chase method. To learn more about TPL, cost avoidance, and collection, see "Websites to Explore" at the end of this chapter.

In the case of TPL, certain blocks of the CMS-1500 form are filled out differently. The health insurance professional must follow the specific Medicaid guidelines in his or her state.

As mentioned, in a case in which the patient has dual eligibility for Medi-Medi, Medicare is primary. In this case, the claim is submitted first to Medicare, which pays its share and then "crosses it over" to Medicaid. More information on Medi-Medi crossover claims is given in Chapter 11.

? What Did You Learn?

1. What is TPL?
2. List some examples of third-party entities that would be primary to Medicaid.
3. True or false: Medicaid pays the bills when due and does not put the burden of collection from a third party on the Medicaid recipient.
4. Explain the difference between "cost avoid" and "pay-and-chase" in reference to Medicaid claims.

MEDICAID REMITTANCE ADVICE

Every time a claim is sent to Medicaid, a document is generated explaining how the claim was **adjudicated**, or how the payment was determined. In the past, this document was referred to as the *EOB*; however, Medicaid now calls it the **remittance advice (RA)**. The RA can be in paper or electronic form (if the medical facility is set up to accept the standard electronic version) and contains information from one or several claims. Fig. 10.5 shows an example of a standard paper remittance notice. The RA typically contains several "remark codes" and "reason codes." The importance of understanding the codes and interpreting this document cannot be stressed enough. Many states generate an RA periodically (e.g., weekly), and the current

status of all claims (including adjustments and voids) that have been processed during the past week is indicated. The RA format may differ from state to state; however, all states furnish basically the same information. It is the health insurance professional's responsibility to interpret this document and reconcile it with patient records. All Medicaid claims and RAs should be maintained for 6 years, or longer if mandated by state statutes of limitation.

? What Did You Learn?

1. Another name for an EOB is a(n) _____.
2. What two types of codes typically appear on an RA?
3. True or false: Although all state RA formats may be different, the information contained in them is basically the same.

SPECIAL BILLING NOTES

The health insurance professional must keep several things in mind when filing Medicaid claims, as described here.

ACCEPTING ASSIGNMENT

As mentioned, Medicaid payments are made directly to the healthcare provider. Some Medicaid contractors require that "YES" is checked in Block 27 if filing a paper claim. Providers participating in Medicaid must accept the Medicaid reimbursement as payment in full. **Balance billing**, billing the recipient for any amount not paid by Medicaid, is not allowed. However, certain population groups can be subject to cost-sharing for some types of services. In addition, according to federal law, a provider who accepts Medicaid payment for services furnished to an ill or injured individual has no right to additional payment from a liable third party even if Medicaid has been reimbursed.

SERVICES REQUIRING PRIOR APPROVAL

Prior approval may be required for certain categories of Medicaid services, products, and procedures to verify medical necessity, with the exception of some emergency situations. If prior approval is required, the provider must request and obtain this approval before rendering the service, product, or procedure to pursue Medicaid payment. Obtaining prior approval *does not* necessarily guarantee payment or ensure recipient eligibility on the date of service. The recipient must be Medicaid eligible on the date that the service, product, or procedure is provided. Requests for prior approval must be submitted as specified by the local HHS office or the Medicaid contractor in the particular state in which the services are rendered.

PREAUTHORIZATION

Most states require 24-hour preauthorization for all inpatient hospitalization, unless the hospitalization is due

PERF PROV	SERV DATE	POS NOS	PROC	MODS	BILLED	ALLOWED	DEDUCT	COINS	GRP /RC-AMT	PROV PD
NAME ALPHA, ALBERT		HIC 699777777A	ACNT 1111111111					ICN 1402065330030	ASG Y MOA MA01	
W88888888	1215 121519	11	1 92547		98.00	27.22	0.00	5.44	CO-42 70.78	21.78
W88888888	1215 121519	11	1 92541		45.00	39.89	0.00	7.98	CO-42 5.11	31.91
PT RESP 13.42			CLAIM TOTALS		143.00	67.11	0.00	13.42	75.89	53.69
										53.69 NET

NAME BAKER, LEEANN		HIC 699123123A	ACNT 0009					ICN 1102025001590	ASG Y MOA MA01 MA18	
W88888888	0113 011320	11	1 J9202 GACC (J9217)		600.00	446.49	0.00	89.30	CO-42 153.51	357.19
W88888888	0121 012120	11	1 J9202 CC (J9217)		600.00	446.49	0.00	89.30	CO-42 153.51	357.19
PT RESP 178.60			CLAIM TOTALS		1200.00	892.98	0.00	178.60	307.02	714.38
										714.38 NET

CLAIM INFORMATION FORWARDED TO: BCBS OF MINNESOTA ④

NAME CHARLIE, CINDY		HIC 699222222A	ACNT 22222222					ICN 1402008151040	ASG Y MOA MA01	
W88888888	0106 010620	11	1 76091 26		80.00	43.76	0.00	8.75	CO-42 36.24	35.01
W88888888	0106 010620	11	1 G0236 26		50.00	0.00	0.00	0.00	CO-B5 50.00	00.00
REM: M58										
PT RESP 8.75			CLAIM TOTALS		130.00	43.76	0.00	8.75	86.24	35.01

ADJS: PREV PD 0.00 INT 0.17 LATE FILING CHARGE 0.00 ②   35.18 NET

NAME BETA, BOB		HIC 699111111A	ACNT 12345678901234567890				ICN 1402063333010		ASG Y MOA MA01 MA72	
W88888888	0304 030420	11	1 99214		180.00	81.99	47.65	6.87	CO-42 98.01	00.00
W88888888	0304 030420	11	1 82010		30.00	0.00	0.00	0.00	CO-B7 30.00	00.00
W88888888	0304 030420	11	1 J1040		10.00	9.39	0.00	1.88	CO-42 00.61	00.00
PT RESP 56.40			CLAIM TOTALS		220.00	91.38	47.65	8.75	128.62	00.00
										00.00 NET

NAME BUMAN, JAMES		HIC 699555555A	ACNT 55555555					ICN 1402065200070	ASG Y MOA MA01	
W88888888	0304 030420	11	1 99214		75.00	0.00	0.00	0.00	PR-B7 75.00	00.00
									OA-71 20.00	
									PR-A3 -20.00	
PT RESP 55.00			CLAIM TOTALS		75.00	0.00	0.00	0.00	75.00	00.00
										00.00 NET

TOTALS: # OF CLAIMS	BILLED AMT	ALLOWED AMT	DEDUCT AMT	COINS AMT	TOTAL RC-AMT	PROV PD AMT	PROV ADJ AMT ❸	CHECK AMT
5	1768.00	1095.23	47.65	209.52	672.77	803.08	108.50	749.56

PROVIDER ADJ DETAILS:	PLB REASON CODE	FCN	HIC	AMOUNT ❶
	CS	1402063333010	699111111A	34.98
	CS	1402065200070	699555555A	20.00
	WO	7101347082956		53.69
	L6			-0.17

GLOSSARY: Group, Reason, MOA, Remark and Adjustment Codes:

CO	Contractual Obligation. Amount for which the provider is financially liable. The patient may not be billed for this amount.
PR	Patient Responsibility. Amount that may be billed to a patient or another payee.
OA	Other Adjustment.
A3	Medicare Secondary Payer liability met.
B5	Claim/Service denied/reduced because coverage guidelines were not met or were exceeded.
B7	This provider was not certified for this procedure/service on this date of service.
42	Charges exceed our fee schedule or maximum allowable amount.
71	Primary Payer amount.
M58	Please resubmit the claim with the missing/correct information so that it may be processed.
MA01	If you do not agree with what we approved for these services, you may appeal our decision. To make sure that we are fair to you, we require another individual that did not process your initial claim to conduct the review. However, in order to be eligible for a review, you must write to us within 6 months of the date of this notice, unless you have a good reason for being late.
MA119	Provider level adjustment for late claim filing applies to this claim.
MA18	The claim information is also being forwarded to the patient's supplemental insurer. Send any questions regarding supplemental benefits to them.
MA72	The beneficiary overpaid you for these assigned services. You must issue the beneficiary a refund within 30 days for the difference between his/her payment to you and the total of the amount shown as patient responsibility and as paid to the beneficiary on this notice.
CS	Adjustment
WO	Withholding
L6	Interest

3/25/02

Fig. 10.5 Standard paper remittance notices, revised format.

to an emergency. In the case of an emergency, most Medicaid contractors require 24-hour notification after the emergency visit, as appropriate. There are typically two options for requesting prior authorization: by telephone or online. Some states have specific forms that must be filled out to get authority from Medicaid to perform specific procedures or services. Normally, a preadmission/preprocedure review is performed by the provider before the patient is admitted to the hospital and the procedure or service is performed. Costs of services that require review will not be paid unless the claim indicates that review has been performed, the admission is medically necessary, and the setting is appropriate. The Medicaid contractor provides a preauthorization number, which should be entered in Block 23 of the CMS-1500 form and is required for electronic claims as well. The health insurance professional should review and be aware of what procedures and services require a preadmission/preprocedure review and preauthorization. This information usually can be found in the Medicaid website or provider manual. The health insurance professional also can contact his or her local Medicaid contractor if unsure whether a particular service or procedure requires prior authorization.

 HIPAA Tip

Paper claim and prior authorization/request form instructions must be consistent with the Administrative Simplification provisions of the federal Health Insurance Portability and Accountability Act (HIPAA) of 1996.

 What Did You Learn?

1. True or false: Obtaining prior approval guarantees payment and ensures recipient eligibility on the date of service.
2. Name two methods that a provider can use to obtain preauthorization to perform a service.
3. True or false: All states require 24-hour preauthorization for all inpatient hospitalization, unless the hospitalization is due to an emergency.

FRAUD AND ABUSE IN THE MEDICAID SYSTEM

We learned in Chapter 3 that **fraud** is an intentional misrepresentation or deception that could result in an unauthorized benefit to an individual or individuals and usually comes in the form of a false statement requesting payment under the Medicaid program. **Abuse** typically involves payment for items or services for which there was no intent to deceive or misrepresent, but the outcome of poor and inefficient methods results in unnecessary costs to the Medicaid program.

WHAT IS MEDICAID FRAUD?

Medicaid fraud and abuse drive up healthcare costs for everyone. Medicaid fraud occurs when a healthcare

Box 10.2 Common Examples of Medicaid Fraud

- Billing for medical services not actually performed
- Billing for a more expensive service than was rendered
- Billing separately for several services that should be combined into one billing
- Billing twice for the same medical service or procedure
- Billing for ambulance runs when no medical service or transport is provided
- Dispensing generic drugs and billing for brand-name drugs
- Giving or accepting something in return for medical services (kickbacks)
- Providing unnecessary services
- Submitting false cost reports
- Transporting multiple passengers in an ambulance and billing a run for each passenger

Note: This list provides common examples of fraud; however, it is not an all-inclusive list. Although states are primarily responsible for detecting, prosecuting, and preventing Medicaid fraud, waste, and abuse, the federal government assists in these efforts by providing information, tools, and training to help states build effective anti-fraud programs. The health insurance professional should contact the Office of Inspector General's National Fraud Hotline at 1-800-447-8477 if he or she has evidence or suspects that a healthcare provider (or patient) is committing Medicaid fraud.

provider (such as a physician, dentist, pharmacist, hospital, nursing home, or other healthcare service) engages in one or more of the practices described in Box 10.2.

PATIENT ABUSE AND NEGLECT

Frequent unexplained injuries or complaints of pain without obvious injury can be indicators of patient abuse and neglect, which is particularly common in nursing homes and other long-term care facilities. In many cases, abuse goes undetected for a time because the victim is unable to communicate the abuse to the proper authorities. Although the signs of patient abuse and neglect are numerous, a few are listed in Table 10.8.

 Imagine This!

Superior Ambulance Company transports patients from the Coast View Convalescent Home to a nearby medical center. The vehicles are equipped to carry four patients at a time. Shirley Holmes, whose father (a Medicaid recipient) resides at Coast View, received a bill for $800 for an emergency transport. She was with her father at the time of transport and noted that two other residents were occupants of the ambulance at the same time her father was taken to the medical center. Mrs. Holmes discussed the charge with Coast View's administrator, and it was discovered that the ambulance company, rather than splitting the cost of the transport among the three patients who were transported on that run, charged each patient the entire $800 fee.

Table 10.8	**Signs of Patient Abuse and Neglect**
Physical abuse	• Frequent unexplained injuries or complaints of pain without obvious injury • Burns or bruises suggesting the use of instruments, cigarettes, etc. • Passive, withdrawn, and emotionless behavior • Lack of reaction to pain • Injuries that appear after the person has not been seen for several days • Patient reports physical abuse
Sexual abuse	• Sexually transmitted infections • Injuries to the genital area • Difficulty in sitting or walking • Fear of being alone with caretakers • Patient reports a sexual assault
Neglect	• Obvious malnutrition • Lack of personal cleanliness • Habitually dressed in torn or dirty clothing • Obvious fatigue and listlessness • Begging for food or water • In need of medical or dental care • Left unattended for long periods • Patient reports neglect

 Stop and Think

Martin Roble received a prescription for a medication that was to be filled using a generic product. The pharmacist filled the prescription with generic drugs, according to Medicaid rules, but charged Medicaid for the more expensive brand-name medication. Would this be considered fraud or abuse?

RECOGNIZING FRAUD AND ABUSE

The health insurance professional should learn how to recognize fraud and abuse and do everything possible to prevent or stop it. There is a Medicaid Fraud Control Unit in every state, which is a federally funded state law enforcement unit located in the state attorney general's office. In addition to investigating fraud committed by healthcare providers, the Medicaid Fraud Control Unit investigates the abuse, neglect, and exploitation of elderly, ill, and disabled residents of long-term care facilities, such as nursing homes, facilities for the mentally and physically disabled, and assisted living facilities. The investigation of corruption in the administration of the Medicaid program is another important responsibility of the Medicaid Fraud Control Unit. To report fraud or abuse, health insurance professionals may use the state's hotline number or contact the Medicaid Fraud Control Unit nearest them.

Extensive information on Medicaid fraud and abuse can be found on the CMS website.

 What Did You Learn?

1. What is the difference between fraud and abuse?
2. What should the health insurance professional do when fraud or abuse is suspected?

MEDICAID QUALITY PRACTICES

"The right care for every person every time" is how CMS defines quality. CMS is responsible for supporting state Medicaid and CHIP programs in their efforts to achieve patient-centered, safe, effective, efficient, timely, and equitable care. CMS partners with states to share best practices, provide technical assistance to improve performance measurement, evaluate current improvement efforts to inform future activities, work together with quality partners, and coordinate activities to en sure efficiency of operations.

MEDICAID INTEGRITY PROGRAM

The **Medicaid Integrity Program (MIP)** is a comprehensive federal policy established to prevent and reduce provider fraud, waste, and abuse in the Medicaid program. CMS has two broad responsibilities under the MIP:

• To hire contractors to review Medicaid provider activities, audit claims, identify overpayments, and educate providers and others on Medicaid program integrity issues
• To provide effective support and assistance to states in their efforts to combat Medicaid provider fraud and abuse

To learn more about the MIP, see "Websites to Explore" at the end of this chapter.

 What Did You Learn?

1. What government entity is responsible for supporting state Medicaid and CHIP programs?
2. What are the two responsibilities CMS has under the MIP?

THE HEALTH INSURANCE PROFESSIONAL'S ROLE

The health insurance professional must learn the specific guidelines for the Medicaid programs offered in the state in which he or she is employed to perform his or her job judiciously. The health insurance professional should contact the Medicaid contractor in his or her state to obtain a guide as to what programs are available and what each one covers in that state. An alternative resource for this information is listed in "Websites to Explore" at the end of this chapter. For a more in-depth discussion of Medicaid, visit the websites listed at the end of the chapter.

 HIPAA Tip

Every health insurance professional who files insurance claims, including Medicaid claims, should be trained in Health Insurance Portability and Accountability Act (HIPAA) policies, procedures, and processes.

 What Did You Learn?

1. What must the health insurance professional learn to perform his or her job judiciously?

SUMMARY CHECKPOINTS

- Medicaid is a combination federal and state medical assistance program designed to provide medical care for low-income individuals and families. Since its beginning, it has evolved into a large insurance program with complex eligibility rules. Today Medicaid is a major social welfare program administered by CMS. The federal government establishes broad national guidelines for Medicaid eligibility and contributes funds to individual states to implement their programs. Population groups eligible for Medicaid include but are not limited to categorically needy, medically needy, and those who qualify for SSI.
- The following are some of the changes that occurred in the Medicaid program since the ACA was enacted:
  - Medically needy groups were expanded.
  - In 2014 people under 65 with income up to 138% of the FPL became eligible for Medicaid.
  - All states that accepted the Medicaid expansion follow uniform eligibility requirements.
  - Expansion almost exclusively covers the working poor and their families.
  - Medicaid expansion helps cover gaps between current Medicaid eligibility and families being able to afford private health insurance using marketplace subsidies.
- Title XIX of the Social Security Act requires that in order for a state to receive federal matching funds for their Medicaid programs, certain basic services (referred to as *mandated [or mandatory] services*) must be offered to the categorically needy population. States can choose to provide other optional benefits. Medically needy is an optional eligibility category. States that allow medically needy individuals to qualify for Medicaid deduct the cost of the person's medical care from his or her income when determining eligibility.
- To qualify for dual eligibility, an individual must meet the requirements for both Medicare and Medicaid. Some people qualify for Medicare and partial dual eligibility, meaning that they have Medicare coverage and can receive Medicaid benefits if they pay a small monthly premium, or cost-share. Others qualify for total dual eligibility, meaning that they can be covered by both Medicare and Medicaid and, because their income and assets are below a certain point, they do not have to pay Medicaid premiums.
- Key Medicaid programs include TANF, which provides temporary funds to needy families, and CHIP, which provides federal matching funds for states to implement health insurance programs for children in families that earn too much to qualify for Medicaid but too little to reasonably afford private health coverage. The EPSDT program was developed to fit the standards of pediatric care and to meet the special physical, emotional, and developmental needs of low-income children, and PACE provides comprehensive alternative care for noninstitutionalized elderly patients who otherwise would be in a nursing home.
- Cost-sharing is when certain groups of beneficiaries are required to pay a portion of the cost of medical services (e.g., copayments, premiums) for Medicaid. Cost-sharing varies by beneficiary category, income level, and the type of service. People who fall in the medically needy category may be required to share in the cost of their medical care. However, premium charges and service-related cost-sharing are prohibited under traditional Medicaid for certain eligibility groups and services (e.g., categorically needy).
- Anyone eligible for Medicaid coverage may also receive the benefit of coverage for their prescription needs unless they are also receiving Medicare. If the Medicaid beneficiary is receiving Medicare, that coverage takes care of prescription needs. Although pharmacy coverage is an optional benefit under federal Medicaid law, all states currently provide coverage for outpatient prescription drugs to all categorically eligible individuals and most other enrollees within their state Medicaid programs. Under Medicaid, states have the ability to use out-of-pocket charges to promote the most cost-effective use of prescription drugs.
- Congress enacted EMTALA in 1996 to make sure that the public has access to emergency services regardless of ability to pay. The law states that if a patient arrives at the emergency department of a Medicare-participating hospital that offers emergency services, the hospital must provide a medical screening examination and/or treatment for any emergent medical condition, including active labor, regardless of an individual's ability to pay. Hospitals are then required to stabilize patients; if the hospital is unable to do so within its capability, or if the patient requests it, he or she should be transported to an appropriate alternative facility.
- Medicaid eligibility can be verified in the following ways:
  - Patient's Medicaid ID card
  - AVR system—uses a touch-tone phone process
  - EDI—involves online interactive clearinghouses
  - Point-of-sale device—eligibility information is on a magnetic strip similar to a credit card
  - Computer software programs—involve keying patient information into a computer
- Medicare is not tied to individual need. Rather, it is an entitlement program. Individuals are entitled to it because they or their spouses paid for it through Social Security taxes withheld from their wages. Medicaid is a federal assistance program for low-income, financially needy individuals set up by the federal government and administered differently in each state. Although an individual may qualify and

receive coverage from Medicare and Medicaid, there are separate eligibility requirements for each program, and being eligible for one program does not mean that an individual is eligible for the other.

- The method for submitting Medicaid claims varies from state to state. Whereas most state Medicaid programs require electronic claim submission, nearly all Medicaid contractors accept paper claims, using either the universal CMS-1500 form or their own form if certain conditions apply. All providers who submit claims electronically must do so using software obtained from an approved vendor. All electronic transactions must be HIPAA compliant. The health insurance professional should contact the Medicaid contractor in his or her state for claims completion instructions. The time limit for filing Medicaid claims varies from state to state and is anywhere from 2 months to 1 year. The health insurance professional should check with the Medicaid contractor in his or her state for the "timely filing" deadline.

- TPL refers to the legal obligation of third parties (other insurance companies) to pay all or part of the expenditures for medical assistance furnished under a state plan. Examples of third parties that may be liable to pay for services before Medicaid pays include group health plans, employment-related health insurance, workers' compensation, and long-term care insurance. The contract language between the individual state Medicaid agency and an MCO dictates the terms and conditions under which the MCO assumes TPL responsibility. Remember: Medicaid is always the payer of last resort.

- Every time a claim is sent to Medicaid, a document is generated explaining how the claim was adjudicated or how the payment was determined; Medicaid now calls this document an *RA*. The RA can be in paper or electronic form and contains information from one or several claims. The RA typically contains "remark codes" and "reason codes," and it is important to be able to understand the codes to interpret this document.

- Several "special notes" are important to understand when filing Medicaid claims; some are described here:
  - *Accepting assignment:* Medicaid payments are made directly to the healthcare provider. Some Medicaid contractors require that "YES" is checked in Block 27.
  - *Balance billing:* Billing the recipient for any amount not paid by Medicaid is not allowed.
  - *Preauthorization:* Most states require 24-hour notice for all inpatient hospitalization, except in an emergency. In the case of an emergency, most Medicaid contractors require 24-hour notification after the emergency visit, as appropriate.

- Medicaid fraud occurs when a healthcare provider engages in illegal or deceptive practices. Abuse typically involves payment for items or services in which there was no intent to deceive or misrepresent, but the outcome of poor and inefficient methods results in unnecessary costs to the Medicaid program. The health insurance professional should learn to recognize fraud and report it to the state's hotline number or contact the Medicaid Fraud Control Unit.

- CMS is responsible for supporting state Medicaid and CHIP programs in their efforts to achieve patient-centered, safe, effective, efficient, timely, and equitable care. CMS partners with states to share best practices, provide technical assistance to improve performance measurement, evaluate current improvement efforts to inform future activities, work together with quality partners, and coordinate activities to ensure efficiency of operations. The MIP is a comprehensive federal policy established to prevent and reduce provider fraud, waste, and abuse in the Medicaid program.

- The health insurance professional must learn the specific guidelines for the Medicaid programs offered in the state in which he or she is employed to perform his or her job judiciously. The health insurance professional should contact the Medicaid contractor in his or her state to obtain a guide as to what programs are available and what each one covers in that state.

Closing Scenario

Nela is proud of the fact that her knowledge of Medicaid has allowed her to help so many patients. Maude Crawford, 76 years old, was concerned about her medical expenses and was sure that she would not qualify for Medicaid because she had too many assets. Nela was able to explain the spend down process and encouraged Mrs. Crawford and her family to talk to their state program representatives about Medicaid. Anna Richardson was convinced that she would not qualify for Medicaid for her children's healthcare expenses, but Nela persuaded her to look into the CHIP program in their state. Being able to assist patients is one of the most rewarding aspects of Nela's job.

Nela's knowledge of Medicaid has also ensured that claims are being submitted properly and preauthorization is being done correctly. This helps her employer to be able to serve more Medicaid patients.

CHAPTER REVIEW QUESTIONS

1. Where does the funding for Medicaid programs come from?
   a. Federal government
   b. State government
   c. Both federal and state governments
   d. None of the above

2. Congress established the Medicaid program under which title of the Social Security Act of 1965?
   a. XVI
   b. XVII
   c. XVIII
   d. XIX
3. State Medicaid programs are required to cover which of the following groups?
   a. Children up to age 19 and pregnant women with family incomes at or below 138% of the FPL
   b. Infants born to Medicaid-eligible pregnant women
   c. Children in foster care or an adoption assistance program
   d. All of the above
4. Someone who is dual eligible is covered by:
   a. Medicaid and TANF.
   b. Medicare and Medicaid.
   c. Medicare and CFC.
   d. Medicaid and MSP.
5. Which of the MSPs pays for both Medicare Part A and Part B premiums?
   a. QMB
   b. SLMB
   c. QI
   d. QDWI
6. Parents receiving TANF must be participating with which of the following activities?
   a. Be pregnant
   b. Be taking classes that increase their long-term employability prospects
   c. Be receiving assistance from Women, Infants, and Children (WIC)
   d. Be eligible for Medicare
7. States have an option to charge higher copayments for a Medicaid recipient who:
   a. Seeks care at an urgent care center.
   b. Seeks care at a health maintenance organization (HMO) for a condition that is considered an emergency.
   c. Seeks care at a chiropractor.
   d. Seeks care at a hospital emergency department for a condition that is not a true emergency.
8. A provider has chosen to not see Medicaid patients or any patients over the age of 65. As the health insurance specialist, what should you tell the provider about this decision?
   a. "Thanks for letting me know. I will make sure that the scheduling staff is aware of this change."
   b. "We can limit the number of Medicaid patients, but we cannot pick and choose which ones we see."
   c. "Would you like me to draft a termination of care letter for the Medicaid patients over the age of 65?"
   d. "Are there any other groups of Medicaid patients you would chose not to treat?"
9. In most states, Medicaid eligibility is determined:
   a. Monthly.
   b. Quarterly.
   c. Weekly.
   d. Annually.
10. When a patient is covered by both Medicare and Medicaid, which one pays the claim first?
    a. Medicare
    b. Medicaid
    c. Whichever one the patient was eligible for first
    d. Whichever one the patient states should pay first

WEBSITES TO EXPLORE

- For live links to the following websites, please visit the Evolve site at http://evolve.elsevier.com/Beik/today.
- To learn about the Medicaid program, visit the website for CMS at http://www.cms.gov/.
- To see a "timeline" illustrating the milestones of Medicare and Medicaid, log on to https://www.cms.gov/About-CMS/Agency-Information/History/Downloads/Medicare-and-Medicaid-Milestones-1937-2015.pdf.
- The *Federal Register,* where you can find an updated guide to the FPL, is available online at https://www.federalregister.gov/articles/2013/01/24/2013-01422/annual-update-of-the-hhs-poverty-guidelines.
- To find the name of the Medicaid program in your state, see https://www.google.com/search?q=medicaid+program1names+by+state&oq=medicaid+program+names&aqs=chrome.1.69i57j0l2.6915j0j7&sourceid=chrome&ie=UTF-8.
- To find the individual state Medicaid and CHIP income eligibility levels, see https://www.kff.org/medicaid/fact-sheet/where-are-states-today-medicaid-and-chip/.
- To find a list of mandatory and optional Medicaid benefits, see https://www.medicaid.gov/medicaid/benefits/index.html.
- To find information about the TANF program in your area, see https://www.benefits.gov/benefit/613.
- For a more in-depth discussion of Medicaid, visit http://www.medicaid.gov/.
- To learn about the Medicaid program in your state, visit http://www.medicaid.gov/ and choose your state from the drop-down menu.
- To see a timeline of Medicare and Medicaid milestones, copy and paste this link into your browser: https://www.cms.gov/About-CMS/Agency-Information/History/Downloads/Medicare-and-Medicaid-Milestones-1937-2015.pdf.
- The following website provides more information on Medicaid dual eligibles: https://www.medicaid.gov/medicaid/eligibility/seniors-medicare-and-medicaid-enrollees/index.html.

- To learn more about the Affordable Care Act, go to http://www.healthcare.gov/.
- For complete information on the Medicare Prescription Drug, Improvement, and Modernization Act of 2003, go to http://www.gpo.gov/fdsys/pkg/PLAW-108publ173/pdf/PLAW-108publ173.pdf or https://www.medicare.gov/drug-coverage-part-d.
- The CMS website provides extensive information on TPL, cost avoidance, and collection at https://www.medicaid.gov/medicaid/eligibility/tpl-cob/index.html, or go to http://www.medicaid.gov and type "third-party liability" into the search box.

- To learn more about SSI benefits, log on to http://www.socialsecurity.gov/.
- For updates on SSI benefits, visit http://www.socialsecurity.gov/ and type "benefits update" and the current year into the search box.
- For more information on the MIP, go to http://cms.gov/MedicaidIntegrityProgram/.

Author's Note: Due to the dynamic nature of the Internet, web addresses and/or links provided in this book may have changed since publication and may no longer be valid. Students can use similar search words to access related sites.

Chapter Outline

Chapter Objectives

After completion of this chapter, the student should be able to:

1. Explain the Medicare program and its structure.
2. Describe the effects the Affordable Care Act (ACA) has on Medicare coverage.
3. List and discuss Medicare combination coverages (i.e., dual eligibles, Medigap, and Medicare secondary policy).
4. Discuss Medicare managed care plans, including their advantages and disadvantages.
5. Outline specific considerations in preparation for the Medicare patient.
6. Recap the Medicare billing process.
7. Summarize the basics for filing Medicare claims electronically.
8. Use established guidelines to complete the CMS-1500 paper form.
9. Compare and contrast Medicare Summary Notices (MSNs) and electronic remittance advices (ERAs) and the information each contains.
10. Discuss the purpose of Medicare audits, and explain the five-level appeal process.
11. Explain the purpose of quality review studies.
12. Identify methods for detecting and reporting Medicare billing fraud.
13. Discuss the function of Clinical Laboratory Improvement Amendments (CLIA) as it pertains to claims processing.

Chapter Terms

5-star plans

adjudicated

advance beneficiary notice (ABN)

allowable charges

appeals process

beneficiary

Beneficiary Complaint Response Program

benefit period

care coordination

Centers for Medicare and Medicaid Services (CMS)

claim adjustment reason code

Clinical Laboratory Improvement Amendments (CLIA)

coordination of benefits contractor (COBC)

cost-sharing

credible (or creditable) coverage

demand bill

disproportionate share

donut hole

downcoding

dual eligibles

electronic funds transfer (EFT)

electronic remittance advice (ERA)

end-stage renal disease (ESRD)

Federal Insurance Contributions Act (FICA)

health insurance claim number (HICN)

HMO with point of service (POS) option

initial claims

initial enrollment period

lifetime (one-time) release of information form

local coverage determination (LCD)

mandated Medigap transfer

medically necessary

Medicare

Medicare administrative contractor (MAC)

Medicare audits

Medicare Beneficiary Identifier (MBI)

Medicare gaps

Medicare limiting charge

Medicare managed care plan

Medicare nonparticipating provider (nonPAR)

Medicare Part A

Medicare Part B

Medicare Part C

Medicare Part D

Medicare participating provider (PAR)

Medicare secondary payer (MSP)

Medicare Summary Notice (MSN)

Medicare Supplement policy

Medicare whistleblowers

Medigap crossover

Medigap insurance

national coverage determination (NCD)

network

noncovered services

observation care

peer review organization (PRO)

Physician Quality Reporting System (PQRS)

Program of All-Inclusive Care for the Elderly (PACE)

provider-sponsored organization (PSO)

quality improvement organization (QIO)

quality review study

recovery audit contractor (RAC)

relative value unit

remittance advice (RA)

remittance remark code

resource-based relative value system (RBRVS)

self-referring

Seniors' Health Insurance Information Program (SHIIP)

small provider

special enrollment period

special needs plan (SNP)

standard paper remittance (SPR)

TrOOP

value-based payment modifier

Opening Scenario

Rita Thomas has been working as a health insurance professional for 2 years at Walden-Martin Family Medical Clinic. She has spent the last year working specifically with Medicare. Rita was encouraged to go into the health insurance field by her grandmother, who she and her 3-year-old son live with. Grandma Nan, as Rita calls her, was very excited when Rita started working with Medicare. Grandma Nan, like many people, finds Medicare to be confusing. Rita found it a bit confusing as well when she started working in that area. She has spent the last year learning the ins and outs of Medicare and has come to realize that is an ever-changing world. She has been working on "conquering Medicare's challenges" and now understand what her teachers meant by lifelong learning.

Rita now knows that she needs to understand not only Medicare, but also how Medicare interacts with Medicaid and commercial insurance carriers. She has found that the Medigap policies can be confusing and has developed a summary of the different policy types for patients to use as a reference. There have also been times when Walden-Martin did not agree with the Medicare payment, and Rita has had to work through the appeals process.

Rita is grateful that she is able to help many people, along with her Grandma Nan, better understand what Medicare is all about. Her employers are grateful that Rita is so dedicated to helping patients and making sure that all Medicare rules and regulations are followed.

THE MEDICARE PROGRAM

Medicare, a comprehensive federal insurance program, was established by Congress in 1966 to give individuals age 65 years and older financial assistance with medical expenses. In 1972 the Medicare program was expanded to include certain categories of disabled individuals younger than age 65 and people of any age who have **end-stage renal disease (ESRD)**, a group of permanent kidney disorders requiring dialysis or transplant. Fig. 11.1 shows important transitions in the Medicare program from its inception to current enrollment. Medicare is administered by the **Centers for Medicare and Medicaid Services (CMS)**, formerly called the *Health Care Financing Administration (HCFA)*. CMS is a federal agency within the US Department of Health and Human Services (HHS) that administers the Medicare program and works in partnership with state governments to administer Medicaid, the Children's Health Insurance Program (CHIP), and health insurance portability standards. To study a timeline of key developments in the Medicare program, log on to the Kaiser Family Foundation's website listed in "Websites to Explore" at the end of this chapter.

Medicare Fact: In 2010 the first "baby boomers" turned age 65 and became eligible for Medicare. In the coming years, it is predicted that the number of patients depending on Medicare will rise from 48 million to more than 90 million Americans.

The **Federal Insurance Contributions Act (FICA)** provides for a federal system of old age, survivor, disability, and hospital insurance. In 2019 the FICA tax rate remained at 6.2% for Social Security taxes and 1.45% for Medicare taxes. This is the employee's contribution withheld from payroll checks. The employer matches the employee's contribution for a total of 12.4% and 2.9%, respectively, that goes to the Internal Revenue Service (IRS) on behalf of each employee. The Social Security part of FICA is taxed on wages up to a certain amount called the *Social Security wage base*. For 2019

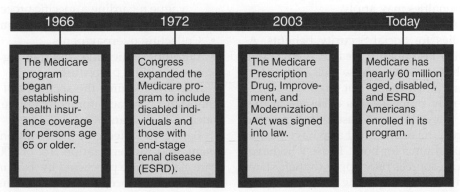

1966	1972	2003	Today
The Medicare program began establishing health insurance coverage for persons age 65 or older.	Congress expanded the Medicare program to include disabled individuals and those with end-stage renal disease (ESRD).	The Medicare Prescription Drug, Improvement, and Modernization Act was signed into law.	Medicare has nearly 60 million aged, disabled, and ESRD Americans enrolled in its program.

Fig. 11.1 The Medicare program. (Modified from Centers for Medicare and Medicaid Services: *World of Medicare.*)

the Social Security wage base was $132,900 and is projected to increase to $191,100 by 2028. There is no wage base for the Medicare tax.

Medicare is not provided free of charge; individuals must meet certain conditions to qualify for benefits. In addition, Medicare requires cost-sharing in the form of premiums, deductibles, and coinsurance, all of which are discussed in this chapter. (See the section on premiums and cost-sharing requirements.)

MEDICARE ENROLLMENT

Before an individual reaches age 65, he or she must decide whether to enroll in Medicare Part A (hospital benefits) or Part B (physician services) or both. If eligible beneficiaries want Medicare coverage to start the month that they reach age 65, they should contact their local Social Security office 3 months before their 65th birthday. There is a 7-month **initial enrollment period** that begins 3 months before the month the individual turns 65, carries through the birthday month, and ends 3 months after the month he or she turns 65. If the individual decides not to sign up for Medicare to start the month they turn age 65 or during the last 3 months of the initial enrollment period, the start day for Medicare coverage will be delayed. The various parts of the Medicare program (A, B, C, and D) are discussed in detail later in this chapter.

Special Enrollment Period

An eligible **beneficiary** (an individual who has health insurance through Medicare or Medicaid) may delay enrollment without a penalty or a waiting period if the individual (or spouse) was still employed and covered by an employer's group health plan at the time of eligibility. Individuals who do not enroll during the initial enrollment period and are not eligible for the **special enrollment period** must wait and enroll during the general election period, which is January 1 through March 31 of each year. Coverage then becomes effective on July 1 of that same year. Unless an eligible person has an employer-provided group health plan, declining Medicare may not be a good idea. If the individual does not enroll when first becoming eligible, "late enrollment" penalties may apply.

Application for Medicare Part A is automatic when an individual applies for Social Security benefits. A husband or wife may also qualify for Part A coverage at age 65 on the basis of the spouse's eligibility for Social Security. If an individual is not eligible for free Part A, he or she may purchase this coverage at the current premium rates. In most cases, if a person chooses to buy Part A, he or she must also have Part B and pay monthly premiums for both. Those who have limited income and resources may apply to their state Medicaid program for help in paying premiums (see Chapter 10). If an individual is not eligible for premium-free Part A and doesn't purchase it when first becoming eligible, the monthly premium may go up 10%. This higher premium will have to be paid for twice the number of years that the individual could have had Part A but didn't sign up. Premiums and cost-sharing requirements are discussed later in this chapter.

 Imagine This!

Sarah Alder was eligible for Medicare Part A for 2 years, but she failed to sign up. As a result, she will have to pay a higher premium for twice the number of years she waited, or 4 years. If she had met certain conditions that allowed her to sign up for Part A during a "special enrollment period" (e.g., if she had been covered by a group health plan [her own, a spouse's, or a family member's] during these 2 years), she could have enrolled without penalty during the 8-month period that began the month after employment ended or the coverage ended, whichever came first.

Medicare Fact: A beneficiary automatically qualifies for Part A if he or she was a federal employee on January 1, 1983.

MEDICARE ADMINISTRATIVE CONTRACTORS

Medicare administrative contractors (MACs), sometimes referred to as *Medicare carriers,* are private organizations that serve as federal government "agents" in the administration and claim processing of Parts A and B for the original (sometimes referred to as *traditional*) Medicare program. MACs also handle durable medical equipment (DME), home health, and hospice claims. Each MAC signs a contract with the federal government to administer the Medicare program in a certain region of the United States. MACs are responsible for various tasks, including:

- Claims processing and reimbursement to Medicare providers for their services
- Making sure services are coded and billed correctly, both before and after payment
- Determining medical necessity of healthcare services billed on Medicare claims

  Note: MACs follow the national coverage determinations set by the CMS, but in cases where there is no such determination or if the rules are too vague regarding a specific procedure, a MAC may develop a local coverage determination (see later).

- Collecting overpayments
- Enrolling, educating, and training Medicare providers on billing procedures

The law requires the secretary of HHS to open up the MAC contracts for competitive bidding at least once every 5 years.

Before the Medicare Prescription Drug, Improvement, and Modernization Act of 2003 (MMA), Medicare claims were processed by *fiscal intermediaries (FIs),* who mostly processed Part A claims, and by *carriers,* who mostly processed Part B claims. Initially, there were 48 separate contracts; however, in recent years the MMA directed the consolidation of MACs for Part

A and Part B to just 12, as well as 4 MAC durable medical equipment (DME) contracts. These MAC Part A and Part Bs are in the process of being consolidated further to 10 contracts. Fig. 11.2 shows a map of these MAC jurisdictions, along with the name of each MAC and the states it covers.

To keep up to date on the MAC implementation schedule, as well as contract awards, visit CMS.gov.

MEDICARE PROGRAM STRUCTURE

Medicare is composed of four parts:
- **Medicare Part A**—hospital insurance
- **Medicare Part B**—medical (providers' care) insurance (original Medicare); includes healthcare provided in clinics
- **Medicare Part C**—Medicare Advantage plans (managed care–type plans, formerly called Medicare+ Choice)
- **Medicare Part D**—prescription drug program

Medicare Part A

Medicare Part A (hospital insurance) helps pay for services for the following types of healthcare (Table 11.1):
- Inpatient hospital care (including critical access hospitals)
- Inpatient care in a skilled nursing facility (SNF)
- Home healthcare
- Hospice care
- Blood

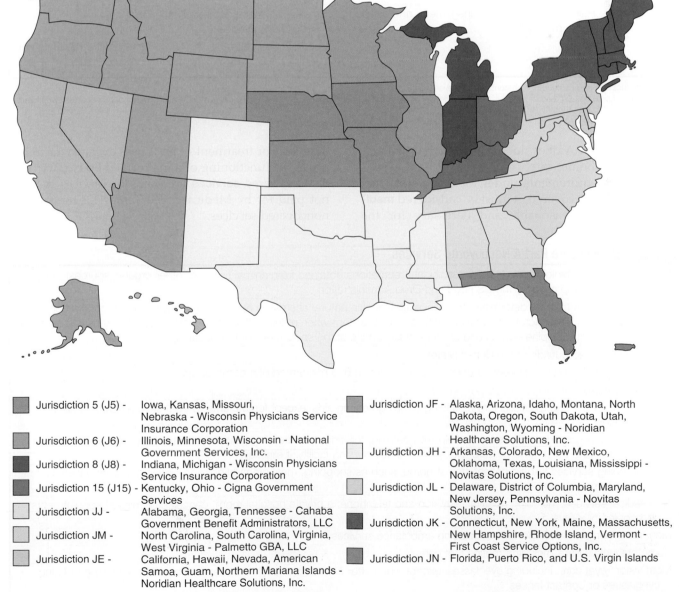

Jurisdiction 5 (J5) - Iowa, Kansas, Missouri, Nebraska - Wisconsin Physicians Service Insurance Corporation

Jurisdiction 6 (J6) - Illinois, Minnesota, Wisconsin - National Government Services, Inc.

Jurisdiction 8 (J8) - Indiana, Michigan - Wisconsin Physicians Service Insurance Corporation

Jurisdiction 15 (J15) - Kentucky, Ohio - Cigna Government Services

Jurisdiction JJ - Alabama, Georgia, Tennessee - Cahaba Government Benefit Administrators, LLC

Jurisdiction JM - North Carolina, South Carolina, Virginia, West Virginia - Palmetto GBA, LLC

Jurisdiction JE - California, Hawaii, Nevada, American Samoa, Guam, Northern Mariana Islands - Noridian Healthcare Solutions, Inc.

Jurisdiction JF - Alaska, Arizona, Idaho, Montana, North Dakota, Oregon, South Dakota, Utah, Washington, Wyoming - Noridian Healthcare Solutions, Inc.

Jurisdiction JH - Arkansas, Colorado, New Mexico, Oklahoma, Texas, Louisiana, Mississippi - Novitas Solutions, Inc.

Jurisdiction JL - Delaware, District of Columbia, Maryland, New Jersey, Pennsylvania - Novitas Solutions, Inc.

Jurisdiction JK - Connecticut, New York, Maine, Massachusetts, New Hampshire, Rhode Island, Vermont - First Coast Service Options, Inc.

Jurisdiction JN - Florida, Puerto Rico, and U.S. Virgin Islands

Fig. 11.2 Medicare Parts A and B Medicare administrative contractor jurisdictions.

Table 11.1   2019 Medicare Part A: Benefits and Gaps Medicare Hospital Insurance (Part A) Covered Services[a]

COVERAGE	BENEFICIARY PAYS	MEDICARE PAYS
Inpatient Hospital Care[b]		
Days 1–60	$1364 deductible	Balance
Days 61–90	$335 per day	Balance
Days 91–150 *(lifetime reserve days)*	$670 per day	Balance
All additional days	All costs	Nothing
Semiprivate room and board, general nursing, and other hospital services and supplies.		
Skilled Nursing Facility Care[b]		
Days 1–20	Nothing	All costs
Days 21–100	$170.50 per day	Balance
All additional days	All costs	Nothing
After 3-day hospitalization and admitted to a skilled nursing facility approved by Medicare within 30 days of discharge		
Home Healthcare		
Part-time or intermittent skilled care, home health aide services	Nothing	Up to 35 hours per week
Other		
Durable medical equipment (DME) or supplies	80% of approved amount	80% of approved amount
Hospice care: Pain relief, symptom management, and support services for the terminally ill	Small copayments for inpatient respite and drugs	Balance
Blood	For first three pints	All but first three pints per calendar year

[a]Hospital deductibles and coinsurance amounts change every year.
[b]A benefit period provides 90 days of hospital care, if needed. A new benefit period begins each time the beneficiary is out of the hospital or has not received skilled nursing care from any other facility for 60 consecutive days.
Data from Centers for Medicare and Medicaid Services (website). http://www.medicare.gov.

Medicare Part A does not cover custodial or long-term (nursing home) care.

Coverage requirements under Medicare state that for a service to be covered, it must be considered **medically necessary**—reasonable and necessary for the diagnosis or treatment of an illness or injury or to improve the functioning of a malformed body part.

Noncovered services are items or services that are not paid for by Medicare. See Table 11.2 for a list of noncovered services.

Table 11.2   Medicare Part A Noncovered Services

Medical devices or biologicals (drugs or medicinal preparations obtained from animal tissue or other organic sources) that have not been approved by the US Food and Drug Administration
Items and services that are determined to be investigational in nature: alternative medicine, including experimental procedures and treatments, acupuncture, and chiropractic services (except when manipulation of the spine is medically necessary to fix a subluxation of the spine—when one or more of the bones of the spine move out of position)
Most care received outside of the United States
Cosmetic surgery (unless it is needed to improve the function of a malformed part of the body)
Most dental care
Hearing aids or the examinations for prescribing or fitting hearing aids (except for implants to treat severe hearing loss in some cases)
Personal care or custodial care, such as help with bathing, toileting, and dressing (unless patient is homebound and receiving skilled care), and nursing home care (except in a skilled nursing facility, if eligible)
Housekeeping services to help patient stay at home, such as shopping, meal preparation, and cleaning (unless patient is receiving hospice care)
Nonmedical services, including hospital television and telephone, a private hospital room, canceled or missed appointments, and copies of x-rays
Most nonemergency transportation, including ambulance services
Some preventive care, including routine foot care
Most vision (eye) care, including eyeglasses (except when after cataract surgery) and examinations for prescribing or fitting eyeglasses or contact lenses

Imagine This!

Eloise Graham went to the Argyle County Mental Health Center for psychiatric counseling. Under Medicare, this is a covered service, but the adult day care services that Eloise receives, which are provided at Argyle County Mental Health Center, are not considered reasonable and necessary. Therefore a claim submitted to Medicare for the adult day care services was denied.

Part A costs and eligibility. Medicare Part A is free to any individual age 65 or older who is:

- Eligible to receive monthly Social Security benefits, or
- Eligible based on wages on which *sufficient* Medicare payroll taxes were paid. ("Sufficient" is 40 or more quarters of Social Security work credits.) Medicare Part A is also free to any disabled individual younger than age 65 who has:
  - Received Social Security disability benefits for 24 months as a worker, surviving spouse, or adult child of a retired, disabled (including ESRD or amyotrophic lateral sclerosis [ALS]), or deceased worker, or
  - Accumulated a sufficient number of Social Security credits to be insured for Medicare and meets the requirements of the Social Security disability program

Medicare Fact: If an individual is diagnosed with ALS (or Lou Gehrig disease), he or she automatically qualifies for both Parts A and B the month that disability benefits begin.

Part A penalty. Normally, individuals don't pay a monthly premium for Part A coverage if they (or their spouse) paid sufficient Medicare taxes while employed. This is referred to as *premium-free Part A.* An individual who is not eligible for premium-free Part A may be able to purchase it if he or she is:

1. Age 65 or older and has (or is enrolling in) Part B and meets the legal requirements of citizenship and residency, or
2. Under age 65 and premium-free Part A coverage ended because of reemployment

Usually if a Medicare-eligible beneficiary chooses to buy Part A, he or she also must have Part B and pay monthly premiums for both. If income and resources are limited, the state may help pay for premiums under the Medicaid program.

Note: Those who are under age 65 and disabled can continue to receive premium-free Part A for up to 8½ years after returning to work. After that, they will have to pay the Part A premium out of pocket unless their income is too low to afford the Part A premium. In that case, there is a program called the *Qualified Disabled and Working Individuals (QDWI)* program that can help (see Chapter 10).

As mentioned, Part A is free for individuals who have worked enough quarters to qualify (40 or more). Penalties may be assessed for failing to enroll at appropriate times. People who are not eligible for premium-free Part A and don't buy it when first eligible may see their monthly premium go up 10% when they decide to enroll. They will have to pay this higher premium for twice the number of years they could have had Part A but didn't sign up. These penalties can be avoided if the individual is eligible for a special enrollment period or if the person is covered by an employer-sponsored group health plan.

Medicare Part B

Medicare Part B is medical insurance financed by a combination of federal government funds and beneficiary premiums that help pay for the following:

- Medically necessary physicians' services
- Some preventive services
- Outpatient hospital services
- Clinical laboratory services
- DME: To qualify as DME, equipment must be ordered by a physician for the patient's use in the home, and items must be reusable (e.g., walkers, wheelchairs, hospital beds).
- Blood (received as an outpatient)

As noted, Medicare typically expands services every year. For a complete up-to-date list of covered and noncovered Part B services, type "Medicare & You" along with the appropriate year in your Internet search engine (e.g., "Medicare & You 2020" [or the most recent publication]).

For a beneficiary who became eligible for Medicare on or after January 1, 2005, Medicare covers a "Welcome to Medicare" physical examination if it is performed within the first 12 months of coverage, if that individual has Part B coverage. Beginning January 2011, Part B also covers a yearly "wellness" examination for those who have had Part B for longer than 12 months to develop or update a personalized prevention plan based on current health and risk factors. This yearly exam is free if the healthcare provider uses the appropriate diagnosis code (ICD-10-CM Z00.00) and accepts assignment. Medicare covers "wellness" exams for healthy beneficiaries every year. Part B also can help pay for many other medical services and supplies that are not covered by Medicare Part A and for home healthcare if the beneficiary is not enrolled in Part A. Medicare Part B covers other preventive healthcare services, such as:

- Bone mass measurements
- Colorectal cancer screening
- Diabetes services
- Glaucoma testing
- Pap tests, pelvic examinations, and clinical breast examinations
- Prostate cancer screening
- Screening mammograms
- Certain vaccinations

The annual *Medicare & You* publication usually has a page in the front titled "What's New & Important in (current year)" so that beneficiaries can learn what services have been added to Medicare's benefits. For example, in 2019 there is a new program, Medicare Diabetes Prevention Program. This program's goal is to help prevent type 2 diabetes in individuals with indications of prediabetes.

Table 11.3 lists additional services and supplies that Medicare Part B helps pay for and services that are not covered by Part B.

All Medicare Part B beneficiaries pay for Part B coverage, which is typically deducted from their Social Security monthly benefits check. Most beneficiaries enrolled in original Medicare paid a monthly premium of $121.80 in 2016. Higher-income beneficiaries are

---

Table 11.3 Services and Supplies Medicare Part B Helps Pay for and Services Not Covered by Part B

Items Medicare Part B Helps Pay For[a]

- Abdominal aortic aneurysm screening
- Alcohol misuse screening/counseling
- Ambulance services
- Ambulatory surgical centers
- Blood
- Bone mass measurements (bone density) (every 2 years)
- Cardiac rehabilitation
- Cardiovascular disease (behavioral therapy)
- Cardiovascular screenings (every 5 years)
- Chemotherapy (doctor's office/freestanding clinics/outpatient)
- Chiropractic services (limited—see *Medicare & You* handbook)
- Clinical laboratory services
- Clinical research studies
- Colorectal cancer screenings
- Defibrillator (implantable automatic)
- Depression screening
- Diabetes screenings
- Diabetes self-management training
- Diabetes supplies (limited insulin coverage)
- Doctor (and other healthcare provider) services
- Durable medical equipment
- ECG screenings
- Emergency room services
- Eyeglasses (limited)
- Federally qualified health center services
- Foot examinations and treatment (diabetes-related nerve damage)
- Glaucoma tests
- Hearing and balance examinations
- Hepatitis B virus (HBV) infection screening
- Hepatitis C screening test
- HIV screening
- Home health services: To qualify for the home health benefit, beneficiary must be under a physician's care; have an intermittent need for skilled nursing care; or require physical, speech-language pathology, or occupational therapy. The beneficiary must be homebound and receive services from a Medicare-approved home health agency (HHA).
- Kidney dialysis services and supplies
- Kidney disease education services
- Laboratory services
- Lung cancer screening
- Medical nutrition therapy services
- Mental healthcare (outpatient)
- Obesity screening/counseling
- Occupational therapy
- Outpatient hospital services
- Outpatient medical/surgical services/supplies
- Physical examination (one-time "Welcome to Medicare" examination)
- Physical therapy
- Prescription drugs (limited)
- Prostate cancer screenings
- Prosthetic/orthotic items
- Pulmonary rehabilitation
- Rural health clinical services
- Second surgical opinions
- Sexually transmitted infection (STI) screening and counseling
- Shots (flu/hepatitis B/pneumococcal)
- Smoking cessation (counseling to stop smoking)
- Speech-language pathology services
- Surgical dressing services
- Telehealth
- Tests (e.g., x-rays, MRI, CT scans, ECGs)
- Transitional care management services
- Transplants and immunosuppressive drugs
- Travel (emergencies when traveling outside United States, in territorial waters, on board a ship)
- Urgently needed care
- Yearly "wellness" visit

Services Not Covered by Medicare Part B[b]

- Acupuncture
- Most chiropractic services
- Cosmetic surgery
- Custodial care
- Deductibles, coinsurance, copayments
- Dental care and dentures
- Eye examinations (routine) and refractions
- Foot care (routine)
- Hearing aids and examinations
- Hearing tests not ordered by doctor
- Laboratory tests (screenings)
- Long-term care (custodial care in nursing homes)
- Orthopedic shoes
- Physical examinations (yearly or routine)
- Prescription drugs (refer to Medicare Part D)
- Shots to prevent illness
- Surgical procedures in ambulatory surgical centers not covered by Medicare Part B
- Syringes or insulin (some diabetic supplies)
- Travel to foreign countries (some exceptions—see *Medicare & You* handbook)

[a]Limitations, deductibles, and copayments may apply.
[b]With exceptions previously listed as being covered.
CT, Computed tomography; *ECG*, electrocardiogram; *HIV*, human immunodeficiency virus; *MRI*, magnetic resonance imaging.

subject to higher premiums. Medicare Part B monthly premiums are subject to an increase every year.

The health insurance professional should become familiar with Medicare's guidelines to determine whether a specific procedure or service is covered. If coverage is questioned, the professional should contact Medicare by phone at 1-800-MEDICARE (1-800-633-4227) or on the Internet at http://www.medicare.gov/.

In addition, "Websites to Explore" at the end of this chapter provides several Internet links to follow for additional help and information.

Part B premiums and cost-sharing requirements. Medicare Part B **cost-sharing** requirements include a monthly premium, which was discussed in a previous section. This premium, which is automatically deducted from the beneficiary's monthly Social Security check, is subject to change every year. The second cost-sharing requirement in original Medicare Part B is an annual deductible of $185 (as of 2019). After the deductible is met, Medicare pays 80% of allowable charges. **Allowable charges** are the fees that Medicare permits for a particular service or supply. Table 11.4 summarizes the Medicare Part B cost-sharing amounts for various types of covered services.

A **benefit period** is the duration of time during which a Medicare beneficiary is eligible for Part A benefits for services incurred in a hospital or SNF or both. A benefit period begins the day an individual is admitted to a hospital or SNF. The benefit period ends when the beneficiary has not received care in a hospital or SNF for 60 days in a row. If the beneficiary is readmitted to the hospital or SNF before the 60 days elapse, it is considered to be in the same benefit period. If the beneficiary is admitted to a hospital or SNF after the initial 60-day benefit period has ended, a new benefit period begins. The inpatient hospital deductible must be paid for each benefit period, but there is no limit to the number of benefit periods allowed.

On a side note, there has been a change in how Medicare pays for services in an SNF when a patient spent time in the hospital under the status of **observation care**. Observation care is when a patient is kept in the hospital for a short time while physicians determine whether the individual is sick enough to require inpatient treatment. Initially, unless a beneficiary was formally admitted to a hospital as an *inpatient*, typically for 3 days or fewer, if that individual was transferred upon hospital discharge directly to an SNF, Medicare would not pay for SNF charges. That was changed in 2013. Now, patients who are in the hospital for at least two "midnights" are considered inpatients and qualify for payment from Medicare for their SNF stay. Patients who are in the hospital for fewer than two "midnights" are still considered observation care patients and do not qualify for SNF benefits.

All Medicare beneficiaries pay the Part B premium each month, which is normally deducted from their Social Security payments. Most beneficiaries pay the standard premium; however, some may pay higher premiums depending on their adjusted gross income (AGI) reported on the tax return from 2 years previous. Currently, the AGI limit for the standard premium is $85,000 ($170,000 for couples filing jointly).

Table **11.4**	Services and Supplies Medicare Part B Helps Pay for and Services Not Covered by Part B for 2020	
COVERAGE	**BENEFICIARY PAYS**	**MEDICARE PAYS**
Medical Expenses		
Doctors' services	$198 deductible[a] plus 20%[b] of Medicare's approved amount	80% of Medicare's approved amount after deductible has been met
Inpatient and outpatient medical services and supplies	$198 deductible plus 20% of Medicare's approved amount	80% of Medicare's approved amount after deductible has been met
Physical and speech therapy, diagnostic tests, and ambulance services	Limited charges above the approved amount may apply for some Part B providers	65% for most outpatient mental health services—will increase each year—80% by 2014
Clinical Laboratory Tests		
Blood tests, urinalysis, and more	Nothing for tests if medically necessary	Generally 100% of approved amount
Home Healthcare		
Part-time or intermittent skilled care, home health aide services	Nothing	Up to 35 hours per week
Other		
Durable medical equipment and supplies	After $198 deductible, you pay 20% of approved amount	80% of approved amount after deductible is met
Outpatient hospital treatment	After deductible, you pay a copayment according to the service	Medicare payment to hospital-based fee schedule
Blood	For first three pints, plus 20% of approved amount (after deductible)	80% of approved amount (after deductible and starting with the fourth pint)

[a]Once the annual deductible amount for Medicare-covered services is met in any year, the Part B deductible does not apply to any further covered services received for the rest of the year.
[b]Part B coinsurance is paid after the annual Part B deductible for covered services is met for the year..

Part B penalty. As with Part A, individuals who don't sign up for Part B when first eligible typically must pay a late enrollment penalty for as long as they have Part B. The monthly premium for Part B may go up 10% for each full 12-month period that they could have had it but didn't sign up. For example, a 2-year delay would be a 20% penalty, a 3-year delay would be a 30% penalty, and so on. This penalty is paid for the remainder of the individual's life. The late enrollment penalty doesn't apply if the beneficiary meets certain conditions that allow him or her to sign up for Part B during a special enrollment period.

 Imagine This!

Part A Late Enrollment Example: Ellen Robinson was eligible for Part A in 2017 but didn't enroll until 2019. As a result, Ellen must pay the higher premium penalty for 4 years.

Part B Late Enrollment Example: Ernesto Perez's initial enrollment period ended on September 30, 2017. He waited to sign up for Part B until the general enrollment period in March 2020. The Part B penalty is 10% for each full 12-month period. His Part B premium penalty is 20% because he waited a total of 30 months to sign up, which included only two full 12-month periods. Ernesto will have to pay this penalty for as long as he has Part B.

Medicare plans typically change every year, and changes include cost, coverage, and which providers and pharmacies are in their networks. For current information, visit Medicare.gov or call 1-800-MEDICARE. *Medicare Fact*: Premiums, deductibles, and penalty amounts are subject to change every year.

Medicare Part C (Medicare Advantage Plans)

The Balanced Budget Act of 1997, which went into effect in January 1999, expanded the role of private plans under what was originally called *Medicare+ Choice* to include managed care plans, such as preferred provider organizations (PPOs), provider-sponsored organizations (PSOs), private fee-for-service (PFFS) plans, and medical savings accounts (MSAs) coupled with high-deductible insurance plans. The Medicare Prescription Drug, Improvement, and Modernization Act of 2003 renamed the Medicare+ Choice program "Medicare Advantage" and created another option: regional PPOs. Medicare Advantage is an alternative to original Medicare that allows the government to pay insurers to manage benefits to seniors. These prepaid healthcare plans offer regular Medicare Parts A and B coverage in addition to coverage for certain other services. Medicare Advantage plans are run by private companies approved by Medicare. Under **Medicare Part C**, individuals who are eligible for Medicare Parts A and B can choose to get their Medicare benefits through a variety of plans (see discussion earlier), with the exception of individuals with ESRD, who must remain on original Medicare. Beneficiaries who get Medicare benefits due to a disability can enroll in a Medicare Advantage plan during the 7-month period that begins 3 months before the 25th month of disability and ends 3 months after the 25th month of disability. Medicare Advantage plans must follow all of Medicare's rules. They cover all services that original Medicare covers except hospice care and some care in qualifying clinical research studies. Original Medicare covers both of these service types even if the individual has a Medicare Advantage plan. Medicare Advantage plans may offer extra coverage, such as vision, hearing, dental, and/or health and wellness programs, and most include prescription drug coverage (Part D). In addition to the Part B premium, an enrollee in a Medicare Advantage plan usually pays a monthly premium.

If the beneficiary moves from a Medicare Advantage plan that has drug coverage to one that does not, he or she may lose prescription drug coverage. The beneficiary must then wait until the next open enrollment period to get drug coverage again and may have to pay a late enrollment penalty.

Types of Part C plans. The different types of Medicare Advantage plans include the following:
- *Medicare managed care plans,* such as health maintenance organization (HMO) plans, PPO plans, and other certified public or private coordinated care plans that meet the standards under the Medicare law. Enrollees in HMO plans can only go to healthcare providers or hospitals in the plan's network except in an urgent or emergency situation. The beneficiary typically will pay more when seeing a provider outside the network.
- *Medicare PFFS plans* allow beneficiaries to see any healthcare provider they choose as long as the provider agrees to see them and accepts the plan's payment terms and conditions. The plan determines how much it will pay and how much the enrollee must pay for care.
- *Special needs plans (SNPs)* that provide specialized healthcare for specific groups of people who are **dual eligibles** (enrolled in both Medicare and Medicaid), who live in nursing homes, or who have certain chronic medical conditions.
- *Medicare MSA plan* combines a high-deductible insurance plan with a medical savings account that can be used to pay for healthcare costs.

The choices listed here are discussed in more detail later in this chapter.

For a Medicare beneficiary to qualify for a Medicare Advantage option, he or she must be eligible for Medicare Parts A and B and must live in the service area of the plan. As mentioned, an individual is generally not eligible to enroll in a Medicare Advantage plan if he or she has been diagnosed with ESRD. There are exceptions to this eligibility rule, however, such as individuals who are already members of a Medicare Advantage plan when they are diagnosed with ESRD and individuals who received a kidney transplant and no longer require a regular course of dialysis treatments. Fig. 11.3 illustrates two main ways in which beneficiaries can get Medicare coverage. Anyone with Medicare can join, switch, or drop a Medicare Advantage plan between October 15 and December 7, and coverage will begin on January 1, as long as the plan receives the request by December 7. In 2019 a new Open Enrollment Period (OEP) started. It runs from January 1 through March 31. The OEP is more limited than the fall open enrollment period. Keep in mind that the plan must be available in the plan's service area. *Medicare Fact:* If a beneficiary enrolls in a Medicare Part C plan, he or she does not need a supplemental plan (Medigap). Furthermore, the beneficiary can join or leave a plan at certain open enrollment times during the year.

5-Star plans. Medicare Advantage plans are rated on performance: how good the care is and the results of care, along with surveys from members. This rating can be between 1 and 5 stars, with a **5-star plan** considered excellent. These ratings help the beneficiary compare plans based on these criteria. A beneficiary can switch to a Medicare Advantage plan or Medicare Cost plan that has a 5-star rating during the annual open enrollment period. This special enrollment period can be used only once during the open enrollment time frame. Star ratings are available at http://www.medicare.gov/find-a-plan.

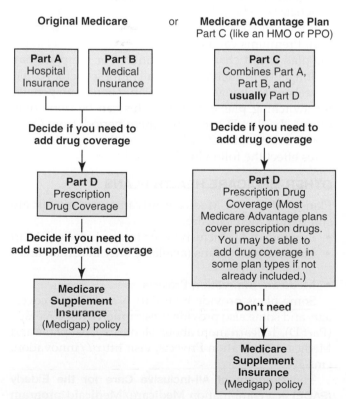

Fig. 11.3 The two main ways in which beneficiaries can get Medicare coverage. *HMO,* Health maintenance organization; *PPO,* preferred provider organization. (Modified from US Department of Health and Human Services, Centers for Medicare and Medicaid Services, Baltimore, MD.)

Medicare Part D (Prescription Drug Benefit Plans)

Medicare Part D offers prescription drug coverage to everyone eligible for Medicare. These plans are run by insurance companies or other private organizations approved by Medicare. The cost of drugs within each plan can vary.

There are two ways to get prescription drug coverage:

1. Medicare prescription drug plans (sometimes called *PDPs*) that add drug coverage to original Medicare, some Medicare Cost plans, some Medicare PFFS plans, and MSA plans.
2. Medicare Advantage plans (e.g., HMOs or PPOs) or other Medicare plans that offer prescription drug coverage as a plan benefit.

When beneficiaries enroll in Medicare Part D, they pay an additional premium, which can be deducted from their monthly Social Security check or paid separately. Premiums vary depending on the plan. In 2020 the lowest-cost PDP premium was $12.20; the highest-cost PDP premium was $76.40, with the mid-range cost of $50.70. Some Medicare Part D or Medicare Advantage plans have an initial deductible where enrollees pay 100% of their prescription costs before Part D benefits begin. Other Medicare Part D or Medicare Advantage plans have no initial deductible, providing coverage as soon as the first prescriptions are purchased. Each drug plan has a formulary (list of prescription drugs) that is covered by the plan. Formularies vary greatly from one PDP to the next, so it is important that the beneficiary choose a plan in which his or her medications are covered. A plan's cost-sharing (copayments or coinsurance) will vary depending on the drug plan selected.

Individual plans, such as group health insurance plans that include prescription coverage, must offer no less than the standard Medicare benefit, which is referred to as **credible (or creditable) coverage**. Medicare's standard benefits under Part D are shown in Table 11.5. These figures are subject to change every

Table 11.5	2020 Medicare Part D Standard Benefit Model Plan Details
Initial deductible	$435
Initial coverage limit	$4020
Out-of-pocket threshold	$6350
Coverage gap (donut hole)	Begins when plan's initial coverage limit of $4020 is reached and ends when a total of $6350 out-of-pocket amount is spent
In 2019 Part D enrollees will receive a 75% discount on the total cost of their brand-name and generic drugs purchased while in the coverage gap.	

Data from Centers for Medicare and Medicaid Services (website). http://www.medicare.gov.

year. It should be noted here that many plans offer more comprehensive coverage than Medicare's basic coverage.

If a Medicare-eligible person elects not to join a Medicare drug plan when first eligible and does not have other credible coverage or doesn't qualify for extra help, he or she will likely pay a late enrollment penalty if they join a plan later. If an individual does not have creditable coverage and does not enroll in a Part D plan at the first opportunity and then later chooses to join, they will be subject to a higher premium based on a late enrollment penalty. CMS sets the initial penalty for the first few years of the program at 1% of the average drug premium per uncovered month. In subsequent years, the amount of the penalty increased with the growth in the base Part D premium. Individuals are subject to the penalty for as long as they remain enrolled in Part D.

What is TrOOP? When you see the acronym **TrOOP**, be aware that it stands for true out-of-pocket costs. TrOOP includes all payments for medications listed on a particular plan's formulary and purchased at a network or participating pharmacy. This includes payments the beneficiary made and payments that were made by others on the beneficiary's behalf. It's important to understand that if a beneficiary switches Medicare Part D plans during the plan year, the TrOOP will be transferred to the new plan.

Medicare Part D and the ACA. The Affordable Care Act (ACA) made some changes to the coverage for Medicare beneficiaries enrolled in a Part D plan. In the "standard" benefit plan, after the deductible is met, the beneficiary pays 25% of covered costs up to total prescription costs meeting the initial coverage limit. At this point the coverage gap (donut hole) begins, and the beneficiary pays 100% of their prescription costs up to the out-of-pocket threshold. (Out-of-pocket threshold is the total out-of-pocket costs including the donut hole.) Catastrophic coverage starts after this point (see Table 11.5). The dollar amounts shown in Table 11.5 are subject to annual change.

Until 2020, the percentage beneficiaries paid while in the donut hole went down. In 2019 the donut closed for brand-name medications but was still in place for generic medications until 2020. Beginning in 2020, Medicare enrollees will pay no more than 25% for all prescriptions.

Medicare Fact: The out-of-pocket threshold is the amount that the individual must pay on his or her own before catastrophic coverage begins. This gap between the initial coverage limit and catastrophic coverage is referred to as the **donut hole**.

Part D and dual eligibles. Since the Medicare Part D Prescription Drug Plan became effective in 2003, state Medicaid programs no longer provide prescription drug coverage for dual eligible individuals, except that states may choose to cover certain drugs that Medicare does not cover. Because of their low-income status, dual eligibles automatically receive premium and cost-sharing subsidies for their covered prescription drugs. Dual eligibles have nominal copayment requirements up to the catastrophic coverage limit, which may be different from state Medicaid requirements. In many states, Medicaid copayment requirements for dual eligibles fall below the levels that most dual eligibles face when they are enrolled in Part D plans. Unlike Medicaid, Medicare Part D does not require pharmacies to provide medications to low-income enrollees regardless of ability to pay. In addition, dual eligibles must pay 100% of the costs of drugs that are not covered by their Part D plans.

Medicare pays the Part D deductible for all dual eligibles and for their monthly premiums if they enroll in an average or low-cost Part D plan. These subsidies eliminate the gap in coverage (donut hole) for dual eligibles that Medicare beneficiaries who do not qualify for Medicare and Medicaid face. As mentioned, dual eligibles can be responsible for small copayments. Dual eligibles residing in nursing homes or other institutions are exempt from copayments because they already are contributing all but a small portion of their income to the cost of their nursing home care.

Changing prescription drug coverage. All Medicare beneficiaries should check every year to make sure that their Medicare Part D PDP remains their best option. Premiums can go up, prescriptions may change, the plan might change its formulary, or the plan may no longer be available. Any or all of these factors could be reasons to change to a new plan. There is no penalty for switching plans; however, this can be done only during the Part D open enrollment period, from October 15 to December 7 each year, and the new plan then takes effect the following January 1.

OTHER MEDICARE HEALTH PLANS

Plans that are not Medicare Advantage plans but are still part of Medicare are:
- Program of All-Inclusive Care for the Elderly (PACE)
- Medicare Cost plans (available only in certain areas of the country)
- Medicare Innovation Projects

Some plans provide both Part A and Part B coverage, and some also provide prescription drug coverage (Part D). To learn more about Medicare Cost plans and Medicare Innovation Projects, visit http://innovation.cms.gov.

The **Program of All-Inclusive Care for the Elderly (PACE)** is a combination Medicare/Medicaid program that provides community-based long-term care services to eligible recipients. If an individual qualifies for Medicare, all Medicare-covered services are paid for by Medicare. If he or she also qualifies for Medicaid, he or she must either pay a small monthly payment or pay nothing for the long-term care portion of the PACE benefit. Those who are not Medicaid eligible must pay a monthly premium to cover the long-term care portion of the PACE benefit and a premium for Medicare Part D drugs. However, there is no deductible or copayment for any drug, service, or care approved by the PACE team.

PACE is available only in areas where a PACE organization is under contract to deliver services. To be eligible for the program, an individual must meet the following criteria:

- Is 55 years or older
- Meets the medical need criteria (needing nursing home level of care)
- Lives in an area serviced by a PACE organization
- Can be safely served in the community according to the PACE organization

To view the fact sheet "Quick Facts About Programs of All-Inclusive Care for the Elderly (PACE)," visit the Medicare.gov website.

GETTING HELP WITH MEDICARE COSTS

"Extra Help" is a Medicare program that helps beneficiaries who have limited income and resources to pay for some healthcare and prescription drug costs. Beneficiaries may qualify for Extra Help if their yearly income and resources meet certain financial guidelines. These dollar amounts are subject to change annually. (See the most recent *Medicare & You* handbook or log on to Medicare.gov and use "Extra Help" as search words.)

WHAT'S IMPORTANT FOR MEDICARE IN 2019

The historic transformation that America's healthcare system has gone through recently has brought about some changes in Medicare benefits. Each year the *Medicare & You* handbook lists important topics regarding what is important for the current year. The topics for 2019 include:

- New Medicare cards
- Finding out if Medicare covers your test, service, or item
- Medicare Advantage plans and other options
- Medicare Supplement Insurance (Medigap) policies
- Getting help paying your health and prescription drug costs

For details on these changes, consult the *Medicare & You* handbook.

It is important to remember that Medicare healthcare benefits and drug plans are subject to annual changes.

SENIORS' HEALTH INSURANCE INFORMATION PROGRAM

Seniors' Health Insurance Information Program (SHIIP) volunteers counsel Medicare beneficiaries and caregivers about Medicare, Medicare supplements, Medicare Advantage, Medicare Part D, Medicaid, and long-term care insurance. The counselors offer free and unbiased information on Medicare healthcare products. SHIIP volunteers also help people recognize and prevent Medicare billing errors and possible fraud and abuse through the Senior Medicare Patrol (SMP) program. Since the program's creation in 1986, SHIIP has become a role model for states and has received two national awards for "innovative" and "exemplary" service. More information on SHIIP is available on individual states' websites.

? What Did You Learn?

1. What is Medicare?
2. Define FICA's role in the Medicare program.
3. Name four common services that Medicare Part B does not cover.
4. List the four parts of the Medicare program structure.
5. True or false: Everyone age 65 can get free Medicare Part A.
6. The fees that Medicare permits for a particular service or supply are referred to as _____.
7. What does TrOOP stand for?
8. List the eligibility requirements for PACE.

THE EFFECTS OF THE ACA ON MEDICARE COVERAGE

The ACA did not adversely affect Medicare coverage for beneficiaries. Options and responsibilities did not change for individuals who are eligible for or insured by Medicare. For those who are Medicare eligible, it does not matter whether they are insured through original Medicare or enrolled in a Medicare Supplement (Medigap) plan, a Medicare Advantage plan, or a Medicare Part D PDP; they will not change their healthcare plan through the health insurance marketplace. As a matter of fact, it is against the law for anyone knowing that a person is on Medicare to sell that individual a "marketplace plan" under the ACA, and beneficiaries cannot enroll in a health or prescription drug plan through the health insurance exchange established by the ACA.

However, there are some benefits for Medicare enrollees established under the healthcare law. They include, for example, specific preventive benefits, cancer screenings, and annual wellness visits, which are available with no cost to patients when furnished by qualified and participating healthcare professionals.

Initiatives under the ACA make it possible for healthcare providers to get additional resources for **care coordination**. The goal of coordinated care is to make sure that patients, especially the chronically ill, get the right care at the right time, while avoiding unnecessary duplication of services and preventing medical errors. Patients benefit when healthcare providers and/or hospitals coordinate care because they work together to provide the right care at the right time in the right setting. Medicare's coordinated care programs include accountable care organizations (local healthcare providers and hospitals that volunteer to work together to provide coordinated care) and the Comprehensive Primary Care Initiative, which is a partnership between Medicare and other insurance programs to help selected primary care providers make additional resources available that can improve the quality of care.

The healthcare law ensures the protection of Medicare for the future. The life of the Medicare trust fund will be extended to at least 2029—a 12-year extension due to reductions in waste, fraud, abuse, and Medicare costs, which will provide Americans with future savings on their premiums and coinsurance.

? **What Did You Learn?**

1. True or false: The ACA drastically changed options for Medicare beneficiaries.
2. List some benefits that were added for Medicare beneficiaries under the ACA.
3. What is the goal of care coordination?

MEDICARE COMBINATION COVERAGES

Because Medicare does not cover all healthcare-related services and there are deductibles and copayments that patients must pay out of pocket for most services, beneficiaries often have added health insurance coverage to help with the gaps in Medicare's coverage. This extra coverage can be one of the following:

- Medicare/Medicaid dual eligibility
- Medicare Supplement policies (Medigap)
- Medicare secondary payer (MSP)

The following sections explain each of these supplemental types of healthcare coverage.

MEDICARE/MEDICAID DUAL ELIGIBILITY

Dual eligibility, as stated earlier, refers to the status of individuals who qualify for benefits under both the Medicare and the Medicaid programs. Most dual eligibles are low-income elderly or individuals younger than 65 years with disabilities. Medicare does not pay for all health services, just basic physician and hospital care. In addition, Medicare beneficiaries must meet a yearly deductible and pay a monthly premium and a 20% copayment (cost-sharing) for all covered services. Dual eligibles rely on Medicaid to pay Medicare premiums and cost-sharing (deductibles and copayments) expenses and to pay for the needed benefits that Medicare does not cover, such as long-term care.

MEDICARE SUPPLEMENT POLICIES

The original Medicare program provides valuable coverage of healthcare needs, but it leaves uninsured areas with which elderly and disabled Americans need additional help. To ensure that they are adequately protected, many seniors may choose to purchase an optional **Medicare Supplement policy** (also referred to as a *Medigap policy*). A Medicare Supplement policy is a health insurance plan sold by private insurance companies to help pay for healthcare expenses not covered by Medicare and Medicare's deductibles and coinsurance. An individual may qualify for supplemental insurance through an employer-sponsored retirement plan or, more commonly, through a Medigap plan.

MEDIGAP INSURANCE

Medigap insurance is designed specifically to supplement Medicare benefits and is regulated by federal and state law. A Medigap policy must be clearly identified as Medicare Supplemental insurance, and it must provide specific benefits that help fill the gaps in Medicare coverage. Other kinds of insurance may help with out-of-pocket healthcare costs, but they do not qualify as Medigap plans.

In June 2010 the types of Medigap plans available changed, adding two new Medigap plans (plans M and N). Plans E, H, I, and J are no longer available to buy; however, beneficiaries who purchased one of these discontinued plans before June 1, 2010, can keep that plan. Each plan has a different set of benefits. Plan A is the basic plan, and it has the least amount of benefits. Plan F, the most comprehensive, provides 100% of the gaps in Medicare; there are no deductibles, no copayments, and no coinsurance with any healthcare provider who accepts Medicare.

For beneficiaries who become eligible in 2020 and after the first-dollar coverage plans, Plans C and F and High Deductible Plan F will no longer be available. First-dollar coverage plans are Medicare Supplement plans that leave the beneficiary with zero out-of-pocket costs. Going forward all beneficiaries will be responsible for the Part B deductible. Beneficiaries who were eligible before 2020 and had a first-dollar coverage plan will not have to change their plan; they will be grandfathered in.

Table 11.6 shows the 10 Medigap plans currently available and what each plan covers.

When an individual buys a Medicare Supplement policy, he or she pays a premium to the private insurance company. This premium is above and beyond the Medicare Part B premium. If the individual has a Medicare Advantage plan, it is not necessary to have a Medicare Supplement policy because these plans typically include many of the same coverages as Medigap.

Standard Medigap Policies

The 10 standard Medigap policies were developed by the National Association of Insurance Commissioners and incorporated into state and federal law. The plans cover specific expenses not covered or not fully covered by Medicare. Insurance companies are not permitted to change the combination of benefits or the letter designations of any of the plans.

Table 11.6   Ten Standard Medicare Supplemental Plans

MEDIGAP BENEFITS	A	B	C[d]	D	F[a,d]	G	K	L	M	N[b]
					MEDIGAP PLANS					
Part A hospital coinsurance	Yes	Yes	Yes	Yes	Yes	Yes	Yes	Yes	Yes	Yes
365 Additional hospital reserve days	Yes	Yes	Yes	Yes	Yes	Yes	Yes	Yes	Yes	Yes
Benefit for blood	Yes	Yes	Yes	Yes	Yes	Yes	50%	75%	Yes	Yes
Part B coinsurance	Yes	Yes	Yes	Yes	Yes	Yes	50%	75%	Yes	Copays
Hospice coinsurance	Yes	Yes	Yes	Yes	Yes	Yes	50%	75%	Yes	Yes
Skilled nursing facility coinsurance	No	No	Yes	Yes	Yes	Yes	50%	75%	Yes	Yes
Medicare Part A deductible	No	Yes	Yes	Yes	Yes	Yes	50%	75%	50%	Yes
Medicare Part B deductible	No	No	Yes	No	Yes	No	No	No	No	No
Medicare Part B excess	No	No	No	No	Yes	Yes	No	No	No	No
Foreign travel benefit	No	No	80%	80%	80%	80%	No	No	80%	80%
Out-of-pocket limit[c]	None	None	None	None	None	None	$5560	$2780	None	None

How to read the chart: If "Yes" appears in a row on this chart, the Medigap policy covers 100% of the described benefit. If a row lists a percentage, the policy covers that percentage of the described benefit. If "No" appears in a row, the policy doesn't cover that benefit.
[a]Plan F also offers a high-deductible plan. If you choose this option, this means you must pay for Medicare-covered costs up to the deductible amount before your Medigap plan pays anything.
[b]Plan N pays 100% of the Part B coinsurance except for a copayment of up to $20 for some office visits and up to $50 copayment for emergency room visits that don't result in an inpatient admission.
[c]After you meet your out-of-pocket yearly limit and your yearly Part B deductible, the Medigap plan pays 100% of covered services for the rest of the calendar year.
[d]Not available after 2020.

From Centers for Medicare and Medicaid Services (website). http://www.medicare.gov.

All states must allow the sale of Plan A, and all Medigap insurers must make Plan A available if they are going to sell any Medigap plans in their state. Although not required to offer any of the other plans, most insurers do offer several of these alternative plans to pick from; some offer all 10. Insurers can decide which of the optional plans they will sell as long as the state in which the plans are sold approves. Although insurers must offer the same coverage in each plan, they do not have to charge the same premium rates; it is strongly suggested that individuals shop around and compare prices before purchasing a Medigap policy. Box 11.1 describes the **Medicare gaps** in various types of care.

Box 11.1   Medicare Gaps by Care Type

During a hospital stay, Medicare Part A does not pay the:

- Yearly deductible
- Coinsurance amount for each day of hospitalization more than 60 days and up to 90 days for any one benefit period
- Coinsurance amount for each day of hospitalization more than 90 days and up to 150 days for any one benefit period past a 150-day hospitalization
- Anything past a 150-day hospitalization
- Cost of three pints of blood, unless replaced
- Medical expenses during foreign travel

During a stay in a skilled nursing facility, Medicare Part A does not pay the:

- Coinsurance amount for each day in the facility more than 20 days and up to 100 days for any one benefit period
- Anything for a stay of more than 100 days

For home healthcare, Medicare Part A does not pay:

- 20% of the approved cost of durable medical equipment or approved nonskilled care
- Anything for nonmedical personal care services

For physicians, clinics, laboratories, therapies, medical supplies, and equipment, Medicare Part B does not pay:

- Yearly deductible
- 20% of the Medicare-approved amount
- 15% above the Medicare-approved amount if provider does not accept assignment
- Acupuncture and cosmetic surgery
- Treatment that is not considered medically necessary
- Prescription medication that can be self-administered
- General dental work
- Routine eye or hearing examinations
- Glasses or hearing aids

Medigap Eligibility

If an individual enrolls in Medicare Part B when he or she turns age 65, federal law forbids insurance companies from denying eligibility for Medigap policies for 6 months. This 6-month period is called the *open enrollment period.* If the individual did not enroll in Medicare Part B when turning 65, he or she can sign up for it later, during the yearly general enrollment period in January to March. The individual has a 6-month open enrollment period for Medigap policies beginning July 1 of that year. Individuals who were covered by a group health insurance plan when they turned 65 have a 6-month open enrollment period for Medigap policies beginning on the date that their Part B coverage begins, regardless of when they sign up for it. An insurance company must sell eligible applicants the policy of their choice without any medical screening, regardless of their medical history. The company is not permitted to place any extra limits on the coverage offered, and they must offer the policy for the same monthly premium as everyone else buying the same policy when first eligible for Medicare.

Medicare Fact: A beneficiary cannot use, and cannot be sold, a Medicare Supplement insurance (Medigap) policy if he or she is enrolled in a Medicare Advantage plan (Medicare Part C).

MEDICARE SECONDARY PAYER

Medicare secondary payer (MSP) is the term used when Medicare is not responsible for paying first because the beneficiary is covered under another insurance policy. The MSP program, enacted in 1980, was created to preserve Medicare funds and to ensure that funds would be available for future generations. Since the program's beginning, a series of federal laws has changed the coordination of benefits provision between Medicare and other insurance carriers. These federal laws take precedence over individual state law and private insurance contracts. For certain categories of individuals, Medicare is the secondary payer regardless of state law or plan provisions. Medicare most likely would be the secondary payer in any of the following situations:

- Workers' compensation (injury or illness that occurred at work)
- Working aged (age 65 years and older) who are covered by a group health plan through their own or their spouse's current employment
- Disabled individuals age 64 years and younger who are covered by a large group health plan (more than 100 employees) through their own or a family member's current employment
- Medicare beneficiaries with ESRD covered under a group health plan
- Individuals with black lung disease covered under the Federal Black Lung Program
- Veterans Administration benefits
- Federal research grant program

It is often the responsibility of the health insurance professional to determine, in cases in which the Medicare beneficiary has other insurance coverage, to which third-party payer the electronic or CMS-1500 paper claim is submitted first. Many medical practices use a structured form, such as an MSP questionnaire, to simplify this process. An example of an MSP questionnaire is shown in Fig. 11.4. Table 11.7 will help health insurance professionals determine who pays first (primary payer) when the beneficiary has other health insurance (OHI).

Table 11.7 Determining Who Pays First

TYPE OF OHI	PRIMARY PAYER
Retiree insurance from the beneficiary or his or her spouse's former employment	Medicare
If beneficiary is age 65 or older and has group health plan coverage from his or her or spouse's current employment of 20 or more employees	Group health plan
If beneficiary is age 65 or older and has group health plan coverage from his or her or spouse's current employment of 20 or fewer employees	Medicare
If beneficiary is under age 65 and disabled, has group health plan coverage based on his or her or a family member's current employment, and the employer has more than 100 employees	Group health plan
If beneficiary is under age 65 and disabled, has group health plan coverage based on his or her or a family member's current employment, and the employer has fewer than 100 employees	Medicare
Beneficiary has Medicare because of ESRD	Group plan pays first for first 30 months. After beneficiary becomes eligible to enroll in Medicare, Medicare pays first after the initial 30-month period has ended.

ESRD, End-stage renal disease; *OHI,* other health insurance.

Medicare Secondary Payer Questionnaire

Date: _____ Patient Name: _____

Patient Date of Birth: _____

Dear Medicare Patient:

Medicare requires that all entities that bill Medicare for services or items rendered to Medicare beneficiaries must determine whether Medicare is the primary payer for those services or items provided. Therefore, Walden-Martin Family Medical Clinic is requesting that the below information be completed so that a determination can be made if Medicare is your primary insurance, please answer all questions.

1. Is the illness/injury due to an automobile accident, liability accident, or
    Workman's Compensation? *If "yes", please complete information below.*   ☐ Yes   ☐ No

2. Is illness covered by the Black Lung Program or Veterans Administration
    Program? *If "yes", please complete information below.*   ☐ Yes   ☐ No

3. Are the services to be paid by a government research/grant program?   ☐ Yes   ☐ No

4. Is the patient covered by an employer group health plan, including
    Federal Employees? *If "yes", please complete information below.*   ☐ Yes   ☐ No

5. Is this patient or his/her spouse actively employed by an employer of 20 or more
    employees? *If "yes", please complete information below.*   ☐ Yes   ☐ No

6a. If under age 65, is your Medicare coverage due to disability?
    If "yes" go to #6b, if "no", go to #7.   ☐ Yes   ☐ No

6b. Is the patient or his/her spouse or parent actively employed by, or is the patient
    considered an employee of an employer having 100 or more employees?
    If "yes", please complete information below.   ☐ Yes   ☐ No

7a. Is the patient entitled to Medicare solely on the basis of End-Stage Renal
    Disease (ESRD)? *If "yes", go to #7b.*   ☐ Yes   ☐ No

7b. Has the patient completed the ESRD coordination period?
    If "no", enter information below.   ☐ Yes   ☐ No

Please complete each question, if applicable.

Name of primary insurance company: _____

Address of primary insurance company: _____

Name of primary insurance policy holder: _____

Primary insurance policy number: _____

Name of policy holder's employer: _____

Address of policy holder's employer: _____

Date benefits began: _____ /_____/_____

Date of accident/injury (If answered "yes" see question #1): _____/_____/_____

_____

Name of research/grant study (If answered yes to question (#3): _____

Patient's signature _____

Fig. 11.4 Medicare secondary payer questionnaire. (From US Department of Health and Human Services, Centers for Medicare and Medicaid Services, Baltimore, MD.)

Some important things to remember:

- The insurance that pays first (primary payer) pays up to the limit of its coverage.
- The insurance that pays second (secondary payer) only pays if there are costs the primary insurance didn't cover.
- The secondary payer (which may be Medicare) might not pay all of the uncovered costs.
- If the employer group insurance is the secondary payer, the beneficiary might need to enroll in Medicare Part B before the group plan will pay.

? What Did You Learn?

1. List three kinds of Medicare combination coverage.
2. What categories of people make up the "dual eligible" classification?
3. How does Medicaid assist Medicare beneficiaries?
4. How many standard Medigap policies are currently available?
5. What do most Medigap plans cover?
6. Name four payers that typically would be primary to Medicare.

MEDICARE AND MANAGED CARE

We have learned that Medicare-eligible individuals have a choice whether to receive Medicare benefits through original Medicare or through a managed care plan. A **Medicare managed care plan** must cover all services that original Medicare covers except hospice care and some care in qualifying for clinical research studies. It also must follow all of Medicare's rules. A Medicare managed care plan can be an HMO, a PPO, a PFFS, or an SNP (see discussion later) that uses Medicare to pay for part of its services for eligible beneficiaries. Medicare managed care plans fill the gaps in basic Medicare benefits like Medigap policies do; however, Medicare managed care plans and Medigap policies function differently. Medigap policies work along with Medicare to pay for medical expenses. Medical claims are sent to Medicare and then crossed over to a Medigap insurer, and each pays a portion of the approved charges. Medicare managed care plans provide all basic Medicare benefits, plus some additional coverages (depending on the plan), to fill the gaps Medicare does not pay. The extent of coverage beyond Medicare, the size of premiums and copayments, and decisions about paying for treatment all are controlled by the managed care plan itself, not by Medicare.

When a patient enrolls in a Medicare managed plan, he or she agrees to receive care only from an approved list of physicians, hospitals, and other providers, called a **network**, in exchange for reduced overall healthcare costs. There are several types of Medicare managed care plans, as discussed earlier in this chapter. Some

have tight restrictions concerning members' visiting specialists or seeing providers outside the network. Others give members more freedom to choose when they see providers and which providers they may consult for treatment. Additional details on the various managed care plans are provided in the following paragraphs.

MEDICARE HMOs

Similar to the structure of the HMOs that we learned about in Chapter 9, Medicare HMOs maintain a network of physicians and other healthcare providers. The HMO member or enrollee must receive care only from the providers in the network, except in emergencies. If a member sees a provider outside the network, the HMO usually pays nothing toward the bill. Because an HMO plan member has technically withdrawn from original Medicare by opting to join the managed care organization (MCO), Medicare also pays nothing. The result in this case is that the plan member usually must pay the entire bill out of pocket.

HMO WITH POINT OF SERVICE OPTION

One type of HMO has a significant modification that makes it more popular, albeit costlier, than the standard HMO plan. This plan offers what is referred to as an **HMO with point of service (POS) option**. A member is allowed to see providers who are not in the HMO network and to receive services from specialists without first going through a primary care physician. This method is called **self-referring**. However, when a member does go outside the network or sees a specialist directly, the plan pays a smaller portion of the bill than if the member had followed regular HMO procedures. The member pays a higher premium for this plan than for a standard HMO plan and a higher copayment each time the self-referral option is used.

PREFERRED PROVIDER ORGANIZATION

A PPO works much the same as an HMO with POS option. If a member receives a service from a PPO's network of providers, the cost to the member is lower than if the member sees a provider outside the network; however, a member does not have to go through a primary care physician for referrals to specialists. PPO patients usually are allowed to self-refer to specialists. PPOs tend to be more expensive than standard HMOs, charging a monthly premium and a higher copayment for non-network services.

PROVIDER-SPONSORED ORGANIZATION

A **provider-sponsored organization (PSO)** is a group of medical providers—physicians, clinics, and hospitals—that skips the insurance company intermediary and contracts directly with patients. As with an HMO, members pay a premium and a copayment each time a service is rendered. Some PSOs in urban areas are large groups of physicians and hospitals that offer a wide choice of providers. Some PSOs are small networks of providers that contract through a particular employer or other large organization or that serve a rural area where no HMO is available.

PRIVATE FEE-FOR-SERVICE PLAN

Under a PFFS plan, the Medicare beneficiary can go to any Medicare-approved physician or hospital that accepts the plan's payment terms and agrees to treat him or her. When joining a PFFS plan that has a network, patients can also see any of the network providers who have agreed to treat plan members.

SPECIAL NEEDS PLANS

A **special needs plan (SNP)** (pronounced "snip") is a type of Medicare Advantage plan designed to attract and enroll Medicare beneficiaries who fall into a certain special needs classification. There are two types of SNPs. The exclusive SNP enrolls only those beneficiaries who fall into the special needs demographic, such as those living in nursing homes or requiring at-home care and dual eligibles. The other type is the **disproportionate share**. (A disproportionate share is a payment adjustment to compensate hospitals for the higher operating costs that they incur in treating a large share of low-income patients.) All SNPs must provide Medicare prescription drug coverage (Part D).

Beneficiaries can join or leave a Medicare Advantage plan even if they have a preexisting condition, except for those with ESRD. This can be done only at certain times during the year. If the plan decides to stop participating in Medicare, the beneficiary can either join another Medicare Advantage plan or enroll in original Medicare. If the beneficiary chooses to join original Medicare, he or she can also enroll in certain Medigap policies if it is done within 63 days. After joining original Medicare, he or she can also join a Medicare PDP.

MEDICARE MEDICAL SAVINGS ACCOUNT PLAN

Medical savings account (MSA) plans allow beneficiaries to enroll in a plan with a high deductible combined with a bank account. Medicare deposits funds into the account (usually less than the deductible), and the enrollee can use the money to pay for medical services received during the year. After the deductible is met, the MSA plan pays providers. Money remaining in the MSA account can be used to pay for future medical care, including some services not usually covered by Medicare Parts A and B, such as dentures.

ADVANTAGES AND DISADVANTAGES OF MEDICARE HMOs

Medicare Advantage plans provide the same benefits as original Medicare. They can charge lower costs because of how HMO plans are structured; however, they cannot charge more than original Medicare for certain services. HMO plans typically provide a managed treatment approach to care that is designed to minimize unnecessary costs and services. This design allows HMO Advantage plan enrollees to pay lower premium rates than those charged by traditional Medicare plans. As well, although insurance rates and coverages vary from state to state, required copayment and deductible amounts under HMO Advantage plans normally are less than those for traditional plans. (It should be noted that even though Medicare Advantage plan enrollees typically pay lower premiums, they still must pay the Medicare Part B monthly premium.)

As with most areas of healthcare insurance, there are advantages and disadvantages to enrolling in a Medicare HMO.

Advantages

- HMOs may cover services that original Medicare does not cover, such as eyeglasses, hearing aids, prescriptions, and dental coverage.
- Enrollees do not need Medigap insurance.
- Paperwork is limited or nonexistent in contrast to original Medicare coverage.
- HMOs often pay additional coverage for hospital stays that exceed the limits set by Medicare.
- There is a yearly cap on how much the enrollee pays for Parts A and B services during the year. (This cap amount varies among plans and is subject to annual change.)

Disadvantages

- Choice of healthcare providers and medical facilities is limited.
- Members or enrollees are covered only for healthcare services received through the HMO, except in emergency and urgent care situations.
- Prior approval is usually necessary from a primary care physician for a specialist's services, surgical procedures, medical equipment, and other healthcare services, which is not required under original Medicare.
- Enrollees who travel out of the HMO's service area do not receive coverage except in emergency and urgent care situations.

If an enrollee decides to switch from the HMO to the original Medicare plan, coverage does not begin until the first day of the month after the disenrollment request. When a Medicare beneficiary has original Medicare and a Medicare Supplement plan (Medigap), this picture changes. Table 11.8 illustrates how original Medicare with a Medigap policy (Plan F) compares with Medicare Advantage.

Medicare Fact: In 2015, of the approximately 50 million people enrolled in Medicare, 16.8 million were enrolled in Medicare Advantage.

Table 11.8 Differences Between Original Medicare and Medicare Advantage Plans

ORIGINAL MEDICARE	MEDICARE ADVANTAGE PLANS
Administered directly through the federal government	Plans sold by private, government-approved companies that provide Medicare benefits
Includes Part A (hospital) and Part B (medical) coverage if enrolled in both	Must cover same Parts A and B benefits as original Medicare (some plans offer extra benefits)
Pay a deductible and/or coinsurance (usually 20%) of the Medicare-approved cost of service	Common plan types are HMOs, PPOs, and PFFS plans
Most pay a monthly premium for Part B; free Part A if work history meets eligibility requirements	Still have Medicare but have different costs and restrictions
Can go to healthcare provider to see specialists; no prior authorization for services	Pay deductible and/or copayment (e.g., $15 per office visit)
Can buy a Medigap plan for supplemental coverage	Still pay Medicare premiums; plan may charge an extra premium
Can buy a separate prescription drug plan from a private insurer if drug coverage is desired	Need prior authorization and/or choose a PCP for referrals to specialists Cannot buy Medigap to pay for out-of-pocket costs Plans must offer annual out-of-pocket limits Usually cannot have a separate Part D plan unless enrolled in a MA-PD or PFFS plan

HMO, Health maintenance organization; *MA-PD,* Medicare Advantage Prescription Drug; *PCP,* primary care physician; *PFFS,* private fee-for-service; *PPO,* preferred provider organization.

Data from Centers for Medicare and Medicaid Services (website). http://www.medicare.gov.

WHY THIS INFORMATION IS IMPORTANT TO THE HEALTH INSURANCE PROFESSIONAL

As a health insurance professional, you will be doing more than sitting at a desk entering data into a computer. In your job, you no doubt will become a liaison between many third-party payers and the entire healthcare team. In addition, you must be able to answer patients' questions about Medicare accurately. The Medicare program and all its various parts and choices can be confusing to people, especially the elderly. Although it is important that the health insurance professional learn all complexities of the Medicare program from the provider standpoint, he or she also must become an expert from the beneficiaries' perspective. The fact alone that the fee-for-service (FFS; or original Medicare) plan covers 80% of *allowed charges* is enough to create confusion. When you present an elderly patient with an **advance beneficiary notice (ABN)** or begin discussing Medicare's lifetime release of information form, you must be prepared to answer questions in layperson's language.

Imagine This!

Arlene Sorensen had been told by her gynecologist when she was younger that it was important to receive a Pap test every year. After she became eligible for Medicare, she told her family practice provider that she wanted to continue this practice. The first Pap test was covered by Medicare; however, a subsequent Pap test a year later was not. When she questioned her physician, he referred her to the health insurance professional, who informed Mrs. Sorensen that Medicare considers Pap tests "medically necessary" only every 2 years, unless the patient is considered at high risk.

? What Did You Learn?

1. Name four kinds of Medicare managed care plans.
2. When patients enroll in a Medicare managed care plan, they typically agree to choose healthcare providers from an approved list called a _____.
3. A type of Medicare Advantage plan designed to attract and enroll Medicare beneficiaries who fall into a certain special needs classification is called a _____.
4. Which type of Medicare plan has a higher enrollment: original Medicare or Medicare Advantage?
5. Explain why it is important for the health insurance professional to be knowledgeable about the specifics of both original Medicare and Medicare Advantage?

PREPARING FOR THE MEDICARE PATIENT

When a Medicare beneficiary comes to the office for an appointment, the procedure for handling the encounter is basically the same as with non-Medicare patients, with a few exceptions.

MEDICARE'S LIFETIME RELEASE OF INFORMATION FORM

The medical facility should maintain a current release of information for every patient. Among other things, this approach allows the health insurance professional to complete and submit the insurance form legally. Typically, a release of information is valid for only 1 year; however, with Medicare, a **lifetime (one-time) release of information form** may be signed by the beneficiary, eliminating the need for annual updates. Fig. 11.5 is an example of a lifetime release of information form.

LIFETIME AUTHORIZATION AND REQUEST FOR MEDICAL INFORMATION

I hereby release Charles H. Shaw, M.D., P.A. DBA Gainesville Orthopaedic Group to release my records to the physician individual I direct verbally or in writing.

RELEASE OF MEDICAL INFORMATION
I, the below named patient, hereby authorize Charles H. Shaw, M.D./D. Troy Trimble, D.O., Gainesville Orthopaedic Group to release to my referring physician and/or family physician and any third party payer (such as an insurance company or government agency; e.g., Blue Cross or Medicare) any medical information and records concerning my treatment when requested or by such third party payer or other entity for use in connection with making or determining claim payment for such treatment and/or diagnosis.

ASSIGNMENT OF BENEFITS AND GUARANTEE OF PAYMENT
I, the below named patient/subscriber, hereby absolutely assign payments directly to Charles H. Shaw, M.D./D. Troy Trimble, D.O., Gainesville Orthopaedic Group and any group and/or individual surgical and/or major medical benefits herein specified and otherwise payable to me for their services as described.

Medicare/Medicaid: I certify that the information given me in applying for payment under title XVIII / XIX of the Social Security Administration or its intermediaries or carriers any information needed for this or a related Medicare claim. I request that payment of authorized benefits be made on my behalf. I assign the benefits payable for physician's services to Charles H. Shaw, M.D./D. Troy Trimble, D.O., Gainesville Orthopaedic Group.

I/We hereby guarantee payment of all charges incurred for the below named patient from the date of the first treatment until discharged from care by Charles H. Shaw, M.D./D. Troy Trimble, D.O., Gainesville Orthopaedic Group. I/We agree that should the amount of insurance benefit to be insufficient to cover the expenses, I/We will be responsible for the entire amount due for services rendered. I/We understand that statements are due when received unless other arrangements have been made with Charles H. Shaw, M.D./D. Troy Trimble, D.O. DBA Gainesville Orthopaedic Group. I/We understand that if there is no response or payment from the insurance company within 60 days of billing, I/we will be responsible for the balance due on account.

_____   _____
Subscriber (insured person) Signature   Date

                                                                          ☐ Checking this box indicates a digital signature.

_____
Subscriber Printed Name

_____   _____
Patient Signature (if different from the subscriber)   Date

_____
Patient Printed Name

Fig. 11.5 Centers for Medicare and Medicaid Services lifetime (one-time) release authorization for Medicare beneficiaries.

DETERMINING MEDICAL NECESSITY

Before Medicare pays for a service or procedure, it must be determined whether it is medically necessary. To meet Medicare's definition of medical necessity, the service or procedure must be:

- Consistent with the symptoms or diagnosis of the illness or injury being treated
- Necessary and consistent with generally accepted professional medical standards
- Not furnished primarily for the convenience of the patient or physician
- Furnished at the most appropriate level that can be provided safely to the patient

CMS has the power to determine whether the method of treating a patient in a particular case is reasonable and necessary on a case-by-case basis. Even if a service is reasonable and necessary, coverage may be limited if the service is provided more frequently than allowed under a national coverage policy, a local medical policy, or a clinically accepted standard of practice.

Claims for services that are not medically necessary are denied, but not getting paid is not the only risk. If Medicare or other payers determine that services were medically unnecessary *after* payment has already been made, the payment is treated as an *overpayment,* and the beneficiary will have to refund the money, with interest. If a pattern of such claims is evident and the provider knows or should have known that the services were not medically necessary, the provider may face large monetary penalties, exclusion from the Medicare program, and possibly criminal prosecution.

One of the most common reasons for denial of Medicare claims is that the provider did not know that the services provided were not medically necessary. Lack of knowledge is not a defense, however, because a general notice to the medical community from CMS or an MAC (including a Medicare report or special bulletin) that a certain service is not covered is considered sufficient notice. This is why it is important for the health insurance professional to attend periodic educational seminars, read all Medicare- and Medicaid-related publications, and make every effort to keep up with these changes. In addition, if a provider fails to read Medicare's publications but delegates that responsibility to others, the physician or the professional corporation may still be held liable for what the physician should have known.

> **⚠ Stop and Think**
>
> Gladys Larson calls the office to schedule an appointment to "have Dr. Clifford remove all these ugly spots on my chest." Looking through her health record, you notice the physician's reference to "benign keratosis." How do you determine whether an advance beneficiary notice (ABN) is necessary?

Health insurance professionals can protect the physicians they work for by obtaining up-to-date information on services covered by Medicare from several sources. CMS publishes a periodical called *The CMS Quarterly Provider Update,* which includes all changes to Medicare instructions that affect physicians, provides a single source for national Medicare provider information, and gives physicians advance notice on upcoming instructions and regulations. (See "Websites to Explore" at the end of this chapter.) In addition, to keep informed, providers can subscribe to the CMS weekly email updates at cmlists@subscriptions.cms.hhs.gov/.

To sign up, go to https://public.govdelivery.com/accounts/USCMS/subscriber/new.

ADVANCE BENEFICIARY NOTICE

If, after checking the coverage rules, the health insurance professional believes that it is likely that Medicare *would not* pay for a test or procedure the provider orders, the patient should be asked to sign an ABN. An ABN should also be offered to a Medicare patient before he or she is provided a service that Medicare ordinarily covers but is likely to be denied on this particular occasion (e.g., when the health insurance professional has good reason to expect the procedure will be denied on the basis of other Medicare denials and/or local coverage determination [LCD; see discussion later] policies, or because the patient's diagnosis or procedure does not meet the Medicare program standards for medical necessity).

The ABN is intended to inform the patient in advance that it is likely that coverage for the procedure will be denied and allows the patient to make an informed decision whether to receive the service for which he or she may be personally responsible to pay.

If the service is denied and a signed ABN is not on file, the physician may not hold the patient responsible for payment. Fig. 11.6 shows Form CMS-R-131 (03/20), which is the most recent ABN form at the time of this writing.

When patients are asked to sign an ABN, they have two options:

- They may choose to receive the test or procedure, agree to be responsible for payment, and sign the ABN.
- They may choose not to receive the test or procedure, refuse to be responsible for payment, and sign the ABN.

When a patient is given an ABN, the health insurance professional should be able to answer questions about financial responsibility and payment options so that the patient can make an informed decision about his or her healthcare.

Medicare Fact: Medicare generally does not pay for healthcare outside the United States except in emergencies or under special circumstances. Certain Medigap policies may offer additional coverage for healthcare services or supplies outside the United States.

> **Imagine This!**
>
> Shelly Jennings, a health insurance professional employed by Medical Specialties, Inc., asked all Medicare patients receiving a "screening" colonoscopy to sign an advance beneficiary notice (ABN) because when she first started working at the facility, Medicare did not cover this procedure unless there were symptoms indicating a problem. After several patients complained, Medicare made an inquiry. Shelly's excuse was that she did not have time to read all of the publications that Medicare sent or attend periodic educational seminars, and she did not realize that Medicare now paid for a colonoscopy screening every 10 years, unless the patient is considered at high risk.

LCDs AND NCDs

A **local coverage determination (LCD)** consists only of information pertaining to when a procedure is considered medically reasonable and necessary. Most of Medicare's policies are established at the local level, giving MACs a great deal of authority over payment policy in a given state. Through development of local Medicare policy, MACs can determine whether a procedure is considered appropriate in an attempt to clarify specific coverage guidelines, particularly when a carrier has identified overutilization of a procedure. These policies were formerly called *local medical review policies.*

A **national coverage determination (NCD)** is a nationwide determination of whether Medicare will pay for an item or service. Medicare coverage is limited to items and services that are considered "reasonable and necessary" for the diagnosis or treatment of an illness

A. Notifier(s):

B. Patient Name: **C. Identification Number:**

ADVANCE BENEFICIARY NOTICE OF NONCOVERAGE (ABN)

NOTE: If Medicare doesn't pay for **D.** _____ below, you may have to pay.

Medicare does not pay for everything, even some care that you or your health care provider have good reason to think you need. We expect Medicare may not pay for the **D.**_____ below.

D. _____	E. Reason Medicare May Not Pay:	F. Estimated Cost:

WHAT YOU NEED TO DO NOW:

- Read this notice, so you can make an informed decision about your care.
- Ask us any questions that you may have after you finish reading.
- Choose an option below about whether to receive the **D.**_____ listed above.
  Note: If you choose Option 1 or 2, we may help you to use any other insurance that you might have, but Medicare cannot require us to do this.

G. **OPTIONS:**   **Check only one box. We cannot choose a box for you.**
☐ **OPTION 1.** I want the **D.**_____ listed above. You may ask to be paid now, but I also want Medicare billed for an official decision on payment, which is sent to me on a Medicare Summary Notice (MSN). I understand that if Medicare doesn't pay, I am responsible for payment, but **I can appeal to Medicare** by following the directions on the MSN**.** If Medicare does pay, you will refund any payments I made to you, less co-pays or deductibles.
☐ **OPTION 2.** I want the **D.**_____ listed above, but do not bill Medicare. You may ask to be paid now as I am responsible for payment. **I cannot appeal if Medicare is not billed**.
☐ **OPTION 3.** I don't want the **D.**_____listed above. I understand with this choice I am **not** responsible for payment, and **I cannot appeal to see if Medicare would pay.**

H. Additional Information:

This notice gives our opinion, not an official Medicare decision. If you have other questions on this notice or Medicare billing, call **1-800-MEDICARE** (1-800-633-4227/**TTY**: 1-877-486-2048). Signing below means that you have received and understand this notice. You also receive a copy.

I. Signature:	J. Date:

According to the Paperwork Reduction Act of 1995, no persons are required to respond to a collection of information unless it displays a valid OMB control number. The valid OMB control number for this information collection is 0938-0566. The time required to complete this information collection is estimated to average 7 minutes per response, including the time to review instructions, search existing data resources, gather the data needed, and complete and review the information collection. If you have comments concerning the accuracy of the time estimate or suggestions for improving this form, please write to: CMS, 7500 Security Boulevard, Attn: PRA Reports Clearance Officer, Baltimore, Maryland 21244-1850.

Form CMS-R-131 (Exp. 03/2020)   Form Approved OMB No. 0938-0566

Fig. 11.6 Example of an advance beneficiary notice.

or injury. In the absence of an NCD, an item or service is covered at the discretion of the Medicare contractors based on an LCD. NCDs can be requested by entities outside of CMS, such as manufacturers, providers, suppliers, medical professional associations, or health plans that identify an item or service as a possible benefit (or to prevent potential harm) to beneficiaries. NCDs can also be internally generated by CMS under various circumstances. A list of NCDs can be found on the CMS website.

MEDICARE BENEFICIARY IDENTIFIERS AND IDENTIFICATION CARD

We know that for years Medicare has used Social Security numbers as the primary means of identifying beneficiaries. Most insurers, including Blue Cross Blue Shield, TRICARE, and CHAMPVA, no longer use Social Security numbers for identification due to the concern over the rising incidence of identity theft. In June 2015, the president signed a law that ended the use of Social Security numbers on Medicare cards. New cards were issued starting in April 2018.

Instead of a **health insurance claim number (HICN)** in the format of nine numerical characters, the cards will show **Medicare Beneficiary Identifiers (MBIs)** in the format of 11 alphanumeric digits. These characters are randomly generated. The MBI's second, fifth, eighth, and ninth characters will always be a letter. Characters 1, 4, 7, 10, and 11 will always be a number. The third and sixth characters will be either a letter or a number. Fig. 11.7 shows an example of a Medicare ID card.

Patients belonging to a Medicare Advantage plan do not have the traditional ID card, but instead use the ID card of the plan in which they are enrolled.

Patients who have both original Medicare and a Medigap policy will have two cards; therefore when they visit the medical office, they should provide both cards. The official Medicare red, white, and blue card has a cardboard-type composition and only has pertinent information on the front. The health insurance professional does not need to make a copy of the back; however, the Medigap card is usually plastic (like a credit card), and it often has pertinent important information on the back (depending on the issuing insurer). If this is the case, a photocopy of both the back and the front of the Medigap card should be made, along with any other photo ID the patient provides.

Replacing the Medicare Card

If a Medicare enrollee loses his or her Medicare card or if it gets worn to such a degree that the information is no longer legible, a replacement can be requested from the local Social Security office. A replacement card also can be requested online on the Social Security website. Once the request has been made, it takes about 30 days for the replacement card to arrive in the mail.

> **[?] What Did You Learn?**
>
> 1. What are the criteria for meeting Medicare's "medically necessary" guidelines?
> 2. What are LCDs?
> 3. When should an ABN be used?
> 4. How is the MBI structured?

MEDICARE BILLING

Billing for services rendered to Medicare beneficiaries is slightly different from that of non-Medicare patients. The health insurance professional should use the Medicare Physician Fee Schedule (MPFS) rather than the regular fee schedule used by the practice. The fees contained in this special fee schedule for the services performed by the healthcare provider are calculated using a complex formula worked out by the federal government and printed periodically.

PHYSICIAN FEE SCHEDULE

CMS publishes an updated MPFS every year. In the past decade, the Medicare fee schedule was changed from FFS to a **resource-based relative value system (RBRVS)**. This means that each of the payment values is found within a range of payments. MPFSs vary from one region to another. Table 11.9 shows a portion of a sample page from an MPFS.

Payment for each service in the fee schedule is based on three factors:

1. A nationally uniform relative value for the specific service calculated with use of components of work, practice overhead, and professional liability—referred to as a **relative value unit**.

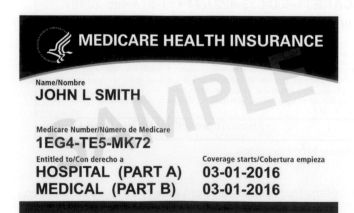

Fig. 11.7 Sample Medicare identification card. (Courtesy Centers for Medicare and Medicaid Services, Baltimore, MD.)

Table **11.9**	Sample Portion of a Medicare Fee Schedule				
PROCEDURE CODE	PAR AMOUNT	NONPAR AMOUNT	LIMITING CHARGE[a]	EHR LIMITING CHARGE[b]	PQRS LIMITING CHARGE[c]
97001	72.80	69.16	79.53	78.74	78.34
97002	40.54	38.51	44.29	43.84	43.62
97003	81.96	77.86	89.54	88.64	88.19
97004	50.47	47.95	55.14	54.59	54.31
97012	15.49	14.72	16.93	16.76	16.68

[a]Limiting charge applied to unassigned claims by nonparticipating providers.
[b]Limiting charge reduced based on the electronic health records (EHRs) negative adjustment program.
[c]Limiting charge reduced based on the Physician Quality Reporting System (PQRS) negative-adjustment program.
nonPAR, Nonparticipating provider; *PAR*, participating provider.
From Centers for Medicare and Medicaid Services.

2. A geographically specific modifier that considers variation in different areas of the country. Each area of the United States has its own geographic practice cost indices for each of the relative value factors of work, practice overhead, and professional liability.

3. A nationally uniform conversion factor that is updated annually.

4. It should be pointed out that although many believe that commercial payers compensate physicians using FFS methodologies that are based on Medicare's RBRVS or the MPFS, these assumptions may not be valid. Commercial payers may not assign the same values that Medicare assigns to the components of RBRVS—work, practice expense, or professional liability insurance (see Chapter 17).

VALUE-BASED PAYMENT MODIFIER

An important provision of the ACA is to reward higher-quality, patient-centered care at a lower cost. The goal of CMS is to pay providers for quality, rather than quantity, of care. To facilitate this shift in approach to payments, Medicare is phasing in the **value-based payment modifier**, which adjusts original Medicare payments to eligible healthcare providers based on the quality and cost of care they furnish to beneficiaries. These adjustments result in payment increases for providers who deliver higher-quality care at a better value, whereas providers who underperform may be subject to a payment reduction.

To help healthcare providers improve quality of care for beneficiaries, CMS released Quality and Resource Use Reports. Healthcare providers can use the reports to improve care coordination and reduce unnecessary services and to improve the quality, effectiveness, and efficiency of care delivered to Medicare beneficiaries—for example, information on where beneficiaries were hospitalized and whether they were readmitted. Additional information on this topic can be found on the CMS.gov website.

MEDICARE PARTICIPATING AND NONPARTICIPATING PROVIDERS

In its simplest explanation, a **Medicare participating provider (PAR)** or supplier is one who has signed a contract with Medicare; a **Medicare nonparticipating provider (nonPAR)** or supplier has not. Medicare PARs agree to accept Medicare's allowed amount as payment in full. Medicare nonPARs and suppliers may choose whether to accept Medicare's approved amount as payment on a case-by-case basis. If they do not accept the approved amount, the beneficiary can be charged the full billed amount. However, the "full billed" amount cannot exceed the **Medicare limiting charge**, which is 115% of Medicare's allowed amount.

After the beneficiary's annual deductible has been met, Medicare pays 80% of the fee schedule amount for a physician's service, and the beneficiary is responsible for 20%. Medicare PARs benefit from the following advantages:

- Their Medicare fee schedule is 5% higher than that of nonPARs.
- They are provided with toll-free lines if they submit claims electronically.
- Their names are listed in the *Medicare Participating Physician/Supplier Directory,* which is furnished to senior citizen groups.
- Medicare automatically forwards Medigap claims to the proper insurer for payment, eliminating the need to submit a separate claim to the supplementary insurer or beneficiary after receiving Medicare's payment.

Participation improves the patient–physician relationship because it helps reduce the beneficiary's out-of-pocket expenses. Medicare providers are generally required to submit claims for beneficiaries whether they are PAR or nonPAR and regardless of whether they accept assignment. Furthermore, the law does not allow the provider to charge for this service. Problems with claims processing can occur when a service has been rendered by a provider who is not enrolled with the Medicare program. The most common service rendered by a nonenrolled provider is an influenza shot. In such cases, beneficiaries must typically submit claims to Medicare on their own behalf. However, some providers who are not enrolled in Medicare will submit claims for beneficiaries.

DETERMINING WHAT FEE TO CHARGE

It is important that the health insurance professional know how to interpret the Medicare fee schedule so that he or she can determine the correct fee to charge the patient. Using the example fee schedule shown in Table 11.9 and choosing Current Procedural Terminology (CPT) code 97001 (a physical therapy evaluation), the amount Medicare allows a PAR to charge the patient is the amount shown in column 3 under the heading "PAR," or $72.80. A Medicare nonPAR accepting assignment can charge the amount in the next column under the heading "NonPAR," or $69.16. The limiting charge for providers *not accepting* assignment is the amount in the next column under the heading "Limiting," or $79.53—15% more than the nonPAR amount. For now, you need not be concerned with electronic health record (EHR) and Physician Quality Reporting System (PQRS) limiting charges. They will be addressed in a later chapter.

? What Did You Learn?

1. Who uses Medicare's "limiting charge"?
2. List three advantages of becoming a Medicare PAR.
3. How does a health insurance professional determine what fee to charge for a Medicare-eligible service?

FILING MEDICARE CLAIMS

Medicare Fact: Beneficiaries who are enrolled in a Medicare Advantage plan do not have to file claims because Medicare pays these private insurance companies a set amount every month.

ELECTRONIC CLAIMS

Medicare claims must be submitted electronically from a provider's office to an MAC or a DME MAC or an FI through the use of computer software that meets two specific electronic filing requirements. The electronic filing requirement established by the Health Insurance Portability and Accountability Act (HIPAA) of 1996 claim standard and the CMS requirements contained in the provider enrollment and certification category (as stated in the Electronic Data Interchange Enrollment page of the CMS website) must be met before claims can be submitted electronically to Medicare. Providers that bill MACs can also submit claims electronically using direct data entry (DDE) screens. (DDE is discussed in detail in Chapter 16.) The complete guide for Medicare enrollment and claim submission guidelines can be found on the Medicare Learning Network website. (See the link under "Websites to Explore" at the end of this chapter.)

ADMINISTRATIVE SIMPLIFICATION COMPLIANCE ACT

The Administrative Simplification Compliance Act (ASCA) requires that all initial claims for Medicare be submitted electronically with limited exceptions. **Initial claims** are those submitted to a Medicare contractor for the first time, including resubmission of previously rejected claims, claims with paper attachments, demand bills, Medicare secondary claims, and nonpayment claims. A **demand bill** is a request form that a beneficiary can send to a Medicare carrier or MAC requesting a review of a rejected claim or noncoverage determination (see Fig. 11.8 for an example of Medicare Reconsideration Request Form, CMS-20033 [12/10]). Initial claims do not include adjustments submitted to contractors on previously submitted claims or appeal requests.

Medicare will not pay on claims submitted on paper that do not meet the limited exception criteria. Claims denied for this reason will contain a **claim adjustment reason code** (an explanation why the claim or service line was paid differently from how it was billed) and a **remittance remark code** (a supplemental explanation for an adjustment already described by a claim adjustment reason code, indicating that the claim will not be considered unless submitted electronically). Claims required to be submitted electronically must comply with the appropriate claim standards adopted for national use under HIPAA.

EXCEPTIONS TO MANDATORY ELECTRONIC CLAIM SUBMISSION

The following is a list of exceptions to ASCA's mandatory electronic claim submission:

- Small provider claims
- Roster billing of inoculations covered by Medicare (except for those companies that agreed to submit these claims electronically as a condition for submission of flu shots administered in multiple states to a single carrier)
- Claims for payment under a Medicare demonstration project that specifies that claims be submitted on paper
- MSP claims when there is more than one primary payer and one or more of those payers made an "obligated to accept as payment in full" adjustment
- Claims submitted by Medicare beneficiaries or Medicare managed care plans
- Dental claims
- Claims for services or supplies furnished outside the United States by non-US providers
- Disruption in electricity or communication connections that are outside a provider's control and expected to last more than 2 business days
- Claims from providers that submit fewer than 10 claims per month on average during a calendar year

SMALL PROVIDERS AND FULL-TIME EQUIVALENT EMPLOYEE ASSESSMENTS

A **small provider** is defined as:

- A provider of services—as defined in section 1861(u) of the Social Security Act—with fewer than 25 full-time equivalent (FTE) employees, or
- A physician, practitioner, facility, or supplier that is not otherwise a provider under the section with fewer than 10 FTEs.

ASCA ENFORCEMENT OF PAPER CLAIM SUBMISSION

MACs are required to monitor and enforce the ASCA regulations and to conduct a quarterly analysis of the number of paper claims received. After the analysis, notices are mailed to any provider who submitted a large number of paper claims the previous quarter, asking the provider to explain which exception is applicable to the practice and to provide documentation to support that exception. If the provider does not respond with an acceptable response to prove eligibility for submitting paper claims, all paper claims will be rejected. This decision cannot be appealed.

Providers can purchase the software required for electronic claims submission from a vendor, contract with a billing service or a clearinghouse that offers software and programming support, or use HIPAA-compliant free billing software supplied by Medicare

DEPARTMENT OF HEALTH AND HUMAN SERVICES
CENTER FOR MEDICARE AND MEDICAID SERVICES

MEDICARE RECONSIDERATION REQUEST FORM — 2ND LEVEL OF APPEAL

1. Beneficiary's name: _____

2. Medicare number: _____

3. Item or service you wish to appeal: _____

4. Date the service or item was received: _____

5. Date of the redetermination notice (please include a copy of the notice with this request):
   (If you received your redetermination notice more than 180 days ago, include your reason for the late filing.)

   _____

   _____

   _____

   5a. Name of the Medicare contractor that made the redetermination (not required if copy of notice attached):

   _____

   5b. Does this appeal involve an overpayment?   ☐ Yes   ☐ No
        (for providers and suppliers only)

6. I do not agree with the redetermination decision on my claim because:

   _____

   _____

   _____

7. Additional information Medicare should consider:

   _____

   _____

8. ☐ I have evidence to submit. Please attach the evidence to this form or attach a statement explaining what you intend to submit and when you intend to submit it. You may also submit additional evidence at a later time, but all evidence must be received prior to the issuance of the reconsideration.

   ☐ I do not have evidence to submit.

9. Person appealing: ☐ Beneficiary   ☐ Provider/Supplier   ☐ Representative

10. Name, address, and telephone number of person appealing: _____

    _____

11. Signature of person appealing: _____

12. Date signed: _____

PRIVACY ACT STATEMENT: The legal authority for the collection of information on this form is authorized by section 1869 (a)(3) of the Social Security Act. The information provided will be used to further document your appeal. Submission of the information requested on this form is voluntary, but failure to provide all or any part of the requested information may affect the determination of your appeal. Information you furnish on this form may be disclosed by the Centers for Medicare and Medicaid Services to another person or government agency only with respect to the Medicare Program and to comply with Federal laws requiring or permitting the disclosure of information or the exchange of information between the Department of Health and Human Services and other agencies. Additional information about these disclosures can be found in the system of records notice for system no. 09-70-0566, as amended, available at 71 Fed, Reg. 54489 (2006) or at http://www.cms.gov/PrivacyActSystemof Records/downloads/0566.pdf

Form CMS-20033 (12/10)

Fig. 11.8 Sample demand bill.

carriers and DME MACs. Medicare contractors maintain a list on their providers' web page that contains the names of vendors whose software is currently being used successfully to submit HIPAA-compliant claims to Medicare.

Medicare Fact: Medicare contractors are allowed to collect a fee to recoup their costs up to $25 if a provider requests a Medicare contractor to mail an initial disk or update disks for this free software.

 HIPAA Tip

Covered entities may disclose protected health information about non-Medicare patients without their permission when the information involves quality-related activities under its contract with the quality improvement organization (QIO). (Under the Health Insurance Portability and Accountability Act [HIPAA], a "covered entity" is a health plan, healthcare clearinghouse, or healthcare provider who transmits information in electronic form.)

The US Department of Health and Human Services (HHS) has posted the final rule for the health insurance reform modifications to the updated version of the HIPAA Electronic Transaction Standards in the *Federal Register,* Vol. 74, No. 11, dated January 16, 2009. Updates are posted to the CMS.gov website periodically.

Medicare Fact: Although the majority of providers and suppliers use electronic claims submission, a significant number of providers meet the ASCA requirement that allows them to submit paper claims.

! **Stop and Think**

You are employed by a two-physician practice. In addition to you, the health insurance professional, there is a medical receptionist, two medical assistants, and a registered nurse. You have just completed transferring all patient accounts over to a computerized patient accounting system. Are you now required to submit all Medicare claims electronically?

CLAIM STATUS REQUEST AND RESPONSE

Providers have several options to obtain claim status information from Medicare contractors. These options allow providers to:
- Use provider help lines to call the local MAC or FI to speak to a customer service representative
- Input data via interactive voice response telephone systems operated by Medicare contractors
- Enter claim status queries via DDE screens maintained by Medicare contractors
- Submit a Health Care Claim Status Request (276 transaction) electronically and receive a Health Care Claim Status Response (277 transaction) back from Medicare

The electronic 276/277 process is recommended if the provider is able to generate and submit 276 queries automatically when necessary. This procedure eliminates the need for manual inquiry entries or phone calls to a contractor to obtain this information. This

electronic process is normally less expensive for both the provider and Medicare. In addition, the 277 response enables automatic posting of the status information directly to patient accounts, eliminating the need for manual data entry. The website for the Medicare electronic claims processing manual can be found under "Websites to Explore" at the end of this chapter.

 HIPAA Tip

With the implementation of the Health Insurance Portability and Accountability Act (HIPAA), it is possible to submit an electronic claim and to submit a separate paper attachment for that claim. When an electronic claim is filed, an attachment control number (ACN) is assigned. The paper attachment is sent with a cover page containing the ACN.

SUBMITTING CLAIMS WITH ATTACHMENTS

With the 5010 version of the ASC X12 837 institutional and professional (electronic healthcare claim transaction) form, electronic billers can use a method for providing additional documentation if it is required for claims processing. Providers now have the option of mailing or faxing paper documentation to support electronically submitted claims using the PWK (paperwork) segment of the claim. The PWK segment is the "electronic staple" that connects paper documentation to an electronic claim and alerts the Medicare contractor that attachment information is being submitted separately. Providers and suppliers submitting claims for which attachments are needed for processing must comply with the ASC X12 attachment reporting instructions required by their Medicare contractor; for example:

1. The provider submits an electronic claim, making sure to complete the PWK segment using the alpha characters BM if mailing the documentation or FX if faxing.
2. After the claim has been accepted, the provider completes the PWK Fax/Mail Cover Sheet (Fig. 11.9), provided by the MAC.
3. The PWK Fax/Mail Cover Sheet with all necessary documentation is sent to the MAC. (The form should include the relevant mailing address and fax number.)
4. The MAC processes the claim and refers to the submitted PWK documentation, if necessary for proper claim adjudication.

Technical information about the use of the PWK segment is available on the CMS website.

Medicare Fact: A Medicare contractor is not permitted to prohibit submission of an electronic claim because there is a paper attachment.

TIMELY FILING RULES FOR MEDICARE CLAIMS

Medicare Fact: Medicare's fiscal year is the same as that of the federal government; it begins on October 1 and ends on September 30 of the following year.

Medicare Part B Fax/Mail Cover Sheet

Complete all fields and fax or mail the form to the applicable address/number provided at the bottom of the page. Complete **ONE (1)** Medicare-Fax/Mail Cover Sheet for each electronic claim for which documentation is being submitted. This form should not be submitted prior to filing the claim.

ACN: (Exactly as entered in the PWK loop on the claim):		ICN:
Beneficiary: Last Name	First Name	HICN:
Date(s) of service: From	To	Total claim billed amount:
Billing provider's name:		Contract and phone number:
NPI:		
State where services were provided:		Total number of documentation pages (including cover sheet):
Additional information/comments		

Fig. 11.9 Fax/mail cover sheet.

The ACA included a provision that limited timely filing of FFS claims to 1 year from the date of services. This change significantly shortens the time providers previously had to file Medicare claims.

Providers should be aware of these timely filing rules, especially if they are holding claims for some reason, because they shorten the time to file claims. If providers have concerns or questions, they should contact their MAC. *MLN Matters Article #MM7080* contains information about timely filing requirements and how CMS implements them. The link to this article is listed in "Websites to Explore" at the end of this chapter. Medicare regulations allow exceptions to timely filing requirements made in case of a Medicare program's administrative error and retroactive entitlements to Medicare coverage.

? What Did You Learn?

1. What does Medicare consider an "initial" claim to be?
2. True or false: Beneficiaries who are enrolled in a Medicare Advantage plan do not have to file claims.
3. List four exceptions to filing electronic claims for Medicare services.
4. Define a small provider.
5. What is the "timely filing" rule?

USING THE CMS-1500 FORM FOR MEDICARE CLAIMS

The CMS-1500 (02/12) form is the most recent updated version of the standard paper claim form used by a noninstitutional provider or supplier to bill MACs and DME MACs when a provider qualifies for a waiver from the ASCA requirement for electronic submission of claims. It is also used to bill some Medicaid state agencies. The CMS-1500 paper claim form was revised to accommodate crosswalking to Version 5010.

CMS does not supply CMS-1500 forms to providers for claim submission. Claim forms can be purchased at the US Government Printing Office (1-866-512-1800), local printing companies, and/or office supply stores. The National Uniform Claim Committee (NUCC) is responsible for the design and maintenance of the CMS-1500 form. NUCC also provides detailed step-by-step instructions for completing the CMS-1500.

The only acceptable claim forms are those printed in the official optical character recognition (OCR) red ink. Although a copy of the CMS-1500 form can be downloaded from the Internet, copies of the form cannot be used for submitting claims. The majority of paper claims are scanned using OCR technology. (See the OCR rules outlined in Chapter 6.)

In July 2013, the NUCC announced the final approval of the CMS-1500 claim form (version 02/12) that accommodates reporting needs for the International Statistical Classification of Diseases and Related Health Problems, tenth revision (ICD-10) and aligns with requirements in the ASC X12 Health Care Claim: Professional (837P) Version 5010 Technical Report Type 3. Initially, two priorities were included in the revisions to the form:

1. The addition of an indicator in Item Number 21 to identify the version of the diagnosis code set being reported (i.e., ICD-9 or ICD-10). The need to identify which version of the code set being reported was important during the implementation period of ICD-10. As of October 2015, ICD-10 was fully implemented, and services rendered on or after that date were no longer to be coded using the ICD-9 structure.
2. The expansion of the number of diagnosis codes that can be reported in Item Number 21 from 4 to 12.

Additional revisions will improve the accuracy of the data reported, such as being able to identify the role of the provider reported in Item Number 17 and the specific dates reported in Item Number 14.

A portable document format (PDF) of the revised 1500 form, including the template and grid versions, can be downloaded from http://www.nucc.org/.

Also, a change log showing all changes between the 08/05 version and 02/12 version of the form is available at http://www.nucc.org, along with the NUCC instruction manual for the CMS-1500 (02/12) claim form.

CMS-1500 COMPLETION GUIDELINES

For those providers who qualify for paper claims submission, the following guidelines will help ensure accurate and quick claim processing:

- Do not staple, clip, or tape anything to the CMS-1500 claim form.
- Place all necessary documentation in the envelope with the claim form.
- Include the patient's name and Medicare number on each piece of documentation submitted.
- Use dark ink.
- Use only uppercase (CAPITAL) letters.
- Use 10- or 12-pitch standard fonts.
- Do not mix character fonts on the same form.
- Do not use italics or script.
- Avoid using old or worn print bands.
- Do not use dollar signs, decimals, or punctuation.[a]
- Enter all information on the same horizontal plane within the designated field.
- Do not print, handwrite, or stamp any extraneous data on the form.
- Ensure that data are in the appropriate fields and do not overlap other fields.
- Remove pin-fed edges at side perforations, if applicable.
- Use only an original red-ink-on-white-paper CMS-1500 claim form.

Submission of paper claims that do not meet the carrier's requirements may delay payments.

The process of completing the CMS-1500 form for Medicare claims is similar to that of a commercial claim with a few exceptions. Complete Medicare claims filing instructions, which are essentially the same as those provided on the NUCC website, can be

---

[a]NUCC alternative guidelines (discussed in Chapter 6) state: "The use of punctuation is noted in the instructions section of each Item Number"; however, this textbook still uses the OCR guideline format disallowing all punctuation.

found in Appendix B. Fig. B.3 in Appendix B shows an example of a completed Medicare "simple" claim—a claim for a patient with Medicare coverage only. In addition, Chapter 26 of the *Medicare Claims Processing Manual* (Pub. 100-04) provides detailed information on completing the CMS-1500 form. Links to both the NUCC and the CMS websites can be found under "Websites to Explore" at the end of this chapter.

> **HIPAA Tip**
>
> The determining factor for the correct place of service (POS) for Medicare beneficiaries is determined by the status of the patient. When a patient is registered as an inpatient (POS 21) or outpatient (POS 22), one of these POS codes must be used to bill Medicare.

COMPLETING A MEDIGAP CLAIM

Completion of Blocks 9 through 9d on the CMS-1500 form is conditional for insurance information related to Medigap. Only PARs are required to complete Block 9 and its subdivisions and only when the patient wishes to assign his or her benefits under a Medigap policy to the PAR. PARs of services and suppliers must enter information required in Block 9 and its subdivisions if requested by the beneficiary. (PARs sign an agreement with Medicare to accept assignment of Medicare benefits for *all* Medicare patients. NonPARs can accept assignment on a case-by-case basis.)

A claim for which a beneficiary elects to assign his or her benefits under a Medigap policy to a PAR is called a **mandated Medigap transfer**. If a PAR and the patient want Medicare payment data forwarded to a Medigap insurer under a mandated Medigap transfer, all information in Blocks 9, 9a, and 9d must be complete and accurate. Otherwise, Medicare cannot forward the claim information to the Medigap insurer.

If the health insurance professional wishes to use the statement "signature on file" in Block 13 in lieu of the patient's actual signature, a statement must be signed and dated by the patient and maintained in the practice's records (Fig. 11.10). Table 11.10 contains instructions for completion of blocks that are affected by Medigap policies. A completed CMS-1500 claim form for a patient with both Medicare and Medigap coverage is shown in Fig. B.5 in Appendix B. Also see the "Medigap Crossover Program" section later in this chapter.

(Name of Beneficiary) (Health Insurance Claim Number) (Medigap Policy Number)

I request that payment of authorized Medigap benefits be made either to me or on my behalf to the provider of service and (or) supplier for any services furnished to me by the provider of service and (or) supplier. I authorize any holder of Medicare information about me to release to (Name of Medigap Insurer) any information needed to determine these benefits payable for related services.

(Signature) (Date)

Fig. 11.10 Example of a "signature on file" statement.

Table 11.10   Modifications to the CMS-1500 Form for a Medigap Claim

BLOCK NUMBER	INSTRUCTIONS
Block 9	Enter the last name, first name, and middle initial of the Medigap enrollee, if it is different from that shown in Block 2. Otherwise, enter the word "SAME." (This field may be used in the future for supplemental insurance plans.)
Block 9a	Enter the policy and/or group number of the Medigap insured preceded by MEDIGAP, MG, or MGAP. Note: Block 9d must be completed if a policy and/or group number is in Block 9a.
Block 9b	Leave blank in CMS-1500 form version 02/12.
Block 9c	Leave blank if Block 9d is completed. Otherwise, enter the claims processing address of the Medigap insurer. Use an abbreviated street address, two-letter postal code, and ZIP code copied from the Medigap insured's Medigap identification card. For example: 1257 Anywhere Street, Baltimore, MD 21204 is shown as "1257 Anywhere St., Baltimore, MD 21204." The NUCC will prove specific instructions for the future use of this block.
Block 9d	Enter the coordination of benefits agreement (COBA) Medigap-based identifier (ID). Refer to Chapter 28, Section 70.6.4 of the Pub 100-04 Medicare Claims Completion Manual for more information.
Block 12	Block 12 must be completed in all Medicare/Medigap claims. The patient or authorized representative must sign and enter a six-digit date (MM | DD | YY), eight-digit date (MM | DD | CCYY), or an alphanumeric date (e.g., January 1, 2014) unless the signature is on file. Failure to include an appropriate signature and date or a "signature on file" statement results in claim rejection. A Medigap authorization signature in Block 13 does not satisfy the Block 12 signature requirement. If a valid signature is on file, no date is necessary. Reminder: For date fields other than date of birth, all fields shall be one or the other format, six-digit: (MM | DD | YY) or eight-digit: (MM | DD | CCYY). Intermixing the two formats on the claim is not allowed.
Block 13	The patient's signature or the statement "signature on file" in this item authorizes payment to the physician or supplier. The patient or his or her authorized representative must either sign this item or the signature must be on file separately with the provider as an authorization. However, when payment is made on an assignment-related basis or when payment is for services furnished by a participating physician or supplier, a patient's signature or a "signature on file" is not required in order for Medicare payment to be made directly to the physician or supplier.

The rest of the form for a Medigap claim is completed using the Medicare guidelines provided in Appendix B and in the Pub. 100-04 *Medicare Claims Processing Manual*. From Centers for Medicare and Medicaid Services.

MEDICARE SECONDARY PAYER

When Medicare is the secondary payer, the claim must be submitted first to the primary insurer. The primary insurer processes the claim in accordance with the coverage provisions in the contract. If, after processing the claim, the primary insurer does not pay in full for the services, the claim may be submitted to Medicare electronically or via a paper claim for consideration of secondary benefits. It is the provider's responsibility to obtain primary insurance information from the beneficiary and to bill Medicare appropriately. Claim filing extensions are not granted because of incorrect insurance information.

Insurance Primary to Medicare

Medicare typically pays second if the beneficiary is injured in an accident or has a workers' compensation case in which OHI is primary. In such cases, Medicare should be notified as soon as possible. Besides the plan types listed in Table 11.7, the following types of insurance are usually primary (pay first) to Medicare:
- No-fault or other liability insurance
- Work-related illness or injury: workers' compensation, black lung, and veterans' benefits

For a paper claim to be considered for MSP benefits, a copy of the primary payer's explanation of benefits (EOB) notice must be forwarded along with the claim form.

Remember: Medicaid never pays first for services that Medicare covers.

Stop and Think

Franklin Elmore is a new patient in your office. When he filled out the patient information form, he indicated that he was born on February 26, 1949, and is employed full-time at Alamo Distributing Company. Under the insurance section, Mr. Elmore lists Medicare as his primary insurer and group coverage with Amax Quality Assurance through his employer as his secondary insurance. Is Mr. Elmore's information form correct? Which insurer should receive the CMS-1500 claim first?

Completing Medicare Secondary Policy Claims

When Medicare is the secondary payer, the primary payer's EOB typically includes the following information:
- Name and address of the primary insurer
- Name of subscriber and policy number
- Name of the provider of services
- Itemized charges for all procedure codes reported
- Detailed explanation of any denials or payment codes
- Date of service

A detailed explanation of any primary insurer's denial or payment codes must be submitted with the claim to Medicare. If the denial or payment code descriptions or any of the previously listed information is not included with the claim, there may be a delay in processing or denial of the claim. If the beneficiary is covered by more than one insurer primary to Medicare (e.g., a working aged beneficiary who was in an automobile accident), the EOB statements from those plans must be submitted with the claim.

To submit MSP claims electronically, refer to the *American National Standards Institute (ANSI) ASC X12N Implementation Guide.* Providers should contact their software vendor to learn how to report MSP claims in the practice's software.

For more information on MSP and required information to submit MSP claims electronically, refer to Chapter 6 of the *Medicare Secondary Payer (MSP) Manual.* The link to this manual is listed under "Websites to Explore" at the end of this chapter.

For submission of a paper claim to Medicare as the secondary payer, the following instructions apply:
- The CMS-1500 form must indicate the name and policy number of the beneficiary's primary insurance in Blocks 11 through 11c.
- Providers, whether they are PAR or nonPAR, must submit a claim to Medicare if a beneficiary provides a copy of the primary EOB.
- The claim must be submitted to Medicare for secondary payment consideration with a copy of the EOB. If the beneficiary is not cooperative in supplying the EOB, the beneficiary may be billed for the amount Medicare would pay as the secondary payer.
- Providers must bill the primary insurer and Medicare the same charge for rendered services. If the primary insurer is billed $50.00 for an office visit

and they pay $35.00, Medicare cannot be billed the remaining $15.00. Medicare also must be billed for the $50.00 charge, and a copy of the primary insurer's EOB must be attached to the completed claim form.

It was stated previously that when paper or electronic claims are submitted for Medicare, Block 11 must be completed. By completing this block, the physician or supplier acknowledges having made a good faith effort to determine whether Medicare is the primary or secondary payer. A claim without this information would be returned.

When there is insurance primary to Medicare, as in the MSP situation, the health insurance professional should enter the insured's policy or group number in Block 11 and proceed to Blocks 11a through 11c. (When there is no insurance primary to Medicare, enter the word "NONE" in Block 11 and proceed to Block 12.) Completion of Blocks 11b and 11c is conditional for insurance information primary to Medicare. Table 11.11 gives instructions for how Blocks 11 through 11d should be completed for MSP claims. A completed CMS-1500 claim for a patient with group coverage primary to Medicare (MSP) is shown in Fig. B.6 in Appendix B.

Medicaid Secondary Payer Conditional Payment
Medicare may make a *conditional* payment if it knows that another insurer is primary to Medicare but that the primary payer has not made prompt payment (within 120 days) or has denied the claim for a reason Medicare considers acceptable. (However, this conditional payment is applicable only for black lung, workers' compensation, liability, and no-fault accidents.) From a reimbursement standpoint, a claim paid

Table 11.11	Modifications to the CMS-1500 for Medicare Secondary Payer Claims
BLOCK NUMBER	**INSTRUCTIONS**
Block 11	This item must be completed; it is a required field. By completing this item, the physician/supplier acknowledges having made a good faith effort to determine whether Medicare is the primary or secondary payer. If there is insurance *primary* to Medicare, enter the insured's policy or group number and proceed to items 11a–11c. Items 4, 6, and 7 must also be completed. NOTE: Enter the appropriate information in item 11c if insurance primary to Medicare is indicated in item 11. If there is no insurance primary to Medicare, enter the word "NONE" and proceed to item 12. If the insured reports a terminating event with regard to insurance that had been primary to Medicare (e.g., insured retired), enter the word "NONE" and proceed to item 11b.
Block 11a	Enter the insured's eight-digit birth date (MM | DD | CCYY) and sex if different from item 3.
Block 11b	Enter employer's name, if applicable. If there is a change in the insured's insurance status (e.g., retired), enter either the six-digit (MM | DD | YY) or the eight-digit (MM | DD | CCYY) retirement date preceded by the word "RETIRED" to the right of the vertical dotted line. (Reminder: Follow specific carrier guidelines.)
Block 11c	For MSP claims, enter the nine-digit PAYER ID number of the primary insurer. If no PAYER ID number exists, enter the *complete* primary payer's program or plan name. If the primary payer's EOB does not contain the claims processing address, record the primary payer's claims processing address directly on the EOB. This is required if there is insurance primary to Medicare that is indicated in Block 11.
Block 11d	Can be left blank. Not required by Medicare.

EOB, Explanation of benefits; *MSP,* Medicare secondary payer.

conditionally pays the same as if there were no insurance other than Medicare. To learn more about how to apply for an MSP conditional payment, contact the local **coordination of benefits contractor (COBC)** by phone or mail. A COBC ensures that the information on the Medicare eligibility database regarding other health insurance primary to Medicare is up to date and accurate. This information can also be found on the CMS website.

MEDIGAP CROSSOVER PROGRAM

Effective October 2007, CMS transferred the mandatory Medicare Supplemental (Medigap) insurance crossover program from its Medicare contractors to the national COBC. The **Medigap crossover** process, which is mandated by the Social Security Act, is activated when (1) a Medicare PAR includes a specific identifier on the beneficiary's claim and (2) payment benefits are assigned to that provider. This process ensures data consistency among the many organizations that transmit Medicare data. A Medigap claim-based coordination of benefits agreements (COBA) ID is a unique identifier associated with each contract. COBA IDs are five-digit numbers in the range 55000 through 59999 that are assigned by the COBC. After a healthcare provider enrolls in this program, an ID is provided. The Medigap policy information should be shown in Blocks 9 through 9d on the CMS-1500 claim form as follows:

- The word *Medigap* (or MG, or MGAP) and the individual Medigap policy number must be present in Item 9a on the CMS-1500 form.
- The Medigap COBA ID number must be present in Item 9d on the CMS-1500 form.

A list of Medigap companies and their corresponding COBA ID numbers is available on the CMS website at https://www.cms.gov/Medicare/Coordination-of-Benefits-and-Recovery/COBA-Trading-Partners/Downloads/Medigap-Claim-based-COBA-IDs-for-Billing-Purpose.pdf.

MEDICARE/MEDICAID CROSSOVER CLAIMS

Modifications must be made on the CMS-1500 form for dual eligible beneficiaries. The claim is sent to Medicare first, which determines its liability portion of the charges. Then the claim is automatically crossed over to Medicaid directly from the Medicare carrier. The following blocks are affected:

Block 1: The Medicare box should be checked. (Only one box can be marked.)

Block 10d: The abbreviation MCD should be entered followed by the beneficiary's Medicaid ID number.

Block 27: PARs and nonPARs should place an "X" in the "YES" box because assignment must be accepted on Medicare/Medicaid crossover claims.

Note: It is a good idea to check with the state Medicaid contractor or FI for any special instructions for submitting claims for dual eligibles.

A completed CMS-1500 claim for a patient with both Medicare and Medicaid coverage is shown in Fig. B.4 in Appendix B.

Other than the blocks noted earlier, the Medicare/Medicaid claim is completed as directed by the Medicare claims completion guidelines listed in Appendix B.

Medicare Fact: Because Medicare Advantage claims do not automatically cross over to Medicaid, plan providers must submit claims to the state Medicaid program to receive payment for any Medicaid cost-sharing obligation.

? What Did You Learn?

1. What entity is responsible for the design and maintenance of the CMS-1500 form?
2. True or false: All providers (PARs and nonPARs) must accept assignment on Medicare claims.
3. What blocks on the CMS-1500 form are typically affected by Medigap claims?
4. Name three circumstances under which Medicare may be the secondary insurer.
5. What must accompany an MSP paper claim?
6. What blocks on the CMS-1500 form are typically affected by MSP claims?
7. What two events activate the Medicare crossover process?

MEDICARE SUMMARY NOTICE AND REMITTANCE ADVICE

Beneficiaries who are enrolled in original Medicare will receive a document called the **Medicare Summary Notice (MSN)** every 3 months. The MSN form is an easy-to-read statement that lists Parts A and B claims information, including what Medicare paid and the patient's deductible status. The MSN shows all services or supplies that providers and suppliers billed to Medicare during the 3-month period, what Medicare paid, and the maximum amount the beneficiary may owe the provider. The health insurance professional should make it clear to the patient that the MSN is not a bill and that he or she should not send any money to the provider or supplier until a statement is received.

Medicare also has a website where beneficiaries can view an electronic MSN online and print copies from their home computers. The electronic MSN does not replace the paper MSN for claims covering services provided to the beneficiary (if any) during that period, but it is a quick and convenient way for beneficiaries to track their claims. Beneficiaries can view their electronic MSNs by visiting http://www.MyMedicare.gov/.

This website provides additional valuable information for Medicare beneficiaries. Seniors who do not own a computer can visit their local library or senior center to look up this information. Another valuable source of information for Medicare beneficiaries is SHIIP. SHIIP's toll-free phone number is printed on the back cover of the *Medicare & You* handbook.

INFORMATION CONTAINED ON THE MSN

The MSN gives a breakdown of Medicare claims billed on the patient's behalf and processed by the MAC. In addition to listing the services received along with the name of the provider, the MSN lists:

- The total amount billed by providers
- Medicare's approved payment amount for services
- Amount paid to the beneficiary or his or her provider
- Costs the beneficiary is responsible for
- Deductible information

If there is a supplemental insurance policy or Medigap, the insurer for this coverage may also need a copy of the MSN to process its share of the bill. This is normally done electronically via the Medicare/Medigap crossover process, which is mandated by the Social Security Act and activated when a participating Medicare provider includes a specific identifier on the beneficiary's claim and the beneficiary assigns benefits to that provider.

The health insurance professional should know how to read the MSN so that he or she can answer any questions beneficiaries might have. To view a sample MSN for both Parts A and B along with detailed instructions on how to read the MSN, visit the CMS website at http://www.medicare.gov/.

Patient's Point of View

Norma Washington, a patient at Walden-Martin Family Medical Clinic, considers herself to be very competent when it comes to understanding Medicare, but after having some significant health issues she was a bit overwhelmed by the Medicare Summary Notice (MSN) she received listing all of the services she had done over the last 3 months. She came in to speak with Rita about it. Norma had services covered under both Part A and Part B. Rita was able to explain how the deductible for each part worked and what the various charges were all about.

Norma mentioned that she is quite proficient with a computer. She stays in contact with her grandchildren through social media and prefers to pay her bills online so that there is no need for envelopes and stamps. Rita told Norma about MyMedicare.gov, where she can check the status of Medicare claims and many other things related to Medicare. Rita was able to walk Norma through the steps to get it set up, and Norma is quite excited to check out just how MyMedicare.gov can help her manage her own healthcare.

MEDICARE REMITTANCE ADVICE

When a claim has gone through the processing stage, Medicare notifies the provider as to how the claim was **adjudicated** (how the decision was made about the payment). This notification is referred to as a **remittance advice (RA)**. The RA is notification that Medicare sends to the provider and includes a list of all claims paid and claims rejected or denied during a particular payment period. A paper RA is generated for all providers whether they file paper or electronic claims. The only exception is when the provider has been approved to receive the RA electronically.

Each RA contains a list of claims that Medicare has cleared for payment since the last RA was generated, as well as any claims that have moved to a "deny status" since the last RA was sent. RAs are generated in a weekly cycle. Each claim listed on the RA contains detailed processing information. A reimbursement amount, claim adjustment reason codes, and remittance remark codes are included for each claim. Claim adjustment reason codes and remittance remark codes are used in the electronic remittance advice (ERA) and the standard paper remittance (SPR) advice to relay information relevant to the adjudication of Medicare Part B claims. Reason codes detail the reason an adjustment was made to a healthcare claim payment by the payer, and remark codes represent nonfinancial information crucial to understanding the adjudication of the claim.

STANDARD PAPER REMITTANCE ADVICE

The **standard paper remittance (SPR)** advice is the standard form that CMS uses for provider payment notification. The form was created to (1) provide a document that is uniform in content and format and (2) ease the transition to the electronic remittance format. The SPR displays the same reason codes, remark codes, messages, and other data as the ERA for Medicare Part A providers.

Fig. 11.11 shows an example SPR along with a list of the various fields depicted on the SPR and their definitions. One claim is listed in each block of the remittance and is separated from other claims with a line. The claims on the remittance are organized in alphabetical order by beneficiary name within each type of claim (i.e., Inpatient, Part A). At the end of each type of claim, there is a subtotal of the information included on the remittance. At the end of the remittance is a total summation. Visit http://www.cms.gov/ to view the Remittance Advice Fact Sheet.

ELECTRONIC REMITTANCE ADVICE

An **electronic remittance advice (ERA)** is one of several different types of electronic formats that are generated in place of a paper document. Information contained in an ERA furnishes basically the same information as that contained on the SPR. An ERA allows automatic posting of claims payment information directly into the facility's practice management computer system. ERAs eliminate the need for manual posting of Medicare payment information, saving the provider time and money. Automatic ERA information transfer also eliminates errors made by manual posting of information from the SPR to the patient ledger accounts.

Medicare provides free software to read the ERA and print an equivalent of an SPR. Institutional and

EXAMPLE OF STANDARD PAPER REMITTANCE

(1)

NHIC, Corp
ADDRESS 1
ADDRESS 2
CITY, STATE ZIP
(999) 111-2222

MEDICARE
REMITTANCE
NOTICE

PROVIDER NAME
ADDRESS 1
ADDRESS 2
CITY, STATE ZIP

PROVIDER #: 1234567890
PAGE #: 1 OF 10
DATE: 06/05/XX
CHECK/EFT #: 12345678901234567890
REMITTANCE #: 12345678901234567890 (NOT A REQUIRED FIELD)

---

(2)

WELCOME TO THE MEDICARE PART B STANDARD PAPER REMITTANCE

---

(3)

PERF PROV	SERV DATE	POS	NOS	PROC	MODS	BILLED	ALLOWED	DEDUCT	COINS	GRP/ RC AMT	PROV PD

NAME: BUNYAN, PAUL   HIC 123456789   ACNT 1234567890234567890   ICN 123456789012345   ASG Y   MOA

| 123456ABC | 0225 0225XX | 11 | 1 | 99213 | | 66.00 | 49.83 | 0.34 | 9.97 | CO-42 16.17 | $39.52 |

| PT RESP | 10.31 | | | CLAIM TOTALS | | 66.00 | 49.83 | 0.34 | 9.97 | 16.17 | **$39.52 NET** |

NAME: FISCHER, BENNY   HIC 999999999   ACNT FISC6123133-01   ICN 0202199306850   ASG Y   MOA MA01 MA07

| 123456ABC | 0117 0117XX | 11 | 1 | 99213 | | 66.00 | 49.83 | 0.00 | 9.97 | PR-96 16.17 | $39.86 |

| PT RESP | 9.97 | | | CLAIM TOTALS | | 66.00 | 49.83 | 0.00 | 9.97 | 16.17 | |

CLAIM INFORMATION FORWARDED TO: MEDICAID   **$39.86 NET**

NAME: HURT, I.M.   HIC 999999999   ACNT HURT5-329   ICN 0202199326870   ASG Y   MOA MA01

123456ABC	0117 0117XX	11	1	90659		25.00	3.32	0.00	0.00	CO-42 21.68	$3.32
123456ABC	0117 0117XX	11	1	G0008		10.00	4.46	0.00	0.00	CO-42 5.54	$4.46
										27.22	**$7.78 NET**

| PT RESP | 0.00 | | | | | | | | | | |

NAME: FINE, R.U.   HIC 999999999   ACNT FINE7-002   ICN 0202199000150   ASG Y   N257 MA130

| 123456ABC | 0526 0526XX | 11 | 1 | 73560 | LT | 79.00 | 0.00 | 0.00 | 0.00 | CO-16 79.00 | |

REM: N257

| PT RESP | 0.00 | | | CLAIM TOTALS | | 79.00 | 0.00 | 0.00 | 0.00 | 79.00 | 0.00 |

---

(4)

TOTALS:	# OF BILLED CLAIMS	ALLOWED AMT	DEDUCT AMT	COINS AMT	TOTAL AMT	PROV PD RC-AMT	PROV AMT	CHECK ADJ AMT	AMT
	4	167.00	107.44	0.34	19.94	59.56	87.16	0.00	$87.16

(5)

PROVIDER ADJ DETAILS:	PLB REASON CODE	FCN	HIC	AMOUNT

---

(6)

GLOSSARY:	Group, Reason, MOA, Remark and Offset Codes
CO-42	Contractual Obligation. Amount for which the provider is financially liable. The patient may not be billed for this amount. Claim/service denied/reduced because this procedure/service is not paid separately. Charges exceed our fee schedule or maximum allowable amount.
M80	We cannot pay for this when performed during the same session as another approved procedure for this beneficiary
MA07	The claim information has also been forwarded to Medicaid for review.
MA28	Receipt of this notice by a physician who did not accept assignment is for information only and does not make the physician a party to the determination. No additional rights to appeal this decision, above those rights already provided for by regulation/instruction, are conferred by receipt of this notice.
MA130	Your clam contains incomplete and/or invalid information, and no appeal rights are afforded.
N257	Missing/incomplete/invalid billing provider/supplier primary identifier.

Fig. 11.11 Example of a standard paper remittance (SPR) advice. (From US Department of Health and Human Services, Centers for Medicare and Medicaid Services, Baltimore, MD.)

professional providers can get this software from their MACs. These software products enable providers to view and print RAs when needed, thus eliminating the need to request or await mail delivery of SPRs. The *Medicare Claims Processing Manual* (Pub. 100-04), Chapters 22 and 24, provides further RA information. Another resource, "Understanding the Remittance Advice: A Guide for Medicare Providers, Physicians, Suppliers and Billers," is also available on the CMS website.

Medicare Fact: Any provider or supplier enrolled in the Medicare program who submits claims electronically may receive ERAs. In addition, providers may allow a billing agent (billing service or clearinghouse) to receive ERAs on their behalf.

Enrolling in Electronic Remittance

Receiving ERAs is not automatic. The provider first must go through an enrollment process, as follows:

1. Providers must contact their software vendor to determine whether ERA capability is available for the facility's practice management system. Special programming is usually required to extract the information from the electronic remittance file and automatically post it to the patient accounts.
2. The provider must complete an ERA enrollment form (Fig. 11.12).

CMS offers free software to providers that will convert the ERA file to a readable and printable format.

ELECTRONIC FUNDS TRANSFER

Payments from Medicare may be automatically deposited to a provider's designated bank account using **electronic funds transfer (EFT)**. Each EFT transaction is assigned a unique number, which functions in the same way as a Medicare check number. The EFT number appears on the RA (paper or electronic) in the same field or location as the Medicare check number. EFT is available to all providers who bill Medicare. Providers must request an EFT enrollment form from their Medicare carrier. A request for an EFT authorization form is shown in Fig. 11.13.

CMS
CENTERS for MEDICARE & MEDICAID SERVICES

HIGHMARK®
MEDICARE SERVICES
A CMS CONTRACTOR

5010 Electronic Remittance Advice (ERA) Migration Form

Submitter Name: _____

Address: _____

Contact Name: _____ Contact Phone Number: _____

Highmark Medicare Services Electronic Data Interchange (EDI) requires a minimum of one business day advance notice to complete your migration request. Business hours are from 8:30AM to 4:30PM. This form should only be used by EXISTING ERA customers requesting to be migrated from version 4010A1 to version 5010.

Effective _____ 20XX, please update my existing submitter number _____ to production version 5010 835 ERA. As of this effective date, I understand that I will no longer receive version 4010A1 ERA.

Signature:

By signing below, I attest to the fact that I am authorized to sign the document on behalf of the party identified above.

Signature _____ Date _____

Printed Name _____ Title _____

Please fax your completed 5010 ERA Migration Form to Highmark Medicare Services EDI at (717) 302-4252.
Your request must be received one business day prior to your requested effective date.
Incomplete 5010 ERA Migration forms, or those signed incorrectly, will not be processed.

Fig. 11.12 Example of an electronic remittance advice (ERA) enrollment form. (From US Department of Health and Human Services, Centers for Medicare and Medicaid Services, Baltimore, MD.)

AUTHORIZATION AGREEMENT FOR ELECTRONIC FUNDS TRANSFER (EFT)

Reason for Submission:
- ❑ New EFT Authorization
- ❑ Revision to Current Authorization *(i.e. account or bank changes)*
- ❑ EFT Termination Request

Chain Home Office:
- ❑ Check here if EFT payment is being made to the Home Office of Chain Organization
  (Attach letter Authorizing EFT payment to Chain Home Office)

Physician/Provider/Supplier Information

Physician's Name _____

Provider/Supplier Legal Business Name _____

_____

Chain Organization Name _____

Home Office Legal Business Name *(if different from Chain Organization Name)* _____

_____

Tax ID Number: *(Designate SSN ❑ or EIN ❑)* ___ ___ ___ ___ ___ ___ ___ ___ ___

Doing Business As Name_____

Medicare Identification Number *(OSCAR, UPIN, or NSC only)* _____

Depository Information (Financial Institution)

Depository Name _____

Account Holder's Name _____

Street Address _____

City _____State_____Zip Code_____

Depository Telephone Number_____

Depository Contact Person _____

Depository Routing Transit Number *(nine digit)* ___ ___ ___ ___ ___ ___ ___ ___ ___

Depositor Account Number _____

Type of Account *(check one)* ❑ Checking Account   ❑ Savings Account

Please include a voided check, preprinted deposit slip, or confirmation of account information on bank letterhead with this agreement for verification of your account number.

Authorization

I hereby authorize the Medicare contractor, _____, hereinafter called the COMPANY, to initiate credit entries, and in accordance with 31 CFR part 210.6(f) initiate adjustments for any credit entries made in error to the account indicated above. I hereby authorize the financial institution/bank named above, hereinafter called the DEPOSITORY, to credit and/or debit the same to such account.

If payment is being made to an account controlled by a Chain Home Office, the Provider of Services hereby acknowledges that payment to the Chain Office under these circumstances is still considered payment to the Provider, and the Provider authorizes the forwarding of Medicare payments to the Chain Home Office.

If the account is drawn in the Physician's or Individual Practitioner's Name, or the Legal Business Name of the Provider/Supplier, the said Physician/Provider/Supplier certifies that he/she has sole control of the account referenced above, and certifies that all arrangements between the DEPOSITORY and the said Physician/Provider/Supplier are in accordance with all applicable Medicare regulations and instructions.

FORM CMS-588 (09/03)

Fig. 11.13 Authorization agreement for electronic funds transfer (EFT). (From US Department of Health and Human Services, Centers for Medicare and Medicaid Services, Baltimore, MD.)

Continued

This authorization agreement is effective as of the signature date below and is to remain in full force and effect until the COMPANY has received written notification from me of its termination in such time and such manner as to afford the COMPANY and the DEPOSITORY a reasonable opportunity to act on it. The COMPANY will continue to send the direct deposit to the DEPOSITORY indicated above until notified by me that I wish to change the DEPOSITORY receiving the direct deposit. If my DEPOSITORY information changes, I agree to submit to the COMPANY an updated EFT Authorization Agreement.

Signature Line

Authorized/Delegated Official Name *(Print)* _____

Authorized/Delegated Official Title _____

Authorized/Delegated Official Signature_____Date_____

PRIVACY ACT ADVISORY STATEMENT

Sections 1842, 1862(b) and 1874 of title XVIII of the Social Security Act authorize the collection of this information. The purpose of collecting this information is to authorize electronic funds transfers.

The information collected will be entered into system No. 09-70-0501, titled "Carrier Medicare Claims Records," and No. 09-70-0503, titled "Intermediary Medicare Claims Records" published in the Federal Register Privacy Act Issuances, 1991 Comp. Vol. 1, pages 419 and 424, or as updated and republished. Disclosures of information from this system can be found in this notice.

Furnishing information is voluntary, but without it we will not be able to process your electronic funds transfer.

You should be aware that P.L. 100-503, the Computer Matching and Privacy Protection Act of 1988, permits the government, under certain circumstances, to verify the information you provide by way of computer matches.

According to the Paperwork Reduction Act of 1995, no persons are required to respond to a collection of information unless it displays a valid OMB control number. The valid OMB control number for this information collection is 0938-0626. The time required to complete this information collection is estimated to average 2 hours per response, including the time to review instructions, search existing data resources, gather the data needed, and complete and review the information collection. If you have any comments concerning the accuracy of the time estimate(s) or suggestions for improving this form, please write to: CMS, Attn: PRA Reports Clearance Officer, 7500 Security Boulevard, Baltimore, MD 21244-1850.

FORM CMS-588 (09/03)

Fig. 11.13 cont'd

What Did You Learn?

1. What is an MSN?
2. Explain the difference between the MSN and the Medicare RA.
3. Who is eligible to receive an ERA?
4. What is an EFT?
5. Who can receive ERAs?

MEDICARE AUDITS AND APPEALS

In January 2013, the Improper Payments Elimination and Recovery Improvement Act of 2012 was signed into law. The purpose of the act is "to intensify efforts to identify, prevent, and recover payment error, waste, fraud, and abuse within Federal spending." The Medicare and Medicaid programs employ a number of contractors to conduct audits of healthcare providers, including MACs, **recovery audit contractors (RACs)**, the Medicaid fraud control units (MFCUs), and the Medicaid audit contractors. The following paragraphs address Medicare audits and appeals.

AUDITS

Medicare audits are generally designed to determine whether a provider has been reimbursed by the Medicare program for services that are properly reimbursable (i.e., medically necessary). These audits are typically based on (1) random reviews, (2) prior problems or unusual billing patterns, or (3) a certain kind of billing problem that the carrier is focusing on.

Medicare audits fall into two broad categories: (1) prepayment audits, which (as the name suggests) review claims before Medicare pays the provider, and (2) postpayment audits, which analyze claims after Medicare reimbursement. Some medical facilities believe that they can avoid audits if they report lower-level evaluation and management codes on claims that result in billing Medicare a lesser fee; this practice is referred to as **downcoding**. Many audits target physicians' offices that practice downcoding because this type of practice "raises a red flag" to auditors. Downcoding on a claim is discouraged when the reason for doing so is simply that documentation in the health record does not meet the carrier's guidelines. If a particular code accurately describes the service or procedure performed, a provider should not voluntarily lower the code simply because he or she fears a documentation deficiency.

Stop and Think

You are having lunch with your friend, Nellie Shumway, who works for a family practice clinic across the courtyard from your building. Over lunch one day, Nellie confides, "In our office, we code all new Medicare patient visits at Level 1 (99201). It's so much easier, and we don't have to worry about Medicare auditing our records." What, if anything, might you tell your friend?

Postpayment audits most commonly are triggered by statistical irregularities. A postpayment audit can result if a provider uses a certain code much more frequently or less frequently than other providers of the same specialty in the same area. Patient complaints can also trigger audits and reviews.

RECOVERY AUDIT CONTRACTOR PROGRAM

The RAC program is a result of the Medicare Modernization Act and the Tax Relief and Health Care Act of 2006. The job of an RAC is to detect and correct past improper payments so that CMS and MACs can implement actions that will prevent future improper payments. Providers who bill Medicare on an FFS basis will be subject to review by RACs.

APPEALS (FEE-FOR-SERVICE CLAIMS)

Medicare regulations allow providers and beneficiaries who are dissatisfied with Medicare's determination of an FFS claim to request that the determination be reconsidered. Through the **appeals process**, Medicare attempts to ensure that the correct payment is made or that a clear and adequate explanation is given supporting nonpayment.

A physician or supplier providing items and services payable under Medicare Part B may appeal an initial determination if:

- He or she accepted assignment
- He or she did not accept assignment on a claim that was denied on the basis of not being reasonable and necessary
- The beneficiary did not know or could not have been expected to know that the service would not be covered, requiring the provider or supplier to refund the beneficiary any payment received for the services
- He or she did not accept assignment but is acting as the authorized representative of the beneficiary and indicates this status in the appeal (attaching a copy of the beneficiary's MSN indicates that the provider or supplier is authorized to act on the beneficiary's behalf)

Claims submitted with incomplete or invalid information are not given appeal rights and are returned as "unprocessable." The provider has two options for correcting the claim:

- Submit an entirely new claim (electronic or paper) with complete, valid information
- Submit corrections in writing

Five levels of appeal action are available if the provider and/or the beneficiary disagrees with a coverage or payment decision made by Medicare (Fig. 11.14). This appeal process is illustrated in the flow chart shown in Fig. 11.15.

Office addresses of where to send the completed forms and appropriate accompanying completed form(s) and/or documentation can be found on the HHS website or the CMS website.

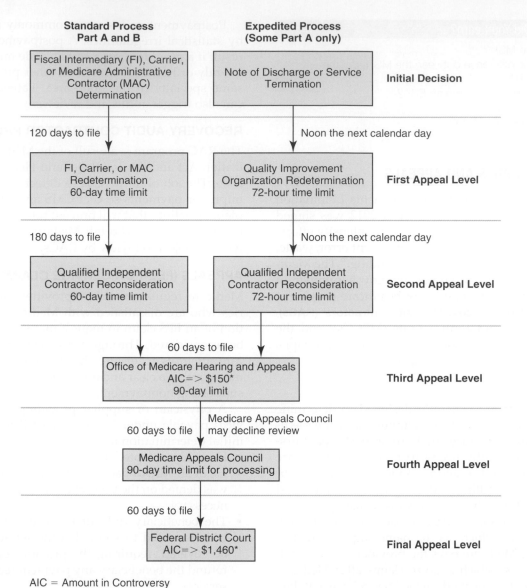

AIC = Amount in Controversy

Fig. 11.14 Original Medicare (Parts A and B fee-for-service) appeals process. *AIC is subject to change periodically. (From US Department of Health and Human Services, Centers for Medicare and Medicaid Services, Baltimore, MD.)

More detailed information regarding the Medicare appeals process can be found in the Medicare Parts A and B Appeals Process brochure on the CMS.gov website. Websites with links to this resource are listed under "Websites to Explore" at the end of this chapter.

The appeals process for prescription drug coverage also has five levels:

Level 1: Redetermination from the plan

Level 2: Reconsideration by an independent review entity (IRE)

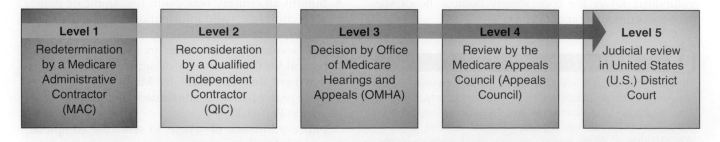

Make all appeal requests in writing.

Fig. 11.15 Original Medicare appeals flow chart.

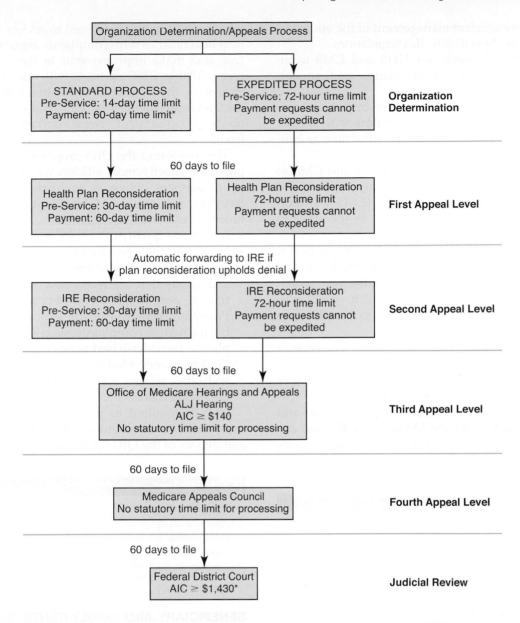

AIC = Amount in Controversy / ALJ = Administrative Law Judge / IRE = Independent Review Entity
*Plans must process 95% of all clean claims from out-of-network providers within 30 days. All other claims must be processed within 60 days.

Fig. 11.16 Flow chart for the Medicare managed care determination/appeals process. Note: AIC is subject to change periodically. (From US Department of Health and Human Services, Centers for Medicare and Medicaid Services, Baltimore, MD.)

Level 3: Decision by Office of Medicare Hearings and Appeals (OMHA)

Level 4: Review by the Medicare Appeals Council (Appeals Council)

Level 5: Judicial review by a federal district court appeals process (Medicare managed care claims)

Medicare Part C (Medicare Advantage) health plans must meet the requirements for grievance and appeals processing under Subpart M of the Medicare Advantage regulations. If a Medicare health plan denies service or payment, the plan is required to provide the enrollee with a written notice of its determination. In addition, Medicare health plan enrollees receiving covered services from an inpatient hospital, SNF, home health agency, or comprehensive outpatient rehabilitation facility have the right to an expedited appeal if they think that their Medicare-covered services are ending too soon. Plans and providers have certain responsibilities related to notifying beneficiaries of Medicare appeal rights.

Fig. 11.16 shows a flow chart for the Medicare managed care determination/appeals process.

THE AUDIT & APPEAL FAIRNESS, INTEGRITY, AND REFORMS IN MEDICARE ACT OF 2015

The Audit & Appeal Fairness, Integrity, and Reforms in Medicare (AFIRM) Act is a bill designed to improve the Medicare audit and appeals process by creating better and more efficient management of the audit and appeals process. Specifically, this legislation:

- Improves the oversight for HHS and CMS to increase the reliability of the claims and appeals process
- Establishes a voluntary alternative dispute process to allow for multiple pending claims with similar issues to be settled as one group rather than as individual appeals
- Coordinates efforts between auditors and CMS to ensure that all parties are receiving accurate and transparent data on audit practices (CMS is also offering incentives and disincentives in the effort to improve auditor accuracy)
- Institutes a new Medicare Magistrate program that allows attorneys with expertise in Medicare law and policies to adjudicate in the same way as administrative law judges (ALJs), which would ultimately free up time for the ALJs to handle more complex cases
- Allows for sampling and extrapolation methods to make the appeals process more efficient

Ideally, the AFIRM Act will alleviate the backlog of Medicare appeals that has been slowing the appeals process, which has become frustrating for seniors and providers alike. Making the Medicare audits and appeals process more efficient will help resolve cases quickly and at the earliest possible step.

? What Did You Learn?

1. Name the two broad categories into which Medicare audits fall.
2. Name two things that might prompt a Medicare audit.
3. What is the job of the RAC?
4. Under what circumstances might a provider initiate an appeal?
5. List the five appeal levels.

QUALITY REVIEW STUDIES

A **quality review study** can be defined as an assessment, conducted by or for a **peer review organization (PRO)**, more recently referred to as a quality improvement organization (QIO), of a patient care problem for the purpose of improving patient care through peer analysis, intervention, resolution of the problem, and follow-up. Quality review studies typically follow a set of related structured activities designed to achieve measurable improvement in processes and outcomes of care. Improvements are achieved through interventions that target healthcare providers, practitioners, plans, or beneficiaries.

QUALITY IMPROVEMENT ORGANIZATIONS

Quality improvement organizations (QIOs) are private, mainly not-for-profit organizations that are staffed by professionals, mostly physicians and other healthcare

professionals, who are trained to review medical care, help beneficiaries with complaints about the quality of care, and make improvements in the entire range of care available. CMS contracts with one organization in each state, the District of Columbia, Puerto Rico, and the US Virgin Islands to serve as that state's or jurisdiction's QIO contractor. These contracts are 3 years in length.

The mission of the QIO program, by law, is to improve the effectiveness, efficiency, economy, and quality of services delivered to Medicare beneficiaries. Based on this mission, CMS identifies the principal functions of the QIO program as:

- Improving quality of care for beneficiaries
- Protecting the integrity of the Medicare trust fund by ensuring that Medicare pays only for services and goods that are reasonable and necessary and that are provided in the most appropriate setting
- Protecting beneficiaries by expeditiously addressing individual complaints, such as beneficiary complaints, provider-based notice appeals, violations of the Emergency Medical Treatment and Labor Act, and other related responsibilities as articulated in QIO-related law

CMS is required to publish a report to Congress every fiscal year that outlines the administration, cost, and impact of the QIO program.

HIPAA Tip

A covered entity can disclose information to a quality improvement organization (QIO) on both Medicare beneficiaries and non-Medicare patients without patient permission when the information is needed for the QIO's quality-related activities under its contract.

BENEFICIARY AND FAMILY-CENTERED CARE (BFCC)–QIOs

BFCC-QIOs improve healthcare services and protect beneficiaries through prompt statutory review functions, including complaints and quality-of-care reviews for Medicare beneficiaries. The BFCC-QIO ensures consistency in the case review process while considering local factors and local needs for general quality of care, medical necessity, and readmissions.

QUALITY INNOVATION NETWORK (QIN)–QIOs

QIN-QIOs improve healthcare services through education, outreach, and sharing practices that have succeeded in other areas, using data to measure improvement, working with patients and families, and organizing community partners for cooperative interaction. QIN-QIOs also work to improve the quality of healthcare for targeted health conditions and specific populations and to reduce the incidence of healthcare-acquired disorders to meet national and local priorities.

BENEFICIARY NOTICES INITIATIVE

Both Medicare beneficiaries and providers have certain rights and protections related to financial liability under the FFS Medicare and Medicare Advantage programs. These financial liability and appeal rights and protections, under the Beneficiary Notices Initiative, are communicated to beneficiaries through notices given by providers.

For example, beneficiaries have the right to:
- Be treated with dignity and respect
- Be protected against discrimination
- Get information they understand
- Get answers to Medicare questions
- Get emergency care when and where it is needed
- Learn about their treatment choices in clear, understandable language

For more detailed information on beneficiaries' rights under this program, go to the CMS website and type "Beneficiary Notices Initiative" into the search box.

BENEFICIARY COMPLAINT RESPONSE PROGRAM

The **Beneficiary Complaint Response Program** handles complaints by Medicare beneficiaries (or their representatives) that are made either in writing or by telephone. When the program receives a complaint, a case manager is assigned who works with the beneficiary from start to finish, keeping him or her informed throughout the review process about the status of the complaint. The program also uses physician peer review to assess clinical quality-of-care issues in a patient's record (referred to as *medical record review*). The focus of the program is on individually based quality improvement efforts that ideally can lead to quality improvements in future care. Typical complaints that beneficiaries file may cite issues such as:
- Received the wrong or an erroneous dose of medication
- Underwent inappropriate surgery
- Experienced an error in treatment
- Received inadequate care or treatment by any healthcare professional
- Was discharged too soon
- Received inadequate discharge instructions

HOSPITAL-ISSUED NOTICE OF NONCOVERAGE AND NOTICE OF DISCHARGE AND MEDICARE APPEAL RIGHTS REVIEWS

When a hospital issues a hospital-issued notice of noncoverage (HINN) or an MCO issues a notice of discharge and Medicare appeal rights (NODMAR), the beneficiary, or his or her representative, may request an immediate review. The purpose of the review is to ensure that the HINN or NODMAR is correct and that the patient is not being discharged prematurely from care. Hospitals provide HINNs to beneficiaries of original Medicare before admission, at admission, or at any point during an inpatient stay if it is determined that the inpatient care the beneficiary is receiving or is about to receive is not covered.

A NODMAR must include the following information:
- The specific reason why inpatient hospital care is no longer needed
- The effective date of the beneficiary's financial liability for continued inpatient care
- The enrollee's appeal rights

THE CENTER FOR MEDICARE AND MEDICAID INNOVATION

As part of the ACA, CMS created the Center for Medicare and Medicaid Innovation (CMMI). The focus of CMMI is to test new models that will reduce costs while maintaining or improving the quality of care for Medicare, Medicaid, and CHIP beneficiaries.

Currently the CMMI is requesting new ideas that it can evaluate on the basis of potential improvements in quality of care and spending reductions. The best proposals are evaluated against CMMI criteria and then tested to see whether they can achieve three critical goals: (1) better care for people, (2) coordinating care to improve health outcomes for patients, and (3) exploring community care models to improve public health. Ideas that do not pass these criteria are terminated. Successful models that meet cost and quality tests may be expanded to all Medicare, Medicaid, or CHIP beneficiaries.

PHYSICIAN REVIEW OF MEDICAL RECORDS

Physician reviewers conduct medical record reviews to determine whether the care received was medically necessary and appropriate. Reviews may include utilization, coding, or quality-of-care issues. The reviewer is generally from the same specialty as the physician who provided the care. This peer review is an important component of the quality-of-care oversight provided by Medicare QIOs and external quality review organizations.

PHYSICIAN QUALITY REPORTING SYSTEM

Physician Quality Reporting System (PQRS) is a quality reporting program that encourages individual eligible professionals (EPs) and group practices to report information on the quality of care to Medicare. PQRS gives participating EPs and group practices the opportunity to assess the quality of care they provide to their patients, helping to ensure that patients get the right care at the right time. By reporting on PQRS quality measures, individual EPs and group practices can also quantify how often they are meeting a particular quality standard. Beginning in 2015 the program will apply a negative payment adjustment to individual EPs and PQRS group practices who did not satisfactorily report data on quality measures for Medicare Part B MPFS–covered professional services in 2013. Those who report satisfactorily for the 2015 program year will avoid the 2017 PQRS negative payment adjustment.

What Did You Learn?

1. List four appeal rights and protections under the Beneficiary Notices Initiative.
2. Explain the purpose of a NODMAR review.
3. Define a "quality review study."
4. What is the purpose of PROs?
5. A quality reporting program that encourages individual EPs and group practices to report information on the quality of care to Medicare describes the _____.

MEDICARE BILLING FRAUD

You might ask yourself: "Where does Medicare billing fraud happen?" The answer is: "It can happen anywhere medicine is practiced." Medicare fraud can involve billing for tests or procedures that were never done, billing for a more complicated procedure than was actually done, or billing a multiple-procedure operation as if several separate procedures were performed. But how do you recognize Medicare billing fraud? First, you must know the rules, and these rules are complex, confusing, and constantly changing. It is possible to misinterpret a rule—this happens a lot, so you must be careful. It may initially appear as if the individual is guilty of Medicare billing fraud, when all that happened was failure to understand a regulation. However, some people break the rules intentionally. This is what should be reported, and Medicare hotlines are posted in most healthcare facilities for this purpose. If you work in a place as either staff or provider and you see potential Medicare billing fraud, you have an obligation to put a stop to it or report it accordingly.

When reporting fraud, follow the procedures posted in your facility or in the facility's procedure manual. There is a website specifically dedicated to reporting Medicare and Medicaid fraud: http://medicarefraudcenter.org.

In addition, there is a wealth of information on both the CMS website and the Medicare.gov website.

MEDICARE WHISTLEBLOWERS

Medicare whistleblowers are typically healthcare professionals who are aware of hospitals, clinics, pharmacies, nursing homes, hospice facilities, long-term care, and other healthcare facilities that routinely overcharge or seek reimbursement from government programs for medical services not rendered, drugs not used, beds not slept in, and ambulance rides not taken. If you have information about a person or a company that is cheating the Medicare program (or any other government-run healthcare program), you may be able to collect a reward for reporting it.

What Did You Learn?

1. Where does billing fraud happen?
2. What is the best practice for reporting Medicare fraud?
3. What is the function of a Medicare "whistleblower"?

CLINICAL LABORATORY IMPROVEMENT AMENDMENTS PROGRAM

Congress established the **Clinical Laboratory Improvement Amendments (CLIA)** program in 1988 to regulate quality standards for all laboratory tests performed on humans to ensure the safety, accuracy, reliability, and timeliness of patient test results regardless of where a test was performed. CMS assumes primary responsibility for financial management operations of the CLIA program. Although all clinical laboratories must be properly certified to receive Medicare or Medicaid payments, CLIA has no direct Medicare or Medicaid program responsibilities.

To enroll in the CLIA program, laboratories (including laboratories located in physician offices) first must register by completing an application, paying a fee, being surveyed if applicable, and becoming certified. CLIA fees are structured according to the type of certificate requested by the laboratory based on the complexity of the tests it performs. After all of these preliminary measures are taken, the laboratory is issued a CLIA certificate number. This information is significant to the health insurance professional because the 10-digit CLIA certificate number must appear in Block 23 of the CMS-1500 paper form for services billed by an entity performing CLIA-covered procedures. For further information on these topics, visit the CMS.gov website.

What Did You Learn?

1. What is the purpose of the CLIA program?
2. True or false: CLIA has no direct Medicare or Medicaid program responsibilities.
3. Where on the CMS-1500 form is the CLIA number entered?

SUMMARY CHECKPOINTS

- Medicare is a comprehensive federal insurance program established by Congress in 1966 to provide limited healthcare to people age 65, certain categories of disabled individuals younger than age 65, and individuals of any age who have ESRD. Medicare is administered by CMS.

- Medicare Part A (hospital insurance) helps pay for medically necessary services for the following types of healthcare:
  - Inpatient hospital care
  - Inpatient care in SNFs
  - Home healthcare
  - Hospice care
- Medicare Part B is medical insurance financed by a combination of federal government funds and beneficiary premiums, which helps pay for:
  - Medically necessary physicians' services (including clinic services)
  - Outpatient hospital services
  - DME
  - Certain other services and supplies not covered by Part A
- Medicare Part C (Medicare Advantage, formerly Medicare+ Choice) is a managed healthcare structure that offers regular Parts A and B Medicare coverage and other services. Primary Medicare Part C plans include:
  - Medicare managed care plans
  - Medicare private, unrestricted FFS plans
  - MSA plans
- Medicare Part C not only includes Parts A and B coverage but also pays for services not covered under the original Medicare plan, such as preventive care, prescription drugs, eyeglasses, hearing aids, and dental care.
- As of January 2006, Medicare Part D (PDP) will pay a portion of prescription drug expenses and cost-sharing for qualifying individuals.
- Medicare combination coverages include:
  - *Dual eligibles* refers to individuals who qualify for benefits under both the Medicare and the Medicaid programs. Most individuals who qualify for this type of coverage are low-income elderly and individuals younger than age 65 with disabilities.
  - *Medigap* is a Medicare Supplement insurance policy sold by private insurance companies to fill "gaps" in the original (FFS) Medicare plan coverage. There are 10 standardized plans. Medigap policies work only with original Medicare.
  - *MSP* is the term used when Medicare is not responsible for payment of healthcare charges first because the beneficiary is covered under another insurance policy. Medicare is a secondary payer when the beneficiary is covered by group insurance, workers' compensation, veterans' benefits, or other third-party liability applies.
- The ACA did not adversely affect Medicare coverage for beneficiaries. Additional benefits were established under the ACA—for example, specific preventive benefits, such as cancer screenings and annual wellness visits, which are available at no cost. Beneficiaries in the "donut hole" get a 55% discount when buying Part D–covered brand-name prescription drugs. The ACA made it possible for healthcare providers to get additional resources for care coordination.
- Medicare managed care (Medicare Part C) is a type of government-subsidized healthcare option to original Medicare. Plans include HMOs, PPOs, PSOs, and PFFS plans. Medicare managed care plans provide basically the same benefits as Medicare, often with additional coverage. When Medicare beneficiaries enroll in a managed care plan, they typically must see healthcare providers within a particular system, must obtain referrals to visit specialists or out-of-network physicians, and have certain other limits on their healthcare benefits. Advantages of Medicare HMOs include the following:
  - HMOs may cover services that original Medicare does not cover, such as eyeglasses, hearing aids, prescriptions, and dental coverage.
  - Enrollees do not need Medigap insurance.
  - Paperwork is limited or nonexistent in contrast to original Medicare coverage.
  - HMOs often pay additional coverage for hospital stays that exceed the limits set by original Medicare.
  - There is a yearly cap on how much the enrollee pays for Parts A and B services during the year. (This cap amount varies among plans and is subject to annual change.)
- Disadvantages of Medicare HMOs include the following:
  - Choice of healthcare providers and medical facilities is limited.
  - Members are covered only for services received through the HMO except in emergency and urgent care situations.
  - Prior approval from a primary care physician is usually necessary for a specialist's services, surgical procedures, medical equipment, and other healthcare services.
  - Enrollees who travel out of the HMO's service area do not receive coverage except in emergency and urgent care situations.
- Office procedures involved in preparing for a Medicare patient are basically the same as with other patients with a few exceptions. First, Medicare accepts a "lifetime release of information." Second, medical necessity must be determined. For a service or procedure to be determined medically necessary under Medicare guidelines, it must meet the following criteria:
  - Consistent with the symptoms or diagnosis of the illness or injury being treated
  - Necessary and consistent with generally accepted professional medical standards
  - Not furnished primarily for the convenience of the patient or physician

- Furnished at the most appropriate level that can be provided safely to the patient
- If it is determined that the service or procedure does not fit the medical necessity guidelines, the patient must be advised. If he or she still wants the service, an ABN must be signed by the patient. The ABN is a form that Medicare requires all healthcare providers to use when Medicare does not pay for a service to ensure that beneficiaries have a choice about their healthcare in the event that Medicare does not pay.
- The Medicare billing process encompasses several considerations. The Medicare fee schedule should be used to determine the amount that Medicare allows PARs and nonPARs accepting assignment to charge a patient for a particular service or procedure.
- Claims should be submitted electronically to MACs using the 5010 electronic standards unless the provider has received a waiver allowing the use of the CMS-1500 paper claim. It is important for all Medicare claims to be submitted within "timely filing" guidelines. Use the CMS or NUCC guidelines (per the MAC instructions) for submitting claims on the CMS-1500 paper claim form. The only acceptable form is the one printed in the official OCR red ink. The OCR rules should be followed when completing the form; however, a recent version of the guidelines allows limited punctuation in some blocks.
- An MSN is an easy-to-read statement sent to the patient that lists Parts A and B claims information, including what Medicare paid and the patient's deductible status. A Medicare RA is the document that Medicare sends to the provider of services explaining how claims were adjudicated. The RA contains detailed processing information, including claim adjustment reason codes, which explain why an adjustment was made to the claim payment, and remittance remark codes, which represent nonfinancial information. The health insurance professional must be able to decipher these codes to understand why the payment is less than that shown on the claim.
- The purpose of Medicare audits is to identify, prevent, and recover payment error, waste, fraud, and abuse within federal spending. Medicare audits are generally designed to determine whether a provider has been properly reimbursed by the Medicare program for services that are medically necessary. Medicare regulations allow providers and beneficiaries who are dissatisfied with Medicare's determination of claim to request that the determination be reconsidered. Through the appeals process, Medicare attempts to ensure that the correct payment is made or that a clear and adequate explanation is given supporting nonpayment. Five levels of appeal action are available if the provider and/or the beneficiary disagrees with a coverage or payment decision made by Medicare.

- Quality review studies are performed to (1) improve the processes and outcomes of patient care, (2) safeguard the integrity of the Medicare trust fund by ensuring that payments are made only for medically necessary services, and (3) investigate beneficiary complaints.
- The health insurance professional has an obligation to report suspected Medicare billing fraud. He or she should be familiar with the rules for billing Medicare to identify fraud. When reporting fraud, the professional should follow the procedures posted in the facility or in the facility's procedure manual. There is also a lot of information on this topic on the Internet.
- The CLIA program was established to set quality standards for all laboratory testing to ensure the safety, accuracy, reliability, and timeliness of patient test results regardless of where a test was performed.

Closing Scenario

Rita enjoys working through the challenges of Medicare and feels that she has learned where to find the answers she needs. She often visits the CMS.gov website to stay current with any updates. She has also found it to be a valuable resource for any questions that come.

Recently a patient came in with a Medicare Summary Notice (MSN) that he did not understand. Rita went through it with the patient, explaining each detail line by line. She also was able to explain the concept of "medical necessity" and the fact that Medicare pays only 80% of "covered charges," not all services and supplies. The light of understanding in the patient's eyes was the only reward Rita needed.

CHAPTER REVIEW QUESTIONS

1. Which of the following groups can qualify for Medicare?
   a. Individuals over the age of 65
   b. Individuals who are disabled
   c. Individuals who have end-stage renal disease
   d. All of the above
2. Claims processing for Part A and Part B is done by:
   a. Centers for Medicare and Medicaid Services.
   b. Medicare administrative contractors.
   c. Program of All-Inclusive Care for the Elderly.
   d. TrOOP.
3. Which part of Medicare covers inpatient hospital services?
   a. Part A
   b. Part B
   c. Part C
   d. Part D
4. The deductible for Part A coverage is:
   a. An annual deductible.
   b. Not part of the Part A cost-sharing.
   c. Paid for each benefit period.
   d. Required every 60 days.

5. The donut hole for Part D closed in:
   a. 1965.
   b. 1972.
   c. 2010.
   d. 2020.
6. Dual eligible refers to people who are covered by both Medicare and:
   a. A spouse's group health plan.
   b. Medicaid.
   c. Medigap.
   d. PACE.
7. A patient covered by Medicare should sign a release of information form:
   a. Every 3 months.
   b. Every 2 years.
   c. Once if it is a lifetime release of information form.
   d. A release of information form is not needed for Medicare.
8. What form is used to inform a patient in advance that it is likely that Medicare will not cover a procedure or service?
   a. ABN
   b. CLIA
   c. ESRD
   d. MAC
9. Medicare Beneficiary Identifiers consist of:
   a. 9 alphabetic characters.
   b. The patient's Social Security number.
   c. The patient's date of birth and a random set of alphabetic characters.
   d. 11 alphanumeric characters.
10. The Medicare appeals process has _____ levels.
    a. 3
    b. 5
    c. 8
    d. 10

WEBSITES TO EXPLORE

- For live links to the following websites, please visit the Evolve site at http://evolve.elsevier.com/Beik/today.
- For extensive information on Medicare, log on to http://www.medicare.gov/.
- For a timeline of key developments of Medicare, log on to http://kff.org/medicare/timeline/medicare-a-timeline-of-key-developments/.
- National Medicare coverage policies are found at http://cms.hhs.gov/.
- For more information about CMS, visit http://www.cms.gov/About-CMS/About-CMS.html.
- Details of the Medicare cost plans and demonstration/pilot programs can be learned by visiting http://www.medicare.gov/find-a-plan.
- To read the fact sheet on PACE, visit https://www.cms.gov/newsroom/fact-sheets/programs-all-inclusive-care-elderly-pace-final-rule-cms-4168-f.

- To peruse an issue of *The CMS Quarterly Provider Update*, visit http://www.cms.hhs.gov/Quarterly-ProviderUpdates/ or http://www.cms.gov/Outreach-and-Education/Medicare-Learning-Network-MLN/MLNProducts/index.html.
- To access the Medicare Provider-Suppier Enrollment information, visit https://www.cms.gov/medicare/provider-enrollment-and-certification/medicareprovidersupenroll/index.html.
- To access the Medicare Claims Submission Guidelines, visit http://www.nacns.org/wp-content/uploads/2016/11/CMS_ReimbursementClaim.pdf.
- *Article MM7080* explaining the new Medicare timely claims filing deadline can be found at http://www.cms.gov/Outreach-and-Education/Medicare-Learning-Network-MLN/MLNMattersArticles/downloads/MM7080.pdf.
- To view the NUCC step-by-step claims completion guidelines, visit http://www.justcms1500forms.com/files/claim_form_manual_v3-0_7-07.pdf.
- The *Medicare Claims Processing Manual* can be found at http://www.cms.gov/Regulations-and-Guidance/Guidance/Manuals/Downloads/clm104c26.pdf.
- The *Medicare Secondary Payer Manual* can be found at https://www.cms.gov/Regulations-and-Guidance/Guidance/Manuals/Internet-Only-Manuals-IOMs-Items/CMS019017.html.
- To submit MSP claims electronically, refer to the *ANSI ASC X12N Implementation Guide:* https://www.cms.gov/Medicare/Billing/ElectronicBillingEDITrans/downloads/5010A1837BCG.pdf. To learn how to report MSP claims in the practice's software, providers should contact their software vendor.
- For a brochure providing more detailed information on the Medicare appeals process, visit http://www.cms.gov/Outreach-and-Education/Medicare-Learning-Network-MLN/MLNProducts/Downloads/MedicareAppealsProcess.pdf.
- For instructions on how to read the beneficiary MSN, log on to https://www.medicare.gov/forms-help-resources/mail-you-get-about-medicare/medicare-summary-notice-msn.
- Information on filing complaints for Medicare beneficiaries is available at https://www.medicare.gov/claims-appeals/how-to-file-a-complaint-grievance.
- For more information on CLIA, see https://www.cms.gov/Regulations-and-Guidance/Legislation/CLIA/index.html?redirect=/clia/.
- To view the electronic version of the *Medicare & You* handbook, visit https://www.medicare.gov/sites/default/files/2020-03/10050-Medicare-and-You_0.pdf.

Author's Note: Due to the dynamic nature of the Internet, web addresses and/or links provided in this chapter may have changed since publication and may no longer be valid. In such cases, students should select comparable search words to access related sites.

12 Military Carriers

Chapter Outline

Chapter Objectives

After completion of this chapter, the student should be able to:

1. Discuss the role of the military health programs.
2. Outline the TRICARE program, including eligibility and enrollment options.
3. Describe TRICARE's additional coverage options.
4. Explain the process of verifying TRICARE eligibility.
5. Distinguish between TRICARE network and non-network providers.
6. Recap TRICARE's cost-sharing requirements.
7. Describe the TRICARE claims process.
8. Explain the CHAMPVA program, including eligibility.
9. List additional CHAMPVA program options and benefits.
10. Summarize the CHAMPVA claims filing process.
11. Analyze the implementation of HIPAA's privacy rules into military treatment facilities.

Chapter Terms

accepting assignment

balance billing

beneficiary

catastrophic cap (cat cap)

CHAMPVA for Life (CFL)

Civilian Health and Medical
    Program of the Department of
    Veterans Affairs (CHAMPVA)

Civilian Health and Medical
    Program of the Uniformed
    Services (CHAMPUS)

claims processor

copayment

cost-share

covered charges

custodial care

Defense Enrollment Eligibility
    Reporting System (DEERS)

Defense Health Agency (DHA)

eZ TRICARE

Military Health System (MHS)

military treatment facilities (MTFs)

minimum essential coverage

network providers

nonavailability statement (NAS)

non-network providers

other health insurance (OHI)

regional contractor

sponsor

TRICARE For Life (TFL)

TRICARE's maximum allowable
    charge (TMAC)

TRICARE Prime

TRICARE Prime Remote

TRICARE provider

TRICARE Regional Office (TRO)

TRICARE Select

TRICARE Supplemental Insurance

XPressClaim

 Opening Scenario

Sally Curtis comes from a long line of military people. Both of her parents are in the Army Reserve, her uncle is currently a Marine stationed in Iraq, her maternal grandfather was a Green Beret, and her great-grandfather was stationed in England during World War II. This background made her very interested in working with TRICARE. When a position became available at the Walden-Martin Family Medical Clinic several years ago, she jumped at the chance to gain a better understanding of TRICARE and to be able to service members and their families. Her personal experiences with TRICARE helped her empathize with her patients who are covered under the various plans offered by TRICARE. She especially likes working with the families of active duty military service members.

MILITARY HEALTH PROGRAMS

The federal government has provided healthcare for the military from the earliest years of US history. In 1884 Congress requested that Army medical officers and surgeons attend to the families of the officers and soldiers free of charge whenever possible. During World War II, Congress authorized the creation of the Emergency Maternal and Infant Care Program, which provided maternity care and care of infants up to 1 year of age for wives and children of service members. During the Korean War in 1956, the Dependents Medical Care Act became law. The 1966 amendments to this law initiated what later became the **Civilian Health and Medical Program of the Uniformed Services (CHAMPUS)**, a military healthcare program that existed for more than 30 years until it was replaced with TRICARE in 1998.

TRICARE

TRICARE (TRI because it offered three different plans) is a worldwide healthcare system for the military. This wide-ranging program combines resources of the uniformed services and supplements them with networks of civilian healthcare professionals, institutions, pharmacies, and suppliers to give enrollees access to cost-efficient, high-quality healthcare. TRICARE serves nearly 10 million beneficiaries worldwide, including

National Guard and Reserve members, retirees, their families, survivors, and certain former spouses. On October 1, 2013, the Department of Defense (DoD) established the **Defense Health Agency (DHA)** to take over management of the **Military Health System (MHS)** activities, replacing the former TRICARE Management Activity (TMA), which ceased operations on that same date.

DEFENSE HEALTH AGENCY

The DHA is a joint, integrated combat support agency that enables the Army, Navy, and Air Force medical services to provide a medically ready force to combatant commands in both peacetime and wartime. The DHA facilitates the delivery of integrated, affordable, and high-quality healthcare services to MHS beneficiaries. The DHA is responsible for improving clinical and business processes across the MHS by:

- Implementing shared services with common ways to measure outcomes
- Enabling rapid adoption of proven practices, helping reduce unwanted variation, and improving the coordination of care across time and treatment settings
- Exercising management responsibility for joint shared services and the TRICARE Health Plan
- Acting as the market manager for the national capital region (NCR) enhanced multiservice market, which includes major treatment centers (e.g., Walter Reed National Military Medical Center)

TRICARE REGIONAL OFFICE

TRICARE is organized into two geographic sections within the United States—West and East regions (Fig. 12.1)—and three overseas "areas": Eurasia-Africa, Latin America and Canada, and the Pacific areas. Each region or area has its own **TRICARE Regional Office (TRO)** and regional contractor. TROs represent the organization for managing regional contractors and overseeing the healthcare delivery system in the two US-based TRICARE regions. Each TRO is led by a regional director who reports to and operates under the authority, direction, and control of the TMA deputy director. Within each region, the regional director is the health plan manager who oversees and coordinates with the service areas to develop an integrated health plan. Specific responsibilities include but are not necessarily limited to:

- Ensuring network quality and adequacy, including provider issues
- Monitoring customer satisfaction outcomes
- Managing TRO customer service issues
- Coordinating appointing and referral of management policies
- Addressing enrollment issues
- Contracting and fiscal management functions
- Establishing and coordinating regional marketing and education functions
- Overseeing contractor credentialing
- Developing TRICARE Maximum Allowable Charge (TMAC) waiver packages

MILITARY HEALTH SYSTEM

MHS is a global, comprehensive, integrated system that includes combat medical services, health readiness futures, a healthcare delivery system, public health activities, medical education and training, and medical research and development. The fundamental mission of the MHS is to provide medical support to military operations. The MHS is constantly responding and adapting to changing demographics, shifting policies, evolving standards for access and quality, advances in science and medicine, complex payment and cost considerations, rapidly evolving communications and information technology capabilities, and fluid patient expectations.

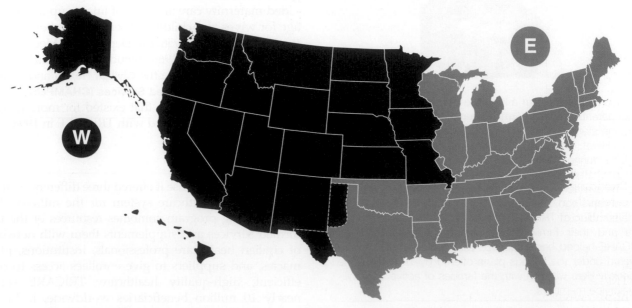

Fig. 12.1 TRICARE healthcare service US regional map. *E*, East region; *W*, West region. (From US Department of Defense, TRICARE Management Activity.)

Military Treatment Facilities

The MHS includes **military treatment facilities (MTFs)**. MTFs are clinics or hospitals operated by the DoD that provide care to military personnel, retirees, and dependents. MTFs are usually located on or near a uniformed service installation where beneficiaries may receive care from military and civilian providers and support staff. Provided the MTF is able to provide the service requested, it is given the *Right of First Refusal (ROFR)* for TRICARE Prime beneficiaries residing in a TRICARE Prime Service Area (PSA) for inpatient admission referrals, specialty appointments, and procedures requiring prior authorization. The MTF staff reviews the referral to determine if they have the specialty capability and an available specialty care appointment within TRICARE access standards. If the MTF accepts the care, the Prime beneficiary must obtain these services at the MTF. If the service is not available at the MTF within the appropriate access standards, the beneficiary is referred to a TRICARE network provider (see discussion later).

Note: ROFR does not apply to TRICARE Prime Remote (TPR) and TRICARE Prime Remote for Active Duty Family Members (TPRADFMs) enrollees seeking care at MTFs.

Pharmacy services also are available at most MTFs (see discussion later). Active duty service members (ADSMs) and TRICARE Prime–enrolled active duty family members (ADFMs) have the highest priority for MTF care. Those not enrolled in TRICARE Prime receive MTF care on a space-available basis.

"Websites to Explore" at the end of this chapter includes a website where you can find the location of the MTF nearest to you.

TRICARE Regional Contractors

As mentioned earlier, TRICARE is administered on a regional basis. Each region is headed by a **regional contractor** who works with the DoD to administer the TRICARE benefits in each region. Responsibilities of the regional contractor include providing beneficiaries with healthcare services and support in addition to the services that are available at MTFs. These responsibilities include:

- Establishing provider networks
- Operating TRICARE Service Centers
- Providing customer service call centers
- Providing administrative support (e.g., enrollment, care authorization, claims processing)
- Distributing educational information to beneficiaries and providers

As of this writing, the regional contractors are as follows:

- TRICARE West, Health Net Federal Services: http://www.tricare-west.com
- TRICARE East, Humana Military: http://www.tricare-east.com
- TRICARE Overseas, International SOS: http://www.tricare-overseas.com

As with Medicare and Medicaid, regional contractors are subject to change periodically.

TRICARE ELIGIBILITY

Enrollment in the following seven branches of the uniformed services determines TRICARE eligibility:

- Army
- Marine Corps
- Navy
- Air Force
- Coast Guard
- Public Health Service
- National Oceanic and Atmospheric Administration (NOAA)

Like recipients of Medicaid and Medicare, TRICARE-eligible individuals are referred to as *beneficiaries*. The service member, whether in active duty, retired, or deceased, is called the **sponsor**. The sponsor's relationship to the **beneficiary** (spouse, child, parent) creates eligibility under TRICARE. In addition, to be eligible for TRICARE, an individual must be registered in the **Defense Enrollment Eligibility Reporting System (DEERS)**. DEERS is a global computerized database of uniformed services members, their family members, and others who are eligible for military benefits. Enrollment in DEERS is the key to using TRICARE benefits. DEERS maintains information about TRICARE eligibility, TRICARE option coverage, primary care manager (PCM) assignment, catastrophic caps, deductibles, enrollment fee totals, and information on other health insurance (OHI). All sponsors are automatically registered in DEERS when they enter the military; however, it is the sponsor's responsibility to register eligible family members. Family members can update personal information such as addresses and phone numbers once they are registered.

It is important to know that registering in DEERS does not determine eligibility, it only reports it. For questions regarding eligibility, beneficiaries may contact the Defense Manpower Data Center Support Office (DSO) or the nearest identification (ID) card–issuing facility at http://www.dmdc.osd.mil/rsl.

Websites for DEERS can be found under "Websites to Explore" at the end of this chapter.

TRICARE-eligible individuals can be classified into the following main categories:

- ADSMs, who are automatically enrolled in TRICARE Prime
- Spouses and unmarried children of ADSMs (ADFMs)
- Uniformed service retirees, their spouses, and their unmarried children
- Medal of Honor recipients
- Un-remarried former spouses and unmarried children of active duty or retired service members who have died

For more details on TRICARE-eligible individuals, visit the TRICARE website at http://www.tricare.mil/.

It is extremely important that DEERS contains up-to-date information on each family member. If eligibility cannot be confirmed, enrollment may be denied. Many life events can change status and require an update to DEERS to maintain eligibility, for example:

- Permanent change of station (PCS)
- Changes in marital status
- Newborn or adopted children
- Retirement

It is the sponsor's responsibility to ensure that family members are registered in DEERS correctly and that all status information is kept current. Only the sponsor can add or delete family members. Adding or deleting family members requires the proper documents, such as a marriage certificate, divorce decree, or birth certificate. DEERS can be notified of status changes in the following ways:

- Visit the DEERS address update website at https://milconnect.dmdc.osd.mil/milconnect/, if applicable.
- Visit a local personnel office that has a uniformed services ID card–issuing facility and provide the necessary documents.
- Call Defense Manpower Data Center Support Office at 1-800-538-9552.
- Fax DEERS at 1-831-655-8317.
- Mail changes to Defense Support Office (DSO), Attention: COA, 400 Gigling Road, Seaside, CA 93955-6771.

Who Is Not Eligible for TRICARE?

Categories of individuals *not* eligible for TRICARE include the following:

- Most individuals who are 65 years or older and eligible for Medicare (except ADFMs). Individuals younger than 65 who are eligible for Medicare because of a disability or end-stage renal disease (ESRD) may retain eligibility until age 65 but must be enrolled in Medicare Part B.
- Parents and parents-in-law of ADSMs or uniformed services retirees or of deceased ADSMs or retirees. They may, however, be able to receive treatment in military medical facilities if space permits.
- Individuals who are eligible for benefits under the Civilian Health and Medical Program of the Department of Veterans Affairs (CHAMPVA) are not eligible for TRICARE.
- Any other person not enrolled in DEERS.

> **Imagine This!**
>
> Alan Workman is a Marine serving on active duty in Iraq. He has a wife and two children (2 years old and 7 years old) at home in the United States. In this scenario, TRICARE considers Alan the sponsor, and his wife and two children are the beneficiaries.

Losing TRICARE Eligibility

Eligibility for TRICARE may end for the following reasons:

- Sponsor separates from active duty; that is, he or she "gets out" of the military before retiring.
- Beneficiary becomes entitled to Medicare Part A but does not purchase Medicare Part B.
- Dependent child reaches age limit: Children remain eligible for TRICARE coverage up to age 21 years, or age 23 years if enrolled in college full-time and the sponsor continues to provide 50% of the child's financial support. Children ages 23 to 26 years who are not married and not eligible for their own employer-sponsored health insurance may qualify for the TRICARE Young Adult (TYA) program, on the basis of the sponsor's eligibility for TRICARE.
- Divorce: A former spouse loses eligibility unless he or she meets specific requirements to maintain eligibility as a former spouse.
- Surviving spouse, widow(er), or former spouse remarries.
- DEERS information is not kept up to date: If eligibility is lost as a result of inaccurate or outdated information, simply updating the information restores coverage.

Note: The preceding list is not intended to be all-inclusive.

TRICARE AND THE AFFORDABLE CARE ACT

The Affordable Care Act (ACA), also known as the *healthcare reform law,* requires that individuals maintain basic healthcare insurance or other health coverage that meets the definition of **minimum essential coverage** beginning in 2014. To qualify as minimum essential coverage, a policy must:

- Cover at least 60% of out-of-pocket costs
- Guarantee coverage—you cannot be denied coverage because of health status or any other reason except ability to pay
- Be renewable
- Offer at least 10 essential benefits (e.g., outpatient care, emergency room visits, prescription drugs, laboratory tests, maternity care, mental healthcare)

View the entire list of benefits at HealthCare.gov.

The TRICARE program meets the minimum essential coverage requirement. TRICARE beneficiaries receive notice when their TRICARE coverage is ending. For more information, visit http://www.tricare.mil/aca.

TRICARE'S TWO BASIC PROGRAM OPTIONS

Depending on the category and location of the beneficiary, he or she may be eligible for different program options. These options may change when the enrollee travels or moves or when he or she becomes entitled to Medicare Part A, which is discussed later in this chapter.

There are two basic options: (1) **TRICARE Prime** and (2) **TRICARE Select**. Upon entering service, ADSMs are enrolled in either TRICARE Prime or **TRICARE Prime Remote (TPR)**, depending on where they live or work. If enrolled in Prime, most care is received at MTFs. If the MTF cannot provide care, the ADSM is referred to a civilian provider. If enrolled in TPR, most care is received from a TRICARE network primary care manager (PCM). If a network provider is not available, TPR enrollees receive care from a TRICARE-authorized provider (see discussion later).

See Table 12.1 for a list of TRICARE program options. Table 12.2 provides program information on the various TRICARE programs—the type of program, enrollment costs, and provider choice.

TRICARE OVERSEAS PROGRAM

The TRICARE Overseas Program (TOP) has one overseas region consisting of three areas:
- TRICARE Eurasia-Africa (Africa, Europe, and the Middle East)
- TRICARE Latin America and Canada (the Caribbean basin, Central and South America, Puerto Rico, and US Virgin Islands)
- TRICARE Pacific (Asia, Australia, Guam, India, Japan, Korea, New Zealand, and western Pacific remote countries)

TOP provides health benefits to beneficiaries living and traveling overseas while they are eligible for TRICARE. TOP allows for significant cultural differences unique to foreign countries and their healthcare practices. The TRICARE Area Office (TAO) director is responsible for the overall management of TOP. For more detailed information on this program, visit http://www.tricare-overseas.com.

TRICARE YOUNG ADULT PROGRAM

Currently, adult children of military members and retirees younger than 26 years who are unmarried and are not eligible for their own employer-sponsored healthcare coverage may become eligible to enroll in the TYA program. TYA offers TRICARE Prime and TRICARE Select coverage worldwide. TYA includes medical and pharmacy benefits but not dental coverage.

Eligibility depends on all of the following:
- A dependent of a TRICARE-eligible uniformed service sponsor
- Unmarried
- At least age 21 (or age 23 if previously enrolled as a full-time student at an approved college and if the sponsor provided at least 50% of financial support) but has not yet reached age 26

If you are married, eligible to enroll in an employer-sponsored health plan (as defined in TYA regulations),

Table **12.1** **TRICARE Program Options**	
BENEFICIARY TYPE	**PROGRAM OPTIONS**
Active duty service members (ADSMs) (includes National Guard and Reserve members activated for more than 30 consecutive days)	TRICARE Prime TRICARE Prime Remote (TPR) TRICARE Select TRICARE Select Overseas TRICARE Active Duty Dental Program
Active duty family members (ADFMs) (includes family members of National Guard and Reserve members activated for more than 30 consecutive days and certain survivors)	TRICARE Prime TRICARE Prime Remote for Active Duty Family Members (TPRADFM) TRICARE Select TRICARE Select Overseas TRICARE For Life (TFL) (ADFMs must have Medicare Part B to participate in TFL) US Family Health Plan (USFHP) TRICARE Dental Program (TDP)
Retired service members and eligible family members, survivors, Medal of Honor recipients, qualified former spouses, and others	TRICARE Prime TRICARE Select TRICARE Select Overseas TFL (If entitled to premium-free Medicare Part A based on age, disability, or end-stage renal disease [ESRD], the beneficiary must have Medicare Part B to keep TRICARE eligibility.) US Family Health Plan (USFHP) TRICARE Retiree Dental Program (TRDP)
National Guard and Reserve members and their family members (qualified non-active duty members of the Selected Reserve, Retired Reserve, and certain members of the Individual Ready Reserve [IRR])	TRICARE Reserve Select (members of the Selected Reserve) TRICARE Retired Reserve (members of the Retired Reserve younger than 60 years) TDP TRDP

Table 12.2   TRICARE Program Descriptions and Enrollment Costs

PROGRAM	DESCRIPTION	ENROLLING	PROGRAM COSTS	GETTING CARE
TRICARE Prime	• Similar to a managed care or health maintenance organization option • Available to active duty service members (ADSMs), active duty family members (ADFMs), retirees, their families, survivors, and qualifying former spouses in specific geographic areas	• Enrollment required • Priority access for military hospitals and clinics • No claims to file (in most cases) • Retirees, their families, survivors, and qualifying former spouses pay annual enrollment fees • Offers lowest out-of-pocket costs	• ADSMs, ADFMs, surviving spouses (during the first 3 years), and surviving dependent children; no enrollment costs • Fiscal year annual fees for retired service members, their families, surviving spouses (after the first 3 years), eligible former spouses, and others	• Receive most care from primary care manager at a military hospital or clinic within the TRICARE network • Referrals and/or prior authorizations for specialty care
TRICARE Prime Remote (includes TRICARE Prime Remote for Active Duty Family Members)	• Benefit similar to TRICARE Prime for ADSMs living and working in remote locations and the eligible family members residing with the sponsor	• Enrollment required • No claims to file (in most cases) • Offers same low out-of-pocket costs as TRICARE Prime	• No enrollment costs	• Receive care from TRICARE network providers (or a TRICARE-authorized non-network provider if a network provider is unavailable) • Referrals and/or prior authorizations required for specialty care
TRICARE Select	• Preferred provider option available in the United States	• Enrollment required • No claims to file	• Annual enrollment costs • Annual deductible and cost-shares apply	• Receive care from TRICARE-authorized non-network providers • No referrals required • Some services require prior authorization
TRICARE Select Overseas	• Provides comprehensive coverage in all overseas areas	• Enrollment required	• Annual outpatient deductible • Cost-shares for covered services	• Receive care from TRICARE-authorized non-network providers • No referrals required • Some services require prior authorization

or otherwise eligible for TRICARE coverage, you cannot enroll in TYA.

Important: The ACA requires that individuals maintain health insurance or other coverage that meets the definition of minimum essential coverage. Examples of minimum essential coverage include but are not necessarily limited to the following:

• Employer-sponsored coverage and retiree coverage
• Coverage purchased in the individual market, including a qualified health plan offered by the health insurance marketplace (also known as an *affordable insurance exchange*)
• Medicare Part A coverage and Medicare Advantage (MA) plans
• Most Medicaid coverage
• Children's Health Insurance Program (CHIP) coverage
• TRICARE and TRICARE Young Adult Program

Patient's Point of View

Pedro Gomez stopped in to talk with Sally. Pedro's father, Daniel, is an active duty Marine. Pedro will soon be 21 years old and will no longer be eligible for TRICARE coverage. Pedro was wondering what his options are for healthcare coverage. Sally explained about the TRICARE Young Adult program. She asked Pedro if he is attending college. Pedro stated that he does not attend college but is working full time. Sally then asked if he is eligible for an employer-sponsored health plan through his employer, and he is not. Sally encouraged Pedro to check into the TRICARE Young Adult program at http://tricare.mil/tya. She also let him know that if he has any further questions, he should come back in and see her again.

WHAT TRICARE PAYS

TRICARE covers treatments, procedures, drugs, or devices (benefits) that are "medically necessary and considered proven." Medically necessary and considered proven means that the benefit is:

- Proven—it isn't experimental
- Safe—it won't hurt the individual, and it's approved by regulatory agencies
- Effective—it works

TRICARE does not cover services that are unproven or experimental and/or specifically excluded by statutes, regulations, or policy.

Certain clinical preventive care services that are intended to promote and maintain good health and are performed as periodic health screenings, health assessments, or health maintenance visits are also covered by TRICARE. In general, TRICARE excludes services and supplies that are not medically or psychologically necessary for the diagnosis or treatment of a covered illness (including mental disorder), for an injury, for the diagnosis and treatment of pregnancy, or for well-child care. In addition, all services and supplies (including inpatient institutional costs) related to a noncovered condition or treatment, or provided by an unauthorized provider, are excluded. For a website that provides a full list of exclusions, see "Websites to Explore" at the end of this chapter.

TRICARE's maximum allowable charge (TMAC), also known as the *CHAMPUS maximum allowable charge (CMAC)*, is the amount on which TRICARE figures a beneficiary's **copayment** or **cost-share**. (Copayments are per occurrence or per visit. Cost-shares are a percentage of allowed amounts for certain types of services. Copayments and cost-shares are subject to change at the beginning of each fiscal year [October 1]). Generally, TMACs are the rates used to set the TRICARE-allowed amount on the claim. These rates are based on the type of service and geographic location. Actual payment may vary by negotiated contracts. Not all services have an established TMAC.

If the health insurance professional does not know what the allowable charge is for a particular service or supply, he or she can telephone the regional claims processor for this information or consult the TRICARE provider handbook. It is advisable to keep a current copy of the handbook on file for information regarding TRICARE billing and claims submission guidelines. For additional information or answers to specific questions regarding TRICARE-covered services, health insurance professionals can consult the *TRICARE Policy Manual*, available at https://manuals.health.mil/pages/DisplayManual.aspx?SeriesId=POLICY; the *TRICARE Reimbursement Manual*, available at https://manuals.health.mil/pages/DisplayManual.aspx?SeriesId=TR15; or the *TRICARE Operations Manual*, available at https://manuals.health.mil/pages/DisplayManual.aspx?SeriesId=TO15.

TRICARE Nonavailability Statement

As discussed previously, military personnel and their TRICARE-eligible dependents typically receive healthcare at an MTF. If the needed treatment is unavailable at an MTF and it becomes necessary for the individual to seek inpatient treatment in a civilian hospital, he or she sometimes must obtain a **nonavailability statement (NAS)**. An NAS is certification from an MTF stating that it cannot provide the care that a TRICARE beneficiary needs. In May 2012 a final rule was adopted eliminating the requirement that an NAS is needed for nonemergency inpatient mental healthcare in order for a TRICARE Select beneficiary's claim to be paid. It was determined that the number of NAS documents issued for nonemergency inpatient mental healthcare was negligible, as most mental health admissions are emergency admissions, and that requiring an NAS for the relatively few nonemergency inpatient mental health admissions was disproportionate to the cost of maintaining the systems necessary to process and coordinate an NAS.

Even though an NAS is no longer required for most care, it might be prudent for beneficiaries enrolled in other TRICARE options to check with their nearby MTF in advance to determine whether an NAS is needed.

An NAS is valid for a hospital admission that occurs within 30 calendar days after the NAS is issued. It will remain valid from the date of admission until 15 days after discharge for any follow-up treatment that is directly related to the admission.

Healthcare providers—whether or not they participate in TRICARE Select—are required to obtain these advance authorizations when needed. The NAS system is now automated, which means that instead of sending a paper copy of the NAS with the TRICARE claim, the MTF enters the NAS electronically into the DEERS computer files.

◎ HIPAA Tip

Health Insurance Portability and Accountability Act (HIPAA) privacy applies to individually identifiable health information, including paper, electronic, and oral communications. This also applies to information that identifies the patient and relates to his or her past, present, or future health condition.

💡 Imagine This!

In February 2003, Kim Sun Hwa, a TRICARE Prime enrollee, sought care for a serious cardiac condition at the military treatment facility (MTF) near the town where she lived. The MTF did not have the facilities to perform the needed quadruple-bypass surgery and referred her to Genesis Cardiac and Rehabilitation Center, which was 150 miles away. The MTF filed an nonavailability statement (NAS) with the Defense Enrollment Eligibility Reporting System (DEERS) for the surgery. After the procedure, Kim experienced postsurgical depression and was readmitted to Genesis for nonemergency mental healthcare. The claim for inpatient treatment of her nonemergency mental health condition at Genesis was refused because an NAS was not filed with DEERS; this happened because such treatment was available at the MTF.

TRICARE'S ADDITIONAL COVERAGE OPTIONS

To review, the two basic program options under TRICARE are TRICARE Select and TRICARE Prime (Fig. 12.2). To use TRICARE Prime, the individual receiving care must live in an area where this option is available and a civilian provider network has been established to support this plan. It is important to keep in mind that active duty, Guard, and Reserve members are automatically enrolled in TRICARE Prime.

TRICARE has many other programs (Box 12.1). Military retirees and their dependents must choose the option that best suits their needs. The website to access information for any of the other TRICARE programs listed in Box 12.1 can be found under "Websites to Explore" at the end of this chapter.

TRICARE DENTAL PROGRAM

TRICARE covers dental care that is medically necessary to treat a covered medical condition. Coverage is based on the beneficiary's status and is separate from TRICARE's medical coverage (Table 12.3).

Topic	TRICARE Prime	TRICARE Select
Definition	TRICARE Prime is a managed care option similar to a health maintenance organization (HMO).	TRICARE Select is similar to a preferred provider organization (PPO) where the beneficiary selects from a network of providers.
Cost vs. Choice	Least out-of-pocket costs with some restrictions on freedom of choice.	Deductible, copay, and coinsurance apply.

Fig. 12.2 TRICARE's two options.

Box 12.1   TRICARE Programs

- TRICARE Prime
- TRICARE Prime Remote (TPR)
- TRICARE Prime Overseas
- TRICARE Prime Remote Overseas
- TRICARE Select
- TRICARE Select Overseas
- TRICARE For Life (TFL)
- TRICARE Reserve Select
- TRICARE Retired Reserve
- TRICARE Young Adult (TYA)
- US Family Health Plan
- TRICARE Pharmacy Program
- Dental Options
- Cancer Clinical Trials
- TRICARE Extended Care Health Option (ECHO)
- TRICARE Comprehensive Autism Care Demonstration (ACD) Program
- Supplemental Health Care Program (SHCP)
- Transitional Health Care Benefits

Table 12.3   TRICARE's Dental Benefits Coverage

Active Duty Service Members	Covered by active duty dental benefits
Active Duty Family Members	Can purchase the TRICARE Dental Program
Guard or Reserve Members	Coverage changes based on sponsor's military status
Guard or Reserve Family Members	Can purchase the TRICARE Dental Program
Retired Service Members and Families	Can purchase the FEDVIP Dental Program
Survivors	Covered by either TRICARE Dental Program or TRICARE FEDVIP Dental Program

FEDVIP, Federal Employees Dental and Vision Insurance Program.

ADSMs receive dental care at military dental clinics or from network providers through the TRICARE Active Duty Dental Program (ADDP). For all other beneficiaries, TRICARE offers two dental programs: the TRICARE Dental Program (TDP) and the TRICARE Federal Employees Dental and Vision Insurance Program (FEDVIP). Separate dental contractors administer each program, and each has its own monthly premiums and cost-shares.

Note: TRICARE may pay for some medically necessary services in conjunction with noncovered dental treatment for patients with developmental, mental, or physical disabilities and children age 5 years and younger. See the TRICARE handbook or visit http://www.tricare.mil for more information.

TRICARE SPECIAL PROGRAMS

TRICARE offers special programs tailored specifically to beneficiary health concerns or conditions. Many of these programs have specific eligibility requirements based on beneficiary category, plan, or status. They include health promotion programs, such as alcohol education, smoking cessation, and weight loss. Some are for specific populations, such as the Foreign Force Member Health Care Option and the Pre-Activation Benefit for National Guard and Reserve. Other programs are for certain health conditions, such as the Cancer Clinical Trials. Many programs are limited to a certain number of participants or a particular geographic location. The following sections discuss four of these special programs. For detailed information on all of these special TRICARE programs, visit the TRICARE website.

Transitional Assistance Management Program

The Transitional Assistance Management Program (TAMP) provides 180 days of premium-free transitional healthcare benefits after regular TRICARE benefits end. TAMP continues to provide the minimum essential coverage that is required under the ACA, but it is temporary. TAMP eligibility is determined by the services and is documented in the DEERS. TAMP eligibility can be viewed online via https://www.dmdc.osd.mil/milconnect/.

Service members should check with their service personnel departments for information or assistance with TAMP eligibility. For those who qualify, the 180-day TAMP period begins upon the sponsor's separation. During TAMP, sponsors and family members are eligible to use one of the following health plan options in addition to military hospitals and clinics:

- TRICARE Prime (where locally available; enrollment required)
- TRICARE Select
- US Family Health Plan (if residing in a designated location; enrollment required)
- TRICARE Prime Overseas (enrollment required)
- TRICARE Select Overseas

A qualifying healthcare option to replace TRICARE benefits should be considered before TAMP ends.

Exceptional Family Member Program

The Exceptional Family Member Program (EFMP) is a mandatory enrollment program based on specifically defined rules. EFMP works with other military and civilian agencies to provide comprehensive and coordinated medical, educational, housing, community support, and personnel services to families with special needs. An *exceptional family member* is a dependent, regardless of age, who requires medical services for a chronic condition; receives ongoing services from a specialist; has mental health concerns, social problems, or psychological needs; or receives education services provided by means of an Individual Education Program (IEP), or is a family member receiving services provided through an Individual Family Services Plan (IFSP). Enrollment updates are required every 3 years or if the condition changes.

Extended Care Health Option

The Extended Care Health Option (ECHO) supplements the basic TRICARE program by providing financial assistance for certain services and supplies. ECHO is offered to beneficiaries who are diagnosed with moderate or severe mental retardation, a serious physical disability, or an extraordinary physical or psychological condition. Children may remain eligible for ECHO beyond the usual age limits in certain circumstances.

To use ECHO, qualified beneficiaries must be enrolled in the EFMP as provided by the sponsor's branch of service and register through ECHO case managers in each TRICARE region.

TRICARE PLUS

TRICARE Plus is an MTF primary care enrollment program that is offered at selected local MTFs. This program allows beneficiaries who normally are able to get care only at MTFs on a space-available basis to enroll and receive primary care appointments at the MTF within the same primary care access standards as beneficiaries enrolled in a TRICARE Prime option. Beneficiaries using TRICARE Select, TRICARE Select Overseas, and TRICARE For Life (TFL) can use TRICARE Plus; however, it is not available to those enrolled in a TRICARE Prime option, civilian health maintenance organization (HMO), or Medicare HMO. Nonenrollment in TRICARE Plus does not affect TFL benefits or other existing programs. (TFL is discussed later in this chapter.)

TRICARE PHARMACY PROGRAM

TRICARE offers comprehensive prescription drug coverage and several options for filling prescriptions. All TRICARE beneficiaries are eligible for the TRICARE Pharmacy Program, administered by Express Scripts, Inc. To fill prescriptions, beneficiaries need written prescriptions or e-prescriptions and valid uniformed services ID cards (see discussion later). TRICARE beneficiaries have the following options for filling prescriptions:

- *Military pharmacies:* This is the least expensive option, but formularies may vary by pharmacy. Note: Military pharmacies will not accept e-prescriptions for controlled substances. Beneficiaries will still need a written prescription for these medications.
- *TRICARE Pharmacy Home Delivery:* This mail-order option is the preferred method when not using a military pharmacy, especially for beneficiaries using maintenance medications.
- *TRICARE retail network pharmacies:* Beneficiaries can access a large network of retail pharmacies in the United States and certain US territories.
- *Non-network retail pharmacies:* This is the most expensive option and is not recommended for beneficiaries.

Effective October 1, 2015, all TRICARE beneficiaries, except ADSMs, are required to get select brand-name maintenance medications through either TRICARE Pharmacy Home Delivery or from a military pharmacy. Beneficiaries who choose to use retail pharmacies for select brand-name maintenance medications will pay full cost. This does not apply to generic medications or to medications taken for acute conditions. Beneficiaries living overseas or who have other health insurance with prescription drug coverage are not affected.

Medicare-eligible beneficiaries can use the TRICARE Pharmacy Program benefits. However, TRICARE beneficiaries who turned age 65 on or after April 1, 2001, must also enroll in Medicare Part B. If they choose not to enroll, their pharmacy benefit is limited to the medications available at military pharmacies. Medicare-eligible beneficiaries are also eligible for Medicare Part D prescription drug plans. However, they do not need to enroll in a Medicare Part D prescription drug plan to keep their TRICARE benefit.

For more information about prescription benefits and costs, visit the TRICARE or Express Scripts websites.

TRICARE AND OTHER HEALTH INSURANCE

If a TRICARE-eligible beneficiary has other healthcare coverage besides TRICARE Select or Prime through an employer, an association, or a private insurer, or if a student in the family has a healthcare plan through his or her school, TRICARE considers this coverage to be **other health insurance (OHI)**. It also may be called *double coverage* or *coordination of benefits.* When there is OHI, follow its rules for filing a claim with them first. If the OHI doesn't cover the entire cost, file a claim with TRICARE. If the OHI denies a claim for failure to follow their rules, such as getting care without authorization or using a non-network provider, TRICARE may also deny the claim.

Any OHI that a TRICARE enrollee has in addition to TRICARE coverage is considered primary health insurance. If a TRICARE beneficiary has OHI, he or she should tell the healthcare provider and regional contractor. Keeping the regional contractor informed about OHI will allow TRICARE to better coordinate benefits and will help ensure that there is no delay in payment of claims.

Remember, *active duty* refers to a person currently serving in the uniformed services. While on active duty, a family member's OHI is primary to TRICARE, but the sponsor's OHI is secondary to TRICARE. Active duty service members cannot use OHI; TRICARE is their only coverage. For TRICARE beneficiaries with Medicare, TRICARE pays last after Medicare and OHI.

When active duty sponsors retire, their OHI becomes primary to TRICARE. An explanation of benefits (EOB) from the primary OHI is required for any claims with dates of service after the retirement date.

TRICARE Fact: OHI does not include TRICARE supplemental insurance or Medicaid. These programs are not primary to TRICARE.

TRICARE SUPPLEMENTAL INSURANCE

TRICARE Supplemental Insurance policies, similar to Medicare supplemental insurance policies, are health benefit plans designed specifically to supplement TRICARE benefits. Unlike OHI, which pays first for healthcare services, supplemental insurance pays *after* TRICARE pays its portion of the bill, generally paying most or all of whatever is left after TRICARE has paid its share of the cost of covered services and supplies. TRICARE Supplemental Insurance plans are frequently available from military associations or other private organizations. Such policies are not specifically for retirees and may be advantageous for other TRICARE-eligible families as well. The healthcare needs of the beneficiary and his or her family members should be considered carefully before purchasing a Supplemental Insurance plan. In some cases, such as with TRICARE Prime, the cost of the supplemental plan may exceed out-of-pocket medical expenses.

TRICARE FOR LIFE

Tricare For Life (TFL) is TRICARE's Medicare-wraparound coverage available to all Medicare-eligible TRICARE beneficiaries, regardless of age or place of residence, provided that they have both Medicare Part A and Medicare Part B. Medicare is the primary insurer, and TRICARE acts as secondary payer, minimizing out-of-pocket expenses. TFL benefits include covering Medicare's coinsurance and deductible. Whether the beneficiary uses a provider who participates in Medicare (participating [PAR] provider) or one who does not (nonparticipating [nonPAR] provider), the provider files claims with Medicare. Medicare pays its portion first and electronically forwards the claim to the TFL claims processor. TFL pays the provider directly for TRICARE-covered services. There are no enrollment fees for TFL and no monthly premium cost other than the Medicare Part B premium.

TFL is available worldwide. It pays after Medicare in the United States and US territories; however, it is the first payer in all other overseas areas. Following are some additional facts about TFL:

- Meets requirements for minimum essential coverage
- Enrollment not required
- Coverage is automatic for those who have Medicare Parts A and B
- Participant must pay Medicare Part B premiums
- Participant may visit any authorized provider

The provider files claims with Medicare. Medicare pays its portion, and then the claim is sent to the TFL claims processor. TFL pays the provider directly for TRICARE-covered services. Participants can receive care at military hospitals and clinics, but only on a space-available basis. There is no enrollment fee, and there are no out-of-pocket costs for services covered by both Medicare and TRICARE, but participants must pay Medicare Part B monthly premiums.

TRICARE For Life Eligibility

TFL is available for *all* dual TRICARE-Medicare–eligible uniformed services retirees, including:

- Retired members of the Reserve Component who receive retirement pay
- Medicare-eligible family members
- Medicare-eligible widow(er)s, certain former spouses, and beneficiaries younger than 65 years who are also entitled to Medicare Part A because of a disability or chronic renal disease

Dependent parents and parents-in-law are not eligible for TRICARE Prime, TRICARE Select, or TFL. However, they are eligible to receive care under the sponsor's TRICARE benefits at an MTF on a space-available basis. Care received outside the MTF must be covered by another form of insurance. They may also be eligible for TRICARE Senior Pharmacy benefits if they are entitled to Medicare Part A; if they turned age 65 on or after April 1, 2001; and if they are enrolled in Medicare Part B. For detailed information on TRICARE, view resources at https://tricare.mil/CoveredServices/BenefitUpdates/Archives/1_2_19_New_to_TRICARE_the_Basics_You_Need_to_Know.

TRICARE Fact: ADFMs are not required to have Medicare Part B to remain eligible for TRICARE. Once the sponsor reaches age 65, Medicare Part B must be in effect no later than the sponsor's retirement date to avoid a break in TRICARE coverage.

? What Did You Learn?

1. List four of TRICARE's additional coverage options.
2. What categories of TRICARE beneficiaries can enroll in TRICARE Plus?
3. What is a "basic core formulary"?
4. True or false: Any OHI that a TRICARE enrollee has in addition to TRICARE coverage is considered primary health insurance.
5. Who is eligible for TFL?

 Imagine This!

Benjamin Hudson, a dual-eligible enrollee under TRICARE and Medicare, visited Dr. Alton Simmons, an ophthalmologist, for vision problems. Benjamin subsequently opted to receive laser surgery to correct his myopia. When he received a statement for the entire fee, he telephoned the health insurance professional in Dr. Simmons' office stating that because he had Medicare and TRICARE coverage, one or the other should pay. Under the impression that an error had been made, Benjamin insisted that the claim be resubmitted; however, the health insurance professional informed him that because laser surgery was a noncovered expense under Medicare, TRICARE would not pay it either. Mr. Hudson refused to pay the bill on the grounds that the health insurance professional should have informed him that this was a noncovered service before the procedure. Dr. Simmons ultimately adjusted the charge off of Benjamin's account.

VERIFYING TRICARE ELIGIBILITY

Patient eligibility for TRICARE must be confirmed at the time of service, and it is the patient's responsibility to provide proof of current coverage. When a patient comes to the office for an appointment and informs the health insurance professional that he or she is eligible for benefits under one of the military's healthcare programs, it should be verified immediately. Identification and enrollment cards are part of the verification process. Every TRICARE-eligible ADSM, family member over age 10, and retiree must have a Common Access Card (CAC), uniformed services ID card (Fig. 12.3), or eligibility authorization letter. Both the uniformed services ID card and the CAC contain a digital photo image of the individual. They also have barcodes containing pertinent machine-readable data and printed ID and entitlement information. ID cards also include an expiration date. If expired, the beneficiary must immediately update his or her information in DEERS and request a new card. The expiration date for retirees should read "INDEF." For civilians, the center section on the ID card should read "YES" under the box titled "Civilian." If the ID card for a TFL patient reads "NO" in this block, TFL can be used only if the patient has both Medicare Part A and Medicare Part B coverage. The beneficiary's valid photo ID presented with a copy of the sponsor's activation orders (when activated for more than 30 consecutive days) serves as proof of the patient's TRICARE eligibility. Because beneficiaries under age 10 are usually not issued ID cards, the parent's proof of eligibility may serve as proof of eligibility for the child. Be sure to check the expiration date and make a copy of both sides of the ID card for your patient files.

It is important to be aware that an ID alone is not proof of eligibility. TRICARE provides enrollment cards for enrollment-based plans. All eligibility is based on DEERS. Beneficiaries can verify their eligibility in DEERS by calling 1-800-538-9552. Providers

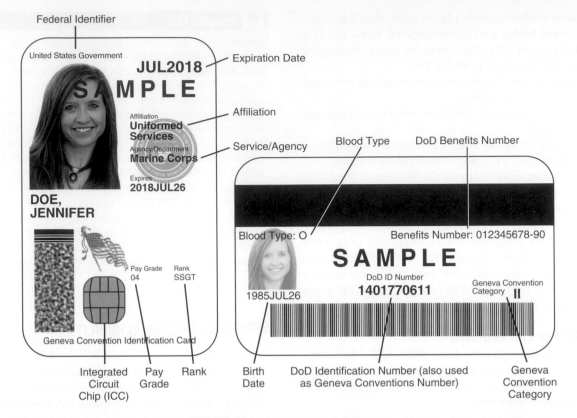

Federal Identifier

United States Government

JUL2018

Expiration Date

Affiliation
Uniformed Services

Affiliation

Agency/Department
Marine Corps

Service/Agency

Expires
2018JUL26

DOE, JENNIFER

Pay Grade 04

Rank SSGT

Geneva Convention Identification Card

Integrated Circuit Chip (ICC)

Pay Grade

Rank

Blood Type

DoD Benefits Number

Blood Type: O

Benefits Number: 012345678-90

DoD ID Number
1401770611

1985JUL26

Geneva Convention Category
II

Birth Date

DoD Identification Number (also used as Geneva Conventions Number)

Geneva Convention Category

Identification (ID) Card example

UNITED STATES UNIFORMED SERVICES

U.S. AIR FORCE

RANK / PAY GRADE
MSGT E8

EXPIRATION DATE
2018JUL26

SIGNATURE
Jennifer Doe

DoD ID NUMBER
1401770611

DOE, JENNIFER

IDENTIFICATION CARD

DATE OF BIRTH	WEIGHT	HEIGHT	HAIR COLOR	EYE COLOR
1985JUL26	125	68	BN	GN

DATE OF ISSUE	BLOOD T		EXP DATE
2017JUL26	O		2018JUL26

DD FORM   OCT 06   PROPERTY OF US GOVERNMENT

Fig. 12.3 Samples of military identification (ID) cards showing the use of Department of Defense (DoD) benefits numbers (DBNs). (From US Department of Defense, TRICARE, and Humana Military Healthcare Services.)

can verify the beneficiary's TRICARE eligibility online through the regional contractor's website (e.g., http://www.tricare-west.com, http://www.tricare-east.com/, or http://www.tricare-overseas.com) or through the interactive voice response (IVR) system at 1-877-TRICARE (1-877-874-2273). Use the sponsor's Social Security Number (SSN) or DoD benefits number (see discussion later) to verify eligibility. Patients must also present an eligibility letter that provides proof of current healthcare coverage under TRICARE. The health insurance professional can also log on to myTRICARE.com to access PGBA's secured portal to check eligibility. (PGBA is the acronym for Palmetto Government Business Administrators, based in South Carolina, which processes claims and provides customer service for much of the nation's TRICARE claims.)

If verification is performed online, the health insurance professional should retain a printout of the eligibility verification screen for the files.

Note: Providers have the right to collect out-of-pocket costs from beneficiaries before seeing the TRICARE patient, or they can file the claim first if that is the customary routine of the medical practice. Both the patient's EOB and the provider remittance will include copayment or cost-share amounts owed.

MILITARY IDENTIFICATION CARDS

To protect beneficiaries' privacy, the DoD had replaced the 9-digit SSN with an 11-digit DoD benefits number

(DBN). The DBN is composed of a unique family identifier number connected to the sponsor, a dash, and then a two-digit number identifiable to each family member. The number is printed on the back of the beneficiary's ID card above the barcode.

Beneficiaries who are dual eligible will have Medicare Part A and Part B and TRICARE. Military ID cards will be similar. An eligibility check will verify TRICARE coverage as secondary. If the ID card does not include a 9-digit sponsor SSN or an 11-digit DBN, ask the beneficiary to provide the two numbers. TRICARE cannot accept or "crosswalk" a 10-digit number in the Member ID field; this causes claims to be rejected. Numbers containing dashes also generate an error.

The transition from SSNs to DBNs on ID cards is expected to take several years, as cards are being replaced as they are renewed. During this period, you can verify eligibility and process claims using either the SSN or the DBN. Ask a beneficiary to provide his or her sponsor's SSN verbally or in writing as required by your office protocol.

Fig. 12.3 shows examples of military ID cards. Box 12.2 describes military ID cards and how to interpret the information on them.

? What Did You Learn?

1. How can TRICARE eligibility be verified?
2. Beneficiaries whose ID cards are expired must update their information in _____.
3. True or false: It is illegal to copy a TRICARE ID card.
4. Why were SSNs replaced with DBNs?

TRICARE PROVIDER TYPES

A **TRICARE provider** is defined as a person, business, or institution that renders healthcare services. There are many provider types; for example, physicians are individual providers, hospitals are institutional providers, and ambulance companies are corporate providers. A provider must be authorized under TRICARE regulations and certified by the TRICARE regional office. Table 12.4 provides an overview of TRICARE provider types.

Note: ADSMs and civilian employees of the federal government who are healthcare providers are generally not authorized to be TRICARE providers in civilian facilities. Only TRICARE-certified civilian providers may receive reimbursement from TRICARE.

TRICARE regional contractors are responsible for verifying a provider's authorized status. Beneficiaries who visit a provider who is not TRICARE authorized may be responsible for the full cost of care. Beneficiaries can contact their regional contractor to find a TRICARE-authorized provider.

Contracted TRICARE providers are obligated to abide by the rules, procedures, policies, and program requirements as specified in the *TRICARE Provider*

Box 12.2 Interpreting the Uniformed Services Identification Card

The Uniformed Services identification (ID) card incorporates a digital photographic image of the bearer, barcodes containing pertinent machine-readable data, and printed ID and entitlement information. The beneficiary category determines the ID card's color:

- Tan: Dependents of active duty and retired service members, 100% Veterans Affairs (VA) disabled veterans and their dependents, as well as Transitional Assistance Management Program (TAMP) beneficiaries
- Red: Retired reservists and dependents of reserve components
- Blue: Retired members of the US armed forces
- Green: Individual Ready Reserves and Inactive National Guard

ID CARD KEY FIELDS

- Department of Defense benefits number (DBN) or sponsor DBN.
  - Providers should use the DBN when verifying the card bearer's eligibility.
- Expiration date.
  - Check the expiration date. It should read "INDEF" (i.e., indefinite) for retirees. If the card is expired, the beneficiary must immediately update his or her information in the Defense Eligibility Enrollment Recording System (DEERS) and get a new card. Eligibility for TRICARE benefits will be determined by the eligibility response received from DEERS and not from the information on the ID card.
- Civilian.
  - Check the back of the ID card to verify eligibility for TRICARE civilian care. The center section of the card should read "YES" under the box titled "CIVILIAN."
  - Note: If a beneficiary using TRICARE For Life (TFL) has an ID card that reads "NO" in this block, the beneficiary is still eligible for TFL if he or she has both Medicare Part A and Medicare Part B coverage.

Handbook, which is a summary of the TRICARE regulations and manual requirements related to the program. TRICARE regulations are available on the Defense Health Agency (DHA) website at http://www.tricare.mil.

 HIPAA Tip

As required by the Health Insurance Portability and Accountability Act (HIPAA) Privacy Rule, provider offices and groups must train all workforce members as necessary to carry out their functions on policies and procedures related to personal health information (PHI). PHI is information created or received by a provider, health plan, or healthcare clearinghouse and can be in any format (electronic, paper, verbal).

Table 12.4	Overview of TRICARE Provider Types[a]

NETWORK PROVIDERS	NON-NETWORK PROVIDERS	
Regional contractors have established networks, even in areas far from military treatment facilities	• Do not have signed agreements with the regional contractor and therefore are considered "out of network" • There are two types: participating and nonparticipating	
TRICARE network providers: • Have signed agreements with the regional contractor to provide care • Agree to file claims and handle other paperwork for TRICARE beneficiaries • Are required to have malpractice insurance • Agree to accept the negotiated payment rate (less any copayments, cost-shares, or deductibles payable by the TRICARE beneficiary) as payment in full	Participating • May choose to participate on a claim-by-claim basis • Agree to accept payment directly from TRICARE and accept the TRICARE allowable charge as payment in full for their services	Nonparticipating • Do not agree to accept the TRICARE-allowable charge or file claims for TRICARE beneficiaries • Have the legal right to charge beneficiaries up to 15% above the TRICARE-allowable charge for services

"TRICARE" is a registered trademark of the Department of Defense, Defense Health Agency. All rights reserved.

[a]TRICARE-authorized providers meet state licensing and certification requirements and are certified by TRICARE to provide care to TRICARE beneficiaries. TRICARE-authorized providers include doctors, hospitals, ancillary providers (i.e., laboratory and radiology providers), and pharmacies. Beneficiaries are responsible for the full cost of care if they see providers who are not TRICARE authorized.

PROVIDER CERTIFICATION AND CREDENTIALING

At a minimum, TRICARE providers must be certified. PGBA conducts the certification process, which includes assigning a TRICARE ID number to the provider. (Being TRICARE certified allows accurate tax reporting to the Internal Revenue Service [IRS].) Providers who are TRICARE certified but have not signed a contract with the TRICARE regional contractor are considered **non-network providers**. Behavioral healthcare providers, skilled nursing facilities, providers in Alaska, and providers who are not Medicare certified must complete and submit certification forms in order for PGBA to process their claims.

In addition to becoming certified, providers interested in signing a contract and becoming a member of the TRICARE network must be credentialed by the TRICARE regional contractor. The credentialing process involves obtaining verification of the provider's education, board certification, license, professional background, malpractice history, and other pertinent data. A provider who is certified, credentialed, and has signed a contract is considered a network provider.

NETWORK AND NON-NETWORK PROVIDERS

Network providers are TRICARE-authorized providers who have signed an agreement with the regional contractors to provide care at prenegotiated rates—usually less than the TRICARE allowable charge—as the full fee for the services they render. In addition, network providers will file claims on the beneficiary's behalf.

Non-network providers are TRICARE-authorized providers who, although they must be certified, do not sign a contractual agreement with the TRICARE regional contractors. There are two types of non-network providers:

• PARs agree to file claims for beneficiaries, to accept payment directly from TRICARE, and to accept the TMAC as payment in full for their services. This is

referred to as **accepting assignment**. Hospitals that participate in Medicare, by law, must participate in TRICARE for inpatient care; however, hospitals may participate on a case-by-case basis for outpatient care. Individual providers may also participate on a case-by-case basis.

• NonPARs do not agree to accept the TRICARE allowable charge or file beneficiary claims, and they may charge up to 15% above the TMAC for services. Beneficiaries who receive care from nonPARs are responsible for those additional charges. A nonPAR may choose whether to file TRICARE claims for beneficiaries. In some cases, beneficiaries may be responsible for paying for services from a nonPAR first, then filing their own claims to receive reimbursement from TRICARE.

Beneficiaries may determine if their provider participates in TRICARE or if their provider is authorized by TRICARE by asking them, by contacting their regional contractor, or by visiting the TRICARE website at http://www.tricare.osd.mil.

When a provider signs a TRICARE Provider Agreement, the provider agrees to follow all contract requirements and all applicable TRICARE program requirements; for example:

• Provider agrees to accept the reimbursement rates (less the amount of any copayments, cost-shares, or deductibles payable by the beneficiary) as the full payment expected from TRICARE and beneficiaries for covered services and for all services paid for by the TRICARE program. (**Balance billing**—billing patients for any remaining amount left after deductibles, coinsurance, and insurance payment have been made—is not allowed.)

• Provider agrees to collect applicable copayments, cost-shares, or deductibles from TRICARE beneficiaries. Provider agrees not to require payment from a TRICARE beneficiary for any excluded service the TRICARE beneficiary received unless the

TRICARE beneficiary has been properly informed that the services are excludable and has agreed, in writing, in advance of receiving the services, to pay for such services.

> ### ? What Did You Learn?
>
> 1. Define and provide examples of a TRICARE provider.
> 2. Providers who are TRICARE certified but have not signed a contract with the TRICARE regional contractor are considered _____.
> 3. NonPARs do not agree to accept the TRICARE allowable charge or file beneficiary claims, and they may charge up to _____ above the TMAC for services.
> 4. True or false: A TRICARE PAR must accept the TRICARE allowable charge as payment in full and cannot balance-bill.

TRICARE BENEFICIARY COST-SHARING

Beneficiaries are responsible for cost-shares and deductibles for care that are covered under TRICARE Select. A **catastrophic cap (cat cap)** is the annual upper limit a family will have to pay for TRICARE Select–covered services in any fiscal year. The cat cap for ADFMs and a family using TRICARE Reserve Select is $1000; for all others it is $3000. The cat cap applies only to allowable charges for covered services—for example, annual deductibles, pharmacy copayments, enrollment fees and premiums, and other applicable cost-shares. It does not apply to services that are not covered or to the total amount of what nonPARs may

charge above the TRICARE allowable charge—the maximum amount TRICARE pays for each procedure or service, which is tied by law to Medicare's allowable charges for services.

Note: Point of service (POS) cost-shares and the POS deductible are not applied to the catastrophic cap.

Table 12.5 provides examples of cost-shares for families who use civilian providers and facilities under each of the three TRICARE options. Table 12.6 provides examples of cost-shares for retirees (younger than 65 years), their family members, and others. The cost-shares shown in Tables 12.5 and 12.6 were current as of this writing; however, cost-shares are subject to change every year. Changes in TRICARE fees have been proposed recently; however, at this writing, they have not been passed. It is important to keep current on TRICARE because changes may occur from year to year.

To view a summary of TRICARE beneficiary costs for other TRICARE programs, visit http://www.TRICARE.mil/costs.

TRICARE CODING AND PAYMENT SYSTEM

TRICARE follows the Centers for Medicare and Medicaid Services (CMS) annual coding and reimbursement updates for claims processing. TRICARE's fiscal year runs from October 1 to September 30, the same as CMS. Annual updates for the TMAC typically occur between February 1 and April 1. New codes are usually implemented on January 1 to align with the Medicare implementation of new Current Procedural Terminology (CPT) codes. Other code structures, such as Healthcare Common Procedure Coding System (HCPCS) codes, are subject to a quarterly update and can undergo code and pricing changes every 3 months during the fiscal year. To view the TRICARE fee schedule/reimbursement file,

Table 12.5 Cost-Shares for Families Using Civilian Providers or Facilities

	TRICARE PRIME	TRICARE SELECT
Annual deductible	None	$51/individual or $102/family for E-4 and below $154/individual or $308/family for E-5 and above
Annual enrollment fee	None	None
Outpatient visit: primary	No cost	Network: $15 Non-network: 20%
Outpatient visit: specialty	No cost	Network: $25 Non-network: 20%
Inpatient admission	No cost	Network: $61 Non-network: 20%
Inpatient mental health	No cost	Network: $61 Non-network: 20%
Civilian inpatient skilled nursing facility (SNF) care	No cost	Network: $25 Non-network: $51

Table 12.6 Cost-Shares for Retirees (<65 Years), Family Members, and Others

	TRICARE PRIME	TRICARE SELECT
Annual deductible	None	Network: $154/individual, $308/family Non-network: $308/individual, $616/family
Annual enrollment fee	$360/individual $720/family	$462/individual $924/family
Outpatient visit: primary	$20	Network: $25 Non-network: 25%
Outpatient visit: specialty	$30	Network: $41 Non-network: 25%
Emergency room visit	$61	Network: $82 Non-network: 25%
Inpatient cost-share	$154 per admission	Network: $179 per admission Non-network: 25%

which posts information on CMAC along with all other reimbursement methodologies defined for TRICARE, visit http://www.tricare.mil.

TRICARE Fact: TRICARE Provider News (published by the TMA) is a periodical that helps keep providers up to date on TRICARE.

◎ HIPAA Tip

Effective October 1, 2015, all healthcare providers, payers, clearinghouses, and billing services who use diagnosis and procedure codes for individuals covered by the Health Insurance Portability and Accountability Act (HIPAA), regardless of whether they file TRICARE or Medicare claims, must update to International Statistical Classification of Diseases and Related Health Problems, 10th revision (ICD-10).

❓ What Did You Learn?

1. True or false: Beneficiaries are responsible for cost-shares and deductibles for care that are covered under TRICARE Select.
2. The cat cap for families of ADSMs is _____ per year.
3. TRICARE's fiscal year runs from _____ to _____, the same as the fiscal year for CMS.

TRICARE CLAIMS PROCESSING

The designated contractor who processes medical claims for care received within a particular state or region is called a **claims processor**. In some regions, such contractors are called *TRICARE contractors* or *fiscal intermediaries (FIs)*. All claims processors have toll-free phone numbers to handle questions that a health insurance professional might have regarding TRICARE claims. It cannot be stressed enough that the health insurance professional should have the latest TRICARE handbook on file or should log on to the TRICARE website and download an electronic version of the handbook. In addition to the handbook, a file that has an up-to-date list of telephone numbers and addresses to assist claims processing should be kept. A website address for downloading a copy of the *TRICARE Provider Handbook* is included under "Websites to Explore" at the end of this chapter, or a hard copy can be requested from the TRICARE contractor in the region. Changes to TRICARE programs are continually made as public law and/or federal regulations are amended, so it is important to keep up to date.

WHO SUBMITS CLAIMS

If the patient is enrolled in TRICARE Prime or TRICARE Select and goes to a participating provider, the provider submits the claim.

Patients using TRICARE Select may be responsible for submitting their own claims to the appropriate claims processor, depending on the status of the provider. If the patient has access to the Internet, the appropriate form (Patient's Request for Medical Payment Form 2642) can be downloaded from the TRICARE website. It may be necessary first to download the Adobe Reader software. Instructions for downloading and installing the software are available on the website. If they receive care from nonPARs, TRICARE Select patients must file their own claims. In this case, the reimbursement check is sent to the patient, and it is his or her responsibility to ensure that the provider's bill is paid.

TRICARE requires that network providers file claims electronically with the appropriate Health Insurance Portability and Accountability Act (HIPAA)–compliant standard electronic claims format, but if a non-network provider must submit claims on paper, TRICARE requires that they be submitted on either a CMS-1500 (for professional charges) or a UB-04 (institutional charges) claim form.

PGBA, based in South Carolina, processes claims and provides customer service for about 65% of the nation's TRICARE claims for medical services. PGBA serves as a claims-processing subcontractor, administering the TRICARE West Region for Health Net Federal Services. In addition to TRICARE, PGBA processes Medicare Advantage claims.

❗ Stop and Think

Ruth Carson is a 36-year-old teacher and a TRICARE Select beneficiary. On March 30, she visits her family physician, Dr. Bennett, for a routine yearly examination. As Dr. Bennett's health insurance professional, you must advise Ruth that Dr. Bennett does not accept assignment on TRICARE claims and Ruth will have to file her own claim. Ruth asks you how to file the claim. What are your instructions?

SUBMITTING PAPER CLAIMS

TRICARE network providers are required to submit claims electronically. Non-network providers still have the option to submit paper claims; however, they are encouraged to consider the benefits of electronic filing options. Providers submitting paper claims should use the standard CMS-1500 claim form. As mentioned, patients who file their own claims must use Form 2642, which can be downloaded from the TRICARE website. If the patient files his or her own claim, the provider's detailed itemized statement and an NAS (if necessary) must be attached. Completed claims are sent to the TRICARE claims processor in the region in which the enrollee resides, rather than where the services were rendered. Beneficiaries may have to pay up front for services if they see a TRICARE-authorized non-network provider who chooses not to accept the TRICARE-allowable charge or file claims. In this case, TRICARE reimburses for the TRICARE-allowable charge, minus any deductible and cost-shares. Keep in mind that nonparticipating providers in the United States may charge up to 15% above the

TRICARE-allowable charge for services in addition to the deductible and cost-share, and the beneficiaries are responsible for this cost. Both stateside regional contractors provide a list of network and non-network providers on their websites. For more information, visit http://www.tricare.mil/costs.

An example of a TRICARE simple (no OHI) CMS-1500 (02/12) paper claim, along with step-by-step completion guidelines, can be found in Appendix B at the back of this book.

ELECTRONIC CLAIMS SUBMISSION

Like other third-party payers, TRICARE prefers claims to be filed electronically. The advantages to electronic claims filing include the following:

- Saves time by sending claims directly into the TRICARE processing system
- Saves money with no-cost or low-cost claims filing options
- Improves cash flow with faster payment turnaround
- Expedites claim confirmation—usually the next day with batch processing
- Reduces postage costs and mailing time
- Reduces paper handling
- Provides a better audit trail (the electronic media claims [EMC] response reports show which claims were accepted for processing and which were denied)

XPressClaim: This is a secure, fast, easy, and free online claims processing system available at http://www.myTRICARE.com. XPressClaim allows providers to submit single TRICARE claims electronically, bypassing a clearinghouse and going directly into the TRICARE system, eliminating time-consuming steps and opportunities for error. As a result, providers receive TRICARE payment much faster, usually within 5 to 15 days. Filing a TRICARE claim with XPressClaim is relatively easy if the provider is already a member of "myTRICARE Claims for Providers." If the provider submits no more than 150 claims a month, XPressClaim may be the best option.

eZ TRICARE: For uploading batches of TRICARE claims directly from a practice management system to the TRICARE claims contractor, eZ TRICARE is available from the Humana military website. With eZ TRICARE, there is no software to install, no data entry, and no cost to the provider. You do not have to rekey claims, but you must be able to create an EMC batch file or have a practice management system that creates print image files. eZ TRICARE can accept a variety of claims formats, including the latest HIPAA National Standard Format, as well as a CMS-1500 print file.

Claims clearinghouses: TRICARE contractors receive claims from a large number of EMC clearinghouses. If this is the preferred method of claims submission, the provider can contact the clearinghouse of choice to find out what is needed to send TRICARE claims to the appropriate contractor.

Electronic data interchange (EDI) Gateway: If the provider's system can create HIPAA-compliant claims formats and it is preferable to send claims directly to the payer, then PGBA's EDI Gateway may be the preferred choice. EDI Gateway can handle all inbound and outbound HIPAA-compliant EDI transactions.

DEADLINE FOR SUBMITTING CLAIMS

It is a good practice to submit TRICARE claims within 30 days from the date of services or as soon as possible after the care is rendered. According to PGBA, initial or new claims must be submitted within 1 year of the date of service; hospital claims must be submitted within 1 year of the date of discharge. The handbook for the West region, however, states that all claims must be submitted within 90 days of service. Therefore it is important to learn and follow the TRICARE claims processor's guidelines in the specific area in question. No payment is made for incomplete claims or claims submitted *more than 1 year* after services are rendered. (For overseas claims-filing addresses by area, visit http://www.tricare-overseas.com/contactus.) PARs are required to participate in Medicare (accept assignment) and submit claims on behalf of TRICARE and Medicare beneficiaries. It is important for TRICARE providers to adhere to specific guidelines in claims preparation to ensure smooth and timely processing and payment of claims.

The sooner the TRICARE contractor receives the claim forms and other papers, the sooner the claim is paid. If the claim covers several different medical services or supplies that were provided at different times, the previously mentioned 1-year deadline applies to each item on the claim. When a claim is submitted on time but the claims contractor returns it for more information, the claim must be resubmitted, along with the requested information, so that it is received by the contractor no later than 1 year after the medical services or supplies were provided, or 90 days from the date the claim was returned, whichever is later.

Medicare network providers must file TRICARE claims electronically even when a patient has OHI. Non-network providers are encouraged to take advantage of the electronic claims features.

For more information on claims processing, visit http://www.myTRICARE.com.

TRICARE EXPLANATION OF BENEFITS

After the claim is submitted and if there are no problems with it, the contractor sends a written notice—an EOB—to both the beneficiary and the provider showing the services performed and the adjudication (the process of an insurance carrier reviewing a claim and deciding on its payment). The EOB shows the following (Fig. 12.4):

- What the provider billed
- The TRICARE allowable charge at the time of care
- How much of the patient's annual deductible has been met

TRICARE *Explanation of Benefits*

PGBA or WPS
TRICARE Claims Administrator for Your Region

TRICARE EXPLANATION OF BENEFITS
This is a statement of the action taken on your TRICARE Claim.
Keep this notice for your records.

1*

3*

4*

2*

5*

Date of Notice:	August 02, 2020
Sponsor SSN:	000-00-0000
Sponsor Name:	NAME OF SPONSOR
Beneficiary Name:	NAME OF BENEFICIARY

7*

Benefits were payable to:

6*

PATIENT, PARENT/GUARDIAN
ADDRESS
CITY STATE ZIP CODE

PROVIDER OF MEDICAL CARE
ADDRESS
CITY STATE ZIP CODE

8*

Claim Number: 919533693-00-00

Services Provided By Date of Services	Services Provided	Amount Billed	TRICARE Approved	See Remarks
9*	10*	11*	12*	13*
PROVIDER OF MEDICAL CARE				
07/08/2020 1	Office/outpatient visit, est (99213)	$ 45.00	$ 38.92	1
07/08/2020 1	Comprehen metabolic panel (88054)	20.00	19.33	1
07/08/2020 1	Automated hemogram (85025)	12.00	12.00	1
Totals:		**$ 77.00**	**$ 70.25**	

Claim Summary	Beneficiary Liability Summary	Benefit Period Summary
	15*	16*

Fiscal Year Beginning:

Amount billed:	77.00	Deductible	0.00	October 01, 2016
TRICARE Approved:	70.25	Copayment:	0.00	
Non-Covered: 14*	6.75	Cost Share	17.56	
Paid by Beneficiary:	0.00			
Other Insurance:	0.00			
Paid to Provider:	52.69			
Paid to Beneficiary:	0.00			
Check Number:				

	Individual	Family
Deductible:	150.00	150.00

Catastrophic Cap:
Enrollment Year Beginning:
December 01, 2016

	Individual	Family
POS Deductible:	300.00	600.00
Prime Cap:		856.32

Remarks 17*

1 – CHARGES ARE MORE THAN ALLOWABLE AMOUNT

1-888-XXX-XXXX 18*

THIS IS NOT A BILL
If you have questions regarding this notice, please call or write us at the telephone number/address listed above.

1.   PGBA or WPS processes all TRICARE claims depending on the region where you live.

2.   Prime Contractor: The name and logo of the company that provides managed care support for the region where you live will appear here.

3.   Date of Notice: PGBA or WPS prepared your TRICARE Explanation of Benefits (TEOB) on this date.

4.   Sponsor SSN/Sponsor Name: Your claim is processed using the Social Security Number of the military service member (active duty, retired, or deceased) who is your TRICARE sponsor.

5.   Beneficiary Name: The patient who received medical care and for whom this claim was filed.

Fig. 12.4 TRICARE example of explanation of benefits. (From US Department of Defense.)

TRICARE Explanation of Benefits

6. Mail To Name and Address: We mail the TRICARE Explanation of Benefits (TEOB) directly to the patient (or patient's parent or guardian) at the address given on the claim. (HINT: Be sure your doctor has updated your records with your current address.)

7. Benefits Were Payable To: This field will appear only if your doctor accepts assignment. This means the doctor accepts the TRICARE Maximum Allowable Charge (TMAC) as payment in full for the services you received.

8. Claim Number: Each claim is assigned a unique number. This helps PGBA or WPS keep track of the claim as it is processed. It also helps them find the claim quickly whenever you call or write us with questions or concerns.

9. Service Provided By/Date of Services: This section lists who provided your medical care, the number of services and the procedure codes, as well as the date you received the care.

10. Services Provided: This section describes the medical services you received and how many services are itemized on your claim. It also lists the specific procedure codes that doctors, hospitals and labs use to identify the specific medical services you received.

11. Amount Billed: Your doctor, hospital, or lab charged this fee for the medical services you received.

12. TRICARE Approved: This is the amount TRICARE approves for the services you received.

13. See Remarks: If you see a code or a number here, look at the Remarks section (17) for more information about your claim.

14. Claim Summary: A detailed explanation of the action taken by PGBA or WPS taken on your claim is given here. You will find the following totals: amount billed, amount approved by TRICARE, non-covered amount, amount (if any) that you have already paid to the provider, amount your primary health insurance paid (if TRICARE is your secondary insurance), benefits we have paid to the provider, and benefits paid to the beneficiary by PGBA or WPS. A Check Number will appear here only if a check accompanies your TEOB.

15. Beneficiary Liability Summary: You may be responsible for a portion of the fee your doctor has charged. If so, you'll see that amount itemized here. It will include any charges that we have applied to your annual deductible and any cost-share or copayment you must pay.

16. Benefit Period Summary: This section shows how much of the individual and family annual deductible and maximum out-of-pocket expense you have met to date. If you are a TRICARE Standard or Extra beneficiary, PGBA or WPS calculates your annual deductible and maximum out-of-pocket expense by fiscal year. See the Fiscal Year Beginning date in this section for the first date of the fiscal year. If you are a TRICARE Prime beneficiary, we calculate your maximum out-of-pocket expense by enrollment and fiscal year. See Enrollment Year Beginning date in this section for the first date of your enrollment year. (Note: the Enrollment Year Beginning will appear on your TEOB only if you are enrolled in TRICARE Prime.)

17. Remarks Explanations of the codes or numbers listed in "See Remarks" will appear here.

18. Toll-Free Telephone Number: Questions about your TRICARE Explanation of Benefits? Please call PGBA or WPS at this toll-free number. Their customer service representatives will assist you.

Fig. 12.4—cont'd

- How much the patient has paid toward the annual cost cap
- The patient's cost-share for the care
- How much TRICARE paid
- Any reasons for denying services on a claim

Note: TRICARE beneficiaries can view their paperless TRICARE EOBs online by logging on to myTRICARE.com and accessing their account.

? What Did You Learn?

1. The designated contractor who processes medical claims for care received within a particular state or region is commonly called a _____.
2. True or false: Patients using TRICARE Select may be responsible for submitting their own claims.
3. List advantages of filing claims electronically.
4. Name two systems commonly used for submitting electronic claims.
5. What is the deadline for filing TRICARE claims?
6. List six items of information contained on a TRICARE EOB.

CHAMPVA

The **Civilian Health and Medical Program of the Department of Veterans Affairs (CHAMPVA)** is a federal healthcare benefits program administered by the Department of Veterans Affairs (VA). Established in 1973, it now provides services for nearly 400,000 qualifying dependents. CHAMPVA is a fee-for-service (indemnity) program. It provides reimbursement for most medical expenses—inpatient, outpatient, mental health, prescription drugs, skilled nursing care, and durable medical equipment (DME)—as well as a limited dental benefit (requires preauthorization) for spouse or widow(er) and the dependent children of veterans who are not TRICARE eligible. CHAMPVA covers most services and procedures that are considered medically necessary. Special rules and/or limitations do apply to certain services. Some services (even when prescribed by a physician) are not covered under CHAMPVA. Although similar in many ways, CHAMPVA is not the same as TRICARE. CHAMPVA is a VA-run program for eligible survivors and dependents, whereas TRICARE is a regionally run, DoD program serving ADSMs, retirees, and their families. In most cases, CHAMPVA pays at rates similar to TRICARE. CHAMPVA typically pays after Medicare and any other insurance have paid their portions.

CHAMPVA AND THE AFFORDABLE CARE ACT

The ACA, also known as *the healthcare law,* was created to expand access to coverage, control healthcare costs, and improve healthcare quality and care coordination. The healthcare law does not change VA health benefits or veterans' out-of-pocket costs. Individuals who are enrolled in any one of the three VA's programs—veterans' healthcare program, CHAMPVA, and the spina bifida program—meet the coverage standards of the law. CHAMPVA-eligible family members who are not enrolled in a VA healthcare program and who do not meet the healthcare law coverage standards should use the marketplace to get coverage. The marketplace remains available during non–open season periods for individuals who have a qualifying life event, such as getting married or having a baby. For more information about the marketplace, visit http://www.healthcare.gov or call 1-800-318-2596.

Beginning in 2016, the VA now sends the IRS, veterans, and eligible beneficiaries forms that provide details of the health coverage provided by VA. These forms are to be used for the income tax process. For more information about ACA and VA healthcare, visit the VA's website at https://www.va.gov/health/aca/ or call 1-877-222-VETS (8387).

CHAMPVA ELIGIBILITY

To be eligible for CHAMPVA, you must be ineligible for TRICARE and meet one of the following conditions:

* You are the spouse or child of a veteran who has been rated permanently and totally disabled for a service-connected disability by a VA regional office.
* You are the spouse or child of a veteran who died from VA-rated service-connected disability.
* You are the surviving spouse or child of a veteran who was 100% disabled at his or her time of death.
* You are the surviving spouse or child of a military member who died in the line of duty, not due to misconduct. (In most of these cases, these family members are eligible for TRICARE, not CHAMPVA.)

The CHAMPVA Dependent Coverage Extension Act allows the VA to extend coverage for veterans' dependents to the age of 26, up from the previous requirement age of 18, or 23 if a full-time student.

An eligible CHAMPVA sponsor may be entitled to receive medical care through the VA healthcare system based on his or her own veteran status. In addition, as the result of a recent policy change, if the eligible CHAMPVA sponsor is the spouse of another eligible CHAMPVA sponsor, both may now be eligible for CHAMPVA benefits. In each instance where the eligible spouse requires medical attention, he or she may choose the VA healthcare system or coverage under CHAMPVA for his or her healthcare needs. If an individual has been denied CHAMPVA benefits previously and believes that he or she would now be qualified, application can be made using the applicable CHAMPVA guidelines.

CHAMPVA Fact: There are no special requirements for foreign spouses or children of veteran sponsors to enroll in CHAMPVA. They must meet the same eligibility criteria as a US citizen beneficiary.

A change in social status, age, or other factors can affect a person's eligibility to receive CHAMPVA benefits. For example, eligibility can be lost if a widow(er) (younger than 55 years) remarries, the spouse divorces the sponsor, or a sponsor or family member becomes eligible for Medicare or TRICARE. Changes in status should be reported immediately to CHAMPVA, ATTN: Eligibility Unit, PO Box 469028, Denver, CO 80246-9028 or call 1-800-733-8387.

CHAMPVA Fact: CHAMPVA is managed by the VA's Health Administration Center (HAC) in Denver, Colorado.

CHAMPVA Fact: There is no cost to CHAMPVA beneficiaries when they receive healthcare treatment at a VA facility.

To see brochures and fact sheets on CHAMPVA eligibility requirements, as well as other information on the CHAMPVA program, go to https://www.va.gov/COMMUNITYCARE/pubs/factsheets.asp.

◎ HIPAA Tip

TRICARE and military treatment facilities (MTFs) are required to give health information about any individual to the US Department of Health and Human Services (HHS) for use in an investigation of a complaint.

❗ Stop and Think

Harold and Patsy Yates were divorced 12 years ago. Harold, a double-amputee Vietnam veteran, was rated by the regional VA office as having a permanent and total service-connected disability. Harold and Patsy are eligible for CHAMPVA; however, Patsy plans to remarry. How, if at all, would marriage affect her eligibility?

❗ Stop and Think

Suppose that Harold Yates had been killed in Vietnam, rather than disabled, and he and Patsy were married at the time of his death, which makes her eligible for CHAMPVA benefits. In this scenario, if Patsy remarries, how would the marriage affect her eligibility?

IDENTIFYING CHAMPVA-ELIGIBLE BENEFICIARIES

Every CHAMPVA-eligible family member is issued a member ID card that looks like the one shown in Fig. 12.5. The practice of displaying the beneficiary's SSN as the member number on the ID card has been discontinued due to the potential risk of identity theft. Note that the sample card in Fig. 12.5 shows that cards are now issued with the phrase "Patient SSN" in the member number space rather than the actual number being displayed. Patients who identify themselves as CHAMPVA beneficiaries should show their CHAMPVA ID, and health insurance professionals should take note of the effective dates on the card. If there is any question as to whether the patient is CHAMPVA eligible, call the VA Administration Center, CHAMPVA Eligibility, in Denver, Colorado. The toll-free number is listed in the CHAMPVA provider handbook. Eligibility can also be confirmed with the use of the CHAMPVA IVR system. CHAMPVA also accepts EDI requests to validate eligibility through its clearinghouse, Emdeon.

 HIPAA Tip

After the date for full compliance with the Health Insurance Portability and Accountability Act's (HIPAA's) final rule is issued by the US Department of Health and Human Services (HHS), the Health Administration Center (HAC) will accept only HIPAA-compliant ASC X12 5010 claims and transactions. The HAC will still maintain its electronic data interchange (EDI) payer IDs with Emdeon as 84146 for medical claims and 84147 for dental claims, and it will support all transactions listed earlier in the same manner.

 Imagine This!

Scott Talbott was an Army corporal stationed in Haiti in 2004 during a civil war. One evening, Scott and two other enlisted men went to a local bar. After an evening of drinking, they got into a brawl with a group of civilian townsmen. During the altercation, Scott sustained a knife wound to the chest and subsequently died of his injuries. Jenny Talbott, his widow, was informed that she and her three children were not eligible for CHAMPVA benefits because Scott's death was due to "misconduct." Jenny appealed but lost.

CHAMPVA BENEFITS

There is no fee for CHAMPVA enrollment, and beneficiaries pay no premiums. They pay only their share of medical expenses as they are incurred. CHAMPVA covers most medically necessary healthcare services, including:

- Ambulance
- Ambulatory surgery
- DME
- Family planning and maternity
- Hospice
- Inpatient services
- Mental health services
- Outpatient services
- Pharmacy
- Skilled nursing care
- Transplants

CHAMPVA pays for covered services and supplies when they are determined to be medically necessary and are received from an authorized provider. When providers perform services within the scope of their license or certification, CHAMPVA considers them to be authorized providers. Beneficiaries do *not* need to see a VA doctor—CHAMPVA covers visits to private providers as long as they are appropriately licensed. No prior approval is necessary for referrals to specialists or for diagnostic tests as long as they are considered medically necessary. Most Medicare providers will also accept CHAMPVA patients. CHAMPVA-eligible patients can go to the US Department of Veterans Affairs website at https://www.va.gov/COMMUNITYCARE/programs/dependents/locate_provider.asp to locate a provider in their area and ask if they also accept CHAMPVA patients.

By accepting assignment, a provider agrees to accept the CHAMPVA allowable amount as payment in full and cannot balance-bill for the difference between the billed amount and the CHAMPVA allowable amount. If a provider does not accept assignment and the beneficiary is informed of this before any services are rendered, the beneficiary is responsible for paying any provider-billed amount up front and then must file a claim to CHAMPVA himself or herself. For care that is not covered by CHAMPVA, the beneficiary pays the entire bill.

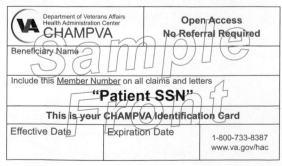

Fig. 12.5 Sample CHAMPVA member identification (ID) card. (From US Department of Veterans Affairs, Health Administration Center, CHAMPVA: *Fact sheet 01-16: for health care providers and office managers* [website]. http://www.va.gov/hac/factsheets/champva/FactSheet01-16.pdf.)

CHAMPVA BENEFICIARY COST-SHARING

Many veterans qualify for cost-free healthcare services on the basis of a service-connected condition or other qualifying factor. In the past, veterans were required to complete an annual financial assessment, or "means test," to determine whether they qualify for cost-free services; however, the VA has discontinued this requirement for enrolled veterans, which eliminates the veteran's annual reporting burden. Along with their enrollment confirmation and priority group assignment, enrollees will receive information regarding their copayment requirements, if applicable.

Beneficiary cost-share (copayment) for professional services is a percentage of the CHAMPVA allowable amount rather than a specific, predetermined dollar amount. There is an annual deductible for covered outpatient medical services and supplies, which is $50 per beneficiary or a maximum of $100 per year per family. After the annual deductible is met, CHAMPVA pays 75% of the allowable amount. There is no deductible for inpatient services, ambulatory surgery, psychiatric day programs, and hospice service provided in VA CHAMPVA In-house Treatment Initiative (CITI) (see discussion later) facilities, or for medications received through the Meds by Mail program.

To provide financial protection against a potential financial crisis of a long-term illness or serious injury, CHAMPVA has established an annual cat cap of $3000 per calendar year. This is the maximum out-of-pocket expense that a beneficiary or a family can incur in 1 year for CHAMPVA-covered services. After the $3000 limit is reached, copayments for covered services are waived for the remainder of the calendar year, and CHAMPVA pays 100% of the allowable amount. Table 12.7 is a cost summary showing what beneficiaries must pay when they have no OHI. Table 12.8 is a cost summary of cost-sharing with OHI. Cost-shares are subject to annual changes.

? What Did You Learn?

1. True or false: The Affordable Care Act drastically changed the health benefits and out-of-pocket costs for veterans.
2. The CHAMPVA Dependent Coverage Extension Act allows the VA to extend coverage for a veteran's dependents to age _____.
3. True or false: There is no fee for CHAMPVA enrollment, and beneficiaries pay no premiums.
4. CHAMPVA pays for covered services and supplies when they are determined to be _____ and are received from a(n) _____.
5. After the CHAMPVA beneficiary's annual deductible is met, CHAMPVA pays _____ of the allowable amount.
6. CHAMPVA has an annual cat cap of _____.

Table 12.7 | Beneficiary Cost-Sharing With No Other Health Insurance

BENEFITS	DEDUCTIBLE	PATIENT/MEMBER PAYS
Ambulatory surgery	No	25% of CHAMPVA allowable amount
Durable medical equipment (DME)	Yes	25% of CHAMPVA allowable amount
Emergency room charges	Depends (on whether the emergency care becomes part of inpatient charges or remains an outpatient charge)	The charges will be included in the inpatient charge if, once stabilized, the patient is admitted to the hospital. The payment will then be based on "inpatient services." If the patient is not admitted, the payment is based on "outpatient services."
Inpatient Mental Health		
High-volume residential treatment centers	No	25% of CHAMPVA allowable amount
Low-volume treatment center	No	Lesser of (1) per-day amount times the number of inpatient days or (2) 25% of billed amount
Inpatient Services		
Diagnosis-related group (DRG)–based	No	Lesser of (1) per-day amount times the number of inpatient days, (2) 25% of billed amount, or (3) DRG rate
Non–DRG-based	No	25% of CHAMPVA allowable amount
Outpatient services (e.g., doctor visits, laboratory/radiology, home health, mental health services, skilled nursing visits, ambulance)	Yes	25% of CHAMPVA allowable amount after deductible is met
Pharmacy services (mail order— Meds by Mail or CITI)	No	Nothing
Pharmacy services (retail)	Yes	25% of CHAMPVA allowable amount
Professional services	Yes	25% of CHAMPVA allowable amount after deductible is met

Table 12.8   Beneficiary Cost-Sharing With Other Health Insurance

SERVICE	OHI PAYS	CHAMPVA PAYS	PATIENT/MEMBER PAYS
All medical services and supplies that are covered by both the OHI and CHAMPVA	Their plan allowable	What is owed up to the CHAMPVA allowable amount	In most cases, $0
Medical services covered by the OHI and *not* covered by CHAMPVA	Their plan allowable	$0	The OHI plan copayment
Medical services *not* covered by the OHI but covered by CHAMPVA (Note: Does *not* pay for services that were determined to be noncovered by the OHI because there was a failure to follow the OHI plan requirements.)	$0	The CHAMPVA allowable amount	The cost-share for the type of service

CHAMPVA, Civilian Health and Medical Program of the Department of Veterans Affairs; *OHI*, other health insurance.

CHAMPVA PROGRAM OPTIONS AND BENEFITS

The following subsections provide a brief description of some of the other programs available under CHAMPVA.

NON-VA MEDICAL CARE PROGRAM

Non-VA medical care is provided to eligible veterans by community-based providers when those services are not "feasibly" available from a VA medical facility. The use of non-VA medical care is governed by federal laws covering eligibility criteria and other policies specifying when and in what situations it can be used. An authorization for treatment in the community is required for non-VA medical care, unless the medical event is an emergency. Costs resulting from emergency events may be reimbursed on behalf of the veteran in certain cases.

IN-HOUSE TREATMENT INITIATIVE

CITI (pronounced "city") is a voluntary program that allows the CHAMPVA beneficiary to be treated at participating VA medical centers with no out-of-pocket cost. Each VA medical center that participates in the CITI program offers different services based on unused capacity. CHAMPVA beneficiaries who are also covered by Medicare cannot participate in the CITI program because Medicare does not pay for services provided by a VA medical center. The VA CITI program does not require authorization. Not all medical centers participate in the CITI program. The decision to participate is made by the medical center's director.

PROGRAM FOR THE PRIMARY FAMILY CAREGIVER

This is a healthcare benefits program in which the VA shares the cost of certain healthcare services and supplies with a veteran's primary family caregiver who is not entitled to care or services under another health plan, including Medicare, Medicaid, Indian Health Insurance, Consolidated Omnibus Budget Reconciliation Act (COBRA), workers' compensation, or TRICARE. The Chief Business Office Purchased Care (CBOPC) is responsible for (1) the administration of primary family caregiver benefits; (2) enrolling the eligible primary family caregiver into CHAMPVA when there is no OHI coverage; (3) processing healthcare claims for eligible primary family caregivers under CHAMPVA; (4) processing reconsiderations; and (5) providing customer service support to primary family caregivers.

FOREIGN MEDICAL PROGRAM

The Foreign Medical Program (FMP) is a healthcare benefits program for US veterans with VA-rated, service-connected disabilities who are residing or traveling abroad (Canada and Philippines excluded). Under FMP, the VA assumes payment responsibility for certain necessary medical services associated with the treatment of those service-connected conditions.

VETERANS AFFAIRS DENTAL INSURANCE PROGRAM

A relatively new dental insurance program is available to any veteran enrolled in VA healthcare or any individual enrolled in CHAMPVA. In 2013 the US government authorized a national voluntary dental insurance program for eligible VA beneficiaries. (Dependents who do not qualify as a CHAMPVA beneficiary are not eligible.) Delta Dental began enrolling eligible VA beneficiaries in its Veterans Affairs Dental Insurance Program (VADIP) program on January 1, 2014. VADIP offers cost-effective dental coverage with three plan options designed to meet the various needs of VA beneficiaries: Standard Plan, Enhanced Plan, and Comprehensive Plan. A link to the website where you can find a benefits booklet that applies to all three VADIP plans (except where otherwise specified) is included under "Websites to Explore" at the end of this chapter.

PRESCRIPTION DRUG BENEFIT

CHAMPVA offers a more cost-effective prescription drug benefit than Medicare Part D, and there is no monthly premium. If CHAMPVA beneficiaries receive their maintenance medications through the CHAMPVA Meds by Mail program and do not routinely use a local pharmacy, their prescriptions will continue to be provided free of charge and delivered directly to their homes.

A website that enables you to view a comparison chart of prescription drug coverages under Medicare, CHAMPVA, and TRICARE is listed under "Websites to Explore" at the end of this chapter.

If there is any question about whether a particular service is payable under CHAMPVA guidelines, the health insurance professional should consult the most recent CHAMPVA handbook, contact the VA HAC using the toll-free phone number, or go to https://www.va.gov/COMMUNITYCARE/programs/dependents/champva/index.asp and follow the directions for submitting an email via the VA's Inquiry Routing and Information System (IRIS). Fact sheets that provide a wealth of information for keeping up to date on CHAMPVA can be viewed at and downloaded from the VA website.

Meds by Mail Program

Prescription medications by mail (Meds by Mail) are free to 100% disabled veterans and their dependent family members who do not have prescription drug insurance. (This includes Medicare Part D.) There are no copayments, no deductibles, and no claims to file. Medications are mailed to the beneficiary's home using a mail-order prescription service. Physicians are requested to prescribe up to a 90-day supply with up to three refills, if possible. However, certain medications may have a 30-day supply limit. CHAMPVA is considered a "creditable prescription drug plan." Medicare Part D (drug program) has no impact on CHAMPVA eligibility; however, individuals who enroll in Part D will not be able to participate in CHAMPVA's Meds by Mail program. Over-the-counter medications are not covered under Meds by Mail.

VETERANS COMMUNITY CARE PROGRAM

The Veterans Access, Choice and Accountability Act of 2014 created the VA Choice Program to provide improved healthcare access and meet the short-term healthcare needs of the nation's veterans. This program allows eligible veterans to elect to receive healthcare from providers in their communities, eliminating a long wait for an appointment at a VA facility. This program has some struggles providing the care needed, and in June 2019 the VA Mission Act of 2018 replaced it with Veterans Community Care Program. The Mission Act's goal is to expand the options to access healthcare for our veterans. If a certain type of service isn't provided by the VA, the veteran may be able to go to a non-VA provider, using VA coverage. For more information on the Veterans Community Care Program, visit https://www.va.gov/COMMUNITYCARE/programs/veterans/index.asp.

DURABLE MEDICAL EQUIPMENT BENEFIT

If a CHAMPVA-eligible beneficiary needs special equipment, such as a hospital bed or a wheelchair, and he or she can prove that it is medically necessary, CHAMPVA will share in its cost. If the equipment is obtained through a VA source, such as a VA medical facility, there is no cost. Getting DME, however, requires a preauthorization from the VA if the cost is $2000 or more to rent or buy.

SERVICES REQUIRING PREAUTHORIZATION

Under CHAMPVA, certain types of care and services require advance approval, commonly known as *preauthorization*. Preauthorization is very important, and failure to obtain it may result in denial of the claim. Preauthorization is required for:

- DME with a purchase price or total rental price of $2000 or more
- Hospice services
- Mental health or substance abuse services
- Organ and bone marrow transplants
- Dental procedures that are directly related to covered medical conditions

When Medicare is the primary payer and authorizes a service typically requiring CHAMPVA preauthorization, CHAMPVA does not require authorization for those same services.

SUMMARY OF CHAMPVA COSTS

To recap CHAMPVA costs, beneficiaries pay nothing to have it; they pay only when they use it, and then payment goes to the provider—not to the veteran. Qualifying services include (but are not limited to) inpatient, outpatient, mental healthcare, substance abuse, prescription medication, and hospice. Veterans have the freedom to receive care from any qualified provider. Out-of-pocket costs include:

- Annual deductible: $50 individual, $100 family
- Cost-share (or copayment) up to the annual cat cap—beneficiary pays 25% of allowable charges, unless care is provided by the VA, such as CITI and Meds by Mail, where CHAMPVA pays 100%
- $3000 annual cat cap
- Any premium paid on OHI coverage, such as a CHAMPVA supplement

There is no deductible for inpatient services, ambulatory surgery services, psychiatric day programs, hospice services, or services provided by VA medical facilities such as CITI and Meds by Mail.

CHAMPVA Fact: Beneficiaries do *not* need to see a VA doctor; CHAMPVA covers visits to private providers as long as they are appropriately licensed. No prior approval is necessary for referrals to specialists or for diagnostic tests as long as they are considered medically necessary.

Long-Term Care

Long-term care, also known as **custodial care**—assistance with activities of daily living (ADLs), such as bathing, dressing, and feeding, or supervision of those who are cognitively impaired—is not a covered

CHAMPVA benefit. Long-term care can be provided in nursing homes, assisted living facilities, adult day care, or a patient's home. Long-term care insurance is sold by private insurance companies and usually covers medical and nonmedical care to help an individual with personal needs such as bathing, dressing, using the bathroom, and eating. Most policies also help with the costs of custodial (nursing home or assisted living) care.

> **! Stop and Think**
>
> Elaine Porter is employed by Harper Products, Inc. She has single coverage under her employer's group healthcare plan. Elaine's husband, a helicopter pilot, was killed when his Chinook helicopter was shot down by an air-to-ground missile during Desert Storm. Because Elaine also is covered under CHAMPVA, which payer in this case would be primary?

TERMINATING CHAMPVA BENEFITS

Benefits will be revoked when the VA HAC receives proof of changes in status resulting in ineligibility. Examples include a divorce certificate between the veteran and spouse, marriage certificate of an eligible child or widow(er) who remarries before age 55, proof of TRICARE eligibility, or death certificate of the beneficiary. Such documents must be sent to the VA Regional Office, as appropriate.

CHAMPVA–TRICARE CONNECTION

Even though CHAMPVA and TRICARE are similar and are both federal healthcare programs, an individual who is eligible for TRICARE is not eligible for CHAMPVA. TRICARE provides coverage to the families of ADSMs, families of service members who died while on active duty, and retirees and their families, whether or not the veterans are disabled. CHAMPVA provides benefits to eligible family members of veterans who officially have been declared 100% permanently disabled from service-connected conditions, eligible survivors of veterans who died from service-connected conditions, and survivors of service members who died in the line of duty who are not otherwise entitled to TRICARE benefits.

HEALTH PLANS PRIMARY TO CHAMPVA

The following list includes (but is not necessarily limited to) other health insurance programs that are primary to CHAMPVA. Unless the beneficiary is covered under one of the following plans, CHAMPVA is the primary payer:

- State Crime Victims Compensation program
- Indian Health Service
- Workers' compensation claim
- Injury due to automobile accident

It is important to note that CHAMPVA does not pay for medical care for the treatment of a work-related illness or injury when benefits are available under a workers' compensation program. In such cases, the individual must apply for workers' compensation benefits. After workers' compensation benefits are exhausted, CHAMPVA will then pay for covered services and supplies. Beneficiaries must provide a copy of the final decision of the workers' compensation claim to avoid any delay in payment of future claims.

Another exception to third-party payer priority is when a CHAMPVA-eligible beneficiary resides or travels overseas. When this is the case, if all eligibility criteria are met, CHAMPVA is the primary payer (unless there is OHI) until the individual returns to the United States. In all other cases, CHAMPVA is the secondary payer. In the case of OHI, either the provider or the beneficiary must file a claim first with the OHI. After receiving an EOB from the primary insurer, a claim may be filed with CHAMPVA for any balance remaining. The EOB from the primary insurer, as well as the provider's itemized statement, must accompany the CHAMPVA claim. Table 12.9 is a cost summary of how CHAMPVA pays if the beneficiary has OHI. CHAMPVA beneficiaries living or traveling overseas (excluding the countries of Iraq, North Korea, and Cuba) have the same benefits as if the service was provided in the United States. Deductibles and cost-shares are also the same as in the United States. Reimbursement for healthcare claims in foreign countries is based on reasonable and customary billed amounts. Claims submitted in English are processed faster because they do not need to be translated. If the billing and/or medical documentation is written in a foreign language,

Table 12.9	Cost Summary of Other Health Insurance and CHAMPVA		
SERVICE	**OHI PAYS**	**CHAMPVA PAYS**	**YOU PAY**
All medical services and supplies that are covered by both the OHI and CHAMPVA	Their plan allowable	What you owe up to the CHAMPVA allowable amount	$0 (in most cases)
Medical services covered by your OHI and *not* covered by CHAMPVA	Their plan allowable	$0	Your OHI plan copayment
Medical services *not* covered by your OHI but covered by CHAMPVA	$0	The CHAMPVA allowable amount	Your cost-share for the type of service

CHAMPVA, Civilian Health and Medical Program of the Department of Veterans Affairs; *OHI*, other health insurance.

translation will be arranged at no cost to the beneficiary. Payment is made in US dollars.

Changes in coverage must be reported to the CHAMPVA office in Denver, Colorado, on VA Form 10-7959c. When submitting this form, the patient or health insurance professional should include a copy of the OHI copayment information or schedule of benefits. A copy of VA Form 10-7959c can be downloaded from https://www.va.gov/vaforms/medical/pdf/10-7959c.pdf.

CHAMPVA SUPPLEMENT PLANS

A number of companies offer CHAMPVA supplemental policies. After CHAMPVA makes a payment for healthcare services, the remaining out-of-pocket expenses (deductibles and copayments) often are payable by the supplemental insurance policy. If the CHAMPVA beneficiary has a policy that was specifically obtained for the purpose of supplementing CHAMPVA, CHAMPVA will compute the allowable amount and pay the claim, and then the beneficiary can submit the balance due on the claim to the supplemental insurer. Further information about supplemental health plans can be obtained from https://champva.us/.

American Military Retirees Association (AMRA) CHAMPVA Supplement Plan

The AMRA CHAMPVA Supplement Plan, when combined with CHAMPVA benefits, is designed to provide beneficiaries with additional protection by paying the cost-share for both covered inpatient and outpatient medical expenses after the calendar year plan deductible ($250 per person, $500 family maximum) is satisfied (Table 12.10). AMRA Supplement pays after CHAMPVA has paid its portion of the claim. This coverage is available to AMRA members and their dependents only.

CHAMPVA–MEDICARE CONNECTION

When a beneficiary is eligible for healthcare benefits under both Medicare and CHAMPVA, Medicare is the primary payer. When Medicare, as the primary payer, authorizes a service, CHAMPVA does not require authorization for those same services.

Medicare status has an impact on eligibility for CHAMPVA benefits. Medicare automatically enrolls most eligible beneficiaries 90 days before their 65th birthday. When the individual receives his or her Medicare card indicating enrollment in Medicare Part A and Part B coverage, a copy of the card must be sent immediately to CHAMPVA (along with the CHAMPVA OHI form, VA Form 10-7959c) so that CHAMPVA benefits can continue without interruption.

When an individual has eligibility for both Medicare and CHAMPVA, billing for healthcare services must be sent first to Medicare and any Medicare Supplement plans (usually referred to as *Medigap plans*) before the bill is sent to CHAMPVA. The claim can be submitted to CHAMPVA after Medicare and any supplement policy pays its portion of the bill. CHAMPVA then processes the remaining portion of the bill when the provider's bill, along with the EOB from Medicare and Medicare Supplemental plans (if applicable), is received.

In most cases, Medicare/CHAMPVA dual coverage results in no out-of-pocket expenses for the individual, and a supplement plan is unnecessary. CHAMPVA does not pay Medicare Part B premiums, however. It is important for the beneficiary to be aware that if he or she has Medicare and CHAMPVA, Medicare's rules and procedures must be followed for covered services. Failure to follow them means that the service would not be covered under CHAMPVA. If Medicare determines that the service is not medically necessary or appropriate, CHAMPVA also will deny coverage. If the beneficiary or the provider disagrees with the Medicare decision, an appeal should be made with Medicare rather than with CHAMPVA. In most cases, beneficiaries who are eligible for Medicare Part A must enroll in Part B also in order to have CHAMPVA eligibility. Individuals not covered under the TRICARE program who purchase Medicare Part B become eligible for CHAMPVA as of the effective date of the Medicare Part B coverage.

Table 12.10   AMRA Supplement Payment Chart

COVERED CARE REQUIRED	CHAMPVA PAYS	CHAMPVA SUPPLEMENT PLAN PAYS
Inpatient services: Confinement in civilian hospital or skilled nursing facility	DRG rate, less the beneficiary cost-share	The lesser of (a) $535 per day times number of inpatient days, (b) 25% of the billed amount, or (c) the DRG rate
Inpatient services: Non-DRG based	75% of the allowable amount	25% of the allowable amount
Inpatient physician services: Visits, surgeons, anesthesiologist, etc.	75% of the allowable amount	25% of the allowable amount
Outpatient services: Office visits, clinics, laboratory and pharmacy services, durable medical equipment (non-VA source)	75% of the allowable amount, after the CHAMPVA annual outpatient deductible	25% of the allowable amount

AMRA, American Military Retirees Association; *CHAMPVA,* Civilian Health and Medical Program of the Department of Veterans Affairs; *DRG,* diagnosis-related group; *VA,* Veterans Affairs.

Stop and Think

Eighty-year-old Jefferson Cabot just became permanently and totally disabled from a service-connected injury. Betty, his wife, is 70 years old, and Betty has Medicare Part A but not Part B. Is Betty eligible for Civilian Health and Medical Program of the Department of Veterans Affairs (CHAMPVA)?

CHAMPVA enrollees who are 65 or over and live overseas must be enrolled in Medicare Part B, even though Medicare does not provide benefits for medical care received overseas. CHAMPVA is the primary payer for the benefits, and beneficiaries will receive the same level of coverage provided to those under age 65.

CHAMPVA Fact: All hospitals that participate in Medicare and hospital-based healthcare professionals who are employed by or contracted to such hospitals are required by law to accept CHAMPVA for inpatient hospital services.

Individuals who are eligible for Medicare Part A also (in most cases) need Medicare Part B to be eligible for CHAMPVA, depending on certain circumstances as follows:

- Individuals who are under age 65 and eligible for Medicare Part A (to include the end-stage renal disease [ESRD] program) must always have Medicare Part B.
- Individuals who are over age 65 and were never eligible for premium-free Medicare Part A do not need Part B.
- Individuals who were eligible for CHAMPVA after June 5, 2001, regardless of their age when they became eligible, must have Medicare Part B.
- Individuals who were over age 65 and eligible for CHAMPVA when the law changed in 2001 to allow CHAMPVA benefits to continue secondary to Medicare might have been "grandfathered in." That means that for individuals who were CHAMPVA eligible as of June 5, 2001, and had only Medicare Part A, the law states that they could continue with CHAMPVA after that date and they did not have to purchase Part B. If they had purchased Part B, however, they could not discontinue their enrollment in it.

Individuals who have Medicare Part B should not cancel it. When Medicare Part B coverage is canceled, eligibility for CHAMPVA benefits will end on the same date Part B coverage ends.

CHAMPVA Fact: CHAMPVA beneficiaries with Medicare cannot use a VA medical center under the CITI program, because Medicare will not pay the VA medical center for the services it provides. If a patient is currently being seen at a VA medical center but will become entitled to Medicare soon, he or she will need to find a different provider.

CHAMPVA AND HMO COVERAGE

If a CHAMPVA-eligible beneficiary has an HMO or preferred provider organization (PPO) plan, CHAMPVA pays any copayments required under the HMO or PPO plan for CHAMPVA-covered services up to the CHAMPVA allowable amount. When medical services are available through the HMO or PPO and the patient chooses to seek care outside the HMO or PPO (e.g., the patient visits a physician who is not associated with the HMO or PPO or does not follow the rules and procedures of the HMO or PPO plan), CHAMPVA will not pay for that care. Likewise, if the beneficiary has Medicare and chooses to receive care from a provider who does not accept Medicare patients, CHAMPVA will not pay. It is very important that the beneficiary follow the primary payer's guidelines when visiting a HMO or PPO network or PARs.

CHAMPVA POLICY ON BALANCE BILLING

Healthcare providers may elect to participate in CHAMPVA simply by agreeing to see the beneficiary and submitting a claim to CHAMPVA on the beneficiary's behalf. As discussed previously, providers who accept CHAMPVA patients also must accept the CHAMPVA allowable rate as payment in full and cannot balance-bill. If the provider chooses not to participate in CHAMPVA—doesn't accept assignment—the patient is obligated to pay the remainder after CHAMPVA has paid its cost-share (75% of the allowable amount). Providers who do not accept assignment may not be willing to submit claims on the beneficiary's behalf. When this is the case, the beneficiary must submit his or her own claim using VA Form 10-7959a. This form can be downloaded from http://www.va.gov/vaforms/.

CHAMPVA Fact: Under CHAMPVA, the patient is responsible for paying the CHAMPVA cost-share and any charges for noncovered services.

CHAMPVA FOR LIFE

The **CHAMPVA for Life (CFL)** program became effective on October 1, 2001. CFL is not separate from CHAMPVA; it is simply an extension of benefits to certain individuals over age 65. CFL serves as the secondary payer to minimize out-of-pocket expenses by covering Medicare's coinsurance and deductibles. Like most health insurance, CFL is not long-term care insurance, but it will cover some of the costs. In addition, it does not pay for custodial care. Much like Medigap insurance, CFL picks up where Medicare leaves off. CFL pays the coinsurance and deductibles but does not pay for the monthly Medicare Part B premium. TFL enrollees do not receive cash or checks from CFL. Benefits cover only medical services and are paid directly to the providers.

CFL does pay for skilled nursing care up to a limit. As with Medicare, there must be a medical condition that was treated in a hospital for 3 consecutive days, and the beneficiary must be admitted to a skilled nursing facility (SNF) within 30 days after hospitalization

Table 12.11	Beneficiary Cost-Shares With Medicare and CHAMPVA For Life			
COVERAGE DAYS	**MEDICARE**	**CFL**	**BENEFICIARY**	
Day 1–20	100%	0%	0%	
Day 20–100	80%	20%	0%	
Day 100+	0%	75%	25%	

CFL, CHAMPVA for Life; *CHAMPVA*, Civilian Health and Medical Program of the Department of Veterans Affairs.

for CFL to be activated. Medicare has a 100-day limit on skilled nursing, after which CFL is the primary payer; however, it does not cover the full amount. The beneficiary should expect to pay a copayment (Table 12.11). Note: CFL beneficiaries cannot use a VA medical center.

CHAMPVA for Life Eligibility

The spouses of veterans must be at least 65 years old to be eligible for CFL. Seniors who turned age 65 before June 5, 2001, need only Medicare Part A to be eligible. Those turning age 65 after that date need both Medicare Parts A and B. The spouse of a veteran qualifies if the veteran meets one of the following conditions:

- Has a service-connected disability rating of 100%, meaning that he or she is permanently and totally disabled or died with that rating
- Has died from a VA-rated service-connected disability
- Has died in the line of duty (does not qualify if eligible for TRICARE)
- Cannot have been dishonorably discharged

A spouse loses eligibility for CFL if he or she divorces the veteran. A widow(er) who remarries also loses eligibility; however, if the remarriage terminates, that person's eligibility is reinstated.

CFL provides benefits if a son or daughter is determined to be a "helpless child" by a VA regional office and if he or she also meets all other eligibility criteria.

CHAMPVA for Life and Medicare

If a service or procedure is covered by both Medicare and CFL, the beneficiary usually will have no out-of-pocket expense.

Medicare usually does not pay for services overseas; therefore CFL will pay for those services after any OHI and/or the beneficiary have paid their share. If there is no OHI, then CFL becomes the primary payer.

Because CHAMPVA does not have an annual deductible for inpatient care, they will cover the Medicare deductible that is paid by the beneficiary. However, CFL does not pay for Medicare Part B premiums.

CHAMPVA Fact: CFL is always the last payer after the claims are paid by Medicare and any OHI.

What Did You Learn?

1. Explain the CITI program.
2. True or false: Prescription medications by mail (Meds by Mail) are free to 100% disabled veterans and their dependent family members who do not have prescription drug insurance.
3. List several types of services that require preauthorization under CHAMPVA.
4. In general, CHAMPVA covers ___% of most healthcare services and supplies that are medically or psychologically necessary.
5. Name CHAMPVA's two cost-sharing responsibilities for outpatient services.
6. What is CHAMPVA's annual cat cap?
7. True or false: An individual can have both TRICARE and CHAMPVA coverage.
8. List four plan types that are primary to CHAMPVA.
9. When a beneficiary is eligible for both Medicare and CHAMPVA, _____ is the primary payer.

FILING CHAMPVA CLAIMS

As with TRICARE, providers accepting assignment for CHAMPVA claims must submit the claim for the beneficiary. Beneficiaries who receive treatment from providers who do not accept assignment usually are required to submit their own claims. When this is the case, the beneficiary should use the CHAMPVA Claim Form, VA Form 10-7959a (available by phone or online at http://www.va.gov/vaforms). All CHAMPVA paper claims should be sent to VA HAC, CHAMPVA, PO Box 469064, Denver, CO 80246-9064.

As stated earlier, if the beneficiary has OHI, claims should be sent to the OHI first. The EOB from the OHI should then be attached to the claim and submitted to CHAMPVA.

CHAMPVA Fact: By law, CHAMPVA is always the secondary payer except to Medicaid and CHAMPVA supplemental policies.

As with TRICARE claims, the status of claims can be checked electronically via the VA HAC's 24-hour IVR system at 1-800-733-8387. A website that lists step-by-step instructions for using IVR is provided under "Websites to Explore" at the end of this chapter. Details on payment methodology and covered benefits for CHAMPVA health plans are covered in the policy manuals on the CHAMPVA website.

ELECTRONIC CLAIMS

The most efficient way to file a claim for CHAMPVA is electronically. The HAC accepts electronically submitted 837 claim transactions, including the 837 Institutional, 837 Professional, and 837 Dental transactions. Transactions are accepted from providers for medical services and supplies provided in the United States, a US commonwealth, or the territories. Providers must submit electronic claims through the clearinghouse Emdeon. Medical claim status and eligibility status also can be checked electronically through Emdeon using the 276 and 270 HIPAA transactions. A provider that is not connected to Emdeon should ask their clearinghouse whether CHAMPVA payer IDs have been added to their system. CHAMPVA also accepts paper claims using the CMS-1500 claim form, but the turnaround time to payment is, on average, an additional 20 days.

Claims sent to Medicare via EDI may be electronically forwarded to the HAC for those CHAMPVA beneficiaries who have Medicare Parts A and B. The provider's valid health insurance claim number must be on file with the HAC for claims to be forwarded automatically.

It is important to remember that for all HAC programs, the beneficiary is always the subscriber. In addition, it is important that claims show the first and last name as it appears on the patient's CHAMPVA ID card. The member ID (patient's SSN or DBN) should also be included.

CLAIMS FILING DEADLINES

CHAMPVA claims follow the same filing deadline specifications as TRICARE—within 1 year from the date of service or 1 year from the date of discharge from an inpatient facility. Claims received after this filing deadline will be denied. CHAMPVA claims are sent to the VA HAC in Denver, Colorado.

A contractor can grant exemptions from the filing deadlines under certain circumstances. Requests for an exception to the claim-filing deadline must be submitted in writing to the HAC along with a complete explanation of the circumstances resulting in late filing, including all available supporting documentation. Each request will be reviewed individually and considered on its own merit. The director of the HAC, or his or her designee, may grant exceptions to the deadline if it is determined that there was good cause for late filing. Box 12.3 lists circumstances that qualify for a timely filing exemption. Delays caused by provider billing procedures do not constitute a valid basis for an exception. When a claim has been denied and the denial was overturned for whatever reason, a retroactive authorization will be made. In such cases, the beneficiary has 180 days after notification of an approved retroactive authorization to file a claim.

❗ Stop and Think

Maria Delgado received care from her family physician, Imari Deili, on July 1, 2019. Anne Jenkins, Dr. Deili's health insurance professional, neglected to file a claim until Ms. Delgado telephoned inquiring about a series of statements she received. Anne completed the claim and mailed it to the Civilian Health and Medical Program of the Department of Veterans Affairs (CHAMPVA) on June 30, 2020. She then told Ms. Delgado that the claim would be paid by TRICARE because it would be postmarked within the 1-year time limit. Is Anne correct?

Box 12.3	**Exceptions to CHAMPVA's Timely Filing Requirements**

Exceptions to CHAMPVA's timely filing requirements may be granted when:

1. There is medical documentation of beneficiary incompetence and the beneficiary did not have a legal guardian.
2. There is evidence of an administrative error (e.g., the beneficiary has been prevented from timely filing due to misrepresentation, mistake, or other accountable action of a Health Administration Center [HAC] employee acting within the scope of that individual's authority). Necessary evidence must include:
   a. A written statement describing how the error caused failure to file within the usual time limit
   b. Copy of an agency letter or written notice reflecting the error
3. The claimant submitted the claim to a primary health insurer and the primary insurer delayed adjudication past the CHAMPVA deadline. In such cases, the following must be established:
   a. The claim was originally sent to the primary health insurer before the CHAMPVA claim-filing deadline or must have been filed with CHAMPVA before the deadline but was returned or denied pending processing by the other health insurer.
   b. The claimant must submit a statement with the claim indicating the original date of submission to the other health insurer, the date of adjudication, any relevant correspondence, and an explanation of benefits (EOB).

CHAMPVA, Civilian Health and Medical Program of the Department of Veterans Affairs.

COMPLETING PAPER CLAIM FORM FOR MILITARY CARRIERS

CHAMPVA allows professional charges to be submitted on paper using a CMS-1500 (02/12) claim form and following TRICARE/CHAMPVA guidelines. These guidelines are provided in Appendix B along with a completed TRICARE simple claim (Fig. B.7), as well as a completed CHAMPVA claim (Fig. B.8). When completing the claim, the health insurance professional should remember that the "sponsor" is the member or was active duty military. The sponsor's dependent (spouse or child) is the "patient" or "beneficiary." (These terms are often used interchangeably.) These instructions are generic and may not be exactly the same as required by the claims processor in each area. The health insurance professional should obtain complete, detailed, and up-to-date claims completion guidelines from the TRICARE claims processor in his or her area or from CHAMPVA to ensure that CMS-1500 forms are completed correctly to expedite reimbursement.

CLAIMS FILING SUMMARY

The following are important points to consider when filing claims:

- Claims should be submitted as soon as services are rendered to expedite the claims process.
- The claims filing deadline is 1 year from the date of service or 1 year from the date of discharge for inpatient hospitalization.
- Copies of all information submitted to the TRICARE claims processor or CHAMPVA should be kept.

- Electronic filing is preferred; however, paper claims are acceptable under certain circumstances, but allow an extra 20 days for processing.

Holding multiple claims over a period of time and submitting them all at once is not beneficial. If numerous claims are submitted and there is a problem with one, it could delay the processing of all claims.

CHAMPVA EXPLANATION OF BENEFITS

On completion of the processing of a CHAMPVA claim, an EOB form is sent to both the beneficiary and the provider if the claim was filed by the provider.

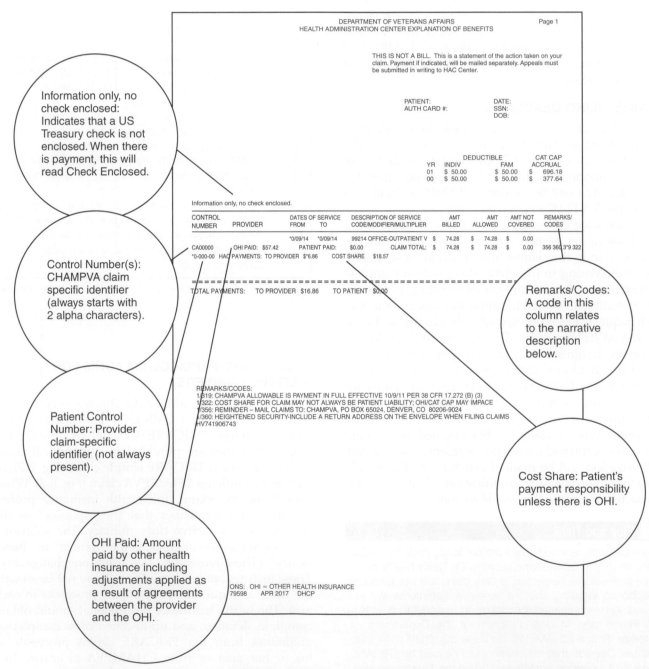

Fig. 12.6 Sample Civilian Health and Medical Program of the Department of Veterans Affairs (CHAMPVA) explanation of benefits (EOB). *OHI,* Other health insurance. (From US Department of Veterans Affairs, Health Administration Center.)

When beneficiaries file their own claims, EOBs are sent only to them. As with a TRICARE EOB, the CHAMPVA EOB is a summary of the action taken on the claim and contains basically the same information (Fig. 12.6).

CLAIMS APPEALS AND RECONSIDERATIONS

As with Medicare, beneficiaries may appeal denials of the following:

- Eligibility determinations
- Benefit coverage
- Authorization requests
- Services
- Second-level mental health appeals (first-level appeals related to mental healthcare are completed by the mental health contractor)

In the event that a provider or beneficiary disagrees with the manner in which a claim was processed and considers it necessary to file a claims appeal or have the processing of a claim reconsidered, such an appeal must be in writing and filed within 1 year of the date of the EOB in the case of a denial of the service or benefit, or 1 year from the date of the letter notifying denial of eligibility or service. (The EOB contains pertinent information on the procedures for filing an appeal.) The appeal request should be in writing and include the following:

- A statement as to why the claim is being appealed
- A copy of the EOB or determination letter
- Any new and relevant information not previously considered

On receipt of the written appeal, all claims for the entire course of treatment are reviewed. After review of the appeal and supporting documentation, a written decision is sent advising of the decision. If the provider or beneficiary still disagrees with the decision, a second review can be requested. Again, the reason(s) it is believed that the decision was made in error should be identified, and any additional information that supports the request included. A second request for review must be sent within 90 days of the date of the initial decision. Second-level decisions are final. Health insurance professionals should contact the CHAMPVA office in Denver, to the attention of Appeals, for information on appeals and reconsiderations. To review a brochure on "how to appeal," go to http://www.bva.va.gov/How_Do_I_Appeal.asp.

 Imagine This!

Dr. Serjio Manya, a psychiatrist, provided psychiatric treatment to Samuel Fortune, a Gulf War veteran, for clinical depression. Samuel, who was determined to be eligible for Civilian Health and Medical Program of the Department of Veterans Affairs (CHAMPVA) after his diagnosis, subsequently was admitted to the Trenton Mental Healthcare Facility because of a suicide attempt, where he remained for 15 months. Because Dr. Manya was a nonparticipating provider (nonPAR) and Samuel's mental condition rendered him incompetent, the claim was not filed within the time limit. Because Samuel's illness was documented by Dr. Manya, however, Samuel was able to get a filing extension and ultimately received CHAMPVA benefits.

 What Did You Learn?

1. Where does the health insurance professional send CHAMPVA claims?
2. True or false: As with TRICARE, providers accepting assignment for CHAMPVA claims must submit the claim for the beneficiary.
3. CHAMPVA accepts paper claims using the _____ form.
4. What is the claim-filing deadline for CHAMPVA claims?
5. Name four types of denials that a CHAMPVA beneficiary can appeal.

MILITARY CARRIERS AND HIPAA

All MTFs have implemented the privacy rules of HIPAA. Although the MHS has always had privacy standards in place to limit unauthorized access to and disclosure of personal health information, HIPAA's rules heighten awareness, raise the level of oversight, and provide a standard set of guidelines to protect the privacy of all patients.

Each MTF has an assigned, trained privacy officer available to respond to any questions or concerns that beneficiaries may have regarding HIPAA's privacy rules. The privacy officers also serve as patient advocates, ensuring that PHI maintained by the MTF remains protected yet accessible to beneficiaries and their providers. The privacy rule is implemented within the MHS by DoD 6025.18-R. A copy of the notice to privacy practice is available on the TRICARE website for sponsors and family members to download; copies are also available for distribution at each DoD MTF. All MTFs now meet HIPAA transaction set standards for all programs. For more information on the HIPAA privacy rule as it relates to the military healthcare system, go to https://tricare.mil/privacy/hipaa.aspx.

 HIPAA Tip

TRICARE and Civilian Health and Medical Program of the Department of Veterans Affairs (CHAMPVA) beneficiaries and providers of care benefit from the Health Insurance Portability and Accountability Act (HIPAA) in the following ways:

- Improves uniformity and efficiency of communication among providers
- Increases protection of patients' protected health information (PHI)
- Makes transferring enrollment between plans easier

HIPAA Tip

The Health Insurance Portability and Accountability Act (HIPAA) requires all employees, contractors, and volunteers of healthcare provider organizations, healthcare insurers, and healthcare clearinghouses, including those associated with TRICARE and the Civilian Health and Medical Program of the Department of Veterans Affairs (CHAMPVA) who come in contact with protected health information (PHI), to be trained annually in the areas of privacy and security.

SUMMARY CHECKPOINTS

- TRICARE is a worldwide healthcare system for the uniformed services, serving nearly 10 million beneficiaries, including National Guard and Reserve members, retirees, their families, survivors, and certain former spouses. On October 1, 2013, the DoD established the DHA to take over management of the MHS activities. TRICARE is organized into five geographic regions: the West and East regions and three overseas areas.
- Categories of eligibility under TRICARE's two plans (Prime and Select) are:
  - ADSMs (automatic enrollment)
  - Spouses and unmarried children of ADSMs
  - Uniformed service retirees, their spouses, and unmarried children
  - Medal of Honor recipients
  - Un-remarried former spouses and unmarried children of active duty or retired service members who have died

  Enrollment in one of the seven branches of the uniformed services determines TRICARE eligibility.
- TRICARE pays for only *allowed* services, supplies, and procedures, which are referred to as **covered charges**. Covered charges include medical and psychological services and supplies that are considered appropriate and are generally accepted by qualified professionals to be reasonable and adequate for the diagnosis and treatment of illness, injury, pregnancy, and mental disorders or for well-child care.
- TRICARE's additional coverage options include the following:
  - *TRICARE's Active Duty Dental Program (ADDP)* that provides private-sector dental care to ADSMs who are unable to receive required care from a military dental treatment facility (DTF)
  - *Transitional Assistance Management Program (TAMP)* that provides the minimum essential coverage temporarily (180 days) of premium-free transitional healthcare benefits after regular TRICARE benefits end
  - *Exceptional Family Member Program (EFMP)* that provides comprehensive and coordinated medical, educational, housing, community support, and personnel services to families with special needs
  - *TRICARE Plus* that allows beneficiaries who normally are able to get care only at MTFs on a space-available basis to enroll and receive primary care appointments at the MTF within the same primary care access standards as beneficiaries enrolled in a TRICARE Prime option
- It is the patient's responsibility to provide proof of current TRICARE coverage at the time of service. TRICARE beneficiaries can verify eligibility by providing the provider with a valid uniformed service ID card. Patients must also present an eligibility letter that provides proof of current healthcare coverage under TRICARE. Providers can also verify eligibility by accessing the applicable regional contractor's website.
- *Network providers* are TRICARE-authorized providers who have signed an agreement with the regional contractors to provide care at prenegotiated rates—usually less than the TRICARE-allowable charge—as the full fee for the services they render. In addition, network providers will file claims on the beneficiary's behalf.
- *Non-network providers* are TRICARE-authorized providers who, although they must be certified, do not sign a contractual agreement with the TRICARE regional contractors. There are two types of non-network providers: PARs and nonPARs. TRICARE PARs agree to accept the TRICARE-allowable charge as payment in full for services provided and not balance-bill. NonPARs can participate in TRICARE on a case-by-case basis. PARs and nonPARs who accept assignment must file the claim for the patient, and TRICARE sends the payment (if any) directly to the provider.
- Beneficiaries are responsible for cost-shares and deductibles for care that is covered under TRICARE Select up to the cat cap—$1000 for ADFMs and Reserve select beneficiaries; $3000 for all others. Cost-sharing amounts are subject to annual changes.
- The designated contractor who processes medical claims for care received within a particular state or region is called *a claims processor, TRICARE contractor,* or *FI*. TRICARE network providers are required to submit claims electronically. Non-network providers still have the option to submit paper claims using the CMS-1500 form. Patients using TRICARE Select may be responsible for submitting their own claims to the appropriate claims processor, depending on the status of the provider. The deadline for filing TRICARE claims is 1 year after services are rendered for both PARs and nonPARs.
- CHAMPVA is a healthcare benefits program for qualifying dependents and survivors of veterans. CHAMPVA is managed by the VA's HAC in Denver, Colorado. Individuals who are entitled to CHAMPVA benefits include:
  - *The spouse or dependent child* of a veteran who has been rated by a VA regional office as having a permanent and total service-connected condition or disability
  - *The surviving spouse or dependent child* of a veteran who died as a result of a VA-rated service-connected condition or who, at the time of death, was rated permanently and totally disabled from a VA-rated service-connected condition
  - *The surviving spouse or dependent child* of an individual who died in the line of duty and where the death did not result from misconduct.

- There is no cost to CHAMPVA beneficiaries when they receive healthcare treatment at a VA facility. The following points further explain the CHAMPVA program:
  - CHAMPVA beneficiaries typically have two cost-sharing responsibilities for outpatient services: (1) an annual deductible and (2) a copayment.
  - An individual who is eligible for TRICARE is not eligible for CHAMPVA.
  - A qualifying beneficiary can be eligible for healthcare benefits under Medicare and CHAMPVA. If Medicare finds that the service is not medically necessary or appropriate, CHAMPVA does not provide coverage either. Medicare is primary to CHAMPVA.
  - Healthcare providers may participate in CHAMPVA by agreeing to see the beneficiary and submitting a claim on the beneficiary's behalf. Providers who accept CHAMPVA patients also must accept the CHAMPVA allowable rate as payment in full and cannot balance-bill.
- Additional CHAMPVA programs and benefits include the following:
  - *Non-VA Medical Care Program* is provided to eligible veterans by community-based providers when those services are not "feasibly" available from a VA medical facility.
  - *In-house Treatment Initiative* (CITI) is a voluntary program that allows the CHAMPVA beneficiary to be treated at participating VA medical centers with no out-of-pocket cost.
  - *Program for the Primary Family Caregiver* is a healthcare benefits program in which the VA shares the cost of certain healthcare services and supplies with a veteran's primary family caregiver, who is not entitled to care or services under another health plan.
  - *Foreign Medical Program* (FMP) is a healthcare benefits program for veterans with VA-rated, service-connected disabilities who are residing or traveling abroad (Canada and Philippines excluded).
  - *Veterans Access, Choice and Accountability Act of 2014* provides quicker access for eligible veterans' short-term healthcare needs by allowing them to receive care from providers in their communities, instead of waiting for an appointment at a VA facility.
- Claims should be submitted as soon as services are rendered to expedite the claims process. Providers accepting assignment for CHAMPVA claims must submit the claim for the beneficiary. Beneficiaries who receive treatment from providers who do not accept assignment usually are required to submit their own claims. Providers filing paper claims should use the standard CMS-1500 claim form and follow the TRICARE/CHAMPVA guidelines for completing the form. Filing claims electronically is the most efficient method. The deadline for submitting CHAMPVA claims is 1 year from the date of service or 1 year from the date of discharge for inpatient hospital claims.
- All MTFs have implemented the privacy rules of HIPAA. Each MTF has an assigned, trained privacy officer available to respond to any questions or concerns that beneficiaries may have regarding HIPAA's privacy rules. The privacy officers also serve as patient advocates, ensuring that PHI maintained by the MTF remains protected yet accessible to beneficiaries and their providers.

Closing Scenario

Sally's understanding of the many plans offered by TRICARE has allowed her to really help her patients. One patient, retired from the Marines, was not aware that he could get his medications by mail from Veterans Affairs (VA). This would be a tremendous cost savings for him because he was taking seven different medications. Sally was able to show another family how to set up an account online to be able to check benefits and claim status. It gave Sally a good feeling to know that she was able to help her patients. One of the most rewarding aspects of her career as a health insurance professional is to help others.

CHAPTER REVIEW QUESTIONS

1. TRICARE has _____ regional offices in the United States and _____ regional offices overseas.
   a. 3, 5
   b. 1, 2
   c. 2, 3
   d. 4, 6
2. The Right of First Refusal affects TRICARE Prime beneficiaries seeking what type of care?
   a. Inpatient admission referrals
   b. Specialty appointments
   c. Procedures requiring prior authorization
   d. All of the above
3. The regional contractor for Wisconsin is:
   a. Health Net Federal Services.
   b. Humana Military.
   c. International SOS.
   d. None of the above.
4. The global computerized database of uniformed services members, their family members, and others eligible for military benefits is:
   a. CFL.
   b. DEERS.
   c. MTF.
   d. NAS.
5. TRICARE-Medicare eligible uniformed services retirees are eligible for:
   a. TRICARE Prime.
   b. TRICARE Select.
   c. TRICARE For Life.
   d. TRICARE Prime Remote.

6. CHAMPVA provides coverage for:
   a. The spouse or child of a veteran who has been permanently and totally disabled for a service-connected disability.
   b. The spouse or child of a veteran who died from a VA-rated service-connected disability.
   c. The surviving spouse or child of a veteran who was 100% disabled at his or her time of death.
   d. All of the above.
7. CHAMPVA cost-share (copayment) is:
   a. A specific dollar amount.
   b. A percentage of the CHAMPVA allowable amount.
   c. A percentage of the provider's billed amount.
   d. There is no copayment for CHAMPVA beneficiaries.
8. The Meds by Mail program through CHAMPVA is:
   a. Free to 100% disabled veterans.
   b. More expensive than Medicare Part D.
   c. A plan that involves copayments and deductibles.
   d. A plan that complements Medicare Part D.
9. The annual deductible for CHAMPVA is:
   a. $300 for a family.
   b. $75 for an individual.
   c. 25% of the allowable charges for both an individual and families.
   d. $100 for a family.
10. When a beneficiary is eligible for both Medicare and CHAMPVA:
    a. Medicare is the primary payer.
    b. CHAMPVA is the primary payer.
    c. The birthday rule is used to determine which is primary.
    d. A beneficiary cannot have both Medicare and CHAMPVA.

WEBSITES TO EXPLORE

- For live links to the following websites, please visit the Evolve website at http://evolve.elsevier.com/Beik/today.
- To locate the MTF nearest you, visit http://www.tricare.mil/mtf/.
- To find the nearest uniformed services personnel office, visit http://www.dmdc.osd.mil/rsl/.
- The website for contacting DEERS for status change is http://www.tricare.mil/DEERS.
- For detailed information on TRICARE, visit http://www.tricare.mil.
- The TRICARE West Region handbook for providers can be found at https://www.tricare-west.com/content/hnfs/home/tw/prov/res/prov_manuals.html (Note: Each TRICARE region publishes its own handbook.)

- For a full list of TRICARE's excluded services, visit http://www.tricare.mil/CoveredServices/IsItCovered/Exclusions.aspx.
- To receive periodic emails from TRICARE, visit https://public.govdelivery.com/accounts/USMHSTMA/subscriber/new.
- To view the *TRICARE Handbook,* visit http://www.tricare.mil/tricarehandbook/.
- Visit the following websites to view TRICARE ID and CACs: http://www.cac.mil/uniformed-services-id-card/ and http://www.cac.mil/common-access-card/.
- For details regarding the cat cap in a particular area, visit http://tricare.mil/contactus/.
- You can access information on the various TRICARE programs at http://www.military.com/benefits/tricare/your-tricare-benefits-explained.html.
- To view the TRICARE fee schedule/reimbursement file, which posts information on CMAC, visit http://www.doc-txt.com/TRICARE-Cmac-Fee-Schedule.pdf.
- For Military Health System coding guidance, visit https://www.health.mil/About-MHS/OASDHA/Defense-Health-Agency/Resources-and-Management/Medical-Coding-Program-Office.
- To view the *CHAMPVA Handbook,* visit http://www.va.gov/COMMUNITYCARE/docs/pubfiles/programguides/champva_guide.pdf.
- Additional information on HIPAA, TRICARE, and the privacy standards is available on the TRICARE website at http://tricare.mil/Privacy/HIPAA.
- To view a comparison chart for prescription drugs under the Medicare, TRICARE, and CHAMPVA programs, visit http://www.military.com/benefits/tricare/outpatient-prescription-drug-coverage-comparison.html.
- View and download CHAMPVA fact sheets at https://www.va.gov/COMMUNITYCARE/pubs/factsheets.asp.
- For more information on Delta Dental's VADIP, you can download the bulletin at http://www.delta-dentalvadip.org/downloads/vadip-combined-benefits-booklet.pdf.
- Step-by-step instructions for using IVR can be found at https://www.tricare-west.com/content/dam/hnfs/tw/prov/resources/pdf/HNFS_West_QRC_Eligibility.pdf.
- To report fraud, waste, or abuse in federal programs, visit https://www.gao.gov/about/what-gao-does/fraudnet/.

Author's Note: Due to the dynamic nature of the Internet, web addresses and/or links provided in this chapter may have changed since publication and may no longer be valid. In such cases, students should select comparable search words to access related sites.

Miscellaneous Carriers

Chapter Outline

I. Workers' Compensation
A. History
B. Federal Legislation and Workers' Compensation
 1. *Division of Federal Employees' Compensation*
 2. *Division of Energy Employees Occupational Illness Compensation*
 3. *Division of Longshore and Harbor Workers' Compensation*
 4. *Division of Coal Mine Workers' Compensation*
 5. *Federal Employers Liability Act*
 6. *The Merchant Marine Act*
 7. *The Patient Protection and Affordable Care Act and Workers' Compensation Premium Determination*
C. Workers' Compensation Requirements
 1. *Eligibility*
 2. *Exemptions*
 3. *Benefits*
 4. *Denial of Benefits and Appeals*
 5. *Time Limits*
D. Workers' Compensation Claims Process
 1. *First Report of Injury*
 2. *Attending Physician's Role*
 3. *Determining Disability*
 4. *Vocational Rehabilitation*
 5. *Waiting Periods*
 6. *Claim Forms*
 7. *Progress Reports*
E. Special Billing Notes
F. Workers' Compensation and Medicare
 1. *Workers' Compensation Medicare Set-Aside Arrangements*
G. Workers' Compensation and Medicaid
H. Workers' Compensation and Managed Care
I. HIPAA and Workers' Compensation
J. Workers' Compensation Fraud

II. Private and Employer-Sponsored Disability Income Insurance
A. Defining Disability
 1. *Short-Term Disability*
 2. *Long-Term Disability*
B. Disability Claims Process
 1. *Employee's Responsibilities*
 2. *Employer's Responsibilities*
 3. *Attending Physician's Statement*
 4. *Health Insurance Professional's Role*

III. Federal Disability Programs
A. Americans With Disabilities Act
B. Social Security Disability Insurance
 1. *History of the SSDI Program*
 2. *Administration and Funding*
 3. *Eligibility*
C. Supplemental Security Income
 1. *Administration and Funding*
 2. *Eligibility*
 3. *Income Limit for SSI*
 4. *Compassionate Allowances Program*
D. State Disability Programs
E. Centers for Disease Control and Prevention
F. Ticket to Work and Self-Sufficiency Program
G. Filing SSDI and SSI Claims
 1. *Patient's Role*
 2. *Physician's Role*
 3. *Health Insurance Professional's Role*

Chapter Objectives

After completion of this chapter, the student should be able to:

1. Discuss the history and purpose of workers' compensation.
2. Identify legislation that provided benefits for various categories of federal workers.
3. Discuss workers' compensation eligibility requirements and exemptions.
4. Explain the major benefit components to workers' compensation, how benefits and appeals can be denied, and the time limits for filing workers' compensation claims.
5. Summarize the workers' compensation claim process.

6. Discuss special billing notes, as well as how workers' compensation works with Medicare, Medicaid, managed care, and HIPAA.
7. Describe workers' compensation fraud and define the purpose of the Online Workers' Compensation Service Center.
8. Define the purpose of disability income insurance and differentiate between a short-term and long-term disability.
9. Describe the role of various parties in the disability claims process.

10. Name and describe the various federal disability programs, discuss the Americans With Disabilities Act, and differentiate between the two major federal disability programs (SSDI and SSI).

11. Discuss the following and their relation to workers' compensation: state disability programs, Centers for Disease Control and Prevention, and the Ticket to Work and Self-Sufficiency Program.

12. Outline the process for filing SSDI and SSI claims.

Chapter Terms

activities of daily living (ADLs)
Americans With Disabilities Act (ADA)
benefit cap
coming and going rule
disability income insurance
earned income
egregious
employment networks
Energy Employees Occupational Illness Compensation Program (EEOICP) Act
exemptions
Federal Black Lung Program
Federal Employees' Compensation Act (FECA)

Federal Employers Liability Act (FELA)
financial means test
instrumental activities of daily living (IADLs)
job deconditioning
Longshore and Harbor Workers' Compensation Act
long-term disability
Merchant Marine Act (Jones Act)
modified own-occupation policy
no-fault insurance
occupational therapy
ombudsman
own-occupation policy
permanent and stationary

permanent disability
permanent partial disability
permanent total disability
progress or supplemental reports
protected health information (PHI)
short-term disability
Social Security Disability Insurance (SSDI)
Supplemental Security Income (SSI)
temporarily disabled
temporary disability
temporary partial disability
temporary total disability
Ticket to Work
vocational rehabilitation
workers' compensation

 Opening Scenario

Jim Lightfoot has been working with patients covered by workers' compensation at Walden-Martin Family Medical Clinic for about 5 years. Working in this area was of personal interest to Jim, as his father had died in a work-related accident when Jim was in high school. He remembers the monthly benefit checks his mother received and how much help it was to his family. Jim works hard to make sure that he completes all of the necessary paperwork so that the patients at Walden-Martin can get their needed benefits in a timely manner.

Along with working with the workers' compensation patients, Jim is also responsible for assisting patient with disability insurance claims. Having a solid understanding of the differences between workers' compensation and disability insurance has allowed Jim to be a great advocate for the patients of Walden-Martin Family Medical Clinic. He has also realized how important it is to understand the Health Insurance Portability and Accountability Act (HIPAA) regulations regarding workers' compensation and other types of disability insurance programs.

WORKERS' COMPENSATION

Workers' compensation is a type of insurance regulated by state laws that pays medical expenses and partial loss of wages for workers who are injured on the job or become ill as a result of job-related circumstances. If death results, benefits are payable to the surviving spouse and dependents as defined by law. Most US workers are covered by the workers' compensation law. Typically the employer, not the employee, pays the premiums. Each state sets up its own workers' compensation laws and regulations; however, they are basically the same from state to state.

HISTORY

Workers' compensation began in Germany in the 1800s when it was determined that something needed to be done to take care of injured workers to limit their physical and financial suffering from injuries or illnesses resulting from their jobs. Workers' compensation became common in the United States in the 1930s and 1940s, and it exists today in all 50 states and territories.

When workers' compensation was first proposed, US companies were hesitant to accept full responsibility for paying the premiums. Their argument was that on top of the premium expense, they still could be financially liable in a worker-initiated lawsuit. A compromise was reached between businesses and workers: companies would pay the premiums for the insurance that protected workers, and the workers would give up the right to sue the employer for damages resulting from a job-related illness or injury. This principle continues essentially intact today. Workers' compensation is not considered a "benefit"; rather, it is a legally mandated right of the worker.

Companies that meet specific state requirements must provide workers' compensation for all employees. Businesses that do not provide coverage as required by law can incur fines and other penalties. Workers' compensation can be purchased from several sources: private insurance companies, state funds, insurance pools, and self-insurance programs. Most states require employers to purchase workers' compensation insurance in the state in which their business operates. State statutes establish the framework and set up the laws for most workers' compensation insurance. As mentioned, these laws provide benefits not only for workers, but also for dependents of workers who are killed or die as a result of job-related accidents or illnesses. Many state laws also protect employers and their fellow workers by limiting the amount an injured employee can recover from an employer and by eliminating the liability of coworkers in most accidents.

For more detailed information on the history of workers' compensation, research the Workers' Compensation Act of 1897 on the Internet.

 Imagine This!

Pirates, contrary to popular myth, proved to be highly organized and entrepreneurial. Before their assignment to the ranks of outlaws, they were considered highly prized allies of the government, plundering and sharing the spoils with governors of the pre-Revolutionary colonies, giving them a safe port.

Privateering (the gentleman's term for piracy) was a dangerous occupation; taking booty away from those who did not want to give it up leads to sea battles, hand-to-hand combat, and injury. Because of the ever-present chance of impairment, a system was developed to compensate injured "employees." There was one catch: he or she (there were female pirates as well) had to survive the wounds to collect because there was no recorded compensation for death.

Piratesinfo.com provides some information on the amount of payment made to the injured: loss of an eye—100 pieces of eight (Spanish dollar); loss of a finger—100 pieces of eight; loss of left arm—500 pieces of eight; loss of right arm—600 pieces of eight; loss of left leg—400 pieces of eight; and loss of right leg—500 pieces of eight.

The average weekly wage for colonial Americans of this period equated to approximately 2 pieces of eight per week. Loss of an eye or finger would merit payment approximating 50 weeks of wages. The right arm was worth 300 weeks (a little less than 6 years). These compare closely with modern compensation schedules.

In addition to being compensated, injured crew members were allowed to remain on board and offered less strenuous duty. The first return-to-work program was created.

FEDERAL LEGISLATION AND WORKERS' COMPENSATION

Workers' compensation programs are offered at the state level. In addition, there are several categories of federal programs for workers who do not fall under the umbrella of covered employees under state laws. The Office of Workers' Compensation Programs (OWCP) administers four major disability compensation programs that provide wage replacement benefits, medical treatment, vocational rehabilitation, and other benefits to certain workers or their dependents who experience work-related injury or occupational disease.

Division of Federal Employees' Compensation

The **Federal Employees' Compensation Act (FECA)** provides workers' compensation coverage to 3 million federal and postal workers around the world for employment-related injuries and occupational diseases. (Workers injured while employed by private companies or by state and local government agencies must contact their state workers' compensation board.)

Division of Energy Employees Occupational Illness Compensation

The **Energy Employees Occupational Illness Compensation Program (EEOICP) Act** provides compensation and medical benefits to employees of the Department of Energy (DOE), its contractors and subcontractors, and employees of DOE-designated atomic weapons employers who became ill as a result of work performed in the production and testing of nuclear weapons. This includes employees who were diagnosed with certain types of cancers caused by exposure to radiation, beryllium, or silica while employed at covered facilities. Uranium miners, millers, and ore transporters (or their eligible survivors) may also be eligible for benefits under this law.

Division of Longshore and Harbor Workers' Compensation

The mission of the **Longshore and Harbor Workers' Compensation Act** is to minimize the impact of employment injuries and deaths on employees and their families by ensuring that the benefits provided under this act and its extensions are paid promptly and properly and to provide information, technical and compliance assistance, support, and informal dispute resolution services to workers, employers, and insurers.

Division of Coal Mine Workers' Compensation

The Division of Coal Mine Workers' Compensation, also known as the **Federal Black Lung Program**, provides compensation to coal miners who are totally disabled by pneumoconiosis (black lung disease) arising out of coal mine employment and to survivors of coal miners whose deaths are attributable to the disease. The act also provides eligible miners with medical coverage for the treatment of lung diseases related to pneumoconiosis.

Federal Employers Liability Act

The **Federal Employers Liability Act (FELA)**, although not a workers' compensation statute, provides that railroads engaged in interstate commerce are liable for on-the-job injuries to their employees if the railroad is negligent. Although the FELA involves employees, the law is different from workers' compensation, which compensates employees for injuries regardless of the employer's liability or negligence. FELA requires the injured railroader to prove that the railroad was "legally negligent," at least in part, in causing the injury. After proving negligence, the injured railroader is entitled to full compensation, which can be many times greater than that provided by state workers' compensation for nonrailroaders.

The Merchant Marine Act

The **Merchant Marine Act** provides seafarers with basically the same protection from employer negligence that FELA provides railroad workers. Also known as the **Jones Act**, this law protects the welfare of the crew of Merchant Marine ships and puts limitations on foreign merchant ships operating between US ports. The purpose of the law was to protect US shipping and ensure the continued existence of a US-based Merchant Marine fleet manned by US citizens.

The Patient Protection and Affordable Care Act and Workers' Compensation Premium Determination

Beginning in 2011, insurers providing health coverage to businesses were required to comply with the medical loss ratio (MLR) provision of the Patient Protection and Affordable Care Act (hereafter referred to as the ACA). This means that they must spend a specific percentage of premium income on healthcare claims and quality improvement activities or pay rebates to consumers. This rule has the potential to affect an employer's workers' compensation premium determination.

National Council on Compensation Insurance (NCCI) rules state that workers' compensation premiums should be calculated based on the total payroll paid by the insured employer for services of individuals who could receive workers' compensation benefits for work-related injuries as provided by the employer's workers' compensation policy.

Under the ACA beginning in 2015, employers with at least a certain number of employees (generally 50 full-time employees or a combination of full-time and part-time employees that is equivalent to 50 full-time employees) are now subject to the employer-shared responsibility provisions as determined by the Internal Revenue Service (IRS). The ACA changed the definition of a full-time employee to increase the number of individuals who qualify for health insurance. As defined by the statute, a full-time employee is an individual employed on average at least 30 hours of service per week. An employer that meets the 50 full-time employee threshold is referred to as an *applicable large employer*. In addition, the

rebates and allowance provisions under the act will affect payroll and thus the premium calculation by workers' compensation insurance providers.

WORKERS' COMPENSATION REQUIREMENTS

Not all employers are required to have workers' compensation coverage. State laws vary, but an employer's responsibility to provide coverage usually depends on how many employees it has, what type of business it is, and what type of work the employees are doing. For example, a few states require only employers with at least three employees to be covered, but most states do not set a minimum. (In these states, an employer that has just one employee must provide coverage.) In addition, some states allow charities to opt out of the workers' compensation system; other states do not. Generally speaking, the vast majority of employers are required to carry coverage.

Typically, employers provide coverage either by purchasing insurance on the private market or, in some states, from a state fund, called *self-insuring*. Many employers purchase workers' compensation insurance even if they are not required to do so. State laws typically allow these exempt employers to "opt in" to the workers' compensation system. This allows the employer to ensure that its employees are compensated for workplace injuries, thus preventing employees from filing a lawsuit against the employer.

Eligibility

In the United States, qualifying employees who are injured on the job or develop an employment-related illness that prevents them from working are likely to be eligible to collect workers' compensation benefits. The benefits also apply to the spouse and dependents of a family member who dies because of a job-related accident or illness. If the disability is permanent or the employee has dependents, benefits include a specific percentage (often two-thirds) of regular wages or salary. Although workers' compensation laws may differ from state to state, there are three basic eligibility requirements for workers' compensation benefits:

1. The person or company where the individual is working must carry workers' compensation insurance or be legally required to do so.
2. The person must be a legal employee of that person or company.
3. The injury or illness must be work related.

As with many rules and regulations, there are exceptions. Benefits are awarded only for disability or death occurring while the employee was in the process of performing lawful duties. If any horseplay, drunken stumbling, or illegal drugs are involved, workers' compensation usually does not pay. Workers' compensation does not pay for self-inflicted injuries and for injuries incurred while a worker is off the job, committing a crime, or violating company policy.

Exemptions

All states require employers to carry workers' compensation insurance coverage for their employees, but **exemptions** exist for certain job categories, high-level employees, and some small businesses. Most states require employers to carry workers' compensation insurance even if it has only one employee, but a few offer exemptions to some very small businesses. The number of employees a business may have without needing insurance varies by state but generally ranges from one to five. In some cases, the type of work employees do may also matter.

Job categories. Each state sets its own workers' compensation laws, so exempt job categories will vary; however, the rules in most states are similar and commonly include the following:

- **Domestic workers.** Someone who works in a home, such as a housekeeper or a babysitter.
- **Agricultural and farm workers.** The majority of states exempt agricultural and farm workers from workers' compensation coverage. Not every person who works on a farm falls into this category, however.
- **Leased or loaned workers.** A leased or loaned worker is one who works for an employer through an agency (e.g., a temp agency). State laws may differ on which company—the one the employee is working for or the agency—has to provide workers' compensation coverage for you.
- **Casual or seasonal workers.** Casual or seasonal workers are those who work only at certain times of the year or work only intermittently or sporadically. Some states do not require that casual or seasonal workers be covered by workers' compensation.
- **Undocumented workers.** Some states (e.g., Arizona, California, Florida, Montana, Nevada, New York, Texas, and Utah) expressly cover undocumented workers in their workers' compensation statutes. Other states expressly exclude undocumented workers.

Business owners and executives. Business owners and other high-level employees may have a choice of participating or opting out of coverage. Again, state rules differ, but here are some workers commonly allowed to opt out:

- **Corporate officers or directors:** Upper-level managers who own a certain percentage of company stock.
- **Limited liability company members:** As with corporate officers and directors, the rules often require a minimum ownership interest and a management role in the company.
- **Construction industry officers:** Some states define construction as an extra-hazardous industry, so may not allow this exemption.
- **Family members:** Family members of sole proprietors may be exempt in some states. (A sole proprietorship is a business with a single owner and not registered as a corporation, partnership, or limited liability company. Examples may be a landscaper, a computer repair business, or a cleaning service.)

The list in Table 13.1 presents various exemption classifications.

| Table **13.1** | Workers' Compensation Exemption Classifications |

EXEMPTION CLASSIFICATION[a]	DESCRIPTION
Independent contractors	People who work for the company but who maintain a greater autonomy than employees. Independent contractors might be freelance workers who do a specific job for the company.
Commissioned employees	For example, salespeople who do not receive a salary, but only a percentage of sales, can be exempt.
Sole proprietors and/or business partners	People who own their own business are eligible for exemption; however, it is recommended, but not required, that they buy workers' compensation insurance on themselves.
Family members	Individuals who work for a family business and live in the same home as their employer can be exempt.
Executive officers	This includes corporate presidents, vice presidents, and chief executive officers (CEOs) of companies, among others.
Employers with a minimum number of full-time employees	Small businesses that employ fewer than three and up to five employees (depending on the state) may be exempt.
Casual employees	Temporary employees or those who are not entitled to paid holiday or sick leave, have no expectation of ongoing employment, and for whom each engagement with the employer constitutes a separate contract of employment.
Volunteers	Those who provide services of their own free will to or on behalf of an organization who neither receive nor expect to receive any kind of pay or compensation for those services.
Part-time domestic employees, agricultural workers, and emergency relief workers	These categories of employees are typically excluded, but employees can obtain workers' compensation and employers' liability insurance coverage by agreement between their employer and an insurance carrier.

[a]The list is not necessarily all-inclusive, and exempt classifications vary from state to state.

Benefits

Workers' compensation insurance is **no-fault insurance**. Benefits are paid to the injured (or ill) worker regardless of who is to blame for the accident or injury, barring the exceptions mentioned previously. Following are some of the major benefit components to workers' compensation. Keep in mind that every state has its own rules and regulations.

1. Medical expenses—This includes initial emergency care and hospitalization (if needed), follow-up visits with physicians, physical rehabilitation treatment, prescriptions and supplies, and (in some cases) transportation expenses.
2. Payment for time off work and recovery (disability pay)—This can be temporary or permanent if it is determined that the worker will never fully recover. Typically, this is a weekly benefit of 66.67% of a worker's average weekly earnings and doesn't last more than 2 years. (See the "Determining Disability" section.) Note: The Family and Medical Leave Act (FMLA) may apply to leave for a work-related injury if the employee had inpatient or continuing medical treatment. The FMLA provides up to 12 weeks of leave; note that it may not be paid time off.
3. Payment for permanent impairment—Many work-related injuries result in a permanent physical impairment that affects the worker's ability to do certain jobs. Even a minor injury can qualify for a small permanent disability payment.
4. Vocational rehabilitation services—If the injury or illness results in the worker being unable to perform the usual duties of his or her occupation, retraining may be necessary for the worker to enter into a new trade or business; also, physical therapy may be necessary.
5. Death benefits—A deceased worker's dependents are entitled to burial expenses and a lump-sum payment in most states.

Because workers' compensation imposes strict liability without inquiry into fault, an employer could be penalized if the cause of injury or illness was **egregious**, meaning that the employer was conspicuously negligent, such as violating federal or state safety standards, failing to correct known defects, or exhibiting other careless conduct.

Most state workers' compensation laws exclude coverage for injuries sustained while an employee is commuting to and from work. This exclusion is referred to as the **coming and going rule**. There are exceptions to this rule, however, such as when the scope of the employee's duties includes travel or when the employee is running an errand for the employer during the commute. Inquiry as to whether the coming and going rule applies to a particular situation should be made before simply ruling out the possibility of coverage for an accident that occurred during a worker's commute to or from work. If an employee is injured during a lunch period, it is usually considered outside the scope of the employment relationship. In the case of an automobile accident, workers' compensation might deny the claim, indicating that the automobile insurance carrier of the at-fault party is the primary payer.

 Stop and Think

Carol Brown, bookkeeper at the Memorial Health Clinic, drops off the bank deposit each evening on her way home from work. One evening, as she is in the process of making the deposit, she slams her hand in the depository door, sustaining a laceration to her middle and index fingers. Several weeks later, as Carol is on her way to the bank to make the daily deposit, she stops at a convenience store for a cup of coffee and a donut. In her haste, she spills the coffee, sustaining second-degree burns to her torso. Does either of these scenarios represent a legitimate workers' compensation claim?

 HIPAA Tip

Health Insurance Portability and Accountability Act (HIPAA) requirements do not apply to certain types of benefit plans known as *excepted benefits*, which include coverage only for accidents (including accidental death or dismemberment) or certain categories of disability income insurance.

Denial of Benefits and Appeals

Workers' compensation insurers may deny legitimate claims. Employees who believe that they have been wrongly denied workers' compensation benefits can appeal or resort to litigation. Some of the main reasons why workers' compensation insurers deny claims include the following:

- The injury was not witnessed.
- The employee did not report the injury immediately.
- There is a discrepancy between the accident report and initial medical records.
- The claim was filed after the employee was fired or laid off.
- The employee failed to give the insurance company a recorded statement or refused to sign medical authorizations.

Some states have an **ombudsman**, who is an individual responsible for investigating and resolving workers' complaints against the employer or insurance company that is denying the benefits.

Most legitimate work injuries result in granted benefits because it is usually obvious when an injury is work related. In these cases, if the claim is filed in a timely manner and according to a company's work rules, benefits are awarded. However, various situations may justify an employer or the insurer contesting a claim for workers' compensation benefits. It may be believed that an injury or resulting disability does not meet one or more of the legal requirements for entitlement to benefits. In these cases, a notice that the claim has been denied, containing reasons for the denial, must be issued promptly to the worker by the employer or by the employer's workers' compensation insurance company.

The appeal process differs from state to state. In many states, if the employee disagrees with the decision to deny the claim, he or she may appeal, but it must be done within a specified time, depending on state statutes. The appeal process can be started by contacting the appropriate state agency or by hiring an attorney. If all attempts at appeal do not reverse the decision and the denial becomes final, the worker is responsible for payment of all medical bills. If the individual has other health insurance, a claim can be submitted to that insurer. Most health insurance companies ask that a copy of the workers' compensation claim denial be included with the claim.

For more detailed information on workers' compensation by state, visit the website listed under "Websites to Explore" at the end of this chapter.

 Imagine This!

Louise Carson has been a teacher at Harrison Junior High School for 10 years. At her yearly physical examination, her healthcare provider informs her that she is dangerously hypertensive. Louise attributes her hypertension to stress from her teaching responsibilities plus increasing pressure from her supervisor to maintain better discipline in the classroom. Louise's blood pressure does not respond to conventional antihypertensive medication, so her physician suggests a 6-week leave of absence from her job. Louise files a workers' compensation claim with the Harrison City School District; however, the claim is denied. The reason for denial, TEL-Abbot, Harrison's insurer, informs her, is that high stress is a normal part of the teaching profession.

 Stop and Think

Benjamin Abbott, owner of Abbott Manufacturing, holds an annual Christmas party in the company cafeteria. Attendance at the party is optional, but Mr. Abbott uses this occasion to hand out the employee Christmas bonuses. A night shift foreman, Ken Carter, sustains a back injury while doing the limbo at the party. Abbott's insurer denies the claim, stating that even though, technically, the injury occurred at work, it was not during regular work hours, and the employee was not engaged in his usual work duties. Can Ken appeal this decision?

Time Limits

Each state has rules established under which an employee is required to file a claim within a certain time limit. Usually, traumatic claims must be brought within a time frame that runs from the date of the accident, date of last medical treatment, or date of the last payment of benefits. In cases where a job-related disease does not manifest immediately (i.e., hearing loss, lung cancer, toxic disease, or mesothelioma [a

type of lung disease caused by asbestos exposure]), the time limit may extend from the date of the last exposure, date of the first symptoms of the disease, or date on which the diagnosis was determined. The time limits for filing claims and issuing appeals are established by individual state statutes and vary from state to state; the health insurance professional needs to become familiar with the workers' compensation regulations in the state in which he or she is employed.

WORKERS' COMPENSATION CLAIMS PROCESS

The workers' compensation claims process can be long and arduous. Various steps must be followed, and report forms must be completed. This process can be facilitated if the individual steps are adhered to carefully and the forms are completed correctly and in a timely manner. The following sections discuss the steps for successful workers' compensation claim processing.

First Report of Injury

Employees who are injured, suspect they have been injured, or have contracted a disease that they believe is related to their job should take immediate steps to protect their rights and to ensure that their claim is processed properly. Failure to seek timely medical treatment within the workers' compensation network may cause a delay in claim processing and perhaps denial of benefits. Injured workers should be transported to a medical treatment facility without delay in the case of an emergency. For nonemergency situations, the employee should take the following steps:

- The injured or ill worker should notify a supervisor of the incident immediately and provide the names of witnesses, if any.
- The injured or ill worker should complete the initial accident report or necessary paperwork. It does not matter whether the injury is severe or minor; it must be documented. The employer should supply the necessary forms (Fig. 13.1).
- The employer should report the incident to his or her workers' compensation carrier.
- The injured or ill worker should be sent to a medical facility for treatment or diagnosis, if not already done.

The procedure for reporting injuries and filing claims may vary from state to state. The injured individual should contact the workers' compensation department in the state in which he or she resides and request specific guidelines for the appropriate state. Until the injury is reported and the claim form is filled out and returned to the employer, the employer is under no obligation to provide the employee with benefits. A common mistake people make is waiting to report the injury until it prevents them from working.

WORKERS COMPENSATION - FIRST REPORT OF INJURY OR ILLNESS

Employer (Name & Address with Zip Code)	Carrier/Administrator Claim Number		Report Purpose Code
	Jurisdiction		Jurisdiction Claim Number
	Insured Report Number		

SIC Code	Employer Fein	Employer's Location Address (If different)	Location #:
			Phone #

CARRIER/CLAIMS ADMINISTRATOR

Carrier (Name, Address & Phone No)	Policy Period To Check if Appropriate ☐ Self-Insurance	Claims Administrator (Name, Address & Phone Number)

Carrier Fein	Policy/Self-Insured Number	Administration Fein

Agent Name & Code Number

EMPLOYEE / WAGE

Name (Last, First, Middle)	Birth Date	Social Security Number	Hire Date	State of Hire
Address (include Zip Code)	Sex	Marital Status	Occupation/Job Title	
			Employment Status	
			NCCI Class Code	
Phone	# Dependents			

Rate Per ☐ Day ☐ Month ☐ Week ☐ Other:	# Days Worked/Week	Full Pay for Day of Injury? ☐ Yes ☐ No Did Salary Continue? ☐ Yes ☐ No

OCCURRENCE/TREATMENT

Time Employee Began Work	Date of Injury/Illness	Time of Occurrence AM PM	Late Work Date	Date Employer Notified	Date Disability Began

Contact Number/Phone Number	Type of Injury/Illness	Part of Body Affected
Did Injury/Illness Exposure Occur on Employer's Premises? Yes ☐ No ☐	Type of Injury/Illness Code	Part of Body Affected Code

Department or Location Where Accident or Illness Exposure Occurred	All Equipment, Materials, or Chemicals Employee Was Using When Accident or Illness Exposure Occurred
Specific Activity the Employee was Engaged in When the Accident or Illness Exposure Occurred	Work Process the Employee Was Engaged in When Accident or Illness Exposure Occurred

How Injury or Illness/Abnormal Health Condition Occurred. Describe the Sequence of Events and Include Any Objects or substances that Directly Injured the Employee or Made the Employee Ill	Cause of Injury Code

Date Return(ed) To Work	If Fatal, Give Date of Death	Were Safeguards or Safety Equipment Provided? ☐ Yes ☐ No Were They Used ☐ Yes ☐ No

Physician/Health Care Provider (Name & Address)	Hospital (Name & Address)	Initial Treatment

Witness (Name & Phone #)

Date Administrator Notified	Date Prepared	Preparer's Name & Title	Phone Number

Fig. 13.1 Sample workers' compensation first report of injury form.

Employer's Instructions
DO NOT ENTER DATA IN SHADED FIELDS

Preferred Formats for Date and Time: Dates should be entered as MM/DD/YYYY, and times as HH:MM a (am)/p (pm)

SIC Code: This is the code which represents the nature of the employer's business which is contained in the Standard Industrial Classification Manual published by the Federal Office of Management and Budget.

Carrier: The licensed business entity issuing a contract of insurance and assuming financial responsibility on behalf of the employer of the claimant.

Claims Administrator: Enter the name of the carrier, third party administrator, state fund, or self-insured responsible for administering the claim.

Agent Name & Code Number: Enter the name of your insurance agent and his/her code number if known. This information can be found on your insurance policy.

Employee/Wage Section: When filling in Social Security Number, do **NOT** include dashes.

Occupation/Job Title: This is the primary occupation of the claimant at the time of the accident or exposure.

Employment Status: Indicate the employee's work status. The valid choices are:

Apprenticeship Full-Time	Apprenticeship Part-Time	Disabled	Full-Time
Not Employed	On Strike	Part-Time	Piece Worker
Retired	Seasonal	Unknown	Volunteer

Date Disability Began: The first day on which the claimant originally lost time from work due to the occupation injury or disease or otherwise deigned by statute.

Contact Name/Phone Number: Enter the name of the individual at the employer's premises to be contacted for additional information.

Type of Injury/Illness: Briefly describe the nature of the injury or illness (e.g. Lacerations to the forearm).

Part of Body Affected: Indicate the part of body affected by the injury/illness (e.g. Right forearm, lower back). Part of Body Affected Code does not allow multiple body parts to be selected. Please choose the most dominant body part affected from the list.

Department or Location Where Accident or Illness Exposure Occurred: (e.g. Maintenance Dept or Client's Office at (address). If the accident or illness exposure did not occur on the employer's premises, enter address or location. Be specific.

All Equipment, Material, or Chemicals Employee Was Using When Accident or Illness Exposure Occurred: (e.g. Acetylene cutting torch, metal plate). List of all the equipment, materials, and/or chemicals the employee was using, applying, handling, or operating when the injury or illness occurred. Be specific, for example: decorator's scaffolding, electric sander, paintbrush, and paint. Enter "NA" for not applicable if no equipment, materials, or chemicals were being used. NOTE: The items listed do not have to be directly involved in the employee's injury or illness.

Specific Activity the Employee Was Engaged in When the Accident or Illness Exposure Occurred: (e.g. Cutting metal plate for flooring). Describe the specific activity the employee was engaged in when the accident or illness exposure occurred, such as sanding ceiling woodwork in preparation for painting.

Work Process the Employee Was Engaged in When Accident or Illness Exposure Occurred:
Describe the work process the employee was engaged in when the accident or illness exposure occurred, such as building maintenance. Enter "NA" for not applicable if employee was not engaged in a work process (e.g. walking along a hallway).

How Injury or Illness/Abnormal Health Condition Occurred. Describe the Sequence of Events and Include Any Objects or Substances That Directly Injured the Employee or Made the Employee Ill:
(Worker stepped back to inspect work and slipped on some scrap metal. As worker fell, worker brushed against the hot metal.) Describe how the injury or illness/abnormal health condition occurred. Include the sequence of events and name any objects or substance that directly injured the employee or made the employee ill. For example: Worker stepped to the edge of the scaffolding to inspect work, lost balance, and fell six feet to the floor. The worker's right wrist was broken in the fall.

Date Return(ed) To Work: Enter the date following the most recent disability period on which the employee returned to work.

Fig. 13.1—cont'd

Megan Fetterly smashed her finger between two file cabinets while at work. Her supervisor was not around, and Megan's fingers began to swell quickly. She told her coworkers what happened and asked them to tell their supervisor that she was going to the clinic to get it checked out. When Megan got to Walden-Martin Family Medical Clinic, the receptionist asked how she had injured her finger. Megan told her it happened at work. Megan was worked into the schedule, and after she was treated Jim Lightfoot stopped in to talk to her. He asked her if she had notified her supervisor before she came to the clinic. Megan explained that her supervisor was not around, and she was really worried about her fingers, so she just left and came to the clinic. Jim explained that she should contact her supervisor as soon as possible to get the first report of injury paperwork started. Jim tried to emphasize the importance of this so that workers' compensation would pay for her treatment. Megan was grateful for Jim's assistance in getting her documentation in order.

Attending Physician's Role

An employee who has been injured on the job has a right to medical treatment. Employees may be required to see the company physician initially, after which it may be possible to choose their own healthcare provider.

The "attending physician" is the doctor or healthcare provider who is primarily responsible for the treatment of a worker's compensable injury. The attending physician must be a licensed medical doctor, doctor of osteopathy, or oral and maxillofacial surgeon. In some states, a chiropractor may also be the attending physician, but usually only for a limited number of days or for a specific number of visits. The attending physician is required to make important decisions that are essential to the progress of the patient's claim.

Physicians have two distinct roles in the workers' compensation process:
1. To diagnose and treat work-related injuries and illnesses
2. To provide claims administrators with opinions in response to specific medical and legal questions about work-related injuries or illnesses

The physician may be asked the following questions:
- Was the injury or illness caused by the employee's work?
- Is the condition **permanent and stationary**, meaning has the employee reached a state of maximal medical improvement?
- If a condition is permanent and stationary, has the injury caused permanent disability that limits the ability to compete in the open labor market?
- Can the employee return to his or her usual and customary work assignment? If not, does he or she need some type of accommodations because of work restrictions, or does the employee need to be retrained for a new job?
- Will the employee who has a permanent and stationary condition require access to future medical treatment for the condition?

Usually, a single physician fills both of these roles in workers' compensation cases; however, an independent medical evaluator may address the specific medical and legal questions. When an injured or ill employee visits the medical facility, the attending physician should:
- Obtain a complete history of the condition, including preexisting conditions or disability
- Obtain a thorough work history, including any exposures as they pertain to the chief complaint
- Perform a physical examination, focusing on the system or systems involved
- Consider restrictions (e.g., no typing for more than 1 hour) before taking the patient off work to prevent **job deconditioning** (i.e., the patient psychologically or physically loses his or her ability to perform normal job duties at the previous level of expertise as a result of being absent from work)
- Make a diagnostic evaluation
- Complete all appropriate paperwork promptly because the patient may have no source of income if the paperwork is delayed (Fig. 13.2)

Determining Disability

When an injured or ill worker visits the healthcare facility for treatment, the provider completes an attending physician statement (as discussed in the previous section), which should indicate any physical or mental impairments resulting from the incident. The classification of workers' compensation disability cases, mandated by federal law, is as follows:
- Medical treatment only: This category comprises minor injuries or illnesses that are resolved quickly, resulting in a minimal loss of work time with no residual limitations. Compensation is made for medical expenses rendered that are necessary to cure and relieve the effects of the injury or illness.
- **Temporary disability**: Benefits in this category are paid as long as the physician's opinion concurs with that claim of status. Temporary disability includes two subcategories:
  - **Temporary total disability**: The worker's ability to perform his or her job responsibilities is totally lost but on a temporary basis.
  - **Temporary partial disability**: An injury or illness that impairs an employee's ability to work is lost only partially and for a limited time. The impairment is such that the individual is able to perform limited employment duties and is expected to recover fully.
- **Permanent disability**: The ill or injured employee's condition is such that it is impossible to return to work. Compensation is awarded to the worker for the loss of value of his or her skills in the open labor

Health Care Provider Report

See Instructions on Reverse Side
(WHEN COMPLETED RETURN TO REQUESTER)

H C 0 1

DO NOT USE THIS SPACE

Please PRINT or TYPE your responses.
Enter dates in MM/DD/YYYY format.

SOCIAL SECURITY NUMBER	DATE OF INJURY	
EMPLOYEE	EMPLOYER	
INSURER/SELF-INSURER/TPA	INSURER CLAIM NUMBER	
INSURER ADDRESS		
CITY	STATE ZIP CODE	

REQUESTER must specify all items to be completed by health care provider. ☐ Items: _____ ☐ MMI (#9) ☐ PPD (#10)

HEALTH CARE PROVIDER TO COMPLETE ITEMS REQUESTED ABOVE

1. Date of first examination for this injury by this office: _____ (date)

2. Diagnosis (include all ICD codes):

3. History of injury or disease given by employee:

4. In your opinion (as substantiated by the history and physical examination) was the injury or disease caused, aggravated, or accelerated by the employee's alleged employment activity or environment? ☐ No ☐ Yes

5. Is there evidence of preexisting or other conditions that affect this disability? ☐ No ☐ Yes If yes, describe:

6. Is further treatment of this injury or referral to another doctor planned? ☐ No ☐ Yes If yes, describe:

7. Has surgery been performed? ☐ No ☐ Yes If yes, date and describe: _____ (date)

8. Attach the most recent Report of Work Ability. Date of report: _____ (date)

9. **Has the employee reached maximum medical improvement?** ☐ No ☐ Yes Date reached: _____
   (If yes, complete item #10) (See definition on back)

10. **Has the employee sustained any permanent partial disability from the injury?** ☐ No ☐ Yes ☐ Too early to determine
    The permanent partial disability is _____ % of the whole body. This rating is based on Minn. Rules:

5223.	%	5223.	%
5223.	%	5223.	%

NAME (Type or Print)	SIGNATURE		DEGREE
ADDRESS	STATE	LICENSE #/REGISTRATION #	
CITY STATE ZIP CODE	AREA CODE	TELEPHONE #	DATE SIGNED

MN HC01 (7/01)

Fig. 13.2 Sample healthcare provider report.

market. As with temporary disability, permanent disability has two subcategories:

- **Permanent partial disability**: Prevents the individual from performing one or more occupational functions but does not impair his or her capability of performing less demanding employment.
- **Permanent total disability**: The employee's ability to work at any occupation is totally and permanently lost.

 Stop and Think

George Meade makes his living as a concert pianist. To relax between concerts, George takes up woodworking and inadvertently severs his right index finger, preventing him from performing. Into what classification would George's disability fall?

Vocational Rehabilitation

When employees cannot return to their previous job because of a workers' compensation injury or illness, they often are entitled to **vocational rehabilitation** services if it is reasonable to assume that these individuals can be trained for some alternative type of employment. The goal of vocational rehabilitation is to return the injured worker to some sort of suitable, gainful employment that he or she can reasonably achieve and that offers an opportunity to restore the injured worker to maximum self-support as soon as practical and as near as possible to what it was before the incident.

Waiting Periods

Workers' compensation benefits normally do not begin immediately. Most states have a waiting period that applies before benefits to the injured (or ill) employee begin. Of the 54 jurisdictions (50 states, District of Columbia, Puerto Rico, Virgin Islands, and Guam), only one jurisdiction, the Virgin Islands, does not have a waiting period. In 24 jurisdictions there is a 3-day waiting period, and the waiting period is 7 days in 23 jurisdictions. Idaho, Massachusetts, Mississippi, and Nevada have a 5-day waiting period. North Dakota and Montana have a 4-day waiting period. (Waiting periods are subject to change; keep current on the statutes in your state.) Most states allow for retroactive compensation when disability continues for a certain period from the date of injury or illness.

Occupational therapy is different from vocational rehabilitation. Occupational therapy is a treatment that focuses on helping individuals achieve independence in all areas of their lives. An occupational therapist works with individuals with varying disabilities and provides treatment for individuals to relearn physical skills lost as a result of an illness or accident—ideally so that they can return to some form of gainful employment or an independent, productive life.

Claim Forms

In contrast to most major third-party payer claims, there is no universal form to use when filing a workers' compensation claim. Some states allow workers' compensation claims to be submitted on the CMS-1500 form. Private insurance carriers typically have their own forms. The health insurance professional should determine whether it is acceptable to submit a workers' compensation claim on the CMS-1500 form; if not, the health insurance professional should ask the patient to request the required form from his or her employer or insurer.

 Imagine This!

Frank Turner sustains a serious cut to his right hand while operating a band saw at work. Frank's injury qualifies him for workers' compensation benefits, which start 1 week after the incident occurred. Larry Boggs, a coworker in the mill room with Frank, becomes ill the same week. Thinking he was just suffering from a minor cold, Larry does not file for workers' compensation; however, 2 weeks later, his cold is no better. Larry returns to his physician, who determines that he has pneumonia. Larry subsequently is hospitalized for 1 week, during which time further tests reveal that Larry's condition is caused by breathing minute particles of sawdust. When Larry is discharged from the hospital, he files a workers' compensation claim. The claim is approved, but Larry's benefits do not begin until 4 weeks after his illness began.

Normally, multiple copies of all workers' compensation reports are essential for proper distribution as follows:

1. Original form to the insurance carrier
2. One copy to the appropriate state agency
3. One copy to the patient's employer
4. One copy to be retained in the healthcare provider's files

When special claim forms are needed, instructions usually are provided—often on the back side of the form. If instructions do not come with the form, the health insurance professional should ask the patient to obtain detailed guidelines from the employer or insurer.

Because thousands of different forms are used for workers' compensation claims in the United States, to avoid confusion, National Uniform Claim Committee (NUCC) instructions for completing the universal CMS-1500 claim form are used. These instructions can be found in Appendix B along with an example of a completed claim for a workers' compensation case. These instructions are generic, and the health insurance professional should obtain exact guidelines from the employer, the insurer, or the state in which the claim occurs to prevent delays or rejections.

Before completing the blocks, the health insurance professional should determine the name and address of the insurer to whom the claim will be sent. This information should appear in the upper-right corner of the claim form.

Progress Reports

Keeping the employer and insurance carrier apprised of the patient's treatment plan, progress, and status is a priority in workers' compensation cases. The health insurance professional should be well versed in the particulars of workers' compensation reporting so that written communications meet all accepted legal standards. After the initial visit to the physician has occurred and the attending physician report has been filed, unless the employee has returned to work full time, periodic reports have to be filed. These are referred to as **progress or supplemental reports** (Fig. 13.3). Often there are no special printed forms for progress reports; copies of clinical notes from the patient's health record or a letter from the attending physician giving a detailed account of the patient's progress is acceptable. When the patient's disability ends and he or she is able to return to work, the physician submits a final report.

SPECIAL BILLING NOTES

Most states have a fee schedule that providers must use when billing a workers' compensation claim, and as long as a workers' compensation claim is pending, the provider cannot bill the patient. In addition, balance billing is not allowed on workers' compensation claims. If the claim has been denied and all efforts for appeal have been exhausted, the health insurance professional should issue a letter of reply immediately, after which direct billing to the patient or the patient's private insurance company for the services rendered is allowed. The workers' compensation fee schedule does not apply to denied claims; instead, the provider's usual and customary fees apply. Workers' compensation claims are handled differently in each state, and the health insurance professional must follow the guidelines set forth by the law in his or her state. Also, rules and regulations and appropriate forms may change from year to year, which makes it vitally important for the health insurance professional to keep up to date with the most current laws in the state in which he or she is employed.

Imagine This!

Sandra Cotter was injured at work when a filing cabinet fell on her foot. The human relations officer advised Sandra to see her own physician because the company did not have a specific workers' compensation physician. Sandra was treated at the Heartland Medical Clinic, which billed her health insurer, Blue Cross and Blue Shield. Blue Cross and Blue Shield refused payment, so Heartland billed Sandra. Sandra refused to pay the bill, stating that it was a workers' compensation case. Heartland argued that they had not received a call from Sandra's employer authorizing treatment. Still, Sandra refused to pay. After sending Sandra statements for 6 months, Heartland sent her a certified letter stating that they were refusing all future medical treatment at the clinic. Sandra filed a complaint with the state workers' compensation board, and the case eventually was resolved; however, Heartland still refused to see Sandra for subsequent visits.

WORKERS' COMPENSATION AND MEDICARE

It is evident that there is normally a delay between when a claim is filed for a work-related illness or injury and when the state workers' compensation insurance decides if it should pay for the medical expenses incurred. If the employee is enrolled in Medicare and the workers' compensation insurer denies payment for medical bills pending a review of a claim (generally 120 days or longer), Medicare may make a conditional payment when there is evidence that the primary plan does not pay promptly based on reimbursement when the primary plan does pay. If the state workers' compensation insurance denies payment, and if the injured (or ill) employee gives Medicare proof that the claim was denied, then Medicare will pay for Medicare-covered items and services.

In some cases, workers' compensation insurance may not pay the entire bill. If, for example, an injury or illness began before the employee started his or her job, workers' compensation may not pay the entire bill if it is determined that the job did not cause the original problem but may have made it worse. In this case, workers' compensation insurance may agree to pay only a part of the medical expenses. If Medicare was paying for the treatment for the initial condition before the job start-up, Medicare may pay its share for part of the medical bills that workers' compensation does not cover.

Workers' Compensation Medicare Set-Aside Arrangements

If a Medicare beneficiary settles a workers' compensation claim in which the employer's workers' compensation insurer pays for medical expenses, the settlement may provide for funds to be set aside to pay for future medical or prescription drug services related to the injury, illness, or disease. In such cases, a Workers' Compensation Medicare Set-Aside Arrangement (WCMSA) can be set up into which these funds can be deposited. It is important to be aware with a WCMSA that:

- Money placed in a WCMSA is for paying future medical and/or prescription drug expenses related to the work injury or illness/disease that otherwise would have been covered by Medicare
- Funds in the WCMSA cannot be used to pay for any other work injury or any medical items or services that Medicare doesn't cover (e.g., dental services)
- Medicare will not pay for any medical expenses related to the injury until after all set-aside money has been used appropriately
- After all WCMSA money has been spent appropriately, Medicare can start paying for Medicare-covered services related to the work-related injury, illness, or disease

WORKERS' COMPENSATION AND MEDICAID

We learned in Chapter 10 that Medicaid is a federal program of healthcare benefits for certain classes of

Workers' Compensation
Medical Progress Report

Claim Number	Health Care Provider

Employee Last Name	First Name

Mailing Address (include zip code) | Telephone (include area code)

Occupation	Date of Birth	Sex

Description of Injury/Illness	Date of Exam	Social Security Number

Employer	Employer Contact Person

Employer Address | Phone #

Insurer Name | Claim Representative

Insurer Address | Phone #

Current Work Ability: ☐ Fit for regular work duties ☐ Unfit for regular work duties

Start date for return to regular work duties (dd/mm/yy)

Duration of modified duties: ☐ 1-7 days ☐ 8-14 days ☐ 15-21 days ☐ More

Start date for modified duties (dd/mm/yy)

Subjective Information

Objective Information

Past Diseases/Injuries

Diagnostics (Lab/x-rays, CT, etc.) | ICD Code:

Prescribed Treatment/Advice/Referrals

Please give details for the following questions when the answer is Yes

Has worker been hospitalized? ☐ Yes ☐ No Dates:_____ to_____

Has an operation been performed? ☐ Yes ☐ No Date(s):

Any factors delaying recovery? ☐ Yes ☐ No Explain:

Is permanent disability probable? ☐ Yes ☐ No

Would you suggest an examination by a WC doctor? ☐ Yes ☐ No

Will worker be seen again? ☐ Yes ☐ No Date:

I hereby certify that the above is a correct statement of services personally rendered by me.

Health Care Professional Signature _____ Date _____

Name of Physician	EIN #
Address	NPI #

Fig. 13.3 Sample workers' compensation medical progress report.

people with limited resources that is administered by the states. Some employees who file workers' compensation claims may be enrolled in Medicaid and receive benefits that cover their non–work-related medical expenses. Before the ACA, Medicaid limited both the assets and the income an enrollee can have. Workers' compensation payments are generally not taxable, so they are not counted in determining Medicaid eligibility. Like Medicare, state Medicaid programs may seek reimbursement for medical expenses paid to a Medicaid beneficiary when that person receives a settlement from workers' compensation. Workers' compensation is considered third-party liability (TPL) under Medicaid rules, and Medicaid is the payer of last resort.

WORKERS' COMPENSATION AND MANAGED CARE

A workers' compensation managed care organization is any entity that manages the utilization of care and costs associated with claims covered by workers' compensation insurance, which must be approved by the state's workers' compensation board. As an alternative to the traditional approach to workers' compensation insurance coverage, some employers choose a managed care system (e.g., health maintenance organization [HMO] or preferred provider organization [PPO]) to provide medical care to injured employees, which can be a cost savings to the employer. Some states, such as New Jersey, have a workers' compensation managed care organization that manages the use of care and costs associated with claims covered by workers' compensation insurance. Employers typically can realize a savings in premium costs by selecting the managed care option if offered in the state and approved by the state workers' compensation board.

HIPAA AND WORKERS' COMPENSATION

The HIPAA Privacy Rule does not apply to workers' compensation insurers, workers' compensation administrative agencies, or employers. The Privacy Rule recognizes the legitimate need for insurers and other entities involved in the workers' compensation system to have access to injured workers' **protected health information (PHI)** as authorized by state or other law. Workers' compensation patients may or may not be required to sign a release of information form for a claim form to be filed. In addition, employers and claims adjusters retain the right of access to workers' compensation files. If the health insurance professional encounters a workers' compensation case for an established patient who already has a health record in that office, a new record should be created and kept separate from that individual's regular health record. Some medical offices

color-code or flag workers' compensation records or file them in a separate area to avoid confusion. The health insurance professional should check the regulations in his or her state regarding PHI regulations.

WORKERS' COMPENSATION FRAUD

As with any type of insurance, fraud occurs in workers' compensation cases. Most states require workers' compensation insurers, self-insured employers, and third-party administrators to report fraud to the state insurance commissioner's office, the local district attorney's office, or both. Anyone can report workers' compensation fraud, however. When fraud is suspected, a report should be made within a reasonable time frame, usually within 30 days from the time the individual reporting knows or reasonably believes that he or she knows the identity of a person or entity that has committed workers' compensation fraud or has knowledge that such fraud has been committed. This report often can be accomplished by a telephone call to either of the previously named offices.

> **? What Did You Learn?**
> 1. How did workers' compensation originate?
> 2. Who is eligible for workers' compensation benefits?
> 3. List four exemption classifications.
> 4. What is no-fault insurance?
> 5. What does an ombudsman do?

PRIVATE AND EMPLOYER-SPONSORED DISABILITY INCOME INSURANCE

Most people think about insurance coverage as it relates to health, life, home, or automobile, but the most crucial aspect of personal and family finances is **earned income**—income from employment. If an illness or injury occurred and this income stopped, most people would quickly find it difficult or impossible to maintain a home and provide for their family. **Disability income insurance** replaces a portion of earned income when an individual is unable to perform the requirements of his or her job because of injury or illness that is not work related.

Disability insurance can be purchased privately through a commercial insurance company, or it is sometimes furnished by the employer. There are two major types of disability coverage:
1. **Short-term disability**, which provides an income for the early part of a disability—typically 2 weeks to 2 years
2. **Long-term disability**, which helps replace income for a longer time—5 years or until the disabled individual turns 65

DEFINING DISABILITY

Disability is commonly defined in one of two ways:

1. An individual is unable to perform in the occupation or job that he or she was doing before the disability occurred. This definition of disability is covered in what is referred to as **own-occupation policies**. A variation is the **modified own-occupation policy**, which covers workers for their own occupation as long as they are not gainfully employed elsewhere.
2. An individual is unable to perform any occupation for which he or she is suited by education and experience.

The distinction between these two definitions can be crucial. If a surgeon loses a hand, he or she may be unable to perform surgery. In the case of an own-occupation policy, the surgeon would be able to recover because he or she was able to work as a physician in a nonsurgical field. With the inability to perform any occupation, there would be no recovery, even if the surgeon could work as a tour guide.

Short-Term Disability

Short-term disability pays a percentage of an individual's wages or salary if he or she becomes **temporarily disabled**, meaning that the individual is unable to work for a short time because of sickness or injury (excluding job-related illnesses or injuries). A typical short-term disability policy pays one-half to two-thirds of salary or wages for a specific number of weeks, depending on the policy. Most short-term disability policies have a **benefit cap**, meaning that there is a maximum benefit amount paid per month.

A worker generally begins receiving money from a short-term disability policy within 1 to 14 days after becoming sick or disabled. The actual time elapsed before payments begin depends on the stipulations in the policy. Often, if the individual sustains an injury, benefits begin immediately. It usually takes longer with an illness because there needs to be enough time to show that the illness is severe enough to be disabling. If the disability insurance is furnished by the employer, there may be additional restrictions as to when the short-term disability benefits begin. The employer may require all sick days to be used up before the employee begins receiving disability payments. Typically, if the condition worsens over time, the individual would receive disability pay retroactive to the first sick day.

Long-Term Disability

As with short-term disability, a long-term disability insurance policy protects an individual from the loss of ability to earn an income because of an illness or injury that is not work related. It pays a monthly amount to help cover expenses when an individual is unable to perform his or her job or function in a chosen occupation or profession.

There are two major types of individual long-term disability insurance: no cancelable and guaranteed renewable. With both no cancelable and guaranteed renewable policies, the insurer cannot cancel or refuse to renew the policy as long as the required premiums are paid on time. The key difference between the two major types of policies is that under a no cancelable contract, the individual has the extra security that premiums can never be increased above those shown in the policy as long as the required premiums are paid. With a guaranteed renewable policy, the premiums can be increased, but only if the change affects an entire class of policyholders. For this reason, initial premiums for guaranteed renewable policies can be less expensive than no cancelable policies.

DISABILITY CLAIMS PROCESS

As with workers' compensation, there are several steps to the disability claims process. To allow this process to work efficiently and effectively, the employee and the employer must attend to certain responsibilities.

Employee's Responsibilities

First, the worker must notify the proper party that he or she intends to file a disability claim. To do this, the individual first needs to submit a claim request. If disability insurance is provided through the employer, a claim form may be obtained from the company's human resources department. Some insurers allow telephone or electronic submission of claims. In this case, the human resources department should provide a toll-free number or website and specific instructions for submitting the claim. In the case of an individual or private disability policy, a claim form may be obtained from the insurance company where the policy was purchased. The claim request should include everything needed to process the claim, including:

- Information that the employee provides (Fig. 13.4)
- Information that the employer provides (Fig. 13.5)
- The attending physician statement (see Fig. 13.2)
- The claimant's authorization to disclose health information (Fig. 13.6)

EMPLOYEE'S CLAIM FOR COMPENSATION

| ANSWER ALL QUESTIONS FULLY - PRINT OR TYPE CLEARLY |

IMPORTANT: Your Social Security Number Must Be Entered:

IMPORTANTE: El Numero de su Seguro Social Debe Ser Indicado:

WCB Case No. (If known)_____ Carrier Case No. (If known)_____

A.
Injured person
	1. Name...
	         First Name Middle Name Last Name
	2. Mailing Address...
	         Number and Street (Include Apartment No.) City State Zip Code
	3. Sex ☐Male ☐Female Date of Birth...Telephone No. ( )...............................
	4. Do you speak English? ☐Yes ☐No If no, what language do you speak?...
	5. Name of union and local number, if member...
	6. State what your regular work/occupation was...
	7. Wages or average earnings per day, including overtime, board, rent, and other allowances................
	8. Were you paid full wages for the day of injury? ☐Yes ☐No
	9. Your work week at time of injury was: ☐Five day ☐Six day ☐Seven day ☐Other..............................

B. Employer(s)	1. Employer..Telephone No. ( ).................................... 2. Employer's Address.. 3. Were you employed by any other employer or employers at the time of your injury/illness? ☐Yes ☐No 4. If yes, did you lose time from work at this other employment as a result of your injury/illness? ☐Yes ☐No
C. Place/Time	1. Address where injury occurred..County......................... 2. Date of Injury..at.....................o'clock, ☐ AM ☐ PM
D. The Injury	1. How did injury/illness occur?... ....
E. Nature and Extent of Injury/ Illness	1. State fully the nature of your injury/illness, including all parts of body injured................................... .... 2. Date you stopped work because of this injury/illness?... 3. Have you returned to work? ☐ Yes ☐ No If yes, on what date?.. 4. Does injury/illness keep you from work? ☐Yes ☐No 5. Have you done any work during period of disability? ☐ Yes ☐ No 6. Have you received any wages since your injury/illness? ☐ Yes ☐ No

F.
Medical Benefits
	1. Did you receive or are you now receiving medical care? ☐Yes ☐No
	2. Are you now in need of medical care? ☐Yes ☐No
	3. Name of attending doctor...
	    Doctor's address...
	4. If you were in a hospital, give the dates hospitalized..
	    Name of hospital...
	    Hospital's address...

G. Comp. Payments	1. Have you received or are you now receiving workers' compensation payments for the injury reported above? ☐Yes ☐No 2. Do you claim further workers' compensation payments? ☐Yes ☐No
H. Notice	1. Have you given your employer (or supervisor) notice of injury? ☐ Yes ☐No 2. If yes, notice was given ☐orally ☐in writing, on... to ....

ANY PERSON WHO KNOWINGLY AND WITH INTENT TO DEFRAUD PRESENTS, CAUSES TO BE PRESENTED, OR PREPARES WITH KNOWLEDGE OR BELIEF THAT IT WILL BE PRESENTED TO, OR BY AN INSURER, OR SELF INSURER, ANY INFORMATION CONTAINING ANY FALSE MATERIAL STATEMENT OR CONCEALS ANY MATERIAL FACT SHALL BE GUILTY OF A CRIME AND SUBJECT TO SUBSTANTIAL FINES AND IMPRISONMENT.

Signed by..Dated..
         (Claimant)

C-3 (2-04)

Fig. 13.4 Employee's statement form.

EMPLOYER'S REPORT OF NON-WORK-RELATED ACCIDENT/OCCUPATIONAL DISEASE

Send this notice directly to the Chair, Workers' Compensation Board at the address shown on the reverse side within ten (10) days after an accident occurs. ANSWER ALL QUESTIONS FULLY. A copy should also be provided to or retained by your workers' compensation insurance carrier.

Any employer who fails to timely file Form C-2, as required by Section 110 of the Workers' Compensation Law, is subject to a fine of not more than $1,000. In addition, the Board or Chair may impose a penalty of up to $2,500.

TYPEWRITER PREPARATION IS STRONGLY RECOMMENDED - INCLUDE ZIP CODE IN ALL ADDRESSES-EMPLOYEE'S S.S.NO. MUST BE ENTERED BELOW ↓

WCB CASE NO.(If Known)	CARRIER CASE NO.	CARRIER CODE NO.	WC POLICY NO.	DATE OF ACCIDENT	EMPLOYEE'S S.S. NO.
		W		m m d d y y	

1.(a) EMPLOYER'S NAME | (b) EMPLOYER'S MAILING ADDRESS | (c) OSHA CASE/FILE NO.

(d) LOCATION (If Different From Mailing Address) | (e) NATURE OF BUSINESS (Principal Products, Services, etc.) | (f) NY UI EMPLOYER REG. NO. | (g) FEIN - if UI Emp. Reg. No. Unknown

2.(a) INSURANCE CARRIER | (b) CARRIER'S ADDRESS

3.(a) INJURED EMPLOYEE (First, M.I., Last) | (b) ADDRESS (Includes No. & Street, City, State, Zip & Apt. No.)

ACCIDENT

4. (a) ADDRESS WHERE ACCIDENT OCCURRED | (b) COUNTY | (c) WAS ACCIDENT ON EMPLOYER'S PREMISES? ☐ Yes ☐ No

5. HOUR EMP. BEGAN WORK h h : m m ☐ AM ☐ PM | 6. TIME OF ACCIDENT h h : m m ☐ AM ☐ PM | 7. DEPT. WHERE REGULARLY EMPLOYED | 8.(a) DATE STOPPED WORK BECAUSE OF THIS INJURY/ILLNESS m m d d y y | (b) WAS EMPLOYEE PAID IN FULL FOR DAY? ☐ Yes ☐ No

INJURED PERSON

9. SEX ☐ Male ☐ Female | 10. DATE OF BIRTH m m d d y y | 11.OCCUPATION (Specific job title at which employed) | 12. DATE HIRED m m d d y y

13.(a) AVERAGE EARNINGS PER WEEK? $, .0 0 | (b) TOTAL EARNINGS PAID DURING 52 WEEKS PRIOR TO DATE OF ACCIDENT (Include bonuses, overtime, value of lodging, etc.) $, , .0 0 | 14. (a) EMPLOYEE IS: ☐ Full Time ☐ Part Time | (b) INJURED EMPLOYEE'S WORK WEEK (Check days usually worked.)

Mon	Tue	Wed	Thu	Fri	Sat	Sun
☐	☐	☐	☐	☐	☐	☐

NATURE OF INJURY

15. NATURE OF INJURY AND PART(S) OF BODY AFFECTED | 16. (a) DID YOU PROVIDE MEDICAL CARE? ☐ Yes ☐ No | (b) IF YES, WHEN?

17. WAS EMPLOYEE TREATED IN AN EMERGENCY ROOM? ☐ Yes ☐ No | 18. WAS EMPLOYEE HOSPITALIZED OVERNIGHT AS AN IN-PATIENT? ☐ Yes ☐ No

19. (a) NAME AND ADDRESS OF DOCTOR | (b) NAME AND ADDRESS OF HOSPITAL

20. (a) HAS EMPLOYEE RETURNED TO WORK? ☐ Yes ☐ No | (b) IF YES, GIVE DATE: m m d d y y | (c) AT WHAT WEEKLY WAGE? $, .0 0

NOTE: FORM C-11 MUST BE FILED EACH TIME THERE IS A CHANGE IN EMPLOYMENT STATUS

CAUSE OF ACCIDENT

21. WHAT WAS EMPLOYEE DOING WHEN INJURED? (Please be specific. Identify tools, equipment or material the employee was using.)

22. HOW DID THE ACCIDENT OR EXPOSURE OCCUR? (Please describe fully the events that resulted in injury or occupational disease. Tell what happened and how it happened. Please use separate sheet if necessary.)

23. OBJECT OR SUBSTANCE THAT DIRECTLY INJURED EMPLOYEE. e.g., the machine employee struck against or which struck him/her, the vapor or poison inhaled or swallowed, the chemical that irritated his/her skin. In cases of strains, the thing (s)he was lifting, pulling, etc.

FATAL CASES

24. (a) DATE OF DEATH m m d d y y | (b) NAME AND ADDRESS OF NEAREST RELATIVE | (c) RELATIONSHIP

PREPARATION

DATE EMPLOYER/SUPERVISOR FIRST KNEW OF INJURY m m d d y y | DATE OF THIS REPORT m m d d y y | IF FORM IS SUBMITTED BY EMPLOYER, COMPLETE A & B BELOW. IF FORM IS SUBMITTED BY THIRD PARTY, COMPLETE A,B,C & D BELOW.

A. EMPLOYEE PREPARING FORM OR SUPPLYING INFORMATION TO THIRD PARTY | B. TITLE | TELEPHONE NUMBER & EXTENSION

C. IF REPORT PREPARED BY THIRD PARTY, COMPANY NAME AND ADDRESS

D. THIRD PARTY CONTACT NAME | TELEPHONE NUMBER & EXTENSION

Fig. 13.5 Sample employer's statement form.

CLAIMANT'S AUTHORIZATION TO DISCLOSE HEALTH INFORMATION
(Pursuant to HIPAA)

INSTRUCTIONS

To the Claimant: The Health Insurance Portability and Accountability Act of 1996 (HIPAA) set standards for guaranteeing the privacy of individually identifiable health information and the confidentiality of patient medical records. By completing and signing this form, you authorize your health care provider to file medical reports with the parties that you choose (such as the Workers' Compensation Board, your employer's insurance carrier, your attorney or representative, etc.) by checking the appropriate boxes below.

You have the right to refuse to sign this Authorization. If you sign, you have the right to revoke this Authorization at any time by mailing a request to revoke to the health care provider. You have the right to receive a copy of this Authorization.

IMPORTANT: Failure to execute this authorization may interfere with your ability to obtain workers' compensation benefits.

CLAIMANT'S NAME	CLAIMANT'S SOCIAL SECURITY NUMBER	CLAIMANT'S DATE OF BIRTH
LIST ALL WCB CASE NUMBER(S) AND CORRESPONDING DATE(S) OF ACCIDENT FOR WHICH YOU ARE GRANTING AUTHORIZATION		

I, _____, hereby authorize my treating health provider,
            Claimant's Name

_____, to disclose the following described health information:
            Health Provider's Name

_____

_____

_____

This information can be disclosed to the following parties: *(check all that apply; give names and addresses, if known)*

☐ New York State Workers' Compensation Board

☐ My current/former employer _____

☐ Workers' compensation insurance carrier(s) _____

☐ Third-party administrator _____

☐ My attorney/licensed representative _____

☐ The Uninsured Employer's Fund (This fund is responsible for paying the medical bills and lost wage benefits when an employer is uninsured.)

☐ Special Funds Conservation Committee (for cases under Section 25-a or 15-8 of the Workers' Compensation Law)

    Section 25-a: If your claim is being reopened after being previously closed, the Special Fund for Reopened Cases may be responsible for paying your medical bills and lost wage benefits.

    Section 15-8: If you had a medical condition that existed prior to this injury, the Special Fund for Second Injuries may be responsible for reimbursing your employer's insurance carrier after a period of time has elapsed.

Redisclosure: I understand that once the above-referenced health care provider discloses health information based on this Authorization, that health information is no longer protected by HIPAA and the Privacy Rule.

Expiration Date: This Authorization expires upon the final closing of the workers' compensation claim(s) for which it is executed.

I have had the opportunity to review and understand the content of this Authorization. By signing this Authorization, I confirm that it accurately reflects my wishes.

_____   _____   _____
Printed Name of Claimant or Legal Representative   Signature of Claimant or Legal Representative   Date

If Authorization signed by a legal representative on behalf of claimant, state relationship to claimant_____and
basis for authority (e.g. claimant is a minor; patient is deceased and representative is the claimant in a workers' compensation proceeding or represents the estate) _____

TO THE HEALTH PROVIDER: Keep the original of this Authorization on file. A copy must be given to the patient/claimant upon request.

Fig. 13.6 Sample disclosure form.

Employer's Responsibilities

If the disability insurance is provided by the employer, a statement that helps identify the benefits available should accompany the claim. The employer also must provide detailed information on the type of coverage, policy number, division/class number, and division/class description.

Attending Physician's Statement

It is important that the injured or ill worker be examined by a physician as soon as possible after the disability has occurred and within the time limit allowed by the insurer. The physician must determine that the individual is disabled as defined by the policy. An attending physician's statement must be completed; it typically includes information such as:

- The diagnosis
- The first day the individual was unable to work
- Whether the illness or injury was work related
- The nature of the treatment or suggested treatment
- Restrictions and limitations

Health Insurance Professional's Role

Frequently, disability claim handling gets tied up in time-consuming tasks, such as document processing, record keeping, written correspondence, telephone inquiries, photocopying, and sending faxes. The process involves a lot of human interaction, which complicates the process, especially if all phases are not properly documented and monitored. Everyone involved can become quickly frustrated and impatient. It is the health insurance professional's responsibility to see that everything possible is done to facilitate the claims process for the benefit of the medical practice and the disabled patient. The health insurance professional attends to this responsibility by seeing to it that claim forms and statements are completed correctly and submitted promptly and all necessary documentation is included.

The health insurance professional's role also might be to educate the patient on disability benefits. With disability insurance, the insurer does not reimburse the patient strictly according to the fees charged for medical services rendered by the attending physician. Disability insurance benefits are paid to compensate for loss of income from wages. Periodic payments (typically monthly) are made directly to the patient to use for expenses as he or she sees fit. Ideally, the patient has a separate health insurance policy to pay the cost of needed healthcare.

❓ What Did You Learn?

1. What do disability income insurance benefits pay?
2. What items should a typical claim request include?
3. List five things the attending physician's statement should address.
4. What is the health insurance professional's role in the disability claims process?

FEDERAL DISABILITY PROGRAMS

Federal disability programs provide services such as cash support, healthcare coverage, and direct supportive services to eligible individuals with disabilities. These programs typically are limited to individuals younger than age 65. There are nine major federal disability programs that include sizable proportions of individuals ages 50 to 64, as follows:

1. Social Security Disability Insurance (SSDI)
2. Supplemental Security Income (SSI)
3. Medicare
4. Medicaid
5. Workers' compensation
6. Federal Black Lung Program
7. Department of Veterans Affairs (VA) Disability Compensation Program
8. VA pension programs
9. VA Health Services Program

An individual may receive benefits from more than one program if he or she meets all eligibility requirements. Specific eligibility requirements typically vary, depending on the purpose of the program, and eligibility requirements may change over time as the result of amendments to the law, new regulations, or court decisions that affect eligibility criteria.

Disability under the federal programs generally is defined as significant difficulty with performing or the inability to perform certain day-to-day functions as a result of a health condition or impairment. For adults age 18 through 64, these functions often involve working or keeping house. For individuals age 65 and older, the functions may involve the inability to carry out routine daily tasks. Some commonly used factors that federal programs look at in assessing disability are:

- Sensory impairments: Difficulty with or the inability to see, hear, or speak

- Cognitive or mental impairments: The presence of or resulting disabilities from cognitive or mental impairments (e.g., Alzheimer disease, mental illness, mental retardation)
- Functioning of specific body systems: Capacity of specific body systems (e.g., climbing stairs, walking three blocks, lifting more than 10 lb)
- **Activities of daily living (ADLs)** and **instrumental activities of daily living (IADLs)**: Difficulty with or the inability to perform, without the help of another person or a device, ADLs (e.g., bathing, dressing, eating, toileting, walking) or IADLs (e.g., using the telephone, shopping, preparing meals, keeping house, managing medications)
- Working: Inability to work; limitations in the amount or kind of work; or ability to work only occasionally, irregularly, or part-time

AMERICANS WITH DISABILITIES ACT

The intent of the **Americans With Disabilities Act (ADA)** of 1990 is to protect the civil rights of individuals with disabilities. Equal opportunity provisions pertain to employment, public accommodation, transportation, state and local government services, and telecommunications. Disability is present for purposes of the ADA if an individual meets one of the following three criteria:

1. The individual has a physical or mental impairment that substantially limits one or more major life activities.
2. A record exists of such an impairment.
3. The individual is regarded as having an impairment.

SOCIAL SECURITY DISABILITY INSURANCE

Social Security Disability Insurance (SSDI) is the primary federal insurance program that protects workers from loss of income as a result of disability. SSDI provides monthly cash benefits to disabled workers younger than age 65 and to certain of their dependents. SSDI is intended for workers who retire before age 65 because of a disability. Disability for SSDI is defined as the inability to do any substantial gainful activity by reason of any medically determinable physical or mental impairment that can be expected to result in death or that has lasted or can be expected to last for a continuous period of not less than 12 months.

History of the SSDI Program

The 1935 Social Security Act established the federal Social Security system to provide old-age benefits for retired workers. The SSDI program was enacted in 1956 to provide benefits to workers ages 50 through 64 who retired early because of a disability. Subsequent amendments broadened SSDI coverage to include certain dependents and workers younger than age 50.

Administration and Funding

SSDI is federally administered by the Social Security Administration (SSA). Funding is provided through the disability insurance (SSDI) portion of the Social Security payroll tax on wages. Generally, the Federal Insurance Contributions Act (FICA) taxes are collected at a rate of 7.65% on gross earnings (i.e., earnings before any deductions). The breakdown of FICA is 6.2% for Social Security (Old-Age, Survivors, and Disability Insurance [OASDI]) and 1.45% for Medicare. The wage base limit in 2016 for Social Security (OASDI parts) was $118,500. This limit is subject to change annually. There is no wage base limit for the Medicare Part A (hospital insurance) payroll tax.

Eligibility

To be eligible for SSDI, there are two tests the individual must pass that involve work credits: the "recent work test" and the "duration of work test."

Recent work test: If you are age 31 or older, you must have worked at least 5 of the past 10 years to pass the recent work test. In other words, you will need to have earned 20 credits (one quarter of work equals one credit) in the 10 years immediately before you became disabled.

If you are between ages 24 and 31, you must have worked at least half the time since turning age 21. For example, if you are age 29, you must have worked at least 4 years of the past 8 years (or have earned 16 credits in the past 8 years).

If you are under age 24, you must have worked at least 1.5 years in the 3-year period before disability (or have earned 6 credits in the past 3 years).

There is an exception to these rules for certain blind applicants.

Duration of work test: The individual must have worked the following number of years (or earned the following number of credits) to qualify for SSDI.

BECAME DISABLED AT AGE	NUMBER OF CREDITS YOU NEED	NUMBER OF YEARS OF WORK
21 through 24	6	1.5
24 through 31	6 to 18	1.5 to 4.5
31 through 42	20	5
44	22	5.5
46	24	6
48	26	6.5
50	28	7
52	30	7.5
54	32	8
56	34	8.5
58	36	9
60	38	9.5
62 or older	40	10

Note: At least 20 work credits must have been earned within the 10 years (40 quarters) immediately before becoming disabled.

Vivian Slattery became disabled at age 50. For the past 6 years she was a schoolteacher at Moorhead Elementary School and did not pay Federal Insurance Contributions Act (FICA) payroll taxes. Before that Vivian worked at BestCo Mattress (a private industry) and did pay FICA taxes for more than 20 years. Vivian is not eligible for SSDI benefits. Although she paid FICA taxes for more than the 28 work credits required, only 16 (4 years) of the work credits were paid in the past 10 years instead of the required 20. (However, Vivian will still be eligible for regular Social Security retirement benefits.)

After it has been established that the applicant has enough quarters and is not earning more than the "substantial gainful activity amount," a state disability determination unit examines medical evidence to determine if the applicant's mental or physical impairment is severe enough to have more than a minimal effect on the applicant's ability to work. If so, the applicant's medical condition is compared with an SSA listing of more than 100 impairments (e.g., loss of two limbs; fracture of vertebra with spinal cord involvement, substantiated by appropriate sensory and motor loss; vision of 20/200 or less after correction). To view the complete list of impairments, log on to http://www.socialsecurity.gov and use "listing of impairments" as search words.

Applicants whose medical conditions are at least as severe as the conditions in the SSA listing are considered disabled. Applicants who are not found disabled at this point must go through two additional evaluation steps. First, a determination is made regarding whether the applicant can do his or her past work. This decision is based on assessments of factors such as physical abilities (e.g., strength, walking, standing) or mental abilities (e.g., the ability to carry out and remember instructions or to respond appropriately in work settings).

For applicants who cannot perform past work, an assessment is done to determine their ability to perform other jobs that exist in the national economy. This assessment is based on the individual's functional capacity, age, education, and work experience. Generally, individuals younger than age 50 are considered to be able to adapt to new work situations.

Dependent coverage and survivor benefits are offered through SSDI to certain qualifying individuals. Disabled individuals can receive SSDI in three ways:
1. On their own as disabled workers (described previously)
2. As widows or widowers (who are ages 50 to 59) of insured individuals
3. As adults ages 18 through 64 who became disabled in childhood whose parents receive SSDI, are Social Security retirees, or are deceased (but had been insured under Social Security)

After teacher Louise Carson had her workers' compensation claim denied, she quit her job and filed for SSDI. SSDI found Louise to be disabled at her teaching position; however, they determined that she could perform at a "new work" situation that was less stressful and suggested that Louise use her education and training to work in a library or become a private tutor.

SUPPLEMENTAL SECURITY INCOME

The **Supplemental Security Income (SSI)** program provides monthly cash payments to low-income aged (65 years and older), blind, and disabled individuals. The SSI program was established by the 1972 amendments to the Social Security Act, which replaced earlier federal grants to the states for old-age assistance, aid to the blind, and aid to the permanently disabled.

Administration and Funding

The SSI program is administered by the SSA. Funding comes from general federal revenues. Many states have chosen the option to supplement federal SSI payments with their own funds.

Eligibility

In contrast to SSDI, individuals receiving SSI because of blindness or disability have no work requirements, but they must meet a **financial means test**, a detailed and comprehensive questionnaire that establishes financial need. The SSI financial means test depends on income and resources. Individuals younger than age 65 must meet disability and financial means criteria, whereas individuals age 65 or older need to meet only the financial means criteria. Individuals may receive SSI payments either as individuals or as couples. Both members of a couple must be aged, blind, or disabled and must meet the financial means criteria to collect payments. Other than these provisions for couples, there are no dependent or survivor benefits in SSI.

The determination of disability under SSI is outlined in Box 13.1. For children younger than age 18, the determination of disability is based on a standard of comparable severity.

Income Limit for SSI

The income limit for the SSI program is based on the federal benefit rate (FBR), which represents both the SSI income limit and the maximum federal monthly SSI payment. In 2019 the FBR was $771 per month for individuals and $1157 for couples. (The FBR increases annually if there is a Social Security cost-of-living adjustment.) To qualify for SSI, an individual's countable monthly income cannot exceed the FBR. Countable income is the amount left over after:
- Eliminating all items that are not considered income
- Applying all appropriate exclusions to the items that are income

Box 13.1 Who Is Eligible for Supplemental Security Income?

ADULTS

Anyone who is 65 or older, blind, or disabled who:

- has limited income;
- has limited resources;
- is a US citizen or national, or in one of certain categories of aliens;
- is a resident of one of the 50 states, the District of Columbia, or the Northern Mariana Islands;
- is not absent from the country for a full calendar month or for 30 consecutive days or more;
- is not confined to an institution (such as a hospital or prison) at the government's expense;
- applies for any other cash benefits or payments for which he or she may be eligible (for example, pensions, Social Security benefits);
- gives the Social Security Administration (SSA) permission to contact any financial institution and request any financial records about you;
- files an application; and
- meets certain other requirements.

CHILDREN

Individuals under age 18 may be considered disabled if they have a medically determinable physical or mental impairment (including an emotional or learning problem) that:

- results in marked and severe functional limitations;
- can be expected to result in death; or
- has lasted or can be expected to last for a continuous period of not less than 12 months.

Blindness in the Supplemental Security Income (SSI) disability programs is "statutory blindness," which means the individual:

1. has a central visual acuity of 20/200 or less in the better eye with use of a correcting lens; or
2. has a visual field limitation in the better eye, such that the widest diameter of the visual field subtends an angle no greater than 20 degrees.

NOTE: Applicants with a visual impairment that is not "statutory blindness" as defined earlier may still be eligible for SSI benefits on the basis of disability.

From Social Security Administration: *Understanding Supplemental Security Income (SSI) eligibility requirements—2019 edition* (website). http://www.socialsecurity.gov/ssi/text-eligibility-ussi.htm.

Countable income is determined on a calendar month basis. It is the amount subtracted from the maximum federal benefit to determine eligibility and to compute the monthly payment amount. However, the SSA counts some income only when it determines eligibility. For instance, people who are earning wages from work have less than half of their monthly earnings counted toward the income limit, so they can make more than the qualifying amount. To know for sure whether a working person's income falls under the SSI income limit and to find answers for any other questions, contact the local Social Security office. SSI allows people who are participating in the Plan to Achieve Self-Support (PASS) program to set aside funds to help them get back to work; these funds do not count toward the income or asset limit for SSI.

A wealth of information regarding the Social Security program, including SSDI and SSI, can be found at http://www.ssa.gov/.

A weblink showing a table comparing the SSDI program with the SSI program is included under "Websites to Explore" at the end of this chapter.

 HIPAA Tip

As a "covered entity" under the Health Insurance Portability and Accountability Act (HIPAA), the Social Security Administration (SSA), which oversees the federal disability programs, such as Social Security Disability Insurance (SSDI) and Supplemental Security Income (SSI), must comply with HIPAA's medical information standards.

Compassionate Allowances Program

In response to complaints about long delays waiting for eligibility determination, SSA now offers a Compassionate Allowances program for disabled workers who have applied for SSDI or SSI. This program provides benefits quickly to applicants whose medical conditions are so serious that they would definitely qualify for disability under an SSA impairment listing. The program allows SSA to quickly identify the most obviously disabled applicants and grants them benefits soon after applying. To automatically qualify for either SSDI or SSI benefits, the individual must prove that he or she has a severe, medically determinable impairment that matches the criteria of a condition included in the SSA's listing of impairments. This listing is commonly known as *the Blue Book, the Listings*, or *the List of Disabilities*. For more information on this program, go to https://www.ssa.gov/compassionateallowances/.

STATE DISABILITY PROGRAMS

A few states (e.g., California, Hawaii, New Jersey, New York, and Rhode Island) and Puerto Rico currently have disability programs that provide short-term benefits for employees. These state programs are set up to supplement Social Security disability benefits. Because Social Security disability benefits do not cover the first 6 months of the disability, these state plans provide benefits to qualifying disabled individuals until Social Security payments begin. The funds are financed by a combination of the employees' payroll deductions and employer contributions. An employee's contributions are based on his or her earnings and are withheld from wages by the employer and transferred to the state fund. There are severe penalties for failing to withhold the contributions. With the exception of Rhode Island, an employer can opt out of the state plan and put the employee's contributions into a private plan. Private plans must meet state requirements regarding coverage, eligibility, contribution amounts, and employee approval.

CENTERS FOR DISEASE CONTROL AND PREVENTION

The Centers for Disease Control and Prevention (CDC) supports 18 state-based disability and health programs to ensure that disabled individuals are included in ongoing state disease prevention, health promotion, and emergency response activities. These programs promote health equity, help prevent chronic disease, and increase the quality of life for people with disabilities. Each program customizes its activities to meet its state's needs, broadening expertise and information sharing among states. Fig. 13.7 shows the states funded by CDC disability and health programs. The programs' goals are to:

- Enhance program infrastructure and capacity
- Improve state-level surveillance and monitoring activities
- Increase awareness of health-related disability policy initiatives
- Increase health promotion opportunities for people with disabilities
- Improve access to healthcare services for people with disabilities
- Improve emergency preparedness for people with disabilities
- Effectively monitor and evaluate program activities

The goals of the state disability and health programs align with those of *Healthy People 2020* related to disability. More information on *Healthy People 2020* can be found by logging on to the CDC's home page at http://www.cdc.gov/ and using the search words "Healthy People 2020."

TICKET TO WORK AND SELF-SUFFICIENCY PROGRAM

The **Ticket to Work** and Self-Sufficiency Program is an employment program for people with disabilities who are interested in going to work. It is part of the Ticket to Work and Work Incentives Improvement Act of 1999, legislation designed to remove many of the barriers that previously influenced people's decisions about going to work because of the concerns over losing healthcare coverage. The goal of the Ticket to Work program is to increase opportunities and choices for Social Security disability beneficiaries to obtain employment, vocational rehabilitation, and other support services from public and private providers, employers, and other organizations.

Under the Ticket to Work program, the SSA provides disability beneficiaries with a ticket that they may use to obtain the services and jobs they need from a new universe of organizations called **employment networks**. You can learn more about the Ticket to Work program by visiting the Choose Work website at http://www.choosework.net/.

FILING SSDI AND SSI CLAIMS

The process for filing an SSDI or SSI claim can be challenging, and assistance and cooperation are needed on several fronts—from the patient, the healthcare provider, and even the health insurance professional. Claims can be initiated online, over the phone, or by going into a local Social Security office. Some individuals hire a lawyer to assist with preparing the initial paperwork. The following paragraphs briefly outline the responsibilities of each party involved in this process.

Patient's Role

The patient must initiate the SSDI or SSI claim process. Often it starts by telephoning the SSA's toll-free

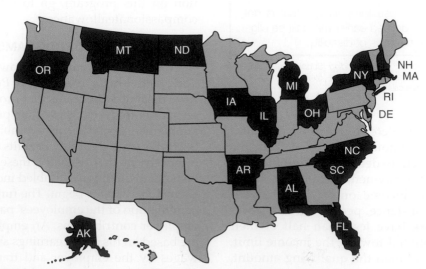

Fig. 13.7 Map showing states (in purple) funded by the Centers for Disease Control and Prevention (CDC) for disability and health programs.

number, 1-800-772-1213, during which a phone meeting with a local Social Security representative will be scheduled. Alternatively, a face-to-face meeting can be set up with a Social Security representative. During either the phone or live meeting, the representative gathers the necessary information regarding the claim and inputs the data into a computer application program. If the information is gathered over the phone, the completed application is sent to the applicant for his or her signature. A Social Security disability claim may also be completed online over the Internet; however, an SSI claim cannot be completed online.

A claim for disability benefits may be filed on the same day that an individual becomes disabled. There is no reason to file a Social Security disability claim for a minor illness or one that is unlikely to last 1 year or more. An individual who has a serious illness or injury and expects to be out of work for 1 year or more should not delay in filing a claim for Social Security disability benefits.

Unless the disability is catastrophic (e.g., terminal cancer, a serious heart condition requiring transplant, total paralysis of both legs), there is no easy way to tell whether an individual would be found disabled by Social Security. Individuals should make the decision about whether to file for Social Security disability based on their own belief regarding their condition. If an individual believes that he or she is truly disabled and is not going to be able to return to work in the near future, the individual should file for Social Security disability benefits.

After a Social Security disability claim is filed, the SSA contracts with a state agency—typically, a medical doctor and a layperson (e.g., a disability examiner)—to evaluate the claim. Similar to a denied Medicare claim, if the SSA denies the claim, a request for reconsideration can be filed, and a separate set of individuals will perform a reevaluation. If the claim is denied a second time, a hearing before an administrative law judge can be requested. The administrative law judge makes an independent decision on the claim, which is usually final.

Applicants for SSI or SSDI benefits should obtain the free booklet *Disability Benefits,* which can be downloaded from the Social Security website at https://www.ssa.gov/pubs/EN-05-10029.pdf. This booklet suggests ways to help shorten the process by knowing what documents to include when applying for benefits.

Physician's Role

In some cases, a patient's own physician may be allowed to conduct the initial assessment in determining disability and then pass on the findings to the disability determination unit. In other cases, a specific physician is designated to carry out the evaluation of a patient claiming disability. This is done to prevent overreporting of injuries and to expedite the claims process.

In addition to making an assessment, the physician normally makes a recommendation for treatment and recovery. Based on these recommendations, a payment plan is set up for the insured. Once payment has begun, patients must continue to communicate with their doctor and follow the recommendations laid out for them. If it is discovered that they have not done so, it is possible that their coverage will be revoked. Updated recommendations from the doctor must be followed as a patient improves. If and when the patient improves, he or she must obtain permission from the physician before returning to work and must inform the insurance company before doing so.

The role of the physician is crucial, not only in making a case for disability claims, but also in getting a fair settlement. Physicians should assess injuries in an unbiased manner, giving patients the best chance of getting the right amount of compensation for their claim. A competent physician can make all of the difference between struggling through a claim and having a streamlined and fair process.

Healthcare providers who serve as medical experts may be asked to give verbal testimony or provide answers to questions on claim reviews. Frequently, the final decision to allow or deny a Social Security disability claim rests on the advice and medical opinions provided by these medical experts.

> **◎ HIPAA Tip**
>
> The Health Insurance Portability and Accountability Act (HIPAA) protects against gaps in insurance coverage, allowing the freedom to move from one job to another or the freedom to move from Supplemental Security Income (SSI) or Social Security Disability Insurance (SSDI) status to employment.

Health Insurance Professional's Role

The health insurance professional needs to know the Social Security regulations so that he or she can provide the exact information needed for evaluation of an individual's disability. There are many steps in the application process, which can be time consuming and challenging, and knowledgeable healthcare team members should do all they can to facilitate this process.

Similar to workers' compensation claims, there is no standard form for billing disability claims. When a patient comes to the medical facility for the purpose of getting the physician's medical opinion regarding disability, the health insurance professional should advise the patient to bring the necessary forms provided by the Social Security office. Additional responsibilities of the health insurance professional include:

- Procuring the patient's authorization to release information
- Acquiring the necessary information for claims processing

- Ensuring that the attending physician forms are complete and signed
- Photocopying all forms for the patient's health record
- Maintaining a well-documented health record
- Answering the patient's questions

The Social Security website has numerous forms available at http://www.ssa.gov/online/.

 Stop and Think

Amy Turner, a health insurance professional for Dr. Laura Nelson, wants to be able to help patients through the often-complicated process of filing for Supplemental Security Income (SSI) or Social Security Disability Insurance (SSDI) benefits. What would you suggest Amy do to become knowledgeable in this area?

? **What Did You Learn?**

1. List six federal disability programs.
2. How do federal programs define disability?
3. The ADA considers disability present if an individual meets what three criteria?
4. What is the difference between SSI and SSDI?
5. List the five states that provide short-term disability benefits.

SUMMARY CHECKPOINTS

- Workers' compensation got its start in Germany in the 1800s to take care of injured workers and limit their physical and financial suffering from injuries or illnesses resulting from their jobs. Workers' compensation became common in the United States in the 1930s and 1940s. Any employee who is injured on the job or develops an employment-related illness that prevents the individual from working is usually eligible to receive workers' compensation benefits. A spouse and dependents of an employee who dies because of a job-related accident or illness are also eligible for benefits.
- The federal government administers several major disability compensation programs that provide wage replacement benefits, medical treatment, vocational rehabilitation, and other benefits to eligible workers or their dependents who experience work-related injury or occupational disease. These programs cover certain federal and postal workers, employees of the DOE and designated atomic weapons employees, longshore and harbor workers, coal mine workers, railroad employees engaged in interstate commerce, and the crew of Merchant Marine ships.
- State laws vary, but an employer's responsibility to provide coverage usually depends on how many employees it has, what type of business it is, and what type of work the employees are doing. Most employers must purchase workers' compensation insurance coverage for their workers; however, there are certain classifications of exemptions, depending on state statutes. Common types of exemptions include but are not limited to the following:
  - Employers with a minimum number of full-time employees
  - Executive officers
  - Individuals who are business partners
  - Sole proprietors
  - Casual employees
- The four major benefit components to workers' compensation are as follows:
  - *Medical expense*: Pays expenses related to hospitalization, physicians' visits, and any necessary medical treatment
  - *Disability pay*: Can be temporary or permanent if it is determined that the worker will never fully recover
  - *Vocational rehabilitation*: If the injury or illness results in the worker being unable to perform the usual duties of his or her occupation, retraining may be necessary for the worker to enter into a new trade or business; also, physical therapy may be necessary
  - *Death benefits*: Paid to surviving dependents
- Each state has rules established under which an employee is required to file a claim within a certain time limit. Usually, traumatic claims must be brought within a time frame that runs from the date of the accident, date of last medical treatment, or date of the last payment of benefits. Time limits for work-related illnesses can vary depending on the onset and duration of the employee's condition.
- The reporting requirements and process for filing a workers' compensation claim include the following steps:
  - Employee notifies a supervisor of the incident immediately and provides the names of any witnesses.
  - Employee completes a detailed accident report on a form furnished by the employer.
  - Employer reports the incident to the company's workers' compensation carrier.
  - Employee is sent to a medical facility for treatment or diagnosis. (In emergencies, this should be the first step.)
  - Attending physician completes statement and distributes copies.
  - Follow-up progress reports are submitted until the employee returns to work, after which a final report is filed.
- When fraud is suspected, a report should be made to the appropriate agency within a reasonable time frame, usually within 30 days from the time the individual reporting knows or reasonably believes that he or she knows the identity of a person or entity that has committed workers' compensation

fraud or has knowledge that such fraud has been committed.

- The purpose of any type of disability income insurance, including private and employer-sponsored disability income insurance, is to replace a portion of salary or wages earned income when an individual is unable to perform the requirements of his or her job because of injury or illness that is not work related.
- SSDI is a federal insurance program that pays monthly cash benefits to disabled workers younger than age 65 and to certain dependents who have lost their income because of disability. Individuals applying for SSDI must meet two criteria:
  - They must have earned a specific number of work credits.
  - They must have a severe impairment that makes them unable to perform their previous work or any other kind of financially gainful activity.
- SSI provides monthly cash payments to low-income aged, blind, and disabled individuals. There are no work requirements for SSI, but individuals must answer a detailed and comprehensive questionnaire that establishes financial need, called a *financial means test*. Disability determination for adults is the same under SSDI and SSI.
- The process for successfully filing an SSDI or SSI claim requires cooperation from several fronts—from the patient, the healthcare provider, and even the health insurance professional. Claims can be initiated online, over the phone, or by going to a local Social Security office. Some individuals hire a lawyer to assist with preparing the initial paperwork.

Closing Scenario

Jim is excited to be working with a new provider at Walden-Martin Family Medical Clinic. Dr. Bonnin has joined the clinic right after completing his residency program. He has not had much experience with workers' compensation cases. Jim has been able to help Dr. Bonnin become familiar with the forms that need to be completed, including the healthcare provider report. They have also had discussions about determining disability and the definitions of temporary partial disability, temporary permanent disability, permanent partial disability, and permanent total disability. Dr. Bonnin recognizes what a great resource Jim is.

CHAPTER REVIEW QUESTION

1. Workers' compensation programs are offered at the _____ level.
   a. Federal
   b. State
   c. County
   d. Both state and federal

2. Coverage for employees of the federal government is provided by which of the following?
   a. Federal Employees' Compensation Act
   b. Energy Employees Occupational Illness Compensation Program
   c. Longshore and Harbor Workers' Compensation Act
   d. All of the above

3. Workers' compensation is no-fault insurance. This means:
   a. If the employee caused the injury, there will be no benefits.
   b. Benefits will only be paid if the employer did not do the proper maintenance on the equipment and an employee is injured.
   c. Regardless of who is to blame for that accident or injury, benefits will be paid.
   d. None of the above.

4. The workers' compensation exclusion that states employees are not covered under workers' compensation when they traveling to and from work is called:
   a. The coming and going rule.
   b. The traveling exclusion.
   c. The to and from addendum.
   d. OSHA Regulation D.

5. Workers' compensation claims are always filed using:
   a. CMS-1500.
   b. The form provided by the insurance carrier.
   c. Both a and b are correct.
   d. None of the above.

6. If an employee whose job requires him or her to stand for 8 hours a day breaks a leg while at work, he or she would have what type of disability?
   a. Temporary total disability
   b. Temporary partial disability
   c. Permanent total disability
   d. Permanent partial disability

7. The HIPAA Privacy Rule does not apply to workers' compensation information. Employers can have access to the employees' health records related to workers' compensation claims.
   a. The first statement is true. The second statement is false.
   b. The first statement is false. The second statement is true.
   c. Both statements are true.
   d. Both statements are false.

8. A patient was unable to work due to a non–work-related illness or injury. He or she could still be eligible for income replacement benefits if:
   a. The employer has a workers' compensation policy.
   b. He or she has a disability income insurance policy.
   c. He or she qualifies for Medicaid.
   d. He or she has health insurance.

9. What information is typically included in an attending physician's statement for disability insurance?
   a. The first day the individual was unable to work.
   b. Whether the illness or injury was work related.
   c. The diagnosis.
   d. All of the above.
10. The federal insurance program that provides monthly cash benefits to disabled workers younger than age 65 is:
   a. SSDI.
   b. SSI.
   c. Medicaid.
   d. Medicare.

WEBSITES TO EXPLORE

- For live links to the following websites, please visit the Evolve website at http://evolve.elsevier.com/Beik/today.
- To find out about the workers' compensations laws in your state, visit https://injury.findlaw.com/workers-compensation/workers-compensation-laws-by-state.html.
- The US Department of Labor provides an overview of state workers' compensation laws in a Portable Document Format (PDF) file at http://www.dol.gov. (Note: You must download and install a free Adobe Acrobat Reader to view and print PDF files.)
- The US Department of Labor also provides general links and information about workers' compensation here: https://www.dol.gov/general/topic/workcomp.
- To learn about SSI and SSDI similarities and differences, visit https://www.ssa.gov/redbook/eng/overview-disability.htm.
- To keep aware of changes in the SSDI and SSI programs, visit http://www.ssa.gov.
- To view a table comparing the SSDI and SSI programs, visit http://www.wceca.org/publications/CurrentSSIvSSD.pdf.

Author's Note: Due to the dynamic nature of the Internet, web addresses and/or links provided in this chapter may have changed since publication and may no longer be valid. In such cases, students should select comparable search words to access related sites.

Diagnostic Coding

14

Chapter Outline

Chapter Objectives

After completion of this chapter, the student should be able to:

1. Identify the meaning of a diagnosis, and state where it can be found in a patient record.
2. Discuss the history and development of diagnostic coding.
3. Describe the process of classifying diseases.
4. Summarize the format and organization of the *International Classification of Diseases,* 10th revision, Clinical Modification (ICD-10-CM) manual.
5. List the coding steps for the Alphabetic Index.
6. Explain the format and structure of codes and conventions in the ICD-10-CM Tabular List.
7. Outline the official guidelines for diagnostic coding and reporting.
8. Describe other coding features in the ICD-10-CM.
9. Document the coding steps for the Tabular List.
10. Explain the connection between the Health Insurance Portability and Accountability Act (HIPAA) and diagnostic coding.
11. Discuss General Equivalence Mappings (GEMs), and state the implementation date of the ICD-10-CM.

Chapter Terms

adverse effects

category

code set

combination code

contraindication

conventions

covered entities

default code

diagnosis

eponym

essential modifiers

etiology

first-listed diagnosis

General Equivalence Mappings (GEMs)

histology

in situ

instructional notes

International Classification of Diseases, 10th revision (ICD-10)

laterality

main term

manifestation

morphology

NEC (not elsewhere classifiable)

neoplasm

nonessential modifiers

NOS (not otherwise specified)

placeholder character

principal diagnosis

puerperium

sequela (pl. sequelae)

seventh (7th) character

subcategory

underdosing

 Opening Scenario

When Park Chalmers was a boy, he had wanted to be a doctor; however, when he fainted after witnessing a bicycle accident that severely injured his best friend's arm, Park realized that the clinical side of medicine was not for him. Still, the field of medicine intrigued him. While in high school Park started looking into other career options within healthcare. He discovered a health insurance program and enrolled. After he completed the program, he got a position working for Walden-Martin Family Medical Clinic, where he does diagnostic coding.

He helped the clinic move from ICD-9-CM to ICD-10-CM and really enjoyed the challenges that presented. With his help, the clinic was able to move to the new system with just a few glitches.

Park is able to work closely with the providers at Walden-Martin to make sure that they are all using the most accurate code for billing. The providers respect Park's expertise in this area. This has had a positive impact on insurance reimbursement.

Park is grateful that he stuck with healthcare and has found a rewarding position. He is able to help the providers as well as the patients by staying current with all changes related to diagnostic coding.

INTRODUCTION TO THE INTERNATIONAL CLASSIFICATION OF DISEASES CODING SYSTEM

In the healthcare profession, there is a recognized process for transforming written descriptions of a patient's disease process, disorder, or injury into universal numerical or alphanumerical formats (i.e., codes) that are understood by all healthcare entities, including providers, government health programs, private health insurance companies, and workers' compensation carriers. In very basic language, a **diagnosis** is the reason that brought the patient to the healthcare facility, such as a rash, sore throat, or chest pain. A final diagnosis, after examination, can be a much more precise statement.

The diagnosis can be taken from various sources within the medical record, such as the clinical notes, laboratory tests, radiological results, and other sources. The diagnosis must be determined by the healthcare professional providing the medical care. Box 14.1 lists examples of medical diagnoses.

When the healthcare insurance professional generates an insurance claim for payment of the provider's services, the written diagnosis itself does not appear on the claim—only the code appears. It is very important that the code describes the diagnosis accurately and to the greatest specificity, to obtain maximum reimbursement for the provider and patient, and that the diagnosis justifies the medical necessity of the procedure codes documented on the insurance claim.

TWO MAJOR CODING STRUCTURES

The US healthcare system currently uses two major coding structures: the *International Classification of Diseases*, *10th revision (ICD-10)* and the *Current Procedural Terminology*, 4th edition (CPT-4) procedure codes (even though the American Medical Association [AMA] refers to this as just CPT, the author will use CPT-4 as in previous editions) (see Chapter 15).

ICD-10 codes are divided into two systems. The *International Classification of Diseases*, 10th revision, Clinical Modification (ICD-10-CM) codes are used in physicians' offices and outpatient settings for the coding of diseases and the signs, symptoms, abnormal findings, complaints, social circumstances, and external causes of injury or diseases, as classified by the World Health Organization (WHO). The *International Classification of Diseases*, 10th revision, Procedure

Coding System (ICD-10-PCS) is used in the inpatient hospital setting for reporting inpatient procedures only; it helps establish diagnosis-related groups (DRGs) that most third-party payers use to determine payment for related services and procedures. (ICD-10-PCS and DRGs are discussed in detail in Chapter 17.)

CPT-4 codes are used to determine third-party payment for related physician services and procedures for reimbursement purposes. These codes also help establish the ambulatory payment classifications (APCs) used by most providers for related services and procedures in the outpatient setting.

This chapter provides the basics of ICD-10-CM diagnostic coding. After completing the assigned readings and exercises, students should have a working knowledge of the ICD-10-CM systems with the ability to generate valid codes for simple diagnoses. Students who wish to pursue a career in coding and become certified should explore the opportunities available in local coding programs or online. Research the Internet using key words such as "becoming a certified professional coder" for more information on becoming certified in coding.

◎ HIPAA Tip

The Health Insurance Portability and Accountability Act (HIPAA) requires that ICD-10-CM diagnosis codes be included on all Medicare claims billed to Part B carriers with the exception of ambulance claims. Providers and suppliers rely on physicians to provide a diagnosis code or narrative diagnostic statement on orders or referrals.

? What Did You Learn?

1. On the most basic level, what is a diagnosis?
2. Where might a patient's diagnosis be located?
3. True or false: Both the written diagnosis and the code must appear on the insurance claim.
4. Name the two major coding structures currently used in US healthcare.

HISTORY AND DEVELOPMENT OF THE INTERNATIONAL CLASSIFICATION OF DISEASES CODING SYSTEM

The history of the International Classification of Diseases (ICD) system dates back to the late 19th century in Europe when it was determined that there was a need for the standardization of medical concepts and terminology. The ICD system was the product of a group effort involving the WHO and 10 international centers. Using this system, medical terms reported on death certificates by physicians, medical examiners, and coroners could be grouped together for statistical purposes. The purpose of the system was to promote a

---

Box **14.1** Examples of Medical Diagnoses
Type 1 diabetic retinopathy
Acute cholecystitis with cholelithiasis
Gastroenteritis due to *Salmonella*
Fracture of neck of scapula
Systemic lupus erythematosus
Acute thyroiditis

Table 14.1 International Classification of Diseases Implementation in the United States

DESIGNATION	YEARS IN EFFECT
ICD-1	1900–1909
ICD-2	1910–1920
ICD-3	1921–1929
ICD-4	1930–1938
ICD-5	1939–1948
ICD-6	1949–1957
ICD-7	1958–1967
ICD-8[a]	1968–1978
ICD-9	1979–2014
ICD-10	1999 (death certificates only); 2015
ICD-11	2022

[a]The United States generally accepted the World Health Organization (WHO) revisions except for the 8th revision; the United States disagreed with some parts of the classification system, specifically some categories in the diseases of the circulatory system. As a result, the United States produced its own version of the ICD, referred to as *ICDA-8*.

means of comparing the collection, classification, processing, and presentation of mortality (death) statistics.

The first ICD system (ICD-1) was put into use in 1900. Since then, the ICD has been modified approximately once every 10 years with the exception of the 20-year period between the last two revisions—ICD-9 and ICD-10 (Table 14.1). The rationale for these periodic revisions has been to reflect advances in medical science and changes in diagnostic terminology. In 1999 the United States replaced ICD-9 with ICD-10 for coding on death certificates; however, the US Department of Health and Human Services (HHS) did not publish the final rule for full adoption of the ICD-10 in the United States until January 2009. Until that time, the United States was one of the few countries that were not using ICD-10. The compliance date for implementation of the ICD-10 coding system was October 1, 2015, for all **covered entities**. *Covered entities* are defined in the Health Insurance Portability and Accountability Act (HIPAA) rules as (1) health plans, (2) healthcare clearinghouses, and (3) healthcare providers who electronically transmit any health information in connection with transactions for which HHS has adopted standards.

Students should visit http://cms.gov/icd10/ periodically to keep abreast of the latest news regarding ICD-10.

KEY NOTE

The ICD-10 Coordination and Maintenance Committee (C&M), composed of representatives from the Centers for Medicare and Medicaid Services (CMS) and the Centers for Disease Control and Prevention's (CDC) National Center for Health Statistics (NCHS), is responsible for approving coding changes, addenda, and other modifications. Requests for coding changes are submitted to the committee for discussion at either the spring or the fall C&M meeting.

USES OF CODED DATA

Coding of healthcare data allows access to health records according to diagnoses and procedures for use in clinical care, research, and education. Following is a list of other common uses of codes in healthcare:
- Measuring the quality, safety, and effectiveness of care
- Designing payment systems and processing claims for reimbursement
- Conducting research, epidemiological studies, and clinical trials
- Setting healthcare policies
- Facilitating operational and strategic planning and the designing of healthcare delivery systems
- Monitoring resource use
- Improving clinical, financial, and administrative performance
- Preventing and detecting healthcare fraud and abuse
- Tracking public concerns and assessing the risks of adverse public health events

WHY THE CHANGE TO ICD-10-CM?

After using ICD-9 for 20 years, one may wonder why the change to ICD-10. In many ways, the ICD-10-CM is comparable to the former ICD-9-CM. The guidelines, conventions, rules, and organization of the codes are very similar. However, many improvements have been made to coding in the ICD-10-CM. For example, a single code can report a disease and its current **manifestation** (signs or symptoms). In fracture care, the code differentiates various outcomes with mandatory use of the appropriate 7th character (in parentheses):
- An initial encounter for fracture (A)
- A subsequent encounter for fracture with routine healing (D)
- A subsequent encounter for fracture with delayed healing (G)
- A subsequent encounter for fracture with nonunion (K)
- A subsequent encounter for fracture with malunion (P)
- A sequela (follow-up) for late effects of a fracture (S)

Similarly, the trimester is designated in obstetrical codes. The episode of care codes (delivery, antepartum, postpartum) have a final character identifying the trimester of pregnancy in which the condition occurred. Because certain obstetric conditions or complications occur during certain trimesters, not all conditions include codes for all three trimesters. For example, preterm labor without delivery can occur in either the second or the third trimester only; therefore the subcategory O60.0 (Preterm labor without delivery) is further subdivided as:
- Preterm labor without delivery, unspecified trimester—O60.00
- Preterm labor without delivery, second trimester—O60.02
- Preterm labor without delivery, third trimester—O60.03

If preterm labor with preterm delivery occurred (subcategory O60.1), a 7th character would be assigned. For example, the 7th character "0" is used for single gestation and multiple gestations in which the fetus is unspecified. Characters 1 through 5 are used for cases of multiple gestations to identify the fetus for which the code applies. Seventh character "9" identifies "other fetus."

Additional documentation is required when a claim is submitted to explain that the injury or condition treated the second time is different from the one that was treated previously.

The number of codes in the ICD-10-CM has increased significantly compared with the number in the ICD-9-CM; the ICD-9 has 13,600 codes, whereas the ICD-10 has more than 70,000. Some of this growth is due to **laterality** (i.e., the side of the body on which surgery was performed or the side of the body affected by the condition). For example, whereas an ICD-9-CM code may identify simply a condition of an ovary, the ICD-10-CM system has four identifying codes: unspecified ovary, right ovary, left ovary, or bilateral (both sides) condition of the ovary(ies). In the ICD-10 diagnosis **code set**, characters within the code identify right versus left, initial encounter versus subsequent encounter, and other more precise clinical information.

Another issue with ICD-9 is that it was running out of available code numbers in some chapters. ICD-10 codes have more characters, which greatly expands the number of codes that are available for use. With more available codes, it is less likely that chapters will run out of codes in the future. Another issue addressed in ICD-10 is the use of full code titles, reflecting advances in medical knowledge and technology. In addition, diagnosis coding under the ICD-10-CM uses three to seven digits (also referred to as *characters*) rather than the three to five digits used in the ICD-9-CM; however, the formats of the code sets are similar. Table 14.2 provides a comparison of the features of

Table **14.2** Comparison of the Diagnosis Code Sets	
ICD-9	**ICD-10**
• Three to five characters in length	• Three to seven characters in length
• Approximately 13,000 codes	• Approximately 68,000 available codes
• First digit may be alpha (E or V) or numeric; digits two to five are numeric	• Digit one is alpha; digits two and three are numeric; digits four to seven are alpha or numeric
• Limited space for adding new codes	• Flexible for adding new codes
• Lacks detail	• Very specific
• Lacks laterality	• Has laterality (codes identifying right and left)

ICD-9, International Classification of Diseases, 9th revision; ICD-10, International Classification of Diseases, 10th revision.

the ICD-9 and ICD-10 code sets. A weblink for a basic introduction to ICD-10 is included under "Websites to Explore" at the end of this chapter. The presentation includes the differences and similarities between ICD-9 and ICD-10.

ICD-10-CM CODING AND REPORTING GUIDELINES

The CMS and the NCHS, two departments of HHS, have provided guidelines for coding and reporting using the ICD-10-CM coding systems. (These guidelines are summarized later in this chapter.) Guidelines for diagnostic coding also can be found on the websites of these two government entities. These guidelines should be used as a companion document to the official version as published by the US Government Printing Office. The CMS website (http://www.cms.gov/) has extensive information and guidelines for the ICD-10 system. To access relevant information on ICD-10, type "ICD-10" in the CMS home page search box.

> **KEY NOTE**
>
> The general guidelines and chapter-specific guidelines are applicable to all healthcare settings unless otherwise indicated. The conventions and instructions of the classification take precedence over guidelines. The **conventions** for the ICD-10-CM are the general rules for use of the classification independent of the guidelines. These conventions are incorporated within the Alphabetic Index and Tabular List of the ICD-10-CM as instructional notes.

> **?** **What Did You Learn?**
>
> 1. When was the first ICD coding system put into use?
> 2. Name the federal entities that maintain ICD-10 codes.
> 3. List five uses of coded data.
> 4. Identify two reasons for the change from ICD-9 to ICD-10.
> 5. How many digits (characters) are used in ICD-10-CM codes?

PROCESS OF CLASSIFYING DISEASES

The first thing the coder must do in the coding process is locate the diagnosis in the patient's medical record. This task can be straightforward sometimes, because many encounter forms (also known as *superbills*) list the more frequently used diagnoses in a certain medical specialty, along with their corresponding diagnosis codes (Fig. 14.1). Other times, the coder may have to refer to the clinical notes in the patient's record to locate the diagnosis. If the notes are handwritten, deciphering the healthcare professional's handwriting sometimes can be challenging (Fig. 14.2). With practice and experience, locating the diagnosis in the clinical notes and translating a physician's handwriting becomes easier.

Pt Name: _____   Date: _____   Time In: _____

Bill # _____   [ ] Care   [ ] Priv.   [ ] MC   [ ] Medicaid   [ ] Cash   Time Out: _____

SYMPTOMS/ DIAGNOSIS

Code	Diagnosis	Code	Diagnosis
R10.9	Abdom. Pain	B02.9	Herpes Zoster
R63.4	Abn. Weight Loss	B00.9	Herpes Simplex
T78.4	Allergic Reaction	K44.9	Hiatal Hernia
G30.9	Alzheimers	E78.5	Hyperlipidemia
D64.9	Anemia	I10	Hypertension
D51.0	Anemia, Pernicious	E03.9	Hypothyroidism
I20.9	Angina	E05.9_	Hyperthyroidism
F41.9	Anxiety	F52.21	Impotence
R06.81	Apnea	J10.1	Influenza
I49.9	Arrhythmia, Cardiac	G47.0	Insomnia
I70.0	Atherosclerosis - Aorta	K58.9	Irr. Bowel Syn
J45.909	Asthma	M32.9	Systemic lupus erythematosus
I48.0	Atrial Fib.	R41.82	Mental Status Change
I48.1	Atrial Flutter	G43.9	Migraine
I47.1	Atrial Tach.	M79.1	Muscle Pain
E53.8	B-12 Defic.	I21.9	Myocardial Infarct/Acute
M54.9	Back Pain	I25.2	Myocardial Infarct/Old
K92.1	Blood - Stool	M54.2	Neck Pain
N40.0_	BPH	G62.9	Neuropathy
R00.1	Bradycardia	R11.0	Nausea, vomiting
I49.5	Brady/Sick Sinus	R11.1	Nausea
J42	Bronchitis, Chronic	E66.9	Obesity
J20._	Bronchitis, Acute	M19.90	Osteoarthritis
M71.9	Bursitis, unspecified	H66.9_	Otitis Media
(site-specific codes available)		G20	Parkinsons
C50.__	CA - breast	J02.9	Pharyngitis
C34.__	CA - lung	R09.1	Pleurisy
C61	CA - prostate	J12.9	Pneumonia, viral
L03.___	Cellulitis	J18.9	Pneumonia
L02.___	Abscess	N41.9	Prostatitis
L03.11_	Cellulitis, Leg	I73.9	PVD
I25.10	CAD	M54.1_	Radiculopathy
R07.89	Chest Discomfort	N19	Renal Failure
R07.9	Chest Pain	M06.9	Rheum Arthritis
K74.60	Cirrhosis of Liver	M54.3_	Sciatica
K51.90	Colitis Ulcerative	G40.909	Seizure Dis.
J00	Common Cold	R06.02	Short. Of breath
R41.0	Confusion	J32.9	Sinusitis
I50.9	CHF	G47.9	Sleep Disorder
K59.00	Constipation	I47.1	SVT
J44.9	COPD	R55	Syncope
R05	Cough	G45.9	T.I.A.
K50.90	Crohn's	R00.0	Tachycardia
I63.9	CVA	M77.9	Tendonitis
L89.___	Decub. Ulcers	K26.9	Ulcer, Duodenal
E86.0	Dehydration	K25.9	Ulcer, Gastric
F03	Dementia	K27.9	Ulcer, Peptic
F32.9	Depression	I20.0	Unstable Angina
E11.9	Diabetes II - non ins.	J06.9	U.R.I.
E10.9	Diabetes I - ins. Dep	N39.0	U.T.I.
R19.7	Diarrhea	R42	Vertigo
K57.92	Diverticulitis	R11.3	Vomiting
K57.90	Diverticulosis	R63.4	Weight Loss
R42	Dizziness	R63.5	Weight Gain
R60.9	Edema		
I38	Endocarditis		
K21.0	Reflux esophagitis		
R53.83	Fatigue		
R50.9	Fever		
K29.70	Gastritis		
K21.9	GERD		
K92.2	G.I. Bleed		
M10.9	Gout		
R51	Headache		
Z00.010	Health Check Up		
R31.9	Hematuria		

RETURN TO OFFICE:

_____ Days Weeks Mos As Needed

OFC	E&M	New	Estab
Level 1	_____	99201	99211
Level 2	_____	99202	99212
Level 3	_____	99203	99213
Level 4	_____	99204	99214
Level 5	_____	99205	99215

Prolonged Svc   99354 _____ min.

CONSULTS

Req. Phys: _____

Consult 1	_____	99241
Consult 2	_____	99242
Consult 3	_____	99243
Consult 4	_____	99244
Consult 5	_____	99245

PROCEDURES

Arthrocentesis	_____	206__
CEM	_____	G000_
Ear Lavage	_____	69210
EKG	_____	93000
Holter - 24 hrs	_____	93224
Inhalation TX	_____	94640
Stress Test	_____	93015
Vascular Study	_____	93923

INJECTIONS

Admin.	_____	90782
B-12 **	_____	J3420
Decadron	_____	J1100
Depo-Testost	_____	J1320
Estradiol	_____	J1390
Influenza Imm	_____	90659
Influ. Admin	_____	G0008/90471
Lincocin	_____	J2010
Nubain	_____	J2300
Phenergan	_____	J2550
Pneumonia Imm.	_____	90732
Pneum Admin.	_____	G0009/90471
Tet. Toxoid	_____	J1670

LABORATORY

Basic Med. Panel	_____	80048
CBC	_____	85024
Comp. Met. Panel	_____	80053
Drug Screen	_____	80100
General Health Panel	_____	80050
Glucose	_____	82947
Hepatic Panel	_____	80076
KOH Wet Prep	_____	87219
Lipid Profile	_____	80061
Liver Profile	_____	80076
Mono Test	_____	86300
Pap Smear [ ] screen	_____	88150
ProTime	_____	85610
PSA	_____	84153
SGOT - blood	_____	84450
Thyroid	_____	87060
Thryoid Profile	_____	80070
Triglycerides	_____	84478
UA	_____	81002
Uric Acid	_____	84550
Venipuncture	_____	36415/G0001
Veni. By phys.	_____	36410

Fig. 14.1 Sample encounter form listing common diagnoses and their ICD-10-CM codes.

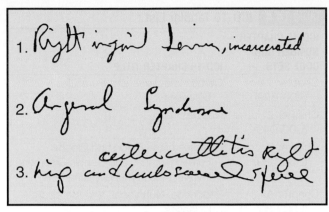

Fig. 14.2 Examples of handwritten diagnoses.

 KEY NOTE

An encounter form (superbill) allows medical practitioners and clinicians to quickly complete and submit the procedures and diagnoses for a patient visit for reimbursement. It is generally customized for the provider's type of practice and contains patient information; the most common CPT (procedure) and ICD (diagnostic) codes used by that office; and a section for items such as follow-up appointments, copayments, and the provider's signature.

After the diagnosis has been determined, the **main term** (sometimes referred to as the *lead term*) in the diagnosis should be identified. For example, if the diagnosis is "breast mass," the main term is "mass." (The anatomic site [e.g., "breast"] is not used in the Alphabetic Index of Diseases.) Fig. 14.3 illustrates how the main term "mass" appears in the Alphabetic Index. (See "Main Terms" later in this chapter.)

 Imagine This!

Marlee Davis, the health insurance professional in Dr. Barnes' office, deciphered one of the physician's handwritten diagnoses as "atrophic arthritis," rather than "aortic arteritis." The error was not caught before the submission of the claim, and the insurance company rejected the claim because the procedures listed on the claim form did not coincide with the diagnosis. When the patient received an explanation of benefits from his insurance carrier that the claim was denied, he phoned the office with a complaint. Marlee apologized to the patient and resubmitted the CMS-1500 claim form.

 HIPAA Tip

Always protect the confidentiality of all ICD-10-CM codes because these codes are part of the patient's record. The Health Insurance Portability and Accountability Act (HIPAA) addresses coding issues and sets standards for their use, along with other issues regarding confidentiality in dealing with patient health records.

 What Did You Learn?

1. What is the first thing the coder should do in the coding process?
2. If the diagnosis is "bronchial constriction," what is the main term?
3. Explain the purpose and use of an encounter form.

Mass
  abdominal R19.00
    epigastric R19.06
    generalized R19.07
    left lower quadrant R19.04
    left upper quadrant R19-02
    periumbilic R19.05
    right lower quadrant R19.03
    right upper quadrant R19.01
    specified site NEC R19.09
  breast —*see also* Lump, breast N63.0
  chest R22.2
  cystic —*see* Cyst
  ear H93.8- ●
  head R22.0
  intra-abdominal (diffuse) (generalized) —*see* Mass, abdomimal
  kidney N28.89
  liver R16.0
  localized (skin) R22.9

Fig. 14.3 Section of the ICD-10 Alphabetic Index showing how the main term "mass" appears in the Index. (From Buck CJ: *2019 ICD-10-CM, standard edition,* St. Louis, 2019, Elsevier.)

OVERVIEW OF THE ICD-10 CODING SYSTEM

As mentioned, the ICD-10 coding system consists of two parts:
1. ICD-10-CM for diagnosis coding (used in all healthcare settings)
2. ICD-10-PCS for inpatient procedure coding (used in inpatient hospital settings only)

This chapter discusses only ICD-10-CM; ICD-10-PCS is addressed in Chapter 18.

ICD-10-CM CODE STRUCTURE

As mentioned, an ICD-10-CM code has three to seven characters (Table 14.3). The first character of an ICD-10-CM code is always an alphabetic letter, and all letters of the alphabet are used in ICD-10-CM coding except for the letter U. Alphabetic characters are not case sensitive.

 KEY NOTE

The letter U has been reserved for future use to assign codes to new diseases for which the **etiology** (cause or origin of the disease) is unknown (U00 through U49) and for bacterial agents that are resistant to antibiotics (U80 through U89). Additional care should be taken in the use of the letters I and O so as not to confuse them with the numerals 1 and 0.

Codes longer than three digits always have a decimal point after the first three characters. Each additional character adds more specificity to the disease or condition. The additional characters augment the clinical detail and address information about previously classified diseases or conditions discovered since the last edition.

FORMAT OF THE ICD-10-CM MANUAL

Before any attempt is made to code a diagnosis, the coder must become familiar with the contents and structure of the coding manual. The format of the

Table 14.3 Code Structure of ICD-10-CM

ICD-10-CM codes may consist of up to seven digits, with the seventh digit extensions representing visit/encounter or sequelae for injuries and external causes

ICD-10-CM Code Format

| X | X | X | . | X | X | X | X |

Category — Etiology, anatomic site, severity — Extension

Examples

B86	Scabies
C02.4	Malignant neoplasm of lingual tonsil
F01.50	Vascular dementia without behavioral disturbance
H81.311	Aural vertigo, right ear
S00.211A	Abrasion of right eyelid and periocular area, initial encounter
S09.91xA	Unspecified injury to ear, initial encounter
S79.131A	Salter-Harris type III physeal fracture of lower end of left femur

Note: When coding fractures, the seventh character classification can indicate type, status, and encounter (initial, subsequent, and sequela). The seventh character can also represent the type of fracture and the present status of the fracture.

ICD-10-CM, International Classification of Diseases, 10th revision, Clinical Modification.

Image from American Health Information Management Association: *ICD-10-CM primer* (website). https://library.ahima.org/doc?oid=106177#.XbhfMmIKiUl. Accessed September 21, 2019.

Table 14.4 ICD-10 Tabular List

ICD-10 CHAPTER NUMBER AND CODE SETS	ICD-10 CHAPTER TITLE
Chapter 1 (A00-B99)	Certain Infectious and Parasitic Diseases
Chapter 2 (C00-D49)	Neoplasms
Chapter 3 (D50-D89)	Diseases of the Blood and Blood-Forming Organs and Certain Disorders Involving the Immune Mechanism
Chapter 4 (E00-E89)	Endocrine, Nutritional, and Metabolic Diseases
Chapter 5 (F01-F99)	Mental and Behavioral Disorders
Chapter 6 (G00-G99)	Diseases of the Nervous System
Chapter 7 (H00-H59)	Diseases of the Eye and Adnexa
Chapter 8 (H60-H95)	Diseases of the Ear and Mastoid Process
Chapter 9 (I00-I99)	Diseases of the Circulatory System
Chapter 10 (J00-J99)	Diseases of the Respiratory System
Chapter 11 (K00-K95)	Diseases of the Digestive System
Chapter 12 (L00-L99)	Diseases of the Skin and Subcutaneous Tissue
Chapter 13 (M00-M99)	Diseases of the Musculoskeletal System and Connective Tissue
Chapter 14 (N00-N99)	Diseases of the Genitourinary System
Chapter 15 (O00-O9A)	Pregnancy, Childbirth, and the Puerperium
Chapter 16 (P00-P96)	Certain Conditions Originating in the Perinatal Period
Chapter 17 (Q00-Q99)	Congenital Malformations, Deformations, and Chromosomal Abnormalities
Chapter 18 (R00-R99)	Symptoms, Signs, and Abnormal Clinical and Laboratory Findings, Not Elsewhere Classified
Chapter 19 (S00-T88)	Injury, Poisoning, and Certain Other Consequences of External Causes
Chapter 20 (V01-Y99)	External Causes of Morbidity
Chapter 21 (Z00-Z99)	Factors Influencing Health Status and Contact with Health Services

ICD-10, International Classification of Diseases, 10th revision.

ICD-10-CM manual may differ among publishers in how the material is arranged in the introduction or preface; however, the basic information is the same. The prefacing instructions used in this chapter follow those in the *2019 ICD-10-CM Standard Edition,* by Carol J. Buck, published by Saunders in 2019, unless otherwise noted. The information, coding instructions, and codes were current at the time of this writing. To keep up to date on ICD-10-CM coding practices, the coder should always consult the most recently published ICD-10-CM coding manual.

Note: The link for the complete ICD-10-CM Official Guidelines for Coding and Reporting is listed under "Websites to Explore" at the end of this chapter.

The first several pages of the ICD-10-CM manual contain the following:
- Table of Contents
- A Guide to Using the (2019) ICD-10-CM
- Symbols and Conventions
- Netter's Anatomy Plates
- Part I—Introduction (containing ICD-10-CM Official Guidelines for Coding and Reporting)
- Part II—Alphabetic Index
- Index to Diseases and Injuries
- Table of Neoplasms
  - Table of Drugs and Chemicals
  - External Cause of Injuries Index
- Part III—Tabular List of Diseases and Injuries (21 Chapters [Table 14.4])

Alphabetic Index

The first main section of the manual is Part II, the Alphabetic Index (hereafter referred to as the Index), which contains a list of terms arranged alphabetically,

Paraspadias Q54.9
Paraspasmus facialis G51.8
Parasuicide (attempt)
  history of (personal) Z91.5
    in family Z81.8
Parathyroid gland —*see* condition
Parathyroid tetany E20.9
Paratrachoma A74.0
Paratyphilitis —*see* Appendicitis
Paratyphoid (fever) —*see* Fever,
  paratyphoid
Paratyphus —*see* Fever, paratyphoid
Paraurethral duct Q64.79
  nonorganic origin F51.5
Paraurethritis —*see also* Urethritis
  gonococcal (acute) (chronic) (with
    abscess) A54.1
Paravaccinia NEC B08.04
Paravaginitis —*see* Vaginitis
Parencephalitis —*see also* Encephalitis
  sequelae G09

Fig. 14.4 Portion of a sample page from the ICD-10-CM Alphabetic Index. (From Buck CJ: *2019 ICD-10-CM, standard edition*, St. Louis, 2019, Elsevier.)

along with their corresponding codes (Fig. 14.4). Each page of the Index is divided into three columns. At the extreme top right (or left) corner of each page is a guide word, similar to guide words on each page of a dictionary, to assist the coder in locating the appropriate page (Fig. 14.5). For example, Fig. 14.6 shows the location of the main term "Paranoid." The guide words on the left-hand page are "Paralysis, paralytic," and the guide word on the right-hand page is "Penetrating wound"; therefore the coder knows that the main term "Paranoid" is located alphabetically within these two pages. Note that "Paranoid" is presented in red boldface type. This indicates a "main term." These guide words may change from year to year, and "Paranoid" may be located on a page between different guide words.

Main terms. As mentioned, the first step in diagnostic coding is to identify the main term of the diagnostic statement. This term typically can be found in the

---

| INDEX TO DISEASES AND INJURIES / **Paralysis, paralytic** | INDEX TO DISEASES AND INJURIES / **Penetrating wound** |

Fig. 14.5 Sample partial page from the ICD-10 Alphabetic Index showing guide terms at the top of the page. (From Buck CJ: *2019 ICD-10-CM, standard edition*, St. Louis, 2019, Elsevier.)

INDEX TO DISEASES AND INJURIES INJURIES / Paralysis, paralytic

Paramyotonia (congenita) G71.19
Parangi —*see* Yaws
Paranoia (querulans) F22
  senile F03
Paranoid
  dementia (senile) F03
    praecox —*see* Schizophrenia
  personality F60.0
  psychosis (climacteric) (involutional)
      (menopausal) F22
    psychogenic (acute) F23
    senile F03
  reaction (acute) F23
    chronic F22
  schizophrenia F20.0
  state (climacteric) (involutional)
      (menopausal) (simple) F22
    senile F03
  tendencies F60.0
  traits F60.0
  trends F60.0
  type, psychopathic personality F60.0
Paraparesis —*see* Paraplegia
Paraphasia R47.02
Paraphilia F65.9
Paraphimosis (congenital) N47.2
  chancroidal A57
Paraphrenia, paraphrenic (late) F22
  schizophrenia F20.0
Paraplegia (lower) G82.20
  ataxic —*see* Degeneration, combined, spinal
    cord
  complete G82.21
  congenital (cerebral) G80.8
    spastic G80.1
  familial spastic G11.4
  functional (hysterical) F44.4
  hereditary, spastic G11.4
  hysterical F44.4
  incomplete G82.22
  Pott's A18.01
  psychogenic F44.4

  abuse F10.182
    dependence F10.282
    use F10.982
  amphetamines
    abuse F15.182
    dependence F15.282
    use F15.982
  caffeine
    abuse F15.182
    dependence F15.282
    use F15.982
  cocaine
    abuse F14.182
    dependence F14.282
    use F14.982
  drug NEC
    abuse F19.182
    dependence F19.282
    use F19.982
  opioid
    abuse F11.182
    dependence F11.282
    use F11.982
  psychoactive substance NEC
    abuse F19.182
    dependence F19.282
    use F19.982
  sedative, hypnotic, or anxiolytic
    abuse F13.182
    dependence F13.282
    use F13.982
  stimulant NEC
    abuse F15.182
    dependence F15.282
    use F15.982
  in conditions classified elsewhere
    G47.54
  nonorganic origin F51.8
  organic G47.50
    specified NEC G47.59
Paraspadias Q54.9
Paraspasmus facialis G51.8

INDEX TO DISEASES AND INJURIES INJURIES / Parrot fever

Parasuicide (attempt)
  history of (personal) Z91.5
    in family Z81.8
Parathyroid gland —*see* condition
Parathyroid tetany E20.9
Paratrachoma A74.0
Paratyphilitis —*see* Appendicitis
Paratyphoid (fever) —*see* Fever, paratyphoid
Paratyphus —*see* Fever, paratyphoid
Paraurethral duct Q64.79
  nonorganic origin F51.5
Paraurethritis —*see also* Urethritis
  gonococcal (acute) (chronic) (with abscess)
    A54.1
Paravaccinia NEC B08.04
Paravaginitis —*see* Vaginitis
Parencephalitis —*see also* Encephalitis
  sequelae G09
Parent-child conflict —*see* Conflict, parent-child
  estrangement NEC Z62.890
Paresis —*see also* Paralysis
  accommodation —*see* Paresis, of
    accommodation
  Bernhardt's G57.1-●
  bladder (sphincter) —*see also* Paralysis, bladder
    tabetic A52.17
  bowel, colon or intestine K56.0
  extrinsic muscle, eye H49.9
  general (progressive) (syphilitic) A52.17
    juvenile A50.45
  heart —*see* Failure, heart
  insane (syphilitic) A52.17
  juvenile (general) A50.45
  of accommodation H52.52-●
  peripheral progressive (idiopathic) G60.3
  ➡ pseudohypertrophic G71.09
  senile G83.9
  syphilitic (general) A52.17
    congenital A50.45
  vesical NEC N31.2
Paresthesia —*see also* Disturbance, sensation,
  skin R20.2

Fig. 14.6 Sample partial Alphabetic Index page showing the guide words between which the main term "Paranoid" can be located. (From Buck CJ: *2019 ICD-10-CM, standard edition*, St. Louis, 2019, Elsevier.)

patient's medical record. After the main term has been identified, it should be located in the Index. Main terms are generally not organized by anatomic site. When locating an anatomic term, such as "shoulder," the Index says "*see* condition." Main terms typically are:

- A disease (bronchitis or influenza)
- A condition (fracture, fatigue, or injury)
- An adjective (double, large, or kinked)
- A noun (a disease, disturbance, or syndrome)
- An **eponym** (diseases, procedures, or syndromes named after the individual who discovered or first used them; for example, Larsen syndrome)

If a patient has a diagnosis of deviated nasal septum, the main term is "deviated," which is found in the Index under "deviation." Remember, main terms in the Index are printed in boldface type (sometimes in color) to assist the coder in locating the desired disease or condition (Fig. 14.7).

For clarification, let's walk through this process with a patient whose diagnosis has been identified as "congestive heart failure." "Heart" is an anatomic site. If you locate it in the Index, the entry will say, "*see* condition." So, we find "congestive" in the Index, and following alphabetically down to "heart," we see the cross-reference "*see* failure—heart, congestive." We now know that "failure" is the correct main term, so we locate "failure" in the Index (Fig. 14.8). Let's look at another example. You locate the diagnosis "breast mass" in Evelyn Hake's medical record. Remember,

anatomic sites are not main terms; therefore "breast" cannot be the main term. This means that the main term is "mass." Locating "mass" in the Index and moving down alphabetically, you locate "breast," followed by the partial code N63. Locating this partial code in the Index is just the first step. The cardinal rule of coding is *never* to code from the Index alone. Before a final code is assigned, it is important that the coder read any special notes or instructions; he or she then turns to the Tabular List (hereafter referred to as the Tabular) to locate the code that defines the diagnosis to the greatest specificity. However, before we explore the Tabular, we have much more to learn about the Index.

Main term (in bold-faced type) **Deviation (in)**

conjugate palsy (eye) (spastic) H51.0
esophagus (acquired) K22.8
eye, skew H51.8
midline (jaw) (teeth) (dental arch) M26.29
 specified site NEC —*see* Malposition
nasal septum J34.2
 congenital Q67.4
opening and closing of the mandible
 M26.53
organ or site, congenital NEC —*see*
 Malposition, congenital
septum (nasal) (acquired) J34.2
 congenital Q67.4
sexual F65.9

Fig. 14.7 Example of the Alphabetic Index showing a main term. (From Buck CJ: *2019 ICD-10-CM, standard edition*, St. Louis, 2019, Elsevier.)

Fabry (-Anderson) disease E75.21
Faciocephalalgia, autonomic (*see also*
 Neuropathy, peripheral, autonomic)
 G90.09
Factor (s)
 psychic, associated with diseases classified
  elsewhere F54
 psychological
  affecting physical conditions F54
  or behavioral
   affecting general medical condition F54
   associated with disorders or diseases
    classified elsewhere F54
Fahr disease (of brain) G23.8
Fahr Volhard disease (of kidney) I12.-
Failure, failed
 abortion —*see* Abortion, attempted
 aortic (valve) I35.8
  rheumatic I06.8
 attempted abortion —*see* Abortion, attempted
 biventricular I50.9
 bone marrow —*see* Anemia, aplastic
 cardiac —*see* Failure, heart
 cardiorenal (chronic) I50.9
  hypertensive I13.2
 cardiorespiratory (*see also* Failure, heart)
  R09.2
 cardiovascular (chronic) —*see* Failure, heart
 cerebrovascular I67.9
 cervical dilatation in labor O62.0
 circulation, circulatory (peripheral) R57.9
  newborn P29.89

heart (acute) (senile) (sudden) I50.9
 with
  acute pulmonary edema —*see* Failure,
   ventricular, left
  decompensation —*see* Failure, heart,
   congestive
  dilatation —*see* Disease, heart
 arteriosclerotic I70.90
 biventricular I50.9
 combined left-right sided I50.9
 compensated I50.9
 complicating
  anesthesia (general) (local) or other
   sedation
   in labor and delivery O74.2
   in pregnancy O29.12-
   postpartum, puerperal O89.1
  delivery (cesarean) (instrumental) O75.4
 congestive (compensated)
  (decompensated) I50.9
  with rheumatic fever (conditions in I00)
   active I01.8
   inactive or quiescent (with chorea)
    I09.81
  newborn P29.0
  rheumatic (chronic) (inactive) (with
   chorea) I09.81
   active or acute I01.8
   with chorea I02.0
 decompensated I50.9
 degenerative —*see* Degeneration,
  myocardial

Fig. 14.8 Portion of the ICD-10-CM Alphabetic Index showing "Failure, heart." (From Buck CJ: *2019 ICD-10-CM, standard edition*, St. Louis, 2019, Elsevier.)

Categories of injuries are arranged alphabetically under the main term "Injury."

Essential and nonessential modifiers. Any relevant subterms, or *essential modifiers,* are indented under the main terms. Indented subterms are always used in combination with the main term. They describe different sites, the *etiology* (cause or origin of a disease or condition), and clinical types. **Essential modifiers** must be a part of the documented diagnosis (Fig. 14.9).

Frequently, a main term is immediately followed by an additional word or words in parentheses, or nonessential modifiers. **Nonessential modifiers** that appear in parentheses do not affect the code number assigned but are provided to assist the coder in locating the correct code (Fig. 14.10).

In our earlier example, diagnosis of heart failure (see Figs. 14.8 and 14.10), note the nonessential modifiers in parentheses immediately after "heart"—(acute) (senile) (sudden). These subterms do not affect the diagnostic code assigned and are given to assist the coder in locating the correct code. They may or may not be a part of the documented diagnosis. Also note that the four-character code I50.9 follows the parenthetical nonessential modifiers. If no other words appear in the stated diagnosis in the patient record, the next step is to cross-reference the code to the Tabular—the section containing diagnosis codes arranged alphanumerically and divided into chapters based on body system (anatomic site) or condition (etiology)—to finalize the process of assigning the correct code. Further steps in locating the correct code in the Tabular are discussed later in this chapter.

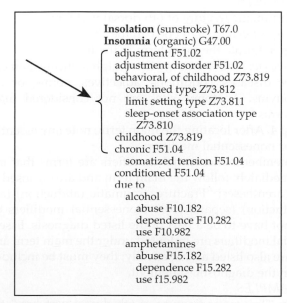

Fig. 14.9 Example from the Alphabetic Index showing main terms with indented essential modifiers. (From Buck CJ: *2019 ICD-10-CM, standard edition*, St. Louis, 2019, Elsevier.)

Fig. 14.10 Partial page from the Alphabetic Index showing the subterm "heart" followed by nonessential modifiers (acute, senile, sudden). (From Buck CJ: *2019 ICD-10-CM, standard edition*, St. Louis, 2019, Elsevier.)

If a code has only three characters (e.g., B03. Smallpox), the coder generally can assume that the category has not been subdivided further.

There are additional indented statements under the subterm "heart." To use any one of these terms, it must be identified in the stated diagnosis. Our example diagnosis was "congestive heart failure," so we must continue our search in the Index and locate this term, which is indented alphabetically under "heart" (see Figs. 14.8 and 14.10). Note, however, that the code after "congestive" does not change; it is still I50.9. For example, if the diagnostic statement in the patient's record is "arteriosclerotic heart failure," without any further description, the code would be I70.90.

KEY NOTE

It cannot be stressed enough that the coder should never code directly from the Index but rather should locate the code found in the Index in the Tabular; this ensures that the diagnosis has been coded to the optimal specificity.

Conventions Used in the Alphabetic Index

The ICD-10 provides *conventions* (i.e., instructions and notations) to further aid the coder in locating the appropriate code. In the Index, conventions include cross-reference terms such as *see* and *see also*. In addition, parentheses have a special meaning. The following subtopics explain these conventions and instructional notations.

Parentheses. Parentheses in the Index have a special meaning. A term that is followed by other terms in parentheses is classified to the given code number, regardless of whether any of the terms in parentheses are reported in the diagnostic statement. For example, Fig. 14.11 shows a partial page on which the term "adrenal abscess" is located in the Index. (Remember, the main term would be "abscess" because "adrenal" is an anatomic site.) Adrenal abscess is classified to E27.8, regardless of any of the terms in parentheses (e.g., capsule, gland).

Cross-references (see** and **see also). Some categories, mainly those subject to notes linking them with other categories, require multiple indexing steps. To avoid repeating multiple steps for each of the additional terms involved, a cross-reference is used. This cross-reference may take several forms, as in the following examples.

❖ *EXAMPLE*

Inflammation bone—*see* Osteomyelitis

The term "Inflammation bone" is to be coded in the same way as the term "Osteomyelitis." Looking up the second term ("bone"), the coder finds various forms of osteomyelitis listed (e.g., acute, acute hematogenous, chronic). When a term has many modifiers that might be listed beneath more than one term, the cross-reference *see also* is used.

❖ *EXAMPLE*

Paraurethritis—*see also* Urethritis

If the term "paraurethritis" is the only term noted in the diagnostic statement in the medical record, the code number is N28.89. If any other information is present that is not found indented below the term, reference should be made to "urethritis." If the diagnosis is gonococcal urethritis (acute) (chronic) (with abscess), the code is A54.1. As stated previously, anatomic sites and broad adjective modifiers are typically not

used as main terms in the Index. Instead, the coder is instructed to look up the disease or injury reported on the medical record and find the site or adjectival modifier under that term.

❖ *EXAMPLE*

Abdomen, abdominal—*see also* condition
  acute R10.0
  angina K55.1
  muscle deficiency syndrome Q79.4

The term "acute abdomen" is coded to R10.0, "abdominal angina" is coded to K55.1, and "abdominal muscle deficiency syndrome" is coded to Q79.4. For other abdominal conditions, the coder should look up the disease or injury documented in the patient record.

? What Did You Learn?

1. Name the two parts of the ICD-10-CM coding system.
2. The first character in an ICD-10 code is always a(n) _____.
3. List the five ways main terms are listed in the ICD-10-CM Alphabetic Index.
4. What do parentheses indicate in the Index?
5. Explain the difference between *see* and *see also*.

CODING STEPS FOR THE ALPHABETIC INDEX

The following are the coding steps for the Index.

Step 1. Locate the diagnostic statement in the patient's medical record.

❖ *EXAMPLES*

Traumatic fracture of 6th dorsal vertebra
Superficial foreign body in the shin

Step 2. Identify the main term in the diagnostic statement.

❖ *EXAMPLES*

Traumatic <u>fracture</u> of 6th dorsal vertebra
Superficial <u>foreign body</u> in the shin

Step 3. Locate the main term in the Index.

(*To review:* Main terms are listed alphabetically and can be diseases, conditions, adjectives, nouns, or eponyms. Anatomic sites are not considered main terms.)

Step 4. After locating the main term, note any essential or nonessential modifiers.

Remember, nonessential modifiers are terms that immediately follow the main term and are enclosed in parentheses: "Fracture, traumatic (abduction) (adduction) (separation)." Nonessential modifiers do not have to be a part of the listed diagnosis. Essential modifiers are indented under the main term and are also listed alphabetically; they must be included in the diagnostic statement.

❖ *EXAMPLES*

In "Traumatic fracture of 6th dorsal vertebra," the essential modifiers are the condition and the anatomic site (traumatic, vertebra, and dorsal).

Abscess *(Continued)*
  abdomen, abdominal
    cavity K65.1
      wall L02.211
    abdominopelvic K65.1
    accessory sinus - *see* Sinusitis
    adrenal (capsule) (gland) E27.8
    alveolar K04.7
      with sinus K04.6
    amebic A06.4
      brain (and liver or lung abscess) A06.6
      genitourinary tract A06.82
      liver (without mention of brain or lung abscess) A06.5
      lung (and liver) (without mention of brain abscess) A06.5
      specified site NEC A06.89
      spleen A06.89

Fig. 14.11 Sample partial page from the Alphabetic Index where "abscess, adrenal" is located. (From Buck CJ: *2019 ICD-10-CM, standard edition,* St. Louis, 2019, Elsevier.)

In "Superficial foreign body in the shin," the essential modifiers are superficial (without open wound) and shin. (Note: The coder can assume that unless it is specifically stated in the diagnostic statement that there is an open wound, the diagnosis would be without open wound.)

Step 5. Scan the main term entry (or applicable essential modifiers) for any instructional or cross-referencing notes (e.g., *see, see also*).

❖ *EXAMPLES*

In "Traumatic fracture of 6th dorsal vertebra," there is an instructional note: "see Fracture, thorax, vertebra." Locating this cross-referenced term with the essential modifiers, the coder finds the code S22.059.

In "Superficial foreign body in the shin," there is an instructional note: "see Foreign body, superficial, leg." When cross-referencing to "Foreign body, superficial, leg," the coder finds "leg (lower) S80.85-."

Step 6. Select the most appropriate code, and verify the selected code by cross-referencing the Tabular.

 KEY NOTE

Using both the Index and the Tabular when locating and assigning a code is important. The Index does not always provide the full code. The full code, including laterality and any applicable seventh character, can be selected only from the Tabular.

 What Did You Learn?

Find the main terms in the following diagnoses, locate them in the Index, and provide the provisional codes found there:
1. Pressure ulcer of right elbow
2. Diffuse interstitial keratitis
3. Eustachian tube obstruction
4. Gestational diabetes mellitus

TABULAR LIST

The second section of the ICD-10-CM manual is the Tabular List (again, also known as the Tabular). This section, which has 21 chapters (see Table 14.4), contains a list of codes arranged alphanumerically and divided into chapters based on body system (anatomic site) or condition (etiology).

 Stop and Think

1. Patient A has an anxiety disorder. In which chapter would the coder find the appropriate code?
2. Patient B has congenital malformation of the bladder. The applicable code for this diagnosis would be located in Chapter ___.
3. Patient C has been diagnosed with acute nephritic syndrome. Search Chapter ___ for the appropriate code for this condition.

FORMAT AND STRUCTURE OF CODES

The Tabular in the ICD-10-CM contains categories, subcategories, and codes comprising three to seven characters. The first character is always a letter. Codes with three characters are included in the ICD-10-CM as the heading of a *category* of codes that may be subdivided further by the use of fourth and fifth digits, which provide greater detail. A three-character **category** that has no further subdivision is equivalent to a code (e.g., see "P09 Abnormal findings on neonatal screening"). A code is invalid if it has not been coded to the full number of characters required for that code, including the seventh character, if applicable. (More information on the use of the seventh character is provided later in this chapter.) Each level of subdivision after a category is a **subcategory**, which can have four or five characters. In the final level of subdivision, a code can have up to seven characters. All codes in the Tabular of the official version of the ICD-10-CM are in boldface type. Codes that have applicable seventh characters are still referred to as codes, not subcategories. The ICD-10-CM uses an indented format for easy reference (Fig. 14.12).

 KEY NOTE

For reporting purposes, only codes are permissible, not categories or subcategories, and any applicable seventh character is required.

Placeholder Character

In the ICD-10-CM coding system, the letter X has two uses: a lowercase x is used in certain codes to allow for future expansion and to fill out empty characters when a code contains fewer than six characters and a 7th character applies. When **placeholder character** "x" applies, it must be used in order for the code to be considered valid. An uppercase X is used at the beginning of a code to denote the code category. For example, in code category X78.0, the X denotes the intention of an injury, exposure, and so on. Codes that start with an X include code series X00 to X99. This series of codes is part of Chapter 20 (External Causes of Morbidity) of the Tabular.

Let's look at the two uses of the lowercase x as a placeholder character.
1. A lowercase x can be used as the fifth character for certain six-character codes. In such instances, the x provides for future expansion without disturbing the six-character structure.

❖ *EXAMPLES*
- T37.0x1A Poisoning by sulfonamides, accidental (unintentional), initial encounter
- T56.0x2S Toxic effect of lead and its compounds, intentional self-harm, sequela
- S03.4xxA Sprain of jaw, initial encounter

In these examples, the letter x serves as a placeholder when the code contains fewer than six

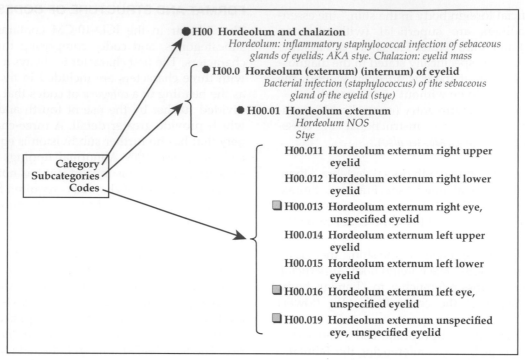

● **H00 Hordeolum and chalazion**
Hordeolum: inflammatory staphylococcal infection of sebaceous glands of eyelids; AKA stye. Chalazion: eyelid mass

● **H00.0 Hordeolum (externum) (internum) of eyelid**
Bacterial infection (staphylococcus) of the sebaceous gland of the eyelid (stye)

● **H00.01 Hordeolum externum**
Hordeolum NOS
Stye

Category
Subcategories
Codes

H00.011 Hordeolum externum right upper eyelid

H00.012 Hordeolum externum right lower eyelid

H00.013 Hordeolum externum right eye, unspecified eyelid

H00.014 Hordeolum externum left upper eyelid

H00.015 Hordeolum externum left lower eyelid

H00.016 Hordeolum externum left eye, unspecified eyelid

H00.019 Hordeolum externum unspecified eye, unspecified eyelid

Fig. 14.12 Sample page from the Tabular List identifying categories, subcategories, and codes. (From Buck CJ: *2019 ICD-10-CM, standard edition,* St. Louis, 2019, Elsevier.)

characters and a seventh character applies. This frequently occurs with poisonings and injuries, as the preceding examples indicate.

2. The lowercase x is used when a code has fewer than six characters and a seventh character extension is required. Here, the x is assigned for all characters fewer than six to meet the requirement of coding to the highest level of specificity.

❖*EXAMPLES*

- W85.xxxA Exposure to electric transmission lines, initial encounter
- S17.0xxA Crushing injury of larynx and trachea, initial encounter
- S01.02xA Laceration with foreign body of scalp, initial encounter

In these examples, a placeholder must be added so that the seventh character is in the correct position. Without this placeholder to ensure that characters appear in the correct positions, codes are invalid. Take, for example, a patient who presents with an accidental poisoning by an antiallergic drug. For the initial encounter, code T45.0x1A should be reported. In this case, the x in the fifth position serves as a placeholder so that the sixth and seventh characters are in the correct position. If a coder unintentionally omits the placeholder, the resulting code would be T45.01A, which is invalid.

 KEY NOTE

Not every ICD-10-CM code with a seventh character has a fourth, fifth, or sixth character.

Seventh (7th) Character

One significant feature of ICD-10-CM coding is the requirement of the addition of a **seventh (7th) character** (also called a *7th character extension*) to codes in certain ICD-10-CM categories. Codes that require a 7th character are used primarily in two chapters: Chapter 15—Pregnancy, Childbirth and the Puerperium and Chapter 19—Injury, Poisoning and Certain Other Consequences of External Causes; however, certain codes found in Chapters 13, 18, and 20 can also require a 7th character. For injuries, poisonings, and other external causes, the 7th character provides information about the episode of care. For pregnancy, childbirth, and the **puerperium** (the 6-week period after childbirth), the 7th character provides information about the fetus. More specifically, the two types of 7th character extensions provide information as follows:

- *Episode of care:* Designates the episode of care as initial, subsequent, or a **sequela** for injuries, poisonings, and certain other conditions, and in some instances provides additional information about the injury.
- *Fetus:* Used for certain complications of pregnancy with multiple gestation to identify which fetus(es) is (are) affected by the condition described by the code.

The applicable *7th character* is required for all codes in the category or, as the notes indicate, in the Tabular instructions. The 7th character always occupies the 7th character data field even for codes that are fewer than 6 characters. If a code that requires a 7th character is not six characters long, placeholder x must be used to fill in the empty characters. (Fig. 14.13 shows a list of 7th characters and their meanings.)

❖ *EXAMPLES of placeholder x in codes requiring a 7th character*
- O65.0xx1 Obstructed labor due to deformed pelvis, fetus 1
- H40.11x2 Primary open-angle glaucoma, moderate stage

For Chapter 19—Injury, Poisoning, and Certain Other Consequences of External Causes (S00 to T88), the appropriate 7th character that needs to be added is one of the following:

A Initial encounter
D Subsequent encounter
S Sequela

● **S52** **Fracture of forearm**

> **Note:** A fracture not identified as displaced or nondisplaced should be coded to displaced
>
> A fracture not designated as open or closed should be coded to closed
>
> The open fracture designations are based on the Gustilo open fracture classification

Excludes1 traumatic amputation of forearm (S58.-)

Excludes2 fracture at wrist and hand level (S62.-)

The appropriate 7th character is to be added to all codes from category S52

> A initial encounter for closed fracture
> B initial encounter for open fracture type I or II
>   initial encounter for open fracture NOS
> C initial encounter for open fracture type IIIA, IIIB, or IIIC
> D subsequent encounter for closed fracture with routine healing
> E subsequent encounter for open fracture type I or II with routine healing
> F subsequent encounter for open fracture type IIIA, IIIB, or IIIC with routine healing
> G subsequent encounter for closed fracture with delayed healing
> H subsequent encounter for open fracture type I or II with delayed healing
> J subsequent encounter for open fracture type IIIA, IIIB, or IIIC with delayed healing
> K subsequent encounter for closed fracture with nonunion
> M subsequent encounter for open fracture type I or II with nonunion
> N subsequent encounter for open fracture type IIIA, IIIB, or IIIC with nonunion
> P subsequent encounter for closed fracture with malunion
> Q subsequent encounter for open fracture type I or II with malunion
> R subsequent encounter for open fracture type IIIA, IIIB, or IIIC with malunion
> S sequela

Fig. 14.13 Partial page from the Tabular List showing S52 under which are listed the seventh characters and their meanings. (From Buck CJ: *2019 ICD-10-CM, standard edition*, St. Louis, 2019, Elsevier.)

❖ *EXAMPLES*
- S41-142A Puncture wound with foreign body of left upper arm
- T17.220D Food in pharynx causing asphyxiation

Note: For aftercare of an injury, the coder should assign the acute injury code with the 7th character "D."

The 7th character to be added to all codes from category S42 (fractures) is selected from the following list as appropriate:

A Initial encounter for closed fracture
B Initial encounter for open fracture
G Subsequent encounter for fracture with delayed healing
K Subsequent encounter for fracture with nonunion
P Subsequent encounter for fracture with malunion
S Sequela

❖ *EXAMPLE of 7th character use in fractures*
- S02.110B Type I occipital condyle fracture, initial encounter for open fracture

TABULAR LIST CONVENTIONS

The ICD-10-CM coding manual contains general guidelines and chapter-specific guidelines, which are applicable to all healthcare settings unless otherwise indicated. The conventions and instructions of the classification take precedence over guidelines. ICD-10-CM uses four types of conventions that provide additional assistance to the coder. Before attempting to assign a code to a given diagnosis, the coder should be familiar with the following conventions and what they mean:
- Abbreviations
- Punctuation marks
- Instructional notes
- Symbols

Instructional notes can appear in both the Index and the Tabular and are similar among publishers. However, symbols can differ from one publisher to the next. In the *2019 ICD-10-CM, Standard Edition* by Buck, the list of symbols and their meanings is illustrated on page xii. Symbols and their meanings are also shown at the bottom of each page in the Tabular (Fig. 14.14). These symbols and their meanings may differ from year to year and from one publisher to another.

Abbreviations

The following sections discuss abbreviations used in the ICD-10-CM.

NEC (not elsewhere classifiable). The abbreviation **NEC (not elsewhere classifiable)** in the Index represents

---

▶ New   ⇒ Revised   ~~deleted~~ Deleted   Excludes 1   Excludes 2   Includes   Use additional   Code first   Code also   Key words

OGCR Official Guidelines   **X** Assign placeholder X   ● Use Additional Character(s)   ▌ Manifestation Code   **Coding Clinic**

Fig. 14.14 Bottom of the Tabular List page showing symbols used in ICD-10. (From Buck CJ: *2019 ICD-10-CM, standard edition*, St. Louis, 2019, Elsevier.)

"other specified." When a specific code is unavailable for a condition in the Index, the coder is directed to the "other specified" code in the Tabular where an NEC entry under a code identifies it as the "other specified" code.

❖ *EXAMPLE*

G93.49 Other encephalopathy
   Encephalopathy NEC

Because all major components of a diagnosis are specified in the ICD-10-CM, there is limited need for an NEC code option.

NOS (not otherwise specified). The abbreviation **NOS (not otherwise specified)** is the equivalent of unspecified, meaning that a more specific diagnosis is unavailable. Let's say that the diagnosis written in the patient's health record is simply "meningitis." Before assigning an NOS code, the coder should examine the medical record more closely or question the physician or provider for more complete documentation.

❖ *EXAMPLE*

G03.9 Meningitis
   Arachnoiditis (spinal) NOS

As with NEC, the use of NOS is restricted in the ICD-10-CM because of the level of specificity that is required.

Punctuation

Various types of punctuation are also used in the ICD-10-CM.

Brackets. Brackets, [ ], are used in the Tabular to enclose synonyms, alternative wording, or explanatory phrases. Brackets are used in the Index to identify manifestation codes.

❖ *EXAMPLES*

B06 Rubella [German measles]
J00 Acute nasopharyngitis [common cold]

Parentheses. Parentheses, ( ), are used in both the Index and the Tabular to enclose supplementary words that may be present or absent in the statement of a disease or procedure without affecting the code number to which it is assigned. The terms enclosed within the parentheses are nonessential modifiers.

❖ *EXAMPLES*

H44.611 Retained (old) magnetic foreign body in anterior chamber, right eye
I10. Essential (primary) hypertension
K51.011 Ulcerative (chronic) pancolitis with rectal bleeding

Colons. Colons, :, are used in the Tabular after an incomplete term that needs one or more of the modifiers after the colon to make it assignable to a given category.

❖ *EXAMPLE*

G73.7 Myopathy in diseases classified elsewhere

Excludes1: myopathy in:
   rheumatoid arthritis (M05.32)
   sarcoidosis (D86.87)
   scleroderma (M34.82)
   sicca syndrome [Sjögren] (M35.03)
   systemic lupus erythematosus (M32.19)

Dashes. Dashes, –, are used in both the Index and the Tabular. A dash is used at the end of a code number in the Index to indicate that the code is incomplete. To determine the additional character or characters, the coder locates the code in the Tabular, reviews the options, and assigns the appropriate code.

❖ *EXAMPLE*

Fracture, pathologic
   ankle M84.47–
   carpus M84.44–

Point dash. In the Tabular, the dash preceded by a decimal point, .–, indicates an incomplete code. To determine the additional character or characters, the coder locates the referenced category or subcategory elsewhere in the Tabular, reviews the options, and assigns the appropriate code.

❖ *EXAMPLE*

J43 Emphysema
Excludes1: tobacco dependence (F17.–)

Instructional Notes

Various **instructional notes** are used in the ICD-10-CM, and it is important that the coder learn what each of them means.

- Use of "and": When the term "and" is used in a narrative statement, it represents "and/or."

❖ *EXAMPLE*

Candidiasis of vulva *and* vagina

- Use of "with": The word "with" in the Index is sequenced immediately after the main term, not in alphabetic order.

❖ *EXAMPLE*

Alzheimer disease *with* behavioral disturbance

- "Other" and "other specified" codes: Codes titled "other" or "other specified" are used when the information in the medical record provides detail for which a specific code does not exist. Index entries with NEC in the line designate "other" codes in the Tabular. These Index entries represent specific disease entities for which no specific code exists, so the term is included within an "other" code. "Other specified" codes that have a ".8" as the fourth character are used for conditions that cannot be classified anywhere else under the relevant three-character category title.

- "Unspecified" codes: Codes (usually those with a fourth-digit 9 or fifth-digit 0 for diagnosis codes) titled "unspecified" are used when the information in the medical record is insufficient to assign a more specific code. For categories in which an unspecified code is not provided, the "other specified" code may represent both other and unspecified (Fig. 14.15).

- **Includes notes:** This note appears immediately under a three-digit code title to define further, or give examples of, the content of the category.
- **Inclusion terms:** A list of terms is included under some codes. These terms are the conditions for which that code is to be used. The terms may be synonyms of the code title; or, in the case of "other specified" codes, the terms are a list of the various conditions assigned to that code. The inclusion terms are not exhaustive. Additional terms found only in the Index may also be assigned to a code.
- **Excludes notes:** The ICD-10-CM has two types of excludes notes. Each type of note has a different definition for use, but they are similar in that they indicate that codes excluded from each other are independent of each other.
  - **Excludes1:** A type 1 excludes note is a pure excludes note. It means "*not coded here!*" Excludes1 indicates that the code identified in the note and the code where the note appears cannot be reported together because the two conditions cannot occur together, such as a congenital form versus an acquired form of the same condition (see Fig. 14.15).

❖ *EXAMPLES*

E10 Type 1 diabetes mellitus
Excludes1 diabetes mellitus due to underlying condition (E08.-)
B06 Rubella

Excludes1 congenital rubella (P35.0)

  - **Excludes2:** A type 2 excludes note means "*not included here.*" An Excludes2 note indicates that the condition excluded is not part of the condition represented by the code, but a patient may have both conditions at the same time. When an Excludes2 note appears under a code, it is acceptable to use both the code and the excluded code together, when appropriate (Fig. 14.16).

❖ *EXAMPLES*

J03 Acute tonsillitis
Excludes2 *chronic tonsillitis* (J35.0)
I70.2 atherosclerosis of native arteries of extremities
Excludes2 *atherosclerosis of bypass graft of extremities* (I70.30-I70-79)

MANIFESTATION CODES

Due to an underlying etiology, certain conditions have manifestations (a sign or symptom of a disease) that affect one or more body systems. ICD-10-CM coding conventions require that the underlying condition (etiology) code be sequenced first, followed by the manifestation code(s). Whenever a condition requires etiology and manifestation codes, there is a "use additional code" note following the etiology code and a "code first" note following the manifestation code. These instructional notes are key to proper sequencing of the codes.

> **KEY NOTE**
>
> The Index in the ICD-10-CM includes the suggestion of some manifestation codes by including the code as a second code, shown in brackets, directly after the underlying or etiology code (which should always be reported first).

❖ *EXAMPLE*

Chorioretinitis—see also Inflammation, chorioretinal
  Egyptian B76.9 [D63.8]
  histoplasmic B39.9 [H32]

  In addition, many common manifestations are included in the etiologic condition by the use of combination codes in the ICD-10-CM (discussed later in this chapter). This element helps the coder sequence the cause of a disease versus the signs and symptoms of a disease.

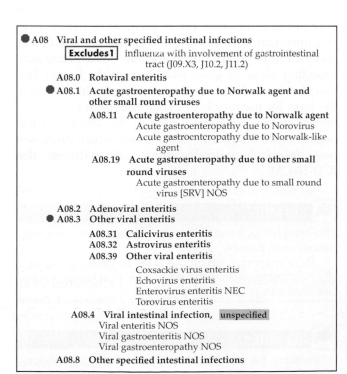

● A08   **Viral and other specified intestinal infections**
  Excludes1 influenza with involvement of gastrointestinal tract (J09.X3, J10.2, J11.2)

A08.0   **Rotaviral enteritis**
● A08.1   **Acute gastroenteropathy due to Norwalk agent and other small round viruses**
    A08.11   **Acute gastroenteropathy due to Norwalk agent**
        Acute gastroenteropathy due to Norovirus
        Acute gastroenteropathy due to Norwalk-like agent
    A08.19   **Acute gastroenteropathy due to other small round viruses**
        Acute gastroenteropathy due to small round virus [SRV] NOS
A08.2   **Adenoviral enteritis**
● A08.3   **Other viral enteritis**
    A08.31   **Calicivirus enteritis**
    A08.32   **Astrovirus enteritis**
    A08.39   **Other viral enteritis**
        Coxsackie virus enteritis
        Echovirus enteritis
        Enterovirus enteritis NEC
        Torovirus enteritis
A08.4   **Viral intestinal infection, unspecified**
        Viral enteritis NOS
        Viral gastroenteritis NOS
        Viral gastroenteropathy NOS
A08.8   **Other specified intestinal infections**

Fig. 14.15 Partial page of the Tabular List showing examples of "other specified" and "unspecified" conventions use. (From Buck CJ: *2019 ICD-10-CM, standard edition*, St. Louis, 2019, Elsevier.)

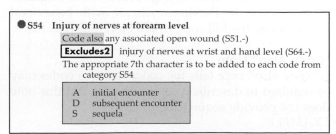

● S54   **Injury of nerves at forearm level**
  Code also any associated open wound (S51.-)
  Excludes2 injury of nerves at wrist and hand level (S64.-)
  The appropriate 7th character is to be added to each code from category S54

A	initial encounter
D	subsequent encounter
S	sequela

Fig. 14.16 Partial page from the Tabular List showing the use of an "Excludes2" note. (From Buck CJ: *2019 ICD-10-CM, standard edition*, St. Louis, 2019, Elsevier.)

❖ *EXAMPLE*

E10.21 Type 1 diabetes mellitus with diabetic nephropathy

KEY NOTE

Combination codes are used for both symptom and diagnosis and etiology and manifestations. An example is K50.013 Crohn disease of small intestine with fistula. The etiology (cause of a disease or condition) is always coded first, and the manifestation (sign or symptom of a disease) is coded second.

Etiology/Manifestation Convention ("Code First," "Use Additional Code," and "In Diseases Classified Elsewhere" Notes)

You've learned that certain conditions have both an underlying etiology and multiple body system manifestations secondary to the underlying etiology. For such conditions, the ICD-10-CM requires that the underlying condition be sequenced first, followed by the manifestation. Wherever such a combination exists, there is a "use additional code" note at the etiology code and a "code first" note at the manifestation code. These instructional notes indicate the proper sequencing order of the codes—etiology followed by manifestation.

Generally, the manifestation codes have the words "in diseases classified elsewhere" in the code title. Codes with this title are a component of the etiology/manifestation convention. The code title indicates that it is a manifestation code. "In diseases classified elsewhere" codes are never permitted to be used as **first-listed diagnosis** (or **principal diagnosis**) codes. They must be used in conjunction with an underlying condition code, and they must be listed after the underlying condition.

❖ *EXAMPLE*

D63 Anemia in chronic diseases classified elsewhere
  D63.0 Anemia in neoplastic disease
  Code first neoplasm (C00-D49)

Another example of the etiology/manifestation convention is *dementia in Parkinson disease*. If the coder looks up "dementia" in the Index and, following down the listed terms, finds "with Parkinson disease," code G20 is listed first, after which the code F02.80 appears in brackets. Code G20 (Parkinson disease) represents the underlying etiology and must be sequenced first. Code F02.80 represents the manifestation of dementia in diseases classified elsewhere (Fig. 14.17). If the diagnosis was dementia in Parkinson disease with behavioral disturbances, the full code would be G31.83 [F02.81].

"Code Also" Note

A "code also" note tells the coder that two codes may be required to describe a condition fully, but this note does not provide sequencing direction.

❖ *EXAMPLE*

D61.82 Myelophthisis
  Leukoerythroblastic anemia
  Myelophthisic anemia
  Panmyelophthisis

> **Dementia** (degenerative (primary) (old age) (persisting) F03.90
> with
>   aggressive behavior F03.91
>   behavioral disturbance F03.91
>   combative behavior F03.91
>   Lewy bodies G31.83 [F2.80]
>   with behavioral disturbance G31.83 [F02.81]
>   Parkinson's disease G20 [F02.80]
>   with behavioral disturbance G20 [F02.81]
>   Parkinsonism G31.83 [F02.80]
>   with behavioral disturbance G31.83 [F02.81]
>   violent behavior F03.91

Fig. 14.17 Portion of the ICD-10-CM Alphabetic Index illustrating etiology and manifestation coding sequencing. (From Buck CJ: *2019 ICD-10-CM, standard edition*, St. Louis, 2019, Elsevier.)

Code also the underlying disorder, such as:
  malignant neoplasm of breast (C50.–)
  tuberculosis (A15.–)

MORPHOLOGY CODES

Morphology is the study of the form and structure of organisms and their specific structural features. If the patient record shows a diagnosis of some type of tumor, the **histology** (microscopic study of the tissue) of the tumor is identified with a *morphology* code. In the ICD-10-CM, morphology codes are no longer listed in the Index alongside the descriptors and standard codes, and they do not have a separate appendix, as was the case in the ICD-9-CM. The Neoplasm Table only distinguishes between malignant, benign, *in situ,* and uncertain behavior. (An *in situ* tumor is one that is confined to its site of origin and has not invaded surrounding tissue or gone elsewhere in the body.) The morphology code can be referenced in the Index under the term for the histology of the **neoplasm** (*new or abnormal growth*). There is a note in the Tabular at the beginning of Chapter 2—Neoplasms, which discusses how morphology codes are dealt with in the ICD-10-CM.

KEY NOTE

The morphology code should be included in the medical record when possible.

There is a note in the Tabular at the beginning of Chapter 2—Neoplasms, which discusses how morphology codes are dealt with in ICD-10-CM.

KEY NOTE

In medicine, the term *morphology* refers to the size, shape, and structure, rather than the function, of a given organ. For example, as a diagnostic imaging technique, ultrasound assists in the recognition of abnormal morphologies as symptoms of underlying conditions.

Stop and Think

Patient Marybelle Sanchez's medical record indicates that she has been diagnosed with basal cell carcinoma of the external ear. Identifying and locating the main term "carcinoma" in the Index, you note the cross-reference (*see also* Neoplasm, skin, malignant). Finding "Neoplasm neoplastic" in the Index, there is another cross-reference (*see also* Table of Neoplasms). Terms in this table are listed by anatomic site, so you must locate "skin" and then "ear."

This is where you need to know the classification of the tissue. Referring back to the patient's record, the histology report indicates that the tissue is a primary malignancy. Therefore the code in the "Malignant, Primary" column C44.21– is the one you select. But you are not finished coding this diagnosis to the greatest specificity. We learned earlier that a dash at the end of a code indicates that the code is incomplete. In addition, the coder should never code directly from the Index.

Locating C44.21 in the Tabular, note a symbol (in Buck 2019, the symbol is a red stop sign) preceding the code. The legend at the bottom of the page tells you that a red stop sign indicates that another character is needed. Ms. Sanchez's record does not indicate which ear, so you would use code C44.211—basal carcinoma of unspecified ear. (Symbols and conventions used in ICD-10-CM and their meanings were discussed earlier in this chapter. They are also listed in the introductory section in the front of the coding manual.

DEFAULT CODES

A code listed next to a main term in the ICD-10-CM Index is referred to as a **default code**. The default code represents the condition that is most commonly associated with the main term or is the unspecified code for the condition. If the details of a condition are not documented in a medical record, such as whether a condition is displaced or nondisplaced, the coder would use "displaced" as the default code. If it is not documented as to whether a fracture is open or closed, the code would be the default code "closed."

 What Did You Learn?

Previously, you identified the main terms and located them in the Index, providing a provisional code. Now, cross-reference to the Tabular and assign the correct code for the following diagnoses to the greatest level of specificity:
1. Pressure ulcer of right elbow
2. Diffuse interstitial keratitis
3. Eustachian tube obstruction
4. Gestational diabetes mellitus

ICD-10-CM OFFICIAL GUIDELINES FOR CODING AND REPORTING

The CMS and the NCHS, under the authority of HHS, provide guidelines for coding and reporting using the ICD-10-CM coding system. These guidelines have been approved by the four organizations that make up the cooperating parties for ICD-10-CM: the American Hospital Association (AHA), the American Health Information Management Association (AHIMA), CMS, and NCHS.

ICD-10-CM conventions, general guidelines, and chapter-specific guidelines are applicable to all healthcare settings unless otherwise indicated. The general guidelines are important for code selection, but chapter-specific guidelines are even more important. Chapter-specific guidelines take precedence over general guidelines. The conventions and instructions of the classification take precedence over guidelines.

The guidelines are organized into sections. Section I includes the structure and conventions of the classification and general guidelines that apply to the entire classification and chapter-specific guidelines that correspond to the chapters as they are arranged in the classification. Section II includes guidelines for selection of principal diagnosis for non-outpatient settings. Section III includes guidelines for reporting additional diagnoses in non-outpatient settings. Section IV is for outpatient coding and reporting. It is necessary to review all sections of the guidelines to fully understand all of the rules and instructions needed to code properly; however, the following sections concentrate on Section IV because most of the encounters the health insurance specialist or biller/coder experiences are in the healthcare provider's office and other outpatient settings.

The complete guidelines can be found in Part I of *2019 ICD-10-CM, Standard Edition* by Buck, and chapter-specific guidelines that correspond to the chapters as they are arranged in the classification are provided. The official guidelines also can be downloaded from the CMS website, which is listed under "Websites to Explore" at the end of this chapter.

SECTION I: CONVENTIONS, GENERAL CODING GUIDELINES, AND CHAPTER-SPECIFIC GUIDELINES

The first section includes the structure and conventions of the classification and general guidelines that apply to the entire classification, much of which has already been discussed in this chapter.

Section I is composed of the following:
A. Conventions for the ICD-10-CM
B. General coding guidelines
C. Chapter-specific coding guidelines

SECTION II: SELECTION OF PRINCIPAL DIAGNOSIS

Section II discusses the circumstances that govern the selection of the *principal diagnosis*. The principal diagnosis is defined in the Uniform Hospital Discharge Data Set (UHDDS) as "that condition established after study to be chiefly responsible for occasioning the admission of the patient to the hospital for care." Because this chapter deals mainly with outpatient services, we will not go into Section II at this time. Chapter 18 addresses hospital coding.

SECTION III: REPORTING ADDITIONAL DIAGNOSES

The UHDDS defines "other diagnoses" as "all conditions that coexist at the time of admission, that develop subsequently, or that affect the treatment received and/or the length of stay." The definitions have been expanded to include all non-outpatient settings. The following three subsections are to be applied in designating "other diagnoses" when neither the Index nor the Tabular provide direction:

A. Previous conditions
B. Abnormal findings
C. Uncertain diagnoses

As noted with Section II, this topic is addressed in Chapter 18.

SECTION IV: DIAGNOSTIC CODING AND REPORTING GUIDELINES FOR OUTPATIENT SERVICES

This is the section that is most applicable to this chapter because the majority of services that physicians and other healthcare professionals provide are on an outpatient basis. Section IV is divided into 17 subsections—A through Q.

A: Selection of First-Listed Diagnosis

In the outpatient setting, the term *first-listed diagnosis* is used rather than the term *principal diagnosis*, which is used for inpatient diagnoses. It is important to take note that a final diagnosis often is not established on the first encounter. It may take two or more visits before a diagnosis is confirmed. Until a diagnosis is established, the coder should report the signs and/or symptoms that brought the patient to the healthcare facility.

> ## ❗ Stop and Think
>
> June 14, 20XX: New 24-year-old patient, Palo Aural, arrives at the clinic with a chief complaint of fatigue, dizziness, and nausea without vomiting for the past week. She also states that she is "late with her period." Dr. Botcher performs a physical exam and orders a pregnancy test. Palo was asked to return in 1 week. Because no definitive diagnosis was reported on this initial visit, only the signs and/or symptoms are coded:
>
> Fatigue, R53.83; dizziness, R42.; nausea w/o vomiting, R11.0
>
> June 21, 20XX: The patient is informed that the pregnancy test is positive. She is referred to Dr. Oppenheim in obstetrics and gynecology. The final diagnosis is:
>
> Positive pregnancy test, Z32.01

1: Outpatient surgery. If the patient is admitted for outpatient (same-day) surgery, which is sometimes referred to as *ambulatory surgery*, code the reason for the surgery as the first-listed diagnosis, even if the procedure is not performed due to a **contraindication**—a condition that makes a particular treatment or procedure potentially inadvisable. In such cases, the reason for the surgery would be coded, and if it was canceled, the code for the reason for the cancellation would follow.

❖ *EXAMPLE*

Diagnosis: Internal derangement of other lateral meniscus due to old tear or injury, right knee, M23.261; Procedure canceled due to other contraindication, Z53.09

2: Observation stay. If a patient is admitted to the hospital for observation of a medical condition, assign the code for the medical condition as the first-listed diagnosis. If a patient reports for outpatient surgery and subsequently develops a complication requiring admission to observation, code the reason for the surgery as the first-listed diagnosis, followed by the code for the complication as the secondary diagnosis.

❖ *EXAMPLE*

Diagnosis: Internal derangement of other lateral meniscus due to old tear or injury, right knee, M23.261
Complication: Intraoperative puncture during musculoskeletal surgery, M96.810

B: Codes From A00.0 Through T88.9, Z00–Z99

The appropriate code or codes from A00.0 through T88.9, Z00–Z99 must be used to identify diagnoses, symptoms, conditions, problems, complaints, or other reasons for the encounter/visit. Detailed guidelines are provided in the ICD-10-CM Official Guidelines for Coding and Reporting document (available on the CMS.gov website) to give the coder further direction in selecting the correct diagnostic code.

C: Accurate Reporting of ICD-10-CM Diagnosis Codes

For accurate reporting of diagnosis codes, the documentation in the patient record should accurately describe the patient's condition using terminology that includes specific diagnoses as well as symptoms, problems, or reasons for the encounter.

D: Codes That Describe Symptoms and Signs

As discussed under "A: Selection of First-Listed Diagnosis," codes that describe symptoms and signs, as opposed to a specific diagnosis, are acceptable for reporting purposes when a related definitive diagnosis has not been established (confirmed) by the healthcare provider.

ICD-10-CM Chapter 18—Symptoms, Signs, and Abnormal Clinical and Laboratory Findings, Not Elsewhere Classified (codes R00.0–R99) contains many, but not all, codes for symptoms.

E: Encounters for Circumstances Other Than a Disease or Injury

The ICD-10-CM provides codes to deal with encounters for circumstances other than a disease or injury.

The Factors Influencing Health Status and Contact with Health Services codes (Z00–Z99) are provided for occasions when circumstances other than a disease or injury are recorded as the diagnosis or problem. (Refer to Section I.C.21 in the ICD-10-CM manual.)

F: Level of Detail in Coding

We learned earlier in this chapter how codes were constructed in the ICD-10-CM diagnosis coding process. If necessary, review the section titled "ICD-10-CM Code Structure" before continuing.

The ICD-10-CM is composed of codes with three to seven digits. Codes with three digits are listed at the heading of a category of codes and may be subdivided further by the use of fourth, fifth, sixth, or seventh digits that provide greater specificity. A three-digit code is to be used only if it is not subdivided further. A code is invalid if it has not been coded to the full number of characters required for that code, including the seventh character extension, if applicable.

G: ICD-10-CM Code for the Diagnosis, Condition, Problem, or Other Reason for the Encounter/Visit

ICD-10-CM guidelines tell the coder to list first the code for the diagnosis, condition, problem, or other reason for the encounter/visit shown in the medical record to be chiefly responsible for the services provided. List any additional codes that describe any co-existing conditions. In some cases, the first-listed diagnosis may be a symptom when a diagnosis has not been confirmed by the healthcare provider.

H: Uncertain Diagnosis

Never code diagnoses documented as "probable," "suspected," "questionable," "rule out," "working diagnosis," or other similar terms indicating uncertainty. Instead, code the condition(s) to the highest degree of certainty for that encounter, such as symptoms, signs, abnormal test results, or other reason for the visit.

I: Chronic Diseases

Chronic diseases treated on a continuing basis may be coded and reported as many times as the patient receives treatment and care for that particular condition. When a condition is described as both acute (subacute) and chronic and separate subentries exist in the Index at the same indentation level, code both, and sequence the acute (subacute) code first. For example, locate the diagnosis "acute and chronic maxillary sinusitis" in the Index. The code for "acute" (J01.00) is sequenced first and "chronic" (J32.0) is second.

J: Code All Documented Conditions That Coexist

Code all documented conditions that coexist at the time of the encounter/visit and require or affect patient care, treatment, or management. Do not code conditions that were previously treated and no longer exist. However, history codes (categories Z80–Z87)

may be used as secondary codes if the historical condition or family history has an impact on current care or influences treatment.

K: Patients Receiving Diagnostic Services Only

For patients receiving diagnostic services only during an encounter/visit, sequence first the diagnosis, condition, problem, or other reason for the encounter/visit shown in the medical record to be chiefly responsible for the outpatient services provided during the encounter/visit. Codes for other diagnoses (e.g., chronic conditions) may be sequenced as additional diagnoses.

L: Patients Receiving Therapeutic Services Only

For patients receiving therapeutic services only during an encounter/visit, sequence first the diagnosis, condition, problem, or other reason for the encounter/visit shown in the medical record to be chiefly responsible for the outpatient services provided during the encounter/visit. Codes for other diagnoses (e.g., chronic conditions) may be sequenced as additional diagnoses. An exception to this rule is when the primary reason for the admission/encounter is chemotherapy or radiation therapy, where the appropriate Z code for the service is listed first and the diagnosis or problem for which the service is being performed is listed second.

M: Patients Receiving Preoperative Evaluations Only

For patients receiving preoperative evaluations only, sequence first a code from subcategory Z01.81-, Encounter for Pre-Procedural Examinations, to describe the preoperative consultations. Assign a code for the condition to describe the reason for the surgery as an additional diagnosis. Code also any findings related to the preoperative evaluation.

N: Ambulatory Surgery

For ambulatory surgery, code the diagnosis for which the surgery was performed. If the postoperative diagnosis is known to be different from the preoperative diagnosis at the time the diagnosis is confirmed, select the postoperative diagnosis for coding because it is the most definitive.

O: Routine Outpatient Prenatal Visits

See Section I.C.15, Routine Outpatient Prenatal Visits, in the guidelines.

P: Encounters for General Medical Examinations With Abnormal Findings

The subcategories for encounters for general medical examinations, Z00.0-, provide codes for encounters with and without abnormal findings. If a general medical examination results in an abnormal finding, the code for general medical examination with abnormal finding should be assigned as the first listed diagnosis. A secondary code for the abnormal finding should also be assigned.

Q: Encounters for Routine Health Screenings

See Section I.C.21, Factors Influencing Health Status and Contact with Health Services, Screening.

! Stop and Think

1. The diagnostic code found in Arnold Banneker's medical chart is E10.311. To assign this six-digit code, what would his documented diagnosis have to read?
2. Football star Edwin McGovern has a diagnostic code of S52.012A. What does the "A" signify?
3. Doris Chambers' diagnostic code is C50.512. What is the diagnosis documented in her medical record?
4. Bernice Soledad is diagnosed with "age-related osteoporosis with current pathologic fracture of the right shoulder, subsequent encounter for fracture with routine healing." What is the correct code for Bernice's condition?
5. Ted Francis's record shows a diagnostic code of T43.1x1. What is the purpose of the "x" in this diagnosis code?

? What Did You Learn?

1. True or false: Coding guidelines for inconclusive diagnoses (e.g., probable, suspected, rule out) were developed for inpatient reporting and do not apply to outpatients.
2. Which chapter in the Tabular provides codes to deal with occasions when circumstances other than a disease or injury are recorded as the reason for the encounter?
3. True or false: A code is invalid if it has not been coded to the full number of characters required for that code, excluding the seventh character extension, if applicable.
4. When a diagnosis is documented as "probable," "suspected," "questionable," or "rule out," what should be coded for that outpatient encounter/visit?
5. True or false: If a general medical examination results in an abnormal finding, the code for the abnormal finding should be assigned as the first-listed diagnosis.

OTHER CODING FEATURES OF THE ICD-10-CM

ICD-10-CM coding offers other features that provide increased detail and greater specificity as discussed in the following paragraphs.

COMBINATION CODES

A **combination code** is a single code used to classify two diagnoses or a diagnosis with an associated secondary process (manifestation). Combination codes are identified by referring to subterm entries in the Index and by reading the inclusion and exclusion notes in the Tabular. The combination code is assigned only when that code fully identifies the diagnostic conditions involved or when the Index so directs.

❖ *EXAMPLES*

I25.110 Arteriosclerotic heart disease of native coronary artery with unstable angina pectoris
K50.013 Crohn disease of small intestine with fistula
K71.51 Toxic liver disease with chronic active hepatitis with ascites

Multiple coding should not be used when the classification provides a combination code that clearly identifies all of the elements documented in the diagnosis. When the combination code lacks necessary specificity in describing the manifestation or complication, an additional code should be used as a secondary code.

! Stop and Think

You note that the diagnosis in patient Lonnie Chadwick's medical record is "type 2 diabetes mellitus with mild nonproliferative diabetic retinopathic macular edema." Given that this is a combination of two diagnoses, a level of severity, and a physical manifestation of one of the diagnoses—type 2 diabetes mellitus, nonproliferative diabetic retinopathy, mild, and macular edema—assign the correct code. (*Hint:* All possible combinations of types of diabetic retinopathy, severity, and presence or absence of macular edema are present under E11.3 Type 2 diabetes mellitus with ophthalmic complications.)

LATE EFFECTS (SEQUELAE)

Sequelae (the plural form of *sequela*) are late effects of injury or illness. Coding of late effects generally requires two codes, with the condition or nature of the late effect sequenced first and the late effect code sequenced second. In ICD-10-CM, these codes appear at the end of each anatomic chapter.

❖ *EXAMPLES*

H59.032 Cystoid macular edema following cataract surgery (left eye)
K91.0 Vomiting following gastrointestinal surgery (digestive system)

IMPENDING OR THREATENED CONDITION

Any condition described at the time of discharge as "impending" or "threatened" should be coded as follows:

- If it did occur, code as confirmed diagnosis.
- If it did not occur, reference the Index to determine whether the condition has a subentry term for "impending" or "threatened," and reference main term entries for "impending" and for "threatened."
- If the subterms are listed, assign the given code.
- If the subterms are not listed, code the existing underlying condition and not the condition described as impending or threatened.

LATERALITY

For bilateral sites, the last character of the six-character diagnostic code indicates laterality (the side of the body affected). An unspecified side code is also provided if laterality is not identified in the medical record. If no bilateral code is provided and the condition is bilateral, assign separate codes for both the left and the right sides.

❖ *EXAMPLES*

C50.212 Malignant neoplasm of upper-inner quadrant of left female breast

H02.835 Dermatochalasis of left lower eyelid

L89.213 Pressure ulcer of right hip, stage 3

Laterality codes are used frequently in the neoplasm and injury chapters.

 KEY NOTE

The coder should always begin the search for the correct code assignment in the Index. Never begin a search in the Tabular because this can lead to coding errors, and never code directly from the Index.

 HIPAA Tip

Version 5010 (the revised set of Health Insurance Portability and Accountability Act [HIPAA] transaction standards, adopted to replace Version 4010/4010A standards) accommodates the ICD-10 code sets and had an earlier compliance date than ICD-10 to ensure adequate testing time for the industry. This rule applies to all HIPAA-covered entities, including health plans, healthcare clearinghouses, and certain healthcare providers.

TABLE OF DRUGS AND CHEMICALS

The Table of Drugs in ICD-10-CM is located after the Table of Neoplasms and includes the following column headings:

- Substance
- Poisoning, accidental (unintentional)
- Poisoning, intentional self-harm
- Poisoning, assault
- Poisoning, undetermined
- Adverse effect
- Underdosing

In the ICD-10-CM, any poisoning that was intentional is classified as "poisoning, intentional self-harm." In the ICD-9-CM, any poisoning that was intentional was classified as a suicide attempt. In the ICD-10-CM, it is recognized that although some people may intentionally poison themselves with a specific drug, they are not necessarily attempting suicide. The ICD-10-CM retains the former "undetermined" category for poisons. If the coder cannot determine whether the poisoning was accidental, intentional self-harm, or an assault, there is still a way to report the

condition as a poisoning. Coders should first report a code from categories T36–T65, followed by the code that specifies the nature of the adverse effect, poisoning, or toxic effect. The Table of Drugs and Chemicals displays the name of the drug alphabetically under the "Substance" column heading and the external cause (T-code).

Adverse Effects

The ICD-10-CM eliminates any potential confusion by adding a column specifically for **adverse effects** (undesirable reaction). Coders report codes from this column when the correct patient took the correct dosage of the correct drug and suffered an adverse effect. For example, if a patient suffered an adverse effect from taking cefmenoxime, coders would report T36.1X5A for an initial visit for the adverse effect.

An instructional note at the beginning of category T36 instructs coders to use additional codes for all manifestations of poisonings and adverse effects. Therefore if a patient overdoses on a substance and suffers a minor adverse event, such as dizziness, coders would report two codes: one for the poisoning and one for the dizziness. Examples of adverse events include the following:

- Tachycardia
- Gastrointestinal hemorrhaging
- Vomiting
- Hypokalemia
- Respiratory failure

! **Stop and Think**

If Laura Phoebes suffers from tachycardia when she drinks too much caffeine, the code for poisoning by adverse effect (unintentional) would be T43.615 followed by a seventh character (A, D, or S) to determine initial encounter, subsequent encounter, or sequela. The adverse effects code for caffeine would be located alphabetically in the Table of Drugs and Chemicals under the column heading "Adverse Effects," or T43.615.

Underdosing

The ICD-10-CM includes a category, *underdosing*, which may require additional documentation. **Underdosing** is defined as taking less of a medication or substance than is prescribed or instructed, whether by a physician or the drug packaging. Underdosing may be intentional or unintentional, and the ICD-10-CM includes codes for both scenarios. The instructional notes at the beginning of category T36 instruct coders to report an additional code for the intent of underdosing. The ICD-10-CM provides specific codes that identify why a patient may be taking less of a drug than instructed or prescribed. Coders choose from codes in categories Z91.12- and Z91.13- as an additional code.

CODING FOR EXTERNAL CAUSES OF MORBIDITY

Diagnostic codes classifying the external cause of death, injury, poisoning, and adverse effects can be found in Chapter 20 (V00–Y99) of the ICD-10-CM. Codes in this chapter define the manner of the death or injury, the mechanism, the place of occurrence of the event, the activity, and the status of the person at the time death or injury occurred:

- Manner refers to whether the cause of death or injury was unintentional/accidental, self-inflicted, or undetermined.
- Mechanism describes how the injury occurred—motor vehicle accident, fall, contact with a sharp object, exposure to fire.
- Place identifies where the injury occurred—personal residence, playground, street, place of employment.
- Activity indicates what the person was doing when the injury occurred—swimming, running, bathing, cooking.
- Status is used to indicate the work or nonwork status of the person at the time death or injury occurred, such as work done for pay (employment), volunteer activity, or leisure activity.

Codes in Chapter 20 are always reported as secondary codes; codes from Chapter 19—Injury, Poisoning, and Certain Other Consequences of External Causes (S00–T98) are reported as first-listed diagnoses. Examples from Chapter 19 include fracture, laceration, abrasion, and so on. Conditions other than injuries may also result from an external cause—for example, a myocardial infarction (heart attack) caused by strenuous activity, such as shoveling snow. In this case, the nature of the condition is the myocardial infarction, reported with codes from categories I21–I22; external cause codes are reported additionally to identify the activity, place, and external cause status.

Although not all third-party payers require reporting of external cause codes, public health departments and other state agencies find them to be a valuable source of information in tracking morbidity and mortality statistics.

> **! Stop and Think**
>
> Billy Helms, a 9-year-old boy, arrives at the clinic with a chief complaint that he fell off of his scooter and hurt his wrist. An x-ray reveals a diagnosis of a fracture of the carpal tunnel bone in the right wrist. How would this be coded? Remember, external causes cannot be first-listed diagnoses.

ALPHABETIC INDEX OF EXTERNAL CAUSES

External causes in the ICD-10-CM have separate alphabetic indexes, which appear immediately after the Table of Drugs and Chemicals. The coder must first identify the external cause code in the Index, after which the Tabular must be reviewed carefully to ensure that the code identified is the correct one. All conventions, instructions, and notes must be taken into consideration.

COMBINATION CODES IN CHAPTER 19

One of the most significant changes in the ICD-10-CM is the addition of combination codes in Chapter 19—Injury, Poisoning, and Certain Other Consequences of External Causes for two code blocks. The code blocks are:

- T36–T50 Poisoning, adverse effects, and underdosing of drugs, medicaments, and biological substances
- T51–T65 Toxic effects of substances chiefly nonmedicinal as to source

These combination codes identify both the substance and the intent, which includes accidental (unintentional), intentional self-harm, assault, undetermined, adverse effect, and underdosing. This means that there are no external cause codes for these conditions in the external cause chapter of the ICD-10-CM.

> **[?] What Did You Learn?**
>
> 1. If a patient comes to the medical office with complaints of a fever of several days' duration and the cause cannot be determined, in what chapter of the ICD-10-CM would the appropriate code be found?
> 2. Coding of late effects generally requires two codes—the condition, or nature, of the late effect and the late effect itself. How are these two codes sequenced?
> 3. Which character of the diagnostic code indicates laterality?
> 4. Provide three examples of adverse events.
> 5. True or false: External causes in ICD-10-CM have their own separate Alphabetic Index.

CODING STEPS FOR THE TABULAR LIST

The condition to be coded must first be located in the Index, following the steps listed earlier in this chapter. The selected term and its corresponding code must then be verified in the Tabular using the following steps:

Step 1. Locate the code in the Tabular List of Diseases and Injuries.

Using the example of the coding steps for the Index for "traumatic fracture of sixth dorsal vertebra," we can locate the code identified in the Index (S22.059) numerically in Chapter 19 (S00–T98) in the Tabular.

Step 2. Read and follow any instructional notes.

Other than "unspecified" as to the type of fracture (wedge compression, stable burst, unstable burst), there are no instructional notes for this diagnosis.

Step 3. Determine whether an additional character must be added.

Note that there is a red bullet symbol preceding code S22.059, which means (according to the legend at the bottom of the page) "use additional character(s)."

Because the code is already six characters, we need a seventh character to code the diagnosis to its greatest specificity. At the beginning of this category (S22), we note the alpha characters and their meanings listed in the shaded box (A, B, D, G, K, S). This tells us that the seventh character must be one of these letters, indicating an initial encounter of a closed or open fracture or the type of healing observed if it is a subsequent encounter—routine, delayed healing, nonunion, or sequela. Going back to the patient record, we see that it is the patient's initial encounter. We have previously discussed that if a fracture is not specifically indicated as "open" in the medical record, it must be assumed that it is closed.

Step 4. Determine laterality (right or left) and any applicable extensions.

Laterality is not applicable in this diagnosis.

Step 5. Assign the correct code to its greatest specificity. S22.059A

 What Did You Learn?

Code the following diagnoses to their greatest specificity beginning in the Index and cross-referencing to the Tabular:

1. Sprain of unspecified ligament of right ankle, initial visit
2. Flexion deformity of the left wrist
3. Arterial fibromuscular dysplasia
4. Measles complicated by pneumonia
5. Sprain of right shoulder joint, subsequent encounter

HIPAA AND CODING

Code sets for medical data are required for data elements in the administrative and financial healthcare transaction standards adopted under HIPAA for diagnoses, procedures, and drugs. Under HIPAA, a code set is any set of codes used for encoding data elements, such as tables of terms, medical concepts, medical diagnosis codes, or medical procedure codes. Medical data code sets used in the healthcare industry include coding systems for the following:

- Diseases, impairments, other health-related problems and their manifestations
- Causes of injury, disease, impairment, or other health-related problems
- Actions taken to prevent, diagnose, treat, or manage diseases, injuries, and impairments
- Any substances, equipment, supplies, or other items used to perform these actions

 HIPAA Tip

Although the Health Insurance Portability and Accountability Act (HIPAA) requirements apply only to electronic claims, to maintain consistency in claims processing, the Centers for Medicare and Medicaid Services (CMS) has mandated that ICD-10-CM requirements be applied to paper claims and electronic claims.

CODE SETS ADOPTED AS HIPAA STANDARDS

Transactions can be defined as electronic exchanges involving the transfer of information between two parties for specific purposes. For example, a healthcare provider sends a claim to a health plan to request payment for medical services. HIPAA named certain types of organizations as covered entities—health plans, healthcare clearinghouses, and certain healthcare providers. In the HIPAA regulations, the HHS adopted certain standard transactions for electronic data interchange (EDI) of healthcare data. These transactions include claims and encounter information, payment and remittance advice, claims status, eligibility, enrollment and disenrollment, referrals and authorizations, coordination of benefits, and premium payment. Under HIPAA, if a covered entity conducts one of the adopted transactions electronically, it must use the adopted standard. Covered entities must adhere to the content and format requirements for each transaction. Under HIPAA, the HHS also adopted specific code sets for diagnoses and procedures to be used in all transactions:

- HCPCS (Ancillary Services/Procedures)
- CPT-4 (Physicians' Procedures)
- CDT (Dental Terminology)
- ICD-10 (as of October 1, 2015)
- NDC (National Drug Codes)

These are the adopted code sets for procedures, diagnoses, and drugs. In addition, the HHS adopted standards for unique identifiers for employers and providers, which must also be used in all transactions.

 HIPAA Tip

Health Insurance Portability and Accountability Act (HIPAA)–compliant claims cannot contain ICD-10-PCS inpatient procedure codes on claims submitted by physicians' offices.

? **What Did You Learn?**

1. Explain what a "code set" is under HIPAA.
2. List the standard code sets adopted by HIPAA.

GENERAL EQUIVALENCE MAPPINGS

Although it may not be vital to students new to coding in general, it may be prudent to introduce the **General Equivalence Mappings (GEMs)** so that the coding student becomes familiar with this term. GEMs were generated through a coordinated effort involving the NCHS, CMS, AHIMA, AHA, and 3M Health Information Systems. The GEM files are designed to give all entities of the healthcare industry that use coded data a tool to migrate and test their coding systems that convert ICD-9 codes to equivalents in the ICD-10 system and vice versa.

Two sets of GEMs have been developed to provide an equivalency crosswalk (link) for mapping: forward mapping, from an ICD-9 code to an ICD-10 code, and backward mapping, from an ICD-10 code to an ICD-9 code.

The mapping entry for the ICD-9-CM diagnosis code for hematuria, 599.7, is highlighted in Table 14.5 as it would appear in the GEM file along with "flags":

- Approximate—There is a direct match between the two systems.
- No map—There is no similar code between the two systems.
- Combination—The source system must be linked to more than one code in the target system to be valid.

> **[?] What Did You Learn?**
>
> 1. What were the GEMs designed to do?
> 2. Name the three "flags" used in GEM and explain what each means.

LOOKING AHEAD TO ICD-11

On May 25, 2019, the member states of the World Health Assembly voted to adopt the eleventh revision of the *International Statistical Classification of Diseases and Related Health Problems* (ICD-11). It will go into effect on January 1, 2022. As of the writing of this textbook, there is no indication of when the United States will adopt ICD-11.

As stated earlier in this chapter, ICD is revised about every 10 years, and this was the case for ICD-11. Below are some of the changes for ICD-11:

- 55,000 unique codes for injuries, diseases, and causes of death, compared to 14,400 in ICD-10
- Stroke will be listed a neurological disorder and not as a disorder of the circulatory system.
- New classification for HIV as a chronic condition
- Attention-deficit/hyperactivity disorder's updated description states that the symptoms no longer must occur within a fixed age range to lead to diagnosis

- Better reporting of antimicrobial resistance
- Special attention has been dedicated to mental health:
  - Posttraumatic stress disorder (PTSD) criteria have been reduced.
  - Addictive conditions, such as gaming and hoarding, have been added.
  - Compulsive sexual behavior has been included as an impulse control disorder.
- More detailed definition of burnout classifying it as an occupational phenomenon
- Improved ability to code for the quality and safety of healthcare and highlights the role of external factors that directly and indirectly contribute to people's health, such as insufficient social welfare support
- New chapters:
  - Disorders of the immune system where allergies will be coded
  - Diseases of blood and blood-forming organs
  - Conditions related to sexual health, where gender incongruence exists, are coded to reflect an understanding that gender incongruence is not a mental health condition, helping to reduce the stigma attached to gender-defined states
  - Sleep-wake disorders
  - Traditional medicine used across many countries, including China, Japan, and the Republic of Korea, can be coded
  - Extension codes
- Codes will look different; there is a minimum of 4 characters, and a letter always will appear in the second position to distinguish a code from ICD-10

As health insurance specialists, it is important that we stay on top of all developments in our field. ICD-11 is one development we should all watch for to see when it will be adopted in the United States. The change in the format of the code itself may require changes to the 5010 electronic claim format as well as to the CMS-1500 paper claim form. Students should periodically check for updated information on ICD-11.

Table **14.5**	Sample from a General Equivalence Mapping File							
ICD-9 CODE	**DESCRIPTION**	**ICD-10 CODE**	**DESCRIPTION**	**APPROXIMATE**	**NO MAP**	**COMBINATION**	**SCENARIO**	**CHOICE LIST**
599.7	Hematuria	R31.0	Gross hematuria	1	0	0	0	0
599.7	Hematuria	R31.1	Benign essential microscopic hematuria	1	0	0	0	0
599.7	Hematuria	R31.2	Other microscopic hematuria	1	0	0	0	0
599.7	Hematuria	R31.9	Hematuria, unspecified	1	0	0	0	0

The complete General Equivalence Mappings (GEMs) file can be found on the Centers for Medicare and Medicaid Services (CMS) website.
ICD-9, International Classification of Diseases, 9th revision; *ICD-10, International Classification of Diseases*, 10th revision.

This information can be accessed on the WHO website at http://www.who.int.

SUMMARY CHECKPOINTS

- Coding is a recognized process of transforming descriptions of a patient's disease process, disorder, or injury into universal numeric or alphanumeric formats that are understood by all healthcare entities. Basically, a diagnosis is the reason that brought the patient to the healthcare facility, such as a rash, sore throat, or chest pains. A final diagnosis after examination can be a much more precise statement.
- The history of the ICD system dates back to the late 19th century in Europe. The first ICD system (ICD-1) was put into use in 1900. Since then, the ICD has been modified approximately once every 10 years, with the exception of the 20-year period between the last two revisions—ICD-9 and ICD-10.
- The first thing the coder must do in the coding process is locate the diagnosis in the health record. The diagnosis typically can be found in the clinical notes or on the encounter form. After the diagnosis has been determined, the main term within the diagnosis should be identified, located in the Index, and cross-referenced to the Tabular to code the diagnosis to its greatest specificity.
- The ICD-10 coding system consists of two parts:
  - ICD-10-CM is used for diagnosis in all healthcare settings.
  - ICD-10-PCS is used for procedure coding in inpatient hospital settings only.
- The format and organization of the ICD-10-CM manual typically includes the following:
  - Table of Contents
  - A Guide to Using the (2019) ICD-10-CM
  - Symbols and Conventions
  - Netter's Anatomy Plates
  - Part I—Introduction (containing ICD-10-CM Official Guidelines for Coding and Reporting)
  - Part II—Alphabetic Index
  - Index to Diseases and Injuries
  - Table of Neoplasms
  - Table of Drugs and Chemicals
  - External Cause of Injuries Index
  - Part III—Tabular List of Diseases and Injuries (21 chapters)
- The essential steps in accurate diagnostic coding for the Index are as follows:
  - **Step 1:** Locate the diagnosis in the health record (or on the encounter form).
  - **Step 2:** Determine the main term of the stated diagnosis.
  - **Step 3:** Find the main term in the Alphabetic Index of the current version of ICD-10-CM.
  - **Step 4:** Read and apply any notes or instructions contained in the Index. *Remember:* Never code directly from the Index.
  - **Step 5:** Scan the main term entry (or applicable essential modifiers) for an instructional or cross-referencing notes.
  - **Step 6:** Select the most appropriate code, and verify the selected code by cross-referencing the Tabular.
- The Tabular in the ICD-10-CM contains categories, subcategories, and codes comprising three to seven characters. The first character is always a letter. Codes with three characters are included in ICD-10-CM as the heading of a category of codes that may be subdivided further by the use of fourth and fifth digits, which provide greater detail. A code is invalid if it has not been coded to the full number of characters required for that code, including the seventh character, if applicable. Each level of subdivision after a category is a subcategory, which can have four or five characters. The final level of subdivision is a code, which can have up to seven characters. All codes in the Tabular of the official version of the ICD-10-CM are in boldface type.
- ICD-10-CM conventions, general guidelines, and chapter-specific guidelines are applicable to all healthcare settings unless otherwise indicated. The guidelines are organized into sections. Section I includes the structure and conventions of the classification and general guidelines that apply to the entire classification, in addition to chapter-specific guidelines that correspond to the chapters as they are arranged in the classification. Section II includes guidelines for selection of the principal diagnosis for non-outpatient settings. Section III includes guidelines for reporting additional diagnoses in non-outpatient settings. Section IV is for outpatient coding and reporting.
- ICD-10-CM coding offers other features that provide increased detail and greater specificity, such as:
  - Combination codes
  - Late effects (sequelae)
  - Impending/threatened conditions
  - Laterality
  - Table of Drugs and Chemicals
  - Alphabetic Index of External Causes
- The term selected from the Index and its corresponding code must be verified in the Tabular using the following steps:
  - **Step 1:** Locate the code in the Tabular List of Diseases and Injuries.
  - **Step 2:** Read and follow any instructional notes.
  - **Step 3:** Determine whether an additional character must be added.
  - **Step 4:** Determine laterality (right or left) and any applicable extensions.

- **Step 5:** Assign the correct code to its greatest specificity.
- Code sets for medical data are required data elements in the administrative and financial healthcare transaction standards adopted under HIPAA for diagnoses, procedures, and drugs.
- GEMs are a tool that coders can use to convert most ICD-9 codes to equivalent ICD-10 codes and vice versa.
- Students should be aware of and periodically check for updated information on ICD-10.

🔍 Closing Scenario

Park Chalmers has found many rewards working as a health insurance specialist, especially as a diagnostic coder. He looks at this whole process as solving a puzzle. He needs to consider all of the options for finding the correct diagnostic statement and then work through the process to assign the correct code. Park is grateful that the providers he works for are willing to listen to his rationale for a particular code even when it differs from what the provider initially indicated. He very much feels like part of the healthcare team.

Park has been following the development of ICD-11 and is excited about the changes that have been made. He also realizes that there is no timeline in place for implementing ICD-11 in the United States. He plans to follow the news of ICD-11 closely so that he can help prepare Walden-Martin when the time comes.

CHAPTER REVIEW QUESTIONS

1. Which of the following letters in the ICD-10-CM is reserved by the World Health Organization to assign new diseases with unknown etiology?
   a. U
   b. X
   c. Y
   d. Z
2. The abbreviation that is the equivalent of "unspecified" is:
   a. NEC.
   b. POS.
   c. NOS.
   d. DOS.
3. At times, the medical assistant must code a(n) _____ if the physician is not yet sure of the diagnosis.
   a. Manifestation
   b. Symptom
   c. Prognosis
   d. Etiology
4. When coding neoplasms, _____ is defined as the absence of invasion of surrounding tissues.
   a. Benign
   b. Carcinoma *in situ*
   c. Malignant primary
   d. Unspecified nature

5. The study of the causes or origin of diseases describes which of the following terms?
   a. Epidemiological
   b. Etiology
   c. Mortality
   d. Sequela
6. The International Classification of Diseases was established by:
   a. Department of Health and Human Services.
   b. World Health Organization.
   c. American Medical Association.
   d. None of the above.
7. ICD-10-CM uses up to ___ characters to identify a disease or injury.
   a. 9
   b. 7
   c. 5
   d. 3
8. When performing diagnostic coding, you should start looking in the:
   a. Table of contents.
   b. Alphabetic Index.
   c. Tabular List.
   d. None of the above.
9. In the Alphabetic Index, main terms appear:
   a. Underlined.
   b. In italics.
   c. Indented.
   d. In boldface.
10. _____ are indented under the main term and must be included in the diagnostic statement.
    a. Main terms
    b. Nonessential modifiers
    c. Essential modifiers
    d. Symptoms

WEBSITES TO EXPLORE

- For live links to the following websites, please visit the Evolve website at http://evolve.elsevier.com/Beik/today/.
- For more information about the HIPAA standardized code sets, visit http://cms.hhs.gov and http://aspe.hhs.gov/admnsimp/faqcode.htm#codesetsadopted.
- An in-depth study of the differences and similarities between ICD-9 and ICD-10 is provided at https://www.ncbi.nlm.nih.gov/pmc/articles/PMC3692324/.
- The CMS website (http://www.cms.gov/) has extensive information and guidelines for the ICD-10 system.
- The American Association of Medical Assistants (AAMA) website (http://www.aama-ntl.org) provides information about coding in the medical office and details about various educational workshops pertaining to this subject. For information on

becoming a certified professional coder, log on to the American Academy of Professional Coders website at http://www.aapc.com.

- The AHIMA website (http://www.ahima.org) also provides information on becoming a certified professional coder.
- To learn the history and development of the ICD, see http://www.who.int/classifications/icd/en/HistoryOfICD.pdf.
- Extensive information on the ICD-10 system can be found on the CMS website at http://www.cms.gov/ICD10/11b1_2011_ICD10CM_and_GEMs.asp#TopOfPage.
- For additional information on the ICD-10, follow the WHO weblink to http://www.who.int/classifications/icd/en/.
- To read an overview of the ICD system, see https://www.cms.gov/Medicare/Medicare-Contracting/ContractorLearningResources/downloads/ICD-10_Overview_Presentation.pdf.
- The ICD-10 Official Guidelines for Coding and Reporting can be found at https://www.cms.gov/Medicare/Coding/ICD10/Downloads/2019-ICD10-Coding-Guidelines-.pdf.
- ICD-10 and HIPAA compliance: https://www.microsoft.com/en-us/industry/health/microsoft-cloud-for-healthcare.
- Find an informative PowerPoint presentation on ICD-10-CM and ICD-CM-PCS at https://www.cms.gov/Outreach-and-Education/Medicare-Learning-Network-MLN/MLNProducts/Downloads/ICD9-10CM-ICD10PCS-CPT-HCPCS-Code-Sets-Educational-Tool-ICN900943.pdf.
- For a free ICD-10 download, visit http://www.cms.gov/icd10.
- For information regarding ICD-11, visit http://www.who.int.

Author's Note: Due to the dynamic nature of the Internet, web addresses and/or links provided in this chapter may have changed since publication and may no longer be valid. In such cases, students should select comparable search words to access related sites.

15 Procedural, Evaluation and Management, and HCPCS Coding

Chapter Outline

Chapter Objectives

After completion of this chapter, the student should be able to:

1. Discuss the purpose and development of the CPT-4 manual.
2. Name and describe the three levels of procedural coding.
3. Explain the format of Current Procedural Terminology (CPT).
4. Interpret the conventions and punctuation used in CPT.
5. List the basic steps in CPT coding.
6. Outline the important rules and regulations for Evaluation and Management (E/M) coding.
7. Discuss the subheadings of the main E/M section.
8. Explain the use of E/M modifiers.
9. List the general principles of medical record documentation.
10. Provide an overview of Healthcare Common Procedure Coding System (HCPCS).
11. Explain the rationale of the National Correct Coding Initiative (NCCI).
12. Discuss the relationship of the Health Insurance Portability and Accountability Act (HIPAA) and HCPCS.

Chapter Terms

adjudication	Healthcare Common Procedure	observation
category	Coding System (HCPCS)	outpatient
Category II codes	HCPCS codes	*Physicians' Current Procedural*
Category III codes	Health Care Financing	*Terminology,* 4th edition (CPT-4)
chief complaint (CC)	Administration (HCFA)	referral
code set	indented codes	section
concurrent care	inpatient	see
consultation	key components	special report
counseling	Level I codes	stand-alone code
critical care	Level II codes	subheading
crosswalk	main terms	subjective information
emergency care	modifiers	subsection
established patient	modifying terms	telehealth consultation
Evaluation and Management	morbidity	transfer of care
(E/M) codes	mortality	unit/floor time
face-to-face time	new patient	

Opening Scenario

As Walden-Martin Family Medical Clinic continued to grow and staff was added to the billing office, Park Chalmers was asked to mentor a new employee who was going to be working in the coding department. Melanie Sanders had just graduated from a program similar to the one that Park went through and was excited and nervous about starting her career as a health insurance specialist.

Park explained to Melanie that accurate coding is the backbone to correct billing. *International Classification of Diseases,* 10th revision, Clinical Modification (ICD-10-CM) codes describe why services were provided, and Current Procedural Terminology (CPT)/Healthcare Common Procedure Coding System (HCPCS) codes describe what services were provided. Walden-Martin's goal is to receive the "maximum" amount of reimbursement that is fair and accurate. Park reminded Melanie that "The secret to coding is in its structure. There is a very systematic method for finding the appropriate code," he explained. "The most important thing is to follow the steps outlined in the chapter and never code from the Alphabetic Index alone."

Park's enthusiasm has motivated Melanie to be the best possible health insurance specialist!

OVERVIEW OF CURRENT PROCEDURAL TERMINOLOGY CODING

The *Physicians' Current Procedural Terminology,* **4th edition (CPT-4)** is a manual containing a list of descriptive terms and identifying codes used in reporting medical services and procedures performed and supplies used by physicians and other professional healthcare providers in the care and treatment of patients. Current Procedural Terminology (CPT) was first developed and published by the American Medical Association (AMA) in 1966. The CPT system is governed by the CPT editorial panel, a group of individuals (made up mostly of physicians representing various specialties of medicine) who have the authority to make final decisions regarding changes to and updates of the content of CPT.

Note: CPT-4 is available in both a standard edition and a professional edition. This chapter uses the CPT (2019) professional edition; however, it is important that students always use the most recent edition available.

Because medicine is constantly changing, the AMA publishes an updated version of the CPT manual every year. It is important that the health insurance professional use the most recent edition of CPT when coding professional procedures and services for claims submissions to avoid rejected claims or incorrect claim **adjudication** (the process of deciding how an insurance claim is paid).

In 1983 CPT was adopted as part of the **Health Care Financing Administration (HCFA) Healthcare Common Procedure Coding System (HCPCS)**. With this adoption, HCFA (now called the *Centers for Medicare and Medicaid Services [CMS]*) mandated the use of HCPCS (pronounced "hick picks") to report services for Part B of the Medicare program. In October 1986 HCFA also required state Medicaid agencies to use HCPCS in the Medicaid Management Information System. In July 1987, as part of the Omnibus Budget Reconciliation Act, HCFA required the use of CPT for reporting outpatient hospital surgical procedures. Today, in addition to its use in federal programs (Medicare and Medicaid), CPT is used extensively throughout the United States as the preferred system of coding and describing healthcare services.

In 2000 the CPT **code set** was designed by the US Department of Health and Human Services (HHS) as the national coding standard for physicians and other healthcare providers to report professional services and procedures under the Health Insurance Portability and Accountability Act (HIPAA). The CPT code set must be used for all financial and administrative healthcare transactions that are transmitted electronically.

Today, not only Medicare and Medicaid, but also most managed care and other health insurance companies, base their reimbursements on the values established by the CMS. As with International Classification of Diseases (ICD) diagnostic coding, it is important that the health insurance professional have a thorough understanding of CPT coding to facilitate accurate claims completion for maximal reimbursement. CPT codes are used instead of a narrative description in claim submission to describe what services or procedures were provided or what supplies were used during the patient encounter.

> ### ◎ HIPAA Tip
>
> Under the Health Insurance Portability and Accountability Act (HIPAA), a code set is any set of codes used for encoding data elements, such as tables of terms, medical concepts, medical diagnosis codes, or medical procedure codes. Code sets for medical data are required for data elements in the administrative and financial healthcare transaction standards adopted under HIPAA for diagnoses, procedures, and drugs.

PURPOSE OF CURRENT PROCEDURAL TERMINOLOGY

The purpose of CPT coding is to provide a uniform language that accurately describes medical, surgical, and diagnostic services, serving as an effective means for reliable nationwide communication among physicians, health insurance carriers, and patients. CPT codes are also used by most third-party payers and government agencies as a record of the activities of an individual healthcare provider.

DEVELOPMENT OF CURRENT PROCEDURAL TERMINOLOGY

As mentioned previously, the AMA developed and published the first CPT in 1966. This first edition contained primarily surgical procedures with limited sections on medicine, radiology, and laboratory procedures.

The second edition was published in 1970 and presented an expanded system of terms and codes to designate diagnostic and therapeutic procedures in surgery, medicine, and other specialties. At that time, the five-digit coding system was introduced, replacing the former four-digit classification. Another significant change was a listing of procedures relating to internal medicine.

The third and fourth editions of CPT were introduced later in the 1970s. The fourth edition, published in 1977, presented significant updates in medical technology. Also, a system of periodic updating was introduced to keep pace with the rapidly changing medical environment.

> ### ? What Did You Learn?
>
> 1. What is CPT?
> 2. What is the purpose of CPT?
> 3. Why were CPT codes developed?
> 4. Who publishes CPT-4?
> 5. How often is CPT updated?

TWO LEVELS OF PROCEDURAL CODING

HCPCS codes are descriptive terms with letters, numbers, or both used to report medical services and procedures for reimbursement. As discussed, the codes provide a uniform language to describe medical, surgical, and diagnostic services. **HCPCS codes** are used to report procedures and services to government and private health insurance programs, and reimbursement is based on the codes reported. A code, in place of a narrative description, can summarize the services or supplies provided when billing a third-party payer. HCPCS codes are grouped into two levels, as follows:

- **Level I codes** contain the AMA Physicians' CPT codes. These are five-digit codes, accompanied by descriptive terms, used for reporting services performed by healthcare professionals. Level I codes are developed and updated annually by the AMA.
- **Level II codes** consist of the HCPCS National Medicare Codes used to report medical services, supplies, drugs, and durable medical equipment not contained in the Level I codes. These codes begin with a single letter, followed by four digits. Level II codes supersede Level I codes for similar encounters, Evaluation and Management (E/M) services, or other procedures and represent the portion of procedures involving supplies and materials. National Level II Medicare Codes are not restricted to Medicare, as their title may suggest. An increasing number of private insurance carriers are encouraging—and some are even requiring—the use of HCPCS National Codes. HCPCS Level II codes are in a separate manual from Level I codes (CPT). Level II codes are developed and updated annually by the CMS and their contractors.

> ### ◎ HIPAA Tip
>
> The combination of Healthcare Common Procedure Coding System (HCPCS) and Physicians' Current Procedural Terminology, 4th edition (CPT-4) (including codes and modifiers) is the Health Insurance Portability and Accountability Act (HIPAA)–adopted standard for reporting physician services and other healthcare services on standard transactions.

CURRENT PROCEDURAL TERMINOLOGY MANUAL FORMAT

INTRODUCTION AND MAIN SECTIONS

Similar to the *International Classification of Diseases,* 10th revision, Clinical Modification (ICD-10-CM) manual, CPT-4 is made up of several sections beginning with a forward and acknowledgements. Next is a table of contents beginning with the Introduction, identified by lowercase Roman numerals. The Introduction contains subheadings titled:

- Section Numbers and Their Sequences
- Instructions for Use of the CPT Codebook

After the Introduction is the Illustrated Anatomical and Procedural Review and a List of (Anatomical) Illustrations followed by the E/M Services Guidelines. The main body of the manual follows the introduction and is organized in six sections. Within each section are subsections with anatomic, procedural, condition, or descriptor subheadings. Table 15.1 lists the CPT sections and their number range sequence. The listed procedures and services and their identifying five-digit codes are presented in numerical order, except for the E/M section. Because E/M codes are used by most physicians for reporting key categories of their services, this section is presented first.

Five-digit CPT codes may be defined further by two-digit modifiers to help explain an unusual circumstance associated with a service or procedure. Appropriate coding modifiers are crucial to getting claims paid promptly and for the correct amount. Missing or incorrect modifiers are among the most common reasons that claims are denied by payers. It is easy to get confused on how to use modifiers correctly, especially because, similar to CPT codes, they are constantly changing. The most important thing to remember when using modifiers is that the health record must

Modifier-22 is used to indicate that there was "something unusual about the procedure, it took longer than usual, or it was harder than usual." The only way you'll get consideration for additional payment is if you use the modifier and have good documentation.

Modifier-59 is used to indicate that a procedure or service was distinct or independent from other services performed on the same day (e.g., not normally reported together) but are appropriate under the circumstances, as documented.

Fig. 15.1 Examples of correct modifier use.

contain adequate documentation to support the modifier (Fig. 15.1). Modifiers are discussed in more detail later in this chapter.

When coding procedures, it is always important to have the most recent edition of the CPT book available to look up current modifier codes. (Modifiers are listed in Appendix A at the back of the CPT manual. Modifiers Approved for Hospital Outpatient Use Level I [CPT] and Level II [HCPCS/National] are listed on the inside cover of the *2019 CPT Professional Edition*.) Also, it is advisable for healthcare providers and their billing staff to read Medicare and other coding newsletters and attend coding workshops periodically to keep up to date.

Each main section of the CPT is preceded by guidelines specific to that section. These guidelines define terms that are necessary to interpret correctly and report the procedures and services contained in that section. The health insurance professional should read and study these guidelines before attempting to assign a code.

CATEGORY II CODES

Category II codes follow the six main sections of the CPT manual. Category II codes are supplemental tracking codes intended to be used for performance measurement. Category II codes provide a method for reporting performance measures. They are intended to facilitate the collection of information about the quality of care delivered by coding numerous services or test results that support performance measures that have been agreed on as contributing to good patient care. Category II codes are alphanumeric, consisting of four digits followed by the letter "F" (e.g., 0503F—Postpartum care visit [Prenatal]). The use of Category II codes is optional, and they should not be used as a substitute for Category I codes.

CATEGORY III CODES

Immediately following the Category II codes are the **Category III codes** (Fig. 15.2). Category III codes were established by the AMA as a set of temporary CPT codes for emerging technologies, services, and procedures for which data collection is necessary to substantiate widespread use or for the approval process of the US Food and Drug Administration (FDA). They are

| Table 15.1 | Current Procedural Terminology Section Numbers and Their Sequence |

SECTION TITLE	NUMBERING SEQUENCE
Evaluation and Management	99201–99499
Anesthesiology	00100–01999, 99100–99140
Surgery	10021–69990
Radiology—Diagnostic Radiology (Diagnostic Imaging)	70010–79999
Pathology and Laboratory	80047–89398
Medicine (except Anesthesiology)	90281–99199, 99500–99607

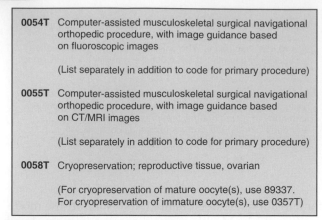

0054T	Computer-assisted musculoskeletal surgical navigational orthopedic procedure, with image guidance based on fluoroscopic images
	(List separately in addition to code for primary procedure)
0055T	Computer-assisted musculoskeletal surgical navigational orthopedic procedure, with image guidance based on CT/MRI images
	(List separately in addition to code for primary procedure)
0058T	Cryopreservation; reproductive tissue, ovarian
	(For cryopreservation of mature oocyte(s), use 89337. For cryopreservation of immature oocyte(s), use 0357T)

Fig. 15.2 Example of Category III codes. *CT,* Computed tomography; *MRI,* magnetic resonance imaging. (Used with permission of the American Medical Association. [AMA, CPT 2019 Professional Edition, 2018.]. © Copyright American Medical Association 2018. All rights reserved.)

composed of four numeric characters followed by the letter "T." To be eligible for a Category III code, the procedure or service must be involved in ongoing or planned research. If a Category III code has not been proposed and accepted into the main body of CPT (i.e., Category I codes) within 5 years, it is archived (note the "sunset" clause following the description of the code), unless a demonstrated need for it develops.

In the Introduction of the CPT manual, users are instructed not to select a code that merely approximates the service provided. The code should identify the service performed accurately. If no such code exists, report the service using the appropriate unlisted procedure or service code. Category III codes are updated semiannually in January and July, and new codes are posted on the AMA website.

CODING NOTE: Any service or procedure must be documented adequately in the patient's medical record.

APPENDICES A THROUGH P

As with ICD-10-CM, CPT-4 contains several appendices, which follow the Category III codes. These appendices and their contents are as follows:
Appendix A—Modifiers
Appendix B—Summary of Additions, Deletions, and Revisions
Appendix C—Clinical Examples
Appendix D—Summary of CPT Add-On Codes
Appendix E—Summary of CPT Codes Exempt From Modifier -51
Appendix F—Summary of CPT Codes Exempt From Modifier -63
Appendix G—Summary of CPT Codes That Include Moderate (Conscious) Sedation
Appendix H—Alphabetical Clinical Topics Listing (AKA—Alphabetical Listing)
Appendix I—Genetic Testing Code Modifiers
Appendix J—Electrodiagnostic Medicine Listing of Sensory, Motor, and Mixed Nerves

Appendix K—Product Pending FDA Approval
Appendix L—Vascular Families
Appendix M—Renumbered CPT Codes-Citations Crosswalk
Appendix N—Summary of Resequenced CPT Codes
Appendix O—Multianalyte Assays With Algorithmic Analyses
Appendix P – CPT Codes That May Be Used for Synchronous Telemedicine Services

CURRENT PROCEDURAL TERMINOLOGY INDEX

Following the appendices is the index, which is an alphabetical listing of main terms. It is important that the index is not used to code; rather, once the correct main term is located in the index, the coder must refer to the main text to ensure that the code selected precisely identifies the service or procedure performed.

Main Terms

In the CPT manual, the index is presented last. As with ICD-10-CM, the CPT index is organized by **main terms** listed alphabetically (Fig. 15.3). Each main term can stand alone, or it can be followed by up to three modifying terms. There are four primary classes of main term entries, as follows:

1. Procedure or service (e.g., colonoscopy, anastomosis, debridement)
2. Organ or other anatomic site (e.g., fibula, kidney, nails)
3. Condition (e.g., infection, pregnancy, tetralogy of Fallot)
4. Synonyms, eponyms, and abbreviations (e.g., ECT, Pean operation, Clagett procedure)

CODING NOTE: Anesthesia-section codes are indexed under the Anesthesia main entry. Only specific codes within the Surgery, Medicine, Category II, and Category III sections that reference the service of anesthesia are indexed under anatomic sites.

Colotomy	
Biopsy	44025
Exploration	44025
Foreign Body Removal	44025
Colpectomy	
See Vaginectomy	
Colpo-Urethrocystopexy	
with Hysterectomy	58152, 58267, 58293
Marshall-Marchetti-Krantz Type	58152
	58267, 58293
Pereyra Type	58267, 58293
Colpoceliocentesis	
See Colpocentesis	

Fig. 15.3 Example of main terms. (Used with permission of the American Medical Association. [AMA, CPT 2019 Professional Edition, 2018.]. © Copyright American Medical Association 2018. All rights reserved.)

! Stop and Think

Surgeon Milford Tramen saw Patrick Lovell, a 34-year-old Illinois farmer, in his office on February 19 for the repair of an injury to the patient's mouth. The presenting problem in the medical record documents that the patient was "kicked in the mouth while vaccinating hogs." The surgeon stitched up the 3.4-cm cut, and the nurse administered a tetanus shot. What would be the main term for the procedure performed by the surgeon?

Modifying Terms

As mentioned previously, each main term can stand alone or be followed by up to three **modifying terms** (Fig. 15.4). Modifying terms are indented under the main term; in some cases, unindented anatomic sites are listed alphabetically first, and modifying terms are indented under them. For example, in Fig. 15.4, "Hip" is listed under the main term "Denervation" (in bold type), after which three indented modifying terms are listed. All modifying terms should be examined closely because these subterms often influence the selection of the appropriate procedural code.

Code Ranges

CPT codes can be displayed in one of the following three ways:
1. Single code (Proetz therapy, nose 30210)
2. Multiple codes (Prolactin 80418, 84146)
3. Range of codes (Prostatotomy 55720–55725)

SYMBOLS USED IN CURRENT PROCEDURAL TERMINOLOGY

The CPT manual uses several symbols that help guide the health insurance professional in locating the correct code. Accurate procedural coding cannot be accomplished without understanding the meaning of each of these symbols (Table 15.2). These symbols are listed on the inside front cover of the CPT manual.

MODIFIERS

Modifiers are important to ensuring appropriate and timely payment. A health insurance professional who understands when and how to use modifiers reduces the problems caused by denials and expedites processing of claims.

A modifier provides the means by which the reporting healthcare provider can indicate that a service or procedure performed has been altered by some specific circumstance, but its definition or code has not been changed. The judicious application of modifiers tells the third-party payer that this case is unique. By using appropriate modifiers, the office may be paid for services that are ordinarily denied. In addition, modifiers can describe a situation that, without the modifier, could be considered inappropriate coding.

Modifiers are not universal; they cannot be used with all CPT codes. Some modifiers may be used only with E/M codes (e.g., modifier -24 or modifier -25), and others are used only with procedure codes (e.g., modifier -58 or modifier -79). Check the guidelines at

---

Denervation
Hip
    Femoral......................27035
    Oburator.....................27035
    Sciatic.......................27035

Denervation, Sympathetic
Chemodenervation...........64650, 64653
Neurolytic Agent.............64680, 64681
Transcatheter Percutaneous...0338T, 0339T

Dens Axis
See Odontoid Process

Denver Shunt
Patency Test......................78291

Deoxycorticosterone
See Desoxycorticosterone

Deoxycortisol............. 80436, 82634

Deoxyribonuclease
Antibody........................86215

Deoxyribonuclease I
See DNAse

Deoxyribonucleic Acid (DNA)
Antibody..................86225, 86226

Depilation
See Removal, Hair

Fig. 15.4 Example of main term with modifying terms. (Used with permission of the American Medical Association. [AMA, CPT 2019 Professional Edition, 2018.]. © Copyright American Medical Association 2018. All rights reserved.)

Table 15.2	Symbols Used in Current Procedural Terminology Manual
SYMBOL	**EXPLANATION**
Bullet (•)	A bullet (•) before a code means that the code is new to the CPT manual for that particular edition.
Triangle (▲)	A triangle (▲) means that the description for the code has been changed or modified since the previous revision of the CPT manual.
Horizontal triangles (►◄)	Horizontal triangles (►◄) placed at the beginning and end of a descriptive entry indicate that it contains new or revised wording.
Plus sign (+)	Add-on codes are annotated by a plus sign (+).
⊘	This symbol is used to identify codes that are exempt from the use of modifier -51.
⚡	The lightning bolt indicates codes for products pending FDA approval.
★	This symbol is used to identify codes that may be used to report telemedicine services
#	The pound sign (#) indicates an out-of-numerical sequence code.

CPT, Current Procedural Terminology; *FDA*, US Food and Drug Administration.

the beginning of each section for a listing or description of the modifiers that may be used with the codes in that section. Appendix A of the CPT manual contains a list of modifiers and their use.

HIPAA Tip

The Health Insurance Portability and Accountability Act (HIPAA) does not mandate the use of modifiers. According to the adopted HIPAA implementation guide, use of modifiers is not required. Their use is "situational," meaning that the use of a modifier is required only when a modifier clarifies or improves the reporting accuracy of the associated procedure code.

UNLISTED PROCEDURE OR SERVICE

Coders must understand the appropriate use of unlisted CPT codes. Unlisted codes are used for services that may be performed by physicians or other healthcare professionals that are not represented by a specific Category I (CPT) code. At the end of each subsection or subheading in question, a code is provided under the heading "other procedures," which typically ends in "-99." In the surgery section, note the "other procedures" code 39499 at the end of the "mediastinum" subsection. This code would be used for any unlisted procedures of the mediastinum.

CODING NOTE: Unlisted procedure codes should be assigned only if no other, more specific CPT code is available. If there is a Category III code that appropriately describes the procedure, it should be used instead of an unlisted code. The use of the unlisted code does not offer the opportunity for collection of specific data.

SPECIAL REPORTS

When a rarely used, unusual, variable, or new service or procedure is performed, many third-party payers require a **special report** to accompany the claim to help determine the appropriateness and medical necessity of the service or procedure. Items that should be addressed in the report, if applicable, include:

- A definition or description of the service or procedure
- The time, effort, and equipment needed
- Symptoms and final diagnosis
- Pertinent physical findings and size
- Diagnostic and therapeutic services
- Concurrent problems
- Follow-up care

? What Did You Learn?

1. List the six main sections of CPT.
2. What is the purpose of the guidelines that appear at the beginning of each main section of CPT?
3. What are Category III codes?
4. Name the first five appendices in the CPT manual and what is contained in each.
5. What are the four primary classes of main term entries?
6. What is the function of a modifier?

CONVENTIONS AND PUNCTUATION USED IN CURRENT PROCEDURAL TERMINOLOGY

There are two types of CPT codes: (1) stand-alone and (2) indented. The terminology of a stand-alone code is complete in and of itself. It contains the full description of the procedure without additional explanation. However, some procedures do not contain the entire written description. These are known as *indented codes*. **Indented codes** refer to the common portion of the procedure listed in the preceding entry, and correct code selection requires careful attention to the punctuation in the description.

IMPORTANCE OF THE SEMICOLON

In the CPT, the semicolon is used to separate main and subordinate clauses in the code descriptions. This method was adopted to save space in the manual where a series of related codes are found. CPT code "38100 splenectomy; total (separate procedure)" is a stand-alone code. The code immediately following it, 38101, is indented and reads "partial (separate procedure)." The semicolon after splenectomy in code 38100 becomes part of the indented code 38101. The full description of code 38101 in effect would read "splenectomy; partial (separate procedure)." See Fig. 15.5 for an example of a **stand-alone code** followed by an indented code used in the previously mentioned example.

SECTION, SUBSECTION, SUBHEADING, AND CATEGORY

Codes in the Tabular section of CPT are formatted using four classifications: (1) section, (2) subsection, (3) subheading, and (4) category. Locate the code "51020" in the Tabular List. At the top right (page 368, 2019 Professional edition), note the code range 50974–51605 followed by the words "Surgery/Urinary System." "Surgery" is the **section**, and "Urinary System" is the **subsection**. Below, in large boldface font, note the word "Bladder." This is the **subheading**.

Hemic and Lymphatic Systems

Spleen

Excision

38100	Splenectomy; total (separate procedure)
38101	partial (separate procedure)
+ 38102	total, en bloc for extensive disease, in conjunction with other procedure (List in addition to code for primary procedure)

Fig. 15.5 Example of a stand-alone code followed by an indented code. Note the use of the semicolon as described in the text. (Used with permission of the American Medical Association. [AMA, CPT 2019 Professional Edition, 2018.]. © Copyright American Medical Association 2018. All rights reserved.)

Section / Subsection

50974–51605 Surgery / Urinary System

Subheading — **Bladder**

Category — **Incision**

51020	Cystotomy or cystostomy; with fulguration and/or insertion of radioactive material
51030	with cryosurgical destruction of intravesical lesion
51040	Cystostomy, cystotomy with drainage

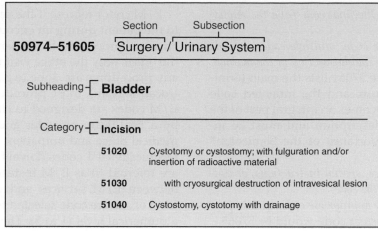

Fig. 15.6 Section of Tabular List illustrating section, subsection, subheading, and category. (Used with permission of the American Medical Association. [AMA, CPT 2019 Professional Edition, 2018.]. © Copyright American Medical Association 2018. All rights reserved.)

Immediately under "Bladder" is the word "Incision," which indicates the **category** (Fig. 15.6).

CROSS-REFERENCING WITH *SEE*

When searching for the correct main term in the Alphabetic Index, the word **see** is frequently encountered. *See* is used as a cross-reference term in the CPT-4 Alphabetic Index and directs the coder to an alternative main term (Fig. 15.7).

? What Did You Learn?

1. Explain the significance of the semicolon in CPT coding.
2. How is a stand-alone code different from an indented code?
3. What does the cross-referencing term *see* indicate?

Desmotomy
See Ligament, Release

Desoxycorticosterone 82633

Desoxycortone
See Desoxycorticosterone

Desoxphenobarbital
See Primodone

Desquamation
See Exfoliation

Fig. 15.7 Example of *see* used as a cross-reference. (Used with permission of the American Medical Association. [AMA, CPT 2019 Professional Edition, 2018.]. © Copyright American Medical Association 2018. All rights reserved.)

BASIC STEPS OF CURRENT PROCEDURAL TERMINOLOGY CODING

CPT coding is a structured process, and it is important for the health insurance professional to follow a few basic steps so that the correct code is identified and assigned.

1. *Identify the procedure, service, or supply to be coded.* These are typically found on the encounter form, in the patient record, in the data in the computerized accounting software, or on the ledger card. A procedure example is "destruction of vaginal lesion, extensive, requiring cryosurgery."
2. *Determine the main term.* The index is located at the back of the CPT manual. Main terms are in boldface type and are listed alphabetically with headings (guide words) located in the top right and left corners, similar to a dictionary (Fig. 15.8). For the purpose of review, main terms are organized by four primary classes of main entries: (1) a procedure or service; (2) an organ or other anatomic site; (3) a condition; or (4) a synonym, eponym, or abbreviation. Subterms (if applicable) are indented under main terms. In this example, the main term is "Destruction."
3. *Locate the main term in the Alphabetic Index and note the code or codes.* For example, if the procedure is "destruction of vaginal lesion, extensive, requiring cryosurgery," the coder first would locate "Destruction" in the Alphabetic Index. Under the main term "Destruction" (in bold), locate the anatomic site "vagina" listed alphabetically, paying attention to the indented modifying terms—in this case, "extensive." Adjacent to "extensive," note the code 57065.

Ankle, Exploration **Antibody, Detection**

Fig. 15.8 Example of guide words at top of page in Index of Current Procedural Terminology (CPT) manual. (Used with permission of the American Medical Association. [AMA, CPT 2019 Professional Edition, 2018.]. © Copyright American Medical Association 2018. All rights reserved.)

Reminder! Do not select the final code from the Alphabetic Index alone.

4. *Cross-reference the single code, multiple codes, or code range numerically in the Tabular section of the manual.* In the Tabular List, code 57061 lists the main terminology of this procedure, and the indented code (after the semicolon) becomes an integral part of the complete procedural description and must be included. (Refer to "Importance of the Semicolon" earlier in this chapter.)

5. *Read and follow any notes, special instructions, or conventions associated with the code.*

6. *Determine and assign the appropriate code.* In this procedure example, the correct code would be 57065.

Before assigning an indented code, refer to the stand-alone code above it. Read the words that *precede* the semicolon, ensuring that the combined description (the portion of the stand-alone code *up* to the semicolon *plus* the wording included in the indented description) corresponds to the documented procedure or service.

? What Did You Learn?

1. What is the first step in CPT coding?
2. What factors should be considered before assigning an indented code?
3. Identify the main term(s) in each of the following:
   - Coronary artery bypass using three arterial grafts
   - Incision and drainage of external abscess, left ear, simple
   - Endoscopy with ablation of colon polyp

EVALUATION AND MANAGEMENT CODING

The **Evaluation and Management (E/M) codes** (99201 to 99499) are found at the beginning of the CPT manual. E/M codes deal with *what the healthcare provider does* during the time spent with the patient, rather than merely with the amount of time spent. The E/M section of the CPT is divided into broad categories, including office visits, hospital visits, and consultations. Most of the categories are divided further. There are two subcategories of office visits (new versus established patients) and two categories of hospital visits (initial versus subsequent visits).

The subcategories list codes that describe differing levels of service provided, ranging from low levels of service to higher and more intense levels of service. Initially, these codes were based on highly subjective factors that were applied inconsistently among carriers. In 1992 new uniform national criteria were established to determine the appropriate level code to be used. Under these criteria, every visit, regardless of location, must include at least two of the following three components—history, examination, and medical decision making—depending on the category of service.

E/M codes represent the services provided directly to the patient during an encounter that do not involve an actual procedure. If a patient has an appointment in the office, only the office visit receives an E/M code. If any procedures are done (e.g., a urinalysis or an electrocardiogram), those procedures receive a CPT code. E/M codes are designed to classify services provided by a healthcare provider and are used primarily in medical office and outpatient settings. E/M codes are technically CPT codes (Level I HCPCS); however, they are referred to as E/M instead of CPT to distinguish between E/M services and procedural coding. The level of service code selected for an office visit is given a numerical level (1 to 5). The code level assigned depends on the complexity of the history, examination, and medical decision making and usually is not affected by the time the provider spends with the patient. The range of codes for office or other outpatient services is 99201 to 99205 for new patients and 99211 to 99215 for established patients. A specific distinction between new and established patients is associated with E/M coding. The exact definitions are discussed in the next section.

VOCABULARY USED IN EVALUATION AND MANAGEMENT CODING

To understand E/M coding more fully, the coder must become acquainted with several terms, as follows:

- **New patient**—An individual who has not received any professional services from the physician or another physician of the same specialty who belongs to the same group practice, regardless of location of service, *within the past 3 years.* (See the "Decision Tree for New vs. Established Patients" flow chart in the CPT-4 manual.)

- **Established patient**—An individual who has been treated previously by the healthcare provider (or one in the same group practice and of the same specialty and subspecialty), regardless of location of service, within the past 3 years. If the provider saw the patient for the first time in a hospital and that individual comes to the office for a follow-up visit after discharge, the individual is considered an established patient to the practice because health record documentation was generated from the hospital visit.

- **Outpatient**—A patient who *has not* been officially admitted to a hospital but receives diagnostic tests or treatment in that facility or a clinic connected with it.

- **Inpatient**—A patient who *has* been formally admitted to a hospital for diagnostic tests, medical care and treatment, or a surgical procedure, typically staying overnight.

- **Chief complaint (CC)**—The primary reason a patient seeks medical care, usually given in the patient's own words.

- **Consultation**—When the attending healthcare provider recommends that the patient see another physician (often a specialist) for a problem usually associated with one major body system. For example, a family practitioner may advise a patient who presents with a suspicious mole to see a dermatologist.

Note: Do not confuse a consultation with a referral. A consultation is usually a one-time visit; the attending physician (or provider) retains control of the patient's healthcare, and the consultation ends when the consulting provider renders his or her opinion. With a **referral**, the original provider relinquishes total care of the patient to the provider to whom the patient has been referred.

- **Counseling**—A discussion with the patient or the patient's family or both. Counseling typically includes one or more of the following:
  - Discussing diagnostic test results, impressions, or recommended studies
  - Discussing prognosis
  - Explaining the risks or benefits of recommended treatment or instruction for management of care
  - Performing patient or family teaching
- **Concurrent care**—When a patient receives similar services (e.g., hospital visits) by more than one healthcare provider on the same day.
- **Critical care**—The constant attention (either at bedside or immediately available) by a physician in a medical crisis.
- **Emergency care**—Care given in a hospital emergency department.
- **Transfer of care**—When the healthcare professional who is providing care for some or all of a patient's problems relinquishes this responsibility to another qualified healthcare professional.

⚠ Stop and Think

Tom Galliger was in the Air Force for 4 years. During that time, he did not see Dr. Boker, his physician in his hometown of Gaithersville. Dr. Boker's office policy is to place any inactive files on microfilm after 2 years of inactivity. After Tom finished his tour of duty, he returned home to Gaithersville. Soon after returning home, he sprained his ankle while hiking in the mountains and subsequently scheduled an appointment with Dr. Boker. Would Tom be considered a new or established patient?

DOCUMENTATION REQUIREMENTS

Because the level of the E/M codes is based on the complexity of the history, examination, or medical decision making performed during the visit, the key to reimbursement is being able to prove the level of complexity of the services rendered. The only valid source of proof is the documentation in the patient's medical record.

Coding E/M services should be based on the extent of documentation in the patient's medical record (Fig. 15.9). The criteria for E/M services must be well understood by the treating provider and documented in the record. Each record needs to show elements of the history, such as the CC; history of present illness (HPI), including location, severity, frequency, and duration; the review of systems (ROS); and past, family, and social history (PFSH). The physical examination should list all systems or organs examined. Medical decision making should discuss the number of options or diagnoses considered in the decision, the amount of data or complexity of data reviewed, and the risk to the patient of the decision made.

6/10/20XX

HX: This 27-year-old white male presents to the clinic today for chief complaint of an abrasion on the right knee following a fall yesterday. According to the patient, he had this soft tissue lesion before the fall; and when he fell, he basically abraded the lower half of the lesion. He is here for reevaluation and possible excision of the lesion.

   PAIN ASSESSMENT: Scale 0-10, one.
   ALLERGIES: DEMEROL
   CURRENT MEDS: None

PE: NAD. Ambulatory. Appears well.
   VS: BP: 120/74   WT: 150#
   RIGHT KNEE EXAMINATION: The patient has a tibial prominence and just above that, there is what appears to be a 1.5-cm epidermal inclusion cyst with an abraded area inferiorly. There is mild erythema and serous drainage but no purulence. There is no appreciable edema. Just lateral to that lesion is a small superficial abrasion. The knee examination was totally within normal limits.

IMP: Epidermal inclusion cyst measuring 1.5 to 2 cm of the right knee, traumatized with abrasion

PLAN: The patient was empirically started on Keflex 500 mg 1 p.o. b.i.d. He was given instructions on home care and is to follow up this week for excision of the lesion. Routine follow-up as noted. RTN PRN.

Frederick Mahoney, MD

Fig. 15.9 Sample documentation.

Definitions for these terms (e.g., HPI, ROS) can be found in the E/M Services Guidelines in the CPT manual.

Imagine This!

Vancil Allen, a 73-year-old white man, was admitted to the hospital with chest pain and shortness of breath after a minor automobile accident. His cardiologist, Dr. Walters, was the admitting physician. While hospitalized, Vancil complained of severe pain in his right lower back. Further examination revealed a kidney stone. Subsequently, Dr. Tomi, a urologist, was called in to take over the care of Vancil's kidney problems.

THREE FACTORS TO CONSIDER

Three factors that would direct the coder to the proper category in the E/M coding section must be determined:

1. Place of service (where the service was provided)
   - Physician's office
   - Hospital
   - Emergency department
   - Nursing home
   - Other
2. Type of service (the reason the service was performed)
   - Office visit
   - Consultation
   - Admission
   - Newborn care
3. Patient status (type of patient)
   - New patient
   - Established patient
   - Outpatient
   - Inpatient

For example, Cindy Carlson recently moved to Jackson City because of a job transfer. Shortly after arriving in Jackson City, Cindy sprained her ankle while jogging in the park. She scheduled an appointment with Dr. Allen Schubert, a family practitioner, for medical treatment. In this scenario:

- The place of service would be the physician's office.
- The type of service would be an office visit.
- The patient status would be "new" because Cindy has never been seen in Dr. Schubert's office before.

After the first three factors have been established, the next step is to determine the three key components of the encounter.

KEY COMPONENTS

The level of service the patient received also must be established. Levels of service are based on the following three **key components**:

- History
- Examination
- Complexity of medical decision making

All three key components must be met or exceeded for new patients; only two must be met for established patients.

History

A patient history is **subjective information**—what the patient tells the healthcare provider in his or her own words. An experienced health insurance professional should be able to identify the various elements and levels of a history by reading the clinical notes entered into the health record. There are four levels of history taking: (1) problem focused, (2) expanded problem focused, (3) detailed, and (4) comprehensive. The health insurance professional should study the detailed E/M Services Guidelines in the front of the CPT manual to become familiar with the key components for choosing the appropriate level of E/M service.

Examination

The second component in determining the correct E/M level is the patient examination. As with history taking, there are four levels, or detailed intensities, involved in a patient examination: (1) problem focused, (2) expanded problem focused, (3) detailed, and (4) comprehensive. The extent of the examination performed depends on clinical judgment and the nature of the presenting problem or problems (also referred to as the *chief complaint* or *CC*).

Medical Decision Making

The last of the three key components is medical decision making. The level of medical decision making is determined by weighing the complexity involved in the healthcare provider's assessment of and professional judgment regarding the diagnosis and care of the patient. In determining the complexity of decision making, the healthcare provider looks at the following three elements:

1. How many diagnostic and treatment options were considered
2. The amount and complexity of data reviewed
3. The amount of risk for complications, morbidity, or mortality

Imagine This!

Sarah Perez, a 55-year-old restaurant manager, was diagnosed with benign essential hypertension in June 2020. Per her physician's orders, Sarah comes to Heartland Medical Clinic every week to have her blood pressure checked. Elizabeth Allen, a medical assistant at Heartland, takes and records Sarah's blood pressure reading in her health record. Sarah does not see a physician for these encounters. Francis Bentley, Heartland's health insurance professional, reports this encounter as 99211, or Level 1, in E/M coding. The visit is documented in the progress notes with the medical assistant's signature or initials, but no further documentation is necessary.

CONTRIBUTING FACTORS

In addition to the three key components used in assigning an E/M code, contributing factors sometimes are considered. Contributing factors help the healthcare provider determine the extent of the three key components (history, examination, and medical decision making) necessary to treat the patient effectively. These contributing factors are as follows:

1. *Counseling:* Services that include the following are provided to the patient or family:
   - Impressions and recommended diagnostic studies
   - Discussion of diagnostic results
   - Prognosis
   - Risks and benefits of treatment
   - Instructions and follow-up
   - Patient and family education
2. *Coordination of care:* A healthcare provider often must arrange for other services to be provided to a patient, such as being admitted to a long-term care facility (LTCF) or home healthcare.
3. *Nature of presenting problem:* The presenting problem (frequently called the *chief complaint* or *CC*) guides the healthcare provider in determining the level of care necessary to diagnose the problem accurately and treat the patient effectively. There are five types of presenting problems:
   - Minimal: Services typically are provided by a member of the medical staff other than the physician, but a physician must be on the premises when the service is rendered. This type may be used only if the patient does not see the physician. *Example:* A 10-year-old girl comes in for an injection based on charted orders by the physician. A medical assistant gives the injection.
   - Self-limiting: Problem runs a definite or prescribed course, is transient in nature, and is not likely to affect the health status of the patient permanently. *Example:* A patient with a sore throat is examined.
   - Low severity: Risk of **morbidity** (incidence or prevalence of a disease) is low, and there is little to no risk of **mortality** (death) without treatment. The patient is expected to recover fully without functional impairment. *Example:* A 16-year-old boy comes in with a case of severe acne.
   - Moderate severity: There is moderate risk of morbidity or mortality without treatment and an increased probability of prolonged functional impairment without treatment. *Example:*

A 40-year-old woman with a 3-month history of severe, recurrent headaches undergoes an initial evaluation.
   - High severity: A patient has a high to extreme risk of morbidity or mortality without treatment and a high probability of severe, prolonged functional impairment without treatment. *Example:* A 10-year-old girl presents with severe coughing fits with wheezing that affect her sleep and other activities. The healthcare provider should document the complexity of the patient's presenting problem in the health record. The health insurance professional must identify the words that correctly indicate the type of presenting problem.

4. *Time:* Time is measured in two ways in E/M coding:
   - **Face-to-face time:** This is the time the healthcare provider spends in direct contact with a patient during an office visit, which includes taking a history, performing an examination, and discussing results.
   - **Unit/floor time:** This includes the time the physician spends on bedside care of the hospitalized patient and reviewing the health record and writing orders.

Note: Time is not considered a factor unless 50% of the encounter is spent in counseling. Time is never a factor for emergency department visits.

Time typically is noted in the E/M section in statements such as the one located under code 99203 shown in Fig. 15.10.

PROLONGED SERVICES

When considering the applicable E/M coding level for a patient encounter, the health insurance professional looks at the history, examination, and medical decision making. Occasionally, the amount of time the healthcare provider spends face-to-face with the patient exceeds the usual length of service associated with the corresponding level in the inpatient or outpatient

> **99203**   **Office or other outpatient visit** for the evaluation and management of a new patient, which requires these three key components:
>
> ■ **A detailed history;**
> ■ **A detailed examination;**
> ■ **Medical decision making of low complexity.**
>
> Counseling and/or coordination of care with other providers or agencies are provided consistent with the nature of the problem(s) and the patient's and/or family's needs.
>
> Usually, the presenting problem(s) are of moderate severity. Physicians typically spend 30 minutes face-to-face with the patient and/or family.

Fig. 15.10 Example from Evaluation and Management (E/M) section showing how time is noted. (Used with permission of the American Medical Association. [AMA, CPT 2019 Professional Edition, 2018.]. © Copyright American Medical Association 2018. All rights reserved.)

setting (Fig. 15.11). When this happens, this extra time is reported in addition to other physician services. The reason for the extra time spent must be documented.

Prolonged Service Without Direct Patient Contact

When a prolonged service is provided that is neither face-to-face time in the office or outpatient setting nor additional unit/floor time in the hospital or nursing facility (NF) during the same session, codes 99358 and 99359 are used.

Standby Services

Code 99360 is used to report healthcare provider standby services that are requested by another individual and that involve prolonged attendance without direct patient contact. An example would be when a surgeon must wait for the results of a biopsy of a frozen section of a tumor. Standby services are reported in 30-minute increments.

> **? What Did You Learn?**
>
> 1. Explain the difference between a new and established patient.
> 2. How does an outpatient differ from an inpatient?
> 3. What are the three factors to consider before assigning an E/M code level?
> 4. Name the three key components in E/M coding.
> 5. What is subjective information?
> 6. Name the four contributing factors that assist the coder in assigning an E/M code.

SUBHEADINGS OF MAIN EVALUATION AND MANAGEMENT SECTION

Following the Office or Other Outpatient Services codes of the main E/M section are additional subheadings. The codes in these various subheadings are used to report services provided to patients who are admitted to a hospital or NF as a result of an encounter in the physician's office or other ambulatory facility.

Note: To better understand the information included in the subsections under the main heading "Evaluation and Management," it is suggested that the student follow along using the most recent version of the CPT-4 coding manual.

OFFICE OR OTHER OUTPATIENT SERVICES

The first subheading under the main E/M section deals with reporting professional services provided in the physician's office or in an outpatient or other ambulatory facility. (An individual is considered an outpatient unless he or she has been formally admitted to a hospital.) In this section, codes are differentiated between "new" and "established" patients. As mentioned, codes for new patient services are 99201 to 99205, and codes for established patients are 99211 to 99215. As the codes increase numerically, the patient's problem becomes more complex or life threatening or both. For new patients, all three key components (history, examination, and medical decision making) must be met or exceeded; however, only two must be met for established patients (Table 15.3).

HOSPITAL OBSERVATION SERVICES

Outpatient **observation** services are short-term services provided in a hospital, including the use of a bed and periodic monitoring by the hospital staff. Observation services are defined as any services that are considered reasonable and necessary to evaluate a patient's illness to determine the need for possible admission to the hospital as an inpatient. When patients are considered "observation status," they receive the same level of care and personal attention as they would receive had they been admitted to the hospital as an inpatient. Initial observation care codes for new or established patients are 99218 to 99220. Subsequent observation care codes are 99224 to 99226. Code 99217 is used to

Total Duration of Prolonged Services	Codes(s)
Less than 30 minutes	Not reported separately
30-74 minutes (30 minutes - 1 hr. 14 min.)	99354 X 1
75-104 minutes (1 hr. 15 min. - 1 hr. 44 min.)	99354 X 1 AND 99355 X 1
105 or more (1 hr. 45 min. or more)	99354 X 1 AND 99355 X 2 or more for each additional 30 minutes

★▲99354   Prolonged evaluation and management or psychotherapy service(s) (beyond the typical service time of the primary procedure) in the office or other outpatient setting requiring direct patient contact beyond the usual service; first hour (List separately in addition to code for office or other outpatient **Evaluation and Management** or psychotherapy service)

(Do not report 99354 in conjunction with 99415, 99416)

★▲99355   **each additional 30 minutes (List separately in addition to code for prolonged service)**

(Use 99355 in conjunction with 99354)

(Do not report 99355 in conjunction with 99415, 99416)

+ 99356   Prolonged service in the inpatient or observation setting, requiring unit/floor time beyond the usual service; first hour (list separately in addition to code for inpatient **Evaluation and Management** service)

(Use 99356 in conjunction with 90837, 99218-99220, 99221-99223, 99224-99226, 99231-99233, 99234-99236, 99251-99255, 99304-99310)

+ 99357   Each additional 30 minutes (List separately in addition to code for prolonged service)

(Use 99357 in conjunction with 99356)

Fig. 15.11 Example of extra time scenario. (Used with permission of the American Medical Association. [AMA, CPT 2019 Professional Edition, 2018.]. © Copyright American Medical Association 2018. All rights reserved.)

Table 15.3	Elements Needed to Substantiate Code Choice

LEVELS OF E/M SERVICE	PROBLEM FOCUSED	EXPANDED PROBLEM FOCUSED	DETAILED	COMPREHENSIVE
History	Presenting problem (CC) Brief HPI	Presenting problem (CC) Brief HPI Problem-focused ROS	Presenting problem (CC) Extended HPI Extended ROS Pertinent PFSH	Presenting problem (CC) Extended HPI Complete ROS Complete PFSH
Examination	Limited to affected body area or organ system	Limited to affected body area or organ system and related organ systems	Extended to all affected body areas and any related organ systems	Multisystem examination or examination of complete single organ system
Medical decision making	Straightforward	Low	Moderate	High
Diagnosis and management	0–1 element	2 elements	3 elements	>3 elements
Data	0–1 element	2 elements	3 elements	>3 elements
Risk	Minimal	Low	Moderate	High

CC, Chief complaint; E/M, Evaluation and Management, HPI, history of present illness; PFSH, past, family, and social history; ROS, review of systems.

report all services provided to a patient on discharge from "observation status" if the discharge is on other than the initial date of observation status. Outpatient observation stay does not count toward the 3-day inpatient stay requirement for admission to a skilled nursing facility (SNF). Observation care is paid under Medicare Part B benefits; hospital inpatient care is paid under Medicare Part A.

When observation status services are initiated at another site, such as the emergency department, physician's office, or SNF, all E/M services provided by the supervising physician in conjunction with initiating the "observation status" are considered part of the observation care, if performed on the same day, and should not be reported separately. It is important that office policies and procedures for reporting observation care services be reviewed and updated annually.

Note: The Notice of Observation Treatment and Implication for Care Eligibility Act passed in 2015 requires hospitals to notify beneficiaries receiving observation services for more than 24 hours of their status as an outpatient under observation. The written notification explains that because the beneficiary is receiving outpatient rather than inpatient services, he or she will be subject to cost-sharing requirements that apply to outpatient services. The notice also must say that the beneficiary's outpatient stay will not count toward the 3-day inpatient stay required for a beneficiary to be eligible for Medicare coverage of subsequent SNF services.

 Imagine This!

Billy Marshall, a 6-year-old boy, was brought to the emergency department after a fall from a jungle gym at the school playground. Billy did not lose consciousness; however, he complained of headache, and his teacher reported an episode of vomiting. Billy was admitted for 24-hour observation to rule out head injury.

HOSPITAL INPATIENT SERVICES

Hospital inpatient services include services provided to hospital inpatients and patients in a "partial hospital" setting. To report E/M services provided to hospital inpatients, use the following codes:

- *Initial hospital care:* The codes in this category (99221 to 99226) are for reporting services provided only by the admitting physician for new or established patients. Other physicians providing initial inpatient E/M services should use consultation or subsequent hospital care codes, as appropriate.
- *Subsequent hospital care:* The codes in this category (99231 to 99233) are for reporting inpatient E/M services provided after the first inpatient encounter (for the admitting physician) or for services (other than consultative) provided by a physician other than the admitting physician. A hospitalized patient may require more than one visit per day by the same physician. Group the visits together and

report the level of service based on the total encounters for the day. Third-party payers vary in their requirements for reporting this service.

- *Observation or inpatient care services (including admission and discharge services):* The codes in this category (99234 to 99236) are used to report observation or inpatient hospital care services provided to patients admitted and discharged on the same date of service. (See the previous section, "Hospital Observation Services.")
- *Hospital discharge services:* These codes (99238, 99239) are used for reporting services provided on the final day of a multiple-day stay.

Time is the controlling factor for assigning the appropriate hospital discharge services code. Total duration of time spent by the physician (even if the time spent is not continuous) should be documented and reported. These codes include final examination, discussion of hospital stay, instructions to caregivers, preparation of discharge records, prescriptions, and referral forms, if applicable.

CONSULTATIONS

By definition, a consultation is a physician's E/M service provided at the request of another physician to recommend care for a specific condition or problem. A physician may not bill for a consultation unless another physician formally requests his or her opinion about the patient's present or future course of treatment. In addition, the consulting physician must communicate that opinion in either a letter or a dictated report. The patient's medical record should include the request by the physician who initiated the consultation and any information (letter, report, or dictation) that was communicated back to this physician.

If a specialist has a patient transferred to his or her care and is going to assume ongoing responsibility for a portion of the patient's care, this is a referral, and office visit or hospital visit codes, not consultation codes, should be used. An example would be a referral from another oncologist for ongoing treatment because of patient choice or geographic transfer.

There are two consultation subheadings in E/M coding:

- Office or other outpatient (new or established patient)
- Inpatient (new or established patient)

These two subheadings define the location where the consultation was rendered: physician's office or other ambulatory facility, codes 99241 to 99245, or inpatient hospital, codes 99251 to 99255. Only one initial consultation is reported by a consultant for the patient on each separate admission. Any subsequent service is reported with applicable codes from Subsequent Hospital Care codes 99231 to 99233 or Subsequent Nursing Facility Care codes 99307 to 99310. A follow-up consultation includes monitoring the patient's progress, recommending management modifications, or advising on a new plan of care in response to the patient's status.

As of January 1, 2010, Medicare no longer recognizes consultation codes (99241 to 99255) for Medicare Part B fee-for-service payment. CMS directs providers to report other E/M codes in lieu of the consultation codes. CMS has preserved telehealth consultations to provide the ability for practitioners to provide and bill for initial inpatient consultations delivered via telehealth where certain services or medical expertise might otherwise not be available to patients. CMS allows providers to report initial inpatient telehealth consultation codes using Level II (HCPCS) codes G0425, G0426, and G0427, depending on the time spent communicating (Fig. 15.12).

The following example can be used as a guideline for coding what previously would have been coded as a consultation visit:

> Surgeon Justin Lang sees Medicare patient Olive Bodkins in his office for a consultation for another provider in the area. Ms. Bodkins is a new patient (one who has not been seen in the previous 3 years by the surgeon or a billing partner); Dr. Lang will bill the consultation as a new patient visit at the appropriate level (1 to 5) using CPT codes 99201 to 99205. If Ms. Bodkins was an established patient (one who was seen during the previous 3 years by the surgeon or a billing partner), Dr. Lang would bill the consultation as an established patient visit at the appropriate level (1 to 5) using CPT codes 99211 to 99215.

✳G0425	Telehealth consultation, emergency department, or initial inpatient, typically 30 minutes communicating with the patient via telehealth
	Problem Focused: Problem-focused history and examination, with straightforward medical decision-making complexity. Typically 30 minutes communicating with patient via telehealth
✳G0426	Initial inpatient telehealth consultation, emergency department, or initial inpatient, typically 50 minutes communicating with the patient via telehealth
	Detailed: Detailed history and examination, with moderate medical decision-making complexity. Typically 50 minutes communicating with patient via telehealth
✳G0427	Initial inpatient telehealth consultation, emergency department, or initial inpatient, typically 70 minutes or more communicating with the patient via telehealth
	Comprehensive: Comprehensive history and examination, with high medical decision-making complexity. Typically 70 minutes or more communicating with patient via telehealth.

Fig. 15.12 Telehealth consultation codes. (From Buck CJ: *2019 HCPCS Level II, professional edition*, St. Louis, 2018, Elsevier.)

The following example represents a **telehealth consultation:**

> The patient selects a provider who reviews his or her clinical information, after which a live conversation begins using video, chat, and/or phone. During the conversation, the provider discusses symptoms and diagnoses, and prescribes medications, as clinically appropriate. A complete record of the interaction is captured automatically and can be shared with the primary care physician, maintaining continuity of care.

> **! Stop and Think**
>
> Dr. Toledo, a family practitioner, has been treating a patient, Alma Cahill, for a rash on her face; however, the medication Dr. Toledo has prescribed is not helping the problem, and the rash is spreading to the neck. With Alma's approval, Dr. Toledo makes an appointment with Dr. Farmer, a dermatologist, for continued treatment of the rash. Is this a consultation or a referral?

EMERGENCY DEPARTMENT SERVICES

E/M codes 99281 to 99288 are used for both new and established patients who have been treated in an emergency department that is part of a hospital. For coding purposes, the CPT-4 manual defines an emergency department as "an organized hospital-based facility for the provision of unscheduled episodic services to patients who present for immediate medical attention." To qualify, the facility must be available for immediate emergency care 24 hours a day for patients not on "observation status." (For E/M services provided to a patient in an observation area of a hospital, see codes 99217 to 99220.)

The single code 99288, for the subheading "Other Emergency Services," is used in physician-directed emergency care and advanced life support when the physician is located in a hospital emergency or critical care department and is in two-way voice communication with ambulance or rescue personnel outside the hospital. The physician directs the performance of necessary medical procedures.

For critical care services provided in the emergency department, see Critical Care notes and codes 99291 and 99292.

CRITICAL CARE SERVICES

The direct delivery of medical care by a physician to a critically ill or critically injured patient is referred to as *critical care*. A critical illness or injury acutely impairs one or more vital organ systems such that there is a high probability of imminent or life-threatening deterioration in the patient's condition. Critical care involves high-complexity decision making to assess, manipulate, and support vital system failure or to prevent further life-threatening deterioration of the patient's condition. Examples of vital organ system failure include, but are not limited to, central nervous system failure,

Total Duration of Critical Care Codes	
Less than 30 minutes	Appropriate E/M codes
30-74 minutes (30 minutes – 1 hr. 14 min.)	99291 X 1
75-104 minutes (1 hr. 15 min. – 1 hr. 44 min.)	99291 X 1 AND 99292 X 1
105-134 minutes (1 hr. 45 min. – 2 hr. 14 min.)	99291 X 1 AND 99292 X 2
135-164 minutes (2 hr. 15 min. – 2 hr. 44 min.)	99291 X 1 AND 99292 X 3
165-194 minutes (2 hr. 45 min. – 3 hr. 14 min.)	99291 X 1 AND 99292 X 4
195 minutes or longer (3 hr. 15 min. – etc.)	99291 and 99292 as appropriate (see illustrated reporting examples earlier)
99291	**Critical care, evaluation, and management** of the critically ill or critically injured patient: first 30-74 minutes
+ 99292	Each additional 30 minutes (list separately in addition to code for prolonged service) (Use 99292 in conjunction with 99291)

Fig. 15.13 Codes for reporting critical care services. (Used with permission of the American Medical Association. [AMA, CPT 2019 Professional Edition, 2018.]. © Copyright American Medical Association 2018. All rights reserved.)

circulatory failure, shock, renal failure, hepatic failure, metabolic failure, and respiratory failure. Fig. 15.13 illustrates the correct reporting of critical care services. Critical care services are discussed in depth in the E/M section of the CPT manual under the heading "Critical Care Services" after "Other Emergency Services."

NURSING FACILITY SERVICES

The Nursing Facility Services category of E/M services includes codes for services provided to both new and established patients in NFs (formerly referred to as *skilled nursing facilities [SNFs], intermediate nursing facilities [ICFs], or long-term care facilities [LTCFs]*). There are two major subcategories of NFs: (1) Initial Nursing Facility Care (codes 99304 to 99306) and (2) Subsequent Nursing Facility Care (codes 99307 to 99310).

Nursing Facility Discharge Services codes 99315 (30 minutes or less) and 99316 (more than 30 minutes) are used to report the total duration of time spent by a physician for the final patient discharge from the NF. This time includes a final examination of the patient; discussion of the NF stay; instructions given to relevant caregivers for continuing care; and preparation of discharge records, prescriptions, and referral forms, as applicable.

Other Nursing Facility Services code 99318 is used to report an annual NF assessment visit on the required schedule of visits if an annual assessment is performed. Refer to the CPT-4 coding manual for additional E/M categories and details on reporting services in these categories.

Additional subheadings follow E/M guidelines for Nursing Facility Services. Students should peruse these subsections thoroughly in the CPT-4 coding manual to acquire a more robust understanding of all aspects of E/M coding.

> **? What Did You Learn?**
> 1. What does "observation status" mean in E/M coding?
> 2. List the two consultation subheadings in E/M coding.
> 3. What level of decision making must be used to assess critical care?
> 4. What services are typically included in the Nursing Facility Discharge Services category?

EVALUATION AND MANAGEMENT MODIFIERS

Before assigning a final E/M code, it is important to check for potential modifiers that should be assigned to report an altered service or procedure (e.g., an unusual or special circumstance that affects the service or procedure). Attaching modifiers to codes provides additional information on the services performed. Some modifiers affect reimbursement; others are for documentation purposes. Leaving off a required modifier can result in denial of payment.

REASONS FOR USING MODIFIERS

A modifier is used to report or indicate that a service or procedure has been altered by some specific circumstance but not changed in its definition or code. In addition, modifiers are used to report if or when:

- A service or procedure has either a professional or a technical component
- A service or procedure was provided more than once
- A service or procedure has been increased or reduced
- Only part of a service was performed
- Unusual events occurred
- A bilateral procedure was performed

A partial list of modifiers can be found on the inside cover of the CPT-4 coding manual. For a complete list of the modifiers and their use applicable to CPT codes, see Appendix A in the CPT-4 manual, which immediately follows the Category III codes.

> **? What Did You Learn?**
> 1. What is the function of a modifier?
> 2. Why is it important to attach a needed modifier to a code?
> 3. Where are modifiers found in the CPT manual?

IMPORTANCE OF DOCUMENTATION

Health record documentation is required to record pertinent facts, findings, and observations about a patient's health history, including past and present illnesses, examinations, tests, treatments, and outcomes. The health record chronologically documents the care of the patient and is an important element contributing to high-quality care.

The appropriately documented health record facilitates:

- The ability of the physician and other healthcare professionals to evaluate and plan the patient's immediate treatment and to monitor the patient's healthcare over time
- Communication and continuity of care among physicians and other healthcare professionals involved in the patient's care
- Accurate and timely claims review and payment
- Appropriate utilization review and quality-of-care evaluations
- Collection of data that may be useful for research and education

An appropriately documented health record can reduce many of the challenges associated with claims processing and serves as a legal document to verify the care provided, if necessary.

PREVENTING MEDICAL BILLING AND CODING ERRORS

Medical coding and billing errors can be the result of common mistakes, such as typographical or data entry errors. Even making a simple mistake can lead to significant time lost tracking down the source of mistakes, and serious delays in payments can result. It is often up to medical billers and coders, and effective communication with the rest of the office staff, to avoid these types of mistakes before they happen.

When medical billing and coding errors occur, a number of problems can result: claims reimbursement is delayed or might not be paid at all, payments could be made incorrectly or to the wrong provider, or fraud and abuse investigations can be initiated. The outcomes can range from simply resubmitting a corrected claim to, in the case of a major error, the provider being charged with violations of the False Claims Act and fined up to $10,000 per error. Fig. 15.14 shows a list of the top 10 coding and billing errors.

Preventing billing and coding errors involves the entire medical office staff. Ideally, the provider should appropriately document the specific service or procedure performed. Second, an experienced health insurance professional or coder should be trained well enough to be able to interpret the documentation in the patient record accurately and provide the correct coding. Codes change every year, and the staff needs to keep up to date with those changes. In addition to using the most current coding manual, it is suggested

1. No documentation for services billed.
2. No signature or authentication of documentation.
3. Always assigning the same level of service.
4. Billing of consult versus outpatient office visit.
5. Invalid codes billed due to old resources.
6. Unbundling of procedure codes.
7. Misinterpreted abbreviations.
8. No chief complaint listed for each visit.
9. Billing of service(s) included in global fee as a separate professional fee.
10. Inappropriate or no modifier used for accurate payment of claim.

Fig. 15.14 Top 10 coding and billing errors.

that the staff attend periodic seminars or Internet webcasts, conduct annual internal updates, and have access to sufficient support material. These measures can go far in preventing lost or delayed revenue due to coding errors.

EVALUATION AND MANAGEMENT DOCUMENTATION GUIDELINES: 1995 VERSUS 1997

In addition to the guidelines found in the CPT manual, HCFA (now CMS) published documentation guidelines. The first set of guidelines became effective in 1995, and the second set became effective in 1997. A third set became effective in 2019 and will be discussed later. The goal was to develop and refine a way to assign a "score" accurately for each level of medical services in the E/M categories. The guidelines specifically identify the elements that must be documented in the medical record to support a particular level of service and a workable method to determine the level of medical decision making. Briefly, the 1995 guidelines are applicable to all medical and surgical services and in all settings. The 1997 guidelines, in addition to incorporating the 1995 guidelines, focus on specialists and outline each component of a typical E/M service. Box 15.1 provides an outline of the general principles to which healthcare practices must adhere when structuring medical records in accordance with the 1995 and 1997 guidelines. The 1995 and 1997 guidelines are still applicable, but the requirements for documentation for each encounter have been simplified.

Evaluation and Management Guidelines 2019

As part of the Patients Over Paperwork Initiative, CMS came up with new documentation guidelines to help streamline the documentation process and keep the focus on the patient. Because patient care has changed to a patient-centered model, CMS felt that the documentation requirements should be updated as well. These changes include:

- Simplifying the documentation of history and examination for established patients by requiring that providers only need to document what has changed

Box 15.1	General Principles of Medical Record Documentation Using 1995 and 1997 Guidelines

1. The medical record should be complete and legible.
2. The documentation of each patient encounter should include:

   - Reason for the encounter and relevant history, physical examination findings, and prior diagnostic test results (this requirement has been simplified in the 2019 guidelines)
   - Assessment and clinical impression or diagnosis
   - Plan of care
   - Date and legible identity of the observer

3. If not documented, the rationale for ordering diagnostic and other ancillary services should be easily understood.
4. Past and present diagnoses should be accessible to the treating or consulting physician.
5. Appropriate health risk factors should be identified.
6. The patient's progress, response to and changes in treatment, and revision of diagnosis should be documented.
7. The Current Procedural Terminology (CPT) and International Classification of Diseases (ICD) codes reported on the health insurance claim form or billing statement should be supported by the documentation in the medical record.

since the last visit rather than redocumenting information that is already contained in the health record.

- When the chief complaint or other historical information has been documented by ancillary staff or even the patients themselves, the provider can review and verify rather than having to reenter the information.
- The need to document the medical necessity of providing visits in the patient's home versus the office has been eliminated.
- The need to duplicate the documentation of certain notations that have been made by residents or other members of the medical team has been removed.

For more information on the 2019 guidelines and the Patients Over Paperwork Initiative, see "Websites to Explore" at the end of this chapter.

DECIDING WHICH GUIDELINES TO USE

Although it is acceptable to use either the 1995 or the 1997 E/M documentation guidelines, it is unacceptable to use them interchangeably on the same document. An extended history may be documented under the 1997 guidelines by identifying three chronic or inactive conditions and the current status of those conditions. The 1995 guidelines do not permit this documentation practice. Under the 1995 guidelines, an extended history requires documentation of at least four HPI elements. The HPI elements include *location*,

quality, severity, duration, timing, context, modifying factors, and *associated signs/symptoms.* For further information on the 1995 and 1997 guidelines, visit the CMS website at http://www.cms.gov/.

 What Did You Learn?

1. Name three ways in which a well-documented health record contributes to high-quality healthcare.
2. What is the principal difference between the 1995 E/M documentation guidelines compared with the guidelines published in 1997?
3. Which set of guidelines does CMS prefer a medical office to use?

OVERVIEW OF HCPCS

HCPCS is a standardized coding system that is used primarily to identify products, supplies, and services not included in the Level I (CPT) codes. HCPCS codes are mandated by CMS (formerly HCFA) for reporting services on Medicare claims and are required by most state Medicaid offices. For general information on HCPCS, visit http://www.cms.gov/medhcpcsgeninfo.

HCPCS quarterly updates are available on the website listed under "Websites to Explore" at the end of this chapter.

To review, Level I (CPT) codes are composed of five digits that describe the service, procedure, or test. CPT codes are developed and maintained by the AMA with annual updates. Level II (national) codes are five-digit alphanumeric codes consisting of one alphabetical character (a letter between A and V) followed by four digits. HCFA (now CMS) created Level II codes to supplement CPT, which does not include codes for nonphysician procedures, such as ambulance services; durable medical equipment, prosthetics, orthotics, and supplies (DMEPOS); and administration of injectable drugs. Level II codes are developed and maintained by CMS with quarterly updates and are a standard component of electronically transmitted claims.

Although thousands of medical products are described by Level II codes, no product brand names are included in the code descriptions. The presence of a Level II code indicates only that the product or service is available within the larger medical system; it does not guarantee payment. Individual payers develop their own reimbursement rules and criteria related to Level II codes, which differ from payer to payer. The following are examples of Level II codes:

A4615—Cannula, nasal

E0147—Walker, heavy duty, multiple braking system, variable wheel resistance

J2250—Injection, midazolam hydrochloride (Versed), 1 mg

If both a CPT code and HCPCS Level II code are available for the service provided, CMS requires that the HCPCS Level II code be used. Medicare has specific requirements for reporting Part B physician office services. These requirements are published in the *Medicare Claims Processing Manual*, Pub. 100-04, available on the CMS website.

HCPCS LEVEL II MANUAL

The HCPCS Level II coding manual, like the CPT-4, is published and updated annually by the AMA. Like CPT, the HCPCS manual is divided into sections; however, they are not like those in the CPT. As stated earlier, they cover such categories as Ambulance Services, Dental Procedures, Injections, Vision Services, and others. Formats may vary somewhat with updated editions, but the basic information remains the same.

Note: Students should always use the most recent versions of all coding manuals for accurate coding.

Index of Main Terms

The first main section of the HCPCS coding manual is an index of main terms, arranged in alphabetical order similar to Level I CPT-4 codes (Fig. 15.15). The index is followed by the 17 alphabetized sections. Level II codes are located in the index using similar guidelines as for CPT-4 codes, as follows:

- Identify the service or procedure performed. *Example:* A patient is provided with a nonprogrammable implantable infusion pump (ambulatory) for chemotherapy treatment.
- Identify the main term and locate the term in the index. In our example, the main term would be "pump." Note in the index that pump is followed by a list of indented subterms, so find "implantable infusion." Tentative codes would be E0782 and E0783.
- Locate these codes in the applicable section of the alphanumeric list and compare the code description with the service provided.
- Eliminate any codes that do not appropriately describe the service provided. In our example, E0783 would be incorrect because it describes a "programmable" pump.
- Check for symbols, notes, and footnotes that clarify code selection further, and review their definitions and other coverage guidelines that apply. In our example, code E0782 cannot be used in an SNF setting. The coding resource may provide a note or symbol to identify this exclusion from Medicare coverage.
- Determine whether any modifiers should be used.
- Assign the appropriate code. In our example, E0783 is the correct code.

Table of Drugs

The Level II (national) code manual also contains a Table of Drugs, which the health insurance professional should use to locate appropriate drug names that correspond with the generic names listed in the J code subsection. The Table of Drugs is arranged alphabetically in column format. The name of the drug is in the first column, the dosage in the second column, the method of administration in the third column, and the HCPCS code in the fourth column (Fig. 15.16).

HCPCS 2013 INDEX / Abatacept

A

Abatacept, J0129
Abciximab, J0130
Abdomen
   dressing holder/binder, A4462
   pad, low profile, L1270
Abduction control, each, L2642
Abduction restrainer, A4566
Abduction rotation bar, foot, L3140-L3170
AbobotulinumtoxintypeA, J0586
Absorption dressing, A6251-A6256
Access, site, occlusive, device, G0269
Access system, A4301
Accessories
   ambulation devices, E0153-E0159
   artificial kidney and machine (*see also* ESRD),
     E1510-E1699
   beds, E0271-E0280, E0300-E0326
   wheelchairs, E0950-E1030, E1050-E1298,
     E2201-/E2295, E2300-E2399, K0001-K0109

Aide, home, health, G0156, S9122, T1021
   bath/toilet, E0160-E0162, E0235, E0240-E0249
   services, G0151-G0156, G0179-G0181, S5180,
     S5181, S9122, T1021, T1022
Air bubble detector, dialysis, E1530
Air fluidized bed, E0194
Air pressure pad/mattress, E0186, E0197
Air travel and nonemergency transportation,
   A0140
Alarm
   not otherwise classified, A9280
   pressure, dialysis, E1540
Alatrofloxacin mesylate, J0200
Albumin, human, P9041, P9042
Albuterol
   all formulations, inhalation solution,
     concentrated, J7610, J7611
   all formulations, inhalation solution, unit
     dose, J7609, J7613
   all formulation, inhalation solution, J7620
Alcohol/substance, assessment, G0396, G0397,
   H0001, H0003, H0049

Fig. 15.15 Example page from HCPCS Index 2019. (From Buck CJ: *2019 HCPCS Level II, professional edition,* St. Louis, 2018, Elsevier.)

2019 TABLE OF DRUGS / AlloSkin

DRUG NAME	DOSAGE	METHOD OF ADMINISTRATION	HCPCS CODE
AlloSkin	per square centimeter		04115
Aloxi	25 mcg		J2469
Alpha 1-proteinase inhibitor, human	10 mg	IV	J0256, J0257
Alphanate			J7186
AlphaNine SD	per IU		J7193
Alprolix	per IU		J7201
Alprostadil			
injection	1.25 mcg	OTH	J0270
urethral suppository	each	OTH	J0275
Alteplase recombinant	1 mg	IV	J2997
Alupent	per 10 mg	INH	J7667, J7668
noncompounded, unit dose	10 mg	INH	J7669
unit dose	10 mg	INH	J7670
AmBisome	10 mg	IV	J0289
Amcort	per 5 mg	IM	J3302
A-methaPred	up to 40 mg	IM, IV	J2920
	up to 125 mg	IM, IV	J2930
Amgen	1 mcg	SC	J9212

Fig. 15.16 Partial page from Table of Drugs in Healthcare Common Procedure Coding System (HCPCS). (From Buck CJ: *2019 HCPCS Level II, professional edition,* St. Louis, 2018, Elsevier.)

Modifiers

As with CPT-4, HCPCS Level II code sets contain modifiers. Modifiers in HCPCS Level II are alphabetical or alphanumeric (e.g., NU, P1). They are used to indicate that a service or procedure that has been performed has been altered by some specific circumstances but not changed in its definition or code. The HCPCS manual contains a complete list of modifiers and their meaning.

SECTIONS OF THE HCPCS MANUAL

HCPCS Level II codes are organized into 17 sections (Fig. 15.17). The D codes, which include dental procedure codes D0000 to D9999, represent a separate category of codes from the Current Dental Terminology (CDT-4) code set, which is copyrighted and updated by the American Dental Association. (Although HCPCS publishers may develop their own format, conventions, and supplemental information, they typically use the same basic formats and conventions.)

APPENDICES

Similar to CPT-4, the HCPCS Professional Edition coding manual contains several appendices. Below are the appendices from Buck's *2019 HCPCS Level II coding manual:*

- Appendix A—Jurisdiction List for DMEPOS HCPCS Codes
- Appendix B—General Correct Coding Policies for National Correct Coding Initiative Policy Manual for Medicare Services

Author's Note: All HCPCS references to appendices are taken from *2019 HCPCS Level II Coding Manual,* Professional Edition, by Carol J. Buck, published by Elsevier, 2018.

? What Did You Learn?

1. How are HCPCS Level II codes structured?
2. What do "J" codes represent in HCPCS coding?
3. What is the function of an HCPCS Level II code modifier?

- **A Codes:** Transportation Services Including
  - Ambulance
  - Medical and Surgical Supplies
  - Administrative, Miscellaneous, and Investigational
- **B Codes:** Enteral and Parenteral Therapy
- **C Codes:** CMS Hospital Outpatient Payment System
- **D Codes:** Dental Procedures
- **E Codes:** Durable Medical Equipment
- **G Codes:** Temporary Codes for Professional Services Procedures
- **H Codes:** Behavioral Health and/or Substance Abuse Treatment Services
- **J Codes:** Drugs Other Than Chemotherapy
- **K Codes:** Temporary Codes Assigned to DME Regional Carriers
- **L Codes:** Orthotics/Prosthetics
- **M Codes:** Other Medical Services
- **P Codes:** Laboratory Services
- **Q Codes:** Temporary Codes Assigned by CMS
- **R Codes:** Diagnostic Radiology Services
- **S Codes:** Temporary National Codes Established by Private Payers
- **T Codes:** Temporary National Codes Established by Medicaid
- **V Codes:** Vision/Hearing Services

Fig. 15.17 Sections of Healthcare Common Procedure Coding System (HCPCS) Level II (national) codes.

NATIONAL CORRECT CODING INITIATIVE

The National Correct Coding Initiative (NCCI) is a system developed by the CMS to promote national correct practices to minimize coding errors that lead to incorrect payment on Medicare Part B claims. NCCI focuses on edits of services billed by the same provider, beneficiary, and date of service. It is based on coding conventions in the AMA CPT manual, national and local policies, coding guidelines from national societies, and analysis of Medicare medical and surgical practices. NCCI edits serve two purposes: (1) to ensure that the most comprehensive group of codes are billed rather than the component parts and (2) to edit two codes that cannot reasonably be performed together on the basis of either the definition or anatomic considerations.

The CMS updates the NCCI policy manual annually for Medicare services. Edits have been incorporated by Medicare carriers for physicians and by Medicare intermediaries for the Hospital Outpatient Prospective Payment System and the Outpatient Code Editor.

The Affordable Care Act requires all state Medicaid programs to incorporate "NCCI methodologies" in their claims processing systems by March 31, 2011. The latest NCCIs can be downloaded from the Internet using the search words "National Correct Coding Initiatives" followed by the current year.

HIPAA AND HCPCS CODING

One HIPAA requirement is that procedure coding be standardized. In October 2003 the secretary of the HHS authorized CMS, under the HIPAA legislation, to maintain and distribute HCPCS Level II codes. In addition, CMS was to establish uniform national definitions of services, codes to represent services, and payment modifiers to the codes. In August 2000 the *Federal Register* published regulations (65 FR 50312) to implement this HIPAA mandate. This regulation called for the elimination of Level III local codes by October 2002, after which only Level I and Level II codes could be used.

CROSSWALK

A **crosswalk** is a procedure by which codes used for data in one database are translated into the codes of another database, making it possible to relate information between or among databases. In coding, a crosswalk is a "link" that refers to a relationship between a medical procedure (CPT code) and a diagnosis (ICD code). Medicare uses CPT/ICD crosswalks to validate or substantiate medical necessity under Local Coverage Determinations/Local Medicare Review Policy. Third-party payers also establish crosswalk tables for validating and auditing medical claims. In brief, physicians dealing in Medicare Part B claims are paid by CPT procedure codes, not diagnoses. To validate proper coding (e.g., the reason for the procedure), providers must specify a diagnosis. If the diagnosis does not support the procedure, the claim may not get paid.

EXPLANATION OF BENEFITS CODE CROSSWALK TO HIPAA STANDARD CODES

Federal privacy regulations of HIPAA require standard national codes used on the electronic remittance advice (ERA) to be crosswalked to Medicaid explanation of benefits (EOB) codes as an informational aid to research adjudicated claims listed on the Remittance and Status Report (RA). The EOB codes are divided into separate crosswalks based on claim types. The EOB Code Crosswalk is compatible with 5010 835 transactions.

> **? What Did You Learn?**
> 1. What does HIPAA require of HCPCS coding?
> 2. Which level of HCPCS codes did HIPAA eliminate?
> 3. What is a crosswalk?

SUMMARY CHECKPOINTS

- The purpose of CPT is to provide a uniform language accurately describing medical, surgical, and diagnostic services, serving as an effective means for reliable communication among physicians, third-party payers, and patients nationwide.
- CPT was developed and published by the AMA in 1966. Originally, it contained mainly surgical

procedures, with limited sections on medicine, radiology, and laboratory procedures. The second edition, published in 1970, expanded codes to designate diagnostic and therapeutic procedures in surgery, medicine, and other specialties. In 1970 the five-digit system was introduced, replacing the former four-digit codes, and internal medicine procedures were added.

- HCPCS codes are grouped into two levels:
  - *Level I codes* contain the AMA Physicians' CPT codes. These are five-digit codes, accompanied by descriptive terms, used for reporting services performed by healthcare professionals. Level I codes are developed and updated annually by the AMA.
  - *Level II codes* are the HCPCS National Medicare Codes used to report medical services, supplies, drugs, and durable medical equipment not contained in the Level I codes. These codes begin with a single letter, followed by four digits, and supersede Level I codes for similar encounters, E/M services, or other procedures and represent the portion of procedures involving supplies and materials.

The CPT manual begins with an introduction, followed by six sections in the main body of the manual. Category III codes follow the main section, after which there are 16 appendices—A to P. The CPT index of main terms appears at the back of the manual.

- The CPT manual uses coding conventions and symbols that help guide the health insurance professional in locating the correct code. Accurate procedural coding cannot be accomplished without understanding the meaning of each of these conventions and symbols.
- The semicolon is important in CPT coding. It is used to separate main and subordinate clauses in the CPT code descriptions. The complete description listed *before* the semicolon applies to that code plus any additional succeeding indented codes. The complete description *after* the semicolon applies only to that code.
- The basic steps for CPT coding are as follows:
  - Step 1: Identify the procedure, service, or supply to be coded.
  - Step 2: Determine the main term.
  - Step 3: Locate the main term in the Alphabetic Index and note the code.
  - Step 4: Cross-reference the single code, multiple codes, or the code range numerically in the Tabular section of the manual.
  - Step 5: Read and follow any notes, special instructions, or conventions associated with the code.
  - Step 6: Determine and assign the appropriate code.
- In E/M coding, a new patient is a patient who has not received any professional services from the physician or another physician of the same specialty, regardless of location, who belongs to the same group practice within the past 3 years.

- An established patient is a patient who has been treated previously by the healthcare provider, regardless of location of service, within the past 3 years. If the provider saw the patient for the first time in a hospital and the patient comes to the office for a follow-up visit after discharge, the patient is considered an established patient to the practice because health record documentation was generated from the hospital visit.
- The three key components that establish the level in E/M coding are as follows:
  - *History*—subjective information based on four elements: (1) presenting problem (in the patient's own words), (2) HPI, (3) ROS, and (4) PFSH. The four levels of history are (1) problem focused, (2) expanded problem focused, (3) detailed, and (4) comprehensive.
  - *Examination*—deals with the degree to which the healthcare provider examines various body areas and organ systems that are affected by the presenting problem. The four levels of examination are the same as in history taking.
  - *Medical decision making*—determined by weighing the complexity involved in the healthcare provider's assessment of and the professional judgment made regarding the diagnosis and care of the patient. The three elements considered are how many diagnostic and treatment options are considered; the amount and complexity of data reviewed; and the amount of risk for complications, morbidity, or mortality. Medical decision making has four levels: (1) straightforward, (2) low complexity, (3) moderate complexity, and (4) high complexity.
- Besides the previously mentioned three key components, the four contributing factors that may affect the level of E/M coding are:
  - Counseling
  - Coordination of care
  - Nature of presenting problem—minimal, self-limiting, low severity, high severity
  - Time
- The subheadings in the E/M section of the CPT-4 manual are used to report services provided in the office (new or established patient), outpatient facility, or other ambulatory facility. Subheadings include hospital inpatient services, consultations, observation care, and emergency department services.
- A modifier provides the means by which the reporting healthcare provider can indicate that a service or procedure performed has been altered by some specific circumstance but its definition or code has not been changed.
- Health record documentation is required to record pertinent facts, findings, and observations about a patient's health history, including past and present

illnesses, examinations, tests, treatments, and outcomes. The health record chronologically documents the care of the patient and is an important element contributing to high-quality care.

- HCPCS is a coding system that is composed of Level I (CPT) codes and Level II (national) codes. CPT codes are composed of five digits that describe procedures and tests. Level II (national) codes are five-digit alphanumeric codes that describe pharmaceuticals, supplies, procedures, tests, and services.

- HCFA created Level II codes to supplement CPT, which does not include codes for nonphysician procedures such as ambulance services, durable medical equipment, specific supplies, and administration of injectable drugs. If a CPT code and HCPCS Level II code for the service are provided, CMS requires that the HCPCS Level II code be used.

- The NCCI is a system developed by the CMS to promote national correct practices to minimize coding errors that lead to incorrect payment on Medicare Part B claims. NCCI edits serve two purposes: (1) to ensure that the most comprehensive group of codes rather than the component parts are billed and (2) to edit two codes that cannot reasonably be performed together on the basis of either the definition or anatomic considerations.

- Because HIPAA requires standardized procedure coding, CMS required healthcare providers and contractors to eliminate any unapproved local procedure or modifier codes. To accomplish this, medical offices were to crosswalk unapproved local procedure and modifier codes to a temporary or permanent national code.

Closing Scenario

Park and Melanie have become quite the coding team at Walden-Martin! They put together a presentation for the providers of Walden-Martin to show the latest changes in both *International Classification of Diseases*, 10th revision, Clinical Modification (ICD-10-CM) and Current Procedural Terminology (CPT). It went over well, and Dr. Khan asked to meet with both of them to further discuss his coding practices.

Melanie suggested a new process for reviewing the coding of insurance claims and has been able to catch errors before the claims are submitted. This process has resulted in faster payment of claims.

Park and Melanie agree that staying on top of all of the changes that occur in the coding world can be a challenge, but it's one that they are up to. Park has found several website bulletin boards where practicing coders write in questions and answers on coding issues, and Melanie has subscribed to the Centers for Medicare and Medicaid Services (CMS) updates and regularly shares them with Park and the others in the billing department. They are both proud that they are contributing to the success of Walden-Martin Family Medical Clinic.

CHAPTER REVIEW QUESTIONS

1. The Current Procedural Terminology (CPT) was developed by:
   a. AMA.
   b. CMS.
   c. HHS.
   d. ICD.
2. An updated version of CPT is published:
   a. Monthly.
   b. Semiannually.
   c. Annually.
   d. Every 5 years.
3. Level I HCPCS codes are also known as:
   a. Diagnostic codes.
   b. CPT codes.
   c. Local codes.
   d. ICD codes.
4. CPT Category II codes are used for:
   a. Emerging technologies.
   b. Coding what the provider does during the time spent with the patient.
   c. Performance measurement.
   d. None of the above.
5. For the full description of an indented code, you must also look at:
   a. The description of the code below the indented code.
   b. The modifiers for the code section.
   c. The essential modifiers for the code.
   d. The description of the code listed above the indented code that comes before the semicolon.
6. Which of the following sections uses the code range between 70000 and 79999?
   a. Anesthesia section
   b. Surgery section
   c. Radiology section
   d. Medicine section
7. Which of the following levels of history includes a review of the systems that relate to the chief complaint?
   a. Problem-focused history
   b. Expanded problem-focused history
   c. Detailed history
   d. Comprehensive history
8. Which HCPCS codes range from A4000 to A8999?
   a. Ambulance transport
   b. Medical supplies
   c. Surgical supplies
   d. Both b and c
9. Which code is assigned to an urgent care facility as the place of service?
   a. 01
   b. 13
   c. 20
   d. 23

10. To find the most accurate code, coders use the following progression:
    a. Categories, subcategories, sections, subsections
    b. Sections, subsections, categories, subcategories
    c. Sections, categories, subsections, subcategories
    d. Subsections, subcategories, sections, categories

WEBSITES TO EXPLORE

- For live links to the following websites, please visit the Evolve website at http://evolve.elsevier.com/Beik/today.
- Access AMA at http://www.ama-assn.org.
- Access Medicare Learning Network (Medlearn) at http://www.cms.gov/Outreach-and-Education/Medicare-Learning-Network-MLN/MLNGenInfo/index.html.
- To visit CMS, see http://www.cms.gov.
- To visit HHS, see http://www.hhs.gov.
- Access NCCI at http://www.cms.gov/NationalCorrectCodInitEd/.
- HCPCS general information is available at http://www.cms.gov/MedHCPCSGenInfo/.
- Access Documentation Guidelines (1995) at http://www.cms.gov/Outreach-and-Education/Medicare-Learning-Network-MLN/MLNEdWebGuide/Downloads/95Docguidelines.pdf.
- Access Documentation Guidelines (1997) at http://www.cms.gov/Outreach-and-Education/Medicare-Learning-Network-MLN/MLNEdWebGuide/Downloads/97Docguidelines.pdf. NOTE: If either this or the previous weblink is unavailable, use "1995 (and/or 1997) documentation guidelines" as search words.
- To visit the Patients Over Paperwork website, see https://www.cms.gov/About-CMS/story-page/patients-over-paperwork.html.
- 2019 documentation guidelines are available at https://www.cms.gov/Research-Statistics-Data-and-Systems/Monitoring-Programs/Medicare-FFS-Compliance-Programs/SimplifyingRequirements.html.
- Guidelines for using the HCPCS Level II codes are posted at http://codingupdates.com.
- See the CMS website at http://www.cms.gov/Manuals/IOM/list.asp for internet-only manuals (IOMs).
- Access NCCI and Additional Edits at http://www.ncdhhs.gov/dma/provider/ncci.htm.
- The General Equivalence Mapping (GEM) Factsheet is available at http://www.scribd.com/doc/39626776/ICD-10-GEM-Factsheet, or use the search words "GEM Fact Sheet." Alternatively, go to the CMS.gov home page and enter "Medicare Learning Network (MLN) product downloads" in the search box.

Author's Note: Due to the dynamic nature of the Internet, web addresses and/or links provided in this chapter may have changed since publication and may no longer be valid. In such cases, students should select comparable search words to access related sites.

The Role of Computers in Health Insurance

16

Chapter Outline

Chapter Objectives

After completion of this chapter, the student should be able to:

1. Explain how computers have affected health insurance.
2. Discuss the role of the Health Insurance Portability and Accountability Act (HIPAA) in electronic transmissions.
3. Describe the essential elements of electronic data interchange (EDI).
4. Discuss the various aspects of electronic claims processing.
5. Explain the final "rule" for electronic submission of Medicare claims mandated under the Administrative Simplification Compliance Act (ASCA).
6. List and describe additional electronic services available to the health insurance professional.
7. Provide a brief response for each of the following.
   - Describe an electronic medical record (EMR).
   - List the two types of EMR hybrids.
   - List potential issues of EMRs.
   - Discuss the future of EMRs, including privacy concerns for patients.
8. Explain interoperability as it applies to healthcare.

Chapter Terms

Administrative Simplification
   Compliance Act (ASCA)
billing service
clearinghouse
code sets
combination records
digital imaging hybrid
direct data entry (DDE)
electronic claims clearinghouse
electronic data interchange (EDI)

electronic funds transfer (EFT)
electronic health record (EHR) (see
   electronic medical record [EMR])
electronic media claim (EMC)
electronic medical record (EMR)
electronic remittance advice (ERA)
enrollment process
evidence-based practice (EBP)
identifiers
mainframe computer

privacy standards
Promoting Interoperability
security standards
small provider of services
small supplier
telehealth
telemedicine
unusual circumstances

Ellie Farnsworth has found that her associate degree in computer technology has really been a benefit in her career as a health insurance specialist. In her years working for Walden-Martin Family Medical Clinic, she has been involved in the implementation of practice management software for billing and then the big move to using electronic health records that completed the clinic's move to tracking patient information electronically.

Her understanding of the Health Insurance Portability and Accountability Act (HIPAA) has helped to ensure that patient information is protected whether it is when a provider is accessing information for patient care or when information is being transmitted for claims submission.

Ellie has attended a workshop to help understand the impact that the Promoting Interoperability Program will have on Walden-Martin. She views all of the changes as an enjoyable challenge.

INTRODUCTION

Computers have influenced every area of society, particularly medicine, which depends on computers as much or perhaps more than any other type of business. Most healthcare facilities use computers in some part of their day-to-day operations. Some systems are basic and perform just a few simple tasks; others are quite sophisticated, incorporating multiple locations and off-site data storage. Computers have changed record keeping in a way that no other advancement has. Many patient records are stored on computer systems; the computer files are backed up and secured to protect them in the event of computer failure. The medical field depends on computers to keep track of financial records as well. It is very important that patient records and financial information be kept highly secured so that no one can access these data without proper authority. This chapter focuses on the role of computers in medicine, specifically their impact on the health insurance claims and billing processes.

IMPACT OF COMPUTERS ON HEALTH INSURANCE

In years past, it was unusual to find a medical office where computers were used for patient accounting and insurance claims submission. As the age of technology evolved, however, the use of computers became more widespread. From a health insurance perspective, computers are now used for:

- Enrolling an individual in a health plan
- Paying health insurance premiums
- Checking eligibility
- Obtaining authorization to refer a patient to a specialist
- Processing claims
- Electronic medical records (EMRs)
- Notifying a provider about the payment of a claim

However, as computer technology advanced, it became clear that the health information being transmitted through computers and the Internet had to be monitored, and laws were needed to protect the security of health information and the privacy of individuals. The US government, under the Health Insurance Portability and Accountability Act (HIPAA) regulations, now mandates that all healthcare information that is electronically transmitted follow specific rules and guidelines to provide this needed security and protection.

 What Did You Learn?

1. List five uses of computers as they relate to healthcare.

ROLE OF HIPAA IN ELECTRONIC TRANSMISSIONS

One of the main reasons Congress enacted HIPAA was to reform health insurance and simplify healthcare administrative processes. The intent of the HIPAA **Administrative Simplification Compliance Act (ASCA)** was to improve the administration of Medicare by taking advantage of the efficiencies gained through electronic claims submission. Provisions of this act require healthcare providers, health plans, and healthcare clearinghouses to use certain standard transaction formats and code sets for the electronic transmission of health information. These requirements also apply to healthcare providers who transmit health information in electronic form in connection with the transactions covered in the ASCA rule. As usage of electronic transmissions of healthcare information increased, privacy and security regulations were adopted to enhance the privacy protections and security measures directed at health information.

One of the goals of ASCA was to reduce the number of forms and methods of completing claims and other payment-related documents and to use a universal identifier for providers of healthcare. Another goal was to increase the use and efficiency of computer-to-computer methods of exchanging standard healthcare information. The five specific areas of administrative simplification addressed by HIPAA are as follows:

- **Electronic data interchange (EDI)** is the electronic transfer of information in a standard format between two entities. EDI allows business entities to exchange

HIPAA Tip

The Administrative Simplification Compliance Act's (ASCA's) compliance date for the "rule" was 2003. The "rule" requires all initial claims for reimbursement under Medicare to be submitted electronically, with limited exceptions. The "rule" further states that no payment may be made under Part A or Part B of the Medicare program for any expenses incurred for items or services for which a claim is submitted in a non-electronic form. Consequently, unless the medical practice fits one of the exceptions (listed later in this chapter), any paper claim that is submitted to Medicare will not be paid. In addition, any medical facility determined to be in violation of this rule may be subject to claim denials, overpayment recoveries, and applicable interest on overpayments.

information and transact business in a rapid and cost-effective way. Transactions included within HIPAA consist of standard electronic formats for enrollment, eligibility, payment and remittance advice (RA), claims, health plan premium payments, health claim status, and referral certification and authorization.

- **Code sets** include data elements used to uniformly document the reasons patients are seen and procedures or services provided to them during healthcare encounters. HIPAA adopted specific code sets for diagnosis and procedures to be used in all healthcare transactions.
  - HCPCS (ancillary services/procedures)
  - CPT-4 (physicians' procedures)
  - CDT (dental terminology)
  - ICD-10-CM (diagnoses codes for physicians and outpatient facilities)
  - ICD-10-PCS (inpatient hospital procedures)
  - NDC (national drug codes)

  A link to the Transaction and Code Sets website can be found under "Websites to Explore" at the end of this chapter.
- **Identifiers** are the numbers used in the administration of healthcare to distinguish individual healthcare providers, health plans, employers, and patients. These identifiers must be used in all transactions, as required by the HIPAA standard. Over time, identifiers are intended to simplify the administrative processes, such as referrals and billing; improve accuracy of data; and reduce costs.
- **Security standards** need to be developed and adopted for all health plans, clearinghouses, and providers to follow and to be required at all stages of transmission and storage of healthcare information to ensure integrity and confidentiality of the records at all phases of the process, before, during, and after electronic transmission.
- **Privacy standards** are intended to define appropriate and inappropriate disclosures of individually identifiable health information and how patient rights are to be protected.

ASCA made it compulsory for all Medicare claims to be submitted electronically with certain exceptions (see "Medicare and Electronic Claims Submission" later in this chapter). These electronic claims must be in a format that complies with the appropriate standard adopted for national use.

What Did You Learn?

1. List the five specific areas of administrative simplification addressed by the Health Insurance Portability and Accountability Act (HIPAA).

ELECTRONIC DATA INTERCHANGE

EDI is the exchange of data in standardized electronic format directly from a computer system in one facility to that in another. EDI offers easy and inexpensive communication of information throughout the healthcare community. In medical facilities, EDI can be used in the conversion and replacement of paper-based documents (e.g., patient records) with electronic equivalents. In the case of insurance claims, EDI is the electronic exchange of information between the provider's office and a third-party payer.

Imagine This!

Electronic transmission began during the 1960s, initially in the transportation industries, when standardization of documents became necessary, and the US Transportation Data Coordinating Committee (TDCC) was formed to coordinate the development of translation rules among four existing sets of industry-specific standards. A further step toward standardization came with the creation of standards for the American National Standards Institute (ANSI), which gradually extended and replaced the standards created by the TDCC.

BENEFITS OF ELECTRONIC DATA INTERCHANGE

EDI leads to faster transfer of data, fewer errors, instant document retrieval, and less time wasted on exception handling, resulting in a more streamlined communication process. Benefits of EDI can be achieved in areas such as inventory management, transport, and distribution; administration and cash management; and, in this case, transmission of healthcare information data. EDI offers the prospect of simple and inexpensive communication of structured information throughout the healthcare community.

HIPAA Tip

The Health Insurance Portability and Accountability Act (HIPAA) has set standards for the electronic transmission of healthcare data. Healthcare service providers have the option of sending client medical billing data electronically to a health plan (or payer), but if so, the data must be in a HIPAA-compliant format. The health plan must be able to receive and process the data and respond electronically, likewise in a HIPAA-compliant format.

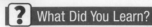
What Did You Learn?

1. What is EDI?
2. List three benefits of EDI.

ELECTRONIC CLAIMS PROCESS

We learned in Chapter 6 that there are two basic methods for submitting health insurance claims: using the universal CMS-1500 paper claim form and submitting claims electronically. Also, with few exceptions, ASCA prohibits payment of services or supplies that a provider did not bill to Medicare electronically. This section discusses various aspects of electronic claims processing.

METHODS AVAILABLE FOR FILING CLAIMS ELECTRONICALLY

The electronic claims process incorporates the use of EDI. There are three ways to submit claims electronically:

1. **Direct data entry (DDE)** (also called *carrier direct*): Accomplished using practice management software to submit electronic claims directly from the provider's office to a specific carrier via a modem. (Practice management software must support this function.) File Transfer Protocol (FTP) is a commonly used method of claims transmission allowing the provider to dial in and transmit a compressed claims file to certain health insurance carriers (e.g., Blue Cross and Blue Shield). With FTP, a provider may also retrieve audit trails and remittances.

2. **Clearinghouse:** The provider sends claims to a clearinghouse electronically. The claim information is entered and edited for errors. The clearinghouse sorts the claims by payer and transmits them to the various insurance companies using the specific formats required by each.

3. **Billing service:** A company files claims on the provider's behalf for a fee, usually a per-claim charge. The provider supplies the billing service with the necessary claims documentation, which the billing service keys into a computer and submits to the appropriate third-party payer electronically. Billing services typically offer other services, such as keeping current with rapidly changing Medicare and insurance laws.

To send claims electronically, the medical practice needs a computer, modem, and HIPAA-compliant software.

Note: Claim submission methods are discussed in more detail in Chapter 6.

ENROLLMENT

Whether the medical practice chooses to use a clearinghouse or submit claims directly to the insurance carrier, it needs to go through an **enrollment process** before submitting claims. This process is necessary so that the business that receives the claims can create a compatible information file about the practice in its computer system to process claims. Most government and many commercial carriers require enrollment. Some also require that the practice sign a contract before sending any claims. The enrollment process usually takes several weeks to complete, and providers usually are required to submit "test" claims before the conversion from paper claims can be completed. The biggest obstacle to getting set up for electronic claims processing is the time that it takes for approval from state, federal, and, in some cases, commercial or health maintenance organization carriers.

ELECTRONIC CLAIMS CLEARINGHOUSE

As discussed in Chapter 6, an **electronic claims clearinghouse** is a business entity that receives claims from several medical facilities and consolidates them so that one transmission containing multiple claims can be sent to each insurance carrier. More specifically, a clearinghouse serves as an intermediary between medical practices and the insurance companies, facilitating the electronic exchange of information between the facilities.

Fig. 16.1 is a flow chart of electronic claims transmission through a clearinghouse.

 Imagine This!

Anthony Skovoski, a radiologist with Mt. Clair Hospital, has an in-house computer set up so that the hospital can transmit x-ray images electronically to him at home. On days that Dr. Skovoski is not at work, the hospital can transmit images directly to his house, and he can read them and generate a written report within minutes, avoiding a 40-minute commute to the hospital. If Dr. Skovoski needs information from the patient's health record, he can also access that from his secure home computer.

DIRECT DATA ENTRY CLAIMS

Submitting claims directly to a specific insurance carrier, referred to as *DDE claims*, is a little more complex. As with a claims clearinghouse, most government carriers and many commercial carriers require enrollment before submitting DDE claims electronically. The medical facility also needs software from each insurance carrier to which it will be submitting claims. Most carriers have their own software or can recommend someone who supports direct transmissions within range of the medical facility. With DDE, the health insurance professional can log on to the website of a specific insurance carrier (e.g., TRICARE) and key claims directly into its system.

CLEARINGHOUSE VERSUS DIRECT

Unless the medical facility submits insurance claims to primarily one carrier and has well-trained staff members to handle multiple carrier software, an electronic

Medical Billing Flow Chart

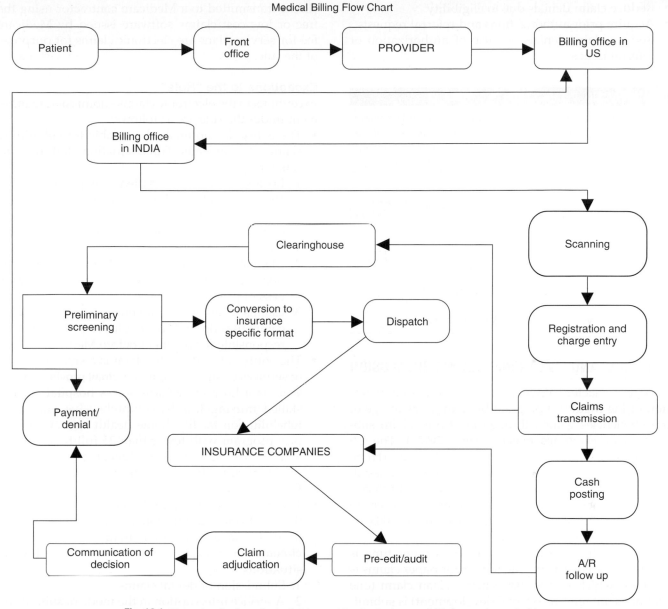

Fig. 16.1 Example of a flow chart of claim sent to clearinghouse. *A/R*, Accounts receivable.

claims clearinghouse might be a better choice than direct carrier submission. If the practice submits claims primarily to one carrier, it may be better off going direct to that carrier. Whichever method the facility chooses, claims are processed much faster and reimbursement time is shortened using electronic claims submission compared with paper claims.

> **! Stop and Think**
>
> Fairview Geriatric Care Center sees only patients on Medicare. Hattie Carmichael, the health insurance professional at Fairview, must make a recommendation at the next staff meeting whether to submit claims through a clearinghouse or use DDE. Which method of claims submission do you think Hattie should choose?

ADVANTAGES OF FILING CLAIMS ELECTRONICALLY

There are many advantages to filing claims electronically. EDI transmissions typically:

- Result in faster, more efficient claim submissions with fewer errors
- Provide immediate notification if a claim has been accepted or rejected and why
- Allow faster processing (and ultimately payment) of claims
- Generate electronic remittance advices (ERAs) from health plans and quickly and accurately post them to the accounting system of the practice automatically
- Provide claims status information reports
- Use a universal set of codes with all health plans

- Reduce claim denials due to eligibility
- Acquire prior authorizations and referral requests
- Reduce claim denials because of authorization or referral issues

---

◎ HIPAA Tip

Under the rules set forth in the Health Insurance Portability and Accountability Act (HIPAA), electronic claims may include only "standard medical code sets" (e.g., ICD-10 diagnostic codes, CPT codes, Medicare HCPCS codes).

? What Did You Learn?

1. What are the two basic ways to submit claims electronically?
2. Name the process that needs to be completed before sending claims electronically.
3. When might direct carrier submission be a better choice than a clearinghouse?
4. List five advantages of filing claims electronically.

MEDICARE AND ELECTRONIC CLAIMS SUBMISSION

Congress enacted ASCA to improve the administration of the Medicare program by taking advantage of the efficiencies gained through electronic claim submission or **electronic media claims (EMCs)**. The US Department of Health and Human Services (HHS) published the final rule for the electronic submission of Medicare claims mandated under ASCA. With certain exceptions, ASCA required that all claims sent to the Medicare program on or after October 16, 2003, be submitted electronically.

When billing electronically, disbursement time is greatly reduced. The payment floor for paper claims is 26 days, which means that when a clean claim (one that does not require external development) is submitted, the provider or beneficiary will be eligible to receive payment on the 27th day. In comparison, electronic claims have a 13-day payment floor, which means that clean claims are eligible for payment on the 14th day. With this faster turnaround, follow-up time is minimized.

MEDICARE CLAIMS AND THE "RULE"

Electronic claims submission is required only for initial Medicare claims, including initial claims with paper attachments, submitted for processing by the Medicare administrative contractor (MAC), fiscal intermediary (FI), or carrier that serves the physician, practitioner, facility, supplier, or other healthcare provider. The rule does not require any other transactions (e.g., changes, adjustments, or appeals to the initial claim) to be submitted electronically.

Claims submitted via DDE are considered electronic claims for purposes of the rule. In addition, claims transmitted to a Medicare contractor using the free or low-cost claims software issued by Medicare fee-for-service plans are electronic claims for purposes of the rule.

Exceptions to the "Rule"

Exceptions to the electronic claims submission requirement under the rule are as follows:

- The entity has no method available for submitting claims electronically. Three situations fall into this category:
  1. Roster billing: A simplified billing process that allows providers who conduct mass immunizations (e.g., influenza and pneumonia) to submit one claim with a list of the Medicare beneficiaries who were immunized.
  2. Claims for payment under Medicare demonstration projects that test and measure the effectiveness of program changes.
  3. Claims where more than one plan (e.g., workers' compensation and/or employer health plan) is responsible for payment before Medicare.
- The entity submitting the claim is a small provider of services or small supplier. A **small provider of services** is a hospital, critical access hospital (CAH), skilled nursing facility, comprehensive outpatient rehabilitation facility, home health agency, or hospice program with fewer than 25 full-time equivalent (FTE) employees. A **small supplier** is a physician, practitioner, facility, or supplier with fewer than 10 FTE employees.
- The Secretary of HHS finds that a waiver of the electronic submission requirement is appropriate because of unusual circumstances. **Unusual circumstances** exist in any one of the following situations:
  1. Submission of dental claims
  2. A service interruption in the mode of submitting the electronic claims that is outside the control of the submitting facility, but only for the period of the interruption and subject to the specific requirements set forth under the rule
  3. On demonstration to the satisfaction of the Secretary of HHS that other extraordinary circumstances exist that prevent the submission of electronic claims

Other than these exceptions, ASCA states that no payment may be made under Parts A and B of the Medicare program for claims submitted in nonelectronic form. Entities that fail to comply with the rule may be subject to claim denial, overpayment recovery, and applicable interest on overpayments. HHS does not intend to broaden these limited exceptions.

To keep up to date on Medicare's electronic claims submission requirements, visit http://cms.gov periodically.

Stop and Think

Margaret Turner, a family practice physician, runs a health clinic in Flint County, which is located in a rural area of the Midwest. Besides herself, Dr. Turner employs a physician assistant, a registered nurse, a laboratory technician, two full-time medical assistants, and a part-time bookkeeper. Dr. Turner hires a private billing service (which has 16 full-time employees) to handle all of the clinic's billing and insurance claims. Based on the US Department of Health and Human Services (HHS) rule, does Dr. Turner's facility qualify as an exempt entity?

 Imagine This!

Clark Emmerson, a health insurance professional with Loveland Health Center, sends all of the center's insurance claims to RapidServ Clearinghouse. RapidServ performs an edit check on each claim and redistributes claims in batches to the appropriate carriers. On one particular batch, a computer error resulted in the employer identification number being left off the claims. RapidServ caught the error, corrected it, and sent the claims on without having to return them to Clark for completion.

 What Did You Learn?

1. To what entities is the ASCA final rule applicable?
2. To what types of claims does the rule not apply?
3. Give an example of an "unusual circumstance" for which waiver of electronic submission might apply.

ADDITIONAL ELECTRONIC SERVICES AVAILABLE

In addition to submitting claims electronically, several other electronic services are available to healthcare professionals.

TELECOMMUNICATION TECHNOLOGIES IN MEDICINE

We talked briefly about **telehealth** in Chapter 5. Although it is a relatively new concept, it is gaining acceptance in the medical community. The Health Resources and Services Administration defines telehealth as the use of electronic information and telecommunications technologies to support long-distance clinical healthcare and administrative services. Technologies include videoconferencing, the Internet, store-and-forward imaging (the transfer of data from one site to another through the use of a camera or similar device), streaming media, and wireless communications.

Telehealth is different from telemedicine because it refers to a broader scope of remote healthcare services than telemedicine. Whereas **telemedicine** refers specifically to remote clinical services, telehealth can refer to remote nonclinical services, such as provider training, administrative meetings, and continuing medical education, in addition to clinical services.

With Medicaid, telemedicine seeks to improve a patient's health by permitting two-way, real-time interactive communication between the patient and the healthcare provider located at a distant site. This type of electronic communication involves the use of interactive telecommunications equipment such as audio and video equipment.

Telemedicine is viewed as a cost-effective alternative to the more traditional face-to-face way of providing medical care (e.g., face-to-face consultations or examinations between provider and patient) that states can choose to cover under Medicaid. It is important to note that the federal Medicaid statute does not recognize telemedicine as a distinct service.

ELECTRONIC FUNDS TRANSFER

Electronic funds transfer (EFT), like direct deposit, is a system whereby data representing money are moved electronically between accounts or organizations. When insurance claims are submitted electronically, many carriers transfer the payments directly into the provider's bank account rather than mailing a check, allowing immediate use of the funds. There are several advantages to receiving insurance payments via EFT rather than paper checks. EFT:

- Reduces the amount of paper
- Eliminates the risk of paper checks being lost or stolen in the mail
- Saves time and eliminates the hassle of going to the bank to deposit checks
- Speeds up funds getting to the provider's bank account, where they can be used or can start earning interest immediately, whereas paper checks can take up to a week to process

To enroll in the Medicare direct deposit program or the direct deposit program of another carrier, the provider must contact the specific payer and ask for an EFT enrollment form, fill it out, and mail it back. To help ensure the validity of deposit information, the form must have original signatures (no copies, facsimiles, or stamped signatures) and include a copy of a canceled or voided check for the bank and the account in which the provider wants the monies deposited. Fig. 16.2 shows a typical form used to authorize EFT.

ELECTRONIC REMITTANCE ADVICE

In addition to EFT, Medicare and other carriers offer an **electronic remittance advice (ERA)**. An ERA allows the provider's office to receive explanations of benefits (EOBs) or RAs electronically. With an ERA, payments can be posted automatically to patient accounts, allowing the health insurance professional to update accounts receivable much more quickly and accurately than if he or she had to post the payments manually. Fig. 16.3 is an example form authorizing the carrier to transmit an RA electronically.

Electronic Funds Transfer (EFT) Form

Please choose one of these options:

☐ Elect EFT payments ☐ Change EFT information ☐ Terminate EFT payments

Name of Brokerage Firm: _____

Name of Broker: _____

Business Address: _____

City: _____ State: _____ Zip Code: _____

Phone Number: _____

Please attach a voided check, if available. When providing the Account and Routing/Transit Numbers, please refer to the series of numbers located at the bottom of your check and insert those numbers located between the symbols shown. For your reference, please see the sample check on the reverse side of this form.

Type of Account: ☐ Business Account   or   ☐ Personal Account   *(check one)*
                   ☐ Checking   or   ☐ Savings   *(check one)*

Name(s) on Account: _____
Please list all names that appear on the account

Account Number: ⑊ _____ ⑊"

Name of Financial Institution: _____

City: _____ State: _____

Routing/Transit Number: ⑊ ☐ ☐ ☐ ☐ ☐ ☐ ☐ ☐ ⑊

__IMPORTANT NOTE:__ It is the applicant's responsibility to ensure that the information provided on this form is complete and accurate. _____ will not be responsible and shall be held harmless for errors made in EFT payments that are a result of inaccurate or incomplete information provided on this form. In no event and under no circumstances will _____ liability exceed the amount of the EFT payments in question.

_____   _____   _____   _____
Signature of Account Owner   Date   Signature of Brokerage Firm Authorized Representative   Date

_____   _____
Print Name   Print Name

_____   _____
Title   Title

To protect the privacy of your financial information, please do not fax or e-mail completed forms. Please mail your signed and completed forms to the following address: **Health Care, Inc., Treasury Department, 93 Fourth Street, Anytown, MA 09080**

For Internal Use Only:	Vendor ID #

Fig. 16.2 Example of an electronic funds transfer (EFT) form.

Authorization for Electronic Transmission
of AHCCCS Fee-For-Service Remittance Advice

I Hereby request and authorize the AHCCCS Administration to transmit my Fee-For-Service Remittance Advice via the Internet to the electronic mail (email) address listed below. I understand that I will no longer receive a paper copy of my Remittance Advice once I begin receiving my Remittance Advice electronically.

I understand that although my Remittance Advice will be transmitted electronically, my reimbursement check(s) will continue to be delivered by the U.S. Postal Service to the pay-to address(es) on file with the AHCCCS Administration Provider Registration Unit.

I understand that it is my responsibility to notify the AHCCCS Administration Provider Registration Unit in writing of any change in my email address.

Provider/Group Name: _____

AHCCCS Provider Identification Number: _____

Street Address: _____

City: _____   State: _____   ZIP Code: _____

Telephone: ( ) _____   Fax: ( ) _____

Name of Contact Person: _____

Email address: _____

Signature of Provider
or Authorized Representative: _____

Date: _____

Mail this form to: AHCCCS Provider Registration Unit
MD 8100
701 E. Jefferson St.
Anytown, XY 85034

or

Fax this form to: AHCCCS Provider Registration Unit
(602) 256-xxxx

Please allow 10 working days for implementation of this change.

Fig. 16.3 Example authorization for an electronic remittance advice (ERA).

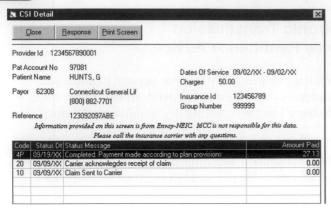

Fig. 16.4 Example of an electronic claims status information advice.

If a medical facility chooses to receive a Medicare ERA, it first must have its computer system programmed using the most recent Centers for Medicare and Medicaid Services (CMS) ANSI specifications (available on the CMS website). When a practice begins receiving payment reports electronically, it may choose to discontinue receiving the paper copy.

The electronic capabilities of many third-party payers and clearinghouses include periodic claim status reports (Fig. 16.4), which give a detailed list of claims that have to be paid, are pending, or have been denied. These reports can be hard copies or electronically transmitted through the practice software.

> **?** **What Did You Learn?**
>
> 1. What occurs when funds are transmitted electronically?
> 2. List two advantages of EFT.
> 3. What is one advantage of receiving an RA electronically compared with a paper RA?

ELECTRONIC MEDICAL RECORD

An **electronic medical record (EMR)** is an electronic file wherein a patient's health information is stored in a computer system. Synonymous terms for EMR include *electronic patient record (EPR), electronic health record (EHR),* and *computerized patient record (CPR).*

The use of EMRs to store patient health information is becoming increasingly prevalent in today's healthcare environment. The information contained in EMRs varies greatly in type—ranging from simple and routine clinical data to sophisticated medical images. An EMR typically includes the following components:

- *Patient demographics*—name, address, telephone numbers, insurance information, etc.
- *Patient's history*—including past encounters, medications, procedures, referrals, and vital statistics
- *Transaction capability*—such as ordering of laboratory tests, medical procedures, and prescriptions

- *Administrative functionality*—including invoice generation, payment requests, payer documentation compliance, and clinical research data compilation

There are obvious benefits to be gained from being able to store, ask questions of, and exchange medical information electronically among various healthcare sites. For example, EMRs can improve patient care by:

- Reducing the incidence of medical error by improving the accuracy and clarity of medical records
- Making the health information immediately available, reducing duplication of tests and delays in treatment
- Keeping both providers and patients better informed to make better decisions

With the advances in technology, some professional offices and hospitals use electronic media to save money and space. The EMR also can support other care-related activities directly or indirectly through various interfaces, including evidence-based decision support (also known as **evidence-based practice [EBP]**, quality management, and outcomes reporting).

Note: EBP is the integration of the healthcare provider's clinical expertise (experience, education, and skills), patient values, and the best research evidence into the decision-making process for patient care.

Despite the alleged advantages, not all offices are ready to change completely over to electronic files. However, many are willing to use one of two types of "hybrid" medical records, which are discussed in the following paragraphs.

COMBINATION RECORDS

Combination records allow the amount of paper records to be reduced because some of the documents are stored electronically and some are kept in paper form. Any record types that can be created electronically, such as chart notes, test results, and prescription records, are stored as electronic records for easy access. Other documents that were originally created on paper—consent forms and correspondence—are kept in paper form. It is up to each office to determine which records are kept on paper and which are kept in electronic form.

DIGITAL IMAGING HYBRID

If the goal of a healthcare office is to migrate completely to an EMR system, a **digital imaging hybrid** may be a good choice. For this type of medical record keeping, many of the documents are maintained in their paper form, but to save space and time when trying to locate a specific record, the paper documentation is scanned and digitally filed into a computer system. In some cases, the paper documentation may be disposed of, or the office may choose to store the physical documents offsite in case they are needed in the future.

Although storing medical records electronically saves space and allows for easier access to the healthcare staff, some professionals worry about the possibility of an electrical outage, viruses, hacking, or other computer issues. If such a problem occurs, no one would be able to access the electronic records. For this reason, some providers are uncomfortable with transferring completely to an electronic system. Using a hybrid system provides the best of both worlds: keeping the paper records just in case but providing the easy access of an electronic system.

POTENTIAL ISSUES

Two of the major disadvantages that some professionals see with changing over to an EMR system are the cost and the amount of time it takes to transfer records. They may be concerned that the transition would disrupt the quality of care they can provide for their patients or concerned about the cost of purchasing, setting up, and maintaining the system and the potential need for additional staff. However, if the transition is planned carefully, it can be a smooth process. The use of a hybrid system allows a facility to take its time transferring records. All records for new patients can be entered immediately into the electronic system; records for established patients can be transferred as each patient is seen or through a gradual, systematic process.

Incompatible Systems

Another issue is that there are many EMR systems on the market. The idea of streamlining patient care across the United States can be achieved only when a single system is used because two or more systems may be incompatible. For example, if a hospital uses a different EMR system than nearby healthcare providers whose patients use that facility, records may not be available to the hospital, or vice versa (records from the hospital may not be available to the providers). Although EMRs may reduce office paperwork, they may not coordinate care between several treating physicians, pharmacies, and allied health workers if different systems are used by each group.

Security Issues

Finally, there is the issue of security of EMRs, which must be completely confidential. Hackers ultimately may be able to penetrate EMRs despite security precautions, and they may release confidential information to others or use it fraudulently. This possibility has both providers and patients worried about how safe EMRs really are.

One of the most significant activities of the healthcare industry is information management. Because of the enormous amount of patient data in existence, computer technology can be an extremely useful tool for the healthcare industry. However, there are obstacles to overcome before computerized patient medical records are used universally in the healthcare environment.

 Imagine This!

The computer system in the Fairview Geriatric Care Clinic was damaged during an electrical storm. Hattie Carmichael, the health insurance professional, had made a digital backup, so no data were lost. However, the computer technical support staff informed her that it would be a week or more before the system would be up and running again. Because this qualified as an "unusual circumstance," Hattie informed InfoData, the local Medicare Part B carrier, that she would be submitting paper claims while the computer was not functional.

FUTURE OF ELECTRONIC MEDICAL RECORDS

Experts predict a bright future for EMRs. Most importantly, it is believed that computerized medical records make it possible to improve the quality of patient care. For example, healthcare providers should be able to make better clinical decisions with immediate access to complete medical histories for their patients—including new patients, returning patients, or patients who see several different providers. Laboratory tests or x-rays downloaded and stored in the patient's EMR make tracking the results easier. Automatic alerts built into the systems can direct attention to possible drug interactions or warning signs of serious health problems. EMR systems allow providers to send prescriptions electronically to pharmacies so patients can get their medications without waiting. It is true that EMRs require an initial investment of time and money; however, providers who have implemented them have reported saving money in the long term. With the efficiencies that EMRs promise, their widespread use has a positive end result—a significant cost savings across our healthcare system.

The ultimate goal in healthcare is an intercommunicative record system, in which an emergency department physician in Florida can treat a vacationing heart patient from the Midwest effectively by "pulling up" his or her records on a computer. This goal has led to the use of the term **electronic health record (EHR)** for those systems that allow for intercommunication. If and when this goal is reached, clinicians would be able to access a timelier and more complete picture of a patient's clinical history, allowing physicians to make better informed healthcare decisions for patients. To be effective, however, the EHR system would have to integrate data from several sources through a linked collection of records and message capabilities. The system also would have to provide decision support, such as reminders, alerts, and clinical pathway information. The EHR must serve as the provider's primary source of information, including orders and test results. With this approach, all the user needs to be fully operational are a browser (Internet Explorer, Firefox, Chrome, etc.) and an Internet service provider.

Need for a Comprehensive Solution

EHRs are a critical tool to support changes necessitated by the massive transformation of the US healthcare system under the Affordable Care Act. Higher initial expenditures, system glitches, and failures are, no doubt, inevitable. Health administrators must stay on top of failures, apply successes, and adapt to challenges to what promises to be an ongoing and developing issue in health administration.

If an EMR system is to provide a comprehensive solution for today's healthcare environment, it should streamline workflow efficiency, improve adherence to treatment standards, provide detailed financial practice analysis, enhance patient education and interaction, and optimize compliance with regulatory and managed care guidelines. Claims submission, physician referrals, patient records, and scheduling information are among the pieces of administrative data that providers could send through a secure central processing hub. This technology would guarantee that data transactions comply with all regulations mandating the privacy of medical data transfer and would allow a non–Web-enabled application to run centrally over the Internet. The software could be operated as though it were local on the remote user's computer.

There are considerable advantages associated with this process. With a mobile device, personal computer, or laptop, users can access and, if authorized, update medical information. Some large medical centers already offer such services to their physician groups. This service allows the emergency department physician to find a patient's chart or laboratory reports immediately.

PRIVACY CONCERNS OF ELECTRONIC MEDICAL RECORDS

As mentioned, both providers and patients want assurances that data transferred electronically would not become vulnerable and would not fall into the wrong hands. To address this, the American Medical Association, in collaboration with microchip maker Intel, has introduced an encrypted identification code that can keep Internet transactions private and patients' rights protected. As consumers explore online EMR possibilities and begin to trust that online healthcare can be kept as confidential as banking accounts, the market can explore its full potential, enabling the healthcare industry to realize its benefits.

 What Did You Learn?

1. What are EMRs?
2. Explain the two options of hybrid medical records.
3. What are two important concerns regarding EMRs?

MEDICARE ACCESS AND CHIP REAUTHORIZATION ACT OF 2015 (MACRA)

This section describes relatively new legislation that went into effect on April 16, 2015, with subsequent deadlines for various phases of the law from HHS and CMS. Referred to as **Promoting Interoperability**, it replaces an earlier program called "Meaningful Use." Meaningful Use was defined by the use of a certified EHR technology in a meaningful manner (e.g., electronic prescribing), ensuring that the certified EHR technology connects in a manner that provides for the electronic exchange of health information to improve the quality of care.

MACRA was designed to eliminate the fee-for-service reimbursement system, replacing it with a structure that rewards high-value patient care and efficiency. MACRA made three important changes to how Medicare pays providers.

- The law repealed the Sustainable Growth Rate formula that determined Medicare payments for providers' services.
- Participating providers are now paid based on the quality and effectiveness of care given.
- MACRA combined existing quality reporting programs into one new system.

CHANGES IN REPORTING THROUGH MACRA

For the 2019 calendar year Performance Period, CMS reduced the types of data that providers need to report from 15 to 10. The remaining 10—to be reported through a new CMS Web Interface—include measures for such things as breast cancer, colorectal cancer, depression, and risk for falls.

MACRA creates a timeline for merit-based reimbursement from 2015 until 2025, when payment adjustments will reach 9% and beyond through alternate payment methods (APMs). APMs introduce new ways for CMS to reimburse healthcare providers for care they provide to Medicare beneficiaries. These include paying new kinds of provider groups and approaches, such as accountable care organizations, patient-centered medical facilities, and bundled payment models, and paying lump sum reimbursement to certain participating providers.

WHAT IS INTEROPERABILITY IN HEALTHCARE?

In the early days of computer usage in healthcare (formerly referred to as information technology, or IT), clinical documentation was done in mainframe computers that acted as a central processing unit for many workstations and terminals connected with it. A **mainframe computer** is used to process large amounts of data. It can control thousands of users. Originally, the data shared from these platforms were typically to billing services. As healthcare IT evolved, competing systems were built on different platforms with various programming languages and by people who had different ideas about what these systems should focus on. Over the years, the number and scope of connected systems has increased considerably. Today, a modern hospital typically has more than 100 systems that need to communicate with each other, as well as an increasing number of devices within the healthcare setting. This means that healthcare IT systems need to become more proficient at exchanging data among numerous devices and other systems. This concept is called clinical interoperability.

THE IMPORTANCE OF PROMOTING INTEROPERABILITY

To review, interoperability is the ability of healthcare IT systems and devices to exchange, interpret, and store data using common standards. For two systems to be considered interoperable, they need to be able to exchange data and present it in a way that is useful to healthcare providers and clinicians. The clinical environment is complex, with different practices in each setting. Interoperability should remove complexity or manual steps on the part of people using the technology. It must bring useful information closer to the point where that information is used to deliver care or make decisions. Otherwise, interoperability is just another catchword.

Recognizing the need to move quickly to overcome the fragmentation of various healthcare technologies, interoperability has been advanced by the Office of the National Coordinator for Health Information Technology (ONC). In 2014 the ONC released a 10-year plan to achieve interoperability in the United States by 2024. The five primary benefits of interoperability in healthcare are:

1. Increases productivity and reduces costs
2. Provides better public health data
3. Results in reduced errors
4. Improves patient privacy
5. Improves the patient experience

> **❗ Stop and Think**
>
> An example of interoperability is the development of infusion pump interfaces. An infusion pump is a medical device that is programmed to deliver fluids or medications at calculated rates through an IV to a patient. The medication formula is programmed into the pump to ensure the correct dosage and duration of the medication formula. Prior to this innovation, the calculations were written on a printed order and then programmed into the device by a nurse. There are now interfaces that transmit the medication calculations from a hospital electronic health record (EHR) system to the pump. The process includes safety checks that require human confirmation of the calculation before the medication is started.
>
> Wearable technology is another effective way to achieve healthcare interoperability. Some examples of such wearable diagnostic and assistive devices are the *cancer-monitoring iTBra patches*, which detect metabolic changes in heat that correlate to breast tumor cellular activity; the *L'Oreal UV sensor*, which measures ultraviolet (UV) exposure; and the *Owlet baby monitoring sock*, which tracks oxygen levels, heart rate, and sleep.

Source: The Journal of mHealth: *The role of wearable technology in healthcare interoperability* (website). http://www.thejournalofmhealth.com/the-role-of-wearable-technology-in-healthcare-interoperability/

FUNDING FOR PROMOTING INTEROPERABILITY

A noncompetitive funding opportunity restricted to Integrating the Healthcare Enterprise USA supports advancements in the technical standards necessary to achieve interoperability among health IT systems and to reach the milestones identified in the Nationwide Interoperability Roadmap. The program will be funded up to $500,000 for the first year. Further funding is subject to the availability of funds.

To learn more about Promoting Interoperability, go to the CMS website and use the search words "Promoting Interoperability" or log on to the applicable website listed under "Websites to Explore" at the end of this chapter.

> **HIPAA Tip**
>
> Health Insurance Portability and Accountability Act (HIPAA) compliance security standards mandate safeguards for physical storage and maintenance, transmission, and access to individual health information. The standards apply not only to the transactions adopted under HIPAA, but also to all individual health information that is maintained or transmitted. HIPAA gives organizations the flexibility to choose the best security solutions to meet the security and privacy mandates.

> **❓ What Did You Learn?**
>
> 1. Define interoperability in your own words.
> 2. List the five primary benefits of interoperability.
> 3. True or false. There is no funding for providers to work toward interoperability.

SUMMARY CHECKPOINTS

- The age of technology has had a great impact on health insurance. Many functions that were previously performed manually are now done faster and with fewer errors using a computer. Processing claims electronically is one of the biggest changes the computer has brought to claims processing. Advanced technology has also created a concern for the security and privacy of health information.
- The five areas of administrative simplification addressed by HIPAA are as follows:
  - *EDI:* Electronic transfer of information in a standard format between two entities. Transactions included within HIPAA consist of standard electronic formats for enrollment, eligibility, payment and RA, claims, health plan premium payments, health claim status, and referral certification and authorization.
  - *Code sets:* Data elements used to uniformly document the reasons patients are seen and the procedures or services provided to them during healthcare encounters. HIPAA adopted the following specific code sets: HCPCS (ancillary services/procedures), CPT-4 (physicians' procedures), CDT (dental terminology), ICD-10-CM (physician diagnoses), ICD-10-PCS (inpatient hospital procedures), and NDC (national drug codes).
  - *Identifiers:* Numbers that HIPAA requires to be used in the administration of healthcare to distinguish individual healthcare providers, health plans, employers, and patients.

- *Security standards:* Required for all health plans, clearinghouses, and providers to follow at all stages of transmission and storage of healthcare information to ensure integrity and confidentiality of the records at all phases of the process before, during, and after electronic transmission.
- *Privacy standards:* To define appropriate and inappropriate disclosures of individually identifiable health information and how patient rights are to be protected.
- EDI is the exchange of documents in standardized electronic form between business entities, in an automated manner, directly from a computer application in one facility to an application in another. The essential elements of EDI include the following:
  - *Electronic transmission medium,* such as magnetic tapes and disks
  - *Structured, formatted messages based on agreed-upon standards* or a set of rules
  - *Fast delivery* of electronic documents from sender to receiver
  - *Direct communication* between applications
- A clearinghouse acts as an intermediary between the medical facility and the insurance carrier. A clearinghouse receives claims from several medical facilities, checks the claims for errors or omissions, consolidates the claims, and transmits them (usually in batches) to individual insurance carriers.
- Advantages of submitting claims electronically include but are not limited to the following:
  - Faster, more efficient claim submissions with fewer errors
  - Immediate claim status notification
  - Quicker processing (and ultimately faster payment) of claims
  - Fast and accurate posting of ERAs automatically to the practice's accounting system
  - Use of universal code sets with all health plans
  - Reduction of claim denials because of eligibility, authorization, or referral issues
- HHS published the final "rule" for electronic submission of Medicare claims mandated under ASCA. With certain exceptions, ASCA requires that all claims sent to the Medicare Program on or after October 16, 2003, be submitted electronically. This rule is applicable only to providers, practitioners, and suppliers who submit claims under Part A or Part B of Medicare.
- Other electronic services available to the health insurance professional include the following:
  - *EFT* allows data representing money to be moved electronically from one bank account to another. In the case of insurance, reimbursement to providers in the form of EFTs is instantaneous, allowing funds to be immediately available to the medical practice.
  - *ERA* allows Medicare and other carriers to transmit the EOBs or RA to the provider electronically, and payments can be posted directly into patient accounts automatically.
  - *EMR* is an electronic file stored in a computer or other electronic medium containing a patient's health information.
- An EMR is an electronic file wherein a patient's health information is stored in a computer system. Synonymous terms for EMR include EPR, EHR, and CPR. The two types of "hybrid" EMRs are combination records and digital imaging hybrid.
- Potential issues with EMRs are the cost of changing over from paper record and the time it takes to make the transition. Other issues include incompatible computer systems and the possibility of a breach in the security of keeping patient records private.
- Experts predict a bright future for EMRs in that computerized medical records can make it possible to improve the quality of patient care. Although it is true that EMRs require an initial investment of time and money, providers who have implemented them have reported saving money in the long term. Some of the problematic issues—incompatible systems and security breaches—must be resolved.
- With the introduction of MACRA, the focus of EHR technology is interoperability. This allows various IT systems to talk to each other in an efficient and meaningful way. The five benefits of interoperability are:
  - Increases in productivity and reduces costs
  - Provides better public health data
  - Reduces errors
  - Improves patient privacy
  - Improves the patient experience

🔍 Closing Scenario

Ellie recognizes that with the Health Insurance Portability and Accountability Act (HIPAA), patients will depend on people in healthcare to ensure that their health information remains confidential and secure. By understanding and implementing the HIPAA administrative and technical requirements, health insurance specialists can assure patients that their electronic claims will be processed in a timely manner and private health information will be safeguarded. Ellie realizes that one of the important reasons HIPAA was created was to protect the privacy and security of healthcare information that is transmitted electronically; they also realize the importance of HIPAA to healthcare in general.

CHAPTER REVIEW QUESTIONS

1. ASCA's compliance for the "rule" required that:
   a. All claims be submitted electronically.
   b. All Medicare claims be submitted electronically, without exception.
   c. All initial claims for Medicare be submitted electronically, with limited exceptions.
   d. All claims for commercial insurance companies be submitted electronically, but Medicare and Medicaid claims are exempted.

2. The electronic transfer of information in a standard format between two entities is the definition of:
   a. RA.
   b. CMS.
   c. DDE.
   d. EDI.

3. A business entity that receives claims from several medical facilities and consolidates them so that one transmission containing multiple claims can be sent to each insurance carrier is an:
   a. Electronic claims clearinghouse.
   b. Electronic data interchange.
   c. Electronic funds transfer.
   d. Electronic medical record.

4. If a healthcare facility submits insurance claims primarily to one carrier, it is recommend that it submit claims using:
   a. An electronic claims clearinghouse.
   b. Direct data entry.
   c. Electronic funds transfer.
   d. Telehealth.

5. Which of the following is not part of the HIPAA standard medical code sets?
   a. ICD-10-CM
   b. CPT-4
   c. HCPCS
   d. All of the above are part of HIPAA's standard medical code sets.

6. When an organization conducts mass immunizations, such as for influenza, it is considered _____ filing Medicare claims electronically for the immunizations.
   a. Exempt from
   b. Excused from
   c. Excluded from
   d. Discharged from

7. The way to provide clinical health services to remote areas is called:
   a. Telehealth.
   b. Electronic medical record.
   c. Evidence-based practice.
   d. Telemedicine.

8. Advantages of using EFT include all of the following except:
   a. Eliminates the risk of paper checks being lost.
   b. Increases the amount of paper.
   c. Saves time and hassle of going to the bank to deposit checks.
   d. Speeds up funds getting into the provider's bank account.

9. The integration of the healthcare provider's clinical expertise, patient values, and the best research evidence into the decision-making process for patient care is:
   a. EDI.
   b. EBP.
   c. EMR.
   d. EFT.

10. When CMS renamed the Meaningful Use incentive program to _____, it also increased the focus on interoperability and improving patient access to health information.
    a. Promoting Interoperability Program
    b. Electronic Data Interchange
    c. Administrative Simplification and Compliance Act
    d. Telehealth

WEBSITES TO EXPLORE

- For live links to the following websites, please visit the Evolve website at http://evolve.elsevier.com/Beik/today.
- You can read the article "5 Ways Technology Is Transforming Healthcare" at http://www.forbes.com/sites/bmoharrisbank/2013/01/24/5-ways-technology-is-transforming-health-care/#69715bd1e261.
- For more information on individual code sets, browse http://cms.hhs.gov.
- http://www.cms.hhs.gov/ElectronicBillingEDITrans/
- For information on Transaction and Code Set Standards, visit http://www.asha.org/practice/reimbursement/hipaa/electronic/.
- The following websites provide more detailed information about EMRs:
  - http://perspectives.ahima.org/tag/electronic-medical-record/
  - http://perspectives.ahima.org/workflow-and-electronic-health-records-in-small-medical-practices/
  - http://perspectives.ahima.org/snomed-ct-survey-an-assessment-of-implementation-in-emrehr-applications/
- The following weblink provides in-depth information on Meaningful Use and Promoting Interoperability, the program that replaced it: https://www.cdc.gov/ehrmeaningfuluse/index.html.
- For more information on Promoting Interoperability, visit https://www.cms.gov/Regulations-and-Guidance/Legislation/EHRIncentivePrograms/index.html?redirect=/EHRincentiveprograms.

Author's Note: Due to the dynamic nature of the Internet, web addresses and/or links provided in this chapter may have changed since publication and may no longer be valid. In such cases, students should select comparable search words to access related sites.

17 Reimbursement Procedures: Getting Paid

Chapter Outline

Chapter Objectives

After completion of this chapter, the student should be able to:

1. List and explain the various types of reimbursement.
2. Discuss the Medicare prospective payment system (PPS) and how it works.
3. Outline various other systems for determining reimbursement: value-based payment modifiers (VBPMs), diagnosis-related groups (DRGs), ambulatory payment classifications (APCs), and resource utilization groups (RUGs).
4. Summarize the transition of Medicare to a resource-based relative value scale (RBRVS).
5. Discuss the reasons reimbursement systems are important to health insurance professionals.
6. Describe the responsibilities of peer review organizations (PROs) as they relate to the PPS.

7. Identify the various functions that most patient accounting software systems can perform.

8. List the advantages of practice management software that is compliant with the Health Insurance Portability and Accountability Act (HIPAA).

Chapter Terms

accounts receivable aging report

ambulatory payment classifications (APCs)

average length of stay (ALOS)

business associate

capitation

case-mix adjustment

comorbidities

contractual write-off

conversion factor (CF)

cost outliers

covered entity

diagnosis-related group (DRG)

discounted fee-for-service

disproportionate share

DRG grouper

fee-for-service (FFS)

geographic practice cost index (GPCI)

home health PPS

inpatient prospective payment system (IPPS)

inpatient psychiatric facility PPS

inpatient rehabilitation facility (IRF) PPS

labor component

long-term care hospital (LTCH) PPS

managed care organizations (MCOs)

nonlabor component

outpatient prospective payment system (OPPS)

packaging

peer review organization (PRO)

per diem rates

principal diagnosis

prospective payment system (PPS)

reimbursement

relative value scale (RVS)

relative weight (RW)

resource-based relative value scale (RBRVS)

resource utilization groups (RUGs)

secondary diagnoses

short-stay outlier

skilled nursing facility (SNF) PPS

standardized amount

Tax Equity and Fiscal Responsibility Act (TEFRA)

usual, customary, and reasonable (UCR)

value-based payment modifier (VBPM)

value-based programs

 Opening Scenario

As a health insurance specialist, Dave Brown has a solid understanding of the various types of reimbursement models being used by the different insurance companies and federal insurance programs. The alphabet soup of acronyms—PPS, APCs, RUGs, DRGs—can be confusing for some, but Dave knows that by taking the time to understand them, he can provide the best service to his employer and the patients.

Dave was talking to one of the new employees in the business office and said, "Reimbursement systems are constantly changing, and new ones are being added. Granted, they may be complicated and confusing, but you have to stay on top of things to really do the job right or you'll find yourself being replaced by someone who is better educated." By taking continuing education classes and attending workshops Dave is prepared to make any needed changes when a new reimbursement model comes along. His supervisor at Walden-Martin Family Medical Clinic appreciates Dave's sense of responsibility when it comes to being a health insurance specialist.

UNDERSTANDING REIMBURSEMENT SYSTEMS

To understand fully the entire health insurance picture and how fees are established, the health insurance professional should be aware of the various reimbursement systems, their structure, and how they affect health insurance in general. Understanding reimbursement systems is important in making the most of payment opportunities. Current reimbursement systems are based on five elements that affect the dollar amount paid:

- Third-party payer
- Healthcare setting and provider
- Coding system (International Classification of Diseases [ICD]/Current Procedural Terminology [CPT])
- Data set used
- Encoder, grouper, and data entry software used

Because reimbursement systems can be challenging, every healthcare facility ideally should assign someone the responsibility of being the "reimbursement expert." The health insurance professional might fit this role best, and he or she should be prepared to take on this responsibility. The rules are constantly changing, with the frequent introduction of new payment formulas, and it takes diligence and dedication to keep current with these changes. Small adjustments in the payment rates can make a big difference in practice income. The following sections describe the various types of reimbursement and their fee structures. The author has attempted to keep these sections brief; however, extensive information on each type is available on the Internet.

TYPES OF REIMBURSEMENT

From an insurance standpoint, the term **reimbursement** means payment to the insured for a covered expense or loss experienced by or on behalf of the insured. More specifically in health insurance, reimbursement is a payment made to a provider or to a patient in exchange for the performance of healthcare services. There are several different types of reimbursement in the healthcare office. Table 17.1 summarizes the common types of reimbursement.

Fee-for-Service

Until the latter part of the 20th century, fee-for-service was the usual method of determining reimbursement in the United States. Chapter 4 defined **fee-for-service (FFS)**, which is a system of payment for healthcare services whereby the provider charges a specific fee (typically the **usual, customary, and reasonable [UCR]** fee) for each service rendered and is paid that fee by the patient or by the patient's insurance carrier. UCR is a fee amount that an insurance carrier accepts based on the prevailing charges made by physicians in a

similar specialty for a particular service or procedure within a specific community or geographic area.

Discounted Fee-for-Service

When a healthcare provider offers services at rates that are lower than UCR fees, that arrangement is called *discounted fee-for-service*. A typical example of **discounted fee-for-service** is when a healthcare provider is a participating provider (PAR) with a preferred provider organization (PPO) and charges patients enrolled in the PPO lower rates in return for certain amenities from the PPO. (See Chapter 9 for details about PPOs.)

Prospective Payment System

A third type of reimbursement is the **prospective payment system (PPS)**. With a PPS, reimbursement is made to the healthcare provider based on predetermined factors (e.g., patient category, type of facility) and not on individual services. PPS is Medicare's system for reimbursing Part A inpatient hospital costs. The amount of payment is determined by the assigned **diagnosis-related group (DRG)**. PPS rates are set at a level intended to cover operating costs for treating a typical inpatient in a given DRG.

The Centers for Medicare and Medicaid Services (CMS) uses a separate PPS for reimbursement to acute inpatient hospitals, home health agencies, hospice, hospital outpatient care, inpatient psychiatric facilities, inpatient rehabilitation facilities, long-term care hospitals (LTCHs), and skilled nursing facilities (SNFs). Payments for each hospital are adjusted for differences in area wages, teaching activity, care to the poor, and other factors. PPS and DRGs are discussed in more detail later. For more detailed information about each specific PPS, see the related link under "Websites to Explore" at the end of this chapter.

Relative Value Units

Many insurance companies reimburse on a fee schedule that is based on relative value units (RVUs). More and more practices are also converting to a provider fee schedule that is based on RVUs. With the use of computers for medical billing, attaching RVUs to each procedure in the system provides the advantage of having a logical explanation for patients who inquire about the cost of their procedure. Patients tend to understand and accept an explanation of how fees based on relative value are arrived at compared with explaining how a UCR fee is determined. In addition, when procedure codes are attached to an RVU, when the practice finds it necessary to increase its charges, staff members can simply increase the conversion factor (CF) rather than go into each procedure in the computer system and reset the charge amount.

Relative Value Scale

The **relative value scale (RVS)**, which was first developed by the California Medical Association in the 1950s, is a method of determining reimbursement for

Table **17.1** Comparison of Reimbursement Methods	
REIMBURSEMENT TYPE	**EXPLANATION**
Fee-for-service	Services or procedures are paid as charged from the Physician Fee Schedule.
Discounted fee-for-service	Services or procedures are paid at insurers' contracted rates.
PPS	Medicare's flat rate reimbursement system for inpatient costs based on predetermined factors for treating a typical patient in a given DRG, such as diagnoses, procedures, or a combination of both. Payments are adjusted for additional variances, such as differences in area wages, teaching activity, and care for the poor.
RBRVS	Payment based on the cost of providing each service divided into three components: physician work, practice expense, and professional liability insurance. Payments are calculated by multiplying the combined costs of a service by a CF (determined by CMS) and adjusted for geographic differences in resource costs.
Capitation	Payment is based on a fixed, per capita amount for each person served without regard to the actual number or nature of services provided.

CF, Conversion factor; *CMS,* Centers for Medicare and Medicaid Services; *DRG,* diagnosis-related group; *PPS,* prospective payment system; *RBRVS,* resource-based relative value scale.

healthcare services based on establishing a standard unit value for medical and surgical procedures. RVS compares and rates each individual service according to the relative value of each unit and converts this unit value to a dollar value. RVS units are based on average charges for a same or similar procedure of all healthcare providers during the time in which the RVS was established and published. The total RVU consists of the following three components:

1. A relative value for *physician work*
2. A relative value for *practice expense*
3. A relative value for *malpractice risk*

Example: For CPT code 29530 (strapping, knee), the physician work RVU is 0.57, the practice expense RVU is 0.41, and the malpractice risk is 0.05.

According to the American Medical Association (AMA), the biggest challenge in developing an RVS-based payment schedule was overcoming the lack of any available method or data for assigning specific values to physicians' work. The Harvard University School of Public Health, in cooperation with CMS, conducted a study that led to the initial relative work values. This nationwide study surveyed physicians to determine the work involved in each of approximately 800 different medical services. More than half of the relative value estimates of almost 6000 services were based directly on findings from the Harvard study.

Values for new and revised procedures that appear in the CPT manual are included in the updated RVS each year. The AMA works in conjunction with national medical specialty societies to develop recommendations for CMS regarding values to be assigned to these new and revised codes.

Resource-Based Relative Value Scale

In 1992 the federal government established a standardized physician payment schedule based on a **resource-based relative value scale (RBRVS)**. In the RBRVS system, payments for services are determined by the resource costs needed to provide them rather than by actual charges. The cost of providing each service is divided into three components: (1) physician work, (2) practice expense, and (3) professional liability insurance (malpractice expense). Payments are calculated by multiplying the combined costs of a service by a CF (a monetary amount that is determined by the CMS). Payments are also adjusted for geographic differences in resource costs. RBRVS is used by many health plans in negotiating fee schedules with in-network physicians. Box 17.1 shows the formula for calculating Medicare RBRVS.

Managed Care Organizations

Managed care organizations (MCOs) vary greatly in their policies and procedures for reimbursement, and laws vary significantly from state to state. Individual MCO contracts have specific restrictions and requirements, and contracts may have rate reductions and discounts of certain types of care (e.g., telephone consultations).

Box 17.1	Formula for Calculating Medicare Resource-Based Relative Value Scale

Work RVU × Work GPCI
+ PE RVU × PE GPCI
+ PLI RVU × PLI GPCI
_____
= Total RVU × CF = Payment

CF, Conversion factor; *GPCI,* geographic practice cost index; *PE,* practice expense; *PLI,* professional liability insurance; *RVU,* relative value unit.

Referral processes typically require prior authorization, and billing procedures with MCOs are often complex.

Capitation

Capitation is a method of payment for healthcare services in which a provider or healthcare facility is paid a fixed, per capita amount for each individual to whom services are provided without regard to the actual number or nature of the services provided to each individual patient. Capitation is a common method of paying physicians in health maintenance organizations (HMOs).

> **? What Did You Learn?**
>
> 1. Define reimbursement.
> 2. List the basic types of reimbursement.
> 3. Explain the difference between fee-for-service and discounted fee-for-service.
> 4. Name the three components that make up the total RVU.
> 5. _____ is a common method of reimbursement in HMOs.

MEDICARE AND REIMBURSEMENT

The **Tax Equity and Fiscal Responsibility Act (TEFRA)** enacted by Congress in 1982 provided for limits on Medicare reimbursement that applied to stays in long-term acute care hospitals. After TEFRA was passed, the fee-for-service–based payment system was replaced with a PPS.

Initially, only Medicare patients were included in the PPS. Later, Medicaid patients were added on a state-by-state basis. As discussed, with the PPS, a predetermined payment level is established primarily based on a patient's diagnoses and services performed, and the healthcare facility receives a set payment. If money spent to care for a patient is less than the PPS payment, the facility is allowed to keep the extra money and makes a profit on the care provided. However, if the money spent to care for a patient is more than the PPS payment, the healthcare organization loses money in caring for the patient.

Medicare presently has three primary reimbursement systems:

- *Prospective payment:* A system of predetermined prices that Medicare uses to reimburse hospitals for inpatient and outpatient services as well as SNFs, rehabilitation hospitals, and home health services.

- *Fee schedules:* Consisting of price lists that Medicare uses to reimburse healthcare providers for the services they provide and other healthcare providers for items and services that are not "bundled" into PPS, such as clinical laboratory tests, durable medical equipment, and some prosthetic devices.
- *Medicare Advantage* (Medicare Part C): Medicare's managed care program in which Medicare pays a set fee to managed care plans to provide care for Medicare beneficiaries.

 Imagine This!

Four different patients visit Dr. Carson Inglewood, a family practice physician, for symptoms of influenza. Dr. Inglewood's charge for an office visit is $150. Tony, a 22-year-old college student, has a commercial policy through the university that accepts fee-for-service charges. Emma, a 36-year-old bank teller, belongs to a preferred provider organization (PPO) that Dr. Inglewood has contracted with at 10% discounted fee-for-service charges. Umberto, a 42-year-old factory worker, has healthcare coverage with a capitated health maintenance organization (HMO). Eunice, a 67-year-old retired teacher, is on Medicare. All four are established patients. Ellen McIntyre, Dr. Englewood's health insurance professional, verifies the individual adjusted charges as follows:

Tony: $150 (usual, customary, and reasonable [UCR] fee)
Emma: $135 (10% discount)
Umberto: $20 (capitation fee per patient per month)
Eunice: $64.50 (Medicare's fee schedule allowed amount)

MEDICARE PROSPECTIVE PAYMENT SYSTEM

A PPS is a method of reimbursement in which payment is made based on a predetermined, fixed amount. The intention of a PPS is to motivate providers to deliver patient care effectively, efficiently, and without overutilization of services. To achieve this, the payment amount for a particular service is calculated based on the classification system of the service (e.g., DRGs for inpatient hospital services). CMS uses a separate PPS for reimbursement to acute inpatient hospitals, hospital outpatient services, SNFs, home health agencies, inpatient rehabilitation facilities, inpatient psychiatric facilities, LTCHs, and hospice.

Congress adopted the PPS to regulate the amount of resources that the federal government spends on medical care for elderly and disabled individuals. The Social Security Amendments of 1983 mandated the PPS for acute hospital care for Medicare patients. The system was intended to encourage hospitals to modify the way they deliver services. Congress had the following four chief objectives in creating the PPS:

1. To ensure fair compensation for services rendered and not compromise access to hospital services, particularly for those who are seriously ill
2. To ensure that the process for updating payment rates would account for new medical technology, inflation, and other factors that affect the cost of providing care

3. To monitor the quality of hospital services for Medicare beneficiaries
4. To provide a method through which beneficiaries and hospitals could resolve problems with their treatment

Under the Medicare PPS, hospitals are paid a set fee for treating patients in a single DRG category, regardless of the actual cost of care for the individual. The DRG system is an inpatient classification structure based on several factors, including principal diagnosis, additional diagnoses, surgical factors, age, sex, and discharge status. In addition to payment adjustments for differences in area wages, teaching activity, care to the poor, and other factors, hospitals may receive payments to cover extra costs associated with atypical patients—patients whose stays are either considerably shorter or considerably longer than average (referred to as **cost outliers**) in each DRG.

Except for acute care hospital settings, Medicare inpatient PPS systems are relatively new and, as a result, will be undergoing gradual revisions.

Some common characteristics of Medicare PPS are the following:

- Prepayment amounts cover defined periods (per diem, per stay, or 60-day episodes).
- Payment amount is based on the unique assessment classifications of each patient.
- It applies only to Part A inpatients (except for HMOs and home health agencies).
- A patient who remains an inpatient can exhaust the Part A benefit and become a Part B case; however, such cases are no longer paid under PPS. (Part B payments for evaluation and treatment visits are determined by the Medicare Physician Fee Schedule.)

 Stop and Think

Referring to the scenario in Imagine This! concerning Dr. Inglewood's practice, what is your reaction to the variation in adjusted charges for the four patients being seen in the same office for the same condition? Do you think it is reasonable that Tony's insurer must pay the full $150, whereas Medicare allows only $64.50 for Eunice's visit?

HOW THE MEDICARE PROSPECTIVE PAYMENT SYSTEM WORKS

In a PPS, payment levels are set ahead of time, or prospectively, and are intended to pay the healthcare provider for a particular group of services. The established payment rate for all services that a patient in an acute care hospital receives during an entire stay is based on a predetermined payment level that is selected on the basis of averages. This means that some providers' actual costs would be above the average payment and some would be below it. Whatever the case, the provider receives only the preset amount, regardless of whether actual costs are more or less than that amount.

Table **17.2** Prospective Payment Systems Comparison

TYPE OF SYSTEM	APPLICABLE SETTING	REIMBURSEMENT BASED ON
DRG	Acute care	Diagnosis and procedures
APC	Ambulatory care	Procedures, using diagnoses to verify medical necessity
RUG	SNFs	MDS, including ADLs index
Home health PPS	Home healthcare	Outcome and assessment information set
IRF PPS	Inpatient rehabilitation facilities	Length of hospital stay and function-related group classification
Hospice	Four levels of care: 1. Routine home care 2. Continuous home care 3. Inpatient respite care 4. General inpatient care	Per diem rate for each level: Geographic wage adjustments determine the only variation in payment rates within each level.

ADLs, Activities of daily living; *APC*, ambulatory payment classification; *DRG*, diagnosis-related group; *IRF*, inpatient rehabilitation facility; *MDS*, minimum data set; *PPS*, prospective payment system; *RUG*, resource utilization group; *SNF*, skilled nursing facility.

CMS has developed several variations of payment systems from the initial PPS currently being used by Medicare and other third-party payers in the United States. Table 17.2 summarizes several of these alternative payment systems for a variety of provider settings. In addition, various PPS systems are discussed briefly in the following paragraphs. Students who want more detailed information about one or more of these PPS systems should visit the website listed under "Websites to Explore" at the end of this chapter.

Acute Inpatient Prospective Payment System

The **inpatient prospective payment system (IPPS)** is the Medicare PPS used for acute care hospital inpatient stays. Under the IPPS, each case is categorized into a DRG with a payment weight assigned to it based on the average resources used to treat patients in that particular DRG. The base payment rate is divided into labor-related and nonlabor shares. The labor-related share is adjusted by the wage index applicable to the area where the hospital is located. This base payment rate is multiplied by the DRG **relative weight (RW)**. Medicare publishes a final rule with revisions to the IPPS every year for the upcoming fiscal year, which goes into effect on October 1, the beginning of the federal government's fiscal year.

Outpatient Prospective Payment System

The **outpatient prospective payment system (OPPS)** is the Medicare PPS used for hospital-based outpatient services and procedures. In most cases, the unit of payment under OPPS is determined by the assignment of ambulatory payment classification (APC) and reimburses a predetermined amount based on similar clinical characteristics and similar costs of the procedure performed. Some new services are assigned to new technology APCs, which are based on similarity of resource use only. As with IPPS, Medicare publishes revisions to OPPS annually that go into effect on January 1 of the following year.

The Affordable Care Act included changes under OPPS regarding certain preventive services for Medicare beneficiaries, which became effective January 1, 2011. This resulted in the elimination of patient cost-sharing requirements (coinsurance and deductible) for most Medicare-covered preventive services, which Medicare now pays in full.

Skilled Nursing Facility Prospective Payment System

The **skilled nursing facility (SNF) PPS** is a per diem reimbursement system for all costs (routine, ancillary, and capital) associated with covered SNF services furnished to Medicare beneficiaries. **Per diem rates** are a hospital's all-inclusive daily rates as calculated by department. SNF payment rates are adjusted for case mix and geographic variation in wages and cover all costs of furnishing covered SNF services.

Home Health Prospective Payment System

The **home health PPS** is the reimbursement system developed by CMS to cover qualifying home health services provided to Medicare beneficiaries. Medicare pays certified home health agencies a predetermined base payment. The payment is adjusted for the health condition and care needs of the beneficiary and for the geographic differences in wages for home health agencies across the United States. The adjustment for the health condition, or clinical characteristics, and service needs of the beneficiary is referred to as the **case-mix adjustment**.

Inpatient Rehabilitation Facility Prospective Payment System

The **inpatient rehabilitation facility (IRF) PPS** is the reimbursement system developed by CMS to cover inpatient rehabilitation services provided to Medicare beneficiaries. To qualify for IRF PPS rates—which are higher than the hospital inpatient PPS rates—an inpatient hospital must establish that at least 60% of its patients meet certain criteria for intensive inpatient rehabilitation. The IRF PPS uses the patient assessment instrument to assign patients to case-mix groups according to their clinical status and resource requirements.

Inpatient Psychiatric Facility Prospective Payment System

Patients who are treated for psychiatric conditions in specialty facilities are covered for 90 days of care per illness with a 60-day lifetime reserve and for 190 days of care in freestanding psychiatric hospitals. Under the **inpatient psychiatric facility PPS**, federal per diem rates include geographic factors, patient characteristics, and facility characteristics. The payment for an individual patient is further adjusted for factors such as the DRG classification, age, length of stay, and the presence of specified **comorbidities** (the presence of one or more disorders or diseases in addition to the primary disorder or disease).

Long-Term Care Hospital Prospective Payment System

The PPS for LTCHs classifies patients into diagnostic groups based on clinical characteristics and expected resource needs of inpatient stays in LTCHs (defined as hospitals with an **average length of stay [ALOS]** greater than 25 days). The patient classification groupings are called *LTC-DRGs*—they are the same DRGs used under the hospital inpatient PPS where each patient stay is grouped into an LTC-DRG based on diagnoses (including **secondary diagnoses**), procedures performed, age, gender, and discharge status. Each LTC-DRG has a predetermined ALOS, or the typical length of stay for a patient classified to the LTC-DRG. Cases assigned to an LTC-DRG are paid according to the federal payment rate, including adjustments.

Hospice Payment System

Under the hospice payment system, each day of care is classified into one of four levels. There is a per diem rate for each of the four levels:

1. Routine home care
2. Continuous home care
3. Inpatient respite care
4. General inpatient care

Geographic wage adjustments determine the only variation in payment rates within each level.

Medicare Advantage Program (CMS Hierarchical Condition Category)

The Medicare Advantage program uses a CMS hierarchical condition category (HCC) risk assessment payment model. This capitation payment model is used to provide payment to MCOs (e.g., HMOs, PPOs) on behalf of Medicare beneficiaries. The CMS HCC risk assessment adjusts beneficiary capitation payments with a risk adjustment methodology using diagnoses to measure relative risk due to health status. Select diagnostic codes are used to define disease groups, which are referred to as *hierarchical condition categories.*

CMS also develops fee schedules for specific providers and services, such as physicians, ambulance services, clinical laboratory services, durable medical equipment, and supplies. You can read more about them on the CMS website at http://www.cms.gov/.

HIPAA Tip

The Health Insurance Portability and Accountability Act (HIPAA) is organized by five subgroups or titles. Titles I and II are the particular HIPAA laws that have the most effect on the healthcare reimbursement process for the medical health insurance professional.

? What Did You Learn?

1. What congressional act provided for limits on Medicare reimbursements for stays in long-term acute care hospitals?
2. List the three primary reimbursement systems for Medicare.
3. Name the federal entity that sets guidelines and rules that affect the entire insurance industry.
4. True or false: Under the Medicare PPS, hospitals are paid a set fee for treating patients in a single DRG category based on the actual cost of care for the individual.
5. Define a *cost outlier.*
6. Identify six types of PPSs.

ADDITIONAL SYSTEMS FOR DETERMINING REIMBURSEMENT

We have learned that until the latter part of the 20th century, fee-for-service was the usual method of determining reimbursement in the United States. As the nation faced an increase in the elderly population and access to healthcare improved, the government enacted legislation to control the increasing cost of healthcare associated with these factors. Out of these federal laws, several new systems of reimbursement appeared (see Table 17.2). In the previous sections, we discussed some of these reimbursement systems. The following paragraphs discuss additional types of systems used today for determining reimbursement.

VALUE-BASED PROGRAMS

The idea behind **value-based programs** is that the provider is rewarded for the quality of care that they provide to patients. CMS's program has a three-part goal:

- Better care for individuals
- Better health for populations
- Lower cost

This concept allows for payment for the quality of care provided, not just the quantity of care provided. CMS has implemented the following value-based programs:

- End-Stage Renal Disease Quality Incentive Program (ESRD QIP)
- Hospital Value-Based Purchasing (VBP) program
- Hospital Readmission Reduction Program (HRRP)

- Value Modifier (VM) Program (also called the Physician Value-Based Modifier or PVBM), discussed next
- Hospital-Acquired Condition (HAC) Reduction Program
- Skilled Nursing Facility Value-Based Program (SNFVBP)
- Home Health Value-Based Program (HHVBP)

Value-Based Payment Modifier

The **value-based payment modifier (VBPM)** adjusts Medicare Physician Fee Schedule (PFS) payments to a physician or group of physicians (identified by their taxpayer identification number [TIN]), based on the quality of care furnished to their Medicare FFS beneficiaries, compared with the cost of care during a performance period.

- The Affordable Care Act requires that the VBPM be applied to specific physicians that the US Department of Health and Human Services (HHS) Secretary determines appropriate starting January 1, 2015, and to all physicians by January 1, 2017.
- The VBPM applies only to physician payments under the Medicare PFS. Reductions in payments to low-performing physicians will fund increases in payments to higher-performing physicians.

Beginning in calendar year 2015, the VBPM affected Medicare payments to physicians in groups of 100 or more eligible professionals (EPs) based on 2013 performance on quality and cost measures. In 2016 the modifier applied to physicians in groups of 10 or more EPs based on 2014 performance. In 2017 the modifier applied to all physicians based on 2015 performance. In addition, for 2015 and 2016, the VBPM did not apply to groups of physicians in which any of the group's physicians participate in the Medicare Shared Savings Program Accountable Care Organizations (ACOs), the testing of the Pioneer ACO model, or the Comprehensive Primary Care Initiative.

DIAGNOSIS-RELATED GROUPS

DRGs have been referred to several times previously in this chapter. This section aids in the understanding of DRGs and their impact on healthcare reimbursement. The DRG used for reimbursement in the PPS of the Medicare and Medicaid healthcare insurance systems is a patient classification system consisting of distinct groupings that provide a means for relating the type of patients that a hospital treats with the costs incurred by the hospital for treating them. DRGs adopted by CMS are defined by diagnosis and procedure codes used in the ICD coding manual, as well as gender, age, sex, treatment procedure, discharge status, and the presence of complications or comorbidities.

The DRG system classifies hospital inpatient cases into categories with similar use of the facility's resources. This system is used as the basis to reimburse hospitals for inpatient services and was established to create an incentive for hospitals to operate more efficiently and more profitably. Under DRGs, a hospital is paid a predetermined, lump-sum amount, regardless of the costs involved, for each Medicare patient treated and discharged. DRGs are organized into major diagnostic categories, which are based on a particular organ system of the body (e.g., musculoskeletal system, nervous system). Only one DRG is assigned to a patient for a single hospital admission. Typically, one payment is made per patient, and that payment is based on the DRG assignment.

The history, design, and classification rules of the DRG system and its application in patient discharge data and updating procedures are published in the *DRG Definitions Manual*, which is available from the CMS, HHS. More detailed information about these different systems is available on the Internet using "DRG Definitions Manual" as search words.

 Imagine This!

Alvin Rictor, a 66-year-old construction worker, underwent a procedure at Mid-Prairie Acute Care Facility to reattach his severed left leg. The hospital's total incurred expense was $12,000 (e.g., staff time, operating room expenses, supplies, anesthesia); however, DRG 209 (major joint and limb reattachment procedures of lower extremity) was assigned, which reimbursed the hospital $9600. As a result, Mid-Prairie Acute Care Facility sustained a $2400 loss on Alvin Rictor's hospital stay.

How Diagnosis-Related Groups Work

We've learned that a patient's DRG categorization depends on the coding and classification of the patient's healthcare information using the ICD coding system, along with other factors. The key piece of information is the patient's **principal diagnosis**—the reason for admission to the acute care facility. The primary procedure to be performed also plays an important part in assigning DRGs. In addition to the coding of the patient's principal diagnosis, the healthcare facility codes and submits information about comorbidities and complications. Also taken into consideration is the patient's principal procedure and any additional operations or procedures done during the time spent in the hospital. The **DRG grouper** (a computer software program that takes the coded information and identifies the patient's DRG category) also considers the patient's age, gender, and discharge status. All of this information together determines the DRG category, which sets the payment dollar amount for the acute inpatient hospital visit.

Assigning a Diagnosis-Related Group to a Patient

To review, the principal diagnosis and principal procedure determine the DRG assignment. Other factors that may play a role in DRG assignment are secondary diagnoses, patient age, the presence or absence of complications or comorbidities, patient sex, and discharge status. Each DRG is assigned an RW and an ALOS.

RWs indicate the relative resource expenditure for the DRG. ALOS is the predetermined number of days of approved hospital stay assigned to an individual DRG. (Referring to the earlier example in Imagine This!, DRG 209 at Mid-Prairie Acute Care Facility has an RW of 2.0782 and an ALOS of 5 days.)

Calculating Diagnosis-Related Group Payments

Calculating DRG payments involves a formula that accounts for the adjustments discussed in the previous section. The DRG weight is multiplied by a **standardized amount**, which is a figure representing the average cost per case for all Medicare cases during the year. The standardized amount is the sum of:

- A **labor component**, which represents labor cost variations in different areas of the United States, and
- A **nonlabor component**, which represents a geographic calculation based on whether the hospital is located in a large urban or other area. The labor component is adjusted by a wage index.

If applicable, cost outliers, **disproportionate share** (payment adjustment to compensate hospitals for the higher operating costs they incur in treating a large share of low-income patients), and indirect medical education payments are added to the formula.

AMBULATORY PAYMENT CLASSIFICATIONS

Ambulatory payment classifications (APCs) were put into effect in August 2000 for hospital outpatient services provided to Medicare beneficiaries as well as enrollees in certain other healthcare plans. Before this system was put into practice, hospital outpatient services were based almost entirely on actual cost. Now, services provided under the hospital OPPS are classified and paid according to APCs. APCs are applied to the full range of ambulatory services, including same-day surgery, hospital emergency department visits, and patient clinics.

APCs are made up of CPT Level I and Health Care Finance Administration (HCFA) Common Procedure Coding System (HCPCS) Level II codes, and each code is assigned to one of the hundreds of individual APCs. Each APC has a prospective (preestablished) payment amount associated with it based on the median cost for all services within that APC group. Hospitals can receive payment on one or more APCs per encounter; however, if no payable code is assigned to the claim, no payment is received.

Services in each APC have similar clinical characteristics, resource use, and cost. Providers receive fixed payments for individual services assigned to the various APC categories. The APC payment rates are adjusted for geographic cost differences, and payment rates and policies are updated annually.

OUTPATIENT CODE EDITOR

The outpatient code editor (OCE) software was developed for the implementation of the Medicare OPPS. The two main functions of the OCE are to assign APCs and identify any errors. In addition, the OCE software performs the following functions when processing a claim:

- Edits claims for accuracy
- Assigns status indicators (SIs)
- Determines if "**packaging**" is applicable[a]
- Applies relevant discount factors

Each claim is represented by a collection of data, which consists of all necessary demographic (header) data, plus all services provided (line items). It is the user's responsibility to organize all applicable services into a single claim record and pass them as a unit to the OCE. The OCE only functions on a single claim and does not have any cross-claim capabilities. The OCE accepts up to 450 line items per claim.

HOW AMBULATORY PAYMENT CLASSIFICATION RATES ARE SET

Payment rates for most medical and surgical services under the APC payment system are determined by multiplying the scaled RW (representing the "relative effort" required to perform a specific procedure that has been prospectively established for the service's clinical APC) by a **conversion factor (CF)** to arrive at a national unadjusted payment for the APC. (The CF is a standard dollar amount that is multiplied by the RW to arrive at the APC-based fee.) The CF translates the weights into payment rates in dollars.

Each CPT/HCPCS code also is assigned an SI, which is a single alpha character (e.g., X, E, S) that specifies how much is paid for a procedure: the full APC payment amount, a discounted payment amount, or no payment (Table 17.3).

Note: Hospital Outpatient Prospective Payment—Final Rule With Comment Period and Final Calendar Year (CY) 2016 Payment Rates, and related links, for each HCPCS code can be found on the CMS.gov website.

Calculating Ambulatory Payment Classification–Based Fees

A unique formula is used to arrive at an APC-based fee. Each APC is assigned an RW. The RW is multiplied by a CF times a discount formula (DF) times the number of paid units:

$$RW \times CF \times DF \times \text{paid units} = \text{APC-based fee}$$

Example:

CPT 71045 (chest x-ray) APC 5521, SI Q3
RW × CF × DF × paid units = APC-based fee
0.7838 (RW) × $45.83 (CF) × 1 (DF) × 1 (paid unit)
= $35.92

APC, Ambulatory payment classification; *CF*, conversion factor; *CPT*, Current Procedural Terminology; *DF*, discount formula; *RW*, relative weight; *SI*, status indicator.

---

[a]The term *packaging* means that reimbursement for certain services or supplies is included in the payment for another procedure or service on the same claim.

Table 17.3   Sample Portion from Addendum B—January 2019

HCPCS CODE	SHORT DESCRIPTOR	CI	SI	APC	RW	PAYMENT RATE	NATIONAL UNADJUSTED COPAYMENT	MINIMUM UNADJUSTED COPAYMENT
G0293	"Non-cov surg proc, clin trial"		Q1	5732	0.4041	$32.12	—	$6.43
G0294	"Non-cov proc, clinical trial"		Q1	5732	0.4041	$32.12	—	$6.43
G0295	Electromagnetic therapy onc		E1					
G0302	Pre-op service LVRS complete		S	5723	5.7274	$455.27		$91.06
G0303	Pre-op service LVRS 10-15 dos		S	5721	1.7103	$135.95		$27.19
G0304	Pre-op service LVRS 1-9 dos		S	5723	5.7274	$455.27		$91.06
G0305	Post op service LVRS min 6		S	5723	5.7274	$455.27		$91.06

APC, Ambulatory payment classification; *CI*, comment indicator; *HCPCS*, Healthcare Common Procedure Coding System; *LVRS*, lung volume reduction surgery; *RW*, relative weight; *SI*, status indicator.

Note: It should be stressed here that although these various payment systems use intricate calculation formulas, health insurance professionals and other auxiliary healthcare staff do not have to calculate fees.

Pass-Through Payments

Pass-through payments are transitional payments established by Medicare for new drugs, biological and radiopharmaceutical agents, and medical devices. Pass-through payment is a temporary way to pay for these items until Medicare determines whether the cost continues to be paid separately or is packaged into an existing APC-based fee.

Health insurance professionals can stay informed of annual changes to the APC system through the annual updates that go into effect each January by logging on to the CMS website or using the key words "APC-based fee schedule" (along with the current year) in an Internet search engine.

RESOURCE UTILIZATION GROUPS

The basic idea of **resource utilization groups (RUGs)** is to calculate payments to an SNF according to the severity and level of care needed by each resident under a Medicare Part A stay. SNFs are nursing homes that provide skilled nursing or skilled rehabilitation services or both to Medicare patients who need a level of medical care that cannot be provided in a custodial-type nursing home or in the patient's home.

When a patient is admitted to a residential healthcare facility or nursing home, the physician is required to prepare a written plan of care for treatment, including rehabilitative therapy. Under this type of PPS, SNFs are required to classify residents into one of the RUG-IV groups based on data from resident assessment, known as the *minimum data set (MDS)*. This classification process is accomplished using the RUG-IV grouper, which groups case types expected to have similar resource use. RUG-IV includes new definitions of RUGs, changes in therapy minutes, and the activities of daily living (ADLs) index.

CMS requires that an MDS be completed for each resident by a registered nurse, and each resident's RUG is based on the MDS. The MDS must be completed periodically during the resident's stay, as appropriate. There are more than 500 items on the MDS, and data from about a quarter of these items are used to determine the RUG—the payment rate for each resident covered in a Medicare Part A stay. CMS conducts oversight activities to monitor the accuracy of the MDS.

RUG categories are divided further into hierarchical groups based on the patient's ability to perform ADLs. ADLs are behaviors related to personal care, including bathing or showering, dressing, getting in or out of bed or a chair, using the toilet, and eating. A qualified registered nurse assessor places each patient into an RUG category by completing a patient review. Each RUG category is assigned a numeric value based on the resources necessary to care for that type of patient with a greater value assigned to categories that require more resources.

> ### ! Stop and Think
>
> Nathan Schnoor, an 84-year-old Medicare patient, was hospitalized at Bestcare Hospital for congestive heart failure. Medicare's average length of stay (ALOS) for this diagnosis-related group (DRG) category was 21 days; however, at the end of this time, Nathan's condition had deteriorated. Bestcare staff informed Nathan's family that, under Medicare rules, he had to be discharged, and arrangements were made to transfer him to a nursing home. What are the ramifications of the Medicare prospective payment system (PPS) and the DRG structure in situations such as this?

> ### ? What Did You Learn?
>
> 1. Provide a brief definition of a DRG.
> 2. The DRG system classifies hospital inpatient cases into _____ with similar use of the facility's resources.
> 3. The key piece of information when assigning a DRG is the _____.
> 4. Explain what APCs consist of and how payment is calculated.
> 5. Name the two main functions of the OCE.
> 6. _____ payments to an SNF are calculated according to the severity and level of care needed by each resident under a Medicare Part A stay.

TRANSITION OF MEDICARE TO A RESOURCE-BASED RELATIVE VALUE SCALE

CMS implemented the Medicare RBRVS physician fee schedule in 1992. The Medicare RBRVS physician fee schedule replaced the Medicare physician payment system of "customary, prevailing, and reasonable" charges from which physicians were paid according to the provision of each service. The current Medicare RBRVS physician fee schedule is calculated using the "relative value" of the service provided (identified by a CPT code) and based on the resources the service consumes. To review, the relative value of each service is based on three components: (1) the amount of physician work that goes into the service, (2) the practice expense associated with the service, and (3) the professional liability expense to provide the service. The relative value of each service is multiplied by the **geographic practice cost index (GPCI)** (pronounced "gypsy") for each Medicare locality and then translated into a dollar amount by an annually adjusted CF. The dollar amount resulting from this calculation is what Medicare will pay to provide that particular service. Many public and private payers, including Medicaid programs, have adopted components of the Medicare RBRVS for calculating physician reimbursement.

For more information on RBRVS and to learn more about how payments are calculated using the Medicare RBRVS formula, see Box 17.1. Use the website listed under "Websites to Explore" at the end of this chapter for more detailed information on Medicare reimbursement under RBRVS.

ESTABLISHING MEDICARE PAYMENT POLICY

Medicare payment rules are made by CMS, which is headquartered in Baltimore. However, the Medicare program is administered largely at the local and regional levels by private insurance companies that contract with CMS to handle day-to-day billing and payment matters. CMS also administers and oversees the Medicaid program.

MEDICARE LONG-TERM CARE HOSPITAL PROSPECTIVE PAYMENT SYSTEM

LTCHs are certified under Medicare as short-term acute care hospitals that have been excluded from the IPPS. Under the Medicare **long-term care hospital (LTCH) PPS**, patients who require hospital-level care for an average of 25 days or longer are classified into distinct diagnostic groups based on clinical characteristics and expected resource needs.

Case-Level Adjustment

One type of case-level adjustment in the LTCH PPS is a **short-stay outlier**, which is an adjustment to the federal payment rate for LTCH stays that are considerably shorter than the ALOS for an LTC-DRG. Without this short-stay outlier adjustment, Medicare would pay an inappropriate amount for cases that did not receive a full episode of care at the LTCH. Cases qualify as a short-stay outlier when the length of stay is between 1 day and up to and including five-sixths ⅚]) of the LOS for the LTC-DRG into which the case is grouped. When a case exceeds the short-stay outlier threshold, Medicare pays a full LTC-DRG payment for that case. For more information on short-stay outliers, visit the CMS website using "short-stay outliers" as search words.

> **HIPAA Tip**
>
> Health Insurance Portability and Accountability Act (HIPAA) regulations do not apply to the format in which data are stored. Computer systems are free to use any format of their choosing to store data. HIPAA applies only to the format in which data are transmitted.

> **? What Did You Learn?**
>
> 1. The current Medicare RBRVS physician fee schedule is calculated using the _____ _____ of a service provided (identified by a given CPT code) and based on the resources the service consumes.
> 2. True or false: Medicare payment rules are made by the AMA.
> 3. What is the IPPS used for?
> 4. Define an LTCH.
> 5. A _____ is an adjustment to the federal payment rate for LTCH stays that are considerably shorter than the ALOS for an LTC-DRG.

SIGNIFICANCE OF REIMBURSEMENT SYSTEMS TO THE HEALTH INSURANCE PROFESSIONAL

A good deal of information has just been presented on various reimbursement systems with a focus mainly on the Medicare PPS. What does all of this information mean to the health insurance professional, and why is it significant? Being a successful health insurance professional does not stop with knowing how to complete and submit insurance claims. To function well on the job, an individual should have a working knowledge of each of the systems discussed in this chapter, to what category of patients each applies, how each is structured, how fees are established within each system, and on what these fees are based. There is a direct correlation between knowledge and capability and job prospects. The more informed a health insurance professional becomes, the better his or her employment prospects and job advancement.

What Did You Learn?

1. True or false: The health insurance professional does not benefit from learning the basics of the various reimbursement systems.
2. Explain why (or why not) the various reimbursement systems are important to the health insurance professional.

PEER REVIEW ORGANIZATIONS AND PROSPECTIVE PAYMENT SYSTEMS

A **peer review organization (PRO)**, now more commonly referred to as a *quality improvement organization*, in this context is an agency typically composed of a group of practicing physicians and other healthcare professionals paid by the federal government to evaluate the services provided by other practitioners and to monitor the quality of care given to patients. PROs were established by TEFRA to review quality of care and appropriateness of admissions, readmissions, and discharges for Medicare and Medicaid patients. These organizations are held responsible for maintaining and lowering admission rates and reducing lengths of stay while ensuring adequate treatment. These organizations sometimes are called *professional standards review organizations*.

> ⚠ **Stop and Think**
>
> Megan Trimble and Bob Shackler are seeking employment after completing a medical insurance and billing program at a career school in their vicinity. Megan did her best to learn all she could about the various reimbursement systems, whereas Bob, considering the information insignificant for his career goals, disregarded it. What advantages might Megan have over Bob in their search for successful employment as health insurance professionals?

RESPONSIBILITIES OF PEER REVIEW ORGANIZATIONS

The basic responsibility of PROs is to ensure that Medicare hospital services are appropriate, necessary, and provided in the most cost-effective manner. PROs have considerable power to force hospitals to comply with HHS admission and quality standards. They may deny payment to hospitals where abusive practices are found and, in some instances, report such practices to HHS for further enforcement action. Congress required HHS to contract with PROs to monitor:

- The validity of diagnostic information supplied by hospitals for payment purposes
- The completeness, adequacy, and quality of care provided to Medicare beneficiaries
- The appropriateness of admissions and discharges
- The appropriateness of care in outlier cases in which additional Medicare payments were made

NONMEDICAL PEER REVIEW ORGANIZATIONS

Not all PROs deal with healthcare. One of the largest and most complex PROs is the one used by the Internal Revenue Service (IRS) to conduct audits through its Coordinated Examination Program. The IRS PRO, comprising teams of senior revenue agents and specialists including computer analysts, engineers, and economists, is the "watch dog" over the Coordinated Examination Program that audits taxpayers. For the purpose of relevancy, however, this section is limited to PROs as they apply primarily to government health programs, such as Medicare and Medicaid.

 What Did You Learn?

1. What federal government act is responsible for the creation of PROs?
2. What are the responsibilities of a PRO?
3. Name two things that PROs monitor.
4. Identify a non–healthcare-related PRO.

UNDERSTANDING COMPUTERIZED PATIENT ACCOUNTING SYSTEMS

In addition to learning about the various reimbursement systems related to medical billing and insurance, a well-rounded health insurance professional should be knowledgeable about computerized patient accounting systems. (Chapter 16 discusses electronic data entry and submitting insurance claims electronically.)

The healthcare office typically uses some kind of computerized patient accounting software. Reimbursement systems address the structure of various fee schedules and the structure and setting for each, whereas computerized patient accounting systems address receiving payment for professional services and report generation. Many different patient accounting systems are available today, and they all are capable of performing the following seven system functions:

1. Input and storage of patient demographic and insurance information
2. Transaction posting
3. Allocation of system control operations
4. Generating patient statements
5. Processing and submitting insurance claims
6. Managing and collecting delinquent accounts
7. Creating reports

Performing these seven functions in a systematic and timely manner is the key to effective and efficient patient accounting.

Chapter 5 suggested that a healthcare practice establish fair policies, practice sound accounting procedures, and maintain a well-trained staff. It is usually the responsibility of the physicians who run the practice to establish accounting policies and procedures of the practice. When the physicians have reached a consensus on these policies and procedures, they should meet with the staff and discuss how the procedures and policies are to be implemented and how to troubleshoot any potential problems that may arise. When a workable system has been established, the patient accounting policies and procedures should be documented. After this process is completed, it is a good idea for the staff to meet periodically to discuss suggested changes, updates, and revisions as needed. Finally, patients must be informed, verbally or through practice brochures, about all established practice policies and procedures.

MANAGING TRANSACTIONS

A successful healthcare practice must maintain control over the many transactions required in the process of providing quality services to patients. Whether the healthcare office is computerized or not, there are numerous transactions to handle throughout the day, such as:

- Posting and tracking patient charges
- Processing payments (cash, checks, or electronic funds transfers)
- Making adjustments to patient accounts

HIPAA Tip

The Health Insurance Portability and Accountability Act (HIPAA) does not require patients to sign consent forms before physicians, hospitals, or ambulances can share information for treatment purposes as long as it pertains to the same case.

Posting and Tracking Patient Charges

The typical process for posting and tracking patient charges is as follows. After the patient has completed the encounter, the charge for the procedure or service is entered into the patient's account ledger from the encounter form. This can be done either manually or using the computerized patient accounting software. Fig. 17.1 illustrates a typical software program screen showing charges and payments for a patient.

Code libraries that integrate with CPT-4 and ICD-10-CM codes that are integrated into the patient accounting software allow fast and accurate selection of applicable diagnostic and procedural coding. Most systems also allow the practice to set up specialty-specific or multiple "code sets" to streamline insurance submissions, assisting in billing the appropriate insurance carrier with the correct, carrier-specific codes.

Processing Payments

As with posting charges, all payments, whether they are in person, received in the mail, or electronic funds transfers, must also be posted to the patient's account. This task can be accomplished manually or by using the computerized patient accounting software. Fig. 17.2 shows how patient accounting software can track patient charges and remittance history.

Insurance Carrier Adjustments (Contractual Write-Offs)

A **contractual write-off** is used when some kind of contract or agreement exists between the provider and an insurance carrier whereby the provider agrees to accept the payer's allowed fee as payment in full

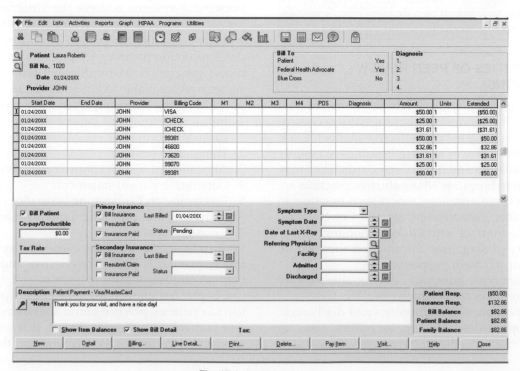

Fig. 17.1 Patient account.

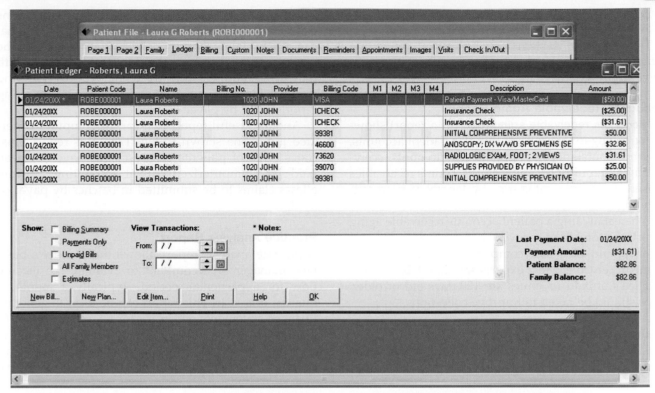

Fig. 17.2 Patient accounting software.

for a particular service or procedure. If the patient has paid the yearly deductible and coinsurance, the provider cannot ask the patient to pay any difference between what is charged and what the insurance carrier allows.

The contractual write-off is the portion of the fee that the provider agrees does not have to be paid. This assumes there is no secondary insurance to which the provider can bill the unpaid (contract write-off) amount from the primary insurer. If there is secondary insurance, a claim (along with the explanation of benefits [EOB] from the primary payer) should be submitted to the secondary carrier, and the remaining amount should be entered as the amount due from the secondary payer, rather than recording it on the patient ledger as a contractual write-off for the primary payer.

Contractual write-offs differ from bad debt write-offs. With a contractual write-off, the healthcare provider has agreed, through a contractual agreement with a third party, not to bill for the remaining amount after the patient has paid his or her deductible and coinsurance and all third-party payers have paid their share. Bad debt write-offs result when patients (or third-party payers) refuse or are unable to pay what is owed. Bad debt write-offs sometimes are used to zero out the balance for a patient's services when it has been determined that the account is uncollectible.

As discussed in Chapter 11, a Medicare nonparticipating (nonPAR) provider or supplier is one who has not signed a contract with Medicare. NonPARs not accepting assignment can charge beneficiaries no more than 115% of the Medicare allowance. In such cases,

the beneficiary must pay the difference between the allowed amount and the limiting charge, and contractual write-offs do not apply. On unassigned claims, the Medicare payment is sent to the beneficiary rather than the healthcare provider. (NonPARs may choose whether to accept Medicare's approved amount as payment on a case-by-case basis.)

> ## ⓘ Stop and Think
>
> Grace Plummer, a 72-year-old Medicare patient, visited dermatologist Harold Grassley on November 17 for removal of a nonmalignant lesion on her left arm. The total fee for the procedure was $125. Medicare's allowed charge for this procedure is $75. Dr. Grassley, a Medicare nonPAR, charged $86.25 (limiting charge). If Grace has met her Medicare deductible for the year, can Dr. Grassley bill her for the balance? Why or why not?

GENERATING REPORTS

Reporting formats vary greatly with different software systems, but all software can generate various standard reports. Some software programs allow the healthcare practice to "self-format" or customize reports; however, this feature often adds to the cost. Typical reporting capabilities that are built into most healthcare accounting software include the following:

- Patient day sheets
- Procedure day sheets
- Patient ledgers
- Patient statements
- Patient account aging

- Insurance claims submission aging reports
- Practice analysis reports

The pegboard system also has report-generating capabilities, although the process is different and involves more extensive manual effort.

Accounts Receivable Aging Report

An **accounts receivable aging report** is a report showing how long invoices, or in this case patient accounts, have been outstanding or unpaid. The accounts receivable aging report is an analysis of accounts receivables broken down into categories by length of time outstanding (Fig. 17.3).

When analyzing a patient accounts receivable aging report, the total money owed that is 120 days old and older should be small compared with the total accounts receivable. Most experts say that if 20% of the practice's unpaid revenues are 120 days old or older, steps should be taken to improve collections.

Insurance Claims Aging Report

A usable report for the health insurance professional is the insurance claims aging report. Chapter 7 discussed keeping a manual register or log of insurance claims submitted so that the health insurance professional can track claims and no claim "falls between the cracks." This process can be done automatically with patient accounting software using report-generating features. Fig. 17.4 shows an example of a claims aging report sorted by payer.

Another useful report that can be computer generated is the one shown in Fig. 17.5. This report illustrates a list of patients whose claims have not been paid yet. Computerized patient accounting software allows claims to be submitted in batches by payer or by date.

Practice Analysis Report

A practice analysis report allows the practice's business manager or accountant to evaluate the income flow for a particular period—typically a month, a quarter, or a year. This report can be used to generate financial statements necessary for tax purposes, profit analysis, and future planning. A typical practice analysis report furnishes a breakdown of total charges, categorized specialty charges, total patient payments,

Happy Valley Medical Clinic
Patient Aging by Date of Service
As of March 30, 20XX

Show all data where the Date From is on or before 3/30/20XX

Chart	Name		Current 0 - 30	Past 31 - 60	Past 61 - 90	Past 91 ---->	Total Balance
AGADW000	Dwight Again		130.00			86.00	216.00
Last Pmt: -200.00	On:3/26/20XX	434-5777					
AUSAN000	Andrew Austin		165.00				165.00
Last Pmt: 0.00	On:	767-2222					
BRIJA000	Jay Brimley					445.00	445.00
Last Pmt: -30.00	On:10/23/20XX	(222)342-3444					
BRISU000	Susan Brimley		8.00			32.00	40.00
Last Pmt: -30.00	On:9/5/20XX	(222)342-3444					
CATSA000	Sammy Catera					71.00	71.00
Last Pmt: 0.00	On:	227-7722					
DOEJA000	Jane S Doe		15.00			79.00	94.00
Last Pmt: 0.00	On:3/11/20XX	(480)999-9999					
JONSU001	Susan Jones					180.00	180.00
Last Pmt: 0.00	On:						
MARRO000	Roberto Marionellio					510.00	510.00
Last Pmt: 0.00	On:						
SIMTA000	Tanus J Simpson					456.00	456.00
Last Pmt: -10.00	On:12/3/20XX	(480)555-5555					
SMIJO000	John Smith					1,095.00	1,095.00
Last Pmt: 0.00	On:						
WAGJE000	Jeremy Wagnew					-1.00	-1.00
Last Pmt: -22.00	On:8/22/20XX	(121)419-7127					
YOUMI000	Michael C Youngblood					85.00	85.00
Last Pmt: 0.00	On:	(602)222-3333					
	Report Aging Totals		$318.00	$0.00	$0.00	$3,038.00	$3,356.00
	Percent of Aging Total		9.5 %	0.0 %	0.0 %	90.2 %	100.0 %

Fig. 17.3 Computer-generated accounts receivable report.

1500 A/R Aging All

SOFTAID DEMO DATA

03/19/20XX 16:11:34

Status Carrier Code	Claim ID	Last Bill	Current	31 to 60	61 to 90
CLAIM STATUS: PRIMARY					
AETNA OF CALIFORNIA–AETNA5					
CLOONEY, GEORGE 58698775501	135741	03/05/20XX	160.00	0.00	0.00
AETNA OF CALIFORNIA			**160.00**	**0.00**	**0.00**
HOME HEALTH AGENCY – AG					
CLOONEY, GEORGE 58698775501	135740	03/05/20XX	60.00	0.00	0.00
HOME HEALTH AGENCY			**60.00**	**0.00**	**0.00**
BLUE CROSS BLUE SHIELD OF FLOR–BCBS					
CLOONEY, GEORGE 59709885501	135735	03/01/20XX	160.00	0.00	0.00
CLOONEY, GEORGE 59709885501	135736	03/01/20XX	240.00	0.00	0.00
CLOONEY, GEORGE 59709885501	135738	03/10/20XX	80.00	0.00	0.00
CLOONEY, GEORGE 59709885501	135739	03/04/20XX	113.00	0.00	0.00
BLUE CROSS BLUE SHIELD OF FLOR			**593.00**	**0.00**	**0.00**
TOTAL: PRIMARY			**813.00**	**0.00**	**0.00**
CLAIM STATUS: SECONDARY					
MEDICAID–MCD					
CLOONEY, GEORGE 58698775501	135737	03/03/20XX	1,580.00	0.00	0.00
MEDICAID			**1,580.00**	**0.00**	**0.00**
TOTAL: SECONDARY			**1,580.00**	**0.00**	**0.00**

Current	31 to 60	61 to 90	91 to 120	> 120
2,393.00	0.00	0.00	0.00	0.00
100.00 %	0.00 %	0.00 %	0.00 %	0.00 %

Fig. 17.4 Claims aging report sorted by payer.

insurance payments, and contractual adjustments (Fig. 17.6).

❓ What Did You Learn?

1. List five functions most patient accounting software systems are capable of performing.
2. Name four important questions to ask a patient accounting software vendor.
3. What are three different ways a healthcare practice receives payment?
4. What is a contractual write-off?
5. List six different reports that patient accounting software systems can generate.
6. What is the purpose of a practice analysis report?

HIPAA AND PRACTICE MANAGEMENT SOFTWARE

Most healthcare practices today are computerized to some extent. The level of computerization may range from simple billing functions and patient scheduling to electronic healthcare records and entire practice management activities. HIPAA *does not* require healthcare practices to purchase computer systems. However, some experts claim that the installation of a HIPAA-compliant software system may help a practice reduce its administrative costs. Two of the principal areas of a physician's practice affected by HIPAA are the practice's billing software and practice management software.

HIPAA includes rules related to the format of electronic transactions; protection of patients' privacy;

Happy Valley Medical Clinic
Primary Insurance Aging

Date of Service	Procedure	Current 0 - 30	Past 31 - 60	Past 61 - 90	Past 91 - 120	Past 121 ---->	Total Balance

Aetna (AET00)   Erik (602)333-3333

SIMTA000   Tanus J Simpson   SSN:

Claim: 1   Initial Billing Date: 3/21/20XX   Last Billing Date: 10/30/20XX   Policy: GG93-GXTA   Group: 99999

Date of Service	Procedure	Current 0 - 30	Past 31 - 60	Past 61 - 90	Past 91 - 120	Past 121 ---->	Total Balance
12/3/20XX	43220	275.00					275.00
12/3/20XX	71040	50.00					50.00
12/3/20XX	81000	11.00					11.00
12/3/20XX	99213	50.00					50.00
	Claim Totals:	386.00	0.00	0.00	0.00	0.00	386.00

Claim: 15   Initial Billing Date: 10/30/20XX   Last Billing Date: 10/30/20XX   Policy: GG93-GXTA   Group: 99999

Date of Service	Procedure	Current 0 - 30	Past 31 - 60	Past 61 - 90	Past 91 - 120	Past 121 ---->	Total Balance
10/25/20XX	99213	60.00					60.00
10/25/20XX	90707	10.00					10.00
	Claim Totals:	70.00	0.00	0.00	0.00	0.00	70.00
	Insurance Totals:	456.00	0.00	0.00	0.00	0.00	456.00

Cigna (CIG00)   Bill S. Preston 234-5678

BRIJA000   Jay Brimley   SSN:

Claim: 16   Initial Billing Date: 10/26/20XX   Last Billing Date: 10/26/20XX   Policy: 98547377   Group: 12d

Date of Service	Procedure	Current 0 - 30	Past 31 - 60	Past 61 - 90	Past 91 - 120	Past 121 ---->	Total Balance
3/25/20XX	99214	55.00					55.00
3/25/20XX	97260	30.00					30.00
	Claim Totals:	85.00	0.00	0.00	0.00	0.00	85.00
	Insurance Totals:	85.00	0.00	0.00	0.00	0.00	85.00

U.S. Tricare (US000)

YOUMI000   Michael C Youngblood   SSN:

Claim: 17   Initial Billing Date: 10/26/20XX   Last Billing Date: 10/26/20XX   Policy: USAA236678   Group: 25BB

Date of Service	Procedure	Current 0 - 30	Past 31 - 60	Past 61 - 90	Past 91 - 120	Past 121 ---->	Total Balance
8/22/20XX	99213	60.00					60.00
8/22/20XX	97128	15.00					15.00
8/22/20XX	97010	10.00					10.00
	Claim Totals:	85.00	0.00	0.00	0.00	0.00	85.00
	Insurance Totals:	85.00	0.00	0.00	0.00	0.00	85.00

		Current 0 - 30	Past 31 - 60	Past 61 - 90	Past 91 - 120	Past 121 ---->	Total Balance
Report Aging Totals		$626.00	$0.00	$0.00	$0.00	$0.00	$626.00
Percent of Aging Total		100.0 %	0.0 %	0.0 %	0.0 %	0.0 %	100.0 %

Page 1

Fig. 17.5 List of patients whose claims have not been paid yet.

Practice Analysis

Code	Description	Amount	Quantity	Average	Cost	Net
01	patient payment, cash	−8.00	1	−8.00		−8.00
02	patient payment, check	−15.00	1	−15.00		−15.00
03	insurance carrier payment	−154.00	2	−77.00		−154.00
04	insurance company adjustment	−10.00	1	−10.00		−10.00
06	OhioCare HMO Charge - $10	10.00	1	10.00		10.00
07	OhioCare HMO Charge - $15	15.00	1	15.00		15.00
29425	application of short leg cast, walking	30.00	1	30.00		30.00
50390	aspiration of renal cyst by needle	38.50	1	38.50		38.50
73510	hip x-ray, complete, two views	90.00	1	90.00		90.00
80019	19 clinical chemistry tests	80.00	1	80.00		80.00
84478	triglycerides test	50.00	2	25.00		50.00
90703	tetanus injection	20.00	1	20.00		20.00
92516	facial nerve function studies	125.00	1	125.00		125.00
96900	ultraviolet light treatment	23.50	1	23.50		23.50
99070	supplies and materials provided	20.00	1	20.00		20.00
99201	OF–new patient, problem focused	280.00	2	140.00		280.00
99211	OF–established patient, minimal	100.00	2	50.00		100.00
99212	OF–established patient, problem focused	200.00	5	40.00		200.00
99213	OF–established patient, expanded	300.00	3	100.00		300.00
99394	established patient, adolescent, per...	90.00	1	90.00	0.00	90.99

Total Procedure Charges	$1,472.00
Total Product Charges	$0.00
Total Inside Lab Charges	$0.00
Total Outside Lab Charges	$0.00
Total Insurance Payments	−$154.00
Total Cash Copayments	$0.00
Total Check Copayments	$0.00
Total Credit Card Copayments	$0.00
Total Patient Cash Payments	$0.00
Total Patient Check Payments	−$23.00
Total Credit Card Payments	$0.00
Total Deductibles	$0.00
Total Debit Adjustments	$0.00
Total Credit Adjustments	−$10.00
Total Medicare Debit Adjustments	$0.00
Total Medicare Credit Adjustments	$0.00
Net Effect on Accounts Receivable	$1,285.00

Fig. 17.6 Practice analysis report.

ensuring the security of patients' health information; and defining universal identifiers for individuals, healthcare providers, and employers. Compliance with two components of HIPAA, the Transactions and Code Set Standard (Transaction Standards) and the Privacy Standards, was required by October 2002 and April 2003, respectively.

According to the *Guide to Medical Practice Software*, there are more than 1500 active practice management software vendors. With this in mind, two questions arise:

1. How does a healthcare practice evaluate its current software system for HIPAA compliance?
2. If a practice is in the market for a new software system, how should it evaluate various vendors in terms of HIPAA compliance?

It is important that the software vendor understands the requirements of the HIPAA Transaction Standards. The Transaction Standards have specified American National Standards Institute (ANSI) 5010 as the standard for electronic transactions, including billing, payment, eligibility verification, and preauthorization. A physician must ensure that the electronic claims sent to third-party payers are in this specific format. Whether a practice is evaluating its current computer vendor or shopping for a new one, it should ensure that the vendor is not only aware of the Transaction Standards but also able to speak intelligently about or show how their systems are compliant with the Transaction Standards.

Ensuring that the vendor can assist the practice in complying with the HIPAA Privacy Rule is also important. The Privacy Rule has imposed numerous requirements on healthcare providers and their practices. Before disclosing a patient's protected health information (PHI) except for the purposes of treatment, payment, or healthcare operations, a practice must obtain the written consent from the patient. A HIPAA-approved authorization form to release PHI is more detailed and specific than many generic authorizations and has a definite expiration date.

A computerized practice management system can alleviate potential administrative problems a healthcare practice may encounter in complying with the Privacy Rule with relative ease, often with just a few simple keystrokes or mouse clicks. Most practice management systems can provide various functions where PHI is concerned, such as:

- Tracking the date that the patient's consent to release PHI was obtained
- Maintaining electronic copies of the signed consent and authorization forms
- Tracking patient requests for restrictions on use and disclosure of PHI, tracking whether the physician agreed to the request, and if so, retaining a copy of the modified consent
- Tracking whether and when the consent was revoked by the patient
- Tracking when patient authorizations were obtained, what they were obtained for, and their expiration dates

The Privacy Standards provide that a patient may request an accounting of all disclosures made by a **covered entity** (which includes healthcare plans, healthcare providers, and healthcare clearinghouses) within the preceding 6 years. The disclosure must include, among other items, the date, name and address (if available) of the person or entity that received the information, and a description of the PHI disclosed. Practice management software designed in compliance with HIPAA Privacy Standards makes all of this information available to the healthcare office by viewing the main "window" or connected "windows" related to that particular patient, rather than having to undertake a manual review of the hard copy in the patient's file.

A software vendor is *not required* to provide all of these services. However, it is in the best interest of the healthcare facility to partner with a vendor who is willing to work with the practice in achieving HIPAA compliance.

If a practice contracts with an entity considered a business associate, as described by the Privacy Standards, the practice should ensure that the agreement between them includes certain protections as defined in the Privacy Standards. HIPAA defines a **business associate** as an individual or corporate "person" who:

- Performs on behalf of the covered entity any function or activity involving the use or disclosure of PHI and
- Is *not* a member of the covered entity's workforce

This definition includes a requirement that the business associate use appropriate safeguards to prevent use or disclosure of PHI other than as provided in the agreement. If a healthcare practice finds that its current vendor is unable or unwilling to meet the HIPAA standards, it may be wise to begin shopping for a new vendor whose products and services can help the practice achieve HIPAA compliance.

 HIPAA Tip

Effective July 1, 2004, Medicare rejects electronic claims that have diagnosis codes, ZIP codes, or telephone numbers that are not compliant with the Health Insurance Portability and Accountability Act (HIPAA). Medical facilities should ensure that their billing systems are modified to generate electronic claims that pass Medicare HIPAA compliancy edits for diagnosis codes, ZIP codes, and telephone numbers.

 Imagine This!

Dr. Agussi uses a computer system that prepares claim information in an electronic file to be submitted to a claims clearinghouse. After the system prepares the electronic file, Dr. Agussi's health insurance professional, Angela Peters, uploads the file to the software provided by the clearinghouse. Later, Angela downloads an electronic remittance file. Dr. Agussi's software reads this file and automatically posts payment information. Dr. Agussi receives maximum value for his computer software if the electronic claim file prepared by the computer system and the electronic remittance file provided by the clearinghouse is in standard American National Standards Institute (ANSI) format. This is possible only if Dr. Agussi's system and the clearinghouse accept and submit standard transactions.

Dr. Benton uses a computer system that prepares claim information in an electronic file to be submitted directly to the payer. Franklin Zetta, Dr. Benton's health insurance professional, dials into the payer's system and uploads the electronic file. Later, Franklin dials back into the payer's system and downloads an electronic remittance file. Dr. Benton's software reads this file and automatically posts payment information. Dr. Benton's system and the payer must support standard transactions because Dr. Benton and the payer are transacting directly with each other.

A healthcare office gets maximum value from patient accounting software or a practice management system if it can prepare, send, receive, and process ANSI standard electronic transactions.

? What Did You Learn?

1. To what four areas of patient accounting software do HIPAA rules relate?
2. Why is it important that a software vendor understand HIPAA requirements?
3. What requirements has HIPAA imposed on healthcare practices that relate to patient privacy?
4. Name the three categories that constitute covered entities.
5. List the two factors that define a business associate.

SUMMARY CHECKPOINTS

- The following paragraphs describe basic types of reimbursement:
  - *Fee-for-service:* The healthcare provider charges a specific fee (typically the RVU multiplied by the current CF) for each service rendered and is paid that fee by the patient or by the patient's insurance carrier.
  - *Discounted fee-for-service:* Although providers typically charge all patients the same amount for the same service (except nonPAR Medicare providers), they accept reimbursement for services at lower rates than their usual fees under certain circumstances, such as when a provider contracts with a PPO. In a PPO with a discounted fee-for-service reimbursement structure, a PAR takes a contractual adjustment according to the PPO contract that results in a discount for member patients.
  - *PPS:* The Medicare reimbursement system for inpatient hospital costs is based on predetermined factors and not on individual services. Rates are set at a level intended to cover operating costs for treating a typical inpatient in a given DRG. Payments for each hospital are adjusted for various factors such as differences in area wages, teaching activity, and care to the poor.
  - *RBRVS:* In the RBRVS system, reimbursement is determined by the resource costs needed to provide the service rather than actual charges. The cost of providing each service is divided into three components: (1) physician work, (2) practice expense, and (3) professional liability insurance. Payments are calculated by multiplying the combined costs of a service by a CF (a monetary amount that is determined by the CMS). Payments are also adjusted for geographic differences in resource costs. RBRVS is used by many health plans in negotiating fee schedules with in-network physicians.
  - *Capitation:* A common method of reimbursement used primarily by HMOs, the provider or healthcare facility is paid a fixed, per capita amount for each person enrolled in the plan without regard to the actual number or nature of services provided.
  - *DRGs* is a system of classifying hospital inpatient cases into categories with similar use of the facility's resources. Under this system, a hospital is paid a predetermined, lump sum amount, regardless of the costs involved, for each Medicare patient treated and discharged.
  - *APC* is a system designed to explain the amount and type of resources used in an outpatient encounter. Under the APC system, Medicare pays hospitals for treating patients in outpatient clinics and physicians for treating patients in their offices. Each procedure or treatment has an APC code. Services in each APC are similar clinically in terms of the resources they require. A fixed payment rate is established for each APC.
  - *RUGs* are used to calculate reimbursement in SNFs according to severity and level of care. Under the Medicare PPS, patients are classified into an RUG that determines how much Medicare would pay the SNF per day for that patient.
- CMS implemented the Medicare RBRVS physician fee schedule in 1992 to replace the Medicare physician payment system of "customary, prevailing, and reasonable" charges from which physicians were paid according to the provision of each service. The Medicare RBRVS Physician Fee Schedule is calculated using the "relative value" of the service provided (identified by a CPT code) and based on the resources the service consumes. The relative value of each service is multiplied by the GPCI (pronounced "gypsy") for each Medicare locality and then translated into a dollar amount by an annually adjusted CF. The dollar amount resulting from this calculation is what Medicare will pay to provide that particular service.
- There are some additional systems for determining reimbursement, including value-based programs developed by CMS. These programs cover a wide range of services with the goal of providing better care for individuals, better health for populations, and lower costs.
- DRGs provide a means for relating the type of patients that a hospital treats with the costs incurred by the hospital for treating them. This system is used for reimbursing inpatient care.
- Being a successful health insurance professional does not stop with knowing how to complete and submit insurance claims. There is a direct correlation between knowledge and capability and job prospects. The more informed a health insurance professional becomes, the better his or her employment prospects and job advancement.
- The responsibilities of a PRO as they relate to the PPS include:
  - Evaluating services provided by practitioners and monitoring the quality of care given to patients
  - Ensuring that Medicare hospital services are appropriate, necessary, and provided in the most cost-effective manner
  - Monitoring the validity of diagnostic information supplied by hospitals for payment purposes
  - Ensuring that the care provided to Medicare beneficiaries is complete, adequate, and of good quality

- Ascertaining the appropriateness of admissions and discharges
- Supervising the care in outlier cases in which additional Medicare payments were made
- Requiring hospitals to comply with HHS admission and quality standards
- Patient accounting software systems have the capability of performing many functions, including:
  - Input and storage of patient demographic and insurance information
  - Transaction posting
  - Allocation of system control operations
  - Generating patient statements
  - Processing and submitting insurance claims
  - Managing and collecting delinquent accounts
  - Creating reports
- A contractual write-off is the process of adjusting or canceling the balance owing (often through a provider's contract agreement with the insuring party) on a patient's account after all deductibles, coinsurance amounts, and third-party payments have been made.
- Advantages gained when a healthcare facility uses HIPAA-compliant software are as follows:
  - Electronic claims are transmitted in the correct ANSI format.
  - Patient privacy is protected.
  - The security of patient health information is ensured.
  - Universal identifiers are defined for individuals, healthcare providers, and employers.
  - Potential administrative problems are alleviated with the use of built-in privacy compliance functions.
  - Electronic records of patient consents and authorizations are tracked and maintained.

Closing Scenario

As a respected member of the business office team, Dave was asked to develop a training manual for new employees that will be working in the business office. He has included information about the different reimbursement models as well as how charges, payments, and adjustments are posted to patient accounts. He was sure to include the policies developed by Walden-Martin about when adjustments should be made to patient's accounts. Dave wants it to be clear to any new employees that Walden-Martin has several different contracts with various insurance companies, as well being a participating provider for Medicare and Medicaid. Each of those situations has different requirements for claims submission as well as the adjustments that are needed.

CHAPTER REVIEW QUESTIONS

1. The payment method that is Medicare's flat rate reimbursement system for inpatient costs based on predetermined factors for treating a typical patient in a given DRG is:
   a. Fee-for-service.
   b. RBRVS.
   c. PPS.
   d. Capitation.
2. The payment method based on a fixed, per capita amount for each person served without regard to the actual number or nature of services provided is:
   a. Fee-for-service.
   b. RBRVS.
   c. PPS.
   d. Capitation.
3. The prospective payment system that reimburses for acute care based on diagnosis and procedures is:
   a. DRG.
   b. APC.
   c. RUG.
   d. IRF PPS.
4. The capitation method or reimbursement is used to provide payment to:
   a. Medicare MCOs.
   b. Fee-for-service.
   c. Inpatient care.
   d. PPS.
5. Which of the following is not one of CMS's value-based programs?
   a. End-Stage Renal Disease Quality Incentive Program
   b. Hospital Readmission Reduction Program
   c. Hospital-Acquired Conditions (HAC) Reduction Program
   d. Medicare Advantage Program
6. The key piece of information in determining a DRG is:
   a. Services provided.
   b. Place of service.
   c. Principal diagnosis.
   d. Length of stay.
7. Resource utilization groups are used to determine payment for:
   a. HMO.
   b. SNF.
   c. OOP.
   d. None of the above.
8. Which of the following would be posted to a patient's account (ledger)?
   a. Payments
   b. Charges
   c. Adjustments
   d. All of the above

9. A nonparticipating Medicare provider is allowed to charge a Medicare patient _____ of Medicare's allowed amount.
   a. 100%
   b. 115%
   c. 130%
   d. 200%

10. A practice's unpaid revenue over 120 days should be below:
   a. 20%.
   b. 40%.
   c. 60%.
   d. 80%.

WEBSITES TO EXPLORE

- For live links to the following websites, please visit the Evolve website at http://evolve.elsevier.com/Beik/today.
- For more detailed information about each specific PPS, visit http://www.cms.gov/Medicare/Medicare-Fee-for-Service-Payment/ProspMedicareFeeSvcPmtGen/index.html.
- To learn more about government acts regulating reimbursement systems, go to https://www.healthit.gov/topic/laws-regulation-and-policy.

- Obtain additional information on RVS from http://www.cdc.gov and http://www.cms.gov.
- For more detailed information on Medicare reimbursement under RBRVS, visit https://www.ama-assn.org/about/rvs-update-committee-ruc/rbrvs-overview.
- For additional examples of calculating ALOS, visit https://www.health.pa.gov/topics/HealthStatistics/Statistical-Resources/UnderstandingHealthStats/Documents/Average_Length_of_Stay_in_Hospitals.pdf.
- For more information on the home health PPS, see http://www.cms.gov/HomeHealthPPS/.
- For more information on value-based programs, visit https://www.cms.gov/Medicare/Quality-Initiatives-Patient-Assessment-Instruments/Value-Based-Programs/Value-Based-Programs.html.

Author's Note: Due to the dynamic nature of the Internet, web addresses and/or links provided in this chapter may have changed since publication and may no longer be valid. In such cases, students should select comparable search words to access related sites.

Chapter Outline

XI. HIPAA–Hospital Connection
    A. The Affordable Care Act's Effect on Hospital
       Charges
    B. Bundled Payments for Care Improvement Initiative

XII. Billing Compliance
    A. Coding Compliance

XIII. Career Opportunities in Hospital Billing
    A. Training, Other Qualifications, and Advancement
    B. Job Outlook

Chapter Objectives

After completion of this chapter, the student should be able to:

1. Differentiate between hospital and physician office billing and coding.
2. Explain modern hospital and health systems.
3. Identify common types of healthcare facilities.
4. Discuss the legal and regulatory environment of today's hospitals.
5. List common hospital payers and how to acquire their claim guidelines.
6. Describe the UB-04 and its relation to the National Uniform Billing Committee (NUBC).
7. Discuss the structure and content of the hospital health record.
8. Outline the inpatient hospital/facility coding process.
9. Discuss outpatient hospital coding.
10. Summarize the hospital billing process.
11. Explain the HIPAA–hospital connection.
12. Provide a rationale for billing compliance.
13. Analyze the career opportunities in hospital billing.

Chapter Terms

72-hour rule
accreditation
Accreditation Association for Ambulatory Health Care (AAAHC)
activities of daily living (ADLs)
acute care
acute care facility
acute condition
ambulatory payment classification (APC)
ambulatory surgery center (ASC)
BCBS member hospitals
benefit period
billing compliance
blockchain technology
case mix
charge description master (CDM)
clinic
coding compliance
cost-sharing
covered entity
critical access hospital (CAH)
Defense Enrollment Eligibility Reporting System (DEERS)
diagnosis-related group (DRG)
electronic claims submission (ECS)
electronic medical record (EMR)
electronic remittance advice (ERA)
Emergency Medical Treatment and Active Labor Act (EMTALA)

emergent medical condition
exacerbation
form locators
for-profit hospitals
general hospital
governance
grouper software
health information management (HIM) system
home health agency
hospice
hospital information system (HIS)
hospital outpatient prospective payment system (HOPPS)
informed consent
integrated delivery system (IDS)
intermediate care facility
The Joint Commission
licensed independent practitioner
long-term care facility
medical ethics
Medicare Severity (MS)–DRG System
multiaxial structure
National Committee for Quality Assurance (NCQA)
National Correct Coding Initiative (NCCI)
National Uniform Billing Committee (NUBC)

nonavailability statement (NAS)
outliers
outpatient prospective payment system (OPPS)
palliative care
pass-throughs
patient centric
Patient Protection and Affordable Care Act (PPACA)
per diems
present on admission (POA)
pricing transparency
principal diagnosis
prospective payment system (PPS)
quality improvement organizations (QIOs)
Registered Health Information Technician (RHIT)
respite care
secondary diagnosis
skilled nursing facility (SNF)
subacute care facility
surrogate
swing bed
transaction set
UB-04
Utilization Review Accreditation Commission (URAC)
vertically integrated hospitals

Brittany Weston is working as a Registered Health Information Technician (RHIT) in the Health Information Management Department of Walden-Martin Family Medical Center. The mission of the Health Information Management Department and Walden-Martin is the total support of the facility's optimal standards for quality care and services through provision of quality information. The functions of Walden-Martin's Health Information Management team support administrative processes; billing through classification systems; medical education; research through data gathering and analysis; utilization, risk, and quality management programs; legal requirements; data security; and release of information to authorized users.

Brittany realizes that her job duties as an RHIT are extremely challenging and include the following:

- Compiling health information (e.g., reviewing, cataloging, and checking medical reports for completeness; organizing medical reports for placement in files; reviewing charts to ensure that all reports and signatures are present)
- Completing health information forms (e.g., preparing charts for new admissions, filling out forms, preparing requests for specific reports or certificates)
- Compiling and filling out statistical reports, such as daily or monthly census, Medicaid days, admissions, discharges, and length of stay
- Filing reports in health records and recording information in logs and files
- Retrieving health information records from filing systems
- Providing information from health records after determining appropriateness of request
- Coordinating health information records procedures with other departments

Brittany enjoys her role as an RHIT. She hopes to return to the classroom eventually and acquire the necessary credentials in health information management, which would allow her career aspirations to grow.

INTRODUCTION

This chapter provides an introduction to hospital billing—the process through which hospitals submit claims to and collect payment from insurance companies for services rendered to patients. Hospital billing procedures are similar to those in other healthcare fields. As a very basic explanation, the hospital sends claims for services rendered to patients to various third-party payers (e.g., Medicare, Medicaid, Blue Shield), which then determine whether the claims are documented correctly and meet all necessary requirements. If so, the insurance carrier sends obligatory payments to the hospital.

HOSPITAL VERSUS PHYSICIAN OFFICE BILLING AND CODING

Everything we have discussed so far in this textbook has applied to billing, coding, and insurance claims processing for physicians' offices and clinics. This final chapter presents some basic information and guidelines for billing, coding, and patient services in inpatient hospital facilities and other hospital-based healthcare. This chapter does not present enough detailed information to enable you to become a hospital biller and coder; that amount of information would fill an entire separate textbook. Instead, this chapter provides an overview of the basics. If you find this information interesting, you may want to explore a career in hospital billing or health information management (HIM).

HOSPITALS AND HEALTH SYSTEMS

The ideal hospital is a place where sick or injured individuals seek and receive care and, in the case of teaching hospitals, where clinical education is provided to the entire spectrum of healthcare professionals. Today's hospital provides continuing education for practicing physicians and increasingly serves the function of an institution of higher learning for entire neighborhoods, communities, and regions. In addition to its educational role, the hospital conducts investigational studies and research in medical sciences.

The construction of today's hospital is regulated by federal laws, state health department policies, city ordinances, the standards of private accrediting organizations such as The Joint Commission, and national and local codes (e.g., building, fire protection, sanitation). These requirements safeguard patients' privacy and the safety and well-being of patients and staff. The popular ward concept of the mid-19th and early 20th centuries, in which multiple patients were housed in one common area, is no longer permissible. Today, hospitals have mainly semiprivate and private rooms. Although permissible in most states, four-bed rooms are the exception.

Beginning in the early 1990s, hospitals became part of the evolution toward **vertically integrated hospitals** (hospitals that provide all levels of healthcare) and other provider networks. It is predicted that inpatient care will gradually diminish with continued advances in medicine and that hospitals, as we once knew them, are likely to continue downsizing. Simultaneously, ambulatory care in physicians' offices and clinics will increase. The hospital, particularly in comparison with its earliest days, will play a different role in the future as part of an integrated collection of providers and sites of care. For more information on the history of hospitals, see "Websites to Explore" at the end of this chapter.

EMERGING ISSUES

A goal of the entire healthcare system is to reduce costs and, at the same time, be more responsive to customers, a trendy designation being given to today's healthcare consumers (i.e., patients). The elderly are the heaviest users of healthcare services, and the percentage of elderly individuals in the population is increasing significantly. Also affecting this scenario are the rapid advances in medical technology, often involving sophisticated techniques and equipment, that are making more diagnostic and treatment procedures available. Other emerging healthcare trends are as follows:

- Movement from hospital-based acute care to outpatient care.
- Trend toward a more holistic, preventive, and continuous care of health and wellness.
- Advent of newer and changing legislative mandates (e.g., Health Insurance Portability and Accountability Act [HIPAA], Medicare Access and CHIP Reauthorization Act [MACRA]) and a growing emphasis on value-based care where compensation is based on outcomes, not on the number of procedures done or the number of patients seen.
- The increasing introduction of highly sophisticated diagnostic and treatment technology.
- A shift to computerized patient information (e.g., electronic health records [EHRs]), including **blockchain technology** that will allow for more patient controlled interoperability. Blockchain technology allows digital information to be distributed but not copied.
- Focus on population health and the management of patient outcomes, including looking at the social determinants of health (e.g., environment, stressors, income, education, level of social interaction, sense of community).

A link to the American Hospital Association (AHA) website, which provides the latest research and analysis of important and emerging trends in the hospital and healthcare field, can be found under "Websites to Explore" at the end of this chapter.

 Imagine This!

When Brittany was going through her orientation, the presenter, the soon-to-be-retired health information manager, told the new recruits about the "ward system," which existed in the large teaching hospital where she was first employed. There were two large wards on each floor—medical was on the third floor, surgical was on the fourth floor, and so forth. The ward on the west end of the third floor was Ward M3A; the ward on the east end was Ward M3B. Each of these wards was a large room with sometimes 30 beds. These beds were occupied by indigent or "state" patients, individuals who did not have insurance or the financial ability to pay for their healthcare. These patients wore dingy hospital gowns with their respective ward identification (ID) stenciled in large digits on the front so as to identify them if they wandered out of the ward.

Patients who had insurance or could pay for their care were housed on the second floor in private or semiprivate rooms and were attended by "staff" physicians. The patients in the wards were attended by medical students, interns, and residents who were overseen by staff physicians. The wards were not air conditioned; they were crowded, malodorous, and noisy. Medical students acquired much of their medical education here, often at the expense of the patients.

The health information manager concluded, "Inpatient medical care as we know it today has improved 200-fold."

COMMON HEALTHCARE FACILITIES

The best-known type of healthcare facility is the **general hospital**, which is set up to handle care of patients experiencing many kinds of disease and injury. It may be a single building or a campus and typically has an emergency department to deal with immediate threats to health and the capacity to provide emergency medical services. A general hospital is usually the major healthcare facility in a region. It typically has a large number of beds for intensive care, skilled nursing care, and long-term care along with specialized facilities for medical care, surgery, childbirth, and laboratories. Big cities may have several different hospitals of various sizes and facilities. Large hospitals are often called *medical centers* and usually conduct operations in virtually every field of modern medicine. Types of specialized hospitals include trauma centers; children's hospitals; seniors' hospitals; and hospitals for dealing with specific medical needs, such as psychiatric problems, pulmonary diseases, orthopedic procedures, and other specialized areas of care.

Some hospitals are affiliated with universities for medical research and the training of medical personnel. In the United States, many facilities are **for-profit hospitals**, meaning that their monetary income must be greater than expenses, whereas elsewhere in the world, most hospitals are nonprofit. Many hospitals have volunteer programs in which individuals (usually students and senior citizens) provide various ancillary services.

? **What Did You Learn?**

1. Describe a typical general hospital.
2. How are today's hospitals regulated?
3. What is meant by *vertically integrated hospital*?
4. List at least three emerging healthcare trends.

A medical facility smaller than a hospital is typically referred to as a *clinic* and is often run by a government agency or a private partnership of physicians. Clinics generally provide only outpatient services.

INTEGRATED DELIVERY SYSTEM

An **integrated delivery system (IDS)** is a healthcare provider or a network of providers created to integrate hospital services with physician services. Under the conventional type of delivery system, hospitals provide services and facilities, such as room and board, emergency care, nursing care, and diagnostic services, for which they are reimbursed by third-party insurers, government programs, or even the patients themselves. Physicians provide medical and surgical services to patients through their private practices, admitting and treating patients in the hospital when necessary, for which they are paid separately by the insurers, government programs, or patients. In an IDS, inpatient hospital and physician services are combined under one entity that provides and bills for both hospital and all physician services, either through the entity itself or through contractual associations.

ACUTE CARE FACILITY

An acute care facility is what most individuals usually think of as a "hospital," although all services provided may not relate directly to an **acute condition** (condition in which a patient's medical state has become unstable). This facility is equipped and staffed to respond immediately to a critical situation.

An **acute care facility** can be defined as a facility offering inpatient, overnight care and services for observation, diagnosis, and active treatment of an individual with a medical, surgical, obstetric, chronic, or rehabilitative condition requiring the daily direction or supervision of a physician. **Acute care** involves assessing and treating sudden or unexpected injuries and illnesses. Acute healthcare settings provide emergency care, sophisticated diagnostic tools, and surgical interventions and can provide patient care 24 hours a day, 7 days a week, and 365 days a year. The staff consists of nurses, doctors, technicians, therapists, and other ancillary staff who have roles in caring for and/or supporting the patient.

After a patient is discharged from the hospital, two different claims typically are generated—one from the hospital for institutional charges (room and board, emergency department, operating room, physical therapy) and the other from the physician for his or her professional services. As we learned in earlier chapters, physician service claims are submitted to the patient's insurance carrier using an **electronic claims submission (ECS)** process or the CMS-1500 paper claim form, if the provider qualifies. Hospital service claims are typically submitted electronically or by using a nationally recognized billing form called the **UB-04**

(short for uniform bill 2004), which is sometimes referred to as the *CMS-1450 form.*

CRITICAL ACCESS HOSPITAL

A **critical access hospital (CAH)** is one that is certified to receive cost-based reimbursement from Medicare. The Critical Access Hospital Program was created by the 1997 federal Balanced Budget Act as a safety net to guarantee Medicare beneficiaries access to healthcare services in rural areas. It was designed to allow more flexible staffing options required by the community, simplify billing methods, and create incentives to develop local integrated health delivery systems, including acute, primary, emergency, and long-term care.

The reimbursement that a CAH receives is intended to improve financial performance, thereby reducing hospital closures. Each hospital must review its own situation to determine whether CAH status would be advantageous. CAHs are certified under a different set of Medicare Conditions of Participation (CoP) that are more flexible than those of acute care hospitals.

AMBULATORY SURGERY CENTERS

An **ambulatory surgery center (ASC)** is a facility where surgical procedures that do not require hospital admission are performed. They provide a cost-effective and convenient environment that may be less stressful than that offered by many hospitals. Particular ASCs may perform surgical procedures in a variety of specialties or dedicate their services to one specialty, such as eye care or orthopedic services.

An ASC treats only patients who already have seen a healthcare provider and who together have selected surgery as an appropriate treatment. All ASCs must have at least one dedicated operating room and the equipment needed to perform surgery safely and to ensure quality patient care. Physician offices and clinics that are not so equipped are not considered ASCs. Patients who elect to have surgery in an ASC arrive on the day of the procedure, undergo the procedure in a specially equipped operating room, and recover under the care of the nursing staff, all without a hospital admission.

ASCs are among the most highly regulated healthcare facilities in the United States. Medicare has certified more than 80% of these centers, and most states require ASCs to be licensed. These states also specify the criteria that ASCs must meet for licensure. States and Medicare survey ASCs regularly to verify that the established standards are being met. All accredited ASCs must meet specific standards that are evaluated during on-site inspections. In addition to state and federal inspections, many surgery centers go through a voluntary accreditation process conducted by peers. As a result, patients visiting an accredited ASC can be assured that the center provides the highest-quality care.

CLINIC

A **clinic** is an organization that provides professional medical or other types of healthcare services in one or more centralized locations, usually on an outpatient basis. A clinic may be similar to the outpatient department of a hospital; however, it is generally distinguishable from a hospital in that it lacks facilities for inpatient or emergency care. A clinic also may be similar in many ways to a multispecialty, private group medical practice. A clinic can also be an IDS, such as when a clinic is owned by, controlled by, or operated in conjunction with a specific hospital.

OTHER TYPES OF HEALTHCARE FACILITIES

Many other types of healthcare facilities exist in addition to acute care hospitals and ASCs (Fig. 18.1). A brief discussion of a few of the more familiar types follows.

Subacute Care Facility

A **subacute care facility** is a comprehensive, highly specialized inpatient program designed for individuals who have experienced an acute event as a result of an illness, injury, or **exacerbation** (worsening) of a disease process. It specifies a level of maintenance care in which there is no urgent or life-threatening condition requiring medical treatment. Subacute care may consist of long-term ventilator care or other procedures provided on a routine basis either at home or by trained staff at a skilled nursing facility (SNF). This type of care often is seen as a bridge between the hospital's acute care units and facilities for patients who require ongoing medical care or who are still dependent on advanced medical technology.

In a subacute care facility, patients have the advantage of constant access to nursing care as they move toward recovery and return to their home, which acute care facilities typically do not provide. If the physician determines that recuperative care is required after an acute hospitalization, the patient may be transferred to a facility that specializes in subacute services; however, a stay in a subacute care facility is generally short term.

Skilled Nursing Facility

A **skilled nursing facility (SNF)** is an institution or a distinct part of an institution that is licensed or approved under state or local law and is primarily engaged in providing skilled nursing care and related services as an SNF, extended care facility, or nursing care facility approved by The Joint Commission or the Commission on Accreditation of Rehabilitation Facilities (CARF), or otherwise determined by the health plan to meet the reasonable standards applied by any of these authorities.

Previously referred to as "nursing homes," SNFs have evolved in the services they provide. They offer 24-hour skilled nursing care; rehabilitation services, such as physical, speech, and occupational therapy; assistance with personal care activities, such as eating, walking, toileting, and bathing; coordinated management of patient care; social services; and activities. Some SNFs offer specialized care programs for patients with Alzheimer disease or other illnesses or short-term **respite care** for frail or disabled individuals when family members require a rest from providing care in the home. Respite care services give individuals, such as family members, temporary relief from tasks associated with caregiving. A crucial element of an SNF is periodic reviews by the state or local department of social and health services.

- Acute Care Facilities
- Ambulatory Surgical Centers
- Assisted Living Residences
- Assisted Living Residences: Residential Care Facilities—Mentally Ill
- Birth Centers
- Community Clinics and Emergency Centers
- Chiropractic Centers
- Community Mental Health Clinics and/or Centers
- Comprehensive Outpatient Rehabilitation
- Designated Trauma Centers
- Freestanding End-Stage Renal Disease Service
- Home/Community-Based Services: Adult Day Care Programs
- Home/Community-Based Services: Personal Care/Homemaker
- Home Health Agencies
- Hospices
- Hospitals (General, Psychiatric, Rehabilitation, Critical Access)
- Intermediate Care Facilities for Developmentally Disabled
- Long-Term Care (Nursing Homes/Nursing Care) Facilities
- Physical Therapy: Outpatient
- Portable X-Ray Services
- Residential Care Facilities—Developmentally Disabled
- Rural Health Clinics
- Skilled Nursing Facilities
- Subacute Care Facilities
- Swing Bed Facilities

Fig. 18.1 List of healthcare facilities.

Imagine This!

Walden-Martin Respite Services offers a wide range of services to caregivers who require temporary relief from their responsibilities. These services include companion services, personal care, household assistance, and skilled nursing care to meet the specific needs of patients with disabilities, patients with chronic or terminal illnesses, and elderly patients. Walden-Martin Respite Services provides overnight, weekend, and longer stays for individuals with Alzheimer disease or a related dementia so that a caregiver can have longer periods of time off. The facility provides meals, helps with activities of daily living (ADLs), and provides therapeutic activities to fit the needs of residents in a safe, supervised environment.

Intermediate Care Facility

An **intermediate care facility** is designed for individuals with chronic conditions who are unable to live independently but who do not need constant intensive care. Intermediate care facilities provide supportive care and nursing supervision under medical direction 24 hours a day but do not provide continuous nursing care. They stress rehabilitation therapy that enables individuals to return to a home setting or to regain or retain as many functions of daily living as possible. A full range of medical, social, recreational, and support services are also provided.

Long-Term Care Facility

A **long-term care facility** provides care for adults who are chronically ill or disabled and are no longer able to manage in independent living situations. Long-term care is the type of care that individuals may need when they no longer can perform **activities of daily living (ADLs)**, such as bathing, eating, and getting dressed, by themselves. It also includes the kind of care an individual would need if he or she had a severe cognitive impairment, such as Alzheimer disease.

When we think of long-term care, we often think of nursing homes. Long-term care can be received in a variety of settings, however, including an individual's own home, assisted living facilities, adult day care centers, and hospice facilities. Long-term care does not refer to the medical care needed to get well from an illness or injury or to short-term rehabilitation from an accident or recuperation from surgery.

Hospice

Hospice is not a specific place; it is a facility or service that provides care for terminally ill patients and support to their families, either directly (including in a patient's home) or on a consulting basis with the patient's physician. Emphasis is on **palliative care** (temporary relief of pain or symptoms without a cure—sometimes called *comfort care*) and support before and after death. Hospice attempts to meet each patient's unique physical, emotional, social, and spiritual needs and the special needs of the patient's family and close friends. The goals of hospice are to keep the patient as comfortable as possible by relieving pain and other discomforting symptoms, to prepare for a death that follows the wishes and needs of the patient, and to reassure the patient and loved ones by helping them understand and manage what is happening. This support assists patients and families through the process of facing, understanding, and accepting death.

Home Health Agency

A **home health agency** provides a wide range of healthcare services that can be given in the patient's home. Home healthcare is usually less expensive and more convenient than, and can be just as effective as, care provided in a hospital or SNF. In general, home healthcare includes part-time or intermittent skilled nursing care and other skilled care services, such as physical and/or occupational therapy and speech-language therapy services. Services may also include medical social services or assistance from a home health aide. A home healthcare agency typically coordinates the services ordered by the patient's physician.

> **? What Did You Learn?**
>
> 1. Name three major types of healthcare facilities.
> 2. How does an acute care facility differ from a CAH?
> 3. In what type of facility might an individual receive long-term care?
> 4. What is hospice?

LEGAL AND REGULATORY ENVIRONMENT

State and federal governments, accrediting organizations, employers, and healthcare plans have developed methods for ensuring quality in managed care plan systems. As physicians and healthcare consumers have become more aware of the need for protection against excessive containment of managed care costs, many state governments have enacted laws designed to protect patients' rights.

All acute care or general hospitals must be licensed by the particular state in which they are located to provide care within the minimum health and safety standards established by regulation and rule. The US Department of Health and Human Services (HHS) enforces the standards by periodically conducting surveys of these facilities. Medicare pays for services provided by hospitals that voluntarily seek and are approved for certification by the Centers for Medicare and Medicaid Services (CMS). CMS contracts with HHS to evaluate compliance with the federal hospital regulations by periodically conducting surveys of these agencies.

A hospital may seek accreditation by nationally recognized accrediting agencies, such as The Joint Commission or the Center for Improvement in Healthcare Quality (CIHQ). Surveys conducted by The Joint Commission and CIHQ are based on guidelines developed by each of these organizations.

The federal **Emergency Medical Treatment and Active Labor Act (EMTALA)**, also known as the *anti–patient dumping law,* was enacted by Congress as part of the Consolidated Omnibus Budget Reconciliation Act of 1985. This act states that Medicare participating member hospitals must respond to an individual's **emergent medical condition** (defined as the onset of a health condition that requires immediate medical attention) by determining the nature of the condition. If an emergent condition exists, it must be treated to the best of the facility's ability, regardless of ability to pay. Patients can then be transferred as appropriate after the condition has been stabilized.

EMTALA applies to virtually all hospitals in the United States with the exception of the Shriners Hospitals for Children and many military hospitals. Its provisions apply to all patients, not just to Medicare beneficiaries.

EFFECTS OF THE AFFORDABLE CARE ACT ON EMERGENCY SERVICES

One of the primary goals of the Affordable Care Act (ACA) is to provide previously uninsured Americans with affordable healthcare coverage. If the ACA remains in force, it is predicted that the number of non-elderly uninsured will decrease considerably, and at the same time there will be an increase in patients insured through expanded Medicaid coverage, as well as state-based health insurance exchanges, thus relieving the burden on emergency departments and freeing them to treat real emergencies. The uninsured rate may drop further due to the healthcare law's provision requiring businesses with 100 or more employees to provide health insurance to 70% of their workers that took effect on January 1, 2016. After this date, companies with 50 or more employees were required to provide health insurance to 95% of their workers.

 Stop and Think

After a fall from his bicycle on his way home from school, Bobby Thaddeus, an 8-year-old boy, complained of pain in his right arm. His mother, fearing that his arm might be fractured, brought Bobby to Meadville Hospital's emergency department. The emergency staff at Meadville refused to treat the child, advising Bobby's mother to take him to their family practitioner for treatment. A spokesman at Meadville defended the hospital's policy, stating that it was put in place to curb misuse of emergency department services. Non-emergencies overloaded staff and facilities with routine medical problems that could be handled as well elsewhere. When routine injuries and illnesses were brought to the emergency department, they cause delayed treatment of true emergencies. Do you agree with the hospital's policy? Why or why not? Was Meadville violating the Emergency Medical Treatment and Active Labor Act (EMTALA) in refusing to treat Bobby's injury?

ACCREDITATION

Accreditation is a voluntary process through which an organization can measure the quality of its services and performance against nationally recognized standards. It is the process by which a private or public agency evaluates and recognizes (certifies) an institution—in this case, hospitals—as fulfilling applicable standards. The Joint Commission evaluates whether hospitals, nursing homes, and managed care organizations (MCOs) meet certain specified requirements. The **Accreditation Association for Ambulatory Health Care**

(AAAHC) and the **National Committee for Quality Assurance (NCQA)** assess and award compliance certifications to MCOs, including health maintenance organizations (HMOs). Public agencies sometimes require accreditation by a private body as a condition of licensure, or they may accept accreditation as a substitute for their own inspection or certification programs. The next section discusses the more commonly known accreditation organizations.

The Joint Commission

The Joint Commission is a private organization created in 1951 to provide voluntary accreditation to hospitals. A panel, called the *Patient Safety Advisory Group,* composed of nurses, physicians, pharmacists, risk managers, clinical engineers, and other professionals who have hands-on experience in addressing patient safety issues in a wide variety of healthcare settings, verifies compliance with the accreditation standards for hospitals and other medical facilities.

National Committee for Quality Assurance

The NCQA is an independent, nonprofit organization that performs quality-oriented accreditation reviews on HMOs and similar types of managed care plans. NCQA is governed by a board of directors that includes employers, consumer and labor representatives, health plan representatives, policymakers, and physicians. The purpose of NCQA is to evaluate plans and provide information that helps consumers and employers make informed decisions about purchasing health plan services. NCQA performs two distinct functions: (1) the evaluation and accreditation of health plans and (2) measurement of performance.

The NCQA accreditation process involves a comprehensive review of health plan structure, policies, procedures, systems, and records. The review includes an analysis of plan documents and an on-site inspection visit by a team of expert reviewers. On the basis of the review, plans are accorded one of several possible accreditation levels: excellent, commendable, accredited, and provisional. Plans that do not meet standards are denied accreditation status.

 Stop and Think

Elena Sanchez, a 42-year-old woman, lived in a large metropolitan area with several large and small hospitals. After a visit to her physician for complications of diabetes, her physician advised her that she should be admitted to one of the local hospitals for some tests and possible surgery. Elena asked her friend Teresa, a health information professional, how she should choose which hospital to go to. She preferred the one located in her neighborhood, Seacrest Memorial. Teresa told Elena that Seacrest might not be the best choice because although it was handy, it was not accredited. Why might this fact be a concern for Elena?

Accreditation Association for Ambulatory Health Care

The AAAHC was formed in 1979 to assist ambulatory healthcare organizations improve the quality of care provided to patients. The accreditation decision is based on assessment of an organization's compliance with applicable standards and adherence to the policies and procedures of AAAHC. AAAHC expects substantial compliance with all applicable standards, which is assessed by at least one of the following means:

- Documented evidence
- Answers to detailed questions concerning implementation
- On-site observations and interviews by surveyors

Utilization Review Accreditation Commission

The **Utilization Review Accreditation Commission (URAC)** is an independent, nonprofit organization. Its mission is to promote continuous improvement in the quality and efficiency of healthcare delivery by achieving a common understanding of excellence among purchasers, providers, and patients through the establishment of standards, programs of education and communication, and a process of accreditation. URAC is nationally recognized as a leader in quality improvement, reviewing and auditing a broad array of healthcare service functions and systems. Their accreditation activities cover health plans, preferred provider organizations, medical management systems, health technology services, healthcare centers, specialty care, workers' compensation, medical websites, and HIPAA privacy and security compliance.

HIPAA

HIPAA provides an extra assurance of privacy for all patients. The rules and regulations involved in the HIPAA law have had an impact on medical billing processes for insurance companies and all medical facilities. The law calls for the electronic processing of all documents between the healthcare provider and the insurance carrier with few exceptions. Hospital billers used to file all claims as paper copies using the UB-04 form. However, billing and coding software that makes the process more accurate and less time consuming has been developed. A few hospitals may still use manual coding and billing processes for some insurance companies, but the third-party payer demand for electronic claims filing is reducing these numbers rapidly. Because of this fact, the author has elected not to discuss the UB-04 form in any detail. A sample copy of the UB-04 form is included in Appendix C, along with step-by-step completion instructions.

PROFESSIONAL STANDARDS

Professional standards that govern US hospitals typically are associated with an accrediting body, such as The Joint Commission, and differ from one organization to the next. The Joint Commission's Medical Staff Standard MS.6.9 requires hospitals to define (e.g., in a policy) the process for supervision of residents by licensed independent practitioners with appropriate clinical privileges. A **licensed independent practitioner** is defined as "any individual permitted by law and by the organization to provide care and services without direction or supervision, within the scope of the individual's license, and consistent with individually granted clinical privileges."

The standard also requires the medical staff to ensure that each resident is supervised in his or her patient care responsibilities by a licensed independent practitioner who has been granted clinical privileges through the medical staff process. Finally, the rules require hospitals to identify in the medical staff rules, regulations, and policies which individuals may write patient care orders, the circumstances under which they may write such orders, and what entries must be countersigned by a supervising licensed independent practitioner.

GOVERNANCE

Governance, in its widest sense, refers to how any organization is run. With reference to healthcare facilities, it involves all of the processes, systems, and controls that are used to safeguard the welfare of patients and the integrity of the institution. The Joint Commission's Revised Governance Standard GO.2 provides that, in addition to providing for the effective functioning of activities related to delivering quality patient care, performance improvement, risk management, medical staff credentialing, and financial management, the governing body must provide for the effective functioning of professional graduate medical education programs (e.g., by adopting policies and bylaw provisions).

CONFIDENTIALITY AND PRIVACY

Most hospital accrediting organizations, specifically The Joint Commission, include strategies for accrediting a hospital on privacy and confidentiality issues that parallel the demands of HIPAA compliance. It is important for hospital staff to understand and abide by HIPAA's Privacy Standards, including such topics as:

- Who qualifies as "covered entities" under the Privacy Standards
- What type of information is protected
- What HIPAA's restrictions are on the use and disclosure of protected health information (PHI)
- How the hospital follows the minimum necessary standard
- How the hospital implements patient rights created by the Privacy Standards
- What administrative requirements the Privacy Standards impose
- What business associates are and when the hospital needs contracts with them to disclose PHI
- What the HIPAA preemption provisions are
- What penalties HHS can impose for failing to comply with the Privacy Standards

A **covered entity** under HIPAA is a health plan, a healthcare clearinghouse, or a healthcare provider that transmits any health information in electronic form in connection with a transaction. The Privacy Rule requires a covered entity (in this case, the hospital) to make reasonable efforts to limit use of, disclosure of, and requests for PHI to the minimum necessary to accomplish the intended purpose. The minimum necessary standard is intended to make covered entities evaluate and enhance protections as needed to prevent unnecessary or inappropriate access to PHI. It is intended to reflect and be consistent with, not to override, professional judgment and standards.

The Privacy Rule is not intended to prohibit providers from talking to other providers and their patients. The following practices are considered permissible, if reasonable precautions are taken to minimize the chance of inadvertent disclosures to others who may be nearby (e.g., using lowered voices, talking apart):

- Healthcare staff may verbally coordinate services at hospital nursing stations.
- Nurses or other healthcare professionals may discuss a patient's condition over the phone with the patient, a provider, or a family member.
- A healthcare professional may discuss laboratory test results with a patient or other provider in a joint treatment area.
- Healthcare professionals may discuss a patient's condition during training rounds in an academic or training institution.

◎ HIPAA Tip

Health Insurance Portability and Accountability Act (HIPAA) regulations state that hospitals are required by law to protect the privacy of health information that may reveal a patient's identity (referred to as *protected health information*, or *PHI*) and to provide the patient with a written Notice of Privacy Practice that describes the health information privacy practices of the hospital.

⚠ Stop and Think

Elizabeth Cotter, a 74-year-old woman, underwent a serious operation after experiencing a cardiac episode. After the surgery was completed, a nurse came to the reception area where Mrs. Cotter's family was waiting and informed them that although the procedure took longer than expected, Mrs. Cotter came through it okay and was now in the recovery room. "You can see her as soon as she is transferred to her room, in about 30 minutes." Has there been a breach of patient confidentiality here? Why or why not?

After Mrs. Cotter returned to her room, her next-door neighbor telephoned the nurses' station to inquire as to her condition. The nurse informed the caller that although the procedure took longer than expected and that it was "touch and go for a while," the patient was back in her room now and was expected to make a full recovery. Has there been a breach of confidentiality here? Why or why not?

FAIR TREATMENT OF PATIENTS

In Chapter 3, we learned about **medical ethics**, which are the moral principles that govern the practice of medicine by physicians and other healthcare practitioners. When dealing with patients or healthcare users, healthcare practitioners are governed by these ethical principles and the law. Breaches of ethical rules may result in disciplinary action by employers and professional staff. Breaches of the law may result in similar disciplinary action and criminal or civil legal action against the healthcare practitioners concerned. Basic principles of medical ethics are usually regarded as:

- Showing respect for patient autonomy
- Not inflicting harm on patients
- Contributing to the welfare of patients
- Providing justice and fair treatment of patients

Ethical principles require healthcare practitioners to become advocates for their patients. The principle of justice or fairness requires medical personnel to ensure that their patients enjoy the constitutional right to equal treatment and freedom from unfair discrimination. The principle of autonomy requires medical personnel to ensure that their patients' constitutional and common law human rights to freedom and security of the individual are respected; this is safeguarded by the ethical and legal requirements of an informed consent. Respect of a patient's right to freedom of religion, beliefs, and opinions is legally required in terms of the US Constitution.

A patient's right to privacy is safeguarded by the ethical and legal rules regarding confidentiality. The principle of not inflicting harm requires medical personnel to ensure that their patients' constitutional human rights to dignity, life, emergency treatment, and an environment that is not harmful to health are upheld. The principle of contributing to the welfare of patients requires medical personnel to ensure that the constitutional imperative against medical malpractice and professional negligence is upheld.

A breach of an ethical principle or of an ethical rule or regulation formally put into effect by a professional council may be used to establish medical malpractice or professional negligence, although the breach itself may not constitute a crime or civil wrong. For a civil wrong to be proved, it would have to be shown that the health professional's conduct was also a breach of a legal obligation.

◎ HIPAA Tip

A hospital billing department is prevented from answering questions from advocates or family members who work on a patient's behalf to help pay medical bills unless the patient has signed a written authorization directing billing department employees to do so.

Imagine This!

If a physician or other healthcare practitioner negligently causes the death of a patient by breaching an ethical rule, he or she may face a criminal charge of culpable homicide or a civil action by the deceased's dependents. Marcus Sherman, a 56-year-old man, saw Dr. Edmund Pithily because of rectal bleeding. Dr. Pithily performed a limited sigmoidoscopy, the results of which were negative. The patient continued to have rectal bleeding but was repeatedly reassured by the physician that he was okay. Eighteen months later, after a 25-pound weight loss, Mr. Sherman was admitted to a hospital for evaluation. He was found to have colon cancer with metastases to the liver. Despite all efforts to combat the spread of the disease, Mr. Sherman died. The physicians who reviewed his medical record judged that proper diagnostic management might have discovered the cancer when it was still curable. They attributed the advanced disease to substandard medical care. The event was considered adverse and due to negligence.

Patient's Bill of Rights Under the Affordable Care Act

The **Patient Protection and Affordable Care Act (PPACA)** was signed into law in March 2010. The main intent of this act is to increase the affordability and rate of health insurance coverage for Americans and reduce the overall costs of healthcare for individuals and the government. The PPACA provides a number of comprehensive reforms, including a patients' bill of rights that:

- Provides coverage to Americans with preexisting conditions
- Protects an individual's choice of doctors
- Allows young adults (under age 26) to be covered under a parent's plan
- Ends lifetime limits for most benefit coverage on new health plans
- Ends preexisting condition exclusions for children under age 19
- Prevents insurers from canceling coverage if the insured made an honest mistake
- Requires insurance companies to publicly justify any unreasonable rate hikes
- Requires premium dollars to be spent primarily on healthcare, not on administrative costs
- Eliminates annual limits on health benefits
- Removes barriers to emergency services outside the health plan's network
- Covers preventive care at no cost for certain eligible groups
- Guarantees the right to appeal if a claim is denied

? What Did You Learn?

1. What governing body licenses acute care and general hospitals?
2. List two nationally recognized organizations that play an important role in hospital accreditation.
3. What function does EMTALA serve?
4. What is the purpose of accreditation?
5. List the principles of medical ethics.

COMMON HOSPITAL PAYERS AND THEIR CLAIMS GUIDELINES

The major payers of hospital costs are much the same as those of physicians' offices and clinics. Government payers (Medicare, Medicaid, and TRICARE/CHAMPVA) typically have the largest share of claims, followed by Blue Cross and Blue Shield (BCBS) and MCOs. Other payers include private or commercial insurance companies, no-fault or liability insurance arrangements, and workers' compensation. These shares differ, however, from state to state. As stated often throughout this text, it is paramount for the health insurance professional to learn and follow the specific guidelines of each individual payer. The following subsections briefly address these major payers. For more detailed information, refer to their specific corresponding chapters.

MEDICARE

Medicare hospital claims are processed by nongovernment organizations or agencies that contract to serve as fiscal agents between providers (hospitals, physicians, and other healthcare providers) and the federal government. These claims processors are commonly referred to as *Medicare carriers, Medicare administrative contractors (MACs),* or *fiscal intermediaries (FIs).* They apply Medicare coverage rules to determine the appropriateness and medical necessity of claims.

Medicare carriers (regional companies that oversee the administration and processing of Medicare policies and claims) process Part A claims (hospital insurance) for institutional services, including inpatient hospital services and those provided by SNFs, home healthcare agencies, and hospice. They also process hospital outpatient claims for Medicare Part B. Examples are BCBS, Noridian, Palmetto, and other commercial insurance companies.

Carriers are required to process claims according to government regulations. In addition, as regional companies, they have the authority to set local policies. A Medicare carrier reviews all Medicare claims and determines whether each claim qualifies for reimbursement. The carrier is then responsible for developing payment policies for the states in its area. Once these local medical review policies (also known as *local coverage determinations*) are established, the Medicare carrier evaluates each Medicare claim to ensure that the services provided are reasonable and necessary. In addition, Medicare carriers are responsible for:

- Maintaining records
- Establishing controls
- Safeguarding against fraud and abuse or excess use
- Conducting reviews and audits
- Assisting providers and beneficiaries as needed

HIPAA Tip

The Centers for Medicare and Medicaid Services (CMS) has instructed their Medicare carriers and intermediaries to make available to providers free or low-cost software that would enable electronic submission of Health Insurance Portability and Accountability Act (HIPAA)–compliant claims.

Quality Improvement Organizations

Quality improvement organizations (QIOs), formerly called *peer review organizations,* are groups of practicing healthcare professionals who are paid by the federal government to overview the care provided to Medicare beneficiaries and to improve the quality of services. QIOs educate and assist in the promotion of effective, efficient, and economical delivery of healthcare services to the Medicare population they serve. QIOs are discussed in more detail in Chapter 11. More information on QIOs can be found on the CMS website.

Keeping Current With Medicare

The Medicare Modernization Act of 2003 brought many changes to the Medicare program. These changes gave beneficiaries more choices in how they get their healthcare benefits, as follows:

- Medicare prescription drug plan (see Chapter 11), which began January 2006 (enrollment started in November 2005)
- New health plan choices, including Medicare Advantage health plans and regional preferred provider organization plans, which began in 2006
- New preventive benefits, first available January 1, 2005, including cardiovascular screening blood tests, diabetes screening tests, and "welcome to Medicare" physical examinations

When the PPACA was first passed into law in 2010, it required that most individuals have minimum health insurance. The legislation created new public plans and expanded the Medicare and Medicaid programs to include more beneficiaries while requiring that all health plans extend coverage to individuals, regardless of health status.

To keep current with Medicare changes, the health insurance professional should log on to the CMS website periodically to research what is new. It is also a good idea to keep on hand a copy of the most recent edition of the beneficiary handbook, *Medicare and You,* which can be downloaded from the Internet.

Medicare Part A: Review

Part A helps provide coverage for inpatient care in hospitals, including CAHs and SNFs, but not extended care in custodial or long-term care facilities. Part A also helps cover hospice care and some home healthcare. Beneficiaries must meet certain conditions to obtain these benefits. Most individuals eligible for Medicare do not have to pay a monthly payment (premium) for Part A because they or a spouse paid Medicare taxes while employed. If Medicare beneficiaries do not get premium-free Part A, they may be able to buy it if:

- They or their spouses are not entitled to Social Security because they did not work or did not pay Medicare taxes while working and are age 65 or older, or
- They are disabled but no longer get free Part A because they returned to work

Qualifying for Medicare Part A

If you or your spouse (or former spouse) has at least 40 calendar quarters (10 years) of work in any job at which you paid Social Security taxes in the United States; or if you are eligible for Railroad Retirement benefits; or if you were a federal employee after December 31, 1982, or a state or local employee after March 31, 1986, you are eligible for premium-free Part A based on your work history or federal employment. You may be eligible for premium-free Part A based on your spouse's work history if you meet certain criteria.

If you do not meet these criteria, you may have to pay the Part A premium. Your monthly Part A premium will depend on how many years you or your spouse worked in any job at which you paid Social Security taxes in the United States.

In 2020 the monthly Part A premium was:	
$0	If you or your spouse worked for 10 years or more or you were a federal employee on January 1, 1983
$240	If you or your spouse worked between 7.5 and 10 years
$437	If you or your spouse worked fewer than 7.5 years

If your income is low, you may be eligible for the Qualified Medicare Beneficiary (QMB) program (see Chapter 10), which pays for your Medicare Part A and B premiums.

What Medicare Part A Pays

All rules about how much Medicare Part A pays depend on how many days of inpatient care the beneficiary has during what is called a **benefit period** or "spell of illness." The benefit period begins on the day the individual enters the hospital or SNF as an inpatient and continues until he or she has been out of the hospital for 60 consecutive days. If the patient is in and out of the hospital or SNF several times but has not stayed out completely for 60 consecutive days, all inpatient charges for that time are figured as part of the same benefit period.

Medicare Part A pays only certain amounts of a hospital bill for any one benefit period, and the rules are slightly different depending on whether the care facility is a hospital, psychiatric hospital, or SNF or whether care is received at home or through hospice.

Table 18.1   2020 Medicare Part A Payment Schedule

Note: Coinsurance per benefit period varies based on the length of the hospital stay.	
Inpatient hospital deductible	$1364 for each benefit period
Inpatient hospital coinsurance	Days 1 through 60 of each benefit period: $0 Days 61 through 90: $341 per day Days 91 and beyond: $682 per day for each lifetime reserve day. (You get 60 lifetime reserve days.) After lifetime reserve days are used up, you pay all costs. Inpatient psychiatric care in a freestanding psychiatric hospital is limited to 190 days in a lifetime.
Skilled nursing facility (SNF) coinsurance	Days 1 through 20 of each benefit period: $0 Days 21 through 100 of each benefit period: $177.50 per day Days 101 and beyond: you are responsible for all costs.

Table 18.1 shows the 2020 Medicare Part A schedule outlining what Medicare pays versus the deductible and coinsurance amounts for which the patient or beneficiary is responsible.

How Medicare Part A Payments Are Calculated

Medicare payments are calculated through the use of the **prospective payment system (PPS)**, which is Medicare's acute care payment method for inpatient care. PPS rates are set at a level intended to cover costs for treating a typical inpatient in a given **diagnosis-related group (DRG)**. DRG is a coding system that groups related diagnoses and their associated medical or surgical treatments. Payments for each hospital are adjusted for differences in area wages, teaching activity, care to the poor, and other factors. Hospitals also may receive additional payments to cover extra costs associated with **outliers** (atypical patients) in each DRG. The CMS uses the DRG system to determine the amount that Medicare would reimburse hospitals and other designated providers for the delivery of inpatient services. Each DRG corresponds to a specific patient condition, and each has a preestablished fixed amount that is paid for any patient in the DRG category. PPS and DRGs are discussed at length in Chapter 17.

Medicare Severity System

One of the most significant changes in DRG methodology since 1983 is the **Medicare Severity (MS)–DRG System**. CMS implemented this modified DRG methodology effective October 1, 2007. The inpatient prospective payment system (IPPS) rule is intended to match hospital payments more closely with the costs of patient care and the patient's condition(s) by placing the most seriously ill patients in the highest-paying DRGs (within the DRG set) for any specific procedure. This change benefits large, urban, and teaching hospitals that have patients whose cases are more complex but provides fewer resources to smaller community and rural hospitals that treat more "routine" patients.

The CMS refined the existing MS-DRG structure to the severity-adjusted DRG (SDRG) system, which better identifies patients with different resource needs and outcomes. SDRGs take into consideration all age ranges, especially the pediatric population, as opposed to just Medicare beneficiaries under MS-DRGs.

To keep current on recent and proposed changes to IPPS, visit http://www.cms.gov/.

Inpatient Prospective Payment System 3-Day Payment Window

Diagnostic outpatient services provided to a patient by the admitting hospital within 3 calendar days prior to and including the date of the inpatient admission are considered inpatient services and should be included in the inpatient MS-DRG payment, unless there is no Part A coverage. The 3-day payment window is discussed in more detail later in this chapter; see "The 72-Hour Rule."

MEDICAID

Each state's Medicaid program determines the method it uses to pay for hospital inpatient services. Most states base reimbursement for hospital inpatient services on a PPS that includes DRGs and **per diems** (actual costs per day), and they provide a single payment to the hospital with no separate payment for specific services, such as imaging agents and other drugs and supplies. Some states use other reimbursement methods, such as cost-based payments, state-specific fee schedules, or a percentage of charges. Many Medicaid programs also adjust payments to reflect a hospital's **case mix** (reported data including patient demographic information such as age, sex, country of residence, and race or ethnicity; diagnostic information; treatment information; disposition; total charges; and expected source of payment) or the intensity of care required by patients treated at the facility.

Medicaid reimbursement for outpatient services varies from state to state as well, and there is a significant variation in Medicaid payment amounts among states; however, Medicaid programs typically pay less than other insurers.

Chapter 10 provides more detailed information on the Medicaid program.

TRICARE

Typically, patients covered under TRICARE (a healthcare program of the US Department of Defense [DoD] Military Health System), which provides civilian health benefits for military personnel, military retirees, and their dependents, including some members of the reserve component, are required to use a military treatment facility if one is located near them. If a military treatment facility is unavailable or cannot provide the inpatient care needed, the patient must, under most circumstances, ask for a **nonavailability statement (NAS)**. As discussed in Chapter 12, an NAS is a certification from a military hospital stating that it cannot provide the necessary care. For all inpatient admissions covered by TRICARE (except bona fide emergencies), an NAS is required. An NAS is valid for a hospital admission that occurs within 30 calendar days after it is issued and remains valid from the date of admission until 15 days after discharge for any follow-up treatment that is related directly to the admission. It is usually the patient's responsibility to provide a copy of the NAS to the hospital and to each physician providing services to the patient. Each paper claim submitted to TRICARE must be accompanied by a copy of the NAS; hospital personnel should advise patients to keep the original of the NAS for their files and provide only copies to the hospital and physician offices as needed.

The NAS system is automated for facilities that use ECS. This means that, instead of mailing paper copies of the NAS to the TRICARE carrier, the treating facility can enter the NAS electronically into the **Defense Enrollment Eligibility Reporting System (DEERS)** computer database.

An NAS is no longer required for outpatient procedures (except for routine maternity cases); however, to avoid claims rejection or delays, the patient or the treating facility should check with the TRICARE carrier for details on obtaining advance authorization before any procedures are done. Providers of care—whether or not they participate in TRICARE—are required to obtain these advance authorizations.

Inpatient TRICARE payments are calculated using the same PPS as Medicare, and the DRG-based payment is the TRICARE allowable charge, regardless of the billed amount. TRICARE also uses the same conversion factors as Medicare; however, the formulas are not identical to those used by the CMS. As a result, the final calculation result may differ slightly from that calculated by Medicare. Reimbursement rates and methods are subject to change per DoD guidelines.

TRICARE patients usually are required to pay a portion of the bill (**cost-sharing**) directly to the hospital at the time of discharge. Copies of the *TRICARE Handbook* should be available from the hospital admitting department or the patient financial services office. For more detailed information on TRICARE, refer to Chapter 12.

CHAMPVA

CHAMPVA (a health benefits program in which the Department of Veterans Affairs [VA] shares the cost of certain healthcare services and supplies with eligible beneficiaries) uses the same DRG-based PPS as that used by TRICARE. As mentioned previously, this reimbursement system is modeled on Medicare's PPS and applies to hospital inpatient services in all 50 states, the District of Columbia, and Puerto Rico. Current DRG weights and ratios are available in the *TRICARE Reimbursement Manual*. The manual also offers a DRG calculator.

CHAMPVA typically pays the allowed amount less the beneficiary cost-share, which is the lesser of:

- The annual adjusted per day amount multiplied by the number of inpatient days, or
- 25% of the hospital's billed charges, or
- The DRG rate (in applicable inpatient facilities)

When the DRG rate does not apply, CHAMPVA pays 75% of the billed amount for covered services and supplies.

Hospitals participating in Medicare must accept the CHAMPVA-determined allowable amount for inpatient services as payment in full. Although many of the procedures in the CHAMPVA DRG-based payment system are similar or identical to those for Medicare, the actual payment amounts differ in some cases. This is because the Medicare program is designed for a beneficiary population older than 65 years, whereas many CHAMPVA beneficiaries are considerably younger than 65 years and generally healthier. Services such as obstetrics and pediatrics are rare for Medicare beneficiaries but common for CHAMPVA beneficiaries.

SNFs also are paid through the use of the Medicare PPS. SNF PPS rates cover all routine, ancillary, and capital costs of covered SNF services. SNF admissions require preauthorization when TRICARE or CHAMPVA is the primary payer. SNF admissions for children younger than 10 years and CAH swing beds are exempt from SNF PPS, and their costs are reimbursed on the basis of billed charges or negotiated rates. The swing bed concept allows a hospital to use its beds interchangeably for acute care or postacute care. A **swing bed** agreement allows a change in reimbursement status. The patient "swings" from receiving acute care services and reimbursement to receiving skilled nursing services and reimbursement, usually without a change of facility.

As with most third-party payers, TRICARE and CHAMPVA reimbursement rates are subject to change on an annual basis. Health insurance professionals working in inpatient hospital facilities should keep current TRICARE and CHAMPVA provider manuals on hand.

BLUE CROSS AND BLUE SHIELD

Inpatient hospitalization reimbursement for patients covered under BCBS policies differs from region to region and depends on the benefit coverage outlined in the individual or group contract. With most BCBS policies, coverage is provided for hospital charges for a semiprivate room and most other customary, or ancillary, inpatient services up to a specific number of days, depending on the policy. Like most commercial policies, patients usually must satisfy an out-of-pocket (deductible) amount on which the PPACA has set limits. Beginning in 2014, qualifying health plans must cover 100% of the costs for medical care once a policyholder has reached the out-of-pocket limit. The out-of-pocket limits for 2020 are up to $8200 on a single policy and $16,400 on a family plan. In the case of a health plan offered in the small group market, the deductible cannot exceed $2000 for a plan covering a single individual and $4000 for any other plan. In addition to the deductible, patients typically must pay a specific percentage, or copayment, of the charges for each occurrence. The copayment or coinsurance amount varies widely—for example, 10% to 40% depending on the policy—before reimbursement begins. BCBS policies typically have an annual out-of-pocket limit—or cap—on the dollar amount for which the patient is responsible.

Under the PPACA, most health plans are required to cover certain preventive care services at no out-of-pocket costs. These services do not require patients to meet their deductible or other limits first. Before the enactment of the PPACA, policies often had a payment cap—a per-incident or lifetime limit on reimbursement. As of 2014, the PPACA prohibits new plans and existing group plans from imposing annual dollar limits on the amount of coverage an individual may receive.

As with most third-party payers, preauthorization is necessary for inpatient hospitalization and some outpatient procedures and diagnostic testing. Although preauthorization is ultimately the patient's responsibility, most healthcare facilities are willing to make the necessary telephone call to obtain preauthorization for the required services. The telephone number to call for preauthorization is generally listed on the back of the patient's healthcare identification (ID) card. That is the main reason for making a photocopy of both sides of the ID card. As with other third-party payers, the health insurance professional should be aware of the guidelines of the BCBS member organization before submitting claims.

Most hospitals in the United States are in the category of **BCBS member hospitals**—that is, they have contracted as participating providers with the BCBS member organization. Member hospitals must accept the BCBS allowable fee as payment in full and, after the initial deductible and copayment are met, cannot bill the patient for any remaining charges. For nonmember hospitals—that is, hospitals that do not contract with BCBS—reimbursement is limited in that way. As with physician charges, nonparticipating hospitals can balance-bill; that is, they can charge the patient for any charges above the allowable fee that BCBS does not pay.

BCBS fees for facility services are established using a variety of methods, as follows:
- Per case allowances (DRG or ambulatory payment classification [APC])
- Per diem allowances
- Percentage of charges
- Resource-based relative value scale (RBRVS)

See Chapter 8 for more details on BCBS. The health insurance professional should refer to the provider payment manual or contact the particular carrier for the specific inpatient and outpatient fee calculations used for the facility in question.

PRIVATE INSURERS

Most private insurers negotiate contracts with facilities regarding hospital inpatient payment methods. These contracts are typically negotiated annually. Many private payers use the DRG system to reimburse hospital inpatient services. Other common payment arrangements used by private insurers are per diems, percentage of allowable charges, and negotiated rates for specific treatments. Table 18.2 summarizes the payment mechanism by type of payer and setting of care.

> **? What Did You Learn?**
> 1. List the major hospital payers.
> 2. What benefits are included in Medicare Part A?
> 3. Many Medicaid programs adjust payments to reflect a hospital's *case mix*. What does this term mean?
> 4. What reimbursement system does CHAMPVA use for inpatient charges?
> 5. Explain the *swing bed* concept.

Table 18.2   Payment Mechanism by Type of Payer and Setting of Care

TYPE OF PAYER	FREESTANDING IMAGING CENTER OR PHYSICIAN SERVICES	HOSPITAL OUTPATIENT DEPARTMENTS	HOSPITAL INPATIENT
Medicare	RBRVS physician fee schedule	APCs	DRGs
Private insurance	RBRVS-based fee schedule Other fee schedule Discounted charges Capitated rates	Percentage of charges Negotiated rates Preset per diem or per-visit rates	DRGs Per diems Percentage of charges Negotiated rates
Medicaid	RBRVS-based fee schedule Other fee schedule	State-specific fee schedule Preset per diem or per-visit rates Percentage of charges	DRGs Per diems Cost-based

APC, Ambulatory payment classification; *DRG*, diagnosis-related group; *RBRVS*, resource-based relative value scale.

NATIONAL UNIFORM BILLING COMMITTEE AND THE UB-04

The UB-04, also known as the *CMS-1450 form,* is the standard paper claim form used by institutional providers (e.g., hospitals, SNFs, home health agencies) for billing third-party payers (Fig. 18.2) when a paper claim is allowed. However, the Administrative Simplification Compliance Act (ASCA) prohibits payment of initial Medicare claims for services or supplies that were not billed electronically unless the provider meets the ASCA "exceptions" or has been granted a

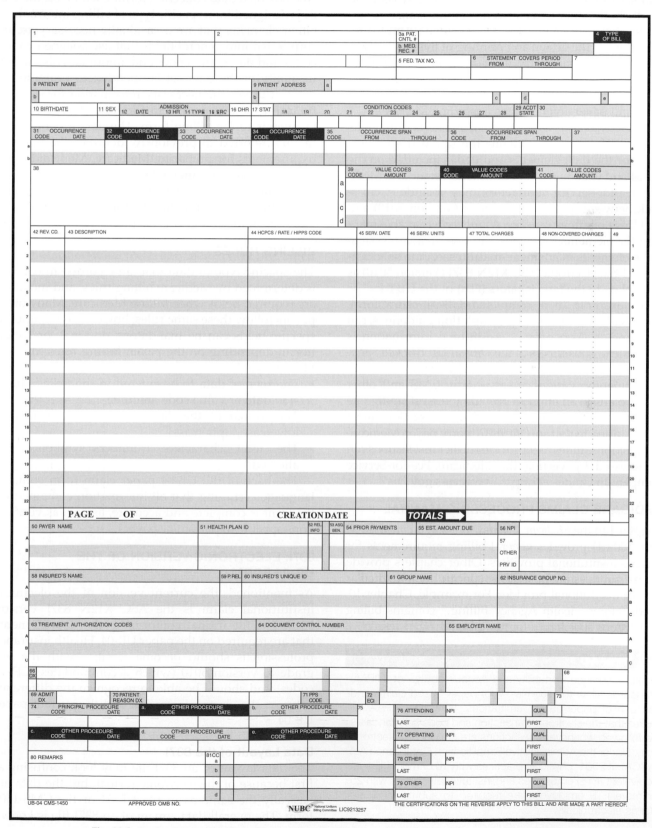

Fig. 18.2 Blank UB-04 claim form. (From Centers for Medicare and Medicaid Services, Baltimore, MD.)

waiver. The ASC X12N 837 Institutional (837I version 5010) claim format is the electronic version of the UB-04 form used by providers who submit claims electronically to various government and some private insurers. Data elements in the CMS uniform electronic billing specifications are consistent with the hard copy data set to the extent that one processing system can handle both paper and electronic submissions.

The **National Uniform Billing Committee (NUBC)** is responsible for the design and printing of the UB-04 form. The NUBC is a voluntary, multidisciplinary committee that develops data elements for claims and claim-related transactions and is composed of all major national provider and payer organizations (including Medicare).

NUBC makes its UB-04 manual available through its website. This manual contains the updated specifications for the data elements and codes included on the UB-04 and used in the 837I transaction standard. Medicare fee-for-service contractors may include a crosswalk between the ASC X12N 837I (Version 5010) and the UB-04 on their websites. A *crosswalk* is a table mapping the elements (or "fields") in one database system to the elements in another—in this case, data specifications of the electronic ASC X12N 837I (Version 5010) as they relate to the **form locators (FLs)** of the UB-04.

An example of a completed UB-04 claim form, along with the step-by-step completion guidelines, can be found in Appendix C. Additional information is available to subscribers of the *Official UB-04 Data Specifications Manual* at http://www.nubc.org/.

Companion Guides are issued by CMS and other health plans in an effort to provide the most up-to-date information related to how standard transactions must be submitted to that specific third-party payer. Medicare Companion Guides that provide further instructions can be accessed by visiting the Medicare Fee-for-Service Companion Guides at http://www.cms.gov/.

MEDICARE CLAIMS PROCESSING MANUAL

Chapter 1 in the *Medicare Claims Processing Manual* (IOM Pub. 100-04) provides general billing requirements for various institutional providers. Other chapters provide claims submission guidelines specific to a particular type of institutional provider. For example, Chapter 10, titled "Home Health Agency Billing," contains billing instructions specifically for home health agencies.

◎ HIPAA Tip

Health Insurance Portability and Accountability Act (HIPAA) standards allow the submission of paper-based claims and the use of paper-based remittances. However, HIPAA requires that the electronic transaction and code set standards be followed whenever transactions are conducted electronically. Under the Administrative Simplification Compliance Act (ASCA) of 2001, physician practices with 10 or more full-time equivalent (FTE) employees and institutional facilities with 25 or more FTE employees are required to submit Medicare claims electronically.

UB-04 DATA SPECIFICATIONS

Data elements, identified as necessary for claims processing, in most cases are assigned designated spaces on the UB-04 form. The designated spaces are referred to as FLs, and each one has a unique number. An FL is a numerical indicator that directs the reader to a specific box on a data collection form. Each FL on the UB-04 is designed for a specific type of billing information. Other elements that are occasionally necessary are incorporated into general fields that use assigned codes, codes and dates, and codes and amounts. This built-in flexibility of the data set is intended to promote the greatest use of the necessary information for successful claim submission and to eliminate the need for attachments to the billing form. The data specifications manual referred to previously identifies the national requirements for preparing Medicare, Medicaid, military, BCBS, and commercial insurance claims. To view an example of a completed UB-04 claim along with instructions for completing the form, see "Websites to Explore" at the end of this chapter.

BILLING RULES

The specific type of data that are recorded in each FL is determined by Medicare billing rules, and most FLs are required fields when billing Medicare. Many other payers follow these same rules; however, data input in specific fields can be mandatory, optional, or conditional, depending on the payer. Billing rules for each FL specify:

- The type of data to be entered in the field (admission date or value code amount)
- The format of the data (numerical/alphabetical; lowercase/uppercase)
- The total characters (numbers/symbols, etc.) allowed

The back of the UB-04 paper claim form contains language certifying that all information contained on the front is complete and accurate, as well as verifications specific to particular payers.

837I: ELECTRONIC VERSION OF THE UB-04 FORM

As mentioned, the current version of the electronic institutional claim is the ASC X12N 837I version 5010. The file format conforms to the data elements that are required on the paper UB-04. Health insurance professionals should become familiar with the upgrade to version 5010 (which accommodates ICD-10 codes) and should be able to recognize the difference between the electronic version and the current paper UB-04.

Data Layout of the 837I

The data layout of an 837I file may look confusing at first because of the electronic format, but the data are basically the same as in the UB-04 or the CMS-1500 form. The overall data stream of an 837I file is known as a **transaction set**, which is divided into sections, with each section providing a specific kind of information.

Every section of the transaction set contains data segments. A segment name is two or three alphabetical characters that begin each line of detail. In the example shown in Fig. 18.3, the segments names are in bold.

Each segment contains data elements that are the same as the data provided by each individual FL position on the UB-04 claim form. The number of elements varies depending on the purpose of the segment. Data elements are separated by asterisks (delimiters). In the example shown in Fig. 18.4, the ST segment has two elements and the BHT segment has six elements.

Electronic claims are typically submitted in batches to the third-party payer, who in turn generates a 997—another type of electronic file. The 997 is an electronic response to the 837I and indicates whether the 837I transmission was accepted or rejected. If the file passed, it contains an "A" for accepted; if it was rejected, it contains an "R" (Fig. 18.5).

To confirm whether batches were accepted or rejected by an insurer, the health insurance professional must be able to identify which batches passed and which batches failed. He or she must also be able to match the claims rejected on the 997 to the 837I file.

National Uniform Billing Committee Codes

Both the 837I and the UB-04 require the use of codes maintained by the NUBC. Examples of these codes include:

- Condition codes
- Occurrence codes
- Value codes
- Revenue codes

The NUBC maintains lists of approved coding for the form in its instruction manual.

> **? What Did You Learn?**
>
> 1. What are the basic function and role of the NUBC?
> 2. Name the standard paper claim form used for inpatient hospitalization.
> 3. What are the designated spaces called on this universal claim form?
> 4. The name of the UB-04 electronic file is _____.
> 5. The overall data stream of the electronic UB-04 file is known as a(n) _____.

STRUCTURE AND CONTENT OF THE HOSPITAL HEALTH RECORD

The information included in a hospital health record is similar to that in a physician's office or medical clinic record. It begins with demographic information—patient's name, address, age, sex, occupation, and insurance information—collected on admission.

Every time a patient receives healthcare, a record of the observations, medical or surgical interventions, and treatment outcomes is generated and maintained. This record includes information that the patient provides concerning symptoms and medical history, the results of examinations, radiology reports, laboratory test results, diagnoses, and treatment plans. Medical records and health information technicians organize

```
ISA*00*                *00*                    *ZZ*000001063         *ZZ*NDDHSMED
*040812*1504*U*00401*000101537*1*P*
GS*HC*000001063*NDDHSMED*20040812*1504*101537*X*004010X096A1
ST*837*0001
BHT*0019*00*101537*20040812*1504*CH
REF*87*004010X096A1
```

Fig. 18.3 Example of a transaction set section.

```
ISA*00*                *00*                    *ZZ*000001063         *ZZ*NDDHSMED
*040812*1504*U*00401*000101537*1*P*
GS*HC*000001063*NDDHSMED*20040812*1504*101537*X*004010X096A1
ST*837*0001
BHT*0019*00*101537*20040812*1504*CH
REF*87*004010X096A1
```

Fig. 18.4 Example showing data elements in a segment.

```
ISA*00*        *00*        *ZZ*NDDHSMED        *ZZ*000001063
*040812*1717*U*00401*000000011*0*P*>
GS*FA*NDDHSMED*000001063*20040812*1717*9*X*004010X096A1
ST*997*0001
AK1*HC*101537
AK2*837*0001
AK5*A   (Accepted File)
AK9*A*1*1*1   (Accepted File)
SE*6*0001
ST*997*0002
```

Fig. 18.5 Example of a 997 electronic file.

and evaluate these records for completeness and accuracy.

The patient health record is the property of the hospital, and hospitals do not automatically provide a copy of a patient's health record upon discharge. If the record (or any part of it) is released, it first must be completed by all physicians involved in the patient's care before being copied and released to the patient. This process can take up to 30 days, after which the patient may receive a copy, normally for a fee. Patient-related information may be released to a physician or medical facility for follow-up care of the patient when needed, usually free of charge.

STANDARDS IN HOSPITAL ELECTRONIC MEDICAL RECORDS

An **electronic medical record (EMR)** is a computerized version of the paper medical record. The EMR is an evolving technology that is being adopted by healthcare facilities as part of an ongoing trend to maximize efficiency and streamline functioning.

The increasing demand for quality care amid rising competition has made hospitals maximize use of technology in the overall processes of day-to-day operations. Not only corporate but also small stand-alone and mid-sized hospitals have become aware that the adoption of a well-functioning and efficient computerized hospital information system (HIS) is an important and integral part of efficient hospital management. Hospitals have been gradually introducing EMRs over the past several years. Until recently, however, only large corporate hospitals were using fully functional EMR applications, whereas most other hospitals use a combination of EMRs and paper-based records.

An EMR system is a complex system consisting of critical information that typically has the following key features:

- Patient's clinical information: Medical history, prescriptions, allergies, diagnosis, reports, etc.
- Clinical decision support databases: Databases that help in making decisions during prescription writing, drug-to-allergy database, etc.
- Order management: Order entry, retrieval, result reviewing, etc.
- Workflow management: Managing processes, such as appointment viewing, check-in of patients, and review
- Security features: For maintaining security and confidentiality of critical information
- Electronic prescription tool: A tool for writing and managing prescriptions
- Patient's financial records: Service bills, receipts, etc.

When EMR is being introduced to the hospital environment, it is critical to establish an HIS, prepare and involve various internal and external individuals and/or groups that have a stake in a successful outcome, and define a clear implementation path for the EMR

system. (The next subsection explains an HIS.) All components of EMR must be able to integrate with other existing information systems in the hospital. Other major factors to consider include the following:

- Ease of use: Most critical, because EMR is used mostly by clinicians, some of whom can be rather hesitant in adopting new technology to be used in parallel with their care services
- System interoperability: Capable enough to interface and interact with other information systems
- Standardization: Standard compliance to avoid data loss or inconsistency when interacting with other systems
- Workflow capacities: Ideally only full-solution systems should be adopted
- The sales team of the vendor: A good fit is crucial for success because the relationship between vendor and institution is frequently long-term
- Vendor services: Good post-sale and maintenance support services are crucial
The EMR benefits a hospital because it:
- Provides faster accessibility to records
- Requires less storage space
- Affords security of information
- Offers anytime, anywhere accessibility (e.g., remote access from handheld devices)
- Is easier to manage than paper-based records

The need to implement basic information systems in hospitals is evident, so more hospitals are adopting them; however, the reluctance of the key users of these systems (e.g., physicians) remains a big challenge for hospitals. Investment cost and personnel training are other key factors impeding widespread adoption of EMR.

ESTABLISHING A HOSPITAL INFORMATION SYSTEM

A **hospital information system (HIS)** is basically a computer system that can manage the information flowing through the facility to allow healthcare providers and ancillary staff to do their jobs efficiently and effectively. Today, a modern hospital can have as many as 200 different systems combined into one HIS, which incorporates a range of applications addressing the needs of various departments in the facility. A well-designed HIS is capable of not only providing immediate access to patients' records, but also managing data in treatment areas; nursing stations; laboratory, pharmacy, radiology, and pathology departments; and even the financial system. Hospitals that use an HIS typically can monitor the diets of patients and the distribution of medications.

Although a well-designed HIS offers many benefits to a healthcare institution, it should not be limited to the delivery of quality patient care and better financial management. The HIS should also be **patient centric** and affordable. Patient centric means putting the patient at the center of the decisions, resources, and desired outcomes and providing the necessary information that empowers patients to become involved in making decisions regarding their own treatment. In addition, an HIS must be flexible so that as technology changes, it is able to quickly accommodate these changes in order to allow hospital growth. Other benefits of an effective HIS are that it can:

- Enhance information integrity
- Reduce transcription errors
- Reduce duplication of information entries
- Optimize report turnaround times

STANDARD CODES AND TERMINOLOGY

Information for inpatient health records consists of many kinds of data, such as narrative progress notes, laboratory test results, radiology reports, history and physical examination reports, operative reports, and discharge summaries. Data come from many sites, including physician offices, hospitals, nursing facilities, public health departments, and pharmacies. Because various providers exist for each kind of data and site of care, standards for terminology are an essential requirement for a computer-based patient record that spans more than one provider's domain.

The important goal is to have an acceptable code system for each kind of data. It is unnecessary (and may be undesirable) to have all codes come from a single master code system because computers can integrate multiple code systems easily.

In addition to a universal coding system, there must be a common language combining data structures and grammar so that meaningful coded messages can be sent between computer-based patient record systems. The federal government and other organizations are working on measures that would make development of such a common language possible.

? What Did You Learn?

1. What is an EMR?
2. List at least five items of demographic information that are typically collected when a patient is hospitalized.
3. What type of information does an inpatient health record consist of?
4. Identify three benefits of an HIS.

INPATIENT HOSPITAL/FACILITY CODING

Hospitals generate insurance claims for many third-party payers. To perform this task effectively, the health insurance professional or the health information technician must have expert knowledge of the coding and payment systems that these payers use. Hospital coding is similar to that done in a physician's office; however, some guidelines differ significantly. The following sections provide a brief overview of the ICD-10-PCS system for coding inpatient hospital procedures.

Correct coding is crucial to submitting valid claims. To ensure that claims are accurate, current diagnosis and procedure codes must be used, and each diagnosis and procedure must be coded to the highest level of specificity (maximum number of digits) available.

ICD-10-CM CODE SETS USED FOR INPATIENT HOSPITAL/FACILITY CLAIMS

Two code sets are included in the revised ICD-10 coding system used for coding hospital/facility claims: (1) ICD-10-PCS is used for reporting inpatient procedures only, and (2) ICD-10-CM is used in all health treatment facilities, including both inpatient and outpatient, for coding diagnoses. The federal government mandates that all payers and providers adopt the ICD-10 coding system for services provided on or after the compliance date, which was put into effect October 1, 2015, or they will be ineligible to receive reimbursement on claims. As mentioned in an earlier chapter, it is strongly recommended that students check the CMS website periodically at http://cms.gov/icd10/ to keep abreast of coding changes. The following paragraphs provide a brief explanation of the ICD-10-PCS coding system. ICD-10-CM was discussed at length in Chapter 14.

◎ HIPAA Tip

All covered entities under the Health Insurance Portability and Accountability Act (HIPAA) (health plans, payers, providers, clearinghouses) were to have implemented the ICD-10 codes by the compliance date. The codes must be supported by medical documentation.

INTERNATIONAL CLASSIFICATION OF DISEASES, 10TH REVISION, PROCEDURE CODING SYSTEM

The International Classification of Diseases, 10th revision, Procedure Coding System (ICD-10-PCS) has been developed as a replacement for Volume 3 of the International Classification of Diseases, 9th revision, Clinical Modification (ICD-9-CM). The development of ICD-10-PCS was funded by the CMS. ICD-10-PCS has a multiaxial, seven-character, alphanumeric code structure that provides a unique code for all substantially different procedures and allows new procedures to be easily incorporated as new codes.

ICD-10-PCS

The ICD-10-PCS is a code set designed by 3M health information management (HIM) for CMS to replace Volume 3 of ICD-9-CM for inpatient procedure reporting. It is significantly different from ICD-9-CM, Volume 3 and from Current Procedural Terminology (CPT) codes. Approximately 79,000 ICD-10-PCS procedure codes will replace the nearly 4000 ICD-9 procedure codes. It is important to keep in mind that ICD-10-PCS will not affect CPT-4 coding of physician services in offices and/or clinics. However, healthcare providers should be aware that documentation requirements under ICD-10-PCS are quite different, so inpatient medical record documentation will be affected by this change.

Like ICD-10-CM codes, ICD-10-PCS codes contain seven characters, which can be numbers or letters and are based on the type of procedure performed, the approach, body part, and other characteristics. Each alphanumeric character has a specific meaning or value, depending on its place in the grouping.

Notable improvements in the ICD-10-PCS coding system include the following:

- Unique codes to differentiate approach (e.g., type of vessel and type of repair)
- Codes that define resource differences and outcomes that describe exactly what was done to the patient
- No diagnostic information is included
- Limited use of the NOS (not otherwise specified) option
- Elimination of the NEC (not elsewhere classifiable) option, except for new devices
- Use of standard terminology; each term is assigned a specific meaning

Structure of ICD-10-PCS Codes

The seven-digit ICD-10-PCS structure provides precision and expandability that is lacking in the former three- to four-digit ICD-9-CM procedure codes. Like ICD-10-CM, which was discussed in Chapter 14, ICD-10-PCS has a **multiaxial structure** with each code character having the same meaning within the specific procedure section and across procedure sections to the extent possible. The first position always indicates one of the 17 procedure section values, the second position always indicates the body system, the third position the root type, the fourth the body type, and so on. Each of the seven characters can **have up to 34 different values or definitions.**

Important Note: ICD-10-PCS defines the term *procedure* as "the complete specification of the seven characters." Each procedure is divided into specific sections that identify the general type of procedure, with the first character (either a number or a letter) designating the section.

The structure of ICD-10-PCS code is as follows:

- Each can be alphabetical (not case sensitive) or numerical.
- Numbers 0 through 9 are valid values.
- Letters O and I are not valid values, eliminating confusion with 0 and 1.
- Each character defines a specific aspect of the procedure. The first character defines the section name related to type or location of service. Characters 2 through 7 have a standard meaning within each section but may have different meanings across sections. As shown next, the character 2 through 7

classification categories change depending on the value of the section in character 1:

Section 0 - Medical and Surgical Categories

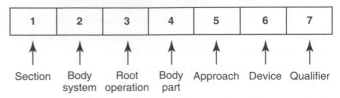

- In Section 5 Imaging Procedures, categories 3, 5, and 6 represent different category types that describe detail aspects relative only to imaging type procedures:

Section 5 - Imaging Procedures

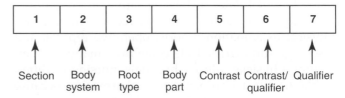

- In Section D Laboratory Procedures, categories 2 through 7 contain values that describe the variants of laboratory procedures:

Section D - Laboratory Procedures

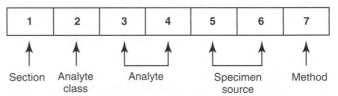

Format of the ICD-10-PCS

There are currently three separate divisions in the ICD-10-PCS system: (1) the Tabular List, (2) the Index, and (3) the List of Codes. Each section of the manual is meant to assist healthcare providers and coders in their search for the correct and complete procedure codes. It is very important that the codes used for billing, reimbursement, and reporting purposes are consistent and accurate, because they are constantly being monitored and audited by both public and private insurers. Fig. 18.6 is a partial page from the ICD-10-PCS index, and Fig. 18.7 is a sample table from the Medical and Surgical section of the ICD-10-PCS manual.

"Websites to Explore" lists several websites where more information on ICD-10-PCS coding can be found, including an informative PowerPoint presentation that describes this coding system. *The ICD-10-PCS Official Guidelines* also can be downloaded from the CMS website. (See "Websites to Explore" at the end of this chapter.)

Selecting the Principal Diagnosis

The health insurance professional or coder must identify key elements or words for possible use as the **principal diagnosis**. The principal diagnosis is

A

Abdominal aortic plexus *see* Nerve, Abdominal
Sympathetic
Abdominal esophagus *see* Esophagus, Lower
Abdominohysterectomy
see Excision, Uterus 0UB9
see Resection, Uterus 0UT9
Abdominoplasty
see Alteration, Wall, Abdominal 0W0F
see Repair, Wall, Abdominal 0WQF
see Supplement, Wall, Abdominal 0WUF
Abductor hallucis muscle
see Muscle, Foot, Right
see Muscle, Foot, Left
Ablation *see* Destruction
Abortion
Products of Conception 10A0
Abortifacient 10A07ZX
Laminaria 10A07ZW
Vacuum 10A07Z6
Abrasion *see* Extraction
Accessory cephalic vein
see Vein, Cephalic, Right
see **Vein, Cephalic, Left**
Accessory obturator nerve *see* **Plexus, Lumbar**
Accessory phrenic nerve *see* Nerve, Phrenic
Accessory spleen *see* Spleen
Acetabulectomy
see Excision, Lower Bones 0QB
see Resection, Lower Bones 0QT
Acetabulofemoral joint
see Joint, Hip, Right
see Joint, Hip, Left
Acetabuloplasty
see Repair, Lower Bones 0QQ
see Replacement, Lower Bones 0QR

Acetabuloplasty *(Continued)*
see Supplement, Lower Bones 0QU
Achilles tendon
see Tendon, Lower Leg, Left
see Tendon, Lower Leg, Right
Achillorrhaphy *see* Repair, Tendons 0LQ
Achillotenotomy, achillotomy
see Division, Tendons 0L8
see Drainage, Tendons 0L9
Acromioclavicular ligament
see Bursa and Ligament, Shoulder, Right
see Bursa and Ligament, Shoulder, Left
Acromion (process)
see Scapula, Left
see Scapula, Right
Acromionectomy
see Excision, Upper Joints 0RB
see Resection, Upper Joints 0RT
Acromioplasty
see Repair, Upper Joints 0RQ
see Replacement, Upper Joints 0RR
see Supplement, Upper Joints 0RU
Activities of Daily Living Assessment F02
Activities of Daily Living Treatment F08
Acupuncture
Breast
Anesthesia 8E0H300
No Qualifier 8E0H30Z
Integumentary System
Anesthesia 8E0H300
No Qualifier 8E0H30Z
Adductor brevis muscle
see Muscle, Upper Leg, Left
see Muscle, Upper Leg, Right
Adductor hallucis muscle
see Muscle, Foot, Left
see Muscle, Foot, Right

Adductor longus muscle
see Muscle, Upper Leg, Right
see Muscle, Upper Leg, Left
Adductor magnus muscle
see Muscle, Upper Leg, Right
see Muscel, Upper Leg, Left
Adenohypophysis *see* **Gland, Pituitary**
Adenoidectomy
see Excision, Adenoids 0CBQ
see Resection, Adenoids 0CTQ
Adenoidotomy *see* Drainage, Adenoids
0C9Q
Adhesiolysis *see* Release
Administration
Blood products *see* Transfusion
Other substance *see* Introduction
Adrenalectomy
see Excision, Endocrine System 0GB
see Resection, Endocrine System 0GT
Adrenalorrhaphy *see* Repair, Endocrine
System 0GQ
Adrenalotomy *see* Drainage, Endocrine
System 0G9
Advancement
see Reposition
see Transfer
Airway
Insertion of device in
Esophagus 0DH5
Mouth and Throat 0CHY
Nasopharynx 09HN
Removal of device from
Esophagus 0DP5
Mouth and Throat 0CPY
Nose 09PK
Revision of device in

Fig. 18.6 Partial page from the Index of the *International Classification of Diseases*, 10th revision, Procedure Coding System (ICD-10-PCS). (From *International Classification of Diseases*, 10th revision, Procedure Coding System [ICD-10-PCS].)

Section	O	Medical and Surgical
Body System	D	Gastrointestinal System
Operation	J	Inspection: Visually and/or manually exploring a body part

Body Part	Approach	Device	Qualifier
0 Upper intestinal tract **6** Stomach **D** Lower intestinal tract	**0** Open **3** Percutaneous **4** Percutaneous endoscopic **7** Via natural or artificial opening **8** Via natural or artificial opening endoscopic **X** External	**Z** No device	**Z** No qualifier
U Omentum **V** Mesentery **W** Peritoneum	**0** Open **3** Percutaneous **4** Percutaneous endoscopic **X** External	**Z** No device	**Z** No qualifier

Fig. 18.7 Sample table from Medical and Surgical section of the *International Classification of Diseases*, 10th revision, Procedure Coding System (ICD-10-PCS). (From *International Classification of Diseases*, 10th revision, Procedure Coding System [ICD-10-PCS].)

defined in the Uniform Hospital Discharge Data Set (UHDDS) as "that condition established after study to be chiefly responsible for occasioning the admission of the patient to the hospital for care." The UHDDS definitions are used by hospitals to report inpatient data elements in a standardized manner. Accurate principal diagnosis selection is critical to ensure that patient encounters are grouped under the proper MS-DRGs and that facilities receive appropriate reimbursement.

Sometimes documentation describes symptoms, signs, and ill-defined conditions that are not linked to a specific disease. Some body system categories include codes for nonspecific conditions. The code for a breast lump is found in the Tabular List under "Diseases of the Genitourinary System" and then under the subcategory "Disorders of the Breast" and would be properly coded as N63, "unspecified lump in breast." These codes, rather than codes for more specific disorders, should be used when the only facts available are the patient's signs and symptoms. Box 18.1 lists guidelines for coding inpatient hospital diagnoses.

It is very important for hospital personnel to properly code the diagnoses and procedures, because that information is what determines what DRG Medicare assigns to the patient. Reimbursement rates are determined by the DRG, so incorrectly coded diagnoses can dramatically affect reimbursement. The importance of consistent, complete documentation in the medical record cannot be overemphasized. Without such documentation, the application of all coding guidelines is a difficult, if not impossible, task. For two good websites that discuss principal diagnosis assignment and secondary diagnosis assignment, see "Websites to Explore" at the end of this chapter.

 Imagine This!

Dr. Ezra Blake admits Paul Faro, who has an inoperable bowel malignancy, to the hospital for acute blood loss anemia. Mr. Faro receives a transfusion of four units of packed cells. In this case, the principal diagnosis is acute blood loss anemia, and the bowel cancer is an additional diagnosis. Later that same day, Dr. Blake admits Imogene Ferrell to the hospital for a local complication due to an ovarian malignancy. In this case, the cancer is the principal diagnosis. When more than one diagnosis meets the criteria for principal diagnosis, the coder should use the diagnosis that accounts for most of the services provided and code that as the primary diagnosis. When more than one condition is listed that pertains to similar and contrasting conditions, the coder should select the diagnosis that is the condition that resulted in the admission and for which most of the services were provided. If one of the diagnoses is ruled out during the hospitalization, it should not be used for coding. When original treatment plans are not completed during the encounter or admission, the reason for admission or encounter is still used as the principal or primary diagnosis.

For clarification, see *International Classification of Diseases*, 10th revision, Clinical Modification, Guideline G: Complications of Surgery and Other Medical Care.

Box 18.1	Guidelines for Coding Inpatient Hospital Diagnoses

- Select the diagnoses that require coding according to current coding and reporting requirements for inpatient services.
- Select the diagnoses that require coding according to current coding and reporting requirements for hospital-based outpatient services.
- Interpret conventions, formats, instructional notations, tables, and definitions of the classification system to select diagnoses, conditions, problems, or other reasons for the encounter that require coding.
- Sequence diagnoses and other reasons for the encounter according to notations and conventions of the classification system and standard data set definitions.
- Determine whether signs, symptoms, or manifestations require separate code assignments.
- Determine whether the diagnostic statement provided by the healthcare provider does not allow for more specific code assignments.
- Recognize when the classification system does not provide a precise code for the condition documented (e.g., residual categories or nonclassified syndromes).
- Assign supplementary codes to indicate reasons for the healthcare encounter other than illness or injury.
- Assign supplementary codes to indicate factors other than illness or injury that influence the patient's health status.
- Assign supplementary codes to indicate the external cause of an injury, adverse effect, or poisoning.

 Stop and Think

Consider the case in which a physician admits a patient with obstruction of the ureter secondary to a metastasis (spread) from a previously resected colon carcinoma. Surgeons place a urinary stent to relieve the obstruction with no other therapy provided for the metastasis. In this case, what would be the principal diagnosis? Would there be a second diagnosis? If so, what would it be?

Secondary Diagnoses

A **secondary diagnosis** is a condition that coexists at the time of admission and/or that develops subsequently and requires one or more of the following:

- Clinical evaluation
- Therapeutic treatment
- Diagnostic procedures
- Extended length of hospital stay (more than 1 day)
- Increased nursing care and/or monitoring

Secondary conditions are either comorbidities or complications, frequently referred to as *CCs*. The MS-DRG system increases the importance of documenting and coding CCs because when patients develop them, the cost and resulting payment of the hospital stay is usually higher.

SKILL REQUIREMENTS FOR ICD-10-PCS CODING

A relatively high degree of knowledge of anatomy, physiology, pharmacology, and medical terminology is an important requirement for acquiring the necessary level of skill to code inpatient procedures accurately and efficiently using the ICD-10-PCS system. In addition, coders need extensive clinical knowledge of conditions and procedures to interpret common medical language (e.g., radial keratotomy, Torkildsen procedure) that do not translate readily into code, as well as an understanding of common Latin roots assigned to medical vocabulary.

ICD-10-PCS coders also must know how to classify surgical procedures in terms of section, body system, root operation, body part, approach, device, and qualifier. An expert knowledge level of various types of surgical approaches, tools and techniques, procedure purposes, codes not identified by eponyms or names, and standardized procedural definitions also tops the list of knowledge base requirements.

Education and training are essential for learning the ICD-10-PCS system. To ensure the quality of ICD-10-PCS education, training must be flexible and provide different options from a variety of sources, including:

- Distance education courses
- Audio seminars or web-based services
- Self-directed learning using printed materials or electronic tools
- Traditional classroom training by a certified trainer

After the initial training is completed, further monitoring for coding accuracy is another critical element to coding accuracy. Subsequent monitoring is important to identify coding errors, after which corrective action should be initiated as necessary. This may require additional education.

THE 72-HOUR RULE

The **72-hour rule** states that all services provided for Medicare patients within 72 hours of the hospital admission are considered part of the inpatient services and are to be billed on one claim. This rule is part of Medicare's PPS.

We learned in the previous chapter that under the Medicare PPS, hospitals are paid a predetermined rate for each hospital admission. Clinical information is used to classify each patient into a DRG. Such information includes the principal diagnosis; complications and comorbidities; surgical procedures; and age, gender, and discharge disposition of the patient.

The 72-hour rule has been amended in accordance with the Preservation of Access to Care for Medicare Beneficiaries and Pension Relief Act of 2010. The CMS "final rule" states that on or after June 25, 2010, all diagnostic services (except for ambulance and maintenance renal dialysis services) provided on the date of the beneficiary's inpatient admission are considered related and must be bundled with the charges for the inpatient stay. Outpatient nondiagnostic services provided during the applicable payment window that are unrelated to the admission and that are covered by Medicare Part B should be billed separately to Medicare Part B.

Acute care hospitals require the 72-hour rule. Other facilities, such as long-term care hospitals, rehabilitation hospitals, and psychiatric hospitals, require a comparable 24-hour rule. CAHs are excluded from both 72-hour and 24-hour provisions.

For more detailed information and updates on the 72-hour rule, visit the CMS website.

HOSPITAL VALUE-BASED PURCHASING PROGRAM

The hospital value-based purchasing (VBP) program is a CMS initiative established by the Affordable Care Act of 2010 that rewards acute care hospitals with incentive payments for the quality of care, not just the quantity of procedures they perform, for Medicare patients. Hospitals are rewarded based on how closely they follow best clinical practices and how well hospitals improve patients' experiences of care while hospitalized. It is believed that when hospitals follow proven best practices, patients receive higher quality care and experience better outcomes.

Hospitals participating in the VBP program were to begin receiving incentive payments for providing higher-quality care or improving care at the beginning of fiscal year 2013 (October 1, 2012).

What Did You Learn?

1. Identify the two code sets used for coding hospital/facility claims.
2. ICD-10-PCS codes contain _____ characters, which can be numbers or letters and are based on the type of procedure performed, the approach, body part, and other characteristics.
3. Explain why the letters O and I are not valid values in ICD-10-PCS coding.
4. The condition established after study to be chiefly responsible for causing the admission of the patient to the hospital for care is referred to as the _____.
5. True or false: Version 5010 accommodates ICD-10 code sets.
6. Name the rule that states that all services provided for Medicare patients within 72 hours of the hospital admission are considered part of the inpatient services and are to be billed on one claim.

OUTPATIENT HOSPITAL CODING

Outpatient hospital coding currently includes ICD-10-CM for coding diagnoses and CPT-4 for coding procedures and services, as well as Healthcare Common Procedure Coding System (HCPCS), when applicable. Section IV of the *ICD-10-CM Official Guidelines for Coding and Reporting* contains the official diagnostic coding and reporting guidelines for outpatient services. These guidelines can be downloaded from the CMS website.

MEDICARE OUTPATIENT PROSPECTIVE PAYMENT SYSTEM

In response to the rapidly rising Medicare expenditures for outpatient services and large copayments being made by Medicare beneficiaries, Congress mandated that the CMS develop an **outpatient prospective payment system (OPPS)** and reduce beneficiary copayments. This payment system was implemented on August 1, 2000, and is used by CMS to reimburse hospitals for services to Medicare patients that are provided on an outpatient basis. Under the Medicare OPPS, hospitals are paid a set amount (called the *payment rate*) to provide certain outpatient services to Medicare beneficiaries. For most services, beneficiaries must pay the annual Part B deductible before Medicare pays its share. Once the deductible has been met, Medicare pays 80% of the allowed amount for the service, and the beneficiary pays the copayment—20%. For certain preventive services, Medicare pays even if the yearly deductible has not been met (e.g., screening mammography). The payment rate is not the same for all hospitals because it is adjusted to reflect what people are paid to work in the area where the hospital is located. The payment rate is adjusted for other factors as well. Part B services paid for under the OPPS include but are not limited to:

- X-rays
- Emergency department or hospital clinic visits (not including the physician's fee)
- Surgery performed on an outpatient basis (e.g., same-day surgery)
- Observation services
- Administration of drugs that cannot be self-administered

Some kinds of hospitals are exempt from the OPPS, including CAHs. A CAH is a hospital certified to receive cost-based reimbursement from Medicare that is intended to improve the financial performance of the facility, thereby reducing the chance that the hospital will close down. A CAH is certified under a different set of rules that are more flexible than those of acute care hospitals.

AMBULATORY PAYMENT CLASSIFICATIONS

Ambulatory payment classification (APC) is the grouping system that the CMS developed for reimbursing acute care facilities for outpatient services (e.g., OPPS). This system of coding and reimbursement for services was introduced by Congress in the 1997 Balanced Budget Act and implemented by CMS in August 2000 in hospital outpatient settings. It is intended to simplify the outpatient hospital payment system, ensure that the payment is adequate to compensate hospital costs, and implement deficit reduction goals of the CMS.

The APC OPPS categorizes outpatient visits into groups according to the clinical characteristics, the typical resource use, and the costs associated with the diagnoses and the procedures performed. All covered outpatient services are assigned to an APC group, and each group of procedure codes within an APC must be similar clinically and with regard to the use of resources. The payment rate associated with each APC is determined by multiplying the relative weight for the APC by a conversion factor, which translates the relative weights into dollar amounts. To account for geographic differences, the labor portion of the payment rate is adjusted by the hospital wage index. The **hospital outpatient prospective payment system (HOPPS)** allows for additional payments for certain pass-throughs and for outlier cases involving high-cost services. **Pass-throughs** are temporary payments for specified new technologies, drugs, devices, and biologics for which costs were unavailable when APC payment rates were calculated.

Ambulatory Payment Classification Payment Rate

The APC payment rate is the total amount the hospital receives from Medicare and the beneficiary. These rates are updated annually and take effect in January of the following year. Under the OPPS, it is possible for more than one APC to be assigned during a single visit, in contrast with the inpatient PPS, in which only one DRG can be assigned per discharge. The importance of capturing, coding, and billing all allowable services provided should be stressed so that no possible revenue goes unbilled. OPPS APC payments are determined totally based on CPT-4/HCPCS code assignment, rather than ICD-10-PCS procedure codes, which are used for coding inpatient PPS.

In November 2000, the *Federal Register* published the OPPS interim final rule (65 FR 67797). CMS publishes the Medicare Physician Fee Schedule and the OPPS annually in the *Federal Register*.

GROUPER SOFTWARE SYSTEM

A **grouper software** system is a computer application interface commonly used in hospitals to send and retrieve data for grouping, editing, and reimbursement outcomes. Capabilities of a grouper system include providing up-to-date claim edits for providers, payers, FIs, and state and federal agencies. With this type of software system, facilities can choose the reimbursement methodology required and calculate the expected payment amount of individual claims based on the group to which it is assigned.

The MS-DRGs grouper software classifies hospital case types into groups expected to have similar hospital resource use. Medicare uses this classification to pay for inpatient hospital care. Hospitals are paid a fixed price by the DRG for treating Medicare patients. The groupings are based on diagnoses, procedures, other demographic information and the presence of complications or comorbidities.

With APCs, grouper software assigns the appropriate payment group to each service on a claim and calculates the anticipated reimbursement before the claim is forwarded to the insurance payer. For every claim processed, each line item is evaluated and assigned an APC if appropriate (not all line items receive an APC), a status indicator, and payment information. The status indicator designates whether the line item is paid by an assigned APC, is paid by a fee schedule, or is not covered by Medicare for outpatient services.

MEDICARE OUTPATIENT CODE EDITOR

The outpatient code editor (OCE) program processes claims for all outpatient institutional providers, including hospitals that are subject to the OPPS as well as those that are non-OPPS. The OCE performs three major functions:

1. Edits the data to identify errors and return a series of edit flags
2. Assigns an APC number for each service covered under OPPS and returns information to be used as input to a PRICER program
3. Assigns an ASC payment group for services on claims from certain non-OPPS hospitals.

Each claim is represented by a collection of data, which consists of all necessary demographic data, plus all services (line items) provided. The OCE only functions on a single claim and does not have cross-claim capabilities. The OCE not only identifies problems (e.g., coding errors, questions regarding medical necessity, gender-specific procedure inconsistencies), but also indicates what actions should be taken and the reasons why these actions are necessary. In general, the OCE performs all functions that require specific reference to the complex procedural and diagnostic coding systems used on claims.

NATIONAL CORRECT CODING INITIATIVE

CMS implemented the **National Correct Coding Initiative (NCCI)** in 1996 to control improper coding that leads to inappropriate increased payment for healthcare services. The agency uses NCCI edits to evaluate billing of HCPCS codes by Medicare providers in postpayment review of providers' claims.

Coding decisions for edits are based on conventions defined in the American Medical Association's (AMA's) *CPT-4 Manual*, national and local policies and edits, coding guidelines developed by national societies, analysis of standard medical and surgical practices, and a review of current coding practices.

Table 18.3 shows commonly used insurer claim forms and coding systems by setting of care. For assistance in billing, providers may access the NCCI edit information online at the CMS website listed in under "Websites to Explore" at the end of this chapter.

> **? What Did You Learn?**
>
> 1. What manuals are used for coding hospital claims?
> 2. Define *principal diagnosis*.
> 3. How is the principal diagnosis determined?
> 4. What are APCs, and in what setting are they used?
> 5. Explain the term *pass-through* in the context it is used in this chapter.
> 6. What is the function of grouper software?

THE HOSPITAL BILLING PROCESS: UNDERSTANDING THE BASICS

The hospital billing process begins when the patient registers for inpatient or outpatient admission. Although this procedure may differ from one institution to another, certain processes remain constant. Registration may be accomplished in person, by telephone, or via the Internet. At the time of registration, the patient typically must provide personal and insurance information. Boxes 18.2 and 18.3 list the data elements for hospital claim forms and outpatient claim forms.

As we learned in previous chapters, preauthorization or precertification is necessary for most inpatient hospital admissions. In the case of emergency admission when preauthorization is impossible, most insurers allow 48 hours for notification of hospitalization.

A certain amount of patient education goes hand in hand with hospital admission. Hospital staff members should inform patients of their rights and responsibilities. Typical patient responsibilities include an obligation for patients to:

- Provide a complete medical history and any information pertaining to their health
- Be responsible for their actions if they refuse any treatment or do not follow physician's orders
- Report perceived risks in their care and unexpected changes in their condition to the physician or other healthcare providers
- Report any perceived or identified safety issues related to their care or the physical environment to the physician or other healthcare providers

| Table 18.3 | Commonly Used Insurer Claim Forms and Coding Systems by Setting of Care |

COMPONENTS OF CLAIMS	FREESTANDING IMAGING CENTER OR PHYSICIAN SERVICES	HOSPITAL OUTPATIENT DEPARTMENTS	HOSPITAL INPATIENT
Claim form	CMS-1500	CMS-1450 (UB-04)	CMS-1450 (UB-04)
Patient diagnoses	ICD-10-CM	ICD-10-CM	ICD-10-CM
Procedures	CPT	CPT revenue	ICD-10-PCS revenue
Drugs, supplies, and certain contrast agents	HCPCS (when appropriate)	HCPCS (when appropriate) revenue	Revenue

CPT, Current Procedural Terminology; *HCPCS*, Healthcare Common Procedure Coding System; *ICD-10-CM*, *International Classification of Diseases*, 10th revision, Clinical Modification; *ICD-10-PCS*, *International Classification of Diseases*, 10th revision, Procedural Coding System.

Box 18.2	**Standard Data Elements: Hospital Claim Forms**

PATIENT CHARACTERISTICS
Patient identifier (unique to each hospital or care facility)
Name (last, first, middle initial)
Address (street, city, state, ZIP code)
Date of birth
Gender
Marital status

PROVIDER CHARACTERISTICS
Hospital/facility identifier (unique)
Physician identifier (unique only for Medicare claims)
Diagnostic and treatment information
Admissions date
Admissions status
Admissions diagnosis code
Condition code
Diagnosis code
Description of service
Service date
Service units
Principal and other diagnoses (up to 6)
Principal and other procedures (up to 5)
Date of procedure
Emergency code

INSURANCE/PAYMENT INFORMATION
Insurance group numbers (differ for each health plan)
Group name
Insured's name
Relationship to insured
Employer name
Employer location
Covered period
Treatment authorization codes
Payer
Total charges
Noncovered charges
Prior payments
Amount due from patient
Revenue codes
Healthcare Common Procedure Coding System (HCPCS)/rates

US Department of Health and Human Services, Centers for Medicare and Medicaid Services.

Box 18.3	**Standard Data Elements: Outpatient Claim Forms**

PATIENT CHARACTERISTICS
Patient identifier (Social Security number or other identifier)
Name (last, first, middle initial)
Address (street, city, state, ZIP code)
Date of birth
Gender
Marital status
Telephone number
Other health insurance coverage

PROVIDER CHARACTERISTICS
Physician identifier (tax identifier or other plan-specific identifier)
Physician's employer identification (ID) number

DIAGNOSTIC AND TREATMENT INFORMATION
Date of encounter
Illness
Emergency
Admission and discharge dates
Diagnosis or nature of illness
Diagnosis code
Place of service
Procedure code
Description of services and supplies
Date patient able to return to work
Date of disability

INSURANCE/PAYMENT INFORMATION
Payer's identifier (e.g., Medicare or Medicaid)
Group name
Insured's name
Insured's ID number
Insured's group number
Address and telephone number of insured
Relationship to insured
Employer name
Employer location
Covered period
Treatment authorization codes
Accept assignment
Total charges
Amount paid
Prior payments
Balance due

US Department of Health and Human Services, Centers for Medicare and Medicaid Services.

- Ask questions when they do not understand what they have been told about their care or what they are expected to do regarding their care
- Ensure that the financial obligations of their hospital care are fulfilled as promptly as possible
- Follow hospital rules and regulations regarding patient care and conduct
- Be considerate of the rights of other patients and hospital personnel

INFORMED CONSENT

Informed consent is the process by which a fully informed patient can participate in choices about his or her healthcare. It originates from the legal and ethical rights a patient has to direct what happens to his or her body and from the ethical duty of the physician to involve the patient in his or her healthcare.

The most important goal of informed consent is that the patient has an opportunity to be a knowledgeable participant in his or her healthcare decisions. Informed consent typically includes a discussion of the following elements:

- Nature of the decision or procedure
- Reasonable alternatives to the proposed intervention

- Relevant risks, benefits, and uncertainties related to each alternative
- Assessment of patient understanding
- Acceptance of the intervention by the patient

For the patient's consent to be valid, he or she must be considered competent to make the decision at hand, and this consent must be voluntary. Ideally, the physician should make it clear to the patient that he or she is participating in a decision, not merely signing a form. With this understanding, the informed consent process should be seen as an invitation to participate in healthcare decisions. The patient's understanding of what is about to occur is equally as important as the information provided; the discussion should be carried out in layperson's terms, and the patient's understanding should be assessed along the way.

If it is determined that a patient is incapacitated or incompetent to make healthcare decisions in his or her best interest, a **surrogate** (someone with legal authority to make decisions or speak on the patient's behalf) decision maker must speak for the patient. A specific hierarchy of appropriate decision makers is defined by law in most states. If no appropriate surrogate decision maker is available, the physician is expected to act in the best interest of the patient until a surrogate is found or appointed.

> **! Stop and Think**
>
> Joseph Mason, a 68-year-old African American man, was admitted to Walden-Martin Medical Center with complaints of "tightness in his chest" and difficulty breathing. Dr. Ethan VanDerVoort, a cardiologist, visited Mr. Mason in his hospital room and informed him that the results of his heart catheterization and other tests showed 80% blockage in a major artery of his heart. "We'll be putting a stent in the artery to open it up, allowing the blood to resume normal flow," Dr. VanDerVoort informed him. "Afterwards, you'll be as good as new." He patted the patient's arm and left the room.
>
> Did Dr. VanDerVoort follow the rules of "informed consent" in this brief conversation with Mr. Mason? If not, what elements of a full informed consent scenario were ignored? How might Dr. VanDerVoort have approached this patient regarding his planned remedy for the patient's heart problem?

PRESENT ON ADMISSION

As required by law, effective October 1, 2007, all general acute care healthcare providers must identify whether a diagnosis was present upon an inpatient admission. This concept was mandated as a result of many concerns about quality healthcare and overpaying by the government because of hospital errors. After many years of planning, the **present on admission (POA)** indicator was added to the UB-04 form for inpatient Medicare claims.

Inpatient acute care hospitals that are paid under the DRG payment system are required to report a POA indicator for every diagnosis on inpatient acute care hospital claims. POA is defined as present at the time the order for inpatient admission occurs. Conditions that develop during an outpatient encounter, including emergency department, are considered POA. (Certain diagnostic codes are exempt from POA reporting.) On the UB-04 paper claim form, the POA indicator is reported in the eighth digit (shaded area) of FL 67 for the principal diagnosis and in the eighth digit (shaded area) of FL 67A-Q for each secondary diagnosis (Fig. 18.8). If the POA indicator is not reported, the claim will be rejected; however, health plans that receive POA information on claims but whose software programs cannot use this information cannot reject these claims.

HOSPITAL CHARGES

Hospital charges are typically divided into two types: (1) facility charges (room and board) and (2) ancillary charges, such as radiology, laboratory, and pharmacy. Professional charges—fees charged by the attending and/or consulting physicians—are billed separately and are not considered a part of the hospital bill.

Hospital Charge Description Master

Hospital charges can be determined in multiple ways, but the main goal is to capture costs for performing procedures and services. To facilitate this goal, every hospital has what is known as a **charge description master (CDM)** or *charge master*. A CDM is a listing of every type of procedure and service the hospital can provide to its patients, including procedures, pharmaceuticals, supplies, and even room charges. CDMs help make the billing process run more smoothly and accurately. Table 18.4 shows an example of a CDM.

Each item on a CDM is precoded with certain information, such as price, procedure code, and revenue codes. Some have modifiers, which are more specific indicators to insurance companies regarding the type of procedure that was performed. Some hospitals are now listing their prices on the Internet in a move known as **pricing transparency**.

Table 18.4   Example of a Charge Description Master

CHARGE DESCRIPTION	CPT/HCPCS CODE	REVENUE CODE	CHARGE	DEPARTMENT CODE	CHARGE CODE	CHARGE STATUS
Nasal bone x-ray	70160	320	150.00	15	2214111000	12/1/2001
Thyroid sonogram	76536	320	250.00	15	2110110000	1/1/2003
Echoencephalogram	76506	320	1500.00	15	2326222111	7/1/2005

CPT, Current Procedural Terminology; *HCPCS*, Healthcare Common Procedure Coding System.

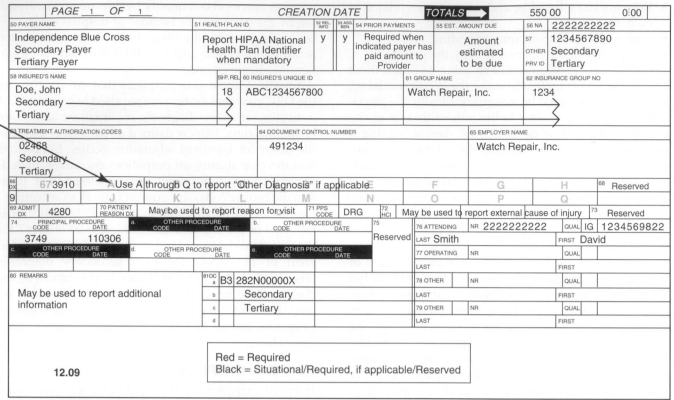

Fig. 18.8 Sample portion of the UB-04 form. The *red arrow* indicates where the present on admission (POA) code(s) should be reported on the UB-04 form. (Modified from Centers for Medicare and Medicaid Services, Baltimore, MD.)

ELECTRONIC CLAIMS SUBMISSION

Most hospitals now submit claims electronically rather than using the UB-04 paper claim. Specifically, claims for Medicare Part A reimbursement must be submitted electronically using the current HIPAA-compliant transaction standards. The HIPAA's Administrative Simplification Compliance Act (HIPAA-ASCA) governs the electronic process of health insurance claims. The purpose of HIPAA-ASCA is to standardize transactions as much as possible. However, each transaction has different data elements that are treated differently by various payers.

Before submitting claims electronically to any payer or clearinghouse, the facility must successfully complete enrollment, certification, and testing processes and obtain the necessary software and identifiers needed for claims submission.

For example, to transmit claims electronically with Wellmark (a BCBS FI), the facility must obtain a Wellmark identifying number (i.e., a submitter number) and preapproval for electronic data interchanges (EDIs). This involves completing registration and authorization forms.

The next step is for the facility to become certified, which involves sending a test transaction for a review of HIPAA-ASCA compliance. If the test is successful, the facility receives a certificate verifying that it was successful in completing a HIPAA-compliant electronic transaction using version 5010 standards.

Providers submitting electronic claims must do so in a format that either is HIPAA compliant or can be translated into a HIPAA-compliant format. Most hospitals submit claims electronically using the 837I electronic version of the UB-04 form.

Benefits of Electronic Claims Submission for Hospital Charges

ECS offers numerous benefits to all participants in the claims submission process. ECS is considered the most efficient and effective means of processing claims, ensuring prompt adjudication and payment to providers, because it reduces claims processing time from start to finish. The ECS process allows providers to use applicable computer software programs to submit claims to a central location, such as a clearinghouse, via a World Wide Web interface that sends the claims to the carriers' system for processing. (Electronic claims also can be sent directly to a third-party payer.)

ECS avoids the sorting and keying process, allowing the claim data to be available immediately to the payer's system. In addition, providers who submit claims electronically can check their claims to ensure that the data have passed basic edits and can resolve any claim data errors that may prevent the claim from being paid. ECS also provides an audit trail of claims that have failed preliminary edits. Providers can receive information about certain problems on submitted claims within a few hours instead of a few weeks.

When problems or errors are detected, they can be corrected, and the claim can be resubmitted immediately. When providers track submissions, make corrections, and resubmit claims online, they receive payment much more quickly than with paper filing.

Providers may use special software created by specific third-party payers or software developed for their particular needs by outside vendors to submit claims electronically. In addition to quicker receipt of payments, some other advantages of ECS are as follows:

- Claims can be submitted 7 days a week (including holidays)
- Providers receive front-end acknowledgement of claims acceptance
- **Electronic remittance advice (ERA)** allows automatic payment posting
- Electronic funds transfer (EFT) makes payments immediately accessible
- Electronic claims reports are provided with each submission

For more detailed information on electronic billing, see "Websites to Explore" at the end of this chapter.

HEALTH INFORMATION MANAGEMENT SYSTEMS

A hospital patient accounting system is a suite of integrated computer applications that allows healthcare facilities to manage patient records more efficiently and optimize reimbursement while ensuring regulatory compliance. This process is commonly referred to as HIM. **Health information management (HIM) systems** are responsible for coding and abstracting all patient charts and releasing them for billing. Integration with other encoder products improves coding accuracy and typically features a specially designed HIM report generator. In addition to ERA management, HIM systems generally include software components that can handle functions such as:

- Patient registration
- Eligibility verification
- Claims management
- Accounts receivable
- Collections

PAYMENT MANAGEMENT

The ERA automates the process of receiving payments from third-party payers. Electronic payments for hospital charges are automatically posted to a patient's file within the hospital financial management system. The ERA automates manual keying of the explanation of benefits (EOB), provides details on how claims were paid and/or why they were denied, and helps improve business office workflow and productivity.

Revenue cycle management systems, used in most hospitals, manage patient information while simultaneously automating the billing process. They allow users to "work" a patient stay from beginning to end, from the initial registration process through the charge entry, patient and insurance billing, payment entry,

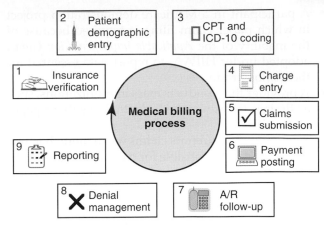

Fig. 18.9 Example of a hospital billing flow chart. *A/R*, Accounts receivable; *CPT*, Current Procedural Terminology; *ICD-10*, *International Classification of Diseases*, 10th revision.

collecting, bad debt management, and reporting phases.

Hospital financial accounting management systems help streamline patient services, minimize rejected claims, and speed up reimbursement while ideally improving patient satisfaction and overall revenue cycle performance. Fig. 18.9 shows a flow chart of the hospital billing process.

> **? What Did You Learn?**
>
> 1. Define a hospital patient accounting system and what it does.
> 2. Name the software components included in a typical HIM system.
> 3. What is an ERA?
> 4. List the steps of the hospital billing cycle.

HIPAA–HOSPITAL CONNECTION

HIPAA's ASCA requires providers, with limited exceptions, to submit all initial Medicare claims for reimbursement electronically on or after October 16, 2003. The act further stipulates that no payment may be made under Part A or Part B of the Medicare program for any expenses incurred for items or services for which a claim is submitted in a nonelectronic form. Consequently, unless a provider fits one of the exceptions listed here, any paper claim submitted to Medicare would not be paid. In addition, if it is determined that the provider is in violation of the statute or rule, he or she may be subject to claim denials, overpayment recoveries, and applicable interest on overpayments. The exceptions to this ECS requirement include the following:

- A small provider: A provider billing a Medicare FI or MAC that has fewer than 25 FTE employees or a physician, practitioner, or supplier with fewer than 10 FTE employees that bills a Medicare carrier
- A dentist

- A participant in a Medicare demonstration project in which paper claim filing is required because of the inability of the *Applicable Implementation Guide,* adopted under HIPAA, to report data essential for the demonstration
- A provider that conducts mass immunizations, such as flu injections, may be permitted to submit paper roster bills
- A provider that submits claims when more than one other payer is responsible for payment before Medicare payment
- A provider that furnishes services only outside the United States
- A provider experiencing a disruption in electricity and communication connections that is beyond its control
- A provider that can establish that an "unusual circumstance" exists and that therefore precludes electronic submission of claims electronically

HIPAA Tip

Hospitals can achieve Health Insurance Portability and Accountability Act (HIPAA) compliance successfully by meeting all of the government guidelines and requirements related to physical security, contingency plans, standard electronic transaction processes, and integrity controls, as well as implementing the most advanced scenario of secure methods of data transmission and storage to ensure proper handling of patient accounts and other health-related information.

THE AFFORDABLE CARE ACT'S EFFECT ON HOSPITAL CHARGES

An important provision in the Affordable Care Act stipulates that hospitals cannot charge uninsured patients more for the same treatment than what those with health insurance are billed. This is to protect uninsured patients from medical bankruptcy. This law applies only to nonprofit institutions, meaning that about 40% of all community hospitals are exempt. In some states (Colorado, for example) the law covers for-profit hospitals also.

As a result of the Affordable Care Act, hospitals are putting more emphasis on quality-based care and encouraging preventive healthcare measures—screening for illness early on at lower costs before they become serious and more expensive to treat. Value-based payment systems are discussed in more detail in Chapter 17. Another goal of the Affordable Care Act is to have people who previously used the emergency department for primary care to seek their healthcare from primary care providers.

BUNDLED PAYMENTS FOR CARE IMPROVEMENT INITIATIVE

In 2011 the HHS announced an initiative known as the *Bundled Payments for Care Improvement (BPCI) initiative* to help improve care for patients while they are in the hospital and after they are discharged. Bundled payments will provide incentives to coordinate care, improve the quality of care, and save money.

The BPCI initiative was introduced by the new CMS Innovation Center, which was created by the Affordable Care Act to carry out the important task of finding new and better ways to provide and pay for healthcare to a growing population of Medicare and Medicaid beneficiaries.

On October 1, 2018, Bundled Payments for Care Improvement Advanced (BPCI Advanced) began. This voluntary initiative combines payments for physician, hospital, and other healthcare provider services into a single bundled payment. Payment is based on the expected costs of all items and services provided during an episode of care (90 days). BPCI Advanced hopes to encourage providers to adopt best practices, reduce variation from standards of care, and provide clinically appropriate levels of services for patients. This initiative is looking at specific inpatient admissions identified by MS-DRGs and at outpatient procedures identified by HCPCS codes. This model hopes to show that a payment system based on quality of outcomes is better for both patients and providers.

What Did You Learn?

1. What is HIPAA's rule on Medicare claims submission?
2. List the exceptions to this rule.
3. How does the Affordable Care Act affect hospital charges?
4. What three things will the BPCI initiative accomplish?

BILLING COMPLIANCE

The creation of a compliance program is a major initiative of the Office of the Inspector General (OIG) in its effort to engage the private healthcare community in preventing the submission of inaccurate claims and combating fraudulent conduct. In the past several years, the OIG has developed and issued compliance program guidelines directed at various segments of the healthcare industry. The development of these types of compliance program guidelines is based on the belief that a healthcare provider can use internal controls to monitor adherence to applicable statutes, regulations, and program requirements more efficiently. A compliance program usually consists of the following elements:

- An internal compliance review, or "legal audit," of the provider's operations (often focused in one or more targeted areas, such as billing practices)
- Identification of practices that are improper, illegal, or potentially abusive
- Drafting of an appropriate code of conduct for management and staff
- Appointment of a compliance officer and compliance oversight committee
- Implementation of a hotline or some other manner of reporting mechanism

- Development and implementation of a training program for relevant staff
- Design of appropriate disciplinary sanctions for violations of the plan
- Securing of continuing compliance through proper dissemination of new regulations and carrier or intermediary directives and statutes
- Periodic audits of the provider's practices and procedures to ensure continued compliance

Depending on the success of this program, providers may wish to expand their compliance review to other areas, such as US Occupational Safety and Health Administration or US Food and Drug Administration compliance, as appropriate.

A meaningful compliance plan addresses more than just billing procedures. Because this chapter focuses on hospital billing, we will take a closer look at **billing compliance, which** begins with the gathering of complete and accurate information during the admission and registration interview. Most problems with claims originate in the claim development process—from the initial physician order, to the moment a patient presents in the facility, to the admission or registration process, to the clinical areas of patient care and the associated documentation, to coding, and finally to billing. A good comprehensive billing compliance program should give hands-on admissions, registration, and billing personnel, as well as others within the organization involved in the claims development process, an appropriate level of information relating to the "full-circle process" and instruction relating to compliance standards.

◎ HIPAA Tip

It is recommended that hospitals periodically evaluate Health Insurance Portability and Accountability Act (HIPAA) rules to ensure that they are still in compliance. Experts suggest that administrative efficiencies gained from compliance would have a positive financial impact on hospitals and health systems in the long run.

CODING COMPLIANCE

Coding compliance is a critical component of a hospital's overall compliance plan. Coding compliance is basically the process of verifying that the diagnoses and procedure codes used on claims comply with all current coding guidelines and rules. For inpatient care, coding compliance relates to the accuracy and completeness of the diagnosis and procedure codes used to assign the applicable DRGs and determine appropriate payment.

A coding compliance program that ensures that Medicare claims are accurate and complete involves five essential components:

- *Detection:* Identifying records with potential coding problems
- *Correction:* Performing audits to locate and correct errors
- *Prevention:* Educating coders to prevent future coding problems

- *Verification:* Providing an audit trail of all coding compliance actions
- *Comparison:* Comparing coding patterns over time and to external standards

Today's computer technology can simplify the process of implementing these coding compliance components.

❓ What Did You Learn?

1. What is the purpose of a billing compliance program?
2. List at least seven of the nine elements of a billing compliance program.
3. Where does billing compliance begin?
4. What three areas should be included in a comprehensive billing compliance program?
5. Name the five components that are essential to the process of coding compliance.

CAREER OPPORTUNITIES IN HOSPITAL BILLING

According to the US Department of Labor's Bureau of Labor Statistics, medical records and health information technicians held more than 215,500 jobs in 2018, and 34% of all jobs were in hospitals. The rest were mostly in offices of physicians, nursing care facilities, outpatient care centers, and home healthcare services. Insurance firms that deal in health matters employ a few health information technicians to tabulate and analyze health information. Public health departments also hire technicians to supervise data collection from healthcare institutions and to assist in research.

TRAINING, OTHER QUALIFICATIONS, AND ADVANCEMENT

Medical records and health information technicians entering the field typically have associate degrees from community colleges or career programs. In addition to general education, coursework includes medical terminology, anatomy and physiology, legal aspects of health information, coding and abstraction of data, statistics, database management, quality improvement methods, and computer science. Applicants can improve their chances of admission into a program by taking biology, chemistry, health, and computer science courses in high school.

Hospitals sometimes advance promising health information clerks to jobs as medical records and health information technicians, although this practice may be less common in the future. Experienced medical records and health information technicians can advance in one of several ways—by specializing, by furthering their education, or by managing. Many senior technicians specialize in coding, particularly Medicare coding, or in cancer registry. More commonly, however, advancement requires 2 to 4 years of job experience, completion of a hospital's in-house training program, or acquiring specialized education or credentialing, such as certification in an HIM program.

Most employers prefer to hire **Registered Health Information Technicians (RHITs)**, who are required to pass a written examination offered by the American Health Information Management Association (AHIMA). To take the examination, an individual must graduate from a 2-year associate degree program accredited by the Commission on Accreditation of Allied Health Education Programs (CAAHEP) of the AMA. Technicians trained in non–CAAHEP-accredited programs or on the job are not eligible to take the AHIMA examination. CAAHEP has accredited 182 programs for health information technicians. Technicians who specialize in coding may obtain voluntary certification.

In medical records and health information departments of large facilities, an experienced technician may advance to section supervisor, overseeing the work of the coding, correspondence, or discharge sections. A senior technician with RHIT credentials may become director or assistant director of a medical records and health information department in a small facility. In larger institutions, the director is usually an administrator with a bachelor's degree in medical records and health information administration.

The AHIMA and the American Academy of Professional Coders (AAPC) offer certification in various coding proficiencies. To learn more about certification, see "Websites to Explore" at the end of this chapter.

JOB OUTLOOK

Job prospects are good. According to the *Occupational Outlook Handbook* published by the Bureau of Labor Statistics in September 2019, employment of hospital billing specialists and medical records and health information technicians is expected to grow much faster than the average for all occupations through 2028, due to rapid growth in the number of medical tests, treatments, and procedures that will be increasingly scrutinized by third-party payers, regulators, courts, and consumers.

Although employment growth in hospitals may not keep pace with growth in other healthcare industries, many new jobs nevertheless will be created. The fastest employment growth and the greatest number of new jobs are expected to occur in offices of physicians, due to increasing demand for detailed records, especially in large group practices. Rapid growth is also expected in nursing care facilities, home healthcare services, and outpatient care centers. Additional job openings will result from the need to replace technicians who retire or leave the occupation permanently. Table 18.5 lists common certifications and their

Table 18.5 Certifications and Their Requirements and Other Career Opportunities in Hospital Billing	
CERTIFICATION	**REQUIREMENTS**
Registered Health Information Administrator (RHIA)	Successfully completing an approved baccalaureate or postbaccalaureate program and passing a national RHIA certification examination
Registered Health Information Technician (RHIT)	Obtaining an associate degree in an approved health information technology program and passing a national certification examination
Certified Coding Specialist (CCS)	Passing a national coding examination measuring medical terminology, disease processes, pharmacology, and the application of ICD diagnostic coding and CPT surgery coding systems
Certified Coding Specialist— Physician-Based (CCS-P)	Passing a national coding examination measuring medical terminology; disease processes; pharmacology; and the application of ICD-10-CM, CPT, and HCPCS level II coding systems
Certified Professional Coder— Hospital Outpatient (CPC-H)	Passing a national coding examination measuring proficiencies in coding procedures and diagnoses on medical claims in the outpatient setting
Certified Coding Associate (CCA)	Passing a national coding examination measuring understanding of entry-level coding applications, including medical terminology, disease processes, pharmacology, and ICD-10-CM and CPT medical record coding
National Healthcareer Association (NHA)	A health career certification provider, providing technology-based educational, assessment, testing, and certification solutions for healthcare and other vocational fields that serve secondary, postsecondary, and professional education markets in nursing, allied health, emergency services, fitness, and many other health science professions.
Other Career Opportunities	
Admissions coordinator Discharge planner Medical records clerk Medical records technician Medical secretary Medical transcriptionist Nutrition educator Transplant coordinator Tumor registrar Unit coordinator	

CPT, Current Procedural Terminology; *HCPCS*, Healthcare Common Procedure Coding System; *ICD-10-CM*, *International Classification of Diseases*, 10th revision, Clinical Modification.

Table 18.6	Quick Facts About Medical Records and Health Information Technicians
QUICK FACT CATEGORY	**QUICK FACT DATA**
2018 median pay	$40,350 per year; $19.40 per hour
Entry-level education	Postsecondary nondegree award
Work experience in a related occupation	None
On-the-job training	None
Number of jobs, 2018	215,500
Job outlook, 2012–2020	11% (Much faster than average)
Employment change, 2018–2028	23,100

US Department of Labor, Bureau of Labor Statistics, 2018.

requirements and other career opportunities in hospital billing.

Table 18.6 lists a summary of "quick facts" from the Bureau of Labor Statistics' most recent census regarding medical records and health information technician jobs. In addition, an Occupational Outlook Handbook for Medical Records and Health Information Technicians can be found on the Bureau of Labor Statistics website. A direct link to this material is included under "Websites to Explore" at the end of this chapter.

? What Did You Learn?

1. What type of coursework should a student expect to complete when entering a medical records or health information technological field?
2. What are the career opportunities for health information clerks or technicians?
3. What is the job outlook for health information clerks or technicians?

SUMMARY CHECKPOINTS

- Today's modern hospital is a place where sick or injured individuals receive healthcare. It also provides continuing education for practicing physicians and serves the function of an institution of higher learning for entire communities. If it is a teaching hospital, clinical education is provided to the entire spectrum of healthcare professionals. The hospital also might conduct investigational studies and perform research in medical sciences.
- A goal of the entire healthcare system is to reduce costs and, at the same time, be more responsive to customers (patients).
- The major types of healthcare facilities include the following:
  - Acute care facilities
  - Subacute care facilities
  - ASCs
  - SNFs
  - Long-term care facilities
  - Hospice
- All acute care or general hospitals must be licensed by the state in which they are located to provide care within the minimum health and safety standards established by regulations and rules. HHS enforces the standards by periodically conducting surveys of these facilities. Hospitals may seek accreditation by nationally recognized accrediting agencies such as The Joint Commission and CARF. Surveys conducted by The Joint Commission and CARF are based on guidelines developed by each of these organizations.
- Common hospital payers are as follows:
  - Medicare
  - Medicaid
  - TRICARE/CHAMPVA
  - BCBS
  - Private (commercial) insurers
- The health insurance professional must be aware of individual payer guidelines for accurate and timely claims completion. Current guidelines can be found on the payers' websites, or provider manuals may be acquired by contacting the payer or its FI/carrier.
- The UB-04 is the standard claim form used for inpatient hospitalization. Data elements necessary for claims processing in most cases are assigned designated spaces on the form called *FLs*. There are 81 FLs, and each has a unique number. Applicable information is entered into these FLs using a numerical, alphabetical, alphanumeric, or text-based format. The electronic equivalent to the UB-04 is the 837I.
- The information included in a hospital health record begins with demographic information—patient's name, address, age, sex, occupation—collected on admission. Every time a patient receives healthcare, a record is maintained of the observations, medical or surgical interventions, and treatment outcomes. This record includes information that the patient provides concerning his or her symptoms and medical history, the results of examinations, radiology reports and laboratory test results, diagnoses, and treatment plans.
- The hospital billing process begins when the patient registers for inpatient or outpatient admission. Hospital charges are recorded for room and board, each procedure performed, medications, laboratory tests, x-rays (if applicable), and miscellaneous service charges.
- Although hospital coding is similar to that done in a physician's office, there are some significant differences. Two code sets are currently used for coding hospital/facility claims: (1) ICD-10-PCS is used for reporting inpatient procedures only, and (2) ICD-10-CM is used in all health treatment

facilities, both inpatient and outpatient, for coding diagnoses. In addition, hospital coders use the "principal diagnosis," which is defined as the condition determined to be chiefly responsible for the patient's admission to the facility. HCPCS codes are used for reporting procedures on Medicare Part B and other claim types. Outpatient hospital coding includes ICD-10-CM and CPT-4/HCPCS codes when applicable. Note: The ICD-10 coding system replaced ICD-9 in October 2015.

- The billing data that are being submitted to Medicare and other payers are examined carefully for accuracy and completeness. It is crucial that the health insurance professional responsible for hospital billing thoroughly understands the instructions relating to the correct completion of the UB-04, possesses insight as to how the data elements interact, and comprehends what the payers do with the data when they are adjudicating a claim. Data quality, coding, and billing compliance are crucial things to consider in the submission of inpatient and outpatient claims. Staying abreast of current rules and regulations is a multidepartment responsibility, as is keeping aware of the quality of documentation, coding, and billing. Compliance cannot be viewed as a one-step process; it must be considered an ongoing effort by every member of the healthcare team.

- Advantages of submitting hospital claims using ECS include the following:
  - Increased cash flow
  - Quicker turnaround for payment than with paper claims
  - Availability to submit claims 7 days a week (including holidays)
  - Availability of ERA for faster posting of payments
  - Availability of EFT for paperless process
  - Ability to generate a variety of reports

- A compliance program typically consists of the following elements:
  - An internal compliance review, or "legal audit," of the provider's operations (often focused in one or more targeted areas, such as billing practices)
  - Identification of practices that are improper, illegal, or potentially abusive
  - Drafting of an appropriate code of conduct for management and staff
  - Appointment of a compliance officer and compliance oversight committee
  - Implementation of a hotline or some other manner of reporting mechanism
  - Development and implementation of a training program for relevant staff
  - Design of appropriate disciplinary sanctions for violations of the plan

- Securing of continuing compliance through proper dissemination of new regulations and carrier or intermediary directives and statutes
- Periodic audits of the provider's practices and procedures to ensure continued compliance

- Many career opportunities may be found under the umbrella of hospital billing. Careers that require completion of a specific program and successful passing of a certification examination include the following:
  - Registered Health Information Administrator (RHIA)
  - Registered Health Information Technician (RHIT)
  - Certified Coding Specialist (CCS)
  - Certified Coding Specialist—Physician-Based (CCS-P)
  - Certified Coding Associate (CCA)
  - Certified Professional Coder (CPC)
  - Certified Professional Coder—Hospital Outpatient (CPC-H)

- Other career opportunities that may or may not require special education or certification (or both) include the following:
  - Admissions coordinator
  - Discharge planner
  - Medical records clerk
  - Medical records technician
  - Medical secretary
  - Medical transcriptionist
  - Nutrition educator
  - Transplant coordinator
  - Tumor registrar
  - Unit coordinator

🔍 Closing Scenario

After working in Walden-Martin Medical Center's Billing Department for several months, Brittany has learned the various stages of hospital billing. Previously, she worked in a small medical office where she was in charge of all billing and claims submission. At Walden-Martin, a much larger facility, work is more specialized, and Brittany's tasks center on Medicare claims submissions.

Walden-Martin's Billing Department is part of the Health Information Management Department, which employs nearly 100 individuals. There are numerous opportunities for advancement within the Health Information Management Department, and after an employee has completed 6 months of orientation and training, he or she can apply for a position that offers better pay; however, a promotion comes with more responsibility. Brittany has decided to continue her education at Deerfield Community College and eventually acquire a bachelor's degree in health information management. She is confident that with all of the job opportunities Walden-Martin Medical Center offers, she will be able to achieve her long-term career goals at this medical facility.

CHAPTER REVIEW QUESTIONS

1. Which piece of legislation is causing a change in focus to value-based care?
   a. HIPAA
   b. MACRA
   c. PPACA
   d. AAAHC

2. A network of healthcare providers that integrated hospital services with physician services is:
   a. An integrated delivery system.
   b. A diagnosis-related group.
   c. A hospital information system.
   d. A quality improvement organization.

3. A facility where surgical procedures that do not require a hospital admission are performed is:
   a. An acute care facility.
   b. A critical access hospital.
   c. An ambulatory surgery center.
   d. An integrated delivery system.

4. The Emergency Medical Treatment and Active Labor Act (EMTALA) states that Medicare-participating hospitals must treat an emergent condition regardless of the patient's ability to pay. It also states that the patient must remain at that facility until he or she is ready to be discharged.
   a. The first statement is false, and the second statement is true.
   b. The first statement is true, and the second statement is false.
   c. Both statements are true.
   d. Both statements are false.

5. Which of the following are accreditation agencies for managed care organizations?
   a. The Joint Commission
   b. The Accreditation Association for Ambulatory Health Care
   c. The National Committee for Quality Assurance
   d. All of the above

6. A benefit period begins:
   a. On the day the patient sees the provider in the medical office.
   b. On the day the patient is discharged from the hospital.
   c. On the day the patient enters the hospital or SNF.
   d. On the day the patient receives payment from Medicare.

7. Medicare Part A payments are based on:
   a. DRGs.
   b. ADLs.
   c. APCs.
   d. IDS.

8. Medicare states that services provided within a certain window of time before admission to the hospital must be included in the inpatient MS-DRG payment. What is that window of time?
   a. 24 hours
   b. 48 hours
   c. 60 hours
   d. 72 hours

9. Most of the time, patients covered under TRICARE receive inpatient care at a military treatment facility, but if that is not available, a(n) _____ must be obtained.
   a. Governance
   b. Billing compliance
   c. Nonavailability statement
   d. None of the above

10. The coding system used for inpatient hospital procedures is:
    a. HCPCS.
    b. CPT.
    c. ICD-10-PCS.
    d. DRG.

WEBSITES TO EXPLORE

- For live links to the following websites, please visit the Evolve website at http://evolve.elsevier.com/Beik/today.
- Visit the CMS home page at http://www.cms.gov/.
- For more information on the history of hospitals in the United States, go to http://www.ncbi.nlm.nih.gov/pmc/articles/PMC1517304/ or use "history of hospitals in the US" as Internet search words.
- For additional information on emerging trends in healthcare, visit the American Hospital Association website at http://www.aha.org and enter emerging trends in the Search window.
- For more information on blockchain technology, go to https://www.ncbi.nlm.nih.gov/pmc/articles/PMC6517629/.
- QIOs are discussed in more detail at http://www.cms.gov/QualityImprovementOrgs/.
- For more information on TRICARE and CHAMPVA reimbursement, visit http://www.tricare.mil/ and peruse the *TRICARE Reimbursement Manual*.
- Refer to the CMS ICD-10-CM official guidelines for coding and reporting at https://www.cms.gov/Medicare/Coding/ICD10/2020-ICD-10-PCS.html.
- An informative PowerPoint presentation on APCs can be accessed at https://www.scribd.com/presentation/249127321/Ambulatory-Payment-Classifications-APCs-ppt.

- For extensive information on hospital compliance and payment monitoring programs, see IPRO's website at http://www.ipro.org/.
- To view a PowerPoint presentation on ICD-10-PCS, go to https://www.cms.gov/Medicare/Coding/ICD10/Downloads/2016-PCS-Slides.pdf.
- For additional information on certification, see the American Association of Professional Coders (AAPC) website at http://www.aapc.com/certification/.
- For further information on the two new HIPAA rules, go to the following CMS websites: http://www.cms.gov/ElectronicBillingEDITrans/18_5010D0.asp and http://www.cms.gov/ICD10/11a_Version_5010.asp.
- Download the Medicare Claims Processing Manual, Chapter 25—Completing and Processing the Form, CMS-1450 Data Set at http://www.cms.gov/Regulations-and-guidance/Guidance/Manuals/downloads/clm104c25.pdf.
- To view an example of a completed UB-04 claim form, go to http://www.ibx.com/pdfs/providers/npi/ub04_form.pdf.
- To learn about recent developments in billing and claims-related transactions, see http://www.nubc.org/.
- To see the entire dialogue of the ASTM standard EMRs, go to http://www.astm.org and enter "E1384" in the website search.
- To learn more about HOPPS and APCs, explore http://www.cms.gov/IdentifiableDataFiles/03_HospitalOPPS.asp.
- The *StandardCompanion Guide, Health Care Claim Payment/Advice (835)* may be downloaded from https://www.cgsmedicare.com/pdf/edi/835_compguide.pdf.
- The CMS 835 Companion Document is available at http://www.cignamedicare.com/.
- Information on HIPAA's transaction code sets can be located at https://www.ama-assn.org/practice-management/hipaa/hipaa-administrative-simplification.
- Peruse the following websites for career opportunities in healthcare technology: http://www.ahima.org/careers/healthinfo?tabid=stories and http://www.ahima.org/careers.
- Two good websites that discuss principal diagnosis assignment and secondary diagnosis assignment are https://acdis.org/system/files/resources/304853.pdf and https://www.fortherecordmag.com/archives/0116p10.shtml.
- The following websites provide additional information about AHIMA and AAPC certification: http://www.aapc.com/certification/ and http://www.ahima.org/certification/default.aspx.
- Detailed information on the job outlook for medical record and health information technicians can be found at http://www.bls.gov/ooh/Healthcare/Medical-records-and-health-information-technicians.htm.

Author's Note: Due to the dynamic nature of the Internet, web addresses and/or links provided in this chapter may have changed since publication and may no longer be valid. In such cases, students should select comparable search words to access related sites.

Sample Blank CMS-1500 (02/12)

HEALTH INSURANCE CLAIM FORM

APPROVED BY NATIONAL UNIFORM CLAIM COMMITTEE (NUCC) 02/12

CARRIER

| | PICA | | | | | | | | PICA | | |

1. MEDICARE (Medicare#) MEDICAID (Medicaid#) TRICARE (ID#DoD#) CHAMPVA (Member ID#) GROUP HEALTH PLAN (ID#) FECA BLK LUNG (ID#) OTHER (ID#)

1a. INSURED'S I.D. NUMBER (For Program in Item 1)

2. PATIENT'S NAME (Last Name, First Name, Middle Initial)

3. PATIENT'S BIRTH DATE MM DD YY SEX M F

4. INSURED'S NAME (Last Name, First Name, Middle Initial)

5. PATIENT'S ADDRESS (No., Street)

6. PATIENT RELATIONSHIP TO INSURED Self Spouse Child Other

7. INSURED'S ADDRESS (No., Street)

CITY STATE

8. RESERVED FOR NUCC USE

CITY STATE

ZIP CODE TELEPHONE (Include Area Code) ( )

ZIP CODE TELEPHONE (Include Area Code) ( )

9. OTHER INSURED'S NAME (Last Name, First Name, Middle Initial)

10. IS PATIENT'S CONDITION RELATED TO:

11. INSURED'S POLICY GROUP OR FECA NUMBER

a. OTHER INSURED'S POLICY OR GROUP NUMBER

a. EMPLOYMENT? (Current or Previous) YES NO

a. INSURED'S DATE OF BIRTH MM DD YY SEX M F

b. RESERVED FOR NUCC USE

b. AUTO ACCIDENT? YES NO PLACE (State)

b. OTHER CLAIM ID (Designated by NUCC)

c. RESERVED FOR NUCC USE

c. OTHER ACCIDENT? YES NO

c. INSURANCE PLAN NAME OR PROGRAM NAME

d. INSURANCE PLAN NAME OR PROGRAM NAME

10d. CLAIM CODES (Designated by NUCC)

d. IS THERE ANOTHER HEALTH BENEFIT PLAN? YES NO If yes, complete items 9, 9a, and 9d.

READ BACK OF FORM BEFORE COMPLETING & SIGNING THIS FORM.

12. PATIENT'S OR AUTHORIZED PERSON'S SIGNATURE I authorize the release of any medical or other information necessary to process this claim. I also request payment of government benefits either to myself or to the party who accepts assignment below.

SIGNED _____ DATE _____

13. INSURED'S OR AUTHORIZED PERSON'S SIGNATURE I authorize payment of medical benefits to the undersigned physician or supplier for services described below.

SIGNED _____

PATIENT AND INSURED INFORMATION

14. DATE OF CURRENT ILLNESS, INJURY, or PREGNANCY(LMP) MM DD YY QUAL.

15. OTHER DATE QUAL. MM DD YY

16. DATES PATIENT UNABLE TO WORK IN CURRENT OCCUPATION MM DD YY FROM TO MM DD YY

17. NAME OF REFERRING PROVIDER OR OTHER SOURCE

17a.

17b. NPI

18. HOSPITALIZATION DATES RELATED TO CURRENT SERVICES MM DD YY FROM TO MM DD YY

19. ADDITIONAL CLAIM INFORMATION (Designated by NUCC)

20. OUTSIDE LAB? YES NO $ CHARGES

21. DIAGNOSIS OR NATURE OF ILLNESS OR INJURY Relate A-L to service line below (24E) ICD Ind.

A. |___ B. |___ C. |___ D. |___
E. |___ F. |___ G. |___ H. |___
I. |___ J. |___ K. |___ L. |___

22. RESUBMISSION CODE ORIGINAL REF. NO.

23. PRIOR AUTHORIZATION NUMBER

24. A. DATE(S) OF SERVICE From MM DD YY To MM DD YY	B. PLACE OF SERVICE	C. EMG	D. PROCEDURES, SERVICES, OR SUPPLIES (Explain Unusual Circumstances) CPT/HCPCS MODIFIER	E. DIAGNOSIS POINTER	F. $ CHARGES	G. DAYS OR UNITS	H. EPSDT Family Plan	I. ID. QUAL.	J. RENDERING PROVIDER ID. #
1									NPI
2									NPI
3									NPI
4									NPI
5									NPI
6									NPI

25. FEDERAL TAX I.D. NUMBER SSN EIN

26. PATIENT'S ACCOUNT NO.

27. ACCEPT ASSIGNMENT? (For govt. claims, see back) YES NO

28. TOTAL CHARGE $

29. AMOUNT PAID $

30. Rsvd for NUCC Use

31. SIGNATURE OF PHYSICIAN OR SUPPLIER INCLUDING DEGREES OR CREDENTIALS (I certify that the statements on the reverse apply to this bill and are made a part thereof.)

SIGNED _____ DATE _____

32. SERVICE FACILITY LOCATION INFORMATION

a. NPI b.

33. BILLING PROVIDER INFO & PH # ( )

a. NPI b.

PHYSICIAN OR SUPPLIER INFORMATION

NUCC Instruction Manual available at: www.nucc.org *PLEASE PRINT OR TYPE* APPROVED OMB-0938-1197 FORM 1500 (02-12)

Fig. A.1 A blank CMS-1500 (02/12) form.

Fig. B.1 Patient, Bertrand: Blue Cross and Blue Shield (BCBS); No Secondary.

HEALTH INSURANCE CLAIM FORM

APPROVED BY NATIONAL UNIFORM CLAIM COMMITTEE (NUCC) 02/12

MEDICAID FISCAL INTERMEDIARY
STREET ADDRESS

CITY STATE AND ZIP

| | PICA | | | | | | | | | PICA | |

| 1. MEDICARE (Medicare#) | MEDICAID [X] (Medicaid#) | TRICARE (ID#DoD#) | CHAMPVA (Member ID#) | GROUP HEALTH PLAN (ID#) | FECA BLK LUNG (ID#) | OTHER (ID#) | 1a. INSURED'S I.D. NUMBER (For Program in Item 1) 92881044PL22 |

| 2. PATIENT'S NAME (Last Name, First Name, Middle Initial) MARSALIS ELOISE A | 3. PATIENT'S BIRTH DATE MM 09 DD 08 YY 2003 SEX M☐ F[X] | 4. INSURED'S NAME (Last Name, First Name, Middle Initial) |

| 5. PATIENT'S ADDRESS (No., Street) 208 OAKLAWN LOT 402 | 6. PATIENT RELATIONSHIP TO INSURED Self☐ Spouse☐ Child☐ Other☐ | 7. INSURED'S ADDRESS (No., Street) |

| CITY MILTON | STATE XY | 8. RESERVED FOR NUCC USE | CITY | STATE |

| ZIP CODE 12345 | TELEPHONE (Include Area Code) (5552347112) | | ZIP CODE | TELEPHONE (Include Area Code) ( ) |

| 9. OTHER INSURED'S NAME (Last Name, First Name, Middle Initial) | 10. IS PATIENT'S CONDITION RELATED TO: | 11. INSURED'S POLICY GROUP OR FECA NUMBER |

a. OTHER INSURED'S POLICY OR GROUP NUMBER

a. EMPLOYMENT? (Current or Previous) YES☐ NO[X]

a. INSURED'S DATE OF BIRTH MM DD YY   SEX M☐ F☐

b. RESERVED FOR NUCC USE

b. AUTO ACCIDENT? YES☐ NO[X] PLACE (State)

b. OTHER CLAIM ID (Designated by NUCC)

c. RESERVED FOR NUCC USE

c. OTHER ACCIDENT? YES☐ NO[X]

c. INSURANCE PLAN NAME OR PROGRAM NAME

d. INSURANCE PLAN NAME OR PROGRAM NAME

10d. CLAIM CODES (Designated by NUCC)

d. IS THERE ANOTHER HEALTH BENEFIT PLAN? YES☐ NO☐ *If yes*, complete items 9, 9a, and 9d.

READ BACK OF FORM BEFORE COMPLETING & SIGNING THIS FORM.
12. PATIENT'S OR AUTHORIZED PERSON'S SIGNATURE I authorize the release of any medical or other information necessary to process this claim. I also request payment of government benefits either to myself or to the party who accepts assignment below.

SIGNED _____ DATE _____

13. INSURED'S OR AUTHORIZED PERSON'S SIGNATURE I authorize payment of medical benefits to the undersigned physician or supplier for services described below.

SIGNED _____

| 14. DATE OF CURRENT ILLNESS, INJURY, or PREGNANCY(LMP) MM DD YY QUAL. | 15. OTHER DATE QUAL. MM DD YY | 16. DATES PATIENT UNABLE TO WORK IN CURRENT OCCUPATION FROM MM DD YY TO MM DD YY |

| 17. NAME OF REFERRING PROVIDER OR OTHER SOURCE DK JAMES A MARTIN MD | 17a. 17b. NPI 1234567890 | 18. HOSPITALIZATION DATES RELATED TO CURRENT SERVICES FROM MM DD YY TO MM DD YY |

| 19. ADDITIONAL CLAIM INFORMATION (Designated by NUCC) | 20. OUTSIDE LAB? YES☐ NO[X] $ CHARGES |

21. DIAGNOSIS OR NATURE OF ILLNESS OR INJURY Relate A-L to service line below (24E) ICD Ind. 0	22. RESUBMISSION CODE ORIGINAL REF. NO.
A. F43.0 B. ___ C. ___ D. ___	
E. ___ F. ___ G. ___ H. ___	23. PRIOR AUTHORIZATION NUMBER
I. ___ J. ___ K. ___ L. ___	

24. A. DATE(S) OF SERVICE From MM DD YY To MM DD YY	B. PLACE OF SERVICE	C. EMG	D. PROCEDURES, SERVICES, OR SUPPLIES (Explain Unusual Circumstances) CPT/HCPCS	MODIFIER	E. DIAGNOSIS POINTER	F. $ CHARGES	G. DAYS OR UNITS	H. EPSDT Family Plan	I. ID. QUAL.	J. RENDERING PROVIDER ID. #
1	01 24 XX	11		99213		A	75 00	1		NPI	1234567890
2										NPI	
3										NPI	
4										NPI	
5										NPI	
6										NPI	

| 25. FEDERAL TAX I.D. NUMBER 421898989 SSN☐ EIN[X] | 26. PATIENT'S ACCOUNT NO. 2644 | 27. ACCEPT ASSIGNMENT? (For govt. claims, see back) YES[X] NO☐ | 28. TOTAL CHARGE $ 75 00 | 29. AMOUNT PAID $ | 30. Rsvd for NUCC Use |

| 31. SIGNATURE OF PHYSICIAN OR SUPPLIER INCLUDING DEGREES OR CREDENTIALS (I certify that the statements on the reverse apply to this bill and are made a part thereof.) J A MARTIN MD SIGNED *J A Martin* DATE 012520XX | 32. SERVICE FACILITY LOCATION INFORMATION a. NPI b. | 33. BILLING PROVIDER INFO & PH # (555) 6567890 WALDEN-MARTIN FAMILY MEDICAL CLINIC 1234 ANYSTREET ANYTOWN AL 12345 6789 a. X100XX1000 b. |

NUCC Instruction Manual available at: www.nucc.org   *PLEASE PRINT OR TYPE*   APPROVED OMB-0938-1197 FORM 1500 (02-12)

Fig. B.2 Patient, Marsalis: Medicaid; No Secondary.

HEALTH INSURANCE CLAIM FORM

APPROVED BY NATIONAL UNIFORM CLAIM COMMITTEE (NUCC) 02/12

MEDICARE CARRIER
STREET ADDRESS OR PO BOX NUMBER

CITY STATE ZIP

| | PICA | | | | | | PICA | |

1. MEDICARE [X] (Medicare#)   MEDICAID [ ] (Medicaid#)   TRICARE [ ] (ID#DoD#)   CHAMPVA [ ] (Member ID#)   GROUP HEALTH PLAN [ ] (ID#)   FECA BLK LUNG [ ] (ID#)   OTHER [ ] (ID#)

1a. INSURED'S I.D. NUMBER   (For Program in Item 1)
181401234A

2. PATIENT'S NAME (Last Name, First Name, Middle Initial)
MARTINSON FREDERICK T

3. PATIENT'S BIRTH DATE   SEX
MM 10 | DD 18 | YY 1940   M [X]   F [ ]

4. INSURED'S NAME (Last Name, First Name, Middle Initial)

5. PATIENT'S ADDRESS (No., Street)
2300 PARNELL AVENUE

6. PATIENT RELATIONSHIP TO INSURED
Self [ ]   Spouse [ ]   Child [ ]   Other [ ]

7. INSURED'S ADDRESS (No., Street)

CITY
MILTON

STATE
XY

8. RESERVED FOR NUCC USE

CITY   STATE

ZIP CODE
12345

TELEPHONE (Include Area Code)
(5552340001)

ZIP CODE

TELEPHONE (Include Area Code)
( )

9. OTHER INSURED'S NAME (Last Name, First Name, Middle Initial)

10. IS PATIENT'S CONDITION RELATED TO:

11. INSURED'S POLICY GROUP OR FECA NUMBER
NONE

a. OTHER INSURED'S POLICY OR GROUP NUMBER

a. EMPLOYMENT? (Current or Previous)
YES [ ]   NO [X]

a. INSURED'S DATE OF BIRTH
MM | DD | YY   SEX   M [ ]   F [ ]

b. RESERVED FOR NUCC USE

b. AUTO ACCIDENT?   PLACE (State)
YES [ ]   NO [X]

b. OTHER CLAIM ID (Designated by NUCC)

c. RESERVED FOR NUCC USE

c. OTHER ACCIDENT?
YES [ ]   NO [X]

c. INSURANCE PLAN NAME OR PROGRAM NAME

d. INSURANCE PLAN NAME OR PROGRAM NAME

10d. CLAIM CODES (Designated by NUCC)

d. IS THERE ANOTHER HEALTH BENEFIT PLAN?
YES [ ]   NO [ ]   If yes, complete items 9, 9a, and 9d.

READ BACK OF FORM BEFORE COMPLETING & SIGNING THIS FORM.

12. PATIENT'S OR AUTHORIZED PERSON'S SIGNATURE I authorize the release of any medical or other information necessary to process this claim. I also request payment of government benefits either to myself or to the party who accepts assignment below.

SIGNED   SIGNATURE ON FILE   DATE

13. INSURED'S OR AUTHORIZED PERSON'S SIGNATURE I authorize payment of medical benefits to the undersigned physician or supplier for services described below.

SIGNED

14. DATE OF CURRENT ILLNESS, INJURY, or PREGNANCY(LMP)
MM | DD | YY   QUAL.

15. OTHER DATE
QUAL.   MM | DD | YY

16. DATES PATIENT UNABLE TO WORK IN CURRENT OCCUPATION
FROM MM | DD | YY   TO MM | DD | YY

17. NAME OF REFERRING PROVIDER OR OTHER SOURCE
DK | JAMES A MARTIN MD

17a.
17b. NPI 1234567890

18. HOSPITALIZATION DATES RELATED TO CURRENT SERVICES
FROM MM | DD | YY   TO MM | DD | YY

19. ADDITIONAL CLAIM INFORMATION (Designated by NUCC)

20. OUTSIDE LAB? $ CHARGES
YES [ ]   NO [X]

21. DIAGNOSIS OR NATURE OF ILLNESS OR INJURY Relate A-L to service line below (24E)   ICD Ind. 0

A. I10   B.   C.   D.
E.   F.   G.   H.
I.   J.   K.   L.

22. RESUBMISSION CODE   ORIGINAL REF. NO.

23. PRIOR AUTHORIZATION NUMBER

24. A. DATE(S) OF SERVICE From MM DD YY To MM DD YY	B. PLACE OF SERVICE	C. EMG	D. PROCEDURES, SERVICES, OR SUPPLIES (Explain Unusual Circumstances) CPT/HCPCS	MODIFIER	E. DIAGNOSIS POINTER	F. $ CHARGES	G. DAYS OR UNITS	H. EPSDT Family Plan	I. ID. QUAL.	J. RENDERING PROVIDER ID. #
1	01 25 XX	11		99213		A	75 00	1		NPI	1234567890
2										NPI	
3										NPI	
4										NPI	
5										NPI	
6										NPI	

25. FEDERAL TAX I.D. NUMBER   SSN EIN
421898989   [ ] [X]

26. PATIENT'S ACCOUNT NO.
2774

27. ACCEPT ASSIGNMENT? (For govt. claims, see back)
[X] YES   [ ] NO

28. TOTAL CHARGE
$ 75 00

29. AMOUNT PAID
$

30. Rsvd for NUCC Use
$

31. SIGNATURE OF PHYSICIAN OR SUPPLIER INCLUDING DEGREES OR CREDENTIALS
(I certify that the statements on the reverse apply to this bill and are made a part thereof.)
J A MARTIN MD
J A Martin
SIGNED   012620XX   DATE

32. SERVICE FACILITY LOCATION INFORMATION

a. NPI   b.

33. BILLING PROVIDER INFO & PH #   (555) 6567890
WALDEN-MARTIN FAMILY MEDICAL CLINIC
1234 ANYSTREET
ANYTOWN AL 12345 6789

a. X100XX1000   b.

NUCC Instruction Manual available at: www.nucc.org   PLEASE PRINT OR TYPE   APPROVED OMB-0938-1197 FORM 1500 (02-12)

Fig. B.3 Patient, Martinson: Medicare (Simple).

HEALTH INSURANCE CLAIM FORM

APPROVED BY NATIONAL UNIFORM CLAIM COMMITTEE (NUCC) 02/12

MEDICARE CARRIER
STREET ADDRESS OR PO BOX NUMBER

CITY STATE ZIP CODE

						CARRIER

PICA | | | | | | | PICA

1. MEDICARE	MEDICAID	TRICARE	CHAMPVA	GROUP HEALTH PLAN	FECA BLK LUNG	OTHER	1a. INSURED'S I.D. NUMBER (For Program in Item 1)
[X] (Medicare#)	[ ] (Medicaid#)	[ ] (ID#DoD#)	[ ] (Member ID#)	[ ] (ID#)	[ ] (ID#)	[ ] (ID#)	233991110D

2. PATIENT'S NAME (Last Name, First Name, Middle Initial)	3. PATIENT'S BIRTH DATE	SEX	4. INSURED'S NAME (Last Name, First Name, Middle Initial)
ATKINSON PRICILLA M	MM 11 DD 04 YY 1934	M [ ] F [X]	

5. PATIENT'S ADDRESS (No., Street)	6. PATIENT RELATIONSHIP TO INSURED	7. INSURED'S ADDRESS (No., Street)
52 SUNSET CIRCLE	Self [ ] Spouse [ ] Child [ ] Other [ ]	

CITY	STATE	8. RESERVED FOR NUCC USE	CITY	STATE
MILTON	XY			

ZIP CODE	TELEPHONE (Include Area Code)		ZIP CODE	TELEPHONE (Include Area Code)
12345	(5552345454)			( )

9. OTHER INSURED'S NAME (Last Name, First Name, Middle Initial)	10. IS PATIENT'S CONDITION RELATED TO:	11. INSURED'S POLICY GROUP OR FECA NUMBER
		NONE

a. OTHER INSURED'S POLICY OR GROUP NUMBER	a. EMPLOYMENT? (Current or Previous) [ ] YES [X] NO	a. INSURED'S DATE OF BIRTH MM DD YY SEX M [ ] F [ ]
b. RESERVED FOR NUCC USE	b. AUTO ACCIDENT? [ ] YES [X] NO PLACE (State)	b. OTHER CLAIM ID (Designated by NUCC)
c. RESERVED FOR NUCC USE	c. OTHER ACCIDENT? [ ] YES [X] NO	c. INSURANCE PLAN NAME OR PROGRAM NAME
d. INSURANCE PLAN NAME OR PROGRAM NAME	10d. CLAIM CODES (Designated by NUCC) MCD678912340	d. IS THERE ANOTHER HEALTH BENEFIT PLAN? [ ] YES [ ] NO If yes, complete items 9, 9a, and 9d.

READ BACK OF FORM BEFORE COMPLETING & SIGNING THIS FORM.

12. PATIENT'S OR AUTHORIZED PERSON'S SIGNATURE I authorize the release of any medical or other information necessary to process this claim. I also request payment of government benefits either to myself or to the party who accepts assignment below.

SIGNED   SIGNATURE ON FILE   DATE

13. INSURED'S OR AUTHORIZED PERSON'S SIGNATURE I authorize payment of medical benefits to the undersigned physician or supplier for services described below.

SIGNED

14. DATE OF CURRENT ILLNESS, INJURY, or PREGNANCY(LMP) MM DD YY QUAL.	15. OTHER DATE QUAL. MM DD YY	16. DATES PATIENT UNABLE TO WORK IN CURRENT OCCUPATION FROM MM DD YY TO MM DD YY
17. NAME OF REFERRING PROVIDER OR OTHER SOURCE DK JAMES A MARTIN MD	17a. / 17b. NPI 1234567890	18. HOSPITALIZATION DATES RELATED TO CURRENT SERVICES FROM MM DD YY TO MM DD YY
19. ADDITIONAL CLAIM INFORMATION (Designated by NUCC)		20. OUTSIDE LAB? [ ] YES [X] NO $ CHARGES

21. DIAGNOSIS OR NATURE OF ILLNESS OR INJURY Relate A-L to service line below (24E)   ICD Ind. 0

A. M08.80   B.   C.   D.
E.   F.   G.   H.
I.   J.   K.   L.

22. RESUBMISSION CODE   ORIGINAL REF. NO.
23. PRIOR AUTHORIZATION NUMBER

24. A. DATE(S) OF SERVICE From MM DD YY To MM DD YY	B. PLACE OF SERVICE	C. EMG	D. PROCEDURES, SERVICES, OR SUPPLIES (Explain Unusual Circumstances) CPT/HCPCS MODIFIER	E. DIAGNOSIS POINTER	F. $ CHARGES	G. DAYS OR UNITS	H. EPSDT Family Plan	I. ID. QUAL.	J. RENDERING PROVIDER ID. #
1	01 24 XX	11		99214	A	115 00	1		NPI	1234567890
2	01 24 XX	11		99214	A	25 00	1		NPI	1234567890
3									NPI	
4									NPI	
5									NPI	
6									NPI	

25. FEDERAL TAX I.D. NUMBER SSN EIN	26. PATIENT'S ACCOUNT NO.	27. ACCEPT ASSIGNMENT? (For govt. claims, see back)	28. TOTAL CHARGE	29. AMOUNT PAID	30. Rsvd for NUCC Use
421898989 [ ] [X]	2340	[X] YES [ ] NO	$ 140 00	$	

31. SIGNATURE OF PHYSICIAN OR SUPPLIER INCLUDING DEGREES OR CREDENTIALS (I certify that the statements on the reverse apply to this bill and are made a part thereof.) J A MARTIN MD SIGNED J A Martin DATE 012520XX	32. SERVICE FACILITY LOCATION INFORMATION a. NPI b.	33. BILLING PROVIDER INFO & PH # (555) 6567890 WALDEN-MARTIN FAMILY MEDICAL CLINIC 1234 ANYSTREET ANYTOWN AL 12345 6789 a. X100XX1000 b.

NUCC Instruction Manual available at: www.nucc.org   PLEASE PRINT OR TYPE   APPROVED OMB-0938-1197 FORM 1500 (02-12)

Fig. B.4 Patient, Atkinson: Medicare/Medicaid.

HEALTH INSURANCE CLAIM FORM

APPROVED BY NATIONAL UNIFORM CLAIM COMMITTEE (NUCC) 02/12

MEDICARE CARRIER
STREET ADDRESS OR PO BOX NUMBER

CITY STATE ZIP

CARRIER →

| | | PICA | | | | | | | | | | | | PICA | | |

1. MEDICARE [X] (Medicare#) MEDICAID [ ] (Medicaid#) TRICARE [ ] (ID#DoD#) CHAMPVA [ ] (Member ID#) GROUP HEALTH PLAN [ ] (ID#) FECA BLK LUNG [ ] (ID#) OTHER [ ] (ID#)

1a. INSURED'S I.D. NUMBER (For Program in Item 1)
343668110A

2. PATIENT'S NAME (Last Name, First Name, Middle Initial)
FREEMAN OZWALD N

3. PATIENT'S BIRTH DATE: MM 10 DD 16 YY 1933 SEX M [X] F [ ]

4. INSURED'S NAME (Last Name, First Name, Middle Initial)

5. PATIENT'S ADDRESS (No., Street)
1111 DOBSON CREEK ROAD

6. PATIENT RELATIONSHIP TO INSURED
Self [X] Spouse [ ] Child [ ] Other [ ]

7. INSURED'S ADDRESS (No., Street)

CITY
MILTON
STATE
XY

8. RESERVED FOR NUCC USE

CITY   STATE

ZIP CODE
12345
TELEPHONE (Include Area Code)
(5552343321)

ZIP CODE   TELEPHONE (Include Area Code)
( )

9. OTHER INSURED'S NAME (Last Name, First Name, Middle Initial)
SAME

10. IS PATIENT'S CONDITION RELATED TO:

11. INSURED'S POLICY GROUP OR FECA NUMBER
NONE

a. OTHER INSURED'S POLICY OR GROUP NUMBER
MGAP 274805022F

a. EMPLOYMENT? (Current or Previous)
YES [ ] NO [X]

a. INSURED'S DATE OF BIRTH MM DD YY   SEX M [ ] F [ ]

b. RESERVED FOR NUCC USE

b. AUTO ACCIDENT?
YES [ ] NO [X] PLACE (State)

b. OTHER CLAIM ID (Designated by NUCC)

c. RESERVED FOR NUCC USE

c. OTHER ACCIDENT?
YES [ ] NO [X]

c. INSURANCE PLAN NAME OR PROGRAM NAME

d. INSURANCE PLAN NAME OR PROGRAM NAME
ABC55000

10d. CLAIM CODES (Designated by NUCC)

d. IS THERE ANOTHER HEALTH BENEFIT PLAN?
[X] YES [ ] NO If yes, complete items 9, 9a, and 9d.

READ BACK OF FORM BEFORE COMPLETING & SIGNING THIS FORM.
12. PATIENT'S OR AUTHORIZED PERSON'S SIGNATURE I authorize the release of any medical or other information necessary to process this claim. I also request payment of government benefits either to myself or to the party who accepts assignment below.

SIGNED SIGNATURE ON FILE   DATE

13. INSURED'S OR AUTHORIZED PERSON'S SIGNATURE I authorize payment of medical benefits to the undersigned physician or supplier for services described below.

SIGNED SIGNATURE ON FILE

PATIENT AND INSURED INFORMATION →

14. DATE OF CURRENT ILLNESS, INJURY, or PREGNANCY(LMP) MM DD YY QUAL.

15. OTHER DATE QUAL. MM DD YY

16. DATES PATIENT UNABLE TO WORK IN CURRENT OCCUPATION FROM MM DD YY TO MM DD YY

17. NAME OF REFERRING PROVIDER OR OTHER SOURCE
DK ANGELA N PEREZ MD

17a.
17b. NPI 2907511822

18. HOSPITALIZATION DATES RELATED TO CURRENT SERVICES FROM MM DD YY TO MM DD YY

19. ADDITIONAL CLAIM INFORMATION (Designated by NUCC)

20. OUTSIDE LAB? [ ] YES [X] NO $ CHARGES

21. DIAGNOSIS OR NATURE OF ILLNESS OR INJURY Relate A-L to service line below (24E) ICD Ind. 0

A. R07.9   B.   C.   D.
E.   F.   G.   H.
I.   J.   K.   L.

22. RESUBMISSION CODE ORIGINAL REF. NO.

23. PRIOR AUTHORIZATION NUMBER

24. A. DATE(S) OF SERVICE From MM DD YY	To MM DD YY	B. PLACE OF SERVICE	C. EMG	D. PROCEDURES, SERVICES, OR SUPPLIES (Explain Unusual Circumstances) CPT/HCPCS	MODIFIER	E. DIAGNOSIS POINTER	F. $ CHARGES	G. DAYS OR UNITS	H. EPSDT Family Plan	I. ID. QUAL.	J. RENDERING PROVIDER ID. #
1	01 24 XX		11	99214	99214		A	115 00	1		NPI	2907511822
2	01 24 XX		11		93350		A	175 00	1		NPI	2907511822
3	01 24 XX		11		93017		A	55 00	1		NPI	2907511822
4											NPI	
5											NPI	
6											NPI	

PHYSICIAN OR SUPPLIER INFORMATION →

25. FEDERAL TAX I.D. NUMBER SSN EIN
421898989 [ ] [X]

26. PATIENT'S ACCOUNT NO.
2544

27. ACCEPT ASSIGNMENT? (For govt. claims, see back)
[X] YES [ ] NO

28. TOTAL CHARGE
$ 345 00

29. AMOUNT PAID
$

30. Rsvd for NUCC Use

31. SIGNATURE OF PHYSICIAN OR SUPPLIER INCLUDING DEGREES OR CREDENTIALS (I certify that the statements on the reverse apply to this bill and are made a part thereof.)
ANGELA N PEREZ MD
Angela N Perez
SIGNED
012520XX
DATE

32. SERVICE FACILITY LOCATION INFORMATION

a. NPI   b.

33. BILLING PROVIDER INFO & PH # (555) 6567890
WALDEN-MARTIN FAMILY MEDICAL CLINIC
1234 ANYSTREET
ANYTOWN AL 12345 6789

a. X100XX1000   b.

NUCC Instruction Manual available at: www.nucc.org   PLEASE PRINT OR TYPE   APPROVED OMB-0938-1197 FORM 1500 (02-12)

Fig. B.5 Patient, Freeman: Medicare/Medigap.

HEALTH INSURANCE CLAIM FORM

APPROVED BY NATIONAL UNIFORM CLAIM COMMITTEE (NUCC) 02/12

EDU BENEFITS INC
15055 144TH AV SUITE 6B

GRANITE FALLS XT 34567

| | PICA | | | | | | | | PICA | |

1. MEDICARE	MEDICAID	TRICARE	CHAMPVA	GROUP HEALTH PLAN	FECA BLK LUNG	OTHER	1a. INSURED'S I.D. NUMBER (For Program in Item 1)
[X] (Medicare#)	[ ] (Medicaid#)	[ ] (ID#DoD#)	[ ] (Member ID#)	[ ] (ID#)	[ ] (ID#)	[ ] (ID#)	222553320A

2. PATIENT'S NAME (Last Name, First Name, Middle Initial)
FRANKLIN ALMA L

3. PATIENT'S BIRTH DATE MM 05 DD 02 YY 1941 **SEX** M [ ] F [X]

4. INSURED'S NAME (Last Name, First Name, Middle Initial)
FRANKLIN JOSEPH P

5. PATIENT'S ADDRESS (No., Street)
89 BRIDGEWAY

6. PATIENT RELATIONSHIP TO INSURED
Self [ ] Spouse [X] Child [ ] Other [ ]

7. INSURED'S ADDRESS (No., Street)
SAME

CITY MILTON   **STATE** XY

8. RESERVED FOR NUCC USE

CITY   **STATE**

ZIP CODE 12345   **TELEPHONE (Include Area Code)** (5552341009)

ZIP CODE   **TELEPHONE (Include Area Code)** ( )

9. OTHER INSURED'S NAME (Last Name, First Name, Middle Initial)

10. IS PATIENT'S CONDITION RELATED TO:

11. INSURED'S POLICY GROUP OR FECA NUMBER
XWT8739995

a. OTHER INSURED'S POLICY OR GROUP NUMBER

a. EMPLOYMENT? (Current or Previous)
[ ] YES [X] NO

a. INSURED'S DATE OF BIRTH MM 06 DD 27 YY 1938 **SEX** M [X] F [ ]

b. RESERVED FOR NUCC USE

b. AUTO ACCIDENT? PLACE (State)
[ ] YES [X] NO

b. OTHER CLAIM ID (Designated by NUCC)

c. RESERVED FOR NUCC USE

c. OTHER ACCIDENT?
[ ] YES [X] NO

c. INSURANCE PLAN NAME OR PROGRAM NAME
EDU BENEFITS INC

d. INSURANCE PLAN NAME OR PROGRAM NAME

10d. CLAIM CODES (Designated by NUCC)

d. IS THERE ANOTHER HEALTH BENEFIT PLAN?
[ ] YES [ ] NO *If yes*, complete items 9, 9a, and 9d.

READ BACK OF FORM BEFORE COMPLETING & SIGNING THIS FORM.

12. PATIENT'S OR AUTHORIZED PERSON'S SIGNATURE I authorize the release of any medical or other information necessary to process this claim. I also request payment of government benefits either to myself or to the party who accepts assignment below.

SIGNED   SOF   DATE

13. INSURED'S OR AUTHORIZED PERSON'S SIGNATURE I authorize payment of medical benefits to the undersigned physician or supplier for services described below.

SIGNED   SOF

14. DATE OF CURRENT ILLNESS, INJURY, or PREGNANCY(LMP) MM 01 DD 16 YY 20XX QUAL.

15. OTHER DATE QUAL. MM DD YY

16. DATES PATIENT UNABLE TO WORK IN CURRENT OCCUPATION
FROM MM 01 DD 16 YY 20XX TO MM 01 DD 24 YY 20XX

17. NAME OF REFERRING PROVIDER OR OTHER SOURCE
DN JAMES A MARTIN MD

17a.
17b. NPI 3256654001

18. HOSPITALIZATION DATES RELATED TO CURRENT SERVICES
FROM MM DD YY TO MM DD YY

19. ADDITIONAL CLAIM INFORMATION (Designated by NUCC)

20. OUTSIDE LAB? $ CHARGES
[ ] YES [X] NO

21. DIAGNOSIS OR NATURE OF ILLNESS OR INJURY Relate A-L to service line below (24E) ICD Ind. 0

A. R09.1 B. C. D.
E. F. G. H.
I. J. K. L.

22. RESUBMISSION CODE ORIGINAL REF. NO.

23. PRIOR AUTHORIZATION NUMBER

24. A. DATE(S) OF SERVICE		B. PLACE OF SERVICE	C. EMG	D. PROCEDURES, SERVICES, OR SUPPLIES		E. DIAGNOSIS POINTER	F. $ CHARGES	G. DAYS OR UNITS	H. EPSDT Family Plan	I. ID. QUAL.	J. RENDERING PROVIDER ID. #
From MM DD YY	To MM DD YY			CPT/HCPCS	MODIFIER						
01 20 XX		11		99203		A	55 00	1		NPI	1234567890
01 20 XX		11		71023		A	90 00	1		NPI	1234567890
										NPI	
										NPI	
										NPI	
										NPI	

25. FEDERAL TAX I.D. NUMBER SSN EIN [X]
421898989

26. PATIENT'S ACCOUNT NO.
3322

27. ACCEPT ASSIGNMENT? (For govt. claims, see back)
[X] YES [ ] NO

28. TOTAL CHARGE
$ 145 00

29. AMOUNT PAID
$

30. Rsvd for NUCC Use
$

31. SIGNATURE OF PHYSICIAN OR SUPPLIER INCLUDING DEGREES OR CREDENTIALS (I certify that the statements on the reverse apply to this bill and are made a part thereof.)
J A MARTIN MD
J A Martin
SIGNED   012520XX DATE

32. SERVICE FACILITY LOCATION INFORMATION
a. NPI b.

33. BILLING PROVIDER INFO & PH # (555) 6567890
WALDEN-MARTIN FAMILY MEDICAL CLINIC
1234 ANYSTREET
ANYTOWN AL 12345 6789
a. X100XX1000 b.

NUCC Instruction Manual available at: www.nucc.org   *PLEASE PRINT OR TYPE*   APPROVED OMB-0938-1197 FORM 1500 (02-12)

Fig. B.6 Patient, Franklin: Group with Medicare Secondary.

HEALTH INSURANCE CLAIM FORM

APPROVED BY NATIONAL UNIFORM CLAIM COMMITTEE (NUCC) 02/12

TRICARE CARRIER NAME
STREET ADDRESS OR PPO NUMBER

CITY STATE ZIP CODE

CARRIER

[ ] [ ] [ ] PICA

PICA [ ] [ ] [ ]

1. MEDICARE	MEDICAID	TRICARE	CHAMPVA	GROUP HEALTH PLAN	FECA BLK LUNG	OTHER	1a. INSURED'S I.D. NUMBER (For Program in Item 1)
[ ] (Medicare#)	[ ] (Medicaid#)	[X] (ID#DoD#)	[ ] (Member ID#)	[ ] (ID#)	[ ] (ID#)	[ ] (ID#)	321549876

2. PATIENT'S NAME (Last Name, First Name, Middle Initial)
SINCLAIR EMILY J

3. PATIENT'S BIRTH DATE
MM 04 | DD 17 | YY 2003   SEX M [ ] F [X]

4. INSURED'S NAME (Last Name, First Name, Middle Initial)
SINCLAIR PARKER L

5. PATIENT'S ADDRESS (No., Street)
1344 ARGYLE COURT

6. PATIENT RELATIONSHIP TO INSURED
Self [ ] Spouse [ ] Child [X] Other [ ]

7. INSURED'S ADDRESS (No., Street)
APO 53555J

CITY
MILTON

STATE
XY

8. RESERVED FOR NUCC USE

CITY
NEW YORK

STATE
NY

ZIP CODE
12345

TELEPHONE (Include Area Code)
(5552344111)

ZIP CODE
22222

TELEPHONE (Include Area Code)
( )

9. OTHER INSURED'S NAME (Last Name, First Name, Middle Initial)

10. IS PATIENT'S CONDITION RELATED TO:

11. INSURED'S POLICY GROUP OR FECA NUMBER
X

a. OTHER INSURED'S POLICY OR GROUP NUMBER

a. EMPLOYMENT? (Current or Previous)
[ ] YES [X] NO

a. INSURED'S DATE OF BIRTH
MM 10 | DD 08 | YY 1984   SEX M [X] F [ ]

b. RESERVED FOR NUCC USE

b. AUTO ACCIDENT?
[ ] YES [X] NO   PLACE (State)

b. OTHER CLAIM ID (Designated by NUCC)

c. RESERVED FOR NUCC USE

c. OTHER ACCIDENT?
[ ] YES [X] NO

c. INSURANCE PLAN NAME OR PROGRAM NAME

d. INSURANCE PLAN NAME OR PROGRAM NAME

10d. CLAIM CODES (Designated by NUCC)

d. IS THERE ANOTHER HEALTH BENEFIT PLAN?
[ ] YES [X] NO   *If yes*, complete items 9, 9a, and 9d.

READ BACK OF FORM BEFORE COMPLETING & SIGNING THIS FORM.

12. PATIENT'S OR AUTHORIZED PERSON'S SIGNATURE I authorize the release of any medical or other information necessary to process this claim. I also request payment of government benefits either to myself or to the party who accepts assignment below.

SIGNED **SIGNATURE ON FILE**   DATE _____

13. INSURED'S OR AUTHORIZED PERSON'S SIGNATURE I authorize payment of medical benefits to the undersigned physician or supplier for services described below.

SIGNED _____

14. DATE OF CURRENT ILLNESS, INJURY, or PREGNANCY(LMP)
MM 01 | DD 18 | YY 20XX   QUAL.

15. OTHER DATE
QUAL.   MM | DD | YY

16. DATES PATIENT UNABLE TO WORK IN CURRENT OCCUPATION
FROM MM | DD | YY   TO MM | DD | YY

17. NAME OF REFERRING PROVIDER OR OTHER SOURCE
DK **ANGELA N PEREZ MD**

17a.
17b. NPI **2907511822**

18. HOSPITALIZATION DATES RELATED TO CURRENT SERVICES
FROM MM 01 | DD 19 | YY XX   TO MM 01 | DD 22 | YY XX

19. ADDITIONAL CLAIM INFORMATION (Designated by NUCC)

20. OUTSIDE LAB? $ CHARGES
[ ] YES [X] NO

21. DIAGNOSIS OR NATURE OF ILLNESS OR INJURY Relate A-L to service line below (24E)   ICD Ind. **0**

A. **J12.9**   B. ____   C. ____   D. ____
E. ____   F. ____   G. ____   H. ____
I. ____   J. ____   K. ____   L. ____

22. RESUBMISSION CODE   ORIGINAL REF. NO.

23. PRIOR AUTHORIZATION NUMBER
0221558766

24. A. DATE(S) OF SERVICE From MM DD YY	To MM DD YY	B. PLACE OF SERVICE	C. EMG	D. PROCEDURES, SERVICES, OR SUPPLIES (Explain Unusual Circumstances) CPT/HCPCS	MODIFIER	E. DIAGNOSIS POINTER	F. $ CHARGES	G. DAYS OR UNITS	H. EPSDT Family Plan	I. ID. QUAL.	J. RENDERING PROVIDER ID. #
1	01 19 XX		21		99221		A	250 00	1		NPI	2907511822
2	01 20 XX		21		99231		A	150 00	2		NPI	2907511822
3	01 22 XX		21		99238		A	110 00	1		NPI	2907511822
4											NPI	
5											NPI	
6											NPI	

25. FEDERAL TAX I.D. NUMBER   SSN EIN
421898989   [ ] [X]

26. PATIENT'S ACCOUNT NO.
2343

27. ACCEPT ASSIGNMENT? (For govt. claims, see back)
[X] YES [ ] NO

28. TOTAL CHARGE
$ **660 00**

29. AMOUNT PAID
$

30. Rsvd for NUCC Use

31. SIGNATURE OF PHYSICIAN OR SUPPLIER INCLUDING DEGREES OR CREDENTIALS (I certify that the statements on the reverse apply to this bill and are made a part thereof.)
ANGELA N PEREZ MD
Angela N Perez
SIGNED   DATE **012520XX**

32. SERVICE FACILITY LOCATION INFORMATION
BROADMOOR MEDICAL CENTER
4990 PINE RIDGE CIRCLE
MILTON XY 12345-0001
a. 0987678912   b. X100XX1111

33. BILLING PROVIDER INFO & PH # (**555**) **6567890**
WALDEN-MARTIN FAMILY MEDICAL CLINIC
1234 ANYSTREET
ANYTOWN AL 12345 6789
a. X100XX1000   b.

NUCC Instruction Manual available at: www.nucc.org   *PLEASE PRINT OR TYPE*   APPROVED OMB-0938-1197 FORM 1500 (02-12)

PATIENT AND INSURED INFORMATION

PHYSICIAN OR SUPPLIER INFORMATION

Fig. B.7 Patient, Sinclair: TRICARE Simple.

HEALTH INSURANCE CLAIM FORM

APPROVED BY NATIONAL UNIFORM CLAIM COMMITTEE (NUCC) 02/12

VA HEALTH ADMIN CENTER
PO BOX 65024

DENVER CO 80206-9024

| | | | | | | | | PICA | | | | | | | | PICA |

1. MEDICARE ☐ (Medicare#) MEDICAID ☐ (Medicaid#) TRICARE ☐ (ID#DoD#) CHAMPVA ☒ (Member ID#) GROUP HEALTH PLAN ☐ (ID#) FECA BLK LUNG ☐ (ID#) OTHER ☐ (ID#)   **1a. INSURED'S I.D. NUMBER** (For Program in Item 1)   223558890

2. PATIENT'S NAME (Last Name, First Name, Middle Initial)   SALISBURY THEODORE V

3. PATIENT'S BIRTH DATE MM 08 DD 11 YY 1957   SEX M ☒ F ☐

4. INSURED'S NAME (Last Name, First Name, Middle Initial)   SAME

5. PATIENT'S ADDRESS (No., Street)   2659 WEST LINCOLN

6. PATIENT RELATIONSHIP TO INSURED   Self ☒ Spouse ☐ Child ☐ Other ☐

7. INSURED'S ADDRESS (No., Street)

CITY   MILTON   STATE XY

8. RESERVED FOR NUCC USE

CITY   STATE

ZIP CODE   12345   TELEPHONE (Include Area Code)   (5552343222)

ZIP CODE   TELEPHONE (Include Area Code) (   )

9. OTHER INSURED'S NAME (Last Name, First Name, Middle Initial)

10. IS PATIENT'S CONDITION RELATED TO:

11. INSURED'S POLICY GROUP OR FECA NUMBER

a. OTHER INSURED'S POLICY OR GROUP NUMBER

a. EMPLOYMENT? (Current or Previous)   YES ☐ NO ☒

a. INSURED'S DATE OF BIRTH MM DD YY   SEX M ☐ F ☐

b. RESERVED FOR NUCC USE

b. AUTO ACCIDENT?   YES ☐ NO ☒   PLACE (State)

b. OTHER CLAIM ID (Designated by NUCC)

c. RESERVED FOR NUCC USE

c. OTHER ACCIDENT?   YES ☐ NO ☒

c. INSURANCE PLAN NAME OR PROGRAM NAME

d. INSURANCE PLAN NAME OR PROGRAM NAME

10d. CLAIM CODES (Designated by NUCC)

d. IS THERE ANOTHER HEALTH BENEFIT PLAN?   YES ☐ NO ☒   If yes, complete items 9, 9a, and 9d.

READ BACK OF FORM BEFORE COMPLETING & SIGNING THIS FORM.

12. PATIENT'S OR AUTHORIZED PERSON'S SIGNATURE I authorize the release of any medical or other information necessary to process this claim. I also request payment of government benefits either to myself or to the party who accepts assignment below.

SIGNED   SOF   DATE

13. INSURED'S OR AUTHORIZED PERSON'S SIGNATURE I authorize payment of medical benefits to the undersigned physician or supplier for services described below.

SIGNED

14. DATE OF CURRENT ILLNESS, INJURY, or PREGNANCY(LMP) MM DD YY   QUAL.

15. OTHER DATE QUAL. MM DD YY

16. DATES PATIENT UNABLE TO WORK IN CURRENT OCCUPATION FROM MM DD YY TO MM DD YY

17. NAME OF REFERRING PROVIDER OR OTHER SOURCE   DN JAMES A MARTIN MD

17a.
17b. NPI 8822343451

18. HOSPITALIZATION DATES RELATED TO CURRENT SERVICES FROM MM DD YY TO MM DD YY

19. ADDITIONAL CLAIM INFORMATION (Designated by NUCC)

20. OUTSIDE LAB? YES ☐ NO ☒ $ CHARGES

21. DIAGNOSIS OR NATURE OF ILLNESS OR INJURY Relate A-L to service line below (24E)   ICD Ind. 0

A. N40.0   B.   C.   D.
E.   F.   G.   H.
I.   J.   K.   L.

22. RESUBMISSION CODE   ORIGINAL REF. NO.

23. PRIOR AUTHORIZATION NUMBER   0221558766

24. A. DATE(S) OF SERVICE From			To			B. PLACE OF SERVICE	C. EMG	D. PROCEDURES, SERVICES, OR SUPPLIES (Explain Unusual Circumstances) CPT/HCPCS	MODIFIER	E. DIAGNOSIS POINTER	F. $ CHARGES	G. DAYS OR UNITS	H. EPSDT Family Plan	I. ID. QUAL.	J. RENDERING PROVIDER ID. #
MM	DD	YY	MM	DD	YY										
01	23	XX				21		52601		A	1200 00	1		NPI	1234567890
														NPI	
														NPI	
														NPI	
														NPI	
														NPI	

25. FEDERAL TAX I.D. NUMBER   421898989   SSN ☐ EIN ☒

26. PATIENT'S ACCOUNT NO.   2466

27. ACCEPT ASSIGNMENT? (For govt. claims, see back) YES ☒ NO ☐

28. TOTAL CHARGE $ 120 00

29. AMOUNT PAID $

30. Rsvd for NUCC Use $

31. SIGNATURE OF PHYSICIAN OR SUPPLIER INCLUDING DEGREES OR CREDENTIALS (I certify that the statements on the reverse apply to this bill and are made a part thereof.)   J A MARTIN MD   *J A Martin*   SIGNED   012520XX DATE

32. SERVICE FACILITY LOCATION INFORMATION   BROADMOOR MEDICAL CENTER 4990 PINE RIDGE CIRCLE MILTON XY 12345-0001
a. 0987678912   b. X100XX1111

33. BILLING PROVIDER INFO & PH # (555) 6567890   WALDEN-MARTIN FAMILY MEDICAL CLINIC 1234 ANYSTREET ANYTOWN AL 12345 6789
a. X100XX1000   b.

NUCC Instruction Manual available at: www.nucc.org   PLEASE PRINT OR TYPE   APPROVED OMB-0938-1197 FORM 1500 (02-12)

Fig. B.8 Patient, Salisbury: CHAMPVA.

HEALTH INSURANCE CLAIM FORM

APPROVED BY NATIONAL UNIFORM CLAIM COMMITTEE (NUCC) 02/12

WORKERS COMP CARRIER
STREET ADDRESS OR PPO BOX NUMBER

CITY STATE ZIP

| | PICA | | | | | | | PICA | |

1. MEDICARE	MEDICAID	TRICARE	CHAMPVA	GROUP HEALTH PLAN	FECA BLK LUNG	OTHER	1a. INSURED'S I.D. NUMBER (For Program in Item 1)
(Medicare#)	(Medicaid#)	(ID#DoD#)	(Member ID#)	(ID#)	(ID#)	[X] (ID#)	C94FPP29930

2. PATIENT'S NAME (Last Name, First Name, Middle Initial)
PORTER JAMES B

3. PATIENT'S BIRTH DATE — MM 03 DD 10 YY 1968 — **SEX** M [X] F [ ]

4. INSURED'S NAME (Last Name, First Name, Middle Initial)
COMPUTER SOLUTIONS LLC

5. PATIENT'S ADDRESS (No., Street)
23411 SOUTH 12TH AVENUE

6. PATIENT RELATIONSHIP TO INSURED
Self [ ] Spouse [ ] Child [ ] Other [X]

7. INSURED'S ADDRESS (No., Street)
4591 PRIME CIRCLE

CITY DODGEVILLE — **STATE** XY

8. RESERVED FOR NUCC USE

CITY LINCOLN — **STATE** XY

ZIP CODE 12367 — **TELEPHONE (Include Area Code)** (5554569981)

ZIP CODE 12470 — **TELEPHONE (Include Area Code)** (5558220010)

9. OTHER INSURED'S NAME (Last Name, First Name, Middle Initial)

10. IS PATIENT'S CONDITION RELATED TO:

11. INSURED'S POLICY GROUP OR FECA NUMBER

a. OTHER INSURED'S POLICY OR GROUP NUMBER

a. EMPLOYMENT? (Current or Previous) [X] YES [ ] NO

a. INSURED'S DATE OF BIRTH MM DD YY — **SEX** M [ ] F [ ]

b. RESERVED FOR NUCC USE

b. AUTO ACCIDENT? [ ] YES [X] NO — PLACE (State)

b. OTHER CLAIM ID (Designated by NUCC)

c. RESERVED FOR NUCC USE

c. OTHER ACCIDENT? [ ] YES [X] NO

c. INSURANCE PLAN NAME OR PROGRAM NAME

d. INSURANCE PLAN NAME OR PROGRAM NAME

10d. CLAIM CODES (Designated by NUCC)

d. IS THERE ANOTHER HEALTH BENEFIT PLAN? [ ] YES [ ] NO *If yes*, complete items 9, 9a, and 9d.

READ BACK OF FORM BEFORE COMPLETING & SIGNING THIS FORM.
12. PATIENT'S OR AUTHORIZED PERSON'S SIGNATURE I authorize the release of any medical or other information necessary to process this claim. I also request payment of government benefits either to myself or to the party who accepts assignment below.

SIGNED _____ DATE _____

13. INSURED'S OR AUTHORIZED PERSON'S SIGNATURE I authorize payment of medical benefits to the undersigned physician or supplier for services described below.

SIGNED _____

14. DATE OF CURRENT ILLNESS, INJURY, or PREGNANCY(LMP) MM 01 DD 25 YY 20XX QUAL. |

15. OTHER DATE QUAL. | MM DD YY

16. DATES PATIENT UNABLE TO WORK IN CURRENT OCCUPATION FROM MM 01 DD 25 YY 20XX TO MM 02 DD 24 YY 20XX

17. NAME OF REFERRING PROVIDER OR OTHER SOURCE
DN JAMES A MARTIN MD

17a. | **17b.** NPI 1234567890

18. HOSPITALIZATION DATES RELATED TO CURRENT SERVICES FROM MM DD YY TO MM DD YY

19. ADDITIONAL CLAIM INFORMATION (Designated by NUCC)

20. OUTSIDE LAB? [ ] YES [X] NO — $ CHARGES

21. DIAGNOSIS OR NATURE OF ILLNESS OR INJURY Relate A-L to service line below (24E) — ICD Ind. | 0

A. G56.02 B. | C. | D. |
E. | F. | G. | H. |
I. | J. | K. | L. |

22. RESUBMISSION CODE — ORIGINAL REF. NO.

23. PRIOR AUTHORIZATION NUMBER

24. A. DATE(S) OF SERVICE From MM DD YY	To MM DD YY	B. PLACE OF SERVICE	C. EMG	D. PROCEDURES, SERVICES, OR SUPPLIES (Explain Unusual Circumstances) CPT/HCPCS	MODIFIER	E. DIAGNOSIS POINTER	F. $ CHARGES	G. DAYS OR UNITS	H. EPSDT Family Plan	I. ID. QUAL.	J. RENDERING PROVIDER ID. #
1	01 25 XX		11		99213		A	75 00	1		NPI	1234567890
2											NPI	
3											NPI	
4											NPI	
5											NPI	
6											NPI	

25. FEDERAL TAX I.D. NUMBER 421898989 — SSN [ ] EIN [X]

26. PATIENT'S ACCOUNT NO. 3451WC

27. ACCEPT ASSIGNMENT? (For govt. claims, see back) [X] YES [ ] NO

28. TOTAL CHARGE $ 75 00

29. AMOUNT PAID $

30. Rsvd for NUCC Use $

31. SIGNATURE OF PHYSICIAN OR SUPPLIER INCLUDING DEGREES OR CREDENTIALS (I certify that the statements on the reverse apply to this bill and are made a part thereof.)
J A MARTIN MD
J A Martin
SIGNED — DATE 012520XX

32. SERVICE FACILITY LOCATION INFORMATION
a. NPI — b.

33. BILLING PROVIDER INFO & PH # (555) 6567890
WALDEN-MARTIN FAMILY MEDICAL CLINIC
1234 ANYSTREET
ANYTOWN AL 12345 6789
a. X100XX1000 — b.

NUCC Instruction Manual available at: www.nucc.org — *PLEASE PRINT OR TYPE* — APPROVED OMB-0938-1197 FORM 1500 (02-12)

Fig. B.9 Patient, Porter: Workers' Compensation.

The guidelines for completion of the claim forms in this appendix are for example only and are intended to be used only as a guide for completing the CMS-1500 (02/12) claim form and not as definitive instructions. They incorporate the current official National Uniform Claim Committee (NUCC) guidelines (Version 1.1 06/13 02/12 1500 Health Insurance Claim Form Reference Manual © 2012 American Medical Association). Although it is the intention of the NUCC to standardize the completion of paper claims, Medicaid simple claims, commercial claims (including Blue Cross/Blue Shield), military claims (TRICARE/CHAMPVA), and workers' compensation may differ from state to state and/or region to region. Instructors and students alike must be aware of these differences and should be cautioned to follow local payer-specific instructions.

Health insurance professionals should request definitive guidelines required by each payer for further clarification of reporting requirements in each block. Optical character recognition (OCR) punctuation rules are used on all examples; however, health insurance professionals should be aware of the punctuation variations allowed by the NUCC. For consistency, eight-digit dates are used in all blocks (except for Block 24A) of the forms in this appendix. Only ICD-10 diagnostic codes are used, because ICD-10 codes completely replaced ICD-9 codes on October 1, 2015. It is important to keep in mind that all diagnostic and procedural codes are subject to annual updates. It is also important to keep up to date on changes in claims completion instructions made by NUCC, clearinghouses, and/or third-party payers.

Table B.1 Step-by-Step Medicaid Claims Instructions

BLOCK NUMBER	DESCRIPTION
Carrier Block	The "carrier block" is located in the upper center-right margin of the form. Enter in the white, open area the name and address of the payer to whom this claim is being sent using the following format: First Line—Name Second Line—First line of address Third Line—Second line of address or blank line Fourth Line—City, State (two digits), and ZIP code
Block 1	Indicate the type of health insurance coverage relevant to this claim by placing an "X" in the appropriate box. (Only one box can be marked.)
Block 1a	Enter the Medicaid recipient's ID number without dashes or spaces.
Block 2	Enter the Medicaid recipient's last name, first name, and middle initial exactly as it appears on the Medicaid ID card using OCR guidelines.
Block 3	Enter the patient's birth date (using the MM I DD I YYYY format), and enter an "X" in the appropriate gender box.
Block 4	This block can be left blank on Medicaid simple claims when the patient and the insured are the same, which is usually the case.
Block 5	The "Patient's Address" must be a permanent residence. A temporary or school address should not be used. "Patient's telephone" does not exist in 5010A1; therefore reporting a phone number is optional, unless the Medicaid payer requires one. Do not use a hyphen or space as a separator within the telephone number.
Blocks 6–9d	These blocks are left blank on Medicaid "simple" claims.
Blocks 10a–c	Type an "X" in the appropriate boxes to indicate whether or not the claim is a result of an auto or other accident or was related to employment. In the case of an auto accident, type the two-letter state code to indicate the state in which the accident occurred. Only one box on each line can be marked. Any item marked "YES" indicates there may be other applicable insurance coverage that would be primary, such as automobile liability insurance. Primary insurance information must then be shown in Block 11.
Block 10d	Claim codes designated by NUCC. When required by payers to provide the subset of Condition Codes approved by the NUCC, enter the Condition Code in this field. The Condition Codes approved for use on the 1500 Claim Form are available at http://www.nucc.org under Code Sets.
Blocks 11–11d	Leave these blocks blank on Medicaid "simple" claims.
Blocks 12–13	Leave these blocks blank. Signatures normally are not necessary on Medicaid claims unless specifically required by the Medicaid payer.

Continued

Table B.1 Step-by-Step Medicaid Claims Instructions—cont'd

BLOCK NUMBER	DESCRIPTION
Blocks 14–16	Leave these blocks blank unless information specific to these blocks is noted in the medical record and required by the Medicaid payer. Some states' Medicaid carriers require an entry here for chiropractic care. If so, enter the date of the most current x-ray.
Block 17	Enter the first name, middle initial, last name, and credentials of the professional who referred, ordered, or supervised the service(s) or supply(ies) on the claim (Block 24). Do not use punctuation within the name except a hyphen for hyphenated names. Enter the applicable qualifier to identify which provider is being reported: DN = Referring Provider; DK = Ordering Provider; DQ = Supervising Provider. Enter the qualifier to the left of the vertical, dotted line.
Block 17a	Leave this block blank unless specifically required by the Medicaid payer, such as provider IDs for MediPASS or state license number per payer guidelines.
Block 17b	Enter the HIPAA-designated NPI of the referring, ordering, or supervising provider reported in Block 17. All providers must report these data.
Block 18	Complete this block when a medical service is furnished as a result of, or subsequent to, a related hospitalization. If the patient is still hospitalized, do not report a date in the "To" blanks. If no hospitalization occurred, leave blank.
Block 19	Reserved for Additional Claim Information designated by NUCC. Check the guidelines of your Medicaid carrier for specific instructions in this field.
Block 20	Enter an "X" in the "NO" block. Outside laboratory facilities must bill Medicaid directly.
Block 21	Enter the patient's diagnosis or diagnoses codes using the most current ICD-10-CM coding manual, listing the primary diagnosis first. There is space for 12 codes (A–L), which should be listed in priority order.
Block 22	If this is a claim resubmission, enter the applicable code provided by the Medicaid payer.
Block 23	If preauthorization was required, enter this number here without spaces or hyphens. Check the guidelines of your Medicaid carrier for specific instructions in this field.
Block 24A	Enter each date of service on a separate line. Enter the month, day, and year in the MMDDYY (no spaces) format for each service. Medicaid normally does not allow "date ranging" for consecutive services. Further instructions on entering supplemental information with qualifiers, including examples, can be found in the NUCC claims instruction manual at http://nucc.org/images/stories/PDF/1500_claim_form_instruction_manual_2012_02.pdf. Accessed June 21, 2014.
Block 24B	Enter the applicable Place of Service code (e.g., 11 for provider's office). A complete list of Place of Service codes are available at: http://www.cms.gov/Medicare/Coding/place-of-service-codes/Place_of_Service_Code_Set.html. Accessed June 21, 2014.
Block 24C	This block is conditionally required. Enter an "X" or an "E" as appropriate for services performed as a result of a medical emergency. If not an emergency service, leave blank.
Block 24D	"Procedures, Services, or Supplies" identify the medical services and procedures provided to the patient. Enter the five-digit CPT or HCPCS code(s) and any applicable modifier(s) from the appropriate code set in effect on the date of service. Do not use a narrative description.
Block 24E	Link the procedure code back to the appropriate diagnosis code in Block 21 by indicating the applicable reference letter(s) A–L assigned to the diagnosis. When reporting multiple letters in the same space (e.g., AB) do not separate them with commas or spaces. **Do not enter ICD codes in 24E.**
Block 24F	Enter the charge for each listed service. Enter numbers right-justified in the dollar area of the field. Do not use dollar signs, decimals, or commas. Negative dollar amounts or "no charges" is not allowed. Enter 00 in the cents area if the amount is a whole number.
Block 24G	Enter the number of days or units left-justified in the field. If only one service is performed per line item, the numeral "1" must be entered.
Block 24H	Medicaid typically requires an "E" if the service was performed under the EPSDT program. Enter an "F" for Family Planning services. Consult your local Medicaid guidelines for correct reporting.
Block 24I	Leave blank or consult your Medicaid carrier for specific guidelines.

Table B.1   Step-by-Step Medicaid Claims Instructions—cont'd

BLOCK NUMBER	DESCRIPTION
Block 24J	Top (shaded) portion is normally left blank. Some states require the provider's legacy number or taxonomy code. Enter the rendering provider's NPI number in the lower (unshaded) portion of this block. The Rendering Provider is the person or company (laboratory or other facility) who rendered or supervised the care. Report the Identification Number in Items 24I and 24J only when different from data recorded in Items 33a and 33b. Check with your Medicaid carrier for more specific guidelines.
Block 25	Enter the nine-digit EIN or Social Security number of the billing provider identified in Block 33. Enter an "X" in the appropriate box to indicate which number is being reported. Only one box can be marked. Enter numbers left-justified in the field without spaces or hyphens. In the case of an unincorporated practice or a sole practitioner, the provider's Social Security number is typically used.
Block 26	Enter the patient's account number left-justified as assigned by the provider's computerized accounting system. (Space is limited to 14 characters.)
Block 27	An "X" in the "YES" box is optional, as Medicaid automatically sends payment to the provider.
Block 28	Enter the total charges without commas, decimals, or dollar signs for all services listed in column 24F. Enter 00 in the cents area for whole numbers.
Blocks 29	If applicable, enter the total amount paid from other insurance sources for covered services only; otherwise, leave blank.
Block 30	Reserved for NUCC use.
Block 31	Enter the provider's legal signature and credentials, or that of his or her official representative and initials, and the original filing date (using the eight-digit format) without spaces. The signature may be typed, stamped, handwritten, or (in some cases) computer generated. Make sure no part of the signature falls outside of the block.
Block 32	Report the name and address of the location where services were provided **only if different from that reported in Block 33,** or if an entry here is specifically required by the Medicaid's claims processing policy.
Block 32a	Report a Service Facility Location NPI when the NPI is different from the Billing Provider NPI in Block 33a, or follow the specific Medicaid's claims processing policy. Otherwise, leave blank.
Block 32b	Usually left blank. If required, enter the two-digit qualifier identifying the non-NPI number followed by the taxonomy code (without spaces) or the Medicaid legacy number associated with the billing provider's NPI. The NUCC defines the following qualifiers—the same as those used in 5010A1: 0B State License Number G2 Provider Commercial Number LU Location Number Consult the specific guidelines of the Medicaid payer in your state for specific instructions.
Block 33	Item 33 identifies the provider that is requesting to be paid for the services rendered and should always be completed. Enter the provider's or supplier's billing name, complete address, nine-digit ZIP code (including the hyphen), and telephone number without a space or hyphen. The phone number is to be entered in the area to the right of the field title.
Block 33a	Report the NPI of the billing provider or group reported in Block 33 here.
Block 33b	Block 33b is normally left blank. If required by the payer, enter the two-digit qualifier identifying the non-NPI number followed by the ID number. Do not enter a space, hyphen, or other separator between the qualifier and number. The following list contains both provider identifiers and the provider taxonomy code: 0B State License Number G2 Provider Commercial Number ZZ Provider Taxonomy Consult the guidelines of your Medicaid carrier to be sure this field is reported correctly.

CPT, Current Procedural Terminology; *EIN,* employer identification number; *EPSDT,* Early and Periodic Screening, Diagnosis, and Treatment; *HCPCS,* Healthcare Common Procedure Coding System; *HIPAA,* Health Insurance Portability and Accountability Act; *ICD-10-CM,* International Classification of Diseases, 10th Revision, Clinical Modification; *ID,* identification; *NPI,* national provider identifier; *NUCC,* National Uniform Claim Committee; *OCR,* optical character recognition.

Table B.2 CMS-1500 Claim Form Instructions for Medicare

Throughout these instructions, the following format is used to report dates:
MMIDDIYY or MMIDDICCYY—indicates that a space must be reported between month, day, and year. This space is delineated by a dotted vertical line on the CMS-1500 claim form.

BLOCK NUMBER	DESCRIPTION
Carrier Block	See instructions in Table B.1.
Block 1	Check the Medicare box for Medicare simple, Medicare/Medicaid, Medicare/Medigap, and Medicare Secondary claims. Only one box can be checked.
Block 1a	Enter the patient's Medicare HICN, without hyphen or spaces, and whether Medicare is the primary or secondary payer.
Block 2	Enter the patient's last name, first name, and middle initial (if any) *exactly* as shown on the patient's Medicare card using OCR guidelines.
Block 3	Enter the patient's eight-digit birth date (MMIDDICCYY), and enter an "X" in the appropriate gender box.
Block 4	If the patient has insurance primary to Medicare through the patient's or spouse's employment or any other source, list the name of the other insured here. When the insured and the patient are the same, enter the word "SAME" or leave blank.
Block 5	Enter the patient's complete, permanent address and phone number. Do not use a hyphen or space within the number. Note: "Patient's telephone" does not exist in 5010A1; therefore reporting a phone number is optional, unless the Medicare administrative contractor (MAC) requires one.
Block 6	Leave blank unless Block 4 is completed indicating other insurance. Enter an "X" in the correct box when there is other insurance to indicate the patient's relationship to insured. Only one box can be marked.
Block 7	Leave this field blank unless Blocks 4, 6, and 11 are completed indicating other insurance. If there is other insurance, enter the other insured's address *if different from that reported in Block 5.* When the address is the same as the patient's, enter the word "SAME."
Block 8	Leave blank. (NUCC will provide instructions for any use of this field.)
Block 9	Complete Blocks 9, 9a, and 9d, when the Medicare beneficiary is covered by other health insurance (OHI) or a supplemental policy secondary to Medicare; otherwise, leave blank. When OHI exists, enter other insured's full last name, first name, and middle initial of the enrollee in the other health plan if it is different from that shown in Block 2. **For Medicare claims with MEDIGAP** supplemental coverage, enter the name of the MEDIGAP enrollee or enter "SAME" if it is the same as reported in Block 2. Only participating providers (PARs) are to complete this block and its subdivisions, and only when the beneficiary assigns benefits under the MEDIGAP policy. Do not list other supplemental coverage at the time Medicare is filed, as other supplemental claims are forwarded automatically to the private insurer if the private insurer contracts with Medicare.
Block 9a	The "Other Insured's Policy or Group Number" identifies the policy or group number for coverage of the insured as indicated in Block 9. Enter the policy or group number of the other insured. Do not use a hyphen or space as a separator within the policy or group number. **For Medicare claims with MEDIGAP,** enter the policy and/or group number of the MEDIGAP insured preceded by MEDIGAP, MG, or MGAP.
Block 9b	Leave blank. (Reserved for NUCC use)
Block 9c	Leave blank. (Reserved for NUCC use)
Block 9d	Report the name of the plan or program of the other insured as indicated in Block 9. Enter the other insured's insurance plan or program name. (This block must be completed even when the provider enters a policy and/or group number in 9a.) **For Medicare claims with MEDIGAP,** enter the Coordination of Benefits Agreement (COBA) MEDIGAP-based identifier. COBA identifiers are listed in the Medicare Claims Processing Manual, which can be found on the www.cms.gov website.
Blocks 10a-10c	If applicable, enter an "X" in the correct box to indicate whether one or more of the services described in Item 24 are for a condition or injury that occurred on the job or as a result of an automobile or other accident. (Only one box on each line can be marked.) The two-letter state postal code where the accident occurred must be reported if "YES" is marked in 10b for "Auto Accident." Any item marked "YES" indicates there may be other applicable insurance coverage that would be primary, such as automobile liability insurance. If any items in this block are checked "YES," identify primary insurance information in Block 11.

Table B.2   **CMS-1500 Claim Form Instructions for Medicare—cont'd**

BLOCK NUMBER	DESCRIPTION
Block 10d	Claim codes designated by the NUCC. When required by payers to provide the subset of Condition Codes approved by the NUCC, enter the Condition Code in this field. The Condition Codes approved for use on the 1500 Claim Form are available at http://www.nucc.org under Code Sets.
Block 11ᵃ	Per Medicare's claims completion manual, this item must be completed for Medicare claims. If there is a name reported in Block 4 that is different from that reported in Block 2, then this field should be completed. By completing this item, the provider acknowledges having made a good faith effort to determine whether Medicare is the primary or secondary payer. If there is insurance primary to Medicare, enter the insured's policy or group number as it appears on the other insured's healthcare ID card. Do not use a hyphen or space as a separator within the policy or group number, and proceed to items 11a–11c. (When this situation occurs Items 4, 6, and 7 must also be completed.) If Medicare is primary, enter NONE and proceed to Block 12.
Block 11a	If there is insurance primary to Medicare, enter the other insured's eight-digit birth date **if different from that reported in Block 3** and check the appropriate box indicating sex (gender). Leave blank on Medicare "simple" claims.
Block 11b	This block must be completed on Medicare claims if there is insurance primary to Medicare that is indicated in Block 11. If payment has been made by the patient's other health insurance, indicate the payment in this field. If the health insurance has denied payment, enter "0.00" in this field. If there is a change in the insured's insurance status (e.g., retired), enter the eight-digit retirement date preceded by the word, "RETIRED." *Provide this information to the right of the vertical dotted line.* **Leave blank on Medicare** "simple" claims.
Block 11c	This block must be reported if there is insurance primary to Medicare that is indicated in Block 11. Enter the nine-digit PAYERID number of the primary insurer (as designated by NUCC). If no PAYERID number exists, enter the **complete** primary payer's program or plan name. If the primary payer's EOB does not contain the claims processing address, record the primary payer's claims processing address directly on the EOB. **Leave blank on Medicare** "simple" claims.
Block 11d	The Medicare claims processing guidelines say to leave this block blank. Consult your MAC to verify this.
Block 12ᵇ	Enter "SIGNATURE ON FILE," "SOF," or legal signature. When legal signature is used, enter date signed. This indicates there is an authorization on file for the release of any medical or other information necessary to process and/or adjudicate the claim. If there is no signature on file, leave blank or enter "NO SIGNATURE ON FILE."
Block 13	If required by Medicare, enter "SIGNATURE ON FILE," "SOF," or legal signature. If there is no signature on file, leave blank or enter "NO SIGNATURE ON FILE." A signature here authorizes payment of mandated MEDIGAP benefits to the participating provider if the required MEDIGAP information is included in Block 9 and its subdivisions.
Block 14	Leave blank on Medicare claims or follow your specific MAC guidelines.
Block 15	Leave blank on Medicare claims or follow your specific MAC guidelines.
Block 16	Leave blank on Medicare claims or follow your specific MAC guidelines.
Block 17	Enter the first name, middle initial, last name, and credentials of the professional who referred, ordered, or supervised the service(s) or supply(ies) on the claim in Block 24. Do not use periods or commas within the name. A hyphen can be used for hyphenated names. Enter the applicable qualifier to the left of the vertical, dotted line to identify which provider is being reported. (DN = Referring Provider; DK = Ordering Provider; DQ = Supervising Provider.)
Block 17a	Leave blank on Medicare claims or follow your specific MAC guidelines.
Block 17b	Enter the NPI of the referring, ordering, or supervising provider listed in Block 17. All providers who order services or refer Medicare beneficiaries must report this data.
Block 18	Enter an eight-digit (MMIDDICCYY) date when a medical service is furnished as a result of, or subsequent to, a related hospitalization.
Block 19	Additional claim information designated by NUCC.
Block 20	Complete this field when billing for purchased services by entering an "X" in "YES." A "YES" indicates that the reported service was provided by an entity other than the billing provider. A "NO" indicates that no purchased services are included on the claim. If "Yes," enter the purchase price under "$Charges" and complete Block 32. When entering the charge, enter the amount in the field to the left of the vertical line. Enter the number right-justified to the left of the vertical line. Enter 00 for cents if the amount is a whole number. Do not use dollar signs, commas, or a decimal point when reporting amounts. Negative dollar amounts are not allowed. Leave the right-hand field blank.

Continued

Table B.2 **CMS-1500 Claim Form Instructions for Medicare—cont'd**

BLOCK NUMBER	DESCRIPTION
Block 21	Enter the appropriate ICD-10-CM diagnosis code(s) in priority order on lines A through L. Between the vertical, dotted lines (next to "ICD Ind." in the upper-right corner), enter "0" to show that you are using ICD-10-CM codes.
Block 22	Leave blank. Not required by Medicare.
Block 23	Follow the specific instructions of your MAC. Typical entries include prior authorization number, referral number, mammography precertification number, or Clinical Laboratory Improvement Amendments (CLIA) number, as assigned by the payer for the current service. Enter the Quality Improvement Organization (QIO) prior authorization number for those procedures requiring QIO prior approval.
Block 24A	Enter a six-digit (MMDDYY) or eight-digit (MMDDYYYY) date, depending on your specific MAC instructions, for each procedure, service, or supply. When "from" and "to" dates are shown for a series of identical services, enter the applicable number of days or units in column 24G.
Block 24B	Enter the appropriate Place of Service Code (11 for provider's office, 21 for inpatient hospital, etc.) for each item used or service performed. The Place of Service codes are available at: http://www.cms.gov/Medicare/Coding/place-of-service-codes/Place_of_Service_Code_Set.html.
Block 24C	Medicare providers are not required to complete this item.
Block 24D	Enter the CPT or HCPCS code(s) and modifier(s) (if applicable) from the appropriate code set in effect on the date of service. Do not report a narrative description. This field allows for the entry of six characters in the unshaded area of the CPT/HCPCS field and up to four sets of two characters each in the Modifier area.
Block 24E	Link the procedure code back to the appropriate diagnosis code in Block 21 by indicating the applicable reference letter(s) A–L assigned to the diagnosis. When reporting multiple letters in the same space (e.g., AB) do not separate them with commas or spaces. **Do not enter ICD codes in 24E.**
Block 24F	Enter the charge for each listed service. Do not use dollar signs, decimals, dashes, or lines. Enter 00 in the cents area for whole numbers. Negative dollar amounts or "no charges" is not allowed.
Block 24G	Enter the number of days or units left-justified in the field. If only one service is performed per line item, the numeral "1" must be entered. This field is also used for multiple visits, units of supplies, anesthesia minutes, or oxygen volume.
Block 24H	Leave this block blank; it is not required by Medicare.
Block 24I	Enter in the shaded area of 24I the qualifier identifying if the number is a non-NPI. For Medicare claims in the examples, the qualifier is 1C. The Other ID# of the rendering provider should be reported in 24J in the shaded area. Refer to the NUCC website for the list of qualifiers used in the 5010A1 Standards.
Block 24J	Enter the individual rendering provider's NPI left-justified in the unshaded area in this field. Enter the non-NPI ID number in the shaded area of the field, if applicable. The Rendering Provider is the person or company (laboratory or other facility) who rendered or supervised the care. Report the Identification Number in Items 24I and 24J only when different from data recorded in items 33a and 33b. Note: More detailed instructions and examples of supplemental information for Block 24 that can be entered on claims can be found in the NUCC guidelines on their website.
Block 25	Enter the nine-digit EIN or Social Security number of the billing provider identified in Block 33. Enter an "X" in the appropriate box to indicate which number is being reported. Only one box can be marked. Enter numbers left-justified in the field without spaces or hyphens. In the case of an unincorporated practice or a sole practitioner, the provider's Social Security number is typically used.
Block 26	Enter the patient's account number as assigned by the provider's computerized accounting system. (Space is limited to 14 characters.) This field is optional to assist the provider in patient identification.
Block 27	Check the appropriate box to indicate whether the provider accepts assignment of Medicare benefits. This indicates that the provider agrees to accept assignment under the terms of the payer's program. If Medigap is indicated in Block 9 and Medigap payment authorization is given in Block 13, the provider shall be considered a Medicare participating provider and accepts assignment for all covered charges.
Block 28	Enter the total charges without commas, decimals, or dollar signs for all services listed in column 24F. Enter 00 in the cents area for whole numbers.
Block 29	Enter the total amount the patient paid on the covered services only. Leave blank if no payment has been made.

Table B.2 **CMS-1500 Claim Form Instructions for Medicare—cont'd**

BLOCK NUMBER	DESCRIPTION
Block 30	Leave blank. The NUCC will provide instructions for any use of this field.
Block 31	Enter the provider's legal signature, or that of his or her official representative and initials, the provider's credentials, and the original filing date (using the eight-digit format). The signature may be typed, stamped, handwritten, or computer generated. Make sure no part of the signature falls outside of the block.
Block 32	Report the name and address of the location where services were provided **only if different from that reported in Block 33,** or if an entry here is specifically required by the MAC's processing policy.
Block 32a	Report a Service Facility Location NPI when the NPI is different from the Billing Provider NPI in Block 33a, or follow the specific MAC's claims processing policy. Otherwise, leave blank.
Block 32b	Leave blank unless otherwise indicated by the MAC.
Block 33	Item 33 identifies the provider that is requesting to be paid for the services rendered and should always be completed. Enter the provider's or supplier's billing name, complete address, nine-digit ZIP code (including the hyphen), and telephone number without a space or hyphen. The phone number is to be entered in the area to the right of the field title.
Block 33a	Enter the HIPAA-assigned NPI number of the billing provider.
Block 33b	This item is not generally reported on Medicare claims; however, the MAC may have specific instructions for completing this block.

[a]*Note:* For a paper claim to be considered for Medicare Secondary Payer benefits, a copy of the primary payer's explanation of benefits (EOB) notice must be attached to the claim form. If a policy or group number is entered, an EOB *must* be attached.

[b]*Note:* In lieu of signing the claim, the patient may sign a "lifetime" release of information statement to be retained in the provider's file. If the patient is physically or mentally unable to sign, a representative may sign on the patient's behalf. In this case, the statement's signature line must indicate the patient's name followed by the representative's name, address, relationship to the patient, and the reason the patient cannot sign. The authorization is effective indefinitely unless the patient or the patient's representative revokes this arrangement. The patient's signature authorizes release of medical information necessary to process the claim. It also authorizes payment of benefits to the provider of service or supplier when the provider of service or supplier accepts assignment on the claim. When an illiterate or physically handicapped enrollee signs by mark, a witness must enter his or her name and address next to the mark.

CLIA, Clinical Laboratory Improvement Amendments; *CPT,* Current Procedural Terminology; *EIN,* employer identification number; *HCPCS,* Healthcare Common Procedure Coding System; *HICN,* health insurance claim number; *HIPAA,* Health Insurance Portability and Accountability Act; *ICD,* International Classification of Diseases; *ICD-10-CM,* International Classification of Diseases, 10th Revision, Clinical Modification; *ID,* identification; *NPI,* national provider identifier; *NUCC,* National Uniform Claim Committee.

From the Centers for Medicare and Medicaid Services (CMS): Available at: http://www.cms.gov/Regulations-and-Guidance/Guidance/Manuals/downloads/clm104c26.pdf. These instructions are somewhat generic. It is important to use the specific, up-to-date CMS-1500 claim form completion instructions of your local Medicare administrative contractor (MAC).

Table B.3 **Instructions for Filing TRICARE/CHAMPVA Paper Claims**

BLOCK NUMBER	DESCRIPTION
Carrier Block	See instructions in Table B.1.
Block 1	Indicate the type of health insurance coverage relevant to this claim by placing an "X" in the appropriate box. Place an "X" in the TRICARE box for TRICARE claims; place an "X" in the CHAMPVA box for CHAMPVA claims. (Only one box can be marked.)
Block 1a	Enter the *sponsor's* member ID/DoD number exactly as it appears on his or her military ID card. (Do not use the patient's ID number unless patient and sponsor are the same). Note: DoD numbers have replaced Social Security numbers on military ID cards.
Block 2	Enter the patient's last name, first name, and middle initial (if any) *exactly* as shown on the TRICARE or CHAMPVA ID card using OCR formatting rules.
Block 3	Enter the patient's birth date (using the MM I DD I YYYY format), and enter an "X" in the appropriate gender box.
Block 4	Enter the *sponsor's* last name, first name, and middle initial, or if the sponsor and the patient are the same, enter the word "SAME."
Block 5	Enter the complete address of the patient's place of residence at the time of service. (Do not use APO/FPO address here.) Enter the telephone number without a hyphen or space within the number. Do not use post office box numbers. Note: "Patient's telephone" does not exist in 5010A1; therefore reporting a phone number is optional, unless the payer requires one.
Block 6	If the patient is the same as sponsor, indicate "SELF"; otherwise, provide the relationship to the sponsor. If patient is a former spouse, check "other."
	Note: Parents, parents-in-law, stepparents, and any grandchildren who are not adopted are not eligible for TRICARE despite the fact that they may have a military ID card. Be sure to check the back of the dependent beneficiary's ID card to ensure it indicates authorization for civilian/TRICARE benefits.

Continued

Table B.3   **Instructions for Filing TRICARE/CHAMPVA Paper Claims—cont'd**

BLOCK NUMBER	DESCRIPTION
Block 7	Enter the address of the TRICARE active duty service member (ADSM) sponsor's duty station or the CHAMPVA retiree's mailing address. If the address is the same as the patient's reported in Block 4, enter "SAME"; however, if "SAME" is entered in Block 4, leave this block blank. If the sponsor resides overseas, enter the applicable APO/FPO address. If no phone number is listed for the sponsor, leave this item blank.
Block 8	Reserved for NUCC use.
Block 9	Leave blank on TRICARE and CHAMPVA "simple" claims. If the patient is covered by OHI under his or her name or covered under a spouse's group or OHI that would likely be primary to TRICARE or CHAMPVA, report this information in Blocks 11a–d. If the patient has supplemental coverage secondary to TRICARE or CHAMPVA, enter the complete name of the supplemental policyholder if different from the patient name reported in Block 2; otherwise, enter SAME.
Block 9a	Provide the policy number/group number of the other insured's policy without spaces or other separators.
Block 9b	Leave blank. Reserved for NUCC use.
Block 9c	Leave blank. Reserved for NUCC use.
Block 9d	Enter the name of the supplemental insurance plan. Note: The information reported in Blocks 9–9d must be other coverage that is actually supplemental to TRICARE, for example, Medicaid or a plan specifically stating it is supplemental to TRICARE or CHAMPVA.
Blocks 10a–c	Check "YES" or "NO" to indicate whether employment, auto liability, or other accident involvement applies to one or more of the services described in Block 24. Provide information concerning potential third-party liability. The claims processor will send a DD Form 2527, "Statement of Personal Injury—Possible Third Party Liability," to the patient if the diagnosis code or codes indicate such.
Block 10d	Claim codes designated by NUCC. When required by payers to provide the subset of Condition Codes approved by the NUCC, enter the Condition Code in this field. The Condition Codes approved for use on the 1500 Claim Form are available at http://www.nucc.org under Code Sets. Some military payers require the word "ATTACHMENT" in this block to indicate that an EOB is attached from any primary OHI.
Block 11	Conditionally required. If the beneficiary has OHI and TRICARE or CHAMPVA is secondary, enter the policy/group number here. Indicate if the beneficiary is covered by Medicare; otherwise, leave blank. Blocks 9a–d should be used to report other coverage held by family members that includes coverage of the beneficiary.
Block 11a	Conditionally required. If the policyholder is different from the patient, enter the primary policyholder's DOB as MM DD YYYY; enter **X** in the appropriate box to indicate gender (otherwise, leave blank).
Block 11b	Leave blank. Applicable claim identifiers are designated by the NUCC.
Block 11c	Conditionally required. Enter the primary OHI plan or program name.
Block 11d	Indicate if there is or is not another health benefit plan that is secondary to TRICARE or CHAMPVA. If this block is checked "YES," Blocks 9a–d must be completed with the information relating to the supplemental coverage.
Block 12	"SIGNATURE ON FILE" or "SOF" can be used here if the patient's signature is on file in the provider's office (and on a document that includes a release of information statement). A date is not required in Block 12.
Block 13	Enter "SIGNATURE ON FILE" or leave blank for TRICARE and CHAMPVA claims. Claims benefits are forwarded to PAR and nonPAR accepting assignment. For nonPAR claims not accepting assignment, benefit checks are mailed to the patient.
Block 14	If required by the payer, enter the date of current illness, injury, or pregnancy, if it is documented in the health record. Remember to be consistent with date format.
Block 15	If required by the payer, and it is documented in the health record that the patient has had the same or similar condition previously, enter that date here.
Block 16	Leave blank.
Block 17	Using OCR formatting, enter the first name, middle initial, last name, and credentials of the professional who referred, ordered, or supervised the service(s) or supply(ies) on the claim (Block 24). Do not use punctuation within the name except a hyphen for hyphenated names. Enter the applicable qualifier to identify which provider is being reported: DN = Referring Provider; DK = Ordering Provider; DQ = Supervising Provider. Enter the qualifier to the left of the vertical, dotted line. If the patient was referred from an MTF, enter the name of the MTF, and attach a copy of the military referral form (DD 2161 or SF 513). If this is not applicable, leave blank.

Table **B.3**	Instructions for Filing TRICARE/CHAMPVA Paper Claims—cont'd
BLOCK NUMBER	**DESCRIPTION**
Block 17a	Leave this block blank unless specifically required by the TRICARE or CHAMPVA payer.
Block 17b	Enter the HIPAA-designated NPI of the referring, ordering, or supervising provider reported in Block 17. All providers must report these data.
Block 18	If the patient was hospitalized as an inpatient, enter the "from" and "to" dates here. If the patient is still hospitalized, leave the "To" block blank. If no hospitalization occurred, leave blank.
Block 19	Reserved for Additional Claim Information designated by NUCC. Check the guidelines of your TRICARE or CHAMPVA for specific instructions in this field.
Block 20	Indicate whether laboratory work was done outside of the provider's office. If so, enter the total amount charged by the laboratory for work being reported on the claim. Check "NO" if no laboratory work was done.
Block 21	Enter the patient's diagnosis or diagnoses codes using the most current ICD-10-CM coding manual, listing the primary diagnosis first. There is space for 12 codes (A–L), which should be listed in priority order. Enter the patient's diagnosis/condition using an ICD-10-CM code number or numbers if more than one diagnosis exists. Between the vertical, dotted lines in the upper-right corner of this block (next to "ICD Ind."), enter "0" to show that you are using ICD-10-CM codes.
Block 22	Not required. Leave blank.
Block 23	Enter the prior authorization number if the services require preauthorization/preadmission review.
Block 24A	Enter each date of service on a separate line. Enter the month, day, and year in the MMDDYY or the MMDDYYYY (no spaces) format for each service. If grouping services, the place of service, procedure code, charges, and individual provider for each line must be identical for that service line. Grouping is allowed only for services on consecutive days. The number of days must correspond to the number of units in 24G. Further instructions on entering supplemental information with qualifiers, including examples, can be found in the NUCC claims instruction manual at http://nucc.org/images/stories/PDF/1500_claim_form_instruction_manual_2012_02.pdf.
Block 24B	Enter the applicable Place of Service code, for example, 11 for provider's office. A list of Place of Service codes are available at: http://www.cms.gov/Medicare/Coding/place-of-service-codes/Place_of_Service_Code_Set.html.
Block 24C	Leave blank.
Block 24D	"Procedures, Services, or Supplies" identify the medical services and procedures provided to the patient. Enter the five-digit CPT or HCPCS code(s) and any applicable modifier(s) from the appropriate code set in effect on the date of service. Do not use a narrative description.
Block 24E	Link the procedure code back to the appropriate diagnosis code in Block 21 by indicating the applicable reference letter(s) A–L assigned to the diagnosis. When reporting multiple letters in the same space (e.g., AB) do not separate them with commas or spaces. **Do not enter ICD codes in 24E.**
Block 24F	Enter the charge for each listed service. Enter numbers right-justified in the dollar area of the field. Do not use dollar signs, decimals, or commas. Negative dollar amounts or "no charges" is not allowed. Enter 00 in the cents area if the amount is a whole number.
Block 24G	Enter the number of days or units left-justified in the field. If only one service is performed per line item, the numeral "1" must be entered.
Block 24H	Not required. Leave blank.
Block 24I	Enter the appropriate qualifier in 24I as required by the TRICARE or CHAMPVA carrier; otherwise, leave blank.
Block 24J	Top (shaded) portion is normally left blank. Enter the rendering provider's NPI number in the lower (unshaded) portion of this block. The rendering provider is the person or company (laboratory or other facility) who rendered or supervised the care. Check with your TRICARE or CHAMPVA for more specific guidelines.
Block 25	Enter the nine-digit EIN or Social Security number of the billing provider identified in Block 33. Enter an "X" in the appropriate box to indicate which number is being reported. Only one box can be marked. Enter numbers left-justified in the field without spaces or hyphens. In the case of an unincorporated practice or a sole practitioner, the provider's Social Security number is typically used.
Block 26	Enter the patient's account number assigned by the provider of service's or supplier's accounting system.
Block 27	PARs and nonPARs accepting assignment should check this box "YES."

Continued

Table B.3   Instructions for Filing TRICARE/CHAMPVA Paper Claims—cont'd

BLOCK NUMBER	DESCRIPTION
Block 28	Enter the total charges without commas, decimals, or dollar signs for all services listed in column 24F. Enter 00 in the cents area for whole numbers.
Block 29	If applicable, enter the total amount paid from other insurance sources for covered services only; otherwise, leave blank.
Block 30	This field is reserved for NUCC use. The NUCC will provide instructions for any use of this field.
Block 31	Enter the provider's legal signature and credentials, or that of his or her official representative and initials, and the original filing date (using the eight-digit format). The signature may be typed, stamped, handwritten, or (in some cases) computer generated. Make sure no part of the signature falls outside of the block. Note: Some TRICAREs require the provider's actual signature or the use of a signature stamp on the printed claim.
Block 32	Report the name and address of the location where services were provided *only if different from that reported in Block 33,* or if an entry here is specifically required by the TRICARE or CHAMPVA claims processing policy. Only report a Service Facility Location NPI when the NPI is different from the Billing Provider NPI. If services were provided at a military treatment facility (MTF), provide the complete address of the MTF in this block.
Block 32a	Enter the NPI of the service facility if the location in Block 32 is different from that reported in Block 33; otherwise, leave blank.
Block 32b	Leave blank.
Block 33	Enter the provider's or supplier's billing name, complete address, nine-digit ZIP code (including the hyphen), and telephone number without a space or hyphen. The phone number is to be entered in the area to the right of the field title.
Block 33a	Report the NPI of the billing provider or group reported in Block 33 here.
Block 33b	Leave blank.

APO, Army Post Office; *CPT,* Current Procedural Terminology; *DoD,* Department of Defense; *EIN,* employer identification number; *EOB,* explanation of benefits; *FPO,* fleet post office; *HCPCS,* Healthcare Common Procedure Coding System; *HICN,* health insurance claim number; *HMO,* health maintenance organization; *ICD-10-CM,* International Classification of Diseases, 10th Revision, Clinical Modification; *ID,* identification; *MTF,* military treatment facility; *nonPAR,* nonparticipating provider; *NPI,* national provider identifier; *OHI,* other health insurance; *PAR,* participating provider.
These instructions are somewhat generic. It is important to use the specific, up-to-date CMS-1500 claim form completion instructions of your TRICARE regional contractor at http://www.humana-military.com/library/pdf/providerhandbook.pdf or CHAMPVA claims Department of Veterans Affairs (VA) center in Denver, Colorado.

Table B.4   Step-by-Step Guidelines for Workers' Compensation Claims

BLOCK NUMBER	DESCRIPTION
Carrier Block	See instructions in Table B.1.
Block 1	"Other" should be checked for workers' compensation claims. "Other" indicates health insurance, including HMOs, commercial insurance, automobile accident, liability, or workers' compensation. For Federal Employees Compensation Act claims, check "FECA BLK LUNG."
Block 1a	Enter the employee ID (e.g., Social Security number) or the workers' compensation claim number, if one has been assigned (if SSN not available, use driver's license # & jurisdiction, green card # + "ZY", visa # +"TA", or passport # + "ZZ") (R). Otherwise, enter the employer's policy number.
Block 2	Use the same guidelines as with all other payers.
Block 3	Indicate the patient's eight-digit birth date and sex.
Block 4	The *employer's name* is entered here as the "insured."
Block 5	Use the same guidelines as with all other payers. Report the patient's 10-digit telephone number, if required by the payer. Do not use a hyphen or space as a separator within the number.
Block 6	Leave blank or check "OTHER."
Block 7	Enter the address of the employer.
Block 8	Reserved for NUCC use.
Blocks 9–9d	Leave these blocks blank or follow state workers' compensations claims completion guidelines. If Block 11d is marked "YES," Blocks 9, 9a, and 9d should be completed.
Block 10a	Check "YES" to indicate that the injury occurred while the patient was on the job.
Blocks 10b–c	Check "NO."
Block 10d	Condition Codes are required when submitting a bill that is a duplicate or an appeal. (Original Reference Number must be entered in Box 22 for these conditions). Note: Do not use Condition Codes when submitting a revised or corrected bill.

Table B.4 Step-by-Step Guidelines for Workers' Compensation Claims—cont'd

BLOCK NUMBER	DESCRIPTION
Blocks 11–11c	If the claim is for a work-related condition under FECA, enter the appropriated nine-digit FECA alphanumeric identifier here. Otherwise, leave blank.
Block 11a	Leave blank.
Block 11b	Enter the workers' compensation insurance carrier (IC) claim number assigned by the payer, if known. Otherwise, leave blank.
Block 11c	Leave blank.
Block 11d	Normally, this is left blank; however, if the workers' compensation case is pending or if the employee has OHI, check with your local state agency's guidelines as to whether or not this box would be checked "YES." Note: Workers' compensation insurance will have no deductible or copayment, and all providers must accept the compensation payment as payment in full. Balance billing of the patient is prohibited. In most states, the state compensation board or commission establishes a schedule of approved fees and can be found on individual state websites. If it is determined that the employee's illness/injury is not a legitimate workers' compensation claim, his or her OHI can be billed.
Blocks 12–13	Patients usually are not required to sign an authorization to release information associated with a work-related illness/injury. Keep in mind that HIPAA privacy rules must be followed, and illness or injuries *unrelated* to a workers' compensation injury should never be billed to the employer.
Block 14	Enter the eight-digit date that the injury occurred or the date on which the illness/injury first was noticed by the patient. (This date must coincide with the employer's First Report of Injury and the provider's First Report of Treatment.) *Note:* Remember to be consistent with the date format.
Block 15	If a date is documented in the patient's record, indicate it in this block; otherwise, leave blank.
Block 16	Enter the first full day the patient was unable to perform his or her job duties to the first day the patient is back to work. (These dates should be documented in the medical record.)
Block 17	Enter the first name, middle initial, last name, and credentials of the professional who referred, ordered, or supervised the service(s) or supply(ies) on the claim (Block 24). Do not use punctuation within the name except a hyphen for hyphenated names. Enter the applicable qualifier to identify which provider is being reported: DN = Referring Provider; DK = Ordering Provider; DQ = Supervising Provider. Enter the qualifier to the left of the vertical, dotted line.
Blocks 17a–b	Leave Block 17a blank unless the payer's or state agency's guidelines say differently. In Block 17b, enter the HIPAA NPI of the professional reported in Block 17.
Block 18	Use the same guidelines as with all other payers.
Block 19	Required based on Jurisdictional Workers' Compensation Guidelines. Consult the payer's or state agency's instructions.
Block 20	Use the same guidelines as with all other payers.
Block 21	Use the same guidelines as with all other payers.
Block 22	Leave blank.
Block 23	Preauthorization, concurrent review, and/or voluntary certification number; refer to CMS instructions for CLIA/IDE or ZIP code for ambulance point of pick-up.
Blocks 24A–J	Use the same guidelines as with all other payers, or consult the appropriate state agency's guidelines. Block 24H is left blank on workers' compensation claims.
Block 25	Use the same guidelines as with all other payers.
Block 26	Use the same guidelines as with all other payers.
Block 27	Leave blank; this is not applicable because workers' compensation payments are sent directly to the provider.
Block 28	Use the same guidelines as with all other payers.
Block 29–30	Leave blank.
Block 31	Use the same guidelines as with all other payers.
Block 32–32b	Use the same guidelines as with all other payers, or follow the specific guidelines of the applicable workers' compensation payer.
Block 33–33b	Use the same guidelines as with all other payers, or follow the specific guidelines of the applicable workers' compensation payer.

NPI, National provider identifier.
These instructions are somewhat generic, as form completion guidelines may differ from state to state. It is important to use the specific, up-to-date CMS-1500 claim form completion instructions of the applicable workers' compensation state agency.

INPATIENT

1 Any Hospital	2 Any Hospital	3a PAT CNTL # 1234		4 TYPE OF BILL
123 Any Street	456 Any Street	b. MED REC. # 98765		0111
Philadelphia PA 19103	Philadelphia PA 19103	5 FED. TAX NO.	6 STATEMENT COVERS PERIOD FROM 11 03 06 THROUGH 11 04 06	7 RESERVED

8 PATIENT NAME a	9 PATIENT ADDRESS a 1234 Main Street		
b Doe, John	b Philadelphia	c PA 19111	Country code if other than USA

10 BIRTH DATE	11 SEX	12 DATE ADMISSION 13 HR 14 TYPE 15 SRC	16 DHR	17 STAT	18 19 20 CONDITION CODES 21 22 23 24 25 26 27 28	29 ACDT STATE	30
03 20 1971	M	11 03 06 08 3 3 12		01	Condition Codes Required Identifying Events	PA	RESERVED

31 OCCURRENCE CODE DATE	32 OCCURRENCE CODE DATE	33 OCCURRENCE CODE DATE	34 OCCURRENCE CODE DATE	35 OCCURRENCE SPAN CODE FROM THROUGH	36 OCCURRENCE SPAN CODE FROM THROUGH	37
Occurrence and Occurrence Span Codes may be used to define a significant event that may affect payer processing						FUTURE USE

38	39 CODE VALUE CODES AMOUNT	40 CODE VALUE CODES AMOUNT	41 CODE VALUE CODES AMOUNT
John Doe 1234 Main Street Philadelphia, PA 19111	a A1 952 00 b Value Codes and amounts required when necessary to process claim c d		

42 REV. CD.	43 DESCRIPTION	44 HCPCS / RATE / HIPPS CODE	45 SERV. DATE	46 SERV. UNITS	47 TOTAL CHARGES	48 NON-COVERED CHARGES	49
1 0129	Semi-Private	200.00		2	400 00	0 00	FUTURE
2 0250	Pharmacy			1	50 00	0 00	USE
3 0360	OR Services				100 00	0 00	
23 PAGE 1 OF 1	CREATION DATE	TOTALS ➡			550 00	0 00	23

50 PAYER NAME	51 HEALTH PLAN ID	52 RES INFO	53 ASG BEN	54 PRIOR PAYMENTS	55 EST. AMOUNT DUE	56 NPI 2222222222
A Independence Blue Cross	Report HIPAA National	y	y	Required when indicated payer has paid amount to Provider	Amount estimated to be due	57 1234567890
B Secondary Payer	Health Plan Identifier					OTHER Secondary
C Tertiary Payer	when mandatory					PRV ID Tertiary

58 INSURED'S NAME	59 P. REL	60 INSURED'S UNIQUE ID	61 GROUP NAME	62 INSURANCE GROUP NO.
A Doe, John	18	ABC1234567800	Watch Repair, Inc.	1234
B Secondary	→			
C Tertiary	→			

63 TREATMENT AUTHORIZATION CODES	64 DOCUMENT CONTROL NUMBER	65 EMPLOYER NAME
A 02468	491234	Watch Repair, Inc.
B Secondary		
C Tertiary		

66 DX 3910	A Use A through Q to report "Other Diagnosis" if applicable	F	G	H	68 RESERVED
9	I J K L M N O P Q				

69 ADMIT DX 4280	70 PATIENT REASON DX	May be used to report reason for visit	71 PPS CODE	72 ECI May be used to report external cause of injury	73 RESERVED
				DRG	

74 PRINCIPAL PROCEDURE CODE DATE	a OTHER PROCEDURE CODE DATE	b OTHER PROCEDURE CODE DATE	75	76 ATTENDING NPI 2222222222 QUAL 1G 1234569822
3749 11 03 06			Reserved	LAST Smith FIRST David
c OTHER PROCEDURE CODE DATE	d OTHER PROCEDURE CODE DATE	e OTHER PROCEDURE CODE DATE		77 OPERATING NPI QUAL
				LAST FIRST

80 REMARKS	81CC a B3 282N00000X	78 OTHER NPI QUAL
May be used to report additional	b Secondary	LAST FIRST
information.	c Tertiary	79 OTHER NPI QUAL
	d	LAST FIRST

UB-04 CMS-1450   APPROVED OMB NO.   THE CERTIFICATIONS ON THE REVERSE APPLY TO THIS BILL AND ARE MADE A PART HEREOF.

Red = Required
Black = Situational/Required, if applicable/Reserved

Fig. C.1 Sample Completed UB-04 form for an Inpatient Claim. (Completion guidelines for the UB-04 may differ slightly from state to state or carrier to carrier.)

OUTPATIENT

1 Any Hospital 123 Any Street Philadelphia PA 19103	2 Any Hospital 456 Any Street Philadelphia PA 19103	3a PAT. CNTL # 1234	4 TYPE OF BILL
		b. MED. REC. # 98765	0131
		5 FED. TAX NO. 221234567	6 STATEMENT COVERS PERIOD FROM 11 03 06 THROUGH 11 04 06	7 RESERVED

8 PATIENT NAME	a	9 PATIENT ADDRESS	a 1234 Main Street
b Doe, John		b Philadelphia	c PA d 19111 Country code if other than USA

10 BIRTH DATE	11 SEX	12 DATE	ADMISSION 13 HR	14 TYPE	15 SRC	16 DHR	17 STAT	18	19	20	21	CONDITION CODES 22 23 24 25 26 27 28	29 ACDT STATE	30
03 20 1971	M	11 03 06	08	3	3	12	01					Condition Codes Required Identifying Events	PA	RESERVED

31 OCCURRENCE CODE/DATE	32 OCCURRENCE CODE/DATE	33 OCCURRENCE CODE/DATE	34 OCCURRENCE CODE/DATE	35 CODE OCCURRENCE SPAN FROM THROUGH	36 CODE OCCURRENCE SPAN FROM THROUGH	37
Occurrence and Occurrence Span Codes may be used to define a significant event that may affect payer processing						FUTURE USE

38		39 CODE VALUE CODES AMOUNT	40 CODE VALUE CODES AMOUNT	41 CODE VALUE CODES AMOUNT
John Doe 1234 Main Street Philadelphia, PA 19111	a	A1 952 00		
	b	Value Codes and amounts required when necessary to process claim		
	c			
	d			

	42 REV. CD.	43 DESCRIPTION	44 HCPCS / RATE / HIPPS CODE	45 SERV. DATE	46 SERV. UNITS	47 TOTAL CHARGES	48 NON-COVERED CHARGES	49
1	0310	Laboratory N40093723106	88173	11 03 06	1	100 00	0 00	FUTURE
2	0402	Ultrasound	76942	11 04 06	1	100 00	0 00	USE
3	0360	OR Services	3749	11 04 03	1	100 00	0 00	
4								
5								
6								
7								
8								
9								
10								
11								
12								
13								
14								
15								
16								
17								
18								
19								
20								
21								
22								
23	PAGE 1 OF 1	CREATION DATE		TOTALS ➡		300 00	0 00	

50 PAYER NAME	51 HEALTH PLAN ID	52 REL INFO	53 ASG BEN	54 PRIOR PAYMENTS	55 EST. AMOUNT DUE	56 NPI 2222222222
A Independence Blue Cross	Report HIPAA National	y	y	Required when	Amount	57 1234567890
B Secondary Payer	Health Plan Identifier			indicated payer has paid amount	estimated	OTHER Secondary
C Tertiary Payer	when mandatory			to Provider	to be due	PRV ID Tertiary

58 INSURED'S NAME	59 P. REL	60 INSURED'S UNIQUE ID	61 GROUP NAME	62 INSURANCE GROUP NO.
A Doe, John	18	ABC1234567800	Watch Repair, Inc.	1234
B Secondary	→	→	→	→
C Tertiary	→	→	→	→

63 TREATMENT AUTHORIZATION CODES	64 DOCUMENT CONTROL NUMBER	65 EMPLOYER NAME
A 02468	491234	Watch Repair, Inc.
B Secondary		
C Tertiary		

66 DX 3910	A	Use A through Q to report "Other Diagnosis" if applicable	F	G	H	68 RESERVED
9	I	J	K	L	M	N	O	P	Q	

69 ADMIT DX 4280	70 PATIENT REASON DX	May be used to report reason for visit	71 PPS CODE	72 ECI DRG	May be used to report external cause of injury	73 RESERVED

74 PRINCIPAL PROCEDURE CODE/DATE	a. OTHER PROCEDURE CODE/DATE	b. OTHER PROCEDURE CODE/DATE	75	76 ATTENDING NPI 2222222222 QUAL 1G 1234569822
3749 11 04 06			Reserved	LAST Smith FIRST David
c. OTHER PROCEDURE CODE/DATE	d OTHER PROCEDURE CODE/DATE	e. OTHER PROCEDURE CODE/DATE		77 OPERATING NPI QUAL
				LAST FIRST

80 REMARKS	81CC a B3 282N00000X	78 OTHER NPI QUAL
May be used to report additional	b Secondary	LAST FIRST
information.	c Tertiary	79 OTHER NPI QUAL
	d	LAST FIRST

UB-04 CMS-1450   APPROVED OMB NO.   THE CERTIFICATIONS ON THE REVERSE APPLY TO THIS BILL AND ARE MADE A PART HEREOF.

Red = Required
Black = Situational/Required, if applicable/Reserved

Fig. C.2 Sample Completed UB-04 form for an Outpatient Claim. (Completion guidelines for the UB-04 may differ slightly from state to state or carrier to carrier.)

Table C.1 UB-04 Data Field Requirements for Inpatient/Outpatient Claims

FIELD LOCATION UB-04	DESCRIPTION	INPATIENT	OUTPATIENT
1	Billing Provider Name and Address	Required	Required
2	Billing Provider's Designated Pay-To Name and Address	Situational	Situational
3a	Patient Control Number	Required	Required
3b	Medical/Health Record Number	Situational	Situational
4	Type of Bill	Required	Required
5	Federal Tax ID Number	Required	Required
6	Statement Covers Period—From/Through	Required	Required
7	Unlabeled—Future Use	N/A	N/A
8a	Patient Name and ID	Situational	Situational
8b	Patient Name	Required	Required
9	Patient Address	Required	Required
10	Patient Birthdate (eight-digit)	Required	Required
11	Patient Sex	Required	Required
12	Admission/Start of Care Date	Required	Required, if applicable
13	Admission Hour	Required	Required, if applicable
14	Priority (Type) of Admission or Visit	Required	Required
15	Point of Origin for Admission or Visit	Required	Required
16	Discharge Hour	Required	N/A
17	Patient Discharge Status	Required	Required
18–28	Condition Codes	Required, if applicable	Required, if applicable
29	Accident State	Situational	Situational
30	Unlabeled—Future Use	N/A	N/A
31–34	Occurrence Codes and Dates	Required, if applicable	Required, if applicable
35–36	Occurrence Span Code/From/Through	Required, if applicable	Required, if applicable
37	Unlabeled—Future Use	N/A	N/A
38	Responsible Party Name and Address	Required, if applicable	Required, if applicable
39–41	Value Codes and Amounts	Required, if applicable	Required, if applicable
42	Revenue Codes	Required	Required
43	Revenue Code Description/IDE Number/ Medicaid Drug Rebate	Required	Required
44	HCPCS/Accommodation Rates/HIPPS Rate codes	Required, if applicable	Required, if applicable
45	Service Rates	N/A	Required
46	Units of Service	Required	Required
47	Total Charges (By Revenue Code)	Required	Required
48	Non-Covered Charges	Required, if applicable	Required, if applicable
49	Unlabeled—Future Use	N/A	N/A
50	Payer ID (Name) Primary, Secondary, and Tertiary	Required	Required
51	Health Plan ID Number	Situational	Situational
52	Release of Information Certification (primary, secondary, tertiary)	Required	Required
53	Assignment of Benefit Certification (primary, secondary, tertiary)	Required	Required
54	Prior Payments (primary, secondary, tertiary	Required, if applicable	Required, if applicable
55	Estimated Amount Due (primary, secondary, tertiary)	Required	Required

Table **C.1** UB-04 Data Field Requirements for Inpatient/Outpatient Claims—cont'd

FIELD LOCATION UB-04	DESCRIPTION	INPATIENT	OUTPATIENT
56	Billing Provider NPI	Required	Required
57	Other Provider IDs	Optional	Optional
58	Insured's Name (primary, secondary, tertiary)	Required	Required
59	Patient's Relation to the Insured (primary, secondary, tertiary)	Required	Required
60	Insured's Unique ID (primary, secondary, tertiary)	Required	Required
61	Insurance Group Name (primary, secondary, tertiary)	Situational	Situational
62	Insurance Group Number (primary, secondary, tertiary)	Situational	Situational
63	Treatment Authorization Codes (primary, secondary, tertiary)	Required, if applicable	Required, if applicable
64	Document Control Number (DCN)	Situational	Situational
65	Insured's Employer Name (primary, secondary, tertiary)	Situational	Situational
66	Diagnosis/Procedure Code Qualifier (ICD Version Indicator)	Required, if applicable	Required, if applicable
67a through 67q	Principal Diagnosis Code and Present on Admission (POA) Indicator	Required	Required
68	Unlabeled—Future Use	N/A	N/A
69	Admitting Diagnosis Code	Required	Required, if applicable
70	Patient's Reason for Visit Code	Situational	Situational
71	Prospective Payment System (PPS) Code	Situational	Situational
72a through 72c	External Cause of Injury (ECI) Code and POA indicator	Situational	Situational
73	Unlabeled—Future Use	N/A	N/A
74	Principal Procedure Code/Date	Required, if applicable	Required, if applicable
74a through 74e	Other Procedure Code/Date	Required, if applicable	Required, if applicable
75	Unlabeled—Future Use	N/A	N/A
76	Attending Provider IDs /Last Name/ First Name	Required	Required
77	Operating Physician IDs	Situational	Situational
78–79	Other Provider IDs/Last Name/ First Name	Situational	Situational
80	Remarks	Situational	Situational
81	Code-Code—QUALIFIER/CODE/VALUE		

DCN, Document control number; *ECI,* external cause of injury; *HCPCS,* Healthcare Common Procedure Coding System; *HIPPS,* Health Insurance Prospective Payment System; *ICD,* International Classification of Diseases; *ID,* identification; *NDC,* national drug code; *NPI,* national provider identifier; *POA,* present on admission; *PPS,* prospective payment system.
Source: Medicare Claims Processing Manual, Chapter 25—Completing and Processing the Form CMS-1450 Data Set (Rev. 2674, 02-07-14) https://www.cms.gov/Regulations-and-Guidance/Guidance/Manuals/downloads/clm104c25.pdf.

Glossary

5-star plans A system used to rate Medicare Advantage plans. Ratings can be between 1 and 5 stars, with a 5-star rating considered excellent. Medicare Advantage plans are rated on performance—how good the care is and the results of care—along with surveys from members. These ratings help the beneficiary compare plans based on these criteria.

7th character (*see also* seventh character) Certain ICD-10-CM categories require an extension to provide further specificity about the condition being coded. The applicable 7th character is required for all codes within the category or as the notes indicate in the Tabular instructions. This extension may be a number or letter and must always be the 7th character. If a code that requires a 7th character is not six characters long, a placeholder "X" must be used to fill in the empty characters.

72-hour rule Part of Medicare's prospective payment system (PPS), which states that all services provided for Medicare patients within 72 hours of hospital admission are considered part of the inpatient services and are to be billed on one claim.

A

abandonment The act of a healthcare provider ceasing to provide care to a patient.

abuse Improper or harmful procedures or methods of doing business that are contradictory to accepted business practices.

acceptance When the insurance company agrees to accept the individual for benefits coverage, or when the policy is issued.

accepting assignment Process wherein healthcare providers agree to accept the amount paid by the carrier as payment in full (after the patient satisfies his or her cost-sharing responsibilities as outlined in the insurance policy).

accountability Responsibility the healthcare profession has to patients so that a feeling of confidence exists between patient and provider.

Accountable Care Organization (ACO) Network of physicians and hospitals that works together and accepts collective responsibility for the cost and quality of care delivered to a specific number of Medicare beneficiaries for a minimum of at least 3 years; similar to a health maintenance organization (HMO).

accounts receivable Total amount of money owed from all patient ledgers.

accounts receivable aging report Report showing how long invoices, or patient accounts, have been outstanding, typically illustrated using variable periods (e.g., 30 days, 60 days).

accreditation Voluntary process through which an organization can measure the quality of its services and performance against nationally recognized standards; the process by which a private or public agency evaluates and recognizes (certifies) an institution as fulfilling applicable standards.

Accreditation Association for Ambulatory Health Care (AAAHC) Organization formed in 1979 to help ambulatory healthcare facilities improve the quality of care provided to patients. An accreditation decision is based on a careful and reasonable assessment of an organization's compliance with applicable standards and adherence to the policies and procedures of the AAAHC.

activities of daily living (ADLs) Behaviors related to personal care, which typically include bathing, dressing, eating, toileting, getting in or out of a bed or a chair, and walking.

acute care Involves assessing and treating sudden or unexpected injuries and illnesses that are potentially severe.

acute care facility Facility that is equipped and staffed to respond immediately to a critical situation.

acute condition When a patient's medical state becomes unstable.

adjudicated How a decision was made regarding the payment of an insurance claim.

adjudication (adjudication process) Process of a carrier reviewing a claim and deciding on its payment.

administrative services organization (ASO) Organization that provides a wide variety of health insurance administrative services for groups that have chosen to self-fund their health benefits.

Administrative Simplification Compliance Act (ASCA) Part of the Health Insurance Portability and Accountability Act (HIPAA) that requires health plans and healthcare clearinghouses to use certain standard transaction formats and code sets for the electronic transmission of health information.

advance beneficiary notice (ABN) Form that Medicare requires all healthcare providers to use when Medicare does not pay for a service. Patients must sign the form to acknowledge that they understand they have a choice about their healthcare procedure or service in the event that Medicare does not pay.

adverse effect An undesirable reaction to a drug.

Affordable Care Act The Patient Protection and Affordable Care Act (PPACA), commonly referred to as the *Affordable Care Act*, is a US federal statute signed into law by President Barack Obama on March 23, 2010. Together with the Health Care and Education Reconciliation Act, it represents the most significant regulatory overhaul of the country's healthcare system since the passage of Medicare and Medicaid in 1965.

allowable charges Fees that Medicare and other third-party payers allow for a particular service or supply.

alternate billing cycle Billing system that incorporates the mailing of a partial group of statements at spaced intervals during the month.

ambulatory payment classification (APC) Service classification system that the Centers for Medicare and Medicaid Services (CMS) developed for facility reimbursement of hospital outpatient services. It is intended to simplify the outpatient hospital payment system, ensure that the payment is adequate to compensate hospital costs, and implement deficit-reduction goals of the CMS.

ambulatory surgery center (ASC) Facility where surgeries that do not require hospital admission are performed; they provide a cost-effective and convenient environment that may be less stressful than what many hospitals offer.

American Standard Code for Information Interchange (ASCII) Most common format used for text files in computers and on the Internet.

Americans With Disabilities Act (ADA) Act that protects the civil rights of individuals with disabilities. Equal opportunity provisions pertain to employment, public accommodation, transportation, state and local government services, and telecommunications.

ancillary Members of the medical team, including nurses, medical assistants, health insurance professionals, and technicians.

annual dollar limit The annual monetary limit that could be applied before the enactment of the Affordable Care Act (ACA) to job-related and individual health plans on yearly reimbursement to patients for covered benefits, after which patients were required to pay the cost of all care exceeding those limits. Now, plans can put an annual dollar limit and a lifetime dollar limit only on spending for healthcare services that are not considered essential health benefits.

appeal To request or petition that a decision be reexamined. Medicare regulations allow providers and beneficiaries who are dissatisfied with a Medicare determination (of a fee-for-service claim) to request that the determination be reconsidered through the appeals process.

appeals process A multistep process available to both provider and patient through which Medicare attempts to ensure that the correct payment is made or that a clear and adequate explanation is given supporting nonpayment.

application (skills) Ability to use computer hardware and software, including Windows and Microsoft Word (or similar word processing software), and the ability to use the Internet.

assign benefits When a patient affixes his or her signature to a document that states that the patient agrees to have the insurance carrier pay benefits directly to the healthcare provider. This also can be done by signing Block 13 of the CMS-1500 claim form.

assignment of benefits Arrangement by which a patient requests that his or her health insurance benefit payments be made directly to a designated person or facility, such as a physician or a hospital.

autonomy Working without direct supervision; having the flexibility of choices. In health insurance, the freedom to choose what medical expenses would be covered.

average length of stay (ALOS) Predetermined number of days of approved hospital stay assigned to an individual diagnosis-related group (DRG).

B

balance billing Practice of billing patients for any balance left after deductibles, coinsurance, and insurance payments have been made.

beneficiary Individual who has health insurance through the Medicare, Medicaid, or TRICARE programs.

Beneficiary Complaint Response Program Program that handles complaints by Medicare beneficiaries (or their representatives) made either in writing or by telephone. A case manager is assigned to work with the beneficiary from start to finish, keeping the beneficiary informed throughout the review process about the status of the complaint.

benefit cap Maximum benefit amount paid for any one incident or any one year.

benefit period Duration of time during which a Medicare beneficiary is eligible for Part A benefits for services incurred in a hospital, a skilled nursing facility (SNF), or both. A benefit period begins on the day an individual is admitted to a hospital or SNF and ends when the beneficiary has not received care in a hospital or SNF for 60 consecutive days.

billing compliance Following a specific set of rules and regulations in the gathering of complete and accurate information leading to patient billing and the claims development process.

billing cycle The period when medical offices send statements to patients, usually every 30 days.

billing service Company that offers services to healthcare facilities, including billing processes and claims filing. Many billing services take on the responsibility of keeping up with rapidly changing Medicare and other healthcare-related laws.

binds When the insurance company agrees to accept the individual for benefits.

birthday rule Informal procedure used in the health insurance industry to help determine which health plan is considered "primary" when individuals (usually children) are listed as dependents on more than one health plan. Under this rule, the health plan of the parent whose birthday comes first in the calendar year is considered the primary plan.

blockchain technology Allows digital information to be distributed but not copied.

Blue Cross and Blue Shield Federal Employee Program (FEP) Program that provides coverage for several million federal government employees, retirees, and their dependents.

Blue Cross and Blue Shield member hospitals Hospitals that have contracted as participating providers with the Blue Cross Blue Shield Association member organization. Member hospitals must accept the Blue Cross and Blue Shield allowable fee as payment in full and cannot bill the patient for any remaining charges after the initial deductible and copayment are met.

breach of confidentiality When confidential information is disclosed to a third party without patient consent or court order.

business associate Defined by the Health Insurance Portability and Accountability Act (HIPAA) as an individual or corporate "person" who performs on behalf of the covered entity any function or activity involving the use or disclosure of protected health information and who is not a member of the workforce of the covered entity.

C

cafeteria plan Type of plan that deducts the cost of the plan (premium) from the employee's wages before withholding taxes are deducted, allowing employees the option of pretax payroll deduction for some insurance premiums, unreimbursed medical expenses, and child or dependent care expenses.

capitation Common method of reimbursement used primarily by health maintenance organizations (HMOs) in which the provider or medical facility is paid a fixed, per capita amount for each individual enrolled in the plan, regardless of how many or few services the patient uses.

care coordination An organized effort initiated under the Affordable Care Act (ACA) to make sure that patients, especially the chronically ill, get the right care at the right time, while avoiding unnecessary duplication of services and preventing medical errors.

carrier Claims processors that apply Medicare coverage rules to determine the appropriateness and medical necessity of claims. Also called *Medicare administrative contractors (MACs)* and *fiscal intermediaries (FIs)*.

carve-out Eliminating a certain specialty of health services from coverage under the healthcare policy.

case mix Reported data that include patient demographic information such as age, sex, country of residence, and race or ethnicity; diagnostic information; treatment information; disposition; total charges; and expected source of payment.

case-mix adjustment The adjustment or modification of the health condition, taking into consideration the clinical characteristics and service needs of the beneficiary.

catastrophic cap (cat cap) Maximum cost limit placed on covered medical bills under TRICARE. The cat cap is the monetary limit that a family of an active duty member would have to pay in any given year.

categorically needy Typically used to describe low-income families with children; individuals receiving Supplemental Security Income (SSI); pregnant women, infants, and children with incomes less than a specified percent of the federal poverty level; and qualified Medicare beneficiaries (QMBs).

category Codes in the Tabular section of Current Procedural Terminology (CPT) are formatted using four classifications: section, subsection, subheading, and category. "Category" is the most definitive classification and aids in selecting the applicable code.

Category II codes Supplemental tracking codes that provide a method for reporting performance measures. They are intended to facilitate the collection of information about the quality of care delivered by coding numerous services or test results that support performance measures that have been agreed on as contributing to good patient care.

Category III codes Established by the American Medical Association (AMA) as a set of temporary Current Procedural Terminology (CPT) codes for emerging technologies, services, and procedures where data collection is necessary to substantiate widespread use or for the US Food and Drug Administration (FDA) approval process.

Centers for Medicare and Medicaid Services (CMS) An agency within the US Department of Health and Human Services (HHS) responsible for administration of Medicare (the federal health insurance program for seniors) and Medicaid (the federal needs-based program). CMS also oversees the Children's Health Insurance Program (CHIP), the Health Insurance Portability and Accountability Act (HIPAA), and the Clinical Laboratory Improvement Amendments (CLIA), among other services.

certification Culmination of a process of formal recognition of the competence possessed by an individual.

CHAMPVA For Life (CFL) Benefits for covered medical services designed for spouses or dependents of veterans who are age 65 or older and enrolled in Medicare Parts A and B. The benefit is payable after Medicare pays its share.

charge description master (CDM) Listing of every type of procedure and service the hospital can provide to patients, including procedures, pharmaceuticals, supplies, and room charges. CDMs help make the billing process run more smoothly and accurately.

charge-to-collection ratio The total amount of money received by a medical practice divided by the total amount charged. Also referred to as *collection ratio*.

chief complaint (CC) The reason why the patient is seeing the physician. Sometimes called the *presenting problem*.

Children's Health Insurance Program (CHIP) Enacted as part of the Balanced Budget Act of 1997, CHIP provides federal matching funds for states to implement health insurance programs for children in families that earn too much to qualify for Medicaid but too little to afford private health coverage reasonably.

Civilian Health and Medical Program of the Department of Veterans Affairs (CHAMPVA) Healthcare benefits program for qualifying dependents and survivors of veterans, whereby the Department of Veterans Affairs (VA) shares the cost of covered healthcare services and supplies with eligible beneficiaries. There is no cost to beneficiaries when they receive healthcare treatment at a VA facility.

Civilian Health and Medical Program of the Uniformed Services (CHAMPUS) Military healthcare program that existed for more than 30 years until it was replaced with TRICARE in 1998.

claims adjustment reason code Code that details the reason an adjustment was made to a healthcare claim payment by the payer. These codes are used in the electronic remittance advice (ERA) and the standard paper remittance advice.

claim attachments Supplemental documents that provide additional medical information to the claims processor that cannot be included within the electronic claim format.

claims clearinghouse Company that receives claims from different healthcare providers and specializes in consolidating the claims so that they can send one transmission containing batches of claims to each third-party payer. A clearinghouse is typically an independent, centralized service available to healthcare providers for the purpose of simplifying medical insurance claims submission for multiple carriers.

claims processor Facility that handles TRICARE claims for healthcare received within a state or region.

clean claim Claim that can be processed for payment quickly without being returned when all information necessary for processing the claim has been entered on the claim form and the information is correct.

clearinghouse Business entity that specializes in consolidating claims received from providers and transmitting them in batches to each respective third-party payer. *See* claims clearinghouse.

clinic A medical facility that is smaller than a hospital and is often run by a government agency or private partnership of physicians. Clinics generally provide only outpatient services.

Clinical Laboratory Improvement Amendments (CLIA) Program that Congress established in 1988 to regulate quality standards for all laboratory testing done on humans to ensure the safety, accuracy, reliability, and timeliness of patient test results, regardless of where the test was performed.

closed-panel HMO Multispecialty group practice in which nonmember healthcare providers in the community generally cannot participate.

CMS-1500 claim form Standard insurance form used by all government and most commercial insurance payers.

code set Data element used to uniformly document the reasons patients are seen and the procedures or services or both provided to them during their healthcare encounters.

coding compliance The process of verifying that the diagnoses and procedure codes used on claims comply with all current coding guidelines and rules.

coinsurance Type of cost-sharing between the insurance provider and the policyholder. After the deductible has been met, the policyholder pays a certain percentage of the bill, and the insurance provider pays the remaining percentage of allowable charges.

collection agency Organization that obtains or arranges for payment of money owed to a third party.

collection ratio Total amount collected divided by the total amount charged. Also called *charge-to-collection ratio*.

combination code A single code that is used when more than one otherwise individually classified disease is combined with another disease and one code is assigned for both, or when a single code is used to describe two diagnoses or conditions that frequently occur together. A combination code can also be used for a diagnosis with an associated secondary process (manifestation) or a diagnosis with an associated complication.

combination record One of two types of "hybrid" medical records that allow the amount of paper records to be reduced because some of the documents are stored electronically and some are kept in paper form.

coming and going rule Rule that coverage for injuries sustained while an employee is commuting to and from work is generally excluded by most state workers' compensation laws.

commercial health insurance Any kind of health insurance paid for by somebody other than the government. Also called *private health insurance*.

communication Sending and receiving of information through mutually understood speech, writing, or signs.

community call plan When two or more hospitals participate in a formal agreement to develop and implement a plan to coordinate on-call physician coverage in a specific geographic area (i.e., community).

Community First Choice (CFC) Option This option was established under the Affordable Care Act (ACA) of 2010 and became available on October 1, 2011. It provides a 6% increase in federal matching payments to states for service expenditures related to this option, gives individuals with disabilities who are eligible for nursing homes and other institutional settings options to receive community-based services, and provides qualifying Medicaid beneficiaries the choice to leave facilities and institutions (e.g., nursing homes) for care in their own homes and communities with appropriate, cost-effective services and supports.

comorbidity Presence of more than one disease or disorder that occurs in an individual at the same time.

comprehension Understanding the meaning (of what you have read).

comprehensive plan Type of policy that combines basic and major medical coverage into one plan.

concurrent care When a patient receives similar services (e.g., hospital visits) by more than one healthcare provider on the same day.

confidentiality Foundation for trust in the patient–provider relationship that concerns the communication of private and personal information from one individual to another.

consideration Binding force in any contract that gives it legal status; the object of value that each party gives to the other.

Consolidated Omnibus Budget Reconciliation Act (COBRA) Law passed by Congress in 1986 that gives workers who lose their health insurance benefits and their dependents the right to continue group coverage temporarily under the same group health plan sponsored by their employer in certain instances where coverage under the plan would otherwise end.

consultation When the primary care provider sends a patient to another provider, usually a specialist, for the purpose of the consulting physician rendering his or her expert opinion on the patient's condition. The primary care provider does not relinquish the care of the patient to the consulting provider.

contractual write-off When the provider agrees, through a contractual agreement, not to be paid the remaining amount of a fee after the patient has paid his or her deductible and coinsurance and all third-party payers have paid their share.

contraindication Issue that makes a certain medical treatment or procedure inadvisable.

convention(s) In healthcare coding, general rules and instructional notes for use of the classification independent of the guidelines.

conversion factor (CF) In medical fee structure, a monetary amount that is determined by the Centers for Medicare and Medicaid Services (CMS) as a standard dollar amount that is multiplied by the relative weight to arrive at the ambulatory payment classification (APC)–based fee.

coordination of benefits (COB) When a patient and spouse (or parent) are covered under two separate employer group policies, the total benefits an insured can receive from both group plans are limited to no more than 100% of the allowable expenses, preventing the policyholder(s) from making a profit on health insurance claims. The primary plan pays benefits up to its limit, and the secondary plan pays the difference up to its limit.

coordination of benefits contractor (COBC) Individual who ensures that the information in the Medicare eligibility database regarding other health insurance primary to Medicare is up to date and accurate.

copayment Amount of money the patient must pay out of his or her own pocket before the insurance company begins to pay.

correct code initiative Part of the National Correct Coding Initiative (NCCI) to develop correct coding methods for the Centers for Medicare and Medicaid Services (CMS). It is intended to reduce overpayments that result from improper coding.

cost avoid(ance) Healthcare provider bills and collects from liable third parties before sending the claim to Medicaid.

cost outliers Atypical patients whose hospital stays are considerably shorter or longer than average.

cost-sharing (share of cost) Situation where insured individuals pay a portion of the healthcare costs, such as deductibles, coinsurance, or copayment amounts.

counseling Service provided to the patient and his or her family that involves impressions and recommended diagnostic studies, discussion of diagnostic results, prognosis, risks and benefits of treatment, and instructions.

covered charges Allowed services, supplies, and procedures for which Medicare and TRICARE (and most other insurers) would pay. Covered charges include medical and psychological services and supplies that are considered appropriate care and are generally accepted by qualified professionals to be reasonable and adequate for the diagnosis and treatment of illness, injury, pregnancy, or mental disorders or for well-child care.

covered entity Health plan, healthcare clearinghouse, or healthcare provider who transmits any health information in electronic form in connection with a transaction.

credible coverage Basic benefits offered by the Medicare Part D Prescription Drug Plan. A Medicare beneficiary who does not choose to enroll in a Part D plan must acquire a "certificate of credible coverage" to avoid a penalty if he or she decides to sign up after the open enrollment period.

critical access hospital (CAH) A hospital that is certified to receive cost-based reimbursement from Medicare.

critical care Constant attention (either at bedside or immediately available) by a physician in a medical crisis.

crossover claims The transfer, usually electronic, of claim data from one insurer to another insurer.

crosswalk A procedure by which codes used for data in one database are translated into the codes of another database, making it possible to relate information between or among databases.

custodial care Nonmedical care that helps individuals with activities of daily living (ADLs), such as bathing, dressing, toileting, preparation of special diets, and self-administration of medication, and that does not require the constant attention of specially trained medical personnel.

D

daily journal Chronological record of all patient transactions, including previous balances, charges, payments, and current balances for that day. Also called a *day sheet*.

data analytics The science of analyzing raw data to make conclusions; certain at-risk patient populations can be determined using this method.

deductible Certain amount of money that the patient must pay each year toward his or her medical expenses before health insurance benefits begin.

default code Code listed next to a main term in the International Classification of Diseases, 10th Revision, Clinical Modification (ICD-10-CM) Index representing the condition most commonly associated with the main term or the unspecified code for the condition.

defendant Party being sued in a lawsuit.

Defense Enrollment Eligibility Reporting System (DEERS) Computerized data bank that lists all active and retired military service members. The data bank is checked before processing claims to ensure that patients are eligible for TRICARE benefits.

Defense Health Agency (DHA) A joint, integrated Combat Support Agency that enables the Army, Navy, and Air Force medical services to provide a medically ready force to combatant commands in both peacetime and wartime. The DHA facilitates the delivery of integrated, affordable, and high quality healthcare services to Military Health System (MHS) beneficiaries.

deidentified When identifiable elements are removed from information that could be linked to a particular individual.

demand bill Under Medicare rules, a beneficiary, on receiving notification of noncoverage, has the right to request that a fiscal intermediary review that determination.

demographic information Information such as name, address, Social Security number, and employment.

diagnosis Determination of the nature of a cause of disease; the process of distinguishing one disease from another by studying the signs and symptoms.

diagnosis-related group (DRG) System of classifying hospital inpatient cases into categories with similar use of the facility's resources. Under this system, a hospital is paid a predetermined lump-sum amount, regardless of the costs involved, for each Medicare patient treated and discharged.

dial-up(s) Form of Internet access to establish a dialed connection to an Internet service provider (ISP) via telephone lines.

digital imaging hybrid A type of medical record keeping in which many of the documents are maintained in their paper form but, to save space and time when trying to locate a specific record, the paper documentation is scanned and digitally filed in a computer system.

diligence Persistence; the ability to stick with a task until it is finished.

direct contract model Health maintenance organization (HMO) similar to an individual practice association except that the HMO contracts directly with the individual physicians. The HMO recruits a variety of community healthcare providers—primary care and specialists.

direct data entry (DDE) claims Claims that are submitted directly to an insurance carrier.

disability income insurance Form of health insurance that replaces a portion of earned income when an individual is unable to perform the requirements of his or her job because of injury or illness that is not work related.

disability insurance Type of insurance that provides a stated weekly or monthly payment for lost income resulting from accidents, sickness, or both that is not work related.

disbursements journal Listing of all expenses paid to vendors, such as building rent, office supplies, and salaries.

discounted fee-for-service When a healthcare provider offers services at rates that are lower than the usual, customary, and reasonable (UCR) fees.

disproportionate share Payment adjustment to compensate hospitals for the higher operating costs they incur in treating a large share of low-income patients.

donut hole Officially referred to as the *Medicare Part D coverage gap,* the donut hole is the difference between the initial coverage limit and the catastrophic coverage threshold. After a Medicare beneficiary exceeds the prescription drug coverage limit, he or she is financially responsible for the entire cost of prescription drugs until the expense reaches the catastrophic coverage threshold.

downcoding When claims are submitted with outdated, deleted, or nonexistent Current Procedural Terminology (CPT) codes and the payer assigns a substitute code it thinks best fits the services performed, resulting in a decreased payment. Also, downcoding can result when Evaluation and Management (E/M) service levels do not match up with diagnostic codes.

DRG grouper A computer software program that takes the coded information and identifies the patient's diagnosis-related group (DRG) category.

dual eligible Patients who are eligible for Medicaid and Medicare coverage.

durable power of attorney Relative (or other person) who has been named as an agent to handle the patient's affairs if the patient becomes incapacitated.

E

Early and Periodic Screening, Diagnostic, and Treatment (EPSDT) program Child health component of Medicaid developed to fit the standards of pediatric care and to meet the special physical, emotional, and developmental needs of low-income children.

earned income Income from employment.

egregious Conspicuously negligent.

electronic claims clearinghouse Business entity that receives claims from several medical facilities and consolidates these claims so that one transmission containing multiple claims can be sent to each insurance carrier. A clearinghouse serves as an intermediary between medical practices and insurance companies, facilitating the electronic exchange of information between the facilities.

electronic claims submission (ECS) Process that allows providers to use computers and applicable software programs to submit claims to a central location, such as a clearinghouse via a web interface. The web interface sends the claims to the carrier system for processing.

electronic data interchange (EDI) Electronic transfer of information in a standard format between two entities. EDI allows business entities to exchange information and transact business in a rapid and cost-effective way.

electronic funds transfer (EFT) System wherein money is moved electronically between accounts or organizations. In the case of insurance claims, when claims are submitted electronically, many carriers transfer the payments directly into the provider's bank account rather than mailing a check, making the funds instantly usable.

electronic media claim (EMC) Instead of filing a claim on a paper claim form, claim information is entered into a computer and electronically transferred to a computer system (e.g., using a modem and a telephone line).

electronic medical record (EMR) Electronic file wherein patients' health information is stored in a computer system. Synonymous terms for an EMR include *electronic patient record, electronic health record,* and *computerized patient record.*

electronic protected health information (ePHI) Identifiable health information that is protected under the Health Insurance Portability and Accountability Act (HIPAA) Privacy Rule in electronic form.

electronic remittance advice (ERA) One of several different types of electronic formats rather than a paper document. Payments can be posted automatically to patient accounts, allowing the health insurance professional to update accounts receivable much more quickly and accurately than if he or she had to post the payments manually.

emancipated minor Individual older than 16 years and younger than 18 years who is living separate and apart from his or her parents and not receiving any financial support from them (except by court order or benefits to which the youth is entitled [i.e., Social Security]), living beyond the parent's custody and control, and not in foster care.

emergency care Care given in a hospital emergency department.

Emergency Medical Treatment and Active Labor Act (EMTALA) Act that requires any hospital to respond to a person's emergent medical condition by determining the nature of the condition. If an emergent condition exists, it must be treated to the best of the facility's ability, regardless of the patient's ability to pay. Patients may be transferred as appropriate after stabilization of the condition.

emergent medical condition Onset of a health condition that requires immediate medical attention.

Employee Retirement Income Security Act (ERISA) of 1974 Federal law that sets minimum standards for pension plans in private industry, which is how most self-insured employers fund their programs.

employer identification number (EIN) Nine-digit number assigned to employers by the Internal Revenue Service (IRS). Business entities that pay wages to one or more employees are required to have an EIN as their taxpayer identifying number.

employment network Public agency or private organization that has agreed to provide services under the Ticket to Work program guidelines.

encounter form Multipurpose billing form used by most providers that can be customized to medical specialties and preprinted with more common diagnoses and procedures. Also called a *superbill, routing form,* or *patient service slip.*

end-stage renal disease (ESRD) Permanent kidney disorders requiring dialysis or transplant.

Energy Employees Occupational Illness Compensation Program Act Provides compensation and medical benefits to employees of the Department of Energy (DOE), its contractors and subcontractors, and employees of DOE-designated atomic weapons employers who became ill as a result of work performed in the production and testing of nuclear weapons.

enrollees Individuals who are covered under a managed care plan.

enrollment process Process through which medical offices usually must go before they can submit claims. The process typically involves completing and returning electronic data interchange setup requirement forms so that the business entity that is to receive the claims can create a compatible information file about the practice in its computer system so that claims can be processed.

enthusiasm Positive motivation to fulfill assigned duties and responsibilities.

entity/entities Individual, business organization, or some kind of economic unit that controls resources, incurs obligations, and engages in business activities.

episode of care (bundled payment) Instead of reimbursing per service as in fee-for-service (FFS), bundled payments give providers a lump sum that represents expected costs for a particular episode of care. Examples of episodes of care for which a single, bundled payment can be made include all physician, inpatient, and outpatient care for such procedures as a knee or hip replacement, pregnancy and delivery, or heart attack.

eponym A disease, procedure, or syndrome named for the individual who discovered or first used it.

Equal Credit Opportunity Act Act stating that a business entity may not discriminate against a credit applicant based on race, color, religion, national origin, age, sex, or marital status.

ERISA plans Certain type of plan typically established by self-insured employers that provides benefits to employees in the form of life, disability, health insurance, severance pay, and pension plans. Benefits are funded through the purchase of insurance policies or through the establishment of trusts, paid for by the employer or the employer and employee together. The money is invested, and the employer takes a tax deduction for its contribution to the trust. If an employer maintains an ERISA pension plan, the federal ERISA law sets strict minimum standards on how the assets are managed and paid out. *See also* Employee Retirement Income Security Act (ERISA) of 1974.

essential health benefits Minimum requirements for all health plans in the insurance marketplace.

essential modifier In ICD coding, an indented term listed under a main term used to describe different anatomic site(s), etiology, or clinical type(s). An essential modifier must be a part of the documented diagnosis.

established patient Person who has been treated previously by the healthcare provider, regardless of location of service, within the past 3 years.

ethics Code of conduct of a particular group of people or culture.

etiology Cause or origin of a disease or condition.

etiquette Following the rules and conventions governing correct or polite behavior in society in general or in a particular social or professional group or situation.

Evaluation and Management (E/M) codes Codes found at the beginning of the Current Procedural Terminology (CPT) manual that represent the services provided directly to the patient during an encounter that do not involve an actual procedure.

evidence-based practice (EBP) The integration of the healthcare provider's clinical expertise (experience, education, and skills), patient values, and the best research evidence into the decision-making process for patient care.

exacerbation Worsening or an increase in the severity of a disease or its signs and symptoms.

exclusions Illnesses or injuries not covered by the health insurance policy.

exclusive provider organization (EPO) A plan composed of a network of individual (or groups of) healthcare providers who have entered into written agreements with a third-party insurer to provide health insurance coverage to those individuals enrolled in the plan. Enrollees are reimbursed only if the medical expenses are rendered by this designated network of providers, who in turn provide patients services at significantly lower rates than what they would have been under more traditional reimbursement models.

exemption(s) When a business organization (or individual) is not required to purchase workers' compensation insurance for employees because of a specific classification of business type or the fact that it has a minimal number of employees. (Exemption criteria vary from state to state.)

explanation of benefits (EOB) Document prepared by the carrier that gives details of how the claim was adjudicated. It typically includes a comprehensive listing of patient information, dates of service, payments, or reasons for nonpayment. *See* remittance advice (RA).

eZ TRICARE Electronic claims filing process wherein providers can upload batches of claims directly from their practice management systems using a variety of claims processing formats.

F

face-to-face time Time that the healthcare provider spends in direct contact with a patient during an office visit, which includes taking a history, performing an examination, and discussing results.

Fair Credit Billing Act (FCBA) Set of procedures or steps that business entities (medical practices) must follow if a customer claims that they made a mistake in their billing.

Fair Credit Reporting Act Law that gives consumers the right to a copy of their credit reports. The law is intended to protect consumers from having their eligibility for credit damaged by incomplete or misleading credit report information.

Fair Debt Collection Practices Act Act that prohibits certain abusive methods used by third-party collectors or bill collectors hired to collect overdue bills.

Federal Black Lung Program The Black Lung Benefits Act provides compensation for miners with black lung (pneumoconiosis). This act requires liable mine operators to award disability payments and establishes a fund administered by the Secretary of Labor that provides disability payments to miners when the mine operator is unknown or unable to pay.

Federal Employees Health Benefits (FEHB) Program Health insurance coverage the government pays for its own civilian employees.

Federal Employees' Compensation Act (FECA) Act that provides workers' compensation for nonmilitary federal employees. FECA covers medical expenses resulting from a disability and provides compensation for survivors of employees who are killed while on the job or who die from a job-related illness or condition.

Federal Employers' Liability Act (FELA) Under this act, states in which railroads are engaged in interstate commerce are liable for injuries to their employees if the railroads have been negligent.

Federal Insurance Contributions Act (FICA) Act that provides for a federal system of old-age, survivors, disability, and hospital insurance.

fee-for-service (FFS) Traditional type of healthcare policy whereby the provider charges a specific fee (typically the usual, customary, and reasonable [UCR] fee) for each service rendered and is paid that fee by the patient or by the patient's insurance carrier.

fee schedule A complete listing of fees set by commercial payers, Medicare, and other government payers to reimburse physicians or other providers or suppliers typically on a fee-for-service basis.

financial means test Detailed and comprehensive question-naire that establishes financial need to receive Supplemental Security Income (SSI).

first-listed diagnosis Main condition treated or investigated during the outpatient (ambulatory) encounter. In cases where there is no definitive diagnosis, the main symptom or sign, abnormal findings, or problem is reported as the first-listed diagnosis; this replaces the outdated term *primary diagnosis.*

flexible spending account (FSA) IRS Section 125 cafeteria plan. The cost of the plan (premium) is deducted from the employee's wages before withholding taxes are deducted, allowing employees the option of pretax payroll deduction for some insurance premiums, unreimbursed medical expenses, and child or dependent care expenses.

form locators Assigned designated spaces on the hospital uniform billing (UB-04) form for data elements necessary for inpatient claims processing. Each one has a unique number.

for-profit hospitals When a hospital's monetary income is greater than its expenses.

fraud Defined by the National Health Care Anti-Fraud Association as an intentional deception or misrepresentation that the individual or entity makes, knowing that the misrepresentation could result in some unauthorized benefit to the individual or the entity or to another party.

full-service HMO A type of health maintenance organization (HMO) that provides physical and mental health services. However, most people who have health insurance receive their mental health services through a different organization known as a *managed behavioral healthcare organization (MBHO).*

G

gatekeepers Primary care physicians (PCPs), typically who are family practice clinicians, internists, or pediatricians, who manage the patient's total care, determine medical necessity, and provide access to specialists when needed.

General Equivalence Mappings (GEMs) Tool developed by various organizations that can be used like a two-way translation dictionary to assist with the conversion of International Classification of Diseases, 9th Revision, Clinical Modification (ICD-9-CM) codes to International Classification of Diseases, 10th Revision (ICD-10) or the conversion of ICD-10 codes back to ICD-9-CM.

general hospital Hospital that is set up to handle the care of many kinds of disease and injury. A general hospital is usually the major healthcare facility in a region and typically has an emergency department to deal with immediate threats to health and the capacity to dispatch emergency medical services.

general journal Chronological listing of transactions with a specific format for recording each transaction. Each transaction is recorded separately and consists of a date, all accounts that receive a debit entry, all accounts that receive a credit entry, and a clear description of each transaction.

general ledger Permanent history of all financial transactions from day one of the life of a practice. A general ledger can be used to prepare a range of periodic financial statements, such as income statements, balance sheets, or both.

geographic practice cost index (GPCI) Used by Medicare to adjust for variance in operating costs of medical practices located in different parts of the United States.

governance Refers to how any organization is run. With reference to healthcare facilities, it includes all processes, systems, and controls used to safeguard the welfare of patients and the integrity of the institution.

grandfathered A provision in a law that exempts an individual or business entity who is already involved in a regulated activity or business from the new regulations established by the law.

grandfathered plans Those that were in effect before March 23, 2010, when the Affordable Care Act was signed into law.

These plans are allowed to offer the same coverage that was in place before the act.

group insurance Contract between an insurance company and an employer (or other entity) that covers eligible employees or members. Group insurance is generally the least expensive kind of insurance, and in many cases the employer pays part or all of the cost.

group model Health maintenance organization (HMO) that contracts with independent, multispecialty physician groups who provide all healthcare services to its members. Physician groups usually share the same facility, support staff, medical records, and equipment.

group plan One insurance policy that covers a group of people.

grouper software A computer application interface commonly used in hospitals to send and retrieve data for grouping, editing, and reimbursement outcomes.

guarantor Person who is responsible for, or agrees to pay, someone else's debt if the individual defaults on a financial obligation. In health insurance, if the patient is a minor, the guarantor typically would be a parent or an adult legally responsible for the patient.

H

hardship exemption When an individual has certain life situations, such as foreclosure of or eviction from the person's home or incurring substantial debt due to high medical expenses, that prevent him or her from being able to afford health insurance, a hardship exemption may be acquired.

HCBS Waivers Program A federally approved Medicaid program authorized by Title XIX of the Social Security Act that provides services in the home for persons who would otherwise require institutional care in a hospital, nursing facility, or intermediate care facility.

HCPCS codes Descriptive terms with letters, numbers, or both used to report medical services and procedures for reimbursement. Healthcare Common Procedure Coding System (HCPCS) codes provide a uniform language to describe medical, surgical, and diagnostic services. These codes are used to report procedures and services to government and private health insurance programs, and reimbursement is based on the codes reported.

Health Care Financing Administration (HCFA) *See* Centers for Medicare and Medicaid Services (CMS).

health information exchange (HIE) An HIE allows healthcare providers and patients to securely access and share a patient's vital medical information electronically, improving the speed, quality, safety, and cost of patient care. HIEs are a key component of the Health Information Technology for Economic and Clinical Health (HITECH) Act of 2009. The purpose of this act was to encourage healthcare providers in the United States to begin using electronic health records (EHRs).

health information management (HIM) system Software system generally made up of components that are responsible for coding and abstracting all patient charts and releasing them for billing.

health insurance claim number (HICN) Number assigned to a Medicare beneficiary that allows the health insurance professional to look at the patient's identification card and immediately determine the level of coverage. The number is in the format of nine digits, usually the beneficiary's Social Security number, followed by one alpha character.

health insurance exchange Model intended to create a more organized and competitive market for health insurance by offering a choice of plans, with common rules governing how the plan is offered and its cost and providing information to help consumers understand better the choices available to them.

health insurance marketplace Also called a *health insurance exchange*, a health insurance marketplace is an organization set up to facilitate the purchase of health insurance in each state in accordance with the Affordable Care Act (ACA).

Health Insurance Portability and Accountability Act (HIPAA) Legislation passed in 1996 that includes a Privacy Rule creating national standards to protect personal health information and that requires most employer-sponsored group health insurance plans to accept transfers from other group plans without imposing a preexisting condition clause.

health maintenance organization (HMO) Organization that provides its members with basic healthcare services for a fixed price and for a given time period.

Health Maintenance Organization (HMO) Act Act passed by Congress in 1973 that provided grants to employers who set up HMOs.

health reimbursement arrangements (HRAs) Also known as *health reimbursement accounts* or *personal care accounts,* HRAs are a type of health insurance plan that reimburses employees for certain qualifying medical expenses. HRAs consist of funds set aside by employers to reimburse employees for "qualified" medical expenses.

health savings account (HSA) Special tax shelter that works in conjunction with a low-cost, high-deductible health insurance policy to provide comprehensive healthcare coverage at the lowest possible net cost for individuals who qualify. HSAs are set up for the purpose of paying medical bills, allowing individuals to make tax-deferred contributions to personal retirement funds. *See also* medical savings account (MSA).

Healthcare Common Procedure Coding System (HCPCS) Developed by the Health Care Financing Administration (HCFA) to provide a uniform language that accurately describes medical, surgical, and diagnostic services, serving as an effective means for reliable nationwide communication among physicians, insurance carriers, and patients.

high-deductible plans (HDPs) Also known as *consumer-directed health plans (CDHPs),* HDPs are becoming increasingly common as employers and health plans are shifting more payment responsibility to the plan member. HDPs include large deductibles for which the family or patient is financially responsible. Once the deductible is met, insurance benefits will begin. (The Affordable Care Act [ACA] mandates that HDPs purchased after March 2010 provide free preventive services even if the deductible has not been met.)

HIPAA-covered entities Consist of healthcare providers, health plans (including employer-sponsored plans), and healthcare clearinghouses (including billing agents). Covered entities must comply with Health Insurance Portability and Accountability Act (HIPAA) rules for any health or medical information of identifiable individuals.

histology The microscopic structure of organic tissues.

HMO with point-of-service (POS) option A health maintenance organization (HMO) member is allowed to see providers who are not in the HMO network and receive services from specialists without first going through a primary care physician; however, the plan pays a smaller portion of the bill than if the member had followed regular HMO procedures. The member also pays a higher premium and a higher copayment each time the option is used.

home health agency A healthcare organization that provides a wide range of healthcare services that can be given in the patient's home. Home healthcare is usually less expensive and more convenient than, and can be just as effective as, care provided in a hospital or skilled nursing facility.

home health prospective payment system (HH PPS) Fixed payment for a home health services PPS.

hospice Facility or service that provides care for terminally ill patients and support to their families, either directly or on a consulting basis with the patient's physician. The emphasis is on symptom control and support before and after death.

hospital information system (HIS) A computer system that can manage the information flowing through the facility to allow healthcare providers and ancillary staff to do their jobs efficiently and effectively.

hospital outpatient prospective payment system (HOPPS) Payment system developed by the Centers for Medicare and Medicaid Services (CMS), sometimes referred to as an *outpatient prospective payment system (OPPS),* that was implemented on August 1, 2000, and is used to reimburse for hospital outpatient services and reduce Medicare beneficiary copayments.

I

iatrogenic effects Symptom or illness in a patient brought on unintentionally by a physician's activity, manner, or therapy.

identifiers Numbers used in the administration of healthcare to distinguish individual healthcare providers, health plans, employers, and patients. Identifiers are intended to simplify administrative processes (such as referrals and billing), improve the accuracy of data, and reduce costs.

implied contract Unwritten contract between a healthcare provider and a patient that has all the components of a legal contract and is just as binding.

implied promises Promises that are neither spoken nor written but are implicated by the individuals' actions and performance.

in situ Existing in a localized state or condition. An in situ tumor is one that is confined to its site of origin and has not invaded surrounding tissue or gone elsewhere in the body.

incidental disclosure Type of privacy exposure that is specifically allowed under the Health Insurance Portability and Accountability Act (HIPAA) (e.g., if two patients in the reception room happen to know each other).

indemnify To reimburse or make payment for a loss.

indemnity insurance The "standard" type of health insurance individuals can purchase. It provides comprehensive major medical benefits and allows insured individuals to choose any physician or hospital when seeking medical care.

indented code Codes that refer to the common portion of the procedure listed in the preceding entry.

independent practice association (IPA) Individual healthcare providers who provide all needed healthcare services for a health maintenance organization (HMO).

indigent People who are poor and deprived, typically without sufficient resources to take care of their daily needs. "Medically indigent" refers to an individual who does not have health insurance and who is not eligible for other healthcare coverage, such as Medicaid, Medicare, or private health insurance.

individual market In the context of healthcare, this means the market for health insurance coverage offered to individuals other than in connection with a group health plan. An individual market policy normally has higher premiums and deductibles than employer-provided plans, and the coverage offered under an individual market is generally less comprehensive.

informed consent The process by which a fully informed patient can participate in choices about his or her healthcare. This concept originates from the legal and ethical rights patients have to direct what happens to their bodies and from the ethical duty of physicians to involve patients in their healthcare.

initial claims Claims submitted for reimbursement under Medicare, including claims with paper attachments; demand bills; claims where Medicare is the secondary payer and there is only one primary payer; claims submitted to a Medicare fee-for-service carrier or fiscal intermediary for the first time, including resubmitted, previously rejected claims; and nonpayment claims.

initial enrollment period The period that begins 3 months before the month in which an individual turns age 65, the birthday month, and ends 3 months after the month in which he or she turns age 65 wherein he or she can sign up for Medicare. If the person decides not to sign up for Medicare in the month he or she turns age 65 or during the last 3 months of the initial enrollment period, the start day for Medicare coverage will be delayed.

initiative Readiness and ability to take action.

inpatient Patient who has been formally admitted to a hospital for diagnostic tests, medical care and treatment, or a surgical procedure, typically staying overnight.

inpatient prospective payment system (IPPS) The Medicare prospective payment system (PPS) used for acute care hospital inpatient stays.

inpatient psychiatric facility PPS A prospective payment system (PPS) in which federal per diem rates include geographic factors, patient characteristics, and facility characteristics.

inpatient rehabilitation facility (IRF) PPS Reimbursement system activated by the Centers for Medicare and Medicaid Services (CMS) in 2001. Reimbursement is based on the hospital stay, beginning with an admission to the rehabilitation hospital or unit and ending with discharge from that facility.

instructional notes In coding, guidelines and general rules for use in identifying or further defining terms, clarifying information, and/or providing additional digit information in the selection of the appropriate diagnosis code.

instrumental activities of daily living (IADLs) Activities that generally include using the telephone, shopping, preparing meals, keeping house, doing laundry, doing yard work, managing personal finances, and managing medications.

insurance Written agreement (policy) between two entities, whereby one entity (the insurance company) promises to pay a specific sum of money to a second entity (often an individual or another company) if certain specified undesirable events happen.

insurance billing cycle Interaction between a healthcare provider and a third-party payer. The cycle begins when a patient visits a healthcare provider, where a medical record is created or an existing one is updated, and can take several days to several months to complete, depending on the number of exchanges in communication required.

insurance claims register (log) Columnar sheet used to record claims information. This is used as an alternative to a suspension file.

insurance marketplace An organization set up to facilitate the purchase of health insurance in each state in accordance with the Affordable Care Act (ACA).

insured Individual who is covered by an insurer.

insurer Insuring party.

intangible Individuals cannot see or feel them.

integrated delivery system (IDS) A healthcare provider or a network of providers created to integrate hospital services with physician services.

integrity Having honest, ethical, and moral principles.

intermediate care facility Designed for individuals with chronic conditions who are unable to live independently but who do not need constant intensive care. Intermediate care facilities provide supportive care and nursing supervision under medical direction 24 hours a day but do not provide continuous nursing care.

International Classification of Diseases, 10th Revision (ICD-10) Updated version of the ICD manual, released in three volumes from 1992 to 1994. ICD-10 provides increased clinical detail and addresses information regarding previously classified diseases and new diseases discovered since the ninth revision. The ICD-10 diagnostic coding system officially went into effect on October 1, 2015, rendering the ICD-9 system obsolete.

J

job deconditioning When an individual psychologically or physically loses his or her ability to perform normal job duties at the previous level of expertise as a result of being absent from work.

Joint Commission, The The private organization created in 1951 to provide voluntary accreditation to hospitals. The purpose of The Joint Commission is to encourage the attainment of uniformly high standards of institutional medical care by establishing guidelines for the operation of hospitals and other health facilities and conducting survey and accreditation programs.

K

key components Main elements that establish the level in Evaluation and Management (E/M) coding (history, examination, and complexity in medical decision making).

L

labor component Represents labor cost variations among different areas of the United States.

laterality Side of the body on which surgery was performed or which side of the body is affected.

Level I codes American Medical Association (AMA) Physicians' Current Procedural Terminology (CPT) codes. Five-digit codes, accompanied by descriptive terms, are used for reporting services performed by healthcare professionals. Level I codes are developed and updated annually by the AMA.

Level II codes National codes used to report medical services, supplies, drugs, and durable medical equipment not contained in the Level I codes. Codes begin with a single letter, followed by four digits. Level II codes supersede Level I codes for similar encounters, Evaluation and Management (E/M) services, or other procedures and represent the portion of procedures involving supplies and materials. Level II codes are developed and updated annually by the Centers for Medicare and Medicaid Services (CMS) and their contractors.

licensed independent practitioner Defined by The Joint Commission as "any individual permitted by law and by the organization to provide care and services, without direction or supervision, within the scope of the individual's license and consistent with individually granted clinical privileges."

lifetime limits A dollar limit on what a patient would spend for covered benefits during the entire time he or she was enrolled in that plan, after which the patient was required to pay the cost of all care exceeding those limits. Under the Affordable Care Act, lifetime limits on essential benefits are prohibited in any health plan or insurance policy.

lifetime (one-time) release of information form Form that the beneficiary may sign, authorizing a lifetime release of information, instead of signing an information release form annually.

litigious Quick to take legal action (bring lawsuits).

local coverage determination (LCD) Medical-necessity documents that focus exclusively on whether a service is reasonable and necessary according to the International Classification of Diseases, 10th Revision, Clinical Modification (ICD-10-CM) code for that particular Current Procedural Terminology (CPT) procedure code.

Longshore and Harbor Workers' Compensation Act Act that provides workers' compensation to specified employees of private maritime employers.

long-term care Custodial care—as opposed to medical care—typically provided in a nursing home setting. Custodial care involves providing an individual with assistance with or supervision of activities of daily living (ADLs) (or both) that he or she no longer can perform.

long-term care facility Facility that provides care for adults who are chronically ill or disabled and are no longer able to manage in independent living situations.

long-term care hospital (LTCH) PPS Discharge-based prospective payment system (PPS) for long-term care hospitals that replaces the former fee-for-service or cost-based system.

long-term disability Helps replace income for up to 5 years or until the disabled individual turns age 65.

M

main term(s) In diagnostic coding, the identifying word (or words) of a diagnosis that, when located in the Index to

Diseases (Volume 2), aids in locating the correct diagnosis code. Main terms are conditions, nouns, adjectives, and eponyms and are always printed in boldface type for ease of reference.

mainframe computer Used to process large amounts of data. It can control thousands of users. Originally, the data shared from these platforms were typically sent to billing services.

maintenance of effort (MOE) A requirement under the Affordable Care Act that states spend at least a specified amount of state funds for federal assistance program purposes.

managed care Medical care that is provided by a corporation established under state and federal laws. This corporation makes medical decisions for its enrollees. Managed care organizations contract with healthcare providers and medical facilities to provide care to their members at a reduced cost. A managed care provider tells patients which physicians they can see, monitors the medications and treatments prescribed, and ensures that their enrollees' costs will remain as low as possible. For these services, enrollees pay a set insurance premium each year and a small copayment with each visit.

managed care organizations (MCOs) Healthcare delivery system that attempts to keep costs down by "managing" the care to eliminate unnecessary treatment and reduce expensive hospital care. The most familiar models are health maintenance organizations (HMOs) and preferred provider organizations (PPOs).

managed healthcare Any system of health payment or delivery arrangement in which the health plan attempts to control or coordinate the use of health services by its enrolled members to contain health expenditures, improve quality, or both. Under managed healthcare plans, patients see designated providers, and benefits are paid according to the structure of the managed care plan.

mandated Medigap transfer Claim for which a beneficiary elects to assign his or her benefits under a Medigap policy to a participating physician or supplier.

mandated (or mandatory) services Certain basic services that must be offered to the categorically needy population in any state Medicaid program.

manifestation A sign or symptom of a disease.

Maternal and Child Health Services Federal–state partnership under the Title V Block Grant enacted to achieve the goal to improve the health of all mothers and children consistent with the health status goals and national health objectives established by the Secretary of the US Department of Health and Human Services (HHS).

meaningful use The practice of physicians and hospitals using certified electronic medical record (EMR) technology in a meaningful manner as an incentive of a program established by congressional legislation.

Medicaid Combination federal and state medical assistance program designed to provide comprehensive and quality medical care for low-income families with special emphasis on children, pregnant women, elderly adults, disabled individuals, and parents with dependent children who have no other way to pay for healthcare. Coverage varies from state to state.

Medicaid contractor (fiscal intermediary) Commercial insurer contracted by the US Department of Health and Human Services (HHS) for the purpose of processing and administering Medicaid claims.

Medicaid expansion The process of increasing the number of people enrolled in Medicaid by making it easier for people to qualify for Medicaid. It is called *Medicaid expansion* because enrolling more people expands the list of those receiving Medicaid benefits.

Medicaid Integrity Program (MIP) A comprehensive federal policy established to prevent and reduce provider fraud, waste, and abuse in the Medicaid program.

Medicaid secondary claim Type of claim that occurs when the beneficiary has two healthcare coverages: medical insurance coverage (e.g., commercial or group policies) or dual coverage with traditional (original) Medicare enrollment. In such cases, Medicaid is the payer of last resort.

Medicaid "simple" claim When the patient has Medicaid coverage only and no secondary insurance.

medical ethics Code of conduct for the healthcare profession. Basic principles usually include showing respect for patient autonomy, not inflicting harm on patients, contributing to the welfare of patients, and providing justice and fair treatment of patients.

medical etiquette Following the rules and conventions governing correct or polite behavior in the healthcare profession.

medical (health) record Clinical, scientific, administrative, and legal document of facts containing statements relating to a patient. It incorporates scientific data and scientific events in chronological order regarding the case history, clinical examination, investigative procedures, diagnosis, treatment of the patient, and his or her response to the treatment.

medical necessity For a procedure or service to qualify for payment under the medically necessary principle, it must be consistent with the diagnosis and in accordance with the standards of good medical practice, performed at the proper level, and provided in the most appropriate setting.

medical savings account (MSA) Special tax shelter set up for the purpose of paying medical bills. Known as the *Archer MSA,* it is similar to an individual retirement account (IRA) and works in conjunction with a special low-cost, high-deductible health insurance policy to provide comprehensive healthcare coverage at the lowest possible net cost for individuals who qualify. MSAs are currently limited to self-employed people and employees of small businesses with fewer than 50 employees. Also called *health savings account (HSA).*

medically necessary Medical services, procedures, or supplies that are reasonable and necessary for the diagnosis or treatment of a patient's medical condition, in accordance with the standards of good medical practice, performed at the proper level, and provided in the most appropriate setting.

medically needy Individuals who do not qualify in the categorically needy program (because of excess income or resources) but need help to pay for excessive medical expenses.

Medicare Comprehensive federal insurance program established by Congress in 1966 that provides financial assistance with medical expenses to individuals 65 years old or older and individuals younger than 65 years with certain disabilities.

Medicare administrative contractor (MAC) Private insurance companies that serve as agents of the federal government in the administration of the Medicare program, including the payment of claims.

Medicare audits Generally designed to determine whether a provider has been reimbursed by the Medicare program for services that are properly reimbursable (i.e., medically necessary). These audits are typically based on (1) random reviews, (2) prior problems or unusual billing patterns, or (3) a certain kind of billing problem that the carrier is focusing on.

Medicare Beneficiary Identifier (MBI) Format of 11 alphanumeric digits. These characters are randomly generated.

Medicare gaps Uninsured areas under Medicare with which elderly and disabled Americans need additional help.

Medicare limiting charge In the original Medicare plan, the highest amount of money a Medicare beneficiary can be charged for a covered service by physicians and other healthcare suppliers who do not accept assignment. The limiting charge is 15% over Medicare's "approved amount." The limiting charge applies only to certain services and does not apply to supplies or equipment.

Medicare managed care plan Health maintenance organization (HMO) or preferred provider organization (PPO) that uses

Medicare to pay for part of its services for eligible beneficiaries. It provides all basic Medicare benefits, plus some additional coverages (depending on the plan) to fill the gaps Medicare does not pay.

Medicare nonparticipating provider (nonPAR) Provider or supplier who has not signed a contract with Medicare and may choose whether to accept Medicare's approved amount as payment on a case-by-case basis. If they do not accept the approved amount, the beneficiary pays the full billed amount.

Medicare Part A Hospital insurance. Medicare Part A helps pay for medically necessary services, including inpatient hospital care, inpatient care in a skilled nursing facility (SNF), home healthcare, and hospice care.

Medicare Part B Medical (physicians' care) insurance financed by a combination of federal government funds and beneficiary premiums.

Medicare Part C (Medicare Advantage Plans) Prepaid healthcare plans that offer regular Part A and Part B Medicare coverage in addition to coverage for other services. Formerly called *Medicare+Choice.*

Medicare Part D (Prescription Drug Plan) Pays a portion of prescription drug expenses and cost-sharing for qualifying individuals.

Medicare participating provider (PAR) Provider or supplier who has signed a contract with Medicare and agrees to accept the allowed amount by Medicare as payment in full.

Medicare savings programs (MSPs) Also known as *Medicare buy-in programs,* all MSPs save the Medicare beneficiary money by paying for the Part B premium. MSPs may also pay for Part A premiums, depending on income and assets. For most people, Part A is free, but if the beneficiary or the beneficiary's spouse has not worked enough to qualify for free Part A, he or she must pay a Part A premium.

Medicare secondary payer (MSP) Term used when Medicare is not responsible for paying first because the beneficiary is covered under another insurance policy.

Medicare secondary payer (MSP) claims When a patient has other health insurance coverage, such as a group health policy, that payer becomes primary, and Medicare becomes the secondary payer. When the primary payer has processed the claim, an MSP claim is submitted to Medicare, along with the explanation of benefits from the primary payer.

Medicare Severity (MS)–DRG System The Centers for Medicare and Medicaid Services' (CMS's) new, restructured diagnosis-related group (DRG) system, which began on October 1, 2007, in which DRG weights are adjusted based on the severity of a patient's condition. This new system is expected to account for the severity of a patient's condition more accurately. Previously, the Medicare system used 538 DRGs; the new system uses 745 MS-DRGs.

Medicare Summary Notice (MSN) Monthly statement that the beneficiary receives from Medicare after a claim is filed. The statement lists Part A and Part B claims information, including the patient's deductible status.

Medicare Supplement plans Private insurance plans specifically designed to provide coverage for some of the services that Medicare does not pay, such as Medicare's deductible and coinsurance amounts and for certain services not allowed by Medicare. Also called *Medigap insurance.*

Medicare supplement policy Health insurance plan sold by private insurance companies to help pay for healthcare expenses not covered by Medicare and its deductibles and coinsurance.

Medicare whistleblowers Typically healthcare professionals who are aware of hospitals, clinics, pharmacies, nursing homes, hospice facilities, long-term care, and other healthcare facilities that routinely overcharge or seek reimbursement from government programs for medical services not rendered, drugs not used, beds not slept in, and ambulance rides not taken.

Medigap Insurance policies sold by private insurance companies to fill "gaps" in the original (fee-for-service) Medicare plan coverage. Policies are specifically designed to supplement Medicare benefits. *See* Medicare Supplement plans.

Medigap crossover program Process whereby beneficiary claims data are automatically transmitted (usually electronically) from a Medicare administrative contractor to a supplemental insurance policy for additional payment after Medicare has determined its obligatory payment. The process is activated when a participating (PAR) Medicare provider (1) includes a specific identifier—a coordination of benefit agreements (COBA) identification (ID) number—on the claim and (2) assigns payment benefits to that provider.

Medigap insurance Designed specifically to supplement Medicare benefits and regulated by federal and state law. A Medigap policy must be clearly identified as Medicare Supplement insurance, and it must provide specific benefits that help fill the gaps in Medicare coverage.

mentally competent Capable of understanding the legal implications of entering into a contract in the eyes of the law.

Merchant Marine Act (Jones Act) Act that provides seafarers (individuals involved in transporting goods by water between US ports) with the same protection from employer negligence that the Federal Employers' Liability Act (FELA) provides railroad workers.

metal plans (metal levels) Health plans that are grouped by levels of coverage—how much the plan will pay for healthcare and what services are covered. Each level is named after a type of metal: bronze, silver, and gold, with a bronze plan providing "basic" coverage, which has the fewest benefits, lowest premium, and highest out-of-pocket costs.

Military Health System (MHS) Total healthcare system of the US uniformed services. The system includes military treatment facilities and various programs in the civilian healthcare market, such as TRICARE.

military treatment facility (MTF) Clinic or hospital operated by the US Department of Defense (DoD) and located on a military base that provides care to military personnel, their dependents, and military retirees and their dependents.

minimum essential coverage The minimum amount that a "large" employer (one with more than 50 full-time employees) must provide to its employees under the Affordable Care Act.

mixed model Describes certain health maintenance organization (HMO) plans in which the provider network is a combination of delivery systems. In general, a mixed-model HMO offers the widest variety of choices and the broadest geographic coverage to its members.

modified adjusted gross income (MAGI) A person's adjusted gross income plus any tax-exempt Social Security, interest, or other income.

modified own-occupation policy Covers workers for their own occupation as long as they are not gainfully employed elsewhere. This policy is a variation of own-occupation policies.

modifier(s) Words that are added to main terms to supply more specific information about a patient's clinical picture. Modifiers provide the means by which the reporting healthcare provider can indicate that a service or procedure performed has been altered by some specific circumstance but has not changed its definition or code.

modifying terms Descriptive words indented under the main term that provide further description of a procedure or service. A main term can have up to three modifying terms. In Current Procedural Terminology (CPT) coding, modifying terms often influence the selection of the appropriate procedural code. *See also* modifier(s).

morbidity Presence of illness or disease.

morphology In medicine, morphology refers to the size, shape, and structure, rather than the function, of a given organ.

For example, as a diagnostic imaging technique, ultrasound assists in the recognition of abnormal morphologies as symptoms of underlying conditions.

mortality Deaths that occur from a disease.

multiaxial structure Code configuration wherein each character has the same meaning within the specific procedure section and across procedure sections to the extent possible, meaning that each seven-character alphanumeric code has a section corresponding to descriptive subsections, such as anatomy or surgical approach. Only the designation of the first character is fixed to a defined section. The roles of the other six characters are assigned depending on the preceding character. For a code in section 0 (medical and surgical), the codes that follow are body system, root operation, body part, approach, device, and qualifier, with an actual set of codes for each succeeding character fixed by the preceding one.

N

National Committee for Quality Assurance (NCQA) Independent, nonprofit organization that performs quality-oriented accreditation reviews on health maintenance organizations (HMOs) and similar types of managed care plans. The purpose of NCQA is to evaluate plans and to provide information that helps consumers and employers make informed decisions about purchasing health plan services.

National Correct Coding Initiative (NCCI) Implemented by the Centers for Medicare and Medicaid Services (CMS) in 1996 to control improper coding that leads to inappropriate increased payment for healthcare services.

national coverage determination (NCD) A nationwide determination of whether Medicare will pay for an item or service. Medicare coverage is limited to items and services that are considered "reasonable and necessary" for the diagnosis or treatment of an illness or injury.

national provider identifier (NPI) Standard unique identifier required by the Health Insurance Portability and Accountability Act (HIPAA) and assigned to all healthcare providers, health plans, and employers that identifies them on standard transactions. The NPI is a 10-digit "intelligence-free" number, meaning that the number does not carry any information about the provider, such as the state in which he or she practices or type of specialization.

National Uniform Billing Committee (NUBC) Created by the American Hospital Association (AHA) in 1975 and includes the participation of all major provider and payer organizations in the United States. NUBC was formed to develop a single billing form and standard data set that could be used nationwide by institutional providers and payers for handling healthcare claims.

NEC (not elsewhere classifiable) Abbreviation in the International Classification of Diseases, 10th Revision, Clinical Modification (ICD-10-CM) Index that represents "other specified." When a specific code is not available for a condition in the Index, the coder is directed to the "other specified" code in the Tabular, where an NEC entry under a code identifies it as the "other specified" code.

negligence Failure to exercise a reasonable degree of care.

neoplasm New growth, often resulting in a tumor.

network Interrelated system of people and facilities that communicate with one another and work together as a unit. An approved list of physicians, hospitals, and other providers is created.

network model Health maintenance organization (HMO) that has multiple provider arrangements, including staff, group, or individual practice association structures.

network providers Healthcare providers who have signed an agreement with third-party payers (or, in the case of TRICARE, the regional contractor) to provide care at prenegotiated rates—usually less than the allowable charge—as the full fee for the services they render.

new patient Person who is new to the practice, regardless of location of service, or one who has not received any medical treatment by the healthcare provider or any other provider in that same office within the past 3 years.

no-fault insurance In workers' compensation insurance, benefits are paid to the injured (or ill) worker, regardless of who is to blame for the accident or injury.

nonavailability statement (NAS) Document of certification from the military treatment facility (MTF) that says it cannot provide the specific healthcare that the beneficiary needs at that facility. The statements must be entered electronically in the US Department of Defense's (DoD's) Defense Enrollment Eligibility Reporting System (DEERS) computer files by the MTF.

noncovered services Situations in which an item or service is not covered under Medicare.

nonessential modifiers Terms in parentheses immediately following the main terms. Typically, these terms are alternative terminology for the main term and are provided to assist the coder in locating the applicable main term. Nonessential modifiers are usually not a part of the diagnostic statement.

nonlabor component One of the two figures used for calculating diagnosis-related group (DRG) payments. The DRG weight is multiplied by a standardized amount, which is the sum of a non-labor component that represents a geographic calculation based on whether the hospital is located in a large urban or other area and a labor component that is adjusted by a wage index.

non-network providers TRICARE-authorized providers who, although they must be certified, do not sign a contractual agreement with the TRICARE regional contractors.

nonparticipating provider (nonPAR) Provider who has no contractual agreement with the insurance carrier; the provider does not have to accept the insurance company's reimbursement as payment in full.

NOS (not otherwise specified) Abbreviation that is the equivalent of "unspecified," meaning that a more specific diagnosis is unavailable. Before assigning an NOS code, the coder should examine the medical record more closely or question the physician or provider for more complete documentation.

O

objectivity Not influenced by personal feelings, biases, or prejudice.

observation When a patient is kept in the hospital for a short time while providers determine whether the individual is sick enough to require inpatient treatment.

observation care The identification of the status of care during the period when a patient is kept in the hospital for a short time while physicians determine whether the individual is sick enough to require inpatient treatment.

occupational therapy Skilled treatment for ill or injured individuals that facilitates their return to ordinary tasks around the home or at work (or both) by maximizing physical potential through lifestyle adaptations, sometimes through the use of assistive devices.

offer In contract law, proposition to create a contract.

ombudsman Individual who is responsible for investigating and resolving workers' complaints against the employer or insurance company that is denying the benefits.

open-panel plan Plan in which the providers maintain their own offices and identities and see patients who belong to a health maintenance organization (HMO) and patients who do not. Healthcare providers in the community may participate if they meet certain HMO or individual practice association standards.

optical character recognition (OCR) Recognition of printed or written text characters by a computer.

other health insurance (OHI) TRICARE-eligible beneficiary has other healthcare coverage besides TRICARE Standard,

Extra, or Prime through an employer, an association, or a private insurer, or if a student in the family has a healthcare plan obtained through his or her school. Also called *double coverage* or *coordination of benefits (COB)*.

outliers Atypical patients.

out-of-pocket maximum After a patient has paid a certain amount of medical expenses, the usual, customary, and reasonable (UCR; allowed) fee for covered benefits is paid in full by the insurer.

outpatient Patient who has not been officially admitted to a hospital but receives diagnostic tests or treatment in that facility or a clinic connected with it.

outpatient prospective payment system (OPPS) The Medicare prospective payment system (PPS) used for hospital-based outpatient services and procedures.

own-occupation policy Covers workers who are unable to perform in the occupation or job that they were doing before the disability occurred.

P

packaging Reimbursement for certain services or supplies is included in the payment for another procedure or service on the same claim.

palliative care Care given to improve the quality of life of patients who have a serious or life-threatening disease. The goal of palliative care is to prevent or treat the symptoms of the disease and side effects caused by treatment of the disease as early and effectively as possible. Also called *comfort care, supportive care,* and *symptom management*.

paraphrase Rephrasing or summarizing important facts in your own words.

partial (blended) capitation A reimbursement model in which only certain categories of services are paid on a capitated basis as opposed to traditional capitated models of reimbursement in which healthcare providers are paid a flat, per-patient fee for all covered services.

participating provider (PAR) Provider who contracts with the third-party payer and agrees to abide by certain rules and regulations of that carrier.

party of the first part (first party) In legal language, the patient in the implied contract between the physician and patient.

party of the second part (second party) In legal language, healthcare provider in the implied contract between the physician and patient.

party of the third part (third party) In legal language, the insurance company in the implied contract between the physician and the patient.

pass-throughs Temporary payments for specified new technologies, drugs, devices, and biologics for which costs were unavailable when calculating ambulatory payment classification payment rates.

patient centric Putting the patient at the center of the decisions, resources, and desired outcomes and providing the necessary information that empowers patients to become involved in making decisions regarding their own treatment.

patient information form Form that medical offices usually require new patients to fill out. The form asks for information, such as name, address, employer, and health insurance information.

patient ledger Chronological accounting of activities of a particular patient (or family), including all charges and payments.

patient ledger card Accounting form on which professional service descriptions, charges, payments, adjustments, and current balance are posted chronologically.

Patient Protection and Affordable Care Act (PPACA) *See* Affordable Care Act.

patient-centered medical home (PCMH) A reimbursement model wherein healthcare practices attempt to improve the quality, effectiveness, and efficiency of the care they deliver while responding to each patient's unique needs and preferences, ideally leading to higher quality and lower costs while improving both patients' and providers' experience of care.

pay for performance A reimbursement model based on the quality and utility of care provided rather than on the sheer volume of services—paying "value over volume" or "paying for performance."

pay-and-chase claims When the state Medicaid agency pays the medical bills and then attempts to recover these paid funds from liable third parties.

payer of last resort After all other available third-party resources meet their legal obligation to pay claims, the Medicaid program pays for the care of an individual eligible for Medicaid.

payroll journal Listing of wages and salaries.

peer review organization (PRO) A group of practicing healthcare professionals that is paid by the federal government to evaluate the care provided to Medicare beneficiaries in each state and to improve the quality of services. PROs act to educate and assist in the promotion of effective, efficient, and economic delivery of health services to the Medicare population they serve.

per diem rates Actual costs per day.

permanent and stationary When a condition reaches a state of maximal medical improvement.

permanent disability Level of disability where the ill or injured employee's condition is such that it is impossible to return to work. There are two classifications of permanent disability: permanent partial disability and permanent total disability.

permanent partial disability When a disability prevents an individual from performing one or more occupational functions but does not impair his or her capability to perform less demanding employment.

permanent total disability When an individual's ability to work at any occupation is totally and permanently lost.

Physician Quality Reporting System (PQRS) A reporting system, previously called the *Physician Quality Reporting Initiative,* established by the Tax Relief and Health Care Act (TRHCA) of 2006, which included an incentive payment for eligible professionals who satisfactorily reported data on quality measures for covered services furnished to Medicare beneficiaries. The Medicare, Medicaid, and State Children's Health Insurance Program (SCHIP) Extension Act of 2007 authorized a financial incentive for participation in this program.

Physicians' Current Procedural Terminology, 4th edition (CPT-4) Manual containing a list of descriptive terms and identifying codes used in reporting medical services and procedures performed and supplies used by physicians and other professional healthcare providers in the care and treatment of patients.

placeholder character ("X") International Classification of Diseases, 10th Revision, Clinical Modification (ICD-10-CM) uses the letter "X" as a placeholder character. It has two uses: (1) as the fifth character for certain six-character codes, "X" provides for future expansion without disturbing the six-character structure; and (2) when a code has fewer than six characters and a seventh character extension is required, "X" is assigned for all characters fewer than six to meet the requirement of coding to the highest level of specificity.

plaintiff Party bringing a lawsuit.

Plan to Achieve Self-Support (PASS) A provision under Supplemental Security Income (SSI) to help individuals with disabilities return to work. PASS allows disabled individuals to set aside money and/or resources or assets to pay for items or services needed to achieve a specific work goal.

point of service (POS) plan "Hybrid" type of managed care that allows patients to either use the health maintenance organization (HMO) provider or go outside the plan and use any provider they choose. Also called *open-ended HMO*.

policy Written agreement between two parties, whereby one entity (the insurance company) promises to pay a specific sum of money to a second entity (often an individual or another company) if certain specified undesirable events occur.

policyholder Individual in whose name the policy is written; the insured.

portability According to the Health Insurance Portability and Accountability Act (HIPAA), people with preexisting medical conditions cannot be denied health insurance coverage when moving from one employer-sponsored group healthcare plan to another.

practice management software Type of software that deals with the day-to-day operations of a medical practice. It allows users to enter patient demographic information, schedule appointments, maintain lists of insurance payers, perform billing tasks, and generate reports.

preauthorization Cost-containment procedure required by most managed healthcare and indemnity plans before a provider carries out specific procedures or treatments for a patient. The insured must contact the insurer before hospitalization or surgery and receive prior approval for the service. Preauthorization does not guarantee payment.

precertification Process whereby the provider (or a member of his or her staff) contacts the patient's managed care plan before inpatient admissions and performance of certain procedures and services to verify the patient's eligibility and coverage for the planned service.

predetermination of benefits Method used by some insurance companies to find out whether a specific medical service or procedure would be covered. Most insurance companies request a written statement from the healthcare provider with the specific Current Procedural Terminology (CPT) codes for the proposed procedures before providing a predetermination of benefits.

preexisting condition A physical or mental condition of an insured individual that existed before the issuance of a health insurance policy or that existed before issuance and for which treatment was received. Preexisting conditions are excluded from coverage under some policies, or a specified length of time must elapse before the condition is covered.

preferred drug (list) Developed to keep drug costs under control. It classifies prescription drugs into three categories, or tiers. Tier 1 consists of generic drugs that can be purchased for the lowest copayment and are equivalent to their nonpreferred brand-name drug counterparts. Tier 2 includes preferred brand-name drugs for which generic equivalents are not available and can be purchased for moderate copayments. Tier 3 drugs are nonpreferred brand-name drugs for which generic equivalents may or may not be available and have the highest copayment.

preferred provider organization (PPO) Group of hospitals and physicians that agree to render particular services to a group of people, generally under contract with a private insurer. These services may be furnished at discounted rates if the members receive their healthcare from member providers, rather than selecting a provider outside the network.

premium A periodic fee that a fee-for-service policyholder must pay to the insurance company in exchange for financial protection against loss.

premium reimbursement arrangement (PRA) An employee health benefits option in which employers allow their employees to reimburse themselves for their individual health insurance costs with pretax wages, resulting in an immediate savings on their health insurance premiums.

present on admission (POA) Present at the time the order for inpatient admission occurs.

preventive medicine Practice that focuses on overall health and the prevention of illness. Some insurance policies pay medical expenses even if the individual is not sick or injured, because it is often less costly to keep a person well or detect an emerging illness in its early stages when it is more treatable than possibly having to pay more exorbitant expenses later on should that individual become seriously ill.

preventive services Certain routine healthcare that includes checkups, patient counseling, and screenings to prevent illness, disease, and other health-related problems—and treatments for adults and children with no out-of-pocket costs such as copayments, coinsurance, or the need to meet a deductible.

pricing transparency Sharing information so that people know up front what their healthcare will cost. For example, some hospitals now put their prices on the Internet.

primary care physician (PCP) In a preferred provider organization (PPO) plan, the specific provider who oversees the member's total healthcare treatment.

primary care preferred provider organizations Point of service (POS) plans that are "hybrids," or a mixture, of the characteristics of the more traditional health maintenance organization (HMO) and preferred provider organization (PPO) models, though they are licensed as PPOs.

principal diagnosis Reason for admission to the acute care facility.

prioritize To organize by importance.

privacy Right to be left alone and to maintain individual autonomy, solitude, intimacy, and control over information about oneself.

privacy standards Intended to define what are appropriate and inappropriate disclosures of individually identifiable health information and how patient rights are to be protected.

privacy statement Statement patients are asked to sign when they visit their healthcare providers. The statement includes information about who the physician or pharmacy shares health information with and why and outlines what rights patients have to access their own health information.

professional ethics Moral principles associated with a specific vocation.

Program of All-Inclusive Care for the Elderly (PACE) Program that provides comprehensive alternative care for noninstitutionalized elderly individuals, 55 years old and older, who would otherwise be in a nursing home. A multidisciplinary team composed of a physician, nurse, therapists, dietitian, social worker, home care coordinator, and transportation supervisor completes an initial and semiannual assessment of each participant with a documented plan of treatment.

progress or supplemental report Report that a physician must file to keep the employer and insurance carrier apprised of a patient's treatment plan, progress, and status in workers' compensation cases.

Promoting Interoperability Replaces an earlier program called "Meaningful Use."

prospective payment system (PPS) Medicare reimbursement system for inpatient hospital costs based on predetermined factors and not on individual services. Rates are set at a level intended to cover operating costs for treating a typical inpatient in a given diagnosis-related group (DRG). Payments for each hospital are adjusted for various factors, such as differences in area wages, teaching activity, and care to the poor.

protected health information (PHI) Identifiable health information that is protected under the Health Insurance Portability and Accountability Act (HIPAA) Privacy Rule.

provider-sponsored organization (PSO) Group of medical providers—physicians, clinics, and hospitals—that skips the insurance company intermediary and contracts directly with patients. Members pay a premium and a copayment each time a service is rendered.

puerperium The 6-week period of time after childbirth.

Q

quality improvement organization (QIO) Program that works with consumers, physicians, hospitals, and other caregivers to refine care delivery systems to ensure that patients get the right care at the right time, particularly among underserved populations. The program also safeguards the integrity of the Medicare trust fund by ensuring that payment is made only for medically necessary services, and it investigates beneficiary complaints about quality of care.

quality review study Assessment of patient care designed to achieve measurable improvement in processes and outcomes of care. Improvements are achieved through interventions that target healthcare providers, practitioners, plans, or beneficiaries.

R

real-time claims adjudication (RTCA) Means of electronic communication that allows instant resolution of an insurance claim, including the third-party insurer's payment, adjustment, and patient responsibility.

reasonable and customary fee Commonly charged or prevailing fee for a specific health procedure or service within a geographic area.

reciprocity When one state allows Medicaid beneficiaries from other states (usually states that are adjacent) to be treated in its medical facilities.

recovery audit contractor (RAC) The job of an RAC is to detect and correct past improper payments so that Centers for Medicare and Medicaid Services (CMS) and carriers, fiscal intermediaries, and Medicare administrative contractors (MACs) can implement actions that prevent future improper payments. Providers who bill Medicare on a fee-for-service (FFS) basis are subject to review by RACs.

referral Request by a healthcare provider for a patient under his or her care to be evaluated or treated (or both) by another provider, usually a specialist.

regional contractor The head of a TRICARE region whose responsibility it is to provide beneficiaries with healthcare services and support in addition to what services are available at military treatment facilities (MTFs).

Registered Health Information Technician (RHIT) Technicians who pass a written examination offered by the American Health Information Management Association (AHIMA).

reimbursement Payment to an insured individual for a covered expense or loss experienced by or on behalf of the insured.

relative value scale (RVS) Method of determining reimbursement for medical services based on establishing a standard unit value for medical and surgical procedures. RVS compares and rates each individual service according to the relative value of each unit and converts this unit value to a dollar value.

relative value unit A nationally uniform relative value for the specific medical service calculated with use of components of work, practice overhead, and professional liability.

relative weight The relative effort required to perform a specific procedure that has been prospectively established for the service's clinical ambulatory payment classification (APC).

release of information Form signed by the patient authorizing a release of medical information necessary to complete the insurance claim form. Typically, a release of information is valid for only 1 year.

remittance advice (RA) Paper or electronic form sent by Medicare to the service provider that explains how payment was determined for a claim (or claims). Formerly called *explanation of benefits (EOB)*.

remittance remark codes Codes that represent nonfinancial information on a Medicare remittance advice (RA).

resource-based relative value system (RBRVS) Method on which Medicare bases its payments for physicians' services. The federal government established RBRVS as a standardized physician payment schedule determined by the resource costs necessary to provide the service or procedure rather than the actual fees typically charged by the physician. It was designed to address the increasing cost of healthcare in the United States and to try to resolve the inequities between geographic areas, time in practice, and the current payment schedule. It replaces the Medicare fee system.

resource utilization groups (RUGs) Used to calculate reimbursement in a skilled nursing facility (SNF) according to severity and level of care. Under the Medicare prospective payment system (PPS), patients are classified into an RUG that determines how much Medicare would pay the SNF per day for that patient.

respite care Provides individuals (such as family members) with temporary relief from tasks associated with providing care in the home for frail or disabled individuals.

respondeat superior Key principle in business law that says that an employer is responsible for the actions of his or her employees in the course of employment.

retroactive eligibility A time period (typically 3 months) when a Medicaid beneficiary can qualify for reimbursement when there is an unpaid medical bill for a service provided immediately before the month of application, providing that the individual meets all eligibility criteria.

S

secondary claim Claim that the secondary insurer (the insurance company that pays after the primary carrier) receives after the primary insurer pays its monetary obligations.

secondary diagnosis A condition that coexists at the time of admission and/or that develops subsequently and requires one or more of the following: clinical evaluation, therapeutic treatment, diagnostic procedures, extended length of hospital stay, and increased nursing care and/or monitoring.

section One of four classifications in the Tabular section (Volume 1) of the Current Procedural Terminology (CPT) manual. This section (e.g., Surgery or Radiology) is one of the six major areas into which all CPT codes and descriptions are categorized.

security standards Standards that need to be developed and adopted for all health plans, clearinghouses, and providers to follow and to be required at all stages of transmission and storage of healthcare information to ensure integrity and confidentiality of the records at all phases of the process, before, during, and after electronic transmission.

see Used as a cross-reference term in the Current Procedural Terminology (CPT) Alphabetic Index and directs the coder to an alternative main term.

self-insured When the employer—not an insurance company—is responsible for the cost of medical services for its employees.

self-pay patient Patient who may have inadequate health insurance coverage or no insurance at all.

self-referring When a member of a managed healthcare group can receive services from specialists without first going through a primary care physician (PCP).

Senior Health Insurance Information Program (SHIIP) A national program through which volunteers counsel Medicare beneficiaries and caregivers about Medicare, Medicare supplements, Medicare Advantage, Medicare Part D, Medicaid, and long-term care insurance. The counselors offer free and unbiased information on Medicare healthcare products. SHIIP volunteers also help people recognize and prevent Medicare billing errors and possible fraud and abuse through the Senior Medicare Patrol (SMP) Program.

sequela (*pl.* sequelae) Residual conditions produced after the acute phase of an illness or injury has ended. Also called *late effects*.

seventh character (*see also* 7th character) Certain International Classification of Diseases, 10th Revision, Clinical Modification

(ICD-10-CM) categories require an extension to provide further specificity about the condition being coded. The applicable seventh character is required for all codes within the category or as the notes indicate in the Tabular instructions. This extension may be a number or letter and must always be the seventh character. If a code that requires a seventh character is not six characters long, a placeholder "X" must be used to fill in the empty characters.

short-stay outlier Adjustment to the federal payment rate for long-term care hospital (LTCH) stays that are considerably shorter than the average length of stay for an LTCH diagnosis-related group (DRG).

short-term disability Coverage that pays a percentage of an individual's wages or salary if and when he or she becomes temporarily disabled.

single or specialty service plans Health plans that provide services only in certain health specialties, such as mental health, vision, or dentistry.

skilled nursing facility (SNF) Institution or a distinct part of an institution that is licensed or approved under state or local law and is primarily engaged in providing skilled nursing or skilled rehabilitation services to patients who need skilled medical care that cannot be provided in a custodial-level nursing home or in the patient's home.

skilled nursing facility (SNF) PPS A per diem reimbursement system for all costs (routine, ancillary, and capital) associated with covered SNF services furnished to Medicare beneficiaries. Per diem rates are a hospital's all-inclusive daily rates as calculated by department. SNF PPS rates are adjusted for case mix and geographic variation in wages and cover all costs of furnishing covered SNF services.

small claims litigation Process administered by the services at local county or district courts that makes it easy for individuals or businesses to recover legitimate debts without using expensive legal advisors. Small claims suits can be for any amount of money up to a limiting threshold that varies by state, usually $3000 to $5000.

small (entity) provider Provider of services with fewer than 25 full-time equivalent employees or a physician, practitioner, facility, or supplier (other than a provider of services) with fewer than 10 full-time equivalent employees.

small provider of services Hospital, critical access hospital, skilled nursing facility (SNF), comprehensive outpatient rehabilitation facility, home health agency, or hospice program with fewer than 25 full-time equivalent employees.

small supplier Physician, practitioner, facility, or supplier with fewer than 10 full-time equivalent employees.

Social Security Disability Insurance (SSDI) (1) Primary federal insurance program that protects workers from loss of income resulting from disability and provides monthly cash benefits to disabled workers younger than age 65 and to certain dependents. (2) Insurance program for individuals who become unable to work. It is administered by the Social Security Administration (SSA) and funded by Federal Insurance Contributions Act (FICA) tax withheld from workers' pay and by matching employer contributions. SSDI pays qualifying disabled workers cash and healthcare benefits.

special enrollment period A time period during which individuals eligible for Medicare coverage who postponed enrollment when first eligible due to specific circumstances (e.g., he or she was covered under a group health plan) can sign up without penalty.

special needs plan (SNP) Type of Medicare Advantage plan designed to attract and enroll Medicare beneficiaries who fall into a certain special needs classification. There are two types of SNPs. The exclusive SNP enrolls only beneficiaries who fall into the special needs demographic. The other type is the disproportionate share SNP.

special report Report that accompanies the claim to help determine the appropriateness and medical necessity of the service or procedure. It is required by many third-party payers when a rarely used, unusual, variable, or new service or procedure is performed.

specialist Physician who is trained in a certain area of medicine.

spend down Depleting private or family finances to the point where the individual or family becomes eligible for Medicaid assistance.

sponsor Under the TRICARE plan, a service member, whether in active duty, retired, or deceased.

staff model Closed panel–type of health maintenance organization (HMO) in which a multispecialty group of physicians is contracted to provide healthcare to members of an HMO and is compensated by the contractor via salary and incentive programs.

stand-alone code Current Procedural Terminology (CPT) code that contains the full description of the procedure without additional explanation.

standard paper remittance (SPR) Product of the standardization of the provider payment notification of the Centers for Medicare and Medicaid Services (CMS). The form was created to provide a document that is uniform in content and format and to ease the transition to the electronic remittance format.

standardized amount Figure representing the average cost per case for all Medicare cases during the year.

subacute care facility Comprehensive, highly specialized inpatient program designed for an individual who has had an acute event as a result of an illness, injury, or worsening of a disease process. It specifies a level of maintenance care in which there is no urgent or life-threatening condition requiring medical treatment.

subcategory In the Current Procedural Terminology (CPT) Evaluation and Management (E/M) section, codes are divided into categories and subcategories. A category would be Office or Other Outpatient Services; a subcategory under it could be either New Patient or Established Patient. In the International Classification of Diseases, 10th Revision, Clinical Modification (ICD-10-CM) coding system, there are three-digit category codes, usually followed by a fourth or fifth digit set of subcategory codes.

subheading One of four classifications in the Tabular section (Volume 1) of the Current Procedural Terminology (CPT) manual. *See* subsection.

subjective information Biased or personal information. For example, a patient's history is based on what the patient tells the healthcare provider in his or her own words.

subpoena *duces tecum* Legal document that requires an individual to appear in court with a piece of evidence that can be used or inspected by the court.

subrogation The process wherein an insurance company pays the policyholder for losses incurred and then attempts to recover claim amounts paid from a negligent third party.

subsection One of four classifications in the Tabular section (Volume 1) of the Current Procedural Terminology (CPT) manual that divides sections further into smaller units, usually by body system.

subsidies Financial assistance from government sources with which individuals can purchase low-cost health insurance.

supplemental coverage Benefit add-ons to health plans, such as vision, dental, or prescription drug coverage.

Supplemental Security Income (SSI) Program established in 1972 and controlled by the Social Security Administration (SSA) that provides federally funded cash assistance to qualifying elderly and disabled poor individuals.

surrogate Substitute.

suspension file Series of files set up chronologically and labeled according to the number of days since the claim was submitted. This type of claims tracking system is used by offices that file paper claims.

swing bed Changes in reimbursement status when patients "swing" from receiving acute care services and reimbursement to receiving skilled nursing services and reimbursement.

T

Tax Equity and Fiscal Responsibility Act (TEFRA) Law enacted by Congress in 1982 to place limits on Medicare reimbursement that applies to stays in long-term acute care hospitals. After TEFRA was passed, the fee-for-service (FFS)–based payment system was replaced with a prospective payment system (PPS).

telehealth (telehealth communication) The use of technology to deliver healthcare, health information, or health education from a distance using an interactive, two-way telecommunications system by an eligible provider who is not at the recipient's location.

telehealth consultation The use of technology to deliver healthcare, health information, or health education from a distance using an interactive, two-way telecommunications system by an eligible provider who is not at the recipient's location.

telemedicine Referring specifically to remote clinical services, telemedicine can refer to remote nonclinical services, such as provider training, administrative meetings, and continuing medical education, in addition to clinical services.

temporarily disabled When an individual is unable to work for a short time as a result of sickness or injury (excluding job-related illnesses or injuries).

Temporary Assistance for Needy Families (TANF) Federal–state cash assistance program for poor families, typically headed by a single parent. Formerly called *Aid to Families With Dependent Children.*

temporary disability Level of disability where the worker's ability to perform his or her job responsibilities is lost for a specific period. There are two subcategories of temporary disability: temporary total disability and temporary partial disability.

temporary partial disability When an injury or illness impairs an employee's ability to work for a limited time. The impairment is such that the individual can perform limited employment duties and is expected to recover fully.

temporary total disability When a worker's ability to perform his or her job responsibilities is totally lost but on a temporary basis.

third-party administrator (TPA) Person or organization that processes claims and performs other contractual administrative services. Often hired by self-insured groups to provide claims-paying functions.

third-party liability (TPL) Legal obligation of third parties to pay all or part of the expenditures for medical assistance furnished under a state plan.

third-party payer Any organization (e.g., Blue Cross and Blue Shield [BCBS], Medicare, Medicaid, commercial insurance company) that provides payment for specified coverages provided under the health plan.

Ticket to Work Voluntary program that gives certain individuals with disabilities a greater choice in selecting the service providers and rehabilitation services they need to help them keep working or get back to work. This program was created with passage of the federal Ticket to Work and Work Incentives Improvement Act of 1999.

tiering What occurs when people with higher incomes can afford a wider range of services than those of the middle- and lower-income classes.

trading partners Any business entity engaging in electronic data interchange (EDI).

transaction set Collection of data that contains all information required by the receiving system to perform a normal business transaction. An example is the overall data stream of an 837 file, which is divided into sections, with each section providing a specific kind of information.

transfer of care When the healthcare professional who is providing care for some or all of a patient's problems relinquishes this responsibility to another qualified healthcare professional.

treatment, payment, or healthcare operations (TPO) To avoid interfering with an individual's access to quality healthcare or the efficient payment for such healthcare, the Health Insurance Portability and Accountability Act (HIPAA) Privacy Rule permits a covered entity to use and disclose protected health information, with certain limits and protections, for treatment, payment, and healthcare operations activities without the patient's written consent, provided that such use or disclosure is consistent with other applicable requirements of the HIPAA privacy rules.

TRICARE Regionally based managed healthcare program for active duty personnel and eligible family members, retirees and family members younger than age 65, and survivors of all uniformed services.

TRICARE For Life (TFL) Comprehensive health benefits program with no monthly premium. TFL is available to uniformed services retirees, their spouses, and their survivors who are 65 or older, are Medicare-eligible, are enrolled in Medicare Part A, and have purchased Medicare Part B coverage. TFL was established by the National Defense Authorization Act.

TRICARE Maximum Allowable Charge (TMAC) The rates used to set the TRICARE-allowed amount on the claim; the amount on which TRICARE figures a beneficiary's copayment or cost share.

TRICARE Prime Health maintenance organization (HMO) type of plan in which enrollees receive healthcare through a military treatment facility primary care manager (PCM) or a supporting network of civilian providers.

TRICARE Prime Remote Provides healthcare coverage through civilian networks or TRICARE-authorized providers for uniformed service members and their families who are on remote assignment.

TRICARE provider A person, business, or institution that renders healthcare services to TRICARE beneficiaries; for example, physicians are individual providers, hospitals are institutional providers, and ambulance companies are corporate providers.

TRICARE Regional Office (TRO) Facilities that represent the new organization for managing regional contractors and overseeing the healthcare delivery system in the three US-based TRICARE regions. Each TRO is led by a regional director who reports to and operates under the authority, direction, and control of the TMA deputy director.

TRICARE Select A fee-for-service insurance plan that allows members to see any doctor using a preferred provider model.

TRICARE Supplemental Insurance A health benefit plan designed specifically to supplement TRICARE benefits.

TrOOP True out-of-pocket costs. TrOOP includes all payments for medications listed on a particular plan's formulary and purchased at a network or participating pharmacy. If a beneficiary switches Medicare Part D plans during the plan year, TrOOP will be transferred to the new plan.

Truth in Lending Act Requires the person or business entity to disclose the exact credit terms when extending credit to applicants and regulates how they advertise consumer credit.

U

UB-04 Basic hardcopy (paper) claim form, also known as *Form CMS-1450,* required by the Centers for Medicare and Medicaid Services (CMS) and accepted only from institutional providers (e.g., hospitals, skilled nursing facilities [SNFs], home health agencies) that are excluded from the mandatory electronic claims submission requirement set forth in the Administrative Simplification Compliance Act (ASCA).

underdosing Taking less of a medication or substance than is prescribed or instructed, whether by a physician or the drug packaging, and may be intentional or unintentional.

unit/floor time Time the physician spends on bedside care of the patient and reviewing the health record and writing orders.

unusual circumstances Situations beyond the control of the submitting provider, such as a service interruption in the mode of submitting electronic claims or other extraordinary circumstances, which prevent claims from being submitted electronically.

urgent care centers A category of walk-in clinics offering immediate outpatient medical care for the treatment of acute and chronic illness and injury in a dedicated medical facility outside a traditional emergency room.

usual, customary, and reasonable (UCR) Use of fee screens to determine the lowest value of physician reimbursement based on (1) the physician's usual charge for a given procedure, (2) the amount customarily charged for the service by other physicians in the area (often defined as a specific percentile of all charges in the community), and (3) the reasonable cost of services for a given patient after medical review of the case. UCR rates are typically what an insurance carrier would allow as covered expenses.

utilization review Method of tracking, reviewing, and giving opinions regarding care provided to patients. Utilization review evaluates the necessity, appropriateness, and efficiency of the use of healthcare services, procedures, and facilities to control costs and manage care.

Utilization Review Accreditation Commission (URAC) Independent, nonprofit organization. Its mission is to promote continuous improvement in the quality and efficiency of healthcare delivery by achieving a common understanding of excellence among purchasers, providers, and patients through the establishment of standards, programs of education and communication, and a process of accreditation.

V

value-based care A type of care wherein providers' payments are based on the "value" of care they deliver as opposed to being paid by the number of visits and tests they order for a patient (as with fee-for-service). The target with value-based care is better healthcare at a lower cost.

value-based healthcare A reimbursement model wherein providers are paid based on patient outcomes. The goal is to provide better care to patients and better health for populations all at a lower cost.

value-based payment modifier (VBPM) VBPM adjusts Medicare Physician Fee Schedule (PFS) payments to a physician or group of physicians (identified by their taxpayer identification number [TIN]) based on the quality of care furnished to their Medicare fee-for-service (FFS) beneficiaries, which is based on the quality of care furnished compared with the cost of care during a performance period.

value-based programs A reimbursement model wherein providers are rewarded for the quality of care they provide to patients.

vertically integrated hospitals Hospitals that provide all levels of healthcare.

vocational rehabilitation Retraining or physical therapy that may be necessary if an injury or illness results in a worker being unable to perform the usual duties of his or her occupation.

W

waiver Formal (sometimes written) release from a particular rule or regulation. For example, the Secretary of the US Department of Health and Human Services (HHS) may grant a waiver for submitting Medicare claims electronically if the provider of services is experiencing "unusual circumstances."

workers' compensation Type of insurance regulated by state laws that pays medical expenses and partial loss of wages for workers who are injured on the job or become ill as a result of job-related circumstances. Commonly referred to as *workers' comp* or *WC*.

X

XPressClaim Secure, streamlined web-based system that allows providers to submit TRICARE claims electronically and, in most cases, to receive instant results.

Resources

AHIMA Practice Brief: *Complete medical record in a hybrid EHR environment* (website). http://campus.ahima.org/audio/2008/RB031808.pdf and http://library.ahima.org/xpedio/groups/public/documents/ahima/bok1_021581.hcsp.

Amatayakul M: Make your telecommuting program HIPAA compliant. *J AHIMA* 73(2):16A–16C, 2002

American Health Information Management Association: *Specialty certifications* (website). https://www.ahima.org/certification/exams?tabid=him. Accessed April 7, 2019.

American Medical Association: *CPT 2019 professional edition*, Chicago, 2018, AMA Press.

American Medical Association: *How to "HIPAA"—top 10 tips* (website). http://www.ama-assn.org/ama1/pub/upload/mm/435/hipaa10tips-opt.pdf. Accessed May 28, 2019.

Appold K: *Top 2018 challenges healthcare executives face* (website). https://www.managedhealthcareexecutive.com/business-strategy/top-2018-challenges-healthcare-executives-face/page/0/7. Accessed July 26, 2019.

Belli P: *Reimbursement systems: an exploration of the literature on reimbursement systems for health providers*, London, 2000, World Bank.

Böhm-Bawerk E: *Value and price: an extract*, ed 2, South Holland, IL, 1973, Libertarian Press.

Bonewit-West K: *Computer concepts and applications for the medical office*, Philadelphia, 1993, Saunders.

Buck CJ: *2013 Step-by-step medical coding*, St. Louis, 2013, Elsevier/Saunders.

Burrill S: *Health care outlook for 2019: five trends that could impact health plans, hospitals, and patients* (website). https://www.modernhealthcare.com/article/20181207/SPONSORED/181209938/health-care-outlook-for-2019-five-trends-that-could-impact-health-plans-hospitals-and-patients. Accessed October 26, 2019.

Burton BK: *Quick guide to HIPAA for the physician's office*, Philadelphia, 2004, Elsevier/Saunders.

Carr RF: *Hospital* (website). http://www.wbdg.org/design/hospital.php#emerg/. Accessed October 30, 2019.

Center for Health Policy Research: *American Medical Association: the impact of Medicare payment schedule alternatives on physicians*, Chicago, 1988, American Medical Association.

Centers for Medicare and Medicaid Services (website). http://www.cms.gov/. Accessed May 28, 2019.

Centers for Medicare and Medicaid Services: *Claim status request and response* (website). http://www.cms.gov/Medicare/Billing/ElectronicBillingEDITrans/ClaimStatus.html. Accessed August 11, 2019.

Centers for Medicare and Medicaid Services: *Electronic health care claims* (website). http://www.cms.gov/Medicare/Billing/ElectronicBillingEDITrans/HealthCareClaims.html. Accessed August 12, 2019.

Centers for Medicare and Medicaid Services: *Form CMS-1500: processing manual* (website). http://www.gerberconsulting.com/CMS%20Updates/R2842CP%20Form%20CMS-1500%20Instructions%20Revised%2012-27-13.pdf. Accessed August 14, 2019.

Centers for Medicare and Medicaid Services: *Important facts for state policymakers: Deficit Reduction Act* (website). http://www.cms.gov/Regulations-and-Guidance/Legislation/DeficitReductionAct/downloads/TOAbackgrounder.pdf. Accessed August 8, 2019.

Centers for Medicare and Medicaid Services: *Medicare & You 2019* (website). CMS Product No. 10050–5410050. http://www.medicare.gov/medicare-and-you/medicare-and-you.html. Accessed August 15, 2019.

Centers for Medicare and Medicaid Services: *Medicare claims processing manual: chapter 26—completing and processing Form CMS-1500 data set* (website). http://www.cms.gov/Regulations-and-Guidance/Guidance/Manuals/downloads/clm104c26.pdf. Accessed October 5, 2019.

Centers for Medicare and Medicaid Services: *Medicare Promoting Interoperability program eligible hospitals, critical access hospitals, and dual-eligible hospitals objectives and measures for 2019* (website). https://www.cms.gov/Regulations-and-Guidance/Legislation/EHRIncentivePrograms/Downloads/TableofContents_EH_Medicare_2019.pdf. Accessed July 26, 2019.

Centers for Medicare and Medicaid Services: *Original Medicare (fee-for-service) appeals* (website). http://www.cms.gov/OrgMedFFSAppeals/. Accessed August 11, 2019.

Centers for Medicare and Medicaid Services: *What are the value-based programs?* (website). https://www.cms.gov/Medicare/Quality-Initiatives-Patient-Assessment-Instruments/Value-Based-Programs/Value-Based-Programs.html.

Covell A: *2012 Coding workbook for the physician's office*, Clifton Park, NY, 2013, Delmar Cengage Learning.

Davis JB: *CPT and HCPCS coding made easy! A comprehensive guide to CPT and HCPCS coding for health care professionals*, ed 6, Downers Grove, IL, 2005, Practice Management Information Corporation.

Davis N, LaCour M: *Health information technology*, ed 3, St. Louis, 2013, Saunders.

Fallon LF Jr.: Advameg, Inc.: *Patient confidentiality. Encyclopedia of surgery* (website). http://www.surgeryencyclopedia.com/Pa-St/Patient-Confidentiality.html/. Accessed April 23, 2019.

Fordney MT: *Insurance handbook for the medical office*, ed 13, St. Louis, 2014, Elsevier/Saunders.

Gallup Well-Being: *Fewer Americans have employer-based health insurance* (website). http://www.gallup.com/poll/152621/fewer-americans-employer-based-health-insurance.aspx. Accessed January 2, 2014.

Green MA, Rowell JC: *Understanding health insurance: a guide to professional billing and reimbursement*, ed 11, Clifton Park, NY, 2013, Delmar Cengage Learning.

Gylya BA: *Computer applications for the medical office*, Philadelphia, 1997, FA Davis.

Hadley J, Berenson RA: Seeking the just price: constructing relative value scales and fee schedules. *Ann Intern Med* 106(3):461–466, 1987.

Hagland M: Electronic record, electronic security. *J AHIMA* 75(2):18–22, 2004.

Henry J. Kaiser Family Foundation: *Total number of Medicare beneficiaries* (website). https://www.kff.org/medicare/state-indicator/total-medicare-beneficiaries/?currentTimeframe=0&sortModel=%7B%22colId%22:%22Location%22,%22sort%22:%22asc%22%7D. Accessed August 13, 2019.

Henry J. Kaiser Family Foundation: *The uninsured and the difference health insurance makes* (website). http://www.kff.org/uninsured/upload/1420-10.pdf/. Accessed January 2, 2014.

Henry J. Kaiser Family Foundation: *Where are states today? Medicaid and CHIP eligibility levels for children, pregnant women, and adults* (website). https://www.kff.org/medicaid/fact-sheet/where-are-states-today-medicaid-and-chip/. Accessed August 6, 2019.

Hodgin S: *The five conceptual templates for value-based reimbursement* (website). http://www.insight-txcin.org/post/the-five-conceptual-templates-for-value-based-reimbursement. Accessed October 14, 2019.

Hsaio WC, Braun P, Becker ER, et al: The resource-based relative value scale: toward the development of an alternative physician payment system. *JAMA* 258:799–802, 1987.

Hsiao WC, Braun P, Goldman P, et al: *Resource based relative values of selected medical and surgical procedures in Massachusetts*, Boston, 1985, Final Report on Research Contract for Rate Setting Commission, Commonwealth of Massachusetts Harvard School of Public Health.

Hsiao WC, Stasson W: Toward developing a relative value scale for medical and surgical services. *Health Care Finance Rev* 1:23–38, 1979.

Humana: *Real-time adjudication* (website). https://www.humana.com/provider/medical-resources/claims-payments/claims-payment/payment-resources. Accessed June 6, 2019.

Karban K: CY 2011 changes to the hospital OPPS. *J AHIMA* 82(4):54–56, 2011.

Keller C, Valerius J: *Medical insurance*, Columbus, OH, 2002, Glencoe/McGraw-Hill.

Kirchner M: Will this formula change the way you get paid? *Med Econ* 65:138–152, 1988.

Lockner A, Walcker C: *INSIGHT: the healthcare industry's shift from fee-for-service to value-based reimbursement* (website). https://news.bloomberglaw.com/health-law-and-business/insight-the-healthcare-industrys-shift-from-fee-for-service-to-value-based-reimbursement. Accessed October 15, 2019.

Medicare Savings Programs (website). https://www.medicare.gov/your-medicare-costs/get-help-paying-costs/medicare-savings-programs. Accessed August 6, 2019.

Mississippi Hospital Association Health Careers Center: *Mississippi health careers guide 2008–2010* (website). http://www.mshealthcareers.com/news/healthcareersguidebook.htm. Accessed April 7, 2019.

Moisio M: *Guide to health insurance billing*, Albany, NY, 2001, Delmar.

Moorhead R: *Here's what's wrong with the relative value scale*, Asheville, NC, 1961, Presented at the 18th Annual Meeting of AAPS, October 12–14.

Moynihan J: Preparing for 5010: internal testing of HIPAA transaction upgrades recommended by December 31. *J AHIMA* 81(1):22–26, 2010. Available from http://library.ahima.org/xpedio/groups/public/documents/ahima/bok1_046274.hcsp?dDocName=¬°bok1_046274. Accessed May 28, 2019.

Quinsey CA: Practice brief: a HIPAA security overview. *J AHIMA* 75(4):56A–556C, 2004.

Quinsey CA, Brandt MD: *AHIMA practice brief: information security—an overview*, Chicago, 2003, AHIMA.

Ranjan D: *4 main objectives of Promoting Interoperability (PI) Program* (website). https://prognocis.com/objectives-of-promoting-interoperability-program/. Accessed October 12, 2019.

Roediger JM: *Use every tool to verify patient eligibility* (website). http://www.obermayer.com/blog/8161/. Accessed June 6, 2019.

Rouse M: *MACRA (Medicare Access and CHIP Reauthorization Act of 2015)* (website). https://searchhealthit.techtarget.com/definition/MACRA-Medicare-Access-and-CHIP-Reauthorization-Act-of-2015. Accessed October 21, 2019.

Rowell J, Green M: *Understanding health insurance*, Albany, NY, 2004, Delmar.

Sabri EH, Gupta AP, Beitler MA: *Purchase order management best practices*, Fort Lauderdale, FL, 2006, J Ross Publishing.

Sanderson SM: *Computers in the medical office*, Columbus, OH, 1998, Glencoe/McGraw-Hill.

Sanderson SM: *Patient billing, using MediSoft Advanced*, Columbus, OH, 2002, Glencoe/McGraw-Hill.

Sheahan K: *How are computers used today in the medical field?* (website), http://www.ehow.com/about_6397797_computers-used-today-medical-field_.html. Accessed October 12, 2019.

study.com: *How to become a medical billing clerk: step-by-step career guide* (website). https://study.com/articles/How_to_Become_a_Medical_Billing_Clerk_Step-by-Step_Career_Guide.html. Accessed April 7, 2019.

United States Bureau of Labor Statistics: *Occupational Outlook Handbook, medical records and health information technicians* (website). https://www.bls.gov/ooh/healthcare/medical-records-and-health-information-technicians.htm. Accessed October 31, 2019.

United States Census Bureau: *Facts for features and special editions* (website). http://www.census.gov/newsroom/facts-for-features.html. Accessed November 9, 2016.

United States Department of Health and Human Services: The 2009 HHS policy guidelines, *Fed Regist* 74(14), 2009. Available from http://aspe.hhs.gov/POVERTY/09poverty.shtml/. Accessed July 7, 2014.

United States Department of Health and Human Services, Centers for Medicare and Medicaid Services: *Transactions and code sets regulations* (website). https://www.cms.gov/Regulations-and-Guidance/Administrative-Simplification/Code-Sets/index.html. Accessed October 29, 2019.

United States Department of Labor: *Notice of changes under HIPAA to COBRA continuation coverage under group health plans* (website). https://www.dol.gov/agencies/ebsa/about-ebsa/our-activities/resource-center/publications/notice-of-changes-under-hipaa-to-cobra-continuation-coverage-under-group-health-plans. Accessed November 3, 2019.

Vola A, Kallem C: A guide to US quality measurement organizations. *J AHIMA* 82(4):41–43, 2011.

Wagner M: *U.S. allocates $1.2 billion for electronic medical records* (website). http://www.informationweek.com/healthcare/electronic-health-records/us-allocates-$12-billion-for-electronic-medical-records/d/d-id/1082464. Accessed October 12, 2019.

Index